EURAIL® GUIDE
How To Travel Europe And All The World By Train

By Kathryn Saltzman Turpin
and
Marvin L. Saltzman

EURAIL® GUIDE   Printed in the U.S.A.

Copyright©1971, 1972, 1973, 1974, 1975, 1976, 1977
1978, 1979, 1980, 1981, 1982, 1983, 1984

by
Kathryn S. Turpin
and Marvin L. Saltzman

All rights reserved under International
and Pan-American Copyright Conventions

Library of Congress Catalog Number 72-83072
ISBN 0-912442-14-X
US ISSN 0085-0330

Published by
Eurail Guide Annual
27540 Pacific Coast Highway
Malibu, California 90265, U.S.A.

Edition	Year	Pages
First Edition	1971	96 pages
Second Edition	1972	168 pages
Third Edition	1973	288 pages
Fourth Edition	1974	384 pages
Fifth Edition	1975	384 pages
Sixth Edition	1976	432 pages
Seventh Edition	1977	432 pages
Eight Edition	1978	768 pages
Ninth Edition	1979	768 pages
Tenth Edition	1980	816 pages
Eleventh Edition	1981	816 pages
Twelfth Edition	1982	816 pages
Thirteenth Edition	1983	816 pages
Fourteenth Edition	1984	816 pages

IMPORTANT NOTES

Always—without exception—before commencing each journey doublecheck the departure and arrival times given in our book or in any timetable, as they are subject to change without prior notice. Changes will usually be minor and have no effect on the trips described in this book. We do not want you to miss a train or to be stranded.

Departure and arrival times in this book are given in 24-hour time. A departure at 1:10 PM is shown as 13:10. Midnight is 24:00. Time between Midnight and 1:00 AM is shown as 0:01 to 0:59.

All schedules shown are daily, unless designated otherwise.

Unless indicated otherwise, the departure and arrival times in our book are for the period of late May to late September. In most cases, these schedules change slightly during September-May.

Where we state that departures from a city are "at frequent times", this means at least once each hour between the 2 time periods indicated.

The schedules for one-day roundtrip excursions do not always reflect *all* the departure times from either the base-city or the destination-city. Only those departure times involved in making a one-day roundtrip are shown. On a particular route, there frequently are later departure times from the base-city and earlier departure times from the destination-city than are shown, none of which would be applicable to a one-day round-trip.

Many cities have 2 or more railstations. Wherever this is so, we note the name of the applicable railstation (in parenthesis) after the name of the city. For Austria, East Germany, Switzerland and West Germany, where no name is shown after the name of the city, the station is always "Hauptbahnhof".

The number appearing at the start of a schedule is the Thomas Cook Timetable number, such as the example below:

Bergen - Oslo   481
    Dep. Bergen   7:20
    Arr. Oslo   14:05

Every year hundreds of readers send us suggestions, each of which is checked and answered. Many are added to the next annually-revised edition. If you have discovered rail travel facts helpful to others, please send them to us.

TWO TABLES OF CONTENTS

The first Table of Contents lists 138 countries alphabetically.

The second Table of Contents lists these 138 countries by geographical areas (Eurailpass Europe, Britain, Eastern Europe, Middle East, Africa, etc.).

INDEX
An index of cities appears on pages 808-812.

TABLE OF CONTENTS #1

495 Afganistan
448 Albania
521 Algeria
526 Angola
734 Argentina
648 Australia
 56 Austria
495 Bahrain
587 Bangladesh
 77 Belgium
528 Benin
744 Bolivia
529 Botswana
748 Brazil
448 Bulgaria
588 Burma
529 Burundi
530 Cameroun
667 Canada
531 Central African Rep.
531 Chad
759 Chile
626 China, People's Rep. of
632 China, Rep. of
     (Taiwan)
766 Colombia
531 Congo
719 Costa Rica
721 Cuba
451 Czechoslovakia
244 Denmark
532 Djibouti
456 East Germany
769 Ecuador
532 Egypt
722 El Salvador
410 England
536 Ethiopia
253 Finland
107 France
537 Gabon
537 Gambia
538 Ghana
139 Greece
724 Guatemala
539 Guinea

772 Guyana
772 Guyane
727 Honduras
590 Hong Kong
465 Hungary
591 India
601 Indonesia
495 Iran
499 Iraq
186 Ireland, Rep. of
502 Israel
191 Italy
539 Ivory Coast
728 Jamaica
604 Japan
505 Jordan
622 Kampuchea
541 Kenya
505 Kuwait
622 Lao People's
     Dem. Rep.
506 Lebanon
543 Lesotho
543 Liberia
543 Libya
 77 Luxembourg
544 Madagascar
546 Malawi
622 Malaysia
547 Mali
547 Mauritania
547 Mauritius
684 Mexico
548 Morocco
552 Mozambique
 77 Netherlands
661 New Zealand
729 Nicaragua
553 Niger
554 Nigeria
625 North Korea
410 Northern Ireland
260 Norway
506 Oman
506 Pakistan
731 Panama
773 Paraguay

775 Peru
631 Philippines
468 Poland
148 Portugal
511 Qatar
556 Reunion
473 Romania
477 Russia (U.S.S.R.)
556 Rwanda
636 Sabah
511 Saudi Arabia
410 Scotland
557 Senegal
557 Sierra Leone
637 Singapore
557 Somali Republic
558 South Africa
639 South Korea
565 South West Africa
148 Spain
641 Sri Lanka (Ceylon)
566 Sudan
780 Surinam
570 Swaziland
276 Sweden
284 Switzerland
511 Syria
570 Tanzania
645 Thailand
573 Togo
574 Tunisia
513 Turkey
580 Uganda
520 United Arab Emirates
696 U. S. A.
581 Upper Volta
781 Uruguay
783 Venezuela
647 Vietnam
410 Wales
344 West Germany
520 Yemen, Arab Republic
520 Yemen, People's Dem.
488 Yugoslavia
581 Zaire
583 Zambia
585 Zimbabwe (Rhodesia)

TABLE OF CONTENTS #2

Chapter 1
13 THE JOY OF TRAIN TRAVEL

Chapter 2
16 WHETHER TO EURAILPASS
- 20 Eurail Youthpass
- 22 Second-Class Space
- 22 Other Discounts
- 25 Eurailpass and Eurail Youthpass Bonuses
- 27 Inter Rail Card
- 27 Senior Inter Rail Card
- 28 Student Travel Discounts

Chapter 3
29 HOW TO PLAN A RAIL ITINERARY
- 30 Reservations — Hotel and Train
- 35 Preparation for Autumn Touring

Chapter 4
37 DON'T MISS THE TRAIN
- 37 Multi-Station Cities
- 38 Timetables
- 40 Train Splitting
- 42 Train Changing

Chapter 5
44 VALUABLE TRAIN TRAVEL TIPS
- 44 Day or Night
- 45 Eating on Trains
- 47 Baggage
- 49 Customs Procedures and Duty-Free Purchases
- 50 Airport-City Rail Connections
- 50 Lost Money and Passports
- 51 Overcoming Jet Lag
- 52 What Weather to Expect
- 52 Last-Minute Checklist
- 52 Signs — The International Language

Chapter 6

56 EURAILPASS EUROPE

    56   Austria
    77   Benelux
              Belgium, Netherlands and Luxembourg
    107 France
    139 Greece
    148 Iberia
              Spain and Portugal
    186 Ireland, Republic of
    191 Italy
    242 Scandinavia
    244   Denmark
    253   Finland
    260   Norway
    276   Sweden
    284 Switzerland
    344 West Germany

Chapter 7

386 EUROPE'S GREATEST TRAINS

         Complete Itineraries — Departure and Arrival Times
    386 Trans Europ Express
    387 International Inter-City
    387 Trains a Grande Vitesse

Chapter 8

410 ENGLAND, WALES, SCOTLAND, NORTHERN IRELAND

    410 British Train Passes
    415 London's Railstations
    416 Days of the Week Variances
    416 Summer and Winter Schedules
    417 Connections with the Continent
    421 One-Day Train Excursions from London
    439 A Day Through Wales
    440 Rail Connections with Ireland
    442 Rail Connections with Scotland
    443 Scotland

Chapter 9
448 EASTERN EUROPE
448 Albania
448 Bulgaria
451 Czechoslovakia
456 East Germany
465 Hungary
468 Poland
473 Romania
477 Russia (U.S.S.R. — Soviet Union)
484   The Trans-Siberian Route
488 Yugoslavia

Chapter 10
495 THE MIDDLE EAST
495 Afghanistan
495 Bahrain
495 Iran
499 Iraq
502 Israel
505 Kuwait
505 Jordan
506 Lebanon
506 Oman
506 Pakistan
511 Qatar
511 Saudi Arabia
511 Syria
513 Turkey
520 United Arab Emirates
520 Yemen, Arab Republic of
520 Yemen, People's Democratic Republic of

Chapter 11
521 AFRICA

521	Algeria	547	Mali
526	Angola	547	Mauritania
528	Benin	547	Mauritius
529	Botswana	548	Morocco
529	Burundi	552	Mozambique
530	Cameroun	553	Niger
531	Central African	554	Nigeria
	Republic	556	Reunion
531	Chad	556	Rwana
531	Congo	557	Senegal
532	Djibouti	557	Sierra Leone
532	Egypt	557	Somali Republic
536	Ethiopia	558	South Africa
537	Gabon	565	South West Africa
537	Gambia		(Namibia)
538	Ghana	566	Sudan
539	Guinea	570	Swaziland
539	Ivory Coast	570	Tanzania
541	Kenya	573	Togo
543	Lesotho	574	Tunisia
543	Liberia	580	Uganda
543	Libya	581	Upper Volta
544	Madagascar	583	Zambia
546	Malawi	585	Zimbabwe

Chapter 12
587 ASIA

587	Bangladesh	625	North Korea
588	Burma	626	People's Republic of China
590	Hong Kong	631	Philippines
591	India	632	Republic of China (Taiwan)
601	Indonesia	636	Sabah
604	Japan	637	Singapore
622	Kampuchea	639	South Korea
622	Lao People's	641	Sri Lanka (Ceylon)
	Democratic Rep.	645	Thailand
622	Malaysia	647	Vietnam

Chapter 13
648 AUSTRALIA

Chapter 14
661 NEW ZEALAND

Chapter 15
667 NORTH AMERICA
      667 Canada
      684 Mexico
      696 U. S. A.

Chapter 16
719 CENTRAL AMERICA and WEST INDIES
      719 Costa Rica   728 Jamaica
      721 Cuba   729 Nicaragua
      722 El Salvador   731 Panama
      724 Guatemala

Chapter 17
732 SOUTH AMERICA
      732 Amerailpass   772 Guyana
      734 Argentina   772 Guyane
      744 Bolivia   773 Paraguay
      748 Brazil   775 Peru
      759 Chile   780 Surinam
      766 Colombia   781 Uruguay
      769 Ecuador   783 Venezuela

Chapter 18
784 EURAIL® GUIDE ROUTE CHART
      785   1984 European Train Ticket Prices

808 INDEX OF CITIES

813 NOTES

816 CALENDARS — 1984 and 1985

TRAVELING SWITZERLAND'S RHONE VALLEY BETWEEN BERNE AND ISELLE

Chapter 1

THE JOY OF TRAIN TRAVEL

The least expensive, safest, most convenient, interesting and pleasant way to travel and really see the world is by train.

We accent "pleasant", because our book is about joyous adventure. Our goal is to make worldwide train travel easy and pleasurable.

When traveling by train, your departure is not delayed by weather, as it can be when traveling by airplane or automobile.

You leave and arrive in the center of a city, saving the time, effort and expense involved with going back and forth to distant airports. In fact, many high-speed trains actually get you from a hotel in one city to a hotel in another city faster than by airplane when the distance is 250-350 miles.

The cost of an uncomfortable and non-airconditioned 2-passenger mini car for 350 miles per day travel can come to as much as $65 (U.S.) per day—daily rental, very high taxes on the rental charge (as much as 20% in Sweden, 18% in Denmark, France, Greece and Holland), mileage charge, gasoline (often at $3.00 per gallon), insurance, servicing, overnight parking fee, substantial drop-off charge, etc.

By contrast, one can travel on high-speed, air-conditioned luxury trains with any of numerous bargain rail passes for $5-$10 per day. (See detailed list on our Inside Front Cover.)

In train travel, you reach thousands of interesting destinations not accessible by airplane. You eliminate the worries, frustrations and delays of socked-in airports, flat tires, the requirement to check-in early at airports, the interminable waiting for baggage to be unloaded, driving into the crowded streets of an unfamiliar city, coping with strange traffic laws and the many other problems, expenses and inconveniences connected with airplane and auto travel.

From London to Tokyo, you find at principal railstations a wide variety of services and goods: food, information on local tours, assistance in obtaining lodging, money exchange, waiting rooms where you can relax shoe repair, etc.

If you plan your routes well, you will see an array of visual delights that airplane passengers never see: indescribable seashores, vineyards tinted by afternoon sunlight, castles that have been straddling their hilltops for centuries, raging rivers, breathtaking waterfalls, Alpine summits, remote villages founded before Christ, fjords, forests, lovely orchards and pastures—a feast of colorful pictures to enjoy long after the trip ends.

At the end of a train trip, you arrive at your destination relaxed and rested.

By selecting special luxury trains, you are able to enjoy not only great scenery en route and interesting destinations but also the added dimension of trains which in themselves are a worthwhile travel experience in the same way that leading steamships of the past were.

There is no waiting for the next city to have the use of lavatory facilities. Usually, a cup of coffee or bottle of beer is only a 2-minute walk away. During the trip you can get up from your seat, stretch, take a stroll through the train.

Only train travel affords the opportunity of meeting and conversing with the people in the area you are visiting and also with tourists from other parts of the world.

Since 1959, among the fellow passengers with whom we have shared train rides have been Amsterdam businessmen, students from California, Italian army officers, gregarious Yugoslav geologists, an Uruguayan cardiologist, North Dakota farmers, a Chinese woman doctor from Canada, a family from Brazil, a young Russian woman returning home from a trade fair in East Germany, and a professor of language from Boston.

Every year since the first Eurail® Guide in 1971, each annually-revised and expanded edition of our book has been the product of a large "family".

Our daughter Kathryn proposed the idea for Eurail® Guide when she was traveling Europe on a 3-month Eurailpass in 1970. We published our first annual edition in early 1971 as 96 pages, and the book has been growing ever since then.

Kathryn and I, in writing each new edition, are aided and abetted by Barbara, who uncovers errors, suggests improvements and causes endless revisions—the classic dissatisfied editor to whom authors become permanently indebted once the travail is over.

Kathryn has traveled at different seasons and has taken different routes than those Barbara and I have traveled, giving each edition a variety of experiences and strikingly different viewpoints. For one thing, no stranger has offered to carry my suitcases or take me to dinner.

Many others have provided information and assistance, for which we express our gratitude: Juergen Arnold, North American Assistant General Manager, German Federal Railroads . . . Walter Bruderer, North American Public

Relations Director, Swiss National Tourist Office . . . Peter Ueltschi, North American Railway Department, Swiss National Tourist Office . . . Andy Lazarus, A.J. Lazarus Associates . . . and Dagobert M. Scher, North American Assistant General Manager, French National Railroads.

Other important members of the Eurail® Guide family are the scores of readers who each Fall write us as we are preparing the next edition to tell us where they have traveled and describe their experiences.

Comments about your train journeys will be greatly appreciate. Write us what you liked and disliked . . . out-of-the-way places you visited and recommend . . . and anything else you believe would help other travelers plan future trips.

Send your notes to: Eurail Guide Annual, 27540 Pacific Coast Highway, Malibu, California 90265, U.S.A.

In the following pages, we identify basic problems in train travel worldwide, show how these can be overcome, and tell you all you need to know in order to travel the world by train safely, economically and pleasantly.

(M.L.S.)

Postscript: Never plan to travel without finding out if the countries you are going to tour have low-price train passes.

And when those countries have train passes, make sure before you leave home to know if any pass you want to buy has to be purchased before you leave home or can be bought only after you arrive in the country you will be touring.

All of the train passes offered when this edition of Eurail® Guide went to press are described in our book.

Chapter 2

WHETHER TO EURAILPASS

Since 1959, Western European railroads have offered the travel bargain called Eurailpass, sold throughout the world except in Europe and North Africa.

Eurailpass and Eurail Youthpass entitle one to unlimited first or second-class train travel plus free or reduced fare on many buses and boats in these 16 countries: Austria, Belgium, Denmark, Finland, France, Greece, Holland, Irish Republic, Italy, Luxembourg, Norway, Portugal, Spain, Sweden, Switzerland and West Germany.

In Europe, first-class cars (and the first-class portion of mixed-class cars) are marked outside by a yellow line running above the windows.

Later in this chapter, we describe the separate Eurail Youthpass, good for unlimited *second-class* train space.

Neither Eurailpass nor Eurail Youthpass can be purchased after you arrive in Europe. Both are non-refundable if lost or stolen. If you present them to a Eurailpass office before they become valid, 85% of the purchase price will be refunded.

There are Eurail Aid Offices in several European cities (listed on the map that is given with each Eurailpass), where a lost Eurailpass or Eurail Youthpass can be replaced if the buyer has retained the purchase authentication slip.

Both passes become valid on the first day they are used, after first having been recorded at the ticket office of the station from where the first journey begins.

Prices in this chapter are U.S. dollars.

The phrase "unlimited travel" means exactly that. You can literally travel 24 hours a day for the entire period a pass is valid. Countless travelers have used 3 and 4 times the price of their pass, saving hundreds of dollars their itinerary would have cost if they had used ordinary tickets.

The bargain does not end there. Tickets for the fast Trans Europ Express, Inter-City and many of the TGV trains cost more than space on an ordinary, slower train on the same route, a supplemental charge ranging from $3.00(U.S.) to $18.00.

Eurailpass includes unlimited use of TEE, IC and TGV trains (described in Chapter 7) without having to pay any supplement. All of the TEE and many of the IC and TGV trains do require reservations. The $2.00(U.S.) fee per reservation must be paid when riding them, even when using a Eurailpass.

In addition to the money-saving feature, Eurailpass adds previous time to a travel schedule. Many travelers feel that never having to stand in a ticket-selling line when you have a Eurailpass or a Eurail Youthpass is enough reason to have the pass. It can take up to 30 minutes for purchasing each ticket along the way.

(With or without a pass, if reserved seats are required or desired it is necessary to allocate time for the separate Seat Reservation Line. More about reservations in Chapter 3.)

On the other hand, Eurailpass is not always an economy. Some European itineraries are less expensive using regular train tickets or using one or a combination of the many national and regional rail passes described in this book (France Vacances, GermanRail Tourist Card, Benelux Tourrail, etc.).

The only way to find out if a Eurailpass or the numerous other passes will save you money on your trip is to compare their price with the total prices of tickets for your particular itinerary.

There are over 100,000 miles of European train travel you can make with a pass. It is impossible for us to give you the fare and travel time for every possible trip in Europe.

However, we provide you in our Chapter 18 ''Route Chart'' a list of more than 700 train trips that most people touring the 16 Eurailpass countries might take, with the first-class fare and travel time for each of them.

If you are considering traveling the heavily-crowded second-class, compute second-class fares at two-thirds of the first-class fares shown. That will come close to actual second-class ticket prices.

The first step in using the Chapter 18 Route Chart is to make a list of your itinerary. It is advisable to schedule any part of your trip that is not in the 16 Eurailpass countries (such as England, Yugoslavia, etc.) either before or after the days you are touring the countries in which Eurailpass is valid so as to avoid consuming Eurailpass days and in order to buy the least expensive Eurailpass for your trip.

Next, consult the Route Chart and note the first-class fare for each leg of your trip that can be covered by Eurailpass or Eurail Youthpass.

Keep in mind that even though you purchase your Eurailpass weeks or months in advance of starting your trip, the Eurailpass validity period does not begin until the first day you actually use the pass.

It's a good idea to protect yourself from having your pass rendered partly or wholly invalid because the validity dates were entered incorrectly. The Eurailpass must be validated at the ticket office of the station at your first departure. At that time, the clerk writes on the pass both the first and last day it can be used. Before he does this, write a note with what you believe are the validity dates, show it to him, and ask him if he agrees with those dates. Only when he says your dates are correct, or explains why they are not, should you hand your pass to him for the dates to be entered on it.

Once the clerk has written any validity dates on the face of your Eurailpass, those dates cannot be changed, since any alteration of the dates invalidates the pass. That is why it is wise to have him agree on the correct dates *before* he writes anything.

If one fails to have the Eurailpass validated before boarding the first train ride, the train conductor can do so. However, there is a $3 fee for a post-departure validation.

After your Eurailpass or Eurail Youthpass has been validated, remove the "proof of purchase" stub from the 3-part pass. From then on, as you would do with a list of traveler's checks after purchasing them, keep that stub separate from the pass. It is this stub that is required for a replacement in case the pass itself is lost or stolen.

Both Eurailpass and Eurail Youthpass are accepted by those trains running between airports and cities: Amsterdam, Barcelona, Bilbao, Brussels, Dusseldorf, Frankfurt, Malaga, Paris, Vienna and Zurich.

The 1984 charge for Eurailpass is $260(U.S.) for 15 days, $330 for 21 days, $410 for one month, $560 for 2 months and $680 for 3 months. Children 4 to under 12 pay half-fare.

An average 21-day itinerary is $150-$250 more expensive with first-class tickets than with a Eurailpass. And, a Eurailpass gives you the convenience of not having to stand in time-consuming lines to purchase tickets.

Depending on the itinerary, it can be the least expensive formula to buy a combination of Eurailpass and train tickets. For example, when traveling by train over a 22-day period with a $40 ride on the last day, it saves $40 to buy a 21-day Eurailpass and a ticket for the 22nd day ($330+$40⁵$370) instead of buying a $410 one-month Eurailpass.

On the other hand, if the trip on the 22nd day is $81 or more, it will save money to buy a one-month Eurailpass even though it is being used only 22 days.

Depending on the circumstances, it can be worthwhile to have any length Eurailpass without using it all the days you are entitled to use it.

The Chapter 18 Route Chart makes it easy for you to compute the ticket price for your trip and then determine *whether* to buy a Eurailpass, which Eurailpass will save you the most money, and how to schedule your train trips so as to fit them into the validity period of your Eurailpass.

Figures in the Route Chart for travel time between 2 cities represent the longest time for each trip. In many distances, the time stated is for a night train and there is a shorter-time day train on which you could make the same journey. Or there may be 2 or more trains running during the day, one of which is a fast express which makes the trip in less time than indicated in the Route Chart.

Despite such differences in travel time, the Route Chart time, as a rule, will be no more than 10% greater than the fastest time between 2 cities.

The Eurail® Guide Route Chart is accurate enough to help you decide whether you want to make a particular trip in one day or break it up into 2 or more shorter trips.

EUROPE'S GREATEST TRAINS

Chapter 7 lists all of Europe's special, very fast TEE, IIC and TGV trains, indicating the itinerary and timetables for each. Seat reservations are mandatory for many of these trains and usually can be made 2 months in advance, some railroads taking reservations only one month before travel date.

The TGV takes only 4 hours 50 minutes to go from Paris to Marseille, traveling at a peak speed of 162 mph on some portions of that route. The running time for a regular train on that route is 7 hours, as noted in our Route Chart. A ticket on the Paris-Marseille TGV costs about $15(U.S.) more than on an ordinary train for the same trip.

The IIC train "Catalan" makes the Barcelona-Geneva run in 9½ hours versus the ordinary train time of 12 hours. A ticket on "Catalan" costs about $10(U.S.) more than a regular, slower train does.

These 2 examples illustrate a major Eurailpass bonus: being able to ride the luxury, high-speed trains at no extra charge over the price you pay for your Eurailpass.

Conversely, the Eurail Youthpass (restricted to travel in second-class space) can be used for travel on all first-class trains only if you pay the difference in fare. On "Aquitane", from Paris to Bordeaux, the extra fare for a passenger traveling with Eurail Youthpass comes to about $37(U.S.).

EURAIL YOUTHPASS

This pass is for unlimited *second-class* train travel in the same 16 countries which honor the first-class Eurailpass. In 1984, the $290(U.S.) price for a one-month Eurail Youthpass is a $120 savings compared to the $410 one-month Eurailpass. The $370 2-month Eurail Youthpass is a $190 savings compared to the $560 2-month Eurailpass.

Second-class space is very acceptable on trains in Austria, Belgium, Denmark, Finland, France, Holland, Irish Republic, Luxembourg, Norway, Sweden, Switzerland and West Germany.

The buyer of a Eurail Youthpass must prove he or she is under 26 years of age on the first day of using the pass.

Both Eurail Youthpass and Eurailpass can be purchased from a travel agent or directly from the following places:

U.S.A. and Canada

BEVERLY HILS, CAL.
French National Railroads
9465 Wilshire Blvd.

BOSTON, MA.
German Federal Railroad
625 Statler Office Bldg.

CHICAGO, ILL.

CIT (Italian State Railways)
765 Route 83

French National Railroads
11 E. Adams St.

German Rail
104 So. Michigan Ave.

CORAL GABLES, FLA.
French National Railroads
2121 Ponce de Leon Blvd. (33134)

DENVER, COL.
German Rail
8000 E. Girard Ave. (80231)

ENCINO, CAL.
CIT (Italian State Railways)
15760 Ventura Blvd. (91436)

HOUSTON, TEX.
German Federal Railroad
1121 Walker St. (77002)

SANTA MONICA, CAL.
GermanRail
520 Broadway (90401)

MONTREAL, P.Q., CANADA

CIT (Italian State Railways)
2055 Peel St. (H3A 1V4)

French National Railroads
1500 Stanley St. (H3A-1R3)

NEW YORK, N.Y.

CIT (Italian State Railways)
666 Fifth Ave.

German Federal Railroad
747 Third Ave. (10017)

French National Railroads
610 Fifth Ave. (10020)

Swiss Federal Railways
608 Fifth Ave.

SAN FRANCISCO, CAL.
French National Railroads
360 Post St. (94108)

GermanRail
1 Hallidie Plaza (94102)

Swiss National Tourist Office
250 Stockton St. (94108)

TORONTO, ONT., CANADA

C.I.T. Tours, Inc.
13 Balmuto St. (M4Y 1W4)

GermanRail
1290 Bay St. (M5R 2Cs)

VANCOUVER, B.C., CANADA
French National Railroads
409 Granville St. (B6C-1T2)

ELSEWHERE

AUSTRALIA: CIT Australia Pty. Ltd., Commercial Banking Co. of Sydney Ltd., Conrode International Travel, Summerland Travel Center Pty, Ltd., Thomas Cook Pty. Ltd.; **BAHREIN:** Thomas Cook Overseas Ltd,; **EGYPT:** Thomas Cook Overseas Ltd.; **HONG KONG:** Hong Kong Student Travel Bureau, Lufthansa German Airlines, Thomas Cook Overseas Ltd.; **INDIA:** Travel Corporation India Pvt. Ltd.; **INDONESIA:** Pantravel Travel & Tourism Service; **ISRAEL:** European Wholesale Tour Representatives; **JAPAN:** Japan Travel Bureau, Travel Plaza International; **KOREA:** Seoul Travel Services, Ltd,; **MALAYSIA:** Thomas Cook Overseas Ltd.; **NEW ZEALAND:** Atlantic & Pacific Travel International, Ltd., Thomas Cook Pty. Ltd.; **PAKISTAN:** American Express International, Inc., **PHILIPPINES:** American Express International Inc., Thomas Cook Inc.; **SAUDI ARABIA:** Tarfa Tours & Travel, Thomas Cook ALRAJHI Ltd.; **SINGAPORE:** American Express International Inc., Lufthansa German Airlines, Thomas Cook Overseas Ltd.; **SOUTH AFRICA:** Global Tours S. Africa (Pty) Ltd., World Travel Agency (Pty) Ltd.; **SRI LANKA:** Aitken Spence Travels Ltd.; **TAIWAN:** American Express International Inc.; **THAILAND:** Diethelm International Transport Services, Ltd.; **U.A.E.:** Thomas Cook A.L. Rostamini (Pvt) Ltd.

SECOND-CLASS SPACE

The 3 price alternatives that passengers 26 or older have when traveling Eurailpass countries by train are: first-class tickets, Eurailpass, or second-class tickets.

Second-class tickets are very close to 66% of the first-class price. Therefore, the cost of the example itinerary using second-class tickets (and that precludes riding on any TEE trains) comes to about $350—more expensive than traveling first-class and TEE trains with a Eurailpass.

OTHER DISCOUNTS

There are alternative economies to use besides Eurailpass and Eurail Youthpass when traveling Europe by train. These are the special discount tickets, coupons, passes, etc. which various countries issue individually. Details on these appear in this book under the listing of each country.

Some of these discount tickets can be purchased outside Europe. Others may be purchased only in the issuing country itself. Since these regulations change frequently, it is suggested that you first contact the office nearest your residence. Those in the U.S. and Canada are listed here:

AUSTRIA
Austrian Federal Railways
200 E. Randolph Dr., Chicago, Ill. 60601
3440 Wilshire Blvd., Los Angeles, Cal. 90010
1010 Ouest Rue Sherbrooke, Montreal, Que. H3A 2R7
545 Fifth Ave., New York, N.Y. 10017
1007 N.W. 24th Ave., Portland, Ore. 97210
2 Bloor Street East, Toronto, Ont. M4W 1A8
736 Granville St., Vancouver, B.C. V6Z 1J2

BELGIUM
Belgian National Railroads
745 Fifth Ave., New York, N.Y. 10151
5801 Ave. Monkland, Montreal, P.Q. H4A 1G4

FRANCE
French National Railroads
9465 Wilshire Blvd., Beverly Hills, Cal. 90212
11 East Adams St., Chicago, Ill. 60603
2121 Ponce de Leon Blvd., Coral Gables, Fla. 33134
1500 Stanley St., Montreal, P.Q., Canada H3A 1R3
610 Fifth Ave., New York, N.Y. 10020
360 Post St., San Francisco, Cal. 94108
409 Granville St., Vancouver, B.C., Canada B6C 1T2

GREAT BRITAIN
BritRail Travel
333 No. Michigan Ave., Chicago, Ill. 60601
510 W. Sixth St., Los Angeles, Cal. 90014
630 Third Ave., New York, N.Y. 10017
55 Eglington Ave. East, Toronto, Ont. M4P 1G8, Canada
409 Granville St., Vancouver, B.C. V6C 1T2, Canada

GREECE
Greek National Tourist Organization
611 W. 6th St., Los Angeles, Cal. 90017
645 Fifth Ave., New York, N.Y. 10022

HOLLAND
Netherlands National Tourist Office
36 So. Wabash Ave., Chicago, Ill.
437 Madison Ave., New York, N.Y. 10022
605 Market St., San Francisco, Cal. 94105

IRELAND
Irish Tourist Board
230 No. Michigan Ave., Chicago, Ill. 60601
590 Fifth Ave., New York, N.Y. 10036
681 Market St., San Francisco, Cal. 94105
10 King St., Toronto, Ont. M5C 1C3

ITALY
Italian State Railways
765 Route 83, Bensenville, Ill. 60106
15760 Ventura Blvd., Encino, Cal. 91436
2055 Peel St., Montreal, P.Q. H3A 1V4
666 Fifth Ave., New York, N.Y. 10103
13 Balmuto St., Toronto, Ont. M4Y 1W4

LUXEMBOURG
801 Second Ave., New York, N.Y. 10017

DENMARK, FINLAND, ICELAND, NORWAY, SWEDEN
Scandinavian National Tourist Offices
75 Rockefeller Plaza, New York, N.Y. 10019

POLAND
Polish Travel Bureau
500 Fifth Ave., New York, N.Y. 10036

SPAIN
Spanish National Tourist Office
845 N. Mighican Ave., Chicago, Ill. 60611
4800 The Galleria, 5085 Westheimer, Houston, Tex. 70056
665 Fifth Ave., New York, N.Y. 10022
Hypolita & St. George Sts., Saint Augustine, Fla. 32084
1 Hallidie Plaza, San Francisco, Cal. 94102
60 Bloor St. West, Toronto, Ont. M4W 1A1

SWITZERLAND
Swiss National Tourist Office
104 S. Michigan Ave., Chicago, Ill. 60603
608 Fifth Ave., New York, N.Y. 10020
250 Stockton St., San Francisco, Cal. 94108
P.O. Box 215, Commerce Court Postal Station, Toronto, Ont. M5L 1E8

WEST GERMANY
625 Statler Office Bldg., Boston, MA 02116
104 So. Michigan Ave., Chicago, IL 60603
8000 E. Girard Ave., Denver, Col. 80231
1121 Walker St., Houston, TX 77002
520 Broadway, Suite 320, Santa Monica, Cal. 90401
747 Third Ave., New York, N.Y. 10017
1 Hallidie Plaza, San Francisco, Cal. 94102
1290 Bay St., Toronto, Ont. M5R 2C3

EURAILPASS AND EURAIL YOUTHPASS BONUSES

In addition to unlimited train travel, the Eurailpass and Eurail Youthpass provide many free bonuses or reduced prices for boat trips, buses and private railways.

AUSTRIA   Two rack railways: (1) Puchberg am Schneeberg-Hochschneeberg and (2) St. Wolfgang-Schafbergspitze. Two cruises: (1) Lake Wolfgang and (2) Danube, between Passau and Vienna. Reduction of 50% on Lake Constance ships.

BELGIUM   Up to 50% reduction on Europabus lines.

DENMARK   These ferry crossings: Aarhus-Kalundborg, Knudshoved-Halskov, Nyborg-Korsor, Fynshav-Bojden, Rodby Farge-Puttgarden, Helsingor-Helsingborg and Frederikshavn-Goteborg. Reduction of 20% on 4 boat trips: (1) Esberg-Harwich, (2) Esberg-Newcastle, (3) Esberg-Faero Islands, and (4) Copenhagen-Oslo.

FINLAND   Three cruises: (1) Helsinki-Stockholm, (2) Turku-Stockholm, and (3) Turku-Aland Island-Stockholm

FRANCE   Irish Continental Line ferry crossings between LeHavre and Rosslare, also between Cherbourg and Rosslare. Port taxes are extra, payable in French francs. The Digne-Nice rail trip. Up to 50% reduction on Europabus lines.

GERMANY   Two cruises: (1) Rhine (between Dusseldorf and Frankfurt), and (2) Mosel (between Trier and Koblenz). Eurail Youthpass holders must pay an extra charge on Express-steamers. One ferry crossing: Puttgarden to Rodby. Most of the Post/Railroad bus lines, including "Romantic Road" (Wiesbaden-Munich and vice versa) and "Castle Road" (Mannheim-Nurnberg and vice versa). Reduction of 50% on (1) Lubeck-Travemunde-Malmo ferry crossing, (2) cruises on Lake Constance, (3) the Freiburg (Breisgau)-Schauinsland private railroad, and (4) the Garmisch-Partenkirchen-Grainau-Zugspitze private railroad. A 20% reduction on some half-day and full-day excursions out of Munich operated by Oberbayern GmbH. A 10% reduction on Munich city sightseeing tours operated by Oberbayern.

GREECE   The ferry crossing from Patras to Brindisi.

ITALY   The ferry crossing from Brindisi to Patras. About 20% reduction on these 7 boat trips: (1) Naples-Palermo, (2) Naples-Malta, (3) Syracuse-Malta, (4) Genoa-Tunis, (5) Genoa-Alicante, (6) Genoa-Malaga, and (7) crossings to Sardinia. Reverse trips are subject to same reduction. A 30% reduction on the boat trip Venice-Piraeus-Haifa, and vice versa on the Adriatica Line.

WARNING !

Don't be diverted at the Patras or Brindisi railstations from Adriatica or Hellenic Mediterranean Lines (the only ferries that honor Eurailpass) to other ships that charge large fees after deceiving passengers into believing their ships accept Eurailpass, extorting the charges when it is too late for passengers to leave their ferry and go to the other docks. The proper lines charge pass holders $12(U.S.) between June 10 and September 30. Reservations are required when using Eurailpass or Eurail Youthpass.

IRELAND   Irish Continental Line ferry crossings between Rosslare and both LeHavre and Cherbourg. Port taxes are extra, payable in Irish pounds.

NORWAY   A 30% reduction on the boat trip between Kristiansand and Hirtshals.

SPAIN   A 20% reduction on Transmediterranean ships that operate between Algeciras and Tangier, Barcelona, Valencia and Palmas de Mallorca.

SWEDEN   These 5 boat trips: (1) Stockholm-Helsinki, (2) Stockholm-Turku, (3) Stockholm-Aland Islands-Turku, (4) Helsingborg-Helsingor, and (5) Goteborg-Frederikshavn. A 50% reduction on the ferry crossing between Malmo and Lubeck-Travemunde.

SWITZERLAND   Boats on the lakes of Geneva, Luzern, Thun, Brienz, Zurich, Neuchatel, Biel and Murten. Boats on the Rhine (Schaffhausen-Kreuzlingen) and on the Aare (Biel Bienne-Solothurn). A 50% reduction on Lake Constance boats Romanshorn-Friedrichshafen and Rorschach-Lindau.

INTER RAIL CARD

Unlimited second-class train travel for one month. (Example: January 14 to February 13.) Can be purchased only in Europe. Sold only to persons under 26 years old who prove they have resided in the issuing country at least 6 months. The bearer can travel half-fare in the issuing country and free on the railways of the other 20 countries. The validity period begins on the first day the card is issued, and that day must be within 2 months after the card is purchased. The card also allows these discounts on boat trips: 50% on Rhine cruises, 50% Lake Constance, 50% Stockholm-Helsinki and 30% Barcelona-Palma de Mallorca.

Must be paid for in the currency of the country that issues it. The 1983 price in French francs is 1,236FF.

Sold at most railstations in Austria, Belgium, Denmark, Finland, France, Great Britain, Greece, Holland, Hungary, Ireland, Italy, Luxembourg, Morocco, Norway, Portugal, Romania, Spain, Sweden, Switzerland, West Germany and Yugoslavia.

SENIOR INTER RAIL CARD

Sold only to persons 65 or older who prove they have resided in the issuing country for at least 6 months. Can be purchased only in Europe. Unlimited first or second-class train travel for one month. Has same bonuses as the Junior Inter Rail Card. The bearer travels half-fare in the issuing country and free on the railways of the other 16 countries.

Must be paid for in the currency of the country that issues it. The 1984 prices in French francs are: First-class 1,663FF. Second-class 1,109FF.

Sold at most railstations in Austria, Belgium, Denmark, Finland, France, Greece, Holland, Italy, Luxembourg, Norway, Portugal, Romania, Spain, Sweden, Switzerland, West Germany and Yugoslavia, plus the privately-owned Bern-Lotschberg Railway in Switzerland.

STUDENT TRAVEL DISCOUNTS

The ISIC (International Student Identity Card) is a passport to low-cost travel for fulltime students and anyone who graduates within the calendar year: lower air fares, tours, accommodations and travel books, plus reduced or free admission to many museums, theaters, cultural attractions, historical sites, etc. More than a million ISIC are issued every year.

It provides entry to special hotels and restaurants in Europe and Asia for low-cost lodging and meals. All intra-European student charter flights, trains and ships offer discounts of 50% or more to holders of this card.

Developed and regulated by the International Student Travel Conference, the card carries the owner's photo. In the U.S.A., it is available through Student Travel Services and hundreds of high schools and college/university campuses authorized by the Council on International Educational Exchange, with offices at:

205 E. 42nd St.
New York, NY 10017

1093 Broxton Ave.
Los Angeles, CA 90024

2511 Channing Way
Berkeley, CA 94704

312 Sutter St.
San Francisco, CA 94108

49, rue Pierre Charron
Paris 75008, France

In recent years, the fee for an ISIC has been $6.00(U.S.). The 1984 ISIC is valid from October 1, 1983 through December 31, 1984.

A free 68-page catalog detailing the services is available before purchasing the card. After buying the card, students receive with it a list of worldwide discounts and benefits.

Chapter 3

HOW TO PLAN A RAIL INTINERARY

There are 4 dimensions to every train tour: the number of days one can allot, interesting destinations, scenic routes, and riding on special trains that are in themselves an attractive travel experience.

Whenever time and budget permit, the minimum trip to Europe should be 23 days. That includes the day you fly away and the day you fly back. Out of the 21 remaining days, you can figure that what is left of your first day in Europe (after going from the airport to your hotel) is good for little more than recovering from the combination whammy of travel fatigue and time change. Very few people are immune to the temporary disablement of jet lag, and most travelers are well advised to go to bed and postpone any appreciable activity until the second day in Europe. That leaves only 20 active days for sightseeing, and it's difficult to really see even a fraction of Europe in that time.

We recommend staying a minimum of 2 or 3 nights in most cities you visit, with only occasional one-nighters mixed in the itinerary. Even the sturdiest develop a psychosis when they spend too many consecutive nights each in a different hotel room. Besides, if you travel mostly by day as we suggest in order to see the countryside and have some opportunity to visit with fellow passengers, you will arrive in a city late in the day. If you leave there the next morning, you certainly are not going to see much in that city.

On a 2-night basis, you can cover 10-11 different cities during your 21 full days in Europe. Reducing a trip to 14 days means reducing the number of cities where you stop to 5 or 6. If 14 days is your limit, the 15-day Eurailpass and some fast footwork will still let you have a happy tour and cover a great deal of Europe.

After deciding on the length of time one has to tour, the next stop in itinerary planning is to pick the places to be visited, and most people have several cities in mind, usually more than time, energy and distance will allow.

The common-sense approach is to consult a map and visualize from it what is practical and what is impractical in putting together a list of places to see. Part of this narrowing-down process depends of course on what interests you the most. Every hamlet in Europe has some art, but if it's the greatest masterpieces you want to see, you go to cities such as Paris and Florence, not to Avignon or Oslo. If your interest is Alpine scenery, you are going to concentrate on Zurich and Salzburg, not on Barcelona or Copenhagen.

Knowing the travel time between each point on your itinerary is essential unless you are indifferent to 15-hour journeys that bring you into a destination after Midnight. The timetables in this book give you that information on more than 9,000 different rail trips.

At this point, you have determined how many days you will be in Europe, where you want to go, and where you can go in that time. You should now consider the combination of using special trains along with the most rewarding routes.

For example, the journey from Paris to Marseille can be made on any one of a dozen ordinary trains instead of riding on a high-speed TGV. A traveler has the same choice on many railway routes all over the world, between riding a commonplace, slow train or having an encounter with extraordinary rail travel. All the information on ''Europe's Greatest Trains'' is provided in Chapter 7.

RESERVATIONS—HOTEL AND TRAIN

Once you have composed the elements of days, cities, trains and routes, you are ready to consider whether you want to reserve hotels in advance.

When traveling to places we haven't been either before or recently, we rely on recommendations by friends who enjoyed particular hotels recently and whose tastes are similar to ours. The ''recently'' qualification is important, because a hotel's quality changes from time to time. We do not recommend hotels or restaurants. Management of both change (and quality along with it) between our annually-revised editions. It is always best to consult a competent travel agent who has current input from clients recently returning.

As in most other things, there is a great deal of luck connected with traveling. We prefer to maximize the odds in favor of our comfort and security when we travel and, as most travel writers urge readers to do, we reserve hotel space well in advance. We also reserve train seats whenever we want to be on a particular train on a certain date.

The objection to such reservations has a great deal of merit. It is that you cannot be a footloose, carefree vagabond, lingering where unexpected attractions are discovered and making impetuous detours as the spirit moves one or abruptly departing sooner than you had planned to do when someplace fails to come up to expectations.

The sturdier one is, physically and psychologically, the stronger that argument is. There is no question that for those of us forced by the circumstances of daily life to lead ordered routines, there are few lawful activities that offer as great an opportunity to achieve freedom from a structured existence as does traveling by train.

While not quite infinite, the random choices one can make spontaneously are considerable. The feature that many people find irresistible about European trains is how easily one can decide an hour after starting a ride to one destination to leave that train and head elsewhere. Depending on how strongly this motive moves you, how fundamentally lucky you are in most matters and what you are willing and able to endure, advance hotel reservations may not be important for you.

On the other hand, if you ever have played an entire night of poker without holding one winning hand, or if you arrive in Copenhagen on the opening day of a World Bank Conference (no room within 20 miles) and your next stop was Paris where the International Motor Salon opened on the day of your arrival and the largest ($250,000) horse race on the Continent was being run the next day (no room within 30 miles), and your next stop was Dijon where the first 2 hotels you phoned ahead to were sold-out even though nothing special was happening that October week in Dijon, you might want to weigh the whole proposition.

From May through early October, European and non-European tourists pack all classes of hotels in leading European cities. Trade shows and business conventions pick up the slack instantly in September, October, March and April. A hotel in Bordeaux (not Paris or Rome, mind you) wrote us on July 13 that it was booked for the 2 nights we had requested: October 2 and 3 !

If you travel Europe without advance room reservations from March through October, it is wise to arrive in your destination city early in the day. Rooms available because of no-shows or last-minute cancellations frequently are taken before mid-afternoon.

Upon arriving without a hotel reservation, go at once to the tourist accommodations desk in the train station. For a fee of 50¢ to $1.00, one of its employees will phone hotels and do his best to find you a room that comes close to your specifications. In certain cities (Amsterdam, Bergen, Brussels, etc.), this convenient service is not offered at the station but can be found at the city tourist office, sometimes only across from the railstation, sometimes quite a distance from it.

In the peak Summer touring months you will find long lines and if, as is usually the case, you stay is brief, you will have to devote previous sightseeing time to obtaining a room.

When traveling in groups of 2 or more, this ploy is effective: one person remains at the station guarding the luggage while the other canvasses the area near the station to find a room. Many non-Europeans are unaware that stations even in the smallest cities have waiting rooms with comfortable, upholstered chairs. If you follow this system, be sure to use the shelter of these waiting rooms. All over Europe, you will find many hotels within a radius of 2 or 3 blocks from the railstation.

A third system has been used successfully by many—to stay in the suburbs and not even attempt to find a hotel room in major cities, provided the suburb is unlinked by train with the city you want to tour.

Pick a town of moderate size about 30-45 minutes train travel time away from a major Metropolis.

Your second consideration is whether to reserve train seats.

Reservations for seats on Europe's greatest trains (see Chapter 7) can be made 2 months in advance, and many Europeans grab spaces on them soon after they become reservable. Casual tourists discover a few days before they want to travel on a special train that it is completely sold-out.

Reservations are mandatory on many of the best trains. That is why we recommend reserving seats even before you arrive in the countries you plan to travel. The worldwide offices of French National Railroads, German Federal Railroad, Italian State Railways and Swiss Federal Railways will obtain seat reservations for special trains within their own countries and in many other (but not all) European countries. Their North American offices are listed in Chapter 2.

Before you pay for a Eurailpass, you or your travel agent should ask the seller to confirm that his or her office will obtain all the seat reservations in all the Eurailpass countries you plan to travel, on those trains which offer reserved seats. If the seller refuses to do this, check with other offices (listed in Chapter 2) that sell Eurailpass. Don't buy your Eurailpass until you find a seller who will obtain all your seat reservations.

It is advisable to have the office that issues you the Eurailpass cable your reservation requests to Europe. The fee for this is $1.00 to $2.00 per reservation. This can result in your obtaining seats which otherwise might have been sold to others if your request had been sent by mail.

If, on the other hand, you wait to reserve train space at each departure station, keep in mind that at most European stations you must get in one line for a ticket and in a different line for a seat reservation. If you have a Eurailpass (described in Chapter 2), you eliminate having to wait in the ticket line, often a long wait.

As a matter of fact, you face long waits in 5 different lines — and part of the trick of making the most of your limited time is to avoid standing in any, and hopefully all, of these lines: information, ticket purchase, seat reservation, hotel accommodation and baggage checkroom.

We will cover how you can avoid needing information in the ''Timetables'' section of Chapter 4. If you use Eurailpass (Chapter 2), you never need to buy a ticket and therefore completely omit the time wasted standing in the ticket purchase line. The solution to the hotel accommodation line, of course, is to make those reservations before you leave home. The baggage check-room problem is discussed in Chapter 5.

There is a way to *reduce* the amount of time spent in either the ticket or seat reservation lines. These lines are far shorter Monday-Thursday than they are on the weekend, when the natives are traditionally restless, and in mid-morning, rather than during the lunch hours or at early evening in the height of the commuter rush hours. During the mid-June to mid-September tourist season, it is often advantageous to have the hotel concierge or the one who runs your pensione get your reservation for you from someone they know at the station.

If you don't make reservations before leaving home and wait to do so until you arrive in the country you are going to tour, be sure to do it as much in advance as possible, preferably upon your arrival in the departure city. Requirements for reservations vary from country to country and, within a country, from city to city. In Italy, for example, reservations cannot be made less than 2 hours before a departure in some cities. Milan requires 3 hours notice. Rome requires 5 hours notice.

Say your trip is New York to Paris, then train to Geneva and train from Geneva to Rome. Make the Paris-Geneva reservation your first day in Paris, and make the Geneva-Rome reservation a few minutes after you arrive at the Geneva depot.

This advice does not mean you *must* have seat reservations. They are *required* only on TEE and a few other trains. However, anyone traveling in peak tourist months without reserved space will probably make the trip standing in the aisle and being brushed-up against approximately every 30 seconds by passengers ambling up and down the corridor. Keep in mind that Europeans can, and do, reserve train seats 2 months in advance.

We rode a very ordinary train from Bordeaux to Tours on an October

Monday morning. It was completely sold-out.

If, as we urge you to do in Chapter 5, you eat your train meals in your compartment rather than in the train dining-room, there is something else you can and should do when you make your seat reservation. Specify the window seat. On most European trains these are the only seats that have a fold-out table. Moreover, you see the sights better from a window seat. In some compartments, the seats next to the sliding door also have a fold-out table.

Another variation in seat reservations is that on nearly all European trains you can reserve seats in a compartment in which smoking is either prohibited or permitted. Depending on what your preference is, this can make a great deal of different in enjoying your trip.

And still another reservation to keep in mind is specifying on which *side* of the train you want to be seated. Often there is a decided sightseeing advantage on one side and a corresponding disadvantage on the alternate side. Obviously, if you are traveling along the Riviera, the view of the Mediterranean is 100 times better on the left side if you are traveling West, and on the right side if your route is going East.

After logic tells you which side of the train offers the best view, the first step is to inquire while making your seat reservation if there is seating on that side. If so, ask for seats accordingly.

Reservation clerks in many European cities speak little or no English. It will save you much time and insure against getting an incorrect reservation if you hand the clerk a note indicating your destination, departure time and day of departure. But be sure to follow the European custom of showing the day of the month first, followed by the number of the month. In Europe, July 8 is 8/7. If you wanted to take a train to Milan, leaving at 1:50 PM on July 8, your note would read "Milan—13:50—8/7".

Finally, here are 7 great tips to keep in mind. Having made a seat reservation, when you leave your compartment to go to the W.C., dining car or merely to stretch, leave some object on your seat—newspaper, hat, something—to inhibit seat-grabbers from settling down in your space during your absence. While it is true that the conductor will aid you in removing an interloper, finding the conductor, explaining the problem and using his intervention is somewhat more bothersome than simply preventing the event.

Do not waste time trying to make a seat reservation for a train trip within Belgium, Holland, Luxembourg or Switzerland. Those countries sell seat reservations only for rides going from them into another country. However, finding a seat on trains of those countries is not a problem except on peak travel days.

Next, on a business day even though the reservation clerk claims all seats on a certain train are taken, you can nevertheless occasionally hop aboard and find an empty seat. This is due to the custome of many European business men, when undecided as to which train they are taking or on which day they are making a trip, to make several advance reservations so as to cover all bases—and then forfeit their reservation fee on all trains other than the one they finally do take. This practice accounts for some seats being marked "reserved" which are not used.

If traveling without seat reservations, be careful you do not take a reserved seat while all the unreserved ones are being occupied.

Check the seat chart outside each compartment before you sit down. If the rightful owners claim your seat later, you may have to stand during the entire ride.

If the required advance time for making a seat reservation has run out, seek the conductor and, in your most charming manner, tell him what your destination is and ask him to help you find a seat. As a class, conductors are remarkably courteous and cooperative and many we have observed welcome the opportunity to use their authority constructively.

Never, never discard a train ticket until after your trip has been completed and you have left the arrival station. You will frequently ride a train for hours without being asked to show a ticket or pass. Then, after you get off the train you discover you are required to show your ticket or pass at the exit of the arrival station. If you have thrown yours away, you will end up having to buy a second one. Best bet is to always hold onto your ticket, whether or not a conductor checks it.

PREPARATION FOR AUTUMN TOURING

One thing that is nearly always overlooked in itinerary planning is to prepare in advance for one very important contingency connected with traveling off-season. If you travel Europe anytime after early September—and Fall is outstanding for touring Europe—you'll find that English-language city sightseeing tours are discontinued as the volume of American tourists decline, particularly in places such as Avignon, Verona, Rouen, Tours, etc.

Autumn travelers can solve that problem by taking advantage of the fact that nearly every city in Europe, even a hamlet such as Honfleur, has a tourist office which will give you a comprehensive folder that includes a fine city map, an interesting description of principal things to see and often a suggested 2 or 3-hour walking tour that allows a visitor to find on his own the worthwhile historic sites, museums, churches, palaces and all the other local highspots he would have been shown on the discontinued motorcoach sightseeing tour.

The only hitch is that by early September many city tourist offices run out of the current year's supply of these useful folders. To insure against the disappointment of arriving somewhere and finding that neither a city tour nor printed material to use in lieu of a tour is available, there is a precaution you can take.

In the early part of the year, write to the cities you plan to visit and ask them while their supply is still good to mail you a copy of all literature and tourist maps they have, and specify you want the English-language (or whatever your preference) version, since this maerial is usually printed in several languages.

Then, if you arrive in a town that Fall after the last bus tour of the season, you're all set to see the sights without a guide, and at your own leisurely pace.

Simply address your request to "Tourist Office". You'll be surprised how much this easy preparation will add to your travel enjoyment.

Chapter 4

DON'T MISS THE TRAIN!

MULTI-STATION CITIES

Determine beforehand whether your departure or transfer city has more than one railstation. If so, next make sure that the train on which you are going to continue your trip will depart from the same station at which you are arriving. The easiest way to do that is to consult Thomas Cook International Timetable. If you are making a transfer, then be certain that there is adequate time to get from one station to the other in the following European cities with more than one railstation:

Antwerp	Dublin	Lodz	Prague
Athens	Dunkerque	London	Ramsgate
Barcelona	Essen	Lyon	Rome
Basle	Exeter	Madrid	Rotterdam
Belfast	Folkestone	Malmo	San Sebastian
Belgrade	Geneva	Manchester	Seville
Berlin	Genoa	Marseille	Southampton
Bilbao	Glasgow	Milan	Stockholm
Boulogne	Halsingborg	Moscow	Tilbury
Brussels	Hamburg	Munich	Tours
Bucharest	Harwich	Naples	Turin
Budapest	Hendaye	Newhaven	Venice
Calais	Irun	Oporto	Vienna
Casablanca	Le Havre	Orleans	Warsaw
Cologne	Leningrad	Oslo	Weymouth
Como	Liege	Paris	Wiesbaden
Copenhagen	Lisbon	Portsmouth	Zurich
Dover	Liverpool		

As can be seen from the preceding list, there are 70 European cities which have 2 or more railroad stations. Immediately upon *arriving* in any of these multi-station cities, find out from which station your train departs for your next destination. Do not rely on getting that information an hour or so before your departure from someone such as your hotel clerk or taxi or bus driver.

TIMETABLES

The venerable Thomas Cook Continental Timetable has been published since 1873 (except from 1939 to 1945). Its younger sibling, the Overseas Timetable, was started in 1981, prompted by the interest in train travel outside Europe that had been generated many years earlier by Eurail® Guide. Both timetables are published in England.

The Continental Timetable (European schedules) is supposed to be published the first day of each month but sometimes misses the mark. The Overseas Timetable, covering the rest of the world, is issued every other month, starting with January.

In addition to train, boat and bus schedules, these publications also provide information on types of food service and sleeping accommodations offered. Their extensive array of symbols for such services and other information are translated into ordinary language at the start of each edition, under "Explanation of Signs".

A key item that even many experienced users of Cooks have failed to note is Table #1000, which lists hundreds of resorts that are not situated on a railway in its timetables. This special list gives the nearest railstation to such resorts, and the distance from that station to the resort. Included in Table #1000 are such places as Delphi (121 miles by road from Athens), Ile de Levant (9 miles by ferry from Le Lavandou) and Offenbach am Main (6 miles by suburban railway from Frankfurt).

Summer European train schedules appear in the June, July, August and September "Continental Timetable" issues. The latter contains an advance Winter supplement. Similarly, the February through May issues contain an advance Summer service supplement.

Both publications can be obtained in North America from Dept. "E", Forsyth Travel Library, P.O. Box 2975, Shawnee Mission, KS. 66201, or by telephoning Dept. "E" at (913) 384-0496 and charging the purchase against a Visa or Master Charge credit card at a service charge of $1.00. Add $2.00(U.S.) for postage on each copy of either timetable that is to be mailed to Canada.

A copy of the "Continental Timetable" costs $16.95(U.S.), postage included. The "Overseas Timetable" costs $20.95, postage included. Cook's "Rail Map of Europe" costs $7.95(U.S.), postage included. A combined purchase of the "Continental" and the "Rail Map" costs $22.95, postage included.FTL has an extensive list of travel publications, maps of all countries and hundreds of cities, atlases, etc.

Because many countries do not offer their own timetables, or run short of them, Cooks is valuable for carrying along on a trip as well as for studying at home while planning an itinerary. Numerous readers tell us that having a copy while touring allows them to make impromptu changes in travel plans on the spur of the moment.

As Cooks says in each edition, the services shown are subject to alteration, and travelers should re-check departure times upon arriving in each station. Our standard train travel procedure upon arriving anywhere is to first provide for shelter, when we have not made advance reservations. The second item we dispose of is deciding what train we are taking to the next city on our itinerary. Third, we make our seat reservation then and there for that departure. Having done this, we are now carefree for the balance of our time in that city.

A "European Timetable for Railway Enthusiasts" lists dozens of "fun railways" in Britain and on the European Continent, including many cable cars, rope railways, horse trams and steam-engine trains. It is published by Schweers+Wall, Lothringerstr. 66, D-5100 Aachen 1, West Germany.

The "Eurail Timetable-Horaire Eurail-Eurail Fahrplan" contains most connections betwen important cities in Western Europe. It is sold at major European railstations.

There are 3 other timetables, specialized and far more condensed than Cooks, that you may find useful. All are distributed free. They can be obtained from travel agents and those railroad offices which sell Eurailpass. One is the very useful 24-page mini-folder put out by French National Railroads, called "Les Trains d'Affairs" ("businessman's trains", not as romantic as it sounds !). Containing May-September schedules, it has timetables for many trains that connect French cities both with each other and with cities in other countries.

A second folder, 34 pages and also very tiny, issued by the French company that runs sleeper cars (Compagnie Internationale des Wagons-Lits), has 40 timetables of trains providing wagons-lits service throughout Europe, including Greece, Hungary, Turkey and Yugoslavia. It is published in both a Summer (June through September) and a Winter (October through May) edition.

The third is a 272-page Intercity timetable issued by the German Federal Railroad.

In most European countries, a Summer timetable goes into effect on the last Sunday of May, remaining in effect until and including the last Saturday in September.

Winter schedules usually start on the Sunday following the last Saturday of September and run until and including the Saturday preceding the last Sunday of May of the following year.

British timetables differ from the Continental pattern. Summer timetables for British rail service begin on the first Monday of May. Changes occur on various dates, first in October and then again in January.

Unless designated otherwise, the departure and arrival times given in this book are for the Summer tourist season and apply to trips that will be made from late May to late September.

CAR-SLEEPER EXPRESS SERVICE

Europe's "Car-Sleeper Express Service" becomes more popular every year. You can sleep in a couchette or sleeping compartment on the same train that carries your auto...or you can ship your car ahead on an "Auto Express" while you ride on another train, and find your car waiting for you at your destination.

Started by French National Railroads in 1957, this service is now offered as well by Austria, Belgium, Britain, Holland, Italy, Spain and West Germany.

It links cities in those countries and also in Portugal, Switzerland and Yugoslavia. In recent years, it annually has moved 500,000 people and more than 160,000 cars.

TRAIN-SPLITTING

How can one fail to admire the superhuman efficiency of Europe's vast international rail systems? Thousands of trains daily transport millions upon millions of people and yet achieve a dependability factor that is nearly perfect. An important part of this remarkable capacity is the technique of avoiding unnecessary duplication of personnel and equipment by the methods of switching cars and timing transfers so that when one must take 2 or more trains to get from one place to another the time between each segment of a trip is very brief.

The foreign tourist is inclined to wrongly regard these positive factors as an undue bother when, actually, only a minimum effort and preparation is required in order to have the advantage of travel speed and flexibiity along with reasonable ticket prices.

This is how simple it is to prevent a mix-up. Before you leave the station to go to the track, find out if the car in which you will be starting your journey is going all the way to your destination without being switched to some other train or if you must transfer from this train to another train en route to your destination.

If your car is to be switched to another train, find out the name of the city where the switching will occur, the time it will take place, and the name of the stop just prior to the switching point.

Next, you're at the correct track, your train is ready to board, and your last step is to get onto the correct car. Where a train originally consists of cars that are eventually going to different destinations, each car is clearly marked with the name of the city where it originated and the name of the city where it will terminate. Frequently, the sign will also designate, as the example below does, some of the cities en route where stops will be made.

VENEZIA

Bologna — Firenze

ROMA

This sign shows that the car began in Venice, stops at Bologna and Florence, and terminates in Rome. Next to the steps leading up into a car, either the numeral "1" or "2" appears, designating first-class or second-class seats. You may find an entirely first-class car coupled to an entirely second-class car, both cars marked with the same origin-destination sign. Or, a single car may be marked "1" at one end and "2" at the other end, indicating that part of this car is first-class and part is second-class.

A car change can occur while you are several cars away from your seat (and from your baggage, since it usually stays either in your compartment or at the end of your car). You may have so little time to get back to your car that you end up going one direction while your suitcases are heading, without you, for the place you had intended to go.

If you have determined in advance when and where your car is being switched and have also boarded the correct car, you are prepared for the change by being in your car when the change occurs. The following story illustrates the hazard we want you to avoid and may induce you to follow some practical recommendations we offer at the end of the vignette.

An officer in the U.S. Army Transportation Corps, who is an expert on both military and personal travel, Lt. Col. Will B. Allanson, wrote us about an experience he suffered when he was a novice: "I and my family had just arrived in France, for our first time in Europe, in the Summer of 1964. Within 5 days of our arrival, my boss asked me to make a busines trip to an army installation in Germany. Thinking it would be nice to let the family catch an initial glimpse of Europe too, I bought tickets for them and off we went from Paris on a rapide headed for Frankfurt.

"At about 11:30, the train stopped at the little town of Bar-le-Duc. My children were beginning to get hungry, and there was no dining-car. Leaning out of the window of our car, the last car on the train, I spied a sandwich hawker up near the locomotive. I jogged up the track to him, bought some sandwiches and, not being certain how long the train would remain stopped, I boarded it near the locomotive. As I started walking through the train, heading back toward my car, the train started up.

"I got about as far as what had been the middle of the train . . . and there was no more train ! It has been split.

"All I knew was that I was heading off towards an unknown direction, without my family, at approximately 80 mph.

"I had done just about everything wrong there was to do. First, of course, was leaving my car. Next, I had most of the travel money on me, leaving my wife practically penniless. But she had the trump¢she had my ticket and my passport.

"Well, my wife was on her way to Frankfurt, heading Northeast, while I was heading due East to Nancy. I borrowed a timetable from the conductor and figured out that I could get off in Nancy and from there take another train to Metz. In Metz, I could then catch a train that would be following my wife's train by 2 hours.

"I did this and, in Metz, found my wife and kiddies (who had gotten off their train to wait for me) practically in a pool of tears. Other passengers in my wife's compartment were Frenchmen who, alarmed at my not returning, had guessed what had happened and urged my wife to get off in Metz and wait for me there."

This experience taught Col. Allanson these rules: Don't stray from your car while stopped in a station. When 2 or more people are traveling together, each should carry his own money, his own passport and his own ticket, or Eurailpass. On our travels, we divvy-up not only U.S. one-dollar bills and the currency of the country we're in, but we also carry separate traveler's checks in each name.

TRAIN-CHANGING

Frequently you will find that while you cannot take a train directly to some point, it is quite easy to get there by using a series of 2 or more trains. And in many cases the connections are very convenient, so that you change from one train to another with only a short waiting period at the transfer station. For example, there is no direct train from Zurich to popular Locarno, but the Zurich-Milan train arrives in Bellinzona at 12:43, and a train for Locarno departs Bellinzona 5 minutes later, at 12:48.

The track for the Bellinzona-Locarno train is next to the trck on which you arrive from Zurich, making this change effortless. Even if the Zurich-Milan train is running a few minutes late—and you will be amazed how rarely trains in Western Europe are even slightly off schedule—your walk from one train to another on this connection is about 10 feet, and they will hold a local train such as the Bellinzona-Locarno one for you to make a train change when the principal train is running late.

On the other hand, international trains from eastern countries (Turkey, Greece, Yugoslavia, etc.) usually arrive late due to delays at border-crossings.

The problem in train-chainging for which you should prepare, by being ready to step off the first train as soon as it pulls into the transfer station, is that if the transfer station is a large one you may find you are arriving on Track #2 and departing from Track #21, a considerable distance and invariably involving first descending into the underground walkway that connects all tracks, passing through it, and then climbing up the steps leading to your departure track. This transfer problem is compounded if your first train arrives late and the second train is an express train which cannot detain its scheduled departure time.

Normally, your first train will arrive on schedule, and you have more than enough time to make the change. However, it is best to inquire on board the first train from its conductor the number of the track on which you are arriving and the number of the track from which your departing train leaves and also to be ready at the exit door of your arriving train some minutes before it pulls into the transfer point.

The word for "track" in Europe is: Gleis (Austria, Germany and Switzerland), Sppor (Holland and Belgium, which also uses Voie), Spor (Norway), Spart (Sweden), Quai (France), Binario (Italy), Anden (Spain), Voie (Luxembourg), and Perron (Denmark).

Most train stops in Europe are efficiently very brief, 2 or 3 minutes. This is one of the reasons you can go from place to place so rapidly on European trains. Where a stop is fairly generous, say 20 minutes or more, it is often because some car on your train is being swtiched to another train and possibly also to another track in that station.

Unwary passengers are apt to get out of the train at a stop and wander away, discovering too late that their train has left without them ! When we have the urge to stretch our legs, get some fresh air and look at the trackside activity, we never go more than a few feet away from the door of the train car. That way, if our car is being switched or the stop is merely a momentary one, we can jump back aboard.

Chapter 5

VALUABLE TRAIN TRAVEL TIPS

We have included in this chapter the many facts we wish we had known when we first traveled by train many years ago. They will make your journeys easier and happier.

DAY OR NIGHT

There are some advantages to traveling by night train. You can hop from one place to another without sacrificing daytime activities in either the departure city or the arrival city. Also, the holder of a Eurailpass (by going at night in a regular sitting compartment, not in an extra-fare couchette or sleeping compartment) can make a substantial contribution to a budget trip by dispensing with room rent.

On some trains the seats in the regular sitting compartments can be adjusted so that you can get your seat and the one facing you to either come together or nearly meet, and many who are fortunate enough to be in a compartment that is not full are able to stretch out, using the facing seat. This is the crafty technique for eliminating room rental at night that many students and other economy prone tourists have used successfully. However, if the seat opposite you has another passenger, both of you are going to spend the night sitting up.

The offsetting drawbacks to taking a night train, however, are considerable. The best way of meeting and conversing with Europeans and tourists from other parts of the world is to be on a train, but that opportunity is slim when you travel at night. And equally important, you miss the scenery en route.

Then, too, if you are in a generally excited state when you travel and don't sleep well on trains, that's another negative to weigh.

Train sleeping accommodations vary from one European country to another, but generally they consist of second-class Couchette, first-class Couchette, Tourist and first-class Wagons-Lit.

In second-class Couchette, you have one of the 6 berths in your compartment (2 vertical rows of 3 berths each). You are provided a blanket encased in a sheet-bag and a pillow. There is no way to tuck the blanket in, it just slides around during the night. You can stretch out, but you may not undress.

First-Class Couchette is a berth in a compartment with 4 berths (2 rows of 2 berths each). Problem: the first-class Couchettes are so rare you not only won't find one, you probably will never meet someone who did !

Wagons-Lit are available in these 3 choices: Single (accommodating one passenger and comparable to the American railroad bedroom), Double (accommodating 2 persons, similar to the American double railroad bedroom), and Special (which accommodates one passenger and is similar to the American railroad duplex bedroom). There are very few Specials.

Tourist is a compartment accommodating 2 or 3 passengers and is second class.

All sleeping facilities cost a supplemental charge over and above a first or second-class ticket. And, these extra charges are *not* included in the Eurailpass. The supplemental charge for a single Wagons-Lit berth in a 2-berth compartment from Paris to Nice is about $50(U.S.) per person in 1981. The extra charge for either a first-class or second-class Couchette berth on this trip (and, strangely, on all overnight train trips in Western Europe) is $13(U.S.) per person.

If you survive the intrusions of the customs officers and conductors, and the vibrations, and you don't mind missing the scenery and camaraderie that goes with daytime travel, you can absolutely count on being awakened sometime between 2:00 AM and 5:00 AM by the voice of a stationmaster bellowing over the public address system at some stations where your train stops along the way.

If we have not yet discouraged you from night travel, ponder this final fact: not one TEE train travels overnight. These marvelous luxury trains are all tucked-away in their station houses before Midnight, getting a good rest.

EATING ON TRAINS

Food in train dining cars is expensive, and the choice is limited. On many TEE trains the lunch is a fixed menu, very good and very caloric, and costs $15(U.S.) to $20 per person. On other trains, the food is adequate quality and also high-priced.

Both budget travelers and many of those who can afford the meals served on trains buy their food at a market or delicatessen (ah, those great French charcuteries !) before they get on the train¢ranging from a hunk of cheese and some bread to a really sensational assortment of salads, meats, pates, fruits and wine.

Before we made the 12-hour ride from Copenhagen to Amsterdam, we bought a dozen, delicious smorre-bord sandwiches a block from the Copenhagen station. The variety included shrimp, ham, chicken and beef, all garnished with tasty cucumbers, asparagus, tomatoes, etc. We ate some of them for lunch and the others for dinner that day. Total cost, 4 meals, 2 persons: $10(U.S.). And we had the convenience of eating when we felt hungry rather than when we could get a table in the dining-car, where lunch and dinner for the 2 of us in that non-TEE dining-car would have cost us over $35.

On the trip from Dijon to Geneva, we feasted on 5 different salads and pates we bought for $6.00 in the supermarket at the big department store in Dijon where we shopped an hour before train time. On another trip, a charcuterie across from the station in Tours was the source for a delightful $5.00 assortment of meat, olives, salads, cheese, bread and custard that 2 of us had for lunch on the way to Rouen.

Some TEE trains such as the Paris to Brussels "Brabant" depart shortly before Noon and arrive in mid-afternoon. Others, like the Paris to Strasbourg "Kleber" start in late afternoon and cut across the dinner-hour. On many of these schedules, you must reserve a seat in the dining-car for the entire trip if you want lunch or dinner.

The meals are larger and heavier than we want, particularly at Noon, and the odor of cooked food for a whole trip is unpleasant to us. We much prefer on such 3-4 hour runs either to wait until we reach our destination and eat a late lunch (or dinner) after arriving there, or to bring your own food onto the train and eat when we are hungry and in our compartment.

If you find the features of "picnicking" attractive, you can ask your hotel or pensione to pack a lunch for you, or you can purchase food either at a store near the station, in a restaurant at the station, from a food market inside the station or, along the way, from vendors that push carts up and down the track at many station stops. Not only is the latter the most inferior food, but our experience is that the train always moves out just as the vendor rolls his cart toward our window.

You will find restaurants and food stores located in many principal railstations. Food stores in the Copenhagen, Stuttgart, Vienna and Zurich railstations offer meat, cheeses, salads, etc. that are excellent.

Whatever your source of bring-along food, don't forget the note in our chapter on "Reservations" to reserve the window-seat, with its convenient fold-out table.

If you train food, make sure before you start the trip that the train you are taking has meal service. You can check this in the Eurail® Guide timetable footnotes and confirm it at the railstation.

BAGGAGE

The criticism we hear most often about rail travel in Europe concerns the problems of storing and handling suitcases. Don't count on being able to get a porter. Many small cities don't have them. Nearly all the large cities with porters have too few. Some stations provide self-service carts, but the stations which do so don't have enough of them at peak times.

An effective procedure if you travel in pairs is for one of you to guard your luggage while the other hurries toward the station to find a cart and returns to the track with it.

When boarding a train, you want to avoid the difficulty of hauling your luggage down the narrow corridors of several cars. Before your train arrives, examine the train diagram on the platform. Sequence of cars and the platform location for each car are shown for all long-distance trains. Then place yourself and your luggage at the correct site for boarding your car.

On some trains, there is a storage area for luggage at one or at both ends of the car. On most trains, you have to store your baggage on a rack above your seat. The racks are very high. Lifting a 30-pound (or heavier) weight above one's head can be a physical strain for the elderly, those who have a physical disability or even for an everage healthy person who weighs less than 140 poundsᶜwhich covers most women.

In some compartments the seat construction is such that a small suitcase can be stored under the seats.

For these reasons, it is much better to travel with 2 small, relatively lightweight suitcases per person than with one monstrous case. The small ones are easier to lift, and there's a better chance of being able to store them on the floor under the seat.

Some trains have a baggage car. Using it is always inconvenient and, although the charge is fairly small, more expensive than having your cases with you in your own car or in your compartment. When your bag is in the baggage car, you don't have access to its contents. Also, you may have to wait up to 30 minutes for your cases to be unloaded if they happen to be in the rear of the baggage car.

Waiting for cases to be unloaded, in turn, delays you in getting to the room reservation desk at the tourist accommodation desk inside the depot—a delay that can cost you getting a decent room that night, since every minute counts in obtaining an available room during peak travel days. Waiting at the baggage car also delays you in getting into what is often a very long line for taxis.

We were riding on the crack Settebello, where it is mandatory to have your luggage in the baggage car. Shortly before arriving at the Milan destination, we strolled down the length of the train, passing through the baggage car as we did so. In the baggage car, a passenger was paying the porter several dollars.

When the train finally reached Milan, and we were outside the baggage car with 60 other people, trying to get our luggage, we then understood the transaction we had observed earlier. The suitcases of the tipping passenger had been placed in advance at the door of the baggage car so that these cases were the first to be unloaded. He had his suitcases a moment after the train stopped. It was 25 minutes later when the last suitcase had been unloaded.

In the interim, some passengers who were trying to make an imminent flight at the Milan airport became so frantic to get their luggage that they had climbed onto the baggage car and began fighting with the baggage clerk.

While some trains equipped with baggage cars require you to store your luggage in them, on other trains it is optional. When that is the case, always keep your luggage with you and avoid using the baggage car.

Another luggage problem is storing suitcases at a railroad station, both necessary and convenient when you want to avoid being burdened either upon arriving, while you search for lodging, or when departing if, as often happens, you must give up your room several hours before your train leaves and you want to sightsee in that interval. Very savvy travelers obtain a locker in the station the night before their departure so as to be sure of having the use of one the following morning.

Although there are baggage check-rooms at nearly all major railstations, using a check-room instead of a rental locker eats up precious time you could have used more pleasantly and productively because there frequently are long lines both when you leave your luggage and then again when you are claiming it. If you use check-rooms instead of rental lockers, be sure to leave yourself adequate time prior to your train's departure to retrieve your suitcases.

The most convenient and safest method of storing luggage is to place it in a 24-hour rental locker. Unfortunately, the lockers present their own set of problems. Several European stations we have checked-out have too few lockers. Every Summer, many travelers report this to be particularly true of Amsterdam.

Often during recent Summers in Amsterdam and other places, travelers lined up for hours waiting for a locker to become available. Furthermore, rental lockers in European stations are usually in 2 sizes. If you are carrying both a small and large case, you may find several small lockers available but not be able to locate one large locker. Again, we urge you to carry small suitcases.

Another wise maneuver is to have small change on hand for each destination. Remember, the lockers in each country are geared to the local coins. You cannot use a kroner for a locker in France, or a franc for one in Denmark!

CUSTOMS PROCEDURES AND DUTY-FREE PURCHASES

Items at "duty-free" shops in major airports are not always a bargain. Often, the merchandise in a duty-free shop is priced higher than in an ordinary store in the same city.

Only by comparison shopping can you be sure whether it is worthwhile buying at the duty-free shops.

Furthermore, upon returning to your home country you will often find that you must pay a duty on your "duty-free" purchases. "Duty-free" means only that the airport store from which you made a purchase did not have to pay a duty when it bought the article.

To know what can and cannot be brought back to the country of your residence and what the duty tax (if any) you will have to pay when returning home with articles purchased abroad, learn about your country's import regulations before you start your trip to another country.

Residents of the U.S.A. can obtain a copy of "Know Before You Go", a helpful booklet, by writing to: U.S. Customs Service, Custom Information Section, 6 World Trade Center, New York, N.Y. 10048.

Only a fool tries to smuggle through customs an article on which there is an embargo or to avoid paying duty for one which is subject to import tax. If caught, the penalty when entering the United States can be a combination of having the article seized, paying a penalty in the amount of the U.S. value, and criminal prosecution.

For example, in trying to avoid a $120 duty on a $1,000 piece of jade, you could lose the jade, be forced to pay a fine of $1,000 and go to jail.

It is almost a certainty that the salesperson who sells you any item of value or one which cannot legally be brought into your country will report your name and your purchase to your country's authorities in that country a few minutes after concluding the transaction. The informer receives a good reward for enabling the customs people at your home port to be expecting you.

To avoid delays and difficulty when you return to your home country, it is advisable before leaving home to register with your Customs Service any major foreign-made items (cameras, watches, etc.) you take on your trip.

Always keep your sales slips, invoices or other evidence of purchase. These are essential when presenting a declaration upon re-entering your home country.

If you carry narcotic medicines or injection needles, have a statement from your physician about them.

Do not try to bring home fruits, vegetables or plants that cannot be cleared by your country's Agriculture Department. Without such clearance, it is a certainty such items will be confiscated.

AIRPORT-CITY RAIL CONNECTIONS

An increasing number of cities in Europe have fast rail service to and from their outlying airports: Amsterdam (6 minutes), Barcelona (11), Brussels (18), Dusseldorf (15), Frankfurt (16), London (50 minutes from Heathrow, 30 minutes from Gatwick), Malaga (20), Paris (20 minutes from De Gaulle, 47 minutes from Orly), Vienna (35) and Zurich (11).

LOST MONEY AND PASSPORTS

Having your money or passport stolen or losing them is certain to spoil your trip.

The best precaution is to carry little cash, have traveler's checks instead, and to keep the record of both your traveler's checks and passport number in a different location than you carry the checks and passport. Also guard your return airport ticket as closely as you guard cash, traveler's checks and passport.

Each year, approximately 3,000 U.S. passports are stolen and another 11,000 are lost. There is a big market for American and European passports in Latin America and Asia.

Here are the steps to take when your passport is taken or missing:

First, notify the police of the country in which you are traveling. At the moment you are without your passport, you are in that country illegally. Next, get a copy of the police report and take it to the local office of your country's consulate. Do not waste time going to your country's embassy. It is your consulate, not your embassy, that will assist you by issuing you a replacement passport.

Obtaining a replacement is expedited if you can provide the passport number. It frequently takes 3-4 business days (up to 6 or 7 days if weekends or holidays intervene) before the consulate receives a reply from a telegram sent to your country's capital, the procedure when you do not know your passport number.

If, in addition to the passport number, you also have a certified copy of your birth certificate or certificate of citizenship, the consulate usually can issue a new passport the same day without cabling your capital.

When your new passport is prepared, you must again provide 2 photos of yourself.

The trip delay, missed connections, taxis (to police, consulate, photographer, return trip to consulate, going to the airline to change your ticket), additional hotel days and various fees to your consulate can amount to a great expense.

OVERCOMING JET LAG

When your trip involves a 5-9 hour time change, many of the early days of your trip to another country can be drastically impaired.

There are ways you can greatly reduce the effects of "jet lag" and have more fun on your trip.

On the flight, drink a great deal of water to overcome dehydration resulting from cabin air conditioning. Do not drink alcoholic beverages. Eat very lightly. Dress comfortably by wearing loose clothing. Exercise as much as possible in flight.

Both SAS and Lufthansa have concise booklets which describe exercises that can be performed on a crowded airplane, while you are sitting. Do the motions involved in rowing a boat and picking apples from an overhead branch. Rise up and sit down repeatedly. Raise your knees to your elbows, alternately. Nod your head and turn it vigorously side to side. Turn your hands at the wrist while spreading and closing your fingers. Lift your heels up and place them down vigorously while placing pressure on your toes. With toes up, rotate your feet in large circles.

WHAT WEATHER TO EXPECT

These descriptions of weather patterns are helpful in planning what season is most comfortable for visiting the areas listed.

NORTH AMERICA AND EUROPE   Spring is April-June, Summer July-September, Fall October-December. Winter January-March.

MEXICO AND CENTRAL AMERICA   Very rainy May-October.

SOUTH AMERICA, AUSTRALIA AND NEW ZEALAND   Spring is October-December, Summer January-March, Fall April-June, Winter July-September.

ASIA   Year-round tropical heat in Hong Kong, India, Indonesia, Malaysia, Philippines, Singapore, Thailand, South Pacific islands, anywhere that is near the Equator. Typhoon season is June-September in Japan, August to mid-October in Taiwan. The monsoon months in India are June-August. The rainy season in most of Asia is May-September (June-November in the Philippines).

NORTH AFRICA   Extremely hot, except December-February in Egypt.

MIDDLE EAST   Israel has mild Mediterranean temperature year round. Iran, Iraq, Jordan, Lebanon and Syria have the same 4 seasons as North America and Europe.

LAST MINUTE CHECKLIST

Here are several important tips that can greatly increase the pleasure of your travel.

Carry as little luggage as possible. You will arrive at many railstations where it is a long walk from the train to the taxis (often requiring walking up and down stairs) and find there are neither porters nor carts.

If the luggage you take is a burden, bring along a folding cart of your own.

Take a container of drinking-water on any long trip. Most trains do not provide drinking-water.

Pack soft-ply toilet paper, wash-and-dry packets, and plastic bags. The bags are useful for storing left-over food items, wet soap and laundry that was not completely dry at the start of that day's journey.

When traveling in pairs, it is easier to pass a suitcase through the train window, into or from your compartment, than it is to carry luggage through the length of a crowded, narrow corridor. Unfortunately, the windows of many new air-conditioned train cars cannot be opened.

SIGNS—THE INTERNATIONAL LANGUAGE

The signs shown on next 3 pages appear in railstations and elsewhere all over the world. They help overcome language problems.

At the Train Station. It won't surprise you to learn that most every station is located in the center of town and is the focal point for all public transportation. A number of hotels are also in the immediate vicinity. What might surprise you is the number and variety of services available on the inside. You can find practically everything—from post office and telegraph bureau to barber and beauty shop, from bookstore and newsstand to gift shop, money exchange, and restaurants. But what will impress the foreign traveler most is the highly efficient information system with which almost every station overcomes the language barrier. Here's the most multi-lingual of visual aids you should look for . . .

Ladies' Rest Room	Men's Rest Room
Barber - Beauty Parlor	Bath

Waiting Room	Telegram
Post office	Telephone
Drinking Water	Restaurant
Smoking permitted	No smoking

Customs

Baggage Claim

Language. Don't worry. Europeans like to practice their conversational English, especially on trains. For detailed information, consult the English-speaking staff at tourist offices, information bureaus, and hotels. At the railroad stations, pictograms lead you not only to the information desk but to any other facility you may be looking for. There are also the highly visible and efficient timetables posted inside the railroad station for get-it-yourself train information. Once you acquire the knack of reading them (and we shall tell you how, later on), they will get you on the right train at the right time on the right track.

Information

Temporary Luggage Storage. At almost every large station you'll find coin-operated lockers. Else, use the special baggage storage indicated by a pictogram and/or the legend: CONSIGNE DES BAGGAGES … GEPAECKAUFBEWAHRUNG … CONSIGNA DE EQUIPAJES … DEPOSITO BAGAGLIO. You'll get a claim check which you have to present when you pick your luggage up again.

Baggage check room

Locker

Checking Your Luggage Through. Time and circumstances permitting, take your bulky luggage or bicycle along on your train, but not with you. Wherever international border crossings and train regulations don't stand in your way, avoid the hassle by checking your extra pieces through to your destination, to ride in the luggage-car. The right counter for this service is indicated by a pictogram.

Luggage registration office

Door-to-Door Luggage Service. If you really want to travel light in France or Germany—with a claim check instead of luggage—find out whether your train station in the city you're in is one of those which pick up your luggage where you're staying and deliver it at your next stay. If that's the case, the small service fee is worth every penny of it.

Border and Customs Control. Be in your seat. Immigration officials will inspect your passport and whatever visa or other required documents right in your compartment, while the train moves across border points. You will be asked whether you have anything to declare, but as a foreign tourist in transit, especially with a EURAILPASS or STUDENT-RAIL-PASS, you will be given the appropriate considerations.

55

Changing Money. A railroad station is a good place to exchange the bills and coins of one currency for another. Look for the sign where the action is: BUREAU DE CHANGE...GELDWECHSEL...WECH-SELSTUBE...OFICINA DE CAMBIO... OFFICIO CAMBEIO...UFFICIO CAMBIO ...or just follow the pertinent picto-gram.

Currency exchange

Which Ticket Window for What. At larger stations tickets for domestic and inter-national travel are purchased at different windows. But as a EURAILPASS or STUDENT-RAILPASS holder, you have your ticket already. So all you'll really want is either the information or reser-vation window or desk—except in Spain, where you must get a boarding pass at the station before you can board a train.

Tickets

Services for Businessmen. If you are combining pleasure with business, there are a number of TEE and Intercity trains on which you can hire a secretary, send telegrams or make telephone calls, make car-rental reservations ahead of ar-rival, or reserve a taxi to pick you up at your destination.

Rent-a-car

Taxi stand

Your Helpful Porter. You'll recognize him by his uniform or official badge. You can usually find one as your cab pulls up to the station. If not, look for him inside. Consult the proper pictogram to find the porters' room. You can rely on your porter to get you to the right track, train, and car. He will put you in a smoker or non-smoker, as you wish, will try his best to find a vacant window-seat, and will place your luggage into the overhead rack.

Call for porter

Washroom Facilities. You can freshen up in a "W.C." (Water Closet) at either end of your car. In most long distance trains next to the "WC" are separate Washrooms. And remember not to drink the tap water; it is not potable.

WC
Rest rooms

A Seat Reservation. Even though you can travel on a European train in most cases without a seat reservation, it's always nice to have a reserved seat—at a win-dow, if possible, or where you want your lunch or dinner served (yes, advance reservations can be made on some TEE trains for meals to be served in your seat). EURAILPASS and STUDENT-RAILPASS holders must pay for seat reservations, but it's very little for a lot of convenience.

Reservation

AUSTRIA

Chapter 6   EURAILPASS EUROPE

AUSTRIA

Children under 6 travel free on Austria's trains.

Austria's fast trains are: "Ex" (International Express Train "Expresszug"), "TS" (Long Distance Express Railcar "Triebwagenschnellzug") and "D" (all other express service). Except for passengers holding tickets issued outside Austria, these trains charge a supplement of 20 Austrian schillings. Special through tickets are required for "privilege trains", those which cross German or Italian borders without border formalities (customs, passport and currency control) when traveling from one part of Austria to another part of Austria. These trains do *not* allow passengers to board or leave the train in Germany or Italy.

The signs you will see at railstations in Austria are:

ABFAHRT	DEPARTURE
ANKUNFT	ARRIVAL
AUSGANG	EXIT
AUSKUNFT	INFORMATION
BAHNHOF	STATION
DAMEN	WOMEN
INGANG	ENTRANCE
FAHRKARTEN-SCHALTER	TICKET OFFICE
FAHRPLAN	TIMETABLE
GARDEROBE	CHECKROOM
GLEIS	TRACK
HERREN	MEN
RAUCHER	SMOKING COMPARTMENT
RESERVIERSCHALTER	RESERVATIONS OFFICE
SCHLAFWAGEN	SLEEPING CAR
SPEISEWAGEN	RESTAURANT CAR
ZU DEN BAHNSTEIGN	TO THE PLATFORMS

AUSTRIAN HOLIDAYS

A list of holidays is helpful because some trains will be noted later in this section as *not* running on holidays. Also, those trains which operate on holidays are filled, and it is necessary to make reservations for them long in advance.

January 1	New Year's Day		Corpus Christi Day
January 6	Epiphany	August 15	Assumption Day
	Easter	October 26	National Holiday
	Easter Monday	November 1	All Saints Day
May 1	May Day	December 8	Immaculate Conception
	Ascension Day	December 25	Christmas Day
	Whit Monday	December 26	St. Stephen's Day

SUMMER TIME

Austria changes to Summer Time on the last Sunday of March and converts back to Standard Time on the last Sunday of September.

AUSTRIA TICKET

Unlimited *second-class* travel for persons 7-26 on all Austrian railroads, buses (except municipal buses and trams), scheduled boats on Lake St. Wolfgang, and the Schaffberg and Schneeberg railways. Also, 50% discount on upstream Danube steamboats and scheduled boats on Lake Constance, 7%-50% discount on many aerial trams and chair lifts, and free admission to any one of the 10 gambling casinos in Austria. Prices until June, 1984: 9 days $56(U.S.), 16 days $79.

The pass can be obtained also at all railstations in Austria and at stations in major cities of West Germany and Switzerland. The first day of travel must be indicated when this pass is purchased.

AUSTRIA'S SENIOR CITIZEN HALF-FARE

Women 60 and over and men who are 65 and older can buy Austria Ticket at half-price after purchasing a Senior Citizen's Identification for $10(U.S.), available at all railstations and major post offices in Austria, and also at the Hauptbahnhof stations in Frankfurt, Munich and Zurich. The ID can also be obtained by mail by sending a travelers check in the amount of $10(U.S.) or equivalent, a photostat of the passport page which has a picture and states the holder's age, plus one passport-size photo to: OeBB-Verkaufsdirektion, Abt. IV/4, Gauernanngasse 2-4, A-1010 Wien, Austria.

AUSTRIA'S BUNDES-NETZKARTEN

Unlimited train travel in *all* of Austria. Prices until June, 1984: First-class AS 1,950 for 9 days, AS 2,640 16 days, AS 4,200 one month. Second-class AS 1,300 9 days, AS 1,760 16 days, AS 2,800 one month.

AUSTRIA'S LAENDER-NETZKARTEN

Unlimited train travel in *only one province* of Austria. Prices until June, 1984: First-class AS 780 for 9 days, AS 1,140 16 days, AS 1,740 one month. Second-class: AS 520 9 days, AS 760 16 days, AS 1,160 one month.

AUSTRIA'S KILOMETERBANK TICKET

May be used by 1-6 persons traveling together on trips of over 70 km. The 1983 prices are: First-class AS 2,250 for 2,000 km, AS 5,400 for 5,000km, AS 10,500 for 10,000 km. Second-class costs AS 1,500 . . . AS 3,600 . . . and AS 7,000.

EURAILPASS BONUSES IN AUSTRIA

Two rack railways: (1) Puchberg am Schneeberg-Hockschneeberg and (2) St. Wolfgang-Schafbergspitze. Two cruises: (1) Lake Wolfgang and (2) Danube, between Passau and Vienna. Reduction of 50% on Lake Constance Ships.

ONE-DAY EXCURSIONS AND CITY-SIGHTSEEING

Here are 17 one-day rail trips that can be made comfortably from 4 major cities in Austria, returning to them in most cases before dinnertime. Notes are provided on what to see at each destination. The number after the name of each route is the Cook's timetable. The 4 base cities are Innsbruck, Linz, Salzburg and Vienna (Wien).

Innsbruck

Marvelous Winter resort. Gateway to many cable railway trips (Hungerburg, Hafelekar, Igls, Patscherkofel). See the 28 bronze statues around the enormous and magnificent tomb of Maximilian I in the 16th century Imperial Church (Hofkirche). Also the effigy of King Arthur there. The roof (2,657 gold plated tiles) on Goldenes Dachl, built in 1500. The Museum of Tyrolean Folk Art, considered the most important collection of costumes and rustic furniture in Austria. The 18th century Triumphal Arch. The paintings and furniture in the 18th century Hofburg Palace. The silver altar at the Silver Chapel.

Linz

The schloss (castle) where Emperor Fredrich III live, with its Upper Austrian State Museum collections of prehistoric and Roman items. Martinskirche, one of Austria's oldest churches.

Salzburg

Do not miss seeing the most amusing place in Europe, the 17th century Hellbrun Palace. The 16th century 200-pipe barrel organ in the 12th century fortress, 500 feet above the town, Festung Hohensalzburg. The traditional Music Festival (last week of July until the end of August). The State Rooms in The Residenz, the 17th century city palace of Salzburg's archbishops. The painted ceilings in the 17th century Festspeilhaus. The collection of Mozart musical instruments and family memorabilia in the Mozart Museum, his birthplace. The vast musical library at Bibliotheca Mozartiana. St. Sebastian's Cemetery at Linzergasse 41. The 17th century Cathedral. The Universitatskirche. The Gothic cloister in the 9th century Benedictine Abbey of St. Peter. The Glockenspiel Tower (particularly at 7:00, 11:00 and 18:00 for the carillon concerts). The ancient marketplace, Alter Markt. The marble Angel Staircase in the 17th century Schloss Mirabell, and the marvelous gardens there. Take the cable car to the top (5,800 feet) of Untersberg for a breathtaking view of Salzburg and the Alps.

Vienna (Wien)

There is 35-minute train service from Vienna (Nord) to the city's Schwechat Airport (Flughafen) daily except Sundays and holidays at 5:13 and 5:51; also daily at 6:15 and hourly from 7:28 to 21:28 (also at 16:00 Monday-Friday, except holidays).

Rail service to Vienna (Nord) departs the Airport daily except Sundays and holidays at 5:31, 6:15, 6:38 and 7:03; also daily at 6:38, 7:24 and hourly from 8:03 to 21:03 (also at 7:12 Monday-Friday, except holidays).

For a glimpse at the world's most beautiful horses and extraordinary riding skill, see the Spanish Riding School. The view from the top of the south steeple of Saint Stephen's Cathedral, or from the top of the Donauturm (Danube Tower). or from the hills in the Vienna Woods. Three-hour boat trips on the Danube Canal operate daily except Monday at 10:00, 13:00 and 16:30 from Schwedenbrucke, a bridge that is a 15-minute walk from St. Stephen's.

See the Opera House, the Art Gallery, the Museum of Natural History, the Burgtheater, the Rathaus (City Hall), the Prater, the amusement park. Take a boat ride on the Danube. See the crown jewels of the Holy Roman Empire and the Austrian Empire, in the Imperial Apartments at the Hofburg (Imperial Palace). The collection of great paintings (Titian, Rubens, etc.) and Egyptian, Greek, Etruscan and Roman antiquities at the Kunsthistorisches Museum. Do not miss visiting some of the 1,400 rooms in Schonbrunn Palace.

The superb collection of prehistoric objects, fossils and meteorites at the Naturhistoriches Museum. The many art museums in Belvedere Palace. The beautiful Austrian National Library at Josefplatz 1. Peterskirche. Karlskirche.

Take trolley car #38 from Schottentor (in central Vienna) to Grinzing, the wine-tasting village. Continue from there on bus #38A to the small Church of St. Joseph on the top of 1,585-feet high Kahlenberg, from where Hungary and Czechoslovakia can be seen on clear days.

In the following timetables, where a city has more than one railstation we have designated the particular station after the name of the city (in parentheses). **Where no station is designated for cities in Austria, Switzerland and West Germany, the station is "Hauptbahnhof".**

Innsbruck - Bregenz - Innsbruck   750

| Dep. Innsbruck | 6:48(1) | Dep. Bregenz | 16:24(1) | 19:28(1) |
| Arr. Bregenz | 10:29 | Arr. Innsbruck | 20:05 | 22:50 |

(1)Light refreshments.

Sights in **Bregenz:** The annual music festival (light opera and ballet on an unusual water stage in the lake) runs mid-July to mid-August. Take the funicular to the top (3,200 feet) of Pfander Mountain for a spectacular view of Bodensee, the town of Lindau and the Rhine.

Innsbruck - Kitzbuhl - Innsbruck   750
Dep. Innsbruck   7:02   8:40   11:00   12:35(1)   14:04
Arr. Kitzbuhl   8:14   10:33   12:13   13:50   15:08
   Sights in **Kitzbuhl:** This is one of the major winter resorts in the Alps.
Cable cars take you from Kitzbuhl to many mountaintops. The city has one
museum, some old churches.
Dep. Kitzbuhl   12:38(1)   14:09   16:03   17:25   18:57(2)
Arr. Innsbruck   13:44   15:28   17:21   19:12   20:12
(1)Meal service. (2)Plus other departures from Kitzbuhl at 19:48(1), 21:45(1)
and 22:50

Innsbruck - Mayrhofen - Innsbruck   758
Dep. Innsbruck   8:55   9:06   11:20   12:55   14:12
Arr. Jenbach   9:20   9:47   11:44   13:32   14:35
   Change to bus or to a narrow-gauge train.
   730
Dep. Jenbach   9:43   10:40(1) 12:30(2) 13:45   15:35(1)
Arr. Mayrhofen   60-70 minutes later
   Sights in **Mayrhofen:** This is a popular Winter resort, with horse sleighs.
   730
Dep. Mayrhofen   12:30(1)   13:30(3) 14:45(4) 14:50(2) 15:45(5+8)
Arr. Jenbach   13:41   14:28   15:48   15:49   16:47
   Change from bus or narrow-gauge train to another train.
   758
Dep. Jenbach   14:43   15:27   16:06   16:13   17:08
Arr. Innsbruck   40 minutes later
(1)Steam train. (2)Train. Runs Sat. and Sun. (3)Bus. Runs daily, except Sun.
and holidays. (4)Bus. Runs Mon.-Fri., except holidays. (5)Train. Runs daily.
(6)Bus. Runs daily. (7)Train. Runs Sat. only. (8)Plus other departures from
Mayrhofen at 17:40(1), 18:35(6) and 19:40(7).

Innsbruck - Munich - Innsbruck   758
Dep. Innsbruck   7:40   8:55(1) 9:01(2+3) 11:20(3)   12:08(4)
Arr. Munich   10:05   11:03   11:16   13:50   13:54
   Sights in **Munich:** The works of Durer, El Greco, Raphael, Holbein, Rem-
brandt and many other great painters at Alte Pinakothek. Frauenkirche Cathedral,
and the view from its north tower . . . and then later see the view of Frauenkir-
che from the top of Neues Rathaus (City Hall). The paintings of Cezanne,
Gauguin, Renoir and other impressionists at the Haus der Kunst. Wittelsbach
Fountain. The fine exhibits and planetarium at Deutsches Museum, considered
the best scientific museum in the world. The view of the Alps from the top of

Peterskirche. The best collection of tapestries and wood carvings in Germany, at the Bavarian National Museum. Munich's most famous beer palace, Hofbrauhaus. The Schatzkammer in the Residenz palace, and the flower gardens in the park north of it.

The decorations in Asamkirche. Schack Gallery. Theatinerkirche. At Schloss Nymphenburger: the porcelain in the showrooms of Nyphenburger Porzellan Manufaktur and in the Residenzmuseum, the enormous Festsaal, and the park outside the castle.

Dep. Munich	15:38(4)	16:26(3)	16:55(1)	19:20(2+3)	20:08
Arr. Innsbruck	17:26	18:36	19:00	21:30	22:35

(1)Meal service. (2)Operates from late May to late September. (3)Light refreshments. (4)TEE. Reservation required. Meal service.

Innsbruck - Zell am See - Salzburg - Innsbruck   750

This is one of the most scenic rides in Austria, as well as a trip to an interesting destination. Exceptionally beautiful views of gorges, lakes, mountains and rivers.

Dep. Innsbruck	7:02(1+3)	7:35(2)	8:40(1)	9:35(2+4)
Dep. Zell-am-See	9:02	-0-	11:35	-0-
Arr. Salzburg	10:32	9:36	13:32	11:36

Sights in **Salzburg:** See notes about sightseeing in Salzburg at the start of this section.

Dep. Salzburg	13:35(1+3)	14:25(1)	16:19(2)	17:22(1+3+5)
Dep. Zell-am-See	15:09	16:25	-0-	18:57
Arr. Innsbruck	17:21	19:12	18:20	20:55

(1)Of the 2 routes between Innsbruck and Salzburg, this train takes the more interesting one (via Zell-am-See), one of the most scenic rail trips in Austria. (2)Via Rosenheim. Special ticket required for car that does not take up or set down passengers in Germany. Meal service. (3)Meal service. (4)Plus another departure from Innsbruck at 11:35(2).   (5)Plus other departures from Salzburg at 18:19(2), 19:22(1+3) and 20:19(2).

Linz - Munich - Linz   61

Dep. Linz	9:54(1)		Dep. Munich	17:20(1)
Arr. Munich	13:34		Arr. Linz	20:42

(1)Meal service.

Sights in **Munich:** See notes about sightseeing in Munich earlier in this section, under "Innsbruck-Munich".

Linz - Salzburg - Linz   750

Dep. Linz	8:00	8:54(1)	9:23	9:54(1)	10:52(1+3)
Arr. Salzburg	9:50	10:15	11:06	11:25	12:13

Sights in **Salzburg:** See notes about sightseeing in Salzburg at the start of this section.

Dep. Salzburg	11:57(1)	12:40(2)	14:40(1)	16:40(1)	17:40(1+6)
Arr. Linz	13:25	14:01	16:01	18:01	19:01

(1)Meal service. (2)Light refreshments. (3)Plus other departures from Linz at 11:54(1), 12:05 and 12:54(1).   (4)Plus other departures from Salzburg at 17:50, 18:40, 19:17(1), 19:40(1), 20:40(1) and 20:58(2).

Linz - Vienna - Linz   750

Most of these trains have meal service or light refreshments.

Dep. Linz	Frequent times from 6:38 to 21:08
Arr. Vienna (Westbf.)	2-2½ hours later

Sights in **Vienna:** See notes about sightseeing in Vienna at the start of this section.

Dep. Vienna (Westbf.)	Frequent times from 7:00 to 22:00
Arr. Linz	2-2½ hours later

Salzburg - Zell am See - Innsbruck - Salzburg   750

This is one of the most scenic rides in Austria, as well as a trip to an interesting destination. Exceptionally beautiful views of gorges, lakes, mountains and rivers.

Dep. Salzburg	8:42(1)	10:19(2)	11:25(1)	12:14(2)
Dep. Zell-am-See	10:29	-0-	13:17	-0-
Arr. Innsbruck	12:40	12:25	15:28	14:12

Sights in **Innsbruck:** See notes about sightseeing in Innsbruck at the start of this section.

Dep. Innsbruck	15:35(2)	16:25(1)	17:35(2)	21:08(1)
Dep. Zell-am-See	-0-	18:51	-0-	23:31
Arr. Salzburg	17:36	20:31	19:36	1:25

(1)Of the 2 routes between Salzburg and Innsbruck, this train takes the most interesting one (via Zell-am-See), one of the most scenic rail trips in Austria. (2)Via Rosenheim. Special ticket required for car that does not take up or set down passengers in Germany. Meal service.

Salzburg - Linz - Salzburg   750
   Most of these trains have meal service or light refreshments.
Dep. Salzburg   Frequent times from 6:40 to 20:58
Arr. Linz   80 minutes later
   Sights in **Linz:** See notes about sightseeing in Linz at the start of this section.
Dep. Linz   Frequent times from 8:00 to 21:59
Arr. Salzburg   80 minutes later

Salzburg - Munich - Salzburg   684
Dep. Salzburg   7:08   7:55   8:22   8:47   9:45   10:12
Arr. Munich   9:18   9:42   10:14   10:52   11:47   12:18
   Sights in **Munich:** See notes about sightseeing in Munich earlier in this section, under ''Innsbruck-Munich''.
Dep. Munich   Frequent times from 12:21 to 23:36
Arr. Salzburg   2-2½ hours later

Salzburg - Vienna - Salzburg   750
Dep. Salzburg   6:40(1)   7:40(1)   8:40   9:40(1)   10:40(1)
Arr. Vienna
   (Westbf.)   3¼ hours later
   Sights in **Vienna:** See notes about sightseeing in Vienna at the start of this section.
Dep. Vienna
   (Westbf.)   13:00(1)   14:00(1)   15:00(1)   16:00(1)   17:00(1+3)
Arr. Salzburg   3¼ hours later
(1)Meal service. (2)Light refreshments. (3)Plus other departures from Vienna at 18:00(1), 19:00(2), 20:00(1) and 21:00(2).

Vienna - Baden - Vienna
   A local tram runs at frequent time from the center of Vienna to Baden and v.v.
   Sights in **Baden:** Famous since the 1st century for the curative powers of its hot sulphur springs. Many of the rooms in hotels here have a faucet in the bathroom that carries mineral water. See the Baroque Trinity Column. Try your luck in the Casino in Kurpark. Visit the house where Beethoven lived, at 10 Rathausgasse, open daily except Thursdays, May-September, 9:00-11:00 and 15:00-17:00.

Vienna - Graz - Vienna   762

Dep. Vienna (Sudbf.)	7:00(1)	8:00(2)	10:00(1)	12:00(1)
Arr. Graz	9:35	10:44	12:35	14:35
	*	*	*	

Dep. Graz	12:20(1)	14:20	16:20(1)	17:05(1+3+4)
Arr. Vienna (Sudbf.)	15:05	17:05	19:05	20:05

(1)Meal service. (2)Light refreshments. (3)Change trains in Bruck an der Mur.
(4)Plus other departures from Graz at 18:20(2) and 19:40(1+3).

Sights in **Graz:** From the main square (Hauptplatz) with its many markets
of vegetables, fruits and flowers, go to the arcades with shops in the 17th
century Luegghaus. Then to the City Hall (Rathaus) to see the city's symbol,
a carved white panther.

Follow Neutorgasse to the Joanneum (State Museum of Styria), one of
the world's oldest museums, to see its archaeological collection, library, paint
ings and exhibits of Styrian crafts (9:00-12:00 daily, 14:30-17:00 Monday,
Wednesday and Friday).

Continue on Landhausgasse and Herrengasse to the splendid Renaissance
Landhaus. Next door, in the Styrian Armory (Zeughaus) is an exhibit of 17th
century armor said to be the best and largest (30,000 weapons) collection in
Europe (same hours as the Joanneum).

Walk on Opernring to the outstanding Opera House and then through
marvelous Stadtpark with its fantastic double-spiral Gothic staircase and cross
the Glacis to visit the city's oldest church, 13th century Leekirche, the Church
of the Teutonic Order.

Pass the castle and see the Diocesan Museum and Treasury in the 15th
century Cathedral. Across a narrow street is the 17th century Mausoleum of
Emperor Ferdinand II (11:00-12:00 and 14:00-15:00 from May to September,
only 11:00-12:00 the rest of the year).

Don't miss the folk dance by carved wood figures performing at 11:00
and 18:00 on the ancient clock in Glockenspielplatz. See the exhibits of regional
costumes, tools, folk art, etc. in the Volkskundemuseum (Folk Art Museum
of Styria) open Monday, Wednesday and Friday 14:30-17:00.

Take the tram to Eggenberg to see the hunting museum in the 17th century
castle there. Go to the top of Castle Hill (Schlossberg) by foot or funicular
for a great view of Graz and tour the Bell Tower and Clock Tower, where
the big hands show the hour and the small hands the minutes.

Drink Schilcher, the local rose wine, and Steiermark beer. Local food
specialties to sample are: Steierische Wurzelfleisch (pork shoulder), Sulmtaler
Krainer (smoked pork sausage) and Steierische Brettljause (a dish of bacon,
sausage, cheese, peppers and tomatoes served on a wooden platter).

Take a local bus to nearby Stubing, which has the largest open-air museum
in Austria (ancient wood churches, peasants' homes). Another tour goes to
Koflach, where a stud farm that is an auxiliary of Vienna's Spanish Riding

School has been breeding thoroughbred horses since 1798.

A 2½-hour motorcoach sightseeing tour of Graz starts from in front of the Opera House weekdays at 10:00, June through September.

Vienna - Linz - Vienna   750

Most of these trains have meal service or light refreshments.

Dep. Vienna (Westbf.)   Frequent times from 7:00 to 22:45
Arr. Linz   2 hours later

Sights in **Linz:** See notes about sightseeing in Linz at the start of this section.

Dep. Linz   Frequent times from 6:42 to 21:08
Arr. Vienna (Westbf.)   2 hours later

Vienna - Melk - Vienna   Train Ride+Danube Boat Trip

Train 750	Danube Steamship 740
Dep. Vienna (Westbf.) 9:20 12:20	Dep. Melk 15:20(1)
Arr. Melk 10:23 13:23	Arr. Vienna
	(Reichsbrucke) 20:15

(1)Operates from early May to late September.

Sights in **Melk:** Walk from the railstation up the hill to the abbey. See the library there and, from the terrace of the abbey, a splendid view of the Danube. For the return trip to Vienna by boat, go to the main river dock, not to the dock below the abbey.

Vienna - Salzburg - Vienna   750

Dep. Vienna (Westbf.)   7:00(1)   8:00(1)   9:00(1)   10:00(1)
Arr. Salzburg   10:15   11:30   12:10   13:25

Sights in **Salzburg:** See notes about sightseeing in Salzburg at the start of this section.

Dep. Salzburg   14:40(1)   16:40(1)   17:40(1)   18:40(2+3)
Arr. Vienna (Westbf.)   17:55   19:55   20:55   21:55

(1)Meal service. (2)Light refreshments. (3)Plus another departure from Salzburg at 19:40(1).

SCENIC RAIL TRIPS

Gmunden - Bad Aussee
There is fine lake scenery on this portion of a circle trip that starts and ends in Salzburg.

750

Dep. Salzburg	9:55	11:57(1)
Arr. Attnang Puchheim	10:50	12:45

Change trains.

760

Dep. Attnang Puchheim	10:57	12:52
Dep. Gmunden	11:16	13:10
Arr. Bad Ausee	12:52	14:40
Arr. Stainach Irdning	13:33	15:30

Change trains.

745

Dep. Stainach Irdning	13:37(2)	16:22(2)
Arr. Salzburg	17:10	19:07

(1)Meal service. (2)Change trains in Bischofshofen.

Innsbruck - Brennero   758
The beautiful mountain scenery here can be seen either on an easy one-day roundtrip from Innsbruck or as a portion of the Innsbruck-Verona route. For the first way:

Dep. Innsbruck	9:05	9:35	10:40	13:15	14:08
Arr. Brennero	9:54	10:11	11:22	14:05	14:58
		*	*	*	
Dep. Brennero	10:20	11:32(1)	12:35	14:41	16:08
Arr. Innsbruck	11:02	12:05	13:28	15:30	16:56

(1)TEE. Reservation required. Meal service.

Here is the schedule for going from Innsbruck to Italy:

381

Dep. Innsbruck	6:38(1)	10:00(2)	10:40(3)	16	:05
Dep. Brennero	7:40(1+3)	10:56(2)	11:42(3)	17	:07
Arr. Verona	11:25	14:25	15:39	20	:56

(1)Operates late May to late September. (2)Meal service. (3)Light refreshments.

Innsbruck - Buchs 750

The excellent mountain scenery here can be seen either on an easy one-day roundtrip from Innsbruck or as a portion of the Innsbruck-Zurich route. For the first way:

Dep. Innsbruck	6:22(1)	8:55(1)	12:30(2)
Arr. Buchs	9:36	12:01	15:05

*   *   *

Dep. Buchs	10:51(2)	12:48(2)	17:48
Arr. Innsbruck	13:24	15:27	20:55

(1)Light refreshments. (2)Meal service.

Here is the schedule for going from Innsbruck to Switzerland.
268

Dep. Innsbruck	6:22(1)	8:55(1+2)	12:30(3)	14:27(3)
Dep. Sargans	10:28(1)	12:46(2)	15:29(3)	17:29(3)
Arr. Zurich	11:26	13:47	16:28	18:28

(1)Light refreshments. (2)Change trains in Sargans. (3)Meal service.

Innsbruck - Bruck an der Mur - Vienna

This indirect route from Innsbruck to Vienna, traveling south of the main line (via Linz), offers excellent mountain scenery.
750

Dep. Innsbruck	7:02(1)	8:40	11:00(1)
Arr. Bischofshofen	9:48	12:40	13:49

Change trains.
745

Dep. Bischofshofen	10:07(1)	12:50	14:25
Arr. Bruck an der Mur	13:02	15:57	18:22

Change trains.
762

Dep. Bruck an der Mur	14:58	16:58(1)	18:58(2)
Arr. Vienna (Sudbf.)	17:05	19:05	21:05

(1)Meal service. (2)Light refreshments.

Innsbruck - Garmisch - Zugspitz 756

The outstanding mountain scenery here can be seen either on an easy one-day roundtrip from Innsbruck or as a portion of the Innsbruck-Munich route.
For the first way:

Dep. Innsbruck	6:33	7:32	9:00	10:54	11:47
Arr. Garmisch	8:27	9:02	10:24	12:22	13:24

Change trains.

The following schedule allows one to ride one cable railway to the summit of Zugspitz and ride a different cable railway en route bck to Garmisch.

693

Dep. Garmisch	9:00	10:00	11:00	13:00	14:00
Arr. Eibsee	9:37	10:37	11:37	13:37	14:37

Change to cable railway.

Dep. Eibsee	9:45(1)	10:45	11:45	13:45	14:45
Arr. Zugspitz	10 minutes later				

(1)Runs every 30 minutes until 17:45.

Use a different cable railway in returning to Garmisch.

Dep. Zubspitz	10:15(1)	11:15	12:15	14:15	15:15
Arr. Scneefernerhaus	10:19	11:19	12:19	14:19	15:19

(1)There are also departures from Zugspitz at 45 minutes after each hour.

Change to train.

* * *

693

Dep. Scneefernerhaus	10:25	11:25	12:25	14:25	15:25
Arr. Garmisch	11:45	12:45	13:45	15:45	16:45

Change trains.

756

Dep. Garmisch	-0-	13:28	15:26	16:24(1)	
					17:31
Arr. Innsbruck	-0-	14:59	16:57	17:46	19:13

(1)Meal Service.

Here is the schedule for continuing on from Garmisch to Munich.

683

Dep. Garmisch	12:30	13:34	14:34	15:34	16:34(1)
Arr. Munich	13:58	14:55	15:55	17:13	17:55

(1)Plus other departures from Garmisch at 17:34, 18:34 and 20:11.

Innsbruck - Salzburg - Innsbruck

The good gorge, lake, river and mountain scenery on this route can be seen either on an easy one-day roundtrip from Innsbruck or as a portion of the Innsbruck-Vienna route.

For the first way, see details earlier in this section, under the "Innsbruck-Zell am See-Salzburg-Innsbruck" one-day excursion.

Innsbruck - Vienna   750

Here are the schedules for going across Austria. All of these trains require a special ticket and have meal service.

Dep. Innsbruck	7:35	9:35	11:35	13:35	15:35
Arr. Vienna (Westbf.)	12:55	14:55	16:55	18:55	20:55

Linz - Vienna   740

Great Danube River scenery on this 10-hour 297km (180-mile) cruise that *is* covered by Eurailpass.

Dep. Linz	10:00(1)	Dep. Vienna	
Arr. Vienna		(Reichsbrucke)	8:00(1)
(Reichsbrucke)	20:15	Arr. Linz	23:50

(1)Operates early may to late September. Runs daily, except Monday.

Salzburg - Zell am See - Innsbruck

Exceptionally beautiful views of gorges, lakes, mountains and rivers on one of the most scenic rides in Austria. Schedules for this trip appear earlier in this section under both "Salzburg-Innsbruck" and "Innsbruck-Salzburg" one-day excursions.

Salzburg - Villach - Salzburg   759

The excellent gorge and mountain scenery on this ride can be seen either on an easy one-day roundtrip from Salzburg or as a portion of the Salzburg-Venice route. For the first way:

Dep. Salzburg	7:50(1)	10:03(1)	11:06(2)	11:46(1)
Arr. Villach	10:50	13:23	14:33	15:00
		*	*	*
Dep. Villach	12:15	14:45(3)	15:21(2)	16:02(1+5)
Arr. Salzburg	15:50	18:10	18:45	19:06

(1)Meal service. (2)Operates late May to late September. (3)Light refreshments. (4)Runs daily, except Saturday. Change trains in Schwarzach St. Veit. (5)Plus other departures from Villach at 17:08(3), 18:50 and 21:12(4).

Here is the schedule for going from Salzburg to Italy:
75

Dep. Salzburg	14:00
Arr. Villach	17:17

Change trains. Be sure to be in a car marked "Venice S.L." when you Depart Villach.

Dep. Villach	18:28(1)
Arr. Venice (S.L.)	23:40

(1)Meal service.

The very scenic Klagenfurt-Udine-Trieste portion of the Vienna-Trieste route is described at the end of this section. A departure from Salzburg can connect with that trip at Villach. Complete schedules appear under the "Vienna-Trieste" trip.

Selzthal - Hieflau

This portion of the easy one-day Linz-Selzthal-Amstetten-Linz circle trip affords fine gorge and mountain scenery.

755

Dep. Linz	7:53	9:50	14:33
Arr. Selzthal	9:45	12:00	16:30

Change trains.

754

Dep. Selzthal	10:05	14:47	16:55
Dep. Hieflau	10:53	15:53	17:36
Arr. Amstetten	12:52	17:42	19:12

Change trains.

750

Dep. Amstetten	14:02	17:58	19:17(1+4)
Arr. Linz	14:58	18:59	19:52

The same trip can be made in reverse, using this schedule:

750

Dep. Linz	7:39(2)	10:08	12:15	14:22
Arr. Amstetten	8:20	11:01	12:10	15:25

Change trains.

754

Dep. Amstetten	9:10	11:35	14:40(3)	16:36
Dep. Hiefflau	10:52	13:42	16:48	18:43
Arr. Selzthal	11:35	14:26	17:37	19:28

Change trains.

755

Dep. Selzthal	13:55(4)	15:26	19:02	19:38
Arr. Linz	15:37	17:15	20:37	21:44

(1)Operates late May to late September. (2)Light refreshments. (3)Daily, except Sundays and holidays. (4)Meal service.

Vienna - Bruck an der Mur - Innsbruck

This indirect route from Vienna to Innsbruck, traveling south of the main line (via Linz), offers excellent mountain scenery.

762

Dep. Vienna (Sudbf.)	7:00(1)	8:00(2)	10:00(1)
Arr. Bruck an der Mur	8:57	10:07	11:57
Change trains.			

745

Dep. Bruck an der Mur	9:00(2)	10:12	13:43
Arr. Bischofshofen	12:16	14:08	16:54
Change trains.			

750

Dep. Bischofshofen	12:24	14:20(1)	17:15
Arr. Innsbruck	15:28	17:21	20:12

(1)Meal service. (2)Light refreshments.

Vienna - Klagenfurt - Udine - Trieste

The marvelous farm and lake scenery on this route includes seeing Worthersee, a lake fed by warm springs that is very popular for swimming and boating, and the beautiful coastline from Udine to Trieste. The great Worthersee resort area is open June through mid-September. Even if you don't stop there, at least watch for that area a few minutes before the stop at Klagenfurt. An early departure from Vienna is recommended in order to be able to see the Adriatic shore approaching Trieste in the afternoon sunlight, as we have done.

The comfortable local train from Udine hurtles downhill too fast to permit picture-taking, but you will have a memory of that truly beautiful scene forever. Be certain to have a seat on the right-hand side of the train for the best possible view.

Not only is Trieste a worthwhile one-day stopover, it is also ideal as a base for several short rail trips into Yugoslavia such as Villa Opicina, Sezana,

Pivka, Postojna and Ljubljana. It is also easy to make a one-day rail excursion to see the sights in Udine while staying in Trieste.

47			388	
Dep. Vienna (Sudbf.)	7:55(1)		Dep. Udine	15:32
Arr. Klagenfurt	12:06		Arr. Trieste	16:43
Arr. Villach	12:33			
Dep. Villach	12:38		(1)Light refreshments.	
Arr. Udine	15:07			
Change trains.				

Sights in **Trieste:** Miramare Castle, Maximilian and Charlotte's lovely seaside palace. Charlotte returned here after their tragic brief time as rulers of Mexico, made insane by Maximilian's death. You will enjoy Trieste's Piazza della Liberta, reminiscent of St. Mark's in Venice. See the 17th century Castello di San Giusto. The 14th century Cathedral of San Giusto. The ruins of a Roman amphitheater. The Civic Museum of History and Art. The Giant Grotto.

If you are originating from Salzburg rather than Vienna, the Udine-Trieste route can be seen by making a connection in Villach, shown here:

759			388	
Dep. Salzburg	7:50		Dep. Udine	15:32
Arr. Villach	10:50		Arr. Trieste	16:43
Change trains.				
47				
Dep. Villach	12:38			
Arr. Udine	15:07			
Change trains.				

Now for the one-day excursion to Udine:

Trieste - Udine - Trieste   388

Dep. Trieste	7:15	9:43	12:26
Arr. Udine	8:37	11:22	13:34

Sights in **Udine:** The collection of paintings in the Civic Museum and Gallery, a 20-minute walk from the railstation. Do they still have in Room 32 Vollett's "Crepuscolo" and Cormaldi's "La Donna e lo Specchio" ? Tiepolo's paintings are featured in both the Bishop's Palace and the Cathedral. Visit Piazza della Liberta.

Dep. Udine	10:52	13:18	15:32	18:44	19:35	21:47
Arr. Trieste	11:50	14:32	16:43	19:55	21:10	22:50

INTERNATIONAL ROUTES FROM AUSTRIA

The Austrian gateways for travel to West Germany (and on to Copenhagen) are both Innsbruck and Salzburg. Vienna is the access point for travel to Poland and Czechoslovakia (and on to Russia), Hungary, Romania and Yugoslavia (and on to Bulgaria, Greece and Turkey). Innsbruck, Salzburg and Vienna are also starting points for trips to Italy. Innsbruck is also the gateway to Switzerland (and on to Belgium, France, Holland and Luxembourg).

Innsbruck - Munich   758
Dep. Innsbruck   7:40   8:55   9:01(1)   11:20(2+6)
Arr. Munich   10:05   11:03   11:27   13:50
(1)Operates late May to late September. (2)Light refreshments. (3)TEE. Reservation required. Meal service. (4)Meal service. (5)Operates mid-July to late September. (6)Plus other departures from Innsbruck at 12:08(3), 12:25(1+4), 14:12(2), 15:00(5), 19:12(1+2), 20:00(4) and 23:35(1).

Salzburg - Munich   684
Arrive at the Salzburg railstation sufficiently in advance of departure time to complete the German Customs clearance that takes place before boarding the train.
Dep. Salzburg   Frequent times from 5:12 to 21:32
Arr. Munich   2 hours later

Vienna - Prague   746
Dep. Vienna (Mitte)   9:30(1)   17:25
Arr. Prague (Main)   15:23   0:10
(1)Meal service.

Vienna - Warsaw (or Kiev) - Moscow
	748	48
Dep. Vienna (Sudbf.)	19:20(1)	22:20(2)
Arr. Warsaw (Gdanska)	-0-	11:56(3)
Arr. Kiev	5:17(3)	-0-
Arr. Moscow (Byel.)	17:30(4)	10:22(4)

(1)Carries sleeping car from late May to late September. (2)Carries sleeping car to Moscow. Couchettes to Warsaw. Meal service 5:44-11:56 on Day 2 and from 19:10 on Day 2 until Moscow arrival on Day 3.   (3)Day 2. (4)Day 3.

Vienna - Budapest and Bucharest

	798	42+ 798	32+ 798
Dep. Vienna (Westbf.)	7:45(1+2)	10:20(3)	16:24(3+5)
Arr. Budapest (Deli)	11:15	-0-	-0-
Arr. Budapest (Keleti)	-0-	14:25	20:30
Dep. Budapest (Keleti)	-0-	15:25(1+4)	21:30(3+5+6)
Arr. Bucharest (Nord)	-0-	8:15	13:17

(1)Operates late May to late Sept. (2)Departs from Sudbahnhof railstation. (3)Meal service. (4)Carries sleeping car. Also has couchettes. Meal service. (5)Carries sleeping car on Monday and Thursday. (6)Has second-class couchette daily.

Vienna - Belgrade and Athens   65

Dep. Vienna (Sudbf.)	18:55(1)	22:50(3)	
Arr. Belgrade	7:44(2)	14:00(2)	
Change trains.			
Dep. Belgrade	9:22(2+5)	14:40(2+6)	23:55(7)
Arr. Athens	9:00(4)	14:41(4)	23:07(4)

(1)Carries sleeping car. Has couchettes. (2)Day 2.   (3)Has couchettes early July to late Sept. (4)Day 3.   (5)Couchettes are replaced by sleeping car on Mon. and Fri. from late May to late Sept. Meal service. (6)Carries sleeping car several days in each week. Has couchettes daily. Meal service on Days 2 and 3.   (7)Supplement charged. Has couchettes. Meal service on Day 3.

Vienna - Belgrade and Istanbul   65

Dep. Vienna (Sudbf.)	18:55(1)
During Summer Time, set your watch back one hour.	
Arr. Belgrade	7:44 Day 2
Change trains.	
Dep. Belgrade	9:32(2)Day 2
All year, set your watch forward 2 hours.	
Dep. Kapikule	4:25(3)Day 3
Arr. IstTanbul	10:30

(1)Carries sleeping car. Also has couchettes. (2)Reservation required. Has couchettes. (3)Meal service.

Innsbruck - Verona and Milan   381

Dep. Innsbruck	1:42(1)	6:38	10:00(3)	17:29(4)
Arr. Verona (P.N.)	6:00	11:25	14:25	21:13(4)
Change trains.				
Dep. Verona (P.N.)	6:40	11:56(2)	14:51	21:24(4)
Arr. Milan	8:35	13:45	16:35	22:50

(1)Carries sleeping car. Has couchettes. (2)Light refreshments. (3)Meal service. (4)TEE. Direct train. No train change in Verona. Reservation required. Meal service.

Innsbruck - Verona - Bologna - Florence - Rome 381

Dep. Innsbruck	1:42(1)	10:00(3)	16:05	18:54(1)	21:48(6)
Arr. Verona	6:00	14:25	20:56	0:14	2:16
Dep. Verona	6:20	14:41(3)	21:32(4)	0:39(1)	2:36(6)
Arr. Bologna	7:47	16:06	23:30	1:56	4:05
Dep. Bologna	8:17(2)	16:24(3)	1:26(4)	2:20(1)	4:27(6)
Arr. Florence	9:38(2)	17:40(3)	2:50(4)	3:47(1)	5:43(6)
Arr. Rome (Ter.)	13:18	21:12	6:30(5)	7:58	9:45

(1)Carries sleeping car. Also has couchettes. (2)Light refreshments. (3)Meal service. (4)Carries sleeping car. (5)Arrives at Rome's Tiburtina railstation. (6)Operates late May to late September. Has couchettes. Carries sleeping car late June to early September.

Salzburg - Venice 75+759

Dep. Salzburg	1:00(1)	7:50(2)	14:00
Arr. Villach	4:05	10:50	17:17
Change trains.			
Dep. Villach	4:45	12:38	18:28
Arr. Venice (S.L.)	9:37	16:54(3)	23:40

(1)Carries sleeping car. Also has couchettes. (2)Meal service. (3)Change trains at Venice's Mestre railstation before taking 9-minute ride to Venice's Santa Lucia railstation.

Vienna - Venice 763

Dep. Vienna (Sudbf.)	7:55(1)	13:00(2)	21:00(3)	23:00(3)
Arr. Venice (S.L.)	16:57	23:40	5:58	9:37

(1)Meal service. (2)Light refreshments. (3)Carries sleeping car. Also has couchettes.

Innsbruck - Zurich 268

There is marvelous Alpine scenery on this route. About 2½ hours before reaching Zurich, the train passes through one of Europe's longest rail tunnels, the 6.3-mile long Arlberg.

Dep. Innsbruck	4:13(1)	6:22(2)	8:55(2+3)	12:30(4+5)
Arr. Zurich	8:33	11:33	13:47	16:33

(1)Carries sleeping car. Also has couchettes. (2)Light refreshments. (3)Change trains in Sargans. (4)Meal service. (5)Plus other departures from Innsbruck at 14:27(4), 16:25(4) and 18:00(4).

BENELUX

BELGIUM, NETHERLANDS and LUXEMBOURG

There is 11-minute train service from Amsterdam (RAI) and 7-minute train service from Amsterdam (Zuid) to the city's Schiphol Airport every 15-30 minutes from 5:29 to 0:45. From the Airport to Amsterdam: 5:15 - 0:12. Tram #4. goes from Amsterdam (Central) to the RAI railstation and v.v.

There is 18-minute train service from Brussels (Central) and 15-minute train service from Brussels (Nord) to that city's National Airport every 20-30 minutes from 5:36 to 23:08. Same schedules (6:00 - 23:37) for the trip from the Airport to Brussels. Bus service is available in the evening when rail transportation is not operating.

The signs you will see at railstations in Belgium, Holland and Luxembourg are:

LUXEMBOURG	BELGIUM and	HOLLAND
Arrival	Arrivee	Aankomst
Departure	Depart	Vertrek
Exit	Sortie	Uitgang
Information	Rensignements	Inlichtingen
Luggage Check-Room	Consignee	Hetbagagedepot
Men	Messieurs	Heren
Restaurant Car	Wagon-Restaurant	Restauratie-Wagen
Sleeping Car	Wagon-Lit	Slaapcoupe
Smoking Compartment	Fumeurs	Rokers
Station	Gare	Station
Timetable	Horaire	Spoorboekje
Track	Quai	Spoor
Women	Dames	Dames

SUMMER TIME
Belgium, Holland and Luxembourg change to Summer Time on the last Sunday of March and convert back to Standard Time on the last Sunday of September.

BENELUX

A list of holidays is helpful because some trains will be noted later in this section as *not* running on holidays. Also, those trains which operate on holidays are filled, and it is necessary to make reservations for them long in advance.

BELGIAN HOLIDAYS

January 1	New Year's Day	August 15	Assumption Day
	Easter	November 1	All Saints Day
	Easter Monday	November 11	Armistics Day
May 1	Labor Day		(World War I)
	Ascension Day	November 15	Dynasty Day
	Whit Monday	December 25	Christmas Day
July 21	Independence Day	December 26	Boxing Day

NOTE: When any holiday falls on Sunday, the following day is also a holiday.

HOLLAND HOLIDAYS

January 1	New Year's Day	May 1	Labor Day
	Good Friday		Ascension Day
	Easter		Whit Monday
	Easter Monday	December 25	Christmas Day
April 30	Queen's Birthday	December 26	Boxing Day

LUXEMBOURG HOLIDAYS

January 1	New Year's Day		Whit Monday
	Shrove Monday	June 23	National Holiday
	Easter	August 15	Assumption Day
	Easter Monday	December 25	Christmas Day
May 1	Labor Day	December 26	Boxing Day
	Ascension Day		

EURAILPASS BONUSES

There are *no* Eurailpass bonuses in Belgium, Holland and Luxembourg.

BENELUX TOURRAIL and JUNIOR TOURRAIL

This pass is for 8 days of unlimited travel (out of any 16-day period from April 1 to October 31) on all the lines of Belgium, Holland and Luxembourg. Sold at the railstations of all 3 countries. The 1983 prices for first-class were: $83(U.S.) for adults 26 and over, $63 for persons 12-25, and $42 for children 6-11.

For second-class: $56, $42 and $28. Children under 6 travel free when not occupying a separate seat.

BELGIAN TOURRAIL

Unlimited train travel in Belgium for either any 5 days out of a 16-day period or for any 8 days out of a 16-day period from April 1 to September 30 The 1983 prices for 5 days first-class were: $40(U.S.) for adults 26 and over, $30 for persons 12-25 years old, and $20 for children 6-11. The 5-day second-class prices were: $26, $19 and $13.

The 1983 prices for 8-day first-class were: $53, $40 and $27. The 8-day second-class prices were: $36, $25 and $18..

BELGIAN 16-DAY CARD

Unlimited train travel for 16 consecutive days. First-class: $70. Second-class: $45.

BELGIAN HALF-FARE CARD

Entitles the traveler to unlimited train travel at half-fare for one month. The 1983 prices were: first-class $14, second-class $10.

ONE-DAY HOLLAND TOURS

Netherlands Railways offers during the Spring and Summer months more than 30 one-day excursions from Amsterdam to interesting destinations. Eurailpass holders pay only for the non-rail portions of these trips and for admission fees.

One example is the day-trip that starts with a train ride from Amsterdam to Rotterdam, entrance to Blijdorp Zoo, a boat ride in the harbor, and the train ride back to Amsterdam.

HOLLAND RETURN

On a same-day roundtrip, the charge for the return ride is 2 guilders, if the return departure is at 20:00 or later.

On a roundtrip that begins with a Saturday train departure, if the return train ride is made anytime the next day, the charge for the return ride on Sunday is 1.50g.

HOLLAND'S ROVER TICKETS

These rail passes are sold in 5 versions. All are available in Holland at railstations and accredited travel agencies. The buyer must provide a passport-size photo or passport number. Prices listed here are valid through the Spring of 1984. Children 4 to under 10 travel at 40% discount. Children under 4 travel free.

One-Day Rover　　One day of unlimited train travel. In 1984, first-class cost 68.50 guilders. Second-class: 45.50g.

3-Day Rover　　Three consecutive days of unlimited train travel. In 1984, first-class cost 99g. Second-class: 66g.

7-Day Rover   Seven consecutive days of unlimited train travel. In 1984, first-class cost 133g. Second-class 91.50g.

One-Month Rover   One month of unlimited train travel. In 1984, first-class cost 490g. Second-class 330g.

Multirover   One day of unlimited train travel. Valid for 2-6 people. Cannot be used from 24:00 Sunday to 9:00 Monday. In 1983, first-class cost 96g for 2 persons, 114.50g for 3, 132.50g for 4, 151g for 5, and 169g for 6. Second-class: 64g for 2 persons, 76.50g for 3,   88.50g for 4,   101g for 5, and 113g for 6.

HOLLAND'S FAMILY CARD (GEZINSTOERKAART)

Unlimited train travel any 4 days in a 9-day period for parents and any number of their children under 18 years old. A passport photo of one of the parents is required. Valid only during June, July and August. Sold at railstations. In 1984, first-class cost 180g, second-class 130g.

LUXEMBOURG'S CARTES D'ABONNEMENT

Unlimited train and bus travel. Prices charged in 1984:

One-Day Carte   Second-class only. Not valid for journeys departing from or arriving at border stations. 179 Luxembourg francs.

5-Day Carte   Valid any 5 days within a 15-day period for either first or second-class. 517FL.

One-Month Carte   Second-class only. Valid from first to last day of one calendar month. 1,375FL.

LUXEMBOURG'S SENIOR CITIZEN HALF-FARE

Presentation of identity card or passport required. People over 65 receive 50% discount on both first and second-class tickets. Not valid for journeys departing from or arriving at border stations.

LUXEMBOURG'S RETURN TRIP DISCOUNT

There is a 50% discount for both weekend and holiday return tickets.

ONE-DAY EXCURSIONS AND CITY-SIGHTSEEING

Here are 39 one-day rail trips that can be made comfortably from 3 major Benelux cities, returning to them in most cases before dinner time. (Five of these trips offer, in addition to interesting destinations, scenic fields of flowers in bloom mid March through May.) Notes are provided on what to see at each destination. The number after the name of each route is the Cook's timetable.

Details on 3 other rail trips recommended for exceptional scenery and schedules for international connections conclude this section.

The 3 base cities are: Amsterdam, Brussels and Luxembourg City.

Amsterdam

Your city-sightseeing in Amsterdam should include the Rijksmuseum (State Museum)collection of Rembrandt, Rubens, Goya and El Greco paintings. Also Dresden china, delftware, tapestries, prints, furniture, dollhouses and sculpture.

The works of Chagall, Cezanne, Picasso, Mondrian, Calder, Pollack, Rodin, Braque and Warhol at the Stedelijkmuseum (Municipal Museum).

A complete spectrum of Van Gogh paintings plus several by Gauguin and Toulousse-Lautrec at the Van Gogh Museum.

All 3 museums are open Tuesday-Saturday 10:00-17:00 and Sunday 13:00-17:00.

Visit the Anne Frank House (263 Prinsengracht), open Monday-Saturday 9:00-17:00 and Sunday 10:00-17:00. Rembrandt's house and, near it, the Flea Market. The Tropical Museum, with its display of Indonesian and Far Eastern art and anthropology. The Amsterdam Historical and Jewish Historical Museum. A 75-minute ride in a glass-roofed canal boat, starting at the piers in front of Central Railstation or at Stadhouderskade, near the Rijksmuseum.

Royal Palace. The Tower of Tears. The altar and organ at the attic church of the Amstelkring Museum. the last of the "hidden" Catholic churches in Holland, with interesting 17th and 18th century furniture. Mint Tower. The Maritime Museum. Free samples when ending the tour of Heineken Brewery, Monday-Friday starting at 10:00.

Brussels

There is rail service between the center of Brussels (Central and Nord stations) and the city's airport every 20-30 minutes 5:36 to 23:08, and from the airport 6:00 to 23:37.

Sightseeing starts in Grand Place, the ornate town square with many gilded buildings. Inside Hotel de Ville (Town Hall), there is a tapestry museum. Next to it is a reproduction of a 17th century brewery. See the 15th century Notre Dame des Victoires church and the 17th century Flemish houses in nearby Place du Grand Sablon.

The marvelous Place Parc de Bruxeles gardens and lakes. The Royal Palace, at one end of this park, is open 9:30-16:00 every day. The Belgian Parliament is located at the other end of the park.

One of the world's best collections of 15th and 16th century Flemish and Dutch paintings (Rubens, Brueghel, Bosch) is exhibited at the Museum of Ancient Art on Rue de la Regence. See the impressive array of African art in The Central Africa Museum.

See the view from the Palais de Justice. The Law Courts. The tapestries in the 13th century Cathedral of St. Michael. The Museum of Modern Art. The Brussels City Museum. The Museum of Arms and Armor. The Postal Museum. The Royal Greenhouses. The Brueghel Museum, in the house where the painter lived his last 6 years. The Railway Museum, on the mezzanine of Brussels' Nord railstation. A bus can be taken 10 miles to Waterloo.

Luxembourg City

The Citadel, with its 53 forts connected by 16 miles of tunnels. Fish Market, site of the city's oldest buildings. The National Museum. The Palace. City Hall. The old quarter, Pfaffenthal, with its medieval buildings. The Fort of Three Acorns. Malakoff Tower. The Church of St. Michael. The Three Towers, marking the outer limits of the town in 1050.

Notre Dame Cathedral. The 4th century Chapel of St. Quirinus, one of the oldest shrines in Christendom. The Museum of History and Art. General Patton's grave in the U.S. Military Cemetery, 3 miles away, at Hamm.

In the following timetables, where a city has more than one railstation we have designated the particular station after the name of the city (in parentheses).

ONE-DAY EXCURSIONS AND CITY-SIGHTSEEING

On day trips from Amsterdam that we have designated "H-L", you will see in the area between Haarlem and Leiden, from mid-March through May, fields of tulips, narcissus, crocus and other bulb flowers in bloom. The region is known as the "Champs de Fleurs" (Fields of Flowers).

Amsterdam - Alkmaar - Amsterdam   224

Dep. Amsterdam   twice each hour
Arr. Alkmaar   32-50 minutes later

Sights in **Alkmaar:** The Friday Cheese Market, from the end of April until the end of September, 10:00-12:00. The organ at St. Lawrence Church. City Hall.

Dep. Alkmaar   twice each hour until 23:51
Arr. Amsterdam   32-50 minutes later

Amsterdam - Alkmaar - Haarlem - Amsterdam   224+223

It is easy to visit both Alkmaar and Haarlem in a single day-trip.

Dep Amsterdam twice each hour	Dep. Haarlem twice each hour.
Arr. Alkmaar 32-50 minutes later.	Arrive Amsterdam 14-18 minutes
Dep. Alkmaar twice each hour.	later
Arr. Haarlem 10-20 minutes later.	

Sights in **Haarlem:** Frans Hals Museum at 62 Groot Heiligland. (Note the address. That is the only mark outside the building !) St. Bavo, Holland's most beautiful church, with its Muller organ. The World Clock at 88 Wagenweg. The collection of 16th to 20th century Dutch, Italian and French paintings exhibited in Teyler's Museum, 16 Spaarne.

Amsterdam - Antwerp - Amsterdam
223

Dep. Amsterdam	7:24(1)	7:48(2)	8:26	8:53(3+4+5)
Arr. Roosendaal	9:09	9:35	10:09	-0-

Change trains.
214

Dep. Roosendaal	9:12	9:43	10:12	-0-
Arr. Antwerp (Cent.)	9:39	-0-	10:39	-0-
Arr. Antwerp (Ber.)	9:46	10:09	10:46	10:55

Sights in **Antwerp:** Visit a diamond firm to watch the cutting of diamonds. The Cathedral, open only in the afternoon. Flemish, Italian, French, Dutch and German masterpieces in the Gallery of Fine Arts. Rubens House, with many of his paintings. The 16th century printing shop in the Plantin-Moretus Museum. The Marine Museum.

The Mayer van den Bergh Museum. The Open-Air Museum of Sculpture. The Folklore Museum. Town Hall. Guild Houses. Vieille Bourse (the Old Stock Exchange). The Rockox Mansion. The view of Antwerp from the 24th floor of Torengebouw.

214

Dep. Antwerp (Ber.)	14:07(4)	14:44(2)	15:44(2+4)	16:44(2+4+6)
Dep. Antwerp (Cent.)	-0-	14:53(2)	15:53(2+4)	16:53(2+4+7)
Arr. Roosendaal	-0-	15:20	-0-	-0-

Change trains.
223

Dep. Roosendaal	-0-	15:23(2)	-0-	-0-
Arr. Amsterdam	16:32	17:05	18:05	19:05

(1)Runs daily, except Sundays and holidays. (2)Light refreshments. (3)TEE. Reservation required. Meal service. (4)Direct train. No train change in Roosendaal. (5)Plus frequent other departures from Amsterdam 8:56 - 20:26. (6)Plus frequent other departures from Antwerp (Berchem) 17:44 - 21:45. (7)Plus frequent other departures from Antwerp (Central) 17:54 - 21:54.

Amsterdam - Arnhem - Amsterdam 235

Dep. Amsterdam (Cent.)	Frequent times from 4:55 to 22:17
Arr. Arnhem	60-70 minutes later

Sights in **Arnhem:** The nearly 3-square-mile Netherlands Open-Air Museum, a collection of several farm villages, depicting rural lifestyles from the 18th to early 20th centuries. Colored arrows direct visitors to one, 2 and 4-hour tours. Open April-October, Monday-Friday 9:00 - 17:00, Sunday 10:00 - 17:00.

At the craft exhibits, wood shoes are chiseled, bread is baked, baskets and paper are made. See a blacksmith at his forge. Don't fail to try the little pancake balls called "poffertjes", and then eat some pannekoeken (traditional Dutch pancakes) and wafelen (waffles).

Also visit the 16th century Grootekerk (Ptotestant Church) and the extensively-restored Eusebiuskerk, a Gothic church. See the Duivelshuis (devil's house).

Dep. Arnhem   Frequent times from 6:28 to 23:11
Arr. Amsterdam   60-70 minutes later

Amsterdam - Brussels - Amsterdam   214

Dep. Amsterdam	7:48(1+2)	8:26(2)	8:53(1+3)	9:26(2)
Arr. Roosendaal	-0-	10:09	-0-	11:09
Change trains.				
Dep. Roosendaal	-0-	10:12	-0-	11:12
Arr. Brussels (Nord)	10:42	11:15	11:26	12:15
Arr. Brussels (Cent.)	-0-	11:19	-0-	12:19
Arr. Brussels (Midi)	10:49	11:23	11:33	12:23

Sights in **Brussels:** See notes about sightseeing in Brussels at the start of this section.

Dep. Brussels (Midi)	13:29(1)	14:09(2)	15:09(2)	16:09(4)
Dep. Brussels (Central)	-0-	14:13(2)	15:13(2)	16:13
Dep. Brussels (Nord)	13:36	14:17(2)	15:17(2)	16:17
Arr. Roosendaal	-0-	15:20	16:20	17:20
Change trains.				
Dep. Roosendaal	-0-	15:23	16:23	17:23
Arr. Amsterdam	16:32	17:05	18:05	19:05

(1)Direct train. No train change in Roosendaal. (2)Light refreshments. (3)TEE. Reservation required. Light refreshments or meal service. (4)Plus other departures from Brussels (Midi) at 17:09(2), 18:09(2), 18:31(2), 19:09(2), 20:09(2), 20:15(1+3) and 21:11(2).

Amsterdam - Delft - Amsterdam   222

Dep. Amsterdam (RAI)   Frequent times from 5:29 to 0:45
Dep. Amsterdam (Zuid)   Frequent times from 5:32 to 0:48
Arr. Delft   55 minutes after departing Zuid station

Sights in **Delft:** The 14th century New Church, where members of the Dutch royal family are buried. The Mausoleum of William the Silent. Prinsenhof Museum. Tetar van Elven Museum, containing the works of Vermeer and Pieter de Hoogh. Old Church. The Grain Market. Town Hall. The Old Delft Canal. The Delft Pottery Factory.

Dep. Delft   Frequent times from 4:44 to 23:25
Arr. Amsterdam (Zuid)   50 minutes later
Arr. Amsterdam (RAI)   3 minutes after arriving at Zuid station

More frequent returns to Amsterdam are possible by taking a local bus from Delft to Den Haag (H.S.), a 9km (5½-mile) ride. Trains leave Den Haag 2-3 times each hour for the 45-minute ride from Den Haag to Amsterdam.

Amsterdam - Den Haag - Amsterdam   223
Dep. Amsterdam   2-3 times each hour from 6:24 to 23:40
Arr. Den Haag   about 45 minutes later

Sights in **Den Haag:** Binnenhof, a complex of palaces and courtyards, including Holland's parliament, the Hall of Knights, and Gevangenpoort, Holland's 14th century prison. Mauritshuis, a great art gallery. The Gemeentemuseum. The Peace Palace. The Hidden Church, at 38 Molenstraat. The Mesdag Museum. The Costume Museum. Municipal Museum. The miniature city of Madurodam, with everything on a scale of 1/25th life size.

There are marvelous paintings in the Johan de Witt Huis at Kneuterdijk 6, open Monday-Saturday 10:00 - 17:00, and on Sundays and holidays 11:00 - 17:00.
Dep. Den Haag   2-3 times each hour until 23:20
Arr. Amsterdam   about 45 minutes later

Amsterdam - Den Haag+Utrecht - Amsterdam (H-L)
It is possible to visit both Den Haag and Utrecht in one day.
223
Dep. Amsterdam   frequent departures from 6:24 to 23:40
Arr. Den Haag (H.S.)   about 45 minutes later
225
Dep. Den Haag   Frequent times from 5:55 to 22:02
Arr. Utrecht   about 40 minutes later

Sights in **Utrecht:** The 13th century Dom Cathedral, and the view from the top of its 465 steps. The museum of mechanical instruments, at 38 Lange Nieuwstraat. The Netherlands Railway Museum, at 6 Van Oldenberneveltlaan. The 11th century St. Peter's Church. The paintings at The Central Museum, 1 Agnietenstraat.
227
Dep. Utrecht   Frequent times from 7:01 to 23:48
Arr. Amsterdam   30 minutes later

For those who prefer the direct trip to Utrecht and to have more time there, refer to notes later in this section under "Amsterdam-Utrecht".

Amsterdam - Gouda - Amsterdam   222a
Dep. Amsterdam   8:21   9:21   10:21   11:21   12:21   13:21
Arr. Gouda   51 minutes later

Sights in **Gouda:** Stained-glass in Sint Janskerk. The 15th century Town Hall. The famous Thursday cheese market.
Dep. Gouda   18 minutes after each hour, from 9:18 to 23:18
Arr. Amsterdam   51 minutes later

Amsterdam - Haarlem - Amsterdam   223
Dep. Amsterdam   twice each hour, from 6:24 to 23:40
Arr. Haarlem   14 minutes later

Sights in **Haarlem:** The Frans Hals Museum at 62 Groot Heiligland (Note the address. That is the only mark outside the building !). St. Bavo, Holland's most beautiful church, with its Muller organ. The World Clock at 88 Wagenweg. Teyler's Museum at 16 Spaarme, for 16th to 20th century Dutch, Italian and French paintings.

Dep. Haarlem   twice each hour, from 7:30 to 23:50
Arr. Amsterdam   14 minutes later

Amsterdam - Hoorn - Amsterdam   Suburban train service.

| Dep. Amsterdam | Frequent times | Dep. Hoorn | Frequent times |
| Arr. Hoorn | 35 minutes later | Arr. Amsterdam | 35 minutes later |

Sights in **Hoorn:** The full-scale enactment of 17th century trades and crafts in Hoorn's "Old Dutch Market" takes place in the Rodesteen Square on Wednesdays mid-June to mid-August: folk dances and stalls with basket weaving, net mending and the making of wood shoes.

Daily from mid-June to mid-August (plus Saturdays and Sundays from mid-August through mid-September), a steam train with antique coaches operates between Hoorn and Medemblik.

See Hoorn's 17th century mansions and warehouses. The collection of paintings and antiques in the West Friesian Museum. The 17th century Weighhouse. The 16th century Hospital of St. John. The 2 medieval churches: Noorderkerk and Oosterkerk. The 16th century St. Mary Tower and East Gate, remains of the original fortification. The 17th century almshouse, St. Pietershof.

Amsterdam - Leiden - Amsterdam   223

Dep. Amsterdam   twice each
                      hour, from
                      6:24 to 23:40
Arr. Leiden   33 minutes later

Sights in **Leiden:** Pieterskerk, the church where the Pilgrim fathers worshipped for 10 years before setting sail for America in 1620. The University. The Royal Arms Museum. The National Museum of Antiquities. The Municipal Museum. The National Ethnicological Museum.

Dep. Leiden   twice each hour
                      until 23:32
Arr. Amsterdam   33 minutes later

Amsterdam - Maastricht - Amsterdam   227

Most of these trains have light refreshments.

| Dep. Amsterdam | 6:28(1) | 7:00(2) | 7:30 | 8:00(1) | 8:28 | 9:00 |
| Arr. Maastricht | 9:02 | 9:40 | 10:02 | 10:40 | 11:02 | 11:40 |

Sights in **Maastricht:** The 6th century St. Servatius Church, oldest church in Holland, where Charlemagne occasionally attended mass. The carved wood columns of the choir in the 10th century Basilica of Our Gracious Lady. The many 17th and 18th century houses on the Stokstraat Quarter. A bus departs from the railstation for the short trip to the Mount St. Peter caves, consisting of 200 miles of labyrinths where people hid during a Spanish invasion in 1570 and where residents sought safety during World War II. It was originally a sandstone quarry, worked from Roman times until the end of the 19th century.

Dep. Maastricht   Frequent times from 5:26 to 21:28
Arr. Amsterdam (Cent.)   2½ hours later
(1)Runs Monday-Friday, except holidays. (2)Runs daily, except Sundays and holidays.

Amsterdam - Paris - Amsterdam   214

Dep. Amsterdam (Cent.)   7:00(1)   7:48(2)   8:53(3)
Arr. Paris (Nord)   12:52   13:52   14:11
                           *   *   *
Dep. Paris (Nord)   15:18(2)   16:45(2+4)   17:41(3)
Arr. Amsterdam (Cent.)   21:33   23:06   22:45

(1)Operates late June to early September. (2)Light refreshments. (3)TEE. Reservation required. Light refreshments or meal service. (4)Change trains in Brussels' Midi station.

Sights in **Paris:** As indicated above, it is possible to make a one-day round-trip from Amsterdam to Paris, although leaving only enough time in Paris to stroll the Champs Elysee from Place Concorde to the Arch of Triumph before having to board the train for the ride back to Amsterdam.

Amsterdam - Rotterdam - Amsterdam (H-L)   223

Dep. Amsterdam   Frequent times from 5:47 to 23:26
Arr. Rotterdam (Cent.) 60 minutes later

Sights in **Rotterdam:** The view from the top of the 365-foot high Euromast. Nearby, Heineken's Brewery (Crookswigksingle 50). The fantastic collection of 15th to 19th century Flemish and Dutch paintings and a wing of modern sculpture and art (Van Gogh and Kandinsky to the present day) in the Boymans-van Beuningen Museum (Mathenesserlaan 18-20). Devices used by smugglers to defraud customs, at the Profesor van der Poel Tax Museum (Parklaan 14).

The collection of globes, ships and atlases in the Maritime Museum (Burgemeester's Jacobplein 8). The 75-minute boat trip in the harbor, one of the world's largest ports, departing every 45 minutes from Willemsplein Landing. Stroll through the noteworthy Lijnbaan shopping center. Hear a free lunchtime concert every day at De Doelen, an enormous complex of music and congress halls, just across from Central Station.

Unwind in the 10,000-acre Zuiderpark, Plaswijck Park, Zuiderparkgordel, Het Park, and the Kralingse Bos (woods). See the wide variety of trees in Arboretum Trompenburg. Visit Blijdrop Zoo. See the many statues located throughout the city, particularly Mastroianni's "Kiss", at the Central Railroad Station.

The collection of folk art of primitive cultures from the non-Western world at the Museum of Georgraphy and Ethnology (Willemskade 25). Complete 17th, 18th and 19th-century interiors at the Rotterdam Historical Museum in the Schielandhus. Many art galleries, including Lijnbaan Centrum (Linjbaan 165) and Kunstzaal (Zuidplein 120).

Nearby, Delfshaven, the port from which the Puritans started their voyage to the New World, sailing from there on July 22, 1620, before boarding the Mayflower off the English coast. That group spent its last night praying in Delfshaven's Reformed Church, now called Pelgrimvaderskerk (Pilgrim Fathers' Church). A stained-glass window and a plaque there commemorate the Pilgrims' sailing.

The Netherlands Tourist Information Bureau (look for its "VVV" sign) has offices all over Holland. The main office in Rotterdam features a "Lunchtime Tour" daily except Sunday (12:00-14:00) that includes visiting Delfshaven, the "De Dubbelde Palmboom" Museum (with everyday objects used centuries ago in Rotterdam), and a pewter workshop in the Sack Carriers guildhouse, plus a typical Dutch lunch, all at a little over 8 Guilders.

Dep. Rotterdam (Cent.)	Frequent times from 5:29 to 23:03
Arr. Amsterdam	60 minutes later

Amsterdam - Rotterdam + Den Haag - Amsterdam (H-L)

This circle trip allows seeing only a few of the sights in Rotterdam (see notes in preceding listing) and in Den Haag (see notes earlier in this section), but one can see something of both Rotterdam and Den Haag in this one-day trip.

222	
Dep. Amsterdam (RAI)	Frequent times from 5:29 to 0:45
Arr. Rotterdam (Cent.)	65 minutes later
222 + 223	
Dep. Rotterdam (Cent.)	Frequent times from 4:25 to 23:11
Arr. Den Haag (Hbf.)	16 minutes later
222 + 223	
Dep. Den Haag	Frequent times from 5:12 to 23:35
Arr. Amsterdam (RAI)	35 minutes later

Amsterdam - Utrecht - Amsterdam (H-L)   235
Dep. Amsterdam   Frequent times from 6:28 to 23:33
Arr. Utrecht   36 minutes later
    Sights in **Utrecht:** see notes earlier in this section under "Amsterdam -
Den Haag + Utrecht - Amsterdam".
Dep. Utrecht   3-4 times each hour until 0:15
Arr. Amsterdam   36 minutes later

Brussels - Amsterdam - Brussels   214
Dep. Brussels (Midi)   6:18   7:09(1)   8:09(1+2)   9:09(1+6)
Dep. Brussels (Cent.)   4 minutes after departing Midi station
Dep. Brussels (Nord)   4 minutes after departing Central station
Arr. Amsterdam   9:43   10:04   11:04   12:04
    Sights in **Amsterdam:** See notes about sightseeing in Amsterdam at the
start of this section.
Dep. Amsterdam   13:26(1)   14:26   15:26(1)   16:26(1+7)
Arr. Brussels (Nord) 16:14   17:22   18:15   19:15
Arr. Brussels (Cent.)   4 minutes after arriving Nord station
Arr. Brussels (Midi)   4 minutes after arriving Central station
(1)Light refreshments. (2)Runs Saturdays, Sundays and holidays. (3)TEE. Reservation required. Meal service, if specified when reserving seat. (4)Runs daily,
except Sundays and holidays. (5)Runs daily, except Saturday. (6)Plus other departures from Brussels at 9:55(3+4) and 10:09(1).   (7)Plus other departures from
Amsterdam at 17:26(1), 17:53(3+5), 18:26(1), 19:26(1) and 20:26.

Brussels - Antwerp - Brussels   214
Dep. Brussels (Midi)   Frequent times from 6:18 to 23:14
Dep. Brussels (Central)   4 minutes later
Dep. Brussels (Nord)   4 minutes after departing Central station
Arr. Antwerp (Central)   45 minutes after departing Brussels (Midi)
    Sights in **Antwerp:** See notes about sightseeing in Antwerp earlier in this
section under "Amsterdam - Antwerp - Amsterdam".
Dep. Antwerp (Central)   Frequent times from 6:36 to 23:18
Arr. Brussels (Nord)   40 minutes later
Arr. Brussels (Central)   4 minutes after arriving Nord station
Arr. Brussels (Midi)   4 minutes after departing Central station

Brussels - Bruges - Brussels   206
Dep. Brussels (Nord)   7:58   8:17   8:51   9:50   10:48   11:25
Dep. Brussels (Cent.)   6 minutes after departing Nord station
Dep. Brussels (Midi)   5 minutes after departing Central station
Arr. Bruges   9:12   9:25   9:57   10:57   11:57   12:36

Sights in **Bruges:** The relic (displayed on Fridays) brought from the Second Crusade to Bruges in 1150, at the 12th century Basilica of the Holy Blood. Also there, a fine display of gold, silver and copper artwork. See the lace, pottery, gold pieces, musical instruments and weapons in the 15th century mansion that houses the Gruuthuse Museum.

The black slate and gilded brass 16th century effigies in the Church of Our Lady. Behind the Church, the Dutch masterpieces at the Groeninge museum (open daily 9:30-12:00 and 14:00-17:00).

The artwork at the Memling Museum, in a section of the 13th century Hospital of St. John (open 9:00-12:30 and 14:00-18:00 in Summer, 9:00-12:00 and 14:00-16:00 the rest of the year). Paintings and silverwork at the Archer's Guild of St. Sebastian.

The famous 47-bell carillon in the city's main square, Markt. The Tourist Office is in the nearby Government Palace. Canal boats leave from several docks for half-hour cruises with English-language guides.

Dep. Bruges	Frequent times from 6:24 to 23:08
Arr. Brussles (Midi)	One hour later
Arr. Brussels (Cent.)	10 minutes after arriving Midi station
Arr. Brussels (Nord)	3 minutes after arriving Central station

Brussels - Cologne (Koln) - Brussels   206

Dep. Brussels (Midi)	6:36(1)	8:12(1)	10:08(2)	
Dep. Brussels (Cent.)4	minutes after departing Midi station			
Dep. Brussels (Nord)	5 minutes after departing Central station			
Arr. Cologne	9:18	10:43	12:48	

Sights in **Cologne:** The Cathedral, above all, that took 600 years to build. The view of Cologne from the top of the Cathedral. The Dionysos Mosaic, on the side of the Cathedral. The luxury shops on Hohestrasse. The Wallraf-Richartz Museum, with its collection of Cologne masters. The 15th century Gurzenich.

The Zoo. The Roman-German Museum. The Metropolitan Historical Museum. Old Town Hall. Praetorium, with its 1st-4th century Roman Palace ruins. The 3rd century Roman Tower. St. Pantaleon Church. St. Andreas Church. Relics and treasures in the Golden Room of the Church of St. Ursula.

Dep. Cologne	13:20(1)	15:08(1)	17:06(2)	18:18(1+4)
Arr. Brussels (Nord)	15:47	17:46	19:49	20:46
Arr. Brussels (Cent.)	-0-	17:53	19:56	20:53
Arr. Brussels (Midi)	15:55	17:56	19:59	20:56

(1)Light refreshments. (2)Meal service. (3)Operates late May to late September. (4)Plus other departures from Cologne at 20:20(1) and 20:50(3).

Brussels - Gent - Brussels 206

Dep. Brussels (Nord)	Frequent times from 5:47 to 23:14
Dep. Brussels (Cent.)	4 minutes after departing Nord station
Dep. Brussels (Midi)	5 minutes after departing Central station
Arr. Gent (St. Pieters)	40-50 minutes after departing Nord station

Sights in **Gent:** The superior collection of paintings at the Fine Arts Museum. The collection of furniture at the Museum of Decorative Arts. The reproductions of medieval Gent homes, ironwork, costumes and weapons at the Byloke Museum.

The fantastic altarpiece in St. Bavo's Cathedral. See the foreboding dungeons and torture chambers in the 12th century Gravensteen (Castle of the Counts), modeled 8 centuries ago on forts visited by Philip of Alsace when he led Crusaders in Syria. Sint Jorishof, built in 1228 and operated as a hotel since the 15th century. It is believed to be the oldest hotel in Europe, with 70 rooms in the original building.

Dep. Gent (St. Pieters)	Frequent times to 23:36
Arr. Brussels (Midi)	30-35 minutes later
Arr. Brussels (Cent.)	6 minutes after arriving Midi station
Arr. Brussels (Nord)	3 minutes after arriving Central station

Brussels - Liege - Brussels 206

Dep. Brussels (Midi)	Frequent times from 6:33 to 22:32
Dep. Brussels (Central)	4 minutes later
Dep. Brussels (Nord)	6 minutes after departing Central station
Arr. Liege (Guillemins)	72 minutes after departing Brussels (Midi)

Sights in **Liege:** There are many museums on and near Rue Feronstree. The wonderful collection of illuminated manuscripts, ancient Roman pottery, tapestries, medieval sculpture and ancient coins in the Musee Curtius (do not miss seeing the enormous twin fireplaces in the large hall on the second floor). In a building at the rear of the Curtius is the Musee du Verre, which has an incredible collection of ancient Egyptian and Roman glassware.

See the exhibit of very beautiful guns in the Musee d'Armes, on nearby Quai de Maestricht. The clocks, tapestries, wood paneling, chandeliers, leather covered walls, porcelain, kitchen utensils and furniture in the Musee d'Ansembourg. The collection of impressionist and expressionist paintings (Courbet, Corot, Chagall, Gauguin and Picasso) at the Musee des Beaux-Arts. The Aquarium.

See the columned courtyard at the Palais des Princes-Eveques. Stroll La Roture, the city's old quarter. Visit the colorful Sunday market at La Batte. Shop the boutiques on Rue Pont de I'lle and Rue Vinave de I'lle.

Dep. Liege (Guillemins)	Frequent times from 6:20 to 23:47
Arr. Brussels (Nord)	60-70 minutes later
Arr. Brussels (Central)	6 minutes after arriving Nord station
Arr. Brussels (Midi)	3 minutes after arriving Central station

Brussels - Luxembourg - Brussels 216

Dep. Brussels (Midi)	6:00(1)	7:19(2)	8:18	8:40(6)
Dep. Brussels (Cent.)	6:05(1)	-0-	8:22	8:44
Dep. Brussels (Nord)	6:10(1)	7:26(2)	8:28	8:50
Dep. Brussels (Q.L.)	6:22(1)	7:36(2)	8:40	9:00
Arr. Luxembourg	8:42	9:49	11:15	11:53

Sights in **Luxembourg:** See notes about sightseeing in Luxembourg at the start of this section.

Dep. Luxembourg	12:08(4)	14:35(1)	15:22	16:59(4+7)
Arr. Brussels (Q.L.)	14:17	17:02	18:02	19:14
Arr. Brussels (Nord)	14:27	17:12	18:13	19:25
Arr. Brussels (Cent.)	-0-	17:24	18:18	-0-
Arr. Brussels (Midi)	14:34	17:28	18:22	19:33

(1)Runs Monday-Friday, except holidays. (2)Reservation required. Meal service. (3)Runs daily, except Sundays and holidays. (4)Meal service. (5)Change trains in Arlon. (6)Plus other departures from Brussels (Midi) at 9:40(1), 10:40, 12:12(2) and 12:40(3). (7)Plus other departures from Luxembourg at 17:30, 17:59(5), 19:21(1), 20:00(5) and 20:16(4).

Brussels - Namur - Brussels 216

Dep. Brussels (Midi)	40 minutes after each hour (8:40-22:40)
Dep. Brussels (Central)	4 minutes later
Dep. Brussels (Nord)	6 minutes after departing Central station
Arr. Namur	One hour after departing Brussels (Midi)

Sights in **Namur:** The silver art in Sisters of Our Lady Convent. The fortress. The baroque 18th century Cathedral. The Diocesan Museum. The extremely elegant Casino, featuring gastronomic feasts.

Dep. Namur	24 minutes after each hour until 22:24
Arr. Brussels (Nord)	47 minutes later
Arr. Brussels (Central)	6 minutes after arriving Nord station
Arr. BRussels (Midi)	4 minutes after arriving Central station

Brussels - Paris - Brussels 106

Dep. Brussels (Midi)	6:41(1+2)	7:30(1+3)	8:15	10:06(4+5)
Arr. Paris (Nord)	9:09	10:05	11:18	12:52

Sights in **Paris:** As indicated here, it is possible to make a one-day round-trip from Brussels to Paris, but not to have enough time to see even a fraction of the sights there. There is sufficient time to stroll the Champs Elysee from Place Concorde to the Arch of Triumph and to sit at a sidewalk cafe and watch the Parisians. For complete notes on city-sightseeing in Paris, see the start of the section on France, later in this chapter.

Dep. Paris (Nord)	15:18(4)	17:41(1)	18:40(1+2)	19:27(6+8)
Arr. Brussels (Midi)	18:17	20:08	21:07	22:30

TEE. Reservation required. Meal service. (2)Operates early September to late June. Runs Monday-Friday, except holidays. (3)Runs daily, except Sunday. (4)Light refreshments. (5)Operates late June to early September. (6)Meal service. (7)Runs daily, except Saturday. (8)Plus another departure from Paris at 20:30(1+7).

Brussels - Tournai - Brussels   201

Dep. Brussels (Nord)	8:04	9:08	10:08	11:08(1)	12:08
Dep. Brussels (Midi)	8:18	9:18	10:18	11:18(1)	12:18
Arr. Tournai		9:25	10:25	11:25	12:25	13:25

Sights in **Tournai:** One of Belgium's leading art towns.

Dep. Tournai	12:27	13:27(2)	14:27	15:27	16:24(4)
Arr. Brussels (Midi)	13:33	14:33	15:33	16:35	17:35
Arr. Brussels (Nord)	11 minutes after arriving at Midi station				

(1)Runs daily, except Sundays and holidays. (2)Runs daily, except Saturday. (3)Runs Monday-Friday, except holidays. (4)Plus other departures from Tournai at 17:27, 18:27, 19:27, 20:21(3), 21:23 and 22:35(3).

Luxembourg - Basel - Luxembourg   176

Dep. Luxembourg	5:38(1)	7:55(1)	10:00(2)
Arr. Basel (S.B.B.)	10:06	12:30	13:39

Sights in **Basel:** Superb Holbein, Delacroix, Gaugin, Matisse, Ingres, Courbet and Van Gogh paintings in the Kunstmuseum on St. Alban Graben. The collection of 18th century clothing, ceramics and watches in the Kirschgarten. The Historical Museum in the Franciscan church in Barfusserplatz. Shop on Freiestrasse. See the 16th century Town Hall. The fishmarket. The 15th century New University. Take a boat excursion from the pier in the back of Hotel Three Kings. See the view of the city from the Wettstein Bridge. Visit Munsterplatz.

Dep. Basel (S.B.B.)	13:20(2)	16:25(2)
Arr. Luxembourg	16:49	20:06

(1)Runs daily, except Sundays and holidays. (2)Meal service.

Luxembourg - Bonn - Luxembourg

625			623		
Dep. Luxembg	6:40(1)	7:27(3)	Dep. Bonn	16:45(2)	18:29(4)
Arr. Trier	7:22	8:10	Arr. Trier	18:58	20:32
Change trains.			Change trains.		
623			625		
Dep. Trier	8:20(2)	8:20(2)	Dep. Trier	19:21	21:33
Arr. Bonn	10:51	10:51	Arr. Luxembg	20:07	22:15

(1)Runs daily, except Sundays and holidays. (2) Light refreshments. (3)Runs Sundays and holidays only. (4)Runs Monday-Friday. Light refreshments.

Sights in **Bonn:** The government buildings in the capital of West Germany. Beethoven's birthplace. The University, in the Electors' Castle. Collegiate Church and Cloister. Poffelsdorf Castle. Jesu Church. The Rhineland Museum. The 13th century Remegius Church. The view from the Alte Zoll.

Luxembourg - Brussels - Luxembourg   216

Dep. Luxembourg	7:01(1)	8:23	9:34(2)	10:19(1)
Arr. Brussels (Q.L.)	9:18	11:02	11:52	13:02
Arr. Brussels (Nord)	9:28	11:12	12:03	13:12
Arr. Brussels (Cent.)	9:32	11:18	-0-	13:18
Arr. Brussels (Midi)	9:36	11:22	12:11	13:22

Sights in **Brussels:** See notes about sightseeing in Brussels at the start of this section.

Dep. Brussels (Midi)	13:40(3)	13:57(2+4)	15:37(2)	16:39(6)
Dep. Brussels (Cent.)	13:44(3)	14:01(2+4)	-0-	16:43(6)
Dep. Brussels (Nord)	13:50(3)	14:06(2+4)	15:44(2)	16:49(6)
Dep. Brussels (Q.L.)	14:00(3)	14:16(2+4)	15:55(2)	17:00(6)
Arr. Luxembourg	16:55	16:34	18:08	19:49

(1)Runs daily, except Sundays and holidays. (2)Meal service. (3)Change trains in Arlon. (4)Runs Monday-Friday, except holidays. (5)Light refreshments. (6)Plus other departures (from all 4 Brussels stations), leaving Midi station at 18:02(2), 18:58(4), 19:40 and 22:23(5).

Luxembourg - Clervaux - Luxembourg   217

The best view (from the viaduct) as you depart Luxembourg City is from the left-hand side of the train.

Dep. Luxembourg	6:05(1)	9:37	10:00	12:08
Arr. Clervaux	7:07	10:28	11:10	12:59

Sights in **Clervaux:** The Benedictine Abbey of St. Maurice. De Lannoi Castle, with its Museum and the World War II U.S. Army tank that is a monument of the "Battle of the Bulge". The Castle is open 10:00-17:00 June through September (13:00-17:00 on Sundays and bank holidays the rest of the year).

Dep. Clervaux	12:45(2)	17:14	19:55
Arr. Luxembourg	13:52	18:05	20:45

(1)Runs Monday-Friday, except holidays. (2)Runs daily, except Sundays and holidays.

Luxembourg - Cologne (Koln) or Dusseldorf - Luxembourg

625			634	
Dep. Luxembourg	6:40(1)	7:27(4)	Dep. Dusseldorf	17:30(3)
Arr. Trier	7:22	8:10	Arr. Cologne	17:52
Change trains.			Change trains.	
623			623	
Dep. Trier	9:50(2)	9:50(2)	Dep. Cologne	18:33
Arr. Cologne	12:32	12:32	Arr. Trier	21:25
Change trains.			Change trains.	
634			625	
Dep. Cologne	13:00(3)	13:00(3)	Dep. Trier	21:33
Arr. Dusseldorf	13:25	13:25	Arr. Luxembourg	22:15

(1)Runs daily, except Sundays and holidays. (2)Light refreshments. (3)Meal service. (4)Runs Sundays and holidays only.

Sights in **Cologne:** See notes about sightseeing in Cologne earlier in this section, under "Brussels - Cologne" one-day roundtrip.

Sights in **Dusseldorf:** Many sensational modern buildings. The Paul Klee collection at Kunstammlung Nordhein-Westfallen. The Goethe Museum, with its firt editions, paintings and over 30,000 manuscripts. The Aquarium at the Museumbunker am Zoo. Hofgarten. The Fine Arts Museum. Jagerhof Castle.

Luxembourg - Frankfurt - Luxembourg

625			662		
Dep. Luxembg	6:40(1)	9:40	Dep. Frankfurt	15:29(3)	18:29(2)
Arr. Koblenz	8:43	11:43	Arr. Koblenz	16:57(3)	19:57
Change trains.			Change trains.		
662			625		
Dep. Koblenz	8:57(1)	11:57(2)	Dep. Koblenz	17:36	20:11
Arr. Frankfurt	10:26	13:26	Arr. Luxembg	20:07	22:15

(1)Runs daily, except Sundays and holidays. (2)Meal service. (3)Change trains in Trier. Light refreshments Koblenz to Trier.

Sights in **Frankfurt:** Goethe's House. Goethe's Museum. The Zoo. The emperor's coronation hall in the Romer complex at medieval Romerberg square. The wonderful doors in the 13th century Leonhardskirche. The 13th century chapel of Saalhof in the remains of the palace of Frederick Barbarossa. Cloth Hall. The Botanical Garden. The pews and murals in the Catherdral of St. Bartholomew. The Church of St. Nicholas.

Luxembourg - Koblenz - Luxembourg 625

Dep. Luxembourg	6:40	9:40
Arr. Trier	7:22	10:22
Arr. Koblenz	8:43	11:43

   Sights in **Koblenz:** Old Town. St. Castor's Church. The Middle Rhine Museum.

Dep. Koblenz	12:11	15:11	20:11
Dep. Trier	13:47	16:47	21:47
Arr. Luxembourg	14:15	17:15	22:15

Luxembourg - Liege - Luxembourg 217

| Dep. Luxembourg | 5:56(1) | 9:37 |
| Arr. Liege (Guillemins) | 9:54 | 12:06 |

   Sights in **Liege:** See notes about sightseeing in Liege earlier in this section, under "Brussels-Liege".

| Dep. Liege (Guillemins) | 15:25 | 18:22 |
| Arr. Luxembourg | 18:05 | 20:45 |

(1)Runs Monday-Friday, except holidays. Change trains in Gouvy.

Luxembourg - Mainz - Luxembourg

625			662		
Dep. Luxembourg	6:40		Dep. Mainz	18:39(1)	19:13(1)
Arr. Koblenz	8:43		Arr. Koblenz	19:35	20:03
Change trains.			Change trains.		
662			625		
Dep. Koblenz	8:49		Dep. Koblenz	-0-	20:11
Arr. Mainz	9:41		Arr. Luxembourg	-0-	22:15

(1)Meal service.

   Sights in **Mainz:** The art collection in the Cathedral. The Museum of the Central Rhineland. The rare books in the World Museum of Printing in the Romischer Kaiser. The restored Baroque mansionns on the Schillerplatz and Schillerstrasse, in the Kirschgarten. Old Town. The sculptures in the Diocesan Museum.

Luxembourg - Metz - Luxembourg   176
Dep. Luxembourg   6:18(1)   7:55(2)   10:00   10:33(2)   12:50(3)
Arr. Metz   50 minutes later

Sights in **Metz:** The oldest church in France, the 4th century Pierre-aux-Nonains. The largest stained-glass windows in the world, in the 16th century Cathedral of Saint Etienne. The Cathedral was formed by the joining of two 12th century churches into a single building. Its contemporary Marc Chagall and Jacques Villon stained-glass are exceptional. There are Gallo-Roman antiquities in the city's Museum. Walk across the 13th century Porte des Allemands (Gate of the Germans).

Dep. Metz   11:13   13:58   16:04   17:05(2)   19:22(5)
Arr. Luxembourg   50 minutes later

(1)Runs Sundays and holidays only. (2)Runs daily, except Sundays and holidays. (3)Change trains in Thionville. (4)Runs Monday-Friday, except holidays. (5)Plus other departures from Metz at 20:01, 21:48(4) and 23:01.

Luxembourg - Paris - Luxembourg   177
Dep. Luxembourg   5:38(1+2)   6:46(3)   7:55(1)
Arr. Paris (Est)   9:22   11:25   11:52

Sights in **Paris:** As indicated above, it is possible to make a one-day round-trip from Luxembourg to Paris, although leaving only enough time in Paris to stroll the Champs Elysee from Place Concorde to the Arch of Triumph before having to board a train for the ride back to Luxembourg. For complete notes on city-sightseeing in Paris, see the start of the section on France, later in this chapter.

Dep. Paris (Est)   17:15(2)   18:52(3)   19:50(4)
Arr. Luxembourg   20:49   23:29   23:52

(1)Runs daily, except Sundays and holidays. (2)Supplement charged. Tray meal service. (3)Light refreshments. (4)Runs daily, except Saturday. Tray meal service.

Luxembourg - Saarbrucken - Luxembourg

625		623	
Dep. Luxembourg	9:40	Dep. Saarbrucken	16:09(1)
Arr. Trier	10:22	Arr. Trier	17:19
Change trains.		Change trains.	
623		625	
Dep. Trier	11:33	Dep. Trier	19:21(2)
Arr. Saarbrucken	12:43	Arr. Luxembourg	20:21

(1)Runs daily, except Saturday. (2)Plus another departure from Trier at 21:33.

Sights in **Saarbrucken:** The Electors' Palace. Ludwigskirche. The Saarland Museum. The City Hall.

Luxembourg - Strasbourg - Luxembourg   176

Dep. Luxembourg	7:55(1)	10:00(2)
Arr. Strasbourg	10:58	12:08

Sights in **Strasbourg:** The famous astronomical clock in the Cathedral. The Alsatian Museum at 23 Quai St. Nicholas. Place Kleber. The Chateau des Rohan museums of archaeology, fine arts and decorative arts.

Dep. Strasbourg	14:39(2)	17:57(2)
Arr. Luxembourg	16:49	20:06

(1)Runs daily, except Sundays and holidays. (2)Meal service.

Luxembourg - Trier - Luxembourg   625

Dep. Luxembourg	9:40	12:40
Arr. Trier	10:22	13:22

Sights in **Trier:** There are more Roman monuments here than in any other German city: the 4th century Porta Nigra gate, 2nd and 4th century baths, a 1st century amphitheater, and a 4th century basilica with its throne room of Roman emperors.

See the "Holy Coat of Trier", said to be Christ's robe, in the Romanesque Cathedral, started in the 6th century. Roman and medieval relics in the Municipal Museum. Peter's Fountain in the market square and, nearby, the 17th century Electoral Palace and 18th century Kasselstatt Palace.

Dep. Trier	13:33	15:36(1)	16:33	17:40(2+4)
Arr. Luxembourg	14:15	16:30	17:15	18:35

(1)Runs daily, except Sundays and holidays. (2)Runs Sundays and holidays only. (3)Runs Monday-Friday, except holidays. (4)Plus other departures from Trier at 18:29(3), 19:21 and 21:33.

SCENIC RAIL TRIPS

Most of the scenic rail trips of the Benelux countries are in Holland, and all of those are included in the list of one-day roundtrips from Amsterdam preceding this section. They are the train rides between Amsterdam and Delft, Den Haag, Leiden, Rotterdam and Utrecht. The scenery on these trips is best from mid-March through May: fields of tulips, narcissus, crocus and other bulb flowers in bloom. The region is known as "Champs de Fleurs" (Fields of Flowers).

Three other scenic trips in the Benelux countries are listed below. All are noteworthy for beautiful river scenery.

Liege - Jemelle

This fine farm and river scenery can be seen by taking an indirect route from Brussels to Luxembourg.

206

Dep. Brussels (Midi)	8:12(1)	10:08(2)	11:10	12:08(2)
Dep. Brussels (Cent.)	4 minutes after departing Midi station			
Dep. Brussels (Nord)	6 minutes after departing Central station			
Arr. Liege (Guillemins)	9:14	11:18	12:22	13:17

Change trains.

218

Dep. Liege (Guillemins)	9:48	11:48	12:48	13:48
Arr. Namur	10:33	12:33	13:33	14:33

Change trains.

216

Dep. Namur	11:41	13:05(1+3)	13:41(4)	14:41(6)
Dep. Jemelle	12:25	-0-	14:25(4)	15:29(5)
Arr. Luxembourg	13:42	14:41	16:05	16:55

(1)Light refreshments. (2)Meal service. (3)Reservation required. (4)Runs daily, except Sundays and holidays. (5)Change trains in Arlon. (6)Plus other departures from Namur at 16:31 and 17:42.

Luxembourg - Liege   217

Excellent farm and river scenery on this easy one-day roundtrip. See page 97 for timetables.

Namur - Dinant

This is a spur off the Brussels-Luxembourg route. The great farm and river scenery here can be seen either by breaking-up the ride from Brussels to Luxembourg (or vice versa), or as an easy one-day roundtrip from Brussels.

For the first way:

216			216	
Dep. Brussels (Midi)	8:18		Dep. Luxembourg	10:19(4)
Dep. Brussels (Cent.)	8:22		Arr. Namur	12:19
Dep. Brussels (Nord)	8:28		Change trains.	
Arr. Namur	9:17		**215**	
Change trains.			Dep. Namur	12:45
215			Arr. Dinant	13:24
Dep. Namur	9:45		Change trains.	
Arr. Dinant	10:23		Dep. Dinant	13:39
Change trains.			Arr. Namur	14:17
Dep. Dinant	11:31(1)	13:39	Change trains.	
Arr. Namur	12:09	14:17	**216**	
Change trains.			Dep. Namur	14:24
216			Arr. Brussels (Nord)	15:12
Dep. Namur	13:05(2)	14:45(3)	Arr. Brussels (Cent.)	15:18
Arr. Luxembrg	14:44	16:55	Arr. Brussels (Midi)	15:22

(1)Runs Monday-Friday, except holidays. (2)Reservation required. Supplement charged. Meal service. (3)Change trains in Arlon. (4)Runs daily, except Sundays and holidays.

Here is the Brussels one-day roundtrip:

216			215	
Dep. Brussels (Midi)	8:18	10:40	Dep. Dinant	13:39
Dep. Brussels (Cent.)	8:22	10:44	Arr. Namur	14:17
Dep. Brussels (Nord)	8:28	10:50	Change trains.	
Arr. Namur	9:17	11:38	**216**	
Change trains.			Dep. Namur	14:24
215			Arr. Brussels (Nord)	15:12
Dep. Namur	9:45	12:45	Arr. Brussels (Cent.)	15:18
Arr. Dinant	10:24	13:24	Arr. Brussels (Midi)	15:22

INTERNATIONAL ROUTES FROM BELGIUM

The Belgian gateway for rail travel to London, Amsterdam, Basel (and on to Zurich and Milan), Cologne (and on to Hamburg and Copenhagen) and Paris (and on to Madrid) is Brussels. (Notes on the route to London appear in Chapter 10.)

Brussels - Amsterdam   214
Dep. Brussels (Midi)	Frequent times from 6:18to 21:11
Dep. Brussels (Cent.)	4 minutes after departing Midi station
Dep. Brussels (Nord)	4 minutes after depsarting Central station
Arr. Amsterdam	3 hours later

Brussels - Basel   63
These trains depart one hour earlier from Late September to early April.

Dep. Brussels (Midi)	7:19(1)	12:12(1)	15:37(1)	18:10(1)	22:23(2)
Dep. Brussels (Nord)	7:26(1)	12:20(1)	15:44(1)	18:19(1)	22:31(2)
Dep. Brussels (Q.L.)	7:36(1)	12:31(1)	15:55(1)	18:30(1)	-0-
Arr. Basel (S.N.C.F.)	13:39	18:25	22:03	1:12	5:20

(1)Meal service. (2)Carries sleeping car. Also has couchettes.

Brussels - Cologne (Koln)   206
Dep. Brussels (Midi)	6:36(1)	7:32(1)	8:12(1)	10:08(2+5)
Dep. Brussels (Cent.)	6:40(1)	-0-	8:17(1)	10:13(2)
Dep. Brussels (Nord)	6:43(1)	7:39(1)	8:22(1)	10:18(2)
Arr. Cologne	9:18	10:20	10:43	12:48

(1)Light refreshments. (2)Meal service. (3)Reservation required. (4)Operates late May to late September. (5)Plus other departures from Midi station at 12:08(2), 15:08(1), 16:00(1+3), 17:44(2), 18:27(1+3), 18:52(4), 20:10(1) and 22:32(1+3).

Brussels - London   via Oostende   (Jetfoil)   52a
Dep. Brussels (Nord)	6:49	9:49(1)	10:24(2)	11:48(4)
Dep. Brussels (Midi)	7:00	10:00(1)	10:34(2)	12:00
Arr. Oostende	8:18	11:15(1)	11:34(2)	13:14
Change to boat.				
Dep. Oostende	8:40	12:00(1)	12:00(2)	13:55

Set your watch back one hour, except from late Sept. to late Oct.

Arr. Dover Docks	9:20	12:40(1)	12:40(2)	14:35
Arr. London (Vict.)	11:17	14:33(1)	14:48(2)	16:36

(1)Runs daily, except Sundays and holidays. (2)Runs Sundays and holidays only. (3)Operates late May to late September. (4)Plus other departures from Brussels (Nord) at 13:42(3) and 16:45(3).

Brussels - London   via Oostende   (Regular Ferry)   52

Dep. Brussels (Nord)	5:47(1)	7:47	8:51(2)	11:48(4)
Dep. Brussels (Midi)	6:00(1)	8:00	9:00(2)	12:00
Arr. Oostende	7:16(1)	9:14	10:14(2)	13:14
Change to boat.				
Dep. Oostende	7:35(1)	10:05	10:45(2)	13:50

Set your watch back one hour, except from late Sept. to late Oct.

Arr. Dover Docks	10:15(1)	12:55	13:35(2)	16:40
Arr. London (Vict.)	13:06(1)	15:10	15:48	18:48

(1)Runs Tuesday-Saturday. (2)Operates early July to late August. Runs Saturday only. (3)Departure time late May to late September. Departs 22:56 late September to late May. (4)Plus another departure from Brussels (Nord) at 23:30(3).

Brussels - Luxembourg   216

Dep. Brussels (Midi)	-0-	8:18(1)	8:40(2)	10:40(7)
Dep. Brussels (Cent.)	-0-	8:22(1)	8:44(2)	10:44
Dep. Brussels (Nord)	6:36	8:28(1)	8:50(2)	10:50
Dep. Brussels (Q.L.)	6:46	8:40(1)	9:00(2)	11:00
Arr. Luxembourg	9:43	11:15	11:53	13:42

(1)Meal service. (2)Change trains in Arlon. (3)Reservation required. (4)Runs daily, except Sundays and holidays. (5)Runs Monday-Friday, except holidays. (6)Light refreshments. (7)Plus other departures from Brussels Midi station at 12:12(1+3), 12:40(2+4), 13:40(2), 13:57(5), 14:40(2+5), 15:37(1), 16:11(5), 16:39, 18:02(1), 18:58(5), 19:40 and 22:23(6).

Brussels - Paris   106

Dep. Brussels (Midi)	0:32(1)	6:41(2+3+4)	7:30(2+5+11)
Arr. Paris (Nord)	6:42	9:10	10:05

(1)Has couchettes. (2)TEE. Reservation required. Meal service. (3)Runs Monday-Friday, except holidays. (4)Operates early September to late June. (5)Runs daily, except Sundays and holidays. (6)Operates late June to early September. (7)Light refreshments. (8)Meal service. (9)Supplement charged. (10)Runs daily, except Saturday. (11)Plus other departures from Brussels at 8:15, 10:06(6+7), 11:03(8), 11:43(2), 14:07(7), 16:08(7), 17:17(2), 17:53(8+9), 18:38(2+3+4), 19:15(8) and 20:42(2+10).

INTERNATIONAL ROUTES FROM HOLLAND

The Dutch gateway for rail travel to London, Basel (and on to Zurich and Milan), Cologne, Hamburg (and on to Copenhagen) and Paris (and on to Madrid) is Amsterdam. (Notes on the route to London appear in Chapter 9.)

Amsterdam - Brussels   214

Dep. Amsterdam	Frequent times from 6:24 to 20:26
Arr. Brussels (Nord)	3 hours later
Arr. Brussels (Cent.)	4 minutes after departing Nord station
Arr. Brussels (Midi)	4 minutes after departing Central station

Amsterdam - Cologne (Koln) - Basle   68

Many castles are seen in the Koblenz-Mainz area as the train travels alongside the Rhine River.

Dep. Amsterdam	7:49(1)	8:38(2)	14:49	19:49(3)
Arr. Cologne	10:46(1)	12:00(2)	18:38	23:39(3)
Arr. Basel (Bad Bf.)	15:25	17:26	0:35	5:28

(1)TEE. Reservation required. Meal service. (2)Meal service. (3)Carries sleeping car. Also has couchettes.

Amsterdam - Hamburg - Copenhagen   67

Dep. Amsterdam	8:01(1)	17:17(2+3)	18:01(3)	20:01(4)
Arr. Hamburg	13:54	22:49	23:16	2:12
Dep. Hamburg	14:02	-0-	-0-	2:21
Arr. Copenhagen	19:29	-0-	-0-	8:09(5)

(1)Light refreshments. (2)Runs daily, except Saturday. (3)Meal service. (4)Has couchettes. (5)Arrives one hour later from late September to late March.

Amsterdam - Luxembourg   63

Dep. Amsterdam	11:51(1)
Arr. Maastricht	14:32
Arr. Luxembourg	18:05

(1)Operates all year. From late September to late May, change trains in Maastricht. Light refreshments until arriving Maastricht.

Amsterdam - London   via Hoek van Holland   (regular ferry)   66
Dep. Amsterdam   9:30(1)   21:16(1)
 Set your watch back one hour.
Arr. London (L'pool)   19:23(2)   9:14
(1)Light refreshments. (2)Arrives 20:18 from late September to late October.

Amsterdam - Paris   76
Dep. Amsterdam   7:00(1)   7:48(2)   8:53(3)   10:53(2)   15:52(2+5)
Arr. Paris (Nord)   12:52   13:52   14:10   16:55   22:06
(1)Operates late June to early September. Light refreshments. (2)Meal service.
(3)TEE. Reservation required. Meal service. (4)Runs daily, except Saturday.
(5)Plus another departure from Amsterdam at 17:53(2+4).

INTERNATIONAL ROUTES FROM LUXEMBOURG

Luxembourg City is a gateway for rail travel to London, Amsterdam, Basel
(and on to Zurich and Milan), Brussels, Cologne, Koblenz (and on to Frankfurt),
and Paris. (Notes on the routes from Amsterdam, Brussels and Paris to London
appear in Chapter 8.)

Luxembourg - Amsterdam   63
Dep. Luxembourg   12:08(1)
Arr. Maastricht   15:21
Arr. Amsterdam   18:03
(1)Operates all year. Change trains in Maastricht from late September to late
May. Light refreshments Maastricht-Amsterdam.

Luxembourg - Basel   176
Dep. Luxembourg   1:18(1)   5:38(2)   7:55(2)   10:00(3)   14:54(3+4)
Arr. Basel (SNCF)   5:20   10:06   12:30   13:39   18:25
(1)Carries sleeping car. Also has couchettes. (2)Runs daily, except Sundays
and holidays. (3)Meal service. (4)Plus other departures from Luxembourg at
18:26(3) and 21:14.

Luxembourg - Brussels   216

Dep. Luxembourg	4:57(1)	7:01(2)	8:23	9:34(3+7)
Arr. Brussels (Q.L.)	7:18	9:18	11:02	11:52
Arr. Brussels (Nord)	7:28	9:28	11:12	12:03
Arr. Brussels (Cent.)	-0-	9:32	11:18	-0-
Arr. Brussels (Midi)	7:37	9:36	11:22	12:11

(1)Light refreshments. (2)Runs daily, except Sundays and holidays. (3)Meal service. (4)Does not stop at Brussels' Cantral railstation. (5)Change trains in Arlon. (6)Runs Monday-Friday, except holidays. (7)Plus other departures from Luxembourg at 10:19(2), 12:08(3+4), 15:20, 16:59(3+4), 17:30, 17:59(5), 19:21(6), 20:00(5) and 20:16(3).

Luxembourg - Cologne
625

Dep. Luxembourg	6:40(1)	7:27(2)	9:40	12:40	14:23(1+5)
Arr. Trier	7:22	8:10	10:22	13:22	15:18

Change trains.
623

Dep. Trier	8:20(3)	9:50(3)	12:50(3)	15:37(1)	16:41(4)
Arr. Cologne	11:11	12:32	15:45	18:39	19:28

(1)Runs daily, except Sundays and holidays. (2)Runs Sundays and holidays only. (3)Light refreshments. (4)Departs Trier at 17:32 on Sunday. (5)Plus another departure from Luxembourg at 15:40.

Luxembourg - Paris   177

Dep. Luxembourg	5:38(1+2)	6:46(3)	7:55(1)	17:20(3+4)
Arr. Paris (Est)	9:22	11:25	11:52	21:56

(1)Runs daily, except Sundays and holidays. (2)Specify meal required when reserving first-class seat. (3)Light refreshments. (4)Supplement charged. (5)Plus another departure from Luxembourg at 17:27(2).

FRANCE

French rail tickets purchased in France are valid for travel any day within 2 months from the date of purchase.

Before boarding a train, passengers are required to validate tickets purchased in France, in one of the many orange-colored machines located at the entrance to the platforms. Tickets are spot-checked on the trains. A person holding a non-validated ticket is subject to a fine.

Train tickets obtained before arrival in France are valid for 6 months, and it is *not* required that a ticket purchased outside France be validated.

The signs you will see at railstaions in France are:

ARRIVEE	ARRIVAL
CONSIGNE	CHECKROOM
DAMES	WOMEN
DEPART	DEPARTURE
ENTREE	ENTRANCE
FUMEURS	SMOKING COMPARTMENT
GARE	STATION
HORAIRE	TIMETABLE
MESSIEURS	MEN
QUAI	PLATFORM
RENSEIGNEMENTS	INFORMATION
SORTIE	EXIT
VOIE	TRACK
WAGON-LIT	SLEEPING CAR
WAGON-RESTAURANT	RESTAURANT CAR

SUMMER TIME

France changes to Summer Time on the last Sunday of March and converts back to Standard Time on the last Sunday of September.

EURAILPASS BONUSES

Ferry crossings on the Irish Continental Line between Le Havre (France) and Rosslare (Ireland) 21 hours, or between Cherbourg (France) and Rosslare 17 hours. Port taxes and cabin accommodations are *not* covered.

The bus (7-franc charge) that transports passengers from le Havre railstation to the boat pier takes people on a first-come-first-served basis. When the bus is filled, people left at the railstation must take a taxi to the pier.

On arrival in Ireland, the bus service there (taking passengers from Rosslare pier to the Rosslare railstation) accommodates all passengers, and at no charge.

Europabus Line #241, Paris to Nice, via Avallon, Lyon and Grenoble (and vice versa).

FRENCH HOLIDAYS

A list of holidays is helpful because some trains will be noted later in this section as not running on holidays. Also, those trains which operate on holidays are filled, and it is necessary to make reservations for them long in advance.

January 1	New Year's Day		Pentecost
	Easter		Pentecost Monday
	Easter Monday	July 14	National Day
May 1	Labor Day		(Bastille Day)
May 8	Victory Day	August 15	Assumption Day
	(World War II)	November 1	All Saints' Day
	Ascension Day	November 11	Armistice Day
	Joan of Arc Day		(World War I)
		December 25	Christmas Day

FRANCE VACANCES

This pass for unlimited train travel is restricted to persons living outside France and its territories.

The first-class prices in 1984 are $170(U.S.) for 7 days, $220 for 15 days, and $345 for one month. For children under 12: $105, $135 and $205. With the 7 or 15-day first-class France Vacances, each pass holder also receives one day of free car rental and 100 kilometers. With the one-month pass this bonus is 2 days of free car rental and 200 kilometers. Car rental is available in 23 cities.

The second-class prices in 1984 are $115 for 7 days, $150 for 15 days, and $230 for one month. For children under 12: $70, $90 and $130.

Both first and second-class passes provide free train transportation between Paris and its airports. The 7-day pass also provides 2 days of subway and bus travel in Paris. The 15-day and one-month passes also provide 4 days of subway and bus travel in Paris.

France Vacances can be purchased from travel agents or from offices of French National Railroad.

FRANCE

WORLD'S FASTEST TRAINS

Since 1981, France has operated the world's fastest trains, the "Trains a Grande Vitesse", which have run at 237 miles per hour and are operated at the top speed of 160mph. The usual composition is 386 seats: 111 in first-class, 275 in second-class.

Reservations are required. Although normal fares are charged at off-peak times, a supplement is charged for those TGV that run at the busiest times. Each TGV has a bar. Meals are brought to seats in some of the first-class cars.

The 1982 service (Paris-Lyon, Paris-Dijon and Paris-Geneva) was expanded in 1983 to include Paris-Marseilles, Paris-Montpelier and Paris-Annecy-Grenoble. A TGV service Paris-Lausanne (with cross-platform transfer in Lausanne for trains to Milan) is scheduled to begin in 1984. Details on TGV schedules appear in Chapter 7.

ONE-DAY EXCURSIONS AND CITY-SIGHTSEEING

Here are 42 one-day rail trips that can be made comfortably from Avignon, Lyon, Nice and Paris, returning to those cities in most cases before dinnertime. Notes are provided on what to see and do at each destination. The number after the name of each route is the Cook's timetable.

Paris

There is rail service from the center of Paris (Nord station) to Charles-de-Gaulle Airport every 15 minutes from 5:26 to 23:26. The rail service from that airport to Paris is every 15 minutes from 5:14 to 23:44

Rail service is also available between 5 Paris stations and Orly Airport at frequent times from 5:32 to 21:02 and every 30 minutes from 21:32 to 0:02 (Blvd. Victor, Invalides, Quai d'Orsay, Austerlitz and Pont de Rungis). There is bus service between Pont de Rungis and Orly from 6:15 to 23:15.

Bus service connects these Paris railstations:
(1) From Austerlitz to Est, Nord and St. Lazare. (2) From Lyon to Est, Nord and St. Lazare. (3) From Nord to Lyon and Austerlitz. (4) From Est to Lyon and Austerlitz.

Your city sightseeing in Paris should include: the Montmartre area and Sacre Coeur. Eiffel Tower. Place Concorde. The Arch of Triumph. The stained-glass at St. Chapelle. Notre Dame Cathedral. Napoleon's Tomb. The Louvre (open daily except Tuesday 9:45-19:00). Luxembourg Palace. Strolling the Champs Elysee. Visit Galleries Lafayette, the most beautiful department store building in the world. The Musee of the Renaissance, in the 16th century Chateau d'Ecouen Castle, with its antique tapestries, ceramics, arms, furniture, outstanding carved white fireplace and painted ceilings. Open daily except Tuesdays 9:45-12:30 and 14:00-17:15.

Marvelous costumes in the Musee de la Mode et du Costume, 10 Ave. Pierre Premier de Serbie. Open daily except Monday 10:00-17:40.

The large poster collection in the Musee de l'Affiche, 18 Rue de Paradis. Open daily except Tuesdays 12:00-18:00.

The Tiepolo ceilings, fantastic staircase, excellent paintings (Rembrandt, Reynolds, Manet, Monet and many other Impressionists) in the Musee Jacquemart-Andre, 12 Rue Louis-Boilly. Open daily except Monday 13:30-17:30.

Paintings and engravings illustrating the history of Paris, along with 17th and 18th century furniture, in the Musee Carnavalet, 23 Rue de Sevigne. Open daily except Monday 10:00-17:40.

The collection of opera costumes, scores and photos in the Museum at the Opera. Open daily except Sunday 10:00-17:00 and during intermissions of performances.

Near the Opera, at 25 Boulevard des Capucines, is the Musee Cognac-Jay, which has an exhibit of lorgnettes, snuff boxes, letter openers and sewing kits, all of them in porcelain, precious metals and jewels. Open daily except Monday and Tuesday 10:00-17:40.

Information about tours sponsored by the Department of Historical Monuments (botanical gardens, the Latin Quarter, churches that are architecturally interesting, private homes) can be obtained at the Caisse Nationale des Monuments Historiques, at 62 Rue Saint-Antoine.

See if you can look through the windows of Fauchon's (finest foods in the world), 26 Place de la Madeleine, and not salivate. There are 2 Fauchon's. One sells extrmely fancy produce (green beans from Kenya, kiwis from New Zealand, breadfruit from Martinique, mangoes from northern Egypt) and canned foods. It also has a wine-liquor section and a delicatessen section with incredible items produced by a staff of 20 cooks: whole glazed ducks decorated with peaches, $50-a-pound fresh foie gras, eggplant stuffed with ground mutton and boiled eggs in watercress sauce, 6 different kinds of ham, a variety of snails, countless salads and every conceivable tidbit.

Across the street from that store is a second Fauchon's. This one, staffed with 20 bakers, offers snacks, beverages and countless sweets. Every year, it sells 18 tons of chocolates, 8 tons of marrons glace and 15 tons of candied fruits (whole melons, strawberries, oranges, prunes). Its prices (prior to franc devaluation in 1983) for chocolates were $14(U.S.) to $16 a pound. The candied fruits were $12 a pound.

For Americans, Fauchon's has all of its 120 salespeople take English-language lessons 3 times a week. (Its total staff numbers 240.) The store stocks such American items as Aunt Jemima's pancake mix, Sarah Lee cheesecake and Fritos. At Thanksgiving, Fauchon's features cans of cranberry sauce and pumpkin pie filling.

Avignon

This walled city, the tourist capital of Provence, can be entered through 14 different gates. You can obtain a city map or a personal guide at the Syndicat d'Initiative (41 Cours Jean-Jaures). During the 14th century, Avignon was briefly the world headquarters of the Catholic Church when it was unsafe for a series of French popes to be in Rome. Take the one-hour tour of the Palace of the Popes. Outside the Palace you can board a trackless 2-car train pulled by a gasoline-powered locomotive and climb to the top of the hill overlooking the Palace for a view of the city and the Rhone Valley.

See the primitive art in the museum in the 14th century Petit Palais. The sculptures in the Lapidary Museum, housed in the 17th century Jesuit Church. The collection of ironwork in the Calvet Museum on Rue Joseph Vernet. The view of Avignon from Villeneuve-les-Avignon, on the other side of the Rhone River.

All-day bus tours from Avignon to many interesting places in this area can be taken from in front of the railstation. One tour includes Roman ruins at St. Remy, the village of Les Baux (sculptured during the Middle Ages from the top of a stone hill), and the Roman theatre in Arles.

Lyon

Occasionally, 2 trains depart from the same track at Lyon's Perrache railstation, heading in opposite directions. Be sure to stand at the correct end (North or South) of the track in order to board the train you want to ride. Check the departure signs at the underground passageway. Do not rely merely on a track number when departing from Perrache railstation !

Next to the North passageway of Track "A" is a take-out restaurant, handy for provisioning your trip.

A metropolitan train connects Lyon's Brotteaux and Perrache railstations. The ride is 15 minutes.

Try to keep from eating at the spectacular Nouvelle Les Halles food market: 65 tantalizing stalls of meat, poultry, fish, produce, cheese, bread, pastry, coffee, tea, spices, wine and candy, plus small restaurants and a florist. Open 7:00-19:00 Monday-Saturday and 7:00-12:00 on Sunday.

Here, you can buy pheasants in plumage, partridges, wild ducks, quail, snipe, frog legs, 4 varieties of oysters, shrimp, eel, cod and sole. There are goose, duck and game pates. Do not fail to sample the 3 Lyon specialties: Morteau de Jesu (pork meat in a pig's foot casing), the peppery pink and white salami, and the garlicky Lyon sausage.

The wine here is magnificent. It has been said that Lyon has 3 rivers: the Rhone, the Saone, and the Beaujolais.

Stroll for a few hours through the winding streets of the 3-block wide half-mile long ancient section (Vieux Lyon) and see the magnificent 15th century Renaissance mansions. Much information is available in the booklet "Guide du Vieux Lyon" sold everywhere in the city.

See the Historical Museum and International Marionette Museum in Lyon's largest Renaissance structure, Hotel de Gadagne. Also in the old town: The tableau of the Cathedral clock at 12:00, 13:00, 14:00 and 15:00. The Roman ruins on the hill atop which the Basilica of Notre Dame de Fourviere is located.

In the modern area, take Bus #13 from the railstation, through the main shopping streets, to the Place de la Croix Rousse and then walk to Place des Terreaux to see City Hall, the 19th century Opera House and The Fine Arts Museum. Do not miss seeing the Italian fountain with its 4 bronze horses, sculptured by the same Bartholdi who created the Statue of Liberty.

Window-shop around Place Bellecourt and along Quai des Celestins. Nearby, see the nearly 2,000-year old collection of Oriental and European silks and velvets in the Musee Historique des Tissus (34 Rue de la Charite). Next door to it, there is a good collection of silver objects, kitchen utensils, furniture, tapestries and enamels in The Museum of Decorative Arts. Also visit The Museum of Printing and Banking (13 Rue de la Poullaillerie) and The Museum of Medicine in Hotel-Dieu on Rue de l'Hopital.

Nice

It is a 15-minute walk South from the railstation to the hotels and casinos along the beach, where boats can be hired. Watch the International Set cavort, and remember that you are now a member of it. Visit the Matisse Museum and the antique shops.

In the following timetables, where a city has more than one railstation we have designated the particular station after the name of the city (in parentheses).

Avignon - Arles - Avignon   151
Dep. Avignon   9:26   12:09   14:50
Arr. Arles   20 minutes later
   Sights in **Arles:** The ancient Roman cemetery, Alyscamps, that contains 400,000 sarcophagi, hand-carved granite caskets. The 21,000-seat Roman arena. The Forum, built during Augustus' rule. The Thermae, from Constantine's era. The 12th century Cloister in the marvelous Romanesque Church of Saint-Trophime.
Dep. Arles   12:35   14:55   16:04(1)   17:54   18:37(2)
Arr. Avignon   20 minutes later
(1)Runs from late June to mid-September. (2)Plus other departures from Arles at 20:14, 22:25 and 22:39.

Avignon - Lyon - Avignon   151
Dep. Avignon   7:03(1)   8:10   10:47   12:57
Arr. Lyon (Perrache)   9:10   10:04   12:46   14:56
   Sights in **Lyon:** See notes about sightseeing in Lyon at the start of this section.
Dep. Lyon (Perrache)   12:16   14:07(2)   17:13(2) 18:43(2+3)
Arr. Avignon   14:46   16:04   19:13   20:39
(1)Light refreshments. (2)Meal service. (3)Plus other departures from Lyon at 20:55(1) and 23:55.

Avignon - Marseille - Avignon   150+151
                151   150   151   150
Dep. Avignon   9:26(1)   11:53(2+3) 12:09(4)   13:40(2+5)
Arr. Marseille
  (St. Ch.)   65 minutes later
   Sights in **Marseille:** Fancy shops on Canebiere, the main street. The dungeon from which the Count of Monte Cristo escaped, at Chateau d'If.
                150   151   150   150
Dep. Marseille
  (St.   13:57(1)   14:44(1)   15:09(2+6) 16:34(2+7+9) Ch.)
Arr. Avignon   65 minutes later
(1)Meal service. (2)TGV. Reservation required. Meal service or light refreshments. (3)Supplement charged. Runs Monday-Friday, except holidays. (4)Light refreshments. (5)Supplement charged only on Saturday. (6)Supplement charged daily, except Saturday. (7)Runs daily, except Saturday. Supplement charged. (8)Supplement charged on Friday and Sunday. (9)Plus other departures from Marseille at 17:08(1), 17:40(2+8), 17:43(4), 19:21(1), 20:27, 21:37, 22:38, 22:55 and 23:54.

Avignon - Monte Carlo - Avignon 151
Dep. Avignon 6:31
Arr. Monte Carlo 11:04

Sights in **Monte Carlo:** The glittering Casino, built in 1865. There is a 12-franc charge to stroll through the huge gaming room, the Salon des Ameriques, where the minimum bet is 10 francs. See the marble pillars in the gilded Hotel de Paris (erected in 1863) and its lovely gardens, next to the Casino. The outstanding Oceanographic Museum and the beautiful Aquarium. The old city, with its Prince's Palace, Palace Museum (Napoleonic items), the collection of dolls in the National Museum, the Museum of Anthropology in the Exotic Garden, and the Zoological Gardens. The changing of the guard at the Palace, daily at 11:55. The array of pleasure boats in the harbor.

Dep. Monte Carlo 18:05 19:19 19:45
Arr. Avignon 22:43 0:04 1:07

Avignon - Nice - Avignon 151
Dep. Avignon 6:31 9:26(1)
Arr. Nice 1033 13:23

It is a 15-minute walk South from the railstation to the hotels and casinos along the beach.

Sights in **Nice:** See notes about sightseeing in Nice at the start of this section.

Dep. Nice 14:58(1) 16:25(1) 18:42 20:00
Arr. Avignon 18:12 20:32 22:43 0:04
(1)Meal service.

Avignon - Nimes - Avignon 162
Dep. Avignon 7:48 9:37 11:49(1) 12:15 12:52(2+3)
Arr. Nimes 30 minutes later

Sights in **Nimes:** Many Roman ruins in excellent condition, such as the 1st century amphitheater (seating 24,000 people) in the center of the city, used in recent years for bullfights to entertain Spanish migrant workers. The construction of the arena was done by fitting large stones together without the use of mortar.

Also see the beautiful 1st century rectangular temple, Maison Carree, and its collection of Roman sculptures. The view of Nimes from the oldest Roman building, Tour Magne, on a hill outside the city. A few miles away is the enormous Pont du Gard Roman aqueduct.

Visit the collection of Iron Age and Roman objects in the Archaeological Museum. Stroll through the 18th century Garden of the Fountain.

Dep. Nimes   12:04   14:25   15:15   15:53(2)   17:02(1+4)

Arr. Avignon   30 minutes later

(1)TGV. Reservation required. Supplement charged. (2)Runs from late June to mid-September. (3)Plus other departures from Avignon at 13:37(1) and 13:59. (4)Plus other departures from Nimes at frequent times from 17:45 to 22:31.

Lyon - Annecy - Lyon   167

En route, the train splits. Some cars go to Annecy, others to Grenoble. Be sure to sit in a car marked "Annecy".

Dep. Lyon (Perrache)   7:24   10:20   12:12

Arr. Annecy   9:27   12:21   14:50

Sights in **Annecy:** This is a beautiful lake resort. See the 12th century Island Palace. The shops in the old quarter.

Dep. Annecy   14:15   16:04

Arr. Lyon (Perrache)   16:36   18:20

Lyon - Dijon - Lyon   151

Dep. Lyon (Perrache)   5:48   6:30(1)   9:16(2)   12:50(3)

Arr. Dijon   7:33   9:30   10:58   14:33

Sights in **Dijon:** Town Hall, formerly the palace of those swashbuckling dukes of Burgundy and now one of the richest museums in France. The Church of Notre Dame. The 13th century Cathedral of St. Benigne archaeological museum. The Palace of Justice. The Magnin Museum. The 14th century Chartreuse de Champmol, with its famous chapel portrait and Moses Fountain. Rude Museum. Don't fail to have lunch in Dijon, France's food and wine capital.

Dep. Dijon   12:14(3)   15:47(3)   16:55(3)   19:17(2+4)

Arr. Lyon (Perrache)   14:02   17:42   18:39   20:51

(1)Change trains in Chagny on Saturday and Sunday. (2)Light refreshments. (3)Meal service. (4)Plus another departure from Dijon at 21:55.

Lyon - Grenoble - Lyon   154

Dep. Lyon (Perrache)	7:10(1)	8:05	11:01(1+2)	12:12
Arr. Grenoble	8:33	9:35	12:27	13:40

Sights in **Grenoble:** The very rich (Utrillo, Picasso, Ruben) art museum in the 16th century Palace of Justice. Take the cable car ride up to Guy Pape Park for a marvelous view of the city below and the fields surrounding Grenoble. While at the top, visit the military museum in the 19th century fort, the Bastille, and the Auto Museum. Walk back to Grenoble, downhill, through the Jardine des Dauphines.

Dep. Grenoble	11:31(3)	12:47	13:20	15:59(5)
Arr. Lyon (Perrache)	13:22	14:20	14:46(2)	17:36

(1)Daily, except Sundays and holidays. (2)Departs/Arrives Lyon's Part-Dieu railstation. (3)Meal service. (4)Daily, except Saturday. (5)Plus other departures from Grenoble at 16:38, 17:08, 18:23(2+4),19:14(1) and 21:14.

Lyon - Marseille - Lyon   151

Dep. Lyon (Perrache)	7:11(1)	9:58(2)	11:55(1)
Arr. Marseille (St. Ch.)	10:33	13:12	14:54

Sights in **Marseille:** See notes about sightseeing in Marseille earlier in this section, under "Avignon-Marseille".

Dep. Marseille (St. Ch.)	14:44(1)	15:18(3)	17:08(1)	17:43(2+4)
Arr. Lyon (Perrache)	17:48	18:37	20:35	2157

(1)Meal service. (2)Light refreshments. (3)Runs from late June to mid-September. (4)Plus other departures from Marseille at 19:21(1), 21:25(3), 21:37 and 21:49.

Lyon - Tours - Lyon   128

Dep. Lyon (Perrache)	6:45(1)	9	:24(1)
Arr. St. Pierre des Corps	11:32	14	:10

Change to suburban train waiting for transfer.

Dep. St. Pierre des Corps	11:33	14	11
Arr. Tours	11:38	14	:16

Sights in **Tours:** The fine collection of paintings in the Musee des Beaux-Arts. Much of the old city was destroyed in the 1944 bombings which forced German occupiers to retreat and resulted in liberation.

Dep. Tours by suburban train	15:53	18	:20
Arr. St. Pierre des Corps	15:58	18	:25

Change to train waiting for transfer.

Dep. St. Pierre des Corps	15:59(1)	18	:26(1)
Arr. Lyon (Perrache)	20:45	23	:12

(1)Light refreshments.

Lyon - Vienne - Lyon   151
Dep Lyon (Perrache)   7:11   9:13   12:16
Arr. Vienne   20 minutes later
   Sights in **Vienne:** Many good Roman ruins. The Temple of Augustus and
Livia, a large amphitheater, and the pyramid which once marked the center
of a Roman coliseum. Ancient jewels and bronze and ceramic relics on exhibit
at the Museum of Fine Arts. Try to dine at one of the world's most famous
restaurants, Pyramide, open daily except Tuesday and closed November through
mid-December.
Dep. Vienne   14:29   17:59   18:16(1)
                                           21:36   22   :32

Arr. Lyon (Perrache)   20 minutes later
(1)Runs from late June to mid-September.

Nice - Cannes (and Grasse) - Nice   151
Dep. Nice   Frequent times from 5:40 to 23:47
Arr. Cannes 40 minutes later
   Sights in **Cannes:** Stroll along Promenade de la Croisette to see the beautiful
beach and splendid yachts, all the way to the Palm Beach Casino. Take boat
rides on the Bay of Cannes or to the St. Honorat and St. Marguerite islands.
On the latter, you can visit the prison that held the Man in the Iron Mask.
There is also a short boat trip to Lerins, where the 5th century Monastery
of the Cistercians is located. It is said that St. Patrick began his evangelical
tour of Europe from there.
   Visit the 10th century castle, Castrum Canois, on a mountain that overlooks
Cannes. It houses the Museum of Mediterranean Civilization.
   La Napoule is a few miles west of Cannes. The attraction there is the
Chateau de la Napoule Art Foundation, one of the finest art galleries on the
Riviera, open daily except Tuesday, with guided tours in the afternoon.
   Sights in **Grasse:** Take the 50-minute bus ride from Cannes' railstation
to nearby Grasse, the perfume capital of France. Many of the 35 perfume fac-
tories there are open to visitors. One of them, Parfumerie Fragonard, is only
a 5-minute walk from the Grasse bus terminal. Near it is a Perfume Museum.
The nearby hillsides are covered with wildflowers and jasmine every Spring.
Dep. CannesFrequent times from 7:31 to 24:00
Arr. Nice   40 minutes later

Nice - Marseille - Nice   151

Dep. Nice   650(1)   8:35(1)   10:32(1)   11:22(1)
Arr. Marseille (St. Ch.)   9:12   11:11   13:10   13:38

Sights in **Marseille:** See notes about sightseeing in Marseille earlier in this section under "Avignon-Marseille".

Dep. Marseille (St. Ch.)   13:22(2)   15:03(1)   15:17   16:49(1+3+4)
Arr. Nice   15:56   17:25   18:09   19:03

(1)Meal service. (2)Light refreshments. (3)Reservation required. (4)Plus other departures from Marseille at 17:25, 18:35, 19:25(1), 20:31(1) and 22:05(1).

Nice - Monte Carlo - Nice   151

Dep. Nice   Frequent times from 7:00 to 23:07
Arr. Monte Carlo   20-25 minutes later

Sights in **Monte Carlo:** See notes about sightseeing in Monte Carlo earlier in this section, under "Avignon-Monte Carlo".

Dep. Monte Carlo   Frequent times from 5:30 to 22:26
Arr. Nice   20-25 minutes later

Nice - Saint Raphael - Nice   151

Dep. Nice   Frequent times from 5:40 to 22:19
Arr. St. Raphael   60 minutes later

Sights in **Saint Raphael:** An excellent Riviera beach resort. Good golfing, hiking and sailing here. To fill the nighttime hours, there is a gambling casino.

Dep. St. Raphael   Frequent times from 6:18 to 23:36
Arr. Nice   60 minutes later

Paris - Amsterdam - Paris   10-B

| Dep. Paris (Nord) | 7:19(1+2) | Dep. Amsterdam | 17:53(1+3) |
| Arr. Amsterdam | 12:30 | Arr. Paris (Nord) | 23:10 |

(1)TEE. Reservation required. Meal service. (2)Daily, except Sunday. (3)Daily, except Saturday.

Sights in **Amsterdam:** As indicated above, it is possible to make a one-day roundtrip from Paris to Amsterdam, although leaving only enough time in Amsterdam for no more than minimal sightseeing. Best bet: take a 75-minute ride in a glass-roofed canal boat, starting at the piers in front of Central Railstation before having to board the train for the ride back to Paris.

Paris - Bayeux - Paris 122

Dep. Paris (St. Lazare)   7:08(1)   9:02
Arr. Bayeux   9:19   11:25

Sights in **Bayeux:** The world-famous 235-foot long tapestry, made in 1077, depicting in 58 scenes the Norman conquest of England. The view of a magnificent seascape from Notre Dame's high center tower.

Dep. Bayeux   14:54(2)   15:22(3)   17:58(4)   19:16(5+6)
Arr. Paris (St. Lazare) 17:09   18:16   20:11   21:58

(1)Late June to mid-September: runs daily. Mid-September to late June: runs daily except Sundays and holidays. (2)Daily, except Sundays and holidays. Runs only mid-September to late June. (3)Daily. Runs only late June to mid-September. (4)Daily, except Sundays and holidays. Supplement charged. Meal service. (5)Sundays and holidays only. (6)Plus other departures from Bayeux at 20:51(5), 21:21 and 21:41(5)

Paris - Bayeux - Caen - Paris 122

As shown below, it is possible to combine a visit from Paris to both Bayeux and Caen in one day.

Dep. Paris (St. Lazare)   7:08(1) | Dep. Bayeux   13:47   14:54(2+3)
Arr. Bayeux   9:30 | Arr. Caen   14:11   15:11

Sights in **Bayeux:** See notes about sightseeing in Bayeux in the listing preceding this.

Sights in **Caen:** Although much was destroyed here during the 1944 Normandy invasion battle, numerous historical buildings have been preserved. Hotel d' Escoville, the "Chateau". The 11th century Abbaye aux Hommes and Abbaye aux Dames. The Museum. The church of Saint Sauveur. The Palace of Justice. For lunch, try these regional specialties: tripes, berlingots, cider, Calvados.

Dep. Caen   17:33(2)   18:18(2+4)   21:15(5)   21:40(2)
Arr. Paris (St. Lazare) 19:38   20:11   23:32   23:42

(1)Late June to mid-September:daily. Mid-September to late June: daily except Sundays and holidays. (2)Daily, except Sundays and holidays. (3)Daily. Runs from mid-September to late June. (4)Supplement charged. Meal service. (5)Sundays and holidays only.

Here are schedules for having more time in Caen.

Dep. Paris (St. Laz.)   708(1)   8:06   9:02   9:17
Arr. Caen   9:01   10:12   11:25   12:18
                                  *   *   *
Dep. Caen   12:03(2) 13:46(3) 14:35(2) 15:14(3+4+7)
Arr. Paris (St. Laz.)   13:57   15:48   16:36   17:09

(1)Late June to mid-September: daily. Mid-September to late June: daily except Sundays and holidays. (2)Meal service. (3)Daily, except Sundays and holidays. (4)Runs mid-September to late June. (5)Runs late June to mid-September. (6)Sundays and holidays only. (7)Plus other departures from Caen at 15:46(5), 16:12(3), 16:25(4), 17:33, 18:18(2+3), 18:56(6), 19:24(6), 19:38(6), 21:15(6), 21:40 and 22:01(6).

Paris - Blois - Paris   136

Dep. Paris (Aust.)	7:09	9:06	10:15(1)	12:06(2)
Arr. Blois	8:46	11:03	11:53	13:37

Sights in **Blois:** Two fine Chateaux: Chambord and Bracieux (Herbault-en-Sologne). St. Louis Cathedral. Church of Saint Nicolas. Church of Saint Vincent. Church of Saint Saturin, and its curious cemetery. The Alluye Manor. The Castle of Blois. For lunch, try regional specialties: Rillettes, Loire fish, great wines and cheeses.

Dep. Blois	13:50(1)	16:17	17:03(2)	18:48(3)
Arr. Paris (Aust.)	15:33	18:13	18:43	20:30

(1)Daily, except Sundays and holidays. (2)Meal service. (3)Plus other departures from Blois at 19:45 and 21:36(2).

Paris - Blois - Tours - Paris   136

As shown below, it is possible to combine a visit from Paris to both Blois and Tours in one day.

Dep. Paris (Aust.)	7:09	Dep. Blois	11:55
Arr. Blois	8:46	Arr. Tours	12:27

Sights in **Blois:** See notes in preceding listing.

Sights in **Tours:** Take a 90-minute walk from the Tours railstation up Boulevard Heurteloup to Rue Nationale, then turn right and go up one side of Rue Nationale to the bridge, come back on the other side of Rue Nationale, cross Boulevard Heurteloup, go one block further, turn left onto Rue de Bordeaux, taking it directly back to the railstation. There are several good restaurants on Rue Nationale and on Boulevard Heurteloup.

Dep. Tours	15:37	16:23	17:29(1)	18:15(4)
Arr. Paris (Aust.)	18:13	18:43	19:39	20:33

(1)Runs late June to mid-September. (2)Supplement charged. (3)Meal service. (4)Plus other departures from Tours at 19:38(2), 20:56(3) and 21:34(3).

Paris - Tours - Paris 136

Here are schedules for having more time in Tours than when combining a trip from Paris to both Blois and Tours.

Dep. Paris				
(Aust.)	7:09	7:47(1+2)	8:04	9:09(3+7)
Arr. Tours	9:16	9:30	10:01	11:11
		*	*	*
Dep. Tours	13:13(6)	14:14(4)	15:37(4)	16:51(4)	17:29(3+4+8)
Arr. Paris				
(Aust.)	15:33	16:16	18:13	19:00	19:39

(1)TEE. Reservation required. Meal service. Runs from early September to late June. (2)Daily, except Sundays and holidays. (3)Meal service. (4)Runs from late June to mid-September. (5)Supplement charged. (6)Daily, except Saturday. (7)Plus other departures from Paris at 10:03(3+4), 11:24(3) and 12:06(3).

(8)Plus other departures from Tours at 18:15(2), 19:28(3+5+6), 19:57(1+6) and 20:56(3).

Paris - Bordeaux - Paris 136

Dep. Paris			
(Austerlitz)	7:47(1+2)	8:04(3)	9:00(3)
Arr. Bordeaux			
(St. Jean)	11:50	13:00	13:24
	*	*	*
Dep. Bordeaux			
(St. Jean)	16:54(3+4)	17:42(1+5)	17:50(3+6)
Arr. Paris			
(Austerlitz)	21:38	21:46	23:12

(1)TEE. Reservation required. Meal service. Runs from early September to early July. (2)Daily, except Sundays and holidays. (3)Meal service. (4)Supplement charged. (5)Daily, except Saturday. (6)Plus other departures from Bordeaux at 18:55(3) and 19:08(3).

Sights in **Bordeaux:** Information about tours of the port and an excellent city map for making a walking tour of Bordeaux are available at the Tourist Office, 12 Cours du 3o Juillet. The opera, parks, hotels, Roman ruins and 18th century mansions are in the northern sector of the city. Museums, churches and fine shops are in the southern part of Bordeaux.

See the Maritime Museum, on the Quai de la Douane. Wonderful Louis XV houses on Rue Fernand Philippart. The modern stained-glass in the 14th century St. Michel Church on Place Dubourg. The view of Bordeaux from the top of that church's tower. The large 15th century belltower, Grosse Cloche. The 13th century Gothic St. Andre's Cathedral. The art in the Musee des Beaux Arts, open daily except Tuesday 10:00-12:00 and 14:00-18:00.

The fans with mother of pearl, ivory and silver handles (plus Medieval furniture, costumes and ceramics) in the Musee des Arts Decoratifs at 39 Rue Bouffard, open 14:00-18:00 daily except Tuesday.

Do not miss seeing the array of fruits, cheeses, wild game and many exotic foods at the market on Place des Grands Hommes. The fantastic carved plants and the swan boat in the Jardin Public. The Maison des Vins at 1 Cours du 30 Juillet, where you can obtain information on visiting nearby famous wineries.

See the lovely 18th century Opera House. The Grand Theatre. The Museum of Painting and Sculpture. The Numismatic Museum. The Museum of Old Bordeaux. The Bonie Museum of Far Eastern Art.

Paris - Brussels - Paris   106

Dep. Paris (Nord)	6:41(1+2)	7:19(1+3)	7:48(4+6)
Arr. Brussels (Midi)	9:11	9:46	10:50

Sights in **Brussels:** The gilded buildings in Grand Place. Town Hall. The Law Courts. The Royal Palace. The tapestries in the 13th century Cathedral of St. Michael. Flemish paintings in the Museum of Ancient Art. The Museum of Modern Art. The Central Africa Museum. The Brussels City Museum. The Museum of Arms and Armour. The Postal Museum. The Brewery Museum. The Royal Greenhouses. The Brueghel Museum, in the house where the painter lived his last 6 years. The view from the Palais de Justice. The Railway Museum on the mezzanine of Brussels' Nord railstation. A bus takes you 10 miles to Waterloo.

Dep. Brussels (Midi)	14:07(4)	16:08(4)	17:17(1+7)
Arr. Paris (Nord)	16:55	18:55	19:44

(1)TEE. Reservation required. Meal service. (2)Operates Monday-Friday except holidays. Runs from early September to late June. (3)Daily, except Sunday. (4)Light refreshments. (5)Meal service. (6)Plus other departures from Paris at 10:23(4) and 11:37(1).   (7)Plus other departures from Brussels at 18:38(1+2), 19:15(5) and 20:42(1+3).

Paris - Chantilly - Paris   SNCF Timetable #B-27

Dep. Paris (Nord)	Frequent times from 4:55 to 0:45
Arr. Chantilly	30-40 minutes later

Sights in **Chantilly:** The chateau and its Living Museum of the Horse, containing a superb collection of furniture and paintings (Delacroix, Fouquet, Ingres, Rembrandt, Clouet, Raphael). Between April 1 and September 30, the chateau is open daily except Tuesday 10:30-18:00 (until 17:00 the rest of the year). Between April 1 and October 31, the Museum is open daily except Tuesday 10:30-17:00 (13:00-17:00 the rest of the year).

Riders wearing 18th century costumes perform at 12:00, 15:00 and 17:00 April 1 to October 31 (at 14:30 and 16:00 the rest of the year). Visit the racetrack. See the spectacle of the Tuesday and Saturday fox hunts.

Dep. Chantilly   Frequent times from 4:41 to 19:22
Arr. Paris (Nord)   30-40 minutes later

Paris - Chartres - Paris

	121	121	123	121	126
Dep. Paris (Montpar.)	7:23	10:48	11:10	11:40	12:57
Arr. Chartres	45 minutes later				

Sights in **Chartres:** The main attraction is the magnificent 13th century Cathedral, third largest in the world, exceeded in size only by St. Peter's and Canterbury. Its stained-glass is unrivalled. Other sights: The Former Collegiate Church. The Church of Saint Aignan. The Church of Saint Martin-au-Val. The Church of Saint Foy.

	126	121	126
Dep. Chartres	14:00	17:30	18:31
Arr. Paris (Montpar.)	45 minutes later		

Paris - Cologne (Koln) - Paris   62

Dep. Paris (Nord)	7:30(1)	Dep. Cologne	16:35(1)
Arr. Cologne	12:41	Arr. Paris (Nord)	21:50

(1)Supplement charged. Meal service.

Sights in **Cologne:** See notes about sightseeing in Cologne on page 350.

Paris - Compeigne - Paris   106

Dep. Paris (Nord)   7:48   12:08
Arr. Compeigne   45 minutes later

Sights in **Compeigne:** Town Hall. Vivenel Museum. Hotel Dieu. The 7th century Beauregard Tower. The "Clairere de l'Armistice" in Compeigne Forest, where Marshal Foch signed the 1918 armistice for France.

Dep. Compeigne   10:32   13:08   19:04   20:10(1)   21:55(2)
Arr. Paris (Nord)   45 minutes later

(1)Sundays and holidays only. (2)Daily, except Saturday.

Paris - Dijon - Paris

	151	151	152	151
Dep. Paris (Lyon)	6:36(1+2)	7:50(3)	8:30(3)	9:52(3)
Arr. Dijon	8:57	10:12	11:03	12:14

Sights in **Dijon:** See notes about sightseeing in Dijon earlier in this section, under "Lyon-Dijon".

	150	151	151	157
Dep. Dijon	14:48(1)	16:44(3)	16:44(3)	17:20(3+5)
Arr. Paris (Lyon)	17:00	19:10	19:10	19:50

(1)TGV. Supplement charged. Meal service. (2)Daily, except Sundays and holidays. (3)Meal service. (4)TEE. Reservation required. Meal service. (5)Plus other departures from Dijon at 18:45(3), 20:28(3) and 21:01(4).

Paris - Evreux - Paris 122

Dep. Paris (St. Laz.)	8:06	9:17	10:50	11:50(1)
Arr. Evreux	8:59	10:26	11:46	12:44

Sights in **Evreux:** The Cathedral of Notre Dame, a jumble of architectural styles due to having been built over a period of 6 centuries — from the 11th to the 17th. Goldsmith work in the Church of Stain Taurin. The ancient Eveche. The tower of The Clock. For lunch, try the Norman cuisine.

Dep. Evreux	13:19	14:53(2)	15:41(1)	17:11(3+6)
Arr. Paris (St. Laz.)	14:14	15:48	16:36	18:16

(1)Meal service. (2)Daily, except Sundays and holidays. (3)Runs from late June to mid-September. (4)Runs from mid-September to late June. (5)Sundays and holidays only. (6)Plus other departures from Evreux at 17:37(2+4), 18:43, 19:24(5), 20:28(5), 22:47 and 23:10(5).

Paris - Fontainebleau - Paris SCNF Timetable #B-50

Dep. Paris (Lyon)	Frequent times from 6:02 to 0:47
Arr. Fontainebleau-Avon	30-40 minutes later

Take the 10-minute bus ride from the railstation to the palace, open 8:00 to sunset, daily except Tuesdays.

Sights in **Fontainebleau:** It is advisable to plan on an entire day here for seeing the magnificent 16th century palace that many kings of France occupied, and the parks and gardens surrounding it. Guided tours of the palace 10:00-12:30 and 14:00-18:00. Many visitors bring a picnic lunch.

Dep. Fontainebleau-Avon	Frequent times from 5:19 to 22:10
Arr. Paris (Lyon)	30-40 minutes later

Paris - Mt. St. Michel - Caen - Paris

From early July to the end of August, there is a direct train on Saturdays. Depart Paris (Montparnasse) at 7:00. Arrive Pontorson at 11:28. Board the bus for Mt. St. Michel. At the end of the day of sightseeing, take the bus from Mt. St. Michel to the Pontorson railstation. Depart Pontorson at 19:10. Arrive at Paris' St. Lazare railstation at 23:50.

The schedules below are for the less direct route.

122		117	
Dep. Paris (St. Lazare)	9:02	Dep. Pontorson	19:12(1)
Arr. Lison	12:07	Arr. Caen	21:28
Change trains.		Change trains	
117		122	
Dep. Lison	14:58	Dep. Caen	21:40
Arr. Pontorson		Arr. Paris (St. Lazare)	23:42
(Mt. St. Michel)	16:32		

(1)Late June to mid-September: daily. Mid-September to late June: daily, except Saturday.

Sights in **Mt. St. Michel:** It is a 10-minute bus ride from the Pontorson railstation to the medieval splendor of the walled town of Mont-Saint-Michel, where there are several hotels. The rushing tides that attract more than 1,400,000 tourists here every year occur 36 hours after the new and full moon, with the fastest tides occurring near March 21 and September 23.

Also worth seeing are the buttressed walls, vaulted halls and colonnaded cloister in the 8th century abbey, which has 90 steps visitors must climb.

One-hour guided tours of the abbey are offered. Those in English-language are conducted daily except Thursday at 10:30, 14:30 and, if a group of at least 15 people is mustered, also at 16:00. Visitors are not allowed to walk through the abbey unescorted.

Columns measuring 16 feet in circumference in a semicircular room called the Crypte des Gros-Piliers support the choir of the sanctuary above that room. Other pillars, in the 115-foot long Knights' Hall, should be seen. A bronze statue of St. Michel, raising his sword to slay a dragon, sits at the top of the main spire of the church, 500 feet above the sea. The mountain is illuminated from nightfall until 23:00.

Do not fail to eat the special omelette made here.

Visitors can see dioramas of this mountain's history and collections of ancient clocks in both the Musee Historique (open all year) and in the Musee Historical du Mont (open from March 1 to November 30).

The last bus from Mt. St. Michel to Pontorson leaves at 18:10, well in advance of the train departures from Pontorson to Paris.

Paris - Limoges - Paris   138
Dep. Paris (Aust.)   6:25(1)   7:41(2+3)   9:33(1)
Arr. Limoges   10:20   10:37   13:08

Sights in **Limoges:** Tours of the porcelain and enamel factories, free by applying to the Syndicat de la Porcelain, 7 Rue du General Cerez. The Adrien Dubouche Museum, with its great collection of ceramics. The Municipal Museum, to see its display of china made in Limoges from the 12th century to the present. The Cathedral of Saint Etienne.

Dep. Limoges   14:34(1)   16:18(4)   17:05   18:04(1+7)
Arr. Paris (Aust.)   18:00   20:39   20:24   21:26

(1)Meal service. (2)Supplement charged. Meal service. (3)Daily, except Sundays and holidays. (4)Light refreshments. (5)Monday-Friday. Runs early September to late June. (6)Sundays and holidays only. (7)Plus other departures from Limoges at 19:38(6) and 20:52(2).

Paris - Lyon - Paris   150
All of these trains are TGV and have meal service.
Dep. Paris (Lyon)   6:15(1)   7:15(2+3)   8:15(3+13)
Arr. Lyon (Part-Dieu)   8:51   10:05   10:51

Sights in **Lyon:** See notes about sightseeing in Lyon at the start of this section.

Dep. Lyon (Part-Dieu)   14:01(4+5)   15:02(2+5)   16:01(5+6+14)
Arr. Paris (Part-Dieu)   16:40   17:41   18:40

(1)Monday-Friday. Suppplement charged every day, (2)Daily. (3)Suppplement charged Monday-Friday. (4)Daily, except Sundays and holidays. (5)Light refreshments. (6)Daily, except Saturday. (7)Suppplement charged Saturday, Sunday and holidays. (8)Suppplement charged every day except Saturday. (9)Suppplement charged every day. (10)Suppplement charged Friday and Sunday. (11)Suppplement charged Sunday. (12)Runs only on Sunday. (13)Plus other departures from Paris at 9:15(2+5+7), 11:15(3+6) and 12:15(4). (14)Plus other departures from Lyon at 17:01(2+5+8), 18:01(2+9), 19:02(2+10), 20:01(2+11) and 21:01(5+12).

Paris - Nancy - Paris   172
Dep. Paris (Est)   6:45(1+2)   7:45(3)   8:35(2)   11:00(1+5)
Arr. Nancy   9:34   10:27   11:56   13:35

Sights in **Nancy:** The Ducal Palace, with its museum of this city's 2,000-year history. The Church of the Cordeliers. The 14th century Porte de la Craffe, oldest monument in Nancy. The wrought-iron grillwork and fountains in Place Stanislas. Lovely 18th century houses on Place de la Carriere.

Dep. Nancy   14:30(2)   17:12(2)   18:09   18:23(5+7)
Arr. Paris (Est)   17:20   20:10   21:43   20:59

(1)Daily, except Sundays and holidays. (2)Meal service. (3)Suppplement charged. Specify meal required when reserving first-class seat. (4)Suppplement charged. Meal service. Runs from early September to late June. (5)TEE. Daily, except Saturday. Reservation required. Meal service. (6)Light refreshments all year. Also tray meal service from early September to late June. (7)Plus other departures from Nancy at 18:53(6), 19:45 and 20:33(3)

Paris - Reims - Paris   177

Dep. Paris (Est)   7:16(1)   8:03(2)   11:06   12:47(2)
Arr. Reims   1½ hours later

Sights in **Reims:** The 13th century Cathedral of Notre Dame. The Porte Mars 13th century Arch. Saint Remi Basilica. The Church of St. Jacquet. The museum at the Church of St. Denis. Seeing champagne processed. The public is invited to visit the Taitinger and Pommery caves.

Dep. Reims   12:25   16:04   17:15(3)   18:09(3+6)
Arr. Paris (Est)   1½ hours later

(1)Light refreshments. (2)Daily, except Sundays and holidays. (3)Monday-Friday, except holidays. (4)Fridays only. (5)Sundays and holidays only. (6)Plus other departures from Reims at 18:57(4), 20:28(1) and 20:51(5).

Paris - Rouen - Paris   120

Dep. Paris (St. Laz.)   7:45(1+2+3)   8:15(3)   9:15   12:00(3)
Arr. Rouen (Rive Dr.)   8:53   9:46   10:26   13:37

Sights in **Rouen:** Walk out of the railstation and then down Rue de Jeanne D'Arc about 1½ miles. Turn right onto Rue de la Grosse Horloge and continue a short distance to the remodeled ancient, large central market, Vieux Marche, the place where Joan of Arc was tied to a stake and burned. This is now the Church of St. Joan, built in 1977. It is in the shape of an upside-down boat and has magnificent stained-glass windows that were saved from the Church of Saint-Vincent, bombed during World War II. Try the regional specialty (terrine of duck) in one of the nearby restaurants.

Then, go back along Rue de la Gross Horloge (crossing Rue de Jeanne D'Arc). Straight ahead is the gigantic, ornate clock for which the street was named. The clock presents a spectacle of moving figures when each hour strikes.

Past the famous clock is the Cathedral, with its renowned Carillon of 56 bells. Nearby, see the sculptures on the doors of the Church of Saint-Maclou and the macabre scenes on the portals of the Cloisters of Saint-Maclou.

Visit the remains of an 11th century building that was either a Jewish school or a synagogue, below the Palace of Justice. See the Hebrew graffiti written on the walls there more than 900 years ago, the elaborate carved columns and the 2 inverted Lions of Judah.

The stained-glass windows in the Church of St. Godard and the Church of St. Patrice.

From Rouen, it is an easy bus trip to either the colorful harbor at Honfleur or to Giverny, to visit the home and spectacular garden of painter Claude Monet.

Dep. Rouen (Rive Dr.)   12:55(2+3) 14:07(3) 14:54 18:03(5)
Arr. Paris (St. Laz.)   14:04   15:37   16:05 19:12

(1)Supplement charged. (2)Specify meal required when reserving first-class seat. (3)Daily, except Sundays and holidays. (4)Sundays and holidays only. (5)Plus other departures from Rouen at 18:47(1+2+3), 19:38, 20:26(4), 21:11(3) and 22:02(4).

Paris - Strasbourg - Paris   172

This ride is along the Marne, with clear views of the area near famous World War I battlefields.

Dep. Paris (Est)   6:45(1+2) 7:45(3) 8:35(2) 11:00(2+4)
Arr. Strasbourg   10:52   11:42   13:40   14:48

Sights in **Strasbourg:** Stroll down Rue du Bain-aux-Plantes, an alley where herbs were once sold. See, smell and taste the brown bread at the almost 300-year old bakery, Boulangerie Winckelsass. Visit the 3 good museums in Chateau des Rohan: the collection of Monet, Renoir, El Greco, Goya and Tintoretto in the Art Gallery; the relics in the Archaeological Museum; and the display of clocks, ironwork, earthenware and porcelain in the Museum of Decorative Arts.

Rooms dating from the early 17th century (furnished with marvelous utensils, stoves, wooden molds and pottery from the same era) at the Musee Alsacien, 23 Quai St. Nicholas. Wonderful 11th to 17th century Alsatian art in the Musee de l'Oeuvre Notre Dame.

On Rue de la Rape, see the city's majestic 12th century Cathedral. All of its windows are 12th, 13th and 14th century stained-glass. Its famous 60-foot high astronomical clock, which calculates eclipses, sunrises and sunsets into eternity, comes alive on the hour and quarter-hour, when figures appear from and return into its interior.

The clock's major performance is at 12:30. It is then that the "Four Ages of Man" pass before "Death", and the 12 Apostles move past the figure of Jesus. As he blesses them, a mechanical rooster flaps its wings and crows 3 times.

There is an extraordinary view of the city from a platform 217 feet above the street, at the top pf the Cathedral's 328-step spiral staircase.

Take a one-hour sightseeing minitrain ride that starts at the south side of the Cathedral. Runs every half-hour, late March to the end of October. There are also cruises on the Rhine (90 minutes, 3 hours and 11 hours, starting in front of the Palais des Rohan, 2 blocks from the Cathedral.

In Summer, a fabulous sound-and-light show is presented inside the Cathedral: illuminated stained-glass windows, bells tolling, organ music.

Walk around Place Kleber. Sample the world's best pate de foie gras.

Dep. Strasbourg   15:49(2)   17:10(5) 17:16(6) 18:24(7+8)
Arr. Paris (Est)   20:10   20:59   22:05   22:24

(1)Runs daily, except Sundays and holidays. (2)Meal service. (3)Supplement charged. Specify meal required when reserving seat. (4)Operates early September to late June. Runs daily, except Sundays and holidays. (5)TEE. Reservation required. Meal service. Operates early September to mid-July. Runs daily, except Saturday. (6)Light refreshments. (7)Runs Sunday only. Supplement charged. Light refreshments. (8)Plus another departure from Strasbourg at 19:17(3).

Paris - Tours - Paris

This one-day excursion appears earlier in this section, immediately following "Paris-Blois-Tours-Paris".

Paris - Trouville and Deauville - Paris   127

Dep. Paris (St. Laz.)	6:50(1+2)	7:55(3)	8:41(4)	10:26(2+7)
Arr. Trou Deau	8:47	9:52	10:53	12:25

Sights in **Trouville:** There is no chance of obtaining hotel rooms here in Summer without advance reservation. One of France's most beautiful swimming beaches. A gambling casino. Marvelous seafood.

Sights in **Deauville:** One of France's most beautiful swimming beaches. Two racetracks. Lovely gardens. To explore the Norman countryside, you can rent a car at the Deauville railstation.

Dep. Trou Deau	13:00(2)	15:47(2)	17:22(3)	17:58(1+2+8)
Arr. Paris (St. Laz.)	15:11	17:40	19:49	19:49

(1)Daily, except Sundays and holidays. (2)Runs from late June to mid-September. (3)Sundays and holidays only. (4)From late June to mid-September:daily. From mid-September to late June: Saturdays and Sundays only. (5)Saturdays only. (6)Supplement charged. (7)Plus other departures from Paris at 10:50(2+5) and 12:15(1+2). (8)Plus other departures from Trou Deau at 18:58(3), 19:17(1+2), 19:57(3) and 20:56(3+6).

Paris - Troyes - Paris   171

Dep. Paris (Est)	6:55(1+2)	7:06(1+3)	8:37(2+4+7)
Arr. Troyes	8:19	9:03	10:08

Sights in **Troyes:** The Cathedral of St. Paul and St. Peter. The mansions of Voluisant, Autry, des Ursins and Marisy. The Museum of Fine Arts, with its solid collection of 17th-18th century paintings and 13th-14th century sculptures.

Dep. Troyes	12:25(1)	16:35(2)	17:33(5+8)
Arr. Paris (Est)	14:11	18:09	19:36

(1)Daily, except Sundays and holidays. (2)Meal service. (3)Light refreshments. (4)Sundays and holidays only. (5)Daily, except Saturday. (6)State meal required when reserving first-class seat. (7)Plus other departures from Paris at 9:07(1+6) and 11:55(3). (8)Plus other departures from Troyes at 19:07(4), 19:24(1), 20:33(4), 21:00(4) and 22:11(6).

Paris - Versailles - Paris   SCNF Timetable #B-37

Dep. Paris (Invalides)   Frequent times from 5:47 to 23:52
Arr. Versailles   30 minutes later

Sights in **Versailles:** The fabulous palace where Louis XVI lived like a king, and the elegant gardens there. The palace is open daily, except Monday. Guided tours are offered from 10:00 to 17:00. Visitors can purchase a book there which makes it possible to see and appreciate the palace interior without a guide.

Dep. Versailles   Frequent times from 5:13 to 23:19
Arr. Paris (Invalides)   30 minutes later

SCENIC RAIL TRIPS

Chamonix - Vallorcine - Chamonix   285

Good mountain scenery on this short ride. It is easy to combine this with the one-day roundtrip from Geneva to Chamonix, described in the Switzerland section of this chapter.

Dep. Chamonix   6:28(1)   8:20   9:50   12:24   14:44(2+3)
Arr. Vallorcine   30 minutes later

                                    *   *   *

Dep. Vallorcine   7:08   8:55   10:59   13:15   14:55(4)
Arr. Chamonix   30 minutes later

(1)Late June to early September: daily. Early September to late June: Monday-Friday. (2)Daily. Runs late June to early September. (3)Plus other departures from Chamonix at 16:18, 17:26 and 18:52.   (4)Plus other departures from Vallorcine at 16:53, 18:06 and 19:28.

Grenoble - Marseille - Grenoble   154

Fine mountain scenery on this easy one-day roundtrip.

Dep. Grenoble	5:51(1)	Dep. Marseille		
Arr. Veynes	7:45	(St. Ch.)	13:20	17:57
Change trains.		Arr. Veynes	16:04	20:53
Dep. Veynes	7:55	Change trains.		
Arr. Marseille		Dep. Veynes	16:14	21:08(1)
(St. Ch.)	10:36	Arr. Grenoble	18:04	22:51

(1)Operates early July to early September.

Limoges - Toulouse - Limoges   138

Recommended for mountain scenery. This can be seen either as an easy one-day roundtrip between Limoges and Toulouse or as a portion of the route from Paris to Toulouse.

Dep. Limoges	10:39)1)	13:13(2)	16:56(2)
Arr. Toulouse (Mat.)	13:48	16:53	20:33

*   *   *

Dep. Toulouse (Mat.)	14:32(3)	17:44(2+4)	21:05
Arr. Limoges	17:58	20:50	1:14

(1)Supplement charged. Runs daily, except Sundays and holidays. Meal service. (2)Meal service. (3)Light refreshments. (4)Supplement charged.

Sights in **Toulouse:**The Basilica of Saint Sernin, displaying the remains of 128 saints, including 6 of the apostles and a thorn from the Crown of Thorns. The museum on the history of art at Saint Raymond. The Roman and medieval sculptures in the des Augustins Museum.

Here is the schedule for the Paris-Toulouse route:
138

Dep. Paris (Aust.)	7:41(1)	9:33(2)	10:24(3)	13:21(2)
Dep. Limoges	10:39(1)	13:13(2)	13:45(3)	16:56(2)
Arr. Toulouse (Mat.)	13:48	16:53	16:57	20:33

(1)Supplement charged. Runs daily, except Sundays and holidays. Meal service. (2)Meal service. (3)Runs late June to late September. Meal service until 14:47. Light refreshments available entire trip.

Lyon - Geneva   155

The Amberieu-Geneva portion of this trip is noted for scenic gorges.

Dep. Lyon (Perrache)	7:05	9:42	14:14	16:05
Dep. Lyon (Part-Dieu)	7:15	9:51	14:23	16:15
Dep. Amberieu	7:41	10:15	-:0-	16:40
Arr. Geneva (Cornavin)	9:23	11:41	16:07	18:08

Marseille - Grenoble - Marseille   154

Excellent mountain scenery on this easy one-day roundtrip.

Dep. Marseille (St. Ch.)	8:00	13:20
Arr. Veynes	10:49	16:04
Change trains.		
Dep. Veynes	11:00	16:14
Arr. Grenoble	12:57	18:04

*   *   *

Dep. Grenoble	13:55	17:49
Arr. Veynes	15:52	19:50

Change trains.

Dep. Veynes	16:00	19:55(1)
Arr. Marseille (St. Ch.)	18:41	22:29

(1)Early July to mid-September: daily. Mid-September to early July: Saturday and Sunday only.

Marseille - Nimes - La Bastide - Clermont Ferrand   148a

The train follows a beautiful river valley between La Bastide and Clermont Ferrand.

Dep. Marseille	7:27(1)	12:12(2)	Dep. Clermont		
Dep. Nimes	8:53(1)	13:47(2)	Ferrand	8:45(1)	12:53(2)
Dep. La Bastide	11:09(1)	15:51(2)	Dep. La Bastide	11:50	15:52
Arr. Clermont			Arr. Nimes	13:46	17:45
Ferrand	14:06	18:45	Arr. Marseille	15:12	19:12

(1)Runs late June to early September. (2)Meal service.

Marseille - Genoa   356

Fine seashore scenery along the Ligure coastline of the Mediterranean.

Dep. Marseille (St. Ch.)	5:22	6:00	8:00	10:35(3)
Arr. Ventimiglia	9:00	9:45	11:40	14:07

Change trains.

Dep. Ventimiglia	9:40)1)	10:20(2)	12:30	15:00
Arr. Genoa (P.P.)	12:37	13:00	15:35	18:10

(1)Meal service. (2)Light refreshments. (3)Direct train to Genoa. No train change in Ventimiglia. (4)Plus another departure from Marseille at 13:22(2+3).

Narbonne - Carcassone

Outstanding farm and vineyard scenery. Easy to make as a one-day round-trip or can be covered in the short route from Narbonne to Toulouse and Bordeaux.

	139	139	139	138	139
Dep. Narbonne	8:40	10:16	11:59	12:50	15:23
Arr. Carcassone	40-45 minutes later				

Sights in **Carcassone:** The most interesting walled city in France and Europe's best preserved relic of the Middle Ages. It is actually double-walled. The inner wall, built by the Romans in the 2nd century, bears 29 towers. The 13th century French outer wall has 17 towers and barbicans (fortified castles).

Nearby are the ruins of 5 other walls, to the South, erected by France in medieval days as additional protection from attack by the Spaniards.

As you stand on the walkways at the top of the French wall, it is easy to imagine yourself shooting arrows through the narrow slits or dropping oil on the marauders below.

Inside the Basilica of St. Nazare are many stone carvings depicting scenes from the fort's history, magnificent stained-glass windows, and the rectangular tombstone of Bishop Radulph.

139

Dep. Carcassone	9:51	11:04	12:54	13:28(1)	14:51(2)
Arr. Narbonne	40-45 minutes later				

(1)Runs late June to mid-September. (2)Plus other departures from Carcassone at 17:55 and 19:33.

Sights in **Narbonne:** The Cloister adjacent to the Palace of the Archbishops. The choir of the incomplete Cathedral of Saint-Just.

Here is the schedule for the Narbonne-Bordeaux route:

139

Dep. Narbonne	8:40(1)	10:16(1)	11:59
Arr. Carcassone	9:11	10:47	12:38
Arr. Toulouse (Matabiau)	9:58	11:38	13:41
Arr. Bordeaux (St. Jean)	12:10	13:55	16:35

(1)Meal service.

Nice - Digne - Nice   185

This is a very scenic line that is operated daily only from late May to late September and weekends from December to Easter. An easy one-day round-trip, this is also the route from Nice to Geneva.

Dep. Nice (C.P.)	8:20	Dep. Digne	16:30
Arr. Digne	11:43	Arr. Nice (C.P.)	19:50

Sights in **Digne:** The 15th century Cathedral of Saint Jerome. Many fruit orchards. Digne is famed for the lavender cultivated here.

Paris - Torino (and Rome)   152

The Culoz-Modane portion of this trip offers outstanding lake and mountain scenery. On this route, the train goes through the 8.5-mile long Mont Cenis Tunnel, constructed in 1871.

Dep. Paris (Lyon)	8:30(1)	Dep. Rome (Ter.)	23:50
Dep. Culoz	13:53	Dep. Torino (P.N.)	11:40
Arr. Modane	16:06	Dep. Modane	14:02(2)
Arr. Torino (P.N.)	18:12	Arr. Culoz	16:10
Arr. Rome (Ter.)	7:07(Day 2)	Arr. Paris (Lyon)	21:24

(1)Meal service until 14:25.   (2)Meal service until Paris arrival.

Toulouse - Limoges - Toulouse 138

Recommended for mountain scenery. This route can be seen either as an easy one-day roundtrip between Toulouse and Limoges or as a portion of the ride from Toulouse to Paris.

Dep. Toulouse (Mat.)	5:46(1)	7:43(2)	9:00(1+3)	10:27(1+6)
Arr. Limoges	9:11	10:47	12:20	14:20
	*	*	*	

Dep. Limoges	10:39(4)	13:13(1)	16:56(1)	20:26(5)
Arr. Toulouse (Mat.)	13:48	16:53	20:33	23:45

(1)Meal service. (2)TEE. Reservation required. Meal service. Runs daily, except Sundays and holidays. (3)Late June to late September: daily. Late September to late June: Friday and Sunday only. (4)Supplement charged. Runs daily, except Sundays and holidays. (5)Daily, except Saturday. (6)Plus another departure from Toulouse at 14:32(1)

Here is the schedule for the Toulouse-Paris ride:

Dep. Toulouse (Mat.)	5:46(1)	7:43(2)	9:00(1+3)	10:27(1+5)
Dep. Limoges	9:25(1)	10:49(2)	12:22(1+3)	14:34(1)
Arr. Paris (Aust.)	13:27	13:45	15:42	18:00

(1)Meal service. (2)TEE. Reservation required. Meal service. Runs daily, except Sundays and holidays. (4)Late June to late September: daily. Late September to late June: Friday and Sunday only. (4)Supplement charged. (5)Plus other departures from Toulouse at 14:32(1) and 17:44(1+4).

INTERNATIONAL ROUTES FROM FRANCE

The French gateway for rail travel to London, Amsterdam, Bern (and on to Zurich and Vienna), Brussels, Cologne, Geneva and Madrid is Paris. (Notes on the route to London appear in Chapter 8.) From Marseille, there is rail service to Barcelona and Genoa (and on to Florence, Milan, Rome and Venice). From Paris, there are trains to Torino and Genoa.

Nice - Marseille - Avignon - Nimes - Narbonne - Barcelona   162

Dep. Nice	-0-	22:19(1)	-0-0	-0-
Dep. Marseille	-0-	1:16(1)	5:56(2)	7:15(2)
Dep. Avignon	1:56(1)	-0-	-0-	7:48(3+6)
Dep. Nimes	2:26(1)	2:44(1)	7:05	8:34(3)
Arr. Narbonne	4:01	4:35	8:35	10:14
Change trains.				
Dep. Narbonne	4:14(1)	4:40(1)	8:53	10:26(4)
Arr. Port Bou	5:47	6:00	10:35	13:01
Change trains.				
Dep. Port Bou	7:10(2)	7:10	11:55	13:45
Arr. Barcelona (Cent.)	9:39	9:39	15:05	15:56

(1)Has couchettes. Direct train to Port Bou. No train change in Narbonne. (2)Meal service until Narbonne. (3)Local train to Nimes. Arrives Nimes 8:22. (4)Change trains in Perpignan. (5)Supplement charged. Meal service. (6)Plus other departures from Avignon at 15:50(5) and 16:12(2).

Marseille - Nice - Genoa - Milan   356

Dep. Marseille (St. Ch.)	-0-	6:00	8:00(3+7)
Dep. Nice	6:200(1)	9:00	10:51(3+8)
Arr. Genoa (P.P.)	10:32(1)	13:00(1)	15:35
Arr. Milan (Cent.)	12:40	15:10	18:05

(1)Light refreshments. (2)Meal service. (3)Change trains in Ventimiglia. (4)Light refreshments 16:52 to 20:38. (5)Carries sleeping car. Also has couchettes. (6)Has couchettes. (7)Plus other departures from Marseille at 10:35, 13:22(4), 16:49(2), 17:25(5) and 20:31(6). (8)Plus other departures from Nice at 13:18, 14:11, 16:09(4), 19:05(2), 20:18(5) and 23:07(6).

Paris - Amsterdam   106

Dep. Paris (Nord)	7:19(1+2)	7:48(3)	10:23(4)	15:18(3+6)
Arr. Amsterdam	12:30	14:13	16:32	21:33

(1)TEE. Reservation required. Meal service. (2)Daily, except Sunday. (3)Light refreshments. (4)Meal service. (5)Runs from early June to early September. Has couchettes. (6)Plus other departures from Paris at 17:41(1) and 23:20(5).

Paris - Bern   56
Dep. Paris (Lyon)   7:41(1)   17:00(2)   23:49(3)
Arr. Bern   13:45   23:06   7:05
(1)Light refreshments. (2)Meal service. (3)Has couchettes.

Paris - Bordeaux - Lisbon   28
Dep. Paris (Austerlitz)   9:00(1)
Dep. Bordeaux   13:28
Dep. Bayonne   15:14
Dep. Irun   17:50
Dep. San Sebastian   18:11
Dep. Salamanca   1:35
   Set your watch back one hour.
Arr. Lisbon (S. Apol.)   9:55
(1)Reservation required. Supplement charged. Carries sleeping car Irun-Lisbon. Has couchettes Paris-Lisbon. A long stop in Hendaye is for changing the wheels on the cars to conform with the wider track in Spain.

Paris - Brussels   106
Dep. Paris (Nord)   6:41(1+2)   7:19(1+3)   7:48(4)   10:23(4+9)
Arr. Brussels (Midi)   9:11   9:46   10:50   13:16
(1)TEE. Reservation required. Meal service. (2)Mon.-Fri., except holidays. Runs only early September to late June. (3)Daily, except Sun. (4)Light refreshments. (5)Sup. charged. (6)Meal service. (7)Daily, except Sat. (8)From early June to early September: daily. From early September to early June: Fri. only. (9)Plus other departures from Paris at 11:37(1), 12:56(4), 15:18(4), 16:45(4+5), 17:41(1), 18:40(1+2), 19:27(6), 20:30(1+7) and 23:20(8).

Paris - Cologne (Koln)   62
Dep. Paris (Nord)   7:30(1)   12:56(2)   16:20(3)   17:10(4+8)
Arr. Cologne   12:41   18:48   22:38   22:33
(1)Sup. charged. Meal service. (2)Sup. charged. Light refreshments. (3)Light refreshments only from mid-June to early September. (4)Light refreshments. (5)Late June to early September: daily. Early September to late June: Monday-Friday. (6)Has couchettes. (7)Carries sleeping car. Also has couchettes. (8)Plus other departures from Paris at 17:44(5), 21:40(6) and 23:15(7)

Paris - Geneva   152

| Dep. Paris (Lyon) | 7:45(1+2) | 12:05(1) | 19:12(1+2) | 23:02(3) |
| Arr. Geneva (Corn.) | 12:00 | 16:25 | 23:33 | 7:25 |

(1)TGV. Reservation required. Meal service. (2)Supplement charged. on certain days. (3)Has couchettes.

Paris - Bordeaux - Madrid   422

Dep. Paris (Aust.)	6:51(1+2)	14:00(3)	17:50(2+4+6)
Dep. Bordeaux (St.J.)	11:20(1+2)	18:36(3)	22:21(2+4+7)
Arr. Madrid (Cham.)	21:47	8:34	10:00

(1)Reservation required. Meal service. (2)Supplement charged. (3)Carries air-conditioned sleeping car. (4)Meal service. Has couchettes. (5)Meal service. Carries sleeping car. (6)Plus other departures from Paris at 20:00(2+5) and 21:55(4).
   (7)Plus other departures from Bordeaux at 0:22(2+5) and 3:50(4).

Paris - Torino - Genoa

	16	24
Dep. Paris (Lyon)	18:50(1+2)	20:39(1+3)
Arr. Torino (P.N.)	3:01(1+2)	5:35(1+3)
Arr. Genoa (P.P.)	4:53	8:10

(1)Carries sleeping car. Also has couchettes. (2)Meal service. (3)Light refreshments.

THE FERRY-CROSSING TO IRELAND

Cherbourg - Rosslar   **Le Havre - Rosslare**
   1022
   These times are for the period April 1 to September 30.

| Dep. Cherbourg | 21:00)1) | Dep. Le Havre | 18:00(2) |
| Arr. Rosslare | 14:00 Day 2 | Arr. Rosslare | 14:00 Day 2 |

(1)Early May to late June and most of September: Tuesday and Saturday. Late June to early September: Tuesday and Sunday. (2)Early May to late June: daily, except Tuesday and Saturday. Late June to early September: Monday, Wednesday, Friday and Saturday. Early October to mid-December: Tuesday, Thursday and Saturday. Mid-December to late December: Monday, Wednesday and Friday.

GREECE

The signs you will see at railstations in Greece are:

ANDRON	MEN
EISODHOS	ENTRANCE
EXODHOS	EXIT
GRAPHEION	TICKET
TON EISTIRON	OFFICE
GYNAIKON	WOMEN
IMATOPHYLAKION	CHECKROOM
PLIROPHORIA	INFORMATION
STATHMO	STATION

GREEK HOLIDAYS

January 1	New Year's Day	May 1	Labor Day
January 6	Epiphany		Holy Spirit Day
	Ash Monday	August 15	Virgin Mary's Day
March 25	Independence Day	Last Mon.	
	Good Friday	in October	National Day
	Good Saturday	December 25	Christmas
	Easter	December 26	Additional Holiday
	Easter Monday		

SUMMER TIME

Greece changes to Summer Time on the last Sunday of March and converts back to Standard Time on the last Sunday of September.

GREECE'S TRAIN PASS

Greek Touring Card Unlimited second-class train travel. Can be purchased only in Greece. The 1984 prices are: 10 days 2,500 drachmas, 20 days 3,900 and 30 days 5,200.

EURAILPASS BONUSES IN GREECE

See details on the Patras-Brindisi ferry-boat trip on page 146.

ONE-DAY EXCUSIONS AND CITY-SIGHTSEEING

Here are 6 one-day rail trips that can be made comfortably from Athens and Thessaloniki, returning to them in most cases before dinnertime. Notes are provided on what to see and do at each destination. The number after the name of each route is the Cook's timetable.

Details on 2 longer rail trips in Greece follow the one-day excursions. Schedules for international connections conclude this section.

GREECE

Athens

From 7:30 to sunset, and from 21:00 to 24:00 on nights of a full moon, visit the Parthenon, the elegant temple of the Wingless Victory and the Erechtheion at the ancient Acropolis. Then walk northwest to the partly restored ancient Agora to see the best preserved Doric temple in Athens, the Hephaistos, also known as the Thesseion.

Also near the Acropolis are: The old theater of Dionyssos. The gravestones and sculptures in Kerameikos, the city's ancient cemetery. The Corinthia-style columns of the Temple of Olympian Zeus. Hadrian's Arch. The all-marble Athenian Stadium, where the Olympic Games were revived in 1896. The Clock of Kyrrestos, showing the prevailing wind on each of its 8 sides, standing in Aerides Square, named for the function of the clock. The Roman Forum.

Walk downhill to the Monastiraki area, where the daily "Flea Market" is held. See the view of Athens from the white chapel of Agios Georgios on the Hill of Lycabettus, climbed either by foot or by cable car.

Athens' best-known museums are the National Archaeological Museum, The Acropolis Museum, the Byzantine Museum (for its collection of icons), the Museum of Greek Popular Art, the Museum of the Ancient Agora excavations in the Stoa (ancient commercial community) at Attalos, and the Fantastic Benaki Museum in central Athens.

The 28 exhibit rooms at the Benaki, arranged chronologically, cover the entire spectrum of Greek culture from the early Bronze Age to the start of the 20th century: gold, ornaments, jewelry, portraits, statues, embroidery, icons, rare 17th and 18th century bibles, and 8 centuries (10th to 18th) of Islamic art that includes ceramics, textiles and wood carvings. Located on Queen Sofias Avenue, opposite the National Garden, the Benaki is open daily except Tuesday 8:00 to 14:00.

There are sound-and-light performances in English at Pnyx Hill every night at 21:00. When it ends, cross the road and see native dances of Greece, performed nightly at 22:15 on the Hill of Filopappos.

For Greek arts and handicrafts (ceramics, hand-woven fabrics, alabaster articles, embroideries, hand-carved wood furniture), shop on the streets around Syntagma Square, the center of the city.

Athens - Arghos - Athens   898

Sit on the right-hand side of the train en route to Arghos in order to see best the view of the canal that connects the Aegean and Ionian Seas, about 80 minutes after leaving Athens. The train crosses a 108-foot long bridge, 200 feet above the water. It is a short walk or inexpensive taxi ride from the Arghos railstation to the town center.

Dep. Athens   7:20(1+2)   9:43(1)
Arr. Arghos   9:50   12:35

    Sights in **Arghos:** The Museum, with its archaeological exhibits. From there, it is a 15-minute walk to the ancient theater, carved into the hillside, and to some Roman ruins. A 5-mile taxi ride to the 800 B.C. ruins of Tiryns is well worth the small fare. At the birthplace of Hercules you will see the ruins of Greece's oldest recognizable temple: underground galleries polished for many centuries by the woolly backs of innumerable sheep who sought shelter there during storms. Massive Cyclopean walls.

Dep. Arghos   12:40(1)   14:38(1)   19:03(1+2)   2:58
Arr. Athens   15:41   17:41   21:36   5:42
(1)Light refreshments. (2)Supplement charged.

Athens - Corinth - Athens   898

    Watch 80 minutes after departing Athens for the same view described above, under "Athens-Arghos". The arrival in Corinth is in the "modern" Corinth, built after the 1858 earthquake.

Dep. Athens   7:20(1+2)   8:36(1+2)   9:43(1)   10:22(3)   12:01(1)
Arr. Corinth   8:54   10:11   11:29   12:13   13:51

    Sights in **Corinth:** The 2500-year old Temple of Apollo. The Kato Pirini Fountain. The rostrum from which St. Paul preached Christianity to the Corinthians.

Dep. Corinth   12:14(1)   13:10(1+2)   13:52(1)   15:48(1)   16:39(3+4)
Arr. Athens   13:59   14:46   15:41   17:41   18:34
(1)Light refreshments. (2)Supplement charged. (3)Meal service. (4)Plus other departures from Corinth at 19:30(3), 19:58(1+2) and 21:03(1+2).

Athens - Kalamata - Athens   898

Dep. Athens   7:20(1) | Dep. Kalamata   15:30(1)
Arr. Kalamata 13:28 | Arr. Athens   21:36
(1)Supplement charged. Light refreshments.

    Sights in **Kalamata:** The exhibits at the Museum in the Kyriakos mansion, ranging from Stone Age weapons to Venetian mirrors and coins as well as relics from the 1821 War of Independence. The Byzantine-style Church of Aghii Apostoli. The splendid view from the Frankish castle and, descending from there, see the handmade silk articles at the Convent. Aghios Haralambos, one of the finest Byzantine churches in the area, is a short distance east of the Convent. Stroll along the seafront.

Athens - Olympia

898			897		
Dep. Athens	8:36(1)	10:22(2)	Dep. Olympia	7:25	10:36(3)
Arr. Pirghos	13:52	17:10	Arr. Pirghos	8:08	11:12
Change trains.			Change trains.		
897			898		
Dep. Pirghos	14:04	18:12	Dep. Pirghos	9:09(1)	11:35(2)
Arr. Olympia	14:45	18:48	Arr. Athens	14:46	18:34

(1)Supplement charged. Light refreshments. (2)Meal service. (3)Plus other departures from Olympia at 13:27 and 16:31 [from Pirghos at 14:57(2) and 17:17(1)].

Sights in **Olympia:** The first Olympic Games (776 B.C.) were held here and continued here every 4 years for the next 12 centuries. See the Stadium. The fine Olympic Museum, with its marvelous Hermes of Praxiteles sculpture. The temples of Hera and Zeus.

Athens - Patras - Athens   898

Dep. Athens	6:39(1)	8:36(2)	Dep. Patras	17:02(1)	18:58(2)
Arr. Patras	10:58	12:15	Arr. Athens	21:20	22:39

(1)Meal service. (2)Supplement charged. Light refreshments.

Sights in **Patras:** Cross the street in front of the railstation to the park. Then walk from the Trion Fountain along Ayiou Nijulauo to the steps that ascend to the Patras Acropolis for a fine view of Patras, the surrounding mountains and the port, third largest of Greece.

After descending the steps, go to the left along Georgiou Street to the old Roman Theater, the Odeon.

Another walk from the Trion Fountain is to the Archaeological Museum to see its collection of exhibits from the Mycenean, Geometric, Archaic and Roman periods. Also worth seeing are the Venetian castle and Greece's largest church, St. Andrews's.

Athens - Piraeus   892a

Subway trains depart every few minutes from the southbound section of a combined north-and-south platform at Athens' Omonia Square railstation for the 20-minute ride to Piraeus. Be certain, at the same platform, you are not boarding the northbound train for Kifissia. There is also ordinary train service from Athens to Piraeus.

Sights in **Piraeus:** One of the largest ports on the Mediterranean. Ships sail daily from here to almost all the Aegean islands and to many other Greek ports. The 2 small adjoining ports of Zea and Mikrolimano are for pleasure craft. Bus #20 (the bus terminal is to the left of the railstation) goes to these ports.

See the neo-classical style Municipal Theater and the exhibits in the Archaeological Museum and the Maritime Museum. Plays are performed at the open-air Theater of Kastella in the Summer.

Athens - Thessaloniki   891

Dep. Athens (Larissa)   7:05(1)   8:00(2)   11:30(1)   14:10(1+11)
Arr. Thessaloniki   14:35   15:50   18:40   22:00

Sights in **Thessaloniki:** Second largest city in Greece. See the ruins of the Roman Baths, north of the Church of Agios Demetrios. The Roman Market and Theater. Nymphaion, the ancient circular building. The Arch of Galerius. The unique mosaics in the 4th century Rotunda, at the intersection of Agiou Georgiou and Filippou streets.

The 2 surviving early Christian churches: the 4th century Ahiropiitos and the 5th century Osios David. The 15th century White Tower. The collection of pre-historic to Byzantine items in the Archaeological Museum on YMCA Square. Articles from the past 3 centuries at the Folklore and Ethnological Museum, 68 Vasilisais Olgas.

Dep. Thessaloniki   5:50(4)   8:14(5)   10:39(1)   13:50(3+12)
Arr. Athens (Larrissa)   14:42   16:08   17:48   21:38

(1)Supplement charged. Light refreshments. (2)Reservation required. Supplement charged. Meal service. (3)Light refreshments. (4)Meal service. (5)Supplement charged. Meal service. (6)Reservation required. Carries sleeping car. Meal service. (7)Reservation required. Has couchettes. (8)From late May to late Sept., couchettes replaced by sleeping car on Tues. and Fri. Carries sleeping car. Also has couchettes. (10)From early June to late September, couchettes replaced by sleeping car on Thurs. and Sun. (11)Plus other departures from Athens at 16:55(1), 19:00(6), 21:10(7+8) and 23:10(9).   (12)Plus other departures from Thessaloniki at 15:06(4), 16:44(1), 21:50(9) and 0:30(7+10).

Thessaloniki - Kavala - Thessaloniki   893

Dep. Thessaloniki   6:14(1)   9:02(1)   15:00(1)   17:55(1+3)
Arr. Drama   10:18   13:41   18:34   22:38

Change to bus for 22-mile ride to Kavala.

Dep. Drama   N/A   N/A   N/A   N/A
Arr. Kavala   N/A   N/A   N/A   N/A

                            *   *   *

Dep. Kavala   N/A   N/A   N/A   N/A
Arr. Drama   N/A   N/A   N/A   N/A

Change to train.

Dep. Drama   7:32   9:55(1)   15:57(1)   18:46(4)
Arr. Thessaloniki   12:06   13:27   20:17   22:24

(1)Light refreshments. (2)Carries sleeping car. Also has couchettes. (3)Plus another departure from Thessaloniki at 23:03(2).   (4)Plus another departure from Drama at 3:11(1+2).

Sights in **Kavala:** The view from the Byzantine Fort. The colossal 16th century aqueduct, Kamares. Imaret, the group of Moslem buildings constructed a short time prior to the 1821 War of Independence. The ancient relics in the Archaeological Museum. Beautiful beaches.

SCENIC TRIPS IN GREECE

Thessaloniki - Katerini - Athens   891

About one hour after departing Katerini, you can see on the right side of the train 9000-foot high Mt. Olympus, home of the ancient Greek gods. Thirty minutes later, the train passes through Tembi Valley and goes along Pinios River. From Domokos to Tithorea, the train winds along Mt. Orthrys and Mt. Iti, providing a panoramic view of many valleys and high mountains and, at one point, of the sea in the distance.

See Thessaloniki-Athens time table on page 144.

Athens - Pirghos

Most of this trip is alongside the sea, through green fields of citrus and olive trees. Between Athens and Corinth, the train goes across the bridge spanning Korinthos Canal, which separates northern Greece from Peloponesia.

898		897	
Dep. Athens	8:36(1)	Dep. Pirghos	14:04
Arr. Corinth	10:11	Arr. Olympia	14:45
Arr. Pirghos	13:52	Sightsee in Olympia	
Change trains.		Dep. Olympia	16:31
		Arr. Pirghos	17:12
		Change trains.	
		898	
(1)Supplement charged		Dep. Pirghos	17:17(1)
Light refreshments.		Arr. Athens	23:39

INTERNATIONAL ROUTES FROM GREECE

Athens is Greece's gateway to Italy and Yugoslavia (and on to Western Europe) as well as to Turkey (and on to the Middle East).

Athens - Belgrad + Munich or Venice

	65	65	40
Dep. Athens	8:00(1+2+3)	19:00(1+2)	21:10(1)

Set your watch back one hour from late September to early April, 2 hours from early April to late September.

Arr. Belgrade	6:35(4)	17:15(4)	19:18(4)
Dep. Belgrade	7:10	17:50	20:00(6)
Arr. Munich	23:30	10:10(5)	-0-
Arr. Venice (S.L.)	-0-	-0-	11:07(5)

(1)Meal service. Has couchettes.   (2)Reservation required.   (3)Supplement charged.   (4)Day 2.   (5)Day 3.   (6)Carries sleeping car. Also has couchettes.

Athens - Patras - Brindis   898

The Patras-Brindisi boat trip is covered by Eurailpass and Eurail Youthpass—but only if you go on Adriatica/Hellenic Mediterranean Lines.

WARNING: The employees of other lines intimate that their ships honor the 2 passes and then charge fees after the boat leaves the pier.

With or without a Eurailpass or Eurail Youthpass, a reservation theoretically can be made on day of departure or day before departure — but it is very unlikely that space will be available (particularly during July and August)unless a reservation is made many weeks in advance of departure date.

Those gambling on making a reservation after arriving in Patras can make application January 1-June 9 and October 1-December 31 only at the Adriatica/Hellenic Mediterranean Lines embarkation office, located at Othonos Amalias 8.

From June 10 to September 30, those without advance reservations can apply also to any Patras travel agency that displays in its window the green badge "Eurail Information - Eurailpass".

Holders of advance reservations must go at all times directly to the A/HM Lines embarkation office to have their tickets checked, settle port taxes due and obtain the required Embarkation Ticket. That office is open 9:00-13:30 and 16:00-22:00.

Advance reservations before you start your trip, at $1.50(U.S.) each, can be made at any office that issues Eurailpass (see pages 20-21) or at travel agencies in countries where Eurailpass is sold. There is also a $12(U.S.) surcharge, in addition to the reservation fee, for travel from June 10 through September 30.

Another fee is charged for such special accommodations as aircraft type seats, pullman berths and cabins. There is also a port tax of 180 Drachmas that is *not* covered by Eurailpass and must be paid in Drachmas.

Passengers without advance reservations must obtain the Embarkation Ticket at least 2 hours prior to the ship's departure time. The ships reserve the right to cancel a reservation when that is not done and to give the space to a standby passenger.

Dep. Athens	6:39(1)	8:36(2)	10:22(1)	13:10(2)	15:42(1)
Arr. Patras	10:58	12:15	14:56	17:00	19:56

For sightseeing in Patras, see notes on page 147.

Walk to Patras Harbor.

For sailing dates, check Cook's Table #1440.

Dep. Patras Harbor	17:00(3)	22:00(4)
Arr. Brindisi	8:30(5)	17:00(5)

(1)Meal service. (2)Supplement charged. Light refreshments. (3)Operates late June to late September. (4)Operates all year. (5)Day 2.

Athens - Istanbul   900

Dep. Athens	23:05 (second-class only)
Arr. Istanbul	6:50 Day 3

IBERIAN PENINSULA (SPAIN AND PORTUGAL)

Spain and Portugal have the broadest gauge railroad tracks in Western Europe (5′ 6″ versus 4′ 8½″ in France and the other Western European countries). It is therefore necessary in most crossings from Spain into France (at Irun/Hendaye, Port Bou/Cerbere, or La Tour-de-Carol) to change trains. A few trains running between Spain and France are adaptable to either gauge.

Many Spanish train tickets include the price of a lunch or dinner. It is wise to determine this in advance of a trip.

For most Spanish trains, it is necessary to reserve a seat and have one's ticket stamped with the train number and departure date. Even when traveling on a Eurailpass or Eurail Youthpass, an endorsed ticket should be obtained for trains requiring them.

Do *not* discard a ticket during the journey. Frequently, the ticket is collected at the termination of a ride. If it is not presented at the destination railstation, the passenger must purchase a second ticket.

It is wise to retain rail tickets all over the world so as to avoid having to pay twice for one journey.

Every year, some tourists using Eurailpass or Eurail Youthpass report being ejected from a Spanish train either just before its departure or at a station en route to their destination for failing to obtain the required endorsed tickets.

A person using a Eurailpass or Eurail Youthpass has been indoctrinated with the idea that he or she need not have either a ticket or (when riding an ordinary train) a seat reservation. This is confirmed on all of one's travels in Europe outside Spain.

Unaware of the Spanish Railway regulation, the passenger blithely steps aboard a train in Spain without having the ticket and seat reservation required there — and a ticket can be obtained without charge upon presenting the Eurailpass or Eurail Youthpass.

If the train is not exceptionally crowded that day and the conductor appears before the train departs, the passenger is told to get off the train, go back into the railstation, and obtain the required endorsed ticket. Frequently, the notice to do this is given so close to the departure time that the train leaves before the passenger is able to return to it.

If the train departs before the conductor has discovered the omission of an endorsed ticket, often the passenger is forced to leave the train at the next stop to obtain a ticket. If that stop is typically brief, the train leaves that station before the passenger is able to return to the train.

SPAIN & PORTUGAL

The justification for the Spanish ticket-and-reservation requirement is that Spain's first-class fares are substantially lower than those of other countries. For example, the charge for the 8-hour Madrid-Barcelona run is about 60% of what French National Railroads charges for the 7-hour trip from Paris to Avignon or what Norwegian State Railways charges for the 8½-hour Bergen-Oslo trip. The demand for Spain's limited number of express train seats far exceeds the supply. Only by issuing endorsed tickets can they control the situation.

The Spanish name for Spanish National Railways is "Red Nacional de los Ferrocarriles Espanoles". Abbreviation: RENFE. Reservations can be made at RENFE offices both in the major railstations and at numerous locations outside the station, as well as at various travel agencies in Spanish cities.

Making train reservations in Spain is very easy. More than 90% of the stations in Spain are hooked-up with a computer in Madrid, making it usually possible to arrange at one time all of your reservations for train trips in Spain. Reservations can be made as much as 2 months in advance. Timetable information can be obtained at offices of RENFE and at Spanish travel agencies.

Tell the clerk at the train information window your departure date, train number (which you can find in the railstation on the list of departures) and/or departure time, destination and number of seats required.

You will be handed a form which you then take to a ticket window, where you will be handed a seat reservation computer card. It will show either an exact seat number or the symbol "SR" ("Seat Reserved") under the column "Asiento".

If it is marked "SR", the conductor will tell you which seat to occupy after you board the car designated on the reservation computer card.

Do *not* board a Spanish non-local train without a seat reservation !

To ride without a Eurailpass on Spanish trains classified "Rap", one must pay a supplement. A higher supplement must be paid when riding a train classified "Talgo", "E.L.T." or "T.E.R.", all of which are air-conditioned.

A Eurailpass entitles the bearer to ride these special trains without having to pay their supplemental charges, the same as when riding Trans-Europ Express trains.

First-class sleeping cars in Spain have single-berth and 2-berth compartments. Second-class sleeping cars have 3-berth tourist compartments, except the Barcelona Talgo, which has tourist compartments with 4 berths. There is a supplemental charge for air-conditioned sleeping cars. Neither berths nor this supplement are covered by Eurailpass. Some Spanish trains have second-class couchette cars, with 6-berth compartments, as are also available in other Western European countries.

First-class sleeping cars in Portugal have single-berth compartments. Second-class Portuguese sleeping cars have 2-berth compartments. The Sud Express also provides 3-berth second-class compartments.

In order to avoid waiting in the wrong line for Spanish tickets and seat reservations, take note of these signs you will find in large Spanish railstations:
TRENES DE SALIDA INMEDIATE (trains ready to depart),
VENTA PARA HOY (trains leaving later in the day), and
VENTA ANTICIPADA (for trains leaving on a future day).

Other **Spanish** railstation signs:

A LOS ANDENNES	TO THE PLATFORMS (TRACKS)
CABALLEROS	MEN
COCHE-CAMA	SLEEPING CAR
COCHE-LITERA	COACHETTES
COCHE-RESTAURANTE	RESTAURANT CAR
ENTRADA	ENTRANCE
ESTACION	STATION
HORARIOS DE TRENES	TIMETABLES
LA CONSIGNA	LUGGAGE CHECK-ROOM
LARGO RECORRIDO	LONG DISTANCE
LLEGADA	ARRIVAL
SALIDA	DEPARTURE (EXIT)
SENORAS	WOMEN
TREN CON SUPLEMENTO	TRAIN WITH SURCHARGE

Signs you will find in **Portuguese** railstations:

CARRUAGEM-CAMA	SLEEPING CAR
CARRUAGEM-RESTAURANTE	RESTAURANT CAR
CHEGADA	ARRIVAL
ESTACAO	STATION
HOMENS	MEN
HORARIO DOS CAMINHOS	TIMETABLES
PARTIDA	DEPARTURE
PLATAFORMA	PLATFORM (TRACK)
SAIDA	EXIT
SENHORAS	WOMEN

SPANISH HOLIDAYS

A list of holidays is helpful because some trains will be noted later in this section as *not* running on holidays. Also, these trains which operate on holidays are filled, and it is necessary to make reservations for them long in advance.

January 1	New Year's Day
January 6	Epiphany
March 19	Saint Joseph's Day
	Maundy Thursday
	Good Friday
	Easter
	Easter Monday (Barcelona)
April 1	Victory Day
May 1	St. Joseph Artisan Day
	Ascension Day
	Corpus Christi Day
June 29	St. Peter and St. Paul
July 18	National Holiday
July 25	Saint James' Day
August 15	Assumption Day
October 12	Columbus Day
November 1	All Saints Day
December 8	Immaculate Conception
December 25	Christmas Day

PORTUGUESE HOLIDAYS

The main public holidays in Portugal are:

January 1	New Year's Day
	Shrove Tuesday
	Good Friday
	Easter
June 10	Day of The Race (Portuguese National Day)
	Saint Anthony's Day (Lisbon)
August 15	Assumption of Our Lady
October 5	Anniversary of the Proclamation of the Portuguese Republic
November 1	All Saints Day
December 1	Restoration of Independence
December 8	Immaculate Conception
December 15	Christmas

SUMMER TIME

Portugal is one hour earlier than Spain all year. Portugal is on the same time as England nearly all year, except for a few weeks in the Spring and Fall. Both Portugal and Spain change to Summer Time on the last Sunday of March and convert back to Standard Time on the last Sunday of September. During Summer Time, when it is 12:00 in England, it is 12:00 in Portugal and 13:00 in Spain.

PORTUGAL'S TRAIN PASSES

All of the following are sold only in Portugal. Children under 4 travel free.

Tourist Ticket   Unlimited train travel for any class. The 1984 prices are: 7 days 3,820 escudos, 14 days 6,100 escudos, 21 days 8,710 escudos.

Kilometric Ticket   Valid for 3 months, covering up to 3,000 km of travel. The 1984 prices for first-class are: 10,015 escudos for express trains, 7,155 escudos for other trains. Second-class: 6,680 and 4,770.

Senior Citizen Discount   Persons 65 or older pay half-fare.

Family Ticket   For 3 or more persons. Valid only for trips of more than 149 km. Passports and documents proving family relationship must be presented. One person must pay full fare. Half-fare for others who are over 12 years old. One-quarter fare for children 4-11. Children under 4 travel free.

Group Ticket   For 10 or more persons, a 20% discount for trips of more than 99 km. One free ticket for a group of 15-50 people. Two free tickets for a group of more than 50.

SPAIN'S TRAIN PASSES

All of the following are sold only in Spain.

Chequetren   1984 prices: 15,000 pesetas of train travel costs 12,750 pesetas, while 20,000 pesetas of train travel costs 17,000 pesetas.

Senior Citizen Discount   For persons 65 or older. Must first purchase a "Tarjeta Dorada" (Gold Card) for less than $1.00(U.S.) at any railstation or Renfe ticket office. Proof of age (Passport, etc.) required. With the Gold Card, there is a 50% discount for trips of more than 100 kilometers (60 miles).

Roundtrip Discount   A 25% discount on trips of more than 100 kilometers. *Not* valid approximately 60 holidays in every years.

EURAILPASS BONUSES

There are *no* Eurailpass bonuses in Spain or Portugal.

ONE-DAY EXCURSIONS AND CITY SIGHTSEEING

Here are 39 one-day rail trips that can be made comfortably from 7 major Spanish and Portuguese cities, returning to them in most cases before dinner-time. Notes are provided on what to see and do at each destination. The number after the name of each route is the Cook's timetable.

This section concludes with details on 12 rail trips recommended for exceptional scenery plus 6 trips to/from Madrid, the schedules for 2 other major routes (Barcelona-Valencia and Lisbon-Seville), and the international rail connections from Portugal and Spain.

The 7 base cities are: Barcelona, Lisbon, Madrid, San Sebastian, Seville, Tarragona and Valencia.

Barcelona

There is rail service between the center of Barcelona (Sants station) and the city's airport every 15 minutes from 6:00 to 22:40. The rail service from the airport to the city is every 15 minutes from 6:30 to 23:00. There is bus service from the city to the airport at 23:15, 23:45, 00:15 and 00:45. Bus service from the airport to the city is offered at 23:45, 00:15, 00:45 and 1:15.

Local trains, not requiring seat reservations, depart from Barcelona's underground Paseo de Garcia and Sants railstations. Faster express trains, requiring seat reservations, also depart from Paseo de Garcia and from Sants, as well as from Barcelona's Termino station.

Your sightseeing here can be divided into covering 4 separate areas of Barcelona. In the Gothic Quarter: The cloisters in the 14th century Cathedral (La Seu), the Episcopal Palace, Palacio de la Generalidad, many elegant 14th and 15th century palaces, the Federico Mares Museum. The Picasso Museum.

In the Montjuich area: the Museum of Catalan Art in the National Palace, the collection of El Greco, Velasquez and Rembrandt paintings at the Archaeological Museum in Palacio Real, handicrafts and architecture representing every region of Spain in the Spanish Village.

In the Tibidado area: Pedralbes Palace, Pedralbes Monastery, the Picasso Museum, and the view all the way to Montserrat and the Pyrenees.

In the modern city center: Stroll the mile-long Ramblas, from Plaza de Cataluna to Plaza Puerta de la Paz, with its Columbus monument at the waterfront. You will enjoy seeing the numerous stalls selling hundreds of varieties of birds, the many stands with flowers and plants, the very large central food market, cafes offering tapas (the local and varied between-meal snacks), and at least half the population of Barcelona.

Another rewarding walk, in the opposite direction, is along beautiful Paseo de Gracia, from Plaza de Cataluna to Avenida del Generalismo Franco (also called "Diagonal", its original name), to see luxury shops, decorative sidewalks designed by Dali, and several buildings created by Barcelona's most radical and inventive architect, Antonio Gaudi.

In Plaza Gaudi, you must see the uncompleted and absolutely unique church, La Sagrada Familia, the architect's most important work. It was started in 1884. Because of lack of funds, Barcelonians believe construction will not be finished until 100 years from now.

What has been constructed in the last 100 years is well worth seeing: the 4 lofty towers (nearly 300 feet tall), the Nativity and Passion facades with the Tree of Life supported by the central arch, and the wrought-iron plants in the side chapels of the completed crypt.

Although public transportation is not available to the Gaudi-designed park, Parque Guell, we suggest you take a taxi there to see it and to see the view of Barcelona from its elevated plaza. The paths in this park are decorated with concrete pillars that imitate trees and vines. Also see the colorful undulating bench surfaced with broken ceramic pieces, on the plaza. And the gigantic tiled frog fountain on the steps leading down from the park's plaza.

Lisbon

Santa Apolonia is Lisbon's railstation for departure to Madrid and beyond (to France and the rest of Europe). It has currency exchange (9:00-21:00) and hotel reservation services (9:30-17:30).

See the beautiful Avenida de Liberdade. The Tower of Belem (monument to Portugal's sailors). The view from the bi-cultural St. George's Castle, built by the Visigoths in the 5th century and by the Moors in the 9th century. The Palace of Queluz.

Largo das Portas do Sol (Sun Gateway), one of the 7 gates into the ancient Arab City. Santa Cruz quarter. Alfama Quarter. Salazar Bridge. The lovely Praco de Rossio. The marvelous collection of tapestries, jewelry, ceramics, and Dutch, Spanish and Italian paintings in the Ancient Art Museum.

The more than 3,000 art treasures (Rembrandt, Fragonard, Corot, many Impressionists, Egyptian sculpture, Persian art) in the Gulbenkian Museum.

Edward VII Park. The Zoological Garden. The Botanical Garden. The Museum of Modern Art. The Municipal Museum. The greatest collection in the world of royal coaches in the Belem Palace at Praca Afonso de Albuquerque. The Flea Market. The Military Museum. The collection of 17th and 18th century Portuguese and Indo-Portuguese furnishings in the Museum of Decorative Arts.

The Maritime Museum, in the West wing of Jeronimos Monastery. Jeronimo's Church. The Cathedral. House of Facets, its front entirely faced with dark stones that have been cut into diamond-like facets.

Madrid

There is train service connecting Madrid's Chamartin and Atocha stations. Eurailpass and Eurail Youthpass can be used on it. At Chamartin, look for the track marked "Linea de Atocha y Guadalajara". At Atocha, go to the separate small station, a short walk from the main station.

The Prado Museum, with its breathtaking collection of great paintings. Puerta del Sol. The Goya Pantheon. Plaza Mayor. San Miguel Basilica. San Isidor Cathedral. The Royal Palace, including: State Apartments and Chapel, Apartments of Queen Maria Cristina of Hapsburg, the Private Apartments, Royal Pharmacy, Armory, Carriage Museum, Library, Numismatic Museum and Music Museum.

Descalzas Reales Convent. The Archaeological Museum. The Folk Museum.

The Americas Museum. The Bullfighting Museum. Retiro Park. University City. Plaza de Espana, with its stone monument to Cervantes. The Royal Tapestry Factory.

For the best food in Spain, and it is moderately priced, dine at Restaurante Botin, at Calle de Cuchilleros 17. Every dish is marvelous. Their specialties are roast suckling pig and roast baby lamb. These and many other foods are cooked there by oak wood in the original 16th century tiled oven. Botin is run by a young and very handsome gentleman, Antonio Gonzalez Jr. His family has operated Botin for more than 80 years.

San Sebastian

Excellent beaches. The Goya and El Greco collection at San Sebastian Picture Gallery. Sta. Maria Church. San Telmo Museum. The Oceanographic museum in Sea Palace. The picturesque fishing village nearby. Mount Urgull.

Seville

The city of Don Juan and Carmen. You must not miss seeing Corpus Christi Cathedral, largest Gothic cathedral in the world and the site of Columbus' tomb.

The 14th century Alcazar Palace with its magnificent chambers, particularly the room where foreign ambassadors were received. Its colorful mosaics and tiles, delicate wrought-iron and carved wood ceilings are spellbinding. You can see nearby Segovia from the tower of Isabella's castle. Allow time to stroll through the elaborate gardens there: bronze and marble statues, lovely fountains and the extraordinary Pavillion of Carlos V.

On one side of the Alcazar is a university, formerly Antigua Fabrica de Tobacos, the tobacco factory Bizet immortalized in his opera, Carmen. On the other side of the Alcazar is Barrio de Santa Cruz, with its ancient buildings and narrow streets. Once a refuge for Jews fleeing the Inquisition, now it is a fashionable residential section of Seville.

You can enjoy spending many hours in Maria Luisa Park, seeing the beautiful buildings, gardens, pools and fountains there. Particularly noteworthy is the magnificent Plaza de Espana.

Other notable sights in Seville: The 12th century La Giralda Tower, a minaret when the Moors ruled here. The 12-sided Tower of Gold. Meander along the city's cobbled streets to see many picturesque homes.

The only way to reach the 200 BC Roman ruins called Italica (a few miles outside Seville) is by auto. Schedule at least one hour to see the third largest arena in Europe (after Rome and Nimes) and many excellent mosaic floors of what had been the houses of those who lived here 2,100 years ago.

Valencia

The Holy Grail, the chalice used at the Last Supper, exhibited in the 13th century Cathedral. The great art collection in the Convent of Pio V. The Orange Court at the 15th century Lonja del Mercado. The popular beaches: Arenas, Nazaret, and Pinedo y Saler. The scent of the vast surrounding orange groves, perfuming the night.

* * *

RESERVATIONS ARE STRONGLY ADVISED ON ALL SPANISH TRAINS.

* * *

In the following timetables, where a city has more than one railstation we have designated the particular station (in parentheses).

Barcelona - Blanes - Barcelona   424

Go to the "Estacion de Cercanias" (suburban section of Barcelona's Termino railstation) to board the train for Blanes. Seat reservations are not required for this ride. Board well before departure time to avoid standing for 1½ hours.

Take a bus or taxi from Blanes' railstation to the center of the village. It is a half-mile walk there from the station.

Dep. Barcelona (Ter.)   Frequent times from 5:45 to 21:45
Arr. Blanes   60 minutes later

Sights in **Blanes:** Stroll the waterfront. See the Aquarium and Botanical Garden, near the location of the daily fish auction, at 17:00. Daily boat excursions go from Blanes to Tossa and Lloret.

Dep. Blanes   Frequent times from 6:10 to 21:40
Arr. Barcelona (Ter.)   60 minutes later

Barcelona - Gerona - Barcelona   424
Dep. Barcelona (Ter.)   7:45(1+2)   9:00(1)   10:20(1+2+3)   10:45(1+4)
Arr. Gerona   8:59   11:00   11:42   12:57

Sights in **Gerona:** The magnificent 14th century Cathedral. The Provincial Archaeological Museum. The 12th century Arab Baths. Sobreportes, the ancient gate. Narrow 17th century streets.

Dep. Gerona   11:36(1)   12:24(1)   13:15(1)   14:20(1+5)
Arr. Barcelona (Ter.)   12:52   14:20   15:05   16:36

(1)Second-class only. (2)Supplement charged. (3)Depart/Arrive Barcelona's Paseo de Gracia railstation. (4)Plus another departure from Barcelona at 13:05(1).
  (5)Plus other departures from Gerona at 14:43(1), 15:38(1), 17:20(1), 18:22(1), 20:17(2+3), 20:47(2+3), 20:58(1) and 22:18(1+2).

Barcelona - Lerida - Barcelona   412

It is advisable to make a reservation for this ride well in advance of departure date. Although departures are from other stations, go to Triunfo station to make this reservation. On boarding, find a seat on the left-hand side so as to have a good view of the restored 13th century hilltop Seo Antiqua Cathedral before the arrival in Lerida.

Dep. Barcelona (Ter.)	-0-	8:30(1)	12:10(1+3)
Dep. Barcelona (P. de G.)	-0-	-0-	12:19(1+3)
Dep. Barcelona (Sants)	8:30(1+2)	-0-	12:27(1+3)
Arr. Lerida	11:44	11:44	14:55

Sights in **Lerida:** The Archaeological Museum, in the Antiguo Hospital de Santa Maria, where the tourist office is located. A walking tour is easy with the city map available there. See the old Byzantine-Gothic-Moorish 13th century Cathedral. The Palacio de la Paheria. Stroll the maze of narrow streets in the interesting old section on the right bank of the Segre River, and visit the 12th century Alcazaba (castle).

Dep. Lerida	14:58(1+3)	18:17(1+2)	20:19(1+3)
Arr. Barcelona (Sants)	17:26	-0-	22:24
Arr. Barcelona (P. de G.)	17:34	-0-	23:33
Arr. Barcelona (Ter.)	17:42	21:23	22:42

(1)Reservation required. Supplement charged. (2)Light refreshments. (3)Meal service.

Barcelona - Montserrat - Barcelona   0000

Dep. Barcelona (P. de Espana)	9:10	11:10	13:10	15:10	17:10
Arr. Montserrat	10:09	12:09	14:09	16:09	18:09

Sights in **Montserrat:** The 9th century Monastery, still occupied by hundreds of Benedictine monks, is 3700 feet above a valley. It ranks with Zaragoza and Santiago de Compostela as one of the most important pilgrimage sites in Spain. See the Grotto of the Virgin, the Mirador, the Chapel of San Miguel and the Chapel of Santa Cecilia. Then take a funicular to the Grotto of San Juan Garin and an aerial tram to the 4,000-foot-high Hermitage of San Jeronimo, from where you will have a view of the Eastern Pyrenees.

Dep. Montserrat	11:41	13:41	15:41	17:41	19:41
Arr. Barcelona (P. de Espana)	12:40	14:40	16:40	18:40	20:40

Barcelona - Sitges - Barcelona   425

Many local trains run from Termino, Paseo de Garcia and Sants stations to Sitges, a 30-minute trip.

Sights in **Sitges:** The 18th century furnishings at Casa Llopis. Antique dolls collected from every part of Europe, in the Lola Anglada Museum. El Greco paintings at the Cau Ferrat Museum.

Barcelona - Tarragona - Barcelona   425

Many local trains run from Termino, Paseo de Gracia and Sants stations to Tarragona, a 90-minute trip.

Sights in **Tarragona:** Relics of pre-Roman, Roman, Visigothic and Moorish cultures.

It is a short, but severely uphill, walk from the railstation to the long promenade, Balcon del Mediterraneo, from which there is a marvelous view of the sea. Two strolling streets start at each end of the "balcony". The first is Rambla del Generalismo. The other is Rambla de San Carlos.

We suggest you rest a while at one of the many sidewalk cafes on either Rambla. Then, start your walking tour of Tarragona by going 2 blocks from the "balcony", down Rambla de San Carlos to where it intersects with San Augustin. Turn right (the street name changes to "Mayor") and walk one-quarter mile to the 12th century Cathedral, worth seeing for its large and architecturally unique Cloisters, influenced by Roman, Gothic and Moorish styles.

Next, return to Rambla de San Carlos and turn right. Walk down it 2 blocks until it intersects with Abalto. Turn right and walk uphill, alongside the Roman wall.

You will then be on the semi-circular Paseo Arqueologico walk, from which there are excellent views of the countryside surrounding Tarragona.

At the end of this walk, bear to the right and come downhill on Avenida de la Victoria for 5 minutes until you reach Plaza del Rey. There, you can visit both the museum in the 1st century B.C. Pretoria and also the marvelous mosaics and ancient coins in the Archaeological Museum.

Across from Plaza del Rey is the Roman Amphitheater. Having completed a circle, you will again be at Balcon del Mediterraneo, and it is all downhill to return to the railstation.

Granada - Malaga - Granada 439

Between Bobadilla and Malaga, the train travels through the spectacular El Chorro gorge.

Dep. Granada	8:30(1)		Dep. Malaga	18:40(1)
Arr. Bobadilla	10:21		Arr. Bobadilla	19:49
Change trains.			Change trains.	
Dep. Bobadilla	10:29(1)		Dep. Bobadilla	19:57(1)
Arr. Malaga	11:30		Arr. Granada	21:55

(1)Reservation required. Supplement charged.

Sights in **Malaga:** Winter sun. The 9th century Alcazaba Moslem palace and the ruins of Gibralfaro Castle, 2 fortresses which made Malaga a major stronghold in the Middle Ages. The Fine Arts Museum. Sagrario, an unusual rectangular church that was originally a mosque. The Cathedral.

Lisbon - Coimbra - Lisbon 445

Dep. Lisbon (S. Apol.)	8:25(1)	8:55(2)	11:35(3)	14:25(1)
Arr. Coimbra	10:27	11:21	14:08	16:33

Sights in **Coimbra:** Almedina Gate. The Cathedral and the Cloisters. The Machado do Castro Museum. The 13th century University. Try the local food specialty, roasted suckling pig (leitao).

Dep. Coimbra	11:11(2)	13:34(2)	16:01(1)	16:32(4)
Arr. Lisbon (S. Apol.)	13:40	16:10	18:10	20:02

(1)First-class only. Reservation required. Light refreshments. (2)Light refreshments. (3)Meal service. (4)Plus other departures from Coimbra at 17:13, 18:26(1), 19:12, 20:26(2) and 22:31(1).

Lisbon - Estoril and Cascais - Lisbon 444a

Dep. Lisbon (Cais do Sodre)	Every 15-30 minutes
Arr. Estoril	28 minutes later
Arr. Cascais	4 minutes after departing Estoril

Sights in **Estoril:** Portugal's major beach resort. Try your luck in the gambling Casino.

Sights in **Cascais:** Bloodless bullfights on Summer Sundays. Surf fishing.

Dep. Cascais	Every 15-30 minutes
Dep. Estoril	4 minutes later
Arr. Lisbon (Cais do Sodre)	28 minutes after departing Estoril

Lisbon - Figueira da Foz   449

Dep. Lisbon (Rossio)	7:40	Dep. Figueira da Foz	18:32
Arr. Figueira da Foz	11:38	Arr. Lisbon (Rossio)	23:00

Sights in **Figueira da Foz:** The Casa do Paco Museum, with what is said to be the world's greatest collection of Delft tiles. Try your luck in the Casino Oceano.

Lisbon - Porto (Oporto) - Lisbon   445

Dep. Lisbon (S. Apol.)	7:25(1)	8:25(1)	8:55(2)	11:00(1)
Arr. Porto (Campanha)	10:25	11:45	13:00	14:00

Sights in **Porto:** The more than 80 wine stores occupying all of the Vila Nova de Gaia quarter. The 12th century Cathedral. Soares dos Reis Museum. The 3 great bridges: Dom Louis, Dona Maria and Ponte da Arrabida. Portugal's oldest chapel, Sao Martinho de Cedofeita. The gilded woodcarvings in the Church of San Francisco. The Church of the Clerigos, with its 10-story tower. The city's many beautiful gardens.

Dep. Porto (Campanha)	14:35(1)	15:30(2)	16:10	17:00(1+4)
Arr. Lisbon (S. Apol.)	18:10	19:45	22:15	20:35

(1)First-class only. Reservation required. Supplement charged. Light refreshments or meal service. (2)Light refreshments. (3)Meal service. (4)Plus other departures from Porto at 18:45(3), 20:15(1) and 21:15(1).

Lisbon - Setubal - Lisbon   450

The start and the end of this trip are a 30-minute ferry boat ride.

Dep. Lisbon (T. de Paco Pier)	6:30	8:10	11:45
Arr. Barreiro (Pier)	7:oo	8:40	12:15

Change to train.

Dep. Barreiro (Stn.)	7:05	8:50	12:25
Arr. Setubal	7:58	9:15	13:12

Sights in **Setubal:** The paintings in the Town Museum. Next to it, the lovely Church of Jesus. The view from Saint Philip's Castle, while having lunch there. Many sardine canneries, some of them open to the public. The Maritime Museum. Take an inexpensive taxi ride to the nearby (5½ miles) Palmela Castle.

Dep. Setubal	12:05(1)	14:42	21:25
Arr. Barreiro (Stn.)	12:33	15:30	21:55

Change to boat.

Dep. Barreiro (Pier)	12:50	15:35	22:10
Arr. Lisbon (T. de Paco Pier)	13:20	16:05	22:40

(1)Light refreshments.

Lisbon - Sintra - Queluz   444a

Dep. Lisbon (Rossio)	Frequent times
Arr. Sintra	41 minutes later

Sights in **Sintra:** Take the "Sintra-Vila" bus from the railstation to the city's tourist office, where guide books and maps are available. Use inexpensive taxis to see the view from the 19th century Palacio de Pena, the Moorish Castle, the Palacio Real and the marvelous gardens at the Palacio de Monserrate.

Dep. Sintra	Frequent times
Arr. Queluz	20 minutes later

Sights in **Queluz:** The beautiful gardens, the monument to Maria I and the exquisite restaurant at the 18th century Palacio de Queluz.

Dep. Queluz	Frequent times
Arr. Lisbon (Rossio)	21 minutes later

Madrid - Aranjuez - Madrid

	416	433	416	433
Dep. Madrid (Atocha)	7:32	-0-	10:30(1)	10:55
Dep. Madrid (Cham.)	-0-	9:12(1)	-0-	-0-
Arr. Aranjuez	8:18	9:49	11:09	12:10

Sights in **Aranjuez:** The Museum of Royal Robes and the luxurious interiors of the Porcelain Room and Throne Room in the Palacio Real. The magnificent furnishings at the Casa del Labrador. The Pastere and Island gardens. The collection of royal ships in the Casa de Marinos.

	433	438	416	433
Dep. Aranjuez	13:33(1)	15:49(1)	16:40	17:54(3)
Arr. Madrid (Cham.)	-0-	16:44	-0-	19:09
Arr. Madrid (Atocha)	14:16	-0-	17:30	-0-

(1)Light refreshments. (2)Reservation required. Supplement charged. (3)Plus other departures from Aranjuez at (#416)19:36(1+2),   (#433)19:40(1) and (#438)20:56(2).

Madrid - Avila - Madrid

	422	420	420	422
Dep. Madrid (Norte)	-0-	8:40	9:20(1+2)	-0-
Dep. Madrid (Atocha-Ap.)	8:35	-0-	-0-	-0-
Dep. Madrid (Cham.)	8:49	-0-	-0-	9:50(1)
Arr. Avila	10:31	10:15	11:05	11:25

Sights in **Avila:** There are bus and inexpensive taxi services from Avila's railstation to the city center, about one mile from the station. Take a stroll on the 1½-mile long 11th century walls that circle Avila to see best the 88 semi-circular towers and more than 2,300 battlements (11:00-13:00 and 16:15-18:00, closed weekday afternoons from October through April).

Also see the El Greco painting and the enormous (nearly 200 pounds) silver monstrance in the fortress Cathedral. The baroque 17th century Convent of St. Teresa. The Basilica of St. Vincent.

	422	422	420	420
Dep. Avila	13:37(1)	15:39	17:58	18:45(1+3)
Arr. Madrid (Cham.)	15:21	17:24	-0-	-0-
Arr. Madrid (Atocha-Ap.)	-0-	17:38	-0-	-0-
Arr. Madrid (Norte)	-0-	-0-	19:39	20:12

(1)Reservation required. Supplement charged. Meal service or light refreshments. (2)Plus another departure from Madrid (Norte) at (#420)12:45(1). (3)Plus other departures from Avila at (#420)19:02(1), (#422)19:44, (#418)20:04(1) and (#422)21:24.

Madrid - Burgos - Madrid   427

	8:45	12:10(1)	12:35(2)
Dep. Madrid (Cham.)	8:45	12:10(1)	12:35(2)
Arr. Burgos	13:24	16:01	16:26

Sights in **Burgos:** The many interesting chapels in the magnificent 13th century Cathedral of Santa Maria, where the remains are of Spain's greatest hero, El Cid, and those of his wife. The Archaeological Museum. Stroll 15 minutes on Paseo del Espolon, from the 14th century Arch of Santa Maria to the statue of El Cid.

To see the Royal Monastery of Las Huelgas, only a few minutes outside Burgos, take a bus from Plaza de Jose Antonio.

	17:05	18:32(3)	-0-
Dep. Burgos	17:05	18:32(3)	-0-
Arr. Madrid	22:01	21:47	-0-

(1)Operates late June to late September. (2)Meal service. (3)Reservation required. Supplement charged. Meal service.

Madrid - Cuenca - Madrid 433

Dep. Madrid			Dep. Cuenca	14:57(2)	17:53(1)
(Cham.)	9:12(1)	10:55(2)	Arr. Madrid		
Arr. Cuenca	11:41	14:46	(Cham.)	19:02	20:23

(1)Depart/Arrive Madrid's Atocha railstation. Reservation required. Supplement charged. Light refreshments. (2)Second-class only.

Sights in **Cuenca:** The old houses hanging from sheer cliffs in this 15th century setting. The best modern art museum in Spain, Museo de Arte Abstrato. Marvelous strolling down the winding lanes and narrow footpaths. Wonderful El Greco paintings and 15th and 16th century altarpieces in the cathedral. A few steps away from the Cathedral, the collection of coins, statues and Roman mosaics at the Archaeological Museum in a restored 14th century granary. Paleolithic red paintings of bison, wild boars, horses and archers at La Pena del Escrito National Monument. The Tourist Information Office at Calderon de la Barca 28 is only a 5-minute walk from the railstation.

Madrid - Escorial - Madrid 422

Dep. Madrid (Atoche-Apeadero)	8:35	13:35	-0-
Dep. Madrid (Chamartin)	8:49	13:49	-0-
Arr. Escorial	9:38	14:38	-0-
	*	*	*
Dep. Escorial	16:37	20:42	22:22
Arr. Madrid (Chamartin)	17:24	21:29	23:09
Arr. Madrid (Atocha-Apeadero)	17:38	21:23	23:23

Sights in **Escorial:** Burial place of Spanish kings and queens. The Royal Monastery of San Lorenzo del Escorial. This enormous granite fortress (300 rooms) has more than 1,600 paintings (many of the finest Velasquez and El Greco) and murals, and it houses the Charter Hall Royal Library, containing 60,000 volumes. See the Phillip II Apartments, the Basilica, the Throne Room, Apartments of the Bourbon kings, Whispering Hall and Casita del Principe. Don't miss seeing the famous cross by Benvenuto Cellini and paintings by El Greco, Ribera and Velasquez in the church.

Do not fail to see the circular, domed Royal Pantheon, crypt for most of the Spanish kings since the 17th century. Thirty feet underground, it contains 26 marble coffins, in 5 tiers, and is illuminated by Italian baroque candelabra.

In planning a visit here, keep in mind that this enormous 16th century building covers 8 acres. It is open 10:00-13:00 and 15:30-18:30 (18:00 in Winter).

Also visit the nearby monumental Valley of the Fallen, memorializing those who died in Spain's civil war. A 492-foot-high cross of concrete faced with stone marks this crypt. You can ride to the top of it in an elevator.

Madrid - Salamanca - Madrid   420

Dep. Madrid (Norte)	8:40	9:20(1)
Arr. Salamanca	12:28	12:50

Sights in **Salamanca:** The Convent of San Sebastian. The House of Shells. The 15th and 16th century houses around the beautiful Plaza Mayor. The oldest university in Spain. The church and cloister at St. Stephens Monastery.

Dep. Salamanca	15:54	17:15(1)
Arr. Madrid (Norte)	19:39	20:38

(1)Reservation required. Supplement charged. Meal service.

Madrid - Segovia - Madrid   419

Frequent departures can be made from Madrid's Chamartin, Atocha, Recoletos and Nuevos Ministerios railstations. A ticket is about $1.00 (U.S.). En route, you can see El Escorial, the enormous granite fortress, and also the gigantic cross that marks Franco's Spanish Civil War monument, the Valley of the Fallen.

Dep. Madrid (Atocha-Apea.)	7:05	8:35	10:05	11:05	12:39
Dep. Madrid (Chamartin)	7:19	8:48	10:19	11:19	12:53
Arr. Segovia	9:15	10:43	12:19	13:14	14:47

*   *   *

Dep. Segovia	13:15	14:48	16:40	17:40	18:40	19:40(1)
Arr. Madrid (Chamartin)	14:59	16:32	18:29	19:26	20:27	21:36

Arr. Madrid (Atocha-Apea.) 12 minutes after arriving Chamartin
(1)Plus another departure from Segovia at 21:24

Sights in **Segovia:** The bus which meets the train goes uphill from the railstation to the main square, Plaza de Franco. Seen on the way is the half-mile long ancient Roman aqueduct, 7 stories high in some places.

A 40-minute stroll from the Plaza includes seeing San Martin Church along Calle de la Juderia Vieja (Old Ghetto), leading to the rear of the immense 16th century Cathedral and, from there, to Alcazar, Isabella's fairy-tale castle, next to the Eresma River.

Across the Eresma is Vera Cruz. where you will find the 13th Century Church of the Knights Templar and the 15th Century Parral Monastery.

Madrid - Toledo - Madrid   438a

Seat reservations are not required or obtainable for this ride. Board well before departure time to avoid standing for 90 minutes. The walk from Toledo's railstation to the center of the city is long. It is best to take a bus or taxi.

Dep. Madrid (Atocha)	8:11	9:15	10:00	12:16	14:10
Arr. Toledo		9:41	10:44	11:19	13:35	15:31

Sights in **Toledo:** The most spectacular Cathedral in Spain (750 stained-glass windows, priceless church clothing, jeweled ornaments, hundreds of tapestries, and paintings by Goya, El Greco, Velasquez, Tintoretto, Murillo and Titian). The house of El Greco, with a superb collection of his paintings. The 15th century Palace of the Duchess of Lerma. The Church of Santo Tome, containing El Greco's "Burial of the Count of Orgaz". The Sefardi Museum in the 14th century El Transito Synagogue. The Provincial Museum of Archaeology and Fine Arts in the 16th century Hospital de Santa Cruz. The Army Museum in the Alcazar (fortress).

The Museum of Santa Cruz. Cristo de la Luz, the church first built in the 11th century as a Mosque (on the site of the ruins of a Visigothic church). It was then converted into a Catholic church in the 12th century. The works of Spain's leading modern sculptor, in the Vitorio Macho Museum.

Dep. Toledo	11:55	13:36	14:25	16:25	18:25(1)
Arr. Madrid (Atocha)	13:20	15:00	15:50	17:50	19:55

(1)Plus other departures from Toledo at 20:05, 20:41 and 22:00.

Madrid - Valladolid - Madrid   422

	422	422	422	418
Dep. Madrid (Atocha-Apea.)	-0-	8:35(3)	-0-	-0-
Dep. Madrid (Cham.)	8:10(1+2)	8:49	9:28(2)	9:50(2)
Arr. Valladolid	11:04	11:50	12:43	12:45

Sights in **Valladolid:** The National Museum of (Wood) Sculpture in San Gregorio College, founded in the 15th century by the confessor to Isabella. The adjacent Church of San Pablo. The Cathedral. Cervantes' House, where he spent the last years of his life. Simancas Castle, 7 miles from Valladolid. Charles V converted the castle into a storehouse for state records. It holds 8,000,000 documents that provide a history of Spanish administration from the 16th through the 20th century.

	422	422	418	422
Dep. Valladolid	14:20	18:25(3)	18:48(1+4)	20:07(3)
Arr. Madrid (Cham.)	17:24	21:29	21:37	23:09
Arr. Madrid (Atocha-Apea.)	17:38	21:43	-0-	23:23

(1)Reservation required. (2)Supplement charged. Light refreshments. (3)Second-class only. (4)Supplement charged. Meal service.

Madrid - Zaragoza - Madrid   412

Dep. Madrid			Dep. Zaragoza	15:30(2)	18:32(2)
(Cham.)	8:30(1)	11:25(2)	Arr. Madrid		
Arr. Zaragoza	13:12	15:10	(Cham.)	19:27	22:07

(1)Light refreshments. (2)Reservation required. Supplement charged. Meal service.

Sights in **Zaragoza:** The Tapestry Museum in the Cathedral. The Exchange. Aljaferia, an 11th century Moorish palace. The Basilica de Pilar. The Goya and El Greco paintings at the Museo de Pintura.

San Sebastian - Bayonne - San Sebastian
422

Dep. San Sebastian (Am.)	7:28	9:08
Arr. Hendaye	8:00	9:42

Change trains.
136

Dep. Hendaye	8:49(1+2)	11:20(1+2+3)
Arr. Bayonne	9:29	11:59

Sights in **Bayonne:** The Cote Basque's leading port and private yacht harbor. The Cathedral. The Basque Museum. The Museum Bonnat. Chateau-Vieux.
136

Dep. Bayonne	10:59(3)	13:05(2+4)	15:14(1)	15:58(2+5)
Arr. Irun	11:53	13:48	16:08	16:54

Change trains.
422

Dep. Irun	12:43	14:50(1)	16:30	17:50
Arr. San Sebastian (Am.)	13:01	15:05	16:59	18:09

(1)Reservation required. Supplement charged. (2)Light refreshments. (3)Operates late May to late September. (4)Reservation required. Runs daily, except Sundays and holidays. (5)Plus other departures from Bayonne at 18:00, 20:35 and 21:04(3).

San Sebastian - Bilbao - San Sebastian   417

This narrow-gauge rail trip is *not* covered by Eurailpass or Eurail Youthpass.

Dep. San Sebastian (Amara)   7:00   11:35
Arr. Bilbao (Achuri)   10:16   14:54

Sights in **Bilbao:** The Fine Arts Museum. The Biscay Historical Museum. The Begona Sanctuary.

Dep. Bilbao (Achuri)   15:10   18:00
Arr. San Sebastian (Amara)   18:28   21:18

San Sebastian - Burgos - San Sebastian   422

Dep. San Sebastian (Norte)   8:46(1)   9:13   10:29(2+3)
Arr. Burgos   12:00   13:47   14:49

Sights in **Burgos:** See notes about sightseeing in Burgos on page 163, under "Madrid-Burgos".

Dep. Burgos   16:06(2) 17:04   17:47(1+4)
Arr. San Sebastian (Norte)   20:03   20:55   21:03

(1)Reservation required. Supplement charged. (2)Operates late June to late September. (3)Meal service. (4)Plus other departures from Burgos at 18:22(1+3) and 21:44(1+3).

San Sebastian - Pamplona - San Sebastian   423

Dep. San Sebastian
  (Norte)   9:46(1+2)
Arr. Pamplona   12:06

Dep. Pamplona   17:17(1)
Arr. San Sebastian
  (Norte)   19:25

(1)Reservation required. Supplement charged. (2)Trip is 137km. Must pay 200km charge for ticket on this train.

Sights in **Pamplona:** The 14th century Gothic Cathedral, with its cloisters and Diocesan Museum. The Navarre Museum. The running of the bulls through the city's streets, every year between July 6 and July 15.

Seville - Cadiz - Seville   416

These trains are second-class only.

Dep. Seville (S.Ber.)   7:42   8:54   10:50   -0-
Arr. Cadiz   9:41 10:37   12:40   -0-

Sights in **Cadiz:** The African environment. The Fine Arts Museum. The Museum of Archaeology and Art. The Cathedral, with its monumental Silver Tabernacle, decorated with almost 1,000,000 jewels. The Historical Museum.

Dep. Cadiz   13:55 15:10   18:30   20:15(2)
Arr. Seville (S.Ber.)   15:46 17:05   20:35   22:35

(1)Reservation required. Meal service (2)Plus another departure from Cadiz at 21:35(1).

Seville - Cordoba - Seville 416

Dep. Seville (P.A.)	6:42(1)	8:05(2)	8:10(1)	10:30(1)	11:57(2+3)
Arr. Cordoba	8:46	9:20	10:12	12:19	13:27

Sights in **Cordoba:** The array of marble, jasper, onyx and granite on the 80 marble columns in the 8th century Mosque, built on top of what was first a Roman temple and later a Catholic church, before the Moors seized Cordoba.

Following the recapture of the city by the Spaniards and in the conversion of the building to a church again, most of the original 1,000 marble columns were removed to provide space for a nave and a high altar.

Called "Mezquita", its interior is illuminated by 4,000 bronze and copper lamps. Its ceiling is carved cedar.

The 6:42 and 8:05 departures are preferable because the Mosque is closed from 12:00 to 16:00, and the Alcazar is closed from 12:00 to 17:00.

Also see the 14th century Synagogue. The Fine Arts Museum. The Museum of Julio Romero de Torres. The Museum of Cordoban art, with its Bullfight Museum. The Provincial Archaeological Museum, one of the most important archaeological collections in Spain. The Roman Bridge, built in the time of Emperor Augustus. The Alcazar.

Dep. Cordoba	13:37(2)	14:05(1)	15:25(1)	16:52(2)	17:55(2+4)
Arr. Seville (P.A.)	15:07	15:59	17:10	18:23(3)	19:15

(1)Second-class only. (2)Reservation required. Supplement charged. Meal serviceor light refreshments. (3)Departs/Arrives Seville's S. Bernardo railstation (4)Plus other departures from Cordoba at 18:30(1), 19:31(2+3) and 20:52(1).

Seville - Granada - Seville 439

Dep. Seville (S.Bernardo)	8:05(1)	Dep. Granada	17:51
Arr. Bobadilla	10:25	Arr. Bobadilla	19:42
Change trains.		Change trains.	
Dep. Bobadilla	10:35	Dep. Bobadilla	19:54(1)
Arr. Granada	12:31	Arr. Seville (S. Bernardo)	22:13

(1)Reservation required. Supplement charged.

Sights in **Granada:** The indescribable Alhambra complex, consisting of the Royal Palace, adjacent Partal Gardens, the 9th century Alcazaba watchtower fortress and, a quarter of a mile away, the Generalife (summer palace of Moorish caliphs).

At the Royal Palace, be sure to see the Court of the Mexuar, the Hall of the Ambassadors, the Court of the Myrtle Trees, the Hall of the Two Sisters, the Court of the Lions, the Royal Baths and the Daraxa courtyard. The Mocarabes Gallery and Abencerrrajes Gallery are near the Court of the Lions.

The Partal Gardens are a series of terraces featuring roses, poinsettias, orange and lime trees, lilies, bouganvillea and carnations. The nearby Generalife is one of Europe's greates gardens.

Also in Granada, see the crypts of Ferdinand and Isabella in the Cathedral's

Royal Chapel. The Fine Arts Museum and Hispano-Moorish Museum in Charles V's Palace. The Royal Hospital. Casa Castril.

Seville - Jerez - Seville   416

Dep. Seville (S.B.)	6:49(1)	7:42(2)	8:54(2)	10:50(2)	14:00(2)
Arr. Jerez	8:10	8:58	9:56	12:00	15:17

Sights in **Jerez:** A 3,000-year old city, famous for its horses, beautiful women and sherry wine. Its renowned Andalusian horses, bred from Spanish mares and stallions which the Moorish invaders brought here more than 1,500 year ago, do not date as far back as the wine does.

Phoenicians started the vineyards here in 1100 B.C. Later Romans began the vinting of sherry. Many of the best wineries offer tours that conclude with tasting.

See the annual September Wine Festival. Its opening ceremony takes place on the steps that lead into the 17th century Collegiate Church of Santa Maria. Next to it is the 11th century Moorish fort, the Alcazar. Also visit the 15th century San Dionisio Church. See the exhibit of Punic, Roman and Arabic pottery, tombstones, household implements and statues in the Archaeological Museum that occupies 2 small rooms inside Chapter House on tiny Plaza de la Asuncion, across from San Dionisio Church. Look for the 7th century BC Corinthian helmet, believed to be the oldest Greek artifact ever found in Spain.

Dep. Jerez	14:35(2)	15:55(2)	19:11(2)	21:03(2)	22:27(3)
Arr. Seville(S.B.)	15:43	17:09	20:30	22:38	23:57

(1)Meal service. (2)Second-class only. (3)Reservation required. Supplement charged.

Seville - Merida   432

These trains require reservation, charge a supplement and have light refreshments.

Dep. Seville (P.A.)	7:30	Dep. Merida	18:15
Arr. Merida	11:02	Arr. Sevile (P.A.)	22:00

Sights in **Merida:** During the 400 years this city was ruled by Romans, the population was 100,000 — nearly 3 times today's population. Come here to see the 2,000-year old antiquities. The longest bridge ever built by Romans (82 arches, more than half a mile long), Puente Romano. The mosaic floors in the restored, large 9th century fort, covering 2 city blocks. The 6,000-seat theater (where plays are still performed) and 14,000-seat amphitheater. Trojan's Arch. The Temple of Diana.

The collection of statues, coins, tombstones, pottery and tools at the Archaeological Museum in the 17th century Santa Clara Church.

Seville - Malaga (via Cordoba) - Seville   416

The 1983 schedules made it impossible to make this roundtrip in one day.

Dep. Seville (P.A.)	10:30(1)	Dep. Malaga	7:00	10:35(2)
Arr. Cordoba	12:22	Arr. Cordoba	9:32	13:34
Change trains.		Change trains.		
Dep. Cordoba	12:45	Dep. Cordoba	10:25	13:47
Arr. Malaga	16:30	Arr. Seville (P.A.)	12:28	15:07

(1)Plus other departures from Seville at 13:10 and 16:07. (2)Plus another departure from Malaga at 14:40.

Sights in **Malaga:** Winter sun. The 9th century Alcazaba Moslem palace and the ruins of Gibralfaro Castle, 2 fortresses which made Malaga a major stronghold in the Middle Ages. The Fine Arts Museum. Sagrario, an unusual rectangular church that was originally a mosque. The Cathedral.

The second route from Seville to Malaga follows:

Sevile - Malaga (via Bobadilla) - Seville   439

Dep. Seville (S. Bernardo)	8:05(1)	-0-
Arr. Bobadilla	10:25	-0-
Change trains.		
Dep. Bobadilla	10:30(2)	-0-
Arr. Malaga	11:29	-0-
	*	*	*
Dep. Malaga	13:50(2)	18:40(1)
Arr. Bobadilla	15:03	19:49
Change trains.		
Dep. Bobadilla	15:13(2)	19:54(1)
Arr. Seville (S. Bernardo)	17:59	22:13

(1)Reservation required. Supplement charged. (2)Second-class only.

Seville - Torremolinos - Seville   439

Dep. Seville (S.B.)	8:05(1)	See "Seville-Malaga" schedule above.
Arr. Malaga	11:29	

(1)Reservation required. Supplement charged.

Change to electric train (Malaga-Fuengirola).
435

Dep. Malaga	Every 30 minutes from 6:00 to 22:30
Arr. Torremolinos	25 minutes later

Sights in **Torremolinos:** Characters from all over the world, on and around this resort's 5-mile beach.

Dep. Torremolinos	Every 30 minutes from 7:29 to 23:59
Arr. Malaga	25 minutes later

Change trains.
439

Dep. Malaga	See preceding "Seville-Malaga" schedules.
Arr. Seville	4-5 hours later

Tarragona - Tortosa - Tarragona   425

Dep. Tarragona	7:26(1)	8:12(2)	10:42(1)	11:44(1+4)
Arr. Tortosa	8:43	9:00	11:47	13:15

Sights in **Tortosa:** St. Louis College, founded in 1554 by Charles V for Moors converting to Christianity. The Cathedral. The Bishop's Palace.

Dep. Tortosa	14:40(2)	16:16(3)	18:26(2)	20:39(1)
Arr. Tarragona	15:32	17:15	19:14	21:40

(1)Second-class only. (2)Reservation required. Supplement charged. Meal service or light refreshments. (3)Operates late May to late September. (4)Plus other departures from Tarragona at 11:48(3) and 13:24(2).

Valencia - Alicante - Valencia   426

Dep. Valencia (Ter.)	7:00(1)	8:22(2)	Dep. Alicante (Ter.)	17:07(2)	19:13(1)
Arr. Alicante (Ter.)	10:09	11:15	Arr. Valencia (Ter.)	20:07	22:30

(1)Light refreshments. (2)Reservation required. Supplement charged. Light refreshments.

Sights in **Alicante:** The avenue lined with date palms, part of the complete African atmosphere. The huge Moorish castle. Take the 26-mile bus trip to Elche to see the only palm forest in Europe.

Valencia - Cuenca - Valencia   433

Dep. Valencia (Ter.)	8:52(1)	Dep. Cuenca	15:06	17:58(1)
Arr. Cuenca	11:42	Arr. Valencia (ter.)	19:16	20:44

(1)Reservation required. Supplement charged. Light refreshments.

Sights in **Cuenca:** See notes about sightseeing in Cuenca earlier in this section, under "Madrid-Cuenca".

Valencia - Murcia - Valencia   426

Dep. Valencia (Ter.)	8:22(1)	Dep. Murcia	15:55
Arr. Murcia	12:30	Arr. Valencia (Ter.)	20:07

(1)Reservation required. Supplement charged. Light refreshments.

Sights in **Murcia:** The Moorish granary. The 14th century Gothic-Romanesque Cathedral. Glass, pottery and leather factories.

Valencia - Tarragona - Valencia   425

Dep. Valencia (Ter.)	5:35(1)	8:35(1)	8:42(1)
Arr. Tarragona	9:46	12:10	13:02

Sights in **Tarragona:** See notes about sightseeing in Tarragona earlier in this chapter, under "Barcelona-Tarragona".

Dep. Tarragona	13:24(2)	13:30(3)	17:32(1)	18:23	20:17(1)
Arr. Valencia (Ter.)	16:37	18:15	21:42	22:10	23:51

(1)Light refreshments. (2)Reservation required. Supplement charged. Meal service or light refreshments. (3)Second-class only.

SCENIC RAIL TRIPS

Here are 11 exceptionally scenic rail trips.

Barcelona - Massanet - Blanes - Barcelona   424

Fine coastline and mountain scenery on this easy one-day circle excursion from Barcelona.

(Via Granollers)

Dep. Barcelona (Ter.)	7:45(1)	8:25	8:44)1+2+3)	10:20(1+4)
Arr. Massanet	8:36	9:43	9:52	11:18
	*	*	*	

(Via Mataro)

Dep. Massanet	9:57	12:53	13:53	14:53(5)
Dep. Blanes	10:12	13:10	14:10	15:10
Arr. Barcelona (Ter.)	11:36	14:20	15:20	16:20

(1)Reservation required. Supplement charged. (2)Departs from Barcelona's Paseo de Gracia railstation. (3)Meal service. (4)Plus another departure from Barcelona at 13:05.   (5)Plus other departures from Massanet at 16:53, 17:53, 19:53 and 21:27.

Barcelona - Madrid   412

Many ancient towns, castles, mountains and gorges to see on this route.

.Dep. Barcelona (Ter.)	-0-	10:43(1)	14:10(1+5)	-0-
Dep. Barcelona (P. de G.)	-0-	10:51(1)	14:18(1+6)	-0-
Dep. Barcelona (Sants)	7:55(1)	11:00(1)	14:25(1)	20:10(2+3+7)
Arr. Madrid (Cham.)	17:57	19:27	22:07	8:00

(1)Reservation required. Supplement charged. Meal service or light refreshments. (2)Light refreshments. (3)Carries sleeping car. Also has couchettes. (4)Supplement charged. (5)Plus another departures from Barcelona (Ter.) at 22:30(3+4). (6)Plus another departure from Barcelona (P. de G.) at 22:21.   (7)Plus another departure from Barcelona (Sants) at 22:30(3+4).

Barcelona - Puigcerda   428+147

There is beautiful Pyrenees mountain scenery on this portion of the BArcelona-Toulouse route. As shown below, this trip also can be made as a one-day excursion from Barcelona.

Dep. Barcelona (Sants)	9:58(1)	14:10(1)
Dep. Barcelona (P. de Cat.)	10:05	14:16
Arr. Puigcerda	13:12	17:20
Arr. La Tour-de-Carol	13:20	17:27

Change trains.

Dep. La Tour-de-Carol	13:46	17:20(2)	17:45(3)	19:05(4)
Arr. Toulouse	16:40	20:40	20:48	22:17

(1)Second-class only. (2)Operates late June to early September. (3)Operates early September to late June. (4)Late June to early September: runs daily. Early September to late June: runs Sunday only.

The easy one-day excursion follows: (428)

Dep. Barcelona (Sants)	5:51	6:53	9:58	11:59
Dep. Barcelona (P. Cat.)	5:58	6:59	10:05	12:06
Arr. Puigcerda	9:59	10:51	13:12	15:57
	*	*	*	
Dep. Puigcerda	12:29	13:57	15:09	16:34	17:28
Arr. Barcelona (P. Cat.)	16:09	17:24	18:54(1)	20:33	20:49
Arr. Barcelona (Cent.)	16:16	17:29	-0-	20:40	20:55

(1)Arrive/Depart Barcelona's Termino railstation.

Barcelona - Tarragona

This trip is noted for excellent scenery along the Mediterranean coastline. City-sightseeing notes for both Barcelona and Tarragona appear earlier in this section. Complete schedules can be found under one-day excursions.

Cordoba - Malaga - Cordoba   416

Scenic gorges can be seen on this trip, an easy one-day excursion from Cordoba. See notes earlier in this section (under "Seville-Cordoba-Seville" excursion) for sightseeing in Cordoba.

Dep. Cordoba	8:05(1)	8:30
Arr. Malaga	11:28	11:50

Sights in **Malaga:** The 9th century Alcazaba Moslem palace and the ruins of Gibralfaro Castle, 2 fortresses which made Malaga a major stronghold in the Middle Ages. The Fine Arts Museum. Sagrario, an unusual rectangular church that was originally a mosque. The Cathedral.

Dep. Malaga	14:40(1+2)			
		18:40	19:00(3)	22:15(1+2)
Arr. Cordoba	17:06	22:15	22:33	1:32

(1)Reservation required. Supplement charged. (2)Meal service. (3)Light refreshments.

Granada - Moreda - Almeria - Granada

Excellent mountain scenery on this trip.

426		441			
Dep. Granada	14:30(1)	Dep. Almeria	6:15(2)	11:40	13:40
Arr. Moreda	15:29	Arr. Moreda	8:45	14:21	15:24
Change trains.		Change trains.			
441		426			
Dep. Moreda	15:39	Dep. Moreda	8:54(2)	16:53(3)	17:37(1)
Arr. Almeria	17:50	Arr. Granada	10:18	18:00	18:40

(1)Reservation required. Supplement charged. Light refreshments. (2)Second-class only. (3)Light refreshments.

Leon - Oviedo - Leon   418

Very good mountain scenery.   Sights in **Leon:** The stained-glass windows in the Cathedral and the 11th century Church of San Isidoro.

Dep. Leon	6:55(1)	14:44(2)		
Arr. Oviedo	10:06	17:19		

*   *   *

Dep. Oviedo	12:38(1)	14:45(2)	15:25(1)	19:11(1)
Arr. Leon	15:41	17:06	19:02	22:25

(1)Second-class only. (2)Reservation required. Supplement charged. Meal service or light refreshments.

The best daytime connections between Madrid and Leon are:

418				
Dep. Madrid			Dep. Leon	17:10(2)
(Chamartin)	8:49(1)	9:50(2)	Arr. Madrid	
Arr. Leon	13:51	14:42	(Chamartin)	21:37

(1)Second-class only. (2)Reservation required. Supplement charged. Meal service or light refreshments.

Leon - Monforte - Vigo   421

The Leon-Monforte portion of this route is recommended for mountain scenery and can be made as an easy one-day roundtrip, as this schedule indicates.

Dep. Leon	7:06(1)	8:30(2)	Dep. Vigo	9:25(3)	14:25(1)
Arr. Monforte	10:43	12:56(2)	Arr. Monforte	12:02	17:26
Dep. Monforte	11:20	14:33	Dep. Monforte	12:07	17:50
Arr. Vigo	14:50	18:23	Arr. Leon	15:30	21:45

(1)Light refreshments. (2)Change trains in Monforte. (3)Reservation required. Supplement charged. Meal service.

Vigo - Santiago de Compostela - Vigo   413

A worthwhile extension of the Leon-Vigo scenic trip is to continue on from Vigo to Santiago de Compostela.

For detailed notes on the marvelous attraction in Santiago de Compostela, please refer to the "Madrid-Santiago" schedule, later in this section, under "The Madrid Routes".

Dep. Vigo	7:00	8:57	12:25	13:55	15:40	18:10(1+2)
Arr. Santiago	2 hours later					

* * *

Dep. Santiago	7:50	10:13	11:04(1)	14:35	16:10	18:57(3)
Arr. Vigo	2 hours later					

(1)Reservation required. Supplement charged. (2)Plus another departure from Vigo at 19:55.   (3)Plus another departure from Santiago at 20:30.

Lisbon - Porto - Vigo

We recommend breaking this trip by staying overnight in Porto.
445

Dep. Lisbon (S. Apol.)	7:25(1)	8:25(1)	8:55(2)	11:00(1+5)
Arr. Porto (Campanha)	10:25	11:45	13:00	14:00

Change trains.
447a

Dep. Porto (Campanha)	7:37	14:08	18:09

Set your watch forward one hour.

Arr. Vigo	12:57	19:22	23:15

Sights in **Porto:** See notes about sightseeing in Porto earlier in this section, under the "Lisbon-Porto" one-day excursion.
447a

Dep. Vigo	7:20	-0-	13:50	20:45

Set your watch back one hour.

Arr. Porto (Campanha)	10:28	-0-	16:51	23:49

Change trains.
445

Dep. Porto (Campanha)	11:00(1)	11:50(2)	17:00(1)	0:20(4+6)
Arr. Lisbon (S. Apol.)	14:00	16:10	20:35	6:50

(1)First-class only. Reservation required. Supplement charged. Meal service or light refreshments. (2)Light refreshments. (3)Meal service. (4)Carries sleeping car. Light refreshments. (5)Plus other departures from Lisbon at 11:35(3), 14:25(1), 15:30(2), 17:00(1), 19:00(2), 20:15(1), 21:15(1) and 0:25(4).   (6)Plus other departures from Porto at 7:15(1), 8:15(1), 9:25(2), 14:35(1), 15:30, 18:45(3), 20:15(1) and 21:15(1).

Madrid - Barcelona   412
Many ancient towns, castles, mountains and gorges to see on this route.

Dep. Madrid (Cham.)	8:30(1+2)	11:25(2+3)	14:45(2+3+5)
Arr. Barcelona (Sants)	18:33	19:40	22:24
Arr. Barcelona (P. de G.)	-0-	19:49	22:33
Arr. Barcelona (Ter.)	-0-	19:59	22:42

(1)Light refreshments (2)Reservation required. Supplement charged. (3)Meal service. (4)Carries sleeping car. Also has couchettes. (5)Plus other departures from Madrid at 20:40(1+4), 22:10(2+3+4) and 22:50(2+4).

Porto - Regua   447
Good river scenery on this easy one-day roundtrip.

Dep. Porto (S. Bento)	7:45	10:45	14:10
Dep. Porto (Campanha)	8:00	10:55	14:24
Arr. Regua	10:09	13:07	16:48
	*	*	*
Dep. Regua	11:15	16:05	21:11
Arr. Porto (Campanha)	13:20	18:21	23:24
Arr. Porto (S. Bento)	13:30	18:38	23:32

Santander - Palencia   419
This trip offers fine mountain views crossing the Cordillera Cantabrica. Santander's seashore is a major Summer resort.

Dep. Santander	8:00	14:55(1)	Dep. Palencia	12:34	16:21(2)
Arr. Palencia	12:09	17:42	Arr. Santander	16:15	20:18

(1)Reservation required. Supplement charged. Light refreshments. (2)Plus another departure from Palencia at 19:03(1).

THE MAJORCA ONE-DAY RAIL TRIP

This narrow-gauge, easy one-day trip goes through olive groves before tunneling through a mountain and emerging high above Soller. At the tunnel exit, the train stops for 10 minutes to allow passengers to enjoy the view before the train spirals downhill to Soller. A quaint tram makes the short ride from Soller to the seaside Puerto de Soller.

This ride is *not* covered by Eurailpass or Eurail Youthpass.

Palma - Soller   437

Dep. Palma	8:00	10:40	13:00	15:15
Arr. Soller	55 minutes later			

*   *   *

Dep. Soller	9:15	11:50	14:10	18:20	21:00(1)
Arr. Palma	55 minutes later			

(1)Runs Sundays only.

THE TRIP TO ANDORRA

La Tour-de-Carol   to   Sant Julia de Loria
428

Dep. Barcelona (P.Cat.)	9:58(1)	14:10(1)		
Arr. La Tour-de-Carol	13:20	17:27		

Change to bus.
192

Dep. La Tour-de-Carol	13:30(2)	17:45(3)		
Arr. Andorra la Vella	15:30	20:00		
Arr. Sant Julia de Loria	15:45	20:20		

*   *   *

Dep. Sant Julia de Loria	7:00(4)	8:00(2)	13:45(3)	-0-
Dep. Andorra la Vella	7:15(4)	8:15(2)	14:00(3)	-0-
Arr. La Tour-de-Carol	10:00	10:55	17:10	-0-

Change to train.
428

Dep. La Tour-de-Carol	-0-	13:49(1)	-0-	9:04
Arr. Barcelona (P.Cat.)	-0-	17:29	-0-	13:09

(1)Operates all year. (2)Operates December 1 to March 1. (3)Operates July 1 to September 30. (4)Operates April 1 to November 30, weather permitting.

THE MADRID ROUTES

Madrid is the hub of the Iberian Peninsula, with spokes going from it to the major cities of Spain and Portugal: Barcelona, Bilbao, Cordoba, Lisbon, San Sebastian, Santiago de Compostela, Seville and Valencia.

Where city sightseeing notes are not indicated in the following schedules, they can be found at the beginning of this section.

Here are the schedules for reaching those cities from Madrid:

Madrid - Barcelona

Covered under the description of scenic trips, earlier in this section.

Madrid - Bilbao   422

Dep. Madrid (Cham.)	8:10(1)	9:28(1+2)	12:35(3+5)
Arr. Miranda de Ebro	13:24	15:07(2)	18:09
Change trains.			
Dep. Miranda de Ebro	13:30	15:12	18:31
Arr. Bilbao (Norte)	15:27	16:49	20:42

Sights in **Bilbao:** This is the largest Basque city. A major port and industrial city.

Dep. Bilbao (Norte)	8:00(1+2)	10:20	15:40(1+2+6)
Arr. Miranda de Ebro	9:38	12:07	17:14
Change trains.			
Dep. Miranda de Ebro	9:55	12:28(3)	17:30
Arr. Madrid (Cham.)	15:21	17:43	21:47

(1)Reservation required. Supplement charged. Meal service or light refreshments. (2)Direct train. No train change in Miranda. (3)Meal service. (4)Reservation required. Supplement charged. Carries air-conditioned sleeping car. Also has couchettes. (5)Plus other departures from Madrid at 15:15(1+2), 22:35(4) and 23:35(2+4).   (6)Plus another departure from Bilbao at 22:50(2+4).

Madrid - Lisbon   448

Dep. Madrid (Atocha)	10:15(1+2)	23:10(1+3)
Set your watch back one hour.		
Arr. Lisbon (S. Apolonia)	19:05	9:35

*   *   *

Dep. Lisbon (S. Apolonia)	7:30(1+2)	21:00(1+3)
Set your watch forward one hour.		
Arr. Madrid (Atocha)	18:38	9:00

(1)Reservation required. Supplement charged. (2)Meal service. (3)Carries air-conditioned sleeping car. Also has couchettes. Light refreshments.

Madrid - San Sebastian   422

Dep. Madrid				
(Cham.)	8:10(1+2)	12:10(3+4)	12:35(3)	15:15(1+3+7)
Arr. San Sebastian	15:42	20:03	20:55	21:34

*   *   *

Dep. San Sebastian	8:47(1)	9:23(3)	10:31(4)	15:07(1+3+8)
Arr. Madrid				
(Cham.)	16:22	17:43	18:57	21:47

(1)Reservation required. Supplement charged. (2)Light refreshments. (3)Meal service. (4)Operates late June to late September. (5)Carries sleeping car. Also has couchettes. (6)Has couchettes. (7)Plus other departures from Madrid at 18:10(1+3), 22:00(5) and 22:35(5).   (8)Plus other departures from San Sebastian at 22:44(5), 23:04(5) and 2:20(1+3+6).

Madrid - Santiago de Compostela   420

There is a good circle trip: Madrid-Santiago-Vigo-Porto-Lisbon-Madrid.

Dep. Madrid			Dep. Santiago	11:39(1)	22:47(2)
(Norte)	12:45(1)	21:30(2)	Arr. Madrid		
Arr. Santiago	21:06	8:07	(Norte)	20:12	9:38

(1)Reservation required. Supplement charged. Meal service. (2)Carries air-conditioned sleeping car. Also has couchettes. Meal service.

Sights in **Santiago de Compostela:** One of the 3 most sacred places in Christendom, ranking equally with Jerusalem and Rome since 812. It is believed that this is the repository of St. James (Santiago), a cousin of Jesus, son of Mary's sister, and the first follower of Jesus to attain martyrdom.

After witnessing the crucifixion, James came to Spain in A.D. 44, converted 9 Iberians to Christianity, was visited at Zaragoza by the Virgin Mary, returned to the Holy Land, and was beheaded there by King Herod Agrippa.

The legend which has generated the pilgrimage to Santiago de Compostela for the past 1100 years is that, after the decapitation in Jerusalem, his body was disinterred and found to have the head intact. The body was brought to Spain's West Coast in A.D. 44.

Eight centuries later, a hermit saw a bright star (stela) over a vacant field (compo). Excavations were conducted, and the remains of James were found. Since that event, pilgrims have come to this shrine by horse and in vehicles, as well as on foot (from as far as Scandinavia) to pray and meditate here.

You would stop here to see the majestic Cathedral built in the 12th century.

See its beautiful Baroque sculptured Obradoire facade. The carved Romanesque 12th century Door of Glory. Touch the grooves left in the central pillar by the fingers of millions of pilgrims over the centuries.

Visit the Archaeological Museum in its basement, the art pieces in its Treasury, the collection of tapestries with designs by Goya and Rubens in the many halls of the Cathedral's Tapestry Museum.

Also see the gigantic 6-foot tall, 118-pound brass censer in the Library of the Cathedral.

In the early pilgrimage years, it was difficult for priests to tolerate the odor of worshippers from afar who had gone unbathed for weeks and months. The censer here is called Botafumeiro (smoke-thrower).

A custom that originated in the early days of pilgraimages here is perpetuated today. On feast days, this censer is brought into the Cathedral, filled with incense, hung by ropes from the dome 104 feet above the floor, and swung in an arc, barely passing over the heads of people standing in the Cathedral.

It is easy to explore Santiago de Compostela on foot. See the marvelous view of the town from Alameda Park. Santa Maria del Sar, one of the more than 40 churches here, is a splendid example of 12th century Romanesque architecture.

Madrid - Seville   416

Dep. Madrid (Atocha)	8:45(1)	10:30(1)	14:35(1+7)
Arr. Seville (P. de Armas)	15:07	-0-	-0-
Arr. Seville (S. Ber.)	-0-	18:23	20:46
	*	*	*
Dep. Seville (S. Ber.)	-0-	11:57(1)	15:19(1+8)
Dep. Seville (P. de Armas)	8:05(1)	-0-	-0-
Arr. Madrid (Atocha)	14:40	20:21	21:27

(1)Reservation required. Supplement charged. Meal service or light refreshments. (2)Supplement charged. (3)Carries air-conditioned sleeping car. Also has couchettes. (4)Meal service. (5)Departs from Seville's Plaza de Armas railstation. (6)Departs from Seville's San Bernardo railstation. (7)Plus other departures from Madrid at 21:40(2+3+4) and 23:00(2+3).   (8)Plus other departures from Seville at 23:00(2+3+5) and 23:57(2+3+4+6).

Madrid - Valencia 438

Dep. Madrid (Chamartin)	7:00(1)	12:00(2)	16:30(1+5)
Dep. Madrid (Atocha)	7:10(1)	12:10(2)	16:40(1+6)
Arr. Valencia (Ter.)	11:47	16:47	21:17

*　　*　　*

Dep. Valencia (Ter.)	6:00(2)	12:00(2)	16:30(1+7)
Arr. Madrid (Atocha)	10:41	16:39	21:09
Arr. Madrid (Chamartin)	10 minutes later		

(1)Light refreshments. (2)Reservation required. Supplement charged that includes meal. (3)Carries air-conditioned sleeping car. Also has couchettes. (4)Arrives only at Madrid's Chamartin railstation. (5)Plus other departures from Madrid Chamartin at 18:30(2) and 23:20(3). (6)Plus another departure from Madrid Atocha at 18:40(2). (7)Plus other departures from Valencia at 18:30(2) and 23:10(3+4).

Barcelona - Valencia 425

Dep. Barcelona (Termino)	-0-	9:10(2+9)	-0-
Dep. Barcelona (P. de G.)	-0-	9:18	10:17(3+10)
Dep. Barcelona (Sants)	7:00(1)	9:24	10:25(11)
Arr. Valencia (Termino)	11:06	14:10	15:23

*　　*　　*

Dep. Valencia (Termino)	1:13(4)	5:04(5)	5:35(5+12)
Arr. Barcelona (Sants)	7:26	10:29	11:26
Arr. Barcelona (P. de G.)	-0-	-0-	-0-
Arr. Barcelona (Termino)	-0-	-0-	-0-

(1)Reservation required. Supplement charged. Meal service or light refreshments. (2)Second-class only. (3)Operates late May to late September. (4)Has couchettes. (5)Light refreshments. (6)Arrives at Barcelona's Sants, Paseo de Gracia and Termino railstations. (7)Arrives at only Barcelona's Sants railstation. (8)Arrives at Barcelona's Sants and Paseo de Gracia railstations. (9)Plus another departure from Barcelona Termino at 11:10(2). (10)Plus other departures from Barcelona Paseo de Gracia at 11:38(2) and 12:00(1). (11)Plus other departures from Barcelona Sants at 11:45(2), 12:09(1), 15:50(5), 17:03(1), 18:45, 20:35(5) and 22:15(4). (12)Plus other departures from Valencia at 7:35(2+6), 8:35(5+7), 8:42(5+7), 12:20(1+8), 13:32(3+8), 16:19(1+7) and 18:15(2+6).

INTERNATIONAL ROUTES FROM PORTUGAL

The route to southern Spain is Lisbon-Seville.

The 2 routes to France and beyond are Lisbon-Madrid (covered in the preceding section under "The Madrid Routes" and Lisbon-Hendaye on the "Sud Express" which goes north of Madrid, via Pampilhosa and Medina del Campo.

Lisbon - Seville   448

Dep. Lisbon (S. Apol.)	7:35	0:10	-0-
Arr. Badajoz	13:40	6:45	-0-

Set your watch forward one hour.
Change trains.

Dep. Badajoz	15:50(1)	7:30(2)	9:15(1)
Arr. Seville (P.A.)	21:19	12:20	16:11

(1)Second-class only. (2)Reservation required. Supplement charged.

Lisbon - Hendaye - Bordeaux - Paris   28

Dep. Lisbon (S. Apol.)	16:20(1)	Arr. San Sebastian	11:29
Dep. Vilar Formoso	23:02	Arr. Irun	11:58
Set your watch forward		Arr. Hendaye	12:17
one hour.		Arr. Bayonne	14:18
Arr. Salamanca	4:03	Arr. Bordeaux	16:00
		Arr. Paris (Austerlitz)	20:54

(1)Reservation required. Supplement charged. Carries sleeping car to Hendaye. Has couchettes from Lisbon to Paris. Meal service Lisbon-Hendaye. The 80-minute stop in Hendaye is for changing the bogies on the couchette cars to conform with the narrower track in France. Departs 2 hours earlier from late September to late May.

INTERNATIONAL ROUTES FROM SPAIN

Reservations for travel from Spain to other countries on night trains are complex, taking often as long as one month to obtain. Normally, day trains are not such a problem. When traveling by train from another country to Spain, if you want to travel later from Spain back into France and/or beyond France, it is advisable to book the trip out of Spain before you enter Spain.

If this is not possible, then we suggest that immediately after you clear Spanish customs (leaving France) that you go as soon as possible to the reservation booth in the Spanish arrival city to reserve space for your train trip back into France.

The Spanish gateway for rail travel to London, Paris, Brussels and Amsterdam is Madrid. (Notes on the route to London, via Paris, appear in Chapter 8).

From Barcelona, there is rail service to southwestern France (via Toulouse) and to southeastern France (Avignon, Marseille and Nice), from where there are connections to Italy, Austria and Switzerland (and on to Germany and Denmark).

Seville - Lisbon   448

Dep. Seville (P.A.)	8:25(1)	Dep. Badajoz	19:25
Arr. Badajoz	15:20	Arr. Entroncamento	21:59
Set your watch back one hour.		Change trains.	
Change trains.		Dep. Entroncamento	22:23
		Arr. Lisbon (S. Apol.)	23:35

(1)Second-class only. Res. required. Supplement charged from Merida to Badajoz.

Madrid - Lisbon

Schedules for this trip appear earlier in this section, under "The Madrid Routes".

Madrid - Paris   422

Unless designated otherwise, the following services require changing trains at the French border (Hendaye).

Dep. Madrid (Cham.)	8:10(1+2)	12:35(3+4)	15:15(1+3+4+8)
Arr. Paris (Aust.)	23:40	7:36	7:36

(1)Reservation required. Supplement charged. (2)Light refreshments. (3)Meal service. (4)Has couchettes. (5)Direct train to Paris. No train change in Hendaye. (6)Inclusive ticket covers sleeping facility (sleeping car or couchette). (7)Carries air-conditioned sleeping car. (8)Plus other departures from Madrid at 18:10(1+3+4+5), 19:40(1+3+5+6), 22:00(4+7) and 22:35(4+7).

Barcelona - Toulouse - Paris   428+147+138

Dep. Barcelona (Sants)	9:58(1)	14:10(1)	-0-
Dep. Barcelona (P. Cat.)	10:05	14:16	-0-
Arr. La Tour-de-Carol	13:20	17:27	-0-
Change trains.			
Dep. La Tour-de-Carol	13:46	17:45(3+4)	19:05(3+5)
Arr. Toulouse (Mat.)	16:40	-0-	-0-
Change trains.			
Dep. Toulouse (Mat.)	17:44(2)	-0-	-0-
Arr. Paris (Aust.)	23:52	6:28	6:48

(1)Second-class only. (2)Supplement charged. Meal service. (3)Direct train to Paris. No train change in Toulouse. (4)Operates early September to late June. Runs daily, except Sunday. Has couchettes. (5)Has couchettes. Early September to late June: runs Sunday only. Late June to early September: runs daily.

Barcelona - Avignon - Geneva 11a

This train requires reservation, charges a supplement, is air-conditioned and has meal service.

Barcelona (Ter.)	9:50	Dep. Avignon	15:29
Arr. Avignon	15:27	Arr. Geneva (Corn.)	19:44

Barcelona - Narbonne - Avignon - Marseille - Nice - Genoa - Rome

	11a	162	424
Dep. Barcelona (Ter.)	9:50(1)	15:00	19:00(5)
Arr. Cerbere	12:30(1)	17:53	21:40
Change trains.			
	11a	162	78
Dep. Cerbere	12:35(1)	18:41(3)	23:40(4+6)
Arr. Narbonne	13:36(1)	20:01(3)	1:20(4)
Change trains.			
	11a	162	78
Dep. Narbonne	13:38(1)	20:18(3)	1:49(4+6)
Arr. Avignon	15:27	-0-	-0-
Change trains.			
	151	162	78
Dep. Avignon	16:08(2)	-0-	-0-
Arr. Marseille (St.Ch.)	17:15	23:17(4)	4:55(4)
Change trains.			
Dep. Marseille (St.Ch.)	17:25(2)	5:28(4)	5:14(4+6)
Arr. Nice	20:07	8:21	8:04
Change trains.			
	151	162	78
Dep. Nice	20:18	8:39	8:19(4+7)
Arr. Genoa (P.P.)	0:03	13:00	12:37(4+7)
Arr. Rome (Ter.)	-0-	-0-	19:55

(1)Direct train to Avignon. No train change in Cerbere or Narbonne. Reservation required. Supplement charged. Meal service. Air-conditioned. (2)Meal service Avignon-Nice. (3)Direct train to Marseille. No train change in Narbonne or Avignon. Meal service. (4)Meal service. (5)Departs from Barcelona's Sants railstation. (6)Has couchettes. (7)Meal service 9:40-19:55.

REPUBLIC OF IRELAND

SUMMER TIME

Ireland changes to Summer Time on the last Sunday of March and converts back to Standard Time on the last Sunday of October.

EURAILPASS BONUSES IN IRELAND

Ferry crossings between Rosslare (Ireland) and Le Havre (France) 21 hours, or Cherbourg (France) 17 hours. Neither port taxes nor cabin accommodations are covered by Eurailpass or Eurail Youthpass.

IRISH TRAIN PASSES

Rambler Pass   Unlimited travel in the Irish Republic. Sold at rail and bus staions throughout Ireland and also at CIE Tours, 590 Fifth Ave., New York, N.Y. 10036. The 1984 prices for only rail *or* bus are: 8 days $51(U.S.), 15 days $76. For *both* rail *and* bus: 8 days $65, 15 days $94. Children under 16 pay half-fare.

Youth Rambler Pass   Available to persons 14-26 years old. Must be purchased from CIE Tours before arriving in Ireland. Covers *both* rail and bus travel. The 1984 prices are approximately 85% of the prices noted above..

Overlander Pass   Covers train and bus travel to Northern Ireland as well as in the Irish Republic. Sold only in Ireland, at the CIE offices in Dublin and Limerick City. The 1984 prices: 15 days $107. Children under 16 pay half-fare.

ONE-DAY EXCURSIONS AND CITY SIGHTSEEING

Here are 5 one-day rail trips that can be made comfortably from Belfast, Cork, Dublin, Galway and Limerick, returning to them in most cases before dinnertime. Notes are provided on what to see at each destination. The number after the name of each route is the Cook's timetable.

Dublin - Belfast   613

Dep. Dublin				
(Con.)	8:00(1+2)	10:30(3)	11:00(1+2)	13:00(1+7)
Arr. Belfast				
(Cent.)	10:20	12:50	13:10	15:20
		*	*	*
Dep. Belfast				
(Cent.)	8:00(1+2)	10:15(3)	11:00(1+2)	15:00(1+2+8)
Arr. Dublin				
(Con.)	9:59(5)	12:40	13:15	17:15

(1)Runs daily, except Sundays and holidays. (2)Meal service. (3)Runs Sundays and holidays only. Light refreshments. (4)Runs daily. (5)Arrives one hour later on Sunday. (6)Light refreshments. (7)Plus other depoartures from Dublin at 15:00(1+2), 18:10(2+4) and 20:00(1+6).   (8)Plus other departures from Belfast at 17:10(1+6) and 18:00(2+4).

Sights in **Dublin:** Capital of the Irish Republic. See the outstanding Bronze Age gold ornaments, the 8th century Ardagh chalice and the 12th century Cross of Cong, in the National Museum, open Tuesday-Saturday 10:00-17:00 and Sunday 14:00-17:00. The collection of paintings (Rubens, Rembrandt, Goya) at the National Gallery, open Monday-Saturday 10:00-18:00 and Sunday 14:00-17:00. The 8th century Book of Kells, a richly illuminated bible regarded as one of the most beautiful books ever made, on view in the Old Library of Trinity College.

The pulpit from which Jonathan Swift preached, at the 12th century St. Patrick's Cathedral, and a performance of the young boys' choir there. The collection of oriental manuscripts at Chester Beatty Library. The Zoo, in the 1,760-acre Phoenix Park. The 13th century Dublin Castle. Leinster House. The restored 12th century Christ Church Cathedral.

The 18th century mansions on St. Stephen's Green. Window-shop on Grafton Street. Stroll on O'Connell Street. See the historic General Post Office, site of the 1916 uprising. The Georgian houses on Parnell Square. The house where George Bernard Shaw was born. Take a tour of the facilities of the Irish Sweepstakes. A tour of Guinness's Brewery.

Sights in **Belfast:** This is the capital of Northern Ireland. A major port. See Queen's University. The collection of antique locomotives and train cars in the Transport Museum.

Dublin - Cork - Dublin   615
The train ride to Ireland's lush southern area.

Dep. Dublin (Heu.)	7:30(1)	8:30(1+2)	8:50(2+3+4+7)
Arr. Cork (Kent)	10:30	12:10	12:10

*   *   *

Dep. Cork (Kent)	7:30(1)	9:00(1)	9:20(3+4+8)
Arr. Dublin (Heu.)	10:32	12:35	12:55

(1)Runs daily, except Sundays and holidays. Meal service. (2)Change trains in Mallow. (3)Runs Sundays and holidays only. (4)Light refreshments. (5)Runs daily. Meal service. (6)Runs daily. (7)Plus other departures from Dublin at 10:05(5), 12:55(1), 14:25(1), 14:40(3), 17:30(1), 18:25(5), 18:45(1), 19:15(3+4) and 21:00 (6).   (8)Plus other departures from Cork at 11:10(1), 14:25(1), 15:05(3+4), 17:35(1), 18:00(3+4), 18:40(3) and 18:45(1).

IRELAND

Cork - Killarney - Tralee   616a
There is much beautiful scenery throughout this fertile area.

Dep. Cork	10:55(1)	12:50(2)	15:40(2+3+4+7)
Arr. Mallow	11:25	-0-(2)	-0-(2)
Change trains.			
Dep. Mallow	11:39(1)	-0-	-0-
Dep. Killarney	12:34	14:30	17:17
Arr. Tralee	13:10	15:15	17:55
	*	*	*
Dep. Tralee	7:45(3+4)	8:00(2+5)	9:50(2+3+8)
Dep. Killarney	8:16	8:34(2)	10:25(2)
Arr. Mallow	9:11	-0-(2)	-0-(2)
Change trains.			
Dep. Mallow	9:18	9:40	11:43
Arr. Cork	30 minutes later		

(1)Runs daily. Meal service Monday-Saturday. Light refreshments on Sundays and holidays. (2)Direct train. No train change in Mallow. (3)Runs daily, except Sundays and holidays. (4)Meal service. (5)Runs Sundays and holidays only. (6)Light refreshments. (7)Plus another departure from Cork at 20:35(2+5).

(8)Plus other departures from Tralee at 14:05(3+4), 14:30(5), 17:20(2+3+6) and 17:50(5).

Sights in **Killarney:** It is 85 miles from Shannon Airport. See the sculpture by Seamus Murphy, called The Shy Woman of Kerry. The marvelous garden and the exhibit of early crafts and housing at Muckross House, a 19th century mansion on the outskirts of Killarney. Shop here for linens, glassware and crocheted women's clothing. Take the 112-mile, all-day "Ring of Kerry" bus sightseeing trip, a popular excursion. You will see many lakes and mountains.

Dublin - Galway   614
Beautiful lakes in this area.

Dep. Dublin				
(Heu.)	8:40(1+2)	9:55(3+4)	12:00(1+3)	14:40(1+3+6)
Arr. Galway	11:00	13:05	14:15	16:50

Sights in **Galway:** The 14th century St. Nicholas' Church. The ruins of a 13th century Franciscan friary. The 13th century town walls.

Dep. Galway	7:50(1+2)	9:25(2+4)	11:30(1+2)	15:10(1+3+7)
Arr. Dublin				
(Heu.)	10:40	12:25	14:30	18:10

(1)Runs Monday-Saturday, except holidays. (2)Meal service. (3)Light refreshments. (4)Runs Sunday only. (5)Departs from Dublin's Connolly railstation. (6)Plus other departures from Dublin at 18:15(2+4), 18:35(1+2) and 20:25(1+5). (7)Plus other departures from Galway at 18:05(1+3) and 18:50(3+4).

Dublin - Limerick 616

There is bus service between Limerick and Shannon Airport.

Dep. Dublin (Heuston)	7:30(1)	8:30(1)	8:50(2+3+7)
Arr. Limerick Junction	9:20	10:37	10:45
Change trains.			
Dep. Limerick Junction	9:25	10:40	11:50
Arr. Limerick	9:55	11:15	11:20

* * *

Dep. Limerick	7:45(1+4)	8:05(1)	9:15(2+5+6+8)
Arr. Limerick Junction	-0-	8:35	-0-
Change trains.			
Dep. Limerick Junction	-0-	8:42	-0-
Arr. Dublin (Heuston)	10:20	10:32	12:15

(1)Runs daily, except Sundays and holidays. Meal service. (2)Runs Sundays and holidays only. (3)Light refreshments. (4)Direct train. No train change in Limerick Junction. (5)Runs daily. Meal service. (6)Meal service. (7)Plus other departures from Dublin at 9:35(2+3+4), 10:05(5), 12:55(1), 14:25(1), 14:40(2), 17:45(1+4), 18:05(2+6) and 19:15(2+3).   ((8)Plus other departures from Limerick at 9:45(1), 10:05(2+6), 11:45(1), 15:10(1), 15:45(1), 17:45(2+3+4), 18:15(1), 19:30(2) and 19:35(1).

THE FERRY-CROSSING TO FRANCE

Rosslare to Le Havre or Cherbourg   1022

Dep. Rosslare	17:00(1)	17:00(3)
Arr. Le Havre	15:00(2)	-0-
Arr. Cherbourg	-0-	11:00(2)

(1)Late June to early September: runs Tuesday, Wednesday, Thursday and Sunday. Most of September: runs daily, except Monday and Friday. Early October to mid-December: runs Wednesday, Friday and Sunday. (2)Arrives one hour earlier from late September to late October. (3)Late June to early September: runs Monday and Saturday. Most of September: runs Monday and Friday.

RAIL CONNECTIONS WITH ENGLAND
See page 440.

ITALY

Italy has 3 types of fast trains: Rapido, Direttissimo (Express) and Diretto. Passengers using individual tickets (not traveling with first-class passes or Eurailpass) must pay a supplemental charge when riding on Rapido trains. Seats should be reserved in advance for all 3 types.

Sleeping-car service is offered by Wagon-Lits Company in first-class compartments, second-class compartments, first-class couchette and second-class couchette. All of these should be reserved in advance.

Food service on Italian trains ranges from FM (full meals served in restaurant car) to TM (tray meals served at one's seat) and S (snacks, sandwiches, fruit, candy and beverages sold by a strolling vendor). Few Italian trains offer full meal service.

The signs you will see at railstations in Italy are:

ARRIVI	ARRIVAL
BINARIO	TRACK
CARROZA RISTTORANTE	RESTAURANT CAR
DEPOSITO	CHECKROOM
DONNE	WOMEN
ORARIO FERROVIARIO	TIMETABLE
PARTENZE	DEPARTURE
SCOMPARTIMENTO PER FUMATORI	SMOKING COMPARTMENT
STAZIONE FERROVIARIO	RAILSTATION
UOMINI	MEN
USCITA	EXIT
VAGONE LETTO	SLEEPING CAR

ITALIAN HOLIDAYS

A list of holidays is helpful because some trains will be noted later in this section as not running on holidays. Also, those trains which operate on holidays are filled, and it is necessary to make reservations for them long in advance.

January 1	New Year's Day		Proclamation of the Republic
January 6	Epiphany		(First Monday in June)
	Easter	August 15	Assumption Day
	Easter Monday		Victory Day (World War I)
April 25	Liberation Day		(First Monday in November)
May 1	Labor Day	December 8	Immaculate Conception
		December 25	Christmas Day
		December 26	St. Stephen's Day

ITALY

SUMMER TIME

Italy changes to Summer Time on the last Sunday of March and converts back to Standard Time on the last Sunday of September. Many Italian trains and international trains originating or terminating in Italy have different schedules during Summer Time than they do the balance of the year.

EURAILPASS BONUSES IN ITALY

The Brindisi-Patras boat trip is covered by Eurailpass and Eurail Youthpass ¢ but only if you go on Adriatica/Hellenic Mediterranean Lines.

WARNING: The employees of other lines intimate that their ships honor the 2 passes and then charge fees after the boat leaves the pier.

With or without a Eurailpass or Eurail Youthpass, a reservation theoretically can be made on day of departure or day before departure ¢ but it is very unlikely that space will be available (particularly during July and August) unless a reservation is made many weeks in advance of departure dates.

Those gambling on making a reservation after arriving in Brindisi can make application January 1-June 9 and October 1-December 31 only at the Adriatica-Hellenic Mediterranean Lines embarkation office, located at Maritime Station, a 15-minute walk from Brindisi's Central railstation, along Corso Umberto and Corso Garibaldi. Taxis are available at the railstation.

From June 10 to September 30, those without advance reservations can apply also to any Brindisi travel agency that displays in its window the green badge "Eurail Information — Eurailpass".

Holders of advance reservations must go at all times directly to the A/HM Lines embarkation office to have their tickets checked, settle port taxes due and obtain the required Embarkation Ticket. That office is open 8:30-13:00 and 15:30-22:30.

Advance reservations before you start your trip, at $1.50(U.S.) each, can be made at any office that issues Eurailpass (see pages 20-21) or at travel agencies in countries where Eurailpass is sold. There is also a $12(U.S.) surcharge, in addition to the reservation fee, for travel from June 10 to September 30.

Another fee is charged for such special accommodations as aircraft type seats, pullman berths and cabins. There is also a port tax of 4,000 Lira that is *not* covered by Eurailpass and must be paid in Lira.

Passengers with advance reservation must obtain the Embarkation Ticket at least 2 hours prior to the ship's departure time. The ships reserve the right to cancel a reservation when that is not done and to give the space to a standby passenger.

The trains from northern Italy to Brindisi, timed to connect with the ferry departures, are frequently late. For that reason, it is advisable to arrive Brindisi the day before a ferry departure to Patras.

For Eurailpass holders, there is about a 20% reduction from the fare for these 7 boat trips: (1) Naples-Palermo, (2) Naples-Malta, (3) Syracuse-Malta, (4) Genoa-Tunis, (5) Genoa-Alicante, (6) Genoa-Malaga, and)7) crossings to Sardinia. Reverse trips are subject to the same reduction. There is a 30% reduction from the fare for the Venice-Piraeus-Haifa boat trip, and vice versa.

Brindisi - Patras - Athens

For sailing dates, see Cook's Table #1440.
Dep. Brindisi Harbor 20:00(1) 22:30(2)
Arr. Patras 13:00 18:00
 Walk to Patras railstation.
898
Dep. Patras 13:47(3) 18:58(4)
Arr. Athens 18:34 22:39
(1)Operates late June to late September. (2)Operates all year. (3)Meal service. (4)Supplement charged. Light refreshments.

ITALIAN RAIL PASSES

Italian Tourist Ticket. (Biglitteo Turistico di Libera Circolazione).
Offers unlimited travel on all Italian trains, including TEE trains, including free seat reservations. Sleeper and couchette services are *not* included. Available at travel agencies worldwide outside Italy. The 1984 prices for first-class are: 8 days $114(U.S.), 15 days $139, 21 days $166, and 30 days $202.   Second-class: 8 days $72, 15 days $87, 21 days $102, and 30 days $127. The 15, 21 and 30-day tickets can be extended to double their initial period. Half-fare for children 4-12 years old.

Kilometric Ticket.   Permits travel up to a maximum of 20 single trips totaling 3,000kms (1,875 miles) within a 2-month period. Can be used by more than one person at a time, to a maximum of 5 persons. When a child travels on this ticket, only half the mileage used is counted. Available before you leave home at both the offices of Italian State Railways and from travel agents worldwide. Also available in Italy at all railstations and from Italian travel agencies. Can be used on TEE and Rapido trains if a supplement is paid when the reservation is made. The 1984 prices are: $140(U.S.) for first-class, $79 for second-class.

Family Ticket.   Allows 30% reduction on train ticket prices when used by at least 4 passengers (father, mother and 2 children, for example). This ticket can be purchased only at railstations in Italy.

ONE-DAY EXCURSIONS AND CITY SIGHTSEEING

Comprehensive maps which make it easy to find the worthwhile sights in an Italian city can be obtained in most cities there in offices marked "Azienda Autonoma di Turismo" or "Ente Provinciale di Turismo", located on a principal street.

Here are 60 one-day rail trips that can be made comfortably from Bologna, Florence, Genoa, Messina, Milan, Naples, Palermo and Rome, returning to those cities in most cases before dinnertime. Notes are provided on what to see and do at each destination. The number after the name of each route is the Cook's timetable.

Bologna

See the dissection theater in the ancient medical school. The fantastic inlaid wood panels in the Chorus at San Domenico Church. (Be sure to turn on the electric lights there in order to get a good look at the marvelous woodwork.) The Church of San Petronio. The Art Gallery. Neptune's Fountain, where Piazza Maggiore and Piazza Nettuno connect.

The 2 leaning towers in Piazza di Port Ravegnana: the 330-foot high Asinelli and the 165-foot tall Garisenda. After climbing the 486 steps of the Asinelli, there is a splendid view from the top of it. Visit the churches on Santo Stefano. The Municipal Archaeological Museum. The Communale, Podesta, Mercanzia, Re Anzio and Bevilacqua palaces. Try the marvelous Bolognese food.

Genoa

The house where Columbus was born. St. Lawrence Cathedral. Do not fail to walk down the 15th century streets near the waterfront, too narrow for a tour bus and unfortunately not seen by many visitors to Genoa. The incredible Monumental Cemetery, with its vast number of dramatic statues of many of the people buried there. The landscaped hillside with colorful plants painting a flowering tapestry of Columbus' fleet: the Nina, the Pinta and the Santa Maria.

Florence (Firenze)

The 14th century Cathedral of Santa Maria del Fiore is where most visitors begin sightseeing in Florence. Ascend its 292-foot high belltower for a great view of the city. Across from the Cathedral, see the magnificent sculptured bronze Ghiberti doors ("Gates of Paradise" was Michelangelo's description) on the octagonal Baptistry of San Giovanni.

There is much more to see, in 2 different directions from the Cathedral-Baptistry complex. Facing the Baptistry, you proceed North on Via Ricasoli to visit Area #1. You go South, toward the Arno River, for the sightseeing in Area #2.

Area #1: See the breathtaking marble floors, walls and crypts at the Medici Chapel. The street behind the Chapel is lined with vendors. On the other side of the street is an enormous food market where game with colorful furs and feathers make an unusual display.

An easy walk from the Chapel is the Academia, housing the stupendous statue of David. Nearby is the Fra Angelico Museum in the Church of San Marco, with its interesting frescoes and monk's cells.

Across the street from the Academia, you can board a city bus for the 20-minute ride uphill to the village of Fiesole, where there are Etruscan ruins, a Roman amphitheater, a 13th century Cathedral, the Convent of St. Francis, and a splendid view of Florence.

Area #2: The Piazza della Signoria and, next to it, the thousands of great art treasures in the 29 exhibit rooms of the Palazzo degli Uffizi. Nearby is the Franciscan Church of Santa Croce, where Michelangelo, Machiavelli, Rossini and Galileo are buried. Also see the sculptures at the Bargello Museum, in a 13th century palace.

Next, cross to the other side of the Arno River, over the Ponte Vecchio (lined with tiny jewelry shops) to visit the outstanding paintings, statues, tapestries and furniture in the 28 exhibit rooms and galleries of the Palazzo Pitti.

Milan

The Duomo Cathedral, holding more than 20,000 people, begun in 1386 and taking 5 centuries to complete. There are more than 3,000 statues on its exterior. Then go through the incredibly beautiful shopping arcade, The Galleries, to La Scala. One of the world's greatest theaters, accommodating 3,600 people, it was first constructed in 1776. Its opera museum is open daily except Sundays 9:00-12:00 and 14:00-18:00.

Exhibited in the museum are old paintings and engravings of the opera house before its destruction by bombs in 1943 and its reconstruction in 1946, portraits of many famous singers, several of Verdi's pianos and such other Verdi memorabilia as his manuscripts and death mask.

Opposite La Scala, behind a statue of da Vinci, is the 16th century Palazzo Marino, now the City Hall. Just past the gate (Porta Nuova) at the end of Via Manzoni are the Museum of Natural History, the Zoo and the Planetarium.

See da Vinci's "Last Supper" at Santa Maria delle Grazie. It can be viewed Tuesday-Saturday 9:00-13:30 and 14:00-18:30, and on Sunday 9:00-15:00. Do not fail to see the enormous and elaborate crypts at the Monumental Cemetery. Visit the Palazzo Dugnani, on Via Manin, to see the Tiepolo ceiling fresco there.

It is a short taxi ride from the Dugnani to the enormous Castello Sforzesco, which has a vast collection of paintings (including Michelangelo's last work, the Rondanini Pieta) and exhibits of harpischords, wrought iron, tapestries and ceramics. The Castle is open daily except Monday 9:30-12:00 and 14:30-17:00.

See the collection of sculpture, Flemish and Persian tapestries, paintings, scientific instruments, glass and armor at Museo Poldi-Pezzoli, at 12 Via Manzoni, open Tuesday-Sunday 9:30-12:30 and 14:30-17:30. Many great paintings (Raphael, Tiepolo, Canaletto) are exhibited in the Accademia di Brera on Via Brera, open Tuesday-Saturday 9:00-14:00, and on Sunday 9:00-13:00.

Both the Modern Art Gallery at 16 Via Palestra and the Archaeological Museum at 15 Corso Magenta are open Wednesday-Saturday 9:30-12:30 and 14:30-17:30, and on Sunday 9:30-13:00. There are marvelous paintings by Raphael, Caravaggi and Botticelli in the Ambrosian Library, open daily except Saturdays, Sundays and holidays 10:00-12:00 and 15:00-17:00, and on Saturdays, Sundays and holidays 15:00-17:00.

Gourmets will want to visit the fantastic food store called Peck's, at No. 9 Via Spadari, opened in 1892 by a Czechoslovak named Franz Peck. It is the Italian equivalent of Fauchon's, described under "Paris" in the section of this chapter on France.

What you will see at Peck's are: large wedges of parmigiano and reggiano cheese, Italian wines, roasts, loins, saddles and breasts of white veal, caviar, numerous cold seafood salads, mussels, langouste, squid, lobster, celery remoulade, pates, head cheese, scampi, sturgeon, hot vegetable dishes (baked fennel, baby zucchini, asparagus milanese), roasted quail skewered with sausages and wrapped in bacon, tripe in tomato sauce, a wide range of pasta (green ravioli al forno, tortellini, ravioli alla contadina), paella with saffron rice, white mushrooms in oil, many sausages and many fish (herring, smoked salmon, smoked eels, smoked trout).

If that is not enough, across the street from Peck's is a famous pork store, La Bottega del Maiale, with an enormous display of whole baby pigs, pork parts (loins, ears, fillets, tongue, liver) and such sausages as sopresa Calabra, salame Toscana, coppa, cacciatorini, stagionata, capocolla and finocchiona.

Next door to the pork store is Peschere Spadari, a great fish store, selling nearly everything that swims: scampi, Channel sole, mackerel, scampi, squid, mussels. A short distance down the street, at No. 1 Via Speroni, is a large cheese store.

Naples

The view from Certosa de San Martino monastery and, inside, its National Museum. The 13th century Castel Nuovo. The National Library. The Archaeological Museum, with its great Grecian and Roman sculptures. The Capodimonte Gallery. The Teatro San Carlo, home of Neapolitan opera. Scores of palaces.

Rome

St. Peter's, the most wonderful work by man in all the world. The Vatican. Capitoline Hill. The Roman Forum. Palatine Hill. The Imperial Fora. Marcellus Theatre. The Jewish Synagogue. The Temple of Avesta. Aventine Hill. St. Paul's Gate. The view of Rome from the Borghese Gardens. The Protestant cemetery, with the graves of Keats and Shelley. The Colosseum. The Arch of Constantine. The Basilica of St. Paul Outside the Walls. Michelangelo's statue of Moses in the Church of St. Peter in Chains. The Pantheon. The mosaics at the Baths of Caracella.

In the following timetables, where a city has more than one railstation we have designated the particular station after the name of the city (in parentheses).

Bologna - Florence - Bologna   374+398

Exceptional mountain scenery on this easy one-day roundtrip.

The train goes through the 11.5-mile long Apennine Tunnel, Italy's longest tunnel.

Dep. Bologna	Frequent times from 1:26 to 23:23
Arr. Florence	70 minutes later

Sights in **Florence:** See notes about sightseeing in Florence at the start of this section.

Dep. Florence	Frequent times from 0:25 to 23:01
Arr. Bologna	70 minutes later

Bologna - Milan - Bologna   374

Dep. Bologna	Frequent times from 3:06 to 21:44
Arr. Milan (Centrale)	2 hours later

Sights in **Milan:** See notes about sightseeing in Milan at the start of this section.

Dep. Milan (Centrale)	Frequent times from 0:30 to 23:15
Arr. Bologna	2 hours later

Bologna - Parma - Bologna   374

Dep. Bologna   7:26   8:18   11:05   13:23
Arr. Parma   65 minutes later

Sights in **Parma:** Corregio's fresco of the Assumption at the Cathedral. The 5-story red marble Baptistry, one of Italy's finest buildings. Italy's most modern museum, in the Palazzo della Pilotta. Also in the Palazzo, more than 40,000 rare manuscripts in the Pallatine Library and the collection of Etruscan, Roman, medieval and Renaissance works of art in the National]Museum of Former Ages.

Dep. Parma   13:22   14:06   14:39   16:05(1)
Arr. Bologna   65 minutes later
(1)Plus other departures from Parma at 16:56, 18:53, 19:44, 20:20, 21:09, 21:25 and 22:38.

Bologna - Pisa - Bologna

374

| Dep. Bologna | Frequent times from 5:36 to 10:30 |
| Arr. Florence (S.M.N.) | 80 minutes later |

Change trains.

364

| Dep. Florence (S.M.N.) | Frequent times from 7:00 to 14:00 |
| Arr. Pisa (1) | 80 minutes later |

*   *   *

| Dep. Pisa | Frequent times to 22:26 |
| Arr. Florence (S.M.N.) | 70-80 minutes later |

Change trains.

374

| Dep. Florence (S.M.N.) | Frequent times to 0:25 |
| Arr. Bologna | 3-3½ hours after departing Pisa |

(1)The #1 Bus at the railstation takes you to the Piazza del Duomo in 10 minutes.

Sights in **Pisa:** The Piazza del Duomo, with 4 major attractions. Walk up the spiral stairs of the Leaning Tower to its roof and see the view from there. A few feet from the base of the Tower is the majestic 11th century striped marble Cathedral. Key features of it are the magnificent bronze entrance doors and, inside, paintings, statues, mosaics, a fantastic pulpit, and Galileo's lamp.

While watching the lamp swing, Galileo timed each arc by his pulse and observed that every swing, long or short, took the same time span. By that, he postulated "the isochronism of the pendular movement".

Next, walk the short distance from the Cathedral to the beautiful, enormous 11th century circular marble Baptistry to see its font and its 6 columns of porphyry, marble and oriental granite. Three of the columns rest on carved lions. Biblical scenes are carved on each panel.

A very short walk from the Baptistry is a large building with a cemetery in its central court. Each section of the building exhibits many frescoes. See the 50-foot by 19-foot "Triumph of Death" in the North Gallery.

Before the train from Florence reaches Pisa, it stops 2 minutes in Campiglia Marittima, which has a large statue of a mongrel dog at its railstation, the dog appearing to watch the procession of coming and going trains.

Lampo ("flash of lightning") liked train travel as much as we do. He learned the train schedules and took a trip every day ¢ more than 3,000 train trips in his lifetime.

Owned by the assistant stationmaster, Lampo escorted his master's daughter to school every morning. For that reason, he made short rail trips on schooldays, longer journeys on weekends. Always, he would go only such distances and make the necessary connections so as to return home every day before dawn.

Prior to Lampo's death in 1961 (under a freight train), he had become known not only by every trainman in Italy but by the Italian public as well, through reports of his love of train travel that appeared on Italian television and in Italy's newspapers.

Local railway workers say only a person with a printed timetable could have equaled the dog's feat, when he once went past his stop on a certain trip and then managed to return hom by taking a complex series of connecting trains to get bck to Campiglia Marittima.

Bologna - Ravenna - Bologna   379

Dep. Bologna	6:13	8:25	9:07(1)	11:01(2)	12:42(1)
Arr. Ravenna	7:47	9:40	11:24	12:13	14:08

Sights in **Ravenna:** The marvelous 5th century monuments, the Mausoleum of Galla Placidia and the Orthodox Baptistry. Just behind the Mausoleum, see the mosaics at the Church of San Vitale. Great mosaics also in Sant'Appollinare Nuovo Church, where it is helpful to use binoculars or even an opera glass in order to see those mosaics that are at the top of the walls. See the ivory pulpit in the Archbishop's Palace. Dante's Tomb. The Museum of Antiquities. The exhibits at the Academy of Fine Arts.

Dep. Ravenna	13:00	14:30	16:20(1)	18:15(2)	18:44(1+3)
Arr. Bologna	14:45	15:45	18:21	19:38	20:35

(1)Change trains in Castel Bolognese. (2)Operates mid-July to late August. (3)Plus another departure from Ravenna at 20:47(1).

Bologna - Siena - Bologna

374

Dep. Bologna	6:18	10:16	10:30
Arr. Florence	7:52	11:30	11:50
Change trains.			

363

Dep. Florence	8:05	11:40	12:15(1)
Arr. Siena	9:39	13:21	14:31

(1)Change trains in Empoli.

Sights in **Siena:** The pervasive color, named for Siena, that dominates this hill town. The view of Italy's most unique square, Piazza del Campo, from the top of the Mangia Tower of the Palazzo Publico (with its marvelous 14th century murals) or from a window of the Palazzo Piccolomini (open 9:00-13:00, except Sundays), where records in unbelievable calligraphy going back to the 12th century are exhibited with 15th century costumes and fine frescoes.

Also see the Pisano sculpture and mosaic floors at the Cathedral, on Piazza del Duomo. The paneled Duccio Crucifixion in the Mureum of the Cathedral. Climb from there to the top of Facciatone, the skeleton for a new cathedral whose construction ceased when the Black Death of 1348 ravished Siena.

Pinacoteca, the art museum, on a street that is down from the Cathedral. Fontebranda, the old fountain with 3 arches. The ancient houses along Via degli Archi, Vicolo della Fortuna, and Vicolo delle Scotto, all of these streets radiating out from the Piazza del Campo.

363

Dep. Siena	13:28	15:40	18:13	19:32
Arr. Florence	15:20	17:28	19:44	21:08

Change trains.

374

Dep. Florence	16:28	18:18(1)	20:08	22:19
Arr. Bologna	17:57	19:40	21:25	0:02

(1)Light refreshments.

Bologna - Venice - Bologna   389

Dep. Bologna	5:58	8:08	11:11
Arr. Venice (S.L.)	8:15	10:30	13:50

Sights in **Venice:** After the obligatory gondola ride, stand at either end of Piazza San Marco and try to cope with the enormity and beauty of the most impressive square in the world. Next visit St. Mark's Cathedral, the most wonderful Byzantine structure in Europe. Next door, see the Doge's Palace. Then relax at one of the outdoor cafes on St. Mark's Square and take in the wonder of it all while waiting for the figures on the enormous 15th century clock to emerge and strike the bell.

For another view of St. Mark's Square and the entire Lagoon, go to the top of the Bell Tower. Walk through the colorful, narrow streets of shops to Rialto Bridge and, standing there, watch the canal traffic. Then cross over the Bridge and walk a short distance to the extraordinary fish market, which should be seen before Noon.

It is a short and inexpensive boat ride to the island of Murano to watch glass-blowing and visit the Glassworks Museum in Palazzo Giustiniani. Among the score of churches to see in Venice are: San Giuliano, Santa Maria Formosa, Santa Maria dei Miracoli, San Giovanni e Paolo, San Francesco della Vigna, San Zaccaria, Santo Stefano, Santa Maria Gloriosa dei Frari, Santa Maria del Carmine, San Sebastiano, Madonna dell'Orto and Santi Apostoli.

There are also 5 synagogues here.

A 15-minute boat ride takes you to the Lido, Venice's beach resort and site of its gambling casino. A 3-minute boat ride takes you to the beautiful, white Church of Santa Maria della Salute, built on more than one million wood pilings.

Dep. Venice (S.L.)	14:04	15:36	16:25(1)	17:05	18:30(2)
Arr. Bologna	16:10	17:47	18:51	19:18	20:39

(1)Meal service. (2)Plus other departures from Venice at 19:55, 20:50 and 22:42.

Bologna - Verona - Bologna 381

Dep. Bologna   8:21   11:14   12:20   12:55
Arr. Verona   9:58   13:14   13:46   14:33

Sights in **Verona:** The large and excellently preserved first century Arena. Then take Via Mazzini (Verona's main shopping street) to Piazza della Herbe (Herb Square), where you will find a marvelous display of fruits, vegetables, live pet birds, and dead game birds. Only a few minutes walk from there, the Veronese marble lobby of the Hotel Due Torri is worth seeing.

At Piazza dei Signori are the tombs of the Della Scala Family, once rulers of Verona. La Scala Opera House in Milan is named after them. See the paintings in the Church of Sant'Anastasia. Visit the Cathedral and the Museum of Art in Castelvecchio, on Corso Cavour.

The main attraction in Verona, since Shakespeare, has always been Juliet's balcony, at Via Cappelo 17-25.

Dep. Verona   13:19   14:15   14:41   15:23   15:55(1)
Arr. Bologna   1½-2 hours later
(1)Plus other departures from Verona at 16:43, 18:45, 19:21 and 21:32.

Florence - Arezzo - Florence 374

Dep. Florence   8:02   9:48(1)   10:13(1)   11:40(1)   11:57(1)
Arr. Arezzo   70-75 minutes later

Sights in **Arezzo:** The 15th century frescoes in the Church of San Francesco. The carvings on the facade of the 11th century Church of Santa Maria della Pieve. Behind Pieve, the marvelous Piazza Grande, with its palaces. There are many other fine palaces on Corso Italia.

The musical scale was invented in the 10th century by Guido of Arezzo. The Piazza Guido Monaco is named for him.

See the 16th century stained-glass in the Cathedral. The collection of Etruscan and Roman artwork in the Archaeological Museum at the Convent. The enormous fortress, Medicea, built in the 16th century by the Medicis. A library and museum is maintained in the home where Petrarch was born.

Dep. Arezzo   12:15(2)   13:35(2)   14:03(1)   15:05(1)   16:57(1-
                                                       +3)

Arr. Florence   70-75 minutes later
(1)Light refreshments. (2)Meal service. (3)Plus other departures from Arezzo at 17:57(2), 18:49(1), 20:53, 21:42 and 23:01.

Florence - Assisi - Florence
374

Dep. Florence			
(S.M.N.)	7:00	9:48(1)	11:40(2)
Arr. Terontola	8:28	11:20	13:07

Change trains.
378

Dep. Terontola	8:41	11:25	13:21
Arr. Assisi	9:59	12:38	14:34

Sights in **Assisi:** St. Francis' tomb in the 13th century Basilica on the Hill of Paradise, and the many outstanding paintings there, considered to be the greatest museum of Italian Renaissance mural painting. St. Claire's Church. The medieval Castle. Piazza del Commune. The upper and lower churches at the Convent of St. Francis, with their many frescos. Prison Hermitage. The 16th century Church of Santa Maria degli Angeli. The 12th century Cathedral of St. Ruffino. The 14th century La Rocca Maggiore fortress.

Dep. Assisi	13:00	14:01	16:30(3)	18:21	19:34(4)
Arr. Terontola	14:09	15:22	-0-(2)	19:40	21:04

Change trains.
374

Dep. Terontola	14:37(1)	16:30(2)	-0-	20:18	21:19
Arr. Florence					
(S.M.N.)	16:18	18:08	19:50	22:09	22:50

(1)Light refreshments. (2)Meal service. (3)Direct train. No train change in Terontola. (4)Plus another departure from Assisi at 21:28.

Florence - Bologna - Florence   374

Exceptional mountain scenery on this easy one-day roundtrip.

The train goes through the 11.5-mile long Apennine Tunnel, Italy's longest tunnel.

Dep. Florence	Frequent times from 5:46 to 23:01
Arr. Bologna	80 minutes later

Sights in **Bologna:** See notes about sightseeing in Bologna at the start of this section.

Dep. Bologna	Frequent times to 23:23
Arr. Florence	80 minutes later

Florence - Livorno - Florence   358a

Dep. Florence	12:00	Dep. Livorno	17:37
Arr. Livorno	13:32	Arr. Florence	19:10

Sights in **Livorno:** The old and new forts, both from the 16th century. The marble statue of Ferdinand. Tacca's 17th century bronze statues of "The Four Moors". Villas once occupied by Shelley and Byron. Italy's Naval Academy. The paintings and the Communal Library, both in the Civic Museum.

Florence - Milan - Florence   374

Dep. Florence (S.M.N.)	5:46	6:45(1)	9:15	10:46(2)
Arr. Milan (Centrale)	9:50	9:55	13:40	13:55

Sights in **Milan:** See notes about sightseeing in Milan at the start of this section.

Dep. Milan (Centrale)	14:25(3)	16:50(2)	17:00	19:40(5)
Arr. Florence (S.M.N.)	18:40	20:02	20:45	23:20

(1)First-class only. Supplement charged. (2)TEE. Reservation required. Meal service. (3)Meal service. (4)Light refreshments. (5)Plus other departures from Milan at 19:50(4), 20:25(1) and 20:30.

Florence - Padua - Florence   389

Dep. Florence (S.M.N.)	6:23	9:50(1)	10:52
Arr. Padua	9:52	12:46	13:56

Sights in **Padua:** The 13th century university on the Via 8 Febraio. Scrovegni Chapel. The Church of Eremitani. The Basilica of Sant'Antonio, with several statues by Donatello.

Dep. Padua	13:15(2)	14:38(2)	16:12	17:21(3+4)
Arr. Florence (S.M.N.)	16:33	18:40	19:36	20:32

(1)Meal service. (2)Change trains in Bologna. (3)Meal service. (4)Plus other departures from Padua at 17:41, 19:04(2), 20:35 and 21:32.

Florence - Parma - Florence   374

Dep. Florence (S.M.N.)	5:51(1)	6:23	9:15	11:27(1)
Arr. Bologna	-0-	7:47	10:46	-0-

Change trains.

Dep. Bologna	-0-	8:18	11:00	-0-
Arr. Parma	8:26	9:22	12:01	14:32

Sights in **Parma:** See notes about sightseeing in Parma earlier in this section, under "Bologna-Parma".

Dep. Parma	14:06(1+2)	14:39(1)	16:05(1+2)	19:44(4)
Arr. Bologna	-0-	-0-	-0-	20:51

Change trains.

Dep. Bologna	-0-	-0-	-0-	21:13
Arr. Florence (S.M.N.)	16:07	17:13	18:40	22:37

(1)Direct train. No train change in Bologna. (2)Meal service. (3)Light refreshments. (4)Plus another departure from Parma at 21:25(1+3).

Florence - Perugia - Florence

374

Dep. Florence (S.M.N.)	7:00	8:02	9:48(1)	11:40(1)
Arr. Terontola	8:28	9:36	11:20	13:07

Change trains.

378

Dep. Terontola	8:41	9:56	11:25	13:21
Arr. Perugia	9:28	10:40	12:12	14:08

Sights in **Perugia:** The Municipal Palace, to see the magnificent carved and inlaid wood panels in the Library, the chapel of the Stock Exchange, and the great paintings in the National Gallery (Pinacoteca). On display to the left of the main door of the Stock Exchange chapel is the white onyx ring with which the Virgin Mary was married.

Also visit the 13th century Church of San Ercolano. Galleng Palace, with its Foreign University. The Pisano sculptures at the Fontana Maggiore in beautiful Piazza 4 Novembre. The fine collection of Tuscan paintings in the museum of the 13th century Palazzo dei Priori.

Stroll along Maesta della Volte, Via dei Priori (to the Oratory of San Bernardino), Via Bagliona and Corso Vannucci, the main street.

Dep. Perugia	13:26	14:34	16:58(2)	18:53	20:10(3)
Arr. Terontola	14:09	15:22	-0-	19:40	21:04

Change trains.

374

Dep. Terontola	14:37(1)	16:30(1)	-0-	20:18	21:19
Arr. Florence (S.M.N.)	16:18	18:08	19:50	22:09	22:50

(1)Light refreshments. (2)Direct train. No train change in Terontola. (3)Plus another departure from Perugia at 22:07.

Florence - Pisa - Florence   364

Dep. Florence	Frequent times from 0:30 to 23:30
Arr. Pisa	1-1½ hours later

Sights in **Pisa:** See notes about sightseeing in Pisa earlier in this section, under "Bologna-Pisa".

Dep. Pisa	Frequent times from 0:07 to 23:26
Arr. Florence	1-1½ hours later

Florence - Ravenna - Florence   397

Dep. Florence (S.M.N.)	6:40	8:15
Arr. Ravenna	10:12	11:10

Sights in **Ravenna:** See notes about sightseeing in Ravenna earlier in this section, under "Bologna-Ravenna".

Dep. Ravenna	15:57	17:23	18:44(1)
Arr. Florence (S.M.N.)	19:04	20:47	21:57

(1)Change trains 3 times en route to Florence.

Florence - Rimini - Florence   358a

| Dep. Florence | 7:12 | Dep. Rimini | 19:17 |
| Arr. Rimini | 10:32 | Arr. Florence | 22:37 |

Sights in **Rimini:** Malatesta Temple. Sigismondo's Castle. The Bridge of Tiberius over the Marecchia River. The Arch of Augustus. Frescoes in St. Augustin's Church. Remains of the Roman amphitheater.

Florence - Siena - Florence   363

| Dep. Florence | 8:05 | 9:45(1) | 11:40 | 12:15(2+3) |
| Arr. Siena | 9:39 | 11:13 | 13:21 | 14:31 |

Sights in **Siena:** See notes about sightseeing in Siena earlier in this section, under "Bologna-Siena".

| Dep. Siena | 13:28 | 15:40 | 18:13 | 19:32 | 21:20(4) |
| Arr. Florence | 15:20 | 17:28 | 19:44 | 21:08 | 22:35 |

(1)Runs Sundays and holidays only. (2)Change trains in Empoli. (3)Runs daily, except Sundays and holidays. (4)Plus another departure from Siena at 22:47(2).

Florence - Verona - Florence
374

| Dep. Florence (S.M.N.) | 6:23 | 9:15(1) | 9:50 | 10:46(2) |
| Arr. Bologna | 7:47 | 10:46 | 11:00 | 11:55 |

Change trains.
381

| Dep. Bologna | 8:21 | 11:14 | -0- | 12:20 |
| Arr. Verona | 9:58 | 13:14 | -0- | 13:46 |

Sights in **Verona:** See notes about sightseeing in Verona earlier in this section under "Bologna-Verona".

| Dep. Verona | 15:23 | 16:43 | 18:45 | 19:21 |
| Arr. Bologna | 17:05 | 19:02 | 20:24 | 21:54 |

Change trains.
374

| Dep. Bologna | 17:17 | 19:32 | 21:13 | 22:01 |
| Arr. Florence (S.M.N.) | 18:40 | 20:55 | 22:37 | 23:20 |

(1)Departs from Florence's Campo di Marte railstation. (2)TEE. Reservation required. Meal service.

Genoa - Bologna - Genoa   357a

| Dep. Genoa (Brignole) | 6:18 | Dep. Bologna | 17:50 |
| Arr. Bologna | 11:07 | Arr. Genoa Brignole | 22:50 |

Sights in **Bologna:** See notes about sightseeing in Bologna at the start of this section.

Genoa - Cremona - Genoa

359

Dep. Genoa (P.P.)	9:15(1)	10:50(2)
Arr. Milan (Centrale)	10:50	12:40

Change trains.

366

Dep. Milan (Centrale)	12:05	14:10
Arr. Cremona	13:15	15:19

Sights in **Cremona:** One of Italy's most impressive squares, the Piazza del Commune, with its octagonal Baptistry, 12th century Duomo Cathedral, Loggia de Militi, and the Gothic Torrazzo (tallest bell tower in Italy).

Cremona is where the art of violin-making reached its apex, with the works of Amati, Stradivari and Guarneri. It is possible to watch young violin makers following that great tradition by visiting La Scuola Internazionale de Liuteria, in a renovated 16th century palace.

At the City Museum every day at 11:00, an outstanding violin made by Stradivari is played by the museum curator. Located near the Liuteria are many shops which will make a special violin to order. On view at the City Hall are 2 original Stradivari, 2 Amatis and a Sacconi.

Dep. Cremona	16:02	17:40(3)	18:25	19:27
Arr. Milan (Centrale)	17:18	20:03	20:40	20:57

Change trains.

359

Dep. Milan (Centrale)	17:52	20:30(1+4)	21:55(2+4)	22:25
Arr. Genoa (P.P.)	20:07	22:04	23:23	0:29

(1)Meal service. (2)Light refreshments. (3)Change trains in Codogno. (4)Reservation required. Supplement charged. First-class only.

Genoa - Milan - Genoa   359

Dep. Genoa (P.P.)	6:37	8:05(1+2)	8:03	8:44(3)	9:15(4+5)
Arr. Milan (Cent.)	8:20	9:25	10:20	10:40	10:50

Sights in **Milan:** See notes about sightseeing in Milan at the start of this section.

Dep. Milan (Cent.)	14:15	15:00	16:08(3)	16:45(3)	17:50(6)
Arr. Genoa (P.P.)	16:00	17:01	18:20	18:49	20:07

(1)Reservation required. (2)First-class only. (3)Light refreshments. (4)Meal service. (5)Plus other departures from Genoa at 10:50(3) and 12:15(4). (6)Plus other departures from Milan at 18:25(1), 18:35(1), 19:45, 20:30(1+4), 21:55(1+2+3) and 22:25.

Genoa - Parma - Genoa   357a

Dep. Genoa (Brignole)	6:18	Dep. Parma	18:59
Arr. Parma	10:02	Arr. Genoa (Brignole)	22:50

Sights in **Parma:** See notes about sightseeing in Parma earlier in this section, under "Bologna-Parma".

Genoa - Pisa - Genoa   355

Exceptional mountain and Mediterranean coastline scenerey on this ride.

Dep. Genoa (P.P.)   6:47   7:51(1)   8:14(2)   8:45(5)
Arr. Pisa (Cent.)   9:55   10:10   10:30   11:50

Sights in **Pisa:** See notes about sightseeing in Pisa earlier in this section under "Bologna-Pisa".

Dep. Pisa (Cent.)   14:51(2)   15:45(2)   17:15(3)   19:45(1+6)
Arr. Genoa (P.P.)   17:35   18:05   19:44   22:00

(1)Operates late May to late September. (2)Meal service. (3)Reservation required in first-class. (4)Supplement charged. (5)Plus other departures from Genoa at 10:08(2+3) and 11:47(2).   (6)Plus other departures from Pisa at 20:48, 21:51(2+4) and 22:23.

Genoa - San Remo - Genoa   356

Dep. Genoa (P.P.)   5:58   6:54   7:00   8:23(1+5)
Arr. San Remo   8:30   9:20   9:37   10:08

Sights in **San Remo:** Bathing beauties (and uglies) on the largest of the Italian Riviera beach resorts.

Dep. San Remo   12:55   13:50   15:20   16:12(2+6)
Arr. Genoa (P.P.)   15:35   17:22   18:10   19:33

(1)Supplement charged. Meal service. (2)Change trains in Savona. (3)Light refreshments. (4)Operates late May to late September. (5)Plus other departures from Genoa at 8:45(3), 9:30(4), 10:00 and 11:40.   (6)Plus other departures from San Remo at 16:43(2), 18:06(3), 18:25, 18:56, 19:27(4), 20:10(1) and 21:53.

Genoa - Torino - Genoa 355

Dep. Genoa (P.P.)	7:30	7:53	9:55	10:37	12:10
Arr. Torino (P.N.)	9:35	10:05	12:00	12:38	14:37

Sights in **Torino:** The beautiful Piazza Carlo Felice park, near the railstation. Piazza San Carlo, considered second only to St. Mark's in Venice. The imposing Palazzo Madama, with its enormous marble staircase and Royal Armory, in Piazza Castello. The museum in Palazzo Carignano, including the third most important (after London and Cairo) Egyptian collection in the world.

The university in Piazzo Carlo, where Erasmus of Rotterdam earned his doctorate in 1506. The view from the top of Mole Antonelliani, on Via Montebello. Parco del Valentino, with its splendid gardens and buildings. Frescos in the Castello del Valentino. The Church of the Great Mother of God, patterned after Rome's Pantheon.

In the black and white marble Chapel of the Holy Shroud, the urn holding what is believed to be the shroud placed on Jesus when he was taken from the cross. The Auto Museum on Corso Unita d'Italia, with models going back to 1893.

Dep. Torino (P.N.)	12:25	13:55(1)	15:20	16:40(2)	17:00(4)
Arr. Genoa (P.P.)	14:18	15:44	17:17	18:29	19:18

(1)Light refreshments. (2)Reservation required in first-class. Meal service. (3)Operates late June to mid-September. (4)Plus other departures from Torino at 18:22, 18:55, 19:55(3), 21:10, 21:23 and 22:00.

Milan - Bologna - Milan 374

Dep. Milan (Cent.)	5:55(1)	7:00(1)	7:55(2)	8:00(3+7)
Arr. Bologna	8:36	9:52	10:08	10:38

Sights in **Bologna:** See notes about sightseeing in Bologna at the start of this section.

Dep. Bologna	12:00(4)	12:30	13:23	14:05(8)
Arr. Milan (Cent.)	13:55	15:20	16:00	16:40

(1)Light refreshments. (2)Meal service. (3)Operates late May to late September. (4)TEE. Reservation required. Meal service. (5)Operates late June to late August. (6)Reservation required. Meal service. (7)Plus other departures from Milan at 8:10(4), 8:30(5), 9:15 and 9:30(4). (8)Plus other departures from Bologna at 15:02(2), 15:42(4), 15:52(3), 16:08, 17:15(4), 17:21(1), 18:20(1+6), 18:55, 19:08(3), 19:32(5), 19:58(2), 20:09(3), 20:44(2), 21:07, 21:44(2) and 22:00.

Milan - Como - Milan

	277	368	277	368	277
Milan (Cent.)	7:10	-0-	9:10	-0-	13:10
Dep. Milan (P. Gar.)	-0-	8:25	-0-	10:20	-0-
Arr. Como (S.G.)	7:49	9:20	9:50	11:20	13:50

Sights in **Como:** Take Bus #4, marked "Piazza Cavour", from the railstation to reach both the lakeshore and the cable car which ascends the 2300-foot high Mount Brunate in 7 minutes. At the peak, there is a wonderful view of Lake Como and the Alps.

Dep. Como (S.G.)   Frequent times from 10:54 to 23:01
Arr. Milan (Cent.)   40 minutes later

Milan - Cremona - Milan   366

Dep. Milan (Cent.)	6:35	8:25(1)	9:05(2)	12:05	14:10
Arr. Cremona	8:02	9:37	11:16	13:14	15:20

Sights in **Cremona:** See notes about sightseeing in Cremona earlier in the section, under "Genoa-Cremona".

Dep. Cremona	12:23	13:21	14:14(1)	16:02	17:40(3+4)
Arr. Milan (Cent.)	13:45	15:17(2)	15:30(1)	17:18	20:03

(1)Depart/Arrive Milan's Lambrate railstation. (2)Depart/Arrive Milan's Porta Garibaldi railstation. (3)Change trains in Codogno. (4)Plus other departures from Cremona at 18:25 and 19:27.

Milan - Florence - Milan   374

Dep. Milan (Cent.)		6:48(1+2)	7:55(3)	8:10(4)
Arr. Florence (S.M.N.)	10:27	11:30	11:13

Sights in **Florence:** See notes about sightseeing in Florence at the start of this section.

Dep. Florence (S.M.N.)	14:23(4)	15:24(2)	16:55(3+5)	17:20(3+7)
Arr. Milan (Cent.)	17:30	20:20	20:30	21:25(6)

(1)Arrive/Depart Milan's Lambrate railstation. (2)Light refreshments. (3)Meal service. (4)TEE. Reservation required. Meal service. (5)Reservation required. (6)Arrive at Milan's Porta Garibaldi railstation. (7)Plus other departures from Florence at 18:18(2), 19:20(3), 19:41(1) and 20:39(4).

Milan - Genoa - Milan   359

Dep. Milan (Cent.)	6:40(1)	6:55	9:00	10:50(2+7)
Arr. Genoa (P.P.)	8:15	8:52	10:55	12:20

Sights in **Genoa:** See notes about sightseeing in Genoa at the start of this section.

Dep. Genoa (P.P.)	14:00	14:40(2)	14:52	16:00(8)
Arr. Milan (Cent.)	1½-2 hours later

(1)Meal service. (2)Reservation required. (3)Light refreshments. (4)Operates late

May to late September. (5)Meal service. (6)Supplement charged. (7)Plus other departures from Milan at 11:08 and 12:15(5). (8)Plus other departures from Genoa at 16:32(5), 17:42(6), 18:37(4), 19:34, 21:15(3), 22:00(1) and 22:50.

Milan - Locarno - Milan

The Camedo-Locarno portion of this trip is one of the 5 most scenic rail trips in Europe, with outstanding mountain, gorge and river scenery.

251

Dep. Milan (Cent.)	-0-	7:05	-0-	10:05
Dep. Milan (P. Gar.)	6:38	-0-	9:05	-0-
Arr. Domodossola	8:58	8:50	11:25	11:50

Change trains. Walk outside the Domodossola railstation and go to the underground track in order to board the Centovalli narrow-gauge local railway.

290

Dep. Domodossola	9:05(1)	10:05(1)	-0-	12:05(1)
Dep. Camedo	10:08(1)	11:08(1)	-0-	13:05(1)
Arr. Locarno	40 minutes later			

Sights in **Locarno:** Stroll the gardens along the shore of lake Maggiore and take the funicular ride to the church high above the village for a fine view of Locarno and lake Maggiore.

An overnight stay in Locarno is worthwhile, in order to have a complete day for touring the Borromean Islands on Lake Maggiore.

Here is our favorite schedule: Depart Locarno Pier 8:30. Arrive Isola Madre 11:25. Take a one-hour walking tour of this fantastic garden island. Depart Isola Madre Pier 12:25. Arrive Isola Pescatori 12:40 for lunch in a restaurant there. (The Swiss-Italian border cuts across Lake Maggiore. This island is on the Italian side. Oddly, restaurants there required Lira on our last visit.)

Depart Isola Pescatori 14:10. Arrive Isola Bella 14:15 and tour the fascinating and very unique palace there, where European leaders met in 1925 to sign the Locarno Pact. Depart Isola Bella Pier on the last boat of the day, at 15:20. Arrive back in Locarno at 18:45.

Dep. Locarno	11:05(1)	13:00(1)	15:00(1)	16:20(2+6)
Dep. Camedo	11:46(1)	13:42(1)	15:42(1)	17:10
Arr. Domodossola	12:44	14:43	16:43	18:25

Change trains. Walk from underground Centovailli track, up to the main Domodossola railstation.

251

Dep. Domodossola	14:04	15:28	17:37(3)	19:32(1)
Arr. Milan (P. Gar.)	-0-	-0-	-0-	-0-
Arr. Milan (Cent.)	15:56	17:00	19:05	21:00

(1)Light refreshments. (2)Change trains in Camedo. (3)Supplement charged. Light refreshments. (4)Arrives at Milan's Centrale railstation. (5)Arrives at Milan's Porta Garibaldi railstation. (6)Plus other departures from Locarno at 17:20(4) and 18:40(5).

Milan - Lugano - Milan   277
Dep. Milan (Cent.)   7:49(1)   9:10(1)   11:10(1)   13:10(2)
Arr. Lugano   8:47   10:40   12:40   14:40

Sights in **Lugano:** Take the cable car from the railstation to Piazza Cioccaro. Walk downhill from there to the city center, Piazza Riforma. See the collection of over 400 masterpieces (Rubens, Goya, Durer) in the gallery of La Villa Favorita. Stroll the shore of lovely Lake Lugano.

Take one of the many boat trips on the lake. Also the cogwheel train to the 5300-foot top of Mt. Generoso and the chair-lift to the slightly higher top of Mt. Lema.

Visit in nearby Melide the Swissminiatur Model Village, a Swiss version of Holland's Madurodam. On the same 1:25 scale as Madurodam, there are excellent reproductions of castles, churches, farmhouses, town squares, etc., in a beautifully landscaped garden setting.

Open mid-March to the end of October 8:00-18:00 (until 22:00 during July and August). The entry fee is reduced one Swiss Franc if you are carrying a copy of Eurail® Guide.

Dep. Lugano   14:13   16:13   17:29   18:13   20:13(4)
Arr. Milan (Cent.)   1½ hours later

(1)Meal service. (2)Light refreshments. (3)Arrives at Milan's Lambrate railstation. (4)Plus other departures from Lugano at 22:06, 22:13 and 0:07(3).

Milan - Torino - Milan   354
Dep. Milan (Cent.)   7:00(1)   -0-   -0-   10:20(1)   11:20(3)
Dep. Milan (P. Gar.) -0-   8:00   9:10   -0-   -0-
Arr. Torino (P.N.)   8:30   9:45   11:09   11:52   13:00

Sights in **Torino:** See notes about sightseeing in Torino earlier in this section, under "Genoa-Torino".

Dep. Torino (P.N.)   12:30   13:30   14:30(2)   15:30   16:30(1+4)
Arr. Milan (P.Gar.)   -0-   -0-   -0-   17:13   -0-
Arr. Milan (Cent.)   14:15   15:10   16:20   -0-   18:00

(1)Supplement charged. Light refreshments. (2)Light refreshments. (3)Plus another departure from Milan's Porta Garibaldi railstation at 12:20.   (4)Plus other departures from Torino at 17:30(2), 18:30, 19:30, 20:08, 21:05, 21:40(1) and 22:40.

Milan - Venice - Milan 390
Dep. Milan (Cent.)   5:55   6:55(1)   7:25   8:05   9:05(4)
Arr. Venice (S.L.)   9:44   9:52   11:00   11:30   12:24
    Sights in **Venica:** See notes about sightseeing in Venice earlier in this section, under "Bologna-Venice".
Dep. Venice (S.L.)   12:55   13:54(1)   15:00   16:05(2)'   17:35(2+5)
Arr. Milan (Cent.)   16:35   16:40   18:34   19:35   21:15
(1)Reservation required. First-class only. (2)Light refreshments. (3)Runs Sundays and holidays only. (4)Plus another departure from Milan at 9:35(1).   (5)Plus other departures from Venice at 18:20, 18:35(1), 18:58(3), 19:50, 20:10(1) and 20:40.

Milan - Verona - Milan 390
Dep. Milan (Cent.)   6:55(1)   7:25   8:05   9:05   9:35(1+4)
Arr. Verona (P.N.)   8:22   9:13   9:14   10:43   11:03
    Sights in **Verona:** See notes about sightseeing in Verona earlier in this section, under "Bologna-Verona".
Dep. Verona (P.M.)   12:50(2)   14:51   15:16(1)   16:40   17:45(2+5)
Arr. Milan (Cent.)   14:35   16:35   16:40   18:34   19:35
(1)Reservation required. Supplement charged. First-class only. Light refreshments. (2)Light refreshments. (3)TEE. Reservation required. Meal service. (4)Plus other departures from Milan at 11:30, 12:15 and 13:00(2).   (5)Plus other departures from Verona at 19:23(2), 20:12(1), 21:24(3), 21:37(1), 21:47 and 22:28.

Naples - Pompeii - Naples 401
    This trip is *not* covered by Eurailpass.
Dep. Naples (F.S.)   Frequent times from 4:53 to 22:54
Arr. Pompeii   30 minutes later
    A travolator connection provides transportation from Naples' Central station to Naples' F.S. station.
    Sights in **Pompeii:** See where 20,000 people were living and how they lived 1900 years ago when this city was buried in a few minutes under a volcanic rain of ashes from nearby (still active) Vesuvius, when it was young and strong.
Dep. Pompeii   Frequent times from 4:43 to 22:49
Arr. Naples (F.S.)   30 minutes later

Naples - Rome - Naples   392

Dep. Naples (Cent.)	-0-	-0-	7:00	-0-	7:58(2+4)
Dep. Naples. (P. Gar.)	-0-	6:45(1)	-0-	-0-	-0-
Dep. Naples (Mer.)	6:23(1)	6:58(1)	-0-	7:55(1)	-0-
Dep. Naples (C. Fle.)	6:28(1)	-0-	-0-	-0-	-0-
Arr. Rome (Ter.)	8:35	9:02	9:20	9:53	10:20
Arr. Rome (Tibur.)	-0-	-0-	-0-	-0-	-0-

Sights in **Rome:** See notes about Rome at the start of this section.

Dep. Rome (Tibur.)	-0-	-0-	-0-	14:53	-0-
Dep. Rome (Ter.)	12:50	13:45(2)	14:30	-0-	15:50(2+5)
Arr. Naples (C. Fle.)	-0-	-0-	-0-	-0-	-0-
Arr. Naples (Mer.)	15:00	-0-	-0-	-0-	-0-
Arr. Naples (P. Gar.)	15:11	-0-	-0-	-0-	-0-
Arr. Naples (Cent.)	-0-	16:02	16:52	17:22	17:52

(1)Supplement charged. (2)Light refreshments. (3)Meal service. (4)Plus other departures from Naples Centrale at 7:58(2), 9:15 and 12:12(2).   (5)Plus other departures from Rome Termini at 16:00(2), 17:15(2), 18:07(2), 18:45(1), 19:15, 19:30(1+3), 20:45 and 22:25.

Rome - Anzio - Rome   380

Dep. Rome (Ter.)	8:05	9:40	12:05	13:00	14:05
Arr. Anzio	50-60 minutes later				

Sights in **Anzio:** This has been a beach resort since ancient times. Many Americans visit the nearby military cemeteries, holding those killed in the January 22, 1944 Allied invasion.

Dep. Anzio	9:29	13:04	15:03	16:04	18:19(1)
Arr. Rome (Ter.)	50-60 minutes later				

(1)Plus other departures from Anzio at 20:15, 21:16 and 23:04.

Rome - Assisi - Rome
395

Dep. Rome (Ter.)	7:05(1)	8:17	9:35(2)	10:38(2)
Arr. Foligno	8:53	10:23	12:29	13:39

Change trains in Foligno.
378

Dep. Foligno	9:10	10:50	12:42	13:43
Arr. Assisi	9:26	11:03	12:58	13:59

(1)Reservation required. (2)Change trains in Orte.

Sights in **Assisi:** See notes about sightseeing in Assisi earlier in this section, under "Florence-Assisi".
378

Dep. Assisi	12:40(1)	15:22(1)	18:22(1)	20:08(1+2)
Arr. Rome (Ter.)	15:35	18:07	21:22	22:38

(1)Change trains in Foligno. (2)Reservation required from Foligno to Rome.

Rome - Florence (Firenze) - Rome 374

Dep. Rome (Termini) 5:42(1) 6:45(2) 7:50(3) 8:00(2+6)
Arr. Florence (S.M.N.) 9:05 9:40 10:36 11:10
    Sights in **Florence:** See notes about sightseeing in Florence at the start of this section.
Dep. Florence (S.M.N.) 13:30 14:22(2+4) 14:54(2) 15:08(3+7)
Arr. Rome (Termini) 17:02 17:10 18:50 17:45
(1)Depart/Arrive Rome's Tiburtina railstation. (2)Meal service. (3)TEE. Reservation required. Meal service. (4)Reservation required. First-class only. (5)Light refreshments. (6)Plus other departures from Rome at 9:35(2) and 11:30(3). (6)Plus other departures from Florence at 15:51(5), 16:17(2), 16:43(2), 17:50(2), 18:50(2), 20:12(3),20:42(2) and 20:57.

Rome - Naples - Rome 392

Dep. Rome (Ter.) 6:42(1) 7:00(2) 7:30 8:15(8)
Arr. Naples (Cent.) 9:03 8:59(3) 10:00 10:45
    Sights in **Naples:** See notes about sightseeing in Naples at the start of this section.
Dep. Naples (Cent.) 12:45(4) 13:38(5) 15:18(3+6) 15:15(9)
Arr. Rome (Ter.) 15:00 16:05 17:25 17:45
(1)Depart from Rome's Tiburtina railstation. (2)Reservation required. Supplement charged. Meal service. (3)Depart from Naple's Mergellina railstation. (4)Meal service. (5)Light refreshments. (6)TEE. Reservation required. Meal service. (7)Arrive/Depart Naples' Garibaldi railstation. (8)Plus other departures from Rome at 8:50(5), 9:08, 9:15 and 11:55(2+7). (9)Plus other departures from Naples at 15:55(2+7), 16:15, 17:15, 17:55, 18:30(5), 18:55(2+7), 19:15, 20:00 and 20:55.

Rome - Orvieto - Rome 374

Dep. Rome (Ter.) 6:25 7:27(1) 10:38(2) 12:23(1)
Arr. Orvieto 7:44 8:45 12:14 13:32
    Sights in **Orvieto:** The gold mosaics, marble pieces, bronze canopies, Fra Angelico and Luca Signorelli frescoes, and rose window in the 13th century Cathedral.
Dep. Orvieto 13:19(1) 14:23(1) 15:50 17:33(2+4)
Arr. Rome (Ter.) 14:38(3) 15:50(3) 17:02 18:50
Light refreshments. (2)Meal service. (3)Arrive at Rome's Tiburtina railstation. (4)Plus other departures from Orvieto at 18:17(1) and 21:21(2).

Rome - Perugia - Rome
395

Dep. Rome (Termini)	7:05(1)	8:17	9:35(2)	10:38(3)
Arr. Foligno	8:53	10:23	-0-	13:39

Change trains.
378

Dep. Foligno	9:10	10:50	-0-	13:43
Arr. Perugia	9:55	11:26	13:25	14:31

Sights in **Perugia:** See notes about sightseeing in Perugia earlier in this section, under "Florence-Perugia".

Dep. Perugia	12:13	14:58	17:52	19:38
Arr. Foligno	12:54	15:37	18:40	20:25

Change trains.
395

Dep. Foligno	13:24	15:42	19:11	20:55(1)
Arr. Rome (Termini)	15:35	18:07	21:22	22:38

(1)Supplement charged. (2)Direct train. No train change in Foligno. (3)Change trains in Orte.

Rome - Pescara - Rome   376

Exceptional mountain scenery on this ride.

Dep. Rome (Termini)	7:00(1)	8:02			
Arr. Pescara (Cent.)	10:30	11:59			

Sights in **Pescara:** A nice beach resort on the Adriatic coast.

Dep. Pescara (Cent.)	13:17	14:14	16:15(1)	18:05	20:25(1)
Arr. Rome (Termini)	17:52	21:01(2)	19:45	22:12	23:54

(1)Supplement charged. (2)Arrives at Rome's Tiburtina railstation.

Rome - Pisa - Rome   355

Dep. Rome (Ter.)	6:40	7:20(1+2)	8:30	10:55(2)	12:08(2)
Arr. Pisa	11:18	10:39	12:35	14:41	15:38

Sights in **Pisa:** See notes about sightseeing in Pisa earlier in this section, under "Bologna-Pisa".

Dep. Pisa	14:37(2)	15:47(2)	16:42	18:38(4)	19:42(5+6)
Arr. Rome (Ter.)	18:35	19:55	20:40(3)	22:15	23:35

(1)Reservation required. (2)Meal service. (3)Arrives at Rome's Tiburtina railstation. (4)Light refreshments. (5)Operates early July to late September. (6)Plus another departure from Pisa at 20:43(1+2).

Rome - Pompeii - Rome   392

Dep. Rome (Ter.)	8:50(1)	Dep. Pompeii	16:16	17:52(1)
Arr. Pompeii	11:41	Arr. Rome (Ter.)	19:45	20:55

Sights in **Pompeii:** See notes about sightseeing in Pompeii earlier in this section, under ''Naples-Pompeii''.

Rome - Siena - Rome
74

Dep. Rome (Ter.)	7:27(1)	9:35(2)
Arr. Chiusi	9:15	11:22

Change trains.
363

Dep. Chiusi	9:20	11:38
Arr. Siena	10:59	13:12

Sights in **Siena:** See notes about sightseeing in Siena earlier in this section, under ''Bologna-Siena''.

Dep. Siena	13:47	14:58	16:49	17:29	19:34
Arr. Chiusi	15:20	16:37	18:34	19:14	21:27

Change trains.
374

Dep. Chiusi	15:25	17:05(2)	18:40(2)	19:44(2)	21:32
Arr. Rome (Ter.)	17:02	18:50	20:07	21:12	23:09(3)

(1)Light refreshments. (2)Meal service. (3)Arrives at Rome's Tiburtina railstation.

Rome - Spoleto - Rome   395

Dep. Rome (Ter.)	7:05(1)	8:17	9:35(2)	10:38(2)
Arr. Spoleto	8:34	10:03	12:09	13:10

Sights in **Spoleto:** Roman ruins. The enormous 14th century Rocca (fortress). The central mosaic, magnificent 15th century Lippi fresco, and 8 rose windows in the Cathedral. The 14th century arched bridge that holds the aqueduct which still supplies Spoleto its water.

The tourist office in Piazza della Liberta hasmany brochures, including a town map and 3 half-day walking itineraries.

Dep. Spoleto	11:11(2)	13:42	16:07	19:30	20:30(2+3)
Arr. Rome (Ter.)	12:55	15:35	18:07	21:22	22:50

(1)Supplement charged. (2)Change trains in Orte. (3)Plus another departure from Spoleto at 21:11(1).

THE TRAIN ROUTES TO THE TOE OF ITALY

Here are the 2 rail routes to Southern Italy: along the Adriatic and Ionian seacoasts from Pescara to Reggio di Calabria, and along the Tyrrhenian seacoast from Naples to Reggio di Calabria.

Pescara - Foggia - Barletta - Bari - Brindisi - Taranto - Catanzaro - Reggio di Calabria
393

Dep. Pescara	0:46	2:36(1)	3:38	4:05	4:45(6)
Arr. Foggia	3:20	5:10	6:16	6:25	7:44
Arr. Barletta	4:21	5:57	-0-	-0-	8:31
Arr. Bari	5:14	6:40	7:51	8:02	9:13
Dep. Bari	5:33	7:14	8:10	8:43	9:33
Arr. Brindisi	7:12	9:01	9:31	10:02	10:46

(1)Carries sleeping car. Also has couchettes. (2)Operates late June to mid-September. (3)Runs daily, except Sundays and holidays. (4)Light refreshments. (5)Reservation required. Supplement charged. Meal service. (6)Plus other departures from Pescara at 5:25(2+3), 9:05, 10:48, 13:10(2), 17:10(4) and 18:00(5).

Change trains.
400

Dep. Brindisi	4:56	6:56	8:49	11:00	12:40	14:24(1)
Arr. Taranto	6:18	8:27	9:48	12:20	14:15	15:43

(1)Plus other departures from Brindisi at 17:43, 19:12 and 21:21.

Change trains.
407

Dep. Taranto	5:05	8:15	9:57(1)	11:13(3+4)
Arr. Catanzaro	11:23	15:35	13:40	16:19
Arr. Reggio (Cent.)	15:56	19:37	16:08	21:31

(1)Supplement charged. (2)Has couchettes. (3)Change trains in Crotone. (4)Plus other departures from Taranto at 16:59 and 22:37(2).

Reggio di Calabria - Catanzaro - Taranto -
Brindisi - Bari - Barletta - Foggia - Pescara
407

Dep. Reggio (Cent.)	6:28	6:53	10:21	15:16(1)	22:36(2)
Dep. Catanzaro	9:11	12:30	15:27	17:39	1:28
Arr. Taranto	12:56	18:47	22:07	21:12	6:16

(1)Supplement charged. (2)Has couchettes.
  Change trains.
  400

Dep. Taranto	6:40	7:51	9:07	10:41	12:54(1)
Arr. Brindisi	8:08	8:44	10:29	11:41	14:10

(1)Plus other departures from Taranto at 14:32, 15:48, 19:36, 21:27 and 23:58
  Change trains.
  393

Dep. Brindisi	6:19	9:41(1)	10:56(2)	12:02(3)	15:19(4)
Arr. Bari	7:50	11:16	12:10	13:26	16:48
Dep. Bari	8:10	11:40	12:37	13:47	17:07
Arr. Barletta	8:55	12:25	-0-	14:26	17:43
Arr. Foggia	9:47	13:13	13:55	15:07	18:32
Arr. Pescara	12:45	16:07	16:40	17:33	21:58

(2)Light refreshments. (2)Operates late June to mid-September. (3)Reservation required. Supplement charged. Meal service. (4)Plus other departures from Brindisi at 16:41, 17:59, 18:56 and 19:26.

Sights in **Bari:** The Picture Gallery. The Archaeological Museum. The relics of St. Nicholas, in the 11th century Basilica of S. Nicola. The rebuilt Norman castle. The 12th century Romanesque Cathedral. Much wine, olive oil and almonds in this area.

Sights in **Barletta:** The 13th century S. Sepolcro Church. The Norman castle. The 12th century Gothic Cathedral.

Sights in **Brindisi:** Many Crusaders set out from here for Jerusalem. See the Roman column that marks the end of the Appian Way. The Civic Museum in the 11th century circular S. Giovanni al Sepolcro Church. Frederick II's 13th century castle. The rebuilt 11th century Cathedral.

Sights in **Catanzaro:** The Baroque S. Domenico Church. The paintings in the Museum.

Sights in **Foggia:** Much wool has been marketed here for centuries. See the ancient records of sheep tax at the Library. The city has an Art Gallery, a Museum and a Cathedral.

Sights in **Pescara:** See notes about sightseeing in Pescara earlier in this section, under "Rome-Pescara-Rome".

(Sightseeing notes continue on page 220)

Sights in **Reggio di Calabria:** A very popular tourist resort. Founded by the Greeks in 720 B.C. See the fine archaeological collection in the Museo Nazionale della Magna Grecia. The reconstructed Romanesque-Byzantine Cathedral. There are many Greek and Roman ruins in this area.

Sights in **Taranto:** The 15th century Aragonese castle. The 14th century S. Domenico Maggiore Church. The exhibit of Greek vases and statues in the Museo Nazionale. The early 19th century Arsenal. The 11th century S. Cataldo Cathedral.

Rome - Naples - Villa San Giovanni - Reggio di Calabria

	398	398	398	392
Dep. Rome (Ter.)	0:40(1)	-0-	-0-	4:33(3+4)
Dep. Rome (Tibur.)	-0-	2:52	3:20	-0-
Dep. Naples (Cent.)	2:47(2)	5:26(2)	5:51(2)	7:17
Arr. V.S. Giovanni	8:35	11:27	12:00	13:00
Arr. Reggio di Cal.	9:15	12:12	12:43	13:43

	392	392	392	392
Dep. Rome (Ter.)	5:40(3+4)	6:03(3)	7:00(5)	8:50(4)
Dep. Rome (Tibur.)	-0-	-0-	-0-	-0-
Dep. Naples (Cent.)	8:30	8:50	8:61(6)	11:21
Arr. V.S. Giovanni	14:44	17:13	14:15	17:30
Arr. Reggio di Cal.	15:23	17:49	14:49	18:18

	392	392	392	392
Dep. Rome (Ter.)	9:08	11:55(5+8)	-0-	-0-
Dep. Rome (Tibur.)	-0-	-0-	13:56(3)	14:53(9)
Dep. Naples (Cent.)	12:55	13:40(6)	16:22	17:34
Arr. V.S. Giovanni	21:04	18:40	22:20	0:10
Arr. Reggio di Cal.	21:40	19:15	22:48	0:48

(1)Has couchettes. (2)Departs from Naples' Campi Flegrei railstation. (3)Departs from Rome's Ostiense railstation. (4)Light refreshments. (5)Reservervation required. Supplement charged. Meal service. (6)Departs from Naples' Mergelina railstation. (7)Carries sleeping car. Also has couchettes. (8)Plus other departures from Rome Termini at 18:07(1+4), 19:40(7), 21:55(7) and 22:25(1).

(9)Plus another departure from Rome Tiburtina at 23:21(7).

Reggio di Calabria - Villa San Giovanni - Naples - Rome

	392	392	392	392
Dep. Reggio di Cal.	0:25(1)	1:09(2)	6:58(2)	10:22(3)
Dep. V.S. Giovanni	1:15	1:53	7:30	11:00
Dep. Naples (Cent.)	7:00	7:58	13:38	16:11(4)
Arr. Rome (Tibur.)	-0-	-0-	-0-	-0-
Arr. Rome (Ter.)	9:20	10:20	16:05	18:00

	392	392	392	398
Dep. Reggio di Cal.	11:24(2)	12:58(5)	13:21	14:18(7)
Dep. V.S. Giovanni	12:08	13:40	13:50	15:02
Dep. Naples (Cent.)	18:30	19:12(4)	21:59	21:34(8)
Arr. Rome (Tibur.)	-0-	-0-	-0-	-0-
Arr. Rome (Ter.)	20:55	21:10	0:26(6)	23:54(6)

	398	392	398	398
Dep. Reggio di Cal.	14:59	15:26(2)	16:37(9)	19:34(9+10)
Dep. V.S. Giovanni	15:53	16:20	17:27	20:18
Dep. Naples (Cent.)	22:20(8)	22:46(8)	23:40(8)	2:38(8)
Arr. Rome (Tibur.)	0:43	-0-	2:05	5:10
Arr. Rome (Ter.)	-0-	1:03(6)	-0-	-0-

(1)Has couchettes. (2)Light refreshments. (3)Reservation required. Supplement charged. First-class only. Meal service. (4)Departs from Naples' Mergelina railstation. (5)Reservation required in first-class. Meal service. (6)Arrives at Rome's Ostiense railstation. (7)Operates mid-July to mid-September. (8)Departs from Naples' Campi Flegrei railstation. ()Carries sleeping car. Also has couchettes. (10)Plus other departures from Reggio di Calabria at (#392)20:07(1), (#392)21:45(9), (#392)22:15(1), (#398)22:24(1) and (#392)23:25(9).

TRAIN RIDES TO SICILY

Rome - Naples - Messina - Catania - Siracusa - Palermo

This trip includes a 35-minute ride on the ferry boat that runs between Villa S. Giovanni and Messina (Maritima).

	392	398	398	398
Dep. Rome (Ter.)	0:40(1)	-0-	-0-	-0-
Dep. Rome (Tibur.)	-0-	0:46(1+2)	2:52	3:20(3)
Dep. Naples (C. Fle.)	2:47	3:11	5:26	5:51
Dep. Naples (Cent.)	-0-	-0-	-0-	-0-
Arr. Messina (Mari.)	10:05	10:40	12:50	13:25
Arr. Taormina	-0-	-0-	-0-	-0-
Arr. Catania	12:34	-0-	15:03	15:44
Arr. Siracusa	-0-	-0-	16:38	17:08
Arr. Palermo	-0-	15:43	17:35	17:57

	60	60	392	392
Dep. Rome (Ter.)	4:33(4)	5:40(4)	7:00(5)	8:50(7)
Dep. Rome (Tibur.)	-0-	-0-	-0-	-0-
Dep. Naples (C. Fle.)	-0-	-0-	8:59(6)	-0-
Dep. Naples (Cent.)	7:17	8:30	-0-	11:21
Arr. Messina (Mari.)	14:20	16:10	15:20	18:50
Arr. Taormina	-0-	17:27	-0-	-0-
Arr. Catania	-0-	18:20	17:17	21:03
Arr. Siracusa	-0-	20:01	18:26	22:43
Arr. Palermo	18:33	-0-	19:00	23:15

	60	60	60	398
Dep. Rome (Ter.)	11:55(5)	18:07(1+7)	19:40(3)	19:58(1+9)
Dep. Rome (Tibur.)	-0-	-0-	-0-	-0-
Dep. Naples (C. Fle.)	13:56(8)	-0-	-0-	22:20
Dep. Naples (Cent.)	-0-	20:44	22:12	-0-
Arr. Messina (Mari.)	19:45	3:50	4:50	6:25(7)
Arr. Taormina	20:47	-0-	-0-	-0-
Arr. Catania	21:35	-0-	-0-	-0-
Arr. Siracusa	22:56	-0-	-0-	-0-
Arr. Palermo	23:22	8:25	10:05	10:58

(1)Has couchettes. (2)Operates mid-July to mid-September. (3)Carries sleeping car. Also has couchettes. (4)Departs from Rome's Ostiense railstation. (5)Reservation required. Supplement charged. Meal service. (6)Departs from Naples' Mergelina railstation. (7)Light refreshments. (8)Departs from Naples' Garibaldi station. (9)Plus other departures from Rome Termini at (#60)21:55(3), (#392)22:25(1), (#392)22:45(1)...and from Rome Tiburtina at (#398)23:21(3).

Palermo - Siracusa - Catania - Messina - Naples - Rome

This trip includes a 35-minute ride on the ferry boat between Messina (Maritima) and Villa San Giovanni.

	392	392	392	398
Dep. Palermo	6:25(1)	6:40(3)	8:55(4)	9:16(5)
Dep. Siracusa	6:58	7:23	9:23	-0-
Dep. Catania	8:09	8:48	10:34	-0-
Dep. Taormina	-0-	-0-	-0-	-0-
Dep. Messina (Mari.)	9:50	10:50	12:25	13:30
Arr. Naples (Cent.)	16:11(2)	18:18	19:12(2)	-0-
Arr. Naples (C. Fle.)	-0-	-0-	-0-	21:24
Arr. Rome (Tibur.)	-0-	-0-	-0-	23:54(6)
Arr. Rome (Ter.)	18:00	20:55	21:10	-0-

	398	398	60	398
Dep. Palermo	10:06	11:48	13:02(7)	14:20(7)
Dep. Siracusa	10:16	12:04	-0-	14:42(9)
Dep. Catania	11:56	13:41	-0-	16:25(9)
Dep. Taormina	-0-	-0-	-0-	-0-
Dep. Messina (Mari.)	14:20	16:05	17:30(3)	18:45
Arr. Naples (Cent.)	-0-	-0-	0:55	-0-
Arr. Naples (C. Fle.)	22:06	23:27	-0-	2:25
Arr. Rome (Tibur.)	0:43	2:05	3:39(6)	5:10
Arr. Rome (Ter.)	-0-	-0-	-0-	-0-

	398	60	60	392
Dep. Palermo	15:08(8)	17:00(7)	19:06(7+9)	-0-
Dep. Siracusa	-0-	-0-	-0-	-0-
Dep. Catania	-0-	-0-	20:33	19:41(8)
Dep. Taormina	-0-	-0-	21:26(9)	-0-
Dep. Messina	19:35(3)	21:15	22:55	22:05
Arr. Naples (Cent.)	-0-	4:23	-0-	-0-
Arr. Naples. (C. Fle.)	3:03	-0-	5:42	5:24
Arr. Rome (Tibur.)	5:30	-0-+	-0-	7:52
Arr. Rome (Ter.)	-0-	6:55	8:15	-0-

(1)Reservation required. Supplement charged. First-class only. Meal service. (2)Arrives at Naples' Mergelina railstation. (3)Light refreshments. (4)Reservation required in first-class. Supplement charged. Meal service. (5)Operates mid-July to mid-September. (6)Arrives at Rome's Ostiense railstation. (7)Carries sleeping car. Also has couchettes. (8)Has couchettes. (9)Plus another departure from Palermo at 20:15(8), Siracusa at 20:04(8), Catania at 21:39(8), and Taormina at 22:29(8).

Sights in **Messina:** The Cathedral and the Annunciata dei Catalani Church, both rebuilt in the 12th century by Norman occupiers. The beautiful astronomical clock in the modern Bell Tower, next to the Cathedral. The art in the Museo Nazionale. The Botanical Gardens.

Sights in **Catania:** Founded 729 B.C. by Greek settlers. Now a very busy seaport and a popular Winter beach resort. Whatever could happen to a city happened here in the 16th and 17th centuries: famines, civil wars, epidemics, pirate raids, earthquakes, and the eruption of Mt. Etna in 1693, after which Catania was almost completely rebuilt. The dark gray color of the city results from the use of volcanic matter in constructing buildings.

See the Greek and Roman theaters, aqueducts and baths. The excellent collection of art and archaeological relics in the Civic Museum of the 13th century Castello Ursino. The tomb of the composer Vincenzo Bellini in the rebuilt 11th century Cathedral, also containing relics of St. Agatha. Sicily's largest church, San Nicolo. Next to it, the Benedictine San Nicolo Monastery, started in the 14th century.

The medieval manuscripts in the library of the University. The royal chapel, Collegiata. The 18th century palaces circling the Piazza del Duomo, with its Elephan Fountain. The museum at the birthplace of Bellini. The Astronomical Observatory.

Sights in **Siracusa:** Settled by Greeks in 734 B.C., 5 years after the founding of nearby Catania. An earthquake that destroyed much of Catania leveled Siracusa in 1693, after which Siracusa was rebuilt.

A comprehensive tour of Siracusa starts by visiting on the hill of Neapolis the Roman Amphitheater (which held 15,000 people attending gladiator fights), constructed during the reign of Augustus, before the birth of Christ. This structure was severely stripped in 1526 for the building of the city's defensive walls.

Above the Amphitheater is the 600-foot-long altar of Hieron II, where 450 oxen were simultaneously sacrificed on pagan religious days. Nearby is an ancient quarry in which the cave called "the ear of Dionysius" is located. Next to it is the 5th century B.C. Greek Theater, where Plato and Aeschylus performed. Behind the Theater is the "Grotto of the Nymphs". Five miles further, on the hill of Epipoli overlooking Siracusa, is the Castle of Euryalus, the mightiest and most complete fortress of Greek times.

Returning downhill, along Corso Gelone, you come to the ruins of the Roman Forum, at Piazzale Marconi. Go along Corso Umberto I and cross the Ponte Nuovo to reach the island of Ortygia. There, in Piazza Pancali, are the remains of the Temple of Apollo, which the conquering Arabs turned into a mosque. Other sights in Ortygia are the 16th century Santa Maria dei Miracoli church, the 15th century arch (Porta Marina), the Maniace Castle, and the 13th century Bellomo Palace, which houses a museum of medieval and modern art.

Other sights: the 17th century Palazzo del Municipo (Tpwn Hall), the 18th century Palazzo Benevantano del Bosco, The National Archaelogical Museum, which has one of the most important collections (Greek, Roman and Byzantine) of sarcophagi, pottery, coins and bronzes in Italy. Its most famous treasure is the 2nd century B.C. Venus Landolina sculpture.

The ancient Cathedral is dominated by the Doric columns of the original Temple of Minerva, where many works of art are exhibited.

Sights in **Palermo:** The capital of Sicily. Severly damaged by bombs in July of 1943. Advisable to plan museum visits for the morning, followed by a long lunch and then touring Palermo's street markets in late afternoon. (Museums here close for the day at 13:00 or 14:00.)

See the carretti (Sicilian horsecarts) exhibits at the Pitre Ethnological Museum. The fine archaeological collection in the Museo Nazionale on Via Roma. The Risorgimento Museum at Piazza San Domenico.

Tombs of important Sicilians, in the San Domenico Church. The 800-year old Cathedral and, next to it, The Archepiscopal Palace, both on Vittorio Emanuele. Nearby, the marvelous Oriental garden at the Church of San Giovanni degli Eremiti.

See statues of former Spanish rulers in the Quattro Canti (Four Corners), a small octagonal piazza. Nearby are 2 very interesting street markets, Vucciria and Il Capo.

Located on a small,twisting street, Vucciria offers Sicilian pastries, cheeses and many foods that are exotic to non-Mediterranean tastebuds: fried lungs and spleen, sea urchins, pork sausage encased in the skin of a pig's foot.

The great array of food at Il Capo (which starts at the intersection of Via Volturno and Via Carini) includes squash, cheese, mounds of tomato paste, grapes, melons, swordfish, eggplant — as well as shirts, blouses, sweaters, leather handbags, etc.

See the antiques sold at Il Papireto, the flea market. Decorative tiles, Italian Victorian furniture, filigree jewelry, coins, religious art.

The Palace of the Norman Kings. Teatro Massimo, an enormous opera house. The 12th century Royal Palace. Martorana Church. The Cuba and Zisa palaces. The catacombs under the Convent of the Capuchin Friars.

Take the #9 bus to see the famous Norman Cathedral and Cloister in Monreale, 5 miles away. Take the #14 or #77 bus to the bathing beach, Mondello. There are half-day bus excursions and local train service to Segesta and Selinunte, sites of substantial Greek ruins.

There is hydrofoil service in the Spring and Summer to 2 interesting islands. Ustica's Blue Grotto attracts many visitors. The Archaeological Museum on Lipari is worthwhile. From Lipari, there is boat service to other nearby islands: Alicudi, Filicudi, Salina, Stromboli (immortalized by Ingrid and Roberto with more passion *off* the silver screen than they invested in the motion picture) and Vulcano. Passenger ships run from Palermo to Tunisia.

It is a short drive to see the excellent mosaics in the 12th century Cathedral at Monreale.

TRAIN ROUTES IN SICILY
(including One-Day Excursions)

Messina - Milazzo - Palermo   405

Dep. Messina (Cent.)	4:40	5:30	5:58	7:15(1)	9:28(7)
Arr. Milazzo	5:10	5:58	6:41	7:56	10:09
Arr. Palermo	8:25	9:07	10:05	10:58	14:00

Sights in **Milazzo:** Founded 7 centuries before Christ. An important naval victory over the Carthaginians was won by the Romans in Milazzo's bay more than 2,200 years ago. See the 13th century Norman castle and the 16th century Spanish walls at the old town, on a hill above the modern city.

Sights in **Palermo:** See notes about sightseeing in Palermo earlier in this section, under "Naples-Messian-Palermo".

Dep. Palermo	6:25(2)	6:40	8:55(3)	9:16(4)	10:06(8)
Dep. Milazzo	8:52	9:39	11:18	12:00	12:51
Arr. Messina (Cent.)	9:25	10:10	11:49	12:44	13:30

(1)Light refreshments. (2)Reservation required. Supplement charged. First-class only. (3)Reservation required in first-class. Supplement charged. (4)Operates mid-July tp mid-September. (5)Operates mid-September to mid-July. (6)Runs Sundays and holidays only. (7)Plus other departures from Messina at 9:50, 11:25(4), 12:22(5), 13:40, 14:10, 14:58, 15:55(3), 19:35 and 20:15(2).   (8)Plus other departures from Palermo at 11:48, 13:02, 14:20, 15:08(1). 17:00, 17:50, 20:15 and 21:16(6).

Messina - Taormina - Catania - Siracusa   406

Dep. Messina (Cent.)	8:10	8:45	9:44	10:40	13:30(4)
Arr. Taormina	8:54	9:27	10:22	11:23	14:08
Arr. Catania	9:50	10:28	11:30	'12:34(1)	15:03
Arr. Siracusa	11:36	12:01	13:08	14:25	16:38

Sights in **Taormina:** A year-around resort, with very mild Winter weather, consisting mainly of 3 streets, each on a different level, connected to each other by many stairways, all on one side of Mont Venere. One funicular provides access to the beaches below the little town (4,000 population).

Stroll and shop for pottery, embroidery and carved wood figures along Corso Umberto, the main street. See the 3rd century Roman theater, facing Mt. Etna. The medieval great halls in the 15th century Palazzo Corvaja. The 14th century Palace of the Duke of St. Stephen. The 13th century Cathedral.

Sights in **Catania:** See notes about sightseeing in Catania earlier in this section, under "Palermo-Siracusa-Catania-Naples".

Sights in **Siracusa:** See notes about sightseeing in Siracusa earlier in this section, under "Palermo-Siracusa-Catania-Naples".

Dep. Siracusa	6:58(2)	7:23	9:23(3)	10:16	11:05(5)
Arr. Catania	8:05	8:35	10:30	11:36	12:24
Arr. Taormina	8:42	9:28	11:10	12:45	13:32
Arr. Messina (Cent.)	9:24	10:10	11:50	13:35	14:20

(1)Change trains in Catania. (2)Reservation required. Supplement charged. First-class only. (3)Reservation required in first-class. Supplement charged. (4)Plus other departures from Messina at 14:05, 16:00(3), 16:50, 19:30 and 20:16(2). (5)Plus other departures from Siracusa at 12:04, 14:42, 15:47(1), 19:06 and 20:04.

Palermo - Agrigento   410

Dep. Palermo	5:27	7:38	9:20	12:36	14:27	17:50(1+4)
Arr. Agrigento	8:07	10:52	12:10	15:18	17:04	21:47

Sights in **Agrigento:** Founded by Greeks in 581 B.C. See the extremely fine Greek ruins: 7 Doric temples, many aqueducts and cemeteries. The 14th century Cathedral. The 13th century churches: S. Nicola, Santa Maria dei Greci and S. Spirito. Baroque palaces. There is an especially good Archaeological Museum here.

Dep. Agrigento	5:30	7:13	8:27	12:56	14:38	17:08(5)
Arr. Palermo	8:07	9:21	10:43	15:32	17:50	19:15

(1)Change trains in Roccapalumba. (2)Runs daily, except Sundays and holidays. (3)Runs Sundays and holidays only. (4)Plus another departure from Palermo at 20:54.   (5)Plus other departures from Agrigento at 19:25(2) and 21:05(3).

Palermo - Caltanisetta   409

Dep. Palermo	6:30	8:42	12:06	15:38	16:53	19:35	20:54
Arr. Caltan. (Xirbi)	9:01	10:27	14:41	17:27	19:04	21:42	22:52

Sights in **Caltanisetta:** The Greek, Arabic and Norman ruins at the Pietrarossa Castle. The excellent archaeological collection in the Civic Museum. The Baroque Cathedral and Palazzo Moncada.

Dep. Caltan. (Xirbi)	6:24	9:03	10:29	14:19	17:04	18:40	21:48
Arr. Palermo	8:15	11:03	12:14	16:35	19:11	20:34	0:03

Palermo - Catania   409

Dep. Palermo	6:30	8:42	15:38	19:35	-0-
Arr. Catania	11:10	12:28	19:55	23:43	-0-

Sights in **Catania:** See notes about sightseeing in Catania earlier in this section, under "Naples-Messina-Catania".

Dep. Catania	6:40	8:10(1)	11:12(1)	16:30	19:18
Arr. Palermo	11:03	12:14	16:35	20:34	0:03

(1)Change trains in Caltanisetta Xirbi.

Palermo - Trapani   405

Dep. Palermo   5:20   7:01   9:07   10:25   12:20   13:45(1)
Arr. Trapani   2½ hours later
(1)Plus other departures at 14:00, 16:55, 18:48, 21:10 and 23:40

Sights in **Trapani:** A major Carthaginian and Roman naval base in the 3rd century B.C. See the outstanding 14th century Santuario dell'Annunziata, rebuilt in the 18th century. The 14th century Santa Agostino Church. The excellent sculpture and paintings in the Museo Nazionale Pepoli. The 17th century Cathedral. The Baroque Palazzo della Giudecca. The 15th century Santa Maria di Gesu Church.

Dep. Trapani   4:47   5:00   6:13   7:43   10:50   12:00(1)
Arr. Palermo   2½ hours later
(1)Plus other departures at 14:05, 15:05, 16:15, 17:38, 20:00 and 22:00.

Agrigento - Caltanisetta   409

Dep. Agrigento   4:16   8:10   14:02   -0-
Arr. Caltanisetta (Cent.)   5:54   10:16   16:20   -0-
Arr. Caltanisetta (Xirbi)   10 minutes after arriving Centrale station

Sights in **Caltanisetta:** See notes about sightseeing in Caltanisetta earlier in this section, under "Palermo-Caltanisetta".

Dep. Caltanisetta (Xirbi)   0:24   10:32   13:54   15:32
Dep. Caltanisetta (Cent.)   0:40   10:44   14:30   15:52
Arr. Agrigento   2:00   12:29   16:41   17:57

Catania - Caltanisetta   409

Dep. Catania   6:40   8:10   11:12   13:00   16:30(1)
Arr. Caltanisetta (Xirbi)   8:57   10:24   13:49   15:28   18:35

Sights in **Caltanisetta:** See notes about sightseeing in Caltanisetta earlier in this section, under "Palermo-Caltanisetta".

Dep. Caltanisetta (Xirbi)   6:02   9:05   10:30   13:26   16:40(2)
Arr. Catania   8:20   11:10   12:28   15:57   19:03

(1)Plus other departures from Catania at 19:18 and 22:12.   (2)Plus other departures from Caltanisetta at 17:31, 18:37 and 21:47.

THE MALTA CRUISE

Reggio di Calabria, Catania and Siracusa are gateways for the boat trip to Malta.

1427

Dep. Reggio	8:30(1)	Dep. Malta	8:45(2)
Dep. Catania	13:00	Arr. Siracusa	14:00
Dep. Siracusa	16:30	Arr. Catania	17:45
Arr. Malta	21:30	Arr. Reggio	22:00

(1)Runs Sunday, Tuesday and Friday. (2)Runs Monday, Wednesday and Saturday.

SCENIC RAIL TRIPS

Arona - Brig   251

There is beautiful lake and mountain scenery on this portion of the Milan-Lausanne route.

Dep. Milan (Cent.)	7:05	9:00(2)	10:05	11:05	12:35
Dep. Arona	7:59	-0-	10:54	12:01	13:44
Dep. Brig	9:46(1)	11:07	12:46(1)	13:46(1)	15:46(1)
Arr. Lausanne	11:26	12:32	14:26	15:26	17:26

(1)Light refreshments. (2)Supplement charged. Light refreshments. (3)TEE. Reservation required. Meal service.

Bologna - Florence   374+398

Excellent mountain scenery on this ride.

The train goes through the 11.5-mile long Apennine Tunnel, Italy's longest tunnel.

Complete schedules appear earlier in this section, under "Bologna-Florence" and "Florence-Bologna" one-day excursions.

Bolzano - Brennero

Exceptional mountain scenery on this portion of the route from Verona to Innsbruck, and on to Munich (see page 230).

Sights in **Bolzano:** Has been Italian since only 1919. The language spoken here (called "Bozen" during the nearly 6 centuries it was ruled by the Hapsburgs, from 1363 until World War I) is German.

Take at least one of the 3 funiculars that climb up the Alps. See the 16th to 18th century house on both Bindnergasse and Silbergasse. The vegetable and fruit market on Piazza delle Erbe. The 18th century Neptune fountain.

The exceptional carved altar depicting the Nativity, in the Holy Virgin Chapel of the Franciscan church. The frescoes at both the Cathedral and the Dominican church.

Stroll along the Talvera River to first the 13th century Maretsch Castle and then to Runkelstein Castle, whose lovely frescoes can be seen on guided tours Tuesday-Saturday, 10:00-12:00 and 15:00-18:00.

Buses are available to make short trips of less than an hour to many vineyard villages. Traminer and Gewurztztraminer are produced in this area.

There is train service to nearby Brixen, which has many interesting churches and lovely arcaded streets.

Verona - Innsbruck - Munich   381

Dep. Verona (P.N.)	8:23(1)	9:08	13:40	14:00(3)	15:00(4)
Dep. Bolzano	10:00	11:23(2)	15:35	15:54	16:54
Arr. Fortezza	10:42	12:16	16:38	17:07	18:04
Arr. Brennero	11:19	13:05	17:25	18:01	18:58
Arr. Innsbruck	12:05	13:59	18:18	19:00	19:52
Arr. Munich	13:54	16:25	-0-	21:26	22:10

(1)TEE. Reservation required. Meal service. (2)Light refreshments. (3)Operates late May to late September. Light refreshments. (4)Meal service.

Fortezza - Dobbiaco

Very good mountain scenery on this spur off the Bolzano-Brennero route, appearing above. The following schedule shows how the Verona-Innsbruck-Munich trip can accommodate this en route detour.

381			383		
Dep. Verona (P.N.)	9:08		Dep. Dobbiaco	14:36	18:30
Arr. Fortezza	12:16		Arr. Fortezza	15:50	19:55
Change trains.			Change trains.		
383			381		
Dep. Fortezza	12:44		Dep. Fortezza	17:09(1)	21:38(1)
Arr. Dobbiaco	14:06		Arr. Innsbruck	19:00	23:27
			Arr. Munich	21:26	1:37(2)

(1)Operates late May to late September. (2)Arrives at Munich's Ost railstation.

Torino - Cuneo - Breil - Nice   370

There is spectacular scenery on the 74-mile-long Cuneo-Nice rail route through the Roya Valley and the Alps, a service that first became operational in 1928. Severe damage during World War II caused it to be closed in 1940, and it was not re-opened until the Winter of 1979.

An outstanding feat of engineering, this line is a succession of very high viaducts, bridges and 60 tunnels that span 27 miles of this route, interspersed with sections that look down into deep valleys. This route has attracted many tourists.

Dep. Torino (P.N.)	8:35(1)	8:55(2)	14:00
Arr. Fossano	9:19(1)	10:00(2)	14:49
Change trains.			
Dep. Fossano	9:21(1)	10:02(2)	14:51
Arr. Cuneo	9:38(1)	10:20	15:09
Change trains.			
Dep. Cuneo	9:41(1)	10:28	16:16(1)
Arr. Breil	11:02	12:00	18:06(1)
Change trains.			
Dep. Breil	11:12	12:10	18:14(1)
Arr. Nice	12:17	13:43	19:27

(1)Direct train to Nice. No train changes en route. (2)Direct train to Cuneo. No train change in Fossano.

The magnificent Cuneo-Breil scenery can also be seen on an easy one-day roundtrip from Torino.

Torino - Cuneo - Torino 370

Dep. Torino			Dep. Breil	12:12(2)	16:49(2)
(P.N.)	8:35	12:26(1)	Arr. Torino		
Arr. Breil	11:02	15:03	(P.N.)	15:05	19:50

(1)Departs from Torino's Porta Susa railstation. (2)Change trains in Cuneo.

Another route for viewing the breathtaking Cuneo-Breil scenery is a one-day roundtrip from Genoa.

Genoa - Torino - Cuneo - Ventimiglia - Genoa and v.v.

355		356	
Dep. Genoa (P.P.)	9:55	Dep. Genoa (P.P.)	8:45
Arr. Torino (P.N.)	12:00	Arr. Ventimiglia	12:05
Change trains.		Change trains.	
370		370	
Dep. Torino (P.N.)	12:40(1)	Dep. Ventimiglia	12:37
Arr. Cuneo	13:53(1)	Dep. Cuneo	14:53
Dep. Ventimiglia	16:10	Arr. Torino (P.S.)	15:58
Change trains.		Change trains **and stations.**	
356		355	
Dep. Ventimiglia	17:41(2)	Dep. Torino (P.N.)	16:40(3)
Arr. Genoa (P.P.)	20:38	Arr. Genoa (P.P.)	18:29

(1)Change trains in Cuneo. (2)Light refreshments. (3)Reservation required in first-class. Supplement charged.

Sights in **Cuneo:** The 10th century Cathedral. The 13th century Church of San Francesco. The Marvelous viaduct over the Stura di Demonte. The Civic Museum in the 18th century Palazzo Audiffredi. The 18th century Town Hall.

Brindisi - Taranto - Reggio

Splendid coastline scenery on this trip.

400		407	
Dep. Brindisi	8:49	Dep. Taranto	9:57(1)
Arr. Taranto	9:48	Arr. Reggio (Cent.)	16:08
Change trains.			

(1)Supplement charged.

Genoa - Pisa

There is exceptional mountain and Mediterranean coastline scenery on this ride. Complete schedules appear earlier in this section under the "Genoa-Pisa" one-day excursion.

Genoa - Nice - Cannes - Marseille   151 + 356

A close look at more than 100 miles of outstanding seashore resorts along the Mediterranean's Ligure coastline: the Savona and San Remo beaches (on the Italian Riviera) and the Monaco, Nice, Antibes, Cannes and St. Raphael beaches (on the French Riviera).

Dep. Genoa (P.P.)	8:23(1)	8:45	9:00(4)	13:24
Arr. Nice	11:18	13:36(2)	16:42	18:04(2)
Dep. Nice	11:22	13:57(3)	16:46	18:19
Arr. Cannes	11:44	14:21	17:27(2)	19:12
Dep. Cannes	11:46	14:24	18:11	19:16
Arr. Marseille (St. Ch.)	13:38	16:19	20:12	21:40

(1)Supplement charged. Meal service. (2)Change trains in Nice. (3)Light refreshments. (4)Operates early July to early September.

Milan - Bern   260

The Brig-Bern portion of this ride is one of the 5 most outstanding scenic rail trips in Europe, with a fabulous array of lakes, mountains and rivers. All of these trains have light refreshments.

Dep. Milan (Centrale)	7:05	9:00	10:05	11:05	12:35
Dep. Brig		9:54	11:12	12:54	13:54	15:54
Arr. Bern		11:34	12:43	14:34	15:34	17:34

Milan - Locarno

The great gorge, mountain and river scenery is on the portion of this route from Domodossola to Locarno by a narrow-gauge local train. This Centovalli (one hundred valley) ride is one of the 5 most outstanding scenic rail trips in Europe. Complete schedules appear earlier in this ection under the "Milan-Locarno" one-day excursion.

Milan - Genoa

Views of marble quarries, mountains, farms and the Mediterranean coast, all in 1½ hours. An easy one-day roundtrip. See schedules earlier in this section, under one-day excursions.

Milan - Zurich   277

This is one of the 5 most outstanding scenic rail trips in Europe. A feast of beautiful farms, lakes, mountains, rivers and vineyards. You go through the 9.3-mile long Gotthard Tunnel. Before it was opened to traffic in 1882, there was no direct rail route from Italy to eastern Switzerland through the Alps.

Prior to entering the Gotthard, the train goes through the beautiful Ticino Valley.

Immediately upon exiting the first of a series of 9 tunnels, you first see the small, white Wassen Church on your right, 170 feet below the track. The next time the church comes into view, after exiting tunnel #4, the church is to your left and nearly level with the track. Later, after exiting tunnel #6, you have a third view of the church, again to your left, this time nearly 230 feet above the track, but you will see it there only if you look far ahead and before being alongside the church. (The train is in the Kirchberg Tunnel when it is directly alongside the church.)

The turns inside 3 semi-circular tunnels in this area (Leggistein, Wattinger and Pfaffensprung) are engineered to well that there is no sensation of the curves that the train is making inside those tunnels.

Try this interesting experiment: make a pendulum of any object, holding the top of a weighted string, chain or handkerchief against the inner face of a train window (a left-hand window when inside Leggistein, and a right-hand window when inside Wattinger and Pfaffensprung). As the train goes around a curve, the weighted bottom will move away from the window.

The Mediterranean climate on the Italian end of the tunnel is usually much warmer than the Alpine temperature on the Swiss end. The train makes 3% gradients at 45-50 miles per hour.

Dep. Milan (Cent.)	7:10(1)	9:10(2)	11:10(2)	13:10(1+4)
Arr. Zurich	11:50	13:50	15:50	17:50

(1)Light refreshments. (2)Meal service. (3)TEE. Reservation required. Meal service. (4)Plus other departures from Milan at 15:10(2) and 16:50(3).

Milan - Sondrio - Tirano - St. Moritz - Chur - Zurich

This is an alternate route from Milan to Zurich. Between Milan and Tirano, you will see many rivers and lakes. The descent from St. Moritz to Chur is spectacular.

357

Dep. Milan (Cent.)	6:35(1)	9:15(3)	12:00(3)
Arr. Sondrio	9:32	-0-	-0-
Change trains.			
Dep. Sondrio	9:41(2)	-0-	-0-
Arr. Tirano	10:18	12:23	14:41
Change trains.			
304			
Dep. Tirano	10:30	12:35	14:55(4)
Arr. St. Moritz	13:03	15:03	17:11(4)
Change trains.			
269			
Dep. St. Moritz	14:08(5)	15:20	18:08(6)
Arr. Chur	16:13	18:33	20:13
Change trains.			
268			
Dep. Chur	16:24	19:16(6)	20:24(6)
Arr. Zurich	17:47	20:47	21:47

(1)Departs from Milan's Garibaldi railstation. (2)Runs daily, except Sunday and Monday. (3)Direct train to Tirano. No train change in Sondrio. (4)Direct train to Chur. No train change in St. Moritz. Light refreshments. (5)Operates mid-June to late September. (6)Light refreshments.

Naples - Brindisi   400

Very good mountain scenery on this route.

Dep. Naples (Cent.)	5:30(1)	8:50(2)	12:15	
Arr. Taranto	10:28	14:22	19:03	
Change trains.				
Dep. Taranto	10:41	15:48	19:36	
Arr. Brindisi	11:41	16:50	20:45	
	*	*	*	
Dep. Brindisi	4:56	6:56	11:00	14:24
Arr. Taranto	6:18	8:27	12:20	15:43
Change trains.				
Dep. Taranto	6:50(1)	9:37(3)	13:03	16:10(1)
Arr. Naples (Cent.)	11:50	18:18	19:50	20:53

(1)Reservation required. Supplement charged. (2)Change trains in Salerno. (3)Change trains in Potenza and Salerno.

Naples - Siracusa

Wonderful Mediterranean coastline scenery on this trip. See details earlier in this section, under "Train Rides To Southern Italy".

Naples - Sorrento 401

Excellent Mediterranean coastline scenery on this ride.

Dep. Naples (Circumvesuviana) and Naples (F.S.) at one or 2 times per hour from 4:53 until 22:54 for the 60 minute ride to Sorrento.

Dep. Sorrento at one or 2 times every hour from 4:23 to 22:29 for the ride back to Naples. (There are stops in both directions at Pompeii.) A travolator provides transportation between Naples' F.S. station and Naples' Centrale station.

Naples - Taranto

Very good mountain scenery on this route.

396			407		
Dep. Naples			Dep. Taranto	7:57	13:13
(P. Gar.)	7:10(1)	10:10(1)	Arr. Bari	9:29	14:32
Arr. Bari	11:12	14:25	Change trains.		
Change trains.			396		
407			Dep. Bari	11:52(2)	14:50(1)
Dep. Bari	12:12	15:26	Arr. Naples		
Arr. Taranto	14:04	16:41	(P. Gar.)	18:24	19:19

(1)Reservation required. Supplement charged. (2)Change trains in Foggia. (3)Arrives at Naples' Centrale railstation.

Pisa - Genoa

Exceptional mountain and Mediterranean coastline scenery. Schedules appear earlier in this section under the "Genoa-Pisa" one-day excursion.

Reggio Calabria - Taranto - Brindisi

Excellent coastline scenery on this ride, which allows a sightseeing stopover in Taranto.

407		400		
Dep. Reggio Cal. (Cent.)	6:28	Dep. Taranto	14:32	15:48(1)
Arr. Taranto	13:13	Arr. Brindisi	15:47	16:50

(1)Plus other departures from Taranto at 19:36, 21:27 and 23:58.

Sights in **Taranto:** See description earlier in this section, under "Reggio di Calabria-Pescara".

Rimini - Pescara - Brindisi 393

The excellent scenery on this route includes olive groves, vineyards and superb beaches on the Adriatic coastline. This can be broken into a 2-day trip by stopping in Pescara one night and then continuing on to Brindisi the next day.

Also, this trip can be extended by continuing on from Brindisi to Reggio, a ride that offers fine coastline scenery (see schedules later in this section under "Taranto-Reggio".

Dep. Rimini	6:42	9:57(1)	12:37(2)
Arr. Pescara (Cent.)	10:38	13:06	15:16
Dep. Pescara (Cent.)	10:48	13:10	15:19(2+4)
Arr. Brindisi	17:35	18:34	21:15

(1)Operates late June to mid-September. (2)TEE. Reservation required. Meal service until 19:25, then light refreshments. (3)Light refreshments. (4)Change trains in Bari at 19:25(3).

Rome - Pescara
Excellent mountain scenery on this trip. Complete schedules appear earlier in this section under the "Rome-Pescara" one-day excursion.

Torino - Paris   152 + 355
The Modane-Culoz portion of this trip offers outstanding lake and mountain scenery.

Dep. Torino (P.N.)	11:40	Dep. Culoz	16:12
Dep. Modane	14:02(1)	Arr. Paris (Lyon)	21:24

(1)Meal service starts at 15:39.

Udine - Trieste
This portion of the Venice-Trieste ride has excellent scenery of the Adriatic coastline. Have a seat on the right-hand side for best viewing. The schedules allow a sightseeing stopover in Udine.

389

Dep. Venice (S. L.)	6:54	9:48	11:32	13:05(1)	14:00	15:32
Arr. Udine	8:52	11:32	13:25	14:58	15:58	17:25

Change trains.

388

Dep. Udine	9:00	10:08	10:52(2)	13:18	15:32	18:44
Arr. Trieste	10:12	11:36	11:50	14:32	16:43	19:55

(1)Change trains in Venice's Mestre railstation. (2)Supplement charged. First-class only.

Udine - Villach   389
This portion of the Venice-Vienna trip offers fine mountain scenery.

Dep. Venice (S. Lucia)	13:05(1)
Dep. Udine	15:13(1)
Arr. Villach	17:34(1)
Arr. Vienna (Sudbf.)	22:25

(1)Meal service.

INTERNATIONAL ROUTES FROM ITALY

The primary Italian gateway for rail travel to Switzerland, western West Germany, Luxembourg, Belgium, Holland and northeastern France (Pairs) is Milan.

A secondary gateway for rail travel from Italy to Switzerland is from Torino, via Aosta, to either Brig or Geneva.

There is rail service to southern France (Nice, Marseille and Avignon), Paris, and to Spain from Genoa.

The gateways for travel to Austria, eastern West Germany and Denmark are Verona and Venice.

Venice is also the starting point for trips to Yugoslavia, Czechoslovakia, East Germany and the rest of Eastern Europe (Bulgaria, Greece, Romania, Hungary, Poland and Russia).

Milan - Zurich   277

Dep. Milan (Cent.)	1:30(1)	4:48(1+2+3)	7:10(4)	9:10(5+7)
Arr. Zurich	6:15	9:50	11:50	13:50

(1)Has couchettes. (2)Carries sleeping car. (3)Departs from Milan's Lambrate railstation. (4)Light refreshments. (5)Meal service. (6)TEE. Reservation required. Meal service. (7)Plus other departures from Milan at 11:10(5), 13:10(4), 15:10(5), 16:50(6) and 18:40(5).

Milan - Luzern - Basel   277

Dep. Milan (Cent.)	1:40(1)	7:10(2)	9:20(2+3)	11:20(2+3+6)
Arr. Luzern	6:29	11:37	13:37	15:37
Arr. Basel (S.B.B)	7:54	12:53	14:53	16:53

(1)Has couchettes. (2)Meal service. (3)Supplement charged. (4)Light refreshments. (5)Carries sleeping car. Also has couchettes. (6)Plus other departures from Milan at 15:10(2), 17:55(2), 18:05(4) and 22:52(5).

Torino - Aosta Gateways to Switzerland

(1) Via San Bernardo Tunnel

Torino - Aosta - Martigny - Brig or Lausanne
362

Dep. Torino (P.N.)	6:40	12:35
Arr. Aosta	8:51	14:40

Change to bus.
337

Dep. Aosta (P. Narbonne)	8:00
Arr. Martigny (CFF)	10:10

Change to train.
251

Dep. Martigny	12:45	19:21
Arr. Brig	13:47	20:17

OR

Dep. Martigny	13:08	18:36	20:08
Arr. Lausanne	14:01	19:26	21:04

(2) Via Mt. Blanc Tunnel

Torino - Aosta - Chamonix - Geneva
362

Dep. Torino (P.N.)	6:40	8:35	12:35
Arr. Aosta	8:51	11:25	14:41

Change to bus.
191

Dep. Aosta	N/A(1)	N/A(1)	N/A(1)
Arr. Chamonix	2½ hours later		

Change to train.
167

Dep. Chamonix	11:34	15:30	17:30
Arr. St. Gervais	12:10	16:06	18:06

Change trains (1)

Dep. St. Gervais	12:30	16:28	18:21
Arr. La-Roche-sur-Foron	13:19	17:12	19:17

Change trains (1)
158

Dep. La-Roche-sur-Foron	13:25	17:20	19:27
Arr. Annemasse	13:44	17:38	19:45

Change trains (1)

Dep. Annemasse	13:50	17:43	20:25
Arr. Geneva (Eaux-Vives)	8 minutes later		

(1)Two departures per day in Winter. Six departures per day in July and August.
(2)All of the Chamonix-Geneva train changes are cross-platform, each taking less than one minute.

ROUTES TO OTHER COUNTRIES

Genoa - Nice - Cannes - Marseille - Avignon - Lyon - Paris   151

Dep. Genoa (P.P.)	2:05(1)	8:23(2+3)	11:40(5+13)
Arr. Nice	8:31(1)	11:18	16:42(5)
Arr. Cannes	9:17(1)	11:44(2+3)	17:27
Change trains.			
Dep. Cannes	9:21(1)	11:46(2+3)	18:13(6)
Arr. Marseille (St. Ch.)	11:38(1)	13:38	20:12
Change trains.			
Dep. Marseille (St. Ch.)	11:47(1)	13:57(4)	20:27(6)
Arr. Avignon	12:53	14:56(4)	22:48
Arr. Lyon (Per.)	14:56	-0-	1:30
Arr. Dijon	16:41	-0-	3:30
Arr. Paris (Lyon)	19:10	19:39	6:36

(1)Has couchettes. Change trains in Ventimiglia at 7:50. Direct train Ventimiglia-Paris. Meal service Nice-Paris. (2)Direct train to Marseille. No train change in Cannes. (3)Supplement charged in Italy. Meal service. (4)TGV. Supplement charged on certain days. Meal service. (5)Operates early July to early September. (6)Operates all year. (7)Direct train to Paris. No train changes en route. (8)Light refreshments Nice-Marseille. (9)From Ventimiglia, carries sleeping car and also has couchettes. (10)Direct train to Dijon. No train changes en route. Terminates in Dijon. (11)Operates late May to late September. (12)Operates early July to late September. Terminates in Nice. (13)Plus other departures from Genoa at 13:24(7+8+9), 15:30(9+10), 16:17(7+9), 17:45(2), 18:40(11) and 22:12(12).

Genoa - Torino - Paris

	24	16
Dep. Genoa (P.P.)	21:25(1+2)	23:57(1+3)
Dep. Torino (P.N.)	23:52	1:53
Arr. Paris (Lyon)	8:57	10:06

(1)Carries sleeping car. Also has couchettes. (2)Meal service on Day 1. Light refreshments on Day 2.   (3)Meal service on Day 2 from 5:01 to 10:06.

Rome - Venice - Budapest - Kiev - Moscow   89+374+806

Dep. Rome (Ter.)	12:23(1)	Day 1
Dep. Venice (S. Lucia)	21:22(1)	Day 1
Arr. Budapest (Keleti)	14:35	Day 2
Dep. Budapest (Keleti)	20:15(2)	Day 2
Arr. Kiev	19:47(2)	Day 3
Arr. Moscow (Kiev)	7:38	Day 4

(1)Carries sleeping car daily except Sat. from Rome and Venice. There is no service in Winter from Rome or Venice. Train also has couchettes Rome-Budapest early June to late September on Mon., Thurs. and Sat. Light refreshments Rome-Venice. (2)Carries sleeping car daily Budapest-Moscow. Meal service from 5:30 (Cop) on Day 3 to Moscow arrival Day 4.

Verona - Innsbruck - Munich 381

Dep. Verona (P.N.)	3:35(1)	3:55	5:34	8:23(2+8)
Arr. Innsbruck	8:41	10:13	11:02	12:05
Arr. Munich (Hbf.)	11:16	-0-	13:50	13:54

(1)Operates mid-June to mid-September. (2)TEE. Reservation required. Meal service. (3)Light refreshments. (4)Terminates in Innsbruck. (5)Meal service. (6)Arrives at Munich's Ost railstation. (7)Carries sleeping car. Also has couchettes. (8)Plus other departures from Verona at 9:08(3), 13:40(4), 14:00(3), 15:00(5), 18:30(3+6) and 0:02(7).

Venice - Belgrade (Beograd) 390

	35	40
Dep. Venice (S. Lucia)	7:04(1)	16:55(2)
Arr. Belgrade	23:10	8:38

(1)Reservation required. Meal service starts at 14:25.   (2)Reservation required. Carries sleeping car. Also has couchettes.

Venice - Salzburg

389

Dep. Venice (S. Lucia)	11:32	13:05	20:14
Arr. Villach	16:54	17:34	1:05

Change trains.

759

Dep. Villach	17:08(1)	18:50	2:40
Arr. Salzburg	20:18	23:30	5:45

(1)Light refreshments.

Venice - Vienna (Wien) 389

Dep. Venice (S. Lucia)	13:05(1)	20:14(2)	23:20(2)
Arr. Vienna (Sudbf.)	22;25	6:52	9:10

(1)Light refreshments. (2)Carries sleeping car. Also has couchettes.

SCANDINAVIA (Denmark, Finland, Norway, Sweden)

SCANDINAVIAN RAIL PASS
Unlimited train travel throughout Denmark, Finland, Norway and Sweden. Can be purchased only at railstations in Scandinavia. The 1984 prices are quoted in Swedish krone. First-class: 1,770SK for 21 days. Second-class: 1,180SK for 21 days. Half-price for children 4-12 years old.

SUMMER TIME
Denmark, Finland, Norway and Sweden change to Summer Time on the last Sunday of March and convert back to Standard Time on the last Sunday of September. Finland is one hour ahead of Denmark, Norway and Sweden all year.

MIDNIGHT SUN CALENDAR
An average June day has over 17 hours of daylight in Copenhagen and almost 19 in Helsinki, Oslo and Stockholm. Above the Arctic Circle, the whole disc of the sun remains visible throughout the night for periods of 30 to 120 days, depending how far north a city is. Some of the best vantage points are:

NORWAY
Green Harbor	April 21-Aug. 23
North Cape	May 14-July 30
Hammerfest	May 17-July 28
Tromso	May 21-July 23
Harstad	May 26-July 19
Narvik	May 26-July 19
Svolvaer	May 26-July 19
Bodo	June 5-July 9
Trondheim	June 8-July 6
Andalsnes	June 5-July 3

SWEDEN
Bjorkliden	May 26-July 19
Abisko	May 31-July 14
Kiruna	May 31-July 14
Gallivare	June 2-July 12
Boden	June 4-July 10

FINLAND
Utsjoki	May 22-July 24
Kilpisjarvi	May 27-July 18
Pallastunturi	May 30-July 15

Gallivare, Kiruna and Abisko are on the rail route from Boden to Narvik. Andalsnes, Trondheim and Bodo can be reached by train service from Oslo. Trondheim also can be reached by rail from Stockholm.

NORWAY
SWEDEN
DENMARK

DENMARK

Denmark's 2 categories of fast trains are "IC" (Intercity Trains) and "L" (Lightning Trains). Reservations are required for "IC" and "L" trains that journey via the Great Belt ferries that cross from Nyborg to Korsor and vice versa. This is the route connecting the island where Copenhagen is located with the rest of Denmark, to Odense and Frederikshavn for ferry service to southern Norway, and to Esbjerg for ferry service to England.

The signs you will see at railstations in Denmark are:

AFGANG	DEPARTURE
ANKOMST	ARRIVAL
BANEGARDEN	RAILSTATION
BILLETKONTORET	TICKET OFFICE
DAMER	WOMEN
GARDROBEN	CHECKROOM
HERRER	MEN
INDANG	ENTRANCE
KOREPLAN	TIMETABLE
LYNTOG	FAST INTERCITY TRAIN
OPLYSNING	INFORMATION
PLADSBESTILLINGEN	RESERVATIONS
PERRON	TRACK
RYGEKUPE	SMOKING COMPARTMENT
SOVEVOGN	SLEEPING CAR
SPISEVOGN	RESTAURANT CAR
TIL PERRONERNE	TO THE PLATFORMS
TOG AFGAR	DEPARTURE TIMETABLE
TOG ANKOMMER	ARRIVAL TIMETABLE
UDANG	EXIT

DANISH HOLIDAYS

A list of holidays is helpful because some trains will be noted later in this section as *not* running on holidays. Also, those trains which operate on holidays are filled, and it is necessary to make reservations for them long in advance.

January 1	New Year's Day	June 5	Constitution Day
	Maundy Thursday		(from Noon)
	Good Friday		Whit Sunday
	Easter		Whit Monday
	Easter Monday		December 24
			(From Noon)
	Prayer Day	December 25	Christmas Day
	(4th Fri. after Easter)	December 26	Boxing Day
	Ascension Day		

EURAILPASS BONUSES IN DENMARK

These ferry crossings: Aarhus-Kalundborg, Knudshoved-Halskov, Nyborg-Korsor, Fynshav-Bojden, Rodby Faerge-Puttgarden, Helsingor-Helsingborg and Frederikshavn-Goteborg.

Reduction of 20% on 4 boat trips: (1) Esbjerg-Harwich, (2) Esbjerg-Newcastle, (3) Esbjerg-Faeroe Islands, and (4) Copenhagen-Oslo.

DENMARK'S TRAIN PASSES

All of Denmark's passes must be purchased in Denmark.

One-Month Ticket   Unlimited travel on trains and ferries for one month. The 1984 prices are: first-class 1,600DK, second-class 1,260DK. Half-price for children 4-11 years old.

Landsrabatkort (National Rebate Card)   Gives 50% discount on train and ferry tickets. The 1984 prices are: 1,400DK for one year, 920DK for half-year. Half-price for children 4-11.

Senior Ticket   Roundtrip tickets at 50% discount for people over 65 after obtaining a free ID card, available at all main railstations. Not valid Friday 14:00-Saturday 14:00 or Sunday 14:00-24:00.

Group Ticket   Three persons or more (need *not* be related) obtain 20%-50% discount, depending on size of the group.

ONE-DAY EXCURSIONS AND CITY-SIGHTSEEING

Here are 13 one-day rail trips that can be made comfortably from Copenhagen, returning there in most cases before dinnertime. Notes are provided on what to see at each destination.

Copenhagen

City tours start from Town Hall Square, in front of the Palace Hotel. To get to the Mermaid or Amalienborg Castle on your own, take bus #1 or #6. For brewery visits, take bus #6 to Carlsberg, or take bus #1 to Tuborg.

Also see Thorvaldsen Museum, with his sculptures and tomb. Tivoli Gardens. Christiansborg Palace, where the Danish Parliament meets. The Danish Resistance Museum. The Zoo. Windowshop in the walking area, Stroget.

The vast collection in the National Museum reflecting Danish life from the Ice Age to today, open daily except Monday. From mid-June to mid-September: 10:00-16:00. From mid-September to mid-June: 11:00-15:00 Tuesday-Friday and 12:00-16:00 on Saturday and Sunday.

An exhibit of superb French Impressionists and also Egyptian, Greek, Roman and French sculptures at Glyptotek (behind Tivoli Gardens), open daily except Monday. From May through September: 10:00-16:00. From October through April: 12:00-15:00 (10:00-16:00 on Sunday).

The Toy Museum is open all year Wednesday-Sunday 10:00-16:00. There is a good collection of weapons and uniforms in the Royal Arsenal. From May through September: 13:00-16:00 on weekdays, 10:00-16:00 on Sunday. From October through April: 13:00-15:00 on weekdays, 11:00-16:00 on Sunday.

The City Museum, at 59 Vesterbrogade. The view from the top of Town Halls' 350-foot-high tower. Borsen, the oldest stock exchange in the world, still functioning.

The gilded spiral staircase of the Old Saviour's Church (Vor Frelsers Kirke), and the view at the top, from its tower. Regensen, a residential university since 1623. Thorvaldsen's marble statues of Christ and the Apostles in Our Lady's Church (Vor Frue Kirke).

The picturesque buildings along Nyhavn Canal. The line of foreign naval ships along Langelinie Promenade.

The crown jewels and other possessions of Danish monarchs in the museum at Rosenborg Palace, particularly the pearl-encrusted saddle of Christian IV. Nearby, the 25-acre Botanical Garden and the National Art Gallery. The Frilandsmuseet open-air museum of Danish houses and farms. The collection of modern art at the Louisiana Museum, 20 minutes away, in nearby Humlebaek, open daily 10:00-17:00.

In the following timetables, where a city has more than one railstation we have designated the particular station after the name of the city (in parentheses).

Copenhagen - Alborg - Copenhagen   452
These trains have light refreshments unless designated otherwise.
Dep. Copenhagen   7:10(1)   9:00(2)
Arr. Alborg   12:58   15:43

Sights in **Alborg**: This thousand-year old town is the most important in the north Jutland area. You will find many medieval houses, down the lanes that wind off the modern boulevards. The early 15th century Monastery of the Holy Ghost. The early 16th century Aalborghus Castle. The outstanding Jens Bang House. The 12th century St. Botolph Cathedral.

Dep. Alborg   13:30(2)   14:30(3)   15:30(2)   16:10(2+4+5)
Arr. Copenhagen   20:15   21:17   22:15   21:56

(1)Runs daily, except Sundays and holidays. All seats are reservable. (2)Reservation required. (3)Does *not* have light refreshments. (4)Runs daily, except Saturday. (5)Plus another departure from Alborg at 17:30(2).

Copenhagen - Aarhus - Copenhagen

There are 2 ways to make this trip. The first is by train between Copenhagen and Kalundborg, then by boat between Kalundborg and Aarhus. The boat has a smorgasbord cafeteria, and the scenery on the cruise is good.

The second way to Aarhus, entirely by train, is via Fredericia.

It makes an interesting day to go to Aarhus by the combination of train and boat via Kalundborg and return to Copenhagen by train via Fredericia.

Boat - via Kalundborg   460

Dep. Copenhagen (H.)	7:30(1)	9:50
Arr. Kalundborg	8:52	11:22
Change to boat.		
Dep. Kalundborg	9:00	11:35
Arr. Aarhus (Stn.)	12:23	14:58
	*	* *
Dep. Aarhus (Stn.)	15:13	19:47(2)
Arr. Kalundborg	18:20	23:15
Change to train.		
Dep. Kalundborg	18:28	23:21
Arr. Copenhagen (H.)	19:49	0:42

(1)Mid-June to late August: runs daily. Late August to mid-June: runs daily, except Sundays and holidays. (2)Mid-June to late August: runs daily. Late August to mid-June: runs daily, except Saturday.

Sights in **Aarhus:** Board the train at the pier and take it to Aarhus' railstation. See the completely furnished medieval houses at the open-air museum (Den Gamle By) in the Botanical Gardens. The 12th century Cathedral. The ancient University. Take bus #6 from the railstation to see the great collection of primitive relics in the Prehistoric Museum at Moesgaard, open daily in Summer 10:00-17:00. It is closed Mondays in Winter.

Train - via Fredericia   452

All of these trains require reservation (unless otherwise designated) and have light refreshments.

Dep. Copenhagen (H.)	6:00	7:00	7:10(1)	9:00
Arr. Aarhus	10:57	11:57	11:21	13:57
	*	*	*	
Dep. Aarhus	13:15	15:15	16:15	17:15(4)
Arr. Copenhagen (H.)	18:13	20:03	21:13	22:13

(1)Runs daily, except Sundays and holidays. (2)Runs daily, except Saturday. (3)Runs Sundays and holidays only. (4)Plus other departures from Aarhus at 17:45(2), 19:15 and 20:15(3).

Copenhagen - Alborg - Aarhus - Copenhagen   452

It is possible to visit both Alborg and Aarhus in one day by using the following schedule.

All of these trains require reservation (unless otherwise designated) and have light refreshments.

Dep. Copenhagen (H.)	6:00	
Arr. Aarhus	10:57	
Sightsee in Aarhus.		
Dep. Aarhus	13:05	14:05
Arr. Alborg	14:43	15:43
Sightsee in Alborg.		
Dep. Alborg	16:10(1)	17:30
Arr. Copenhagen (H.)	21:57	0:13

(1)Runs daily, except Saturday.

Copenhagen - Helsingborg - Copenhagen

	465	465	466	465
Dep. Copenhagen (H.)	7:34	8:19(1)	9:34	10:34(2+7)
Arr. Helsingborg	8:50	9:35	10:50	11:50

Sights in **Helsingborg:** Stained-glass windows, depicting the city's 900 years of history, in the Radhuset (Town Hall). Karnan, the 14th century fort with walls up to 15 feet thick, one of the best preserved Medieval buildings in Scandinavia. To reach it, take the elevator at the left of The Terrace, from the Main Square.

See the view of the Sound from Rosengarden, and the beautiful roses there. The Municipal Museum. The magnificent pulpit in the 15th century Mariakyrkan (Church of St. Mary). The handsome Concert Hall in Stadsbiblioteket (Town Library). The bronze statue in Hamntoget (Harbor Square).

	466	465	465	466
Dep. Helsingborg	13:35(3)	14:20(4)	16:05(4)	17:35(3+8)
Arr. Copenhagen (H.)	14:51	15:35	17:21	18:51

(1)Operates late May to late September. (2)Departs at 10:19 late September to late May. (3)Light refreshments. (4)Reservation required. (5)Departs 12:19 late September to late May. (6)Meal service. (7)Plus other departures from Copenhagen at (#466)11:49, (#466)12:34(3+4+5) and (#465)12:53.   (8)Plus other departures from Helsingborg at (#465)18:35(4+6), (#466)19:35(3), (#465)20:35(1+6), (#466)21:35(3) and (#465)22:05(4).

Copenhagen - Helsingor - Copenhagen   455

Dep. Copenhagen (Central)	Frequent times from 5:23 to 0:38
Arr. Helsingor	40-50 minutes later

Sights in **Helsingor:** Kronborg Castle (of Shakespeare's Hamlet). The stained-glass, depicting the town's history, in the Council Chamber of the Radhus (Town Hall). If time allows you to visit only Helsingor or Hillerod (described in the next listing), do *not* choose Helsingor. Fredericksborg Castle at Hillerod is by far the more interesting of the 2.

Dep. Helsingor   Frequent times from 5:04 to 0:02
Arr. Copenhagen (Central)   40-50 minutes later

Copenhagen - Hillerod - Copenhagen

This is an excellent one-day trip by local commuter train on which Eurailpass is valid. We recommend leaving Copenhagen (Central) at 8:42 or 9:42 for the 40-minute ride. It is a 25-minute walk from the Hillerod railstaion, through the village, past the lake and market square, to Fredericksborg Castle and its National Historic Museum of both worldwide art and Danish history. You could spend many days enjoying its contents. A full morning will fly by.

The Castle is open 10:00-17:00 May through September, 10:00-16:00 in October, and 11:00-16:00 November through March.

Market days in Hillerod are Monday, Thursday and Saturday (9:00-13:00).

You can eat lunch at the Castle's restaurant or in the village on your walk back to the railstation, for departures to Copenhagen every hour at 17 minutes past the hour.

If you depart Hillerod at 13:17 or 14:17, there is time to stop in Humlebaek to see the Louisiana Museum of Modern Art on the return trip to Copenhagen.

Copenhagen - Malmo - Copenhagen   1203b

This ferry-boat ride to Sweden's West Coast is popular and requires a small additional charge if you are using a Eurailpass. Depart Copenhagen (Havnegade) and Malmo hourly from 7:00 to 24:00, and Malmo from 8:00 to 23:45.

Sights in **Malmo:** The Art, Archaeology, Military, Technical and Carriage Museums, all in the Castle. Town Hall. St. Peter's Church. The Sailor's House (3 Fiskehamnsgatan). The 17th and 18th century houses on Lilla Torg (Small Square).

Copenhagen - Odense - Copenhagen   453

En route, the train drives onto a ferry for the 65-minute boat ride between Korsor and Nyborg. Passengers can leave the train and stroll on the boat for fine views of the shoreline.

All of these trains require reservation and have light refreshments.

Dep. Copenhagen (H.)   Every hour, on the hour, 6:00-21:00(1)
Arr. Odense   3 hours later

Sights in **Odense:** The home of Hans Christian Andersen, now a museum, on Hans Jensenstraede. You can visit another Andersen Museum at Munkemollestraede 3. Also see the National Railway Museum in the Dannebrogsgade. The 13th century Cathedral of St. Knud.

Dep. Odense   16 minutes after each hour, 7:16-21:16(1+2)
Arr. Copenhagen (H.)   3 hours later

(1)Additional trains run during almost every hour daily except Sundays and holidays, *not* requiring reservation and *not* having light refreshments. (2)Plus an additional departure from Odense on Sunday at 22:16

Copenhagen - Roskilde - Copenhagen

	460	456	460	4 5-6	456
Dep. Copenhagen (H.)	7:30(1)	9:12(2)	9:50	11:12(2)	12:12(6)
Arr. Roskilde	20minutes later				

Sights in **Roskilde:** The 40 tombs of Denmark's kings and queens, a 500-year old clock, and the post on which such royalty as Peter the Great and the 20th century Duke of Windsor marked their heights (some of them with humorous exaggeration), all in the red brick Cathedral. Open for tours weekdays April-September 9:00-17:45 and October-March 10:00-15:45. Also on Sundays and holidays 12:30-17:45 June-August and 12:30-15:45 September-May.

Also see the exhibits in the Viking Ship Museum. Open 9:00-18:00 June-August, 9:00-17:00 September and October, 10:00-16:00 November-March, and 9:00-17:00 April and May.

	456	456	460	4 5 6	456
Dep. Roskilde	10:38	11:38(2)	12:07	12:38(4)	14:38(7)
Arr. Copenhagen (H.)	20 minutes later				

(1)Mid-June to late August: runs daily. Late August to mid-June: runs daily except Sundays and holidays. (2)Runs daily, except Sundays and holidays. (3)Late May to late August: runs daily. Late August to late May: runs daily, except Saturday. (4)Runs Sundays and holidays only. (5)Runs daily, except Saturday. (6)Plus other departures from Copenhagen at (#460)14:12 and (#460)14:52(3). (7)Plus other departures from Roskilde at (#460)17:07(3), (#456)17:38(5), (#456)18:38, (#460)19:27, (#456)20:38, (#456)21:38(5) and (#456)23:38

Copenhagen - Vordingborg - Copenhagen 456

Dep. Copenhagen (H.)	6:43(1)	9:10(2)	11:10(2)	12:10	14:10
Arr. Vordingborg	8:06	10:39	12:39	13:39	15:39

Sights in **Vordingborg:** An interesting old town.

Dep. Vordingborg	10:32(2)	11:37(3)	13:32	16:32(4)	17:32(5)
Arr. Copenhagen (H.)	11:59	12:59	14:59	17:59	18:59

(1)Light refreshments. (2)Runs daily, except Sundays and holidays. (3)Runs Sundays and holidays only. (4)Runs daily, except Saturday. (5)Plus other departures from Vordingborg at 19:32, 20:32(4) and 22:32.

SCENIC RAIL TRIPS

Odense - Fredericia - Odense 453

There is fine coastline scenery on this easy one-day roundtrip. This can also be seen as a portion of the Copenhagen-Frederickshavn route.

All of these trains require reservation.

Dep. Odense	56 minutes after each hour, from 7:56 to 23:56
Arr. Fredericia	39 minutes later

*   *   *

Dep. Fredericia	35 minutes after each hour, from 7:35 to 20:35
Arr. Odense	39 minutes later

INTERNATIONAL ROUTES FROM DENMARK

Copenhagen is the gateway for travel from Denmark, Norway and Sweden to Western Europe, starting with its connections to Berlin and Hamburg, and then on from those cities to the rest of Western Europe.

Copenhagen - Berlin 769

Dep. Copenhagen (H.)	6:43(1+2)	11:12(2+3)	22:12(5)
Arr. Berlin (Ost.)	16:12	21:59(4)	7:42
Arr. Berlin (Fried.)	16:25	-0-	8:18
Dep. Berlin (Zoo)	16:53	-0-	8:46

(1)Light refreshments available on ship. (2)Runs Monday-Friday. (3)Second-class only. Meal service. (4)Arrives at Berlin's Lichtenberg railstation. (5)Carries sleeping car.

Copenhagen - Hamburg 648

Light refreshments are available on most of the boats.

Dep. Copenhagen (H.)	7:20	9:25(1)	10:10(2)	13:20(8)
Arr. Hamburg (Hbf.)	12:29	15:01	15:07	18:28
Arr. Hamburg (Altona)	12:46	-0-	-0-	-0-

(1)Operates late May to late September. (2)Supplement charged. (3)Operates mid-June to early September. (4)Light refreshments. (5)Operates late June to early September. (6)Carries sleeping car. Also has couchettes. (7)Has couchettes. (8)Plus other departures from Copenhagen at 15:10(3), 16:40(4), 17:45, 19:48(5), 21:10(6), 22:10(7) and 23:45(7).

Copenhagen - Oslo 466

Dep. Copenhagen (H.)	1:05(1)	9:34(2)	12:34(2+3)	20:34(4+5+6)
Arr. Oslo (Cent.)	13:19	19:30	22:05	6:46

(1)Operates late May to late September. Runs daily, except Sundays and holidays. Has couchettes. (2)Light refreshments. (3)Reservation required. (4)Operates late June to early September. (5)Carries sleeping car. Also has couchettes.(6)Plus another departures from Copenhagen at 23:00(5).

Copenhagen - Stockholm 465

Dep. Copenhagen (H.)	7:34(1)	8:19(1+2)	10:34(3+4+9)
Arr. Stockholm (Cent.)	16:25	16:47	18:47

(1)Meal service. (2)Operates late June to early September. (3)Departs 10:19 late September to late May. (4)Light refreshments all year. Meal service late June to early September. (5)Meal service late May to late September. (6)Late May to late September: runs daily. Late September to late May: runs daily, except Saturday. Departs at 21:19.   (7)Carries sleeping car. Also has couchettes. (8)Operates late May to late September. (9)Plus other departures from Copenhagen at 12:53(5), 15:19(1), 21:34(6+7), 23:34(7) and 1:05(7+8).

FINLAND

Travel on Finnish trains titled "Rap" requires payment of a small supplement. The tracks in Finland are constructed with the wide Russian gauge of 5′0″. This makes for spacious cars. The rail service extends as far north as Lapland. Service is maintained during severe Winter weather.

All major Finnish name express trains are equipped with radiotelephones for passengers to use. Long-distance express trains, stopping only at main railstations, are called Erikoispikajuna and Pikajuna. Both charge supplemental fares. Local trains, stopping at all stations, are called Henkilojuna. Finland's national timetable is called Suomen Kulkuneuvot.

The signs you will see at railstations in Finland are:

AIKATAULUT	TIMETABLE
LAHTO	DEPARTURE
LAITURILTA	TRACK
LIPPULUUKKU	TICKET OFFICE
MAKUUVAUNU	SLEEPING CAR
MATKALIPPUJEN	RESERVATIONS
MIEHILLE	MEN
NAISILLE	WOMEN
NEUVONTATOIMIST	INFORMATION
ODOTUSSALI	CHECKROOM
RAUTATIEASEMALLE	RAILSTATION
RAVINTOLAVAUNU	RESTAURANT CAR
SAAPUMINEN	ARRIVAL
SISAAN	ENTRANCE
TUPAKOITSEVILLE	SMOKING COMPARTMENT
ULOS	EXIT

FINLAND'S TRAIN PASSES

Finnrailpass   Unlimited rail travel. Can be purchased at railstations in Finland. The sales agent in North America is Holiday Tours of America (1290 Ave. of the Americas, New York, N.Y. 10019). The 1984 first-class prices are $90(U.S.) for 8 days, $132 for 15 days, $177 for 22 days. Second-class: $60 for 8 days, $88 for 15 days, $118 for 22 days.

Senior Citizens Rail Card   Available at railstations. Buyer must pay about $1.50(U.S.) and provide photo. Allows persons over 65 to purchase up to 6 tickets for trips of at least 48 miles at half-fare. *Not* valid on holidays.

Group Reduction   Discounts of 20%-30% for groups of 3 or more people. Available only at Finnish railstations.

Return Ticket   Allows 10%-15% discount. For trips over 45 miles, allows up to one month to make the return trip.

FINLAND

FINNISH HOLIDAYS

A list of holidays is helpful because some trains will be noted later in this section as *not* running on holidays. Also, those trains which operate on holidays are filled, and it is necessary to make reservations for them long in advance.

January 1	New Year's Day		Midsummer's Day
	Epiphany		(Saturday nearest
	Good Friday		to June 24)
	Easter	June 21	Finnish Flag Day
	Easter Monday		All Saint's Day
	Ascension Day	December 6	Independence Day
May 1	Labor Day	December 25	Christmas Day
		December 26	Boxing Day

EURAILPASS BONUSES IN FINLAND

These cruises: Helsinki-Stockholm, Turku-Stockholm, and Turku-Aland Islands-Stockholm

ONE-DAY EXCURSIONS AND CITY-SIGHTSEEING

Here are 6 one-day rail trips that can be made comfortably from Helsinki, returning there in most cases before dinnertime. Notes are provided on what to see at each destination. The number after the name of each route is the Cook's timetable.

Helsinki

Helsinki's single most inspiring sight is Temppeliaukio Church, knwon since its 1969 dedication as the "Rock Church". This fantastic structure was quarried on its site, out of the bedrock in the middle of one of the oldest residential districts of Helsinki. Because the area occupied by worshipers is below the street level, all that can be seen as you walk toward the church is a low rock wall and the massive (70-foot diameter) copper dome.

Also see the large tubular steel sculpture, symbolizing music, in Sibelius Park. Tapiola, the model "new town". Finlandia Hall. The National Museum. The floral cemetery. The onion towers on the Greek Orthodox Uspenski Cathedral.

You should visit Market Square, before Noon, to see the flowers, fish and mountains of berries. The Town Hall. The Empress Stone obelisk. (Ferries from a pier near the obelisk go every hour to the island Suomenlinna Fortress.) See the impressive columns of Parliament House. The University Library and the Cathedral, in Senate Square.

The paintings and sculptures in the National Art Gallery. The National Theater. The Elaintarhantie shopping complex, opposite the railstation. The Botanical Gardens. The Linnanmaki amusement center.

The collection of Finnish wood houses at the open-air Museum of Seurasaari. The Ateneum Art Gallery. The Gallen-Kallela Museum. The art and furniture at the Helsinki Municipal Museum. Old-fashioned and modern farm tools and implements in the Agricultural Museum. The Military Museum. Take the #6 tram to Arabia and see the original site of Helsinki, Old Town.

Helsinki - Hameenlinna - Helsinki   492

Dep. Helsinki	6:05	10:00(1)	14:00(1)
Arr. Hameenlinna	7:26	11:14	15:13

Sights in **Hameenlinna:** The medieval castle. Ahvenisto Tower. The Art Museum. The City Museum.

Dep. Hameenlinna	14:15(1)	19:45(1)	22:18(1)
Arr. Helsinki	15:30	21:00	23:30

Helsinki - Hanko - Helsinki   493

A beautiful ride through woods and along lakes,

Dep. Helsinki	7:32(1)	9:10(2)	12:40(1)
Arr. Karjaa	8:40	10:18	13:50

Change to local train.
000

Dep. Karjaa	8:55	10:30	14:00
Arr. Hanko	9:50	11:25	14:55

Sights in **Hanko:** Take a 2-hour cruise, leaving from the eastern harbor, operating June through September. There is good fishing here. See the statue dedicated to the many Finns who disembarked from here to migrate to the United States between 1880 and 1930. Dance or try your luck at the Casino.

Dep. Hanko	15:50	17:50	21:15
Arr. Karjaa	16:45	18:45	22:10

Change to standard train.

Dep. Karjaa	17:20(2)	19:10(1+3)	22:20(1)
Arr. Helsinki	18:27	20:22	23:32

(1)Meal service. (2)Light refreshments. (3)Runs daily, except Saturday.

Helsinki - Lahti - Helsinki   498

Dep. Helsinki	7:05(1)	9:25(2)	10:30(3)	13:10(2)	
Arr. Lahti	8:36	10:52	11:57	14:37	

Sights in **Lahti:** The Art Gallery. The Ethnographic Museum. The Radio Museum. See the view from the top of the ski-jump, elevators operating June-September 10:00-19:30.

Dep. Lahti	11:27(2)	12:04(2+4)	15:03(2)	18:00(3)	18:47(2+6)
Arr. Helsinki	12:55	13:30	16:30	19:30	20:30

(1)Early June to late August: runs daily. Late August to early June: runs daily, except Sundays and holidays. (2)Meal service. (3)Light refreshments. (4)Reservation required. Supplement charged. (5)Early June to late August: runs daily. Late August to early June: runs daily, except Saturday. (6)Plus other departures from Lahti at 21:03(2+4) and 21:17(2+5).

Helsinki - Riihimaki - Helsinki

	497	498	497	498	497	498
Dep. Helsinki	8:00	9:25	10:00	10:30	11:00	13:10
Arr. Riihimaki	30minutes later					

Sights in **Riihimaki:** The wood-working mills of H. G. Paloheimo. The glass factories of Riihimaen Lasi Oy. The Museum Peltosaari. The Municipal Museum.

	498	497	497	498	497	497
Dep. Riihimaki	12:05	12:10	13:06	15:42	16:03	17:41(1)
Arr. Helsinki	20minutes later					

(1)Plus other departures from Riihimaki at frequent times from 18:40 to 22:00.

Helsinki - Tampere - Helsinki   497

All of these trains have meal service, unless designated otherwise.

Dep. Helsinki	8:00	9:05	10:00	11:00(1)
Arr. Tampere	10:10	11:15	12:10	13:07

Sights in **Tampere:** The aquarium, planetarium, children's zoo, amusement park, observation tower and planetarium at the Sarkanniemi Recreation Center. The more than 30,000 objects exhibited in the Hame Museum, particularly the handwoven rugs and tapestries. Many excellent artworks, frescoes and the altarpiece in the Cathedral, completed in 1907. The fine modern architecture of Kaleva Church. The National history Museum. The Haihara Doll Museum. The largest church bells in Finland, at the Orthodox Church.

See a performance at Tampere's Summer Theater in Pyynikki Park, from a seat in the unique bowl-shaped auditorium that rotates 360 degrees. Everyone sitting in the last row at the beginning of a performance also has a front-row seat during the show.

Dep. Tampere	11:40	14:45(1)	16:15	17:40	18:45(4)
Arr. Helsinki	14:00	16:55	18:30	19:55	21:00

(1)Light refreshments. (2)Runs Monday-Friday, except holidays. (3)Runs Sunday only. *No* meal service. (4)Plus other departures from Tampere at 19:20, 20:30(2) and 21:50(3).

Helsinki - Turku - Helsinki   493
All of these trains have light refreshments.
Dep. Helsinki   7:32   9:10   12:40
Arr. Turku (Stn.)   10:10   11:51   15:20

Sights in **Turku:** The Museum and the marvelous Banquet Hall in the 13th century Castle, a short walk from the Silja Lane railstation, only a few minutes ride past the Main railstation. The 13th century Cathedral. See the 2 old sailing ships from St. Martins Bridge: Sigyn and Soumen Joutsen. Qwensel House, the oldest residence in Turku, now housing the Apothecary Museum. The handicrafts center, a complex of 17 charming 18th century houses, located on Luostarinmaki (Cloister Hill).

Dep. Turku (Stn.)   12:15   15:45   17:20(1)   20:56
Arr. Helsinki   14:55   18:27   20:22   23:32
(1)Runs daily, except Saturday.

INTERNATIONAL ROUTES FROM FINLAND

Helsinki is the gateway both to Russia (Leningrad, and on to Moscow) and Western Scandinavia (Stockholm, and on to Oslo and Copenhagen). Oulu is the starting point for trips to northern Sweden (Boden) and northern Norway (Narvik).

Helsinki - Leningrad   495
Dep. Helsinki   12:00(1) | Arr. Leningrad   20:05
(1)Reservation required. Meal service.

Helsinki - Moscow   495+855
Dep. Helsinki   17:00(1) | Arr. Moscow   9:30
(1)Carries sleeping car. Also has couchettes. There is a stop in Viborg for meal service at 22:44.

Helsinki - Stockholm   493+1238
Dep. Helsinki   7:32(1)   16:02(1)   18:02(1)
Arr. Turku (Harbor) 10:20   19:08   20:55
Walk to Abo Pier.

The price for the cruise across the Bay of Bothnia on the comfortable and pleasant Silja Line ships is about $44(U.S.). This passage *is* covered by Eurailpass. The fare for a sleeping cabin is *not* covered by Eurailpass. Food on the ship is varied and delicious.

We recommend the daytime sailing in order to see the thousands of tiny islands on the ride through this extremely interesting archipelago. During the daytime cruise, there is a good smorgasbord for both lunch and dinner.

A small band plays music in a delightful bar area. Movies are shown in a small theater. There is a duty-free shop on board. The ships ferry autos.

Dep. Turku (AbO)   10:30(2)   18:00(3)   21:30
Arr. Stockholm (Vartan)   20:30   9:00   7:00

(1)Meal service. (2)Late April to the end of August: runs daily. First of September to late April: runs daily, except Monday. (3)Departs from Helsinki's South Harbor.

Helsinki - Oulu - Haparanda - Boden - Narvik
   492

Dep. Helsinki   22:00(1+2)   7:00(1)   10:00(1)   16:00(3+6)
Arr. Oulu   7:38   14:24   18:06   23:10

   Sights in **Oulu:** The Art Museum. The Zoological Museum.

Dep. Oulu   8:00(1)   14:35   18:20
Arr. Kemi   9:15   15:50   19:30

   Change trains.
   496

Dep. Kemi   9:15

   Set your watch back one hour.

Arr. Haparanda   8:55

   Change trains.

Dep. Haparanda   9:47
Arr. Boden   12:08

   Change trains.

   We recommend stopping-over in Boden for the night so as to travel Boden-Narvik during the daylight hours in order to be able to see the fine mountain scenery on that route. You cross the Arctic Circle going from Boden to Narvik.
   476

Dep. Boden   14:45(1)   6:36(3)   10:00(1+4)
Arr. Narvik   22:00   13:55   17:26

(1)Meal service. (2)Carries sleeping car. (3)Reservation required. Supplement charged. Meal service. (4)Late June to early September: runs daily. Early September to late June: runs daily, except Saturday. (5)Operates late May to late August. Runs daily, except Saturday. Light refreshments. (6)Plus other departures from Helsinki to Oulu at 16:00(3), 19:00(2) and 21:10(2+5).

NORWAY

Norway has the most number of scenic rail trips of any Scandinavian country. Its trains are classified Expresstog (express trains stopping only at main railstations), Hurtigtog (fast), and Persontog (slow, local trains, usually stopping at all railstations.

Norwegian State Railways has one coach on the Oslo-Bergen and Bergen-Oslo runs (and similar service on other long-distance routes) designed for conveying handicapped persons and other passengers requiring special care, such as mothers traveling with young children.

These special cars have a compartment accommodating 2 wheel chairs that are lifted aboard. An 8-seat compartment in these cars, equipped for mothers and their infants, is provided with a baby-chair, bottle heater, and other equipment helpful when caring for small children. This compartment is adjacent to a space with fitted toilets and a diaper-changing table. The car also has oxygen tanks, a stretcher and a small wheel chair for handicapped persons to use in moving about inside the train.

From Dombas and on north, you are in the land of the Midnight Sun. (See "Midnight Sun Calendar" at the start of the Scandinavia section.)

The signs you will see at railstations in Norway are:

ANKOMIST	ARRIVAL
AVGANG	DEPARTURE
BANESTASJONEN	RAILSTATION
BILLETLUKEN	TICKET OFFICE
DAMER	WOMEN
GARDEROBEN	CHECKROOM
HERRER	MEN
INFORMASJON	INFORMATION
INGANG	ENTRANCE
RESERVASJONSLUKEN	RESERVATIONS
ROKERE	SMOKING COMPARTMENT
SOVEVOGN	SLEEPING CAR
SPISEVOGN	RESTAURANT CAR
SPOR	TRACK
TIL PLATTFORMENTE	TO THE PLATFORMS
TOGTABELL	TIMETABLE
UTGANG	EXIT
VEKSLIGSKONTOR	CURRENCY EXCHANGE
VINDUSPLASS	WINDOW SEAT

NORWEGIAN HOLIDAYS

A list of holidays is helpful because some trains will be noted later in this section as *not* running on holidays. Also, those trains which operate on holidays are filled, and it is necessary to make reservations for them long in advance.

January 1	New Year's Day		Ascension Day
	Maundy Thursday	May 17	Constitution Day
	Good Friday		Whit Monday
	Easter	December 25	Christmas Day
	Easter Monday	December 26	St. Stephen's Day
May 1	Labor Day		

EURAILPASS BONUSES

A 30% reduction on the fares of the Steamship Company KDS for the cruise between Kristiansand and Hirtshals.

NORWAY'S TRAIN PASSES

All of Norway's passes must be purchased in Norway.

Norwegian Bargain Rail Pass   Sold at all Norwegian railstations. Available in 2 versions. Both are valid for 7 days and allow unlimited stopover. Cannot be used on Friday, Sunday or a major holiday. The 1984 prices are quoted in Norwegian Krone. For a one-way ticket not exceeding 465 miles: 220NK. For unlimited mileage: 300NK.

Family Reduction   One adult pays full fare. Other family members traveling with that adult, including children up to 25 years old, pay half-fare. Minimum journey is 90 miles.

Senior Citizen Discount   A person over 67 and the spouse (even if younger) can buy tickets at half-fare. Must obtain an ID card, available at railstations.

ONE-DAY EXCURSIONS AND CITY-SIGHTSEEING

Here are 5 one-day rail trips that can be made comfortably from Oslo, returning there at or shortly after dinnertime. Notes are provided on what to see at each destination. The number after the name of each route is the Cook's timetable.

In the following timetables, where a city has more than one railstation, we have designated the particular station after the name of the city (in parentheses).

Oslo

Walk from the railstation, up Karl Johansgate, to the Royal Palace. En route, you will pass the National Theater. Behind it is the underground suburban train station. See the massive mural, in the post World War II City Hall, commemorating the Nazi occupation of Norway. From the pier behind City

Hall, take a 4-minute boat ride to Bygdoy to see the 4 interesting museums there: Viking ships, the balsa Kon Tiki raft, Amunden's polar expedition ship Fram, and the 80,000 exhibits in the Norwegian Folk Museum.

Later, see the bronze and granite sculptures of Gustav Vigeland in Frogner Park. Also the Vigeland Museum at Nobelsgate 32. The Munch Museum. The Historical Museum. The National Gallery. Oslo Cathedral. The Museum of Applied Art. Gamle Aker Church. The 14th century Akershus Fortress. The Sonja Henie-Nils Onstad collection of modern paintings at Henie-Onstad Art Center. The Ski Museum at Holmenkollen. Take the trolley to the Merchant Marine Academy at Sjomannsskolen.

Take Bus #36 from Town Hall Square for a one-hour ride to Sundvollen. Beautiful Tyri Fjord scenery.

Oslo - Goteborg - Oslo 487

| Dep. Oslo (Sent.) | 7:40(1) | Dep. Goteborg | 17:20(2) |
| Arr. Goteborg | 12:18 | Arr. Oslo(East) | 22:05 |

(1)Reservation required. Meal service. (2)Light refreshments.

Sights in **Goteborg:** A great seaport. The one-hour sightseeing bus tour leaves from Stora Teatern. There are one-hour boat trips covering the 7-mile harbor and its canals, leaving from Kungsportsbron. See the view of the harbor and city from the Sailor's Tower near the Maritime Museum at Gamla Varvsparken. The Liseberg amusement park. The magnificent City Theater and Concert House.

Oslo - Hamar - Oslo 483

Be sure to sit on the right-hand side for the best view of the fantastic scenery along the western shore of Lake Mjosa. Norway's largest lake (75 miles long).

| Dep. Oslo (Sent.) | 8:00(1+2) | 9:13(2) | 10:00(3) |
| Arr. Hamar | 9:26 | 11:02 | 11:39 |

Sights in **Hamar:** The enormous outdoor Hedmark Museum complex of more than 40 buildings, most of them from the 18th and 19th century, brought here from other places. One of the buildings is a house built in 1871 in North Dakota, U.S.A., by a Norwegian emigrant.

Also visit the 7½-acre Railway Museum, open May-September, to see many early coaches and locomotives as well as Norway's first railstation.

| Dep. Hamar | 11:50(2) | 13:55(1+3) | 14:49(1+2) | 17:43(3+4) |
| Arr. Oslo (Sent.) | 13:38 | 15:25 | 16:38 | 19:38 |

(1)Reservation required. (2)Light refreshments. (3)Meal service. (4)Plus other departures from Hamar at 19:50(2) and 20:48(1+2).

Oslo - Lillehammer - Oslo 483

Dep. Oslo			Dep.		
(Sent.)	8:00(1)	10:00(2)	Lillehammer	13:10(1)	14:01(3+4)
Arr.			Arr. Oslo		
Lillehammer	10:11	12:32	(Sent	15:25	16:38

(1)Reservation required. Meal service. (2)Meal service. (3)Reservation required. Light refreshments. (4)Plus other departures from Lillehammer at 16:40(2) and 20:04(1)

Sights in **Lillehammer:** The Sandvig collection of more than 100 old buildings and craftwork demonstration at the 100-acre open-air Maihaugen Museum, open daily 11:00-19:00 from late June to early August and 11:00-14:00 the rest of the year. See the "White Swan" paddle-wheel steamboat, Skibladner, at the city's dock.

Oslo - Vinstra - Oslo 483

Dep. Oslo (Sent.)	8:00(1)	10:00(2)
Arr. Vinstra	11:09	13:52

Sights in **Vinstra:** A mountain resort. Home of the legendary Peer Gynt. See the memorial over his grave in the village church. Cross-country skiing is popular here.

Dep. Vinstra	12:11(1+3)	12:57(1+3)	15:21(2)	19:06(1)
Arr. Oslo (Sent.)	15:25	16:38	19:38	22:17

(1)Reservation required. Meal service. (2)Meal service. (3)Operates mid-June to mid-August. Runs daily, except Sunday.

(THE NEXT SCHEDULE IS TO BE READ ON PAGE 264,
UNDER "OSLO-NORDAGUTU-OSLO")

Here are schedules for taking a different route in returning to Oslo from Nordagutu, by making it a circle trip, via Kongsberg.

Nordagutu - Kongsberg - Oslo 482

Dep. Nordagutu	14:05(1)	16:22(1)	20:03(2)
Dep. Kongsberg	14:55	17:10	20:42
Arr. Oslo (West)	16:23	18:35	21:55

(1)Light refreshments. (2)Reservation required. Meal service.

THE FJORD TRAIN ROUTE

Oslo - Drammen - Tonsberg - Sandefjord - Larvik - Skien - Nordagutu - Oslo   488

This one-day excursion offers great views of several fjords (starting with the Oslofjord), wooded countryside, and lovely lakes. As the schedules indicate, stops can be made for sightseeing in several of the towns on this route.

Dep. Oslo (West)	7:25	9:25(1)	11:25(1)
Arr. Drammen	8:00	10:00	12:00
Arr. Tonsberg	8:56	10:56	12:56
Arr. Sandefjord	9:18	11:18	13:18
Arr. Larvik	9:37	11:37	13:37
Arr. Skien	10:20	12:20	14:20
Dep. Skien	-0-	13:30	15:35
Arr. Nordagutu	-0-	14:00	16:09

* * *

(See page 263 for alternate return trip to Oslo)

* * *

Dep. Nordagutu	10:05(1)	14:03(1)	20:04
Arr. Skien	10:35	14:35	20:30
Dep. Skien	10:40	14:40	20:40
Dep. Larvik	11:23	15:23	21:23
Dep. Sandefjord	11:40	15:40	21:40
Dep. Tonsberg	12:03	16:03	22:03
Dep. Drammen	13:00	17:00	23:00
Arr. Oslo (West)	13:35	17:35	23:35

(1)Light refreshments.

Sights in **Drammen:** The activity along the busy docks. Many attractive old buildings. Watching the Drommensfjorden meet the Drammen River.

Sights in **Tonsberg:** Norway's oldest town. See today's whaling ships and the ruins of an ancient Viking castle, Tonsberghus. Also, the Vestfold Museum, the 12th century St. Michael's Church, the 12th century Sem Church, and the 13th century Royal Castle.

Sights in **Sandefjord:** The main port for Norway's whaling ships. See the whaling monument in the square. The Whaling Museum. Nearby are the mouth of the Oslofjorden and the head of the Sandefjorden.

Sights in **Larvik:** The Museum. The fjord.

Sights in **Skien:** The large sawmill operations. The meeting of Skien River and Lake Hjelle.

SCENIC RAIL TRIPS

Bergen to Oslo . . . The Stalheim-Flam Detour

Indisputably, the most scenic rail route in Europe. There are several ways to make this detour, either in a single day or by adding one or 2 days to the Bergen-Oslo trip. After describing the sights to see in Bergen, we detail both directions for this splendid journey: Bergen-Oslo and Oslo-Bergen.

Bergen

Visit Torget, a fish market that has been operating for 9 centuries (weekdays: 8:30-15:00). See Bergenhus Fortress, with its 13th century Hakon Hall. The 12th century Mariakirken (St. Mary's Church). Europe's most modern aquarium and the collection of 19th century houses in Gamle Bergen (Old Bergen). Edvard Grieg's home in Troldhaugen. Take the 5-minute funicular ride to the top of Mt. Floien. See the Hanseatic Museum. The Maritime Museum. The Arts and Crafts Museum. Take the cable car to the top of Mt. Ulriken. It's only 22 minutes for the bus ride and short walk to see the 13th century Fana Church and Fantoft, the old stave church.

Bergen to Oslo

There are train departures from Bergen to Voss at 7:20 (reservation required), 8:35 (*not* a through train to Oslo) and 9:50, arriving Voss at 8:36, 10:05 or 11:03. If you are eliminating the Stalheim-Flam detour and going direct to Oslo, the 7:20 departure arrives Oslo at 14:05. The 9:50 departure arrives Oslo at 17:40 (Cook's Table #481). When departing at 9:50, you can take the Myrdal-Flam-Myrdal detour and arrive Oslo at 22:00. The first 40 minutes after leaving Bergen is along the lovely Sorfjorden.

The complete Bergen-Oslo line was opened in 1909 as the only year-round land transportation between Norway's 2 larges cities. It was electrified in 1964. Terrain and climate both caused construction problems which prior to then had never been encountered in building a railway line. The 300-mile length of track must pass through 200 tunnels and 18 miles of snow sheds in addition to also crossing more than 300 bridges.

Travelers are frustrated by the interruptions of viewing the scenery caused by the many snow sheds. However, it would be impossible for the trains to operate daily year round and stick to a strict timetable if it were not for these structures.

You omit the 63-minute Voss-Myrdal portion of the main line route when taking the Voss-Stalheim-Flam-Myrdal detour we have been recommending since 1971.

Upon arriving Voss at 8:36, 10:05 or 11:03, you leave the train and continue on to Stalheim by the bus waiting at the Voss railstation. The one-hour bus ride from Voss to Stalheim passes (on your left) the spectacular Tvinde waterfall. You arrive Stalheim at 10:00, 11:00 or 12:00.

At Stalheim there is only a Norwegian village museum and a hotel. But what an elegant place Stalheim Hotel is, managed superbly by handsome Reidar Chris Thomassen. There is a view here of such magnificence that Kaiser Wilhelm II came to Stalheim annually for 25 years to look at it. Then there is a smorgasbord lunch that alone makes taking a trip from anywhere in the world to this Scandinavian oasis worthwhile. We always allow 2½ hours for this outstanding meal.

The land here has been farmed since 400 A.D. Some facility for food and lodging has existed here since 1647 when mail was carried by Norway's "pony express" from Bergen to Oslo, and Stalheim was one of the stations for changing horses and riders, right up until 1900.

An inn was operated at Stalheim before 1700. The first hotel here, constructed in 1885, burned in 1900. A second hotel, built in 1901, met the same fate in 1902. Another hotel, constructed and used first in Voss, was moved to Stalheim in 1906, enlarged in 1912, and burned down in 1959.

The present Stalheim Hotel was built in the Winter of 1959-60 and enlarged in 1967 to its present capacity of 130 units, ranging from single rooms to doubles and then suites consisting of a double room plus sitting-room with fireplace. Stalheim can accommodate 219 guests, and it is filled nearly every day in its April-September operation.

The terrace of the hotel provides a view over the Naro, Brekke and Jordal valleys, the Sivle and Stalheim waterfalls, and the conical peak of Mt. Jordal.

Two mounds on the right-hand side of the hotel's terrace date from 800 A.D. These were opened in 1890, revealing the remains of a woman who had been buried with her frying-pan, loom, bronze brooches and bracelets ϛ and the remains of a man, with his sword, axes and other utensils.

These relics were given to the museum in Bergen. The mounds have been reconstructed, and photos of the relics are displayed in the hotel's entrance hall.

Of those who start lunch at Stalheim at 12:30, few finish before 14:30. The remainder of the afternoon can be used enjoying the after-lunch euphoria in the spacious main lobby or on the large terrace. A leisurely stroll through the Open Air Museum on the hill behind the hotel is an enjoyable way to fill part of the afternoon and prepare oneself for dinner.

A walk down the narrow country road in September when delicious and accessible wild raspberries are in profusion is another pleasant diversion.

The hotel will arrange a tour of the ancient village museum. The owner of Stalheim, Kaare Tonneberg, gives an excellent commentary on the old log buildings, the lives that were led in them, the white mansion of the landowner who built it in 1726, and the contents of all the structures.

These objects dramatize the contrasting life-style between the rich and the poor of that era. Among the contents are antique Norwegian furniture, arms, glass, silver, pewter and brass, some of which are also displayed in the hotel lobby.

If your schedule does not allow staying overnight at Stalheim, from mid-June to mid-August a boat leaves Gudvangen (only a 30-minute bus ride from Stalheim) at 20:05 for a cruise along the Sognefjord, all in Midnight Sun daylight, arriving Flam at 21:45. This is one of the most scenic fjord trips in Norway.

To get the most out of the Stalheim-Flam detour, remain at Stalheim for an excellent dinner that night and have the enormous "cold table" breakfast the next morning. The traditional Norse breakfast (cereals, fruits, fish, cold and hot meats, salads, cheeses, breads and beverages) originated in the days when a farmer doing heavy physical work in sub-freezing temperatures had to be sustained by one meal from dawn until sunset.

We tourists are fortunate that most Norwegian hotels have perpetuated this eating tradition long after most of the people in Norway have come to work in heated factories or offices 7 hours a day !

You can leave Stalheim by bus on Day 2 at 10:35 to connect with the Gudvangen-Flam boat ride on the Sognefjord, starting at 11:10 for arrival in Flam at 13:30. Snacks and beverages are available on the boat, or you can have lunch after you reach Flam at either the excellent Hotel Fretheim or the fine Heimly Pensjonat.

Short strolls from either of these bring you to the foot of several interesting waterfalls, or you can swim in Fretheim's heated pool.

On the morning of the following day, take the ride on the 12½-mile "Flam Line" railroad to Myrdal (Cook's Table 481a) to connect with the train that left Bergen at 9:50, and then continue from Myrdal to Oslo.

The "Flam Line" is one of the 5 most beautiful train rides in Europe.

Departing Flam at 10:15, this 45-minute ride goes along the Aurlandsfjord, a branch of the Sognefjord. Watch for sturdy, wild mountain goats that often cluster on huge granite boulders only a few feet from the track.

This railway has the greatest incline of any Norwegian track, 5.5 percent at one stretch. The descent is so steep that the train takes a longer time to go downhill than it does to go up. It has 5 different braking systems, any one of which is sufficient to stop the train.

The mountainside is so steep along one stretch that the train has to go through reverse tunnels. In one particular short distance, the track must go on 3 different levels on one side of Kjosfossen Gorge and on 2 levels on the other side of the Gorge. There are 20 tunnels with a combined length of 3.7 miles in the 12½-mile route.

The train proceeds slowly or stops completely at the finest scenic sections in order for passengers to have the best possible views of magnificent scenery and of a road that was built in 1895 to supply materials for building the railway. This road has 21 hairpin bends. Along another stretch, the train crosses a 110-yard-long embankment and stops there for several minutes so that passengers can get off and walk closer to an enormous raging waterfall that cascades close to the train. Its force is marvellous to see and hear.

Arrival in Myrdal at 10:56 is timed to transfer to the Oslo-Bergen train that connects with "Flam Line" in Myrdal at 12:02.

The first stop en route from Myrdal to Oslo is at Finse, highest elevation (4,267 feet) of the entire Bergen-Oslo line. Workers are stationed permanently at Finse to fight snow on the tracks 9 months out of the year and repair the snow sheds during the 3-month Spring-Summer-Autumn there.

Between Finse and Oslo, the scenery changes from glacier to ski resorts, waterfalls, and then beautiful valley farms and fast-moving rivers. You arrive at Oslo at 17:40.

If time does not permit going to Stalheim, you can leave Bergen (June, July and August, reservation required) by fjord boat at 8:00. Arrive Flam at 13:50. Depart on the "Flam Line" train at 14:55 or also (late May to late August only) at 15:25. Arrive Myrdal at 15:36 or 16:10. Connect in Myrdal with the train that departed Bergen at 15:05. Depart Myrdal on that train at 17:10 (reservation required). Arrive Oslo at 22:00.

Despite the late arrival, you will see all of the interesting scenery between Myrdal and Oslo in daylight if you are taking this trip in Summer.

Oslo to Bergen   481

Depart Oslo (Sentrum) at 7:30, 10:05 or 15:45. If you eliminate the Myrdal-Flam-Stalheim-Voss detour, you arrive Bergen at 14:10, 18:30 or 22:30. The 7:30 and 15:45 Oslo departures require reservation and have meal service.

If you take the Myrdal-Flam-Myrdal detour, depart Oslo at 7:30, change trains in Myrdal at 12:15, return to Myrdal at 15:36, arrive Bergen at 18:30.

For taking the 2 or 3-day Myrdal-Flam-Stalheim-Voss detour, depart Oslo at either 7:30 or 10:05. The 15:45 Oslo departure does *not* stop at Myrdal.

The 7:30 and 10:05 Oslo departures arrive Myrdal at 12:10 and 15:52. Change trains. "Flam Line" departs Myrdal at 12:15 and also at 16:20 (late May to late August), 17:12 and 19:00 for the splendid 40-minute ride to Flam. Spend the night in Flam.

On the morning of Day 2, leave Flam Pier at 8:45 for the boat trip on Sognefjord. Arrive Gudvangen at 10:45. Take a bus to Stalheim for the great Smorgasbord lunch there. Either the same day or (if you stay overnight in Stalheim) the next day, go by bus from Stalheim to Voss, and then by train from Voss to Bergen.

Dep. Voss	8:40(1)	12:54(2+3)	16:58(3)	19:10	21:12(2+3)
Arr. Bergen	10:10	14:10	18:30	20:55	22:30

(1)Runs daily, except Sundays and holidays. (2)Reservation required. (3)Light refreshments.

Hotel Grand Terminus is a 2-minute walk from the Bergen railstation.

If time does not permit going to Stalheim on Day 2, you can depart Flam by fjord boat at 15:15 (June, July and August, reservation required), arriving Bergen at 21:15 the same day.

Oslo - Dombas - Andalsnes   483

This 71-mile "Rauma Line" detour off the "Dovre Line" (Oslo to Trondheim) is, mile for mile, one of the 5 greatest scenic rides in Europe.

Even for one who is not going further north than Dombas, the 2-day round-trip is well worth the time involved. There is no question that the route is worth seeing twice, and from 2 perspectives.

Be sure to obtain a free brochure at Oslo's Sentrum railstation before beginning the trip. We would enjoy riding "Rauma Line" every day of our lives. Depart Oslo (Sentrum) at 10:00. Arrive Andalsnes at 17:00. In the Summer, you can read a newspaper there by sunlight at Midnight.

Soon after the train leaves Dombas it crosses the granite Jora Bridge, which spans a 120-foot deep gorge. At Bjorli, the Romsdal Valley comes into view, and you will see (at least in late Spring and early Summer) unmatched foaming torrents of thawed-glacier water, rushing at 80 miles an hour down vertical mountain slopes and through the boulder-strewn Rauma River bed.

The descent from Bjorli involves a double spiral through 2 circular mountain tunnels ¢ first the 1,550-yard-long Stavem Tunnel, then through the 500-yard-long Kylling Tunnel.

Between these 2 tunnels, at Verma railstation, there is a monument that commemorates the opening of the Rauma Line by King Haakon in 1924. Along the opposite side of the Rauma River are small, well-kept farms, lush from the benefit of the warmth of the Gulf Stream, which keeps temperatures moderate along most of the coast of Norway.

The train next crosses Kylling Bridge, 200 feet above a thundering run of the Rauma River through a steep, narrow gorge. You are now approaching the valley floor.

Near Flatmark, you cross Foss Bridge and see Bridal Veil, best known of the numerous waterfalls on this route. At Marstein railstation, the sun is visible only 7 months of the year due to the combination of the tall surrounding mountains and the arc of the sun at this latitude.

After passing along the glaciated foot of the majestic Romsdalshorn Montain, whose peak rivals the Matterhorn as a climber's challenge, one can see on the left the highest vertical rock face in northern Europe, the "Troll's Wall" (Trollveggen), which is 3,000 feet high.

The "Rauma Line" reaches sea level in the Romsdall Valley before ending at Andalsnes (population 2,500) on the shore of Isfjord, at the head of the Romsdallfjord.

There is a bus connection between Andalsnes and Alesund. At Alesund, one can make flights to Oslo, Bergen or Trondheim, or make coastal express boat trips to Bergen or Trondheim.

The Rauma River is fished by sportsmen for salmon and trout.

To return to Oslo, depart Andalsnes at 9:45 daily except Sundays and holidays. Change trains in Dombas. Depart Dombas at 11:17 (reservation required). Arrive Oslo at 15:25. Or, depart Andalsnes on a through train at 12:00.

Arrive Oslo at 19:38. The Oslo-Andalsnes-Oslo roundtrip can be made without stopping overnight in Andalsnes. There is a night departure from Andalsnes at 22:30, arriving Oslo the next morning at 7:11. What a shame, to take this ride at night !

The only overnight lodging we know of in Andalsnes is at the excellent 65-room Grand Hotel Bellevue. Advance room reservations are recommended.

There is a 2-hour bus/ferry connection from Andalsnes to Molde, Norway's "town of roses" located on a fjord and surrounded by 87 beautiful snowcapped peaks. In Molde, see the many ancient wood buildings from the 11th century. The Romsdal Museum, largest Norwegian provincial museum. The floral decorations in the modern concrete and glass Town Hall. The view of the Norwegian Sea and the countryside from the Varden Restaurant, 1300 feet above the town. An International Jazz Festival (music, art, poetry and theatrical events) has been held in Molde the first week of August every year since 1960.

Take the Eide bus 18 miles to visit the grottos and daves at the Troll's Church and the waterfall that tumbles against a marble mountain.

Oslo - Andalsnes - Trondheim - Bodo - Narvik

This is a marvelous 5-day rail trip up Norway's Gulfstream-warmed coastline. Keep in mind when reading the timetables that there is constant daylight on this route during June and July.

A transplanted herd of gigantic musk oxen live along the Dombas-Trondheim route, Day 2 of this journey. On one of our trips, we saw a mother and baby grazing on a grassy slope near the train track.

The scenery of forests, rich valleys, waterfalls, rivers and farms is lovely almost all the way to the crossing of the Arctic Circle, on the ride from Trondheim to Bodo.

Passengers are given a brochure with details about the Arctic Circle trip. Announcements during the ride over a public address system alert passengers to approaching points of interest. A steward or hostess is on board to provide information. Upon reaching the stone monument that marks the Arctic Circle, the train stops there for 5 minutes, allowing passengers adequate time to take photographs.

We were fortunate that it was snowing on our first crossing of the Arctic Circle one June, giving the trip the feeling of a polar environment. A few hours later, as the train's route came close to the coastline, and when we were considerably north of the Arctic Circle, the weather was sunny and warm. At that time there was no sensation of being so far north, nor was there in Narvik the next day, by which time we were 700 miles above the Arctic Circle.

The northernmost rail service from Oslo is to Bodo. Passage from Bodo to Narvik is via an all-day bus trip through beautiful countryside interspersed by 3 ferry-boat crossings. There is train service from Narvik across northern Norway, to Sweden.

Here are the schedules for a recommended rail trip from Oslo to Narvik, and then to Stockholm. On the trip from Narvik to Boden, you cross the Arctic Circle again, although without the interesting ceremony that is presented on the Trondheim-Bodo ride.

Day 1
  483
Dep. Oslo (Sent.)   10:00(1)
Arr. Andalsnes   17:11

Day 2   (Bus trip to Dombas)
  483
Dep. Andalsnes   16:00
Arr. Dombas   18:00
  Change to train
Dep. Dombas   18:45(2)
Arr. Trondheim   21:30

Day 3   In Trondheim

Day 4
  489
Dep. Trondheim   8:15(3)
  Cross the Arctic Circle   17:15
Arr. Bodo   19:30

Day 5 Bus trip to Narvik
Dep. Bodo   7:50(4)
Arr. Narvik   15:00

(1)Operates all year. Meal service. (2)Operates mid-June to mid-August. Plus another departure from Dombas at 19:38(1).   (3)Reservation required. Meal service. (4)Food is available at occasional stops.

Keep in mind that during June, July and August the Midnight Sun allows you to see all the scenery to Trondheim, despite the 21:30 arrival time there. The light is not blinding, but you can read a newspaper by it at 24:00.

Sights in **Trondheim:** This is the gateway for northern cruises. See the old Nidaros Cathedral. The 18th century rococo Striftsgarden royal residence. The Bishop's Palace.

Sights in **Narvik:** The second (after Murmansk) most northern rail passenger terminus in the world.

Founded in 1901 at the western tip of Ofot Fjord to provide an ice-free port for the mid-Winter export of iron ore from Swedish mines which cannot ship via the frozen Bay of Bothnia during Winter.

For the most breathtaking view of Midnight Sun sky, fjords, mountains and the town of Narvik, take the 10-minute walk from Grand Hotel Royal to the base of the cable that lifts you 2,000 feet in 13 minutes to the top of Mt. Fagernsefjell.

Food and beverages are sold in the Fjellsheimen restaurant on the peak, an ideal site for taking spectacular photos and watching the sun revolve clockwise around the horizon.

A crucial British-German naval battle (commemorated at a small museum in the center of town) was fought in Narvik's fjords during World War II. Destroyed in 1940, Narvik was completely rebuilt after the war.

Narvik - Boden - Stockholm   476

The way to see most of the Narvik-Stockholm route during what are the average person's awake hours is to take the 5:45 departure from Narvik, spend the night in Boden, and take the 6:30 departure from Boden the next day. Day 6

Dep. Narvik	5:45(1)	9:25(7)	14:50(1+3+6)
Arr. Boden	13:00	18:00	22:02
Dep. Boden	13:20(1)	18:20(7+10)	22:25(1+3+6)
Arr. Langsele	20:04(2)	-0-	-0-
Dep. Langsele	21:40(3)	0:45(4)	5:12(4)
Arr. Stockholm	7:20(4)	8:20(4)	13:00(4)

(1)Meal service. (2)Change trains in Langsele. (3)Carries sleeping car. Also has couchettes. (4)Day 7 of the Oslo-Stockholm trip. (5)Late May to late June: runs Saturday and Sunday. Late June to early September: runs daily. Early September to late May: runs daily, except Saturday. (6)Reservation required. (7)See footnotes 1+3+5+6.   (8)See footnotes 1+3+6.   (9)Reservation required. Light refreshments. (10)Plus another departure from Boden at 6:30(9).

Oslo - Kritiansand - Stavanger 482

There is excellent mountain scenery between Kristiansand and Stavanger.

Dep. Oslo (West)	8:05(1)	10:05(2)	22:30(3)
Arr. Kristiansand	12:55	15:50	4:00
Arr. Stavanger	16:17	19:50	7:40

Sights in **Stavanger:** Many old streets and houses in this 1100-year old town. See the market of fruits, vegetables, flowers and fish. The 11th century Cathedral. Outside the city, see the prehistoric Viste Cave. Try a deep-sea fishing trip.

Dep. Stavanger	8:45(4)	13:40(1)	22:00(3)
Arr. Kristiansand	12:15	16:55(1)	1:27
Arr. Oslo (West)	18:35	21:55	7:15

(1)Reservation required. Meal service Oslo-Kristiansand and v.v. (2)Reservation required. Light refreshments. (3)Reservation required. Carries sleeping car. (4)Light refreshments.

Here is the schedule for the short coastline roundtrip, returning to Oslo at the end of the day:

488		482			
Dep. Oslo (West)	9:25(1)	Dep.			
Arr. Drammen	10:00	Nordagutu	14:05(1)	16:22(1)	20:03(2)
Arr. Larvik	11:37	Arr.			
Arr. Nordagutu	14:00	Oslo (West)	16:23	18:35	21:55

(1)Light refreshments. (2)Reservation required. Meal service.

Stavanger - Kristiansand - Stavanger 482

From Stavanger, it is an easy one-day roundtrip to see the fine mountain scenery en route to Kristiansand.

Dep. Stavanger	8:45(1)	Dep. Kristiansand	13:05(2)	16:15(1)
Arr. Kristiansand	12:15	Arr. Stavanger	16:17	19:50

(1)Light refreshments. (2)Reservation required. Meal service.

Voss - Granvin

This spur off the Bergen-Oslo route affords great farm, mountain and river scenery. It is an easy one-day roundtrip.

481			485		
Dep. Bergen	9:50(1)	12:50(2)	Dep. Granvin	12:30	15:55
Arr. Voss	11:08	14:36	Arr. Voss	13:20	16:45
Change trains.			Change trains.		
485			481		
Dep. Voss	11:15	14:45	Dep. Voss	-0-	16:58(2)
Arr. Granvin	12:05	15:35	Arr. Bergen	-0-	18:30

(1)Light refreshments. (2)Runs daily, except Sundays and holidays.

INTERNATIONAL ROUTES FROM NORWAY

Bergen is Norway's starting point for cruises to England and Holland. Oslo is the gateway for rail trips to Sweden (Stockholm, and on to Finland) and Denmark (Copenhagen, and on to Germany and the rest of Western Europe).

Bergen - Newcastle   1107

Dep. Bergen	11:00(1)	13:00(2)	16:00(3)	19:30(4)
Arr. Newcastle (Tyne)	9:00	12:30	11:30	15:00

(1)Operates early September to early October. Runs Wednesday only. (2)Mid-May to early September: runs Tuesday and Friday. Early September to early October: runs Friday only. (3)Operates early September to early October. Runs Monday only. (4)Operates mid-May to early September. Runs Sunday only.

Bergen - Amsterdam   1107

These boat schedules are early July to early September.

Dep. Bergen	14:30(1)	17:30(2)
Dep. Stavanger	20:30	-0-
Arr. Amsterdam (Suezhaven)	18:30(3)	20:30(3)

(1)Runs Thursday only. (2)Runs Tuesday only. (3)Day 2.

Narvik - Boden - Stockholm

Schedules for this trip appear earlier in this section, under "Scenic Rail Trips".

Narvik - Boden - Haparanda - Kemi - Oulu - Helsinki

476			496		
Dep. Narvik	5:45	14:50	Dep. Haparanda	17:30(1)	12:18
Arr. Boden	13:00	22:02	Set your watch forward one hour.		
Change trains.			Arr. Kemi	22:25	14:10
496			Change trains.		
Dep. Boden	15:00	8:15	492		
Arr. Haparanda	17:28	10:37	Dep. Kemi	22:47(2)	14:29(3)
Change trains.			Dep. Oulu	0:20(2)	16:00(3)
			Arr. Helsinki	8:55	23:30

(1)Change trains in Tornio. (2)Carries sleeping car. Meal service. (3)Meal service.

This is the way to see all of the Narvik-Helsinki route during what are the average person's awake hours: take the 5:45 departure from Narvik, spend that night in Boden, take the 8:15 departure from Boden, spend that night in Oulu, and on Day 3 depart Oulu at either 7:00 or 12:20, arriving Helsinki the afternoon or night of Day 3.

Oslo - Stockholm   471
Dep. Oslo (Sent.)   8:40(1)   12:55(2)   15:55(1+3)   22:55(3+4)
Arr. Stockholm   15:00   21:55   22:20   8:00
(1)Reservation required. Light refreshments (2)Change trains in both Karlstad
and Hallsberg. (3)Late May to late September: runs daily. Late September to
late May: runs daily, except Saturday. (4)Reservation required. Carries sleeping
car all year. Has couchettes only from late June to early September.

Oslo - Copenhagen   466
Dep. Oslo (Sent.)   7;40(1)   11:00(1)   20:00(2+3)   22:40(3)
Arr. Copenhagen (H.)   17:21   20:51   6:21   9:07
(1)Light refreshments. (2)Operates late June to early September. (3)Carries sleeping car. Also has couchettes.

SWEDEN

In Sweden, passengers not holding reserved seats, and who board a train in which reserved seats are required, are charged twice the reservation fee on board the train.

The signs you will see at railstations in Sweden are:

ANKOMST	ARRIVAL
AVGANG	DEPARTURE
BILJETTLUCKAN	TICKET OFFICE
DAMER	WOMEN
GARDEROBEN	CHECKTOOM
HERRAR	MEN
JARNVAGSSTATIONEN	RAILWAY STATION
INGANG	ENTRANCE
INFORMATIONSDISKEN	INFORMATION
LIGGPLATSVAGN	COUCHETTE CAR
PLATSBILJETTER	RESERVATIONS
RESTAURANGVAGN	RESTAURANT CAR
SOVVAGN	SLEEPING CAR
SPAR	TRACK
TILL SPAREN	TO THE PLATFORMS
UTGANG	EXIT
VAXELKONTORET	CURRENCY EXCHANGE

SWEDISH HOLIDAYS

A list of holidays is helpful because some trains will be noted later in this section as *not* running on holidays. Also, those trains which operate on holidays are filled, and it is necessary to make reservations for them long in advance.

January 1	New Year's Day		Ascension Day
	Epiphany		Whit Monday
	Good Friday		Midsummer Day
	Easter		All Saint's Day
	Easter Monday	December 25	Christmas Day
May 1	Labor Day	December 26	Boxing Day

EURAILPASS BONUSES IN SWEDEN

These boat trips: Goteborg-Fredrickshavn, Helsingborg-Helsingor, Stockholm-Helsinki, Stockholm-Turku and Stockholm-Aland Islands-Turku. There is also a 50% reduction of the fares of the ferry between Malmo and Lubeck-Travemunde (West Germany).

SWEDEN'S TRAIN PASSES

All of Sweden's passes must be purchased in Sweden.

Family Reduction   Allowed for 3 or more relatives traveling together. A 45% discount for adults, 50% discount for children 6-16. Children under 6 travel free.

Senior Citizen Discount   Persons over 65 can buy first or second-class tickets at 40% discount irrespective of distance traveled, but not allowed on Easter, Christmas or weekends in June, July and August.

Lagpriskort   Valid 12 months. Allows 45% discount on *second-class* ticket prices. Sold at railstations. Photo required. Prices are quoted in Swedish krone. The 1984 price is: 110SK.

ONE-DAY EXCURSIONS AND CITY SIGHTSEEING

Here are 9 one-day rail trips that can be made comfortably from Stockholm and Goteborg, returning to them in most cases before dinnertime. Notes are provided on what to see at each destination. The number after the name of each route is the Cook's timetable.

Goteborg

A great seaport. The one-hour sightseeing bus tour leaves from Stora Teatern. There are one-hour boat trips covering the 7-mile harbor and its canals, leaving from Kungsportsbron. See the view of the harbor and city from the Sailor's Tower near the Maritime Museum at Gamla Varvsparken. The Liseberg amusement park. The magnificent City Theater, Concert House and Art Museum, all in the large square, Gotaplatsen. Antikhallarna, Scandinavia's largest permanent antiques and collectors market.

The view from Ramberget, highest point on the Hisingen side of Goteborg. The Botanical Garden. The 7:00 fish auction, weekdays, at Scandinavia's largest fish market. The 17th century Elfsborg Fortress. The Museum, located in the city's oldest (1643) building. The view of the harbor and city from the top of Sjomanjtornet, a 193-foot high tower. The Slottsskogen Zoo.

Stockholm

Bus connections to the city's airport are available at a terminal across the street from the Central railstation. Stockholm's subways depart from the same level as the Tourist Information Office in Central railstation. A Tourist Ticket, good for rides on both buses and subways, is sold for 2 periods: one day and 3 days. These can be purchased at the Tourist Information Office in Central railstation.

Bus #47 can be taken from across the street from Central railstation to the Wasa Museum, where the 17th century battleship is on exhibit. This ancient ship sank in Stockholm harbor at the moment she set forth on her first voyage as flagship of the Swedish Navy and rested in 100 feet of water from 1628 until it was raised in 1956, restored and turned into a museum.

Also see the historic and art treasures in Chapel Royal, the king's silver throne in the Hall of State, the palace museum, and the Bernadotte and Festival suites, all in the Royal Palace. Changing of the guard is Wednesday and Saturday at 12:00, Sunday at 13:00, every day at 12:00 during July and August.

Other sights: the 13th century Cathedral, across from the Palace. The tall old houses and Stock Exchange on Stortorget, the city's oldest square. Both the outdoor museum of life in early Stockholm and the zoo, at Skansen, an amusement park. The collection of Carl Milles statues at Millesgarden.

Do not miss seeing the Golden Hall, Blue Hall, Prince's Gallery, Terrace and the view from the Tower, all at Town Hall. You can obtain maps, literature and advice at the Stockholm Tourist Association, in Sweden House located at Hamngatan 27, in the central business-shopping district. The casino connected to the restaurant (Centalens Restaurang) at the Central Railstation.

Goteborg - Kalmar - Goteborg   467

| Dep. Goteborg | 7:55(1) | Dep. Kalmar | 17:40(2) |
| Arr. Kalmar | 13:20 | Arr. Goteborg | 22:53 |

(1)Runs daily, except Sundays and holidays. (2)Runs daily, except Saturday.

Sights in **Kalmar:** The moat, courts and towers of the Castle. A bus trip to the nearby glassworks.

Stockholm - Eskilstuna - Stockholm

Swedish State Railways Timetable #65.

| Dep. Stockholm | 8:02(1) | 8:17(2) | 10:02 | 10:30(1) | 12:30 |
| Arr. Eskilstuna | 9:40 | 11:15 | 11:40 | 13:15 | 15:15 |

Sights in **Eskilstuna:** The 6 Rademacher Forges that are more than 300 years old, on display in the center of town. Eskilstuna is the capital of Sweden's steel industry. Also see the wooden Fors Church and the statue of the 10th century English missionary, Saint Eskil, for whom the town was named in 1659, one year after Reinhold Rademacher built the forges which launched the local industry.

The Zoo and Amusement Park. The 12th century church. The wonderful collection of Scandinavian art in the Art Museum. Take a local bus 8 miles to Sundbyholm Castle. Shop for gold, iron and copper souvenirs.

| Dep. Eskilstuna | 14:33(1) | 14:33(3) | 16:33 | 18:33(1) | 20:20(4) |
| Arr. Stockholm | 16:13 | 17:42 | 18:13 | 20:13 | 21:58 |

(1)Runs Monday-Friday, except holidays. (2)Runs daily, except Saturday, Good Friday, May 1, Ascension Day, Whit Monday and the day before Midsummer Day. (3)Runs daily, except Saturdays and holidays. Via Vasteras. (Runs Sunday only, except Easter and the last 2 Sundays of December.

Stockholm - Gavle - Stockholm   476+478
Dep. Stockholm (Cent.)   7:45(1)   8:15(2)   10:15(3)   12:15(3)
Arr. Gavle   2 hours later
   Sights in **Gavle:** The Swedish Railway Museum.
Dep. Gavle   10:59(1)   13:56(3+4)   15:56(3)   17:56(3+6)
Arr. Stockholm (Cent.)   2 hours later
(1)Reservation required. Meal service. (2)Reservation required. Light
refreshments. (3)Light refreshments. (4)Runs Monday-Friday, except holidays.
(5)Runs daily, except Saturday. (6)Plus other departures from Gavle at
19:56(2),20:19(1) and 22:00(3+5).

Stockholm - Goteborg - Stockholm   469
   All of these trains require reservation and have meal service, unless other-
wise designated.
Dep. Stockholm (C.)   6:05(1)   7:30(2)   8:05   9:05(1)
Arr. Goteborg   10:42   11:55   12:42   13:42
   Sights in **Goteborg:** See notes about sightseeing in Goteborg at the start
of this section.
Dep. Goteborg   13:18   14:18(3)   15:18   16:18(3+6)
Arr. Stockholm (C.)   17:55   18:55   19:55   20:55
(1)Runs daily, except Sundays and holidays. (2)Operates early August to late
June. Runs Monday-Friday. (3)Runs daily, except Saturday. (4)Operates early
September to late June. (5)Early August to late June: runs daily, except Satur-
day. Late June to early August: runs Sunday only. (6)Plus other departures
from Goteborg at 16:49(1+4), 17:18 and 18:18(5).

Stockholm - Malmo - Stockholm   465
Dep. Stockholm (Cent.)   6:13(1+2)   8:13(1)
Arr. Malmo (Cent.)   13:00   14:55
   Sights in **Malmo:** See notes about sightseeing in Malmo earlier in this
chapter, in the "Denmark" section, under "Copenhagen-Malmo".
Dep. Malmo (Cent.)   15:00(3+4)   16:00(1)   17:00(1+3)
Arr. Stockholm (Cent.)   21:47   22:47   23:17
(1)Reservation required. Meal service. (2)Runs daily, except Sundays and
holidays. (3)Change trains in Hassleholm. (4)Meal service.

Stockholm - Mora - Stockholm   480

Dep. Stockholm		Dep. Mora	15:09	19:09(1)
(Central)	8:38	Arr. Stockholm		
Arr. Mora	12:52	(Central)	19:20	23:25

(1)Runs daily, except Saturday.
   Sights in **Mora:** The outdoor museum of 40 timber buildings, some 600
years old. The collection of Anders Zorn, Sweden's most famous painter.

Stockholm - Norrkoping - Stockholm 465

All of these trains require reservation and have meal service, unless other-wise designated.

Dep. Stockholm (C.) 13 minutes after each hour from 6:13 to 12:13
Arr. Norrkoping 2 hours later

Sights in **Norrkoping:** The amazing collection of more than 25,000 cactus plants in beautiful Karl Johans Park. Take the short sightseeing trip by boat, from the pier at the end of this park.

See the 3,000-year old Bronze Age carvings and also the display of roses in Himmelstalund Park, to the right of the railstation. On the other (east) side of the railstation, visit the ruins of the star-shaped Johannisborg Fort. See the Lindo Canal.

Hear the bell-chiming at 13:00 in front of the Radhuset (Council House). See Hedvigs Kyrka, the German Church.

See the demonstration of antique textiles (from rugs to doilies) and textile machinery in the museum of old factory buildings and tour the restored residence of the factory owner, the Stadsmuseet, a short walk from the railstation. Also exhibited there are interesting scale models of the city as it was in various past centuries.

Dep. Norrkoping 12:50 13:50(1) 14:20(2) 15:50(4)
Arr. Stockholm (C.) 2 hours later

(1)Reservation *not* required. (2)Departs at 14:50 from late September to late May. (3)Runs daily, except Saturday. (4)Plus other departures from Norrkoping at 16:50, 17:50(1+3), 18:50, 19:50, 20:50 and 21:24.

Stockholm - Rattvik - Stockholm 480

Dep. Stockholm (Cent.)	8:38	Dep. Rattvik	15:38 19:38(1)
Arr. Rattvik		Arr. Stockholm	
		(Cent.)	19:20 23:25

(1)Runs daily, except Saturday.

Sights in **Rattvik:** The rustic arts museum.

Stockholm - Uppsala - Stockholm

Most of these trains have meal service or light refreshments.

	478	478	478	478
Dep. Stockholm (Cent.)	8:15(1)	10:15	12:15	14:15(2)
Arr. Uppsala	40-50 minutes later			

Sights in **Uppsala:** The largest church in Scandinavia, Uppsala Cathedral, a short walk from the railstation. Sweden's largest library, Carolina Rediviva, with more than 20,000 hand-illuminated medieval manuscripts, including the only book in existence that is written in pure Gothic, the famous Codex Argentus, the 5th century Silver Bible. The Great Hall of State in the old red Castle, open 11:00-16:00 from mid-May to mid-September. Take a bus marked "Gamla Uppsala" for a 2-mile ride to see relics of heathen worship going back to the 5th century.

	478	476	480	478
Dep. Uppsala	12:15(1)	13:06	14:40	15:06(3+5)

Arr. Stockholm (Cent.)   40-50 minutes later

(1)Reservation required. (2)Runs daily, except Sundays and holidays. (3)Runs Monday-Friday, except holidays. (4)Runs daily, except Saturday. (5)Plus other departures from Uppsala at (#480)16:40(4), (#478)17:06(1), (#480)18:40, (#478)19:16, (#480)20:40(4), (#476)21:06(1), (#478)21:43(1) and (#478)23:22(4)

SCENIC RAIL TRIPS

Ostersund - Trondheim   478

There is fine mountain scenery on this portion of the Stockholm-Trondheim route.

Dep. Stockholm (Cent.)	22:10(1)
Dep. Ostersund	7:37
Arr. Trondheim	12:35

(1)Carries sleeping car. Also has couchettes.

INTERNATIONAL ROUTES FROM SWEDEN

Stockholm is the gateway for rail trips to northern Norway (Trondheim and Narvik) and to northern Finland (Oulu), as well as by boat to Helsinki (and on to Leningrad). It is also the gateway for travel to southern Norway (Oslo, and on to Bergen or Stavanger). Malmo is the starting point for rail travel to Denmark (Copenhagen, and on to Germany and the rest of Western Europe).

Stockholm - Trondheim   478

Dep. Stockholm (Cent.)	7:45(1)	22:10(2)
Arr. Storlien	16:52	-0-
Change to bus.		
Dep. Storlien	17:10	-0-
Arr. Trondheim	20:05	12:35

(1)Reservation required. Meal service 7:40-14:06. (2)Direct train to Trondheim. No change to bus in Storlien. Carries sleeping car. Also has couchettes.

Stockholm - Copenhagen   465

All of these trains require reservation and have meal service, unless otherwise designated.

Dep. Stockholm (C.)   7:13   9:13   11:13   13:13(1+2+6)
Arr. Copenhagen (H.)   15:37   17:21   19:51   21:51

(1)Operates late May to late September. (2)Reservation *not* required. (3)Carries sleeping car. Also has couchettes. (4)Late May to late September: runs daily. Late September to late May: runs daily, except Saturday. (5)Carries sleeping car. Light refreshments.

Stockholm - Helsinki (Boat and Train)

The price for the cruise across the Bay of Bothnia on the comfortable and pleasant Silja Line ships is about $44(U.S.). This passage *is* covered by Eurailpass. The fare for a sleeping cabin is *not* covered by Eurailpass. Food on the ship is varied and delicious. We recommend the daytime sailing in order to see the thousands of tiny islands on the ride through this extremely interesting-archipelago. During the daytime cruise, there is a good smorgasbord for both lunch and dinner. A small band plays music in a delightful bar area. Movies are shown in a small theater. There is a duty-free shop on board. The ships ferry autos.

    1238   Boat
Dep. Stockholm (Vartan)   8:30(1)   18:00   21:30
Arr. Turku (Abo)   20:15   -0-   8:10
    Walk to either railstation.
    493
Dep. Turku (Harbor)   20:30(2)   -0-   8:30(2)
Dep. Turku (Stn.)   20:46(2)   -0-   8:42(2)
Arr. Helsinki   23:32   9:00   11:35

(1)Runs daily, except Monday. (2)Meal service.

Stockholm - Narvik   476

The most scenic portion of this trip is from Boden to Narvik, best seen on the 17:00 or 20:15 departures from Stockholm.

Dep. Stockholm (Cent.)	8:15(1)	17:00(5)	20:15(7)	22:10(9)
Arr. Boden	23:13(2)	6:20	9:36	14:24
Dep. Boden	2:23(3)	6:36(6)	10:00	14:45
Arr. Kiruna	6:30(2)	10:30	13:54	18:38
Dep. Kiruna	6:55(4)	11:00	14:20(8)	18:58
Arr. Narvik (Day 2)	10:18	13:55	17:26	22:00

(1)Reservation required. Light refreshments available until 19:11. (2)Change trains in Boden. (3)Runs daily, except Sundays and holidays. (4)Light refreshments Kiruna-Narvik. (5)Carries sleeping car. Also has couchettes. Meal service until 22:10. (6)Meal service Boden-Kiruna. (7)Reservation required. Carries sleeping car. Also has couchettes. Meal service Stockholm-Kiruna. (8)Late May to late June: runs Saturday and Sunday. Late June to early September: runs daily. Early September to mid-September: runs Saturday and Sunday. (9)Carries sleeping car. Change trains in Langsele at 7:19 on Day 2. Light refreshments 7:53-10:38 on Day 2.

Stockholm - Oslo   471

Dep. Stockholm (Cent.)	7:00(1+2)	15:30(1+3+4)	23:10(4+5)
Arr. Oslo (Sent.)	13:25	21:44	7:55

(1)Reservation required. (2)Meal service 7:00-10:10. Light refreshments 11:32-13:25. (3)Light refreshments. (4)Late May to late September: runs daily. Late September to late May: runs daily, except Saturday. (5)Carries sleeping car all year. Has couchettes only from late June to early September. Departs Stockholm one hour earlier on Saturday.

Stockholm - Oulu - Helsinki

476		496	
Dep. Stockholm (Cent.)	17:45(1)	Dep. Haparanda	12:18(2)
Arr. Boden	7:48	Set your watch forward one hour.	
Change trains.		Arr. Kemi	14:10
496		Change trains.	
Dep. Boden	8:15(2)	492	
Arr. Haparanda	10:37	Dep. Kemi	14:29(2)
Change trains.		Arr. Oulu	15:47
		Dep. Oulu	16:00(2+3)
		Arr. Helsinki	23:30

(1)Late June to early September: runs daily. Early September to late June: runs daily, except Saturday. Carries sleeping car. Also has couchettes. (2)Runs daily. (3)Meal service.

SWITZERLAND

The signs you will see at railstations in Switzerland are those you would see in France, Germany or Italy, depending on the section. French is the language south and southwest of Bern. Italian is dominant in the southeast corner of the country. Elsewhere, the prevailing language is German. There are free timetables at the railstations.

A traveler with a confirmed flight reservation for a departure from Zurich's or Geneva's aiport can check bags at a special counter in the railstation at nearly 100 Swiss cities. Unencumbered with luggage, the passenger using "Fly Luggage Service" rides a train from places such as Bern, Locarno and Luzern directly to the airport, checks-in at the airport's "Express" counter, boards the airplane, and claims the luggage at the end of the flight. The time required for baggage deposit in advance of train departure varies from one Swiss railstation to another. Be sure to obtain that information before departure day.

SWISS TRAIN PASSES

Must be purchased before arriving in Switzerland.

Swiss Holiday Card.   Good for unlimited travel on trains, lake steamers and postal buses. Also provides discounts up to 50% on many extremely scenic and very expensive privately-owned mountain railroads and aerial cable cars that are *not* covered by Eurailpass.

The 1984 first-class prices are: $77(U.S.) for 4 days, $103 for 8 days, $129 for 15 days, and $182 for one month. Second-class: $56 for 4 days, $71 for 8 days, $93 for 15 days, and $129 for one month. Half-fare for children 6 to under 16.

Half-Fare Travel Card.   Honored on both first and second-class space, allowing purchase of tickets at 50% discount: 15 days $27(U.S.), one month $35.

Senior Citizen Half-Fare Travel Card.   May be purchased by women over 62 and men over 65. The 1984 price is $52(U.S.). In addition to 50% discount on tickets, this card also entitles the bearer to reduced prices at participating Swiss hotels. Valid for one year.

Junior Half-Fare Travel Card.   For persons 16-26 years old. The 1984 price for one month is $16(U.S.).

SUMMER TIME

Switzerland changes to Summer Time on the last Sunday of March and converts back to Standard Time on the last Sunday of September.

EURAILPASS BONUSES IN SWITZERLAND

Boat trips on the Rhine from Schaffhausen to Kreuzlingen and also on the Aare from Biel/Bienne to Solothurn and on the lakes of Biel, Brienz, Geneva, Luzern, Murten, Neuchatel, Thun and Zurich.

SWITZERLAND

SWISS HOLIDAYS

A list of holidays is helpful because some trains will be noted later in this section as not running on holidays. Also, those trains which operate on holidays are filled, and it is necessary to make reservations for them long in advance.

January 1	New Year's Day		Ascension Day
	Good Friday		Whit Monday
	Easter	August 1	National Independence
	Easter Monday		Day
		December 25	Christmas Day

ONE-DAY EXCURSIONS AND CITY-SIGHTSEEING

Here are 56 one-day rail trips that can be made comfortably from 6 major cities in Switzerland, returning to them in most cases before dinnertime. Notes are provided on what to see at each destination. The number after the name of each route is the Cook's timetable. The 6 base cities are: Basel, Bern, Geneva, Interlaken, Luzern and Zurich.

When no station is designated for cities in Austria, Switzerland and West Germany, the station is "Hauptbahnhof".

Basel

The superb Holbein, Delacroix, Gauguin, Matisse, Ingres, Courbet and Von Gogh paintings in the Kunstmuseum. The Historical Museum in the Franciscan Church in Barfusserplatz. The Municipal Casino. The collection of 18th century clothing, ceramics and watches in the Kirschgarten mansion. Shop on Freiestrasse. See the 16th century Town Hall. The fishmarket. The 15th century New University. Take a boat excursion from the pier in the back of the Hotel Three Kings. See the view of the city from the Wettstein Bridge. The beautiful Munsterplatz.

Munster, the 13th century Cathedral. The more than 100,000 rarities from every continent (particularly those from New Guinea and the South Seas) in the Ethnological Museum at Augustinerstrasse 2. In the same complex, the extraordinary geological section at the Museum of Natural History.

The Jewish Museum of Switzerland, at Kornhausgasse 18, where Theodore Herzl presided over the first Zionist Congress, in 1897. The Zoo, Switzerland's largest, is a short stroll from the SNCF and SBB railstations. Or, take Trolleys #4 and #7 from the stations.

Bern

The comic antics of the denizens of the Bear Pit. How they love figs ! The performance every hour of the clock tower, the Zytglockenturm. The nearby old arcaded streets. Lunch on the terrace of the Casino restaurant and enjoy the view from there of the River Aare. The Art Museum, with the largest Klee collection in the world. The Cathedral. The elaborate statue honoring the world postal system, without which it would be impossible to have one country handle and deliver to an addressee a mailing for which another country had been paid the postage by the addressor.

One of the world's largest stamp collections, at the Swiss PTTT Museum. The view of the Alps from the terrace of the Federal Palace, and the nearby open-air flower and produce market (Tuesday and Saturday mornings). The Swiss Alpine Museum. The Natural History Museum. Prison Tower. Holy Ghost Church. The Botanical Gardens. The many window-boxes with flowering geraniums throughout the streets in the city center.

Geneva

Walk from the railstation, down Rue du Mont Blanc, to the shore of Lake Leman. See the monument to international Protestantism and the fabulous clock of living flowers and plants in the park across the lake. It is on that side of the lake you will find the city's old narrow streets and, in St. Peter's Cathedral, the pulpit from which Calvin preached. See the view from the top of the Cathedral's North Tower.

In modern Geneva: Palais des Nations, today the European headquarters of the United Nations Organization. The chinaware collection in the Ariana Museum.

The Art and History Museum, 2 rue Charles-Galland (Bus #1 from the railstation) has an archaeological collection, paintings, decorative art and sculptures, open 10:00-12:00 (except Monday) and 14:00-18:00 daily. The National History Museum, 11 route de Malagnou (Bus #5 from the railstation), one of the most modern museums in Europe, open daily 10:00-12:00 and daily except Monday 14:00-17:00. Nearby, at 15 route de Malagnou, is the Watch and Clock Museum, open daily except Monday 10:00-12:00 and 14:00-16:00 daily.

The Voltaire Museum, 25 rue des Delices (Bus #6 from the railstation), open Monday-Friday 14:00-17:00. The world-famous Davidoff's Cigar Store on rue de Rive, open Monday-Friday 8:00-18:00 and Saturday 8:00-18:30, where the No. 2 coronas sold for $6.60(U.S.) each in 1982. Also in stock there: enormous ebony and mahogany humidors.

Luzern

Walk across the 14th and 15th century bridges spanning the Reuss River and see the 120 paintings on the ceiling of Kappelbrucke depicting Luzern's history and the 45 "Dance of Death" paintings inside the Spreuerbrucke. See the immense 30-foot high, 42-foot long Lion of Luzern, carved in 1821 into a sandstone cliff at what is now the entrance to the Glacier Gardens outdoor museum. The lion commemorates the bravery of those Swiss soldiers who defended Marie Antoinette during the French Revolution. The Glacier Museum, in operation since 1872, is well worth visiting. You will see there the absolute proof that palm trees once grew here, when this area was tropical. The old railway cars, locomotives, trolley cars, buses and autos at the Swiss National Transport Museum, the largest museum of its kind in Europe. The exhibit of model railways nearby. The Art Museum, near the railstation. The August music Festival. The giant (12,000 square foot) canvas Grand Panorama, depicting war in Winter.

Zurich

Here is a great 2-hour walk: Upon arriving at the main Zurich railstation, take the escalator down one level and enjoy a snack or meal in Shopville, the enormous underground shopping center beneath Bahnhof Platz, the square in front of the station. Come up from Shopville on the other side of Bahnhof Platz. Walk one mile down one side of Bahnhofstrasse, lined with smart stores. When this city's Fifth Avenue ends at the shore of Lake Zurich, take in the lakeside promenade before returning to the railstation by walking along the opposite side of Bahnhofstrasse that you walked earlier. Upon returning to the station, go all the way through it, cross Museumstrasse, and visit the National Museum. Other sights: The Bellevue Platz amusement center. The paintings and sculptures at the Kunsthaus. African and Asian art at the Rietberg Museum. Kunstgewerbemuseum. The Museum of Applied Arts (handicrafts, architecture and industrial design).

The 5 Chagall stained-glass windows (red, blue and green) in the 13th century Fraumunsterkirche. The great toy museum on the top floor of the marvelous Franz Carl Weber Toy Shop, on Bahnhofstrasse.

A cruise on Lake Zurich is covered by Eurailpass. Board the boat at the lake end of Bahnhofstrasse.

There is rail service from Zurich's Hauptbahnhof railstation to the Zurich airport and v.v. every 24-30 minutes from 5:30 to 23:00.

Basel - Baden Baden - Basel   664

Dep. Basel	8:08(1)	10:08(1)	-0-	-0-
Dep. Basel	8:14(1)	10:14(1)	10:34	11:52
Arr. Baden Baden	9:35	11:35	12:47	14:04

Sights in **Baden Baden:** Praised for its hot salt springs since the Romans discovered the curative water in this area nearly 2,000 years ago. The illnesses treated here include rheumatism, abnormal blood pressure, metabolic disturbances, respiratory ailments, and problems caused by lack of physical exercise.

Nearly 300 prominent European families once had their permanent homes here. Fantastic landscape. The Oos Valley has been called the most beautiful valley in the world. Exotic trees include the Japanese maple, American tulip, East Asian ginkgo, Chinese trumpet, magnolia and fig. The colors of many deciduous trees make Autumn glorious here.

See the Louis XIII and Louis XIV decor of the halls in the casino. The fancy boutique shops. Exhibitions of international art in the Staatliche Kunsthalle (City Art Gallery).

Motorized vehicles are not permitted in the core area of Baden Baden. There is a constant schedule of balls, fashion shows and concerts. Food specialties here are Grunkernsuppe (a vegetable soup), game pate, pike dumplings, Blaufelchen (a kind of whitefish, from Lake Constance), raspberry schnapps and kirsch with smoked bacon, bread baked by charcoal, and pate of truffled goose-liver from nearby Strasbourg.

Dep. Baden Baden   13:15   14:03(2)   14:49(1)   16:15(1+6)
Arr. Basel (Bad Bf.)   14:39   15:25   16:28   17:39
Arr. Basel (S.B.B.)   7-12 minutes later

(1)Meal service. (2)TEE. Reservation required. Meal service. (3)Light refreshments. (4)Daily, except Sat. (5)Terminates at Bad. Bf. station. (6)Plus other departures from Baden Baden at 16:50(3), 18:15(1+4), 19:50(3), 21:00(5), 22:16(1+5) and 23:07.

Basel - Bern - Basel   260

All of these trains have light refreshments.

Dep. Basel (S.B.B.)   6:56   7:46   8:56   9:46   10:56(1)
Arr. Bern   8:09   9:09   10:09   11:09   12:09

Sights in **Bern:** See notes about sightseeing in Bern at the start of this section.

Dep. Bern   11:45   12:45   13:45   14:45   15:45(2)
Arr. Basel (S.B.B.)   13:08   13:58   15:08   15:58   17:08

(1)Plus other departures from Basel at 11:46, 12:56 and 13:46.   (2)Plus other departures from Bern at frequent times from 16:45 to 22:41.

Basel - Interlaken - Basel   260

All of these trains have light refreshments.

Dep. Basel (S.B.B.)   6:56   7:46   8:56   9:46(1)
Arr. Interlaken (West)   9:15   10:15   11:27   12:15
Arr. Inerlaken (Ost)   5 minutes later

Sights in **Interlaken:** A fine Summer resort and health spa. Take the funicular to Heimwehfluh for a marvelous view of the mountains.

Dep. Interlaken (Ost)   12:24   13:24   14:34   15:24(2)
Dep. Interlaken (West)   5 minutes later
Arr. Basel (S.B.B.)   15:08   15:58   17:08   17:58

(1)Plus other departures from Basel at frequent times from 10:56 to 20:56.   (2)Plus other departures from Interlaken (Ost) at 16:34, 17:34, 18:34, 19:27 and 20:27.

Basel - Luxembourg - Basel   176

Dep. Basel (SNCF)   5:03   8:21(1)
Arr. Luxembourg   9:05   11:56

Sights in **Luxembourg:** See notes about sightseeing in Luxembourg on page 82.

Dep. Luxembourg   14:54(1)   18:26(1)   21:14
Arr. Basel (SNCF)   18:25   22:03   1:28

(1)Meal service.

Basel - Luzern - Basel   277

Most of these trains have meal service or light refreshments.

Dep. Basel (S.B.B.)   6:22   7:00   8:01   9:00   10:01   11:00(1)

Arr. Luzern   70 minutes later

Sights in **Luzern:** See notes about sightseeing in Luzern at the start of this section.

Dep. Luzern   9:44   10:37   11:44   12:37   13:44   14:37(2)

Arr. Basel (S.B.B.)   7 minutes later

(1)Plus other departures from Basel on the hour from 12:00 to 21:00, plus 22:31.   (2)Plus other departures from Luzern at frequent times from 15:44 to 22:40.

Basel - Rheinfelden - Basel   268

Dep. Basel (S.B.B.)   6:31   7:13   7:52   8:33   10:33   11:13(1)

Arr. Rheinfelden   15 minutes later

Sights in **Rheinfelden:** Tours of the Cardinal and Feldschlosschen breweries. The island park in the Rhine River.

Dep. Rheinfelden   8:06   9:06   10:23   11:06   12:23   13:06(2)

Arr. Basel (S.B.B.)   15 minutes later

Plus other departures from Basel at 12:33, 14:33, 15:13 and 16:33.   (2)Plus other departures from Rheinfelden at frequent times from 15:06 to 0:06.

Basel - Strasbourg - Basel   176

Dep. Basel (SNCF)   5:10)1)   8:21(2)   9:17(3)   11:12(5)

Arr. Strasbourg   6:40   9:45   10:47   12:40

Sights in **Strasbourg:** See very lengthy notes about sightseeing in Strasbourg in the "France" section, under "Paris-Strasbourg".

Dep. Strasbourg   11:03(4)   12:11(2)   13:15   17:02(2+6)

Arr. Basel (SNCF)   12:30   13:39   14:46   18:25

(1)Light refreshments. (2)Meal service. (3)Mon.-Fri., except holidays. (4)Daily, except Sun. and holidays. (5)Plus another departure from Basel at 13:20(2). (6)Plus other departures from Strasbourg at 17:43(3), 20:37(2), 23:46(1) and 0:05.

Basel - Zurich - Basel   268

All of these trains have light refreshments.

Dep. Basel (S.B.B.)   6:09   6:58   7:52   8:12(1)   8:58(2)

Arr. Zurich   60 minutes later

Sights in **Zurich:** See notes about sightseeing in Zurich at the start of this section.

Dep. Zurich   Frequent times from 10:57 to 23:09

Arr. Basel (S.B.B.)   60 minutes later

(1)Reservation required. Meal service. (2)Plus other departures from Basel at frequent times from 9:54 to 22:25.

Bern - Basel - Bern   260

All of these trains have light refreshments.

Dep. Bern   6:45   7:45   8:45   9:45   10:45(1)
Arr. Basel (S.B.B.)   70 minutes later

Sights in **Basel:** See notes about sightseeing in Basel at the start of this section.

Dep. Basel (S.B.B.)   10:56   11:46   12:56   13:46   14:56(2)
Arr. Bern   70 minutes later

(1)Plus other departures from Bern at frequent times from 11:45 to 21:45.

(2)Plus other departures from Basel at frequent times from 15:52 to 22:18.

Bern - Geneva - Bern   256

Dep. Bern   6:34(1)   7:16(1)   7:34   8:16(2)   9:16(2+3)
Arr. Geneva (Corn.)   8:28   8:58   9:28   9:58   10:58

Sights in **Geneva:** See notes about sightseeing in Geneva at the start of this section.

Dep. Geneva (Corn.)   12:56(2) 13:26   13:56(2) 14:56(2) 15:56(2+4)
Arr. Bern   14:38   15:20   15:38   16:38   17:38

(1)Light refreshments. (2)Meal service. (3)Plus other departures from Bern at frequent times from 9:34 to 13:16.   (4)Plus other departures from Geneva at frequent times from 16:56 to 20:56 plus 22:26.

Bern - Interlaken - Bern   260

Dep. Bern   6:40   7:27   8:27   9:27(1)
Arr. Interlaken (West) 7:28   8:15   9:15   10:15
Arr. Interlaken (Ost)   5 minutes later

Sights in **Interlaken:** See notes about sightseeing in Interlaken at the start of this section.

Dep. Interlaken (Ost)   7:34   8:24   9:34   10:24(2)
Dep. Interlaken (West) 5 minutes later
Arr. Bern   8:27   9:27   10:27 11:27

Plus other departures from Bern at frequent times from 10:27 to 22:21.   (2)Plus other departures from Interlaken at frequent times from 11:34 to 22:30.

Bern - Lausanne - Bern   256

Dep. Bern   Frequent departures from 6:34 to 22:16
Arr. Lausanne   70 minutes later

Sights in **Lausanne:** The Cathedral. The Castle of St. Maire. City Hall. The Federal Palace of Justice.

Dep. Lausanne   Frequent departures from 5:27 to 23:09
Arr. Bern   70 minutes later

292

Bern - Fribourg - Lausanne - Bern 256

It is possible to stop and sightsee in both Fribourg and Lausanne on the same one-day excursion.

| Dep. Bern | 8:16 | 9:16 | 10:16 | 11:16 | 12:16 |
| Arr. Fribourg | 8:37 | 9:37 | 10:37 | 11:37 | 12:37 |

Sights in **Fribourg:** The world-famous organ in the 18th century Church and Convent of the Cordeliers was missing in 1982. See the 17th century altar in the Church of the Augustines. Farmers and their wives in traditional local dress, at the Wednesday and Saturday markets. The many stone fountains in the winding streets that lead to the 16th century Town Hall.

| Dep. Fribourg | 10:38 | 11:38 | 12:38 | 13:38 | 14:38 |
| Arr. Lausanne | 11:22 | 12:22 | 13:22 | 14:22 | 15:22 |

Sights in **Lausanne:** See notes in preceding listing.

| Dep. Lausanne | 13:32 | 14:09 | 14:32 | 15:32 | 16:09(1) |
| Arr. Bern | 60 minutes later |

(1)Plus other departures from Lausanne at frequent times from 16:32 to 23:09.

Bern - Fribourg - Bern 256

Here are the schedules for a one-day excursion involving only Fribourg.

| Dep. Bern | Frequent times from 6:34 to 22:16 |
| Arr. Fribourg | 20 minutes later |

Sights in **Fribourg:** See notes in preceding listing.

| Dep. Fribourg | Frequent times from 6:14 to 23:58 |
| Arr. Bern | 20 minutes later |

Bern - Luzern - Bern 262

Outstanding farm and forest scenery as you travel through Switzerland's beautiful Emmental (valley of the Emme River).

Most of these trains have light refreshments.

| Dep. Bern | 6:44 | 7:44 | 9:44 | 10:00 | 11:44 | 13:44 |
| Arr. Luzern | 8:01 | 9:01 | 11:01 | 11:49 | 13:01 | 15:01 |

Sights in **Luzern:** See notes about sightseeing in Luzern at the start of this section.

| Dep. Luzern | 11:51 | 13:51 | 15:51 | 16:51 | 17:51 | 18:51(1+2) |
| Arr. Bern | 13:10 | 15:10 | 17:10 | 18:10 | 19:10 |

(1)Sundays and holidays only. (2)Plus other departures from Luzern at 19:51, 20:51 and 22:03.

Bern - Langnau - Luzern - Bern   262

It is possible to stop and sightsee in both Langnau and Luzern on the same one-day excursion.

Most of these trains have light refreshments.

Dep. Bern   7:44   9:44   10:00   11:44   13:44
Arr. Langnau   17 minutes later

Sights in **Langnau:** The antique household utensils and local industry products (linen-weaving, tanning, embroidery) in the museum housed in a 16th century wood building.

Dep. Langnau   10:45   12:15   14:15
Arr. Luzern   11:49   13:01   15:01

Sights in **Luzern:** See notes about sightseeing in Luzern at the start of this section.

Dep. Luzern   11:51   13:51   15:51   16:51   17:51(1)
Arr. Bern   13:10   15:10   17:10   18:10   19:10

(1)Plus other departures from Bern at 18:51, 19:51, 20:51 and 22:03.

Bern - Langnau - Bern   262

Here are the schedules for a one-day excursion involving only Langnau.

Dep. Bern   7:44   9:44   10:00   11:44   13:44
Arr. Langnau   30 minutes later

Sights in **Langnau:** See notes about sightseeing in Langnau at the start of this section.

Dep. Langnau   10:41   12:41   14:41   16:41   17:41(1)
Arr. Bern   30 minutes later

(1)Plus other departures from Langnau at 18:41, 19:41, 20:41, 21:41 and 23:25.

Bern - Neuchatel - Bern   253

Dep. Bern   8:40   9:20   9:40   10:40   11:20   11:40(1)
Arr. Neuchatel   40-60 minutes later

Sights in **Neuchatel:** After many years of recommending a visit to the Suchard chocolate factory, we received a letter from the Suchard people telling us it does *not* offer tours during July and August when its employees take vacations and it slows down production during those months. At any time of year, Suchard requires advance notice "of at least a couple of days" before it can provide a factory tour. For chocolate maniacs such as we are, if a tour of Suchard is imperative try phoning them at (038) 21-11-55. Failing the Suchard tour, see the city's museum of mechanical dolls and music boxes. Take a stroll up winding streets, past elegant Renaissance and 17th century houses, to the hilltop Castle. Visit the Fine Art Museum. Take the funicular to the top (3,839 feet) of Chaumont for a view of the Alps.

Boat rides on the 3 lakes (Neuchatel, Biel and Morat) are covered by Eurailpass.

Try the great Fondue Neuchatelois, made from white wine and kirsch schnapps. On the first Sunday of October, the local grape harvest is celebrated with a colorful Parade and Battle of Flowers. On this day, wine flows from the city's outdoor fountains instead of water.

Dep. Neuchatel   10:56 11:28 13:08 13:28 14:56 15:28(2)
Arr. Bern   40-60 minutes later
(1)Plus other departures from Bern at 12:40, 13:20, 13:47 and 14:40.   (2)Plus other departures from Neuchatel at frequent times from 16:20 to 23:20.

Bern - Zurich - Bern   256

All of these trains have meal service or light refreshments.

Dep. Bern   7:50   8:41   9:41 10:41 11:41 12:41
Arr. Zurich   9:29   9:54 10:54 11:54 12:54 13:54

Sights in **Zurich:** See notes about sightseeing in Zurich at the start of this section.

Dep. Zurich   Frequent times from 6:33 to 23:00
Arr. Bern   1-1½ hours later

Geneva - Annecy - Geneva   158

Dep. Geneva (Eaux-Vives)	7:04	10:30	12:27
Arr. Annemasse	7:12	10:38	12:35
Change trains.			
Dep. Annemasse	7:17	10:45(1)	12:41
Arr. La Roche-sur-Foron	7:38	11:06(1)	13:00
Change trains.			
167			
Dep. La Roche-sur-Foron	8:46(2)	11:11(1)	13:30
Arr. Annecy	9:35	11:45	14:08

Sights in **Annecy:** This is a beautiful lake resort. See the 12th century Island Palace. The shops in the old quarter.

Dep. Annecy	12:25	14:55	18:05
Arr. La Roche-sur-Foron	13:03	15:26	18:53
Change trains.			
158			
Dep. La Roche-sur-Foron	13:25	15:35	19:27
Arr. Annemasse	13:44	15:53	19:45
Change trains.			
Dep. Annemasse	13:50	16:10	20:25
Arr. Geneva (Eaux-Vives)	8 minutes later		

(1)Direct train. No train change in La Roche-sur-Foron. (2)Bus.

Geneva - Basel - Geneva   266
Dep. Geneva (Corn.)   6:26   8:03(1)   9:26(2)   11:03(2)
Arr. Basel (S.B.B)   9:33   10:54   12:33   13:54
   Sights in **Basel:** See notes about sightseeing in Basel at the start of this section.
Dep. Basel (S.B.B.)   14:18   15:18(2)   16:18(2)   17:18(3)
Arr. Geneva (Corn.)   17:28   18:28   19:28   20:28
Meal service. (2)Light refreshments. (3)Plus other departures from Basel at 17:59(1), 19:15 and 20:18

Geneva - Bern - Geneva   256
   All of these trains have meal service or light refreshments.
Dep. Geneva (Corn.)   6:56   7:56   8:56   9:56   10:56   11:56(1)
Arr. Bern   8:38   9:38   10:38   11:38   12:38   13:38
   Sights in **Bern:** See notes about sightseeing in Bern at the start of this section.
Dep. Bern   12:16   13:16   14:16   15:16   16:16   17:16(2)
Arr. Geneva (Corn.)   13:58   14:58   15:58   16:58   17:58   18:58
(1)Plus another departure from Geneva at 12:56.   (2)Plus other departures from Bern at frequent times from 18:16 to 22:16.

Geneva - Dijon - Geneva   152
   Both of these trains have meal service.

| Dep. Geneva (Corn.) | 7:23(1) | Dep. Dijon | N/A |
| Arr. Dijon | 10:58 | Arr. Geneva (Corn.) | N/A |

(1)Departs 6:26 from early September to late October.
   Sights in **Dijon:** Town Hall, formerly the palace of those swashbuckling dukes of Burgundy and now one of the richest museums in Grance. The Church of Notre Dame. The 13th century Cathedral of St. Benigne archaeological museum. The Palace of Justice. The Magnin Museum. The 14th century Chartreuse de Champmol, with its famous chapel portrait and Moses Fountain. Rude Museum. Don't fail to have lunch in Dijon, France's food and wine capital.

Geneva - Grenoble - Geneva   165
Dep. Geneva (Corn.)   8:12(1)   9:24   10:30(2)   11:27(3)
Arr. Grenoble   10:29   11:21   12:28   13:34
   Sights in **Grenoble:** See very lengthy notes about sightseeing in Grenoble in the "France" section, under "Lyon-Grenoble".
Dep. Grenoble   15:07   17:36(3)   19:03(1)   21:05(4)
Arr. Geneva (Corn.)   17:12   19:44   21:27   23:33
(1)Runs late June to mid-September. (2)Runs late May to late September. Tray meal availableif ordered in advance. (3)Supplement charged. Meal service. (4)Change trains in Bellegarde.

Geneva - Lausanne - Geneva   256
Dep. Geneva (Corn.)   Frequent times from 4:46 to 23:46
Arr. Lausanne   40 minutes later
   Sights in **Lausanne**: See notes about sightseeing in Lausanne earlier in this section, under "Bern-Lausanne".
Dep. Lausanne   Frequent times from 7:49 to 23:30
Arr. Geneva (Corn.)   40 minutes later

Geneva - Lyon - Geneva   155
   Occasionally, 2 trains depart from the same track at Lyon's Perrache railstation, heading in opposite directions. Be sure to stand at the correct end (North or South) of the track in order to board the train you want to ride. Check the departure signs at the underground passageway. Do not rely merely on a track number when departing from Perrache railstation !
   Next to the North passageway of Track "A" is a take-out restaurant, handy for provisioning your trip.
   A metropolitan train connects Lyon's Brotteaux and Perrache railstations. The ride is 15 minutes.
Dep. Geneva (Corn.)   6:30   10:47   12:51
Arr. Lyon (Part-Dieu)   8:29   12:50   14:36
Arr. Lyon (Per.)   11 minutes later
   Sights in **Lyon**: See very lengthy notes about sightseeing in Lyon at the start of the "France" section.
Dep. Lyon (Per.)   14:14   16:05   18:18
Dep. Lyon (Part-Dieu)   11 minutes later
Arr. Geneva (Corn.)   16:07   18:08   20:33

Geneva - Montreux - Geneva   251
Dep. Geneva (Corn.)   8:03(1)   8:45   9:45(1)   10:45(1)   11:45
Arr. Montreux   70 minutes later
   Sights in **Montreux**: Chillon Castle, about 1½ miles from Montreux, immortalized by Byron. Its dungeon, used as a model for many movies, is the attraction. Board the bus to Chillon across from the Montreux railstation.
Dep. Montreux   11:06   11:43(1)   13:06   13:43   14:06(1+3)
Arr. Geneva (Corn.)   70 minutes later
(1)Light refreshments. (2)Plus other departures from Geneva at 11:56, 12:56(1), 13:45, 13:56(1) and 14:56.   (3)Plus other departures from Montreux at frequent times from 14:43 to 23:06.

Geneva - Neuchatel - Geneva   266
Dep. Geneva (Corn.)   7:26(1+2)   8:03(3)   8:26   9:26(1+2+4)
Arr. Neuchatel   1½ hours later
   Sights in **Neuchatel:** See notes about sightseeing in Neuchatel earlier in
this section, under ''Bern-Neuchatel''.
Dep. Neuchatel   10:54   11:54(1+2)   12:24(1)   12:54(1+5)
Arr. Geneva (Corn.)   1½ hours later
(1)Light refreshments. (2)Change trains in Lausanne. (3)Meal service. (4)Plus
other departures from Geneva at 10:26(3), 11:03(1), 11:26(1+2), 12:26(1) and
13:26(1+2).   (5)Plus other departures from Neuchatel at frequent times from
13:54 to 21:54.

Geneva - Zurich - Geneva   256
   All of these trains have meal service, unless otherwise designated.
Dep. Geneva (Corn.)   5:47   6:56   7:56   8:56(1)   9:56
Arr. Zurich   8:54   9:54   10:54   11:54   12:54
   Sights in **Zurich:** See notes about sightseeing in Zurich at the start of this
section.
Dep. Zurich (Hbf.)   13:00   14:00(1)   15:00   16:00   17:00(2)
Arr. Geneva (Corn.)   15:58   16:58   17:58   18:58   19:58
(1)Light refreshments. (2)Plus other departures from Zurich at 18:00, 19:00,
20:00 and 21:00.

Interlaken - Bern - Interlaken   260
Dep. Interlaken (Ost)   7:34   8:24   9:34   10:24   11:34
Dep. Interlaken (West)   5 minutes later
Arr. Bern   8:27   9:27   10:27   11:27   12:27
   Sights in **Bern:** See notes about sightseeing in Bern at the start of this section.
Dep. Bern   12:27   13:27   14:27   15:27   16:27(1)
Arr. Interlaken (West)   13:27   14:27   15:15   16:27   17:15
Arr. Interlaken (Ost)   5 minutes later
(1)Plus other departures from Bern at frequent times from 17:27 to 23:28.

Interlaken - Lausanne - Interlaken   260

Dep. Interlaken (Ost)	6:34	7:34	8:24	9:34	10:24
Dep. Interlaken (West)		5 minutes later			
Arr. Bern	7:34	8:27	9:27	10:27	11:27

Change trains.
256

Dep. Bern	8:16(1)	9:16(1)	10:16(1)	11:16(1)	12:16(1)
Arr. Lausanne	9:22	10:22	11:22	12:22	13:22
	*	*	*		
Dep. Lausanne	11:32(1)	12:32(1)	13:32(1)	14:32(1)	15:32(1+2)
Arr. Bern	12:38	13:38	14:38	15:38	16:38

Change trains.
260

Dep. Bern	13:27	14:27	15:27	16:27	17:27(3)
Arr. Interlaken (West)	14:27	15:16	16:27	17:15	18:15
Arr. Interlaken (Ost)		5 minutes later			

(1)Meal Service. (2)Plus other departures from Lausanne at 16:32(1), 17:32(1), 18:32(1), 19:32(1) and 20:32(1).   (3)Plus other departures from Bern at 18:27, 19:27, 20:27, 21:27 and 22:21.

Interlaken - Murren - Jungfraujoch - Interlaken

This one-day trip covers the heart of the Bernese Oberland area. (It is *not* covered by Eurailpass or Eurail Youthpass.) There have been top ski resorts in this area since 1906. Jungfraujoch is the highest (11,333 feet) railstation in Europe. From there, you can see the Jungfrau, Eiger and Monch peaks. It is great to see the fabulous views from the revolving restaurant, which rotates every 50 minutes. The highest waterfall in Europe (2,000-foot drop) is spectacular in late Spring and early Summer.

287

Dep. Interlaken (Ost)	9:40
Arr. Lauterbrunnen	10:05
Change to funicular.	
Dep. Lauterbrunnen	10:15
Arr. Murren	10:43
Change funiculars.	
Dep. Murren	11:13(1)
Arr. Lauterbrunnen	11:41
Change to train.	
Dep. Lauterbrunnen	12:10
Arr. Scheidegg	12:54
Change trains.	
Change trains.	

288

Dep. Scheidegg	13:05
Arr. Jungfraujoch	13:56
Change trains.	
Dep. Jungfraujoch	14:05(1)
Arr. Scheidegg	14:50
Change trains.	

287

Dep. Scheidegg	14:57
Arr. Interlaken (Ost)	16:23

(1)There are other departures from Brunnen at frequent times.

Interlaken - Luzern - Interlaken   264

Dep. Interlaken (Ost)	6:37	7:39	8:37	9:39	10:37
Arr. Luzern	8:56	9:37	10:56	11:37	12:56

Sights in **Luzern:** See notes about sightseeing in Luzern at the start of this section.

Dep. Luzern	11:17	11:57	13:17(1)	13:57	15:17(1+2)
Arr. Interlaken (Ost)	13:17	14:19	15:17	16:19	17:17

(1)Light refreshments. (2)Plus other departures from Luzern at 15:57, 17:17, 17:57, 18:57 and 20:02.

Lausanne - Sion - Lausanne   251

Dep. Lausanne	7:50	8:22(1)	Dep. Sion	10:53	11:38(2)
Arr. Sion	8:59	9:14	Arr. Lausanne	12:04	12:32

(1)Plus other departures from Lausanne at frequent times from 8:50 to 22:28.
(2)Plus other departures from Sion at frequent times from 12:16 to 22:21.

Sights in **Sion:** Ruins of the 13th century Valere Castle. The world's oldest operable pipe organ, carved and painted wood chests and 15th century frescoes in the Church of Our Lady of Valere, open daily except Monday, 9:00-12:00 and 14:00-18:00.

The collection of Roman antiquities in the Cantonal Archaeological Museum. Paintings by artists of this area in the Majorie Fine Arts Museum. Both museums are open daily except Monday 9:00-12:00 and 14:00-18:00. The astronomical clock and carved doors of the 17th century City Hall. The ancient Tour de Sorciers (Tower of the Wizards). The 9th century Romanesque bell-tower of the Cathedral. Supersaxo, the mansion of a Renaissance nobleman.

Luzern - Andermatt - Luzern

The Goschenen-Andermatt-Goschenen portion of this one-day excursion is by rack railway and is *not* covered by Eurailpass.

277

Dep. Luzern	8:04(1)	9:04(1)	10:04(2)	12:04(2)	14	:04(1)
Arr. Goschenen	9:42	10:37	11:47	13:47	15	:47

Change trains.
295

Dep. Goschenen	9:55	10:48	11 :52	13:55	15	:55
Arr. Andermatt	10:10	11:03	12:07	14:10	16	:10

Sights in **Andermatt:** A great ski resort.

Dep. Andermatt	12:40	13:30	14:40	15:29	16	:18(3)
Arr. Goschenen	12:55	13:45	14:55	15:44	16	:33

Change trains.
277

Dep. Goschenen	13:04(2)	14:44	15:05	16:40	17	:01
Arr. Luzern	15:37	16:21	16:29	18:21	18	:29

(1)Light refreshments. (2)Change trains in Arth Goldau. (3)Plus other departures from Andermatt at 16:37, 17:43, 18:40, 19:25, 19:47 and 21:12.

Luzern - Basel - Luzern   277

| Dep. Luzern | 6:37 | 7:37 | 8:37 | 9:44(3) |
| Arr. Basel (S.B.B.) | 7:54 | 8:54 | 9:54 | 10:53 |

Sights in **Basel:** See notes about sightseeing in Basel at the start of this section.

| Dep. Basel (S.B.B.) | 11:00(1) | 12:01(1) | 13:00(2) | 14:01(2+4) |
| Arr. Luzern | 12:16 | 13:10 | 14:16 | 15:10 |

(1)Meal service. (2)Light refreshments. (3)Plus other departures from Basel at 10:37(2), 11:44(1), 12:37(2) and 13:44(1).   (4)Plus other departures from Basel at frequent times from 15:00 to 22:31.

Luzern - Bern - Luzern   262

| Dep. Luzern | 6:51 | 7:51 | 9:51 | 11:51 | 13:51 |
| Arr. Bern | 8:10 | 9:10 | 11:10 | 13:10 | 15:10 |

Sights in **Bern:** See notes about sightseeing in Bern at the start of this section.

| Dep. Bern | 9:44(1) | 10:00 | 11:44(1) | 13:44(1) | 15:44(1+2) |
| Arr. Luzern | 11:01 | 11:49 | 13:01 | 15:01 | 17:01 |

(1)Light refreshments. (2)Plus other departures from Bern at 16:44, 17:44(1), 19:44(1) and 21:44.

Luzern - Interlaken - Luzern   264

| Dep. Luzern | 6:05 | 7:17 | 8:00(1) | 9:17(1) | 9:57(2) |
| Arr. Interlaken (Ost) | 8:19 | 9:17 | 10:00 | 11:17 | 12:19 |

Sights in **Interlaken:** See notes about sightseeing in Interlaken at the start of this section.

| Dep. Interlaken (Ost) | 8:37 | 9:39 | 10:37 | 11:39(1) | 12:37(3) |
| Arr. Luzern | 10:56 | 11:37 | 12:56 | 13:37 | 14:56 |

(1)Light refreshments. (2)Plus other departures from Luzern at 11:17, 11:57, 13:17(1) and 13:57.   (3)Plus other departures from Interlaken at frequent times from 13:39 to 20:37.

Luzern - Zurich - Luzern   254

Most of these trains have light refreshments.

| Dep. Luzern | Frequent times from 6:20 to 22:07 | |
| Arr. Zurich | minutes later | 50 |

Sights in **Zurich:** See notes about sightseeing in Zurich at the start of this section.

| Dep. Zurich | Frequent times from 6:12 to 23:10 | |
| Arr. Luzern | minutes later | 50 |

Luzern - Schwyz - Luzern   277
Dep. Luzern   8:31   9:31
Arr. Schwyz   40 minutes later
    Sights in **Schwyz:** The Staatsarkivmuseum (National Archive Museum), to
see the 13th century Oath of Eternal Alliance, the document which marks the
founding of Switzerland. This village's name became the name of the country
(Schweiz). The Museum is one mile (uphill) from the railstation. A bus meets
every train.
Dep. Schwyz   10:40 11:40 13:37 15:40 16:40 17:36(1)
Arr. Luzern   40 minutes later
(1)Plus other departures from Schwyz at 18:40, 19:40, 20:40, 21:30 and 22:29.

Zurich - Andermatt - Zurich
    The Goschenen-Andermatt-Goschenen portion of this one-day excursion is
by rack railway and is *not* covered by Eurailpass.
    277
Dep. Zurich   6:27   8:04(1)   9:04(1)   10:04(2)
Arr. Goschenen   8:06   9:42   10:37   11:47
    Change trains.
    295
Dep. Goschenen   8:24   9:55   10:48   11:52
Arr. Andermatt   15 minutes later
    Sights in **Andermatt:** A great ski resort.
Dep. Andermatt   10:42   12:40   14:40   16:37
Arr. Goschenen   11:02   12:55   14:55   16:52
    Change trains.
    277
Dep. Goschenen   11:04(2) 13:04   15:05(1+2) 17:10
Arr. Zurich   12:50   14:50   16:50   18:50
(1)Light refreshments. (2)Change trains in Arth Goldau.

Zurich - Arosa - Zurich
268

| Dep. Zurich | 6:24 | 7:07(1) | 8:07(2) | 9:07(1) | 10:07(1) |
| Arr. Chur | 7:55 | 8:38 | 9:30 | 10:38 | 11:30 |

Change trains.
303

The cogwheel train to Arosa leaves from the front of the Chur railstation. This is a very scenic ride.

| Dep. Chur | 8:00 | 8:50 | 9:50 | 10:50 | 11:50 |
| Arr. Arosa | 9:01 | 9:51 | 10:51 | 11:51 | 12:51 |

Sights in **Arosa:** Great Summer and Winter sports. Fantastic mountain scenery.

| Dep. Arosa | 10:00 | 11:00 | 12:00 | 13:00 | 16:00(3) |
| Arr. Chur | 11:01 | 12:01 | 13:01 | 14:011 | 16:01 |

Change trains.
268

| Dep. Chur | 11:16(1) | 12:24(1) | 13:16(1) | 14:24(2) | 16:24(1) |
| Arr. Zurich | 12:47 | 13:47 | 14:47 | 15:47 | 17:47 |

(1)Light refreshments. (2)Meal service. (3)Plus other departures from Arosa at 17:00, 18:00 and 19:00 that connect with Chur-Zurich service.

Zurich - Basel - Zurich   268
Most of these trains have light refreshments or meal service.

Dep. Zurich   Frequent times from 6:43 to 23:09
Arr. Basel (S.B.B.)   60-70 minutes later

Sights in **Basel:** See notes from sightseeing in Basel at the start of this section.

Dep. Basel (S.B.B.)   Frequent times from 4:50 to 22:41
Arr. Zurich   60-70 minutes later

Zurich - Bern - Zurich   256
Most of these trains have meal service.

Dep. Zurich   Frequent times from 6:33 to 23:00
Arr. Bern   1½ hours later

Sights in **Bern:** See notes about sightseeing in Bern at the start of this section.

Dep. Bern   Frequent times from 4:50 to 22:41
Arr. Zurich   1½ hours later

Zurich - Chur - Zurich 268

Most of these trains have light refreshments or meal service.

Dep. Zurich   Frequent times from 6:24 to 22:07
Arr. Chur   1½ hours later

Sights in **Chur:** This 2100-year old village is located at what has been a strategic pass in the Alps since Roman times. Walk from the station up through the small business area to a hilltop church and see the unusual cemetery there. The modern portion of it has rows of graves that are solidly decorated with living, blossoming plants. Also see the fine stained-glass and the 12th century altar in the 15th century St. Martin's Church. The Bishop's Palace. A one-hour walking tour of Chur is made easy by following red and green footprints painted on the sidewalks. The footprints are matched to a map available at the city's tourist office.

Dep. Chur   Frequent times from 6:08 to 21:08
Arr. Zurich   1½ hours later

Zurich - Davos - Zurich 268

Dep. Zurich	7:20(1)	8:07(2)	9:07(1)	10:07(1+4)
Arr. Landquart	8:32	9:19	10:27	11:19

Change trains.

301

The Landquart-Davos-Landquart trips are *not* covered by Eurailpass or Eurail Youthpass.

Dep. Landquart	8:40	9:30	10:35	11:30(3)
Arr. Davos (Platz)	9:48	10:42	11:45	12:41

Sights in **Davos:** One of the world's most popular ski resorts. Also popular for its skating rinks, hiking trails, a sled run, horse-drawn sleigh rides, indoor swimming, hang-gliding, horseback riding and ice hockey.

Take the 22-minute ride on the Parsenn cable railway, once described by Vogue Magazine as "the Rolls Royce of mountain railways", to the ridge of Weissfluh. A cable car ascends from there to the summit, the start of the different ski runs to Serneus, Sass and Klosters.

Davos has 35 mountain railways and ski lifts with a capacity for transporting 32,000 people every hour. A general-fare ticket, costing about $80 (U.S.) allows unlimited use of the entire network of funicular railways, ski lifts and cable cars for 6 days. There is also bus service every 15 minutes from one end of Davos to the other.

Dep. Davos (Platz)	12:11	12:56	14:10(3)	15:13(5)
Arr. Landquart	13:20	14:20	15:20	16:27

Change trains.

268

Dep. Landquart	13:27(1)	14:35(2)	15:27(1)	16:35(1)
Arr. Zurich	14:47	15:47	16:47	17:47

(Timetable notes appear on next page.)

(1)Light refreshments. (2)Meal service. (3)Rund mid-June to late September. (4)Plus other departures from Zurich at 11:07(1) and 13:07(1). (5)Plus other departures from Davos at 16:10(1), 17:06(1+3), 18:13(1) and 19:15 that connect with Landquart-Zurich service.

Zurich - Frankfurt - Zurich 73

Both of these trains charge a supplement and have meal service.

| Dep. Zurich | 6:57 | Dep. Frankfurt | 17:37 |
| Arr. Frankfurt | 11:17 | Arr. Zurich | 21:57 |

Sights in **Frankfurt:** Goethe's House. The Goethe Museum. The Zoo. The emperor's coronation hall in the Romer complex at medieval Romberberg square. The wonderful doors in the 13th century Leonhardskirche. The 13th century chapel of Saalhof in the remains of the palace of Frederick Barbarossa. Cloth Hall.

The Botanical Garden. The pews and murals in the Cathedral of St. Bartholomew. The Church of St. Nicholas. The Church of St. Paul. Senckenberg Natural History Society's Museum. Stadel Museum and Liebighaus (sculpture). The Museum of Plastic Art. Sachsenhausen, the old quarter of the city, across the Main River from the commercial district. The major shopping streets: Zeil and Kaiserstrasse.

Zurich - Geneva - Zurich 256

Most of these trains have meal service.

Dep. Zurich   Frequent times from 7:00 to 21:00
Arr. Geneva (Corn.)   3 hours later

Sights in **Geneva:** See notes about sightseeing in Geneva at the start of this section.

Dep. Geneva (Corn.)   Frequent times from 5:47 to 20:56
Arr. Zurich   3 hours later

Zurich - Lugano - Zurich   277

Dep. Zurich	6:27	7:04(1)	8:04(2)	8:39(3)	9:04(2+4)
Arr. Lugano	9:46	10:03	11:17	11:35	12:10

Sights in **Lugano:** See lengthy notes about sightseeing in Lugano in the "Italy" section under "Milan-Lugano".

Dep. Lugano	10:43(1)	11:26(2)	12:43(1)	14:43(2)	15:32(2+5)
Arr. Zurich	13:50	14:50	15:50	17:50	18:50

(1)Meal service. (2)Light refreshments. (3)TEE. Reservation required. Meal service. (4)Plus another departure from Zurich at 11:04(1).   (5)Plus other departures from Lugano at 16:43(1), 17:55(3), 18:36(1) and 20:05(1).

Zurich - Luzern - Zurich   254

Most of these trains have light refreshments.

Dep. Zurich	Frequent times from 6:12 to 23:10
Arr. Luzern	50 minutes later

Sights in **Luzern:** See notes about sightseeing in Luzern at the start of this section.

Dep. Luzern	Frequent times from 6:20 to 22:07
Arr. Zurich	50 minutes later

Zurich - Milan - Zurich   277

Dep. Zurich	7:46(1)	8:39(2)	9:17(3)
Arr. Milan (Cent.)	12:00	12:40	13:40

Sights in **Milan:** The Duomo Cathedral, holding more than 20,000 people, begun in 1386 and taking 5 centuries to complete. There are more than 3,000 statues on its exterior. Then, through the beautiful shopping arcade to La Scala, one of the world's greatest theaters, constructed in 1776-78. During the day, you can visit its opera museum and, if your timing is right, see a moment of a rehearsal.

You will also want to see Da Vinci's "Last Supper" at Santa Maria della Grazie. Do not miss the enormous crypts at the Monumental Cemetery.

Dep. Milan (Cent.)	15:10(2)	16:50(2)	18:40(3)
Arr. Zurich	19:50	20:53	22:59

(1)Light refreshments. (2)TEE. Reservation required. Meal service. (3)Meal service.

Zurich - Munich - Zurich 256

| Dep. Zurich | 7:04(1) | Dep. Munich | 16:03(2) | 17:35 |
| Arr. Munich | 12:06 | Arr. Zurich | 20:37 | 22:50 |

(1)Light refreshments. (2)Meal service.

Sights in **Munich:** The works of Durer, El Greco, Raphael, Holbein, Rembrandt and many other great painters at Alte Pinakothek. Frauenkirche Cathedral, and the view from its north tower . . . and then later get a view of Frauenkirche from the top of the Neues Rathaus (City Hall). The paintings of Cezanne, Gauguin, Renoir and other impressionists at the Haus der Kunst.

Wittelsbach Fountain. The fine exhibits and planetarium at Deutsches Museum, considered the best scientific museum in the world. The view of the Alps from the top of Peterskirche. The best collection of tapestries and wood carvings in Germany, at the Bavarian National Museum. Munich's most famous beer palace, Hofbrauhaus.

The Schatzkammer in the Residenz palace, and the flower gardens in the park north of it. The decorations in Asamkirche. Schack Gallery. Theatinerkirche. At Schloss (Castle) Nymphenburg: the porcelain in the showrooms of Nymphenburger Porzellan Manufactur and, in the Residenzmuseum, the enormous Festsaal, and the park outside the castle.

Zurich - Rheinfelden - Zurich 268

| Dep. Zurich | 6:57(1) | 7:09 | 8:09(2) | 10:09(3) |
| Arr. Rheinfelden | 60-70 minutes later |

Sights in **Rheinfelden:** Tours of the Cardinal and Feldschlosschen breweries. The island park on the Rhine River.

| Dep. Rheinfelden | 10:45 | 12:45 | 14:45(2) | 16:45(2+4) |
| Arr. Zurich | 60-70 minutes later |

(1)Meal service. (2)Light refreshments. (3)Plus other departures from Zurich at 10:57(2), 11:57(1), 12:09, 12:57(1), 13:57(2) and 14:09. (4)Plus other departures from Rheinfelden at 18:45, 20:45, 22:37 and 23:48.

Zurich - St. Moritz - Zurich

268			269		
Dep. Zurich	7:20(1)	8:07(2)	Dep. Chur	8:50	9:38
Arr. Chur	8:44	9:30	Arr. St. Moritz	10:52	11:41
Change trains.					

Sights in **St. Moritz:** The lovely scenery of the Alps, reflected on the Lake of St. Moritz. The curative waters. Great Summer (swimming, sailing, fishing, golf, mountain climbing) as well as Winter sports. The creme de la creme of the international jet set December to April.

See the collection of porcelain stoves, furniture and carved woodwork in the Engadine Museum, open Monday-Saturday 9:30-12:00 and 14:00-17:00, also on Sunday 10:00-12:00. Many paintings of this beautiful area by Giovanni Segantini in the Segantini Museum, open Monday-Saturday 9:30-12:00 and 14:00-16:00, on Sunday 14:30-16:00. Also visit the marvelous Engadin Museum.

269

Dep. St. Moritz	10:55(1)	12:08(2+3)	12:55	14:08(3+4)
Arr. Chur	13:02	14:13	15:02	16:13

Change trains.

268

Dep. Chur	13:16(1)	14:24(2)	15:16(1)	16:24(1)
Arr. Zurich	14:47	15:47	16:47	17:47

(1)Light refreshments. (2)Meal service. (3)Runs from mid-June to late September. (4)Plus other departures from St. Moritz at 17:16(1), 18:24(1), 19:16(1) and 20:24.

Zurich - Schwyz - Zurich   277

Dep. Zurich	8:31	9:31	Dep. Schwyz	11:40(1)	13:37(1+2)
Arr. Schwyz	9:10	10:10	Arr. Zurich	12:50	14:50

(1)Change trains in Arth Goldau. (2)Plus other departures from Schwyz at frequent times from 15:40 to 21:30.

Sights in **Schwyz:** See notes about sightseeing in Schwyz earlier in this section, under "Luzern-Schwyz".

Zurich - Solothurn - Zurich   266

All of these trains have light refreshments.

Dep. Zurich	Frequent times from 6:04 to 21:04
Arr. Solothurn	60 minutes later

Sights in **Solothurn:** Switzerland's oldest town. (It and Trier, in Germany, are the 2 oldest towns north of the Alps.) See the outstanding ancient art here. Holbein's Madonna in the Museum. The marvelous Assumption over the high altar in the Jesuit church. The bulb domes on the twin towers of the Town Hall. The comprehensive collection of arms and armor in the old Arsenal. The Italian belltower of the Cathedral. The town's many fine statues and fountains.

Dep. Solothurn	Frequent times from 6:45 to 21:47
Arr. Zurich	60 minutes later

Zurich - Stuttgart - Zurich   668

Dep. Zurich	6:31	8:10(1)	10:10(1)
Arr. Stuttgart	10:04	11:24	13:47

*   *   *

Dep. Stuttgart	12:31(1)	15:18(1)	17:13(1)	20:18(2)
Arr. Zurich	15:44	18:44	20:44	23:44

(1)Light refreshments. (2)Reservation required.

Sights in **Stuttgart:** Outstanding contemporary architecture, built since World War II. Liederhalle, with its 3 concert halls. The Schillerplatz flower and vegetable market (Tuesday, Thursday and Saturday).

Zurich - Winterthur - Zurich   266
Dep. Zurich   Frequent times from 7:07 to 22:04
Arr. Winterthur   22 minutes later
  Sights in **Winterthur:** More art treasures than any other place in Switzerland, at the country's National Gallery in the Am Roemerholz mansion. Great Austrian, German and Swiss paintings.
Dep. Winterthur   Frequent times from 6:29 to 22:22
Arr. Zurich   22 minutes later

Zurich - Zug - Zurich   254+277
Dep. Zurich .   Frequent times from 6:12 to 23:10
Arr. Zug   26 minutes later
  Sights in **Zug:** This village is located on the northeast shore of the 14-mile long Lake Zug. See the spires and massive towers of the 15th century Church of St. Oswald. The stained-glass for which this area is noted and also gold and silver work, embroidery and wood carvings in the Museum at the 16th century Town Hall.
  The view from the peak of the Zugerberg, 4000 feet above the town. From there, one can see the peaks of Rigi, Pilatus, Jungfrau, Eiger, Monch and Finsteraarhorn.
  Try the local specialties: rotel, a tasty salmon-like fish from the lake, the local cherries that are used for producing the liqueur kirsch, and the local cake, kirsch-torte, laced with the cherry liqueur.
Dep. Zug   Frequent times from 5:51 to 22:35
Arr. Zurich   26 minutes later

SCENIC RAIL TRIPS

Basel - Schaffhausen - Basel   674
  An easy one-day roundtrip, to see the marvelous Rhine Falls.

Dep. Basel (Bad Bf.)	7:06	8:36	12:04	14:01	17:10
Arr. Schaffhausen	8:26	9:50	13:20	15:21	18:23
	*	*	*		
Dep. Schaffhausen	10:10	12:57	14:50	16:46	19:01
Arr. Basel (Bad Bf.)	11:34	14:06	16:01	18:06	20:19

Bern - Brig - Bern   260

An easy one-day roundtrip that affords a view of Rhone Valley and Lonza Valley farms, gorges, lakes and mountains plus the Lake Thun scenery at Spiez about which we enthuse in the "Geneva-Spiez" trip described later in this section . . . and going through the 9-mile Lotschberg Tunnel and over the Bietschtal Bridge. This structure takes the train 255 feet above the ravine it crosses. We recommend a stop in Spiez and a stroll there on either the outbound or homebound leg of the trip.

Most of these trains have light refreshments.

Dep. Bern	6:21	7:21	8:13	8:21	9:21(1)
Arr. Spiez	6:52	7:52	8:43	8:52	9:52
Dep. Spiez	6:54	7:54	8:45	8:54	9:54
Arr. Brig	8:00	9:00	9:43	10:00	11:00

Sights in **Brig:** Switzerland's largest private residence, the 17th century Stockalper Castle, built by a very successful businessman.

Dep. Brig	8:54	9:54	10:54	11:12	11:54(2)
Arr. Spiez	10:01	11:01	12:01	12:10	13:01
Dep. Spiez	10:03	11:03	12:03	12:12	13:03
Arr. Bern	31 minutes later				

(1) Plus other departures from Bern at frequent times from 10:21 to 20:21.
(2)Plus other departures from Brig at frequent times from 12:54 to 21:54.

Bern - Brig - Domodossola - Bern   260

To see all of the scenery and Lotschberg Tunnel noted above under "Bern-Brig" plus having the experience of going through the 12-mile Simplon, longest main line rail tunnel in the world, make the Bern-Domodossola portion of the Bern-Milan trip. The Simplon is actually 2 tunnels, one southbound and a 65-foot longer bore for the separate northbound tunnel.

Dep. Bern	6:21	8:13	9:21(1)	11:21(1)	13:21(1)
Arr. Domodossola	8:49	10:27	11:49	13:49	16:00
		*	*	*	
Dep. Domodossola	9:05(1)	10:32(1)	12:05(1)	15:05	17:05(1)
Arr. Bern	11:34	12:43	14:34	17:34	19:34

(1)Light refreshments.

Bern - Interlaken - Brienz - Interlaken - Bern

Fine gorge, lake and mountain scenery on this easy one-day roundtrip.
260

Dep. Bern	7:27	8:27	9:27	10:27	11:27(1)
Arr. Interlaken (Ost)	8:20	9:20	10:20	11:32	12:20

Change trains.
264

Dep. Interlaken (Ost)	8:37	9:39	10:37	11:39	12:37
Arr. Brienz	8:58	9:55	10:58	11:55	12:58
	*	*	*		
Dep. Brienz	8:59	9:56	10:59	11:56	12:59
Arr. Interlaken (Ost)	9:17	10:19	11:17	12:19	13:17

Change trains.
260

Dep. Interlaken (Ost)	9:34	10:24	11:34	12:24	13:24
Arr. Bern	10:27	11:27	12:27	13:27	14:27

(1)Plus other departures from Bern (that allow the same roundtrip) at 12:27, 13:27, 14:26, 15:27, 16:27 and 17:27.

Bern - Interlaken - Jungfraujoch - Wengen - Interlaken - Bern

This easy one-day trip covers the heart of the Bernese Oberland area and offers very good gorge, lake and mountain scenery. The Interlaken-Jungfraujoch portion of this excursion is *not* covered by Eurailpass or Eurail Youthpass. There have been popular ski resorts in this area since 1906.

Jungfraujoch is the highest (11,333 feet) railstation in Europe. Fabulous views of the Jungfrau, Eiger and Monch peaks can be seen from the revolving restaurant, which rotates completely every 50 minutes. The highest waterfall in Europe (2,000-foot drop) is spectacular in late Spring and early Summer.

We suggest, for variety, you go from Interlaken to Jungfraujoch via Wengen and then return to Interlaken via Grindelwald.

260			288		
Dep. Bern	7:27	8:27	Dep. Jungfraujoch	12:10	13:05
Arr. Interlaken (Ost)	8:20	9:20	Arr. Scheidegg	12:52	13:50
Change trains. Go to			Change trains. Go to		
Jungfraujoch via Wengen.			Interlaken via Grindelwald.		
287			287		
Dep. Interlaken (Ost)	8:40	9:40	Dep. Scheidegg	12:57	13:57
Arr. Scheidegg	10:02	11:02	Arr. Interlaken (Ost)	14:23	15:36
Change trains.			Change trains.		
288			260		
Dep. Scheidegg	10:07	11:58	Dep. Interlaken (Ost)	14:34	16:34
Arr. Jungfraujoch	10:58	11:58	Arr. Bern	15:27	17:27

Bern - Lausanne - Brig - Spiez - Bern

Excellent gorge, lake and mountain scenery on this eacy one-day circle trip. This is a portion of the "Geneva-Spiez-Geneva" trip listed later in this section. There is time for a stopover in Lausanne and/or Spiez. You go through the 9-mile Lotschberg Tunnel after leaving Brig.

256

Dep. Bern	6:34(1)	7:34	8:16(2)	9:34(2)	10:16(2+3)
Arr. Lausanne	7:45	8:45	9:22	10:45	11:22

Change trains.

251

Dep. Lausanne	7:50	8:50(1)	9:28(2)	10:50	11:28(1)
Arr. Brig	9:40	10:47	11:08	12:47	13:08

Change trains.

260

Dep. Brig	9:54(1)	10:54(2)	11:12(1)	12:54	13:54
Arr. Spiez	11:01	12:01	1210	14:01	15:01
Dep. Spiez	11:03(1)	12:03(2)	12:12(1)	14:03	15:03
Arr. Bern	11:34	12:34	12:43	14:34	15:34

(1)Light refreshments. (2)Meal service. (3)The same circle trip can be made in daylight by leaving Bern at frequent times from 11:16 to 14:16.

Bern - Locarno - Bern

Complete notes on the Domodossola-Locarno portion of this easy one-day roundtrip appear later in this section, under "Brig-Domodossola-Locarno".

260

Dep. Bern	7:21	9:21
Arr. Domodossola	9:49	11:49

Change trains. Walk outside the Domodossola station and go to the underground Centovalli track.

290

Dep. Domodossola	10:05	12:05
Arr. Locarno	11:50	13:48

290

Dep. Locarno	15:00	17:20(1)
Arr. Domodossola	15:43	19:00

Change trains. Walk from the underground Centovalli track, up to the main Domodossola station.

260

Dep. Domodossola	17:05	19:15
Arr. Bern	19:34	21:34

(1)Plus another departure from Locarno at 18:40, arriving Bern at 23:34.

Sights in **Locarno:** Stroll the gardens along the shore of Lake Maggiore and take the funicular ride to the church high above the village for a fine view of Locarno and Lake Maggiore.

312

Bern - Mt. Pilatus - Bern

Very nice gorge, lake and mountain scenery on this easy one-day roundtrip that can include a stopover in Luzern.

The Pilatus Rack Railway trip (Alpnachstad-Pilatus-Alpnachstad) operates only April 1 to October 31. It is *not* covered by Eurailpass or Eurail Youthpass. Costs about 34 Swiss Francs for the roundtrip. There are good views and several restaurants at the peak of Pilatus.

262

Dep. Bern	6:44	7:44	10:00	11:44(1)
Arr. Luzern	8:01	9:01	11:49	13:01

Change trains.

264

Dep. Luzern	8:09	9:57	11:57	13:57
Arr. Alpnachstad	8:28	10:13	12:13	14:13

Change to rack railway for the ride to the top of Mt. Pilatus.

292

Dep. Alpnachstad	8:45	10:20	12:25	14:40
Arr. Pilatus Kulm	9:25	11:00	13:05	15:20

* * *

Dep. Pilatus Kulm	9:36	11:35	13:52	15:55
Arr. Alpnachstad	10:16	12:15	14:36	16:35

Change trains.

264

Dep. Alpnachstad	10:38	12:38	14:38	16:38
Arr. Luzern	10:56	12:56	14:56	16:56

Change trains.

262

Dep. Luzern	11:51(1)	13:51	15:51	17:51(1+2)
Arr. Bern	13:10	15:10	17:10	19:10

(1)Light refreshments. (2)Plus other departures from Luzern at 19:51(1), 20:51(1) and 22:03.

Bern - Spiez - Bern 260

Great gorge, lake and mountain scenery on this easy one-day roundtrip. This is a portion of the "Geneva-Spiez-Geneva" trip listed later in this section. Plenty of time to stroll in Spiez and enjoy the beauty of Lake Thun and the mountains above it.

Dep. Bern   Frequent times from 6:40 to 22:21
Arr. Spiez   30 minutes later

* * *

Dep. Spiez   Frequent times from 6:00 to 23:03
Arr. Bern   30 minutes later

Bern - Spiez - Brig - Lausanne - Bern

Marvelous gorge, lake, mountain and river scenery on this easy one-day circle trip. This is the reverse of the "Bern-Lausanne-Spiez-Bern" ride listed earlier in this section. A stroll in Spiez is a nice way to break the journey. You go through the 10-mile Lotschberg Tunnel after leaving Spiez.

260

Dep. Bern	7:21(1)	8:21(1)	9:21(1)	10:21(1)	11:21(1)
Arr. Spiez	7:52	8:52	9:52	10:52	11:52
Dep. Spiez	7:54	8:54	9:54	10:54	11:54
Arr. Brig	9:00	10:00	11:00	12:00	13:00

Change trains.

251

Dep. Brig	9:06(1)	10:06(1)	11:07(2)	12:06	13:46(1)
Arr. Lausanne	11:04	12:04	12:32	14:04	15:26

Change trains.

256

Dep. Lausanne	11:32(3)	12:09(1)	13:32(3)	14:09(1)	15:32(3+4)
Arr. Bern	12:38	13:20	14:38	15:20	16:38

(1)Light refreshments. (2)Supplement charged. Light refreshments. (3)Meal service. (4)Plus other departures from Lausanne at frequent times from 16:09 to 23:09.

Brig - Andermatt - Disentis - Brig   315

Fine gorge and mountain scenery on this easy one-day roundtrip. A stopover can be made (11:06-14:10) in Andermatt, a great ski resort. This trip is *not* covered by Eurailpass or Eurail Youthpass.

The luxury "Glacier Express" presents gourmet meals in an elegant paneled restaurant car. Wine is served in special glasses that have bent stems. Spilling is avoided by careful turning of the glass. Sit on the left-hand side for best views from Brig, on the right-hand from Disentis.

Dep. Brig	8:18(1)	9:20	11:44(2)	11:58(1+3)	13:44(1+4)
Arr. Andermatt	10:09(1)	11:08	13:25	14:10(1)	15:27(1)
Arr. Disentis	11:25	12:32	14:40	15:28	16:45
		*	*	*	
Dep. Disentis	12:17(2)	13:09	15:09	16:29(1)	
Dep. Andermatt	13:28(2)	14:30	16:56	18:22	
Arr. Brig	15:12	16:35	18:45	20:16	

(1)Change trains in Andermatt. (2)"Glacier Express" Meal service. (3)Daily, except Sundays and holidays. (4)Light refreshments.

Brig - Arona - Brig   251

Beautiful lake and mountain scenery on this easy one-day roundtrip, which can also be seen as a portion of the Lausanne-Milan route. This ride takes you through Europe's longest (19.8km or 11.9 miles) tunnel, the Simplon. It is the second longest tunnel in the world, after Japan's Daishimizu Tunnel (22.3km or 13.4 miles) between Tokyo and Niigata.

Dep. Brig	8:18	9:17	9:55	11:17	13:17	14:41
Arr. Arona	9:54	10:56	11:29	12:56	14:56	16:13
			*	*	*	
Dep. Arona	10:54	12:01	13:44	15:55	17:41	18:11(1)
Arr. Brig	12:37	13:37	15:37	17:37	19:27	19:45

(1)Plus other departures from Arona at 20:02 and 22:56.

Here is the schedule for the Lausanne-Milan route.
251

Dep. Lausanne	6:30	8:22	9:28	11:28(1)	12:52(1+2)
Dep. Brig	8:18	9:55	11:17	13:17	14:41
Arr. Arona	9:54	11:29	12:56	14:56	16:13
Arr. Milan (Centrale)	50-60-minutes later				

(1)Light refreshments until Brig. (2)Plus another departure from Lausanne at 15:22 that allows daylight viewing.

Brig - Bern - Brig   260

An easy one-day roundtrip that affords a view of Rhone Valley and Lonza Valley farms, gorges, lakes and mountains plus the Lake Thun scenery at Spiez about which we enthuse in the "Geneva-Spiez" trip described later in this section . . . and going through the 10-mile Lotschberg Tunnel and over the Bietschtal Bridge. This structure takes the train 255 feet above the ravine it crosses. We recommend a stop in Spiez and a stroll there on either the outbound or homebound leg of this trip.

All of these trains have light refreshments.

Dep. Brig	6:46	7:49	8:54	9:54	10:54	11:12(1)
Arr. Spiez	8:01	9:01	10:01	11:01	12:01	12:10
Dep. Spiez	8:03	9:03	10:03	11:03	12:03	12:12
Arr. Bern	30 minutes later					

	*	*	*			
Dep. Bern	9:21	10:21	11:21	12:21	12:54	13:21(2)
Arr. Spiez	9:52	10:52	11:52	12:52	13:25	13:52
Dep. Spiez	9:54	10:54	11:54	12:54	13:27	13:54
Arr. Brig	66 minutes later					

(1)Plus other departures from Bern that allow daylight viewing at frequent times from 11:54 to 17:54.   (2)Plus other departures from Bern at frequent times from 14:21 to 20:21.

Brig - Domodossola - Locarno - Domodossola - Brig

We call the Domodossola-Locarno portion of this one-day roundtrip one of the 5 most scenic rail trips in Europe. It is a spectacular narrow-gauge local train ride offering great gorge, mountain and river scenery on the Centovalli (one hundred valleys) route. Be sure to have your passport with you. On this trip, you go from Switzerland to Italy, then Switzerland, back to Italy, and then again to Switzerland. In Locarno, take the chairlift to Cimetta for a magnificent view of Lake Maggiore and the Alps.

This ride takes you through Europe's longest (19.8km or 11.9 miles) tunnel, the Simplon (between Brig and Domodossola). It is the second longest tunnel in the world, after Japan's Daishimizu Tunnel (22.3km or 13.4 miles) between Tokyo and Niigata.

The 90-minute, 35-mile Locarno-Domodossola trip does not start from the Locarno railstation. You catch what looks like a trolley car at the central Locarno bus stop, across from the train station. Stops en route include Camedo, Intragna with its many churches, Verdasio which has a train connection to the mountain town of Rasa, Palagnedra which has a lake, and Druogno, highest point on this scenic route.

See detailed notes about Locarno on page 211, under "Milan-Locarno-Milan".

260

Dep. Brig	8:18	11:17
Arr. Domodossola	8:49	11:49

Change trains. Walk outside the Domodossola station and go to the underground Centovalli track.

290

Dep. Domodossola	9:05	12:05
Arr. Locarno	10:50	13:48

290

Dep. Locarno	13:00	16:20
Arr. Domodossola	14:43	18:25

Change trains. Walk from the underground Centovalli track up to the main Domodossola station

260

Dep. Domodossola	15:05	18:55
Arr. Brig	15:37	19:27

Brig - Spiez - Interlaken - Brienz - Interlaken - Brig

Very good gorge, lake and mountain scenery on this easy one-day roundtrip.

260			264		
Dep. Brig	9:54	10:54	Dep. Brienz	12:59	14:59
Arr. Spiez	11:01	12:00	Arr. Interlaken (Ost)	13:17	15:17
Change trains.			Change trains.		
260			260		
Dep. Spiez	11:07	12:00	Dep. Interlaken (Ost)	13:24	15:24
Arr. Interlaken (Ost)	11:32	12:20	Arr. Spiez	13:53	15:53
Change trains.			Change trains.		
264			260		
Dep. Interlaken (Ost)	11:39	12:37	Dep. Spiez	13:54	15:54
Arr. Brienz	11:56	12:59	Arr. Brig	15:05	17:00

Brig - Interlaken - Jungfraujoch - Interlaken - Brig

Excellent gorge, lake and mountain scenery on this easy one-day roundtrip. Jungfraujoch is the highest (11,333 feet) railstation in Europe. The Interlaken-Jungfraujoch-Interlaken portion of this trip is *not* covered by Eurailpass or Eurail Youthpass.

We suggest, for variety, you go from Interlaken to Jungfraujoch via Wengen and then return to Interlaken via Grindelwald.

260			288		
Dep. Brig	7:49	8:54	Dep. Jungfraujoch	14:05	15:07
Arr. Spiez	8:59	9:59	Arr. Scheidegg	14:50	15:50
Change trains.			Change trains. Go to Interlaken		
260			via Grindelwald.		
Dep. Spiez	9:00	10:00	287		
Arr. Interlaken (Ost)	9:20	10:20	Dep. Scheidegg	14:57	15:57
Change trains. Go to Jungfrau-			Arr. Interlaken (Ost)	16:23	17:23
joch via Wengen.			Change trains.		
287			260		
Dep. Interlaken (Ost)	9:40	10:40	Dep. Interlaken (Ost)	16:34	17:34
Arr. Scheidegg	10:54	11:54	Arr. Spiez	16:53	17:53
Change trains.			Change trains.		
288			260		
Dep. Scheidegg	11:33	12:07	Dep. Spiez	16:54	17:54
Arr. Jungfraujoch	12:32	12:58	Arr. Brig	18:00	19:00

Brig - Lausanne - Brig   251

Nice gorge, lake, mountain and river scenery on this easy one-day roundtrip.

Dep. Brig   Frequent times from 5:29 to 21:46
Arr. Lausanne   1½-2 hours later

*   *   *

Dep. Lausanne   Frequent times from 6:30 to 20:28
Arr. Brig   1½-2 hours later

Brig - Zermatt - Gornergrat - Zermatt - Brig

Great gorge and mountain scenery on this easy one-day roundtrip that includes an outstanding cogwheel train ride to Gornergrat (10,200 feet) for a close view of the Matterhorn (14,692 feet) and more than 50 other peaks. This trip is *not* covered by Eurailpass or Eurail Youthpass. The cost of the roundtrip is approximately 50 Swiss francs per person.

280
Dep. Brig   Frequent times from 5:08 to 19:23
Arr. Zermatt   90 minutes later
  Change trains.
281
Dep. Zermatt   Frequent times from 7:10 to 17:35 (18:00 from
                 late June to late September)
Arr. Gornergrat 45 minutes later

*   *   *

Dep. Gornergrat Frequent times from 7:55 to 18:20 (18:45 from
                 late June to late September)
Arr. Zermatt   45 minutes later
  Change trains.
280
Dep. Zermatt   Frequent times from 6:04 to 21:05
Arr. Brig   90 minutes later

Chur - Brig - Zermatt - Gornergrat - Zermatt

There is fabulous Rhone Glacier scenery on this ride plus crossing Oberalp Pass (6,700 feet) and Furka Pass (7,100 feet) on the Chur-Brig portion. This trip crosses the highest bridges in Europe and includes the outstanding cogwheel train ride to Gornergrat (10,200 feet) for a close view of the Matterhorn (14,692 feet) and more than 50 other Alpine peaks. This trip is *not* covered by Eurailpass or Eurail Youthpass. The cost of the roundtrip is approximately 50 Swiss francs per person.

Table 315

| Dep. Chur | 8:53(1) |
| Arr. Zermatt | 14:46 |

Change to narrow-gauge train.

281

| Dep. Zermatt | 15:05(2) | 15:30 | 16:20 | 17:10(2) | 17:35(3) |
| Arr. Gornergrat | 15:50 | 16:15 | 17:05 | 17:55 | 18:15 |

* * *

| Dep. Gornergrat | 17:05 | 17:45(2) | 18:20 | 18:45(2) | -0- |
| Arr. Zermatt | 45 minutes later | | | | |

(1)Light refreshments. (2)Runs from late June to late September. (3)Plus another departure from Zermatt at 18:00(2).

Chur - St. Moritz - Chur 346

Marvelous gorge, lake and mountain scenery on this easy one-day bus round-trip. It is a very scenic ride involving going through double spiral tunnels and across the amazing Landwasser Viaduct.

Dep. Chur	7:15(1)	9:00	11:50	15:10
Arr. St. Moritz (Stn.)	9:51	11:33	14:26	17:44
Arr. St. Moritz (Post)	5 minutes later			

* * *

Dep. St. Moritz (Post)	8:30	13:30(1)	16:05	17:25
Dep. St. Moritz (Stn.)	5 minutes later			
Arr. Chur	11:10	16:10	18:50	20:08

(1)Runs from late June to late September.

Geneva - Lausanne - Brig - Spiez - Bern - Geneva

One of the 5 most scenic rail trips in Europe. The succession of beautiful scenes defy verbal description: 15 miles of terraced vineyards and Lake Geneva shoreline between Geneva and Lausanne. Great river scenery en route from Martigny to Brig. After leaving Brig, you go through the 10-mile Lotschberg Tunnel. Take a seat on the side of the train that faces the Brig railstation.

Upon emerging from the tunnel, there is such beautiful farm and mountain scenery around tiny Kandersteg and Fruitigen that you want to get off the train and spend the rest of your life there.

We urge you to arrive Spiez near Noon and have the local specialty for lunch. Walk only 5 minutes from the Spiez railstation down a short hill to the dining-room of the little Hotel Krone, and order the delicious Geschnetzeltes und Rosti.

After lunch, it is only a 15-minute walk to the castle overlooking Lake Thun, the most beautiful lake scene on this planet. If the view of Lake Thun and the mountains reflected on its surface does not thrill you, pack up and go home because you will not find any landscape more beautiful to see in this world.

You can return to Geneva (via Bern) either by boarding a train in Spiez or by first taking the 45-minute boat ride (covered by Eurailpass) from Spiez to Thun village and then boarding the train in Thun. The lake steamer ties up 100 feet from Thun's railstation. If you resume the train ride in Spiez, look for the steamer when the train pulls into Thun. Look out the right side of the train.

It is possible to schedule a brief stop-over in Bern.

On the way back to Geneva from Bern, you pass through the same lake and vineyard scenery you saw between Lausanne and Geneva that morning, at the start of this fabulous one-day trip.

251

Dep. Geneva (Corn.)	7:45	8:45	9:45(1)	11:45	
Dep. Lausanne	8:22	9:28	10:28(1)	11:28(1)	12:28
Arr. Brig	9:47	11:08	12:17	13:08	14:17

Change trains.

260

Dep. Brig	9:54(1)	11:12(1)	12:54(1)	13:54(1)	14:54(1)
Arr. Spiez	11:01	12:10	14:01	15:01	16:01
Dep. Spiez	11:03(1)	12:12(1)	14:03(1)	15:03(1)	16:03(1)
Dep. Thun	11:14(1)	12:23(1)	14:14(1)	15:14(1)	16:14(1)
Arr. Bern	11:34	12:43	14:34	15:34	16:34

Change trains.

256

Dep. Bern	12:16(2)	13:16(2)	15:16(1)	16:16(2)	17:16(3)
Arr. Lausanne	13:22	14:22	16:22	17:22	18:22
Arr. Geneva (Corn.)	13:58	14:58	16:58	17:58	18:58

)1)Light refreshments. (2)Meal service. (3)Plus other departures from Bern at 17:34(1), 18:16(2), 19:16(2), 19:34, 20:16(2), 21:16(2) and 22:16.

Here are the Lake Thun (Spiez-Thun) boat schedules (covered by Eurailpass) to combine with departures from Thun village for Bern.

321

Dep. Spiez	11:46(1)	13:17(2)	14:02	15:03(2)	16:02(2+3)
Arr. Thun (Pier)	12:29	14:02	14:56	15:46	16:46

It is a 2-minute walk from the boat pier to the train.

260

Dep. Thun (Stn.)	13:07	14:07	15:07	16:07	17:07
Arr. Bern	20 minutes later				

(1)Light refreshments. (2)Meal service. (3)Plus other boat departures from Spiez at 17:04(1), 18:01(2), 19:23(2) and 20:10, connecting in Thun with trains to Bern.

Geneva - Chamonix (Mt. Blanc) - Geneva

Be sure to have your passport with you on this trip filled with fantastic mountain scenery, as you will be going from Switzerland to France. From Chamonix, you should take the 2-mile-high cable-car ride that goes nearly to the top of the tallest mountain in Europe, the 15,771-foot Mt. Blanc, towering almost 10,000 feet above Chamonix, for a view of Alpine peaks extending 80 miles.

After descending, there is just time to also take the narrow-gauge train to see the "Sea of Ice" glacier bed. The tombstones in the small cemetery, a 5-minute walk from the railstation, are fascinating. Nearly one-fourth of the headstones read "died on the mountain". Climbers and their rescuers.

The train changes on this trip are easy cross-platform transfers taking only a minute.

158			167		
Dep. Geneva (Eaux-Vives)	9:32		Dep. Chamonix	15:30	17:30
Arr. Annemasse	9:40		Arr. St. Gervais	16:06	18:06
Change trains.			Change trains.		
Dep. Annemasse	9:53		Dep. St. Gervais	16:28	18:21
Arr. La Roche-sur-Foron	10:11		Arr. La Roche	17:12	19:17
Change trains.			Change trains.		
167			158		
Dep. La Roche-sur-Foron	10:25		Dep. La Roche	17:20	19:27
Arr. St. Gervais	11:17		Arr. Annemasse	17:38	19:45
Change trains.			Change trains.		
Dep. St. Gervais	11:43		Dep. Annemasse	17:43	20:25
Arr. Chamonix	12:22		Arr. Geneva		
			(Eaux-Vives)	17:51	20:33

Geneva - Lausanne - Geneva

Here is a short trip packed with fine scenery of 15 miles of terraced vineyards, nearly the entire route following the lovely shoreline of Lake Geneva. Complete schedules are listed earlier in this section, under the "Geneva-Lausanne" one-day excursion.

Geneva - Lyon - Geneva   155

The Geneva-Amberieu portion of this easy one-day roundtrip is noted for scenic gorges.

Occasionally, 2 trains depart from the same track at Lyon's Perrache railstation, heading in opposite directions. Be sure to stand at the correct end (North or South) of the track in order to board the train you want to ride. Check the departure signs at the underground passageway. Do not rely merely on a track number when departing from Perrache railstation !

Next to the North passageway of Track "A" is a take-out restaurant, handy for provisioning your trip.

A metropolitan train connects Lyon's Brotteaux and Perrache railstations. The ride is 15 minutes.

Dep. Geneva (Corn.)	6:30	10:47	12:51	16:43
Dep. Amberieu	8:06	12:26	14:15	18:10
Arr. Lyon (Part-Dieu)	8:29	12:50	14:36	18:32
Arr. Lyon (Perrache)	8:40	13:00	14:47	18:43
	*	*	*	
Dep. Lyon (Perrache)	9:42	14:14	16:05	18:18
Dep. Lyon (Part-Dieu)	9:51	14:23	16:15	18:28
Dep. Amberieu	10:15	-0-(1)	16:40	-0-(1)
Arr. Geneva (Corn.)	11:41	16:07	18:08	20:33

(1)Does not stop in Amberieu.

Geneva - Martigny - Geneva   251

This is a scenic trip of intermediate length, longer than the Geneva-Lausanne ride and shorter than the Geneva-Brig-Bern-Geneva circle trip. Very good gorge, lake, mountain and vineyard scenery.

Dep. Geneva (Corn.)	6:45	8:45	9:45(1)	10:45(1+3)
Arr. Martigny	8:16	10:16	11:19	12:16
	*	*	*	
Dep. Martigny	8:36(1)	12:31	13:08(2+4)	
Arr. Geneva (Corn.)	10:08	12:08	14:08	14:58

(1)Light refreshments. (2)Change trains in Lausanne. (3)Plus other departures from Geneva at 11:45(1), 12:56(2), 13:45(1) and 14:56(1+2).   (4)Plus other departures from Martigny at frequent times from 13:36 to 22:36.

Geneva - Montreux - Zweisimmen - Spiez - Bern - Geneva

This variation on the scenic trip described earlier (Geneva-Brig-Bern-Geneva) runs parallel and north of the Martigny-Brig route. You miss going through the Lotschberg Tunnel, but you are able to see all of the Geneva-Lausanne vineyard and Lake Geneva scenery plus Lake Thun (Spiez) and a possible stopover in Bern, en route back to Geneva. See earlier notes about Spiez and taking a boat on Lake Thun from Spiez to Thun village.

The ascent from Montreaux to Sweisimmen is very scenic as the train climbs from the shore of Lac Leman to Les Avants in a series of hairpin bends. The funicular ride from Les Avants to Sonloup is worthwhile.

251

Dep. Geneva (Corn.)	8:45	9:45(1)	10:45(1)	11:45	12:56(1+4)
Arr. Montreux	9:47	10:47	11:47	12:47	14:10

Change trains.

255

Dep. Montreux	9:58(2)	10:53	12:20	12:53	14:20(2)
Arr. Zweisimmen	11:38	12:55	14:07	14:55	16:07

Change trains.

Dep. Zweisimmen	12:20	13:00	14:20	15:00	16:20
Arr. Spiez	12:57	13:50	14:57	15:50	16:57

Change trains.

260

Dep. Spiez	13:03(1)	14:03(1)	15:03(1)	16:03(1)	17:03(1+5)
Dep. Thun	13:14(1)	14:14(1)	15:14(1)	16:14(1)	17:14(1)
Arr. Bern	13:43	14:34	15:34	16:34	17:34

Change trains.

256

Dep. Bern	13:16(3)	15:16(1)	16:16(3)	17:16(3)	18:16(3+6)
Arr. Geneva (Corn.)	14:58	16:58	17:58	18:58	19:58

(1)Light refreshments. (2)"Panoramic Express". Has special observation cars. (3)Meal service. (4)Plus another departure from Geneva at 13:45(1) that allows daylight viewing. (5)Plus other departures from Spiez at frequent times from 18:03 to 23:03. (6)Plus other departures from Bern at 19:34, 20:16(3), 21:16(3) and 22:16.

Interlaken - Mt. Pilatus - Interlaken

Great gorge and mountain scenery on this easy one-day roundtrip. The Alpnachstad-Pilatus-Alpnachstad rack railway portion operates only from May to end of October and is *not* covered by Eurailpass or Eurail Youthpass. Costs about 34 Swiss francs for roundtrip. There are good views and several restaurants at the peak of Pilatus.

264

Dep. Interlaken (Ost)	6:37	8:37	10:37	12:37
Arr. Alpnachstad	8:36	10:36	12:36	14:36

Change to rack railway for the ride to the top of Mt. Pilatus.

292

Dep. Alpnachstad	8:45	11:00	13:17	14:40
Arr. Pilatus Kulm	9:25	11:40	13:57	15:20
	*	*	*	
Dep. Pilatus Kulm	10:55	13:12	15:15	17:13
Arr. Alpnachstad	11:35	13:52	15:55	17:53

Change to standard train.

264

Dep. Alpnachstad	12:15	14:15	16:15	18:15
Arr. Interlaken (Ost)	14:19	16:19	18:19	20:22

Interlaken - Spiez - Bern - Spiez - Interlaken 260

Excellent gorge, lake and mountain scenery on this easy one-day roundtrip that includes visiting Lake Thun and a possible stopover in Bern. See earlier notes about Spiez and taking a boat on Lake Thun from Spiez to Thun village, under the ''Geneva-Brig-Bern-Geneva'' scenic trip.

Dep. Interlaken (Ost)	7:34	8:24	9:34	10:24
Dep. Interlaken (West)	5 minutes later			
Dep. Spiez	7:56	8:56	9:56	10:56
Dep. Thun	8:07	9:07	10:07	11:07
Arr. Bern	20 minutes later			
	*	*	*	
Dep. Bern	Frequent times from 6:40 to 22:21			
Arr. Interlaken (West)	45-60 minutes later			
Arr. Interlaken (Ost)	5 minutes after arriving West station			

Interlaken - Spiez - Brig - Spiez - Interlaken 260

Nice gorge, lake and mountain scenery on this easy one-day roundtrip which includes visiting Lake Thun and going through the 10-mile Lotschberg Tunnel. There is time to stoppover in Spiez. See earlier notes about Spiez under the "Geneva-Brig-Bern-Geneva" scenic trip.

Dep. Interlaken (Ost)	7:34	8:24	9:34	10:24	11:34	12:24
Dep. Interlaken (West)	5 minutes later					
Arr. Spiez	7:53	8:53	9:53	10:53	11:53	12:53
Change trains.						
Dep. Spiez (1)	7:54	8:54	9:54	10:54	11:54	12:54
Dep. Brig	9:00	10:00	11:00	12:00	13:00	14:00

*   *   *

Dep. Brig (1)	Frequent times from 9:54 to 21:54
Arr. Spiez	70 minutes later
Change trains.	
Dep. Spiez	Frequent times from 11:07 to 23:04
Arr. Interlaken (West)	15 minutes later
Arr. Interlaken (Ost)	5 minutes after arriving West station

(1)Most of these trains have lightrefreshments.

Interlaken - Jungfraujoch - Interlaken

Great gorge and mountain scenery on this easy one-day roundtrip. This spectacular route ends at Europe's highest (11,333 feet) railstation. It includes 2 stops in the tunnel through Mount Eiger, for viewing through "windows" which the railroad's builders cut in the face of the cliff.

At Jungfraujoch, passengers alight to look down on the great Jungfrau glacier and stroll in the "Ice Palace" carved inside the glacier.

None of this trip is covered by Eurailpass or Eurail Youthpass.

For variety, we suggest you go from Interlaken to Jungfraujoch via Wengen, and then return to Interlaken via Grindelwald.

Grindelwald sits at 3400-feet altitude. The majestic peaks that rise around this village are: Jungfrau (13,642 feet), Eiger (13,026), Wetterhorn (12,142), Breithorn (12,409), Monch (13,449), Schreckhorn (13,380), Gspaltenhorn (11,277) and Tschingelhorn (11,736).

287

Dep. Interlaken (Ost)						
(Via Wengen)	7:40	8:40	9:40	10:40	11:40	12:40
Arr. Scheidegg	9:02	10:02	11:02	12:02	13:08	14:31
Change trains.						
288						
Dep. Scheidegg	9:07	10:07	11:07	12:07	14:05	15:05
Arr. Jungfraujoch	9:58	10:58	11:58	12:58	15:02	15:58

*   *   *

Dep. Jungfraujoch   10:05   12:10   13:05   14:05   15:07   16:05(1)
Arr. Scheidegg   10:52   12:52   13:50   14:50   15:50   16:46
    Change trains.
    287
Dep. Scheidegg
    (via Grindelwald)   11:14   12:57   13:57   14:57   15:57   16:57
Arr. Interlaken (Ost)   13:08   14:23   15:36   16:23   17:23   18:23
(1)Plus other departures from Jungfraujoch at 16:58 and 17:58 for connections
in Scheidegg with trains to Interlaken.

Lausanne - Brig - Lausanne   251
    Fine gorge, lake, mountain and river scenery on this easy one-day roundtrip.
Dep. LausanneFrequent times from 6:30 to 21:28
Arr. Brig   1½-2 hours later
                 *   *   *
Dep. Brig   Frequent times from 5:29 to 21:46
Arr. Lausanne 1½-2 hours later

Lausanne - Brig - Spiez - Bern - Lausanne
    Marvelous gorge, lake, mountain and river scenery on this easy one-day
roundtrip, a portion of the ''Geneva-Lausanne-Spiez-Bern-Geneva'' scenic trip
listed earlier in this section and to which you should refer for complete schedules
and sightseeing details.

Locarno - Camedo - Locarno   290
    One of the 5 most scenic rail trips in Europe. Fantastic gorge, river and
mountain scenery. You will see some hillside farms that are nearly vertical.
The ride is called "Centovalli", and you *will* see a hundred valleys. This trip
can be made either as an easy one-day roundtrip or as a portion of the Locarno-
Milan or Locarno-Brig routes.
    Please note that this trip does *not* start from the Locarno railstation. You
catch what looks like a trolley car at the central bus stop, across from the
train station.
    At Camedo, there is only a tiny restaurant-bar and absolutely nothing to
do while you wait for the return ride to Locarno.
Dep. Locarno   7:10   9:00   10:05(1)   12:00   13:00(1)   15:00(1+2)
Arr. Camedo   7:50   9:47   10:45   12:47   13:41   15:41
                    *   *   *
Dep. Camedo   7:55   10:08(1)   11:08(1)   13:05(1)   15:05(1)   16:34
Arr. Locarno   45 minutes later
(1)Light refreshments. (2(Plus another departure from Locarno at 16:20 that
allows a roundtrip.

Locarno - Domodossola - Brig - Domodossola - Locarno

Very good gorge, mountain and river scenery on this one-day roundtrip that includes the wonderful Centovalli ride described in the previous trip plus going through the 12-mile Simplon, longest main line rail tunnel in the world. Be sure to take your passport on this trip from Switzerland to Italy, Switzerland, back to Italy and then again to Switzerland.

The Domodossola-Brig (and v.v.) portion of this route takes you through Europe's longest (19.8km - 11.9 miles) tunnel, the Simplon. It is the world's second-longest tunnel, after Japan's Daishimizu Tunnel between TokyoT and Niigata (22.3km - 13.4 miles).

The 90-minute, 35-mile Locarno-Domodossola trip does *not* start from the Locarno railstation. You catch what looks like a trolley car at the central Locarno bus stop, across from the train station. Stops en route includes Camedo, Intragna with its many churches, Verdasio which has a train connection to the mountain town of Rasa, Palagnedra which has a lake, and Druogno, highest point on this scenic route.

252			251	
Dep. Locarno	11:05(1)		Dep. Brig	14:41
Arr. Domodossola	12:44		Arr. Domodossola	15:13
Change trains. Walk from the underground Centovalli track, up to the main Domodossola station.			Change trains. Walk outside the Domodossola station and go to the underground Centovalli track.	
251			251	
Dep. Domodossola	13:05		Dep. Domodossola	15:30
Arr. Brig	13:37		Arr. Locarno	17:13

(1)Light refreshments.

Luzern - Brunnen - Luzern   319

Here is an excellent one-day roundtrip boat ride on Lake Luzern, covered by Eurailpass.

Dep. Luzern (Stn. Quay)	9:00	9:30	10:30	11:30	13:25(1)
Arr. Brunnen	10:54	11:59	12:47	13:58	15:29
		*	*	*	
Dep. Brunnen	12:36	13:52	14:36	15:43	17:26(2)
Arr. Luzern (Stn. Quay)	14:52	16:15	16:52	18:20	19:29

(1)Plus other departures from Luzern at 14:25 and 15:25.   (2)Plus another departure from Brunnen at 18:19

Luzern - Interlaken - Luzern

Great gorge and mountain scenery on this easy one-day roundtrip. Complete schedules are listed earlier in this section, under the "Luzern-Interlaken--Luzern" one-day excursion.

Luzern - Interlaken - Brig - Domodossola - Locarno - Luzern

This route includes going through the 9-mile Lotschberg Tunnel, the 12-mile Simplon and the 9-mile St. Gotthard, as well as seeing the beautiful Centovalli scenery between Domodossola and Locarno.

264		290		
Dep. Luzern	8:00(1)	Dep. Domodossola	14:05(1)	
Arr. Interlaken (Ost)	10:00	Arr. Locarno	15:47	
Change trains.		Change trains.		
260		**261**		
Dep. Interlaken (Ost)	10:24(1)	Dep. Locarno	15:53	18:31
Arr. Spiez	10:53	Arr. Bellinzona	16:22	18:31
Change trains.		Change trains.		
Dep. Spiez	10:54	**277**		
Arr. Brig	12:00	Dep. Bellinzona	17:20(2)	19:05(2)
Change trains.		Arr. Luzern	19:37	21:37
251				
Dep. Brig	13:17			
Arr. Domodossola	13:49			

(1)Light refreshments. (2)Meal service.

Luzern - Interlaken - Jungfraujoch - Interlaken - Luzern

Marvelous gorge, lake and mountain scenery on this easy one-day round-trip. See details about Jungfraujoch earlier in this section, under "Interlaken-Jungfraujoch".

For variety, we suggest you go from Interlaken to Jungfraujoch via Wengen, and then return to Interlaken via Grindelwald. This portion is *not* covered by Eurailpass or Eurail Youthpass.

264			288		
Dep. Luzern	7:17	8:00(1)	Dep. Jungfraujoch	12:10	13:05(2)
Arr. Interlaken			Arr. Scheidegg	12:52	13:50
(Ost)	9:17	10:00	Change trains		
Change trains.			**287**		
287			Dep. Scheidegg (via		
Dep. Interlaken			Grindelwald		
(Ost)	9:40	10:08	Arr. Interlaken		
(via Wengen)			(Ost)	14:23	15:36
Arr. Scheidegg	10:54	11:27	Change trains.		
Change trains.			**264**		
288			Dep. Interlaken		
Dep. Scheidegg	11:07	12:07	(Ost)	14:37	15:39(1)
Arr. Jungfraujoch	11:58	12:58	Arr. Luzern	16:56	17:37

(1)Light refreshments. (2)Plus other departures from Jungfraujoch at frequent times from 14:05 to 17:58 that allow connections for returning to Luzern.

Luzern - Interlaken - Spiez - Brig - Andermatt - Goschenen - Luzern

Here is a marvelous one-day circle trip, crammed with outstanding scenery. Although this schedule allows only 50 minutes in Spiez, if you take a packed lunch from Luzern there are benches outside the Spiez railstation where you can sit while eating and have a fabulous view of the village, Lake Thun and the mountains reflected on its surface. From Spiez to Brig, there is a good view of the Matterhorn from the right side of the train. Walk to the front of the Brig railstation to board the train to Andermatt. En route from Brig to Andermatt, you see the beautiful Rhone Valley, pass the face of the Rhone Glacier, and cross Furka pass (7,100 feet).

The Brig-Andermatt-Goschenen portion of this trip is *not* covered by Eurailpass or Eurail Youthpass.

264		315	
Dep. Luzern	9:17(1)	Dep. Brig	14:28
Arr. Interlaken (Ost)	11:17	Arr. Andermatt	16:26
Change trains.		Change trains.	
260		295	
Dep. Interlaken (Ost)	11:34	Dep. Andermatt	16:37
Arr. Spiez	11:52	Arr. Goschenen	16:52
Change trains.		Change trains.	
260		277	
Dep. Spiez	12:54	Dep. Goschenen	17:01(1)
Arr. Brig	14:00	Arr. Luzern	18:29
Change trains.			

Luzern - Mt. Pilatus - Luzern   264+292

Fine gorge and mountain scenery on this easy one-day roundtrip. The Alpnachstad-Pilatus-Alpnachstad rack railway portion operates only from May to end of October and is *not* covered by Eurailpass or Eurail Youthpass. Costs about 34 Swiss francs for the roundtrip. There are good views and several restaurants at the peak of Pilatus.

Dep. Luzern	8:09	9:57	11:57	13:57	14:57
Arr. Alpnachstad	8:28	10:13	12:13	14:13	15:13

Change to rack railway for the ride to the top of Mt. Pilatus.

Dep. Alpnachstad	8:45	10:20	12:25	14:40	15:20
Arr. Pilatus Kulm	9:25	11:00	13:05	15:20	16:00
		*	*	*	
Dep. Pilatus Kulm	9:36	11:35	13:12	15:55	16:35
Arr. Alpnachstad	10:16	12:15	13:52	16:35	17:15
Change trains.					
Dep. Alpnachstad	10:38	12:38	14:38	16:38	17:38
Arr. Luzern	18 minutes later				

Luzern - Mt. Titlis - Luzern 291

Very good gorge and mountain scenery on this easy one-day roundtrip. The Engelberg-Titlis-Engelberg rack railway is *not* covered by Eurailpass or Eurail Youthpass and does *not* operate the month of November. The cost for that roundtrip is 41 Swiss francs. Engelberg is a popular ski resort. It also has more than 20 miles of level walking and hiking paths, toboggan runs, a gambling casino and indoor swimming pools. There are great views from the restaurant on the top of Mount Titlis.

Dep. Luzern	7:17(1)	7:55	9:27	9:53	11:17(2)
Arr. Engelberg	8:12	8:46	10:22	10:49	12:12

Change to the funicular.

Dep. Engelberg	Frequent times
Arr. Mt. Titlis	60 minutes later

         *   *   *

Dep. Mt. Titlis	Frequent times
Arr. Engelberg	60 minutes later

Change to the train.

Dep. Engelberg	Frequent times from 6:24 to 20:50
Arr. Luzern	60-65 minutes later

(1)Change trains in Hergiswil. (2)Plus other departures from Luzern at frequent times from 12:09 to 21:17.

Luzern - Mt. Titlis - Luzern - Mt. Pilatus - Luzern

May through October, both mountains can be ascended in one day by following this schedule.

291		264	
Dep. Luzern	7:55(1)	Dep. Luzern	13:57
Arr. Engelberg	8:46	Arr. Alpnachstad	14:13
Change to the funicular.		Change to the rack railway.	
000		292	
Dep. Engelberg	9:30(1+2)	Dep. Alpnachstad	14:40(1)
Arr. Mt. Titlis	10:30(2)	Arr. Pilatus Kulm	15:20
	*	* * * *	
Dep. Mt. Titlis	11:00(1+2)	Dep. Pilatus Kulm	15:55(1+3)
Arr. Engelberg	12:00(2)	Arr. Alpnachstad	16:35
Change to the train.		Change to the train.	
291		264	
Dep. Engelberg	12:30(1)	Dep. Alpnachstad	16:38
Arr. Luzern	13:37	Arr. Luzern	16:56

(1)*Not* covered by Eurailpass or Eurail Youthpass. (2)Estimated. (3)Plus another departure from Alpnachstad at 17:15, arriving Luzern at 18:56.

Luzern - Mt. Rigi (via Arth-Goldau) - Luzern

The excellent gorge and mountain scenery on this route is, unlike the route that follows, entirely by train. This is an easy one-day roundtrip. The rides between Arth-Goldau and Rigi are *not* covered by Eurailpass or Eurail Youthpass.

272+277

Dep. Luzern	9:02	10:24	11:02	12:24	13:02	14:24(1)
Arr. Arth-Goldau	9:26	10:48	11:26	12:48	13:26	14:48

Change to rack railway.

294

Dep. Arth-Goldau	10:05	11:05	12:05	13:05	14:05	15:05
Arr. Rigi Kulm	10:40	11:40	12:40	13:40	14:46	15:40
		*	*	*		
Dep. Rigi Kulm	11:00	12:00	13:00	14:00	14:54	16:00(2)
Arr. Arth-Goldau	11:45	12:45	13:45	14:45	1545	16:45

Change to standard train.

272+277

Dep. Arth-Goldau	11:52	13:11	14:04	15:11	15:52	16:52
Arr. Luzern	30-40 minutes later

(1)Plus other departures from Luzern at 15:17, 15:31 and 16:24.   (2)Plus other departures from Rigi Kulm at 17:00. 18:00 and 19:00.

Luzern - Mt. Rigi (via Vitznau) - Luzern

The very nice gorge, lake and mountain scenery on this easy one-day round-trip includes a boat ride, covered by Eurailpass, on Lake Luzern. All boats serve food. From Vitznau to Mt. Rigi, the train climbs 4,000 feet in 4¼ miles. Over 450,000 passengers take this ride every year. There is good skiing at Rigi in the Winter. This line was constructed in 1871. The Vitznau-Rigi ride is *not* covered by Eurailpass or Eurail Youthpass.

319 (Boat)

Dep. Luzern (Stn. Quay)	9:00	9:30	10:30	12:05	13:25
Arr. Vitznau (Pier)		9:53	10:28	11:46	12:53	14:26

Change to rack railway. *Not* covered by Eurailpass or Eurail Youthpass.

293

Dep. Vitznau	10:00	10:40	12:oo	13:00	14:35
Arr. Rigi Kulm	10:35	11:15	12:35	13:35	15:10

		*	*	*		
Dep. Rigi Kulm	10:40	11:45	12:45	14:20	16:25(1)	
Arr. Vitznau	11:20	12:25	13:25	15:00	17:05	

Change to boat.
319

Dep. Vitznau (Pier)	11:40	12:55	13:40	15:15	17:14
Arr. Luzern (Stn. Quay)	55-70 minutes later				

Plus other departures from Rigi Kulm at 17:40 and 19:20 that connect in Vitznau with boat departures to Luzern.

St. Moritz - Tirano - St. Moritz   304

Great mountain scenery on this easy one-day roundtrip. Take your passport ! The track reaches the height of 7,405 feet, making this Europe's highest main rail line.

Dep. St. Moritz	7:40	8:55	11:35	13:30	
Arr. Tirano	10:12	11:30	14:11	16:13	
		*	*	*	
Dep. Tirano	10:30	12:35	14:55(1)	15:40	16:57
Arr. St. Moritz	13:03	15:03	17:11	18:11	19:19

(1)Light refreshments.

St. Moritz - Chur - Brig - Zermatt

Marvelous gorge, mountain and Rhone Glacier scenery on this ride, which crosses 291 bridges (including Europe's highest ones) and goes through 91 tunnels, including the 8-mile-long Furka, as the train traverses both the 6,700-foot Oberalp Pass and the 7,100-foot Furka Pass.

The luxury "Glacier Express" presents gourmet meals in an elegant paneled restaurant car. Wine is served in special glasses that have bent stems. Spilling is avoided by careful turning of the glass.

The Chur-Brig and Brig-Zermatt trips are *not* covered by Eurailpass or Eurail Youthpass. Sit on the right-hand side for the best views from St. Moritz, on the left-hand from Zermatt.

269

Dep. St. Moritz	6:00	8:55(1)
Arr. Chur	7:56	11:01

Change trains.
315

Dep. Chur	8:53(2)	-0-(1)
Arr. Brig	13:13	-0-(1)

Change trains.
280

Dep. Brig	13:22	15:18(1)
Arr. Zermatt	14:46	16:45

(1)Direct train to Zermatt. No train changes en route. (2)Change trains in Disentis.

Zermatt - Brig - Disentis - Chur - St. Moritz

280

Dep. Zermatt	6:04	7:23	10:05(1)	12:05
Arr. Brig	7:30	8:46	11:34	13:33

Change train.

315

Dep. Brig	8:18	9:20	-0-(1)	13:44(2)
Arr. Disentis	11:25	12:32	-0-	-0-

Change trains.

Dep. Disentis	11:32	12:45	-0-(1)	-0-(2)
Arr. Chur	12:56	14:07	-0-	18:04

Change trains.

269

Dep. Chur	13:50(3)	14:50(4)	15:45	18:50
Arr. St. Moritz	15:49	16:54	17:52	20:49

(1)Direct train to St. Moritz. No train change en route. Meal service. (2)Direct train to Chur. Light refreshments. (3)Runs from mid-June to late September. (4)Light refreshments.

Zermatt - Gornergrat - Zermatt   281

This is a great cogwheel train ride to 10,200-foot high Gornergrat for a close view of the Matterhorn (14,692 feet) and more than 50 other Alpine peaks. This ride is *not* covered by Eurailpass or Eurail Youthpass. Cost is approximately $43 (U.S.) per person for the roundtrip.

Dep. Zermatt   Frequent times from 7:10 to 17:35(1)

Arr. Gornergrat   minutes later   45

*   *   *

Dep. Gornergrat   :20   Frequent times from 7:55 to 18

Arr. Zermatt   minutes later   45

(1)Plus another departure from Zermatt at 18:45 from late June to mid-September.

Zurich - Buchs - Zurich   268

Fine lake scenery on this easy one-day roundtrip.

Dep. Zurich	6:24	7:20(1+2)	8:07(3)	9:26(2+4+5)
Arr. Sargans	7:31	8:18(2)	9:08	10:24(2)

Change trains.

Dep. Sargans	7:46	8:26	9:21	10:26
Arr. Buchs	10-15 minutes later			

                    *   *

Dep. Buchs	10:14(2)	11:15	12:20	13:15(6)
Arr. Sargans	10:26(2)	11:33	12:31	13:33

Change trains.

Dep. Sargans	10:28	11:40(3)	12:46(1)	13:40(1)
Arr. Zurich	11:26	12:47	13:47	14:47

(1)Light refreshments. (2)Direct train. No train change in Sargans. (3)Meal Service. (4)Reservation required. Meal service. (5)Plus other departures from Zurich at 10:07(1), 11:26(3), 12:16(1) and 13:26(2+3).   (6)Plus other departures from Buchs at 14:15(3) and 15:15(2+3) that connect in Sargans with trains to Zurich.

Zurich - Chur - Arosa - Chur - Zurich

Very good gorge, lake and mountain scenery on this easy one-day roundtrip. There is time for a stopover in Chur.

All of the Zurich-Chur and Chur-Zurich trains have light refreshments or meal service.

268

Dep. Zurich	7:07	8:07	9:07	10:07	11:07(1)
Arr. Chur	8:38	9:30	10:38	11:30	12:38

Change trains.

303

Dep. Chur	8:50	9:50	10:50	11:50	12:50
Arr. Arosa	61 minutes later				

                    *   *   *

Dep. Arosa	10:00	11:00	12:00	13:00	14:00(2)
Arr. Chur	11:01	12:01	13:01	14:01	15:01

Change trains.

268

Dep. Chur	11:16	12:24	13:16	14:24	15:16
Arr. Zurich	12:47	13:47	14:47	15:47	16:47

(1)Plus other departures from Zurich at frequent times from 12:07 to 19:07. (2)Plus other departures from Arosa at 16:00, 17:00. 18:00, 19:00 and 20:00 that connect in Chur with trains to Zurich.

Zurich - Chur - Desentis - Andermatt - Brig - Zermatt - Gornergrat - Zermatt

There is fabulous Rhone Glacier scenery on this ride plus crossing Oberalp Pass (6,700 feet) and Furka Pass (7,100 feet) on the Chur-Brig portion. This trip includes going over the highest bridges in Europe and, by departing Zurich at 7:07 or 9:07, you can include the outstanding cogwheel train ride to Gornergrat (10,200 feet) for a close view of the Matterhorn (14,692 feet) and more than 50 other Alpine peaks.

Only the Zurich-Chur portion of this trip is covered by Eurailpass and Eurail Youthpass. The rest of this itinerary costs about $100(U.S.).

Do not let this timetable discourage you. This trip is easier to make than it was for us to prepare the table !

268
| Dep. Zurich | 7:07(1) | 9:07(1) | 10:07(1) |
| Arr. Chur | 8:38 | 10:38 | 11:30 |

Change trains.
315
| Dep. Chur | 8:53 | 10:53(2) | 11:41 |
| Arr. Disentis | 10:05 | 12:09(2) | 13:01 |

Change trains.
| Dep. Disentis | 10:15 | 12:17(2) | 13:09 |
| Arr. Brig | 13:13 | 15:12 | 16:35 |

Change trains.
280
| Dep. Brig | 13:22 | 15:18(2) | 17:18 |
| Arr. Zermatt | 14:46 | 16:45 | 18:45 |

Change trains.
281
| Dep. Zermatt | 15:30 | 17:35 | -0- |
| Arr. Gornergrat | 16:15 | 18:20 | -0- |

*　　　*　　　*

| Dep. Gornergrat | 17:05 | 18:20 | -0- |
| Arr. Zermatt | 17:50 | 19:05 | -0- |

(1)Light refreshments. (2)"Glacier Express". Direct train. No train changes en route to Zermatt. Light refreshments.

Zurich - Landquart - Davos - Landquart - Zurich

Excellent gorge, lake and mountain scenery on this easy one-day roundtrip. The Landquart-Davos-Landquart portion of this trip is *not* covered by Eurailpass or Eurail Youthpass.

268

Dep. Zurich	7:07(1)	8:07(2)	9:07(1)	10:07(1+3)
Arr. Landquart	8:27	9:19	10:27	11:19

Change trains.
301

Dep. Landquart	8:45	9:30	10:35	12:35
Arr. Davos Platz	10:00	10:42	11:45	13:45
		*	*	*
Dep. Davos Platz	10:00	10:57	12:11	13:47(4)
Arr. Landquart	11:12	12:28	13:20	15:15

Change trains.
268

Dep. Landquart	11:27(2)	12:35(1)	13:27(1)	15:27(1)
Arr. Zurich	12:47	13:47	14:47	16:47

(1)Light refreshments. (2)Meal service. (3)Plus other departures from Zurich at frequent times from 11:07 to 22:07. (4)Plus other departures from Davos at 16:10, 16:40, 18:13 and 19:15 that connect in Landquart with trains to Zurich.

Zurich - Lugano - Milan   277

The Zurich-Lugano portion of the Zurich-Milan route can be seen on a one-day roundtrip from Zurich. That portion is a major part of one of the 5 most scenic rail trips in Europe (Zurich-Milan). A feast of beautiful farms, lakes, mountains, rivers and vineyards. You go through the 9.3-mile long Gotthard Tunnel.

Before the Gotthard was opened to traffic in 1882, there was no direct rail route from eastern Switzerland through the Alps to Italy. For 7 years and 5 months, 2500 men worked in 3 shifts day and night to build this engineering marvel.

Immediately after exiting the third of a series of 9 tunnels, the train passes the small, white Wassen Church to your right, and about 230 feet above the track. The next time the church comes into view, after leaving Wassen Station, it is also to your right, and nearly level with the track. Later, after exiting tunnel #7, you have a third view of the church, this time to your left and 170 feet above the track.

The turns inside 3 semi-circular tunnels in this area (Pfaffensprung, Wattinger and Leggistein) are engineered so well that there is no sensation of the curves that the train is making inside those tunnels.

Try this interesting experiment: make a pendulum of any object, holding the top of a weighted string, chain or handkerchief against the inner face of a train window (a left-hand window when inside Pfaffensprung and Wattinger, a right-hand window when inside Leggistein). As the train goes around a curve, the weighted bottom will move away from the window.

Climate on the Swiss side of the tunnel is usually much cooler than the Mediterranean temperature on the Italian end. There is a beautiful descent from the Italian end of the tunnel down the Ticino Valley. The train makes 3% gradients at 45-50 miles per hour.

At Bellinzona, the line forks. One branch goes to Locarno, the other to Lugano and Milan.

Dep. Zurich	7:04(1)	8:04(2)	8:39(3)	9:04(2)	11:04(1)
Arr. Lugano	10:03	11:17	11:35	12:10	14:10

                                         *   *   *

Dep. Lugano	11:26(2)	12:43(1)	14:43(2)	15:32(2)	16:43(1+4)
Arr. Zurich	14:50	15:50	17:50	18:50	19:50

(1)Meal service. (2)Light refreshments. (3)TEE. Reservation required. Meal service. (4)Plus other departures from Lugano at 17:26(2), 17:55(3), 18:36(1) and 20:05(1).

Zurich - Milan   Schedules for the complete Zurich-Milan trip appear later in this section, under "International Routes From Switzerland".

Zurich - Luzern - Mt. Pilatus - Luzern - Zurich

Fine gorge and mountain scenery on this easy one-day roundtrip. The Alpnachstad-Pilatus-Alpnachstad rack railway portion operates only from May to the end of October and is *not* covered by Eurailpass or Eurail Youthpass. Costs about 34 Swiss francs for the roundtrip. There are good views and several restaurants at the top of Pilatus.

254

Dep. Zurich	6:58	8:58	10:58	12:58(1)	13:58(1)
Arr. Luzern	7:46	9:46	11:46	13:46	14:46

Change trains.

264

Dep. Luzern	8:09	9:57	11:57	13:57	14:57
Arr. Alpnachstad	8:28	10:13	12:13	14:13	15:13

Change to rack railway.

292

Dep. Alpnachstad	8:45	10:20	12:25	14:40	15:20
Arr. Pilatus Kulm	9:25	11:00	13:05	15:20	16:00
		*	*	*	
Dep. Pilatus Kulm	9:36	11:35	13:12	15:55	16:35(2)
Arr. Alpnachstad	10:16	12:15	13:52	16:35	17:15

Change to standard train.

264

Dep. Alpnachstad	10:38	12:38	14:38	16:38	17:38
Arr. Luzern	10:56	12:56	14:56	16:56	17:56

Change trains.

254

Dep. Luzern	Frequent times from 6:20 to 22:07
Arr. Zurich	50 minutes later

(1)Light refreshments. (2)Plus another departure from Pilatus Kulm at 17:13 that connects with a train arriving Luzern at 18:56.

Zurich - Romanshorn - St. Gallen - Zurich

Very good lake and mountain scenery on this easy one-day roundtrip that visits Lake Konstanz.

Sights in **St. Gallen:** The history of lacemaking and embroidery from the 16th century to the present, and lacework worn by European nobility, at the Gewerbemuseum (Embroidery Museum). The 100,000 volumes (including illuminated manuscripts), more than 1,000 years old, in the rebuilt rococo library of the ancient abbey. The twin-towered baroque 18th century Cathedral. Near it, many old houses decorated with frescoes and oriel windows, in the city's old quarter.

266

Dep. Zurich	7:07	8:07	10:07(1)	11:07(1+3)
Arr. Romanshorn	8:16	9:16	11:16	12:16

Take time for a boat on Lake Konstanz.

272

Dep. Romanshorn	9:02	10:02	12:02	13:02(4)
Arr. St. Gallen	9:30	10:30	12:30	13:30

Change trains.

256

Dep. St. Gallen (1)	9:40(2)	10:40(2)	12;40(1)	13:40(2)
Arr. Zurich	11:00	12:00	13:50	14:50

(1)Light refreshments. (2)Meal service. (3)Plus other departures from Zurich at 12:07, 14:07(2), 15:07(1) and 16.07. (4)Plus other departures from Romanshorn at 14:02, 16:02, 17:02 and 18:02 that connect in St. Gallen with trains to Zurich.

Romanshorn - Friedrichshafen   323

There is ferry service between Romanshorn and Friedrichshafen (50% discount with Eurailpass).

Dep. Romanshorn	9:31	11:31	13:31	15:55	17:31
Arr. Friedrichshafen	40-45 minutes later				

* * *

Dep. Friedrichshafen	10:48	12:48	15:00	16:50	18:50
Arr. Romanshorn	40-45 minutes later				

Zurich - Schaffhausen - Zurich   668

To see the marvelous Rhine Falls.

Dep. Zurich	8:10	9:10	11:10	14:10(1)
Arr. Schaffhausen	42 minutes later			

* * *

Dep. Schaffhausen	10:03	12:03	14:03	15:03	17:03(2)
Arr. Zurich	42 minutes later				

(1)Plus other departures from Zurich at 15:10, 16:10 and 18:10. (2)Plus other departures from Schaffhausen at frequent times from 18:03 to 23:03.

Here is a great 7-day circle itinerary of Switzerland that gives you in the span of one week a visit to most of the country's major cities plus a view of much of Switzerland's great scenery:

Day 1 Geneva, Montreux, Zweisimmen, Spiez (Lunch). Lake Thun boat to Interlaken.
Day 2 Interlaken, Jungfraujoch, Grindelwald (lunch), Interlaken.
Day 3 Interlaken, Luzern.
Day 4 Luzern, Vitznau, Mt. Rigi (lunch), Arth-Goldau, Lugano.
Day 5 Lugano, Bellinzona, Locarno.
Day 6 Locarno, Domodossola, Bern.
Day 7 Bern To Geneva Or Zurich.

INTERNATIONAL ROUTES FROM SWITZERLAND

The Swiss gateways for travel to West Germany are Basel (to Cologne) and Zurich (to Munich). Zurich is also the starting point for the train trip to Austria (Innsbruck, and on to Vienna and East Europe) and for train travel to Italy (Milan and beyond).

Basel is also a starting point for trips to Belgium, Holland and France (Paris, and on to London or Madrid).

Geneva (via Aosta, and on to Torino) as well as Bern and Brig (via Domodossola) are also departure cities for rail rides to Italy (Milan, and beyond).

There is also rail service from Geneva to Paris, and from Geneva to southern France (Avignon) and on to Spain (Barcelona).

Basel - Cologne   662

All of these trains charge a supplement and have meal service.

Dep. Basel (S.B.B)	-0-	7:08(2)	8:08(2)	9:08(2+6)
Dep. Basel (Bad Bf.)	6:14(1)	7:14(2)	8:14(2)	9:14(2)
Arr. Cologne	10:57	11:57	12:57	13:57

(1)Daily, except Sundays and holidays. Meal service. (2)Meal service. (3)Daily, except Saturday. Meal service. (4)TEE. Reservation required. Meal service. (5)Carries sleeping car. Also has couchettes.

Zurich - Munich 685
Dep. Zurich   7:04(1)   9:19(2)   12:04(1)   14:19(1)   16:19(1)
Arr. Munich   12:06   13:45   17:06   19:09   21:13
(1)(Light refreshments. (2)Meal service.

Zurich - Innsbruck - Vienna 268
About 2½ hours out of Zurich, the train passes through one of Europe's largest tunnels, the 6.3-mile long Arlberg. There is a very beautiful view of Alpine scenery as the train comes out of the tunnel.
Dep. Zurich   7:20(1)   9:26(2)   11:26(1)   13:26(1)   16:07(3+5)
Arr. Innsbruck   11:56(1)   13:24(2)   15:27(1)   17:30(1)   20:55
Arr. Vienna
  (Westbf.)   19:55   18:55   20:55   22:55   6:10
(1)Meal service. Reservation required. Meal service. (3)Light refreshments. (4)Carries sleeping car. Also has couchettes. (5)Plus another departure from Zurich at 21:20(4).

Bern - Brig - Milan
This trip takes you on the marvelous scenic route via Spiez (noted earlier in this section under "Scenic Trips") and through both the 10-mile long Lotschberg Tunnel and the 11.9-mile long Simplon, longest tunnel in Europe and world's second longest, after Japan's 13.4-mile long Daishimizu Tunnel, between Tokyo and Niigata.
  260
Dep. Bern   6:21(1)   8:13(1)   9:21(2)   11:21(1+2)   12:54(1+9)
Arr. Brig   8:00(1)   9:43(1)   11:00   13:00(1)   14:30(1)
  Change trains.
  251
Dep. Brig   8:18   9:55   11:17   13:17   14:41(3+11)
Arr. Milan
  (Cent.)   10:55   12:25   13:55   15:56   17:00
(1)Direct train to Milan. No train change in Brig. (2)Light refreshments. (3)Departs 15:29 from early September to late October. (4)Supplement charged. (5)Meal service. (6)Carries sleeping car from late May to late September. Has couchettes all year. (7)Has couchettes. (8)Carries sleeping car. Also has couchettes. (9)Runs from early September to late October. (10)Plus other departures from Bern at 14:21(2), 16:21(5), 17:13, 19:21(2+7), 20:21(2) and 23:28.
  (11)Plus other departures from Brig at 16:50(2+4), 18:50(5), 19:17, 21:17, 23:21, 1:45(6), 2:17(8) and 2:50(9).

Zurich - Milan   277

Dep. Zurich	7:04(1)	8:39(2)	9:04(3)	10:04(4+9)
Arr. Milan (Cent.)	11:35	12:40	13:40	15:00

(1)Meal service. (2)TEE. Reservation required. Meal service. (3)Light refreshments. (4)Meal service 10:52-13:54. (5)Meal service 11:49-14:36. (6)Meal service 13:49-16:36. (7)Change trains in Chiasso. (8)Has couchettes. (9)Plus other departures from Zurich at 11:04(5), 13:04(6), 14:04(3), 15:04(3), 16:04(3+7), 17:03(3) and 18:04(7+8).

Basel - Amsterdam

You see many castles in the Mainz-Koblenz area as you travel alongside the Rhine River.

	68	68	63	68	68
Dep. Basel (S.S.B.)	0:15(1)	4:51	8:21(2)	12:22(3)	13:16(4)
Dep. Basel (Bad Bf.)	0:21(1)	5:18	-0-	12:29(3)	13:40(4)
Arr. Amsterdam	9:36	14:26	18:03	20:03	22:26

(1)Carries sleeping car. Also has couchettes. (2)Departs from Basel's SNCF railstation. Change trains in Maastricht from late September to late May. Light refreshments 15:29-18:03. (3)TEE. Reservation required. Meal service. (4)Meal service.

Basel - Brussels   63+216

Dep. Basel (S.N.C.F.)	0:35(1)	5:03(2)	8:21(2)	13:20(2)	16:25(2)
Arr. Brussels (Q.L.)	7:17	11:42	14:17	19:14	22:30
Arr. Brussels (Nord)	7:28	11:52	14:27	19:25	22:40
Arr. Brussels (Cent.)	-0-	-0-	-0-	-0-	22:46
Arr. Brussels (Midi)	7:37	12:02	14:34	19:33	22:51

(1)Carries sleeping car. Also has couchettes. (2)Meal service.

Basel - Paris   171

Dep. Basel (S.N.C.F.)   8:13(1)   11:25(2)   12:44(2)   16:32(3+4+6)
Arr. Paris (Est)   12:59   16:16   18:09   21:16

(1)Supplement charged. Light refreshments. State meal required when reserving first-class seat. (2)Meal service. (3)Daily, except Saturday. (4)Supplement charged. Meal service. (5)Carries sleeping car. Also has couchettes. (6)Plus other departures from Basel at 18:30(2) and 0:10(5).

Geneva - Paris   150 + 152

Dep. Geneva (Cornavin)   7:09(1+2)   7:23(3)   13:15(1+4)   18:09(1+5)
Arr. Paris (Lyon)   11:35   13:35   17:36   22:33

(1)TGV. Reservation required. Meal service. (2)Supplement charged on Monday. (3)Meal service. (4)Supplement charged on Saturday. (5)Supplement charged every day.

Geneva - Avignon - Barcelona
   77

Dep. Geneva (Corn.)	8:12(1)	11:27(2)	21:28(3)
Arr. Avignon	12:50(1)	15:48(2)	1:54(3)
Dep. Avignon	12:52(1)	15:50(2)	1:56(3)
Arr. Narbonne	15:07(1)	17:39(2)	4:01(3)
Dep. Narbonne	15:11(1)	17:41(2)	4:14(3)
Arr. Port Bou	16:46	19:03(2)	5:47
424			
Dep. Port Bou	17:05	19:22	7:10(4)
Arr. Barcelona (Plaza de G.)	-0-	21:20	9:33
Arr. Barcelona (Sants)	-0-	11:26	9:39
Arr. Barcelona (Ter.)	19:52	-0-	-0-

(1)Runs late June to mid-September. (2)Supplement charged. Meal service. (3)Has couchettes. (4)Light refreshments.

Aosta - Torino Gateways to Italy

(1) Via San Bernardo Tunnel
Lausanne or Brig - Martigny - Aosta - Torino

251			251		
Dep. Lausanne	6:50	14:50	Dep. Brig	6:37	15:14
Arr. Martigny	7:43	15:43	Arr. Martigny	7:29	16:06

Change to bus.
337

Dep. Martigny (Stn.)	8:00	16:15
Arr. Aosta (P. Narbonne)	10:10	18:25

Change to train.
362

Dep. Aosta	12:18	19:37
Arr. Torino (Piazza Narbonne)	15:55	21:35

(2) Via Mt. Blanc Tunnel
Geneva - Chamonix -Aosta - Torino   158

Dep. Geneva (Eaux-Vives)	9:32	12:27
Arr. Annemasse	9:40	12:35

Change trains. (All of the train changes Geneva-Chamonix are cross-platform, taking only one minute.)

Dep. Annemasse	9:53	12:41
Arr. La Roche-sur-Foron	10:11	13:00

Change trains.   167

Dep. La Roche-sur-Foron	10:25	13:07
Arr. St. Gervais	11:17	13:51

Change trains.

Dep. St. Gervais	11:43	14:01
Arr. Chamonix	12:22	14:36

Change to bus.   191

Dep. Chamonix	N/A(1)
Arr. Aosta	2 hours later

(1)Two departures per day in Winter. Six departures per day during July, August and early September.

Change to train.   362

Dep. Aosta (Piazza Narbonne)	14:15	16:15	19:37
Arr. Torino (Piazza Narbonne)	16:20	19:42	21:35

A good break in this journey is to spend the night in Aosta and continue on to Torino the next day. Here are the schedules for the early departures from Aosta:

Dep. Aosta (Piazza Narbonne)	5:15	6:12	9:10	12:18
Arr. Torino (Piazza Narbonne)	7:32	9:00	11:15	15:55

WEST GERMANY

The German Federal Railroad operates over 20,000 passenger trains every day, linking 6,500 destinations. **Where no station is designated for cities in West Germany, the station is "Hauptbahnhoff".**

West Germany's fast Intercity trains, connecting 50 important cities along 4 major rail routes, are identified by the abbreviation "IC". These trains have easy cross-platform connections in such cities as Cologne, Wurzburg, Mannheim, Dortmund, etc.

A small supplement is charged for both first-class and second-class IC tickets. However, there is no additional charge for making a seat reservation on them. The supplement is *not* charged to passengers using a Eurailpass, Eurail Youthpass or GermanRail Tourist Card. (All of those passes are also valid on all commuter rail services in major German cities.) The IC supplement must be paid when using the Inter Rail Card.

Some of the Intercity trains have top speeds of 125 mph. A "conference compartment" in them can be rented for the cost of 4 first-class tickets. Worldwide telephone calls can be made from all IC trains.

When entering or leaving West Germany on an international train, the customs, passport and currency control are usually performed in the train. Because of this, passengers traveling across West Germany (such as from Amsterdam to Copenhagen) are required to travel in a special car or compartment.

Porter service may be reserved in advance.

The signs you will see at railstations in West Germany are the same as those listed earlier in this chapter, under "Austria".

SUMMER TIME

West Germany changes to Summer Time on the last Sunday of March and converts back to Standard Time on the last Sunday of September.

WEST GERMAN HOLIDAYS

A list of holidays is helpful because some trains will be noted later in this section as not running on holidays. Also, those trains which operate on holidays are filled, and it is necessary to make reservations for them long in advance.

January 1	New Year's Day	June 17	Commemorating East Berlin Uprisings
	Good Friday		
	Easter		
	Easter Monday	August 15	Assumption Day
May 1	Labor Day	November 1	All Saints Day
	Ascension Day	December 25	Christmas
	Whit Monday	December 26	Holiday

WESTERN GERMANY

EURAIL BONUSES IN WEST GERMANY

Two cruises: (1) Rhine (between Dusseldorf and Frankfurt), and (2) Mosel (between Trier and Koblezn). Eurail Youthpass holders must pay an extra charge on Express-steamers. One ferry crossing: Puttgarden to Rodby. Most of the Post/Railroad bus lines, including "Romantic Road" (Wiesbaden-Munich and vice versa) and "Castle Road" (Mannheim-Nurnberg and vice versa). Reduction of 50% on (1) Lubeck-Travemunde-Malmo ferry crossing, (2) cruises on Lake Constance, and (3) the Freiburg (Breisgau)-Schauinsland private railroad. A small reduction (only for Eurailpass, *not* for Eurail Youthpass) is allowed on the Garmisch-Partenkirchen-Grainau-Zugspitze private railroad.

GERMANY'S TRAIN PASSES

GermanRail Tourist Card   Sold all over the world and also at many railstations and airports in West Germany. Unlimited train travel, valid for the Romantic Road and Frankfurt-Moselle bus rides, and also allows reduced fares on Rhine and Moselle Rivers excursion steamboats. First-class prices in 1984: 9 days $165(U.S.), 16 days $215. Second-class: 9 days $120, 16 days $155. Half-fare for children 4 to under 12.

Travelers arriving in West Germany by airplane can validate the GermanRail Tourist Card, Eurailpass or Eurail Youthpass at the airport ticket office, after exiting the customs area, and use any of those passes for the rail trip from the airport to the city.

Another benefit of the GermanRail Tourist Card is that it entitles the holder to a greatly reduced roundtrip rail ticket across part of East Germany to West Berlin plus a free sightseeing tour in West Berlin.

NOTE: The reduced-price ticket to Berlin can be purchased in West Germany either at GermanRail ticket offices or at an authorized DER travel agency.

National Netzkarte   Sold only in West Germany. Unlimited train travel through *all* of West Germany for one month. The 1984 prices are: first-class DM-1,128, second-class DM-752.

Area Netzkarte   Sold only in West Germany. Unlimited train travel in *one specified area* of the country. The 1984 prices are: first-class DM-680, second-class DM-453.

Tourenkarte   Sold only in West Germany, after presentation of a roundtrip ticket that covers a distance of at least 201 km. Allows unlimited second-class train travel within 10 consecutive days over a network of approximately 1,000 km of rail lines. The 1984 prices are: 1 person DM-45, 2 persons DM-60, one family DM-75.

THE ISLAND OF WEST BERLIN

The city of West Berlin is a virtual island within the sometimes stormy sea of East Germany. Travelers to West Berlin must cross through East Germany. The portion of the train trip through East Germany is *not* covered by Eurailpass, Eurail Youthpass or GermanRail Tourist Card.

In order to avoid being in East Berlin by mistake, be certain to leave the train only at Berlin's Zoo railstation.

Tickets from Berlin to East German destinations must be paid in West German marks. The East Germany rail authorities will *not* accept East German currency.

Sightseeing tours can be arranged from West Berlin to such East German cities as Potsdam, Dresden and Karl Marx Stadt. For reservations, write to: Deutsches Reiseburo, Kurfurstendamm 17, Berlin W. 30, West Germany.

The key cities in West Germany for rail connections to and from West Berlin are Frankfurt, Hamburg, Hannover and Munich.

Two-hour and 4-hour tours of West Berlin begin at 10:00 and occur at frequent intervals during the day, from 220 Kurfurstendamm, 216 Kurfurstendamm, and opposite from the bombed-out Gedachtniskirche (Memorail Church).

Sights in **West Berlin:** The stroll down tree-lined Kurfurstendamm is almost mandatory, to observe the city's fine stores, theaters, cafes, movie houses and bars. See the Zoo and Aquarium, one of Europe's oldest and best animal exhibits. The New National Gallery. The bust of Nefertiti and other important items in the Egyptian Museum at 70 Schloss Strasse. The rooms and gardens of Charlottenburg Castle, opposite the Egyptian Museum. The 1936 Olympic Stadium. The reconstructed Reichstag Building. The tent-shaped Philharmonic Hall. Take a boat ride on the Havel River.

Visit the sixth floor (called Feinschmecker Etage c "the gourmet's floor") of Kaufhaus des Westens, a large department store on Tauentzienstrasse. It is the largest food store in Europe: 500 sales clerks dispensing 25,000 different products. Fruits and vegetables sold there include limes from Brazil, rare wild mushrooms from France and Poland, avocados from Israel, tiny beans from Kenya, tomatoes from Spain, apples from Hungary. The meats available there go far beyond the 1,000 kinds of wurst and 250 varieties of salami. Then there are eels, crawfish, catfish and carp. Live lobsters are delivered to the store in tank trucks. You will also find hundreds of pastries and breads. Three separate cheese counters for items from France, Italy and from all other countries. Eighteen kinds of herring salad. And much more.

The Weissbierstube Restaurant in the Berlin Museum is acclaimed for its bounteous buffet tables. Both the Restaurant and the Museum are open daily except Mondays 11:00-18:00.

To see East Berlin, take the elevated railway from West Berlin's Zoo station to the Friedrichstrasse station, where entry visas can be obtained.

On leaving Friedrichstrasse station, turn right and walk 3 blocks to reach Berlin's famous boulevard, Unter den Linden. A few blocks further, at the end of the boulevard, is the classical Brandenburg Gate and the Berlin Wall. Also see the Museum of German History. The State Opera. The tiny 14th century church, Marienkirche. The archaeological exhibits in the Pergamon Museum.

GATEWAYS TO BERLIN

Here are the schedules for the major routes to and from Berlin.

Frankfurt - West Berlin   776

Dep. Frankfurt	8:51(1)	15:26(2)	22:35(3)
Arr. Berlin (Zoo)	16:13	22:36	6:19

* * *

Dep. Berlin (Zoo)	6:39(2)	13:05(1)	23:08(3)
Arr. Frankfurt	13:56	20:27	7:13

(1)Meal service. (2)Light Refreshments. (3)Carries sleeping car. Also has couchettes.

Hamburg - West Berlin   775

Dep. Hamburg (Hbf.)	8:01(1)	13:40(2)	17:30(2)	20:11(2+3)
Arr. Berlin (Zoo)	11:41	17:20	21:22	23:48
	*	*	*	
Dep. Berlin (Zoo)	8:04(2)	9:43(4)	12:57(2)	17:06(1)
Arr. Hamburg (Hbf.)	11:42	14:03	16:52	21:02

(1)Light refreshments. (2)Meal service. (3)Operates Sundays and holidays all year. Also on Friday from late June to late July. (4)Operates Saturday all year. Also on Sunday from mid-June to late July.

Hannover - West Berlin   764

Dep. Hannover	1:33(1)	2:39(2)	3:04(2)	8:10(3)	10:11(4+5)
Arr. Berlin (Zoo)	5:10	6:34	7:07	11:30	13:51
	*	*	*		
Dep. Berlin (Zoo)	0:31(1)	6:49(4)	7:58(4)	10:50(4)	12:54(4+6)
Arr. Hannover	4:06	10:27	11:42	14:38	16:44

(1)Runs late May to late September. Carries sleeping car. (2)Carries sleeping car. Also has couchettes. (3)Light refreshments. (4)Meal service. (5)Plus other departures from Hannover at 13:13(4), 14:15(4), 17:06(4) and 19:10(4).   (6)Plus other departures from Berlin at 15:44(4), 16:49(4), 23:33(2) and 23:56(2).

Munich - West Berlin   771

Dep. Munich	7:44(1)	12:45(1)	22:25(2)
Arr. Berlin (Zoo)	16:51	21:55	7:32
	*	*	*
Dep. Berlin (Zoo)	7:03(1)	9:06(1)	21:50(2)
Arr. Munich	16:08	18:20	7:27

(1)Meal service. (2)Carries sleeping car. Also has couchettes.

ONE-DAY EXCURSIONS AND CITY-SIGHTSEEING

Here are 60 one-day rail trips that can be made comfortably from 4 major cities in West Germany, returning to them in most case before dinnertime. Notes are provided on what to see at each destination. The number after the name of each route is the Cook's timetable.

Details on 11 other rail trips recommended for exceptional scenery and schedules for international connections conclude this section.

The 4 base cities are Cologne (Koln), Frankfurt/Main, Hannover and Munich (Munchen).

Cologne (Koln)

It is a 10-minute bus ride from the Cologne/Bonn Airport to the center of Cologne.

Your city-sightseeing in Cologne should include, above all, the Cathedral. Started in 1248 and not completed until 1880, it houses the world's largest reliquary, containing relics of the 3 kings, the Magi. See the view of Cologne and the Rhine Valley from the top of the Cathedral, very close to the railstation.

Near the Cathedral, explore ancient Cologne. The Praetorium, a palace for Roman governors several centuries before Christ. The 3rd century Dionysus mosaic (once the dining hall floor of a Roman house) in the Roman Museum, open Tuesday-Sunday 10:00-20:00. Also on view there is an outstanding collection of Roman glass and 4th century jewelry. See the 3rd century Roman tower.

All museums in Cologne are closed on Monday. See the collection of paintings by Cologne masters of the Middle Ages, also Impressionists, Expressionists and post World War II art at the Wallraf Richartz Museum, open 10:00-17:00 (until 20:00 on Tuesday and Thursday).

See the Zoo. The 15th century Gurzenich. The Metropolitan Historical Museum. The Town Hall. St. Pantaleon Church. St. Andreas Church. Relics and treasures in the Golden Room at the Church of St. Ursula. The luxury shops on Hohestrasse and Schildergasse.

Frankfurt

There is frequent rail service from Frankfurt's Hauptbahnhof railstation to the city's airport and vice versa (16-minute travel time) every 25-30 minutes from 5:00 to 23:30. One train per hour continues beyond the airport station to Mainz and Wiesbaden. Trains also depart the Airport at 9:19, 13:09 and 20:58 for Darmstadt (20 minutes), Mannheim (60 minutes) and Ludwigshafen (66 minutes).

See Goethe's house. The Goethe Museum. The Zoo. The emperor's coronation hall in the Romer complex at medieval Romerberg Square. The wonderful doors in the 13th century Leonhardskirche. The 13th century chapel of Saalhof in the remains of the palace of Frederick Barbarossa. Cloth Hall. The Botanical Garden. The pews and murals in the Cathedral of Bartholomew. The Church of St. Nicholas. The Church of St. Paul. Senckenberg Natural History Society's Museum. Stadel Museum and Liebighaus (sculpture). The Museum of Plastic Art. Sachsenhausen, the old quarter of the city, across the Main River from the commercial district. The major shopping streets: Zeil and Kaiserstrasse.

Hannover

The bus ride between Langenhagen Airport and Hannover's railstation takes 30 minutes. The bus terminal is located next to Track #14.

For an interesting 2-hour walking tour of Hannover, obtain the detailed brochure available at both of the railstation's 2 tourist information offices. Walk out of the station to the statue in front of it and start to follow the painted red line which leads to Passerelle (a pedestrian mall), the 19th century Opera House, the old city wall, Town Hall, and Hannover's oldest (16th century) half-timbered structure.

See the bronze doors by Marcks at Market Church. The outstanding collection of Egyptian antiquities in the Kestner Museum. The prehistorical objects in the Museum of Lower Saxony. Take streetcars #5 or #16 from the Central railstation to the absolutely fantastic baroque Royal Gardens of Herrenhausen. Its ornamental fountains perform in Summer Monday-Friday 11:00-12:00 and 15:30-16:30. On Saturdays and Sundays, they can be seen 10:00-12:00 and 15:30-17:30. Next to Herrenhausen is the natural park, Georgengarten. Nearby, see the exotic plants in the greenhouses at Berggarten.

Take streetcar #6 from the Central railstation to Hannover's outstanding Zoo.

Munich (Munchen)

A metropolitan train connects Munich's Hauptbahnhof and Ostbanhof railstations. It is a 10-minute bus ride between Munich's Reim Airport and the Hauptbahnhof railstation, where the city's monthly program of events (theaters, museums, exhibits, concerts, plays, etc.) can be obtained. The program is also sold at newsstands.

See the works of Durer, El Greco, Raphael, Holbein, Rembrandt and many other great painters at Alte Pinakothek. Frauenkirche Cathedral, and the view from its north tower . . . and then later the view of Frauenkirche from the top of Neues Rathaus (City Hall). The paintings of Cezanne, Gauguin, Renoir and other impressionists at the Haus der Kunst. Wittelsbach Fountain.

The fine exhibits and planetarium at Deutsches Museum, considered the best scientific museum in the world. The view of the Alps from the top of Peterskirche. The best collection of tapestries and wood carvings in Germany, at the Bavarian National Museum. Munich's most famous beer palace, Hofbrauhaus.

The Schatzkammer in the Residenz palace, and the flower gardens in the park north of it. The decorations in Asamkirche. Schack Gallery. Theatinerkirche. At Schloss (Castle) Nymphenburg: the porcelain in the showrooms of Nymphenburger Porzellan Manufaktur and in the Residenzmuseum, the enormous Festsaal. The park outside the castle. Closed on Mondays. A short ride from the center of Munich by streetcars #17 or #21, or by buses #41 or #42.

On the island in the river, visit the Deutsches Museum (science and engineering). See the history of Munich in the Isartorplatz Museum. The 19th and 20th century art in the Neue Pinakothek. The collection of Klee, Kandinsky and Marc paintings in the Stadtische Galerie on Lenbachplatz.

Infamous Dachau is a 40-minute ride by Subway train #3 or bus #11. Although there are no guides at Dachau, an exhibit there details the operation of the concentration camp, and an English-language film is shown at 11:30 and 15:30.

Since 1870, an Alois Dallmayr food store has offered gourmet delicacies in Munich. It added a restaurant in 1978. As Fauchon's in Paris does, Dallmayr has a vast section of imported foods. Its most notable feature, however, is the enormous array it offers of West Germany's finest lunch meats, 22 varieties of smoked fish, and 27 types of bread.

Nearly everything edible can be found at Dallmayr's: local and imported fruits, cooked meats and poultry, fresh fish, wines, more than 50 different salads, chocolates, 18 types of ham, and they also sell special cigars.

If you eat none of the splendid food there, at least see the statues, marble pillars and mounted deer heads that decorate the interior of the store.

An excursion bus departs at 8:30 from Lenbachplatz 1 for Neuschwanstein and Hohenschwangau Castles, returning to Munich at 18:30. Fantastic Alpine and lake scenery.

In the following timetables, where a city has more than one railstation we have designated the particular station after the name of the city (in parentheses). **Where no station is designated for cities in Austria, Switzerland and West Germany, the station is "Hauptbahnhoff".**

It is not necessary to be staying in East Germany in order to tour that area. Sightseeing tours to Potsdam, Dresden and Karl Marx Stadt start in West Berlin at Parkplatz Rankestrasse, near the Kurfurstendamm. For reservations, contact Deutsches Reiseburo, Berlin W.30, Kurfurstendamm 17, West Germany.

Cologne - Amsterdam - Cologne 221

Dep. Cologne	6:17	7:27	9:31(1)	10:46	12:22
Arr. Amsterdam	9:36	10:42	12:26	14:26	15:42

Sights in **Amsterdam:** The Rijksmuseum collection of Rembrandt paintings. Rembrandt's house and, near it, the Flea Market. Anne Frank's house at Prisengracht 263. The Tropical Museum, with its display of Indonesian and Far Eastern art and anthropology. The Amsterdam Historical and Jewish Historical Museum. A 75-minute ride in a glass-roofed canal boat, starting at the piers in front of Central Railstation or at Stadhouderskade, near the Rijksmuseum. Royal Palace. The Tower of Tears. The attic church of the Amstelkring Museum. Mint Tower. The Maritime Museum.

Dep. Amsterdam	13:17	14:25(1)	14:53	17:19(2)	18:17(3)
Arr. Cologne	16:29	17:30	18:38	20:42	21:36

(1)Supplement charged. Meal service. (2)Light refreshments. (3)Plus other departures from Amsterdam at 19:19 and 19:49.

Cologne - Bonn - Cologne   637+662

Dep. Cologne   Frequent times from 5:36 to 23:52
Arr. Bonn   22 minutes later

Sights in **Bonn:** The government buildings in the capital of West Germany, including Bundeshaus where its legislature meets. Beethoven-Halle and the museum at Bonngasse 20, where Beethoven was born in 1770. Drachenfels Mountain and the castle ruins that Byron immortalized. The 13th century Remigius Church. Jesu Church. The view of the Rhine and Siebengebirge from Alte Zoll. The university in the Electors' Castle. The Rhineland Museum.

Dep. Bonn   Frequent times from 4:08 to 24:00
Arr. Cologne   22 minutes later

Cologne - Brussels - Cologne   206

Dep. Cologne	4:47(1)	5:12(2)	7:05(1)	8:09(3+6)
Arr. Brussels (Nord)	7:55	8:07	9:47	10:22
Arr. Brussels (Cent.)	- 0 -	-0-	9:53	10:26
Arr. Brussels (Midi)	8:04	8:19	9:57	10:31

Sights in **Brussels:** The gilded buildings in Grand Place. Town Hall. The Law Courts. The Royal Palace. The tapestries in the 13th century Cathedral of St. Michael. Flemish paintings in the Museum of Ancient Art. The Museum of Modern Art.

The Central Africa Museum. The Brussels City Museum. The Museum of Arms and Armor. The Postal Museum. The Brewery Museum. The Royal Greenhouses. The Bruegel Museum, in the house where the painter lived his last 6 years. The view from the Palais de Justice. A bus takes you 00 miles to Waterloo.

Dep. Brussels (Midi)	12:08(4)	15:08(1)	16:00(5)	17:44(3+7)
Dep. Brussels (Cent.)	12:13(4)	15:13(1)	-0-	17:49(3)
Dep. Brussels (Nord)	12:18(4)	15:18(1)	16:07(5)	17:54(3)
Arr. Cologne	14:48	17:49	18:48	20:17

(1)Light refreshments. (2)Runs mid-June to late August. (3)Supplement charged. Meal service. (4)Meal service. (5)Reservation required. Light refreshments. (6)Plus other departures from Cologne at 9:06(1) and 11:12(1).   (7)Plus another departure from Brussels Midi at 20:10(1).

Cologne - Dortmund - Cologne   633+634

Dep. Cologne   Frequent times from 5:54 to 23:26
Arr. Dortmund   70 minutes later

Sights in **Dortmund:** The view of the city from the top of the Television Tower. Westphalia Park. The Ostwall Museum.

Dep. Dortmund   Frequent times from 5:15 to 22:39
Arr. Cologne   70 minutes later

Cologne - Dusseldorf - Cologne   634

There is frequent rail service between Dusseldorf's railstation and the Lohhausen Airport. Travel time is 15 minutes.

Dep. Cologne   Frequent times from 5:55 to 0:37
Arr. Dusseldorf   24-28 minutes later

Sights in **Dusseldorf:** Many sensational modern buildings. The Paul Klee collection at Kunsttammlung Nordhein-Westfallen. The Goethe Museum, with its first editions, paintings and over 30,000 manuscripts. The Aquarium at the Museumbunker am Zoo. Hofgarten. The Fine Arts Museum. Jagerhof Castle.

Dep. Dusseldorf   Frequent times from 6:33 to 23:44
Arr. Cologne   24-28 minutes later

Cologne - Essen - Cologne   634

Dep. Cologne   Frequent times from 5:55 to 0:37
Arr. Essen   48-52 minutes later

Sights in **Essen:** The Folkwang Museum. The 10th century Cathedral and its collection of priceless 10th and 11th century processional crosses, the crown of the Gold Madonna, and the sword of Cosmas and Damian, the martyr saints. The museum and park at Villa Hugel.

Dep. Essen   Frequent times from 6:02 to 23:06
Arr. Cologne   48-52 minutes later

Cologne - Frankfurt - Cologne   662

Dep. Cologne   7:03(1)   7:27(2)   8:03(1+2)   8:16(2+6)
Arr. Frankfurt   9:26   9:56   10:26   10:43
   Sights in **Frankfurt:** See notes about sightseeing in Frankfurt at the start
of this section.
Dep. Frankfurt   12:29(1)   13:29(1+3)   14:29(1+4)   15:21(5+7)
Arr. Cologne   14:51   15:51   16:51   17:56
(1)Supplement charged. Meal service. (2)Meal service. (3)Daily, except Sundays and holidays. (4)Daily, except Saturday. (5)Light refreshments. (6)Plus other departures from Cologne at 8:36, 9:03(1), 9:32(5), 10:03(1) and 11:03(1). (7)Plus other departures from Frankfurt at 15:29(1), 15:40(2), 16:24(5), 16:29(1), 17:03(5), 17:29(1), 18:11(2), 18:29(1), 19:29(1), 20:29(1+4) and 21:42(1).

Cologne - Hamburg - Cologne   638

Dep. Cologne   5:32(1+2)   7:00(1)   7:15(3)   9:00(1)
Arr. Hamburg   9:47   11:14   12:04   13:14
   Sights in **Hamburg:** The port, one of the busiest in the world. Hagenbeck Zoo. St. James Church, with its famous organ, built in 1693. Rathausmarkt Square. The models of Old Hamburg, the port and the city's railway system, in the Historical Museum. The Counting Houses in the business quarter, around Burchardplatz. The notorious Reperbahn.
Dep. Hamburg   13:40(1)   14:40(1+4)   15:40(1)   16:40(1+4+5)
Arr. Cologne   17:53   18:53   19:53   20:53
(1)Supplement charged. Meal service. (2)Daily, except Sundays and holidays. (3)Light refreshments. (4)Daily, except Saturday. (5)Plus other departures from Hamburg at 17:40(1), 18:40(1+4) and 19:40(1).

Cologne - Heidelberg - Cologne   662

Dep. Cologne   7:38(1)   7:57(2)   8:57(2+3)   10:57(2)
Arr. Heidelberg   10:29   10:39   11:39   13:39
   Sights in **Heidelberg:** The gardens, Library, Great Terrace, Fat Tower, Elizabeth Gate, Freidrich's Wing, the Otto-Heinrich Wing and the Mirror Room Wing at Heidelberg Castle. Germany's oldest (13th century) university, immortalized in "The Student Prince" opera. The astounding 16th century carved wood Altar of the Twelve Apostles in the Kurpfalzisches Museum. The Jesuit

Church. The Church of the Holy Ghost. The German Pharmaceutical Museum. The Electors of The Palatinate Museum. Knight's Mansion. Student's Gaol.

Dep. Heidelberg   13:14(2) 14:14(2) 15:14(2) 15:51(1) 16:42(1+5)
Arr. Cologne   15:57   16:57   17:57   19:17   19:35

(1)Meal service. (2)Supplement charged. Meal service. (3)Daily, except Sundays and holidays. (4)Daily, except Saturday. (5)Plus other departures from Heidelberg at 17:14(2), 18:14(2), 20:14(2+4) and 21:14(2+4)

Cologne - Koblenz - Cologne   662

(There is a description later in this section of a marvelous scenic trip from Cologne to Koblenz and Bullay and back to Koblenz which does not permit much time for sightseeing in Koblenz.)

Dep. Cologne   Frequent times from 5:36 to 0:29
Arr. Koblenz   One hour later

Sights in **Koblenz:** Old Town. St. Castor's Church. The Middle Rhine Museum.

Dep. Koblenz   Frequent times from 5:06 to 23:18
Arr. Cologne   One hour later

Cologne - Luxembourg - Cologne

662			625		
Dep. Cologne	7:57(1)	11:03(1)	Dep.		
Arr. Koblenz	8:49	11:55	Luxembourg	17:40	19:20(2)
Change trains.			Arr. Koblenz	19:43	21:43
625			Change trains.		
Dep. Koblenz	9:11	12:11	662		
		Arr.	Dep. Koblenz	19:59	21:59(3)
Luxembourg	11:15	14:15	Arr. Cologne	20:51	22:51

(1)Supplement charged. Meal service. (2)Change trains in Trier. (3)Daily, except Saturday. Plus other departures from Koblenz at 22:05(3), 23:05(3) and 23:18.

Sights in **Luxembourg:** The Citadel, with its 53 forts connected by 16 miles of tunnels. Fish Market, site of the city's oldest buildings. The National Museum. The Palace. City Hall. The old quarter of Pfaffenthal, with its medieval buildings. The Fort of Three Acorns. Malakoff Tower. The Church of St. Michael. The Three Towers, marking the outer limits of the town in 1050. Notre Dame Cathedral. The 4th century Chapel of St. Quirinus, one of the oldest shrines in Christendom. The Museum of History and Art. General Patton's grave in the U.S. Military Cemetery, 3 miles away, at Hamm.

Cologne - Mainz - Cologne   700

Here is a way to combine a cruibe on the Rhine with a scenic rail trip.

Dep. Cologne (Frankenwerk) by boat	7:00(1)	9:00(2)
Dep. Bonn	9:15(1)	9:40(2)
Dep. Koblenz	14:00(1)	11:05(2)
Arr. Mainz	21:00	13:10

(1)Covered by Eurailpass. Runs daily from early May to mid-September. Ticket buyers must pay a supplement for the Koblenz-Mainz portion. (2)Hydrofoil boat express service. *Not* covered by Eurailpass. Operates daily, except Monday. Runs from early May to early October.

During the Koblenz-Bingen portion of this cruise, you will see the best scenery on the Rhine, many hilltop castles, and the Lorelei. Have lunch and Rhine wine on board just before arriving Mainz. Early in the trip, you can see Drachenfels Castle, near Bonn.

Sights in **Mainz:** The art collection in the Cathedral. The Museum of the Central Rhineland. The rare books in the World Museum of Printing in the Romischer Kaiser. (Also called Gutenberg Museum. A movie on the inventor's life can be seen there.) The restored Baroque mansion on the Schillerplatz and Schillerstrasse, in the Kirschgarten. Old Town. The sculptures in the Diocesan Museum.

Then for the train ride back to Cologne:

662

Dep. Mainz	Frequent times from 6:52 to 22:18
Arr. Koblenz	50 minutes after departing Mainz
Arr. Bonn	1½ hours after departing Mainz
Arr. Cologne	2 hours after departing Mainz

Here is the schedule for visiting Mainz by taking the train both ways:

662

Dep. Cologne	Frequent times from 6:57 to 22:36
Arr. Mainz	2 hours later

*   *   *

Arr. Cologne	Frequent times from 7:07 to 22:18
Dep. Mainz	2 hours later

Cologne - Siegen - Cologne   636

Dep. Cologne	8:06	9:15	10:05(1)	11:06(2)	12:08
Arr. Siegen	9:58	11:24	11:35	12:36	14:01

Sights in **Siegen:** The Upper Castle, with its Reubens paintings. (He was born here.) The crypts of the Princes of Nassau-Orange in the Castle.

Dep. Siegen	11:19	11:57	12:44	14:17	14:59(2+3)
Arr. Cologne	12:45	13:48	14:48	15:36	16:33

(1)Light refreshments. (2)Daily, except Sundays and holidays. (3)Plus other departures from Siegen at frequent times from 15:28 to 20:30.

Cologne - Mannheim - Cologne 662

Dep. Cologne   6:57(1)   7:57(1)   8:24(2)   8:57(1+3+7)
Arr. Mannheim   9:24   10:24   11:10   11:24

Sights in **Mannheim:** The first thing that strikes you about Mannheim is its "Squareness". Built to be a fortified town, it was designed as a chessboard of 144 residential blocks, each known by a letter and number that identifies its position on the grid. The Squared Town. See the Fine Arts Museum. The Reiss Municipal Museum. The Cathedral, Europe's largest Romanesque church. The Water Tower. The old Town Hall and parish church in the Marketplatz. The Castle.

Dep. Mannheim   12:30(1)   13:30(1)   13:48(2)   14:30(1+8)
Arr. Cologne   14:57   15:57   16:36   16:57

(1)Supplement charged. Meal service. (2)Meal service. (3)Daily, except Sundays and holidays. (4)Light refreshments. (5)TEE. Reservation required. Meal service. (6)Daily, except Saturday. (7)Plus other departures from Cologne at 9:20(2), 9:26(4), 9:57(1), 10:49(5), 10:57(1) and 11:57(1). (8)Plus other departures from Mannheim at 14:51(5), 16:05(2), 16:30(1), 17:30(1), 18:30(1), 19:04(4), 19:30(1), 20:30(1+6) and 21:30(1+6).

Frankfurt - Baden Baden - Frankfurt 664

Dep. Frankfurt   7:25(1)   7:37(2)   9:37(2)
Arr. Baden Baden   9:26   9:13   11:13

Sights in **Baden Baden:** See very lengthy notes about sightseeing in Baden Baden earlier in this chapter ("Basel-Baden Baden", under "Switzerland").

Dep. Baden Baden   13:37(1+3)   15:37(4)   16:59(3+5)   20:09(1+6)
Arr. Frankfurt   15:17   17:17   19:17   22:18

(1)Light refreshments. (2)Supplement charged. Meal service. (3)Daily, except Saturday. (4)Change trains in Mannheim. (5)Change trains in Karlsruhe. (6)Plus another departure from Baden Baden at 21:54(5).

Frankfurt - Basel - Frankfurt 664

Dep. Frankfurt   6:30(1+2)   7:37(1)   9:37(1)   10:37(1+2)
Arr. Basel (Bad Bf.)   9:39   10:39   12:39   13:39
Arr. Basel (S.B.B.)   7 minutes later

Sights in **Basel:** The Cathedral, with the tombs of Queen Anne and Erasmus of Rotterdam. The superb Holbein, Delacroix, Gauguin, Matisse, Ingres, Courbet and Van Gogh paintings in the Kunstmuseum. The Historical Museum in the Franciscan church in Barfusserplatz. The Municipal Casino.

The collection of 18th century clothing, ceramics and watches in the Kirschgarten mansion. The 16th century Town Hall. The fishmarket. The 15th century New University. Take a boat excursion from the pier in the back of Hotel Three Kings. The beautiful Munsterplatz. See the view of the city from the Wettstein Bridge. Shop on Freiestrasse.

Dep. Basel (S.B.B.)	14:08(1+3)	15:08(1)	16:08(1+4)	17:29(5+6)
Dep. Basel (Bad Bf.)	6 minutes later			
Arr. Frankfurt	17:17	18:17	19:17	22:18

(1)Supplement charged. Meal service. (2)Daily, except Sundays and holidays. (3)Change trains in Mannheim. (4)Daily, except Saturday. (5)Light refreshments. (6)Plus other departures from Basel at 18:08(1), 19:08(1+4), 19:23 and 20:08(1).

Frankfurt - Bremen - Frankfurt 664

Dep. Frankfurt	7:23(1+2)	8:23(2)	9:23(1)
Arr. Hannover	10:44	11:43	12:43
Change trains.			
Dep. Hannover	11:04	11:49(1)	13:05
Arr. Bremen	12:31	12:50	14:35

Sights in **Bremen:** It is an easy walk, down Bahnhofstrasse, from the railstation to the fine buildings in Market Square and to the 17th century Rathaus (Town Hall), Liebfrauenkirche, and the 11th century Cathedral, with its ancient crypt. From Market Square, walk down Bottcherstrasse to see the Porcelain Carillon and the Atlantis House, decorated with Zodiac signs.

Visit the Overseas Museum. Rampart Walk. The Focke Museum of Folklore. The Municipal Weights and Measures Office. Martini Church, from which 75-minute harbor cruises depart frequently every day in Summer. See the old workshops, inns and houses in the Schnoor residential area.

Dep. Bremen	16:09(2+3)	17:12
Arr. Hannover	17:05	18:42
Change trains.		
Dep. Hannover	17:10(2)	19:10(2+3)
Arr. Frankfurt	20:31	22:32

(1)Daily, except Sundays and holidays. (2)Supplement charged. Meal service. (3)Daily, except Saturday.

Frankfurt - Brussels - Frankfurt 64

Dep. Frankfurt	6:25(1)	8:29(2+3)		
Arr. Cologne	8:48(1)	10:51		

Change trains.

Dep. Cologne	9:06(1)	11:12(4)		
Arr. Brussels (Nord)	11:42	13:45		
Arr. Brussels (Midi)	10 minutes later			

Sights in **Brussels:** See notes about sightseeing in Brussels earlier in this section, under "Cologne-Brussels".

Dep. Brussels (Midi)	15:08(4)	16:00(2)	17:44(2)	18:27(1+6)
Dep. Brussels (Nord)	15:18(4)	16:07(2)	17:54(2)	18:35(1+6)
Arr. Cologne	17:49	18:48	20:17	21:23(1)

Change trains.

Dep. Cologne	18:03(2)	19:03(2+5)	21:03(2+5)	21:35(1+6)
Arr. Frankfurt	20:26	21:26	23:14	24:00

(1)Direct train. No train change in Cologne. Light refreshments. (2)Supplement charged. Meal service or light refreshments. (3)Daily, except Sunday and Monday. (4)Light refreshments. (5)Daily, except Saturday. (6)Reservation required.

Frankfurt - Cologne - Frankfurt 662

Dep. Frankfurt	6:25(1)	7:09(2)	7:24(1)	8:29(2+3+7)
Arr. Cologne	8:48	9:29	9:44	10:51

Sights in **Cologne:** See notes about sightseeing in Cologne at the start of this section.

Dep. Cologne	12:03(2)	13:03(2+4)	14:03(2)	14:14(1+8)
Arr. Frankfurt	14:26	15:26	16:26	16:56

(1)Light refreshments. (2)Supplement charged. Meal service. (3)Daily, except Sundays and holidays. (4)Monday-Friday, except holidays. (5)Daily, except Saturday. (6)Meal service. (7)Plus other departures from Frankfurt at 9:29(2), 9:40, 10:29(2), and 11:29(2+3).   (8)Plus other departures from Cologne at 15:03(2+5), 15:06, 16:03(2), 17:03(2), 17:33(2), 18:03(2), 19:03(2+5), 19:21, 20:03(2+5), 21:03(2+5) and 21:35(6).

Frankfurt - Dusseldorf - Frankfurt 662
Dep. Frankfurt   7:09(1)   7:24(2)   8:49   9:29(3)
Arr. Dusseldorf   9:55   10:14   12:45 12:26
    Sights in **Dusseldorf:** See notes about sightseeing in Dusseldorf earlier in this section, under "Cologne-Dusseldorf".
Dep. Dusseldorf 12:30(1+4) 13:44(2) 14:31 17:07(1+5)
Arr. Frankfurt   15:26   16:56   17:52 19:51
(1)Supplement charged. Meal service. (2)Light refreshments. (3)Supplement charged. (4)Monday-Friday, except holidays. (5)Plus other departures from Dusseldorf at 17:30(1), 18:45, 19:30(1) and 20:18(2).

Frankfurt - Essen - Frankfurt 662
Dep. Frankfurt   7:24(1)   9:29(2)
Arr. Essen   11:02   12:53
    Sights in **Essen:** See notes about sightseeing in Essen earlier in this section, under "Cologne-Essen".
Dep. Essen   13:08(1) 17:02(3) 18:10 19:31(1+4)
Arr. Frankfurt   16:56   20:26 22:02 23:25
(1)Light refreshments. (2)Supplement charged. (3)Supplement charged. Meal service. (4)Runs late May to late September.

Frankfurt - Hamburg - Frankfurt 664
Dep. Frankfurt   7:23(1+2) 8:23(1) 9:23(1)
Arr. Hamburg   12:09   13:09   14:09
    Sights in **Hamburg:** See notes about sightseeing in Hamburg earlier in this section under "Cologne-Hamburg".
Dep. Hamburg   15:45(1)   16:45(1) 17:45(1+3)
Arr. Frankfurt   20:31   21:31   22:32
(1)Supplement charged. Meal service. (2)Daily, except Sundays and holidays. (3)Daily, except Saturday.

Frankfurt - Hannover - Frankfurt   664

All of these trains charge a supplement and have meal service.

Dep. Frankfurt   7:23(1) 8:23   9:23   10:25
Arr. Hannover   10:44   11:43   12:43   13:43

Sights in **Hannover:** See notes about sightseeing in Hannover earlier in this section at the start of "One-Day Excursions".

Dep. Hannover   14:10   15:10   16:10   17:10   18:10(2)
Arr. Frankfurt   17:31   18:31   19:31   20:31   21:31

(1)Daily, except Sundays and holidays. (2)Plus another departure from Hannover at 19:10(1).

Frankfurt - Heidelberg - Frankfurt   662+664

Dep. Frankfurt   Frequent times from 7:19 to 23:47
Arr. Heidelberg   One hour later

Sights in **Heidelberg:** See notes about sightseeing in Heidelberg earlier in this section, under "Cologne-Heidelberg".

Dep. Heidelberg   Frequent times from 6:46 to 23:03
Arr. Frankfurt   One hour later

Frankfurt - Luxembourg - Frankfurt

657		625	
Dep. Frankfurt	7:07	Dep. Luxembourg	17:40
Arr. Koblenz	8:52	Arr. Koblenz	19:43
Change trains.		Change trains.	
625		657	
Dep. Koblenz	9:11	Dep. Koblenz	20:03
Arr. Luxembourg	11:15	Arr. Frankfurt	21:58

Sights in **Luxembourg:** See notes about sightseeing in Luxembourg earlier in this section, under "Cologne-Luxembourg".

Frankfurt - Mainz - Frankfurt

	662	622	622	662
Dep. Frankfurt	8:49	10:45	12:48	15:21
Arr. Mainz	30 minutes later			

Sights in **Mainz:** See notes about sightseeing in Mainz earlier in this section, under "Cologne-Mainz".

Dep. Mainz   Frequent times from 7:39 to 0:49
Arr. Frankfurt   30 minutes later

Frankfurt - Mannheim - Frankfurt   664

All of these trains charge a supplement and have meal service.

Dep. Frankfurt   7:37   8:37   9:37   10:37(1)   11:37
Arr. Mannheim   50 minutes later

Sights in **Mannheim:** See notes about sightseeing in Mannheim earlier in this section, under "Cologne-Mannheim".

Dep. Mannheim   11:33   12:33   13:33   14:33(2)   15:33(3)
Arr. Frankfurt   50 minutes later

(1)Daily, except Sundays and holidays. (2)Daily, except Saturday. (3)Plus other departures from Mannheim at 16:33(2), 17:33, 18:33(2), 19:33, 20:33, 21:33(2) and 22:33

Frankfurt - Munich - Frankfurt   663

All of these trains charge a supplement and have meal service.

Dep. Frankfurt   6:32(1)   8:32   9:32
Arr. Munich   10:28   12:22   13:42

Sights in **Munich:** See notes about sightseeing in Munich at the start of this section.

Dep. Munich   12:30   13:15   14:15   15:30(3)
Arr. Frankfurt   16:23   17:23   18:23   19:23

(1)Daily, except Sundays and holidays. (2)Daily, except Saturday. (3)Plus other departures from Munich at 16:30(2), 17:15 and 19:30(2).

Frankfurt - Nurnberg (and Bayreuth) - Frankfurt 663

Dep. Frankfurt   7:32(1)   7:54(2)   9:32(1)   10:06(2)   11:32(1)
Arr. Nurnberg   9:57   10:51   11:56   12:42   13:56

Sights in **Nurnberg:** The bronze and silver Sebaldusgrab in the 13th century St. Sebaldus Church. The Kaiserburg (Imperial Castle), Burggrafenburg and Imperial Stables in the fort. Albrecht Durer Haus, with copies of his paintings. The Rosette window, wood carving and statues in St. Lorenz Church. The 14th century Frauenkirche. The Alstadt Museum. The collection of toys, doll houses and other works in the Germanic National Museum. The 40 gold figures of artists, emperors, philosophers, prophets and popes around the Schoner Brunnen (Beautiful Fountain).

On the little island in the Pegnitz River, the Holy Ghost Hospital, locale of the legendary Till Eulenspiegel. Disguised as a doctor, this is where the 14th century peasant clown told the man in charge of the hospital that he could cure all the patients in one day.

The hospital authorities believed Till was a miracle worker when the patients rose from their beds and left the hospital after he whispered in each one's ear. "Those of you who are the most sick are going to be burned into a powder the hospital will use to heal the others," he told the patients.

See, every Noon, the moving figures in the clock on the front of the Church of Our Lady in the marketplace, and then lunch at a bratwurst restaurant. One is next to St. Sebaldus Church; another is behind the rebuilt 17th century Rathaus (City Hall). In the Rathuas, there are guided tours of the 14th century catacombs.

In St. Sebaldus, see the carved tomb of the Saint for whom the church is named. Visit the collection of porcelains at Fembo House (The City Museum), 15 Burgstrasse.

From Nurnberg, it's a short trip to Bayreuth, site of a 5-week annual (over 100 years) Wagner opera festival at Festspielhaus, every year from late July to late August at 16:00. See Haus Wahnfried, Wagner's home. Marvelous sights in **Bayreuth:** The breathtaking opera house. The Orangerie castle, open daily 10:00-11:30 and 13:30-15:00. Eremitage Park.

Dep. Nurnberg   13:01(1)   14:05(3)   15:01(1)   15:25(2)   16:01(1+4)
Arr. Frankfurt   15:23   16:54   17:23   18:02   18:23

(1)Supplement charged. Meal service. (2)Meal service. (3)Light refreshments.
(4)Plus other departures from Nurnberg at 19:01(1), 19:09 and 20:05(1).

Here are the connections between Nurnberg and Bayreuth:
678

Dep. Nurnberg	13:04	15:04	Dep. Bayreuth	16:30	20:37
Arr. Bayreuth	14:21	16:21	Arr. Nurnberg	17:53	21:53

Frankfurt - Siegen - Frankfurt 636

Dep. Frankfurt	7:45(1)	9:31(4)	12:20(2)
Arr. Siegen	9:25	11:17	14:11

                                  *   *   *

Dep. Siegen	14:37(2)	18:32(3)	20:37
Arr. Frankfurt	16:30	20:09	22:24

(1)Daily, except Sundays and holidays. (2)Light refreshments. (3)Daily, except Saturday.

Sights in **Siegen:** The Upper Castle, with its Reubens paintings. (He was born here.) The crypts of the Princes of Nassau-Orange in the Castle.

Frankfurt - Strasbourg - Frankfurt 670

Dep. Frankfurt	7:25	9:37	Dep. Strasbourg	16:20(1)	19:33(2)
Arr. Strasbourg	10:05	12:24	Arr. Frankfurt	20:17	22:26

(1)Change trains in Offenburg. (2)Daily, except Saturday. Supplement charged. Change trains in Offenburg.

Sights in **Strasbourg:** See notes about sightseeing in Strasbourg on page 129, under "Paris-Strasbourg".

Frankfurt - Stuttgart - Frankfurt 662

Dep. Frankfurt	6:09	7:52(1)	8:37(2)	9:17(1+4)
Arr. Stuttgart	8:45	10:17	10:51	11:29

Sights in **Stuttgart:** Outstanding contemporary architecture, built since World War II. Liederhalle, with its 3 concert halls. The Schillerplatz flower and vegetable market (Tuesday, Thursday and Saturday).

Dep. Stuttgart	11:26	13:13	15:03(2+3)	16:49(1+5)
Arr. Frankfurt	14:12	15:20	17:17	19:20

(1)Light refreshments. (2)Supplement charged. Meal service. (3)Daily, except Saturday. (4)Plus another departure from Frankfurt at 9:40. (5)Plus other departures from Stuttgart at 18:03(2), 19:44(1) and 21:03(1).

Frankfurt - Wiesbaden - Frankfurt   657+662
Dep. Frankfurt Frequent times from 7:07 to 20:08
Arr. Wiesbaden 30-40 minutes later
  Sights in **Wiesbaden:** One of Europe's top mineral bath resorts. See the
longest colonnade in Europe: Brunnenkolonnade.
Dep. WiesbadenFrequent times from 6:21 to 21:29
Arr. Frankfurt 30-40 minutes later

Hannover - Berlin - Hannover   764
Dep. Hannover   8:10(1) 10:11(2)
Arr. Berlin (Zoo)   11:30   13:51
  Sights in **Berlin:** See lengthy notes about sightseeing in Berlin earlier in
this section, under "The Island of West Berlin".
Dep. Berlin (Zoo)   15:44(2) 16:49(2)
Arr. Hannover   19:27   20:15
(1)Light refreshments. (2)Meal service.

Hannover - Bremen - Hannover   645
Dep. Hannover   7:48   9:15   11:04   11:49(1) 13:05
Arr. Bremen   9:01   10:44   12:31   12:50   14:35
  Sights in **Bremen:** See notes about sightseeing in Bremen earlier in this
section, under "Frankfurt-Bremen".
Dep. Bremen   13:09(2) 13:15   14:10   15:04   16:09(3+4)
Arr. Hannover   14:05   14:46   15:33   16:35   17:05
(1)Daily, except Sundays and holidays. (2)Supplement charged. Meal service.
(3)Daily, except Saturday. (4)Plus other departures from Bremen at 16:12,
17:04(3), 17:12, 19:05, 19:49, 20:53, 22:29 and 23:54.

Hannover - Celle - Hannover   658
Dep. Hannover   9:21   9:49   11:51   12:46   14:08
Arr. Celle   25 minutes later
  Sights in **Celle:** The 13th century Duke's Castle. The marvelous 16th-19th
century homes in the old section. The 14th century Church and Town Hall.
The Museum, with its Lower Saxon exhibits.
Dep. Celle   12:07   13:12(1) 14:30   15:41(2) 16:34(3)
Arr. Hannover   25 minutes later
(1)Monday-Friday, except holidays. (2)Supplement charged. (3)Plus other depar-
tures from Celle at frequent times from 19:45 to 0:11.

Hannover - Frankfurt - Hannover   664

Dep. Hannover   6:10(1)   7:10(1)   8:10(1)   8:35(2+5)
Arr. Frankfurt   9:31   10:31   11:31   12:51

Sights in **Frankfurt:** See notes about sightseeing in Frankfurt at the start of this section on West German "One-Day Excursions".

Dep. Frankfurt   12:23   13:23(3)   14:23(3)   15:05(2+6)
Arr. Hannover   15:43   16:43   17:43   18:32

(1)Daily, except Sundays and holidays. Supplement charged. Meal service. (2)Light refreshments. (3)Supplement charged. Meal service. (4)Daily, except Saturday. (5)Plus other departures from Hannover at 9:10(3) and 10:10(3).

(6)Plus other departures from Frankfurt at 15:23(3+4), 17:23(3+4), 18:23(3), 19:23(3+4) and 20:23(3+4).

Hannover - Goslar - Hannover   653

Dep. Hannover   7:23(1)   7:55(2)   10:45
Arr. Goslar   8:37   9:09   11:57

Sights in **Goslar:** The many 13th-16th century half-timbered buildings and 19th century houses. The Eagle Fountain. The five 13th century churches. The chandeliers of reindeer horns in the 15th century Town Hall. The 16th century towers and old city walls. The 11th century Imperial Palace. The museums of natural science and antiquities. Goslar is a popular base for touring the Harz Mountains.

Dep. Goslar   12:27   13:17   15:15   17:23   18:38(3)
Arr. Hannover   13:48   14:33   16:33   18:52   20:02

(1)Sundays and holidays only. (2)Daily, except Sundays and holidays. (3)Plus another departure from Goslar at 21:35.

Hannover - Hamburg - Hannover   658

Dep. Hannover   6:21   7:17   7:43   9:21(1+5)
Arr. Hamburg (Hbf.)   8:19   9:09   9:39   11:09

Sights in **Hamburg:** See notes about sightseeing in Hamburg earlier in this section, under "Cologne-Hamburg".

Dep. Hamburg   12:45(2)   13:00(1)   13:45(2)   14:45(2+6)
Arr. Hannover (Hbf.) 14:07   14:56   15:07   16:07

(1)Light refreshments. (2)Supplement charged. Meal service. (3)Daily, except Sundays and holidays. (4)Daily, except Saturday. (5)Plus other departures from Hannover at 10:46(2+3), 11:46(2) and 12:51(2).   (6)Plus other departures from Hamburg at 15:45(2), 16:45(2), 17:45(2+4), 18:00, 18:50(1), 19:55 and 20:55.

Hannover - Hameln - Hannover 654
Dep. Hannover   7:38 10:35 12:34 12:55
Arr. Hameln   35-50 minutes later

Sights in **Hameln:** Every Sunday at Noon (mid-May through mid-September), see the reenactment of the Pied Piper leading children through the Town Square. Take the 90-minute guided walking tour (10:00-11:30) from the tourist information office. A stroll through the surrounding woods is pleasant. Or, try a steamboat trip on the Weser River.
Dep. Hameln   13:37 14:49 15:52 19:23 20:27(1)
Arr. Hannover   35-50 minutes later
(1)Plus another departure from Hameln at 21:52.

Hannover - Hildesheim - Hannover 653
Dep. Hannover   7:23(1) 7:55(2) 10:45 13:20 14:19
Arr. Hildesheim   25-30 minutes later

Sights in **Hildesheim:** The supposedly 1,100-year old rose tree (probably 300-500 years old) which survived World War II bombings that literally destroyed the city, on the grounds of the Cathedral which houses marvelous 11th century art. Also see the Egyptian and Greco-Roman objects in the Roemer und Pelizaeus Museum. The 12th century painted ceiling in St. Michael's Church. The 15th century Tempelhaus. The Gothic Town Hall.

Take a local train for the short ride to Nordstemmen and then it is a 20-minute walk from that railstation to see the medieval castle, Schloss Marianburg.
Dep. Hildesheim   11:42   13:20   14:09 16:03 18:21(3)
Arr. Hannover   25-30 minutes later
(1)Sundays and holidays only. (2)Daily, except Sundays and holidays. (3)Plus other departures from Hildesheim at 19:36 and 22:32.

Hannover - Kassel - Hannover 664
There is beautiful Fulda River Valley scenery 20 minutes before arriving in Kassel.

All of these trains have light refreshments, unless designated otherwise.
Dep. Hannover   7:51   8:35 10:35
Arr. Kassel   9:49 10:35 12:35
Sights in **Kassel:** Take the bus #13 to see the enormous 233-foot high statue of Hercules, the 19th century Wilhelmshohe Castle, and the art museums

inside the Castle. Open daily except Monday, March-October, 10:00-17:00. Also see the collection of Brothers Grimm memorabilia in the City Museum. They wrote their fairy tales here. Other interesting sights are the 18th century Orangery Palace in Karlsaue Park. The paintings in the Landesmuseum. The Tapestry Museum. The Fredericianum Museum.

| Dep. Kassel | 13:10 | 14:45 | 16:45 | 19:21 |
| Arr. Hannover | 15:24 | 17:04 | 19:02 | 21:20 |

Hannover - Luneburg - Hannover   658

| Dep. Hannover | 7:43 | 9:21(1) | 9:49 | 11:51(1) | 12:51(2) |
| Arr. Luneburg | 9:00 | 10:32 | 11:17 | 13:06 | 13:49 |

Sights in **Luneburg:** The twisted-brick cornices on many old buildings. Fine art pieces in the churches: St. Nicholas, St. John and St. Michael. The 18th century crane at the waterfront. Guided tours of Town Hall, constructed over 5 centuries (1300-1800). The 17th century Ducal Palace.

| Dep. Luneburg | 11:06 | 12:00(3) | 12:57(4) | 13:35(1) | 15:02(2+5) |
| Arr. Hannover | 12:35 | 13:47 | 14:41 | 14:56 | 16:03 |

(1)Light refreshments. (2)Supplement charged. Meal service. (3)Monday-Friday, except holidays. (4)Saturday and Sunday. (5)Plus other departures from Luneburg at 15:33, 18:39, 19:27(1), 20:32 and 21:32.

Munich - Augsburg - Munich   662

| Dep. Munich | Frequent times from 6:55 to 23:30 |
| Arr. Augsburg | 30-40 minutes later |

Sights in **Augsburg:** An ancient castled city, complete with splendid Gothic gate, moat, tower and ramparts. The oldest (12th century) Romanesque stained-glass in the world, great 11th century bronze doors and an altar painting by Holbein in the 10th century Cathedral. The city's three 16th century fountains. The Mozart Museum in the house where the composer's father lived. The collection of manuscripts and drawings in the Municipal Library. The best Renaissance street in Germany is Augsburg's Maximilianstrasse.

| Dep. Augsburg | Frequent times from 8:23 to 0:34 |
| Arr. Munich | 30-40 minutes later |

Munich - Bayreuth - Munich

658

Dep. Munich	10:08	12:19
Arr. Nurnberg	12:42	14:49

Change trains.

678

Dep. Nurnberg	13:04	15:04
Arr. Bayreuth	14:21	16:21

Sights in **Bayreuth:** See notes about sightseeing in Bayreuth earlier in this section, under "Frankfurt-Bayreuth".

Dep. Bayreuth	16:30	20:37
Arr. Nurnberg	17:53	21:53

Change trains.

658

Dep. Nurnberg	18:11	22:02(1)
Arr. Munich	20:26	23:46

(1)Supplement charged. Meal service.

Munich - Frankfurt - Munich   662

All of these trains charge a supplement and have meal service.

Dep. Munich	6:30	7:15(1)	8:30	9:15(1)
Arr. Frankfurt	10:23	11:23	12:23	13:23

Sights in **Frankfurt:** See notes about sightseeing in Frankfurt at the start of this section.

Dep. Frankfurt	14:32	15:32(2)	16:32	17:32(3+4)
Arr. Munich	18:25	19:43	20:22	21:45

(1)Daily, except Sundays and holidays. (2)Monday-Friday, except holidays. (3)Daily, except Saturday. (4)Plus other departures from Frankfurt at 18:32 and 19:32.

Munich - Heidelberg - Munich   662

Dep. Munich	6:43(1+2)	6:55(3)	7:43(1)	8:43(1+5)
Arr. Heidelberg	10:12	11:06	11:12	12:12

Sights in **Heidelberg:** See notes about sightseeing in Heidelberg earlier in this section, under "Cologne-Heidelberg".

Dep. Heidelberg	13:41(1)	14:41(1)	15:41(1)	16:41(1+6)
Arr. Munich	17:10	18:10	19:10	20:10

(1)Supplement charged. Meal service. (2)Daily, except Sundays and holidays. (3)Light refreshments. (4)Daily, except Saturday. (5)Plus another departure from Munich at 9:43(1).   (6)Plus other departures from Heidelberg at 17:41(1+4), 17:46(3), 18:41(1), 19:41(1) and 20:49(3).

Munich - Innsbruck - Munich   758

Dep. Munich	7:40(1)	8:00(2+3)	8:24(3+4)
Arr. Innsbruck	9:50	10:20	10:30

Sights in **Innsbruck:** Marvelous Winter resort. Gateway to many cable railway trips (Hungerburg, Hafelekar, Igls, Patscherkofel). See the gilded copper shingles on Goldenes Dachl (Golden Roof). The 18th century Roman style Triumphal Arch. The paintings and furniture in the 18th century Hofburg Palace. The enormous and magnificent tomb of Maximilian I and the effigy of King Arthur in the 16th century Imperial Church. The silver altar at the Silver Chapel. Costumes and rustic furniture in the Tyrolean Folk Art Museum.

Dep. Innsbruck	12:08(5)	12:25(1+3)	14:12(2)	15:00(6+7)
Arr. Munich	13:54	14:33	16:25	17:19

(1)Meal service. (2)Light refreshments. (3)Runs late May to late September. (4)Depart/Arrive Munich's Ost railstation. (5)TEE. Reservation required. Meal service. (6)Runs mid-July to late September. (7)Plus other departures from Innsbruck at 18:38(2+3), 19:12(2+3), 20:00(1) and 23:35(3+4).

Munich - Mainz - Munich 662

All of these trains charge a supplement and have meal service, unless otherwise designated.

Dep. Munich   6:43(1)   8:43   9:43
Arr. Mainz   11:11   13:11   14:11

Sights in **Mainz:** See notes about sightseeing in Mainz earlier in this section, under "Cologne-Mainz".

Dep. Mainz   13:43   14:43   15:43   16:43(2+4)
Arr. Munich   18:10   19:10   20:10   21:13

(1)Daily, except Sundays and holidays. (2)Daily, except Saturday. (3)No supplement. Light refreshments. (4)Plus other departures from Mainz at 17:43 and 19:31(3).

Munich - Mannheim - Munich 662

All of these trains charge a supplement and have meal service.

Dep. Munich   5;43(1)   6:43(2)   7:43   8:43(5)
Arr. Mannheim   9:27   10:27   11:26   12:27

Sights in **Mannheim:** See notes about sightseeing in Mannheim earlier in this section, under "Cologne-Mannheim".

Dep. Mannheim   13:27   14:27   15:27   16:27(6)
Arr. Munich   17:10   18:10   19:10   20:10

(1)Monday-Friday, except holidays. (2)Daily, except Sundays and holidays. (3)Daily, except Saturday. (4)Light refreshments. (5)Plus other departures from Munich at 9:43 and 10:43. (6)Plus other departures from Mannheim at 17:27(3), 18:27, 19:28 and 20:32(4).

Munich - Nurnberg - Munich 663

All of these trains charge a supplement and have meal service, unless otherwise designated.

Dep. Munich   7:15(1)   8:15   9:15(1)   10:15(2+6)
Arr. Nurnberg   8:55   9:55   10:55   11:55

Sights in **Nurnberg:** See notes about sightseeing in Nurnberg earlier in this section, under "Frankfurt-Nurnberg".

Dep. Nurnberg   13:02   14:02   14:08(2)   15:02(7)
Arr. Munich   14:45   15:45   16:08   16:43

(1)Daily, except Sundays and holidays. (2)Daily, except Saturday. (3)No supplement. (4)Monday-Friday, except holidays. (5)No supplement. No meal service. (6)Plus other departures from Munich at 11:15 and 12:15. (7)Plus other departures from Nurnberg at 16:02, 17:02, 18:02(4), 18:11(5), 19:02, 20:02(2), 21:02 and 22:02.

Munich - Oberammergau - Munich

683

Dep. Munich	7:30(1)	9:00	10:00	11:00	12:00
Arr. Murnau	8:28	9:58	10:55	11:55	12:56

Change trains.

682

Dep. Murnau	8:33	10:03	11:03	12:15	13:12
Arr. Oberammergau	9:13	10:45	11:45	12:55	13:54

Sights in **Oberammergau:** Every year ending in zero (1980, 1990, etc.), the famous Passion Play. Three hundred years ago the villagers here promised to produce this play every 10 years if the Black Plague ended. In the interval between decades, you can still see the unique theater and enjoy this interesting woodcarving capital of Bavaria. There is time to take a bus trip and see the lapis lazuli, gilt and crystal in King Ludwig II's glorious palace, Schloss Linderhof.

682

Dep. Oberammergau	10:05	11:05	12:11	13:10	15:13(3)
Arr. Murnau	10:45	11:45	12:52	13:52	15:53

Change trains.

683

Dep. Murnau	11:02	12:02(2)	12:58	13:59	16:04
Arr. Munich	11:58	12:58	13:59	14:55	17:13

(1)Light refreshments. (2)Suuplement charged. Meal service. (3)Plus other departures from Oberammergau at 16:12, 17:10, 18:19 and 19:55.

Munich - Salzburg - Munich   684

Dep. Munich	6:47(1)	7:47(2)	9:02(2)	9:27(2)	9:48(1+6)
Arr. Salzburg	8:27	9:30	10:42	11:10	11:30

Sights in **Salzburg:** The most amusing place in Europe, the 17th century Hellbrun Palace. The 16th century 200-pipe barrel organ in the 12th century fortress 500 feet above the town, Festung Hohensalzburg. The traditional Music Festival (last week of July until the end of August). The State Rooms in The Residenz, the 17th century city palace of Salzburg's archbishops. The painted ceilings in the 17th century Festspeilhaus. The collection of Mozart musical instruments and family memorabilia in the Mozart Museum, his birthplace. The vast musical library at Bibliotheca Mozartiana. St. Sebastian's Cemetery at

Linzergasse 41. The 17th century Cathedral. The Universitatkirche. The Gothic cloister in the 9th century Benedictine Abbey of St. Peter. The Glockenspiel Tower, particularly at 7:00, 11:00 and 18:00 for the Carillon concerts. The ancient marketplace, Alter Markt. The marble Angel Staircase in the 17th century Schloss Mirabell, and the garden there. Take the cable car to the top (5,800 feet) of Untersberg for a breathtaking view of Salzburg and the Alps.

Dep. Salzburg   13:45   14:47   15:32(3)   16:13   17:14(4+7)
Arr. Munich   15:33   16:58   17:28   18:24   19:59

(1)Meal service. (2)Light refreshments. (3)Supplement charged. Meal service. (4)Monday-Friday, except holidays. (5)Runs early July to late August. (6)Plus other departures from Munich at 10:24 and 11:30.   (7)Plus other departures from Salzburg at 18:52(1), 19:05, 19:54(5) and 20:47.

Munich - Stuttgart - Munich   662

Dep. Munich   Frequent times from 6:55 to 23:30
Arr. Stuttgart   2-3 hours later

   Sights in **Stuttgart:** See notes about sightseeing in Stuttgart earlier in this section, under ''Frankfurt-Stuttgart''.

Dep. Stuttgart   Frequent times from 5:53 to 22:26
Arr. Munich   2-3 hours later

Munich - Tegernsee and Schliersee - Munich   1000

   Take a local train from Holzkirchner Bahnhof, a wing of Munich's Hauptbahnhof, for this 36-mile ride.

   At the northern end of Tegernsee (an exceptionally beautiful lake) is Gmund, not to be confused with the 2 Austrian villages also named Gmund. A mile away from this Gmund is a smaller lake, Schliersee. It is only a 4-mile walk around Schliersee. There is a lovely view of the lake from the ruins of Hohenwaldeck Castle and also from one of the many benches along the lake's shore. Also much sports (tennis, sailing, swimming) in this area. The Taubenstein mountain railway goes to an area that provides extensive mountain hiking. Wandering through the Weissachau Wildlife preserve, with its rare flowers, is worthwhile. Local food specialties in this region are white sausage, liver loaf, big white radishes and spicy Miesbacher cheese.

   Sights in **Tegernsee:** The concerts (May-September) in the enormous Baroque dining hall of the Castle. The large collection of rustic furniture, weapons, craft utensils, traditional costumes and ancient books in the Tegernsee Museum. The drawings, illustrations, sketches and caricatures by Olaf Gulbransson at the Kurpark Museum. The lakeside gambling casino. The 10-minute boat trip (every half hour) across the lake to Wiessee. Both Tegernsee and Wiessee have been popular for centuries for their curative mineral waters, laden with iodine and sulphur. Swimming in the pure lake is marvelous.

Take the cable car from nearby Rottach-Egern to the top of Wallberg for a view of the Tegernsee Valley and Austria's highest peak, the Grossglockner.

Munich - Wurzburg - Munich   658

All of these trains charge a supplement and have meal service.

| Dep. Munich | 6:30(1) | 7:30(1) | 9:30 | 10:30 |
| Arr. Wurzburg | 8:57 | 9:57 | 11:57 | 12:57 |

Sights in **Wurzburg:** Vineyards and wineries galore. The tourist information center is located in Falcon House, on the square where bratwurst, vegetables, fruits and flowers are sold. See the Main-Franconia Museum (sculptures, wine presses, etc.) in the 13th century Miarienberg Fortress. The view of the city from the restaurant at the Fortress. The roccoco garden in the nearby Schloss Veitshochheim. The 12 statues of saints on the Old Main Bridge. Pilgrimage Church. The Tiepolo ceiling and the Emperor's Hall, in the Residenz. Neumunster Church. The Cathedral. The fine sculptures in the Mainfrankisches Museum at the Festung. Take a boat trip on the River Main to see Randersacker and Sommerhausen.

| Dep. Wurzburg | 12:59 | 13:59 | 14:59 | 15:59(4) |
| Arr. Munich | 15:45 | 16:43 | 17:45 | 18:45 |

(1)Daily, except Sundays and holidays. (2)Monday-Friday, except holidays. (3)Daily, except Saturday. (4)Plus other departures from Wurzburg at 16:59(2), 17:59, 18:59(3), 19:59 and 20:59.

Munich - Ulm - Munich   662

| Dep. Munich | Frequent times from 6:55 to 23:30 |
| Arr. Ulm | 70-80 minutes later |

Sights in **Ulm:** The Bakery Museum (tools, library, artwork pertaining to bread) on Fuersteneckerstrasse. The display there includes breads made in ancient Egypt and in the Middle Ages. Open Monday-Friday 10:00-12:00 and 15:00-17:30.

The 14th century Gothic Cathedral, which has one of the highest towers (528 feet) in the world. The 17th century Schworhaus, where Town Council members once took their oaths to perform their duties (where they were "sworn in").

| Dep. Ulm | Frequent times from 7:13 to 23:39 |
| Arr. Munich | 70-80 minutes later |

Munich - Zurich - Munich   685

All of these trains have light refreshments.

| Dep. Munich | 7:00 | 9:07 | Dep. Zurich | 14:19 | 16:19 |
| Arr. Zurich | 11:37 | 13:50 | Arr. Munich | 19:09 | 21:13 |

Sights in **Zurich:** Here is a great 2-hour walk. Upon arriving at the Zurich railstation, take the escalator down one level and enjoy a snack or meal in Shopville, the enormous underground shopping center under Bahnhof Platz, just alongside the station. Come up from Shopville on the other side of Bahnhof Platz, and then walk one mile down one side of Bahnhofstrasse, lined with smart stores, until this city's Fifth Avenue ends at the shore of Lake Zurich. After viewing the lakeside promenade, return to the railstation down the opposite side of Bahnhofstrasse that you walked earlier. Upon returning to the station, go all the way through it, cross Museumstrasse, and visit the National Museum. Other sights to see: the Bellevue Platz amusement center. The paintings and sculptures at the Kunsthaus. African and Asian art at the Rietberg Museum. Kunstgewerbemuseum (The Museum of Applied Arts: handicrafts, architecture and industrial design).

SCENIC RAIL TRIPS

Cologne - Koblenz - Bullay - Cologne

There is beautiful farm, mountain and vineyard scenery on this easy one-day trip through the Moselle Valley.

662

| Dep. Cologne | 7:57(1) | 9:03(1) | 10:57(1) | 12:57(1) | |
| Arr. Koblenz | 8:49 | 9:55 | 11:49 | 13:49 | |

Change trains.

625

Dep. Koblenz	9:11	10:11	12:11	14:11(2)	
Arr. Bullay	9:51	10:51	12:51	14:51	
		*	*	*	
Dep. Bullay	12:59	14:59	17:02	19:02	20:59
Arr. Koblenz	13:43	15:43	17:43	19:43	21:43

Change trains.

662

| Dep. Koblenz | 13:59(1) | 16:05(1) | 17:59(1) | 20:05(1) | 21:59(1+3) |
| Arr. Cologne | 14:51 | 16:05(1) | 17:59(1) | 20:05(1) | 21:59(1+3) |

(1)Supplement charged. Meal service. (2)Monday-Friday, except holidays. (3)Daily, except Saturday.

Cologne - Mainz

Fine mountain, vineyard and Rhine river scenery. Complete schedules appear under the "Cologne-Mainz-Cologne" one-day excursion.

Cologne - Siegen - Frankfurt - Koblenz - Cologne

Excellent mountain scenery on this ride, which can be made as a circle trip from either Cologne or Frankfurt.

636

Dep. Cologne	7:06(1)	10:05(2)	13:16(2)
Arr. Siegen	8:24	11:37	14:37
Arr. Frankfurt	9:58	13:24	16:30

Change trains.

662

Dep. Frankfurt	10:29(3)	14:29(3+4)	17:03(2)
Dep. Koblenz	11:59	15:59	18:27
Arr. Cologne	12:51	16:51	19:32

(1)Daily, except Sundays and holidays. (2)Light refreshments. (3)Supplement charged. Meal service. (4)Daily, except Saturday. There is a Saturday departure at 15:21(2).

Here is the Frankfurt version of this circle trip:

662

Dep. Frankfurt	7:09(1)	10:29(1)	13:29(2)
Dep. Koblenz	8:37	11:59	14:59
Arr. Cologne	9:29	12:51	15:51

Change trains.

636

Dep. Cologne	10:05(3)	13:16(3)	17:16(4)
Dep. Siegen	11:37	14:37	18:32
Arr. Frankfurt	13:24	16:30	20:09

(1)Supplement charged. Meal service. (2)Daily, except Sundays and holidays. There is a Sunday departure at 14:29(1). (3)Light refreshments. (4)Daily, except Saturday. There is a Saturday departure at 19:06.

Freiburg - Donaueschingen

The train runs through the heart of the Black Forest. Very good mountain scenery on this spur of the Frankfurt-Basel route.

664

Dep. Frankfurt	9:01	16:01
Arr. Freiburg	9:01	16:01

Change trains.

690

Dep. Freiburg	9:48(2)	16:09
Arr. Don.	11:28	17:46

690

Dep. Don.	12:54	17:50
Arr. Freiburg	14:30	19:31

Change trains.

664

Dep. Freiburg	15:03(1)	20:03(1)
Arr.		
Basel (S.B.B.)	15:46	20:46

(1)Supplement charged. Meal service. (2)Daily, except Sundays and holidays.

Koblenz - Giessen

There is fine river scenery on this easy one-day roundtrip. This area can also be seen by taking an indirect route from Koblenz to Frankfurt. For the first way:

650

Dep. Koblenz	7:01(1)	9:12(1)	11:12(1)	14:19(2)
Arr. Giessen	9:09	11:23	13:06	16:18
		*	*	*
Dep. Giessen	10:52(1)	11:38(1)	13:28	17:52
Arr. Koblenz	12:42	14:18	15:42	20:00

Here is the long route to Frankfurt that offers the same scenery:

650

Dep. Koblenz	7:01(1)	9:12(1)	11:12(1)	14:19(2)
Arr. Giessen	9:09	11:23	13:06	16:18

Change trains.

664

Dep. Giessen	9:39	11:26	14:06	17:05(2)
Arr. Frankfurt	10:24	12:12	14:46	17:50

(1)Daily, except Sundays and holidays. (2)Daily, except Saturday.

The schedule for the reverse trip:

664

Dep. Frankfurt	9:31(1)	10:42	12:31	14:31(1)	17	:02
Arr. Giessen	10:15	11:26	13:10	15:10	17	:45

Change trains.

650

Dep. Giessen	10:52(2)	11:38(2)	13:28	16:14(3)	17	:52
Arr. Koblenz	12:42	14:18	15:42	18:32	20	:00

(1)Light refreshments. (2)Daily, except Sundays and holidays. (3)Daily, except Saturday.

Munich - Innsbruck - Garmisch - Zugspitz - Munich

Fine mountain scenery on this easy one-day circle trip.

758

Dep. Munich	7:40(1)	8:00(2)	8:24(2)	10:06(3)	13:38(4)
Arr. Innsbruck	9:50	10:20	10:30	12:20	15:49

Change trains.

756

Dep. Innsbruck	10:54	11:47(5)	13:55	14:55(5)	16:54(7)
Arr. Garmisch	12:22	13:24	15:25	16:23	18:25

(1)Meal service. (2)Runs late May to late September. (4)Light refreshments. (5)Privilege train (no border formalities). Special ticket required. (6)Change trains in Mittenwald. (7)Plus other departures from Innsbruck at 18:30(5) and 20:31(6).

The following schedule allows one to ride one cable railway to the summit of Zugspitz and ride a different cable railway en route back to Garmisch.

693

Dep. Garmisch	13:00	14:00	15:00	16:00
Arr. Eibsee	13:38	14:38	15:38	16:38
Change trains.				
Dep. Eibsee	13:45	14:45	15:45	16:45
Arr. Zugspitz	13:55	14:55	15:55	16:55
Change trains.				
Dep. Zugspitz	14:00	15:00	16:00	17:00
Arr. Schneefernerhaus	14:04	15:04	16:04	17:04
Change trains.				
Dep. Schneefernerhaus	14:25	15:25	16:25	17:25
Arr. Garmisch	15:45	16:45	17:45	18:45
Change trains.				

683

Dep. Garmisch	16:34	17:34	18:38	20:11
Arr. Munich	17:55	18:55	20:14	21:35

Munich - Nurnberg - Heilbronn - Heidelberg

This schedule follows the route of the "Castle Road" and "Romantic Road" bus trips.

663

Dep. Munich	7:15(1+2)	13:15(1)
Arr. Nurnberg	8:55	14:55
Change trains.		

679

Dep. Nurnberg	9:06	15:22
Arr. Heilbronn	11:11	17:24
Change trains.		
Dep. Heilbronn	11:21	17:30
Arr. Heidelberg	12:27	18:36

(1)Supplement charged. Meal service. (2)Daily, except Sundays and holidays.

Munich - Salzburg

This route offers good mountain scenery and is an easy one-day roundtrip. See schedules earlier in this section, under "One-Day Excursions".

380

Offenburg - Konstanz - Offenburg   675

This trip is recommended for exceptional mountain scenery.

Dep. Offenburg	8:07	8:42(1)	10:37	12:43	13:32(2)	14:45
Arr. Konstanz	10:37	11:16	13:02	15:34	16:06	17:13
		*	*	*		
Dep. Konstanz	11:50	13:40	14:42	16:34	18:18	21:00(3)
Arr. Offenburg	14:10	16:08	17:08	19:06	20:50	23:23

(1)Daily, except Sundays and holidays. (2)Meal service. (3)Daily, except Saturday.

Offenburg - Singen - Schaffhausen

Excellent Black Forest scenery on this route. This trip can also be made as a detour en route from Frankfurt to Basel.

675

Dep. Offenburg	8:07	10:37
Arr. Singen	10:10	12:36

Change trains.

668

Dep. Singen	10:38	14:39	17:38	19:38
Arr. Schaffhausen	11:54	14:54	17:54	19:54

Here is the detour from the Frankfurt-Basel ride:

664

Dep. Frankfurt	7:25(1)
Arr. Offenburg	9:49

Change trains.

675

Dep. Offenburg	10:37
Arr. Singen	12:36

Change trains.

674

Dep. Singen	12:41
Arr. Schaffhausen	12:55
Dep. Schaffhausen	12:57
Arr. Basel (Bad Bf.)	14:06

(1)Light refreshments.

Wurzburg - Zurich

Exceptional Black Forest scenery on this ride.

672

Dep. Wurzburg	9:59	12:22	13:02
Arr. Stuttgart	12:16	14:45	15:36

Change trains.

668

Dep. Stuttgart	12:31(1)	15:18(1)	17:13(1)
Arr. Zurich	15:44	18:44	20:44

(1)Light refreshments.

RHINE RIVER CRUISES

A variety of cruising on the Rhine is offered. The complete 5-day downstream route (from Basel to Amsterdam or Rotterdam) and the complete 6-day upstream route (Amsterdam or Rotterdam to Basel) are offered April to October.

A shorter portion (Rotterdam-Strasbourg and vice versa) is also available April to October. It is 4 days downstream and 5 upstream.

Still another service (3 days downstream and 4 upstream), between Amsterdam or Rotterdam and Mainz, is offered April to September.

On any of these, passengers may stop-over at points en route and resume the journey later (Dusseldorf, Cologne, etc.).

The most popular stretch of the Rhine, Dusseldorf to Frankfurt, is covered by the Eurailpass. This is the portion famed for scenic vineyards and hilltop castles. The entire Rhine trip is *not* covered by Eurailpass. With a Eurailpass, there is no charge for either the Mainz-Cologne boat trip or for the Cologne-Mainz train ride.

The scenery between Mainz and Koblenz can be seen as well from a train as from a boat because the track on this run goes along the river bank.

Here are the schedules for taking the boat Mainz-Cologne and returning to Mainz by train the same day:

700 (Boat)		662 (Train)		
Dep. Mainz	8:45(1)	Dep. Cologne		
Arr. Koblenz	13:20	(Hbf.)	18:46(2)	19:21(5)
Arr. Cologne		Dep. Koblenz	19:48(2)	20:31
(Frankenwrft.)	18:00	Arr. Mainz	20:59	21:30

(1)Runs early May to early October. (2)Light refreshments. (3)Supplement charged. Meal service. (4)Daily, except Saturday. (5)Plus other departures from Cologne at 20:47(2), 21:03(3+4), 21:35(2) and 22:36(2).

THE ONE-DAY HYDROFOIL CRUISE

Dusseldorf - Mainz - Dusseldorf   700

Operates daily except Monday, from early May to early October.

Dep. Bonn	9:00	Dep. Mainz	14:25
Dep. Koblenz	11:05	Dep. Koblenz	16:20
Arr. Mainz	13:10	Arr. Bonn	17:30

SCENIC BUS TRIPS COVERED BY EURAILPASS

Both of these extremely popular bus trips are covered by Eurailpass: "Romantische Strasse" (Romantic Road) and "Burgenstrasse" (Castle Road). Advance seat reservations should be made. They can be obtained at no cost by writing to: Bahnbusverkehrstelle, Hauptbahnhof, Augsburg, West Germany. Be sure to indicate the dates you want to journey, which of the 2 different lines you want to travel, where you will start and end your trip, and the number of seats you want.

Passengers are allowed to break the journey at as many stops as they desire on both bus lines, and we recommend some specific places to do so in the text that follows. If that is your plan, be sure to provide all the specific dates this will involve when requesting a reservation.

The 2 lines connect in **Rothenburg,** making it easy to ride on all or part of both trips. Lodging in Rothenburg is good quality, but the supply is small and the demand very great. The Encyclopedia Britannica calls Rothenburg "probably the finest surviving example of a medieval town". It has been there for 1,000 years. Its 30 watchtowers and many dungeons, churches, patrician homes, ornamental fountains and market squares are perfectly preserved.

The town's most important buildings are on the old Market Square: Town Hall, Virgin's Pharmacy (Marienapotheque), the lovely stone fountain (Herterichbrunnen), the ancient city council drinking hall, and the mechanical clock that performs at 11:00, 13:00 and 14:00 the Meistertrunk legend.

When the town was under siege in the 17th century, the commander of the victorious Imperial Army was given his first taste of wine by the inhabitants. He offered to spare the lives of the city officials if any of them could empty in one drink the content of a tankard holding almost one gallon. One burgermeister rose to the challenge, accomplished the feat, and even quaffed more.

The 3.24 liter Meistertrunk tankard is on display in the town's Reichstadt Museum. The legend is recreated every year in a pageant held on Whitsunday, 7 weeks after Easter.

Statues of the 7 deadly sins and 7 virtues adorn the Baumeisterhaus, on Schmiedgasse, near Market Square. This chiseled house is well worth seeing. The torture museum at the Dominican Nunnery is another attraction in the town.

Rothenburg has 15 hotels with 11 to 145 rooms each. It is an ideal stopover either for breaking the Romantische Strasse ride into 2 days or for transferring from or to the Burgenstrasse ride.

Also a recommended stopover on the Romantische Strasse ride is **Dinkelsbuhl,** another finely preserved medieval town with a surfeit of gates, bastions, towers, a moat equipped with floating swans and a sharp sense of ancient history. Its major pageant is every July, complete with sword dances and historic tableaux.

Augsburg is an ancient castled city, complete with splendid Gothic gate, moat, bridge, tower and ramparts. The oldest (12th century) stained-glass in the world, an 11th century bronze door and an altar painting by Holbein are features worth seeing in the 10th century Cathedral. The best Renaissance street in Germany is Augsburg's Maximilianstrasse.

Romantic Road

The portion of this trip that has the principal sights is Wurzburg-Augsburg (and v.v.). A stewardess-guide is provided for this part of the 2 schedules shown below.

	1635	1636		1635	1636
Dep. Wiesbaden	7:05(1)	-0-	Dep. Fussen	-0-	8:15(4)
Dep. Frankfurt	8:15	-0-	Dep. Munich	9:00(1)	-0-
Dep. Wurzburg	10:15(2)	9:00(4)	Dep. Augsburg	10:15	11:30
Arr.			Arr.		
Rothenburg	11:35(3)	12:00(3)	Dinkelsbuhl	12:35(3)	13:15(3)
Dep.			Dep.		
Rothenburg	13:45	13:10	Dinkelsbuhl	14:15	14:45
Arr.			Arr.		
Dinkelsbuhl	14:45(3)	14:10(3)	Rothenburg	15:15(3)	15:45(3)
Dep.			Dep.		
Dinkelsbuhl	15:30	14:45	Rothenburg	17:00	17:00
Arr. Augsburg	17:35	16:45	Arr. Wurzburg	18:09	19:20
Arr. Munich	18:55	-0-	Arr. Frankfurt	19:55	-0-
Arr. Fussen		-0-	Arr. Wiesbaden	20:40	-0-

(1)Runs from late March to early November. (2)No boarding or leaving this bus in Wurzburg from mid-June to late September. (3)Meal stop. Time to stroll. (4)Runs from mid-June to late September.

Castle Road   1636

Dep. Mannheim	7:15(1)	Dep. Rothenburg	16:50(1)
Dep. Heidelberg	7:45(1)	Arr. Heidelberg	20:25(1)
Arr. Rothenburg	12:00	Arr. Mannheim	20:45

(1)Runs from early June to late September.

INTERNATIONAL ROUTES FROM WEST GERMANY

The West German gateway for travel to Amsterdam and Brussels (and on to London) and Paris (and on to Barcelona and Madrid) is Cologne. Notes on the route to London appear in Chapter 10. Frankfurt is the access point for travel to Basel and Zurich (and on to Milan and Genoa). Munich is the nearest starting point for trips to Vienna (and on to Belgrade and Budapest), Venice and Rome. Hamburg is the gateway to Copenhagen (and on to Oslo and Stockholm).

Cologne - Amsterdam 68

Dep. Cologne	6:17	10:46	17:18(1)	19:17(2)
Arr. Amsterdam	9:36	14:26	20:03	22:26

(1)TEE. Reservation required. Meal service. (2)Meal service.

Cologne - Brussels 62+64+206

Dep. Cologne	4:47	5:12(1)	7:05(2)	8:09(3)	9:06(6)
Arr. Brussels (Nord)	7:55	8:07	9:47	10:22	11:42
Arr. Brussels (Cent.)	-0-	-0	9:51	10:26	-0-
Arr. Brussels (Midi)	8:04	8:19	9:57	10:31	11:49

(1)Runs mid-June to late August. (2)Light refreshments. (3)Supplement charged. Meal service or light refreshments. (4)Meal service. (5)Runs late May to late September. (6)Plus other departures from Cologne at 11:12(2), 13:20(3), 15:08(2), 17:06(4), 18:18(4), 20:20(2) and 20:50(2+5).

Cologne - Paris 62

Dep. Cologne	3:18(1+2)	7:15(3)	8:13	13:20(4+6)
Arr. Paris (Nord)	8:40	12:30	14:34	18:55

(1)Reservation required. Supplement charged. (2)Has couchettes. (3)From late June to early September: daily. From early September to late June: Monday-Friday, except holidays. Light refreshments. (4)Supplement charged. Meal service or light refreshments. (5)Carries sleeping car. Also has couchettes. (6)Plus other departures from Cologne at 16:35(4) and 23:37(5).

Frankfurt - Basel and Zurich 73

All of these trains charge a supplement and have meal service.

Dep. Frankfurt	9:37	12:37	14:37	17:37
Arr. Basel (S.B.B.)	12:46	15:46	17:46	20:46
Arr. Zurich	70 minutes later			

Hamburg - Copenhagen   648

All of these trains charge a supplement.

Dep. Hamburg	2:21(1)	3:20(2)	4:27(3)	7:00(6)
Arr. Copenhagen (Cent.)	8:09	9:09	10:17	12:09

(1)Has couchettes. (2)Carries sleeping car. Also has couchettes. (3)From late June to early September: daily. From early September to late June: Monday-Friday. Light refreshments. (4)Supplement charged. (5)Runs late May to late September. (6)Plus other departures from Hamburg at 8:39, 11:32, 14:02, 14:43(4), 17:30, 19:32(5) and 23:48(2).

Munich - Rome   74

Dep. Munich	7:40(1)	13:38	16:26(3+4)	19:20(4+5+7)
Arr. Rome (Ter.)	21:12	6:30(2)	7:58	9:45(2)

(1)Meal service. (2)Arrives at Rome's Tiburtina railstation. (3)Light refreshments until 18:36. (4)Carries sleeping car. Also has couchettes. (5)Runs mid-June to mid-September. (6)Light refreshments on Day 2. (7)Plus another departure from Munich at 23:20(4+6).

Munich - Vienna   61

Dep. Munich	6:47(1+2)	9:48(2)	17:20(2)	23:36(3)
Arr. Vienna (Westbf.)	11:55	15:36	22:50	6:10

(1)Runs late May to late September. (2)Meal service. (3)Has couchettes.

Munich - Venice   381

Dep. Munich	7:40(1)	8:00	13:38	16:26	19:20(2)
Arr. Verona (P.N.)	14:25(1)	15:39	20:56	0:14	2:16

Change trains.

Dep. Verona (P.N.)	15:10	16:39	22:08	3:20	2:44
Arr. Venice (S.L.)	16:45	18:14	23:48	5:08	4:32

(1)Direct train to Venice. No train change in Verona. (2)Runs late May to late September. Has couchettes to Verona.

Munich - Zurich   685

All of these trains have light refreshments.

Dep. Munich	7:00	9:07	11:19	16:03	17:35
Arr. Zurich	11:37	13:50	16:18	20:37	22:50

Chapter 7

EUROPE'S GREATEST TRAINS

For train travel that is the ultimate in speed, comfort and service, nothing in the world equals the 21 Trans-Europ Express trains, the 24 International Inter-City trains and the French Trains a Grande Vitesse (trains of great speed). Those which have an international route provide on-board customs inspection during transit.

The complete itineraries for all of these trains appear in this chapter. The name in parenthesis after a city-name refers to the correct station where a city has 2 or more railstations. Unless designated otherwise all stations in Austria, Switzerland and West Germany are "Hauptbahnhof".

Trans Europ Express Trains

All TEE trains charge first-class fare plus a supplement. Holders of Eurailpass need not pay the supplemental charge but must pay the same $2(U.S.) reservation fee required of any passenger traveling by a regular ticket.

If you board a TEE train without a seat reservation and there is vacant space, the conductor can allocate space after collecting the reservation fee. If all the seats are taken, you can be required to leave the train at the next stop.

A special telex network exists between the principal cities served by TEE trains. Except where a return ride begins in Spain, both outward and return reservations can be made quickly at the same time.

Holders of Eurail Youthpass can ride TEE trains by paying the difference between the second-class fare for a particular route and the TEE fare (first-class price plus supplemental charge).

Space on TEE trains can be reserved 2 months in advance of travel date. It is advisable to reserve TEE space before arriving in Europe. All of these special trains have a fixed maximum capacity. They do *not* add cars beyond that limit in peak travel periods, as many ordinary trains do. Often, demand for seats is greater than capacity.

For example, the outstanding "Settebello" consists of only 4-8 cars, with 144-384 seats. It was sold-out on many rides we made on it. (Don't fail to seek the conductor as early as possible so as to reserve time in the limited area of the locomotive's unique glass nosecone.)

As noted in Chapter 3, you can make reservations on TEE trains either through travel agents or directly with those offices of European railroads that sell Eurailpass which we list in Chapter 2.

The numeral following the name of each TEE train refers to the following index:

(1) 6-12 cars, 230-460 seats in compartments and open saloons. Meals are served at passengers' own seats in the open saloons. Passengers desiring meals should specify so when ordering seats.

(2) 6-9 cars, 300-461 seats in compartments and open saloons. Meals are served in a 42-seat restaurant car.

(3) 5 cars, 168 seats in open saloons. Meals are served in a 48-seat restaurant car.

(4) 7-9 cars, 230-320 seats in compartments. Meals are served in a 48-seat restaurant car.

(5) 4-10 cars, 144-452 seats in compartments and open saloons. Meals are served in a restaurant car.

International Inter-City Trains

These comprise the second stage of quality train service that began with the introduction of the marvelous TEE trains in the 1960's. Many former TEE trains ("Catalan", "Ligure", "Prinz Eugen", etc.) have been converted to IIC status, fast day trains having the newest coaches.

Unlike the first-class-only TEE trains, the IIC trains have offered since their introduction in 1980 both first *and* second-class coaches.

A supplement is charged by most IIC trains, and most IIC trains are air-conditioned. Most IIC trains do *not* require reservation.

Trains a Grande Vitesse

The third, and most revolutionary, stage in the modern development of European train transportation was the 1982 introduction of France's air-conditioned TGV service — the fastest trains on earth, capable of 236 miles-per-hour and often operated at 162 mph.

The previous 3 hours 30 minutes time to travel the 265 miles between Paris and Lyon has been reduced to 2 hours 30 minutes. The ordinary train ride of 7 hours from Paris to Marseille now takes only 4 hours 50 minutes on the TGV. The usual 6 hours to go from Paris to Geneva requires only 4 hours 15 minutes aboard a TGV.

Each TGV train is a single 660-foot-long unit with an engine at both ends, consisting of 8 passenger cars that accommodate 111 persons in first-class and 275 in second-class.

Advance reservation on TGV's are essential since French National Railways often cannot handle all the people who have switched from either airplane or auto travel to the TGV. Where a TGV has not been sold-out, a reservation can be made at an automatic machine in the railstation.

On a TGV, no one sits over the wheels. These trains ride smoothly due to running on continuous-welded rails that were specially built for the TGV. Seating in first-class consists of a single place on one side of the aisle and 2 seats on the other side. Second-class is 2 by 2 seating.

Each car has its own galley. The meals a passenger desires must be stated when reserving a first-class seat and are served to the passenger's seat airline style in 2 of the first-class cars, an attendant wheeling a cart down the aisle. Some TGV's offer light refreshments. Every TGV has a bar mid-train.

Normal fares are charged at off-peak times. A supplement is charged on peak travel days and at peak travel times.

Departure and arrival times shown in this chapter are for the Summer period (late May to September).

All times given in this chapter and throughout our book should be verified, as they are subject to change.

INDEX OF EUROPE'S GREATEST TRAINS

AMSTERDAM
Antwerp 13, 21
Basel 49
Bonn 11, 48, 49, 57
Brussels 13, 21
Cologne 11, 48, 49, 57
Den Haag 40
Dusseldorf 11, 48, 49, 57
Frankfurt 11, 57
Heidelberg 48
Innsbruck 11
Koblenz 11, 48, 49, 57
Mainz 48, 49
Munich 11
Nurnberg 11
Paris 13, 21
Rotterdam 13, 21
Stuttgart 48
Wiesbaden 57

BASEL
Amsterdam 49
Baden-Baden 49
Bern 29
Bonn 29, 33, 49, 50
Bremen 29, 50
Brig 29
Brussels 22
Chur 22
Cologne 29, 33, 49, 50
Dortmund 29, 33, 50
Dusseldort 29, 33, 49, 50
Frankfurt 20, 35, 47, 56
Geneva 35
Hamburg 20, 29, 35, 47, 50, 56
Hannover 20, 35, 47, 56
Interlaken 29
Koblenz 29, 33, 49, 50
Lausanne 35
Lugano 33, 56
Luxembourg 22
Luzern 33, 56
Mainz 29, 33, 49, 50
Mannheim 29, 33, 35, 49, 50
Milan 33, 56
Paris 5
Strasbourg 22
Zurich 5, 20, 22, 50

BRUSSELS
Amsterdam 13, 21, 40
Antwerp 13, 21, 40
Basel 22
Chur 22
Cologne 53
Den Haag 13, 21, 40
Luxembourg 22
Paris 7, 13, 21, 31, 38, 40, 52
Rotterdam 13, 21, 40
Strasbourg 22
Zurich 22

COLOGNE
Amsterdam 48, 49, 57
Baden-Baden 2, 49
Basel 29, 33, 49, 50
Bern 29
Bonn 2, 15, 17, 19, 29, 32,
    33, 37, 48, 49, 50, 57
Bremen 29, 32, 50
Brig 29
Brussels 53
Copenhagen 32
Dortmund 2, 15, 17, 19, 29,
    32, 33, 34, 37, 50
Dusseldorf 2, 15, 17, 19, 29, 32,
    33, 37, 48, 49, 50, 57
Frankfurt 2, 15, 17, 19, 57
Hamburg 29, 32, 50
Heidelberg 2, 15, 37, 48
Innsbruck 37
Interlaken 29

Karlsruhe 32
Koblenz 2, 15, 17, 19, 29, 32,
        33, 37, 48, 49, 50, 57
Lugano 33
Luzern 33
Mainz 2, 15, 17, 19, 29, 32, 33,
        37, 48, 49, 50
Mannheim 29, 32, 33, 37, 49, 50
Milan 33
Munich 37
Paris 34
Strasbourg 2
Stuttgart 2, 15, 37, 48
Wiesbaden 57
Zurich 50

GENEVA
Avignon 9, 51
Barcelona 9
Basel 35
Brig 27
Frankfurt 35
Grenoble 9, 51
Hamburg 35
Hannover 35
Lausanne 27, 35
Mannheim 35
Marseille 51
Milan 27
Narbonne 9
Paris 43

FRANKFURT
Amsterdam 11
Basel 20, 35, 47, 56
Bonn 6, 11, 17, 19
Chur 47
Cologne 6, 11, 17, 19
Dortmund 6, 17, 19
Dusseldord 11, 17, 19
Geneva 35
Hamburg 20, 35, 47, 56
Hannover 20, 35, 47, 56
Innsbruck 11
Koblenz 6, 11, 17, 19
Lausanne 35
Lugano 56
Luzern 56
Mainz 17, 19
Mannheim 35, 42
Milan 56
Munich 6, 11
Nurnberg 6, 11, 23
Paris 42
St. Moritz 47
Salzburg 6
Wiesbaden 6
Vienna 23
Zurich 20, 47

HAMBURG
Basel 20, 29, 35, 47, 50, 56
Bern 29
Bonn 29, 32, 50
Bremen 29, 32, 50
Brig 29
Chur 47
Cologne 29, 32, 50
Copenhagen 32
Dortmund 29, 32, 50
Dusseldorf 29, 32, 50
Frankfurt 20, 35, 47, 56
Geneva 35
Interlaken 29
Karlsruhe 32
Koblenz 29, 32, 50
Lausanne 35
Linz 46
Lugano 56
Luzern 56
Mainz 29, 32, 50
Mannheim 29, 32, 35, 50
Milan 56
Nurnberg 46
St. Mortz 47
Vienna 46

MILAN

Bari 1
Basel 33, 56
Bolgona 1, 3, 54, 58
Bonn 33
Brig 10, 27
Cannes 28
Cologne 33
Como 18
Dijon 10
Dortmund 33
Dusseldort 33
Florence 3, 54, 58
Frankfurt 36
Geneva 27
Genoa 28
Hamburg 56
Hannover 56
Innsbruck 30
Koblenz 33
Lusanne 10, 27
Lugano 18, 33, 56
Luzern 33, 56
Lyon 36
Mainz 33
Mannheim 33
Mmarseille 28
Modane 36
Manaco 28
Munich 30
Naples 3, 54, 58
Nice 28
Paris 10
Pescara 1
Rimini 1
Rome 3, 54, 58
Stresa 27
Torino 36
Verona 30
Zurich 18

MUNICH

Amsterdam 11
Bonn 6, 11, 37
Bremen 35
Cologne 6, 11, 37
Dortmund 6, 37
Dusseldorf 11, 37
Frankfurt 6, 11
Hannover 35
Heidelberg 37
Innsbruck 11, 30, 35, 37
Koblenz 6, 11, 37
Mainz 37
Mannheim 37
Mmilan 30
Nurnberg 6, 11, 35
Salzburg 6
Stuttgart 37
Verona 30
Wiesbaden 6
Wurzburg 6, 35

PARIS

Amsterdam 13, 21, 40
Annecy 39
Antwerp 13, 21, 40
Avignon 45-B
Basel 5
Bordeaux 4, 12
Brig 10,44
Brussels 7, 13, 21, 31, 38, 40, 52
Cologne 34
Den Haag 13, 21, 40
Dijon 10,41
Dortmund 34
Frankfurt 42
Geneva 43
Grenoble 39
Lausanne 10
Lille 14, 16, 59
Limoges 8
Lyon 45-A
Marseille 45-B

Milan 10
Nancy 26, 55
Nantes 24
Rotterdam 13, 21, 40
Strasbourg 26, 55
Toulouse 8
Tourcoing 14, 16, 59
Zurich 5

ROME
Bologna 3, 54, 58
Florencd 3, 54, 58
Milan 3, 54, 58
Naples 58

VIENNA
Frankfurt 23
Hamburg 46
Hannover 46
Linz 23, 46
Nurnberg 23, 46

ZURICH
Basel 5, 20, 22, 47, 50
Bonn 50
Bremen 50
Brussels 22
Chur 22, 47
Cologne 50
Como 18
Dusseldorf 50
Frankfurt 20, 47
Hamburg 20, 47, 50
Hannover 20, 47
Koblenz 50
Lugano 18
Luxembourg 22
Mainz 50
Mannheim 50
Milan 18
Paris 5
St. Mortz 47
Strasbourg 22

1 ADRIATICO   TEE Type #5

Arr.	Dep.		Arr.	Dep.
	9:30	Milan (Centrale)	19:05	
11:22	11:27	Bologna	17:10	17:15
12:35	12:37	Rimini	15:55	15:58
13:36	13:41	Ancona	14:49	14:53
15:16	15:19	Pescara (Centrale)	13:08	13:11
17:36	17:39	Foggia	10:51	10:54
18:56		Bari		9:40

2 ALBERT SCHWEITZER   TEE Type #2
Discontinued in 1983.

3 AMBROSIANO   TEE Type #5

Arr.	Dep.		Arr.	Dep.
	16:50	Milan (Centrale)	17:30	
18:47	18:53	Bologna	15:34	15:42
20:02	20:12	Florence	14:13	14:23
23:00		Rome (Termini)		11:30

4 AQUITANE   TEE Type #4
This is one of Europe's fastest trains (125 mph in open country, averaging 87 mph on its 360-mile run). Gourmet food is served on this beautiful train. Meals desired must be specified when reserving seat. Operates early September to late June. From Paris: runs Mon.-Thurs.. From Bordeaux: runs Tues.-Fri.

Arr.	Dep.		Arr.	Dep.
	17:47	Paris (Austerlitz)	12:33	
20:03	20:04	Poitiers	10:18	10:19
20:52	20:53	Angouleme	9:24	9:25
21:52		Bordeaux (St. Jean)		8:25

5 ARBALETE   IIC   (Meal service)

Arr.	Dep.		Arr.	Dep.
	17:04	Paris (Est)	12:59	
	20:57	Belfort		9:09
	21:25	Mulhouse		8:35
21:46	22:00	Basel (S.B.B.)	7:56	8:13
23:02		Zurich		6:57

6 BLAUER ENZIAN IIC (Meal service)

Arr.	Dep.		Arr.	Dep.
	5:40	Dortmund	22:14	
	6:04	Hagen	21:51	
	6:22	Wt. Elberfeld	21:34	
6:52	7:03	Cologne	20:51	21:03
	7:23	Bonn		20:31
	7:57	Koblenz		19:59
	9:00	Wiesbaden		19:02
	9:32	Frankfurt		18:29
	10:59	Wurzburg		17:02
	12:02	Nurnberg		16:01
13:42	13:52	Munich	14:02	14:15
	15:26	Salzburg		12:26
	18:52	Villach		9:08
19:30		Klagenfurt		8:25

7 BRABANT TEE Type #1

One of Europe's fastest trains. Averages 78 miles per hour.

Arr.	Dep.		Arr.	Dep.
	17:17	Brussels (Midi)	14:05	
19:44		Paris (Nord)		11:37

8 CAPITOLE TEE Type #4

From Paris to Toulouse: daily, except Saturday. From Toulouse to Paris: daily, except Sundays and holidays.

Arr.	Dep.		Arr.	Dep.
	18:00	Paris (Austerlitz)	13:54	
20:51	20:53	Limoges	11:01	11:03
21:52	21:53	Brive-la-Gaillarde	10:02	10:03
22:54	22:55	Cahors	8:58	8:59
23:32	23:33	Montauban	8:20	8:21
23:59		Toulouse (Matabiau)		7:55

9 CATALAN   IIC

Supplement charged. Meals are served in a 48-seat restaurant car. Also has bar. All cars are air-conditioned.

Arr.	Dep.		Arr.	Dep.
	11:27	Geneva (Cornavin) ▲	19:44	
11:54	11:55	Bellegarde	19:11	19:13
12:45	12:55	Chambery	18:12	18:22
13:32	13:34	Grenoble	17:33	17:35
14:32	14:35	Valence	16:27	16:36
15:46	15:48	Avignon	15:25	15:27
16:14	16:16	Nimes	14:57	14:59
16:41	16:43	Montpellier	14:29	14:31
17:21	17:23	Beziers	13:50	13:52
17:35	17:41	Narbonne	13:34	13:36
18:14	18:16	Perpignan	13:00	13:02
18:43	18:48	Cerbere	12:30	12:35
19:03	19:22	Port Bou	11:53	12:15
20:15	20:17	Gerona	10:59	11:01
21:20	21:21	Barcelona (P. de G.)	9:54	9:56
21:26		Barcelona (Sants) ▼		9:50

10-A CISALPIN   TGV   (Meal service)

Arr.	Dep.		Arr.	Dep.
	12:34	Paris (Lyon) ▲	21:31	
14:10	14:13	Dijon	19:46	19:50
15:36	15:37	Vallorbe	18:16	18:17
16:10		Lausanne ▼		17:43

10-B CISALPIN   IIC   (Light refreshments)

Arr.	Dep.		Arr.	Dep.
	15:45	Geneva ▲	18:12	
16:18	16:22	Lausanne	17:33	17:37
20:05		Milan (Centrale) ▼		13:52

11 ERASMUS   IIC

Supplement charged. Meal service. Mid-April to late September: runs daily. Early October to mid-April: runs Friday and Saturday.

Arr.	Dep.		Arr.	Dep.
	6:57	Amsterdam ▲	20:52	
9:32	9:35	Dusseldorf	18:18	18:20
9:59	10:03	Cologne	17:51	17:54
10:21	10:23	Bonn	17:29	17:31
10:55	10:57	Koblenz	16:57	16:59
12:26	12:32	Frankfurt	15:23	15:29
14:56	15:02	Nurnberg	12:55	13:01
16:43	16:55	Munich	11:03	11:15
19:00		Innsbruck ▼		8:55

12 **ETENDARD** TEE Type #4

From Paris to Bordeaux: runs Monday-Friday. From Bordeaux to Paris: runs daily, except Saturday. Specify meals desired when reserving seat.

Arr.	Dep.		Arr.	Dep.
	7:47	Paris (Austerlitz)	21:48	
9:20	9:21	St. Pierre des Corps	20:10	20:11
9:59	10:00	Poitiers	19:32	19:33
10:48	10:49	Angouleme	18:40	18:41
11:50		Bordeaux (St. Jean)		17:42

13 **ETOILE DU NORD** TEE Type #1

Arr.	Dep.		Arr.	Dep.
	8:53	Amsterdam	22:45	
9:32	9:33	Den Haag	22:07	22:08
9:50	9:52	Rotterdam	21:50	21:52
10:29	10:30	Roosendaal	21:15	21:16
10:56	10:57	Antwerp (Bercham)	20:49	20:50
11:26	11:28	Brussels (Nord)	20:20	20:21
11:33	11:43	Brussels (Midi)	20:08	20:15
14:10		Paris (Nord)		17:41

14 **FAIDHERBE** TEE Type #4

Runs Monday-Friday, except holidays.

Arr.	Dep.		Arr.	Dep.
	7:27	Paris (Nord)	9:03	
8:55	8:56	Arras	7:34	7:35
9:10	9:11	Douai	7:20	7:21
9:30	9:36	Lille	6:56	7:02
9:46	9:47	Roubaix	6:44	6:45
9:52		Tourcoing		6:39

15 **GAMBRINUS** TEE Type #2

Ceased operating in 1983.

16 GAYANT   De-classified as TEE in 1983.

Runs Monday-Friday, except holidays. Supplement charged. Meal service.

Arr.	Dep.		Arr.	Dep.
	11:55	Paris (Nord) ↑	14:04	
13:23	13:25	Arras	12:30	12:31
13:39	13:41	Douai	12:16	12:17
14:00	14:06	Lille	11:50	11:57
14:20	14:21	Roubaix	11:38	11:39
14:26		↓ Tourcoing		11:33

17 GOETHE   TEE Type #2
Ceased operating in 1983.

18 GOTTARDO   TEE Type #3

Arr.	Dep.		Arr.	Dep.
	8:39	Zurich ↑	20:53	
11:08	11:10	Bellinzona	18:23	18:25
11:35	11:38	Lugano	17:52	17:55
12:04	12:06	Como	17:23	17:25
12:40		↓ Milan (Centrale)		16:50

19 HEINRICH HEINE   TEE Type #2
Ceased operating in 1983.

20 **HELVETIA** IIC
Supplement charged. Meal service.

Arr.	Dep.		Arr.	Dep.
	12:31	Hamburg (Hbf.)	16:09	
14:07	14:10	Hannover	14:43	14:46
17:31	17:37	Frankfurt	11:17	11:23
20:39	20:41	Basel (Bad. Bf.)	8:13	8:14
20:46	20:58	Basel (S.B.B.)	7:56	8:08
21:57		Zurich		6:57

21 **ILE DE FRANCE**   TEE Type #1

Arr.	Dep.		Arr.	Dep.
	17:53	Amsterdam	12:30	
18:32	18:34	Den Haag	11:48	11:49
18:51	18:53	Rotterdam	11:31	11:33
19:29	19:30	Roosendaal	10:55	10:56
19:55	19:56	Antwerp (Berchem)	10:29	10:30
20:26	20:27	Brussels (Nord)	9:58	9:59
20:32	20:42	Brussels (Midi)	9:46	9:53
23:10		Paris (Nord)		7:19

22 **IRIS** IIC
Meal service.

Arr.	Dep.		Arr.	Dep.
	12:12	Brussels (Midi)	19:33	
12:15	12:20	Brussels (Nord)	19:25	19:29
14:44	14:54	Luxembourg	16:49	16:59
17:00	17:03	Strasbourg	14:39	14:41
18:25	18:35	Basel (S.N.C.F.)	13:05	13:20
18:40	18:58	Basel (S.B.B.)	12:56	13:01
19:57	20:07	Zurich	11:47	11:57
21:30	-0-	Chur	10:19	10:24
-0-	-0-	St. Moritz		7:33

23 **JOHANN STRAUSS**   IIC
Supplement charged in Germany. Meal service.

Arr.	Dep.		Arr.	Dep.
	7:32	Frankfurt	22:27	
	8:59	Wurzburg		21:04
	9:59	Nurnberg		20:05
	11:02	Regensburg		18:59
12:08	12:12	Passau	17:37	17:51
13:21		Linz		16:20
15:29		Vienna (Westbf.)		14:20

24 JULES VERNE   TEE Type #4
Runs Monday-Friday.

Arr.	Dep.			Arr.	Dep.
	18:30	↓	Paris (Montparnasse) ↑	9:22	
20:49	20:50		Angers-St. Laud	6:59	7:00
21:33			Nantes		6:19

25 KARWENDEL   IIC
Runs the Garmisch-Innsbruck and v.v. portion only from late May to late September. Meal Service.

Arr.	Dep.			Arr.	Dep.
	7:09		Bremen ↑	19:45	
	8:15		Hannover	18:38	
	9:13		Gottingen		17:40
	10:07		Bebra		16:48
	11:59		Wurzburg		15:07
	13:02		Nurnberg		14:01
14:45	14:58		Munich	11:58	12:15
16:11	16:24		Garmisch	10:24	10:38
16:44			Mittenwald		10:03
17:46		↓	Innsbruck		9:00

26 KLEBER   TEE Type #4
Kleber was reduced to a Rapide train in 1982.

27 LEMANO   IIC
Supplement charged in Italy. Light refreshments.

Arr.	Dep.			Arr.	Dep.
	14:45	↓	Geneva (Cornavin) ↑	13:08	
15:19	15:22		Lausanne	12:32	12:35
16:15	16:16		Sion	11:37	11:38
16:47	16:50		Brig	11:04	11:07
17:22	17:37		Domodossola	10:22	10:32
18:01	18:02		Stresa	9:54	9:55
19:05		↓	Milan (Centrale)		9:00

28 LIGURE IIC

Supplement charged in Italy. Meal service.

Arr.	Dep.		Arr.	Dep.
	6:40	Milan (Centrale) ↑	23:30	
8:15	8:23	Genoa (P.P.)	21:50	22:00
8:51	8:53	Savona	21:19	21:21
9:45	9:47	Imperia P. Maurizio	20:29	20:31
10:08	10:10	San Remo	20:08	20:10
10:25	10:44	Ventimiglia	19:43	19:56
10:54	10:56	Menton	19:31	19:33
11:04	11:06	Monaco-Monte Carlo	19:20	19:22
11:20	11:24	Nice	19:02	19:05
11:37	11:39	Antibes	18:47	18:49
11:47	11:49	Cannes	18:37	18:39
12:10	12:12	St. Raphael	18:14	18:16
12:57	12:59	Toulon	17:29	17:31
13:42	↓	Marseille (St. Ch.)		16:48

29 LOTSCHBERG IIC

Meal service. From Hamburg to Munster: runs daily, except Sundays and holidays. From Munster to Hamburg: runs daily, except Saturday. From Dortmund to Brig and v.v.: runs daily.

Arr.	Dep.		Arr.	Dep.
	5:26	Hamburg (Altona) ↑	23:35	
	5:40	Hamburg (Hbf.)	23:16	
	6:40	Bremen	22:16	
	8:03	Munster	20:53	
	8:37	Dortmund	20:18	
	9:02	Essen		19:54
	9:30	Dusseldorf		19:27
9:53	9:57	Cologne	18:57	19:00
	10:17	Bonn		18:37
	10:51	Koblenz		18:05
	11:43	Mainz		17:13
	12:29	Mannheim		16:30
	13:00	Karlsruhe		15:56
	14:03	Freiburg (Breisgau)		14:52
	14:39	Basel (Bad. Bf.)		14:14
14:46	14:56	Basel (S.B.B.)	13:58	14:08
16:09		Bern		12:45
17:20		Interlaken (Ost)		11:34
18:00	↓	Brig		10:54

30 **MEDIOLANUM** TEE Type #5

Arr.	Dep.			Arr.	Dep.
	15:38	Munich	↑	13:54	
16:38	16:43	Kufstein		12:51	12:53
17:26	17:29	Innsbruck		12:05	12:08
18:04	18:17	Brennero		11:19	11:32
19:33	19:36	Bolzano		9:57	10:00
20:08	20:09	Trento		9:24	9:26
21:12	21:24	Verona (P.N.)		8:11	8:23
21:58	21:59	Brescia		7:34	7:35
22:50	↓	Milan (Centrale)			6:50

31 **MEMLING** TEE Type #1
Runs Monday-Friday, except holidays.

Arr.	Dep.			Arr.	Dep.
	18:38	Brussels (Midi)	↑	9:11	
21:06	↓	Paris (Nord)			6:41

32 **MERKUR** IIC
Departs Freiburg Monday-Friday, except holidays. Runs from all other cities daily. Meal service Hamburg-Karlsruhe and v.v.

Arr.	Dep.			Arr.	Dep.
	10:10	Copenhagen (H.)	↑	19:45	
	12:10	Rodby Ferry		17:30	
	13:34	Puttgerden		16:22	
	14:30	Lubeck		15:21	
15:07	15:40	Hamburg		14:14	14:43
	16:40	Bremen			13:18
	17:36	Osnabruck			12:21
	18:03	Munster			11:55
	18:37	Dortmund			11:23
	19:02	Essen			10:54
	19:30	Dusseldorf			10:27
19:53	19:57	Cologne		9:57	10:00
	20:17	Bonn			9:37
	20:51	Koblenz			9:05
	21:43	Mainz			8:13
22:24		Mannheim			7:30
22:58		Karlsruhe			6:56
-0-	↓	Freiburg (Breisgau)			5:31

33 METROPOLITANO IIC Meal service.

Arr.	Dep.		Arr.	Dep.
	5:37	Dortmund	23:18	
	6:02	Essen	22:52	
	6:30	Dusseldorf	22:25	
6:53	6:57	Cologne	21:57	22:00
	7:17	Bonn		21:37
	7:51	Koblenz		21:05
	8:43	Mainz		20:13
	9:29	Mannheim		19:30
	10:00	Karlsruhe		18:56
	11:03	Freiburg (Breisgau)		17:52
11:39	11:41	Basel (Bad. Bf.)		17:14
11:46	12:01	Basel (S.B.B.)	16:53	17:08
13:10		Luzern		15:44
15:34		Bellinzona		13:20
16:03		Lugano		12:50
16:29		Chiasso		12:25
17:35		Milan (Centrale)		11:20

34 MOLIERE IIC
Discontinued in 1983.

35 MONT-BLANC IIC
Meal service. Connects in Geneva with trains to and from Barcelona.

Arr.	Dep.		Arr.	Dep.
	9:31	Hamburg (Altona)	19:24	
9:41	9:45	Hamburg (Hbf.)	19:09	19:13
11:07	11:10	Hannover	17:43	17:46
12:05	12:07	Gottingen	16:43	16:45
14:31	14:37	Frankfurt	14:17	14:23
15:21	15:29	Mannheim	13:25	13:33
15:58	16:00	Karlsruhe	12:54	12:56
17:01	17:03	Freiburg (Breisgau)	11:50	11:52
17:39	17:41	Basel (Bad. Bf.)	11:13	11:14
17:46	17:59	Basel (S.B.B.)	10:54	11:08
19:02	19:04	Biel	9:49	9:51
19:23	19:24	Neuchatel	9:28	9:29
20:10	20:16	Lausanne	8:37	8:43
20:50	21:29	Geneva (Cornavin)	7:25	8:03

	CONNECTION	TO BARCELONA/GENEVA		
23:26	23:30	Lyon (Brotteaux)	5:15	5:19
9:39		Barcelona		19:00

36 **MONT-CENIS**   IIC

Supplement charged in Italy. Light refreshments.

	17:03	Lyon (Perrache)	13:00	
17:12	17:13	Lyon (Part Dieu)	12:51	12:52
18:28	18:30	Chambery	11:30	11:32
19:40	19:52	Modane	10:15	10:27
21:30	21:40	Torino (P.N.)	8:30	8:40
23:10		Milan (Centrale)		7:00

37 **NYMPHENBURG**   IIC

Meal service. The Munich-Innsbruck portion and v.v. runs daily late May to
late September. Also runs occasional days in October, December and January.
Runs Friday and Saturday mid-January to early April.

Arr.	Dep.		Arr.	Dep.
	6:37	Dortmund	22:18	
	7:02	Essen	21:52	
	7:30	Dusseldorf	21:25	
7:54	7:57	Cologne	20:57	21:00
	8:17	Bonn		20:37
	8:51	Koblenz		20:05
	9:43	Mainz		19:13
	10:27	Mannheim		18:30
	10:41	Heidelberg		18:14
	11:57	Stuttgart		17:03
	12:55	Ulm		15:59
14:10	14:21	Munich	14:33	14:43
	15:40	Kufstein		13:31
16:40		Innsbruck		12:25

38 **OISEAU BLEU**   TEE Type #1

From Brussels to Paris: runs daily, except Sunday. From Paris to Brussels:
runs daily, except Saturday.

	7:13	Brussels (Nord)	23:12	
	7:30	Brussels (Midi)	23:03	
10:05		Paris (Nord)		20:30

39 PARIS-ANNECY   TGV

Dep. Paris (Lyon)	7:34(1)	13:09(2)	14:32(3)	19:13(4)
Arr. Annecy	11:07	16:38	18:16	22:57
		*	*	*
Dep. Annecy	7:07(1)	11:57	18:19(2+4)	19:29(5)
Arr. Paris (Lyon)	10:55	15:46	21:53	23:09

(1)Supplement charged Mon.-Fri., except holidays. (2)Runs daily mid-December to mid-April. (3)Light refreshments. (4)Supplement charged, except on Sat. (5)Mid-December to late April: runs daily. Late April to mid-December: runs daily, except Sat. Supplement charged on Sun. and holidays.

40 PARIS-BRUSSELS   IIC

Supplement charged. Runs daily, except Sat. Light refreshments or meal service.

Arr.	Dep.		Arr.	Dep.
	16:45	Paris (Nord) ↑	20:34	
	19:30 ↓	Brussels (Midi)		17:53

41 PARIS-DIJON-LAUSANNE   TGV

These trains have light refreshments or tray meal service.

Dep. Paris (Lyon)	627(1)	7:18(2)	8:16(2)	12:34(1+3+9)
Arr. Dijon	8:09	8:56	9:54	14:10
Arr. Lausanne	-0-	11:10	-0-	16:10
	*	*	*	
Dep. Lausanne	-0-	-0-	7:38(2+10)	-0-
Dep. Dijon	6:56(4)	9:45(1)	9:45	11:35(2+11)
Arr. Paris (Lyon)	8:43	11:26	11:26	13:16

(1)Runs Mon.-Fri. (2)Runs daily. (3)Supplement Mon.-Fri., except holidays. (4)Runs daily, except Sundays and holidays. Supplement Mon.-Thurs., except holidays. (5)Terminates in Dijon. (6)Supplement on Fri. (7)Supplement, except Sat. (8)Supplement on Mon., Fri., Sun. and holidays. (9)Plus other departures from Paris at 14:26(2), 16:17(1+5+6), 17:19(2+5+7), 18:08(2+7) and 19:46(2+6). (10)Plus other departures from Lausanne at 12:40(2), 17:43(2+8) and 19:43(2). (11)Plus other departures from Dijon at 14:43(2), 16:59(2+3), 18:34(2+6), 19:50(2+8) and 21:45(2)

42 PARIS-FRANKFURT   IIC

Supplement charged. Meal service.

Arr.	Dep.		Arr.	Dep.
	17:15	Paris (Est) ↑	14:06	
	20:03	Metz		11:16
	20:47	Forbach		10:25
20:54		Saarbrucken		10:09
22:19		Mannheim		8:43
23:08 ↓		Frankfurt		7:55

43 PARIS-GENEVA   TGV
All of these trains run daily and have tray meals or light refreshments.

Dep. Paris (Lyon)	7:34(1)	10:41	14:32	19:13(2)
Arr. Geneva (Corn.)	1104		14:23	18:14	22:55

*   *   *

Dep. Geneva (Corn.)	7:10(1)	11:59	16:46(2)	19:31(3)
Arr. Paris (Lyon)	10:55	15:46	20:33	23:09

(1)Supplement charged Mon.-Fri., except holidays. (2)Supplement charged, except Sat. (3)Supplement charged on Sun. and holidays.

44 PARIS-LAUSANNE   TGV
See "Paris-Dijon-Lausanne"

45-A PARIS-LYON   TGV
Supplement for these trains are charged on various days. Tray meals or light refreshments.

Dep. Paris (Lyon)	6:15(1)	7:00(2)	7:30(3)	8:00(2+9)
Arr. Lyon (P. Dieu)	8:23	9:02	9:30	10:02
Arr. Lyon (Per.)	10 minutes later			

*   *   *

Dep. Lyon (Per.)	5:45(1)	6:15(1)	6:50(4)	7:50(2+10)
Dep. Lyon (P. Dieu)	10 minutes later			
Arr. Paris (Lyon)	8:05	8:35	9:04	10:10

(1)Runs Mon.-Fri. (2)Runs daily. (3)Runs Mon.-Thurs. (4)Runs daily, except Fri. (5)Runs daily, except Sun. and holidays. (6)Runs daily, except Sat. (7)Runs Fri. and Sun. (8)Runs Sun. and holidays. (9)Plus other departures from Paris at 8:30(5), 10:00(2), 11:00(1), 12:00(2), 13:00(2), 14:00(2), 15:00(2), 16:00(1), 17:00(2), 17:27(1), 18:00(2), 19:00(2), 20:00(2), 21:00(6), 21:50(7). (10)Plus other departures from Lyon (Per.) at 8:50(5), 9:50(2), 10:50(6), 11:50(2), 13:20(2), 13:49(2), 14:50(2), 15:50(6), 16:50(2), 17:16(1), 17:50(2), 18:28(8), 18:49(2), 19:50(2), 19:58(8) and 20:50(6).

45-B PARIS-AVIGNON-MARSEILLE   TGV
These trains have tray meals or light refreshments.

Dep. Paris (Lyon)	6:55(1)	7:44(2)	10:10(2)	11:42(2+6)
Arr. Avignon	10:46	11:45	14:05	15:33
Dep. Avignon	10:49(1)	11:51(2)	14:07(2)	15:36(2+7)
Arr. Marseille (St. Ch.)	11:48	12:51	15:07	16:35

*   *   *

Dep. Marseille (St. Ch.)	6:29(1)	7:58(2)	8:45(2)	11:54(2+8)
Arr. Avignon	7:27	8:55	9:42	12:52
Dep. Avignon	7:34(1)	8:59(2)	9:49(2)	12:59(2+9)
Arr. Paris (Lyon)	11:33	12:54	13:54	16:58

See footnotes to this timetable on page 406.

406

(1)Runs Monday-Friday. (2)Runs daily. (3)Runs daily, except Saturday. (4)Supplement charged on Monday. (5)Supplement charged on Monday, Friday, Sunday and holidays. (6)Plus other departures from Paris at 12:48(2), 15:10(2+4), 16:49(2), 17:46(2) and 18:40(3). (7)Plus other departures from Avignon at 16:41(2), 19:11(2+4), 20:54(2), 21:49(2) and 22:40(3). (8)Plus other departures from Marseille (St. Ch.) at 14:00(2), 14:51(2+5), 16:39(2), 17:29(2) and 18:23(3). (9)Plus other departures from Avignon at 15:00(2), 15:51(2+5), 17:39(2), 18:29(2), and 19:28(3).

46 **PRINZ EUGEN**   IIC

Supplement charged in Germany. Meal service.

Arr.	Dep.		Arr.	Dep.
	9:16	Hamburg (Altona)	19:38	
	9:30	Hamburg (Hbf.)	19:24	
	11:15	Hannover		17:51
	12:13	Gottingen		16:40
	13:07	Bebra		15:48
	15:03	Wurzburg		14:07
	16:04	Nurnburg		12:56
	17:06	Regensburg		11:52
18:11		Passau		10:46
19:25		Linz		9:23
21:28		Vienna (Westbf.)		7:20

47 **RATIA**   IIC

Meal service.

Arr.	Dep.		Arr.	Dep.
	9:37	Frankfurt	16:17	
	10:29	Mannheim		15:33
	11:00	Karlsruhe	14:56	
	12:03	Freiburg		13:52
12:39	12:41	Basel (Bad Bf.)	13:13	13:14
12:46	12:58	Basel (S.B.B.)	12:56	13:08
13:57		Zurich		11:57
15:19		Landquart		10:35
16:40		Davos		9:00
15:30		Chur		10:24
		St. Moritz		7:33

48 **REMBRANDT** IIC

Supplement charged. Meal Service.

Arr.	Dep.			Arr.	Dep.
	14:25	Amsterdam	↑	12:26	
14:54	14:58	Utrecht		11:54	11:58
15:33	15:37	Arnhem		11:17	11:22
15:59	16:12	Emmerich		10:47	10:58
16:50	16:52	Duisburg		10:09	10:11
17:05	17:07	Dusseldorf		9:55	9:57
17:30	17:33	Cologne		9:29	9:31
17:51	17:53	Bonn		9:07	9:09
18:25	18:27	Koblenz		8:35	8:37
19:17	19:19	Mainz		7:39	7:41
19:37	19:38	Frankfurt Airport		7:20	7:21
19:51		Frankfurt	↓		7:09

49 **RHEINGOLD** TEE Type #2

Arr.	Dep.			Arr.	Dep.
	7:49	Amsterdam	↑	19:57	
8:17	8:21	Utrecht		19:25	19:28
8:50	9:01	Arnhem		18:50	18:52
9:20	9:33	Emmerich		18:18	18:29
10:09	10:10	Duisburg		17:43	17:44
10:23	10:24	Dusseldorf		17:30	17:31
10:47	10:49	Cologne		17:03	17:06
11:07	11:08	Bonn		16:41	16:42
11:40	11:41	Koblenz		16:10	16:11
12:32	12:34	Mainz		15:18	15:20
13:15	13:19	Mannheim		14:36	14:38
13:47	13:48	Karlsruhe		14:06	14:07
14:02	14:03	Baden-Baden		13:49	13:50
14:49	14:50	Freiburg		13:04	13:05
15:25	15:27	Basel (Bad. Bf.)		12:27	12:29
15:32		Basel (S.B.B.)	↓		12:22

50 **RHEINPFEIL** IIC
Change trains in Basel, en route to and from Zurich. Meal service.

Arr.	Dep.		Arr.	Dep.
	12:26	Hamburg (Altona)	18:28	
	12:40	Hamburg (Hbf.)	18:14	
	13:40	Bremen	17:16	
	15:03	Munster	15:53	
	15:37	Dortmund	15:18	
	16:02	Essen		14:54
	16:30	Dusseldorf		14:27
16:54	16:57	Cologne	13:57	14:00
	17:17	Bonn		13:37
	17:51	Koblenz		13:05
	18:43	Mainz		12:13
	19:29	Mannheim		11:30
	20:00	Karlsruhe		10:56
	21:03	Freiburg (Breisgau)		9:52
21:39		Basel (Bad. Bf.)		9:14
21:46	22:00	Basel (S.B.B.)	8:56	9:08
23:02		Zurich		7:57

51 **RHODANIEN** IIC
Meal Service.

Arr.	Dep.		Arr.	Dep.
	15:50	Geneva	12:38	
18:01	18:03	Grenoble	10:18	10:20
20:14		Avignon		8:04
21:18		Marseille		7:03

52 **RUBENS** TEE Type #1
Runs Monday-Friday, except holidays.

Arr.	Dep.		Arr.	Dep.
	6:41	Brussels (Midi)	21:07	
9:09		Paris (Nord)		18:40

53 **SAPHIR** IIC
Supplement charged. Meal service.

Arr.	Dep.		Arr.	Dep.
	16:43	Oostende	11:34	
17:41	17:44	Brussels (Midi)	10:31	10:34
	17:54	Brussels (Nord)	10:22	
20:17		Cologne		8:09

54 SETTEBELLO TEE Type #5

Sitting in the nosecone of Settebello's locomotive is one of the world's greatest train travel experiences.

Arr.	Dep.		Arr.	Dep.
	8:10	Milan (Centrale)	13:55	
9:59	10:04	Bologna	11:55	12:00
11:13	11:23	Florence	10:36	10:46
14:05		Rome (Termini)		7:50

55 STANISLAS TEE Type #4 Discontinued in 1983.

56 TIZIANO IIC

Supplement charged. Meal service from Hamburg to Chiasso and v.v.

Arr.	Dep.		Arr.	Dep.
	7:45	Hamburg (Hbf.)	23:09	
9:07	9:10	Hannover	21:43	21:46
12:31	12:37	Frankfurt	18:17	18:23
15:39	15:41	Basel (Bad Bf.)	15:13	15:14
15:46	16:01	Basel (S.B.B.)	14:53	15:08
17:10		Luzern		13:44
20:03		Lugano		10:50
20:29		Chiasso		10:25
21:40		Milan (Centrale)		9:20
0:29		Genoa		6:37
2:01		Bologna		5:02
3:39		Florence		3:30
7:40		Rome (Ter.)		23:30

57 VAN BEETHOVEN IIC Discontinued in 1983.

58 VESUVIO TEE Type #5

Arr.	Dep.		Arr.	Dep.
	11:55	Milan (Centrale)	23:40	
13:42	13:47	Bologna	21:47	21:52
14:58	15:08	Florence	20:29	20:39
17:45	18:00	Rome (Termini)	17:25	17:42
20:10		Naples (Mergellina)		15:18

59 WATTEAU TEE Type #4

Runs Monday-Friday, except holidays.

Arr.	Dep.		Arr.	Dep.
	18:05	Paris (Nord)	20:05	
19:46	19:47	Douai	18:21	18:22
20:06	20:12	Lille	17:56	18:02
20:22	20:23	Roubaix	17:45	17:46
20:28		Tourcoing		17:40

Chapter 8

ENGLAND, WALES, SCOTLAND, NORTHERN IRELAND

On British trains, first-class sleeping cars have single compartments; second-class cars have 2-berth compartments. Passengers are served morning tea and biscuits free of charge. Generally, overnight passengers may remain in sleeping cars at destinations the next morning until 7:30.

British trains continually increase speed as a result of the country's rail modernization program. Its 1,800 "Inter-City" trains, linking more than 200 towns each weekday, average 98 to 100 miles per hour on some routes.

Reservations are required on the fast day trains. If there are vacant spaces, the conductor at the departure platform can allocate available places.

BritRail Pass

The BritRail Pass, similar to Eurailpass (which does *not* cover Britain), provides unlimited rail travel in England, Scotland and Wales. Youth-Pass, limited to ages 16 to under 26, is for Economy-class space. Prices in U.S. dollars April 1, 1984 to March 31, 1985 are:

	First-class	Economy	Youth
1 week	$155	$115	$ 95
2 weeks	230	175	150
3 weeks	290	220	190
4 weeks	335	260	225

Children from 5 to under 16 are charged half of either the First-class or Economy fare.

These passes do *not* cover travel in the Irish Republic or in Northern Ireland. They cannot be purchased in Britain. They can be purchased through the offices of BritRail Travel International, its representatives, and travel agencies outside Britain.

Validate these passes at the railstation's "Travel Centre" before starting your first trip with them. The rail official will mark your pass with that day's date and also the appropriate expiration date.

It is a good idea to protect yourself from having your pass rendered partly or wholly invalid because the validity dates were entered incorrectly.

Before the rail official writes on the pass the first and last day it can be used, you should write a note with what you believe are the correct validity dates, show it to the seller, and ask if he or she agrees with those dates.

(Be sure to follow the European custom of showing the day of the month first, followed by the number of the month. In Europe, July 8 is 8/7. If you wanted to take a train to Edinburgh, leaving London at 2:00 PM on July 8, your note for a reservation would read: "Edinburgh — 14:00 — 8/7".)

Only when the official says your dates are correct, or explains why they are not, should you have the dates entered on your pass.

BritRail Seapass

Can be purchased only as an addition to a Britrail Pass.

The Britrail Seapass covers travel by train from London and then by economy class on either ordinary ships or on hovercraft from several British ports (Dover, Folkestone, Harwich, Newhaven or Weymouth) to various European ports (Boulogne, Calais, Cherbourg, Dieppe, Dunkerque, Hoek van Holland, Oostende).

The 1984 price for BritRail Seapass is $26(U.S.) for each crossing of the Channel, a savings of up to 50% compared to buying ordinary tickets. Valid for 6 months after issue date.

Irish Seapass

Can be purchased only as an addition to a BritRail Pass. Good for rail service from London to Fishguard and Holyhead, plus the boat passage (economy class) from those English ports to Rosslare and Dun Laoghaire on the Irish coast.

The 1984 price for Irish Seapass is $38(U.S.) for each one-way trip. Valid for 6 months after issue date.

Young Person's Railcard

Can be purchased only in Britain and available only to a bona-fide student aged 18-30 registered for the scholastic year at a British establishment of higher education. The current Young Person's Railcard is valid from September 15, 1983 to September 30, 1984. Its price is 10 Pounds. Entitles the bearer to 50% discount on second-class space.

Senior Citizens BritRail Pass

Can be purchased only outside Britain. For people over 65. Alows first-class space at the economy price. The 1984 prices are : $115(U.S.) for 1 week, $175 for 2 weeks, $220 for 3 weeks, and $260 for 4 weeks.

Scottish Highland and Islands Travel Pass

Allows unlimited travel on most train, bus and ship routes in Scotland. Both the pass for 5 consecutive days at $68(U.S.) and another for 10 consecutive days at $113 can be purchased either outside Britain or in Britain. Two other versions (for 7 days and for 12 days) are sold only in Scotland.

Northern Ireland Rail Runabout

Unlimited rail travel in Northern Ireland for 7 consecutive days. Valid April 1 to September 30. Sold at principal railstations. The 1984 prices are: 17 British Pounds for adults, 8.50 Pounds for both children under 16 and adults over 65.

Family Railcard

Sold only to families resident in the U.K. Valid for one year from date of issue. Covers up to 4 adults plus 4 children. A child is anyone under 16. Price is 10 Pounds. Adults then travel at half-fare while each child pays only 1 Pound for each trip.

North Wales Rideabout Ticket

Can be purchased only in Britain. Covers 7 days of rail and bus travel. Provides a substantial savings. Costs 6 Pounds.

Southwest Wales Runabout Ticket

Can be purchased only in Britain. Covers 7 days of rail and bus travel. Provides a substantial savings. Costs 10.70 Pounds.

Day Return

When buying rail tickets for a one-day roundtrip rail excursion, be sure to use this economy. The price of the return ride will be about only 12% of the cost of the outgoing ride. However, there is a severe limitation: this discount is *not* given for departures prior to 10:00.

Weekend Return

Another good discount, if your outbound train ride is on a Friday, Saturday or Sunday—and your return trip is Saturday, Sunday or Monday of the same weekend.

Makes the cost of the return ride a fraction of the outgoing ride.

Monthly Return

Makes the cost of the return ride a fraction of the outgoing ride, if both rides are within one month of each other.

BRITAINSHRINKERS

Available March 1 to October 31. Guided one-day excursions from London by train and bus to Bath and Stonehenge, Canterbury and Dover, Stratford-upon-Avon, York, Brighton, Oxford and the Cotswolds. Cambridge and Ely, Leeds Castle and Cantebury, Devon, and Stratford and Oxford.

From the time you board a specially marked car on the designated train, a red-uniformed escort accompanies you to the day's destination: onto a waiting deluxe motorcoach, that day's sightseeing (including admission fees), and on the ride back to London. Lunch at a pub is included. Purchased in conjunction with a BritRail Pass and taken during the BRP's validity period, these tours are priced at a great discount. The 1983 prices range from U.S.$41 ($29 with a BRP) to $65 ($35 with a BRP) per adult, and 30%-40% less for a child. A $201 Scotland overnight tour is only $149 with a BRP, and a 2-night $289 York-and-Scotland tour is $237 with a BRP.

Three overnight (2-day) tours are also offered: Scotland, a combination of York and Scotland, and Shakespeare Country.

When planning to travel both in Britain and on the Continent, keep in mind that the maximum value of combining a British pass with Eurailpass is achieved by scheduling Britain for either the start or end of a tour.

For example, to start a tour in Amsterdam and have one's itinerary then go to Paris, London and then return to the Continent for additional Eurailpass traveling would require a longer and therefore more expensive Eurailpass since the time spent in Britain consumes Eurailpass days.

Conversely, to start a tour in London, followed by travel on the Continent, and then concluding with more travel in Britain will require a longer and therefore more expensive BritRail Pass since the time spent on the Continent will consume BritRail Pass days.

In either direction, the "bridge" for using both the BritRail Pass and a Eurailpass is to also have a BritRail Seapass.

We present in this chapter descriptions of 4 categories of rail service. First, the train connection services between London and the Continent (Paris, Brussels and Amsterdam). Next, 43 one-day rail trips that can be made comfortably out of London, with details as to departure and arrival times plus what to see in each destination before returning to London, in most cases, at dinnertime.

Third, you will find itineraries for 3 long trips from and to London: Shannon Airport, Dublin and Edinburgh. This chapter concludes with details on many rail trips in Scotland.

Several of the routes are noted for outstanding scenery.

START HERE

Always — without exception — before commencing each journey doublecheck the times given here or in any published timetable, as they are subject to change without prior notice. Eurail® Guide has made every effort to publish correct departure and arrival times, but schedules are constantly changed.

Changes will usually be minor and have no effect on the trips recommended in this book. However, in being one-minute late for a connection, the proverbial "a miss is as good as a mile" applies. WE DO NOT WANT YOU TO BE STRANDED!

The extensive notes on train connections in this book are intended to help you plan your itinerary before you start your trip. These notes are also useful after your trip begins (if you bring Eurail® Guide along !) for making impromptu, last-minute travel plans.

WARNING: Many cities have 2 or more railstations. London has 8 railstations. We take pains to tell you for every trip in this book the name of the railstation from which your train departs, by noting the station in parenthesis immediately after the name of the city.

PAY HEED !

BRITAIN

All of London's railstations are interconnected by subway service, providing far easier and quicker transfers than by surface streets. For example, when entering England by rail from France, at Dover, you will come into Victoria station. To continue directly to Edinburgh, it is necessary to take a train from King's Cross station, on the opposite side of London from Victoria station.

A brief description of the areas served by London's 8 major railstations:

CHARING CROSS STATION

This station services suburban commuters between London and Folkestone, and between London and Hastings. It connects at Dover (Priory station) with Hovercraft service to and from France.

EUSTON STATION

A part of Central England and the Northwestern area of Britain are reached from Euston station, starting with Coventry and Birmingham, and then running through Stafford, Chester, Liverpool, Manchester and Blackpool, on into Glasgow. Also, Holyhead, gateway to Dublin.

KING'S CROSS STATION

Northeastern England (Leeds, York, Hull, Newcastle) and Edinburgh are reached by trains from King's Cross station. Newcastle is the gateway to Norway. Hull is a gateway to Denmark, Germany and Holland.

LIVERPOOL STREET STATION

This station services the area immediately Northeast of London: Colchester, Cambridge, Ipswich, Harwich (gateway to Holland, Germany, Austria, Yugoslavia and Norway), Norwich and King's Lynn.

PADDINGTON STATION

The area in Southern England, West from Weymouth (Exeter, Plymouth and Penzance), is reached out of Paddington station—as is also that portion of Southwestern England running North to Bristol, Swansea, Fishguard (gateway to Rosslare, at the Southeastern tip of the Republic of Ireland), Gloucester, Worcester, Hereford and Oxford.

ST. PANCRAS STATION

Trains going due North from London to Leicester, Derby, Nottingham and Sheffield leave from St. Pancras station.

VICTORIA STATION

The London airport for charter flights is Gatwick, which is serviced from 6:00 to 24:00 by a train every 15 minutes (and hourly from 1:00 to 5:00) for the 40-minute ride to London's Victoria station.

The transfer from airplane to train, or vice versa, is entirely indoor as the railstation at Gatwick is a part of the airport.

Victoria station services the small area of Southern England just East of but not including Portsmouth: Worthing, Brighton, Newhaven, Eastbourne, Hastings and Dover (gateway to France, Spain, Belgium, Switzerland, Italy, Austria and Yugoslavia).

WATERLOO STATION   Services South Central England: Southampton, Bournemouth and Weymouth.

London Underground Connection with Heathrow

Opened in mid-1977, the direct subway service between Heathrow Airport and central London allows one to take a direct train from and to any station on Piccadilly Line and London's airport for scheduled airlines.

SUMMER TIME

Britain changes to Summer Time on the last Sunday of March and converts back to Standard Time on the last Sunday of October.

Days of the Week Variances

For the time schedules given in this book, "daily" means Monday through Sunday. Where Sunday departure and arrival times are specified in conjunction with a list of daily schedules, this refers to additional service on Sunday, not to substitute service.

In other words, if a daily schedule lists departures at 10:00 and 11:12, and the Sunday schedule indicates a departure at 13:05, there are 3 departures on Sunday: at 10:00, 11:12 and 13:05.

Conversely, if Monday-Friday or Monday-Saturday schedules show departures at 10:00 and 11:12, and there is a listing of a Sunday departure at 13:05, then the only departure on Sunday for that trip is 13:05.

The same treatment applies to "Saturday only" schedules in connection with times given as "Monday-Friday" or as "daily".

Summer and Winter Schedules

You'll use

In most European countires, a Winter timetable goes into effect on the last Saturday in September. Outside Britain, Winter schedules usually start on the Sunday following the last Saturday of September and run until and including the Saturday preceding the last Sunday in May of the following year.

British timetables differ from the Continental pattern.

Summer timetables for British rail service begin on the third Monday in May. The change to a Winter schedule occurs on the first Monday in October and on the first Monday in January.

Unless designated otherwise, the departure and arrival times given in this chapter are for the Summer season and apply to trips that are made from early May to October.

So — use the following with caution!

LONDON

The capital of England. See the changing of the guard at Buckingham Palace. Downing Street, official residence of the Prime Minister. The Tower of London. London Bridge. The Houses of Parliament. The Wellington Museum. Hyde Park.

The Kensington Gardens complex of Royal Albert Hall, the Science Museum and the Natural History Museum. Globe Theater. Piccadilly Circus. The National Gallery. The British Museum. Dickens' House. St. Paul's Cathedral. Gray's Inn. The Imperial War Museum. Kew Gardens. Regent's Park.

Westminster Abbey. The Geological Museum. The National Portrait Gallery. Nelson's Monument in Trafalgar Square. The Victoria and Albert Museum. St. James Palace. The 53-acre Green Park. The Wellington Arch. Admiralty Arch. The Sunday orators at Speaker's Corner. Marble Arch. Lambeth Palace, the residence of the Archbishop of Canterbury. The newspaper offices along Fleet Street.

The dragon at Temple Bar Memorial. Mansion House, the residence of the Lord Mayor of London. Tower Bridge. The South Bank Arts Centre complex of National Theatre, Queen Elizabeth Hall, Royal Festival Hall, and Hayward Gallery. The Victoria Tower. Whitehall, the compound of government offices. The beautifully uniformed sentries outside The Horse Guards. Piccadilly Circus.

One of the world's greatest food stores, in Harrods Department Store, presents a spectacle of more than 500 cheeses, 120 different breads, 21 kinds of butter, produce from California, and a meat hall 90 feet long by 60 feet wide containing hams, pork, sausages, beef and lamb. There is also venison, shellfish, poultry, salmon (smoked and fresh), tinned foods from all over the world, eggs, teas from everywhere, caviars, wine, and the list goes on forever.

CONNECTIONS WITH THE CONTINENT

The shortest route from England to the Continent is Dover (Marine) to Calais, or Dover (Priory) to Boulogne.

The validity of one's BritRail Pass stops or starts, as the case may be, at the British shore. Similarly, the validity of one's Eurailpass stops or starts at the Continental port where your boat ride begins or ends.

In all cases, the channel boat fare is *not* covered by either pass.

Regular ferries run the following routes: Dover-Boulogne, Dover-Calais, Dover-Dunkerque, Dover-Oostende, Folkestone-Boulogne, Folkestone-Calais, Harwich-Hoek van Holland and Newhaven-Dieppe.

Hovercraft service, faster and more expensive, is provided Dover-Boulogne, Dover-Calais, Dover-Zeebrugge, Newhaven-Dieppe, Portsmouth-Cherbourg, Porsmouth-Le Havre, Ramsgate-Calais, Ramsgate-Dunkerque, Southampton-Cherbourg and Southampton-Le Havre.

Both regular ferries and hovercraft carry autos.

London - Paris vis Dieppe (regular ferry)   51

Dep. London (Vict.)	7:50(1)	8:34(3)	11:10(4)	20:10(5)
Dep. Gatwick Airport	8:28(1)	9:12(3)	11:46(4)	20:46(5)
Arr. Newhaven Harbour	9:12	10:03	12:28	21:29
Change to ferry.				
Dep. Newhaven Harbour	10:00	11:00	13:00	22:00
Set your watch forward one hour, except from late Sept. to late Oct.				
Arr. Dieppe	15:00	15:00	18:00	3:00
Change to train.				
Dep. Dieppe	15:50(2)	15:50(2)	18:40	4:00
Arr. Rouen (Rive Dr.)	16:42	16:42	-0-(4)	4:56
Arr. Paris (St. Laz.)	18:07	18:07	21:05	6:25

*   *   *

Dep. Paris (St. Laz.)	10:55(1+2)	10:45(3)	13:45(6)	22:36(7)
Dep. Rouen (Rive Dr.)	12:17(1+2)	12:17(3)	15:14(6)	0:03(7)
Arr. Dieppe	13:10	13:10	16:28	0:56
Change to ferry.				
Dep. Dieppe	13:45	13:45	17:00	2:00
Set your watch back one hour, except from late Sept. to late Oct.				
Arr. Newhaven Harbour	16:45	17:45	20:00	5:00
Change to train.				
Dep. Newhaven Harbour	17:26	18:26	20:27	5:40
Arr. Gatwick Airport	18:09	19:09	22:16	6:20
Arr. London (Vict.)	18:46	19:46	22:33	6:57

(1)Runs late May to late September. (2)Light refreshments. (3)Runs late September to late October. No time change during this period. (4)Runs mid-June to mid-September. Only the Sunday departure stops in Rouen. (5)Runs from mid-June to mid-September. (6)Operates only on Saturday. Runs early June to late ·September. (7)Runs late June to mid-September.

The other Channel-crossing schedules are:

London - Paris (regular ferry)   50
Dep. London (Vict.)   8:00(1)   9:58(2)   13:58   20:58(3)
  Set your watch forward one hour, except from late Sept. to late Oct.
Arr. Paris (Nord)   16:15   18:03   22:28   8:43
          *   *   *
Dep. Paris (Nord)   8:10(2)   10:37(2)   12:20(4)   14:25(2+5)
  Set your watch back one hour, except from late Sept. to late Oct.
Arr. London (Vict.)   14:17   16:55   19:02   21:33
(1)Runs late July to late August. (2)Runs late May to late September. Light refreshments available Boulogne to Paris and v.v. (3)Light refreshments available Boulogne to Paris and v.v. (4)Meal service Paris to Calais. (5)Plus another departure from Paris at 22:35(3).

London - Paris (hovercraft)   49
Dep. London
  (Charing X)   7:48(1)   10:00(1)   12:00(1)   14:00(1)   16:00(2)
  Set your watch forward one hour, except from late Sept. to late Oct.
Arr. Paris
  (Nord)   14:15   16:32   18:25   20:40   23:02
          *   *   *
Dep. Paris
  (Nord)   6:52(3)   9:20(1)   11:25(1)   13:00(1)   14:20(1+4)
  Set your watch back one hour, except from late Sept. to late Oct.
Arr. London
  (Charing X)   11:40   13:40   15:40   17:43   19:40
(1)Light refreshments available Boulogne to Paris and v.v. (2(Runs late May to late September. Operates Monday, Friday and Sunday. Also on Saturday, from early July to early September. (3)Monday-Friday. Light refreshments. (4)Plus another departure from Paris at 16:37(2).

London - Brussels   via Oostende (Jetfoil)   52a

Reservations are advisable on all of these trains.

Dep. London (Vict.)   8:44   11:30(1)   13:44   15:58
Dep. Dover Docks   10:35   13:20   15:40   17:50

Set your watch forward one hour, except from late Sept. to late Oct.

Arr. Oostende   13:15   16:00   18:20   20:30
  Change to train.
Dep. Oostende   13:53   16:53   18:53   21:08
Arr. Burssels (Midi)   15:04   18:06   20:06   22:25
Arr. Burssels (Nord)   12 minutes later

(1)Late May to late September: runs daily. Late September to mid-November: runs Monday-Friday. Mid-November to mid-December: does *not* operate. Mid-December to early January: runs Monday-Friday. Early January to mid-March: does *not* operate. Mid-March to late May: runs Monday-Friday.

London - Brussels   via Oostende (regular ferry)   52

Dep. London (Vict.)   9:30   13:30   21:44(1)

Set your watch forward one hour, except from late Sept. to late Oct.

Arr. Brussels (Midi)   18:06   22:10   7:05
Arr. Burssels (Nord)   12 minutes later

(1)Runs late May to late September.

London - Amsterdam   via Hoek van Holland (regular ferry)   66

All of these trains have light refreshments.

Dep. London (L'pool)   9:40   19:40

Set your watch forward one hour, except from late Sept. to late Oct.

Arr. Amsterdam (C.S.)   20:55   9:01

                  *   *   *

Dep. Amsterdam (C.S.)   9:30   21:16

Set your watch back one hour, except from late Sept. to late Oct.

Arr. London (L'pool)   19:23   9:14

One-Day Excursions from London

The notation "frequent times" in these schedules means at least one (and usually more) departures every hour.

London - Arundel - London   520

Dep. London (Victoria)   *Frequent times from 8:26 to 13:26
Arr. Arundel   80 minutes later

Sights in **Arundel:** A lovely town, dominated by the magnificent Castle of the Dukes of Norfolk, open late March to late October, Monday-Friday plus Sundays in August, 12:00-17:00.

Dep. Arundel   Frequent times from 12:38 to 20:38
Arr. London (Victoria)   80 minutes later

London - Bath - London   535

Dep. London (Pad.)   Mon.-Sat. Frequent times from 7:25
             Sunday   8:20   9:15   10:35   11:35
Arr. Bath   60-80 minutes later

Sights in **Bath:** The Roman baths. Antique shops around Abbey Green. The Costume Museum in the Assembly Rooms. The Pump Room. The Royal Crescent row of town houses. Queen Square. The shops on Pulteney Bridge. The Circus.

The American Museum at Claverton Manor, open daily except Monday 14:00-17:00. The collection of Eltonware and Nailsea glass in the 14th century Clevedon Court manor house, open Wednesday, Thursday and Sunday 14:30-17:30. There is much elegant 18th century architecture here.

Bath is a great base for seeing much of the best sights in England. Several good, inexpensive motorcoach tours go to Gloucester, Salisbury, Stonehenge and Cheddar Gorge. These buses stop for photo-taking along the way.

Dep. Bath   Mon.-Sat.   Frequent times to 21:31
           Sunday   Frequent times to 21:17
Arr. London (Pad.)   60-80 minutes later

London - Bournemouth - London 522

Dep. London (Waterloo) Mon-Sat Frequent times from 5:45
                        Sunday   Frequent times from 8:30
Arr. Bournemouth 2 hours later

Sights in **Bournemouth:** A large seaside resort. Stroll through Pavillion Rock Garden. There are 3 gambling casinos. Many lovely parks and gardens.

Dep. Bournemouth Mon.-Sat. Frequent times to 21:41
                  Sunday   Frequent times to 21:58
Arr. London (Waterloo) 2 hours later

London - Brighton - London 518

Dep. London (Victoria) Frequent times from 6:18
Arr. Brighton 55-70 minutes later

Sights in **Brighton:** The Aquarium at Palace Pier. Antique shops in the many alleys, called "The Lanes". Plenty of Regency architecture. The Royal Pavillion. The ornate chandelier in Banquet Hall.

Dep. Brighton Frequent times to 23:10
Arr. London (Victoria) 55-70 minutes later

London - Bristol - London 535

Dep. London (Paddington) Frequent times from 6:35
                          (from 8:20 on Sundays)
Arr. Bristol (Temple Meads) 90 minutes later

*   *   *

Dep. Bristol (Temple Meads) Frequent times to 21:25 (21:05 on Sun.)
Arr. London (Paddington) 90 minutes later

Sights in **Bristol:** A famous seaport. Everything here is either a short walk or can be reached by bus. The city operates 1½-hour guided walking tours June, July and August from the Exchange on Corn Street at 11:00 on Monday and Tuesday, at 14:30 on other days. Some of Bristol can be seen from a tour boat at the harbor. That tour operates daily at 12:00, 14:00, 15:00 and 16:00.

See the many excellent Georgian buildings on Royal York Crescent, Cornwallis Crescent, Windsor Terrace, West Mall, Caledonia Place, Queen Square and Berkeley Square. The Christmas Steps, built in 1669. The 12th century St. James' Church.

The John Wesley Chapel, world's first Methodist preaching house, with a bronze statue of Wesley in the courtyard. The 11th century St. Mary-le-Port Church. St. John's Church. The 13th century St. Mary Redcliffe, one of England's largest churches. The 12th century Cathedral.

The exhibit of period furniture in the 18th century Georgian House. The view from the top of Cabot Tower, on Brandon Hill. The collection of porcelain, models of early sailing ships and paintings of the waterfront in the Bristol

Museum and Art Gallery, open every day 10:00-17:00. See the rare animals (including white tigers) at the Zoo. Brunel's Clifton Suspension Bridge, built in 1864, striding Avon Gorge, 245 feet above the water. Tour Brunel's iron steamship, The Great Britain (the first ocean screw steamship, launched in 1843). returned to Bristol in 1970 from the Falkland Islands. It is open to visitors 10:00-18:00.

London - Cardiff - London   540
Dep. London (Pad.)   Frequent times from 6:55 (8:48 on Sun.)
Arr. Cardiff (Cent.)   2 hours later
    Sights in **Cardiff:** Llandaff Cathedral. Cardiff Castle. The National Museum of Wales, featuring Welsh handicraft and art.
Dep. Cardiff (Cent.)   Frequent times to 21:25 daily
Arr. London (Pad.)   2 hours later

London - Bristol - Cardiff - London
    As these schedules indicate, it is easy to visit both Cardiff and Bristol in one day. These schedules are only for Monday-Friday travel.

535		540	
Dep. London (Pad.)	8:15	Dep. Cardiff (Central)	16:25(1)
Arr. Bristol (T.M.)	9:57	Arr. London (Pad.)	18:25
Sightsee in Bristol.			
Change trains.			
539			
Dep. Bristol (T.M.)	13:15		
Arr. Cardiff (Cent.)	14:07		

(1)Plus other departures from Cardiff at 17:25, 18:25, 19:25 and 21:25.

London - Cambridge - London   589
Dep. London (L'pool)   7:32(1)   8:35(2+3)   9:35(4)   10:35(4+5)
Arr. Cambridge   70-80 minutes later
    Sights in **Cambridge:** To see buildings that have housed great colleges for more than 700 years, take bus #101 to Market Street. See King's College Chapel and Queen's College. Visit the Wren Library at Trinity College, the tapestries and manuscripts in the Fitzwilliam Museum, and the Botanical Gardens. Hire a boat at Mill Bridge or Anchor Inn, and paddle along the idyllic Cam River. Four miles away is the American Cemetery.
Dep. Cambridge   Frequent times to 21:50
Arr. London (L'pool)   70-80 minutes later
(1)Monday-Friday, except holidays. (2)Light refreshments. (3)Daily, except Sundays and holidays. (4)Daily. (5)Plus other departures from London at 11:35(3), 13:35(3) and 14:35(4).

London - Canterbury - London

The easiest way to make a one-day excursion to Canterbury is to start by departing from either London's Waterloo or Charing Cross railstations. Trains running frequently arrive 70 minutes later at Canterbury's West railstation. The walk from it to the famous Cathedral allows you to view interesting buildings.

For the ride back to London, depart from Canterbury's East railstation, nearer to the Cathedral than the West staion. A departure from Canterbury's East station will take you to London's Victoria station. Or, you can depart from Cantebury's West station, arriving London's Waterloo or Charing Cross stations.

Sights in **Canterbury:** The great Cathedral, housing the tomb of Thomas a Becket. Medieval inns (Falstaff, Beverlie, Olive Branch). The cemetery, where Christopher Marlowe and Joseph Conrad are buried. Shops, plays, ballet, cricket, excavated Roman ruins.

London - Chester - London   557

Dep. London (Euston)	8:05(1)	8:50(2)	9:55(3)	10:00(1+4)
Arr. Chester	11:25	12:27	12:36	12:55
	*	*	*	
Dep. Chester	14:16(1+4)	15:10(2)	16:28(2+4)	18:10(5)
Arr. London (Euston)	17:10	18:14	19:22	21:43

(1)Daily, except Sunday. (2)Sunday only. (3)Monday-Friday. Runs mid-July to early September. (4)Light refreshments. (5)Daily.

Sights in **Chester:** The excellent collection of Roman artifacts (glass, tools, coins, weapons, tombstones) at Grosvenor Museum. The "Rows", long covered balconies (to protect shoppers from rain) that are full-length streets above the streets of Chester. These are lined with shops. Also see the Cathedral. The castle overlooking the River Dee. The ancient city walls. The marvelous carving of animals and historic scenes on the front of the 17th century Bishop Lloyd's House. The 16th century mansion, Stanley Palace. The 30-minute slide show of Chester's history, in the British Heritage Centre. The Tourist Office at City hall offers a free guided 2½-hour walking tour.

London - Chartwell - London

There are many departures daily from London's Charing Cross railstation for the 45-minute ride to Sevenoakds. Take a taxi for the 7-mile trip from Sevenoaks to Chartwell.

Sights in **Chartwell:** The country house that Winston Churchill bought in 1922, where he painted and wrote his books during the years he was out of power. You will see here the best collection of Churchilliana in the world: his collection of eccentric hats, his World War II "jump suit", Knight of the Garter uniform, many of his paintings, and a model of the Invasion Day harbor at Arromanches. Also the brick wall and cottage he built with his own hands on a small part of the 79 acres there. The main house is open Wednesday, Thursday, Saturday and Sunday from April to mid-October.

London - Chichester - London   520

Dep. London (Victoria)   6:48(1)   8:26(2)   9:26(2)   10:26(3+4)
Arr. Chichester   2 hours later

Sights in **Chichester:** The museum and mosaic floors in the Palace at Fishbourne, one mile away, the largest Roman residence in Britain, built in the 3rd century.

Dep. Chichester   Mon-Sat   Frequent times from 13:19 to 21:39
Arr. London (Victoria)   2 hours later

(1)Daily, except Saturday. (2)Daily. Light refreshments Monday-Friday. (3)Daily. (4)Plus other departures from London at 11:26(3), 12:26(3) and 13:26(3).

London - Coventry -London   552

Dep. London (Euston)   Mon-Sat Frequent times from 6:02 to 23:10
                       Sunday   Frequent times from 10:00 to 23:20
Arr. Coventry   1-1½ hours later

Sights in **Coventry:** Completely rebuilt since the Nazi air attacks, Coventry was the site of Lady Godiva's notorious horseback ride. See the Graham Sutherland tapestry, the abstract stained-glass windows and the enormous engraved glass wall at the new (1962) Cathedral.

Dep. Coventry   Frequent times to 21:58 (21:06 on Sundays)
Arr. London (Euston)   1-1½ hours later

London - Dover - London   512

Dep. London (Victoria)   Frequent times from 6:25 to 21:23
Arr. Dover (Priory)   2 hours later

Sights in **Dover:** The legendary white cliffs. The mighty castle. The busy harbor.

Dep. Dover (Priory)   Frequent times from 5:41 to 22:18
Arr. London (Victoria)   2 hours later

London - Exeter - London   #1
530

Dep. London (Pad.)

Mon-Fri	Frequent times from 8:05 to 20:15	
Sat	Frequent times from 8:05 to 23:25	
Sun	Frequent times from 8:20 to 23:00	

Arr. Exeter
(St. David's)   2½ hours later

Sights in **Exeter:** The 11th century Cathedral, with its 300-foot nave and row of statutes. Rougemont Castle. The Mint. The underground water channel at Princesshay. The paintings and oak paneling in Exeter Guildhall.

The exhibit of boats from all parts of the world at the very interesting Maritime Museum.

Dep. Exeter

(St. David's)	Mon-Fri	Frequent times from 7:00 to 20:06
	Sat	Frequent times from 6:57 to 19:54
	Sun	Frequent times from 8:33 to 22:20

Arr. London (Pad.)   2½ hourslater

OR

London -Exeter -London   #2
523

Dep. London (Waterloo)	6:50(1)	8:37(2)	9:10(3)	
Arr. Exeter (Central)	10:33	11:44	12:26	
Arr. Exeter (St. David's)	5 minutes later			
	*	*	*	

(Monday-Saturday)

Dep. Exeter (St. DAvid's)	14:13(4)	16:18(4)	17:33(5)	19:34(6)
Dep. Exeter (Central)	5 minutes later			
Arr. London (Waterloo)	17:48 .	19:47	20:52	23:12

(Sundays)

Dep. Exeter (St. David's)	15:25(4)	16:05	17:39	18:25
Dep. Exeter (Central)	5 minutes later			
Arr. London (Waterloo)	18:43	19:30	20:56	21:43

(1)Monday-Saturday. (2)Late May to early October: Monday-Saturday. Early October to late May: Monday-Friday. (3)Daily. Light refreshments, except Sunday. (4)Light refreshments. (5)Departs 18:16 on Saturdays. (6)Departs 20:20 on Saturdays.

London - Greenwich - London 0000

There is commuter train service from London to Blackheath, from where it is a short walk through Greenwich Park to the Observatory, the Cutty Sark and the Royal Navy College. Allow 3 hours for the walk and sightseeing.

Greenwich

Dep. London (Charing X)   On the half-hour
Arr. Blackheath   20 minutes later   *upon hill*

Sights in **Greenwich:** The location of the world's prime meridian, from which all distances and hours worldwide are measured. See the 1870 clipper chip, Cutty Sark, at Greenwich Pier. Nearby, the 53-foot Gypsy Moth sailboat which Chichester sailed around the world in 1966-67. The Royal Navy College, and its magnificent Painted Hall. The Royal Observatory. The Marvelous exhibits in the National Maritime Museum. The Meridian Building.

Dep. Blackheath   Frequent times
Arr. London (Charing X)   20 minutes later

I would NOT put this trip as a 1st priority as it takes minimum of 1/2 day. But going by boat is worthwhile for sights along the Thames. Consider one way by boat, return by train (but not using your rail pass & prob. not your London pass —

London - Hampton Court - London 0000

Dep. London (Waterloo)   Frequent times
Arr. Hampton Court   35 minutes later

Sights in **Hampton Court:** The riverside Palace built by Cardinal Wolsey and then given to Henry VIII. Walk through the ancient maze.

Dep. Hampton Court   Frequent times
Arr. London (Waterloo)   35 minutes later

Again — this would be out of reach of your London pass but is nice.

London - Hastings - London 516

These trains have light refreshments daily, except Sundays and holidays.

Dep. London (Vict.)   8:52   9:52 10:52 11:52
Arr. Hastings   2 hours later

Sights in **Hastings:** This is where William became the Conqueror, of the Saxons. Visit the old fishing harbor.

Dep. Hastings   28 minutes after each hour, from 6:28 to 21:28
Arr. London (Vict.)   2 hours later

London - Hatfield - London 0000

Dep. London (King's Cross) Frequent times
Arr. Hatfield 35 minutes later

Sights in **Hatfield:** The fine state rooms in the 17th century Hatfield House, open from late March to early October, Tuesday-Saturday 12:00-17:00 and Sundays 14:00-17:30.

Dep. Hatfield Frequent times
Arr. London (King's Cross) 35 minutes later

London - Isle of Wight - London (via Portsmouth) #1
521

Dep. London (Waterloo)	7:48(1)	8:48(1)	9:48(1)
Arr. Portsmouth (Harbour)	9:19	10:19	11:19
Change to boat.			
Dep. Portsmouth (Harbor)	9:33	10:30	11:33
Arr. Ryde Pier Head	9:58	10:58	11:58
Change to train.			
Dep. Ryde Pier Head	10:07	11:07	12:07
Arr. Shanklin	10:28	11:31	12:28

Three different bus tours on the Isle of Wight operate on different Sundays from June through early September. These are offered as a package that includes the roundtrip train fare from London (the 9:50 departure). The bus tours end in Ryde, connecting with the hovercraft departure from there for Portsmouth that is timed for the train that arrives back in London at 20:25.

Dep. Shankin Frequent times from 12:41 to 21:11
Arr. London (Waterloo) 3 hours later

(1)Meal service Monday-Friday. Light refreshments on Saturday.

OR

London - Isle of Wight - London (via Lymington) #2

522		522a	
Dep. London (Waterloo)	8:45(1)	Dep. Yarmouth	14:00
Arr. Brockenhurst	10:28	Arr. Lymington Pier	14:30
Change trains.		Change to train.	
522a		Dep. Lymington Pier	14:58
Dep. Brockenhurst	10:41	Arr. Brockenhurst	15:11
Arr. Lymington Pier	10:54	Change trains.	
Change to ferry.		522	
Dep. Lymington Pier	11:00	Dep. Brockenhurst	16:21(1)
Arr. Yarmouth	11:30	Arr. London (Wat.)	18:04

(1)Meal service Monday-Friday. Light refreshments on Saturday.

London - Leicester - London   570

Dep. London (St. Pancras)   Frequent times from 7:45 to 23:00
Arr. Leicester   1½-2 hours later

Sights in **Leicester:** The Jewry Wall, to see outstanding Roman ruins. The Church of St. Mary de Castro.

Dep. Leicester   Frequent times from 6:14 to 21:45
Arr. London (St. Pancras)   1½-2 hours later

London - Lincoln - London   576

Change trains in Newark.

Dep. London (King's X)	8:04(1)	9:50(2+3)	10:04(1+4)
Arr. Lincoln (St. Marks)	10:09	11:37	12:29

Sights in **Lincoln:** The wonderful Cathedral. Newport Arch. Roman relics in the City and County Museums. The houses on High Bridge.

Dep. Lincoln (St. Marks)	14:21(1+2)	16:32(1+2)	18:27(1+5)
Arr. London (King's X)	16:41	18:41	20:41

(1)Runs Monday-Saturday. (2)Runs Monday-Friday. (3)Meal service. (4)Plus another departure from London at 12:04(1+2).   (5)Plus another departure from Lincoln at 20:23(1+2).

London - Norwich - London   590

Dep. London (Liverpool)	8:30(1+2)	9:30(1+3)	10:30(4+5+7)
Arr. Norwich	10:47	11:32	12:40

Sights in **Norwich:** Norwich Grammar School. (Its alumni include Lord Nelson.) The Cathedral. The collection of lace, pottery, teapots, paintings and coins at the Museum in the Castle, and the view of Norwich from the Castle. Assembly House. The Strangers Hall. Walk down the Elm Hill alley.

Dep. Norwich	14:25(1+3)	15:40(1+3)	16:25(1+3+8)
Arr. London (Liverpool)	16:45	17:45	18:45

(1)Runs daily. (2)Runs Monday-Saturday. Meal service. (3)Meal service, except on Saturday and Sunday. Light refreshments on Saturday. (4)Runs Monday-Saturday. (5)Meal service Monday-Friday. Light refreshments on Saturday. (6)Runs Sunday only. (7)Plus other departures from London at 11:30(4) and 12:30(1+3).   (8)Plus other departures from Norwich at 17:45(1+3), 18:45(1), 19:33(6) qnd 19:54(4).

London - Notthingham - London 570

Dep. London (St. Pan.)   8:20(1)   9:00(2)   9:20(3+13)
Arr. Nottingham   10:08   11:31   11:03

Sights in **Nottingham:** The Duke of Newcastle's castle. which was a new Newcastle castle in 1679, with its art collection. The great council house. The Natural History Museum in Wollaton Hall.

Dep. Nottingham   12:55(5)   14:27(6)   15:10(7+14)
Arr. London (St. Pan.)   14:47   16:06   16:58

(1)Daily. (2)Sundays only. (3)Runs Monday-Saturday. Light refreshments Monday-Friday. (4)Runs Monday-Saturday. Meal service Monday-Friday. (5)Daily. Meal service Monday-Friday. (6)Runs Monday-Saturday. Meal service. (7)Runs Monday-Saturday. Meal service Monday-Friday. Light refreshments on Saturday. (8)Daily. Meal service Monday-Friday. Light refreshments on Saturday. (9)Daily. Light refreshments, except Saturday. (10)Runs Monday-Saturday. Light refreshments, except Saturday. (11)Light refreshments. (12)Daily. Light refreshments on Sunday only. (13)Plus other departures from London at 10:10(4), 11:30(8) and 12:10(9).   Plus other departures from Nottingham at 15:50(4), 16:18(2), 16:57(10), 17:46(2+11), 18:12(12), 19:22(1) and 20:17(2).

London - Leicester - Nottingham - London 570

As these schedules indicate, it is easy to visit both Leicester and Nottingham in one day. Monday-Saturday service is shown here.

Dep. London (St. Pancras)	7:45	Dep. Nottingham	16:57(1)
Arr. Leicester	9:01	Arr. London (St. Pan.)	18:39
Sightsee in Leicester.			
Dep. Leicester	13:32	(1)Plus other departures at	
Arr. Nottingham	14:02	18:12 and 19:22	

London - Oxford - London   527+538

Dep. London (Pad.)	Frequent times from 5:50 to 23:40
Arr. Oxford	60-75 minutes later

*   *   *

Dep. Oxford	Frequent times from 8:30 to 23:05
Arr. London (Pad.)	60-75 minutes later

Sights in **Oxford:** This is the home of one of the greatest universities in the world, comprising 28 different colleges. Start your stroll at the center of Oxford, Carfax Tower, where the Information Center is located and from which a 2-hour guided tour can be taken at 10:45 and 14:15 Monday-Saturday. There is bus service from the railstation to Carfax Tower.

Begin by walking south from Carfax Tower, down St. Aldates Street, to Folly Bridge, Christ Church and Pembroke College.

Later, see Merton College and Corpus Christi before continuing on to Oriel and then into High Street. See Bodleian Library, which has a copy of every book published in England. Most popular among visitors is Magdalen College, with its beautiful main quadrangle.

Nearby Blenheim Palace   Churchill's Birthplace

To see lovely Blenheim Palace, take a bus in Oxford from Gloucester Green bus station for the 8-mile trip to Woodstock. This magnificent 18th century structure was the birthplace of Winston Churchill in 1874.

A gift from Britain to the Duke of Marlborough after this ancestor of Churchill defeated the French in 1704 at Blenheim in Bavaria, the beautiful 300-room mansion is open daily March-October, with guided tours 11:30-17:00.

Letters, documents, photos, even a lock of Churchill's hair (at the age of 5) are exhibited in the tiny room where he was born prematurely and unexpectedly on November 30, 1874, in his mother's seventh month of pregnancy. Other rooms throughout the palace have more memorabilia: some of Churchill's paintings (see "London-Chartwell", earlier in this chapter), recordings of his speeches, his letters, etc. A visit here is worthwhile if only to see the 180-foot-long library, with its marvelous Willis pipe organ.

There is time in the same day to visit nearby Bladon Churchyard. A simple tombstone there that reads merely "Winston Leonard Spencer Churchill 1874/1965" marks the burial place, alongside his American mother Jenny Spencer, of the greatest Englishman of the last 1,000 years.

London - Penzance - London   530

All of the day trains have meal service or light refreshments.

Dep. London (Pad.)	7:45(1)	8:05(2)	8:45(3)	9:45(4)	10:45(3+9)
Arr. Penzance	5 hours later				

*   *   *

Dep. Penzance	5:07(2)	6:10(4)	7:35(1)	8:27(7)	9:33(7+10)

(Footnotes appear on next page.)

(1)Sat. only. (2)Mon.-Fri. (3)Sat. and Sun. (4)Mon.-Sat. (5)Sun. only. (6)Daily, except Sat. (7)Daily. (8)Carries sleeping car. (9)Plus other departures from London at 11:45(4), 12:45(3), 13:45(4), 14:45(5), 15:45(4), 16:45(6), 17:45(4), 18:45(5), 23:25(1+8) and 23:59(2+8). (10)Plus other departures from Penzance at 10:30(7), 11:15(3), 12:35(1), 13:35(3), 14:50(1), 15:35(3), 16:25(4), 18:40(5), 20:45(1+8) and 21:35(6+8).

Although it is possible to visit Penzance on a one-day train excursion from London, Penzance and the rest of Cornwall deserve a stay of several days.

Sights in **Penzance:** Take the walk described in the free brochure called "A day in Chapel Street, Abbey Street and Quay Street" and visit Egyptian Shop, the Admiral Benbow Inn, the Nautical Museum and Morrab Gardens. See the view of Mount's Bay from Bolitho Gardens and from Terry and Sheila Knowles' outstanding Mount Prospect Hotel, which we recommend highly.

It is only a 10-mile bus trip to Land's End, the westernmost edge of England and a beautiful seascape of waves crashing against the granite cliffs. In another direction, it is also only a 10-mile bus ride to St. Ives, a quaint fishing village and the location of The Hepworth Gallery, containing the work of Britain's best-known sculptress. (Both buses leave from the terminal next to the railstation.)

Go a mere 3 miles by city bus to Marazion to visit St. Michael's Mount, a small island only a half-mile offshore. There has been a church at the summit since 1135. The castle has been occupied by the St. Aubyn family from 1659 to the present day. Visitors are allowed to enter most of the rooms of the castle and are provided a brochure describing its history and the many interesting contents: furniture, costumes, guns, maps, portraits, banners.

St. Mary's, the largest (3 miles by 2 miles) of the Isles of Scilly, can be reached daily except Sunday either by a 20-minute helicopter flight or a 2½-hour boat ride. Many beautiful gardens of sub-tropical plants, coastal walks and nature trails are the attractions there. Small launches offer transportation to the other inhabited islands: Tresco, Bryher, St. Agnes and St. Martin's.

London - Portsmouth - London   520

Dep. London (Victoria)	26 minutes after each hour, from 8:26 to 20:26
	Also frequent times 5:20-23:20 from Waterloo station
Arr. Portsmouth (Hbr.)	2 hours later

Sights in **Portsmouth:** England's great naval base. See Lord Nelson's flagship, H.M.S. Victory, which won the battle of Trafalgar over the combined Spanish and French fleets. The nearby Victory Museum. The Dickens Museum at the house where the author was born, 393 Commercial Road.

Dep. Portsmouth (Hbr.)	50 minutes after each hour, from 8:50 to 19:50(1)
	Also frequent times 5:30-22:20, arriving Wat.station
Arr. London (Victoria)	2 hours later

(1)On Sundays, depart Portsmouth 2 minutes after each hour = 9:02 to 21:02

London - Portsmouth - Isle of Wight - London   521

As these schedules indicate, it is easy to visit both Portsmouth and the Isle of Wight in one day by stopping-over in Portsmouth from 9:19 to 11:20 or 12:30.

Dep. London			Dep. Shanklin	15:41(2)	
(Wat.)	7:48(1)	8:48(1)	Arr. Ryde Pier Head	16:03	
Arr. Portsmouth			Change to hovercraft.		
(Hbr.)	9:19	10:19	Dep. Ryde Pier Head	16:10	
Sightsee in Portsmouth. Then take			Arr. Portsmouth (Hbr.)	16:45	
hovercraft to Isle of Wight.			Change to train.		
Dep. Portsmouth			Dep. Portsmouth (Hbr.)	16:53(1)	
(Hbr.)	11:20	12:30	Arr. London (Wat.)	18:25	
Arr. Ryde					
Pier Head	11:50	12:58			
Change to train.					
Dep. Ryde					
Pier Head	11:55	13:07			
Arr. Shanklin	12:16	13:28			

(1)Meal service Monday-Friday. Only light refreshments on Saturday. (2)Plus frequent other departures from Shanklin until 21:11.

London - Rochester - London   512

Dep. London (Vict.)	MON-FRI	Frequent times from 6:25 to 23:23
	SAT & SUN	Frequent times from 5:23 to 23:39
Arr. Chatham	60 minutes later	

Change to suburban train for the 1-mile ride from Chatham to Rochester.

Sights in **Rochester:** The 17th century Bull Hotel, where Dickens' characters, Pickwick and his friends, spent the first night of their long and memorable trip. The house where Dickens lived his last 10 years and where he died is here, a red brick mansion. The cemetery has many markers from which Dickens took the names for the people he cast in his stories. Alongside the cemetery is the 15th century Gatehouse Tea-shoppe.

Visit the City Museum in Eastgate House, open daily except Friday 14:00-17:30. See the little house at 11 Ordinance Terrace, where Dickens lived from the time he ws 4 until he was 9 years old.

Dep. Chatham	MON-FRI	Frequent times from 5:57 to 23:21
	SAT & SUN	Frequent times from 6:21 to 23:21
Arr. London (Vict.)	60 minutes later	

London - Rye - London 0000

Dep. London (Charing Cross)	Frequent times
Dep. London (Waterloo)	Frequent times
Arr. Rye	1½ hours later

Sights in **Rye:** The old houses and inns along the cobbled streets in this delightful little hilltop town, once an important seaport but now 2 miles from the sea.

Dep. Rye	Frequent times
Arr. London (Waterloo)	1½ hours later
Arr. London (Charing Cross)	1½ hours later

London - Salisbury - Stonehenge - London 523

Dep. London (Wat.)	7:45(1+2)	8:37(3)	9:10(4)	10:10(1+9)
Arr. Salisbury	9:21	9:54	10:34	11:53

Sights in **Salisbury:** The Cathedral, with its tombs of Crusaders and one of the 4 existing copies of the Magna Carta. Take a bus from Salisbury to Stonehenge to view the mysterious oval of huge stones there, about 4,000 years old. This is the most important prehistoric relic in Britain. How were these stupendous weights moved many miles from their quarry, and why ?

Dep. Salisbury	12:10(3)	13:10(5)	14:15(4)	15:10(5+10)
Arr. London (Wat.)	13:48	14:48	15:47	16:48

(1)Monday-Saturday. (2)Change trains in Basingstoke. (3)Saturdays only. (4)Light refreshments. (5)Monday-Friday, except holidays. (6)Saturday and Sunday. (7)Sundays only. (8)Daily, except Saturday. (9)Plus another departure from London at 11:10(4).   (10)Plus other departures from Salisbury at 16:20(4+5), 17:10(6), 17:30(5), 18:00(7), 18:20(1+4), 19:26(8), 20:20(6), 21:20(2+7), 21:35(5), 22:15(2+7) and 22:17(3).

London - Salisbury - Exeter - London 523

As these schedules indicate, it is easy to visit both Salisbury and Exeter in one day.

Dep. London (Waterloo)	9:10	Dep. Exeter (St. Davids)		17:33
Arr. Salisbury	10:34	Dep. Exeter (Central)		17:38
Sightsee in Salisbury		Arr. London (Waterloo)		20:52
Dep. Salisbury	12:39			
Arr. Exeter (Central)	14:27			
Arr. Exeter (St. Davids)	14:32			

London - St. Albans - London 570

Dep. London (St. Pancras)   6:00(1)   7:00(1)
Arr. St. Albans   14 minutes later
   Sights in **St. Albans:** The beautiful Cathedral. The Roman ruins.
Dep. St. Albans   17:36   23:13
Arr. London (St. Pancras)   14 minutes later
(1)Monday-Saturday, except holidays.

London - Stratford on Avon - London   527

Dep. London (Pad.)	6:45(1)	9:00	10:30(2)
Arr. Leamington Spa	8:52	10:53	12:56
Change trains.			
Dep. Leamington Spa	9:05(1)	11:00	13:05(2)
Arr. Stratford	9:36	11:31	13:36

Many people prefer fully-escorted day tours to Stratford that start and end in London. Details are available from British Tourist Authority, 64 St. James Street, near Piccadilly Circus.

A special "Shakespeare Connection" train departs from London's *Euston* station at 8:40 Monday-Saturday (9:40 on Sundays), arriving Coventry about one hour later. A special bus transfers passengers from Coventry to Stratford-on-Avon, a one-hour ride. This bus stops near the Stratford office that books various local tours. After 7 hours of leisurely sightseeing, passengers leave Stratford at 17:30 for the train departing Coventry at 18:30 for London. Those wishing to attend a performance at the Royal Shakespeare Theater are provided a bus at 11:38 for the 0:38 train from Coventry, arriving back in London, reaching there at 1:25.

There are many restaurants and pubs in Stratford, and visitors may picnic either by the theater or in the garden along the river.

It is a 10-minute walk from the railstation to Shakespeare's birthplace. See the house of Mary Arden, his mother. The cottage of Anne Hathaway, his wife. Shakespeare's tomb in Trinity Church. The home of John Harvard, founder of America's great university. There are afternoon performances at the Royal Shakespeare Theater on some Thursdays and Saturdays.

Dep. Stratford	15:32(1)	18:26(1)	20:40(1)
Arr. Leamington Spa	15:55	18:58	21:12
Change trains.			
Dep. Leamington Spa	17:25(1)	19:04(1)	21:28(1)
Arr. London (Pad.)	19:17	21:13	23:31

(1)Monday-Saturday. (2)Sundays only.

London - Torquay - London 530

Most of these trains have meal service or light refreshments.

Dep. London (Pad.)   9:15(1)   9:20(2)   9:45(3+4+9)
Arr. Torquay   13:01   12:10   13:30

Sights in **Torquay:** An 11-mile coastline that resembles a Mediterranean resort, palm trees and all.

Dep. Torquay   13:01(6) 13:36(3) 15:03(2+4+10)
Arr. London (Pad.)   16:08   16:35   18:10

(1)Saturdays only. Reservation required. (2)Monday-Saturday. Meal service. (3)Sundays only. Light refreshments or meal service. (4)Change trains in Newton Abbot. (5)Saturdays only. Reservation required. Light refreshments. (6)Monday-Friday. Meal service. (7)Saturdays only. (8)Sundays only. (9)Plus other departures from London at 10:10(5) and 10:45(2+4). (10)Plus other departures from Torquay at 16:05(7), 16:57(3+4), 17:26(8), 18:55(4+8) and 19:19(4+6).

London - Winchester - London 522

Dep. London (Wat.)   MON-SAT   Frequent times from 5:45 to 23:46
                    SUN   Frequent times from 8:45 to 22:46
Arr. Winchester   65 minutes later

Sights in **Winchester:** King Arthur's roundtable in the Great Hall at the Castle. The 11th century Cathedral, with the tombs of King Alfred, Jane Austen and Izaak Walton.

Dep. Winchester   MON-SAT   Frequent times from 10:01 to 22:55
                    SUN   Frequent times from 7:02 to 23:04
Arr. London (Wat.)   65 minutes later

London - Windsor - London 525

Dep. London (Waterloo)   Frequent times from 6:11 to 22:42
Arr. Windsor (Riverside) 50-60 minutes later

Sights in **Windsor:** Windsor Castle with its collection of Da Vinci drawings and, occasionally, members of the Royal Family. See the Changing of the Guard there, at 10:25. Queen Mary's Doll House. St. George's Chapel.

In the town, stroll down the 3-mile "Long Walk". See Eton College, where once it did not matter if you won or lost, in the days when observing amenities was more important than the final score.

Dep. Windsor (Riverside) Frequent times from 6:10 to 22:40
Arr. London (Windsor)   50-60 minutes later

London - York - London   575

Most of these trains have meal service.

MONDAY-SATURDAY

Dep. London (King's X)	7:30	8:00	8:50	9:30(1)
Arr. York	9:46	10:10	11:22	11:47
	*	*	*	
Dep. York	14:46	15:17	16:46	17:17(2)
Arr. London (King's X)	16:50	17:24	18:54	19:26

SUNDAYS

Dep. London (King's X)	8:45	9:30	10:00	10:30(3)
Arr. York	11:49	11:58	12:35	13:06
	*	*	*	
Dep. York	14:38	15:14	15:38	16:13(4)
Arr. London (King's X)	16:48	17:25	18:00	18:27

(1)Plus other Mon.-Sat. departures from London at 10:00, 11:00, 11:30 and 12:00.   (2)Plus other Mon.-Sat. departures from York at 17:46, 17:55, 19:17, 19:44 and 20:52.   (3)Plus other Sunday departures from London at 11:00, 12:00 and 12:30.   (4)Plus other Sunday departures from York at 17:13, 17:27, 18:13, 18:45, 19:44 and 20:52.

Sights in **York:** York Minister, the Cathedral with fantastic 15th century stained-glass. The collection of antiques at York Castle Museum. Walk down "The Shambles".

National Railway Museum, to which there are special excursion trains a few days in August, September, October and November. The all-day event includes roundtrip train service from London and 4 hours at the Museum.

SCENIC TRAIN TRIPS

There is much fine scenery on nearly every rail route in England. The next 3 train rides offer exceptional scenic views.

London - Pwllheli - London

There is fine coastal scenery plus a splendid view of Harlech Castle on this ride. It is not possible to make this trip without staying overnight in Pwllheli.

552
Dep. London (Euston)   9:30(1)
Arr. Wolverhampton   11:34
  Change trains.
547
Dep. Wolverhampton   11:50
Arr. Shrewsbury   12:34
  Change trains.
554
Dep. Shrewsbury   14:36
Arr. Pwllheli   18:42

	*	*	*
Dep. Pwllheli	8:00	12:15(2)	15:05(2)
Arr. Shrewsbury	12:30	16:11	19:28
Change trains.			
547			
Dep. Shrewsbury	12:37	16:40(3)	19:50(3)
Arr. Wolverhampton	13:20	-0-	-0-
Change trains.			
552			
Dep. Wolverhampton	13:30(1)	-0-	-0-
Arr. London (Euston)	15:33	19:31	22:48

(1)Meal service. (2)Change trains in Machynlleth. (3)Direct train to London. No train change in Wolverhampton.

London - Windermere - London   565

These trains run Monday-Saturday, except holidays.

Dep. London (Euston)	7:45(1)	10:20(2)
Arr. Preston	10:32	-0-(2)
Change trains.		
Dep. Preston	11:00	-0-
Arr. Oxenholme	11:35	13:45
Change trains.		

563

Dep. Oxenholme	11:50	14:08
Arr. Windermere	12:15	14:33

Sights in **Windermere:** Breathtaking lake scenery.

Dep. Windermere	14:38	17:10
Arr. Oxenholme	15:01	17:33
Change trains.		

565

Dep. Oxenholme	15:21(2)	17:38
Arr. Preston	-0-(2)	18:17
Change trains.		
Dep. Preston	-0-	19:02
Arr. London (Euston)	19:10	22:12

(1)Meal service. (2)Direct train. No train change in Preston.

A DAY THROUGH WALES

There is a marvelous one-day circle train trip from London that takes you through the incredibly beautiful rural scenery in the heart of Wales, between Swansea and Shrewsbury. As shown below, this trip can be made either clockwise or counter-clockwise.

London - Swansea - Shrewsbury - London

These trains run Monday-Saturday, except holidays.

540		552	
Dep. London (Pad.)	9:00	Dep. London (Euston)	7:35
Arr. Swansea	11:46	Arr. Wolverhampton	9:39
Change trains, (548)		Change trains. (547)	
Dep. Swansea	12:27	Dep. Wolverhampton	9:45
Arr. Shrewsbury	16:07	Arr. Shrewsbury	10:21
Change trains. (547)		Change trains. (548)	
Dep. Shrewsbury	16:23	Dep. Shrewsbury	10:50
Arr. Wolverhampton	17:17	Arr. Swansea	14:36
Change trains. (552)		Change trains. (540)	
Dep. Wolverhampton	17:30	Dep. Swansea	15:30
Arr. London (Euston)	19:28	Arr. London (Pad.)	18:25

RAIL CONNECTIONS WITH IRELAND

London - Limerick (Shannon Airport) or Dublin via Fishguard 504

Dep. London (Pad.)	9:22(1)	21:00(2)	21:10(5)
Arr. Fishguard (Hbr.)	14:10	2:00	2:00
Change to boat.			
Dep. Fishguard (Hbr.)	15:00(1)	3:15(3)	3:15
Arr. Rosslare (Hbr.)	18:30	6:50	6:50
Change to train.			
Dep. Rosslare (Hbr.)	19:15(1)	7:15(3)	7:50(1)
Arr. Dublin (Con.)	-0-	-0-	10:50
Arr. Limerick (Colb.)	23:00(1)	11:15(3)	-0-
	*	*	*
Dep. Limerick (Colb.)	-0-	15:55(1)	-0-
Dep. Dublin (Con.)	18:00(2)	-0-	18:20(1)
Arr. Rosslare (Hbr.)	21:05	20:10	21:20
Change to boat.			
Dep. Rosslare (Hbr.)	21:40(2)	21:40(1)	21:40(1)
Arr. Fishguard (Hbr.)	1:10	1:10(4)	1:10(4)
Change to train.			
Dep. Fishguard (Hbr.)	1:50(3)	1:50(4)	1:50(4)
Arr. London (Pad.)	7:00(3)	7:00(4)	7:00(4)

(1)Monday-Saturday. (2)Sundays only. (3)Mondays only. (4)Tuesday-Sunday. Arrives London at 9:03 on Sundays. (5)Late June to mid-September: runs daily. Mid-September to late June: Runs Monday-Saturday.

London - Dublin   via Holyhead   501

Dep. London (Euston)	8:50(1+3)	10:00(2+3+4)	12:40(5+13
Arr. Holyhead	14:18	14:29	18:00
Change to boat.			
Dep. Holyhead	15:00	15:00	19:00
Arr. Dun Laoghaire	18:30	18:30	22:30
Change to bus.			
Arr. Dublin (Con.)	19:35	19:35	23:00
	*	*	*
Dep. Dublin (Con.)	8:00(3+6)	12:40(3+8)	13:05(3+14)
Change to boat.			
Dep. Dun Laoghaire	8:45	14:00	14:00
Arr. Holyhead	12:15	17:30	17:30
Change to train.			
Dep. Holyhead	12:46	18:10	18:05
Arr. London (Euston)	17:10(7)	22:56	22:38

(1)Sundays only. (2)Monday-Saturday, except holidays. (3)Change trains in both Crewe and Chester. (4)Light refreshments. (5)Monday-Friday. Runs late July to early September. Meal service. Change trains in Chester. (6)Daily, except Saturday. Light refreshments Monday-Friday. (7)Arrive London 18:14 on Sundays. (8)Sundays only. Runs early July to late September. (9)Monday-Saturday. Runs late July to early September. Change trains in both Chester and Crewe. (10)Saturdays only. Runs late July to early September. (11)Daily, carries sleeping car. Light refreshments. Change trains in Crewe. Departs Dublin 21:25 on Sundays. (12)Daily. Change trains in Chester. (13)Plus other departures from London at 14:00(3+10) and 21:45(1). (14)Plus another departure from Dublin at 19:30(12).

RAIL CONNECTIONS WITH SCOTLAND

These are the schedules for rail travel between London and the capital of Scotland.

London - Edinburgh 575

MONDAY-SATURDAY

Dep. London (King's Cross)
  1:55(1)   8:00(2)   9:00(3)   10:00(3)   10:35(2)   11:00(3+9)
Arr. Edinburgh
  9:15   12:54   13:53   14:50   15:09   15:50

  *   *   *

Dep. Edinburgh
  7:00(3)   8:00(3)   9:00(3)   10:00(2)   11:00(3)   12:00(3+10)
Arr. London (Kind's Cross)
  11:59   12:55   13:51   14:48   15:52   17:07

(1)Carries sleeping car. (2)Limited accommodation. Reservation advisable. Meal service. (3)Meal service. (4)Reservation required. (5)Monday-Friday. (6)Train has only sleeping cars. (7)Carries sleeping car. (8)Saturdays only. (9)Plus other departures from London on the hour from 12:00(3) to 18:00(3), plus 22:50(3+4), 23:00 and 23:20(5).   (10)Plus other departures from Edinburgh on the hour from 13:00(3) to 18:00(3), plus 21:10(5+7), 21:40(6), 22:30(7), 23:00(6+8), 23:20(5+6), 23:30(7+8), 23:40(3) and 23:59(7).

SUNDAYS

Most of these trains have meal service.

Dep. London (King's Cross)
  9:30   10:00   11:00   12:00   13:00   14:00(3)
Arr. Edinburgh
  15:14   15:47   16:37   17:32   18:37   18:44

  *   *   *

Dep. Edinburgh
  9:30   10:00   11:00   12:00   13:00   14:00(4)
Arr. London (King's Cross)
  15:52   16:07   16:48   17:25   18:27   19:20

(1)Train has only sleeping cars. (2)Carries sleeping car. (3)Plus other departures from London at 15:00, 16:00, 17:00, 18:00, 22:50, 23:00 and 23:20(1). (4)Plus other departures from Edinburgh at 15:00, 16:00, 17:00, 18:00, 21:10(2), 22:30, 23:20(1), 23:40 and 23:59(2).

SCOTLAND

The 2 rail trips north from Edinburgh (to Dundee-Aberdeen and to Perth-Inverness) are very scenic. There is also train service between Aberdeen and Inverness.

From Inverness, there is a rail route to Wick in northernmost Scotland, and to Kyle of Lochalsh on the west coat of Scotland. Other train routes to the same coastal area are from Glasgow to both Oban and to Mallaig. The other principal rail service in Scotland is between Edinburgh and Glasgow.

Edinburgh

The capital of Scotland. Most of the 25-acre railstation is under glass. Visit Edinburgh Castle, sitting on a cliff 270 feet above the city, on a site where there have been forts since the 6th century. A cannon has been fired from there every day since 1858. The Castle is open every day in the Summer: 9:30-18:00 Monday-Saturday, 11:00-18:00 on Sundays. The panoramic view of Edinburgh from the Castle is breathtaking. At the Castle, see the hammer-beamed timbered ceiling in the Great Hall of James IV, the Scottish Crown Jewels, the small St. Margaret's Chapel, and the State Apartments, including the rooms once occupied by Mary Queen of Scots.

Below the Castle is the 37-acre Princess Street Gardens, with the city's main rail tracks running through it, at a lower level than the surface of the park.

Also visit the 17th century Palace of Holyrood House to see the Throne Room and also the portraits of 110 Scottish kings (painted by the same artist) in the gallery. You will notice that all 110 noses are the same ! Stroll through 648-acre Holyrood Park, which has 3 lakes.

Other interesting sights in Edinburgh: the paintings at both the National Gallery of Scotland and in the National Portrait Gallery. The National Museum of Antiquities. The collection of technology, art, archaeology, geology and natural history in the Royal Scottish Museum. The Museum of Childhood (historic books, toys and materials about child rearing), closed on Sundays. The adaptation of Athens' Temple of Thesus. The month-long International Festival of Music and Drama.

Edinburgh - Dundee - Aberdeen   606

This is a very scenic rail trip.

Dep. Edinburgh	7:00(1+2)	7:30(1)	9:05(3+4+9)
Arr. Dundee	8:11	9:00	10:41
Arr. Aberdeen	9:24	10:34	12:48

* * *

Dep. Aberdeen	6:05(1+5)	7:30(1+6)	8:30(1+2+10)
Arr. Dundee	7:28	8:42	9:42
Arr. Edinburgh	8:51	9:52	10:55

(1)Monday-Saturday. (2)Meal service. (3)Sundays only. (4)Change trains in Dundee. (5)Light refreshments. (6)Limited accommodations. Reservation advisable. (7)Change trains in Dundee on Sundays. (8)Daily. (9)Plus other departures from Edinburgh at 9:17(1+4), 10:35(5+8), 11:17(1+4), 12:35(1+5), 13:17(1+4), 15:00(1+2), 15:17(1+4), 15:30(3), 17:00(1), 17:17(1+4), 17:40(2+3), 18:00(5+7+8), 19:08(4+5+8), 20:00(1+2) and 20:30(2+3). (10)Plus other departures from Aberdeen at 10:30(1+2), 11:50(1+5), 12:55(1+4), 13:05(2+3), 13:50(1+5), 14:55(1+4), 15:25(3+4), 16:30(1+5), 16:55(3+5), 17:25(3+4), 18:30(2+7) and 19:20(8).

Sights in **Dundee:** A very ancient city, predating Roman occupation. Mountains of jam and preserves are processed here.

Sights in **Aberdeen:** A very popular tourist center and busy seaport. The center of Scotland's fishing industry. Straddles 2 rivers. See the 15th century Cathedral of St. Machar. Streets that were laid out in the 13th and 14th centuries. The local history museum in the 17th century Provost Skene's House.

The 16th century Provost Ross's House. The 18th century St. Nicholas Church. Two very old bridges: the 14th century Brig o'Balgownie and the 16th century Old Bridge of Dee. The 19th century Music Hall. The 19th century Marischal College, considered the world's largest and finest granite building.

Edinburgh - Perth - Inverness   611

A very scenic train ride.

Dep. Edinburgh	9:22(1)	13:22(1)	17:10(2)	23:10(3)
Dep. Perth	10:50(1)	14:50(1)	18:41(2)	1:10(4)
Arr. Inverness	13:35	17:30	21:40	4:50

* * *

Dep. Inverness	8:30(1)	16:30(1)	17:05(5)	23:50(3)
Dep. Perth	11:15(1)	19:25(1)	20:19(5)	3:55(4)
Arr. Edinburgh	12:36	20:48	21:43	6:45(6)

(1)Monday-Saturday. Light refreshments. (2)Sundays only. Light refreshments. (3)Daily, except Saturday. Carries sleeping car. (4)Daily, except Sunday. (5)Sundays only. (6)Passengers may remain in bed until 7:30.

Sights in **Perth:** A popular tourist center. There is much whiskey distilling and weaving of tartans here. Good Winter sports. Sailing and water skiing in the Summer.

Sights in **Inverness:** Located in the mountainous Highlands. Very cold Winters and cool Summers here. A popular tourist resort for hunting of grouse and deer, hiking, fishing, sailing, camping and Winter sports. Many whiskey distillers in this area. Nearby is Great Britain's highest mountain, Ben Nevis (4,406 feet).

Aberdeen - Inverness   605

Dep. Aberdeen	7:55(1+2)	9:55(1)	11:55(1+2)	12:51(3+4)
Arr. Inverness	10:15	12:15	14:15	15:05
		*	*	*

Dep. Inverness	5:48(1)	8:48(1+2)	9:48(2+3)	10:48(1+2+5)
Arr. Aberdeen	8:15	11:08	12:00	13:08

(1)Monday-Saturday. (2)Light refreshments. (3)Sundays only. (4)Plus other departures from Aberdeen at 13:55(1+2), 15:55(1+2), 16:40(2+3), 17:55(1+2) and 20:55(1).   (5)Plus other departures from Inverness at 12:48(1+2), 14:48(1+2), 16:05(2+3), 17:48(1+2) and 20:48(1).

Inverness - Wick   610

Dep. Inverness	6:40(1)	8:05(2)	11:40(1)	17:40(1)
Arr. Wick	11:03	13:05	15:45	21:45
		*	*	*

Dep. Wick	6:00(1)	11:10(2)	12:00(1)	18:00(1)
Arr. Inverness	10:10	15:10	16:10	22:15

(1)Monday-Saturday. Light refreshments. (2)Sundays only. Runs mid-June to mid-September.

Inverness - Kyle of Lochalsh - Inverness   610

This is one of the most scenic train trips in Britain. The track climbs and descends, turns and twists through the Wester Ross mountains as it often goes along the shoreline of lovely lakes through the heart of the Highlands. In the Spring, there are fields of red and orange rhododendrons. The fields of purple heather can be seen all year.

In the high Luib Summit area there are forests and snowcapped mountains. It is only an 8-minute ferry-boat ride from Kyle to the Isle of Skye.

All of these trains run Monday-Saturday, except holidays.

| Dep. Inverness | 6:55(1) | 9:30(2) | 10:45(1+3) | 17:55(1) |
| Arr. Kyle | 9:40 | 12:10 | 13:40 | 20:40 |

*   *   *

| Dep. Kyle | 7:10(1) | 11:10(1) | 14:10(2) | 17:10(1+3) |
| Arr. Inverness | 9:50 | 13:50 | 16:45 | 19:50 |

(1)Monday-Saturday. (2)Sundays only. Runs early July to late August. Supplement charged. Carries an observation car. (3)Runs all year. Has light refreshments and an observation car from early June to late September. Supplement charged.

Edinburgh - Dunbar - Edinburgh 575

| Dep. Edinburgh | 7:05(1) | 9:00(1) | 9:30(2) | 12:00(1) |
| Arr. Dunbar | 25-40 minutes later | | | |

Sights in **Dunbar:** A small fishing port, the birthplace of naturalist John Muir (128 High Street). See the Castle ruins at the harbor. Take the 45-minute walk and visit the Old Harbor with its lifeboat museum, the roost for domesticated pigeons in Friar's Croft, and the Georgian houses (Castellau and Lauderdale). This walk is detailed in a guidebook available at the town's tourist information center in the 17th century Town House on High Street.

Also visit the 1,667-acre John Muir Country Park, containing a wide variety of birds and plants. Near it are the restored 17th century Preston watermill and many old towns and villages: Gifford, Haddington, Dirleton and North Berwick.

A list of hotels, guest houses and bed-and-breakfast places can be obtained by writing to the Dunbar Tourist Information Centre, if sufficient international reply coupons are enclosed.

| Dep. Dunbar | 8:33(1) | 9:51(1) | 11:48(1) | 12:28(2) | 13:28(1+4) |
| Arr. Edinburgh | 25-40 minutes later | | | | |

(1)Monday-Saturday. (2)Sundays only. (3)Daily. (4)Plus other departures from Dunbar at 20:44(2) and 21:23(3).

Edinburgh - Glasgow - Edinburgh 600

| Dep. Edinburgh | Frequent times from 7:00 to 23:00 |
| Arr. Glasgow | 45 minutes later |

Sights in **Glasgow:** A major seaport. Largest city in Scotland. See the 12th century Cathedral. The fine collection in Kelvingrove Art Galleries and Museum. The Hunterian Museum.

| Dep. Glasgow | Frequent times from 6:20 to 23:00 |
| Arr. Edinburgh | 45 minutes later |

Glasgow - Oban - Glasgow 604

Marvelous Highland scenery on this route. The train service is Monday-Saturday except holidays. As indicated below, a one-day excursion (Glasgow-Oban-Glasgow) is possible.

Dep. Glasgow (Queen St.)	8:04(1)	12:55	18:23
Arr. Oban	11:16	16:00	21:30

Sights in **Oban:** This has been a holiday resort for nearly a century, and a fishing port for even longer.

Dep. Oban	7:40	12:55(1)	17:58(1)
Arr. Glasgow (Queen St.)	10:55	15:28	20:55

(1)Light refreshments.

Glasgow - Mallaig - Glasgow 604

A very scenic rail trip. The train service is Monday-Saturday except holidays. As indicated below, a one-day excursion (Glasgow-Mallaig-Glasgow) is possible.

Dep. Glasgow (Queen St.)	6:00(1)	8:34(1+2+3)	16:34(1+4)
Arr. Mallaig	11:38	14:30	22:33

* * *

Dep. Mallaig	7:00(1+4)	12:25(1+3)	16:10(1+2)
Arr. Glasgow (Queen St.)	13:13	18:55	22:28

(1)Light refreshments. (2)Supplement charged. (3)Runs early June to early September. (4)Change trains in Fort William.

Glasgow - Stranraer - Glasgow 603

A trip through the beautiful moor of southwest Scotland.

Dep. Glasgow (Cent.)	8:35(1)	9:00(2)	11:35(1+3+4+10)
Arr. Stranrear	11:32	11:44	14:09

* * *

Dep. Stranrear	7:32(1)	13:06(2+4)	13:15(1+11)
Arr. Glasgow (Cent.)	10:23	15:57	15:54

(1)Mon.-Sat. (2)Sun. only. (3)Sat. only. (4)Runs late June to mid-September. (5)Runs early June to early September. Change trains in Ayr. (6)Runs mid-September to late June. (7)Change trains in Ayr. (8)Mon.-Fri. (9)Fri. and Sat. (10)Plus other departures from Glasgow at 13:00(3+5), 15:05(2), 15:35(1+7), 17:25(8), 18:00(3) and 22:00(1)   (11)Plus other departures from Stranrear at 14:25(1+6), 18:38(1), 19:05(2) and 21:25(9).

Stranrear - Belfast Boat 505

The boat connection with Northern Ireland.

Dep. Stranrear (Hbr.)	7:00(1+2)	7:30(3)	12:00(4+5)
Arr. Belfast (York Rd.)	10:46	11:00	15:28

(1)Sundays only. (2)Runs late June to mid-September. (3)Monday-Saturday. (4)Daily. (5)Plus other departures from Stranrear at 14:30(2+3) and 19:00(4).

Chapter 9

EASTERN EUROPE

ALBANIA

There are *no* rail connections between Albania and other countries. The really long train ride in little Albania is 43 miles, from Durres to Elbasan, taking nearly 2 hours.

Durres - Elbasan   838

Dep. Durres	8:20	16:25		Dep. Elbasan	7:35	16:45
Arr. Elbasan	10:45	19:10		Arr. Durres	9:45	19:00

Sights in **Durres:** Albania's Adriatic port. Excellent sand beaches. Bus tours go to such interesting villages as Apollonia. Kruja (ruins of the 15th century Skanderbeg fortress), Shkodra (great Moslem mosques and bazaars), and Gjirokastra.

Sights in **Elbasan:** Many interesting ruins.

Durres - Tirana   837

This 23-mile ride takes about 62 minutes.

Dep. Durres   5:50   8:20   9:45   12:40   16:35   19:00   21:00

Sights in **Tirana:** This is Albania's capital. The prehistoric and Illyrian objects and folk art in the Museum. Tours of the textile factory and film studio. Moslem mosques and bazaars.

Dep. Tirana   6:00   7:15   8:30   14:05   15:20   17:55   21:00

BULGARIA

Back in the 1930's, American humorist Robert Benchley said: "Traveling with children corresponds roughly to traveling third-class in Bulgaria. They tell me there is nothing lower in the world than third-class Bulgarian travel."

In the 1980's, even first-class travel in Bulgaria is awful.

Bulgaria's express trains are called Ekspresen. The name for its fast trains is Brzi, and the slow trains are Putnichki.

BULGARIAN HOLIDAYS

January 1	New Year's Day	June 2	Memorial Day
May 1 and 2	Labor Day	Sept. 9 and 10	Liberation Day
May 24	Education Day	November 7	Revolution Day

SUMMER TIME

Bulgaria changes to Summer Time on the last Sunday of March and converts back to Standard Time on the last Sunday of September.

ONE-DAY EXCURSIONS AND CITY-SIGHTSEEING

Here are 2 one-day rail trips that can be made comfortably from Sofia and one longer ride. Notes are provided on what to see at each destination. The number after the name of each route is the Cook's timetable.

Schedules for one other train route and international connections conclude this section.

Sofia

The capital of Bulgaria. See the beautiful icons at Alexander Nevsky Memorial Church. Relics from the Stone Age to the Roman Empire at the Archaeological Museum, in Bouyouk, the city's largest mosque. The Georgi Dimitrov Mausoleum. The Byzantine Sancta Sophia Church. The 14th century frescos at the Church of St. Georgi.

The delicate murals in the medieval Boyanna Church, a 10-minute drive outside the city. There is an extensive art collection at the Rila Monastery, 74 miles from Sofia.

Sofia - Burgas - Sofia   823

Dep. Sofia	6:14(1)	7:00(2)	10:00(2)	14:30(2)	16:10(3+5)
Arr. Burgas	12:14	13:30	17:09	20:45	21:49
		*	*	*	
Dep. Burgas	5:00(3)	9:19(2)	9:49(2)	16:04(2)	16:45(1+6)
Arr. Sofia	10:35	16:15	17:09	23:00	22:45

(1)Reservation required. Light refreshments. (2)Meal service. (3)Reservation required. Meal service. (4)Carries sleeping car. Also has couchettes. (5)Plus another departure from Sofia at 22:05(4).   (6)Plus another departure from Burgas at 22:44(4).

Sights in **Burgas:** A good beach resort.

Sofia - Plovdiv - Sofia   823

Dep. Sofia	6:14(1)	10:00(2)	15:50(1)	22:05
Arr. Plovdiv	8:23	12:43	17:52	0:43

Sights in **Plovdiv:** This city has been a commercial center for more than 2,000 years, serving the early caravans that moved between Europe, Asia and Africa. There are excellent exhibits of Thracian gold utensils in the Archaeological Museum. See the Bachkovo Monastery and, near it, the ruins of Tsar Ivan Asen II's fort. The Roman ruins. The Church of Constantine and Helina. The Turkish Imaret Djamiya.

Dep.Plovdiv	3:15	6:50(1)	14:24(2)	20:35(1)
Arr. Sofia	6:06	9:02	17:09	22:45

(1)Reservation required. Light refreshments. (2)Meal service.

Sofia - Varna   823

Dep. Sofia   6:15(1+2)   9:20(2)   16:10(1+2)   22:18(3)   22:50(3)
Arr. Varna   14:51   19:16   22:56   7:54   6:56

Sights in **Varna:** An important seaport and a very popular beach resort. Many museums and art galleries.

Dep. Varna   7:50(2)   9:26(2)   13:45(1+2)   21:35(3)   21:17(3)
Arr. Sofia   16:15   19:30   22:25   5:50   8:18

(1)Reservation required. (2)Meal service. (3)Carries sleeping car. Also has couchettes.

INTERNATIONAL ROUTES FROM BULGARIA

Sofia is the gateway for train travel to Yugoslavia (and on to Western Europe), Romania and Greece (and on to Turkey).

Sofia - Belgrade   821

There is great mountain scenery on the Dragomagoman-Crveni Krst portion of this route.

Dep. Sofia   7:10(1)   8:40(2)   11:25(3)
Arr. Belgrade   14:38   17:15   19:08

(1)Reservation required. (2)Operates late September to late May. (3)Operates late May to late September.

Sofia - Bucharest   822

Dep. Sofia   8:14(1)   11:30(1)   21:49(1+2)
Arr. Bucharest   19:15   22:30   8:27

(1)Carries sleeping car. (2)Has couchettes.

Sofia - Athens   88

Dep. Sofia   11:42(1)
Arr. Athens   6:55

(1)Carries sleeping car. Also has couchettes.

CZECHOSLOVAKIA

A supplement is charged when traveling on Czechoslovakia's express trains, except for passengers holding tickets purchased outside the country.

Prague is the rail center for Czechoslovakia. International trains depart from both its Hlavni (Main) and Stredni (Central) railstations. The city's 2 other stations are Liben and Smichov (for suburban trains).

Reservations can be made at the office of CEDOK, the State Tourist Organization, a short walk from Hlavni station.

The volume of rail service in Czechoslovakia is evidenced by the fact that its timetable book has 683 pages of tables.

CZECHOSLOVAKIAN HOLIDAYS

January 1	New Year's Day	May 9	Liberation Day
	Easter	October 28	Nationalization Day
	Easter Monday	December 25	Christmas Day
May 1	Labor Day	December 26	Additional Holiday

SUMMER TIME

Czechoslovakia changes to Summer Time on the last Sunday of March and converts back to Standard Time on the last Sunday of September.

ONE-DAY EXCURSIONS AND CITY-SIGHTSEEING

Here are 7 one-day rail trips that can be made comfortably from Prague, returning there in most cases before dinnertime. Notes are provided on what to see at each destination. The number after the name of each route is the Cook's timetable.

Details on 3 other rail trips recommended for exceptional scenery and schedules for international connections conclude this section.

Prague

See the beautiful frescos in the 18th century St. Nicolas Church. the 13th century Synagogue. The statue of John Huss at Staromestke Namesti (Old Town Square). The ceremony performed by the 15th century Town Hall Clock. Dalibor Tower, a medieval prison.

The complex of interesting buildings on Castle Hill: The thousand-year old Hradcany Castle. The illuminated manuscripts and ancient globes in the library of Strahov Monastery, near Loretanski Square. The burial place of many Czech kings and the exhibit of crown jewels at St. Vitus Cathedral, in the Castle's third courtyard. The changing of the guard, outside the Cathedral.

Also visit the 14th century Charles Bridge with its 30 statues of saints, straddling the Vltava River. The 14th century Tyn Cathedral. The 17th century Wallenstein Palace.

The Prague House of Artists. The memorial to Mozart at Bertramka. The Laterna Magica. The hall at Vladislav Palace, so large that knights on horseback once jousted in it. The tiny houses on Zlata Ulicka (Golden Lane). The 7 centuries of art exhibited in the 5 wings of the National Gallery, in Sternbeck Palace. Near Sternbeck is Lookout Point, a paved terrace that offers a good view of the city below. Then, see Belevedere, the royal Summer Palace, and visit the tiny museum across from it. See the Old Jewish Cemetery and Museum.

Ten minutes south, at Pruhonice, is one of the largest and most beautiful arboretums in Europe, open May-October. This 625-acre park features more than 1,200 trees, 900 varieties of roses, thousands of azaleas, tulips and rhododendrons and 18 water lily ponds.

Prague - Bratislava - Prague   812

Dep. Prague (Hlavni)   4:01(1+2)   6:07(2)   8:20(2)
Arr. Bratislava   10:04   11:44   13:56

Sights in **Bratislava:** An important Danube port in ancient Roman times. See the 14th-15th century castle. The Hussite House. The Old City Hall. The Cathedral. The palaces on Mirove Square, Michalska Street and Gottwald Square.

Dep. Bratislava   14:38(2)   16:36(2)   18:28(2+4)
Arr. Prague (Hlavni)   20:57(3)   22:19   0:17

(1)Operates late May to late September. (2)Meal service. (3)Arrives at Prague's Stredni railstation. (4)Reservation required.

Prague - Brno - Prague   812

Dep. Prague (Hlavni)   6:07(1)   8:20(1+2)   8:53(1+3)
Arr. Brno   9:40   11:56   12:52

Sights in **Brno:** The folk-art exhibit of woodcarving, laces, pottery and costumes in the Moravian Museum. Brno Castle. Take a cruise on one of the underground rivers to see the Macocha and Sloup grottos. The outstanding 13th century Pernstejn Castle, near Brno.

Dep. Brno   14:05   16:52(1)   18:29(1+2)   20:38(1+2)
Arr. Prague (Hlavni)   18:25   20:57(3)   22:19   0:17

(1)Meal service. (2)Reservation required. (3)Depart/Arrive Prague's Stredni railstation.

Prague - Ceske Budejovice - Prague   810a

Dep.			Dep.		
Prague (Hlavni)	6:00	13:15	Ceske Budejovice	12:50	18:20
Arr.			Arr.		
Ceske Budejovice	9:05	16:35	Prage (Hlavni)	16:20	21:40

Sights in **Ceske Budejovice:** A city that appears as it did in the Middle Ages. Visit the Budvar brewery.

Prague - Karolovy Vary - Prague   810

Dep. Prague (Stredni)   6:20(1)   9:22(2)
Arr. Karlovy Vary   11:05   14:18

Sights in **Karlovy Vary:** Once called Carlsbad, still famous for its curative waters. An international film festival, held here every July. The Moser crystal glass factory. An interesting porcelain factory in nearby Slakov.

Dep. Karlovy Vary   13:13(2)   16:57
Arr. Prague (Stredni)   18:01   21:40

(1)Departs from Prague's Hlavni railstation. (2)Meal service.

Prague - Marianske Lazne - Prague   809

Dep. Prague (Hlavni)   8:22   11:00(1)
Arr. Marianske Lazne   12:04   14:33

Sights in **Marianske Lazne:** Once called Marienbad, still a famous health spa.

Dep. Marianske Lazne   15:13   17:15
Arr. Prague (Hlavni)   18:41   21:03

(1)Reservation required.

Prague - Plzen - Prague   809

Dep. Prague (Hlavni)   8:22   11:00(1)
Arr. Plzen   10:35   13:04

Sights in **Plzen:** Visit the enormous Urquell brewery, where more than 200 million pints of beer are bottled annually. They have been producing beer here (hence "Pilsener") for over 800 years.

Dep. Plzen   14:00   16:36   18:42
Arr. Prague (Hlavni)   16:12   18:41   21:03

(1)Reservation required.

Prague - Tabor - Prague   810a

Dep. Prague (Hlv.)   6:00   13:15 | Dep. Tabor   14:01   19:26
Arr. Tabor   7:59   15:31 | Arr. Prague (Hlv.)   16:20   21:40

Sights in **Tabor:** A museum town, preserved to immortalize the unusual Hussite 14th century reform movement which held that all people are brothers and equal.

SCENIC RAIL TRIPS

Bratislava - Kosice   811

Very good mountain scenery, through the Low and High Tatras Mountains.

Dep. Bratislava	9:18(1)	13:40(1)	15:50(1+2)	22:25	23:25(3+5)
Arr. Kosice	17:31	22:00	23:03	6:45	7:14

* * *

Dep. Kosice	0:45(3)	6:20(1)	13:10(1)	15:30(1+2)	21:15(6)
Arr. Bratislava	8:43	14:15	21:18	22:30	5:55

(1)Meal service. (2)Late May to late September: runs daily. Late September to late May: runs daily, except Saturday. (3)Carries sleeping car. (4)Also has couchettes. (5)Plus another departure from Bratislava at 23:50(3+4).   (6)Plus another departure from Kosice at 23:25(3+4).

Poprad - Tatry to Stary Smokovec   815

This spur off the Prague-Kosice route is the most scenic rail trip in Czechoslovakia. Forty minutes of the spectacular Tatras Mountains. Then, you can continue on to the Tatranska Lomnica ski resort and take a funicular to the top of 8,645-foot Lomnicky Stit.

Dep. Prague (Hlavni)	0:20	12:35(1)	15:52(2)	16:32(3+6)
Arr. Poprad-Tatry	11:39	21:39	1:32	2:05

* * *

Dep. Poprad-Tatry	1:00(2+4)	3:16(3)	8:01(2)	10:42(1+7)
Arr. Prague (Hlavni)	11:55	12:38	17:36	19:46

(1)Reservation required. Meal service. (2)Meal service. (3)Train of only sleeping cars. (4)Carries sleeping car. Also has couchettes. (5)Arrive/Depart Prague's Stredni railstation. (6)Plus other departures from Prague at 18:07(4), 19:00(2+4), 20:15(3) and 21:15(4+5).   (7(Plus other departures from Poprad-Tatry at 17:59, 19:55(4+5), 21:47(3) and 22:21(4).

Change trains.
814

Dep. Poprad-Tatry	26 times daily
Arr. Stary Smokovec	40 minutes later
Change trains.	
Dep. Stary Smokovec	Frequent times
Arr. Tatranska Lomnica	15 minutes later

Dep. Poprad-Tatry	1:36	5:03	6:30	6:46	7:11	11:43(4)
Arr. Kosice	3:14	6:45	8:20	8:28	8:51	13:24

(1)Meal service. (2)Reservation required. (3)Late May to late September: runs daily. Late September to late May: runs daily, except Saturday. (4)Plus other departures from Poprad-Tatry at 15:49(1), 20:16(1), 21:32(1+3) and 21:41(1+2).

Strba - Strbske Pleso

This is another great Tatras Mountain scenic rail trip. Much winter sports in this area.

815

Dep. Prague (Hlavni)	0:20	12:35(1)	19:00(2+3+6)
Arr. Strba	11:22	21:22	6:25

Change trains.

814

Dep. Strba	25 times daily in Summer
	20 times daily in Winter
Arr. Strbske Pleso	16 minutes later

(1)Reservation required. Meal service. (2)Carries sleeping car. Meal service. (3)Has couchettes. (4)Train of only sleeping cars. (5)Departs from Prague's Stredni railstation. (6)Plus other departures from Prague at 20:15(4) and 21:15(3+4+5).

INTERNATIONAL ROUTES FROM CZECHOSLOVAKIA

Prague is Czechoslovakia's gateway to Vienna (and on to Budapest, Bucharest and Athens), Berlin (and on to Copenhagen and all of Scandinavia), Warsaw (and on to Moscow), and Nurnberg (and on to the rest of Western Europe).

Prague - Budapest   812

Dep. Prague (Hlavni)	0:38(1+2+3)	-0-	6:07(3+6)
Dep. Prague (Liben)	-0-	4:01(3+4)	-0-
Arr. Budapest (Nyugati)	11:25	-0-	-0-
Arr. Budapest (Keleti)	-0-	14:20	15:53

(1)Operates mid-June to mid-September. (2)Has couchettes. (3)Meal service. (4)Operates late May to late September. (5)Carries sleeping car. (6)Plus other departures from Prague at 8:20(3), 14:07(3), 19:13(2+5) and 22:04(2+5).

Prague - Vienna   746

Dep. Prague (Hlavni)	0:21(1)	7:33(2)	15:31(3)
Arr. Vienna (Franz Josefs Bf.)	8:10	16:05	21:27

(1)Carries sleeping car. (2)Change trains in Veseli N. Luznici and in Gmund. (3)Meal service.

Prague - Berlin   87+780
Dep. Prague (Stredni)   0:54(1)   5:41(2)   9:02(3)   10:31(5+7)
Arr. Berlin (Ost)   7:56   12:28   16:30(4)   17:42(4)

(1)Carries sleeping car. Also has couchettes. (2)Reservation required. Carries sleeping car. Meal service. (3)Operates mid-June to mid-September. Meal service. (4)Arrives at Berlin's Lichtenberg railstation. (5)Meal service. (6)Reservation required. Meal service. (7)Plus other departures from Prague at 15:38(6), 16:44(6) and 23:01(1).

Prague - Warsaw   819
Dep. Prague (Hlavni)   18:51(1)   23:00(2)
Arr. Warsaw   8:57   11:44

(1)Carries sleeping car. Also has couchettes. (2)Train of only sleeping cars.

Prague - Nurnberg   809
Dep. Prague (Hlavni)   7:40(1)   11:00(1+2)   20:03
Arr. Nurnberg   14:47   18:53   5:51

(1)Meal service. (2)Reservation required.

EAST GERMANY

The signs you will see at railstations in East Germany are the same as those listed in Chapter 6, under the section on "Austria".

Supplements are charged for East Germany's 3 categories of fast trains: Ex (Express diesel trains), D (ordinary express trains) and E (semi-fast trains). Local trains, stopping at all stations, are called Personnenzug. Reservations are essential on the routes from East Berlin to Poland. Most Hauptbahnhof (main) railstations have food facilities.

Train trips from Berlin to West Germany are *not* covered by Eurailpass. Tickets for trips from Berlin to West Germany must be paid in West German marks. The East Germany rail authorities will *not* accept East German currency for tickets from Berlin to West Germany.

There is 23-minute suburban train service between Schonefeld Airport and East Berlin every 20 minutes from 4:22 to 1:02. Bus service to West Berlin is hourly from 5:00 to 23:00 and takes 60 minutes.

Where no station is designated for cities in East Germany, the station is Hauptbahnhof.

EAST GERMAN HOLIDAYS

January 1	New Year's Day	October 7	Republic Day
	Easter	December 25	Christmas Day
	Easter Monday	December 26	Additional Holiday
May 1	Labor Day		

ONE-DAY EXCURSIONS AND CITY-SIGHTSEEING

Here are 19 one-day rail trips that can be made comfortably from 3 major cities in East Germany, returning to them in most cases before dinnertime. Notes are provided on what to see at each destination. The number after the name of each route is the Cook's timetable.

The 3 base cities are: Dresden, East Berlin and Leipzig.

It is not necessary to be staying in East Germany in order to tour that area. Sightseeing tours to Potsdam, Dresden and Karl Marx Stadt start in West Berlin at Parkplatz Rankestrasse, near the Kurfurstendamm. For reservation, contact Deutsches Reisebüro, Berlin W. 30, Kurfurstendamm 17.

Schedules for international connections conclude this section.

Dresden

Major works of Raphael, Rembrandt, Rubens, Tintoretto, Van Eyck, Vermeer and other great 16th and 17th century painters at the Picture Gallery in the Semper Building of Zwinger Palace. Another excellent collection of paintings in the National Gallery.

Hear the Silberman organ (229 years old in 1984) at the cathedral, Hofkirche. Visit the baroque Opera House. The Zoo in Stadtpark (also called Volkspark). The Block House. Dresden Palace. The Japanese Castle. The treasures at the Albertinium Museum. The Palace of Culture. Take the cable car to Weisser Hirsch for the view of Dresden from the top of that hill.

It is a 17-mile ride by suburban railway from Dresden to Meissen. See the 15th century castle (Albrechtsburg) and the Cathedral there. Shop in Meissen for Dresden china and Albrecht porcelain.

East Berlin

The reconstructed St. Hedwig's Cathedral, National Gallery and 18th century State Opera. The tremendous collection of Near East monuments, the Market Gate of Milet and the impressive Pergamon Altar, all at the Pergamon Museum. The enormous Soviet Embassy on Unter den Linden. Palace of the Republic. Bode Museum. The Altes Museum.

Leipzig

Concentrate on the area around Market Place. Visit the Museum of the History of Leipzig in the Renaissance Old Town Hall. The 17th century stock exchange (Alte Bourse), rebuilt in 1963. The weighinghouse (Alte Waage), where taxes were levied on imported goods. Auerbachs Keller, the old tavern on which Goethe based the locale of his Faust drama. Bach's tomb, at St. Thomas Church. The Museum of Fine Arts.

West of Market Place is the church where Johann Sebastian Bach is buried. Bach composed in that church the last 27 years of his life. Also see Gohliser Schlosschen, a rococo palace. Gohlis, the home of the poet Schiller. The Opera House in Karl Marx Platz. It is impossible to find a room in Leipzig during the semi-annual (March and September) trade fairs that attract visitors from all over the world.

Dresden - East Berlin - Dresden   780

Dep. Dresden	6:01(1)	9:55(1)
Arr. Berlin (Ost)	8:46	12:28

Sights in **East Berlin:** See notes on sightseeing in East Berlin at the start of this section.

Dep. Berlin (Ost)	12:39(1+2)	14:19(1+3)	16:38(1)	19:08(1+4)
Arr. Dresden	15:09	17:13	19:07	21:49

(1)Meal service. (2)Reservation required. (3)Departs from Berlin's Lichtenberg railstation. (4)Plus another departure from Berlin at 21:36(1).

Dresden - Karl Marx Stadt - Dresden

	774	777	777
Dep. Dresden	8:00	8:24	13:18
Arr. Karl Marx Stadt	9:15	9:37	14:37

Sights in **Karl Marx Stadt:** An East German post-World War II showplace new city.

	774	777	774	777	774
Dep. Karl Marx Stadt	11:36	12:53	14:39	15:53	17:00(1)
Arr. Dresden	12:51	14:08	16:00	17:06	18:13

(1)Plus other departures from Karl Marx Stadt at 17:23 and 19:59.

Dresden - Leipzig - Dresden   768

Dep. Dresden (Hbf.)	-0-	7:57	8:34	9:00(1+7)	-0-
Dep. Dresden (Neu.)	7:26	8:06	8:43	9:08(1)	9:58(8)
Arr. Leipzig		8:44	9:28	10:11	10:35	11:20

Sights in **Leipzig:** See notes about sightseeing in Leipzig at the start of this section.

Dep. Leipzig	14:09	15:02	16:05	16:12(3)	17:08(4+9)
Arr. Dresden (Neu.)	15:38	16:22	17:32	17:38	18:26
Arr. Dresden (Hbf.)	15:46	-0-	-0-	17:49	18:34

(1)Light refreshments. (2)Operates late May to late September. (3)Operates mid-June to early September. (4)Late May to mid-September: runs daily. Mid-September to late May: runs daily, except Saturday. (5)Arrives only at Dresden's Neustadt railstation. (6)Operates late May to late September. (7)Plus another departure from Dresden Hbf. at 10:58(2).   (8)Plus another departure from Dresden Neustadt at 11:06(2).   (9)Plus other departures from Leipzig at 17:54, 19:02(5), 20:10(4), 21:29(6) and 22:03

East Berlin - Dresden - East Berlin   780

Dep. Berlin (Ost)   6:38(1)   8:33(1)   11:10(2+3)
Arr. Dresden   9:18   11:02   13:39

Sights in **Dresden:** See notes about sightseeing in Dresden at the start of this section.

Dep. Dresden   12:00(3)   14:56(3)   15:49(3)   19:40(1)   20:57(1)
Arr. Berlin (Ost) 14:48(2)   17:42(2)   18:28   22:12   23:40

(1)Reservation required. Meal service. (2)Departs/Arrives Berlin's Lichtenberg railstation. (3)Meal service.

East Berlin - Erfurt - East Berlin   776

Dep. Berlin (Lichtenberg)   6:10(1)   6:58(2)   -0-
Dep. Berlin (Schoneweide)   -0-   -0-   9:39(1)
Dep. Berlin (Schonefeld)   6:34(1)   7:22   9:52(1)
Arr. Erfurt   9:59   11:00   13:33

Sights in **Erfurt:** The exquisite Gothic and German Renaissance houses. The Cathedral, where Martin Luther was ordained in 1507. The bridge, on which 33 houses stand. St. Severin Church.

Dep. Erfurt   13:27(3)   17:20(1)
Arr. Berlin (Schonefeld)   17:09   20:39
Arr. Berlin (Schoneweide)   17:24   -0-
Arr. Berlin (Lichtenberg)   -0-   21:06

(1)Meal service. (2)Operates late May to late September. (3)Light refreshments.

East Berlin - Karl Marx Stadt - East Berlin   772a

All of these trains have light refreshments.

Dep. Berlin (Schoneweide)   6:09   -0-
Dep. Berlin (Lichtenberg)   -0-   9:30
Dep. Berlin (Schonefeld)   6:22   9:58
Arr. Karl Marx Stadt   9:57   13:38

Sights in **Karl Marx Stadt:** This is an East German post-World War II showplace new city.

Dep. Karl Marx Stadt   13:56   17:48
Arr. Berlin (Schonefeld)   17:33   21:15
Arr. Berlin (Lichtenberg)   -0-   21:42
Arr. Berlin (Schoneweide)   17:48   -0-

East Berlin - Leipzig - East Berlin   776

Dep. Berlin				
(Lichtenberg)	6:16(1)	6:45(2)	7:27(3)	8:49(2)
Dep. Berlin				
(Schonefeld)	6:40(1)	7:10(2)	7:58(3)	9:22(2)
Arr. Leipzig	8:52	9:24	9:47	11:44

Sights in **Leipzig:** See notes about sightseeing in Leipzig at the start of this section.

Dep. Leipzig	13:22(3)	13:40(3)	15:42(1)	16:06(2+5)
Arr. Berlin				
(Schonefeld)	15:27	15:57	17:45	18:27
Arr. Berlin				
(Schoneweide)	15:42	-0-	-0-	-0-
Arr. Berlin				
(Lichtenberg)	16:01	16:24	18:12	18:54

(1)Runs Monday-Friday, except holidays. Meal Service. (2)Meal service. (3)Light refreshments. (4)Late May to mid-September: runs daily. Mid-September to late May: runs daily, except Saturday. (5)Plus other departures from Leipzig at 18:19(3), 19:41(3+4) and 21:08(3).

East Berlin - Potsdam - East Berlin

There is inexpensive local suburban train service (50 minutes) from the center of East Berlin to Potsdam, and v.v.

Sights in **Potsdam:** The Concert Room and the great paintings in the Picture Gallery at the 18th century Sanssouci Palace. The 17th century Palace, Cecillienhof, where Truman, Attlee and Stalin signed the Potsdam Agreement in 1945.

East Berlin - Rostock - East Berlin   769

Dep. Berlin (Zoo)	8:38(1)	Dep. Rostock	18:22(2)	22:39
Dep. Berlin (Fr'str.)	9:06	Arr. Berlin (Licht.)	21:57	1:56
Dep. Berlin (Ost)	9:34	Arr. Berlin (Fr'str.)	-0-	-0-
Arr. Rostock	12:56	Arr. Berlin (Zoo)	-0-	-0-

(1)Reservation required. (2)Meal service

Sights in **Rostock:** East Germany's largest seaport. St. Mary's Church. the ancient Town Hall.

East Berlin - Stralsund - East Berlin   765a

Dep. Berlin (Ost)	7:19(1+2)	12:33(2)
Arr. Stralsund	10:41	15:59

Sights in **Stralsund:** Many old red-brick buildings and churches along the city's quaint Hanseatic streets.

Dep. Stralsund (Rotterdam)   14:56(3) 18:49(3)
Arr. Berlin (Ost)   18:42   22:38
(1)Departs from Berlin's Lichtenberg railstation. (2)Light refreshments. (3)Meal service.

East Berlin - Warnemunde - East Berlin 769

Dep. Berlin (Zoo)	8:38(1)	Dep. Warnemunde	16:27(2)	22:15(3)
Dep. Berlin (Fr'str.)	9:06(1)	Arr. Berlin (Ost)	21:59	1:56
Dep. Berlin (Ost)	9:34(1)	Arr. Berlin (Fr'str.)	-0-	-0-
Arr. Warnemunde	13:26	Arr. Berlin (Zoo)	-0-	-0-

(1)Reservation required. (2)Change trains in Rostock. Meal service. (3)Operates late May to late September.

Sights in **Warnemunde:** A famous beach resort. A ferry connection to Denmark.

East Berlin - Weimar - East Berlin 776

Dep. Berlin (Lichtenberg)	6:10(1)	6:58(2)	9:39(1+3)
Dep. Berlin (Schonefeld)	6:34(1)	7:22(2)	9:52
Arr. Weimar	9:44	10:46	13:31

Sights in **Weimar:** The marvelous atmosphere of the era when German princes lived here.

Dep. Weimar	13:42(4)	17:35(1)
Arr. Berlin (Schonefeld)	17:09	20:39
Arr. Berlin (Lichtenberg)	17:24(3)	21:06

(1)Meal service. (2)Operates late May to late September. (3)Deprts/Arrives Berlin's Schoneweide railstation. (4)Light refreshments.

Leipzig - Dresden - Leipzig 768

Dep. Leipzig	8:03	8:45	9:30	11:06(1+4)
Arr. Dresden (Neustadt)	9:27	10:06	10:45	12:29
Arr. Dresden (Hbf.)	9:38	-0-	10:55	12:37

Sights in **Dresden:** See notes about sightseeing in Dresden at the start of this section.

Dep. Dresden (Hbf.)	13:06	15:00	16:00	16:53(2)	18:24(5)
Dep. Dresden (Neustadt)	8 minutes later				
Arr. Leipzig	14:38	16:32	17:27	18:14	19:53

(1)Light refreshments. (2)Late May to late September: runs daily. Late September to late May: runs daily, except Saturday. (3)Meal service. (4)Plus another departure from Leipzig at 12:52. (5)Plus other departures from Dresden Hbf. at 20:18(3) and 22:00(2).

462

Leipzig - East Berlin - Leipzig 776

Dep. Leipzig	7:01(1+2)	7:43(2)	8:20(3)	8:54(3)
Arr. Berlin (Schonef.)	9:09	10:03	10:33	10:57
Arr. Berlin (Licht.)	9:36	10:28	10:58(4)	11:22(5)

Sights in **East Berlin:** See notes about sightseeing in East Berlin at the start of this section.

Dep. Berlin (Licht.)	13:34(3)	14:03(5)	15:28(1+2)	15:36(3+6)
Dep. Berlin (Schonef.)	13:58(3)	14:26(3)	15:52(1+2)	16:05(3+7+8)
Arr. Leipzig	16:30	16:41	18:07	18:30

(1)Runs Monday-Friday, except holidays. (2)Meal service. (3)Light refreshments. (4)Arrives at Berlin's Ost railstation. (5)Depart/Arrive Berlin's Schoneweide railstation. (6)Plus another departure from Berlin Lichtenberg at 21:32(3).

(7)Plus another departure from Berlin Schoneweide at 16:57(2). (8)Plus other departures from Berlin Schonefeld at 17:10(2) and 21:58(3).

Leipzig - Erfurt - Leipzig 776

Dep. Leipzig	7:28	8:28	10:30	12:09(1)
Arr. Erfurt	8:56	9:53	11:54	13:37

Sights in **Erfurt:** The exquisite Gothic and German Renaissance houses. The Cathedral, where Martin Luther was ordained in 1507. The bridge, on which 33 houses stand. St. Severin Church.

Dep. Erfurt	13:16	14:01	16:33	18:11	19:57	20:22
Arr. Leipzig	14:52	15:28	18:10	19:40	21:34	21:48

(1)Runs daily, except Sundays and holidays.

Leipzig - Karl Marx Stadt - Leipzig 768a

Dep. Leipzig	7:50	9:57	Dep. Karl Marx Stadt	14:23	17:25
Arr. Karl Marx Stadt	9:31	11:28	Arr. Leipzig	15:41	18:58

Sights in **Karl Marx Stadt:** An East German post-World War II showplace new city.

Lepzig - Naumberg - Leipzig 776

Dep. Leipzig	7:28	8:28	12:09(1)	13:35
Arr. Naumberg	40 minutes later			

Sights in **Naumberg:** A gem of a Medieval village.

Dep. Naumberg	11:30	14:00	14:46	17:24	18:56(2)
Arr. Leipzig	40 minutes later				

(1)Runs daily, except Sundays and holidays. (2)Plus other departures from Naumberg at 20:43 and 21:05

Leipzig - Rostock - Leipzig   767

Dep. Leipzig	6:27(1)	Dep. Rostock	15:43(2)	18:01()
Arr. Rostock	12:36	Arr. Leipzig	21:58	0:07

(1)Light refreshments. (2)Meal service.

Sights in **Rostock:** East Germany's largest seaport. St. Mary's Church. The ancient Town Hall.

Leipzig - Schwerin - Leipzig   767

Dep. Leipzig	6:27(1)	8:06(1)	Dep. Schwerin	17:04(2)	19:21(1)
Arr. Schwerin	11:21	12:44	Arr. Leipzig	21:58	0:07

(1)Light refreshments. (2)Meal service.

Sights in **Schwerin:** The Opera House. The fine castle.

INTERNATIONAL ROUTES FROM EAST GERMANY

Berlin is East Germany's principal gateway to Copenhagen (and on to the rest of Scandinavia), Frankfurt/Main (and on to the rest of Westarn Europe), Munich (and on to Western Austria, Switzerland and Italy), Prague (and on to Eastern Austria, Italy, Romania, Yugoslavia, Greece and Turkey), and Warsaw (and on to Russia).

Berlin - Copenhagen   769

Dep. Berlin (Zoo)	8:38(1)	22:00(2)
Dep. Berlin (Fr'str.)	9:06(1)	22:28(2)
Dep.Berlin (Ost)	9:34(1)	23:49(2)
Arr. Copenhagen	18:59	9:41

(1)Reservation required. Light refreshments on train. Meal service on ship 14:05-16:10. (2)Carries sleeping car. Also has couchettes.

Berlin - Frankfurt/Main   776

Dep. Berlin (Fr'str.)	5:51(1)	12:31(1)	21:44(2)
Dep. Berlin (Zoo)	6:39(1)	13:05(1)	23:08(2)
Arr. Frankfurt/Main	13:56	20:27	7:13

(1)Meal service. (2)Carries sleeping car. Also has couchettes.

Berlin - Munich   771

Dep. Berlin (Fr'str.)	6:42(1)	8:48(1)	21:17(2)
Dep. Berlin (Zoo)	7:03(1)	9:06(1)	21:50(2)
Arr. Munich	16:08	18:20	7:27

(1)Meal service. (2)Carries sleeping car. Also has couchettes.

B⁄lin - Prague   780

₣p. Berlin (Ost)	-0-	6:38(3+4)	8:33(3+4+6)
⟩ep. Berlin (Licht.)	2:10(1+2+7)	-0-	-0-
Dep. Berlin (Schoef.)	2:34(1+2)	7:03(3+4)	8:58(3+4+8)
Arr. Prague (Hlavni)	9:57	13:38	15:13

(1)Operates late May to late September. (2)Has couchettes. (3)Reservation required. (4)Meal service. (5)Carries sleeping car. (6)Plus other departures from Berlin Ost at 12:39(3+4), 16:38(4) and 21:38(2+4+5).

(7)Plus other departures from Berlin Lichtenberg at 11:10(4) and 23:52(2+3).

(8)Plus other departures from Berlin Schonefeld at 11:34(4), 13:04(3+4), 17:03(4), 22:04(2+4+5) and 0:16(2+3).

Berlin - Vienna   746

Dep. Berlin (Ost)	8:33(1)	16:38(2)
Arr. Vienna (F. Josef Bf.)	21:27	8:10

(1)Meal service. (2)Carries sleeping car.

Berlin - Warsaw   847

Dep. Berlin (Ost)	0:32(1+2)	6:20(1+3)	7:50(1)	8:43(1)	10:12(3+4)
Arr. Warsaw (Centralna)	9:30	-0-	-0-	-0-	-0-
Arr. warsaw (Gdanska)	-0-	14:47	16:14	17:10	19:40

(1)Meal service. (2)Carries sleeping car. (3)Operates late May to late September. (4)Plus other departures from Berlin at 15:05(1), 20:28(1+2) and 22:06(2).

HUNGARY

Timetables (Hivatalos Menetrend) can be purchased at Hungary's main railstations. The larger stations in Hungary have food service.

Budapest's railstations are: Keleti (Eastern, for arrivals from and departures to Berlin, Prague and Vienna), Nyugati (Western, for arrivals from and departures to Berlin, Prague and Stockholm), and Deli (Southern, for arrivals from and departures to eastern Yugoslavia).

HUNGARIAN HOLIDAYS

January 1	New Year's Day	August 20	Constitution Day
	Easter	November 7	Revolution
	Easter Monday		Remembrance Day
April 4	Liberation Day	December 25	Christmas Day
May 1	Labor Day	December 26	Additional Holiday

SUMMER TIME

Hungary changes to Summer Time on the last Sunday of March and converts back to Standard Time on the last Sunday in September.

ONE-DAY EXCURSIONS AND CITY-SIGHTSEEING

Here are 3 one-day rail trips that can be made comfortably from Budapest, returning there in most cases before dinnertime. Notes are provided on what to see at each destination. The number after the name of each route is the Cook's timetable.

Schedules for international connections conclude this section.

Budapest

The capital of Hungary. Actually 2 cities, there is the dominant Buda on the west side of the Danube and the youthful Pest, extending east of the river.

In **Buda,** be sure to see the 112-acre garden island, Margitziget (Margaret Island). The Celtic and Roman ruins. The 250-foot Gothic tower at the 14th century Mathias Church. The view of the Danube and Pest from the tower of the nearby Fisherman's Bastion. The State Opera House. Heroes' Square. The National Gallery and Art Museum. The Railway Museum. The old stone fort.

The display of pottery, weaving, wood-carving, embroidery and costumes in the Ethnographical Museum. The 13th century Coronation Church. The exhibits of pre-history, Roman, medieval and Turkish objects in the National Museum. The Aquincum Museum. The tomb of the 16th century Turkish poet, Gul-Baba. The collection of medieval art in the museum at the Royal Palace

The view of mountains, Buda Castle, Parliament, Pest and all of the Danube bridges from the top of the 770-foot hill called Gellerthegy. Take the cogwheel railway to the tops of Varhegy (Castle Hill) and Rozadomb (Hill of Roses).

In **Pest:** The 12th century church, Belvarosi Templom. Windowshop on Vaci Ucta. The great Zoo and Central Europe's largest amusement park, both in Varosliget Park. The city's best restaurants and shops are in Pest.

Budapest - Kecskemet - Budapest 803
All these trains have meal service.

Dep. Budapest (West)	7:05 14:05	Dep. Kecskemet	15:00 19:00
Arr. Kecskemet	8:24 15:31	Arr. Budapest (West)	16:30 20:20

Sights in **Kecskemet:** Home of the ancient art of distilling barack, apricot brandy.

Budapest - Lake Balaton (Siofok and Balantonszentgyorgy) - Budapest
It is a short train and bus ride to reach Hungary's most popular resort area, the 46-mile long Lake Balaton, circled with spas, motels and campgrounds along its 118 miles of shoreline. Great sailboating and fishing here. Frequent ferries link the many towns on both sides of the lake.

Sights in **Siofok:** Many resort hotels and sidewalk cafes.

Sights in **Balatonszentgyorgy:** The attraction here is the curative carbonated water from the town's 11 mineral springs.

Sights in **Keszthely:** The Balaton Museum of the lake's natural history and the large collection of paintings and rare books in the Helicon Library at the 18th century Festetics mansion.

Sights in **Heviz:** The thermal waters. This has been famous as a health spa for more than 600 years.

799

Dep. Budapest (South)	6:45(1)	7:15	8:00(2)	11:05(2)
Arr. Siofok	8:30	9:05	10:02	13:28
Arr. Balatonszentgyorgy	9:44	-0-	12:05	15:16
	*	*	*	
Dep. Balatonszentgyorgy	14:35(1)	15:27	16:51	17:38(1)	18:43(1)
Dep. Siofok	15:51(1)	17:17	18:09	18:50(1)	20:45(1)
Arr. Budapest (South)	17:30	19:20	19:55	20:30	22:45

(1)Meal service. (2)Light refreshments.

Budapest - Szeged - Budapest 803
All of these trains have meal service.

Dep. Budapest (Ny.)	7:05(1)	Dep. Szeged	13:50 18:00(1)
Arr. Szeged	9:20	Arr. Budapest (Ny.)	16:30 20:15

(1)Reservation required.

Sights in **Szeged:** Many Summer festivals.

INTERNATIONAL CONNECTIONS FROM HUNGARY

Budapest is Hungary's gateway for rail travel to Belgrade (and on to Athens and Istanbul), Moscow, Prague (and on to Berlin and Scandinavia), Vienna (and on to the rest of Western Europe), and Zagreb (and on to Italy).

Budapest - Belgrade   791

Dep. Budapest (Keleti)	6:50(1)	16:25(1)	23:20(1+2)
Arr. Belgrade	12:50	22:36	7:53

(1)Reservation required. (2)Departs from Budapest's Nyugati railstation. Carries sleeping car. Also has couchettes.

Budapest - Moscow   806

Dep. Budapest (Keleti)	20:15(1)	23:10(2)
Arr. Moscow	7:15(3)	13:05(3)

(1)Carries sleeping car. (2)Late May to late September: runs daily. Late September to late May: runs Tuesday, Friday and Sunday. (3)Day 3.

Budapest - Prague   812

Dep. Budapest (Keleti)	-0-	-0-	14:25(2+7)	-0-
Dep. Budapest (Nyugati)	8:00	13:00(1)	-0-	15:10(3+8)
Arr. Prague (Hlavni)	16:23	22:19	0:17	4:15

(1)Meal service. (2)Reservation required. Meal service. (3)Operates mid-June to mid-September. (4)Operates late May to late September. (5)Carries sleeping car. Also has couchettes. (6)Operates late June to early September. (7)Plus other departures from Budapest Keleti at 21:15(1+4+5) and 23:30(5).   (8)Plus other departures from Budapest Nyugati at 18:05(1+5+6) and 22:25(1+3+5).

Budapest - Vienna   798

Dep. Budapest (Keleti)	9:20(1)	16:10(1)	18:30(1+2)
Arr. Vienna (Westbf.)	13:25	20:15	22:00(3)

(1)Meal service. (2)Departs from Budapest's Deli railstation. Late May to late September: runs daily. Late September to late May: runs Saturday and Sunday. (3)Arrives at Vienna's Sudbahnhof railstation.

Budapest - Zagreb   805

These trains require reservation.

Dep. Budapest (Keleti)	12:35(1)	23:25(2)
Arr. Zagreb	19:34	6:51

(1)Departs 13:05 late September to late May. (2)Operates late June to early September.

POLAND

POLISH HOLIDAYS

January 1	New Year's Day	July 22	National Day
	Easter	November 1	All Saints' Day
	Easter Monday	December 25	Christmas Day
May 1	Labor Day	December 26	Additional
	Corpus Christi		Holiday

SUMMER TIME

Poland changes to Summer Time on the last Sunday of March and converts back to Standard Time on the last Sunday in September.

POLRAILPASS

Unlimited train travel. Non-transferable. Can be purchased in Poland at any office of Polish Travel Bureau (Orbis). Also sold at Orbis offices in London, Cologne, Stockholm and New York (500 Fifth Ave., New York, N.Y. 10036). The 1984 prices for first-class are: 8 days 45(U.S.), 15 days 60, 21 days 75, one month 90. Second-class: 30, 40, 50 and 60. Children under 10 pay half-fare.

ONE-DAY EXCURSIONS AND CITY-SIGHTSEEING

Here are 9 one-day rail trips that can be made comfortably from Warsaw, returning there in most cases before dinnertime. Notes are provided on what to see at each destination. The number after the name of each route is the Cook's timetable.

Warsaw

See the priceless collection of coins, jewelry, paintings and Polish crown jewels in 15 large rooms on the second floor of the rebuilt (1974) 16th century Royal Castle, destroyed during World War II. Also, see the Sigismund Column at the Castle.

Visit the churches, houses, Barbicon Wall, Blacha Palace and the ancient market in the reconstructed Old Quarter. The University in Casimir Palace. The reconstructed "Chopin Family Drawing Room" in the side wing of the former Raczynski Palace. The very colorful changing of the guard (Sundays) in Victory Square. Lazienki, the wonderful park with its enormous Chopin monument and Island Palace. Belvedere Palace. Wilanow Park and its 18th century Palace. Contemporary art in Zacheta Museum, located in Malachowskiego Palace. The Monument to the Heroes of the Ghetto.

In the city center: The 37-story Palace of Culture and Science, highest building in Warsaw, and the view of the city and the Vistula River from the top of it. Amfora, a strolling street. The National Philharmonic Hall. Warka, the museum devoted to General Pulaski and to the Polish emigration to America. The collection of picturesque folk costumes and hand-painted furniture and dishes in the Lowicz Museum.

The Zoological Gardens. The ancient Polish weapons at the Army Museum. The Jewish Historical Museum. The Curie Museum. The City Historical Museum.

Warsaw - Czestochowa - Warsaw 845

Dep. Warsaw (Cent.)	6:29(1+2)	12:16(1)
Arr. Czestochowa	9:40	15:28

Sights in **Czestochowa:** The Black Madonna in the 14th century Jasna Gora Monastery. The 2,600-year old cemetery.

Dep. Czestochowa	12:08(2)	16:40(2)	18:05(1)	19:23(2+3)
Arr. Warsaw (Cent.)	15:52	20:21	21:19	23:29

(1)Reservation required. Meal service. (2)Meal service. (3)Operates late June to early September.

Warsaw - Gdansk - Warsaw 846

Dep. Warsaw (Cent.)	5:45(1)	Dep. Gdansk	14:37(2)	17:28(1)
Dep. Warsaw (Wsch.)	6:00(1)	Arr. Warsaw		
Arr. Gdansk	10:20	(Wsch.)	19:50	22:13
		Arr. Warsaw		
		(Cent.)	20:23	22:23

(1)Reservation required. Meal service. (2)Meal service.

Sights in **Gdansk:** A major Polish seaport. See the reconstructed Old Town. The immense Church of St. Mary. Town Hall. The Armory. Artus Mansion. The 600-pipe organ in nearby Oliwa.

Warsaw - Gdynia - Warsaw 846

Dep. Warsaw (Cent.)	5:45(1)	Dep. Gdynia	14:05(2)	17:00(1)
Dep. Warsaw (Wsch.)	6:00(1)	Arr. Warsaw		
Arr. Gdynia	10:51	(Wsch.)	19:50	22:13
		Arr. Warsaw		
		(Cent.)	20:23	22:23

(1)Reservation required. Meal service. (2)Meal service.

Sights in **Gdynia:** A leading Polish seaport.

Warsaw - Krakow - Warsaw   842

Dep. Warsaw (Cent.)	6:00(1)	Dep. Krakow	16:25(2)	18:22(1)
Arr. Krakow	10:31	Arr. Warsaw		
		(Cent.)	21:29	22:50

(1)Reservation required. Meal service. (2)Meal service.

Sights in **Krakow:** Undamaged in World War II, it is one of Europe's most beautiful Medieval towns. See such historical monuments at Wawel-Castle, with its priceless collection of tapestries. The unique 15th century carved wood altar in St. Mary's Church. The very interesting library in the 14th century Jagiellonian University.

The interior of the old Remuh Synagogue. The tombs of all of Poland's kings and queens, plus many national heroes and poets, in the 14th century Cathedral. The gold dome of Sigismund Chapel.

There are 3 guided half-day bus tours: The Museum of Martyrdom at the death camp in Oswiecim (Auschwitz). The underground sculptures, great hall, chapels, lakes and even tennis courts and a sanitarium in the 10th century salt mines at Wieliczka. The Ethnological Museum at Zubrzyca Gorna, a collection of houses typifying the lifestyles of several centuries of both peasants and wealthy people (primitive cooking utensils, elegant inlaid wood chests, furniture, etc.).

Warsaw - Lublin - Warsaw   844

All of these trains have meal service.

Dep. Warsaw (Centralna)	6:17	7:43	
Dep. Warsaw (Wschodnia)	6:39	8:20	
Arr. Lublin	9:17	11:47	

Sights in **Lublin:** One of Poland's oldest cities. Many outstanding churches. The Castle, above Lublin. The Gothic Krakowski Gate.

Dep. Lublin	11:15	18:00	20:00
Arr. Warsaw (Wschodnia)	14:55	21:58	22:44
Arr. Warsaw (Centralna)	15:27	22:19	23:02

Warsaw - Poznan - Warsaw   847

Dep. Warsaw (Gdanska)   -0-
Dep. Warsaw (Centralna)   6:59(1)
Arr. Poznan   10:38

Sights in **Poznan:** Przemyslaw Castle. The sculptures at Dzialynski Castle. Gorki Palace. Parish Church. Franciscan Church. The State Ballet School. The stained-glass at the Church of the Holy Virgin. The Cathedral. The 12th century Church of St. John of Jerusalem.

Dep. Poznan   15:10(2)   18:47(1)
Arr. Warsaw (Centralna)   -0-   22:19
Arr. Warsaw (Gdanska)   19:40   -0-

(1)Meal service. (2)Operates late May to late September.

Warsaw - Sopot - Warsaw   846

Dep. Warsaw (Cent.)	5:47(1)	Dep. Sopot	14:15(2)	17:14(1)
Dep. Warsaw (Wsch.)	6:02	Arr. Warsaw		
Arr. Sopot	10:38	(Wsch.)	19:50	22:13
		Arr. Warsaw		
		(Cent.)	20:23	22:23

(1)Reservation required. Meal service. (2)Meal service.

Sights in **Sopot:** The International Music (Jazz) Festival, every August. This is a popular beach resort on the Baltic, with concerts on the half-mile pier.

Warsaw - Torun - Warsaw   852a

These trains have meal service.

Dep. Warsaw (Cent.)	6:25	Dep. Torun	18:04
Arr. Torun	9:47 ·	Arr. Warsaw (Cent.)	21:55

Sights in **Torun:** A 13th century town on the banks of the Vistula River. The birthplace of Nicholas Copernicus in 1473. See the house where he was born. The instruments he used to determine that the earth revolves around the sun are exhibited there. Visit the ancient 3-story Town Hall. The Church of St. John contains one of the largest bells in Poland.

Warsaw - Krakow - Zakopane   842

Dep. Warsaw (Cent.)	6:00(1)	8:40(2)	17:18(1)	20:45(3+4+7)
Arr. Krakow (Gl.)	10:31	15:42	21:47	2:19(3+4)
Change trains.				
Dep. Krakow (Gl.)	10:50	17:30(6)	23:10	2:24(3+4+8)
Arr. Zakopane	15:52	21:51	4:22	6:51

Sights in **Zakopane:** Good mountain scenery. Great Winter and Summer sports. Poland's most popular health resort. Take a ride on a horsedrawn sleigh. Ride the chairlift to the top of Mt. Kasprowy.

(Timetable continues on next page.)

Dep. Zakopane	0:05	9:00	12:40	18:54(3+5+9)
Arr. Krakow (Gl.)	5:30	13:11(6)	17:25	23:35(3+5)
Change trains.				
Dep. Krakow (Gl.)	8:55(2)	16:25(2+6)	18:20(1)	23:50(3+5+10)
Arr. Warsaw (Cent.)	15:30	21:30	22:54	5:45

(1)Reservation required. Meal service. (2)Meal service. (3)Direct train. No train change in Krakow. (4)Carries sleeping car. Also has couchettes. (5)Has couchettes Warsaw-Zakopane and v.v. Carries sleeping car only Warsaw-Krakow and v.v. (6)Change trains in Krakow Plasow. (7)Plus another departure from Warsaw at 22:10(3+5). (8)Plus another departure from Krakow at 4:05(3+5). (9)Plus another departure from Zakopane at 20:50(3+4). (10)Plus another departure from Krakow at 1:00(3+4).

INTERNATIONAL CONNECTIONS FROM POLAND

Warsaw is Poland's gateway for rail travel to Berlin (and on to both Scandinavia and northwestern Europe), Moscow, and Vienna (and on to Italy, southeastern Europe and southwestern Europe).

Warsaw - Berlin   847

Dep. Warsaw (Wsch.)	6:45(1)	10:48(1)	-0-	-0-
Dep. Warsaw (Gdan.)	-0-	-0-	14:23(2)	-0-
Dep. Warsaw (Cent.)	6:59	10:56	-0-	22:49(1+3)
Arr. Berlin (Ost)	14:22	20:01	23:32	8:52

(1)Meal service. (2)Operates late May to late September. (3)Carries sleeping car.

Warsaw - Moscow

	847	48	847	847
Dep. Warsaw (Cent.)	9:32(1)	-0-	14:22(1)	-0-
Dep. Warsaw (Gdan.)	-0-	13:05(1+2)	-0-	16:50(1+4)
Dep. Warsaw (Wsch.)	10:00(1)	-0-	14:31(1)	-0-
Set your watch forward 2 hours.				
Arr. Moscow (Byel.)	8:36	10:22	11:12	15:03

(1)Carries sleeping car. Meal service. (2)Reservation required. (3)Operates late May to late September. Carries sleeping car. (4)Plus other departures from Warsaw Gdanska at (#847)17:50(1) and (#847)20:06(3).

Warsaw - Vienna   845

Dep. Warsaw (Wschodnia)	6:15(1+2)	-0-
Dep. Warsaw (Centralna)	6:30(1+2)	17:58(1+3)
Arr. Vienna (Sudbf.)	21:20	8:25

(1)Reservation required. Meal service. (2)Operates late June to early September. (3)Departs from Warsaw's Gdanska railstation. Carries sleeping car. Also has couchettes.

ROMANIA

Romania has 3 classes of trains: Rapide (the fastest), Accelerate and Personal. Avoid travel on the very slow, very crowded, very filthy "Personal" trains. Supplements are charged for travel on "Rapide" and "Accelerate" trains, except for passengers holding tickets purchased outside Romania. Reservations are required for the fast trains. To buy a Romanian timetable, ask for "Mersul Trenurillor".

ROMANIAN HOLIDAYS

January 1	New Year's Day	August 23	Liberation Day
January 2	Additional Holiday	August 24	Additional Holiday
May 1	Labor Day	December 30	Republic Day
May 2	Additional Holiday		

SUMMER TIME
Romania changes to Summer Time on the last Sunday of March and converts back to Standard Time on the last Sunday in September.

ONE-DAY EXCURSIONS AND CITY-SIGHTSEEING
Here are 5 one-day rail trips that can be made comfortably from Bucharest, returning there in most cases before dinnertime. Notes are provided on what to see at each destination. The number after the name of each route is the Cook's timetable.

Schedules for international connections conclude this section.

Bucharest
See the lakes and fountains at Cismigiu Gardens on Gheorghiu-Dej Blvd. Great paintings at the Arth Museum in the Royal Palace, the lovely Athenaeum Concert Hall, and the Folk Art Museum, all on Calea Victoriei. Near that museum, in Herastrau Park, is the city's major attraction, Village Museum (on Kisselef Ave.), featuring perfect replicas of 17th-20th century peasant homes, workplaces, shops, barns and churches, which have been moved from all over Romania to this site.

On Piata Victoriei, you will find the Statue of Soviet Heroes, the Geological Institute, the Natural Science Museum, and the Council of Ministers. Other interesting places: The Zoo. Fine paintings at the National Gallery of Art, in the former Royal Palace. A great collection of gold treasures and crown jewels in the Museum of Romanian History. The Technical Museum. The Art Collection Museum. The vast Northern Train Station, built in 1870 and restored in 1945, after World War II.

Guides at the Jewish Federation office, Strada Dmitri Rakovita 8, escort visitors to the well-preserved 200-year-old synagogue located at Strada Sfintul Veneri 9, to the kosher "soup kitchen" that is subsidized by American Jewish charities, and to the Jewish Museum.

Bucharest - Brasov - Bucharest   831

Dep. Bucharest (Nord)	6:43(1)	9:20(1+2)	10:15(1)
Arr. Brasov	9:25	12:05	13:20

Sights in **Brasov:** Excellent Transylvania Mountain scenery in this area. See the 14th century Black Church. The Museum of History. The Art Museum. The Museum of the Romanian School. A popular Winter resort, Poiana Brasov, is 9 miles from here.

Dep. Brasov	16:30(1)	17:36(1)	18:56(1)
Arr. Bucharest (Nord)	18:59	20:20	21:20

(1)Meal service. (2)Reservation required.

Bucharest - Constantza (Eforie, Mangalia) - Bucharest   827

Dep. Bucharest (Nord)	5:25(1+2)	5:45(3)	7:25(3)	
Arr. Constantza	8:11	9:05	10:40	
Dep. Constantza	8:25(1+2)	9:19(3)	-0-	
Arr. Eforie Nord	8:37	9:45	-0-	
Arr. Mangalia	9:45	10:35	-0-	
	*	*	*	
Dep. Mangalia	12:20(3)	15:35(4)	-0-	19:15(2)
Dep. Eforie Nord	13:02(3)	16:34(4)	-0-	19:59(2)
Dep. Constantza	13:35(3)	17:14(4)	18:40(3)	20:32(2)
Arr. Bucharest (Nord)	17:20	20:50	22:25	23:25(1)

Depart/Arrive Bucharest's Baneasa railstation. (2)Operates early June to early September. Meal service. (3)Light refreshments. (4)Meal service.

Sights: **Constantza** is a very large resort. **Eforie** and **Mangalia** are popular Black Sea beach resorts. In **Constantza,** see the Museum of Archaeology Parvan. The Open Air Museum of Archaeology. The Roman Mosaic. The Museum of the Black Sea.

Bucharest - Galati - Bucharest   836

These trains have light refreshments.

Dep. Bucharest (Nord)	6:10	13:30
Arr. Galati	9:35	17:18

Sights in **Galati:** The most splendid array of birdlife in all of Europe.

Dep. Galati	15:09	19:40
Arr. Bucharest (Nord)	18:48	22:47

Bucharest - Sighisoara - Bucharest 826
These trains have meal service.

Dep. Bucharest (Nord)	6:43	Dep. Sighisoara	14:44	18:33
Arr. Sighisoara	11:17	Arr. Bucharest		
		(Nord)	18:53	22:37

Sights in **Sighisoara:** The birthplace of Count Dracula. This is an interesting medieval fortress city. See the Museum of the Walled Town. Stroll through the old section.

Bucharest - Sinaia - Bucharest 831
All of these trains have meal service.

Dep. Bucharest (Nord)	6:43	9:20	10:15
Arr. Sinaia	8:25	11:03	12:22

Sights in **Sinaia:** This is a major Winter resort.

Dep. Sinaia	11:44	18:34	19:49
Arr. Bucharest (Nord)	12:17	20:10	21:20

INTERNATIONAL ROUTES FROM ROMANIA

Bucharest is Romania's gateway for rail travel to Belgrade (and on to Yugoslavia's Adriatic cities), Budapest (and on to Western Europe), Kiev (and on to Moscow and Leningrad), and Sofia (and on to Athens and Istanbul).

Bucharest - Belgrade 795
Dep. Bucharest (Nord)   22:37(1)
Arr. Belgrade (Dunav)   10:24
(1)Carries sleeping car.

Bucharest - Budapest   826+831

	831	826	826	831
Dep. Bucharest (Nord)	0:01(1+2)	-0-	-0-	9:20(5+10)
Dep. Bucharesti	-0-	6:00(3+9)	-0-	-0-
Dep. Bucharest (Chitila)	-0-	-0-	8:25(4)	-0-
Arr. Budapest (Nyugati)	-0-	21:40	-0-	-0-
Arr. Budapest (Keleti)	14:33	-0-	-0-	22:33
Arr. Budapest (Zuglo)	-0-	-0-	23:10	-0-

(1)Operates late May to late September. (2)Reservation required. Carries sleeping car. Also has couchettes. Meal service. (3)Operates mid-June to mid-September. Reservation required. (4)Operates early July to late September.

(5)Reservation required. Meal service. (6)Arrives at Budapest's Keleti railstation. (7)Reservation required. Carries sleeping car. Light refreshments. Arrives at Budapest's Nyugati 'railstation. (8)Operates mid-June to mid-September. Arrives at Budapest's Nyugati railstation.

(9)Plus another departure from Bucharesti at (#826)23:45(8).   (10)Plus other departures from Bucharest Nord at (#831)18:23(5+6) and (#826)21:45(7).

Bucharest - Kiev - Moscow

	833	834	834
Dep. Bucharest (Nord)	20:00(1)	20:28(1)	22:15(1)
Arr. Ungeni (Romanian Time)	-0-	4:18(2)	7:05(2)

Set your watch forward 2 hours.

Ungeni is the Russian border station where the wheels of the trains are changed to fit the wider Soviet rail gauge.

	833	834	834
Dep. Ungeni (Moscow Time)	-0-	7:16(2)	10:05(2)
Arr. Kiev	18:13(2)	21:00(2)	23:09(2)
Arr. Moscow	6:00(3)	9:35(3)	11:11(3)

(1)Train is sleeping cars only. (2)Day 2.   (3)Day 3.

Bucharest - Sofia - Istanbul   834

	834	834
Dep. Bucharest (Nord)	8:03(1)	22:10(2)
Arr. Sofia	18:00	8:31
Arr. Istanbul	10:30	-0-

(1)Train is sleeping cars only. (2)Carries sleeping car.

RUSSIA (U.S.S.R.—SOVIET UNION)

Children under 5 travel free. Half-fare for children 5-9. Children 10 and over must pay full fare.

There are 2 classes of trains in Russia: Soft Class (upholstered seats, which convert to large 4-berth couchette compartments) and Hard Class (plastic or leather seats, which convert to bunks either in 4-berth compartments or open non-compartment coaches). Bedding, including mattresses, is available at an extra charge for both classes.

A few important trains provide a third category of service: Sleeping Cars, with 2-berth compartments which have a folding table at the window, a closet and a speaker carrying both recorded music, which can be shut off, and announcements, which cannot be shut off. One car on the Trans Siberian Express is in this category. On these trains, for which reservations are required, conductors in each car serve Russian tea to passengers.

Through sleeping cars going to Western Europe, Scandinavia, Greece, Turkey and Iran have single and double compartments in First Class and 3-berth compartments in Second Class, all with full bedding included in the ticket price.

The only timetables available in Russia are printed in the Cyrillic alphabet. All timetables show Moscow Time, even though Russia has 9 different time zones.

Because Soviet rail tracks are 5 feet wide (along with Finland, whose rail system was constructed while Russians dominated that country), their passenger cars and compartments are considerably roomy. Good road maintenance and excellent engineers make Russian trains smooth-running.

As with all travel in Russia, your rail routes and travel dates must be predetermined and are limited to the provisions of the visa with which you enter the country. Tourists are *not* permitted to travel on many routes. For example, although the Trans Siberian Express terminates its run in Vladivostock, foreign passengers must leave the train 460 miles earlier, in Khabarovsk.

RUSSIAN HOLIDAYS

January 1	New Year's Day	November 7	Victory Day
March 8	Women's Day		(World War II)
May 1	Labor Day	November 8	Additional
May 2	Additional Holiday	Holiday	
May 9	Revolution Day	December 5	Constitution Day

478

LONG-DISTANCE TRIPS FROM LENINGRAD

Here are schedules for rail trips from Leningrad to 5 other interesting cities, with notes on what to see at each destination.

Leningrad

Russia's most interesting city. The Hermitage Museum has the world's largest exhibition of fine arts, over 2,500,000 articles. See the 112 columns, gold cupola and priceless paintings and mosaics at St. Isaac's Cathedral. The park and palace at Petrodvorets. The Winter Palace. The 600-ton, 154-foot high Alexandrovskaya Column, marking Russia's victory over Napoleon. The Peter-Paul Fortress and Cathedral. The Summer Gardens. The Museum of the History of Religion and Atheism, in Kazansky Cathedral.

Leningrad - Kiev   867

| Dep. Leningrad (Viteb.) | 11:25 | Dep. Kiev | 23:29 |
| Arr. Kiev | 16:28(1) | Arr. Leningrad (Viteb.) | 6:10(2) |

(1)Day 2.   (2)Day 3.

Sights in **Kiev:** The 11th century catacombs at the Pecherskaya Lavra Monastery. The frescos and mosaics at the 11th century St. Sophia Cathedral. The Golden Gate (Zolotiya Vorota) at the intersection of Sverlovskaya and Vladimirskaya. The Museum of Russian Art. The Museum of Western and Oriental Art.

Below are schedules for continuing on from Kiev to Odessa:

Kiev - Odessa   865

| Dep. Kiev | 8:51(1) | 21:43 | Dep. Odessa | 15:32(1) | 22:20 |
| Arr. Odessa | 18:22 | 8:32 | Arr. Kiev | 1:34 | 9:06 |

(1)Meal service.

Sights in **Odessa:** A sea resort and Russia's second largest port. See the beautiful Opera and Ballet Theater. The Potemkin Stairway, descending 455 feet from Primorsky Boulevard to the waterfront.

Leningrad - Moscow   859

| Dep. Leningrad (Mos.) | 0:10(1) | 1:20(2) | 6:44(3) | 10:36(3+6) |
| Arr. Moscow (Len.) | 8:50 | 10:12 | 14:03 | 19:04 |

(1)Meal service. (2)Second-class only. (3)Operates early June to late September. (4)Operates July 1 - August 31.   (5)Carries sleeping car.

(6)Plus other departures from Leningrad at 11:30(3), 12:52(4), 12:56, 15:38(1), 15:42(1), 20:12, 20:40(2), 21:12, 21:17, 21:53(2), 23:00, 23:10(2), 23:33, 23:55(5) and 23:59.

Sights in **Moscow:** See notes about sightseeing in Moscow under "Long-Distance Trips From Moscow", next in this section.

Leningrad - Murmansk 860

Murmansk is the world's northernmost passenger rail terminus. All arrivals shown below are on Day 2.

Dep. Leningrad			Dep. Murmansk	10:10	21:20
(Mos.)	9:12	18:59	Arr. Leningrad		
Arr. Murmansk	11:05	21:25	(Mos.)	12:30	22:55

Sights in **Murmansk:** The largest city in the world north of the Arctic Circle. Founded in 1915 as a supply post in the First World War. Valuable in World War II as Russia's principal port for receiving war supplies from Britain and the U.S. Its ice-free harbor has made Murmansk a major ship repair center and commercial fishing base.

Leningrad - Tallinn 862

Dep. Leningrad			Dep. Tallinn	7:06(1)	17:00(1+3)
(Var.)	7:00(1)	16:15(2)	Arr. Leningrad		
Arr. Tallinn	15:44	22:55	(Var.)	16:37	23:27

(1)Second-class only. (2)Plus another departure from Leningrad at 23:30.   (3)Plus another departure from Tallinn at 22:40.

Sights in **Tallinn:** A fortified town for more than 2,000 years. Once the capital (1918-1940) of Estonia, before that country was annexed by Russia. In the walled Lower Town, see the 13th century Toom Church. The 13th century Great Guildhall. The 14th century Town Hall. Ruins of the 13th century fort built by invading Danes on Toompea Hill. The Gothic churches, Niguliste and Oleviste. The old castle.

LONG-DISTANCE TRIPS FROM MOSCOW

Here are schedules for rail trips from Moscow to 10 other interesting cities, with notes on what to see at each destination.

Moscow

Red Square, with Lenin's Mausoleum. The 15th century Cathedrals: Uspensky, Blagoveshchensky and Archangelsky. The priceless jewelry,costumes, gold and silver objects, Faberge eggs, carriages and weapons in the Armory Museum (Oruzheinaya Palata). The 16th century gigantic 38-ton canon, Czar Pushka. The Grand Kremlin Palace. The 32-story Moscow University skyscraper. The Saturday and Sunday trading of birds and other pets on Kalitnikovskaya Street.

The Bolshoi Theater. The Tretyakov Gallery, with its more than 50,000 paintings and sculptures. The Lenin State Library, containing over 19 million books, magazines and manuscripts in over 160 different languages. The Zoo. The Lenin Central Museum. The Pushkin Museum of Fine Arts. Dozens of other museums.

Moscow's 9 railstations are: Byelorussian (trips to Warsaw, and on to Western Europe), Kazanski (to Tashkent and Samarkand), Kievski (to the city of Kiev, and on to Eastern Europe), Kurski (to Sochi, and on to the Caspian Sea), Leningradski (to the city of Leningrad, and on to Helsinki), Paveletski (for which Cook's lists no trains), Riga (to the city of Riga and the Baltic area), Savelovski (for which Cook's lists no trains), and Yaroslavski (across Siberia to Russia's Far East area, and to Pekin).

Moscow - Kiev   865

Dep. Moscow (Kiev.)	0:43(1)	9:21	9:47(2)	19:36(3+4)
Arr. Kiev		12:49	22:35	23:27	7:20

Sights in **Kiev:** See notes about sightseeing in Kiev earlier in this section, under "Leningrad-Kiev".

Dep. Kiev	1:51(2)	3:12(3)	5:04(2)	10:58(5)
Arr. Moscow (Kiev.)	14:00	15:02	17:23	23:48

(1)Carries sleeping car. Meal service. (2)Meal service. (3)Operates mid-May to late September. Second-class only. Meal service. (4)Plus other departures from Moscow at 20:15(2), 21:25(1), 22:10(2) and 23:01(1).   (5)Plus other departures from Kiev at 15:28(2), 18:24(1), 21:21(1) and 23:18(1).

Moscow - Leningrad   859

Dep. Moscow (Len.)	0:28(1)	7:12(2)	9:01(2)	11:31(2+5)
Arr. Leningrad (Mos.)	9:11	14:56	17:55	19:55

(1)Meal service. (2)Operates early June to late September. (3)Operates July 1 to August 31.   (4)Carries sleeping car. (5)Plus other departures from Leningrad at 12:30(3), 13:20, 16:06(1), 16:53(2), 20:38, 21:47, 23:00 and 23:55(4).

Sights in **Leningrad:** See notes about sightseeing in Leningrad earlier in this section, under "Long-Distance Trips from Leningrad".

Moscow - Riga   863

Dep. Moscow			Dep. Riga	18:01(1)	18:53(2)
(Riga)	20:20(1)	21:30(2)	Arr. Moscow		
Arr. Riga	10:26	12:15	(Riga)	9:00	10:05

(1)Carries sleeping car. Meal service. (2)Meal service.

Sights in **Riga:** An important Baltic port. The great pipe organ at the 13th-15th century Cathedral. The 14th century Riga Castle.

Moscow - Sochi - Sukhumi   874

Dep. Moscow (Kurski)	14:46(1)	19:50(1)	23:25(1)	23:59(1)
Arr. Sochi	0:35(2)	4:56(2)	9:21(2)	8:54(2)
Arr. Sukhumi	4:56(2)	8:17(2)	-0-	13:12(2)

*   *   *

Dep. Sukhumi	2:18(1)	-0-	13:35(1)	23:12(1)
Arr. Sochi	5:54(1)	9:33(4)	16:20(1)	2:10(1+3)
Arr. Moscow (Kurski)	15:05(3)	20:05(3)	4:50(2)	10:25(2)

(1)Carries sleeping car. Meal service. (2)Day 3.   (3)Day 2.   (4)Meal service.

Sights in **Sochi:** A popular Black Sea resort. Over 800 species of trees at the Dendrarium. Scenic Lake Ritsa is a 5-hour bus trip away.

Sights in **Sukhumi:** This is the heart of Russia's subtropical area: citrus fruits, tobacco, etc. See the monkey farm used by Russian scientists in their program of studying human behavior.

Moscow - Tashkent - Samarkand
5031

Dep. Moscow (Kaz.)	13:30(1)	14:00(1)	20:50(3)	22:20(1)
Arr. Tashkent	0:45(2)	5:30(2)	21:47(4)	8:10(4)

Change trains.
5032

Dep. Tashkent	10:40(5)	13:35(5+6)	16:30(5)	17:05(5)
Arr. Samarkand	18:44	21:35	1:53	0:50

(1)Meal service. (2)Day 5. (3)Operates July 1 to August 31. Second-class only. Meal service. (4)Day 4.   (5)Second-class only. (6)Train used by Intourist for foreign tourists.

Sights in **Tashkent:** This has been an important center of trade and handcraft on the major caravan route (the "silk road") between Europe and China and India for nearly 2,000 years. Many 15th and 16th century churches. Heavy Muslim cultural influence here. See: The Academy of Sciences. The Navoi Public Library. The Navoi Theater of Opera and Ballet.

Sights in **Samarkand:** One of the oldest cities in Central Asia. Alexander the Great captured Samarkand 2300 years ago. Heavy Turkish cultural influence here since the 6th century. Uninhabited from 1720 to 1770 due to an economic decline at that time caused by constant attacks by nomad tribes. The inception of train service in 1896 revived the city. See: The enormous colored domes of the 14th century mausoleums, decorated in marble and gold. The 14th century mosque. The ruins of a 16th century aqueduct.

Moscow - Sevastopol   874

Dep. Moscow (Kur.)	11:55(1)		Dep. Sevastopol	19:21(1)
Arr. Sevastopol	10:56(2)		Arr. Moscow (Kur.)	19:45(2)

(1)Operates June, July and August. Second-class only. Meal service. (2)Day 2.

Sights in **Sevastopol:** A Russian naval base since 1784. A commercial port since 1808. A railway terminal since 1875. Totally destroyed by Germans in July, 1942. Reconstructed after 1944. See the 377-foot wide panorama of the 1854 Crimean War siege by English and French forces.

Moscow - Volgograd - Rostov   Rostov - Moscow

Here is a great combination train and boat trip: from Moscow to Volgograd by train, and from Volgograd to Rostov by ship on the Volga-Don Canal. Then, return to Moscow by train.

869

Dep. Moscow (Kaz.)	14:30(1)	14:45(2)
Arr. Volgograd	10:40	11:50

(1)Carries sleeping car. Meal service. (2)Meal service.

Change to a ship. Check Intourist for current Volga-Don Canal timetables for this cruise. The complete 2,000 mile ship trip runs from Moscow to Rostov.

874   Train

Dep. Rostov	12:33(1)	13:26(1)	17:49(1)	18:51(1+3)
Arr. Moscow (Kur.)	9:35	10:25	15:05	15:45

(1)Carries sleeping car. Meal service. (2)Meal service. (3)Plus another departure from Rostov at 22:47(2).

Sights in **Volgograd:** Renamed (from Stalingrad) after being destroyed during a 7-month battle in 1942-43. See: the enormous 63-mile canal. The huge industrial complex, particularly the Tractor Factory.

Sights in **Rostov:** Another post-World War II metropolis based on heavy industrial manufacturing. See the enormous theater on Teatralnaya Square. Window-shop on Engels Street.

Here is the reverse route for this circle trip:

874

Dep. Moscow (Kur.)	8:50(1)	14:46(1)	19:50(1)	23:25(1+3)
Arr. Rostov	5:11	10:15	16:26	19:28

(1)Carries sleeping car. Meal service. (2)Meal service. (3)Plus another departure from Moscow at 23:54(2).

Change to a ship for the cruise from Rostov to Volgograd. Change to a train in Volgograd.

869

Dep. Volgograd	13:05(1)	13:55(2)
Arr. Moscow (Kaz.)	10:08	11:10

(1)Carries sleeping car. Meal service. (2)Meal service.

INTERNATIONAL ROUTES FROM RUSSIA

Here are the schedules for rail trips from Leningrad to Helsinki (and on to the rest of Scandinavia) and to Warsaw (and on to Western Europe).

Also, from Moscow to Bucharest (and on to the rest of Eastern Europe as well as to Athens and Istanbul), Khabarovsk (and on to Nakhodka, and from there to Yokohama and Hong Kong), Pekin, Tehran and Warsaw (and on to Western Europe).

Leningrad - Helsinki   855
Dep. Leningrad (Finlandski)   11:10 (Second-class only. Meal service.)
   Set your watch back one hour.
Arr. Helsinki   17:00

Leningrad - Warsaw   853
Dep. Leningrad (Varshavski)   23:45(1)
Dep. Vilnius   12:00 Day 2
   During Poland's Summer Time, set your watch back one hour (2 hours in Winter.)
Arr. Warsaw (Gdanska)   21:18
(1)Carries sleeping car. Meal service.

Moscow - (Warsaw) - Amsterdam   23+67

Dep. Moscow (Byel.)	19:19(1)		Dep. Hannover	7:04(2)
Dep. Brest	11:25		Arr. Amsterdam	11:30
Arr. Warsaw (Gdan.)	13:03			
Arr. Berlin (Zoo)	23:49			
Arr. Hannover	4:06			

   Change trains.
(1)Carries sleeping car Moscow-Hannover. Also has couchettes Warsaw-Hannover. Meal service Moscow-Brest and Warsaw-Berlin. (2)Meal service 9:34-11:30.

Moscow - Bucharest

	833	834	834
Dep. Moscow (Kiev.)	0:45(1)	21:27(1)	23:00(1)
Set your watch back 2 hours.			
Arr. Bucharest (Nord)	9:45(2)	7:35(3)	9:20(3)

(1)Train is only sleeping cars. (2)Day 2.   (3)Day 3.

Moscow - Pekin   879
Dep. Moscow (Yar.)   21:10(1) | Arr. Pekin   6:20(2)
(1)Runs Friday only. Carries sleeping car. Meal service. (2)The following Friday.

Moscow - (Warsaw - Frankfurt - Berlin - Cologne) - Paris

	847	847	847	23
Dep. Moscow (Byel.)	12:38(1)	16:00(3)	17:25(4)	19:19(5)
Dep. Brest	3:55(2)	7:30(2)	8:57(2)	11:25(2)
Arr. Warsaw (Wsch.)	-0-	8:48	10:45	-0-
Arr. Warsaw (Gdan.)	5:47	-0-	-0-	13:03
Arr. Warsaw (Cent.)	-0-	8:57	10:55	-0-
Arr. Frankfurt	14:52	-0-	18:26	-0-
Arr. Berlin (Ost)	15:59	-0-	20:01	22:52
Arr. Berlin (Zoo)	-0-	-0-	-0-	23:49
Arr. Cologne	-0-	-0-	-0-	8:08(6)
Arr. Aachen	-0-	-0-	-0-	8:53
Arr. Paris (Nord)	-0-	-0-	-0-	14:42

(1)Operates late May to late September. Carries sleeping car. (2)Day 2.
(3)Carries sleeping car. (4)Carries sleeping car. Meal service Brest-Berlin.
(5)Carries sleeping car Moscow-Paris. Also has couchettes Warsaw-Paris. Meal
service Moscow-Brest and Warsaw-Berlin Ost. Light refreshments Aachen-Paris.
(6)Day 3.

Moscow - Pyongyang   5000

Dep. Moscow (Yar.)   21:10(1) | Arr. Pyongyang   15:55(2)
(1)Runs Friday only. Carries sleeping car. Meal service. (2)The following Friday.

Moscow - Tabriz - Tehran

5025		4500	
Dep. Moscow (Kurski)	21:35(1)	Dep. Djulfa (USSR)	12:00
Arr. Baku	19:35)2)	Dep. Djulfa (Iran)	15:00
Arr. Djulfa (USSR)	7:50(3)	Dep. Tabriz	18:50(4)
		Arr. Tehran	9:45(5)

(1)Meal service daily to Baku. Carries sleeping car to Tehran on Saturday only.
This train is used by Intourist for foreign tourists. (2)Day 3.   (3)Day 4. (4)Meal
service. (5)Day 5.

Moscow - Khabarovsk - Yokohama - Hong Kong

This is the Trans-Siberian rail route.

It is advisable to stopover in Novosibirsk (population 1,500,000) and Irkutsk on the 7½-day Moscow-Khabarovsk trip. The Hotel Novosibirsk has better accommodations than are available in either Irkutsk or Khabarovsk. It is always recommended to bring toilet paper and soap when traveling on Soviet trains, including the Trans-Siberian Express.

878 (Train)		
Dep. Moscow		
(Yar.)	10:00(1)	
Arr. Novosibirsk	15:50	Day 3
Arr. Irkutsk	0:12	Day 5
Arr. Khabarovsk	0:30	Day 8
Change trains.		
Dep. Khabarovsk	18:25(2+3)	
Arr. Nakhodka	9:25(4)	Day 9
Change to boat.		
1480		
Dep. Nakhodka	12:00(5)	Day 9
Arr. Yokohama	16:00	Day 11
Dep. Yokohama	11:00(5)	Day 12
Arr. Hong Kong	16:00(6)	Day 16

1480 (Boat)		
Dep. Hong Kong	11:00(5)	
Arr. Yokohama	16:00(6)	Day 5
Dep. Yokoham	11:00(5)	Day 6
Arr. Nakhodka	17:00	Day 8
Change to train.		
878		
Dep. Nakhodka	19:50(3+7)	
Arr. Khabarovsk	11:10	Day 9
Change trains.		
Dep. Khabarovsk	13:55(1)	Day 9
Arr. Irkutsk	1:00	Day 12
Arr. Novosibirsk	9:35	Day 13
Arr. Moscow		
(Yar.)	15:05	Day 15

(1)Runs daily. Carries sleeping car. Also has second-class couchettes. Meal service. (2)Runs only on days prior to sailings from Nakhodka to Yokohama. Carries sleeping car. (3)Has only second-class coach cars for seat passengers. Meal service. (4)Day 2 after depoarture from Khabarovsk. (5)For specific sailing dates, check Cook's Continental Timetable. (6)Fifth day of boat trip. (7)Runs only on days that salings from Yokohama arrive in Nakhodka. Carries sleeping car.

Sights in **Novosibirsk:** The Theater of Opera and Ballet, which is larger than Moscow's Bolshoi Theater. Take the 18-mile bus ride to Akademgorodok, the "Science Town", located along the Ob Sea, a man-made reservoir. There, top Soviet scientists and technicians live, work and shop in the USSR's most modern apartments, office buildings and stores.

Sights in **Irkutsk:** A large industrial city with no major tourist attraction. *However,* Irkutsk is the gateway for visiting the most unique place in the Soviet Union: Lake Baykal. Buses take tourists through a virgin forest to the shore of the world's deepest (6,365 feet) lake, 380 miles long and 12 to 50 miles wide, containing one-fifth of the fresh water on the earth's surface (four-fifths of the fresh water in the U.S.S.R.). Its waves sometimes measure over 15 feet.

Formed nearly 30,000,000 years ago by a rupture in the earth's crust, it is fed by 336 rivers and streams. There are 1,800 species of animals and plants in the lake. About three-quarters of them are found nowhere else in the world.

The day-trip includes a stop at the Limnological Museum, where hundres of local flora and fauna are exhibited. The excursion to Baykal ends with a 90-minute hydrofoil ride from the Museum, up the Angara River, to Irkutsk.

Sights in **Khabarovsk:** Named after Yerofei Khabarov, a Slavak Daniel Boone who led a Cossack expedition to explore this area in the 17th century. Khabarovsk was first settled in 1858 by a handful of people living in tents along the banks of the Amur River.

When the Bolsheviks came into power in 1917, Khabarovsk was too far from Moscow for the embryonic Soviet regime to defend it, and the city was grabbed by Manchuria. Soviet rule here was re-established in 1922. By then, the old Khabarovsk had been reduced to ruins by the Manchurians. The city that exists today was started from scratch in 1922.

Its commercial air connections with Japan make Khabarovsk the Eastern gateway to the Soviet Union. Japanese tourism to Moscow and Leningrad begins and ends in Khabarovsk. The city is so geared to Japanese tourism and has so little tourism from elsewhere that several of its tourist brochures are printed only in the Japanese language.

There is a good museum here, with exhibits on the natural and political history of this area.

THE TRANS-SIBERIAN TIMETABLE

The times shown here are Moscow Time, considerably different than actual arrival and departure times as this route covers 9 time zones. For example, the real arrival time in Khabarovsk is 8 hours later than the Moscow Time listed. Also the real departure time from Khabarovsk (for the westward trip to Moscow) is 8 hours earlier than indicated. The number of travel days is represented by capital letters: A=Day 1, B=Day 2, etc.

Moscow - Khabarovsk 5020

Dep. Moscow (Yar.)	4:30 A	14:30(1) A	14:45(3) A	19:15 A
Dep. Kirov	5:13 B	9:00(2) B	9:05 B	15:35 B
Arr. Sverdlovsk	3:57 C	19:25	0:57 C	7:17 C
Dep. Sverdlovsk	5:06	19:40	1:12	7:32
Arr. Omsk	5:25 D	N/A C	17:24	22:19
Dep. Omsk	6:32	N/A	17:39	22:40
Dep. Novosibirsk	21:53	19:58	5:10 D	8:50 D
Dep. Krasnoyarsk	17:58 E	8:49 D	19:30	23:06
Arr. Irkutsk	18:54 F	4:33 E	17:22 E	21:05 E
Dep. Irkutsk	20:14	4:45	17:39	21:25
Dep. Ulan Ude	7:00 G	13:07	3:03 F	6:50 F
Dep. Chita	20:42	2318	13:50	17:53
Dep. Skovorodino	22:10 H	N/A F	14:05 G	19:10 G
Dep. Belogorsk	10:30 I	N/A G	2:13 H	7:30 H
Arr. Khabarovsk	2:10 J	22:06	15:40 H	22:40 H
	*	*	*	
Dep. Khabarovsk	2:00 A	3:55 A	6:55(1) A	21:05(3) A
Dep. Belogorsk	19:05	18:20	19:50	10:55 B
Dep. Skovorodino	8:40 B	6:35 B	7:10 B	23:52
Dep. Chita	11:35 C	7:56 C	6:54 C	0:29 D
Dep. Ulan Ude	0:02 D	19:20	17:00	11:34
Arr. Irkutsk	10:35	4:09 D	1:00 D	20:35
Dep. Irkutsk	12:16	4:27	1:15	20:50
Dep. Krasnoyarsk	14:20 E	2:54 E	20:50	18:59 E
Dep. Novosibirsk	8:32 F	18:05	9:55 E	9:18 F
Arr. Omsk	20:38	4:15 F	19:34	19:47
Dep. Omsk	21:38	4:36	19:50	20:05
Arr. Sverdlovsk	21:41 G	19:51	9:33 F	11:28 G
Dep. Sverdlovsk	23:00	20:14	9:48	11:43
Dep. Kirov	22:26 H	11:21 G	0:17 G	3:13 H
Arr. Moscow (Yar.)	0:35 J	7:20 H	15:05 G	20:50 H

(1)"Rossia". Carries sleeping car. Meal service. (2)Estimated. (3)Operates June 1 to August 31.

YUGOSLAVIA

Yugoslavian trains are classified Exspresni (express), Poslovni (rapid), Brzi (fast), and Putnicki (slow). Supplements are charged for internal express trains, except to passengers holding tickets that were issued outside Yugoslavia. Yugoslavia stays on Standard Time all year.

YUGOSLAVIAN HOLIDAYS

January 1	New Year's Day	May 9	Victory Day
January 2	Additional		(World War II)
	Holiday	July 4	Veterans Day
May 1	Labor Day	November 29	Republic Day
May 2	Additional	November 30	Additional
	Holiday		Holiday

SUMMER TIME

Yugoslavia changes to Summer Time on the last Sunday of March and converts back to Standard Time on the last Sunday of September.

ONE-DAY EXCURSIONS AND CITY-SIGHTSEEING

Here are 4 one-day rail trips that can be made comfortably from 3 major cities in Yugoslavia, returning to them in most cases before dinnertime. Notes are provided on what to see at each destination. The number after the name of each route is the Cook's timetable.

The 3 base cities are: Belgrade, Split and Zagreb.

Details on 9 other rail trips recommended for exceptional scenery and schedules for international connections conclude this section.

Belgrade

The collection of monuments to Serbian heroes in the Cathedral of the Holy Archangel Michael. The National Museum. The Kalemegdan fortress. Daman Pasha's Dome. The Museum of Medieval Frescos. The Ethnographic Museum. Many Turkish-style houses.

Split

This is a popular resort. See: The 2220-year old immense (7 acres) Palace of Diocletian, with its 7-foot thick, 72-foot high walls. Sacked in 615, only 3 of its 16 original towers remain. It is considered the largest and best preserved example of Roman palace architecture. Do not miss the fine frescos, marble pulpit and carvings in the Cathedral, which had been a mausoleum until it was converted to a church in 653. The Temple of Jupiter. The Museum of Ethnography in the Venetian Gothic Town Hall. The 12th century belfry at Our Lady of the Belfry Church.

Sarajevo

Turkish houses and mosques. The 16th century arched bridge over the Neretva River. The oriental handicrafts offered along Bascarsija, a row of small shops (silver, copper and other works).

Zagreb

Many medieval palaces. The Modern Gallery. St. Mark's Church. St. Stephen's Cathedral. The cable-car ride to Mount Sljeme.

Belgrade - Zagreb - Belgrad   781

Dep. Belgrade   5:10   7:00(1)   7:10(1)
Arr. Zagreb   11:23   12:06   12:15

Sights in **Zagreb:** See notes about sightseeing in Zagreb immediately preceding these schedules.

Dep. Zagreb   16:55   17:20(1)   18:00(1)
Arr. Belgrade   23:02   23:10   23:18

(1)Reservation required. Meal service.

Zagreb - Belgrade - Zagreb   781

| Dep. Zagreb   5:05(1) | Dep. Belgrade   15:05(1)   16:25(2)   17:40(3) |
| Arr. Belgrade   10:10 | Arr. Zagreb   19:55   22:29   23:58 |

(1)Reservation required. First-class only. Meal service. (2)Meal service. (3)Plus other departures from Belgrade at 17:50(2) and 19:50.

Sights in **Belgrade:** See notes about sightseeing in Belgrade at the start of this section.

Zagreb - Ljubljana - Zagreb   781

Dep. Zagreb   7:14(1)   8:50   8:56(1)   11:45   12:39(3)
Arr. Ljubljana   9:30   11:10   11:55   14:20   14:50

Sights in **Ljubljana:** Sampling (free) hundreds of different Yugoslav wines at the Autumn Wine Fair. Interesting Baroque churches. The Castle. Several good museums.

Dep. Ljubljana   14:00   14:25(3)   15:30(4)   16:30(1)   18:15(5)
Arr. Zagreb   16:25   16:43   17:41   18:50   20:28

(1)Operates late May to mid-October. (2)Second-class only. (3)Reservation required. Meal service. (4)Meal service. (5)Plus other departures from Ljubljana at 19:00(4), 22:15 and 22:25.

LONG-DISTANCE RAIL TRIPS IN YUGOSLAVIA

Here are some longer trips in Yugoslavia to interesting destinations:

Belgrade - Split   788

Dep. Belgrade   18:00(1)   20:25(2)
Arr. Split   7:38   8:10

Sights in **Split:** See notes about sightseeing in Split at the start of this section.

Dep. Split   19:30(2)   19:42(1)
Arr. Belgrade   8:12   9:44

(1)Operates early September to mid-June. Carries sleeping car. (2)Operates all year. Carries sleeping car. Also has couchettes.

Split - Zadar 788

| Dep. Split | 9:25 | 15:35(1) |
| Arr. Knin | 11:47 | 17:31 |

Change trains.

| Dep. Knin | 11:57(1) | 19:40(2) |
| Arr. Zadar | 13:20 | 21:40 |

* * *

| Dep. Zadar | 6:48(2) | 15:03(2) |
| Arr. Knin | 8:57 | 17:11 |

Change trains.

| Dep. Knin | 11:22(1) | 19:29(1) |
| Arr. Split | 12:14 | 21:25 |

(1)First-class only. Meal service. (2)Second-class only.

Sights in **Zadar:** One of the most beautiful towns on the Adriatic. Many Roman monuments are well-preserved here. See the 9th century St. Donat's Church. The 12th century Cathedral.

Zagreb - Split 788

| Dep. Zagreb | 6:20(1+2) | 7:12(1) | 14:30(1+2) | 21:05(3+4) |
| Arr. Split | 13:14 | 16:10 | 21:25 | 6:26 |

Sights in **Split:** See notes about sightseeing in Split at the start of this section.

| Dep. Split | 5:45(1+2) | 9:25(1) | 15:35(1+2) | 20:55(3+5) |
| Arr. Zagreb | 13:13 | 18:49 | 22:32 | 5:58 |

(1)Meal service. (2)First-class only. (3)Carries sleeping car. (4)Plus another departure from Zagreb at 21:55(3). (5)Plus another departure from Split at 22:42(3).

SCENIC RAIL TRIPS

Belgrade - Bar   793

This is the most scenic rail route in Yugoslavia. Steep canyons, turbulent rivers and mountains. The 325-mile line has 254 tunnels and 234 concrete and steel bridges. The trip climbs from the Danube to heights of 4,000 feet before descending to sea level on the Adriatic coast.

Dep. Belgrade   9:05(1)   10:20(2)   14:20(3)   20:55(4+5+6)
Arr. Bar   16:39   18:31   21:30   4:22

Sights in **Bar:** A seaport and popular tourist resort.

Dep. Bar   8:21(1)   9:52(2)   14:10(3)   20:43(4+5+7)
Arr. Belgrade   15:55   17:33   21:23   4:20

(1)Operates late June to early September. Meal service. (2)Meal service. (3)First-class only. Meal service. (4)Operates mid-June to mid-September. (5)Carries sleeping car. Also has couchettes. Light refreshments. (6)Plus another departure from Belgrade at 22:00(5). (7)Plus another departure from Bar at 22:33(5).

Belgrade - Sarajevo   786

This route involves 120 tunnels and many bridges. It gives a view of Ovcar Gorge, the Kablar Mountains and Zapadna River. Many monasteries can be seen on the hillsides. The line from Priboj is narrow-gauge as the train descends to the valley of the Rzav River.

Dep. Belgrade   7:20(1)   10:25(2)   15:15(1)   21 :45(3+4)
Arr. Sarajevo   13:06   17:30   20:55   4 :45

Sights in **Sarajevo:** See notes about sightseeing in Sarajevo at the start of this section.

Dep. Sarajevo   6:27(1)   11:40(2)   15:15(1)   21 :50(3+5)
Arr. Belgrade   12:25   18:47   21:14   5 :05

(1)Reservation required. First-class only. Meal service. (2)Meal service. (3)Carries sleeping car. Also has couchettes. Meal service. (4)Plus another departure from Belgrade at 23:35(3). (5)Plus another departure from Sarajevo at 23:00(3).

Belgrade - Skopje   790

This ride passes along many rivers and ancient Roman towns. The picturesque Juzna Morava Valley can be seen after leaving Nis.

Dep. Belgrade   9:22(1)   10:00   14:30(1)   21:30(2)   21:50(2+3+4)
Dep. Nis   13:04)1) 14:12   18:10(1)   -0-   2:03(2+3)
Arr. Skopje   16:35   17:44   21:34   8:04   5:55

Sights in **Skopje:** Daut-Pasha's Bath. St. Spas' Church. The Clock Tower. The 12th century Nerezi Monastery, with its beautiful frescos.

Dep. Skopje   9:30(1)   9:55   11:35(1)   14:45(1)   20:55(2+3+5)
Dep. Nis   13:10(1) 13:38   15:33(1)   18:05(1)   0:35(2+3)
Arr. Belgrade   17:15   18:15   19:18   21:58   5:40

(1)Meal service. (2)Carries sleeping car. (3)Has couchettes.

492

Ljubljana - Postojna - Ljubljana   785

The longest and most beautiful river cave of Europe is near Postojna, where the Pivka River flows through an underground passage. Tourists, traveling through the cave on a small train, are able to see wonderful rows of stalactites and stalagmites, gigantic underground rooms, chasms and little lakes. A 16th century castle is at the entrance to the cave.

Dep. Ljubljana   7:30   10:15   12:05   13:35(1)
Arr. Postojna   60-65 minutes later

*   *   *

Dep. Postojna   11:36   12:20   15:05   17:28   19:15   20:48(2)
Arr. Ljubljana   60-65 minutes later

(1)Runs daily, except Sundays and holidays. (2)Plus another departure from Postojna at 21:31.

Ljubljana - Jesenice - Sezana - Ljublana

There are many interesting ski resorts between Ljubljana and Jesenice in this region of the Slovenian Alps. Kranj is noted for fishing, water sports and mountaineering. Lesce-Bled (Lake Bled) is popular both Summer and Winter. All through this area there is fine scenery of evergreen forests and picturesque pastures. The most beautiful region of the Slovenian Alps is the route from Jesnice to Sezana. Here is the one-day circle trip that takes in all this area.

781			796		
Dep. Ljubljana	9:35	12:19	Dep. Nova Gorica	15:33	18:45
Arr. Kranj	10:05	12:50	Arr. Sezana	16:30	19:54
Arr. Lesce-Bled	10:29	13:18	Change trains.		
Arr. Jesenice	10:43	13:34	783		
Change trains.			Dep. Sezana	18:20	20:00
796			Arr. Ljubljana	20:15	22:00
Dep. Jesenice	11:10	14:20			
Arr. Nova Gorica	13:05	16:12			
Change trains.					

Sarajevo - Dubrovnik   786

There is scenery reminiscent of Norway's fjords and one of the most beautiful train rides in Yugoslavia on the Mostar-Kardeljevo portion of the trip from Sarajevo to Dubrovnik.

Dep. Sarajevo	5:15(1)	7:05(1)	8:40	15:00(3)	18:30(1+4)
Dep. Mostar	7:25(1)	9:12(1)	10:49	16:40(3)	20:31(1)
Arr. Kardeljevo	8:23	10:18	11:47'	17:27	21:32

Change to the local bus for the trip from Kardeljevo to Dubrovnik.

Dep. Kardeljevo	8:55	10:35	12:35	19:50	23:35
Arr. Dubrovnik	10:50	12:30	14:30	21:45	1:30

Sights in **Mostar:** The Old Quarter is very Turkish, with an open-air market, a mosque and cobblestoned streets. See the arched bridge the Turks built in 1566, using a mortar of eggs, butter and cheese ! Dine and drink at the Labyrinth Bar, under the bridge.

Sights in **Dubrovnik:** One of Europe's most popular beach resorts. See the 4 ancient forts. The 15th century Rector's Palace. Prince's Court. St. Blaise's Cathedral. Sponza Palace. St. Vlah's Church. The Dominican and Franciscan Cloisters. The beautiful 600-year old pharmacy at St. Francis' Monastery. Shop on Stradun (a pedestrian mall) for sheepskin coats, coral jewelry, hand-woven rugs, filigree, lace, embroidery and leather items. Walk on the top of the city walls.

Bus

Dep. Dubrovnik	5:00	11:00	14:00	16:00
Arr. Kardeljevo	6:55	12:55	15:55	17:55

Change to train.

Dep. Kardeljevo	7:45(2)	13:50(1)	17:15(1)	18:05(1)
Dep. Mostar	9:13(2)	14:59(1)	18:32(1)	19:16(1)
Arr. Sarajevo	12:07	17:11	20:28	21:15

(1)Meal service. (2)Second-class only. (3)First-class only. Meal service. (4)Plus another departure from Sarajevo at 22:25(2).

Split - Sunja - Zagreb

Between Knin and Sunja, this route passes through gorges and the valley of the Una River. There is excellent scenery of thick forests as the train passes from one bank of the river to the other.

Schedules for this trip appear earlier in this section, under "Long-Distance Trips".

INTERNATIONAL ROUTES FROM YUGOSLAVIA

There are rail connections from Belgrade to Athens (and on to Istanbul), Bucharest (and on to Kiev and Moscow), Budapest (and on to Moscow, Prague, Vienna and Warsaw), Salzburg (and on to the rest of Western Europe and to Scandinavia), Sofia (and on to Athens and Istanbul), and to Venice (and on to the rest of Italy and Southern Europe).

Belgrade - Athens   15+891
Dep. Belgrade   9:22(1)   14:40(1+3)   23:55(4)
    Set your watch forward one hour.
Arr. Athens (Larissa)   9:00(2)   14:41(2)   23:06(2)
(1)Meal service on Day 2. Carries sleeping car some days. (2)Day 2.   (3)Has couchettes. (4)Meal service on Day 2 15:06-23:06. Supplement charged in Greece. Has couchettes.

Belgrade - Bucharest   795
Dep. Belgrade (Dunav)   18:00   Carries sleeping car.
    Set your watch forward one hour.
Arr. Bucharest (Nord)   8:29

Belgrade - Budapest   791
Dep. Belgrade   7:28   15:25   21:25(1)
Arr. Budapest (Keleti)   13:20 21:43   6:12(2)
(1)Carries sleeping car. Also has couchettes. (2)Arrives at Budapest's Nyugati railstation.

Belgrade - Sofia   792
Dep. Belgrade   9:32(1)   13:20   14:40(2)
    Set your watch forward one hour.
Arr. Sofia   19:30   23:15   23:54
(1)Operates mid-April to late September. (2)Operates late September to mid-April.

Belgrade - Venice   783
Dep. Belgrade   7:00(1)   20:00(2)
Arr. Venice (S.L.)   21:52   11:07
(1)Reservation requirted. Meal service until 14:50.   (2)Reservation required. Carries sleeping car. Also has couchettes.

Chapter 10

THE MIDDLE-EAST

AFGHANISTAN

There are no passenger trains in Afghanistan.

BAHRAIN

There are no passenger trains in Bahrain.

IRAN

Five rail routes radiate from Tehran: (west to Tabriz (and on to both Russia and Turkey), south to Khorramshahr on the Persian Gulf (and on to Iraq), southeast to Zarand (with a spur to Isfahan, a popular tourist resort), and west to both Mashhad and Gorgan. A short line runs from Zahedan into Pakistan.

The country's oldest rail line has been operating only 50 some years. The rail service to Turkey was completed in 1971. Engineering and equipment are both highly modern.

First-class rail fares are nearly double the price for second-class tickets and 3 times the price of third-class. Third-class has only wood or plastic seats. Children under 7 travel free. Half-fare for children 7-13. Children 14 and over must pay full fare. Sleeping cars and couchettes are available on trains to Turkey and to the USSR.

Tehran

See: The museums in the fantastic Shahyad Monument, built to commemmorate Iran's 2500th anniversary, only a few years ago. The 6-mile labyrinth of the city's Bazaar. The House of Strength. Gulistan Palace. The 19th century Sepahsalar Mosque. Shah Mosque. The Crown Jewels Museum in Markazi Bank.

The gardens and museums of Golestan Palace. The Ethnological Museum. The Archaeological Museum. The Mausoleum of Reza Shah The Great. The Marble Palace. The Decorative Art Museum. The National Art Museum.

Take a one-day excursion to the Shemshak ski resort or to see carpet-washing in the Cheshmeh Ali Stream.

Tehran - Tabriz   4500

There is much mountain scenery on this ride. Tabriz is the gateway for rail travel to Turkey (see "International Routes From Iran" later in this section).

Dep. Tehran	18:00(1)	Dep. Tabriz	18:50(1)
Arr. Tabriz	8:25	Arr. Tehran	9:45

(1)Meal service. Air-conditioned in first-class. Carries sleeping car on Wednesday from Tehran, on Tuesday from Tabriz.

Sights in **Tabriz:** This is one of the major carpet producing areas in Iran. A popular Summer resort. Do not fail to see the fantastic 15th century Blue Mosque.

Tehran - Khorramshahr   4506

Fine mountain scenery on this journey. Khorramshahr is the gateway for rail travel to Iraq (see "International Routes From Iran" later in this section).

Dep. Tehran	12:20(1)
Arr. Andimeshk	3:15
Arr. Karun	6:35
Arr. Khorramshahr	N/A(2)

Sights in **Khorramshahr:** An important port. Many date palm groves in this area.

Dep. Khorramshahr	N/A(2)
Dep. Karun	10:25(1)
Dep. Andimeshk	13:40
Arr. Tehran	5:05

(1)Second-class only. (2)Service on the 73-mile trip Karun-Khorramshahr and v.v. was "temporarily" suspended in 1981.

Tehran - Zarand   4505

Dep. Tehran	17:00(1+2)	Dep. Zarand	17:55(1+3)
Arr. Zarand	10:00	Arr. Tehran	11:25

(1)Air-conditioned in first-class. (2)Monday, Wednesday and Friday. (3)Tuesday, Thursday and Saturday.

Tehran - Esfahan   4505

This is the schedule for the spur to Esfahan off the Tehran-Zarand route.

Dep. Tehran	21:10(1+2)	Dep. Esfahan	21:25(1+3)
Arr. Esfahan	6:15	Arr. Tehran	7:05

(1)Air-conditioned. (2)Tuesday, Thursday and Sunday. (3)Monday, Wednesday and Friday.

Sights in **Esfahan:** A popular tourist resort. See: The blue enameled domes of the mosques. Ali Qapu Palace. The breathtaking frescoes at the Palace of Four Columns. The ancient Friday Mosque. The Theological School. The Bazaar. The tiered bridges. Wonderful textiles, rugs and tiles can be purchased here. Esfahan carpets are magnificent.

Tehran - Neyshabur - Mashhad   4504

Excellent mountain scenery on this trip.

Dep. Tehran	12:45(1)	15:45(2)
Dep. Meyshabur	4:20	5:45
Arr. Mashhad	7:00	7:50

Sights in **Neyshabur:** The birthplace and burial site of Omar Khayyam, Persia's famous astronomer, mathematician and poet.

Sights in **Mashhad:** The holiest city in Iran. Its great gold-domed shrine contains the Tomb of Imam Reza. Also see: Gowhar Shad Mosque. The Tomb of Nader Shah. Mashhad Museum.

Dep. Mashhad	10:45(1)	14:30(2+3)
Dep. Neyshabur	13:20	16:40
Arr. Tehran	5:00	6:55

(1)Third-class only. (2)Second-class only. (3)Runs Monday, Wednesday and Friday.

Tehran - Gorgan   4503

Dep. Tehran	7:30(1)	20:15(2)	Dep. Gorgan	5:55(3)	18:10(4)
Arr. Gorgan	19:40	7:20	Arr. Tehran	18:40	6:00

(1)Runs Monday, Wednesday and Saturday. (2)Air-conditioned. Runs Tuesday, Thursday and Sunday. (3)Runs Tuesday, Thursday and Sunday. (4)Air-conditioned. Runs Monday, Wednesday and Friday.

Sights in **Gorgan:** This city was rebuilt after being destroyed in an earth-quake during the 1930's.

Tabriz - Djulfa   4500

Dep. Tabriz	8:00(1)	Dep. Djulfa	15:00(1)
Arr. Djulfa	11:45	Arr. Tabriz	18:30

(1)Air-conditioned.

INTERNATIONAL ROUTES FROM IRAN

The gateway for train travel from Iran to both Turkey and Russia is Tabriz. The route to Iraq begins at Khorramshahr. A line starting in Zahedan leads into Pakistan.

Tehran - Tabriz - Haydarpasa - Istanbul   4021

Dep. Tehran	N/A(1)	Dep. Tatvan Pier	N/A(3)
Dep. Tabriz	N/A(1)	Dep. Tatvan	6:35(4)
Set your watch back 30 minutes.		Arr. Ankara	15:50(5)
Dep. Kapikoy	N/A(2)	Dep. Ankara	16:25
Arr. Van Pier	N/A(2)	Arr. Haydarpasa	5:16(6)
Change to ferry.			
Dep. Van Pier	N/A(3)		
Arr. Tatvan Pier	N/A(3)		
Change to train.			

Boat to Istanbul
4025

Dep. Haydarpasa   Frequent times from 6:00 to 24:00 for the 20-minute boat trip to Istanbul. When making connections for trains, allow at least 4 hours.

(1)Service "temporarily" suspended in 1981. (2)Service "temporarily" suspended in 1983. (3)No information about this service was available in 1983. (4)Runs Tuesday, Thursday and Saturday. Has couchettes. Also carries sleeping car on Tuesday and Thursday. Meal service. (5)Day 2 from Tatvan. (6)Day 3 from Tatvan.

Tehran - Tabriz - Moscow

4500		Arr. Djulfa (USSR)	15:00(2)
Dep. Tehran	18:00(1)	Change your watch	
Dep. Tabriz	8:00(2)	to Moscow time.	
Arr. Djulfa (Iran)	11:45(2)	5025	
		Dep. Djulfa (USSR)	21:00(3)
		Arr. Moscow	5:45(4)

(1)Air-conditioned in first-class. Meal service. Carries sleeping car on Wednesday. (2)Day 2. (3)Wednesday only. Carries sleeping car. (4)Day 4 from Djulfa.

Khorramshahr - Abadan - Seeba - Basra - Baghdad   4506+4507+4150

See notes earlier in this section with "Tehran-Khorramshahr" schedules. The 14-mile bus service from Khorramshahr to Abadan was suspended in 1981. A motor launch used to make the 15-minute boat trip from Abadan to Seeba, Iraq. From Seeba, there once was bus service for the 25-mile ride to Basra. There was a 4-hour bus service from Basra to Kuwait (for which times have not been available since 1981) and also a boat that operated according to demand, without a regular schedule. The Basra-Baghdad services appear in the next section, on Iraq.

Zahedan - Quetta   5942

This is the rail route from Iran into Pakistan. The Zahedan railstation is 2 miles east of the city.

Dep. Zahedan   7:00   Fridays only. Meal service.
Arr. Quetta   19:15   Day 2 (Saturday)

IRAQ

Iraq's 2 rail routes are the standard-gauge line extending south from Baghdad to Basra and north to Mosul, plus a narrow-gauge line running north from Baghdad to Jalawla. The latter line forks at Jalawla, one line running further north to Khankin, the other going northwest to Erbil.

Iraqi trains have 3 classes of space: first, tourist and second on standard gauge lines; and first, second and third on metre (narrow) gauge lines. First-class and second-class seats convert into berths for overnight travel. Children under 4 travel free. Half-fare for children 4-9. Children 10 and over must pay full fare.

Baghdad

More than 100 mosques and minarets here, including the spectacular gold-domed Kazimayn Mosque. The 13th century Abbasid Palace and its museum. The 13th century Mustansiriyah law college. The selection of copper, cloth and silver in the many bazaars. The collection of Arabic history and literature at the Library of Waqfs. The Central Library of Baghdad University__The Costumes and Ethnographic Museum. The Iraq Museum. The Iraq Natural History Museum. The Museum of Arab Antiquities. The National Museum of Modern Art. Nearby, the tombs of 2 imams.

Baghdad - Basra   4157

This scenic route follows the Tigris River to the Persian Gulf.

Dep. Baghdad (West)   20:30(1)   21:30(2)
Arr. Basra (Ma'qil)   5:03   6:15

Sights in **Basra:** This is a prominent river harbor. Many date palm groves in this area.

Dep. Basra (Ma'qil)   20:30(1)   21:30(2)
Arr. Baghdad (West)   5:15   6:15

(1)Air-conditioned space available at extra charge in both first-class and tourist-class. (2)Second-class only.

Baghdad - Mosul 4155

Dep. Baghdad (West)	22:00(1)	Dep. Mosul	22:00)1)
Arr. Mosul	6:35	Arr. Baghdad (West)	6:35

(1)Air-conditioned space available at extra charge in both first-class and tourist-class.

Sights in **Mosul:** The ruins of ancient Nineveh are near here. The word "muslin" came from the production here once of fine cotton goods. See: The Great Mosque and its leaning minaret. The 13th century Red Mosque.

Baghdad - Kirkuk - Erbil 4156

A very scenic trip through the Iraqi mountains. Tourists are not permitted beyond Kirkuk, as Erbil is a military installation.

Dep. Baghdad (East)	7:35	Dep. Erbil	12:00(1)
Arr. Kirkuk	18:45	Arr. Kirkuk	16:00
Change trains.		Change trains.	
Dep. Kirkuk	5:30(1)	Dep. Kirkuk	7:00
Arr. Erbil	9:30	Arr. Baghdad (East)	17:45

(1)Second and third-class space only.

Sights in **Erbil:** This area has been inhabited continuously since 3,000 B.C. There is a famous fortress here, on a high mound.

INTERNATIONAL ROUTES FROM IRAQ

There is train service from Iraq to Turkey, Syria and Iran.

Baghdad - Haydarpasa   4020

Dep. Baghdad (West)	21:00(1)	Monday and Friday
Dep. El Yaroubieh	12:26	Tuesday and Saturday
Dep. Gaziantep	8 :10(2)	Wednesday and Sunday
Dep. Ankara	8 :40	Thursday and Monday
Arr. Haydarpasa	18:25	Same day as Ankara departure

(1)Carries sleeping car. (2)Meal service from Gaziantep to Haydarpasa

Baghdad - Kamechlie - Halab (Aleppo)   4075

Dep. Baghdad (West)	21:00	Monday and Friday
Arr. Kamechlie	11:33	Tuesday and Saturday
Arr. Halab (Aleppo)	19:14	Same day as Kamechlie arrival

Baghdad - Basra - Tehran   4157

Dep. Baghdad (West)	20:30(1)	21:30(2)
Arr. Basra (Ma'qil)	5:03	6:15

Sights in **Basra:** This is a prominent river harbor. Many date palm groves in this area.

From Basra, there once was bus service for the 25-mile ride to Seeba. A motor launch used to make the 15-minute boat trip from Seeba to Abadan. The 14-mile bus service from Abadan to Khorramshahr was suspended in 1981. Fine mountain scenery on the ride from Khorramshahr to Tehran.

4506

Dep. Khorramshahr	N/A(1)
Arr. Tehran	N/A(1)

(1)Service was "temporarily" suspended in 1981.

ISRAEL

Plan carefully rail trips in Israel to avoid the crowded conditions on public holidays and Friday afternoons and the suspension of nearly all transportation service from Friday sunset to Saturday sunset in conformance with the Jewish sabbath, which causes heavy traffic on Friday afternoons.

The country's principal train route is south from Haifa, to Tel Aviv, Beer-sheva and Dimona. Its west-east line goes from Tel Aviv to Lod and Jerusalem.

There are *no* rail connections between Israel and countries adjacent to it.

The heaviest passenger train traffic in Israel is during August. Lightest is in February. Israel Railways urges tourists to make advance seat reservations at all times. Children under 4 travel free. Half-fare for children 4-9. Children 10 and over must pay full fare.

Although Israel is very small in size, there are more than 40 railstations on its routes. Summer timetables are in effect from late June to early September. All times given here are Summer schedules.

ISRAELI PRICE REDUCTIONS

There are several price reductions on Israeli trains: to organized groups of 20 or more adults (25%), to organized groups of 10 or more children up to the age of 18 (50%), to students having an International Student Card (25%), for women over 60 and men over 65 (25%), and for children from the age of 4 to 9 (50%). Children under 4 years of age travel free.

In order to obtain the various reductions, application must be made in writing at least 3 days in advance of travel date to the Station Master of the starting station or to the office of Traffic and Commercial Manager, Israel Railways, P.O. Box 44, Haifa, Israel.

Seats can be reserved for trips from Haifa, Jerusalem and Tel Aviv.

Railrover   Unlimited train travel for one calendar month. Costs $12(US). Can be purchased only *outside* Israel.

Haifa - Tel Aviv   4004
All of these trains have meal service.
Dep. Haifa (Merkaz)   5:54(1)   6:24(1)   7:24(1)   8:24(1+3)
Dep. Haifa (Bat Galim)6   minutes later
Arr. Tel Aviv (Merkaz)   80 minutes after departing Merkaz station

Sights in **Haifa:** This is Israel's main port. See the Bahai Shrine and Gardens, open 9:00-12:00. The Museum of Prehistory, a Nature Museum and Zoo complex, open Sunday-Thursday 8:00-14:00, Fridays 8:00-12:00, Saturdays 9:00-14:00. The collection of Islamic folk art and costumes at the Museum of Ethnology, open 10:00-13:00 every day, plus 17:00-19:00 on Monday and Wednesday.

Sights in **Tel Aviv:** One of the oldest cities in the world. See: The Helena Rubenstein Pavillion. The art at the Tel Aviv Museum. The exhibit of coins, folklore, science and technology at the Ha-aretz Museum complex. The view from the observation terrace of the Shalom Building. The fascinating museum of the Jewish underground movement of the 1930's and 1940's, in the Bet Jabotinsky Building on King George Street.

The Museum of the Diaspora, recounting the cultural, social and religious events of those Jews who settled in different countries all over the world between 70 A.D. and the 20th century. Open daily, except Friday and Saturday, 10:00-17:00. There are guided tours in English, Hebrew and many other languages. The exhibits are in the categories of Family, Community, Faith, Culture, Among The Nations, Return and Martyrdom.

Located on the campus of Tel Aviv University, this museum is reached by Bus #25 from the beachfront hotels, or by taxi.

Models of 20 famous synagogues (including the 18th century one in Newport, Rhode Island) are part of the "Faith" exhibit. One of the dioramas in the "Community" section is an array of more than 100 figures re-enacting life in a 13th century German village.

Take a 20-minute bus ride to Jaffa, the ancient port, and browse in the artists' colony there.

One-day bus tours from Tel Aviv go to the occupied Golan Heights (Thursday); the northwestern frontier at Rosh Hanikra, the ruins at Caesarea, and remains of the Crusaders at Acre (Tuesday, Friday and Sunday); Christian holy sites (Monday, Wednesday and Saturday); and to the Dead Sea plus a 1,000-foot ascent by cable car to the Masada fortress (daily except Fridays).

Dep. Tel Aviv (Merkaz)	6:00(1)	7:00(1)	8:00(1)	9:00(1+4)
Arr. Haifa (Bat Galim)	74 minutes later			
Arr. Haifa (Merkaz)	6 minutes after departing Bat Galim station			

(1)Daily, except Sat. (2)Daily, except Fri. and Sat. (3)Plus other departures from Haifa at 9:54(1), 11:24(1), 12:24(1), 13:24(1) 14:24(1), 15:24(2), 16:24(2), 17:24(2) and 19:24(2).   (4)Plus other departures from Tel Aviv at 10:30(1), 12:00(1), 13:00(1), 14:00(1), 15:00(2), 16:00(2), 17:00(2), 18:30(2) and 20:00(2).

Tel Aviv - Beersheva - Dimona   4005

All of these trains have meal service.

Dep. Tel Aviv (Benei Beraq)	8:18(1)	-0-	-0-
Dep. Tel Aviv (Darom)	-0-	11:30(2)	16:00(3)
Arr. Naan	9:19	11:59	16:32
Change trains.			
Dep. Naan	N/A(4)	N/A(4)	N/A(4)
Arr. Beersheva	N/A(4)	N/A(4)	N/A(4)
Arr. Dimona	N/A(4)	N/A(4)	N/A(4)

Sights in **Beersheva:** This modern desert town is the location where Abraham rested on his way south.

Dep. Dimona	N/A(4)	N/A(4)	N/A(4)
Dep. Beersheva	N/A(4)	N/A(4)	N/A(4)
Arr. Naan	N/A(4)	N/A(4)	N/A(4)
Change trains.			
Dep. Naan	8:49(3)	12:43(2)	17:11(3)
Arr. Tel Aviv (Darom)	9:30	-0-	-0-
Arr. Tel Aviv (Benei Beraq)	-0-	13:38	18:03

(1)Daily, except Friday and Saturday. (2)Friday only. (3)Daily, except Saturday. (4)Service "temporarily" suspened in 1981.

Tel Aviv - Lod - Jersualem   4005

This ride through the Judean wilderness, in operation since 1892, is the most scenic train trip and most exciting travel experience in Israel.

The train winds from the Mediterranean coast through orange groves before climbing into the Judean mountains, covered with pine and cypress trees. Then it passes Zor'a and Eshtaol and the Valley of Sorek, where Samson lived and met Delilah, according to the Bible.

Next, this route goes through a breach in the wall the Romans built around Bittir (called Beitar in biblical days), where Simeon Bar Kochba in 135 A.D.led the unsuccesful second Jewish revolt against the Romans, marking the begin ning of the long Jewish diaspora.

All of these trains have meal service.

Dep. Tel Aviv (Darom)	8:18(1+2)	11:30(3)	16:00(4)
Dep. Lod	9:00(2)	11:47(3)	16:17(4)
Arr. Jerusalem	10:35	13:20	17:45
	*	*	*
Dep. Jerusalem	7:30(4)	11:30(3)	16:00(4)
Dep. Lod	9:05(4)	12:57(3)	17:27(4)
Arr. Tel Aviv (Darom)	9:30	13:38(1)	18:03(1)

(1)Depart/Arrive Tel Aviv's Benei Beraq railstation. (2)Daily, except Friday and Saturday. (3)Fridays only. (4)Daily, except Saturday.

Sights in **Jerusalem:** The Western (Wailing) Wall of the Temple Mount. The Dome of the Rock (Mosque of Omar). The el-Aska Mosque. The Church of the Holy Sepulchre. The 14 stations of the cross, along Via Dolorosa. Colorful oriental markets.

Mount Zion, with the Tomb of the House of David, Cenacle (the room of the Last Supper), and the Abbey of the Dormition.

The Tombs of the Sanhedrin. En Karem, birthplace of John the Baptist. The Chagall stained-glass windows, depicting the Tribes of Israel, at the Synagogue of the Hadassah Medical Center.

The Bezalel National Art Museum, Samuel Bronfman Biblical and Ar chaeological Museum, and Billy Rose Art Garden, all in the Israel Museum complex. Alongside it, the Shrine of the Book, housing the Dead Sea Scrolls, open Sun., Mon., Wed. and Thurs. 10:00-17:00 and Tues. 10:00 to sunset.

The Knesset (Israel's Parliament) and the President's Garden, opposite the Israel Museum. The Biblical Zoo. The Kennedy Memorial. Yad Vashem Holocaust Memorial, open Sunday-Thursday 9:00-16:45 and Friday 9:00-14:00. The Middle-East archaeology collection in the Rockefeller Museum, open Sunday, Tuesday and Thursday 10:00-17:00 and Saturday 10:00-14:00

Southwest of the city are the ancient Jewish cemetery at the Mount of Olives and the Christian shrines at the Garden of Gethsemane. Below the Mount of Olives: Absalom's Pillar, the Tomb of Zechariah, and the toms of Bnei Hezir.

Northeast of the city are the Tombs of the Kings of Judah, the Garden Tomb, the Tomb of Simon the Just, the Cave of King Zedekiah (also known as Solomon's Quarries).

Haifa - Lod - Jerusalem   4005
All of these trains have meal service.

Dep. Haifa (Merkaz)	6:54(1)	-0-	-0-
Dep. Lod	9:00(1)	11:47(2)	16:17(3)
Arr. Jerusalem	10:35	13:20	17:45
	*	*	*
Dep. Jerusalem	7:30(3)	11:30(2)	16:00(3)
Dep. Lod	9:05(3)	12:57(2)	17:27
Arr. Haifa (Merkaz)	-0-	15:03	19:30

(1)Daily, except Fri. and Sat. (2)Fri. only. (3)Daily, except Sat.

KUWAIT
There are no passenger trains in Kuwait.

JORDAN
Children under 4 travel free. Half-fare for children 4-9. Children 10 and over must pay full fare.

Jordan's only national railway (Amman to Ma'an), has not operated regularly since British and Arab armies destroyed it in 1917.

There is Syrian-operated rail service from Amman to Damas (Damascus), which continued on to Beirut(Lebanon)prior to 1982. There is no other rail connection between Jordan and countries adjacent to it. The rail route from Ma'an to Aqaba is primarily for freight. However, Jordan provides small 8-seat railcars on this line under "charter" arrangements.

Amman   See the remains of the ancient fort. Next to it, the Archaeological Museum and the Roman Amphitheater.

Amman - Damas (Damascus)   4079

Dep. Amman	8:00(1)	Dep. Damas	8:10(1)
Arr. Damas	13:37	Arr. Amman	14:14

(1)Runs Monday and Friday. (2)Runs Thursday and Sunday.

LEBANON

Beirut
Lebanon's major port. There are many art galleries and public gardens here.

Beirut - Damascus   4103   Bus

Dep. Beirut	N/A(1)	Dep. Damascus	N/A(1)
Arr. Damascus	N/A	Arr. Beirut	N/A

Beirut - Tripoli - Aleppo (Halab)   4076

Dep. Beirut (St.M.)	N/A(1)	Dep. Aleppo (Halab)	11:30(2)
Dep. Tripoli	N/A(1)	Arr. Homs	16:51(2)
Dep. Homs	13:50(2)	Arr. Tripoli	N/A(1)
Arr. Halab (Aleppo)	19:00(2)	Arr. Beirut (St. M.)	N/A(1)

(1)Service was suspended in 1978. (2)Service was suspended in 1982.

Sights in **Tripoli:** A major port. Popular beach resort. See: The 14th century Teynal Mosque. The 13th Century Great Mosque. The 15th century Tower of the Lions.

OMAN
There are no passenger trains in Oman.

PAKISTAN
There are 3 classes of train travel here: air-conditioned, first-class and second-class. The first 2 classes are convertible into sleeping compartments for night travel. Advance application is recommended to reserve bedding rolls in air-conditioned class. Higher fares are charged for second-class space in fast trains than for second-class in ordinary trains. Reservations are recommended for all overnight and long-distance journeys. All of Pakistan's express trains have meal service. Children under 3 travel free. Half-fare children 3-11. Children 12 and

over must pay full fare. Most trains in Pakistan provide "special ladies' accommodation" which both male and female children under 12 may use if they are traveling with a female relative.

Passengers in air-conditioned coaches can obtain (at extra charge) bedding, soap, toilet paper and a towel.

Private cars can be rented. They are air-conditioned and have a dining-room, kitchen and servants' quarters as well as private bedrooms and drawing rooms.

The 3 major train routes in Pakistan are from Karachi: northeast to Lahore, north to Peshawar, and northwest to Quetta.

Karachi

This is a natural harbor. See: Burns Gardens. The Ghanshyam Art Center. The Zoo in Ghandi Gardens. Good swimming and fishing beaches.

The 270-acre Botanical Garden. The National Museum, with its Greco-Buddhist art, near Cantonment Railstation. Adamji Mosque. The Memorial Museum. Mamon Mosque. The Hindu Temple. Jahangir Park. You will find every thing from mangos to silver anklets in these typical Eastern bazaars: Juna, Khajoor, Jodia, Sarafa and Bahri. See Fire Temple. Islamia College. "Mazaar", the Mausoleum of Quaid-E-Azam Mohammad Ali Jinnah, who guided Pakistan to independence.

Karachi - Hyderabad   5905

Dep. Karachi (Canton.)	4:30	10:00(1)	10:46(1+2+5)
Arr. Hyderabad	7:32	12:22	13:35

Sights in **Hyderabad:** Much lacquerware, ornamented silks and items of gold and silver are made here. See the large 18th century fort. The 1½-mile-long Shahi Bazaar, running from the fort to the Market Tower. The old palaces. The tombs of ancient rulers.

Dep. Hyderabad	2:48(3)	4:02(1+4)	5:04(1+4+6)
Arr. Karachi (Canton.)	6:40	7:25	8:33

(1)Reservation required. Meal service. (2)Carries air-conditioned coach car. (3)Reservation required. (4)Carries air-conditioned restaurant car. (5)Plus other departures from Karachi at 11:31(1+2), 16:30(1+2), 17:00(1+2+4), 17:20, 19:26(1+2), 21:00(1+2) and 21:30.   (6)Plus other departures from Hyderabad at 6:06(1+2+4), 7:12(1+2), 9:40(1), 13:12(1+2), 13:46(1), 15:25 and 16:00(1+2).

Karachi - Lahore   5905

| Dep. Karachi (Canton.) | 6:00(1+2+3) | 10:00(1+8) |
| Arr. Lahore | 22:00 | 5:15 |

* * *

| Dep. Lahore | 6:00(1+2+4) | 9:30(1+5+6+9) |
| Arr. Karachi (Canton.) | 22:00 | 7:25 |

(1)Reservation required. Meal service. (2)Carries only air-conditioned coach cars. (3)Runs Wednesday and Saturday. (4)Runs Monday and Friday. (5)Carries air-conditioned sleeping car. (6)Air-conditioned coach space, at an extra charge, can be reserved. (7)Carries air-conditioned restaurant car. (8)Plus other departures from Karachi at 10:46(1+5+6), 16:30(1+2), 17:00(1+6) and 21:00(1+5+6).   (9)Plus other departures from Lahore at 14:20(1+5+6+7), 16:30(1+2), 17:25(1), 19:40(1) and 21:08(1+5+6).

Sights in **Lahore:** Pakistan's second-largest city. Often called "the city of gardens". This is a busy rail center, with 10,000,000 passengers handled here every year.

See the complex of 16th-18th century palaces and halls inside Lahore Fort. The Shish Mahal (Palace of Mirrors) with its fretted screens, colored mirrors and marble. The museum of 18th and early 19th century maps, drawings and weapons. The small Moti Masjid Mosque. The royal apartments and throne room. The marble hall, Diwan-i-Khas.

At one of the world's largest places of worship, across from the Fort (on the other side of Hazuri Bagh Square), see the marble ornamentation at the Badshahi (Imperial) Mosque. Its courtyard can hold 100,000 people, and the view of Lahore from its minarets is worth climbing the more than 200 stairs to them.

Take the 2-mile walk from the Fort through many colorful bazaars (jewelry, leather, copper, brass, cloth). Also see the mirrored ceilings and glass mosaics in the mausoleum of the 18th century playboy, Maharajah Ranjit Singh. The ashes of his 4 wives and 7 concubines, cremated at his death, are also stored there.

The marvelous collection of Gandhara and Greco-Buddhist art (particularly the "starving Buddha") at the Lahore Museum. The many marble ornaments and mosaics of flowers with Arabic and Persian inscriptions at Jehangir's Mausoleum, 3 miles north of the city.

Without fail, go 6 miles east of Lahore to the incredibly magnificent 40-acre Shalimar Gardens, one of the greatest gardens in the world. It was designed in the 17th century to rival the one of the same name at Srinigar in Kashmir.

Karachi - Peshawar   5905

This is a 1,100-mile journey.

Dep. Karachi (Canton.)
    10:00(1)   10:16(1)   19:26(1+3)   21:00(1+3)

Arr. Peshawar (Canton.)
    16:35(2)   20:25(2)   9:30(4)   6:15(4)

Sights in **Peshawar:** Stroll down the ancient Qissah Khwani Bazar (Street of Storytellers), with its stores selling dried fruits, rugs, sheepskin coats and lambskin (karacul) caps. See the 17th century pure white Mahabat Khan Mosque. The 16th century Bala Hisar Fort. The shoes sold at Mochilara Bazaar. The central square, Chowk Yaad Gar. The former Buddhist Monastery, Gor Khatri. The famed Khyber Pass, 10 miles from Peshawar.

Dep. Peshawar (Cent.)
    6:20(1)   7:29(1)   18:45(1+3)   22:10(1+3)

Arr. Karachi (Canton.)
    12:45(2)   17:10(2)   8:33(4)   7:25(4)

(1)Reservation required. Meal service. (2)Day 2. (3)Carries air-conditioned sleeping car. Air-conditioned coach space, at extra charge, can be reserved. (4)Day 3.

Lahore - Peshawar   5905

Dep. Lahore	5:45(1)	8:30(1)	19:00(1+2)	21:10
Arr. Peshawar (Canton.)	16:35	20:25	6:15	8:30
	*	*	*	
Dep. Peshawar (Canton.)	6:20(1)	7:20(1)	18:15	22:00(1+2)
Arr. Lahore	16:55	19:10	5:40	8:55

(1)Reservation required. Meal service. (2)Carries air-conditioned sleeping car. Air-conditioned coach space, at extra charge, can be reserved.

Peshawar - Landi Kotal   5922

This route is via the fabled Khyber Pass. The service operates only on Fridays. Landi Kotal is 8 miles east of the Afghan border.

Dep. Peshawar (Cant.)	9:40	Dep. Landi Kotal		14:40
Arr. Landi Kotal	13:10	Arr. Peshawar (Cant.)		17:50

Sights in **Landi Kotal:** The "smuggler's bazaar", shops that are tucked away in rock caverns and along hilly sidestreets.

510

Lahore - Quetta 5904

Dep. Lahore	12:00(1+2)	Dep. Quetta	14:25(1+3)
Arr. Quetta	12:45(4)	Arr. Lahore	15:15(4)

(1)Reservation required. Carries air-conditioned sleeping car. Air-conditioned coach space, at extra charge, can be reserved. (2)Meal service on first day: Lahore-Sibi. (3)Meal service on second day: Sibi-Lahore. (4)Day 2.

Sights in **Quetta:** A popular Summer resort. This town developed around a fort occupied by British troops in 1876. It is a market center for western Afghanistan, eastern Iran and part of Central Asia. See: The Geological Survey of Pakistan (there was severe earthquake damage here in 1935). Sandeman Library.

Karachi - Quetta 5904

Dep. Karachi (Cant.)	11:55(1)	Dep. Quetta	15:50(1)
Arr. Quetta	8:40	Arr. Karachi (Cant.)	13:15

(1)Reservation required. Meal service. Carries air-conditioned sleeping car. Air-conditioned coach space, at extra charge, can be reserved.

INTERNATIONAL ROUTES FROM PAKISTAN

The Pakistani rail gateway to Iran is Quetta. Lahore is the departure point for train travel to India.

Quetta - Zahedan 5942

Dep. Quetta   7:50 Wednesday. Meal service.
Arr. Zahedan 15:40 Thursday

Lahore - Delhi - New Delhi 6026

Dep. Lahore   14:45
Arr. Amritsar 18:20
  Change trains.   6006+6030

Dep. Amritsar	6:35(1+2+3)	9:35(4)	12:55	16:20(5+7)
Arr. Delhi Junct.	-0-		-0-	5:25
Arr. New Delhi	14:40	20:05	22:00	-0-

(1)Daily, except Wednesday. (2)Air-conditioned coach space available, at extra charge. (3)Meal service only on Thursday, Friday and Saturday. (4)Meal service. (5)Second-class only. (6)Runs Monday, Wednesday, Friday and Saturday. (7)Plus other departures from Amritsar at 18:45(2+6) and 20:50(2).

Sights in **Amritsar:** This is the holiest city of the Sikh Religion.

QATAR

There are no passenger trains in Qatar.

SAUDI ARABIA

The only passenger rail route in Saudi Arabia is from the port of Dammam on the Persian Gulf to Riyadh, the inland capital. There are no train connections between Saudi Arabia and countries adjacent to it. The trains are modern air-conditioned diesels. Children under 4 travel free. Half-fare for children 4-11. Children 12 and over must pay full fare.

Dammam - Riyadh   4200

These trains are air-conditioned and provide meal service.

Dep.	8:45(1)	14:10(2)	Dep. Riyadh	8:10(3)	14:00(2)
Arr. Riyadh	15:39	21:07	Arr. Dammam	15:05	21:08

(1)Runs Monday, Tuesday, Saturday and Sunday. (2)Runs Wednesday, Thursday and Friday. (3)Runs Wednesday, Friday, Saturday and Sunday.

Sights in **Riyadh:** The Museum of Antiquities. The Zoo.

SYRIA

Syria's rail lines are the north-south standard-gauge from Halab (Aleppo) to Akkari (and on to Lebanon), the north-south special 3'5¼" gauge Hedjaz Railway from Damas (Damascus) to Deraa (and on to Jordan), a narrow-gauge from Damas to Beirut, the west-east route from Halab to Deir ez Zor and Kamechlie (and on to Baghdad), and 2 short lines running north from Halab: one to Karkamis (and on into eastern Turkey), the other to Fevzipasa (and on into central and western Turkey, en route to Ankara and Istanbul). Children under 3 travel free. Half-fare for children 3-9. Children 10 and over must pay full fare.

All of Syria's train routes become international connections.

Passenger train service was once possible from Europe, through Istanbul, via Turkey, Syria and Jordan all the way to Aqaba on the Red Sea. The interruption of service in Jordan from Amman to Ma'an, has made that intercontinental train travel impossible since 1917.

Halab (Aleppo)

Founded before 2,000 B.C. See: The remains of the ancient Cathedral of St. Helena, converted into a mosque in the 12th century A.D. The 11th century minaret on the 8th century Great Umayyad Mosque. The ancient Citadel, built before the 13th century. Fantastic 16th and 17th century bazaars. The archaeological exhibits in the National Museum.

Damas (Damascus)

"The pearl of the east." Oldest inhabited city in the world, founded about 3,000 B.C. See: Great Umayyad Mosque. Al-Marjah Square, in the center of the city. The National Museum. The Qasr al-'Azm Museum. The Arab Academy, containing the national library. The fabulous orchards of the Ghutah.

Deraa

The ancient Greco-Roman ruins. The 13th century mosque.

Halab (Aleppo) - Akkari - Tripoli - Beirut 4076

Dep. Halab	11:30(1)	Dep. Beirut	N/A(2)
Arr. Homs	16:51(1)	Arr. Tripoli	N/A(2)
Arr. Akkari	N/A(2)	Dep. Tripoli	N/A(2)
Arr. Tripoli	N/A(2)	Arr. Akkari	N/A(2)
Dep. Tripoli	N/A(2)	Dep. Homs	13:50(1)
Arr. Beirut	N/A(2)	Arr. Halab	19:00(1)

(1)Service "temporarily" suspended in 1982. (2)Service "temporarily" suspended in 1981.

Damas (Damascus) - Beirut 4103 (Bus)

Dep. Damas	N/A(1)	Bep. Beirut	N/A(1)
Arr. Beirut	N/A(1)	Arr. Damas	N/A(1)

(1)Times not available since 1981.

Damas (Damascus) - Deraa - Amman 4079

Dep. Damas (Kanawat)	8:10(1)	15:00
Dep. Deraa	11:26	17:54
Arr. Amman	14:14	-0-
	*	* *
Dep. Amman	-0-	8:00(2)
Dep. Deraa	5:40	10:41

(1)Runs Thursday and Sunday. (2)Runs Monday and Friday.

Halab (Aleppo) - Mosul - Baghdad 4075

Dep. Halab	5:00(1)	6:00(2)	15:00(2)
Arr. Kamechlie	13:05(1)	13:46	22:52
Arr. Mosul	20:25(1)	-0-	-0-
4155			
Dep. Mosul	22:00(3)	-0-	-0-
Dep. Samara	4:12(3)	-0-	-0-
Arr. Baghdad (West)	6:35	-0-	-0-

(1)Service was "temporarily" suspended in 1982. (2)Second-class only. (3)Air-conditioned first-class and tourist-class space available at extra charge.

Halab (Aleppo) - Ankara - Haydarpasa - Istanbul   4020+4055

Dep. Halab	5:45(1)	Sundays only
Arr. Ankara	7:50	Mondays only
Dep. Ankara	8:40	Monday and Thursday
Arr. Haydarpasa	18:25	Same day as Ankara departure

(1)Carries sleeping car. Meal service.

When making connections for trains in Istanbul, allow 8 hours from arrival in Haydarpasa even though the boat trip from Haydarpasa to Istanbul is only a 20-minute ride.

Halab (Aleppo) - Malataya - Tabriz - Tehran

4055			4051		
Dep. Halab	5:45(1)		Dep. Narli	13:30(2)	
Arr. Fevzipasa	13:40		Arr.		
Change trains.			Malataya	17:35	
Dep. Fevzipasa	12:00(2)		Change trains		
Arr. Narli	13:28		4062		
Change trains.			Dep.		
			Malataya	N/A(3)	
			Arr. Tabriz	N/A(4)	
			Change trains		
			4500		
			Dep. Tabriz	8:10(5)	18:50(2+6)
			Arr. Tehran	22:25	9:45

(1)Sundays only. (2)Runs daily. (3)Service was "temporarily" suspended in 1982. (4)Day 2 from Malataya. (5)Saturdays only. (6)Air-conditioned. Meal service.

TURKEY

The first-class sleeping cars here have single compartments. Second-class sleeping cars have 2-berth and 3-berth compartments. Named trains also have first-class 6-berth couchette cars or first-class reclining-seat cars (designated "Pullman") for which a special fare is charged. Express trains charge higher fares than local or mail trains. Children under 7 travel free. Half-fare for children 7-11. Children 12 and over must pay full fare.

Turkish trains in Asia are liable to cancellation or change.

Most of the train trips in Turkey for which we provide schedules are also the international rail routes to countries adjacent to Turkey. For that reason, we do not show a separate International Route list in this section.

Ankara

Capital of the Turkish Republic. See: The collection of relics from prehistoric times until the present in the magnificent Ataturk Mausoleum, and the view of Ankara from there. The Museum of the National Assembly. The third century Roman Baths. The Columns of Julian. The Temple of Augustus. The Byzantine Citadel. The finest collection of Hittite and pre-Hittite artifacts in Turkey can be seen in the Museum of Anatolian Civilizations. Visit the exhibits of ancient clothing, jewelry, manuscripts, tapestries, wood carving, musical instruments and weapons in the Ethnographic Museum. Next to it is the Museum of Modern Art and Sculpture. Nearby, the Zoo at Ataturk's Farm. Ankara has several fine mosques: Haci Bayram, Alaettin, Ahielvan, Arslanhane and Yeni.

Istanbul

Colonized 2,600 years ago. First called Byzantium, then Constantinople. The city that links Europe and Asia.

See several exceptional mosques: The 17th century Blue Mosque (Sultanahmet), the rich tiles and stained-glass in the 16th century Suleymaniye, the enormous Fatih, the 15th century Eyup, the extraordinary jasper columns in the 15th century Beyazit, lovely tile decorations in the 17th century Yeni and in the 16th century Rustempasa.

One of the world's richest museums, Topkapi Sarayi, palace of sultans from the 15th to mid 19th century. The turbans, swords and tea cups encrusted with emeralds, rubies and diamonds as well as the satins embroidered with pearls will dazzle you. The kitchens there contain what is said to be the world's finest collection of Chinese porcelain.

The 19th century white marble Palace of Dolmabahce. Two other splendid palaces: Yildiz and Beylerbeyi. The blue and green tiled interior of the 15th century Cinili kiosk.

Istanbul's churches are outstanding: Ayasofia (St. Sophia), first built in 325, reconstructed in 532, later converted to a mosque, now a museum with fine Byzantine mosaics. The 4th century Church of St. Irene. The Byzantine frescoes and mosaics depicting the life of Christ and Old Testament scenes in the ancient Church of St. Saviour, now called Kaariye Mosque. The 14th century beautiful gilded mosaics in the old Church of St. Mary. Penmakaristos, now called Fethiye Mosque.

The Summer open-air folklore performances at Rumeli Castle. The 4th century fortification. The Ramparts. Tour the great underground cistern, Yerebatan Sarayi. This storage facility, connected to the 4th century Aqueduct of Valens, supplied water to the Imperial Palace. It is built with 336 columns that have corinthian capitals.

Visit the Grand Bazaar. See the ancient Hippodrome of Constantinople, where chariot races took place. One of the 3 tall columns there was taken from the Egyptian Temple of Karnak. Another was removed from the Greek Temple of Apollo at Delphi.

The views of the Bosphorus from the luxury restaurant on Galata Tower and from the top of the Tower of Leander, and the view of Istanbul from the top of the white marble Beyazit Tower.

There are 2 incredibly beautiful fountains: Ahmet II (behind St. Sophia Cathedral) and the marble Tophane.

Istanbul has many excellent museums: The immense Greco-Roman collection at the Archaeological Museum. Next to it, the Assyrian, Babylonian, Sumerian and Hittite treasures in the Museums of the Ancient Orient. The Museum of Mosaics. The Museum of Turkish and Islamic Art. The Municipal Museum.

Istanbul - Haydarpasa (Boat Trip)   4025
The boat departs both piers frequent times from 6:00 to 24:00 for the 20-minute journey. Allow at least 12 hours for making connections with trains.

Istanbul - Athens   900
Dep. Istanbul   20:40
Arr. Athens   7:00 Day 3

Istanbul - Edirne - Svilengrad - Sofia - Belgrade - Munich   901

Dep. Istanbul (Sirkeci)	17:00(1)	20:30(2)
Arr. Edirne	22:44	0:22 Day 2
Dep. Edirne	22:48(1)	0:28(2)
Set your watch back one hour.		
Arr. Svilengrad	1:07	4:52
821		
Dep. Svilengrad	2:30(1)	5:54(2)
Arr. Sofia	7:30	10:55
Set your watch back one hour.		
Arr. Belgrade	17:15	19:08
Arr. Munich	10:10	12:18 Day 3

(1)Runs late September to late March. Carries sleeping car on Saturday departure from Istanbul. (2)Runs late March to late September. Carries sleeping car on Sunday departure from Istanbul. Has couchettes daily.

Sights in **Edirne:** There is bus service from the railstation for the 10-minute ride to Hurriyet Square, the center of Edirne. See: The fine blue tiles in Ucserefeli Mosque. The 13-domed Eski (Old) Mosque. Nearby, the fantastic Selimiye Mosque. The 16th century Turkish Bath, still operating and worth using. The Municipal Museum.

Istanbul - Bandirma - Manisa - Izmir

Travel between Istanbul and Bandirma is by boat.

4031		4015	
Dep. Istanbul	9:00	Dep. Izmir (Basmane)	8:20
Arr. Bandirma	13:30	Dep. Manisa	9:54
Change to train.		Arr. Bandirma Quay	15:05
4015		Change to boat	
Dep. Bandirma Quay	16:00	4031	
Dep. Manisa	21:14	Dep. Bandirma	16:00
Arr. Izmir (Basmane)	22:40	Arr. Istanbul	20:30

Sights in **Manisa:** The 14th century Ulu Cami (Great Mosque) and the 16th century Muradiye Mosque.

Sights in **Izmir:** Third largest city in Turkey and its largest Aegean port. Once known as Smyrna. Walk along Ataturk Caddesi on the seafront. See: The elegant Moorish-style clock tower at Konak Meydani. The Bazaar. Three very attractive mosques: Kemeralti, Hisar and Sadirvan. Remains of the second-century Roman Agora. The Archaeological Museum in Culture Park. The magnificent view of the city from Velvet Castle, on Mount Pagos.

Izmir - Balikesir - Ankara   4042

Dep. Izmir (Basmane)	7:50(1)	18:10(2)
Dep. Balikesir	12:22	23:00(2)
Arr. Ankara	21:50	9:40
	*	*	*
Dep. Ankara	7:25(1)	18:05(2)
Arr. Balikesir	16:32(1)	3:34(2)
Arr. Izmir (Basmane)	21:00	8:15

(1)First-class only. Meal service. (2)Carries sleeping car. Meal service.

Ankara - Fevzipasa - Baghdad

4042	
Dep. Ankara	20:50(1)
Arr. Fevzipasa	14:46
Arr. Gaziantep	18:59
Dep. Gaziantep	N/A(2)
Arr. Mosul	N/A(2)
Dep. Mosul	21:00
Arr. Baghdad (West)	5:40

(1)Runs Thursday and Sunday. Carries sleeping car. Meal service Ankara-Gaziantep. (2)Service suspended in 1983.

Fevzipasa - Halab (Aleppo)   4055

| Dep. Fevzipasa | 15:20(1) | Dep. Halab | 5:45(2) |
| Arr. Halab | 21:25 | Arr. Fevzipasa | 13:35 |

(1)Runs Monday and Friday. (2)Sundays only.

Ankara - Kars - Leninakan - Rostov - Kharkov - Moscow
4050

Dep. Ankara	9:30(1)	18:55(8)
Dep. Kayseri	17:50	2:36(2)
Dep. Erzurum	10:06(2)	17:25(2)
Arr. Kars	14:45(2)	21:50(2)

Change trains.

| Dep. Kars | 9:00(3) | 9:00(3) |
| Arr. Leninakan | 14:50 | 14:50 |

Change trains.

5025   These trains are used by Intourist for foreigners.

| Dep. Leninakan | 19:15(4) | 12:17(9) |
| Arr. Rostov | 8:17(5) | 17:37(5+9) |

Change trains.

| Dep. Kharkov | 9:00(6) | 2:58(7+9) |
| Arr. Moscow (Kurski) | 5:15(7) | 15:05(7) |

(1)Carries sleeping car. Meal service to Kars. (2)Day 2 from Ankara. (3)Runs Tuesday and Friday. (4)Second-class only. (5)Day 2 from Leninakan. (6)Daily. Carries sleeping car only on Saturdays. (7)Day 3 from Leninakan. (8)Meal service to Kars. Has only coach cars. (9)Operates late May to late September. Meal service. Carries second-class sleeping car only on Tuesday and Saturday. Direct train. No train change in Rostov.

Sights in **Kayseri:** Called Caesarea when it was the capital of a Roman province. See: The Byzantine Citadel and, in it, the Faith Mosque. East of the Citadel, the 13th century Huand Mosque and College, and the geometric designs in the Baths of Princess Mahperi. Nearby, the beautifully decorated 13th century Doner Kumbet (Mausoleum). West of the Citadel is the interesting covered market. Also see the Archaeological Museum. The 13th century Koluk Mosque.

Sights in **Erzurum:** The Seljuk fort. The collonaded courtyard at the 12th century Ulu Cami Mosque. The Cifte Minareli Madrese Museum. The Hatuniye Medrese Mausoleum.

Sights in **Kars:** The 10th century Church of the Holy Apostles, now a museum. The ancient Georgian fort. The Kumbet Mosque. The 11th century Cathedral. The murals in the Church of St. Gregory. The Evliya Mosque.

Sights in **Rostov:** A post-World War II Russian metropolis, designed for heavy industrial manufacturing. See the enormous theater on Teatralnaya Square. Window-shop on Engels Street.

Sights in **Kharkov:** Almost totally reconstructed after World War II with wide streets. Sixth largest city in the USSR. Among the few old treasures that survived Nazi destruction are the 17th century Pokrovsky Cathedral, a belltower commemorating the 1812 victory over Napoleon, the 19th century Patriarchal Cathedral, and an 18th century theater. Modern sights include the large Park of Physical Culture, the Botanical Garden, several museums and a planetarium.

Ankara - Haydarpasa 4040

Dep. Ankara	8:00(1)	8:40(2)	13:30(1+3+9)
Arr. Haydarpasa	17:05	18:25	21:00
	*	*	*
Dep. Haydarpasa	9:20(1)	10:35(4)	13:30(1+3+10)
Arr. Ankara	19:00	20:18	21:00

(1)First-class only. Meal service. Has cars with reclining seats. (2)Runs Monday, Thursday and Saturday. (3)Reservation required. Supplement charged. (4)Runs Tuesday, Thursday and Sunday. Meal service. (5)Reservation required. (6)Train carries only sleeping cars. (7)Meal service. (8)Carries both sleeping cars and coach cars. (9)Plus other departures from Ankara at 21:05(1), 21:40(5+6), 22:25(6+7) and 23:00(1+3). (10)Plus other departures from Haydarpasa at 21:05(1), 21:35(5+6+7), 21:50(8) and 22:50(1+3).

Haydarpasa - Ankara - Kayseri - Van - Tabriz - Tehran 4021

Dep. Haydarpasa	19:25(1)	Dep. Van (Pier)	N/A(3+4)
Dep. Ankara	7:20(2)	Arr. Tabriz	N/A(4)
Dep. Kayseri	N/A(2)	Arr. Tehran	N/A(4)

Carries sleeping car on Monday and Saturday. Has couchettes and meal service on Monday, Wednesday and Saturday.. (2)Day 2. (3)Day 3. (4)Service was "temporarily" suspended in 1981.

Sights in **Van:** This city is on a lake. See: The old fort. The 2 small Seljuk mosques.

Ankara - Samsun 4059

Dep. Ankara	N/A(1)	Dep. Samsun	N/A(1)
Arr. Samsun	N/A(1)	Arr. Ankara	N/A(1)

(1)This service is approximately hourly. Times have not been available since 1980.

Sights in **Samsun:** Birthplace of the Turkish Republic, in 1919. This is the largest Turkish port on the Black Sea.

Haydarpasa - Ankara - Mersin   4020 + 4055

Dep. Haydarpasa	10:35(1+2)		Dep. Mersin	16:15	
Arr. Ankara	20:18		Arr. Yenice	18:00	
Dep. Ankara	20:50		Change trains.		
Arr. Yenice	10:07	Day 2	Dep. Yenice	18:10	(2+4)
Change trains.			Arr. Ankara	7:50	Day 2
Dep. Yenice	10:13(3)	Day 2	Dep. Ankara	8:40	Day 2
Arr. Mersin	11:09	Day 2	Arr. Haydarpasa	18:25	Day 2

(1)Runs Tuesday, Thursday and Sunday. Carries sleeping car Thursday and Sunday. (2)Meal service. (3)Second-class only. (4)Runs Tuesday, Friday and Saturday.

Sights in **Mersin:** This is Turkey's principal port on the Mediterranean, surrounded by citrus groves. See: Eski Cami (the Old Mosque) and Yeni Cami (New Mosque). Crusaders' castles. Roman ruins.

Haydarpasa - Ankara - Adana   4020

Dep. Haydarpasa	10:35(1)	Dep. Adana	17:35(2)
Arr. Ankara	20:18	Arr. Ankara	7:50
Dep. Ankara	20:50(1)	Dep. Ankara	8:40(3)
Arr. Adana	10:39	Arr. Haydarpasa	18:25

(1)Runs Tuesday, Thursday and Sunday. Carries sleeping car Thursday and Sunday. Has couchettes on Tuesday. (2)Runs Tuesday, Friday and Saturday. Carries sleeping car Tuesday and Saturday. Has couchettes on Friday. (3)Runs Wednesday, Saturday and Sunday.

Sights in **Adana:** This city was founded about 1,000 B.C. See: The second-century stone bridge, Tas Kopru. The 16th century Ulu (Great) Mosque. The 15th century Akca and Ramazanoglu mosques. The Archaelogical Museum.

Haydarpasa - Izmit   4020 + 4040

| Dep. Haydarpasa | 5:35(1) | 8:00(2) | 9:20(2+3) | 10:35(4+5+8) |
| Arr. Izmit | 7:05 | 9:15 | 10:40 | 11:56 |

Sights in **Izmit:** The remains of the ancient Roman walls. The Clock Tower. The Museum. The Pertev Pasha Mosque.

| Dep. Izmit | 3:17(4+6) | 5:15(2+7) | 6:10(2+3) | 6:53(4+9) |
| Arr. Haydarpasa | 5:16 | 6:50 | 7:55 | 8:45 |

(1)First-class only. (2)Supplement charged. First-class only. Meal service. (3)Has cars with reclining seats. (4)Supplement charged. Has both first and second-class space. Meal service. (5)Runs Tuesday, Thursday and Sunday. (6)Runs Monday, Thursday and Saturday. (7)Reservation required. (8)Plus other departures from Haydarpasa at 13:30(2+3+7), 15:55(1), 18:25(1), 19:00(4), 21:05(3+4), 21:30(1), 21:50(4) and 22:50(2+3).   (9)Plus other departures from Izmit at 7:14(1), 7:50(4), 8:40(1), 13:54(4), 14:10(1), 15:22(2+3), 16:41(4+6), 17:48(1), 18:10(2), 19:13(1) and 19:44(2+3+7).

Haydarpasa - Konya   4042

Dep. Haydarpasa	8:00(1)	Dep. Konya	6:45(1)
Arr. Konya	20:39	Arr. Haydarpasa	19:45

(1)Supplement charged. First-class only. Meal service.

Sights in **Konya:** The 13th century Mevlana Mausoleum, ancient monastery of the Whirling Dervishes, with its greenish-blue tiles, now a museum. The ebony pulpit, 42 Roman columns and sarcophagi of many sultans in the 13th century Alaeddin Mosque. Nearby, the 13th century Karaty College and the interesting ceramics in the ruins of the Seljuk Palace. The 13th century Iplikci Mosque and Sircali College. The 16th century Selimiye Mosque. The Archaeological Museum. The collection of Islamic Art in the Koyunoglu Museum.

Haydarpasa - Ankara - Adana - Fevzipasa - Halab (Aleppo)   4020

Dep. Haydarpasa	10:35(1)	Dep. Adana	11:10(3)
Arr. Ankara	20:18	Arr. Fevzipasa	14:46
Dep. Ankara	20:50(1)	Change trains.	
Arr. Adana	10:39(2)	Dep. Fevzipasa	15:26(4)
		Arr. Halab	21:25(5)

(1)Runs Tuesday, Thursday and Sunday. Meal service to Fevzipasa on Thursday and Sunday. Carries sleeping car to Fevzipasa on Thursday and Sunday. Has couchettes on Tuesday, but only to Adana. (2)Day 2. (3)Runs Monday and Friday. Meal service. (4)Runs Fridays only. (5)Friday. Same day as departure from Fevzipasa.

Haydarpasa - Ankara - Mosul - Baghdad   4020

Dep. Haydarpasa	10:35(1+2)	Thursday and Sunday
Dep. Ankara	20:50(1)	Thursday and Sunday
Dep. Gaziantep	21:25(1)	Friday and Monday
Dep. El Yaroubieh	16:30(1)	Saturday and Tuesday
Dep. Mosul	21:00(1)	Saturday and Tuesday
Arr. Baghdad	5:40	Sunday and Wednesday

(1)Carries sleeping car. (2)Meal servce to Gaziantep

UNITED ARAB EMIRATES

There are no passenger trains in the United Arab Emirates.

YEMEN ARAB REPUBLIC

There are no passenger trains in the Yemen Arab Republic.

YEMEN, PEOPLE'S DEMOCRATIC REPUBLIC

There are no passenger trains in the People's Democratic Republic of Yemen.

Chapter 11   AFRICA

ALGERIA

The train lines here are standard-gauge. Algeria's rail system consists of one east-west route (connecting Tunisia with Morocco) from which there are 4 spurs heading north to Mediterranean ports and 3 routes going south from the transcontinental main line.

The 2 principal southern routes, Constantine (via El Gourzi) to Touggourt, and Mohammadia to Colomb Bechar, go through the Atlas Mountains to the Sahara Desert. The third southerly route is the short run from Annaba (via Souk-Ahras) to Tebessa.

The 3 very short spurs heading north are Constantine to Skikda, Boudjellil to Bejaia, and Tlelat to Oran.

Children under 4 travel free. Half-fare for children 4-9. Children 10 and over must pay full fare.

Algiers

See the shops, cafes and unique narrow streets of the Kasbah. The Marechal Franchet d'Esperey Museum. The fabulous palaces (Summer and Winter) of the Governor-General. Many fine mosques. The view of little islands, harbor and city from Notre-Dame d'Afrique Church.

The splendid Jardin d'Essai du Hamma botanical gardens. The view from Saint-Raphael Park. Nearby, several good seashore resorts: Moretti, Zeralda, etc.

Constantine

Located on the eastern edge of the Kabylia mountain area. The ancient section of the city is on top of a steep rock. See: The elaborate Ahmed Bey Palace. Medina, the Moslem Quarter. The Gustav Mercier Museum. Nearby: restored ruins of ancient Roman towns: Tebessa, Timgad, Djemila. Several Berber villages.

There is much good Berber handicraft in this area: pottery, carved furniture, enamel-inlaid jewelry.

Transcontinental Algerian Rail Routes

The 3 services listed below are Algeria's only train connections with countries adjacent to it, Tunisia and Morocco.

Algiers - Constantine - Annaba - Tunis
2540

Dep. Algiers	8:55(1+2)	12:30(1)	18:00(3+4)	21:05(4)
Arr. Constantine	16:05	19:50	2:10	5:55
Dep. Constantine	-0-	20:00	2:20(3+4)	-0-
Arr. Annaba	-0-	22:45	5:17(3)	-0-

Change trains.
2550 + 2611

Dep. Annaba	-0-	-0-	7:10(5)	-0-
Arr. Ghardimaou	-0-	-0-	10:55	-0-

Set your watch forward one hour.

Dep. Ghardimaou	-0-	-0-	11:30	-0-
Arr. Tunis	-0-	-0-	14:52	-0-

(1)Meal service. (2)Air-conditioned. (3)Direct train to Tunis. No train change in Annaba. Light refreshments. (4)Has couchettes. Light refreshments. (5)Supplement charged.

Sights in **Annaba:** This old city was settled by Phoenicians in the 12th century B.C. See: The narrow streets of the old town. The 11th century Sidi Bou Merouan Mosque. (Its columns were taken from Roman ruins.) The Hippo Museum. The 18th century Salah Bey Mosque. The Place d'Armes.

Algiers - Oran   2530

Dep. Algiers	7:25(1)	10:30(1+2)	12:10(1)	17:45(1)	21:30(3)
Arr. Oran	12:38	15:21	17:21	22:54	6:02
		*	*	*	
Dep. Oran	7:15(1)	10:50(1+2)	12:20(1)	17:25(1)	21:20(3)
Arr. Algiers	12:34	15:43	17:36	22:45	6:22

(1)Meal service. (2)Air-conditioned. Supplement charged. (3)Has couchettes. Light refreshments.

Algiers - Rabat - Casablanca - Marrakech

Schedules appear later in this chapter, in the section on Morocco.

Northern Algerian Rail Routes

Here are the schedules for the 4 short spurs heading north from the transcontinental train route.

Constantine - Skikda 2542

Dep. Constantine	16:50	Dep. Skikda	5:35
Arr. Skikda	18:45	Arr. Constantine	7:37

Sights in **Skikda:** Ruins of the largest Roman theater in ATgeria. Roman antiquities in the City Museum.

Annaba - Skikda

2540

Dep. Annaba	6:10(1)	18:45(2)	-0-
Arr. Ramdane Djamal	7:20	20:00	-0-

Change trains.
2542

Dep. Ramdane Djamal	18:24	21:30	3:53
Arr. Skikda21		minutes later	
	*	*	*
Dep. Skikda	3:20	5:35	19:40
Arr. Ramdane Djamal	3:39	5:46	20:00

Change trains.
2540

Dep. Ramdane Djamal	3:50(2)	-0-	21:28(1)
Arr. Annaba	5:17	-0-	22:45

(1)Meal service. (2)Light refreshments.

Algiers - Bejaia 2540

Dep. Algiers	6:00	7:15	16:04	17:00
Arr. Bejaia	10:47	12:13	21:11	21:44
		*	*	*
Dep. Bejaia	5:55	7:00	15:15	17:00
Arr. Algiers	10:50	11:52	20:11	21:54

Sights in **Bejaia:** Many Roman ruins in this area.

Oued Tlelat - Oran

	2530	2525	2530	2525	2530
Dep. Oued Tlelat	5:28	6:50	8:55	9:12	12:22(1)
Arr. Oran	30 minutes later

*   *   *

	2525	2530	2525	2530	2525
Dep. Oran	6:45	7:15	10:06	12:20	17:00(2)
Arr. Oued Tlelat	30	minutes later

(1)Plus other departures from Oued Tlelat at 16:53, 17:05, 20:17 and 22:38.
 (2)Plus other departures from Oran at 17:25, 18:20, 18:45 and 21:20

Sights in **Oran:** This city has 3 sections: La Blanca (the 16th century Spanish city on the hill), La Marine (near the Mediterranean) and La Ville Nouvelle (on the right bank of the Raz el-Ain River).

See: The Turkish Citadel, Santa Cruz. The early 19th century Cathedral of Saint-Louis. The fountain in the 18th century Place Emerat. The 18th century Porte de Canastel. The Great Mosque.

The Sidi al-Hawwari Mosque. Nearby, the Kasbah. Chateau Neuf, once the residence of the rulers and later the headquarters of the French colonial army. The harem of the rulers. The 18th century Jewish cemetery.

The Roman and Punic exhibits at the Municipal Museum. The collection of Islamic art in the Tlemcen Museum. The Aubert Library.

Southern Algerian Rail Routes

The following schedules are for the 3 Algerian train lines going south from the transcontinental route.

Annaba - Souk Ahras - Tebessa 2550

Dep. Annaba	16:44	Dep. Tebessa	4:20
Arr. Souk-Ahras	18:47	Arr. Souk-Ahras	6:41
Change trains.		Change trains.	
Dep. Souk-Ahras	19:22	Dep. Souk-Ahras	6:42
Arr. Tebessa	21:42	Arr. Annaba	8:59

Sights in **Tebessa:** The walled Byzantine Citadel, with 4 gates and 12 towers. The second century Roman Arch of Caracalla. Only one mile north, the ruins of the Roman Temple of Minerva, thermal baths and an amphitheater at the same site as a beautiful Christian basilica. Much carpet-weaving here.

Constantine - Biskra - Touggourt 2541

Dep. Constantine	5:30	18:50	Dep. Touggourt	7:27	-0-
Arr. Biskra	9:22	22:40	Arr. Biskra	11:15	-0-
Change trains.			Change trains.		
Dep. Biskra	16:22	-0-	Dep. Biskra	17:20	5:30
Arr. Touggourt	20:06	-0-	Arr. Constantine	21:07	9:10

Sights in **Biskra:** An ancient Roman outpost, now a popular Winter resort. Five miles to the west is the hot sulphur spring famous for medicinal value, Hamman Salahin ("Bath of the Saints"). Many oases here.

Sights in **Touggourt:** A typical Saharan town. There are many dried mud buildings here. See: The tremendous fortress minaret. The clock tower in the Kasbah. The tombs of the kings. Many date palms in this oasis. Nearby, the tomb of Sidi el-Hadj Ali.

Mohammadia - Bechar 2535

Dep. Mohammadia	7:15(1)	18:45(2)
Arr. Bechar	21:41	9:22

*   *   *

Dep. Bechar	6:00(1)	17:40(2)
Arr. Mohammadia	20:12	7:54

(1)Runs mid-October to mid-April. (2)Runs mid-April to mid-October. Meal service.

Sights in **Bechar:** The city lies at the base of 1,600-foot high Djebel Bechar. Many date palm groves in this area. There are interesting covered narrow streets in the Arab section. Good leatherwork and jewelry are produced here.

ANGOLA

Children under 3 travel free. Half-fare for children 3-11. Children 12 and over must pay full fare.

The 3 parallel west-to-east rail lines in Angola start at seaports on the South Atlantic coastline and run inland. One of these, beginning in Lobito, connects at Dilolo with a train service in Zaire and ultimately provides also a train link with Zambia (at Ndola) and then on to Tanzania, Rhodesia, Mozambique, Botswana and South Africa. This route is part of the trans-African railway line.

Luanda - Malanje   3420

This line has 2 short spurs, one to Dondo and another to a hill station, Golungo Alta.

Dep. Luanda   6:00(1)   9:00(3)   -0-
Arr. Malanje   19:10(2)   16:54   -0-

                                 *   *   *

Dep. Malanje   6:00(1)   9:00(5)   13:00(6)
Arr. Luanda   19:14(4)   17:00   20:18

(1)Runs daily, except Sunday. Meal service. (2)Arrives 20:32 on Tuesday, Wednesday and Saturday. (3)Runs Tuesday and Thursday. Light refreshments. (4)Arrives 20:05 on Wednesday. (5)Runs Thursday only. (6)Runs Sunday only. Light refreshments.

Sights in **Luanda:** The capital of Angola. A major harbor. See the Angola Museum. The Bunda Museum. The old Sao Miguel Fort. The 17th century Chapel of Nazareth. The Zoological Museum.

Sights in **Malanje:** The 350-foot high Duque de Braganca Falls. The Pungo Andongo stones, enormous black monoliths that figure in tribal legends. To the south, the Game Reserve.

Lobito - Dilolo - Lubumbashi

The Benguela Railway is a major segment of Africa's only transcontinental rail line. When operating, there is service from Lobito (on the Atlantic Ocean) to Dilolo on the Zaire border, where the Benguela joins other lines that pass through the copper fields of Zaire and Zambia, terminating at the Indian Ocean cities of Beirain (Mozambique) and Dar es- Salaam (Tanzania).

Construction of the Benguela line took from 1903 to 1928.

There is outstanding scenery in the first 40 miles and an ascent from sea level to 6,000 feet in the first 250 miles, after which the train descends to 4,000 feet and goes through eucalyptus forests.

Passenger service over the complete Lobito-Dilolo route was first suspended in 1977 due to anti-government guerrillas attacking the trains by bombing

3421

| Dep. Lobito | N/A(1) | N/A(1) | N/A(1) |
| Arr. Dilolo | N/A(1) | N/A(1) | N/A(1) |

Change trains.

3228

| Dep. Dilolo | 9:00(2+3) | 15:00(5) | 23:00(2+7) |
| Arr. Lubumbashi | 7:25(4) | 5:00(6) | 3:10(6) |

(1)Since 1980, it has been reported that daily service is in operation, circumstances permitting. Times have *not* been available. (2)Has couchettes. Meal service. (3)Runs Wednesdays only. (4)Day 2. (5)Third-class only. Runs Thursdays only. (6)Day 3. (7)Runs Fridays only.

Mocamedes - Lubango - Jamba - Menongue   3422

The train ascends from sea level to 5,000 feet on this route. One spur from it goes to Chibia, another spur to Cassinga.

Dep.		Dep. Menongue	N/A(3)
Mocamedes	23:05(1)	Dep. Jamba	6:00(1)
Dep. Lubango	6:05(2)	Dep. Lubango	15:15(3)
Arr. Jamba	15:20(3)	Arr.	
Arr. Menongue	N/A(3)	Mocamedes	22:00

(1)Runs Thursday and Sunday. (2)Runs Monday and Friday. (3)Service Jamba-Menongue and v.v. was "temporarily" suspended in 1977.

Mocamedes - Lubango - Chibia   3422

Dep. Mocamedes	7:29(1)	Dep. Chibia	N/A(2)
Arr. Lubango	13:08	Arr. Lubango	N/A(2)
Change trains.		Change trains	
Dep. Lubango	N/A(2)	Dep. Lubango	9:01(3)
Arr. Chibia	N/A(2)	Arr. Mocamedes	14:29

(1)Runs Tuesday and Saturday. (2)Service was "temporarily" suspended in 1981. (3)Runs Tuesday and Friday.

Mocamedes - Dondo - Cassinga   3422

Dep. Mocamedes	23:05(1)	Dep. Cassinga	N/A(2)
Arr. Dondo	N/A(2)	Arr. Dondo	N/A(2)
Change trains.		Change trains.	
Dep. Dondo	N/A(2)	Dep. Dondo	N/A(2)
Arr. Cassinga	N/A(2)	Arr. Mocamedes	22:00(3)

(1)Runs Thursday and Sunday. (2)Time has *not* been available since 1979. (3)Runs Tuesday and Saturday.

BENIN

Previously called Dahomey. Children under 4 travel free. Half-fare for children 4-9. Children 10 and over must pay full fare.

Cotonou - Ouidah   3027

Dep. Cotonou   8:04   13:50   17:42
Arr. Ouidah   9:21   15:10   19:08

Sights in **Ouidah:** This was a European slave trade center in the 18th century. See the 16th century Portuguese fort. The Cathedral. The streets lined with colorful blossoming plants and fruit trees. There is an interesting temple of the local traditional religion. Nearby coconut and coffee plantations.

Dep. Ouidah   5:52   11:50   17:50
Arr. Cotonou   7:36   13:12   19:12

Cotonou - Parakou   3025

Dep. Cotonou   8:44(1)   13:35(1+2)   17:00(3)
Arr. Parakou   17:12   20:45   8:14
                             *   *   *
Dep. Parakou   9:20(1)   13:55(1+4)   17:40(5)
Arr. Cotonou   18:04   21:10   7:54

(1)Light refreshments. (2)Runs Tuesday, Friday and Saturday. (3)Runs Tuesday, Thursday, Friday and Sunday. (4)Runs Wednesday, Saturday and Sunday. (5)Runs Monday, Wednesday, Friday and Sunday.

Sights in **Cotonou:** Many interesting markets. The Supreme Court. The National Assembly. Nearby are Abomey and Ouidah.

Sights in **Abomey:** The 30-foot high walls of the ancient 100-acre fortified palace and the interesting Museum, Jewelry Hall and Statuary Hall in the palace, with good exhibits of weapons, furniture and textiles.

Cotonou - Pobe   3026

Dep. Cotonou   17:02 | Dep. Pobe   6:00
Arr. Pobe   20:55 | Arr. Cotonou   9:54

BOTSWANA

The one rail trip in landlocked Botswana (operated by Rhodesian Railways) leads north from Ramatlhabama near South Africa's border to Plumtree and into Rhodesia. It is one of the 2 routes from Johannesburg (South Africa) to Harrare (formerly Salisbury) Zimbabwe (formerly Rhodesia]).

Johannesburg - Mafiking - Plumtree - Harrare (Salisbury)

3475

Dep. Johannesburg	12:30(1)	-0-
Dep. Mafiking	21:00(1)	14:05
Dep. Ramatlhabama	21:30(1)	16:10(3)
Dep. Plumtree	12:09(2)	10:05(2)
Arr. Bulawayo	14:10(2)	12:45(2)

Change trains.

3455

Dep. Bulawayo	19:30(3)	20:00
Arr. Harrare	6:00	7:00

(1)Runs Thursdays only. Reservation required. Meal service. (2)Day 2. (3)Runs Friday and Sunday. Third and fourth-class only.

BURUNDI

There are no passenger trains in Burundi.

CAMEROUN

Children under 3 travel free. Half-fare for children 3-9. Children 10 and over must pay full fare.

Douala - Nkongsamba   3128

Dep. Douala	7:10(1)	Dep. Nkongsamba	8:25(1)
Arr. Nkongsamba	14:50	Arr. Douala	15:55

(1)Second-class only.

Sights in **Douala:** The 13,000-foot high Mount Cameroun, tallest mountain in West Africa. The beautiful view of the enormous bridge over the Wouri River.

Sights in **Nkongsamba:** Pleasant climate. A popular tourist resort. Many banana, coffee and palm-oil plantations.

Douala - Yaounde   3128

Dep. Douala	8:00	13:30(1)	20:00(2)
Arr. Yaounde	17:58	19:40	5:40

Sights in **Yaounde:** Capital of Cameroun. Many streams and shaded avenues. Nearby: The cocoa plantations in a very large forest. The Ekom Waterfalls and the Dschang health resort at the 4,000-foot high Bamileke Plateau. Nachtigal Falls. The Grottos of the Pygmies.

Dep. Yaounde	7:30	14:30(3)	21:00(2)
Arr. Douala	17:35	20:40	6:00

(1)Runs Monday, Tuesday, Thursday and Saturday. (2)Runs daily. Has couchettes. (3)Runs Monday, Wednesday, Friday and Saturday.

Yaounde - N'gaoundere   3125

Dep. Yaounde	7:30	20:20(1+2)	Dep.	
Arr.			N'gaoundere	7:00 19:00(1+3)
N'gaoundere	18:42	8:50	Arr. Yaounde	18:40 7:20

(1)Second-class only. (2)Daily. Has first-class couchettes. Monday, Wednesday and Friday. (3)Daily. Has first-class couchettes Tuesday, Thursday and Sunday.

Sights in **N'gaoundere:** Big-game hunting and photography is the attraction here. There are large game reserves nearby.

CENTRAL AFRICAN REPUBLIC
There are no passenger trains in Central African Republic.

CHAD
There are no passenger trains in Chad.

CONGO
Children under 5 travel free. Half-fare for children 5-9. Children 10 and over mus pay full fare.

The rail system in Congo starts at the South Atlantic seaport of Pointe Noire and runs inland to Loubomo, where it forms the two top arms of a "Y", one fork heading north to M'Binda, the other going east to Brazzaville, the nation's capital. Kinshasa, across the border in Zaire, has a rail line running to Matadi.

Pointe Noire - Brazzaville   3172
This is the principal Congo-Ocean Railway.

Dep. Pointe Noire	6:25	12:32(1)	18:10(3+4)
Arr. Brazzaville	20:40	15:15(2)	6:10(2)
		*	*

Dep. Brazzaville	6:15	11:15(1)	18:50(3+5)
Arr. Pointe Noire	20:03	11:20(2)	6:30(2)

(1)Only third-class space. (2)Day 2. (3)Meal service. (4)Has couchettes on Monday, Thursday and Saturday. (5)Has couchettes on Tuesday, Friday and Sunday.

Pointe Noire - M'Binda   3172

Dep. Pointe Noire	6:25	12:32(1)	18:10(2)
Arr. Loubomo	11:32	21:28	22:35
Change trains.			
Dep. Loubomo	14:46	17:40(1)	-0-
Arr. M'Binda	22:29	8:37	-0-
		*	*

Dep. M'Binda	4:40	17:27	-0-
Arr. Loubomo	12:44	11:02	-0-
Change trains.			
Dep. Loubomo	14:54	2:06(3)	3:56(1)
Arr. Pointe Noire	20:03	6:30	11:20

(1)Third-class only. (2)Meal service. (3)Runs daily. Has couchettes Monday, Wednesday and Saturday.

DJIBOUTI

This was formerly the northwestern corner of Somalia. Its only passenger rail service is the 186-mile portion of the line running from its Gulf of Aden seaport, Djibouti, to Ethiopia's Addis Abeba.

Djibouti - Dire Daoua - Addis Abea   3255

Dep. Djibouti	20:00	-0-		Dep. Addis Abeba	7:30	19:30(2)
Arr. Dire Daoua	6:55(1)	-0-		Arr. Dire Daoua	17:24	8:45(1)
Change trains.				Change trains.		
Dep. Dire Daoua	7:30	19:30(2)		Dep. Dire Daoua	19:30	-0-
Arr. Addis Abeba	17:27	8:50(1)		Arr. Djibouti	7:40	-0-

(1)Day 2. (2)Carries sleeping car.

Sights in **Djibouti:** A major seaport. See the Palace, on Menelik Square. The Great Mosque, on Place Rimbaud, where a large camel market is conducted.

EGYPT

Most Westerners prefer to visit Egypt November-March.

Egyptian trains charge a supplement for traveling in air-conditioned cars. First-class sleeping cars have single-berth compartments. Second-class sleeping cars have 2-berth compartments. All sleeping cars are air-conditioned. Passengers in sleeping cars must pay 2 supplemental charges: for the sleeping-car and for air-conditioning.

Children under 4 travel free. Half-fare for children 4-9. Children 10 and over must pay full fare.

From Cairo, there is one rail line south, to Sadd-el-Ali, where a connection can be made for train travel across the desert in Sudan. This is the only international rail route between Egypt and countries adjacent to it.

The 3 other Egyptian rail routes from Cairo are northwest to Alexandria, northeast to Ismailia (and on to Port Said), and east to Suez.

There is also train service along the Suez Canal, from the city of Suez to Ismailia. Egypt's Mediterranean coastline train trip is between Alexandria and Mersa Matruh.

Cairo

See the world's greatest collection of pharaonic treasures, covering the 30 dynasties of ancient Egypt from the dawn of civilization to the coming of the Romans, in the Egyptian Antiquities Museum at Tahrir Square, near the Nile Hilton Hotel. The more than 3,000 world-famous treasures of Tutankhamun are on the second floor.

The 12th century Citadel and, at its top, the 19th century Mohammad Ali Mosque (also called the Alabaster Mosque for its marble interior). Near the Citadel is the Mosque of Sultan Hassan, which has the tallest minarets in Cairo and is a veritable fortress.

The ornate 10th century Al Azhar Mosque is the oldest university in the Moslem world. Nearby is Wekalet el Ghouri, where local craft from different parts of Egypt are exhibited.

The 9th century Mosque of Ibn Toulon, oldest in Cairo and noted as the world's finest example of pure Islamic architecture, is near Anderson House, a museum on how a prosperous Cairo family would have lived in the 17th century. Cairo has several hundred mosques that are open to visitors except during Friday prayers. Women are not allowed to enter mosques after sunset. See King Farouk's tomb, at El Rifai Mosque.

Visit the Coptic Museum. Nearby, the 4th century Church of Abu Serga (St. Sergius) where, according to legend, the Holy Family stayed when fleeing from Herod. The ancient El Mollaqa Church. The 10th century gate, Bab Zuweilla. The Papyrus Museum, in houseboats near the Sheraton Hotel, has an exhibit on making the early writing material. Nearby, the work of one of Egypt's best sculptors, in the Mukhtar Museum.

The view of the city and the Nile from the revolving restaurant on the top of Cairo Tower. The Khan al-Khalili Market's tinsmiths, tentmakers, hand-hammered copper and brass trays, cotton caftans, and local inexpensive perfumes. The Ben Ezra Synagogue. Thousands of bazaars.

Nine miles west of Cairo, a 25-minute taxi ride from the city center, is the largest pyramid, Cheops, and the Sphinx, in Giza. A visit to the pyramids at sunset is recommended and also the Sound and Light Pageant (19:30-20:30) in an outdoor theater at the Sphinx. An English-language commentary on the history of the pharaohs is performed Monday, Wednesday and Saturday.

A one-hour sailboat ride in the evening on the Nile costs about $10(U.S.). The boats leave from the Shepheards and Meridien hotels.

Alexandria

Egypt's most important port and second-largest city. Very popular beach resort.

Cairo - Alexandria - Cairo   2660

Those trains which are air-conditioned require reservations.

Dep. Cairo (Main)	Frequent times from 6:05 to 20:25
Arr. Alexandria	3 hours later

*   *   *

Dep. Alexandria	Frequent times from 5:25 to 20:00
Arr. Cairo	3 hours later

Alexandria - El Alamein   2664

These trains have only second-class and third-class space.

Dep. Alexandria	6:55	9:30(1)		Dep. Al Alamein	14:18(1)	15:46
Arr. El Alamein	13:18	17:08		Arr. Alexandria	2:00	22:15

(1)Air-conditioned in second-class.

Sights in **El Alamein:** There is a small museum commemorating General Montgomery's defeat of Field Marshal Rommel in one of the most famous battles of World War II. More than 8,000 soldiers are buried in large cemeteries in this area.

Cairo - Ismailia - Port Said   2655

These trains have only second and third-class space.

Dep. Cairo (Main)	6:25(1)	9:55(2)	11:50	15:30	18:45(2)	21:40
Arr. Ismailia	9:15	12:25	14:35	18:25	21:32	0:40
Arr. Port Said	10:55	-0-	-0-	-0-	23:10	-0-

*   *   *

Dep. Port Said	-0-	5*;15*)2)	-0-	12*;45*)1)16*;50		-0-
Dep. Ismailia	5:10	7:00	12:50(2)	14:30	18:40	21:05
Arr. Cairo (Main)	8:40	9:55	15:30	17:10	21:25	23:50

(1)Light refreshments. (2)Air-conditioned in second-class.

Sights in **Ismailia:** Many parks and gardens. The Suez Canal. The Sweet Water Canal, built in 1863 to provide thousands of canal workers with drinking water. There are several ancient ruins 10 miles west of here.

Sights in **Port Said:** This is Egypt's second most important seaport.

Cairo - Suez   2656

These trains have only second and third-class space.

Dep. Cairo (Pont Limoun)	5:50	10:00	15:35	19:35
Arr. Suez	8:35	13:05	18:20	22:40

*   *   *

Dep. Suez	5:50	9:40	14:50	19:15
Arr. Cairo (Pont Limoun)	9:00	12:25	18:05	22:00

Sights in **Suez:** The Canal and this city's 2 harbors. This is a departure point for pilgrimages to Mecca.

Cairo - Luxor - Aswan   2663

Pyramids, ancient temples and camel trains can be seen on this route.

Dep. Cairo (Main)	7:30(1)	7:40(2)	12:00(1)	12:25(2+3)
Arr. Luxor	18:20	0:50	0:20	1:20
Arr. Aswan	23:20	-0-	-0-	-0-

Dep. Cairo (Main)	16:20(2)	19:00(4)	19:35(4)	20:30(5+7)
Arr. Luxor	7:10	5:56	8:20	14:12
Arr. Aswan	12:12	10:,0	12:35	14:12

	*	*	*	
Dep. Aswan	-0-	-0-	5:15(1)	5:40(2)
Dep. Luxor	4:15(2+3)	5:15(1)	10:14(1)	12:42(2)
Arr. Cairo (Main)	17:30	16:35	20:55	5:35

Dep. Aswan	-0-	14:45(4)	17:45(4)	20:08(5)
Dep. Luxor	15:10(2)	19:30(4)	22:25(4)	1:02(5)
Dep. Cairo (Main)	6:00	6:40	9:50	14:30

(1)Reservation required. Air-conditioned. Meal service. (2)Has only second and third-class space. (3)Air-conditioned only in second-class. (4)Carries only air-conditioned sleeping cars, both first and second-class. Meal service. (5)Second-class only. (6)Third-class only. (7)Plus another departure from Cairo at 22:50(6).

Sights in **Luxor:** In 2133 B.C. this was Thebes, capital of the Egyptian empire, and on the opposite side of the Nile it was Karnak, the "city of the dead", with the kings' mortuary temples. The ruins of the great temples of Karnak, Amon, Mont, Mut and Khons, and the complex of temples called Amon-Re are the interesting places to see here today. Also, the Colossi of Memnon, more than 60 tombs in the Valley of the Kings.

Sights in **Aswan:** A Winter resort. You can see the ancient quarries from which granite was taken for building the pharaohs' monuments. Four miles north is the Aswan High Dam, completed in 1970, one of the greatest engineering accomplishments in the world. It is 1½ miles long and has 180 sluices.

Nile Cruises

Several cruise firms provide boat service on the Nile. These cruises are so popular that reservations for the high season (September to May) have to be made as much as 3 years in advance.

There are 14-day Nile trips Cairo-Awan-Cairo, September to April, calling at the principal monuments on the river. There are also 10-day, 14-day and 16-day roundtrip cruises between Luxor and Aswan. One cruise is a one-day (5:15-17:00) hydrofoil service between Aswan and the temple complex at Abu Simbel, operated daily, but generally available only to groups.

The Rail Route to Sudan

Egypt's train connection with Sudan starts with a Nile boat trip from Sadd el Ali to Wadi Halfa.

Sadd el Ali - Wadi Halfa   2690

Dep. Sadd el Ali 16:00(1)	Dep. Wadi Halfa 16:00(2)
Arr. Wadi Halfa 8:00 Day 3	Arr. Sadd el Ali 8:00 Day 3

(1)Runs Monday and Thursday. (2)Runs Tuesday and Friday.

Wadi Halfa - Khartoum   2700

This trip crosses the Nubian Desert.

Dep. Wadi Halfa   16:40(1) | Arr. Khartoum   16:45 Day 2
(1)Runs Wednesday and Saturday. Carries sleeping car. Meal service.

ETHIOPIA

Ethiopia's 2 rail lines are the route between 8,000-foot high Addis Abeba and Dire Daoua (which continues to Djibouti on the Gulf of Aden), and the line from Agordat to Massawa, a port on the Red Sea.

Children under 4 travel free. Half-fare for children 4-9. Children 10 and over must pay full fare.

Addis Abeba - Dire Daoua - Djibouti   3255

The ride descending from Addis Abeba to Dire Daoua is very scenic, similar to Colorado mountain scenery in the United States.

Dep. Addis Abeba	7:30	Dep. Djibouti	20:00
Arr. Dire Daoua	17:24	Arr. Dire Daoua	6:55
Change trains.		Change	trains.
Dep. Dire Daoua	19:30	Dep. Dire Daoua	7:30
Arr. Djibouti	7:40	Arr. Addis Abeba	17:27

Sights in **Addis Abeba:** The depiction of Africa's past struggles, present problems and future progress in the magnificent stained-glass window at All Africa Hall. The lavishly decorated National Palace. The mosaics, ceiling carvings and stained-glass at Holy Trinity Cathedral. The obelisk on Miazia 27 Square.

The Natural History Museum. The Imperial Lion House. The handicrafts for sale in the Empress Menen Handicraft School. The view of the city from Mount Entoto. Haile Selassie I Square. The National Museum's archaeology exhibits. The paintings in the Institute of Ethiopian Studies. The activities every Saturday at Mercato, the city's large marketplace. The heavy traffic of domestic animals on some of the downtown streets. The imperial lions in the small zoo at Jubilee Palace. Several other palaces. St. George's Cathedral.

Sights in **Dire Daoua:** The Mosque. The Muslim cemeteries. Prehistoric paintings in the nearby caves. The Palace.

Massawa - Asmara - Agordat   3250

The train makes an amazing climb on this route, similar to some of the steepest gradients in Peru.

Dep. Massawa	N/A(1)	Dep. Agordat		N/A(1)
Dep. Asmara	N/A(1)	Dep. Asmara		N/A(1)
Arr. Agordat	N/A(1)	Arr. Massawa		N/A(1)

(1)Service was suspended in 1977.

Sights in **Massawa** (also called Mitsiwa): This is one of the hottest places in the world, with an annual average temperature of 87 degrees Fahrenheit (31 degrees Celsius). Despite this, it is an important tourist center. Massawa is a seaport and is used as a naval base. The Ethiopian Orthodox Church is worth seeing. There is an ice factory here.

Sights in **Asmara** (also called Asmera): The Coptic Church. The Grand Mosque. The Palace. There is good deep-sea fishing off this shore.

GABON

Children under 4 travel free. Half-fare for children 4-11. Children 12 and over must pay full fare.

Owendo (Libreville) - Franceville   3150

Dep. Owendo	7:00(1+2)	17:00(4+5)	-0-
Arr. Ndjole	10:02	20:15	-0-
Arr. Franceville	N/A(3)	N/A(3)	-0-
	*	*	*
Dep. Franceville	N/A(3)	N/A(3)	N/A(3)
Arr. Ndjole	6:50(5+6)	13:00(1+7)	17:00(1+2)
Arr. Owendo	10:01	15:56	20:05

(1)Air-conditioned in first-class. (2)Runs Tuesday, Thursday, Saturday, Sunday and holidays. (3)The 293-mile track between Ndjole and Franceville, under construction since 1980, is scheduled to open in 1988. (4)Runs Wednesday, Saturday, Sunday and holidays.)5)Second-class only. (6)Runs Wednesday only. (7)Runs Saturday, Sunday and holidays.

GAMBIA

There are no passenger trains in Gambia.

GHANA

This country's rail system forms the letter "A", with the western arm running from the Atlantic seaport of Takoradi north to inland Kumasi, the eastern segment going from the port of Accra north to Kumasi, and the cross-arm extending from Tarkwa (on the western route) to the eastern route. The cross-arm is the Takoradi-Accra route.

The sleeping cars have 8 first-class compartments, each with a single bed. Couples can obtain adjoining compartments that have a common door. Second-class sleeping compartments have 8 berths.

Ghana's rail authorities advise travelers that its engines "are old and not wholly reliable" and therefore "breakdowns may occur during the course of travel." They also state: "The situation is being ameliorated but will definitely take some time."

Applicants for visas to travel in Ghana are required to purchase from the Ghana Consulate in their own country travel vouchers for use in purchasing food, lodging and transportation in Ghana. The price varies according to length of stay in Ghana. The price required for 14 days in Ghana is about $305(U.S.).

Accra

See the port longshoremen carrying crates and bundles on their heads. The spirited nightlife here. The Arts Council of Ghana. The Ethnological Museum. The Science Museum. Nearby: The enormous Volta Dam and, behind it, the largest manmade lake in the world, Lake Volta.

Tarkwa

There is much mining here for gold, diamonds, manganese and bauxite. Because of the sand that is found in this area, there is a substantial glass industry here.

Kumasi

The "Garden City of West Africa". The Ashanti kings rule from here. The area is dense forest. See: The Ghana Regiment Museum in the old British fort. The museum, zoo and library at the Ashanti Cultural Center. Good textiles are available here.

Takoradi - Tarkwa - Kumasi 3066

Dep. Takoradi	6:15	21:00(1)	Dep. Kumasi	6:40	21:00(1)
Dep. Tarkwa	9:12	23:21	Dep. Tarkwa	13:15	3:35
Arr. Kumasi	15:45	5:56	Arr. Takoradi	15:31	5:48

(1)Carries sleeping car.

Takoradi - Tarkwa - Accra 3065

Dep. Takoradi	19:30	-0-	Dep. Accra	5:20	19:30
Dep. Tarkwa	21:28	6:00	Dep. Tarkwa	17:00	2:45
Arr. Accra	4:57	17:26	Arr. Takoradi	-0-	4:42

Accra - Kumasi 3061

Dep. Accra	6:20	21:00	Dep. Kumasi	6:20	21:00
Arr. Kumasi	16:25	5:47	Arr. Accra	15:42	5:38

GUINEA

Guinea's 2 rail lines are from Conakry and Kamsar on the Atlantic seacoast to inland Kankan and Sangaredi.

Conakry - Kankan 2852

All of these trains provide light refreshments.

Dep. Conakry	6:30 Tues.	19:40 Fri.
Arr. Kankan	22:25 Tues.	8:43 Sat.

* * *

Dep. Kankan	4:50 Wed.	19:40 Sat.
Arr. Conakry	21:23 Wed.	8:39 Sun.

Sights in **Conakry:** Good beaches. The Corniche, a lovely promenade along the seashore. The African exhibits at the Museum. The Mosque. The monument to anti-colonial martyrs. The picturesque Boulbinet fishing harbor. Nearby, the Botanical Garden in Camayenne.

Sights in **Kankan:** This was an 18th century caravan center. The ambience is very Moslem. Many mosques. Much wood, gold and ivory craftsmanship here. A center for trading in reptile skins, sesame, cattle, rice.

Kamsar - Sangaredi 2853

These trains are second-class only.

Dep. Kamsar	12:45(1)	Dep. Sangaredi	16:15(1)
Arr. Sangaredi	15:20	Arr. Kamsar	19:15

(1)Runs daily, except Tuesday and Wednesday.

IVORY COAST

This country's single passenger rail route is the 725-mile narrow-gauge Abidjan-Niger Line (constructed by France), running from Abidjan on the shore of the Gulf of Guinea to Bobo Dioulasso and then on to Ouagadougou in the grasslands of landlocked Upper Volta.

In 1979, the price of a roundtrip ticket for the 195-mile Abidjan-Bouake portion of this line (5½ hours in each direction) was $21 (U.S.). The cost for a one-way first-class seat from Ouagadougou to Abidjan was then $70 (U.S.). Children under 4 travel free. Half-fare for children 4-11. Children 12 and over must pay full fare.

The train's 38 first-class seats are in an air-conditioned section of the turbine-powered locomotive. The back of each seat is fitted with a pull-down meal tray. Food can be purchased near Abidjan's railstation. Sandwiches and beverages are sold in a section of the locomotive. During the trip, a waiter sells a full hot lunch. At several stops, women vendors sell meat snacks, stews and fresh fruit.

People from several different tribes make this trip. Many of the women passengers wear very high-heeled shoes, colorful long dresses and turban-style hats.

The ride was said in 1981 to be quite smooth due to the modern rails and good roadbed.

En route to Ougadougou, the train goes through a heavily-foliaged rain forest before arriving at Dimbokro. After leaving Dimbokro, the train travels alongside a village of dirt streets and many thatched-roof huts. Women can be seen in that village walking with lumber, large packages and trays balanced on their heads.

Next seen on the route are large banana plantations and a jungle with bright flowers.

Adjacent to the Bouake railstation is a 66-room hotel built in 1975, with swimming pool and a restaurant that at least once featured French cuisine in a pleasant dining-room.

Abidjan - Bouake - Bobo Dioulasso - Ouagadougou   3105

Dep. Abidjan	7:08(1)	10:28(2+3)	12:38(4)	14:28(3+6)
Arr. Bouake	12:36	15:32	19:40	20:30
Dep. Bouake	-0	15:55(2+3)	-0-	20:55(3)
Arr. Bobo Dioulasso	-0-	1:25(2+3)	-0-	8:40(3)
Arr. Ougadougou	-0-	7:00	-0-	15:15
	*	*	*	
Dep. Ougadougou	-0-	-0-	-0-	7:15(3+7)
Dep. Bobo Dioulasso	-0-	-0-	6:00(1)	14:20(3)
Arr. Bouake	-0-	-0-	14:40	1:18
Dep. Bouake	6:00(5)	11:22(1)	15:10(1)	1:45(3)
Arr. Abidjan	11:05	17:32	21:01	7:57

(1)Light refreshments. (2)Supplement charged. (3)Carries sleeping car. Meal service. Air-conditioned in first-class. (4)Second-class only. (5)Supplement charged. Light refreshments. Air-conditioned in first-class. (6)Plus another departure from Abidjan (to Bouake) at 16:28(5).   (7)Plus another departure from Ouagadougou (to Abidjan) at 18:35(2+3).

Sights in **Abidjan:** Chief port and largest city in the Republic of Ivory Coast. See: The exhibits of traditional Ivorian art in the National Museum. The handicrafts at Plateau Market in the enormous Square Bressoles. The 2-story bazaar in Treichville, a suburb. The Adme market. The extravagant President's Palace. The wonderful tropical rain forest, Parc National du Banco, north of the city.

Sights in **Bouake:** Many mosques here. Good textile products for sale. You cannot miss seeing the brilliant-colored clothing worn by the crowds at the open-air market.

Sights in **Bobo Dioulasso:**This is an Islamic center, with many mosques. There are good buys here in ivory and bronze products, also traditional jewelry.

Sights in **Ouagadougou:**This is the capital of Upper Volta.

KENYA

Kenya's one train line is from Mombasa on the Indian Ocean, inland to Nairobi. From there, the rail route forks, one tine running to Kisumu at Lake Victoria and a second tine going to Tororo on the Kenya-Uganda border, and on into landlocked Uganda.

Children under 3 travel free. Half-fare for children 3-15. Children 16 and over must pay full fare.

Passengers have a view of Tsavo National Park, teeming with African game. West of Nairobi, there are extraordinary views of flamingos and of tea and coffee plantations.

Mombasa - Nairobi - Kisumu   3275

Dep. Mombasa	17:00(1)	19:00(5)	Dep. Kisumu	17:30(3)	18:30(1)
Arr. Nairobi	7:50(2)	8:15(2)	Arr. Nairobi	5:30(2)	7:30(2)
Change trains.			Change trains.		
Dep. Nairobi	17:30(3)	18:00(1)	Dep. Nairobi	17:00(1)	19:00(5
Arr. Kisumu	6:10(4)	8:05(4)	Arr. Mombasa	7:20(6)	8:00(6)

(1)Light refreshments. (2)Day 2. (3)Runs when required. (4)Day 3 after departing Mombasa. (5)Meal service. (6)Day 3 after departing Kisumu.

Sights in **Mombasa:** The city sits on an offshore island, linked to the mainland by causeway, bridge and ferry. Mombasa was founded by Arab traders in the 11th century and has been an important seaport since then.

See the porcelain and other artifacts in the museum at the 2-acre, 16th century Fort Jesus. The silver door at Lord Shiva Temple. The Moorish-style Anglican Memorial Cathedral, with its silver roof. The exhibit of elephant tusks, hippopotamus teeth and rhinoceros horns in the Game Department Ivory Room, and the semi-annual auctions there.

The stalls of ivory carvers, perfumemakers, goldsmiths, spice merchants and silk dealers in the winding, narrow streets of Old Town. The 16th century Manadhara/Mandhry Mosque. Sheikh Jundani Mosque. Kilindini Mosque. The 4 enormous sheet-metal elephant tusks forming an arch over Kilindini Road, the main street. Take a cruise of Kilindini Harbor.

Sights in **Nairobi:** This city is almost on the equator. However, it is one mile high, making for temperate climate. See the treasures of Kenya's past and the exhibits of a vast number of birds, insects, mammals, fish, musical instruments, ornaments and tribal weapons in the National Museum of Kenya, a 15-minute walk from the center of Nairobi, open daily 9:30-18:00.

Across the street from the museum is Snake Park. Its collection of 200 varieties of snakes, crocodiles and alligators is open daily 9:30-18:00. Visit the Sorsbie Art Gallery. Jeevanjee Gardens.

See the trees and flowering plants in the 100-acre Arboretum. Tribal dances performed 14:30-16:00 weekdays and 15:30-17:30 weekends, as well as tribal jewelry, baskets and 16 replicas of tribal villages at the Bomas of Kenya cultural center. Near it, the 44-square-mile Nairobi Game Park. A fantastic collection of African railway relics at the Railway Museum, a 5-minute walk from the railstation.

African and Western contemporary art at Paa-ya-Paa Gallery. The fruit, vegetable, flower and curio stalls in Municipal Market. Jamia Mosque. The African exhibits at McMillan Memorial Library. The fascinating rust-red and white International House.

The tapestries, murals, tribal shields and the conference table made from 33 kinds of Kenya wood, in the National Assembly. The Tuesday morning coffee auction at Kahawa (''coffee'') House. City Nurseries, with its enormous number of different species of bougainvillaea.

Mombasa - Nairobi - Nakuru - Eldoret - Tororo - Kampala 3275+3286

Carries sleeping cars and has meal service Mombasa-Nairobi and vice versa. Light refreshments are available Nairobi-Kampala and vice versa. The first-class sleeping car was very good quality in 1979. Third-class cars (made in Sweden) had comfortable, padded seats.

Dep. Mombasa	19:00(1)	Dep. Kampala	16:00(6)
Arr. Nairobi	8:15(2)	Arr. Tororo	22:50(5)
Change trains.		Dep. Malaba	16:00(1+2+7)
Dep. Nairobi	9:30(3)	Dep. Eldoret	21:00(1+2+7)
Dep. Nakuru	15:20(3)	Dep. Nakuru	3:35(1+4+8)
Dep. Eldoret	22:30(3)	Arr. Nairobi	8:45(4+8)
Arr. Malaba	2:50(4+5)	Change trains.	
Dep. Tororo	6:00(6)	Dep. Nairobi	19:00(1)
Arr. Kampala	12:25(4)	Arr. Mombasa	8:00(9)

(1)Meal service. (2)Day 2. (3)Runs Tuesday, Friday and Sunday. Meal service. (4)Day 3. (5)There is frequent taxi service Malaba-Tororo and v.v. (6)Runs daily, except Monday. (7)Runs Monday, Wednesday and Saturday. (8)Runs Tuesday, Thursday and Sunday. (9)Day 4.

Sights in **Nakuru:** The pelicans on the inland saline Lake Nakuru. Lake Nakuru National Park.

Sights in **Eldoret:** The temperate climate here is due to the 6,800-foot altitude, which attracted many European settlers in the period this was an English colony.

LESOTHO
There are no passenger trains in Lesotho.

LIBERIA
There are no passenger trains in Liberia.

LIBYA
There are no passenger trains in Libya.

MADAGASCAR

There are 3 short rail lines in north Madagascar: Antananarivo-Moramanga-Tamatave, Moramanga to Ambatosoratra, and Antananarivo to Antsirabe. (Antananarivo is also called Tananarive.)

The southern train route is Finanarantsoa to Manakara.

Children under 4 travel free. Half-fare for children 4-6. Children 7 and over must pay full fare.

Antananarivo - Moramanga - Tamatave   3330

All of these trains are air-conditioned in first-class.

Dep. Antananarivo	6:30	Dep. Tamatave	11:35
Dep. Moramanga	10:50	Arr. Moramanga	19:32
Arr. Tamatave	18:58	Change trains.	
		Dep. Moramanga	10:09(1) 14:44(1)
		Arr. Antananarivo	14:26(1) 19:05(1)

(1)Day 2.

Sights in **Antananarivo:** Capital of Madagascar (Malagsay Republic). See the 19th century towered palaces of the Imerina kings on the royal estate, above the city. The exhibits of Malagsay culture and archaeology in The Organisation pour la Recherche Scientifique et Technique. The collection of lemurs and other Malagsay animals in the Zoo.

The stupendous Friday outdoor marked (called Zoma), on Independence Avenue. Thousands of booths and "blanket shops" offering leather goods, semiprecious stones, woven baskets, etc. This is the place to flex your bargaining muscles. Most items in this market are intended to sell for half the asking price, and buyers are expected to start bidding below that figure.

Sights in **Tamatave:** This is the country's chief seaport, on the Indian Ocean. Stroll down tree-lined Avenue Poincare.

Moramanga - Ambatosoratra   3330

All of these trains are air-conditioned in first-class.

Dep. Moramanga	11:00	14:53
Arr. Ambatosoratra	16:20	20:24

*   *   *

Dep. Ambatosoratra	3:40	8:30
Arr. Moramanga	9:19	14:06

Sights in **Ambatosoratra:** Lake Alaotra.

Antananarivo - Antsirabe   3330

This is a very scenic 92-mile ride to 4,000-foot high Antsirabe. All of these trains are air-conditioned in first-class.

Dep. Antananarivo	5:20	10:53	-0-
Arr. Antsirabe	9:17	14:45	-0-

       * * *

Dep. Antsirabe	4:50	12:00	17:06
Arr. Antananarivo	8:48	16:30	21:00

Sights in **Antsirabe:** This is a thermal springs resort, situated under 8,674-foot high Mt. Tsiafajavona, the top of the Ankaratra volcanic mass.

Fianarantsoa - Ranomena - Manakara   3335

Dep. Fianarantsoa	5:30	13:30(1)	17:47(2)
Dep. Ranomena	6:41	14:42	19:52
Arr. Manakara	11:04	19:05	-0-

       * * *

Dep. Manakara	-0-	5:20(4)	13:23
Dep. Ranomena	5:40(3)	10:20	18:24
Arr. Fianarantsoa	6:20	11:33	19:38

(1)Runs Tuesday, Thursday and Saturday. (2)Runs Monday-Friday, except holidays. (3)Runs daily, except Sundays and holidays. (4)Runs Monday, Wednesday and Friday.

MALAWI

Landlocked Malawi's rail system consists of 2 routes that start at Chipoka on Lake Malawi. The first goes east, across Mozambique, to Nacala on the Indian Ocean. The other runs south through central Mozambique, ending at Beira, another Indian Ocean seaport.

Children under 3 travel free. Half-fare for children 3-13. Children 14 and over must pay full fare.

Chipoka - Nkaya - Nacala

3384		3345			
Dep.		Dep.			
Chipoka	6:15(1)	Entre Lagos	21:30(3)		
Arr.		Arr. Cuamba	0:41		
Nkaya	12:40	Change trains.			
Change trains.		Dep. Cuamba	6:00(4)	16:15(5+7)	17:00(6+7)
3376		Arr. Nampula	18:23	3:36	5:21
Dep.		Change trains.			
Nkaya	9:26(2)	Dep. Nampula	-0-	4:00(8)	16:00(8)
Arr. Entre		Arr. Nacala	-0-	11:58	23:58
Lagos	12:00				
Change trains.					

(1)Third-class only, except Thursday and Sunday, when this train also has second-class. (2)Second-class only. Runs only Tuesday and Friday. A third-class only train runs daily at 11:00, arriving Entre Lagos at 16:05. (3)Third-class only. (4)Runs Thursday only. (5)Runs Monday only. (6)Runs Wednesday and Saturday. (7)Carries sleeping car. (8)Runs daily.

Chipoka - Blantyre - Limbe - Inhaminga - Beira

3384		3350	
Dep. Chipoka	6:15(1)	Dep. Dona Ana	17:58(4+5)
Dep. Blantyre	16:55	Arr. Inhaminga	8:39(6)
Arr. Limbe	17:30	Change trains.	
Change trains.		Dep. Inhaminga	9:20(6+7)
Dep. Limbe	6:10(2+3)	Arr. Beira	20:10
Arr. V.N. Fronteira	15:50(3)		

(1)Runs daily. Third-class only, except Thursday and Sunday, when this train also has second-class. (2)Third-class only. (3)Day 3. Walk ½ mile along railway track to Dona Ana. (4)Runs Wednesday, Friday and Sunday. (5)Day 3. (6)Day 4. (7)Second and third-class only.

Sights in **Blantyre:** The Museum of Malawi. Jubilee Gardens. Rangely Gardens.

MALI

The 2 rail lines in landlocked Mali are from its capital, Bamako, east to Sikasso (and then on to Upper Volta) and west to Kidira (and then on to Senegal). Children under 3 travel free. Half-fare for children 3-9. Children 10 and over must pay full fare.

Bamako - Sikasso   2758

Dep. Bamako	16:00(1)	Dep. Sikasso	16:00(3)
Arr. Bougouni	19:00	Arr. Bougouni	20:30
Change trains.		Change trains.	
Dep. Bougouni	8:00(2)	Dep. Bougouni	8:00(4)
Arr. Sikasso	13:30	Arr. Bamako	12:00

(1)Runs Monday, Tuesday and Friday. (2)Runs Tuesday, Wednesday and Saturday. (3)Runs Monday, Thursday and Saturday. (4)Runs Tuesday, Friday and Sunday.

Bamako - Kayes - Kidira - Dakar   2760

Dep. Bamako	8:00(1+2)	Dep. Dakar	12:00(2+3)
Dep. Kayes	19:10	Dep. Kidira	4:10 Day 2
Arr. Kidira	2:10	Dep. Kayes	7:35
Arr. Dakar	13:17 Day 2	Arr. Bamako	18:15

(1)Runs Wednesday and Saturday. (2)Carries sleeping car. Meal service. (3)Runs Tuesday and Friday.

Sights in **Bamako:** This city is on the Niger River. See: The fine display of prehistoric-to-modern exhibits in the National Museum. The handicraft (weaving, jewelry, ironwork, sculpture, leatherwork) in Maison des Artisans (Artisans' House). The interesting marketplaces. The excellent Zoo. The Botanical Gardens. Nearby, the forests at Lake Mandingues, La Boule National Game Reserve, Lake Ouegna, the Korounkorokale Grottoes, Oyako Waterfalls.

MAURITANIA

The only passenger rail service in Mauritania is a second-class, limited facility on an overnight iron-ore freight train that runs the 392 miles between Nouadhibou, a West African Atlantic fishing and freight port, and Zouerate, a mining town.

Nouadhibou-Zouerate   2800

Dep. Nouadhibou	15:00	18:20	Dep. Zouerate	12:55	16:55
Arr. Zouerate	5:18	9:04	Arr. Nouadhibou	6:03	10:00

MAURITIUS

There are no passenger trains in Mauritius.

MOROCCO

Moroccan trains are all standard gauge. A substantial supplement is charged for air-conditioned trains. Sleeping cars are first-class and have single and double compartments. The country's 3 classes of trains are: first-class, second-class and economy. Children under 4 travel free. Half-fare for children 4-11. Children 12 and over must pay full fare.

Morocco's rail system runs east from Marrakech to Casablanca and Rabat. It then forks at Sidi Kacem, one tine going to Tangier, the other to Oujda (and on to Algeria).

Tangier

Excellent beaches. Extensive night life. See: Grand Socco, the colorful square in the Old Town, and the market stalls by walking through the twisting alleys to the Petit Socco.

Marrakech

A popular Winter resort. Good skiing at the nearby 8,000-foot Atlas Mountains. This area is a vast 30,000-acre date palm grove. See: Africa's most famous mosque: the 12th century Koutoubia, with its pale green 220-foot high minaret and the thrilling voice of its muezzin. The 16th century Sa'di Mausoleum. The 18th century Dar el-Beida Palace.

The Moorish gardens at the 19th century Bahia Palace. Marvelous fountains: El Mouasine and Eshrob ou Shouf. The fantastic scenes (dancers, acrobats, musicians, snake charmers, costumed water boys) in the tremendous square, Place Djemaa el-F'na. The gardens of the Hotel Mamounia. The casino. The olive orchards of the walled 1,000-acre Agdal gardens and the Menara gardens, at the edge of which the Sahara Desert begins.

The costumes of the mountain and desert people, on a shopping visit. The green and blue tiles on the walls of the central court of the 16th century Medersa of Ben Yussef. The monumental palace, El-Badi, with its small museum and nesting storks. Take a ride around the Old City in a horse-drawn carriage.

Casablanca

Morocco's major seaport. See: The stained-glass at the white Cathedral of the Sacre Coeur. The gardens in the Park of the Arab League. Busy Muhammad V Square. The Municipal College of Fine Arts. Many good beaches.

Rabat

This has been a military post since the 12th century. There are many splendid gardens here: Belvedere, Essai, Udayia, Triangle de Vue. See: The Kasbah. The Museum of Moroccan Art. Tour Hassan, largest Arabian minaret, once part of a now ruined mosque. The collection of Moroccan art in the King Muhammad V Memorial, and the view from its roof.

The Old Town. G'Naoua, the old fort. The Royal Palace, built in the 1950's. The Friday procession of the king, from his palace to Djamaa Abel Fez Mosque. Fine work is done here in carpets, blankets and leather handicrafts.

Nearby, the Roman ruins at Sala Colonia. The 12th century Bab ar-Rouah (Gate of the Wind) and the Archaeological Museum.

Meknes

Founded in the 10th century. See: The 25 miles of 17th century walls that circle the city. The heavily decorated gate, Bab el Mansour. The large Royal Palace. Many big gardens, irrigated by a 10-acre artificial lake, and several other large artificial lakes here. The shops with outstanding rugs.

The exhibit of handicrafts at Dar Jamai, the art museum. The bronze doors of Bou Inania Medersa (school for studying the Koran). Nearby, the ruins of the Roman Volubilis.

Fez

Founded in the 8th century. See: The hundreds of columns in Karaouine Mosque. Dar Batha Museum. The fascinating gate of Andalusian Mosque. The Bon Jelud gardens. Karaouine University. Qarawiyin Mosque, oldest in North Africa, housing a 9th century university and the tomb of Idris II. The Royal Palace and the multi-colored minaret on the Great Mosque, both in the 13th century Fes Jalid complex.

Nearby, the olive groves. The extremely high dam, Bin el Widane.

Marrakech - Casablanca - Rabat - Meknes - Fez - Oujda - Algiers

2510

Dep. Marrakech	1:20	6:51	17:27(1+2)
Arr. Casablanca (Voy.)	5:30	10:47	20:58
Arr. Casablanca (Port)	5:53	-0-	21:21

Change trains.

2502

Dep. Casablanca (Port)	6:20(2+3)	12:28(1+2)	16:13(1+2+8)
Dep. Rabat (Ville)	7:59(2)	13:57(1+2)	17:39(1+2)
Dep. Meknes	11:06(2)	17:17(1+2)	20:50(1+2)
Arr. Fez	12:01	18:11	21:47
Arr. Oujda	-0-	0:28	-0-

Change trains. Set your watch forward one hour.

2525

Dep. Oujda	N/A(6)	N/A(6)
Arr. Maghnia	N/A(6)	N/A(6)
Dep. Maghnia	5:45	13:22
Arr. Oued Tlelat	9:10	16:51

Change trains.

/ 2530

Dep. Oued Tlelat	7:35(7)	12:40(7)	17:45(7+9)
Arr. Algiers	12:34	17:36	22:45

(1)Supplement charged. Air-conditioned. (2)Light refreshments. (3)Departs from Casablanca's Voyageurs railstation. (4)Carries sleeping car. Also has couchettes. Light refreshments. (5)Has couchettes. Light refreshments. (6)Service was "temporarily" suspended in 1981. (7)Meal service. (8)Plus another departure from Casablanca (Port) at 20:20(2+4), arriving Oujda at 7:38...and another departure from Casablanca (Voyageurs) at 21:51(2+5), arriving Oujda at 10:17. (9)Plus another departure from Oued Tlelat at 21:50(2+5), arriving Algiers at 6:22.

Algiers - Oujda - Fez - Meknes - Rabat - Casablanca - Marrakech

2530

Dep. Algiers	7:25(1)	12:10(1)	17:45(1)	21:30(2)
Arr. Oued Tlelat	12:20	17:03	22:36	5:26

Change trains.

2525

Dep. Oued Tlelat	-0-	17:00	-0-	6:45
Arr. Maghnia	-0-	21:02	-0-	10:51
Dep. Maghnia	-0-	N/A(3)	-0-	N/A(3)
Arr. Oujda	-0-	N/A(3)	-0-	N/A(3)

Change trains. Set your watch back one hour.

2502

Dep. Oujda	11:55(4)	18:27(2)	21:05(6)	-0-
Dep. Fez	18:15(4)	0:34(2)	3:13(6)	-0-
Dep. Meknes	19:11(4)	1:40(2)	4:14(6)	-0-
Dep. Rabat (Ville)	22:20(4)	5:20(2)	7:13(6)	-0-
Arr. Casablanca (Port)	23:50	7:07(5)	8:45	-0-

Change trains.

2510

Dep. Casablanca (Port)	1:00	8:00(4)	-0-	-0-
Dep. Casablanca (Voy.)	1:25	8:20	17:10	-0-
Dep. Marrakech	5:35	11:47	21:10	-0-

(1)Meal service. (2)Has couchettes. Light refreshments. (3)Service was "temporarily" suspended in 1981. (4)Air-conditioned, at an extra charge, in both first and second-class. (5)Arrives at Casablanca's Voyageurs railstation. (6)Carries sleeping car. Also has couchettes. Light refreshments.

Casablanca - Rabat - Tangier   2502

Dep. Casablanca (Port)	7:30(1+2)	12:28(1+3)	21:51(4+5)
Dep. Rabat	8:50(1+2)	13:57(1+3)	23:26(4)
Arr. Tangier	13:31	20:31	7:14

* * *

Dep. Tangier	6:10(1+3)	15:45(1+2)	21:30(4)
Dep. Rabat	11:38(1+3)	20:41(1+2)	5:20(4)
Arr. Casablanca (Port)	13:00	22:12	7:07(5)

(1)Air-conditioned. Supplement charged. (2)Meal service. Light refreshments. (4)Has couchettes. Light refreshments. (5)Departs/Arrives Casablanca's Voyageurs railstation.

MOZAMBIQUE

This country's 3 major rail terminals are its Indian Ocean seaports: Nacala, Beira and Maputo.

Children under 3 travel free. Half-fare for children 3-9. Children 10 and over must pay full fare.

Nacala - Nkaya - Chipoka
3345

Dep. Nacala	4:00	15:20
Arr. Nampula	12:04	22:57
Change trains.		
Dep. Nampula	15:30(1)	17:10(2)
Arr. Cuamba	3:43	3:38
Change trains.		
Dep. Cuamba	16:00(3)	-0-
Arr. Entre Lagos	18:18	-0-
Change trains.		

3376

Dep. Entre Lagos	12:35(4)	15:00(3)
Arr. Nkaya	15:06	22:30
Change trains.		

3384

Dep. Nkaya	9:00(5)	-0-
Arr. Chipoka	15:04	-0-

(1)Runs Monday, Wednesday and Saturday. Carries sleeping car on Monday and Saturday. (2)Runs Thursday only. Carries sleeping car. (3)Runs daily. Third-class only. (4)Runs Tuesday and Friday. (5)Runs daily. Has both second and third-class coach cars on Tuesday and Friday. Only third-class cars on other days.

Beira - Inhaminga - Limbe - Blantyre - Chipoka

3350		3384	
Dep. Beira	3:30	Dep. V.N. Fronteira	8:10(4)
Arr. Inhaminga	12:25	Arr. Limbe	19:34(2)
Change trains.		Change trains.	
Dep. Inhaminga	13:07(1)	Dep. Limbe	4:30(5+6)
Arr. Dona Ana	4:22(2+3)	Dep. Blantyre	5:15(5+6)
Change trains.		Arr. Chipoka	15:14(5)

(1)Runs Monday, Wednesday and Friday. (2)Day 3. (3)Walk ½ mile along the railway track to Vila Nova Fronteira. (4)Third-class only. (5)Day 4. (6)Runs daily. Has both second and third-class coach cars on Tuesday and Friday. Only third-class cars on other days.

Sights in **Beira:** The ultra-modern railstation.

Beira - Machipanda - Mutare - Harare (Salisbury)

3350		3450	
Dep. Beira	7:30	Dep. Mutare	21:00
Arr. Machipanda	20:33(1)	Arr. Harare	6:00
Arr. Mutare	N/A(1)		
Change trains.			

(1)Rail service between Machipanda and Mutare has been suspended since 19:77.
Passengers travel this 12km trip by taxi or bus.

Maputo - Chicualacuala - Somabula - Harare (Salisbury)

3355		3455	
Dep. Maputo	6:10(1)	Dep. Somabula	23:21(4)
Arr. Chicualacuala	21:59	Arr. Harare	7:00
Change trains.			
3452			
Dep. Chicualacuala	N/A(2)		
Dep. Mbizi	17:15(3)		
Arr. Somabula	4:00		
Change trains.			

(1)Runs Monday, Wednesday and Friday. Second and third-class only. (2)Service
was suspended in 1981. It is 5km by road to Mbizi. (3)Third and fourth-class
only. (4)Runs daily.

Maputo - Pretoria - Johannesburg   3510

Both of these trains require reservations.

Dep. Maputo	16:35		Dep. Johannesburg	18:15	
Arr. Pretoria	7:49	Day 2	Dep. Pretoria	19:53	
Arr. Johannesburg	9:30		Arr. Maputo	11:05	Day 2

NIGER

There are no passenger trains in Niger.

NIGERIA

The 2 classes on Nigerian trains are first and third. Third-class has padded leather seats. Children under 3 travel free. Half-fare for children 4-13. Children 14 and over must pay full fare.

Lagos - Ibadan - Ilorin - Minna - Kaduna - Kano   3005

All of these trains have meal service.

Dep. Lagos (Term.)	8:30	11:00(2)
Dep. Ibadan	13:52	16:42(2)
Dep. Llorin	19:50	22:21(2)
Dep. Minna	6:00(1)	8:25(1+3)
Arr. Kaduna	9:43(1)	12:02(1+3)
Arr. Kano	-0-	17:45(1)
	*	* *
Dep. Kano	8:00(4)	-0-
Dep. Kaduna	13:05(4)	18:30
Dep. Minna	17:00(4)	22:20
Dep. Llorin	2:54(1+5)	8:17(1)
Dep. Ibadan	8:32(1+5)	13:47(1)
Arr. Lagos (Term.)	14:45(1)	20:00(1)

(1)Day 2. (2)Runs daily. Has air-conditioned first-class coach on Wednesday, Friday and Sunday. (3)Runs daily. Has air-conditioned first-class coach on Thursday, Saturday and Monday. (4)Runs daily. Has first-class coach on Monday, Tuesday and Friday. (5)Runs daily. Has air-conditioned first-class coach on Tuesday, Wednesday and Saturday.

Sights in **Lagos:** Capital of Nigeria. Second largest city in tropical Africa (after Kinshasa, Zaire). Settled more than 300 years ago. It is a complex of lagoons, sandbars and islands. The islands are: Iddo, Lagos, Ikoyi and Victoria. They are connected to each other and to the mainland by bridges. In a population of over 1,000,000 there are about 10,000 who are European, American and Asian.

See: The large harbor. The Zoo. The Iga Idungaran Palace, occupying 10 acres. The Obun Edo and Ebute Ero markets. The exhibit of Nigerian arts and crafts at the National Museum. Holy Qur'an Mosque. The Government Handicraft Center. The contemporary and historic sculptures in the Orhoghua Art Gallery. The Benin art in the Unikon Museum.

Sights in **Ibadan:** Many streams flow through this ancient city. There are teak forest reserves on the outskirts. Much weaving and pottery here. See: Iba Market. The 130-acre Agodi Garden. Four zoological and botanical gardens. The Central Mosque. Ansar ad-Din Mosque.

Sights in **Ilorin:** The Moorish-style concrete palace and the canopied Mallim Alimi Well, both near the Central Market. Traditional single-story, red-mud houses. The ancient mud wall. Much dyeing of cotton cloth with local indigo, weaving, pottery and leathergoods here. Nearby, the Borgu Game Reserve. There are roads from Ilorin to Ogbomosho, Kabba, Jebba and Kaiama.

Sights in **Minna:** This is a major collecting point for peanuts, cotton, indigo, yarns, tobacco, kola nuts, goats and chickens. Much raffia mats and baskets, brassware, pottery and woven and dyed cloth for sale here.

Sights in **Kaduna:** The name of the city is the word for "crocodile". See: The stately Lugard Hall, in Muslim architecture, housing the state legislature. The Geological Survey of Nigeria headquarters. Much manufacturing here: explosives, furniture, soft drinks (kola nuts are collected in this area).

Sights in **Kano:** This city has been a tribal capital since the 11th century. A camel caravan center for many centuries. Kano was the greatest commercial power in West Africa in the 1820's, its leather and cotton goods shipped north, across the Sahara, by camel caravan to Morocco, Algeria and Tunisia where its red goatskin products were called "morocco leather".

The Encyclopedia Britannica carries a photo of tall pyramids built from peanuts harvested here. Kano is divided into 100 hamlets, each having its own mosque.

See: The Kurmi Market and Juma'at Mosque, both built in the 15th century. The 15th century Palace. Next to it, the Central Mosque (built in 1951), Nigeria's largest mosque. The collection of Hausa and Fulani artifacts at the museum in Gidan Makama ("Makama's House").

Lagos - Maiduguri   3002

Both of these trains have meal service.

Dep. Lagos (Iddo)	8:30(1)	Dep. Maiduguri	16:30(2)
Arr. Maiduguri	11:30 Day 3	Arr. Lagos (Iddo)	20:00 Day 3

(1)Runs Monday, Tuesday, Thursday and Saturday. (2)Runs Monday, Wednesday, Thursday and Saturday.

Sights in **Maiduguri:** This city is on the historic pilgrimage path from Senegal to Mecca and is a major gathering center for many agricultural products. See: The Palace. The Mosque. The very large Monday market and the procession of nomads bringing crocodile skins, cattle hides, goats and sheep as well as finished leather products to the market by donkey and oxen. Chewinggum and peanut butter are manufactured here, and the tall pyramids of bagged peanuts is something to see.

Lagos - Jos 3001

This trip involves a short spur off the Lagos-Maiduguri line. Both of these trains offer meal service.

Dep. Lagos (Ter.)	8:30(1)	Dep. Jos	9:00(2)
Arr. Jos	19:10 Day 2	Arr. Lagos (Ter.)	20:00 Day 2

(1)Runs Wednesday, Friday and Sunday. (2)Runs Monday, Wednesday and Saturday.

Sights in **Jos:** Its high elevation makes this a cool resort. See the 60-acre park with the Zoo. The Arboretum. The open-air museum of traditional architecture. The Nok terra-cotta figurines and wood, brass, bronze and pottery artifacts in the Museum, the oldest in Nigeria. The Nok culture flourished in this area from 900 B.C. to 200 A.D.

Lagos - Kafanchan - Port Harcourt

3002			3007		
Dep. Lagos	8:30(1)		Dep. Port Harcourt		
Arr. Kafanchan				11:00(1)	
	15:38	Day 2	Arr. Kafanchan		
Change trains.				8:55	Day 2
3007			Change trains.		
Dep. Kafanchan			3002		
	22:15(1+2)	Day 2	Dep. Kafanchan		
Arr. Port Harcourt				12:10(1)	Day 2
	20:45	Day 3	Arr. Lagos	20:00	Day 3

(1)Runs daily. Meal service. (2)Plus another departure from Kafanchan at 19:30 on Tuesday, Friday and Sunday.

Sights in **Port Harcourt:** Nigeria's second largest port. Much manufacturing here: cigarettes, tires, paper. Also offshore oil drilling.

REUNION

The one rail line on this tiny Indian Ocean island is the 38-mile route along its picturesque seacoast, from Pointe des Galets to St. Benoit. Reunion advised Thomas Cook in 1978 that this service no longer operates regularly.

RWANDA

There are no passenger trains in Rwanda.

SENEGAL

Senegal's 2 rail lines are the short ride from Dakar to St. Louis and the long route from Dakar to Kidira and on to Bamako in landlocked Mali. Chidren under 3 travel free. Half-fare for children 3-9. Children 10 and over must pay full fare.

Dakar

A major seaport. Capital of Senegal. There are good museums here on the sea, ethnography and archaeology. Also see: The Zoo. The outstanding uniforms of the sentries at the President's Palace. The great Mosque. The beautiful Church of Our Lady of Fatima in the Cathedral du Souvenir Africain. The collection of African art in the National Museum. The array of gold, silver, exotic musical instruments, produce, spices, jewelry and embroidered African garments sewn to order in a few minutes, all at the Sandaga central market. Nearby, the picturesque fishing village, Cayar.

Take the 20-minute ferry ride to Goree Island for a tour of the Slave House Museum. Goree was once the main port for the slave trade. You can see the cells where chained slaves were held before they were moved onto crowded ships.

Dakar - St. Louis   2812

| Dep. Dakar | 7:25(1) | 13:40 | Dep. St. Louis | 6:20 | 14:30(1) |
| Arr. St. Louis | 12:00 | 18:37 | Arr. Dakar | 11:02 | 19:10 |

(1)Runs Monday, Wednesday and Friday.

Dakar - Kidira - Bamako   2815

Dep. Dakar	12:00(1+3)	Dep. Bamako	8:00(2+3)
Arr. Kidira	3:10(4)	Dep. Kidira	22:20
Arr. Bamako	18:15(4)	Arr. Dakar	13:17(4)

(1)Runs Tuesday and Friday. (2)Runs Wednesday and Saturday. (3)Carries sleeping car. Meal service. (4)Day 2.

SIERRA LEONE

There are no passenger trains in Sierra Leone.

SOMALI REPUBLIC

There are no passenger trains in Somali Republic.

SOUTH AFRICA

Summer climate here is November to mid-April. The peak Summer holiday period is December 12 to January 30.

All rail lines in South Africa are narrow-gauge ($3'6+_0$) because so much track is over mountain terrain. However, carriages are only slightly narrower than those used on British, European and North American railways.

Reservations can be made up to 6 months in advance, with 2 exceptions: up to 3 months for "Drakensberg" (Johannesburg-Durban), up to 11 months for "Blue Train" (Pretoria-Johannesburg-Cape Town).

First-class coupes carry 2 passengers. First-class compartments carry 4. Second-class coupes carry 3, and second-class compartments accommodate 6. By paying a surcharge, one person can reserve a first-class coupe, and first-class compartments can be reserved for the use of 2 or 3 people.

On night trains, first-class compartments convert to 4 couchette berths and second-class compartments to 6 couchette berths. There is a charge for sterilized bedding, packed in a sealed canvas bag. The seal is broken in the passenger's presence, when the attendant makes up the berth.

Travel is free for children under 7 years old accompanied by an adult who has paid the full advertised ticket price. Half-fare for children under 12 either who are traveling alone or when with an adult who has paid a reduced ticket price. Also half-fare for children 3-12 who are either unaccompanied by an adult or who are accompanied by an adult paying reduced fares. Children 12 and over must pay the full price.

Holders of first-class tickets are permitted up to 100 pounds of free luggage. Passengers arriving by boat may have their baggage collected at the dock and either shipped from there by train to any destination, or delivered to a local address, or placed in the railstation check-room to be collected later.

A similar service is offered for taking luggage from a local address to a railstation or dock. Luggage also can be sent on in advance to await one's arrival at a destination. There is free porterage at all main railstations.

An inexpensive, large timetable published by South African Railways is very useful, containing altitudes, distances and much other interesting information.

The country's extensive rail system connects inland Johannesburg with 5 seaports: Durban, East London, Port Elizabeth, Mossel Bay and Cape Town. There is train service from South Africa to all of the 4 countries adjacent to it: Mozambique, Zimbabwe (formerly Rhodesia), Botswana and South West Africa (Namibia).

Johannesburg

There are many museums here on archaeology, costumes, transportation, Judaica, geology, medicine and South African history.

See the collection of European and South African paintings at the Art Gallery. The Mosque. The Money Museum. The Zoo. Jan Smuts House. Nearby, tour the Simmer and Jack gold mine.

Pretoria - Johannesburg - Pietermaritzburg - Durban   3525

Dep. Pretoria	8:35(1)	-0-	17:40	-0-	18:40(8)
Dep. Johannesburg	10:15	17:45(3+4)	18:30(5)	18:05(6)	20:00(8)
Dep. Pietermaritzburg	4:00(2)	5:58(3+4)	6:28(5)	7:31(7)	8:50(8)
Arr. Durban	7:00	8:45	9:15	10:15	11:45
		*	*	*	
Dep. Durban	11:45	15:30(8)	17:45(9)	18:00(5)	20:00(6)
Dep. Pietermaritzburg	14:38	18:17	20:40(9)	20:18(5)	22:49(6)
Arr. Johannesburg	5:50	6:20	7:35	8:30(5)	16:00
Arr. Pretoria	6:34	-0-	-0-	9:33	-0-

(1)Runs Monday, Wednesday, Friday and Saturday. (2)Runs Tuesday, Thursday, Saturday and Sunday. (3)Reservation required. Supplement charged. Air-conditioned train. Carries only sleeping cars. Meal service. (4)Runs Fridays only. (5)Meal service. (6)Runs Tuesday, Thursday, Friday and Sunday. (7)Runs Wednesday, Friday, Saturday and Monday. (8)Carries only second and third-class coach cars. (9)Runs Sundays only.

Sights in **Pretoria:** The streets lined with jacaranda trees. Paul Kruger's house. The National Cultural History and Open Air Museum. The sunken gardens at Venning Park. The National Zoological Gardens. The Voortrekker Monument.

Sights in **Pietermaritzburg:** Called "City of Flowers" for its many fine botanical gardens and parks. See the Voortrekker Museum. The Natal Museum. The model native village in nearby Mountain Rise. Many nearby mountain resorts and game preserves.

Sights in **Durban:** This is South Africa's largest port. See the Botanical Gardens. The Bantu Market. Snake Park. Japanese Water Gardens. The rose gardens in Jameson Park. The Oceanarium. The Indian Market. The nearby game and nature reserves.

Johannesburg - Bloemfontein - East London   3550

Dep, Johannessburg	-0-	-0-	14:00(3)	14:20(1+4)
Dep. Bloemfontein	0:15(1+2)	8:15	21:45(3)	22:40(1+4)
Arr. East London	16:15	6:20	12:35	13:40
		*	*	*
Dep. East London	3:30(1+5)	11:15(6)	13:35(1+8)	21:25
Arr. Bloemfontein	19:59	2:37(7)	4:47(1+9)	17:10
Arr. Johannesburg	-0-	11:15	13:20	-0-

(1)Runs daily. Has only second and third-class coach cars. (2)Runs Monday and Friday. (3)Reservation required. Runs Tuesday, Thursday, Friday and Sunday. Meal service. (4)Reservation required. Runs daily, except Saturday. Light refreshments. (5)Runs Wednesday and Thursday. (6)Runs Nonday, Wednesday, Friday and Sunday. Meal service. (7)Runs Tuesday, Thursday, Saturday and Monday. (8)Reservation required. Runs daily, except Sunday. Light refreshments. (9)Reservation required. Runs daily, except Monday. Light refreshments.

Sights in **Bloemfontein:** The beautiful 300-acre King's Park. The Franklin Game Reserve. Two astronomical observatories: Lamont-Hussey and Boyden Station. The enormous dinosaur and other fossils at the National Museum.

Sights in **East London:** The 80-acre Queen's Park. This seaport's Museum has a coelacanth, a primeval fish.

Johannesburg - Bloemfontein - Port Elizabeth

3550		3573	
Dep. Johannesburg	14:00(1+2)	Dep. Port Elizabeth	17:00(3)
Dep. Bloemfontein	22:25(1+2)	Arr. Noupoort	1:10
Arr. Noupoort	3:56	3550	
3573		Dep. Noupoort	1:35(4)
Dep. Noupoort	4:25(3)	Arr. Bloemfontein	7:19(4)
Arr. Port Elizabeth	13:10	Arr. Johannesburg	15:30

(1)Reservation required. (2)Runs Tuesday, Thursday, Friday and Sunday. Meal service. (3)Runs Monday, Wednesday, Friday and Saturday. Meal service. (4)Runs Tuesday, Thursday, Saturday and Sunday. Meal service.

Sights in **Port Elizabeth:** Many fine parks, including St. George's Park. The oceanarium in Settler's Park Nature Preserve. Nearby is Addo Elephant National Park.

Port Elizabeth - Mosselbaai (Mossel Bay) - Cape Town   3572

The most scenic train ride in South Africa, called "the Garden Route". This trip offers mountain and seashore scenery. Watch for thousands of ostriches near Oudtshoorn.

Dep. Port Elizabeth	18:40(1)		Dep. Cape Town	15:45(1)
Dep. Oudtshoorn	10:20 Day 2		Arr. Mosselbaai	8:40 Day 2
Dep. Mosselbaai	15:10		Dep. Oudtshoorn	14:03
Arr. Cape Town	8:40 Day 3		Arr. Port Elizabeth	6:15 Day 3

(1)Runs daily, except Saturday. Meal service.

Sights in **Mosselbaai:** A very nice seashore resort.

Sights in **Cape Town:** The Malay Quarter. The Municipal Botanic Garden, South African Library, Museum and National Gallery, all at what was once the garden of the East India Company. The Africana collection at both the Library of Parliament and the Castle. The Cultural History Museum. Koopmans de Wet House. Groote Kerk (the "Great Church"). See the marvelous coastal scenery, either by taking the bus tour along Chapman's Peak Drive or the cable car to the top of Table Mountain. Other bus tours go to the many wineries near Stellenbosch.

Pretoria - Johannesburg - Kimberley - Cape Town   3500+3570

This is the route of the wonderful, all first-class Blue Train, which provides 4 categories: Super-Luxury (a suite consisting of a bedroom with twin beds, private lounge and a bathroom with tub and toilet), Luxury (compartment with one or 3 berths, with its own bathroom having a tub and toilet), Semi-Luxury (compartment with one or 3 berths, private shower and toilet), and Standard (compartment with one or 2 berths that can be converted to 3 berths). There is only one Super-Luxury compartment. Passengers traveling in a Standard Compartment have use of a shower in the carriage.

Blue Train is so popular that advance seat reservations are nearly always necessary. Due to the heavy demand for travel on this train, space on it can be reserved as much as 11 months in advance of travel date.

Air-conditioning with individual controls. Electrically operated venetian blinds sealed between windows. Suites equipped with refrigerator, wine rack and FM radio reception. Double insulation and advanced construction techniques make this train vibrationless and noiseless. The seats are upholstered in leather. At 16:30, the "valet" brings tea and the afternoon newspaper.

The schedule provides daytime viewing in both directions of the scenic area between Touws River and Cape Town, during which the line descends or ascends 2,352 feet within one 36-mile section, into or out of De Doorns Valley.

Dep. Pretoria	6:45(1+2)	10:00(1+4)	19:18(5)	20:15(7)
Dep. Johannesburg	9:00(1+2)	11:30(1+4)	20:30(5)	22:00(7)
Arr. Kimberley	16:32(1+2)	18:31(1+4)	-0-	7:38(8)
Arr. Cape Town	10:50(3)	12:00(3)	6:30(6)	6:30(6)

*　　*　　*

Dep. Cape Town	9:00(1+7)	10:30(1+4)	22:00(11)	-0-
Dep. Kimberley	2:00(1+3+10)	3:35(1+3+4)	21:00(3+11)	-0-
Arr. Johannesburg	10:10(3)	11:00(3)	6:07(6)	-0-
Arr. Pretoria	11:56(3)	12:30(3)	8:02(6)	-0-

(1)Reservation required. Meal service. (2)Runs daily, except Monday and Wednesday. (3)Day 2. (4)"Blue Train". Reservation required. Supplement charged. Has only sleeping cars. Air-conditioned. See Cooks Table #3500 for days that "Blue Train" runs in 1984. (5)Runs Tuesday, Thursday, Saturday and Sunday. Meal service. (6)Day 3. (7)Runs daily, except Monday and Wednesday. Meal service on Day 2. (8)Runs daily except Tuesday and Thursday. Meal service. (9)Daily, except Monday and Wednesday. (10)Daily, except Tuesday and Thursday. (11)Daily, except Monday and Wednesday. Meal service all of Day 2.

Sights in **Kimberley:** Many diamond mines in this area. See the collection of Bushman artifacts in both the Duggan-Cronin Bantu Gallery and in McGregor Memorial Museum.

Cape Town - Bitterfontein   3577

Dep. Cape Town	20:15(1)	Dep. Bitterfontein	13:40(4)
Arr. Bitterfontein	11:19(2+3)	Arr. Cape Town	6:00(2)

(1)Runs Tuesday, Thursday, Friday and Sunday. (2)Day 2. (3)Arrives 12:10 on Saturday. (4)Runs Monday, Wednesday and Friday.

Johannesburg - Pretoria - Maputo   3510
The train route to Mozambique.

Dep. Johannesburg	6:48	16:45(1)	18:15
Arr. Pretoria	8:33	18:20	19:43
Arr. Maputo	-0-	-0-	11:05
	*	*	*
Dep. Maputo	-0-	-0-	16:35
Dep. Pretoria	18:20	6:42	7:59
Arr. Johannesburg	20:10	8:15(2)	9:30

(1)Departs at 16:30 on Sunday. (2)Arrives at 9:17 on Sunday.

Johannesburg - Harare (Salisbury)
The train route through Botswana to Rhodesia.

3475		3455	
Dep. Johannesburg	12:30(1)	Dep. Bulawayo	20:00
Dep. Mafikeng	21:00	Arr. Harare	7:00(3)
Arr. Bulawayo	14:10(2)		
Change trains.			

(1)Runs Thursday only. Reservation required. Mea; service. (2)Day 2.   (3)Day 3 from Johannesburg.

Johannesburg - De Aar - Windhoek
3570

Dep. Johannesburg	10:30(1)	11:30(2)	20:30(3)	22:00(4)
Arr. De Aar	22:44	22:01	14:05	13:34
Change trains.				

3600

Dep. De Aar	3:25(5)	17:55(7)	18:55	-0-
Arr. Windhoek	6:30(6)	21:16(6)	4:15(8)	-0-

(1)Daily, except Monday and Wednesday. Reservation required. Meal service. (2)"Blue Train". Reservation required. Supplement charged Air-conditioned. Carries only first-class sleeping cars. Suites and staterooms are available. See pages 561 and 562 for detailed description of luxury services provided. See Cooks Table -3500 for days that "Blue Train" runs in 1984.   (3)Runs Tuesday, Thursday, Saturday and Sunday. Meal service (4)Runs daily, except Monday and Wednesday. (5)Runs Wednesday only. Meal service. (6)Day 2 from De Aar. (7)Runs Friday only. Meal service. (8)Day 3 from De Aar.

Cape Town - De Aar - Windhoek

The other train route to South West Africa (Namibia).

3570

Dep. Cape Town	9:00(1)	9:30(2)	18:00(3)	18:15(4 + 10)
Arr. De Aar	22:15	0:58	8:45	12:50

Change trains.

3600

Dep. De Aar	3:25(6)	17:55(8)	18:55	-0-
Arr. Windhoek	6:30(7)	21:16(7)	4:15(9)	-0-

(1)"Blue Train". Reservation required. Supplement charged. Air-conditioned. Meal service. Carries only first-class sleeping cars. Suites and staterooms available. For description of luxury services aboard "Blue Train", see pages 561 and 562. See Cooks Table –3500 for exact days "Blue Train" runs in 1984. (2)Reservation required. Runs daily, except Monday and Wednesday. Meal service. (3)Reservation required. Runs Monday and Friday. Meal service. (4)Runs daily. Has light refreshments on Tuesday, Thursday and Sunday. (5)Reservation required. Meal service. (6)Runs Wednesday only. Meal service. (7)Day 2 from De Aar. (8)Runs Friday only. Meal service. (9)Day 3 from De Aar. (10)Plus another departure from Cape Town at 21:00(5).

SOUTH WEST AFRICA (NAMIBIA)

These services are run by South African Railways.

Otavi - Windhoek - Keetmanshoop - De Aar

3606   (Bus)

Dep. Otavi	-0-	10:00(1)	-0-
Arr. Windhoek	-0-	16:00	-0-

Change to train.

3600

Dep. Windhoek	8:00(1+2)	19:00(2+4)	21:00(6)
Dep. Keetmanshoop	17:50(1+2)	4:40(2+3+5)	9:00(3+6)
Arr. De Aar	11:05(3)	22:13(3)	8:05(7)
	*	* *	
Dep. De Aar	3:30(2+8)	18:00(2+9)	19:15(6)
Dep. Keetmanshoop	21:00(2+8)	11:05(2+3+10)	16:07(3+6)
Arr. Windhoek	7:00(3)	21:25(3)	3:50(7)

Change to bus.

3606

Dep. Windhoek	9:30(11)	10:00(12)	-0-
Arr. Otavi	18:00	19:00	-0-

(1)Runs Saturday only. (2)Meal service. (3)Day 2.   (4)Runs Monday only. (5)Runs Tuesday only. (6)Runs daily. (7)Day 3. (8)Runs Wednesday only. (9)Runs Friday only. (10)Runs Saturday only. (11)Reservation required. Runs Thursday only. (12)Reservation required. Runs Sunday only.

Sights in **Windhoek:** The capital of South West Africa (Namibia). Many hot springs in this area. Karakul (Persian lamb) graze here, and the furs are processed in this area. See the State Museum. The lovely gardens around Christus Church.

Walvisbaai - Swakopmund - Windhoek - Tsumeb

3602

Dep. Walvis	19:00	-0-
Dep. Swako	20:10	-0-
Arr. Windhoek	6:05	-0-

Change trains.

3606

Dep. Windhoek	9:30(1)	10:00(2)
Arr. Tsumeb	18:00	19:00

3606

Dep. Tsumeb	7:00(3)	-0-
Arr. Windhoek	16:00	-0-

Change trains.

3602

Dep. Windhoek		
Dep. Swakop	5:55(5)	8:15(7)
Arr. Walvis	7:00	9:20

(1)Reservation required. Runs Thursday only. (2)Reservation required. Runs Sunday only.(3)Reservation required. Runs Monday and Friday. (4)Runs daily, except Saturday. (5)Runs daily, except Sunday. (6)Runs Saturday only. (7)Runs Sunday only.

Sights in Swakopmund: The government moves here from Windhoek, the capital, during the Summer (December and January) because it is cooler here than in Windhoek. This is South West Africa's principal seaside resort. Good fishing. See the exhibits of natural history, marine life and mineralogy in the Swakopmund Museum.

Luderitz - Keetmanshoop   3601

Dep. Luderitz	18:00(1)	Dep. Keetmanshoop	18:30(1)
Arr. Keetmanshoop	6:19(2)	Arr. Luderitz	6:20(2)

Sights in **Luderitz:** There is much diamond mining in this area. One cannot enter the prohibited area outside the town without a permit. Rock lobster fishing and processing is extensive here. See the small museum's collection of Bushman tools and other archaeological objects.

SUDAN

Sudan's rail system links Port Sudan on the Red Sea with the inland capital, Khartoum. From Haiya, there are 2 possible train routes to Khartoum. A northern one goes vis Atbara, and a southern route runs via Kassala.

There is rail service north from Khartoum to Wadi Halfa and, from there, on to the Nile and to Cairo by a combination of boat and train. This is the only rail connection between Sudan and a country adjacent to it. A short spur from this route goes west to Karima.

Two lines run south from Khartoum, one to Ed Damazine and the other to Kosti (from which there is a slow, 11-day boat trip to Juba) and to Babanousa.

A short spur runs from Kosti northwest to El Obeid. Two spurs continue from Babanousa. One goes northwest to Nyala, another southwest to Wau.

Children under 3 travel free. Half-fare for children 3-11. Children 12 and over must pay full fare. When available, the air-conditioned first-class space is advisable. Routes in Sudan are very dusty.

Little vegetation is seen in Sudan. Grass fires engulf more than half the country every year.

Bur Sudan (Port Sudan) - Khartoum   2710
Via Atbara

Dep. Bur Sudan	18:00(1+3)	Dep. Khartoum	11:00(2+3)
Arr. Khartoum	17:45	Arr. Bur Sudan	10:35

(1)Runs Wednesday and Saturday. (2)Runs Tuesday and Thursday. (3)Carries sleeping car.

Sights in **Khartoum:** It is very hot here. The temperature reaches more than 100 degrees Fahrenheit every month and goes as high as 117 degrees. The city was founded by Egyptians as an army camp in 1824. See: The Republican Palace. The Sudan Museum. The Ethnographical Museum. The Natural History Museum. The Zoo, along the river. The meeting of the White Nile and Blue Nile, viewed from the White Nile Bridge. Across the bridge is the sister town, Om Durman, with its fabulous Mosque Square that holds 100,000 people. The silver Khalifa's Mosque. The Mahdi-Khalifiana Museum.

Sights in **Bur Sudan:** African Moslems stop here en route on their pilgrimage to Mecca. This is Sudan's principal port.

Bur (Port) Sudan - Khartoum   2710
Via Kassala

Dep. Bur Sudan	18:00(1)	Dep. Khartoum	13:00(3)
Arr. Khartoum	8:45(2)	Arr. Bur Sudan	9:05(2)

(1)Runs Friday only. (2)Day 3. (3)Runs Thursday only.

Khartoum - Ed Damazine   2705

Both of these trains carry sleeping cars.

Dep. Khartoum	17:00	Monday only
Arr. Ed Damazine	11:20	Tuesday

*   *   *

Dep. Ed Damazine	8:00	Wednesday only
Arr. Khartoum	3:05	Thursday

Khartoum - Nyala 2705

Dep. Khartoum	10:30(1)	Dep. Nyala	10:00(2)
Arr. Nyala	13:25 Day 3	Arr. Khartoum	11:15 Day 3

(1)Runs Monday and Friday. Carries sleeping car. Meal service only on Monday. (2)Runs Tuesday and Saturday. Carries sleeping car. Meal service only on Saturday.

Khartoum - Waw 2705

Dep. Khartoum	10:30(1)	Dep. Waw	18:00(3)
Arr. Waw	10:30(2)	Arr. Khartoum	11:15(2)

(1)Runs Saturday only. Meal service. (2)Day 4. (3)Runs Friday only. Meal service.

Khartoum - Kosti - Juba

The Khartoum-Juba trip takes 9 days, the Juba-Khartoum trip 6 days.

2705 (Train)		2707 (Boat)	
Dep. Khartoum	10:30(1)	Dep. Juba	N/A(2)
Arr. Kosti	2:20	Dep. Malakal	N/A(2)
Change to boat.		Arr. Kosti	N/A(2+4)
2707		Change to train	
Dep. Kosti	N/A(2)	2705	
Dep. Malakal	N/A(2)	Dep. Kosti	20:35(5)
Arr. Juba	N/A(2+3)	Arr. Khartoum	11:15

(1)Runs Monday-Friday. Carries sleeping car. Meal service only on Monday. (2)Service operates "about every 2 weeks". Schedules vary according to depth of water in river. Meal service. (3)Day 6 from Kosti. (4)Day 5 from Juba. (5)Runs Tuesday and Saturday. Carries sleeping car. Meal service only on Saturday.

Wadi Halfa - Khartoum 2700

This train carries sleeping cars and has meal service.

Dep. Wadi Halfa 16:40 Wednesday and Saturday
Arr. Khartoum 16:45 Day 2

Sights in **Wadi Halfa:** This area was the center of archaeological activities in the 1970's to save Egyptian monuments from being covered by the Aswan High Dam reservoir. Egyptian ruins from 2,000 B.C. (the ruins of Buchen) are across the river from Wadi Halfa. An Egyptian colony was here until the Roman invasion.

The Rail Route to Egypt

Sudan's train connection with Egypt from Khartoum involves a Nile boat trip from Wadi Halfa to Sadd el Ali.

Khartoum - Wadi Halfa - El Sadd el Ali - Cairo

This trip crosses the vast Nubian Desert.

2700 (Train)

Dep. Khartoum	6:45(1)
Arr. Wadi Halfa	5:40(2)

Change to boat.

2690

Dep. Wadi Halfa	16:00(3)
Arr. El Sadd el Ali	8:00

Change to train.

2665

Dep. El Sadd el Ali	18:00(5)	19:30(7)
Arr. Cairo (Main)	13:30(6)	14:30(6)

(1)Runs Wednesday and Sunday. Carries sleeping car. Meal service. (2)Day 2 from Khartoum. (3)Runs Thursday and Monday. (4)Day 3 from Wadi Halfa (Saturday and Wednesday. (5)Runs daily. Has only second and third-class coach cars. (6)Day 2 from El Sadd el Ali. (7)Runs daily. Has only second-class coach cars.

SWAZILAND
There are no passenger trains in Swaziland.

TANZANIA
This country's rail system is the modern Tanzam Line that was completed in 1976, running from the seaport of Dar es-Salaam to Tunduma (and on into Zambia), plus 2 routes going north from Dar es-Salaam and 2 that head west from there. One of the northern lines connects another of Tanzania's seaports, Tanga, with Dar es-Salaam.

There is also train-ferry service on Lake Victoria.

Tanzania has many excellent national parks, offering splendid viewing of monkeys, elephants, rhinos, antelopes, lions, zebras and giraffes: Arusha (45 minutes from Dar es-Salaam), Ngorongoro Crater, Lake Manyara, Tarangire, Mikumi, Gombe and the 5,000-square-mile Serengeti.

Children under 3 travel free. Half-fare for children 3-13. Children 14 and over must pay full fare.

First-class seats convert to 2-berth compartments and second-class seats convert to 6-berth compartments for overnight travel.

Dar es-Salaam - Tunduma - Kapiri Mposhi   3310
During this ride, the train climbs as high as 6,000 feet altitude. If you do not like curry and local maize cuisine, it is advisable to bring your own food for this 37-43 hours of travel.

First-class compartments have seats and sleeping berths for 4 persons. Second-class compartments are for 6 people. Both classes share restaurant car services.

All of the trains on this route have meal service.

Dar es-Salaam	10:45(1)	Dep. Kapiri Mposhi	16:50(1)
Arr. Tunduma	12:32(2)	Arr. Tunduma	13:00(2)
Change trains.		Change trains.	
Dep. Tunduma	13:30(3)	Dep. Tunduma	16:00(3)
Arr. Kapiri Mposhi	8:42(4)	Arr. Dar es-Salaam	17:22(4)

(1)Runs Wednesday only. Meal service. (2)Day 2.   (3)Runs Thursday only. Meal service. (4)Day 3.

Sights in **Dar es-Salaam:** Means "Haven of Peace" in Arabic. This is Tanzania's main Indian Ocean seaport. See the 1,700,000-year old skull at the National Museum, as well as abstract Makonde wood carving, Masai weapons, drums and Zanzibar chests and elaborately carved doors. The Botanical Gardens. The Askari Monument. The picturesque boats at Dhow Wharf. The Asian Bazaar, called "Uhindini". Fifteen miles north of here is an extensive complex of seaside resorts.

Dar es-Salaam - Korogwe - Tanga 3300

Dep. Dar es-Salaam	15:10	Dep. Tanga	19:30
Arr. Korogwe	2:25	Arr. Korogwe	21:55
Change trains.		Change trains.	
Dep. Korogwe	3:00	Dep. Korogwe	23:35
Arr. Tanga	5:30	Arr. Dar es-Salaam	9:20

Dar es-Salaam - Moshi

This train trip goes to the southern foot of Mt. Kilimanjaro, highest mountain (over 19,000 feet) in Africa.

	3300	3305	3305
Dep. Dar es-Salaam	15:10	16:30	19:00
Arr. Moshi	8:55	5:05	6:55
	*	*	*

	3300	3305	3300
Dep. Moshi	15:00	16:00	18:30
Arr. Dar es-Salaam	4:05	9:20	6:45

Tanga - Korogwe - Moshi 3305

Dep. Tanga	19:30	Dep. Moshi	16:00
Arr. Korogwe	21:55	Arr. Korogwe	23:35
Change trains.		Change trains.	
Dep. Korogwe	2:25	Dep. Korogwe	3:00
Arr. Moshi	8:55	Arr. Tanga	5:30

Dar es-Salaam - Tabora - Mwanza 3305

This rail trip goes to Lake Victoria. All of these trains have meal service.

Dep. Dar es-Salaam	20:00	Dep. Mwanza	21:10
Arr. Tabora	18:20 Day 2	Arr. Tabora	6:45 Day 2
Change trains.		Change trains.	
Dep. Tabora	20:15	Dep. Tabora	8:45 Day 2
Arr. Mwanza	5:25 Day 3	Arr. Dar es-Salaam	7:20 Day 3

Dar es-Salaam - Morogoro - Dodoma - Tabora - Kigoma   3305

Here are the schedules for the train ride to Lake Tanganyika. There is boat service across the lake, from Kigoma to Kalemie (Zaire).

On this 900-mile trip, Dodoma and Tabora are fine stopping places en route, which at least recently had good and picturesque railway hotels near both stations. There is taxi service for the 7-mile trip from Kigoma to Ujiji, the village where Henry Stanley, after many months of ordeal, found Dr. David Livingstone. A small monument marks the site.

Dep. Dar es-Salaam	20:00(1)	Dep. Kigoma	18:45	
Dep. Morogoro	2:30 Day 2	Arr. Tabora	5:30 Day 2	
Dep. Dodoma	9:30	Change trains.		
Arr. Tabora	18:20	Dep. Tabora	8:45(1)	
Change trains.		Dep. Dodoma	18:30	
Dep. Tabora	21:00	Dep. Morogoro	1:15 Day 3	
Arr. Kigoma	6:50 Day 3	Arr. Dar es-Salaam	7:20	

(1)Meal service.

From Dar es-Salaam to Morogoro is only 7 hours by train. It took Stanley 29 days to walk this 121-mile distance. As at many stations in Africa, here one can buy hard-boiled eggs, peanuts, tea, oranges and samosas (spicy meat knishes) from vendors along the platform.

Sights in **Tabora:** Long avenues, shaded by mango trees that grew from seeds spitted by endless lines of slaves who were herded down these streets. There is a small Livingstone museum in nearby Kwihara (reached by taxi from Tabora), where Stanley rested many weeks during his 1871 search for Livingstone.

Mpanda - Tabora - Kigoma   3305

This is the train route from Mpanda to Lake Tanganyika.

Dep. Mpanda	13:15(1)	Dep. Kigoma	18:45(2)
Arr. Tabora	2:50 Day 2	Arr. Tabora	5:30 Day 2
Change trains.		Change trains.	
Dep. Tabora	21:00(2)	Dep. Tabora	19:40(3)
Arr. Kigoma	6:50 Day 3	Arr. Mpanda	9:55 Day 3

(1)Runs Tuesday, Thursday and Saturday. (2)Day 2.   (3)Runs Monday, Wednesday and Friday.

TOGO

The 2 classes of trains are first and third. Upholstered seats are available only in first-class. Children under 5 travel free. Half-fare for children 5-9. Children 10 and over must pay full fare. The official language in Togo is French.

Lome - Aneho   3052
All of these trains are third-class, unless otherwise designated.

Dep. Lome	7:03(1)	11:45	16:10(2)	-0-
Arr. Aneho	8:45	13:20	17:46(3)	-0-

*   *   *

Dep. Aneho	6:00(4)	9:00(1)	14:05	18:00(5)
Arr. Lome	8:06	10:35	15:40	19:35

(1)Runs Saturday and Sunday. (2)Runs Monday, Tuesday, Thursday and Friday. (3)Arrives 18:33 on Tuesday and Friday. (4)Runs Wednesday and Saturday. (5)Has a first-class coach. Runs Wednesday, Saturday and Sunday.

Sights in **Lome:** Luxury hotels on the beach of this popular resort. The German Cathedral. Nearby, Moslems wearing embroidered robes, selling beads, baskets and bracelets. Many stalls stocked with bolts of bright patterned cloth. Many French restaurants. See the fetish market (black roots, crudely carved dolls, iron objects, etc., all used in the local religion).

Lome - Kpalime   3051

Dep. Lome	6:30(1)	15:15	Dep. Kpalime	6:10	14:20(1)
Arr. Kpalime	11:00	19:08	Arr. Lome	10:35	18:45

(1)Runs daily. Has only third-class space on Tuesday, Thursday and Saturday.

Sights in **Kpalime:** The ride from Lome is through many small villages and tropical forest. Experience the Friday night frivolities before each Saturday's market day, where thousands of people from the outlying area come here to do their weekly shopping. Do not fail to see the famous fantastic kente cloth that has irridescent silk and cotton threads woven into geometric patterns.

Lome - Blitta   3050

Dep. Lome	5:45	7:22(1)	13:20(2)
Arr. Blitta	11:49	18:38	19:27

*   *   *

Dep. Blitta	5:07(3)	6:40(4)	12:30
Arr. Lome	17:14	12:47	18:30

(1)Runs Monday, Wednesday and Friday. Third-class only. (2)Runs Saturday only. (3)Runs Tuesday, Thursday and Saturday. Third-class only. (4)Runs Sunday only.

TUNISIA

Because Tunisia is only 2 hours by air from Paris and one hour from Rome, it is a popular vacation place for Europeans.

Tunisia's rail system is 2 lines running west from Tunis (one to Bizerte and the other to Ghardimaou, and on to Algeria) and one heading south from Tunis, to Gabes. An 11-mile spur from Bir-bou-Rekba on this southern line goes to Hammamet and Nabeul.

The 3 classes of seats are first, second and luxury-class. All luxury-class and some first-class space are air-conditioned. Children under 3 travel free. Half-fare for children 3-9. Children 10 and over must pay full fare.

Tunis

There are more than 700 exceptional monuments to see here. The finest and largest collection of Roman mosaics in the world are on exhibit at the National Museum of the Bardo, as well as Punic, Byzantine, Arab and other Roman objects (open daily except Monday 9:00-12:00 and 14:00-17:30).

See the fantastic 9th century Great Mosque Zitouna (Mosque of the Olive Tree). A marvelous collection of illuminated Korans and other Arabic manuscripts in the National Library. The beautiful interior of the Zaouia (temple) of Sidi Mahrez. The marble and sculptured wood in the lovely Dar Ben Abdullah, an example of Tunis' many 19th century "great houses".

The Lapidary Museum of Sidi Bou Krissan. The valuable objects from Egypt, Persia and Turkey at the Dar Hussein Museum of Islamic Art, in an 18th century mansion. The 17th century Mosque of Hamouda Pasha. The 16th century Mosque El Youssefi (Mosque of the Kasbah). The Belvedere Zoo. The many beach resorts south of Tunis.

There are half-day tours to Carthage, Sidi Bou Said and the Bardo Museum. A full-day tour goes to Dougga.

Dougga

It is a short drive from Tunis to Dougga. See the 2nd century B.C. Dougga Mausoleum, a prince's tomb. Many temples and an ancient Market Place, all very well preserved. The Comedie Francaise often performs in the large open-air theater. Dougga is Tunisia's largest archaeological site, one of the best-preserved Roman towns in Tunisia.

Kerkouane

This city is near Tunis. It is the only unmutilated Punic town, the only one that was not built upon by succeeding generations.

Thuburo Majus

Near both Tunis and Sousse. Many fabulous ruins here: temples, a Forum, and public buildings. An excellently-preserved Roman town.

Utica

Near both Tunis and Bizerte. This was a Phoenician port in the 11th century B.C. Some vaults from that period and many fine Roman ruins can be seen here. The Museum has a fine collection of ancient jewels and funeral furniture.

Tunis - Bizerte   2610

All of these trains have light refreshments.

Dep. Tunis (Bizerte)	5:35	13:50	17:18(1)	18:25
Arr. Bizerte	7:27	15:42	18:48	20:17
		*	*	*
Dep. Bizerte	5:40	8:45(1)	13:30	18:05
Arr. Tunis (Bizerte)	7:29	10:16	15:21	20:01

(1)Air-conditioned in first and luxury-class.

Sights in **Bizerte:** A seaport and naval base. This city has been ruled by Punic, Roman, Byzantine, Arab and Turkish leaders. See: The Er-Rimel beach. The Old Port, with docks for fishing boats. Nearby there are many interesting villages: Tabarka, Utica, Raf-Raf, Ain Draham, Ghar El Melh (Porto Farina), Ras Djebel, Metline, Sounine, Aousdja, Zouaouine, El Alia, Kalaat El Andalous, Sedjenane.

Tunis - Carthage   2600

It is a short ride from Tunis to Carthage on a 1908 wooden train which starts at Place d'Afrique in the center of Tunis and stops at several fashionable seaside resorts.

Get off at Carthage's Hannibal station to visit the birthplace of Hannibal. This city was founded in 814 B.C. There are many outstanding Punic and Roman ruins here. Plays, dances, musical performances and sound and light performances are presented every July and August in both the Roman Theater and in the Baths of Antonin.

See: The very large and beautifully decorated 2nd century Roman baths, nearly 700 feet long. The National Museum of Carthage. The ancient Theater, built in a marble quarry. The pink marble columns and the mosaic floor (depicting birds in the leaves of a tree) at the Villa de la Voliere in the Carthage Antiquarium. The Basilica of St. Cyprian.

Get off at Carthage's Salammbo station to see The Tophet, now an open-air museum, where humans were sacrificed.

Dep. Tunis (Nord)	Frequent times from 3:05 to 1:10
Arr. Carthage	25 minutes later
	* * *
Dep. Carthage	Frequent times from 3:05 to 1:10
Arr. Tunis (Nord)	25 minutes later

Tunis - Ghardimaou   2611

Dep. Tunis	4:48(1)	8:10(1+2)	11:25(3)	13:28(1+4)
Arr. Ghardimaou	8:42	11:20	14:35	16:51

* * *

Dep. Ghardimaou	5:35(1)	10:00(1+2)	11:30(3)	12:45(1+5)
Arr. Tunis	9:11	13:05	14:52	16:07

(1)Light refreshments. (2)Air-conditioned in luxury and first-class. (3)Supplement charged. (4)Plus other departures from Tunis at 16:15(1+2) and 17:52(1).
(5)Plus other departures from Ghardimaou at 15:40(1+2) and 17:50(1).

Ghardimaou - Algiers
2550

Dep. Ghardimaou	11:05	14:55
Arr. Annaba	14:32	17:55

Change trains.
2540

Dep. Annaba	18:45(1)	6:10(2)
Dep. Constantine	22:10(1)	9:30(2)
Arr. Algiers	6:35	16:46

(1)Light refreshments. (2)Meal service.

Tunis - Jerba   2618 (Bus)

Dep. Tunis	5:30	Dep. Jerba		5:15
Dep. Sfax	9:55	Dep. Gabes		7:30
Dep. Gabes	12:40	Dep. Sfax		10:15
Arr. Jerba	14:55	Arr. Tunis		14:30

Sights in **Sfax:** Archaeological collections of mosaics, lamps and glass and bronze objects in the Municipal Museum.

Sights in **Sfax** and **Gabes:** see page 579.

Sights in **Jerba:** This heavenly island garden-oasis is one of Tunisia's most popular resorts. See the fine 3rd century mosaics. The massive white 15th century fort. La Ghriba, one of the oldest synagogues in the world. The magnificent Museum. Marvelous handicrafts (enameled jewelry, blankets) are sold in small shops.

Tunis - Kairouan   2602 (Bus)

Dep. Tunis	5:30	10:00	13:45
Arr. Kairouan	8:30	13:00	18:30

* * *

Dep. Kairouan	4:45	10:30	15:15
Arr. Tunis	8:45	13:30	18:15

Sights in **Kairouan:** The unbelievably beautiful carved wood panels of the Minibar (pulpit) and gilded 9th century tiles in the massive 9th century Great Mosque of Okba Ibn Nafaa, the founder of Kairouan. The splendid collection of parchment manuscripts of the Koran, 9th century bookbindings, ceramics and glassware in the Museum of Islamic Art, opposite the Great Mosque.

The 17th century Zaouia of Abou Zamaa El Balaoui (Mosque of the Barber). The 9th century reservoirs, Bassins Aghlabides. Narrow streets that are 1,000 years old. The 9th century facade on the Mosque of Three Doors. The Museum of Rugs. The ruins of nearby Rakada.

Taste the date cakes, dipped in honey. Famous piled rugs are made here. Also outstanding copperware: coffee and tea pots, jars, plates, cooking pots.

Tunis - Hammamet - Nabeul   2605

A one-day roundtrip from Tunis to Hammamet and/or Nabeul is possible, as these schedules indicate.

Dep. Tunis (East)	6:00(1)	7:10(2+3)	12:30(2+3+7)
Arr. Bir-bou-Rekba	7:06	8:01	13:21
Change trains.			
Dep. Bir-bou-Rekba	7:08(1)	8:32(2)	13:58(2)
Arr. Hammamet	7:15	8:39	14:05
Arr. Nabeul	7:30	8:54	14:20

* * *

Dep. Nabeul	5:34(1+5)	6:15(1)	7:36(1+8)
Dep. Hammamet	5:50(1+5)	6:31(1)	7:52(1)
Arr. Bir-bou-Rekba	5:52(1+5)	6:37	7:58
Change trains.			
Dep. Bir-bou-Rekba	5:57(1+5)	6:40(1)	8:30
Arr. Tunis	7:16	7:46	9:20

(1)Second-class only. (2)Air-conditioned in luxury and first-class. (3)Light refreshments. (4)Runs Friday and Saturday (5)Direct train. No train change in Bir-bou-Rekba. (6)Runs daily, except Friday and Saturday. (7)Plus other departures from Tunis at 14:05(1+4+5), 15:10(1), 18:08(1+5+6) and 18:30(1).

(8)Plus other departures from Nabeul at 10:11(1+2+3), 12:52(1), 15:45(1) and 18:28(1+2+3).

Sights in **Hammamet:** A popular seashore resort. See: The medieval fortress. Fantastic gardens of flowers and fruit trees.

Sights in **Nabeul:** Many fine mosaics. Excellent straw and pottery porducts are made here.

Tunis - Sousse - El Jem - Sfax - Gabes

2605

Dep. Tunis (East)	7:10(1)	13:05	14:00(1)	17:05(1)
Dep. Sousse	9:09(1)	14:58	15:54(1)	19:01(1)
Dep. El Jem	-0-	15:45	-0-	19:52(1)
Arr. Sfax	10:42(1)	16:29	17:25	20:39

2615

Dep. Sfax	10:46(1)	-0-	-0-	20:45(1)
Arr. Gabes	12:49	-0-	-0-	22:50

*   *   *

Dep. Gabes	5:50(1)	-0-	-0-	15:48(1)
Arr. Sfax	7:50	-0-	-0-	17:50

2605

Dep. Sfax	7:55(1)	12:05(1)	13:15(2)	17:55(1)
Dep. El Jem	-0-	-0-	14:06(2)	18:42(1)
Dep. Sousse	9:40(1)	13:39(1)	14:59(2)	19:32(1)
Arr. Tunis (East)	11:27	15:46(1)	17:07	21:33

(1)Air-conditioned in luxury and first-class. (2)Second-class only.

Sights in **Sousse:** Exhibits of prehistoric objects as well as Punic, Roman and early Christian mosaics and statues at the Museum, in the Kasbah. The 9th century Ribat (fort), 2 rooms of which are devoted to exhibits of Islamic textiles, ceramics, miniatures, Koran manuscripts, jewelry and glassware. The 9th century Grand Mosque.

Sights in **Maktar:** Near Sousse. Outstanding Roman ruins: the Great Baths and Trajan's Triumphal Arch. Also Punic and Roman marble and bronze statues at the Museum.

Sights in **Mahdia:** Near Sousse. An important vacation resort. The presently restored 10th century Mosque of Mahdia. Fantastic mosaics and Roman architecture. Fine wool embroidery is done here.

Sights in **Sbeitla:** Near Sousse. A truly magnificent ancient capital. See: The Triumphal Arch, Forum, and the mosaics on the floor of an old Christian basilica.

Sights in **Moknine:** Near Sousse. This is a pottery center. Its little museum has ancient gold jewelry, still a specialty of local artisans. Much spectacular weaving is done here.

Sights in **Monastir:** A short ride from Sousse. The remarkably well-preserved 8th century Ribat, one of the largest Arab forts in North Africa, 3 rooms of which have exhibits of Islamic textiles, ceramics, miniatures, Koran manuscripts, jewelry and glassware.

Sights in **El Jem:** A marvelous 3rd century amphitheater, one of the largest and best preserved Roman colosseums. Near it are many statues, mosaics and bronze objects from the Punic, Roman and early Christian periods. Great wool embroidery here.

Sights in **Sfax;** Archaeological collections of mosaics, lamps and glass and bronze objects in the Municipal Museum.

Sights in **Gabes:** This town consists of 2 large villages: Djara and Menzel. It is a 3½-mile oases along the seashore. There are many date palm groves here. Try the palm wine. Good palm leaf basket-work, jewelry and forged iron are offered in the shops of Djara. See the Sidi Driss Mosque. The Sidi Boulbaba Mosque is on the road to nearby Matmata.

Sights in **Matmata:** Near Gabes. People live here in holes, both to get out of the sun and because of the lack of building materials in this locale. However, the interior of some of these underground homes are beautifully furnished. One hotel, with a bar and restaurant, is completely underground.

Sights in **Zarzis:** Near Gabes. A dense green oasis resort, with a forest of 50-year old olive trees. There is exceptional fishing in nearby Biban Lake.

UGANDA

Landlocked Uganda's rail lines radiate from Tororo: northwest to Pakwach, west to Kasese, and southeast to Nairobi (and on to Mombasa). Children under 3 travel free. Half-fare for children 3-13. Children 14 and over must pay full fare.

Tororo - Gulu - Pakwach   3285

Dep. Tororo	4:00(1)	Dep. Pakwach	14:00(2)
Arr. Gulu	18:00	Arr. Gulu	19:08
Change trains.		Change trains.	
Dep. Gulu	6:00(2)	Dep. Gulu	7:00(3)
Arr. Pakwach	10:15	Arr. Tororo	20:35

(1)Runs Monday, Wednesday and Friday. (2)Runs Saturday only. (3)Runs Tuesday, Thursday and Saturday.

Tororo - Jinja - Kampala - Kasese

This line touches the northern shore of Lake Victoria at Kampala.

3286		3289	
Dep. Tororo	6:00(1)	Dep. Kasese	18:30
Dep. Jinja	9:32(1)	Arr. Kampala	9:20(2)
Arr. Kampala	12:25	Change trains.	
Change trains.		3286	
3289		Dep. Kampala	16:00(1+2)
Dep. Kampala	19:00	Dep. Jinja	19:04(1+2)
Dep. Kasese	10:20(2)	Arr. Tororo	22:50(2)

(1)Daily, except Monday. (2)Day 2.

Sights in **Kampala:** The capital of Uganda. See the collection of African musical instruments in the Uganda Museum. Several Hindu temples. Rubaga Cathedral. The white Kibuli Mosque. The "apocalypse" ceiling of St. Francis' Chapel at Makerere University. The Botanical Garden in Entebbe, 20 miles away.

Tororo - Nairobi - Mombasa   3275

Dep. Tororo	N/A(1)	Dep. Mombasa	19:00(4)
Dep. Malaba	16:00(2)	Arr. Nairobi	8:15(3)
Arr. Nairobi	8:45(3)	Change trains.	
Change trains.		Dep. Nairobi	9:30(6)
Dep. Nairobi	19:00(4)	Arr. Malaba	2:50(1+5)
Arr. Mombasa	8:00(5)	Arr. Tororo	N/A(1)

(1)Travel 14km (8½ miles) by road Tororo-Malaba and v.v. (2)Runs Monday, Wednesday and Saturday. Meal service. (3)Day 2.   (4)Meal service. (5)Day 2 from Nairobi. (6)Runs Tuesday, Thursday and Sunday. Meal service.

UPPER VOLTA

Landlocked Upper Volta has one train route, from Ouagadougou to Bobo Dioulasso, and on into Ivory Coast. Schedules appear earlier in this chapter, under "Ivory Coast".

ZAIRE

Children under 3 travel free. Half-fare for children 3-9. Children 10 and over must pay full fare.

This country's rail system is Y-shaped, with Lubumbashi at the bottom of the vertical South-North line and Kamina at the point that one route goes northwest to Ilebo, where there is boat service to Kinshasa and train facility from there to the ports of Banana and Pointe Noire on the coastline of Congo. Another route goes northeast from Kamina to Kalemie (on the west shore of Lake Tanganyika), where there is boat service across the lake to Kigoma in Tanzania, and trains from Kigoma to Dar es-Salaam.

Rail facilities operate south from Lubumbashi to Kapiri Moshi and on through Zambia, Zimbabwe and Botswana into South Africa and all the way to Cape Town. Another major rail line runs west from Tenke (on the Lubumbashi-Kamina route) to Lobito on the coastline of Angola. This is a segment of Africa's only transcontinental rail line, running from Lobito on the Atlantic Ocean to the Indian Ocean cities of Beirain (Mozambique) and Dar es-Salaam (Tanzania).

Lubumbashi - Tenke - Kamina   3225

Dep. Lubumbashi	9:00(1+2)	12:00(2+4)	20:00(5+6)
Dep. Tenke	15:25(1+2)	21:10(2+4)	13:00(6+7)
Arr. Kamina	2:50(3)	10:00(3)	15:00(8)

*   *   *

Dep. Kamina	0:15(2+7)	4:50(2+9)	7:15(2+10+12)
Dep. Tenke	13:10(2+7)	16:25(2+9)	20:45(2+10+13)
Arr. Lubumbashi	22:05	22:50	6:00(3)

(1)Runs Monday, Tuesday and Thursday. (2)Has couchettes. Meal service. (3)Day 2.   (4)Runs Wednesday and Saturday. (5)Runs Saturday only. (6)Third-class only. (7)Runs Sunday only. (8)Day 3.   (9)Runs Thursday only. (10)Runs Tuesday only. (11)Runs Wednesday only. (12)Plus other departures from Kamina at 8:50(2+5), 9:00(6+9) and 22:00(2+10).   (13)Plus other departures from Tenke at 20:25(2+5), 15:20(6+9) and 9:35(2+11).

Kamina - Ilebo - Kinshasa - Brazzaville

This route involves a 4-day boat ride from Ilebo to Kinshasa.

3225			3209		
Dep. Kamina	11:00(1)	Sun.	Dep. Ilebo	15:00(2)	Tues.
Arr. Ilebo	6:00	Tues.	Arr. Kinshasa	7:00	Sat.
Change to boat.			Change to another boat.		
			3171		
			Dep. Kinshasa	N/A(3)	
			Arr. Brazzaville	N/A(4)	

(1)Has couchettes. Meal service. (2)Reservation required. Meal service. (3)Operates daytime only. Runs every 30 minutes. (4)Twenty minutes after departing Kinshasa.

Sights in **Kinshasa:** The capital of Zaire. Largest city in Black Africa (1,400,000 population). See the Kinshasa Museum.

Kamina - Kalemie - Kigoma - Tabora - Dar es-Salaam

This is the train trip to Lake Tanganyika and on into Tanzania.

3220			3305	
Dep. Kamina	11:00(1)	Fri.	Dep. Kigoma	18:45
Arr. Kalemie	6:00	Sat.	Arr. Tabora	5:30(2)
Change to boat.			Change trains.	
3215			Dep. Tabora	8:45(1)
Dep. Kalemie	16:30(1)	Sun.	Dep. Dodoma	18:30(1)
Arr. Kigoma	7:00	Mon.	Dep. Morogoro	1:15(1+3)
Change to train.			Arr. Dar es-Salaam	7:20(3)

(1)Meal service. (2)Day 2 from Kigoma. (3)Day 3 from Kigoma.

Lubumbashi - Ndola - Kapiri Mposhi

3401			3405		
Dep. Lubum	N/A(1)	N/A(1)	Dep. Kapiri	16:53(3)	20:38(2)
Arr. Ndola	N/A(1)	N/A(1)	Arr. Ndola	20:00	22:40
Change trains.			Change trains.		
3405			3401		
Dep. Ndola	10:00(2)	21:40(3)	Dep. Ndola	N/A(1)	N/A(1)
Arr. Kapiri	12:02	0:15	Arr, Lubum	N/A	N/A(1)

(1)Time has *not* been available since 1980. (2)First-class only. Meal service. (3)Light refreshments.

Lubumbashi - Sakania   3229

Both of these trains have light refreshments.

Dep. Lubumbashi	9:00(1)	Dep. Sakania	24:00(2)
Arr. Sakania	21:00	Arr. Lubumbashi	15:00

(1)Runs Wednesday only. (2)Runs Thursday only.

Lubumbashi - Tenke - Dilolo - Lobito
The rail service to Angola.

3228

Dep. Lubumbashi	17:00(1+2)	17:00(1+4)	20:00(1+3)
Dep. Tenke	23:25(1+2)	2:10(1+5)	13:00(1+6)
Arr. Dilolo	15:25(3)	20:50(5)	11:00(7)

Change trains.

3421

| Dep. Dilolo | N/A(8) | -0- | -0- |
| Arr. Lobito | N/A(8) | -0- | -0- |

(1)Has couchette. Meal service. (2)Mon. only. (3)Tues. only. (4)Thurs. only. (5)Fri. only. (6)Wed. only. (7)Thurs. only. Daily service, circumstances permitting. Times have *not* been available since anti-government guerrillas began bombing and derailing the trains in 1980.

ZAMBIA
On a map of landlocked Zambia, the outline of its rail system is a sloppy "Y", with Livingstone in the south at the bottom of the "Y". The right-arm runs east from Kapiri Mposhi to Tunduma and on into Tanzania. This is Zambia's portion of the Tanzam Railway, which terminates at the port of Dar es-Salaam.

The left-arm of the "Y" goes from Kapiri Mposhi to Ndola and on into Zaire. A small spur runs off this route, from Ndola to Kitwe.

South of Livingstone is the border with Zimbabwe and a connection to Victoria Falls, and on to Bulawayo, a junction for continuing southwest to South Africa or heading southeast to Mozambique. There is also service from Bulawayo northeast to Harare (Salisbury).

First-class seats are upholstered. Second-class seats have leather covering. Children under 3 travel free. Half-fare for children 3-15. Children 16 and over must pay full fare.

Livingstone - Victoria Falls - Bulawayo - Salisbury

3458

Dep. Livingstone	N/A(1)
Arr. Victoria Falls	N/A(1)
Dep. Victoria Falls	17:30(2)
Arr. Bulawayo	7:15 Day 2

Change trains.

3455

| Dep. Bulawayo | 20:00 Day 2 |
| Arr. Harare | 7:00 Day 3 |

Dep. Bulawayo	19:00(2)
Arr. Victoria Falls	7:30 Day 2
Dep. Victoria Falls	N/A(1)
Arr. Livingstone	N/A(1)

(1)Service was "temporarily" suspended in 1979. (2)Meal service.

Sights in **Livingstone:** This is the most popular tourist center in Zambia. See the flowers and aviary in Barotse Gardens. The Livingstone Museum's archaeological, historical and ethnological exhibits. Traditional dances, performed at Maramba Cultural Center.

Nearby, Lake Kariba, Livingstone Game Park, Kafue National Park and Wankie National Park. Take a cruise on the Zambesi River.

The most important sight here is seen by taking an excursion to the nearby majestic Victoria Falls, which are more than 5,500 feet wide and have a minimum drop of 355 feet. The falls are the border between Zambia and Zimbabwe (formerly Rhodesia). There is a great view from Knife Edge Bridge. However, the best view is from the Zimbabwe side, looking at the two-thirds of the falls owned by Zambia.

Livingstone - Lusaka - Kapiri Mposhi - Dar es-Salaam

The Tansam Railway is the portion from Kapiri Mposhi to Dar es-Salaam. Much wildlife can be seen as the train passes through Mkumi National Park.

The train climbs as high as 6,000 feet altitude during this ride. If you do not like curry and local maize cuisine, it is advisable to bring your own food for this 37-43 hours of travel.

3405		
Dep.		
Livingstone	8:00(1)	23:40(2)
Dep. Lusaka	17:10(1)	11:40(2)
Arr. Kapiri	20:33	16:48
Change trains.		
3310		
Dep. Kapiri	-0-	16:50(3)
Arr. Tunduma	-0-	13:00
Change trains.		
Dep. Tunduma	-0-	16:00(4)
Arr.	-0-	17:25(5)

331		
Dep. Dar	-0-	10:45(3)
Arr. Tunduma	-0-	12:32(6)
Change trains.		
Dep. Tunduma	-0-	13:30(4+6)
Arr. Kapiri	-0-	8:42(7)
Change trains.		
3405		
Dep. Kapiri	0:25(2)	12:07(1)
Dep. Lusaka	6:05(2)	15:45(1)
Arr.		
Livingst'n	17:45	0:45 Dar

(1)First-class only. Meal service. (2)Carries sleeping car. Light refreshments. (3)Runs Wednesday only. Meal service. (4)Runs Thursday only. Meal service. (5)Day 2 from Tunduma. (6)Day 2 from Dar es-Salaam. (7)Day 3 from Dar es-Salaam.

Sights in **Lusaka:** The capital of Zambia. See the large copper cross over the altar in the Anglican Cathedral of the Holy Cross. Luburma Central Market. The Tobacco Auction Floor. The 8-acre Twickenham Road Archaeological Site in Olympia Park, a suburb. Nearby, Munda Wanga Park and Botanical Gardens, Kafue Gorge. The Ayrshire Farm Rock Engravings national monument. Blue Lagoon National Park.

Kapiri Mopshi - Ndola - Lubumbashi
This is the train route into Zaire.

3405			3401		
Dep. Kapiri	16:53(1)	20:38(3)	Dep. Lubum	N/A(2)	N/A(2)
Arr. Ndola	20:00	22:40	Arr. Ndola	N/A(2)	N/A(2)
Change trains.			Change trains.		
3401			3405		
Dep. Ndola	N/A(2)	N/A(2)	Dep. Ndola	10:00(3)	21:40(1)
Arr. Lubum	N/A(2)	N/A(2)	Arr. Kapiri	12:02	0:15

(1)Light refreshments. (2)Time has not been available since 1980. (3)First-class only. Meal service.

Livingstone - Mulobezi 3410
This is a spur off the Victoria Falls-Kapiri Mposhi line.

Dep. Livingstone	9:00(1)	Dep. Mulobezi		8:00(2)
Arr. Mulobezi	17:55	Arr. Livingstone		17:45

(1)Runs Thursday and Sunday. (2)Runs Monday and Friday.

ZIMBABWE (formerly RHODESIA)
There are 4 classes of seats. First-class compartments convert to 4 couchettes at night. Second-class compartments convert to 6 couchettes. There is a charge for bedding. Children under 3 travel free. Half-fare for children 3-11. Children 12 and over must pay full fare.

There are rail connections between Harare (formerly Salisbury) in landlocked Zimbabwe and Zambia, Mozambique and Botswana.

Harare (Salisbury) - Bulawayo - Victoria Falls - Livingstone

3455		3458	
Dep. Harare	20:00	Dep. Livingstone	N/A(2)
Arr. Bulawayo	7:00	Dep. Victoria Falls	17:30(1)
Change trains.		Dep. Thomson Junction	20:50(1)
3458		Arr. Bulawayo	7:15
Dep. Bulawayo	19:00(1)	Change trains.	
Dep. Thomson Junction	4:35(1)	3455	
Arr. Victoria Falls	7:30	Dep. Bulawayo	20:00
Arr. Livingstone	N/A(2)	Arr. Harare	7:00

(1)Meal service. (2)Service between Victoria Falls and Livingstone was "temporarily" suspended in 1979.

Sights in **Salisbury:** The capital. See the Queen Victoria Memorial Library and Museum. The Rhodes National Gallery.

Sights in **Bulawayo:** The National Museum. Nearby, Rhodes' Tomb in the Matapo Hills and the Khami Ruins.

Sights in **Victoria Falls:** These spectacular falls are more than 5,500 feet wide and have a maximum drop of 355 feet. This is the border between Zimbabwe (formerly Rhodesia) and Zambia. The best view is from the Zimbabwe side, looking at the two-thirds of the falls that is in Zambia.

Harare (Salisbury) - Mutare - Beira

3450		3350	
Dep. Harare	21:30	Dep. Beira	7:30
Arr. Mutare	6:00	Arr. Machipanda	20:33
Change trains.		Arr. Mutare	N/A(1)
3350		Change trains.	
Dep. Mutare	N/A(1)	3450	
Dep. Machipanda	7:00	Dep. Mutare	21:00
Arr. Beira	18:44	Arr. Harare	6:00

(1)Service Mutare-Machipanda (12km) en route to Beira and Machipanda-Mutare en route to Harare was "temporarily" suspended in 1977.

Sights in **Umtali:** The Museum. Nearby, many national parks which attract tourists.

Harare (Salisbury) - Bulawayo - Mafikeng - Johannesburg

3455 (Bus)

Dep. Harare	19:30(1)	20:00		
Arr. Bulawayo	6:00	7:00		

Change to train.
3475

Dep. Bulawayo	11:45(2)	13:30(4)		
Arr. Mafikeng	5:30(2)	11:40		

Change trains.
3545

Dep. Mafikeng	6:15(3)	9:00(5)	10:00(6)	20:30(7)
Arr. Johannesburg	14:45	17:50	16:40	20:30(7)

(1)Runs Friday and Sunday. (2)Runs Tuesday only. Reservation required. Meal service until 23:00. Direct train to Johannesburg. No train change in Mafikeng. (3)Runs Wednesday only. Reservation required. Meal service. (4)Meal service until 11:04 on Day 2. (5)Runs Sunday only. (6)Bus. (7)Runs daily.

Chapter 12   ASIA

BANGLADESH

Bangladesh offers 6 classes of train space: air-conditioned, first-class, second-express-class, second-ordinary-class, third-mail-class and third-ordinary-class. The first 3 convert to 2-berth or 4-berth compartments at night. Children under 3 travel free. Half-fare for children 3-9. Children 10 and over must pay full fare.

The principal cities in Bangladesh having train service are Chittagong and Dacca.

Chittagong

This is Bangladesh's largest port. See the slab believed to bear the imprint of Mohammed's foot, in the Qadam Mubarik Mosque. The Chandanpura Shahi Jame Mosque. The tortoises at the tomb of Hazrat Bayazid Bostami.

Dhaka (Dacca)

This is the nearly 400-year old capital of Bangladesh. See the 17th Century Lalbagh Fort and the tomb of Pari Bibi. the 4 bazaars in the Chowk (old market). The 17th century Chowk Mosque. Other notable mosques: The Star, Kar Talab, Baidul Mukarram, and Sat Gumbad. The collection of coins, painting, and stone, wood and metal sculptures in the Museum of Antiquities.

There are many interesting archaeological digs at Mainamati and Lalmai, 5 miles west of Comilla, which is on the Chittagong rail route. Although not on Cook's timetable #2530, Comilla is 50 miles east of Dhaka, about a one-hour train ride.

Dhaka (Dacca) - Chittagong   6605

All of these trains charge a supplement.

Dep. Dhaka	7:30(1+2)	10:00	14:30(1+2)	22:30(1+3)
Arr. Chittagong	15:50	18:55	21:00	7:10

*   *   *

Dep. Chittagong	7:00(1+2)	12:30(1+2)	21:20(2+3)	22:30(1+3)
Arr. Dhaka	15:55	18:45	5:35	7:25

(1)Has air-conditioned compartments. (2)Meal service. (3)Seats convert to couchettes.

Dhaka (Dacca) - Sylhet   6605

Dep. Dhaka	20:00(1)	21:30(2)	Dep. Sylhet	11:00(1)	20:00(2)
Arr. Sylhet	5:40	9:00	Arr. Dhaka	20:50	6:35

(1)Seats convert to couchettes. Meal service. (2)Seats convert to couchettes. Has air-conditioned compartments.

Sights in **Sylhet:** This is the tea estates area of the beautiful Surma Valley. Much small-game hunting here.

BURMA

Burma does not publish timetables. Those timetables that are posted at railstations are in Burmese script, including the numerals.

An English-speaking duty officer at the Information Office in Rangoon's railstation will assist foreigners with ticket purchases and will provide information about train connections.

Tickets may be purchased up to 3 days in advance of travel date, and it is usually necessary to make reservations 2 days in advance for First-Class space on the Rangoon-Mandalay ride. Lower class space is very unsatisfactory.

Only tea and soft drinks are served on Burma's trains. Vendors at many stations sell food. This is Burmese food and does not appeal to all Westerners. It is advisable to bring your own food and a container of water. Both Burma Airways and Tourist Burma's office in Rangoon arrange tours of Burma and a 3-hour guided tour of Rangoon.

Children under 3 travel free. Half-fare for children 3-9. Children 10 and over must pay full fare.

Rangoon

The 320-foot high stupa of the enormous 2400-year old Shwe Dagon Pagoda is completely covered with gold leaf. Value of the 8,688 foot-square gold plates on the plantian bud at the top has been computed as over $2,500,000(U.S.). There are 5,448 diamonds and more than 2,000 other precious stones at the top of the bud.

A 25-ton bell is located at one corner of the platform. The British took the bell, as a prize of war, and dropped it into the Rangoon River as they were attempting to load it onto a ship. Unable to raise the bell, the British abandoned it. Burmese workers raised it by tying enough bamboo poles to it until it floated.

In central Rangoon, see: The 2300-year old Sule Pagoda. The National Museum. Burmese students learning their dances at the State School of music and Drama in Jubilee Hall. Bogyoke Market on Park Road, only a few minutes' walk from the town center, has many shops and stalle selling handcrafts. Also visit the Zoo, which has an excellent collection of monkeys. North of the city's center is the contemporary Kaba Aye Pagoda, built in 1956. In nearby Regu, a 2-hour auto ride, there is a 180-foot long reclining Buddha.

Rangoon - Mandalay   6700

The 7:00 departures are usually less crowded than the other departures.

Dep. Rangoon	7:00	11:45	18:45(1)
Arr. Mandalay	15:20	6:05	7:45

*   *   *

Dep. Mandalay	7:00	11:00	18:45(1)
Arr. Rangoon	19:30	5:50	7:45

(1)Carries sleeping car.

Sights in **Mandalay:** This is one of Burma's youngest cities, existing since only 1857. Great Buddhist carvings here. Fine Burmese timber architecture. Many interesting monasteries, beautiful small pagodas.

Mandalay - Pagan   6702   Bus

Dep. Mandalay	4:00	Dep. Naungu	4:00(1)
Arr. Nyaungu	14:00(1)	Arr. Mandalay	14:00

(1)Taxi serviceis available for the 7km ride Nyaungu-Pagan and v.v.

Sights in **Pagan:** Once a fantastic city of many millions and called City of Four Million Pagodas, before Kublai Khan sacked it in the 13th century. Now, there are splendid ruins of more than 5,000 structures to see: great temples and pagodas.

Here are schedules for 3 other possible long train trips from Mandalay:

Mandalay - Lashio   6701

This route has fine scenery.

Dep. Manadalay	5:20	Dep. Lashio	7:00
Arr. Lashio	17:00	Arr. Mandalay	19:40

Mandalay - Myitkyina   6701

Dep. Mandalay	15:00	16:00(1)	Dep. Myitkyina	7:00	8:00(1)
Arr. Myitkyina	14:45(2)	16:05(2)	Arr. Mandalay	6:05(2)	9:10(2)

(1)Carries sleeping car. (2)Day 2.

Mandalay - Thazi - Shwenyaung - Taunggyi   6700

Dep. Mandalay	11:00	18:45	Dep. Shweyaung	10:05	-0-
Arr. Thazi	15:15	21:21	Arr. Thazi	21:45	-0-
Change trains.			Change trains.		
Dep. Thazi	-0-	4:20(1)	Dep. Thazi	1:37	5:01
Arr. Shwenyaung	-0-	16:35	Arr. Mandalay	6:05	7:45

(1)Carries sleeping car.

It is an 11-mile taxi ride from Shwenyaung to Taunggyi, a hill station located at 4712 feet.

HONG KONG

Children under 3 travel free. Half-fare for children 3-9. Children 10 and over must pay full fare.

This country owns the Kowloon-Canton Railway, which operates 40 passenger trains daily between Kowloon and Lo Wu, the border station for rail trips into the People's Republic of China. Nearly 2,000,000 people make this ride every year. There is ferry service from Hong Kong to Kowloon.

Prior to 1979, it had always been necessary to go through customs formalities in Lo Wu and then walk across the bridge spanning the Shum Chun River to the Chinese railstation on the north side of the river before boarding a second train in Shenzhen and proceeding on to Canton.

Since 1979, 2 trains per day make a direct ride from Kowloon to Canton, without requiring passengers to change trains at Lo Wu-Shenzhen.

Kowloon - Lo Wu   5400

Dep. Kowloon	Frequent times from 5:30 to 21:14
Arr. Lo Wu	One hour later.

* * *

Dep. Lo Wu	Frequent times from 5:50 to 21:29
Arr. Kowloon	One hour later.

Kowloon (Hong Kong) - Canton   5400

Dep. Kowloon	6:44	8:54	10:44	13:03(3)	14:55(3)
Arr. Lo Wu	7:55(1)	10:07(1)	11:57(1)	13:54(3)	15:46(3)
Change trains.					
Dep. Lo Wu	-0-	-0-	-0-	13:57	15:52
Arr. Shenzhen	-0-	-0-	-0-	14:02	15:57
Dep. Shenzhen	9:54(2)	11:34(2)	13:07(4)	14:09	16:00
Arr. Canton	13:05	14:21	15:04	15:59	17:50

(1)Walk across the frontier bridge and board another train in Shenzhen. (2)Second-class only. (3)Reservation required. Direct train to Canton. No train change in Lo Wu. First-class only. Air-conditioned. Meal service. (4)First-class only. Air-conditioned.

Hong Kong

See the art objects in Fung Ping Shan Museum at the University of Hong Kong. Take the cruise to Yaumati Typhoon Shelter to see the "floating people" who live their entire lives on small boats. Go on the bus tour to Aberdeen and several interesting villages. The bus also stops at the unique Tiger Balm Gardens.

INDIA

Children under 3 travel free. Half-fare for children 3-11. Children 12 and over must pay full fare.

Every day, more than 9,000,000 people ride India's 11,000 trains, connecting 7,085 railstations. This is Asia's largest railway system.

The 5 classes of space on Indian Railways are: air-conditioned, first-class, air-conditioned chair, second-class sleepercoach and second-class. The air-conditioned class converts at night to 2 to 4 berths. First-class converts at night to 4, 5 or 6 berths. Second-class sleepercoaches convert into sleeping berths between 21:00 and 6:00, with 4 or 6 berths in each compartment. The fare for air-conditioned class includes bedding. Passengers in first-class and in sleeper-coaches must pay a supplement for bedding.

Foreign tourists can reserve Air Conditioned and First-Class space up to 180 days in advance of travel date. To determine which of the 7 rail offices in India you need contact for advance reservations, first communicate your itinerary to any Government of India Tourist Office. That office will advise you whether to direct your reservation order to the Central, Eastern, North Eastern, Northern, South Central, South Eastern or Western offices of Indian Railway.

Breaking of a journey at any station en route is permitted with single journey tickets when the entire trip is more than 200 miles, at the rate of one day for every 100 miles. However, the first break of journey cannot be made until the passenger has traveled at least 150 miles from his or her starting station.

There are restaurants at important railstations. The leading passenger trains have restaurant cars which offer both Indian and Western food. India Government Tourist Offices provide a "Tourist Timetable".

INDIA'S TRAIN PASSES

Indrail Pass. Unlimited rail travel. Available to citizens of countries other than India and to those Indians residing outside India who hold valid passports. The bearer is not required to pay for reservations. Indrail Pass must be purchased *in* India, either at the Tourist Guide Office at a railstation or from a travel agent, and must be paid in the currency of a country other than India. The 1984 prices (in U.S. dollars) are:

	Air-conditioned	First-class	Second-class
7 days	$160	$ 80	$ 35
15 days	200	100	45
21 days	240	120	55
30 days	300	150	55
60 days	450	225	100
90 days	600	300	130

Children 5-12 years old pay half-fare.

Student Discounts.   Students of educational institutions and art schools of foreign countries are allowed substantial discounts when traveling for educational purposes or when visiting places of artistic importance. The letter of authority required in order to obtain this concession can be obtained from the Chief Commercial Superintendent in each major city upon presenting a passport and either a Student Identity Card or a letter from one's embassy certifying that the bearer is a student. See the Deputy Superintendent at the railstation in order to obtain the address of the local C.C.I.

India's 4 principal cities (Bombay, Calcutta, Delhi and Madras) are connected by rail routes.

Bombay

This is a fantastic seaport. See: The Zoo and the Victoria and Albert Museum at Victoria Gardens. The Mahatma Phule Market. Jehangir Art Gallery. The collection of Chinese jade and porcelain and the Tata Collection of paintings at The Prince of Wales Museum. The Rajabal Tower.

Calcutta

A major seaport. See: The many alleys with shops called Bara Bazaar. The stone carvings in the India Museum. The large Nakhoda Mosque. The Botanical Gardens. The Kali Temple. The Jain Temple. The white tigers at the Zoo. The assortment of both great art objects and junk in the Marble Palace.

Delhi

See: the 16th century Lodi Tombs. The Great Mosque. Teen Murti's House, once the home of Nehru and his daughter, Indira Gandhi. The Pearl Mosque. The 2200-year old Ashoka Pillar. The 17th century Red Fort. Humayon's Tomb. The view from the top of the 13th century. 238-foot high, red sandstone Qutb Minar Tower.

The Zoo. The National Museum. For shopping, stroll Connaught Place and see the marvelous jewelry assortment (emeralds, diamonds, rubies and sapphires) in both the leading stores and at the Sundar Nagar Market. Visit the Central Cottage Industries Emporium on Janpath and the silver and cloth stores on Chandni Chowk.

The 43 locomotives and 17 coaches in New Delhi's enormous Rail Transport Museum, including the world's oldest (1855) and still operational steam locomotive. This museum also has a model train for children and a floating restaurant.

Madras

See: the collection of weapons, chinaware and costumes in the Fort Museum. The view of the harbor from the top of the lighthouse. The fine beach. The Government Museum's archaeological exhibit. The South Indian bronzes at the National Art Gallery. Fort St. George, the oldest Anglican church in the Orient. San Thome Basilica, where the remains of the apostle Thomas are said to lie.

Bombay - Ahmadabad   6066

Dep. Bombay (Central)	5:40	7:45	21:15(1)
Arr. Ahmadabad	15:50	19:50	6:30

Sights in **Ahmadabad:** The 250 beautifully carved pillars at the lovely 15th century Jumma Masjid Mosque. The exquisite filligree marble windows at Sidi Said's Mosque. The promenades, boating, gardens and museums at Lake Kankaria.

Dep. Ahmadabad	7:10	7:45	22:00(1)
Arr. Bombay (Central)	16:10	19:30	7:00

(1)Air-conditioned in first-class. Has couchettes in both air-conditioned class and in first-class.

Bombay - Allahabad
6080

Dep. Bombay (Victoria)	6:40(1+2)	16:30(3)	21:10(2+4)
Arr. Itarsi	-0-(2)	5:50(5)	-0-(2)

Change trains.
6081

Dep. Itarsi	-0-(2)	9:42(6)	-0-(2)
Arr. Allahabad	7:30(5)	18:20	20:45(5)

Sights in **Allahabad** (City of God): The Pillar of Asoka at the 16th century fort. The Jami Masjid (Great Mosque). The Museum. The beautiful Victorian Nehru House.

Dep. Allahabad	10:45(7)	11:15(2+4)	17:00(2)
Arr. Itarsi	19:40	-0-(2)	-0-(2)

Change trains.
6080

Dep. Itarsi	20:40	-0-(2)	-0-(2)
Arr. Bombay (Victoria)	13:45(5)	11:25(5)	20:05(1)

(1)Arrive/Depart Bombay's Dadar station. (2)Direct train. No train change in Itarsi. (3)Air-contioned. Meal service. (4)January-June: Has air-conditioned class daily that converts to berths at night. July-December: Has air-conditioned class only on Monday, Thursday and Saturday that convert to berths. (5)Day 2. (6)Runs Wednesday and Friday. (7)Runs Tuesday and Sunday.

Bombay - Bangalore

6140			6155		
Dep. Bombay			Dep. Bagalore	6:00	15:55(1)
Victoria	7:55(1)	20:25	Arr. Miraj	22:10	-0-
Arr. Miraj	-0-	5:55(2)	Change trains.		
Change trains.			6140		
6155			Dep. Miraj	22:40	-0-
Dep. Miraj	-0-	6:25	Arr. Bombay		
Arr. Bangalore	11:55(2)	22:15	(Victoria)	8:15(2)	20:55(2)

(1)Direct train. No train change in Miraj. Carries second-class sleeping car. Also has second-class Air-conditioned class coach. (2)Day 2.

Sights in **Bangalore:** The palace of the Maharajah of Mysore. The 18th century Lal Bagh botanic garden. The Mysore Government Museum. The Nandi Hill Station summer resort, 38 miles from here. The nearby Hesaraghatta Lake.

Bombay - Calcutta   6011

Dep. Bombay (Victoria)	6:00(1+2)	19:10(4)	21:10(6+9)
Arr. Calcutta (Howrah)	13:55(3)	8:05(5)	12:40(5)

Sights in **Calcutta:** See notes about Calcutta at the start of this section.

Dep. Calcutta (Howray)	12:40	14:00(2+7)	19:45(4+10)
Arr. Bombay Victoria	6:25(5)	22:05(3)	7:40(5)

(1)Daily, except Tuesday and Saturday. (2)Meal service. Has air-conditioned class that converts to berths. Has only second-class coach cars. (3)Day 2. (4)Meal service. Has air-conditioned class that converts to berths at night. (5)Day 3   (6)January-June: Has air- conditioned class daily that converts to berths. July-December: Has air-conditioned class only Monday, Wednesday and Saturday that converts to berths. (7)Runs daily, except Thursday and Sunday. (8)January-June: Has air-conditioned class daily that converts to berths. July-December: Has air-conditioned class only Monday, Thursday and Saturday that converts to berths. (9)Plus another departure from Bombay at 21:30, arriving Calcutta at 14:30(5).   (10)Plus another departure from Bombay at 20:40(8), arriving Bombay at 11:25(5).

Bombay - Madras   6095

Dep. Bombay (Victoria)	7:55(1)	14:25(3+4+5)	22:10(6)
Arr. Madras (Central)	13:35(2)	17:05(2)	5:10(7)

Sights in **Madras:** See notes about sightseeing in Madras at the start of this section.

Dep. Madras (Central)	9:30(5+8)	13:55(1)	22:15(6)
Arr. Bombay (Victoria)	11:50(2+3)	20:55(2)	5:10(7)

(1)Second-class only. (2)Day 2.   (3)Arrive/Depart Bombay's Dadar railstation. (4)Has air-conditioned class that converts to berths only on Saturday. (5)Has air-conditioned class that converts to berths daily. (6)Runs daily. Has both air-conditioned class and first-class that convert to berths. (7)Day 3.   (8)Has air-conditioned class that converts to berths only on Monday.

Bombay - New Delhi   6070

Dep. Bombay (Central)	6:10(1+2)	10:50(5)	16:00(6+7+12)
Arr. New Delhi	1:47(3)	10:25(3)	9:20(3)

Sights in **Delhi:** See notes about sightseeing in Delhi at the start of this section.

Dep. New Delhi	2:56(1+8)	8:21(1)	16:20(6+11+13)
Arr. Bombay (Central)	23:10	8:05(3)	10:25(3)

(1)Has air-conditioned class and first-class that both convert to berths. Also has air-conditioned chair class. (2)Runs Monday and Friday. (3)Day 2. (4)Second-class only. (5)Has air-conditioned class and first-class that both convert to berths. (6)Reservation required. Supplement charged. Entire train is air-conditioned. Has both air-conditioned class that converts to berths and air-conditioned chair class. (7)Runs Monday, Tuesday, Thursday, Friday and Sunday. (8)Runs Wednesday and Sunday. (9)Has first-class that converts to berths. (10)Day 3.   (11)Runs Monday, Tuesday, Wednesday, Friday and Saturday. (12)Plus other departures from Bombay at 20:15(1) arriving New Delhi at 19:03(3), and 21:40(9) arriving New Delhi at 5:45(10).   (13)Plus other departures from New Delhi at 16:40(5) and 22:25(9)

Bombay - Pune   6095

The first double-deck passenger train in India started operating in 1978 on the 115-mile long Bombay-Pune line. Its coaches seat 148 (versus 90 in ordinary second-class coaches).

Dep. Bombay (Victoria)	6:45	7:55(1)	8:45	12:35	14:25(2+4)
Arr. Pune		11:05	12:10	13:20	17:10	18:35

Sights in **Pune:** Many ancient palaces and temples. This route involves 25 tunnels and many high bridges and viaducts. Can be made as a one-day roundtrip. The very picturesque narrow-gauge Matheran Hill Railway is near this route and can be visited during the day.

Dep. Pune	0:50	2:10(1)	4:00	6:10(1)	7:10(3+5)
Arr. Bombay (Victoria)	5:10	6:10	8:15	10:15	10:40

(1)Second-class only. (2)Departs from Bombay's Dadar railstation. (3)Meal service. (4)Plus other departures from Bombay at 14:35(1), 17:10(3), 17:50, 20:25, 21:55(1) and 22:10.   (5)Plus other departures from Pune at 7:35, 9:35, 15:10, 16:25(1) and 16:40.

Calcutta - Allahabad   6060

Dep. Calcutta (Howrah)	9:40(1+2)	19:20(3)	21:00(3)
Arr. Allahabad	0:15	9:03	16:10

Sights in **Allahabad:** See notes about city sightseeing in Allahabad earlier in this section, under "Bombay-Allahabad".

Dep. Allahabad	2:20(2+4)	18:18(3)	21:15(5)
Arr. Calcutta (Howrah)	17:10	8:15	12:40

(1)Runs daily, except Monday and Friday. Meal service. (2)Has air-conditioned class and first-class that both convert to berths. Also has air-conditioned chair class. (3)Has air-conditioned class and first-class that both convert to berths. Meal service. (4)Runs daily, except Wednesday and Saturday. (5)Runs daily. January-June: has air-conditioned class daily that converts to berths. July-December: Has air-conditioned class only on Monday, Wednesday and Saturday that converts to berths.

Calcutta - Darjeeling
6120

Dep. Calcutta (Howrah)	12:30(1)	18:55(2)	19:00(3)	21:05
Arr. New Jalpaiguri	6:35	7:25	7:50	19:15

Change trains.
6121

Dep. New Jalpaiguri	-0-	8:15	9:00	-0-
Arr. Darjeeling	-0-	15:15	16:30	-0-

Sights in **Darjeeling:** At 7,000 feet, this is a cool and beautiful area. Many famous tea plantations. The interesting items to purchase here are jewelry, carvings, colorful fabrics. There is a large population of Tibetans in Darjeeling.

One can walk or take a jeep to Tiger Hill to see the sunrise. There is a hotel at Tiger Hill, and the preferred visit is to spend the night there, see the sunrise the next morning, and then catch the 11:00 train from Darjeeling for the ride back to Calcutta.

Excursions by 4-wheel drive vehicles are made from Darjeeling to Nepal, Sikkim and Bhutan.
6121

Dep. Darjeeling	7:00	11:00	-0-	-0-
Arr. New Jalpaiguri	13:55	17:50	-0-	-0-

Change trains.
6120

Dep. New Jalpaiguri	9:50	17:55(2)	19:20	21:40(1)
Arr. Calcutta (Howrah)	4:40	6:30	8:45(3)	13:35

(1)Second-class only. (2)Runs daily. Has air-conditioned class and meal service only on Monday, Wednesday and Friday from Calcutta...only on Tuesday, Thursday and Sunday from New Jalpaiguri. (3)Arrive/Depart From Calcutta's Sealdah railstation.

Calcutta - Madras   6150

Dep. Calcutta (Howrah)   15:20(1)   20:00(3)   23:10(5)
Arr. Madras (Central)   18:45(2)   4:50(4)   18:00(4)

Sights in **Madras:** See notes at the start of this section.

Dep. Madras (Central)   8:00(1)   9:05(5)   22:25(3)
Arr. Calcutta (Howrah)   11:30(2)   4:10(4)   6:05(4)

(1)Supplement charged. Meal service. Has air-conditioned class and first-class that both convert to berths. (2)Day 2.   (3)Has first-class daily that converts to berths. Also has only on Monday, Wednesday and Saturday air-conditicned class that converts to berths. (4)Day 3   (5)Second-class only.

Calcutta - New Delhi   6060

The train passes through several different regions on this trip. Climate, language and clothing change every few hours.

Dep. Calcutta (How.)   9:40(1+2+3)   17:00(5)   19:20(2+6+9)
Arr. New Delhi   10:15(4)   10:40(4)   -0-
Arr. Delhi   -0-   -0-   19:30(4)

Sights in **Delhi:** See notes about Delhi at the start of this section.

Dep. Delhi   8:15(2+6)   -0-   -0-
Dep. New Delhi   -0-   16:30(2+3+8)   17:10(5+10)
Arr. Calcutta (How.)   8:15(4)   17:10(4)   10:50(4)

(1)Runs daily, except Mon. and Fri. Meal service. (2)Has air-conditioned class and first-class that both convert to berths. (3)Also has air-conditioned chair class. (4)Day 2.   (5)Supplement charged. Reservation required. Runs Mon. Thurs., Fri. and Sun. from Calcutta; Mon., Tues., Fri. and Sat. from New Delhi. (6)Meal service. (7)Day 3.   (8)Runs daily, except Wed. and Sat. Meal service. (9)Plus another Calcutta departure at 21:00(2).   (10)Plus another Delhi departure at 22:15(2).

Delhi - Agra   6073

The 7:05 departure from New Delhi is "Taj Express". It is met on 10:15 arrival in Agra by an air-conditioned government-operated tourist bus and an official guide. Its tour includes the 17th century Taj Mahal and Fatehpur Sikri Fort. Avoid private guides. They do not provide as complete a tour as the government does. Another interesting sight in Agra is the tomb of Hmad-ud-Daulah. The bus brings you back to the Agra station for the 18:55 departure of "Taj Express", arriving New Delhi at 22:15.

As the following schedules indicate, it is not necessary to spend a night in Agra in order to see the Taj by moonlight.

Dep. New Delhi   7:05(1)   7:55(2)   9:20(3+4+5+12)
Arr. Agra   10:15   11:06   12:16

                        *   *   *

Dep. Agra   16:03(2)   17:08(6)   18:55(1+13)
Arr. New Delhi   19:50   20:25   22:15

(Timetable footnotes appear on next page.)

(1)"Taj Express". Reservation required. Meal service. Has air-conditioned class and air-conditioned chair class. (2)Has air-conditioned class. (3)Arrive/Depart Delhi's Nizamudin railstation. (4)Daily, except Tuesday and Friday. (5)Second-class only. (6)Has first-class and air-conditioned chair class.

(7)Runs Monday, Wednesday, Friday and Sunday. (8)Runs daily. Has air-conditioned class. Also has air-conditioned chair class on Tuesday and Friday. (9)Runs Wednesday, Friday and Sunday. (10)Runs daily, except Monday and Thursday. (11)Runs Monday, Tuesday, Thursday and Saturday.

(12)Plus other departures from New Delhi at 11:27(6), 11:55(7), 15:18(5), 19:10(8), 20:40(3) and 21:44. (13)Plus other departures from Agra at 1:55(3), 4:20(8), 7:00(3), 9:20(9), 10:23(3+10), 12:00(3+11) and 13:50.

Delhi - Allahabad   6060

Dep. Delhi	- 0 -	-0-	8:15(4+16)	-0-
Dep. New Delhi	5:15(1+2)	7:15(3+4)	-0-	9:40(17)
Arr. Allahabad	16:01	16:28	18:08	20:33

Sights in **Allahabad:** See notes under "Bombay-Allahabad".

Dep. Allahabad	0:25(5+6)	2:14(7)	4:00(8)	6:00(18)
Arr. New Delhi	10:15	12:00	14:35	16:55
Arr. Delhi	-0-	12:25	- 0 -	-0-

(1)Runs Tuesday, Thursday, Saturday and Sunday. (2)Has air-conditioned class. (3)Runs Tuesday, Thursday and Sunday. (4)Has air-conditioned class. Meal service. (5)Has air-conditioned class and air-conditioned chair class. Meal service. (6)Runs Monday and Friday. (7)Runs daily, except Monday and Friday. Is only second-class on Wednesday and Saturday. Has first-class that converts to berths and air-conditioned chair class on Tuesday, Thursday and Sunday.

(8)Runs Monday, Wednesday and Saturday. Has first-class that converts to berths and air-conditioned chair class. (9)Runs daily. Has first-class that converts to berths daily, except Thursday and Sunday. Has air-conditioned chair class on Monday, Wednesday and Friday. (10)Runs daily. Has air-conditioned class and first-class that both convert to berths.

(11)Runs Monday, Wednesday and Friday. (12)Has air-conditioned chair class. (13)Runs daily, except Wednesday and Saturday. Has air-conditioned class and first-class that both convert to berths. (14)Runs Monday, Wednesday and Saturday. (15)Runs Tuesday, Thursday, Friday. and Monday.

(16)Plus other departures from Delhi at 18:35(9), 20:10 and 22:15(10). (17)Plus other departures from New Delhi at 12:05(11+12), 16:30(12+13) and 19:05(9). (18)Plus other departures from Allahabad at 8:27(10+14), 8:45(10+15), 16:20(10), 17:40 and 19:51(12).

Delhi - Jaipur   6061

Pink City Express (one of India's fastest trains) colored pink, departs from a station that is a few miles away from the main Delhi station. Provide extra time to get there.

Dep. Delhi	5:55(1)	9:35	12:30	19:20	22:10
Arr. Jaipur	11:00	17:55	20:45	7:58	5:35

Sights in **Jaipur:** This city is noted for the unusually colorful clothes worn by its people. See the pink Palace of the Winds.

Dep. Jaipur	0:13	6:27	10:32	17:00(1)	-0-
Arr. Delhi	7:25	14:10	18:55	22:00	-0-

(1)"Pink City Express". Meal service.

Delhi - Madras   6013

Dep. New Delhi	6:15(1)	15:18(3)	19:10(5)
Arr. Madras (Central)	14:00(2)	21:30(4)	6:50(4)

Sights in **Madras:** See notes about city-sightseeing in Madras at the start of this section.

Dep. Madras (Central)	7:05(1)	14:20(3)	18:15(5)
Arr. New Delhi	16:00(2)	21:53(4)	7:50(4)

(1)Runs Tuesday, Wednesday, Friday and Sunday. Meal service. Has air-conditioned class and first-class that both convert to berths. Also has air-conditioned chair class. (2)Day 2.   (3)Second-class only. (4)Day 3.   (5)Runs daily. Meal service. Has air-conditioned class and first-class that both convert to berths. Also has air-conditioned coach class on Tuesday and Friday from New Delhi and on Wednesday and Sunday from Madras.

Madras - Cochin   6170

It is possible to leave the train in Ernakulum, sightsee there, and then later the same day take the trip of a few minutes to Cochin either by ferry boat or by bus across the bridge that connects the 2 cities.

Dep. Madras (Cent.)	19:20(1)	Dep. Cochin	16:05(1)
Arr. Ernakulam	9:05	Dep. Ernakulam	16:35
Arr. Cochin	9:40	Arr. Madras (Cent.)	6:45

(1)Has first-class that converts to berths.

Sights in **Cochin:** This is actually a conglomerate of several islands and 3 cities. See the 16th century Santa Cruz Cathedral. The 16th century synagogue. The 16th century tomb of the great Spanish explorer Vasco de Gama. The blue willow-patterned tiles on the floor of a second synagogue. The Dutch Palace. Picturesque palm-lined beaches.

Sights in **Ernakulam:** The week-long festival at the Siva temple, in January. Performances of the unusual Kathakali dance.

INTERNATIONAL ROUTES FROM INDIA

New Delhi is the gateway for train travel to Pakistan. The rail route to Sri Lanka (Ceylon) is via Madras and Rameswaram.

New Delhi - Amritsar - Lahore - Hyderabad - Karachi

6030

Dep. New Delhi	7:36(1)	11:40(2)	12:40	19:17(3+4)
Arr. Amritsar	17:55	19:45	21:15	7:15(5)

Change trains.

6026

Dep. Amritsar	-0-	-0-	-0-	9:15(5)
Arr. Lahore	-0-	-0-	-0-	12:15(5)

Change trains.

5905

Dep. Lahore	9:30(3+6)	14:20(3+6)	16:30(7)	17:25(7+10)
Dep. Hyderabad	4:02(8)	6:06(8)	7:10(8)	9:40(8+11)
Arr. Karachi	7:25(8)	9:20(8)	10:00(8)	12:45(8)

(1)Meal service. (2)Runs daily, except Tuesday. Has air-conditioned class. Also has air-conditioned chair class, except on Thursday. Meal service on Wednesday, Thursday, Friday and Saturday. (3)Has air-conditioned class and first-class that both convert to berths. (4)Also has air-conditioned chair class. (5)Day 2 from New Delhi.

(6)Reservation required. Meal service. Carries air-conditioned sleeping car. (7)Reservation required. Meal service. Has air-conditioned class *or* first-class, either of which converts to berths. (8)Day 2 from Lahore. (9)Reservation required. Meal service. (10)Plus other departures from Lahore at 19:40(7) and 21:08(7). (11)Plus other departures from Hyderabad at 13:46(8+9) and 16:00(8+9).

Madras - Rameswaram - Talaimannar - Colombo Fort

6182		6300	
Dep. Madras (Egmore)	10:45	Dep. Talaimannar (Pier)	20:43(3)
Arr. Rameswaram	10:10(1)	Arr. Colombo Fort	8:36(4)
Change to ferry.			
6180			
Dep. Rameswaram (Port)	12:00(2)		
Arr. Talaimannar (Pier)	15:00		
Change to train.			

(1)Day 2 from Madras. (2)Runs Monday, Wednesday and Friday. (3)Runs daily. Carries sleeping car. Meal service. Departs at 22:30 on Monday, Wednesday and Friday. (4)Arrival time every day on Day 3 from Madras.

INDONESIA

Nearly every train ride in Indonesia offers views of extinct volcanoes, mountains, water buffalo and rain forests.

Children under 3 travel free. Half-fare for children 3-7. Children 8 and over must pay full fare.

Jakarta

The main railstation is Kota. See Bali dancing at Gedun Kesenian. The collection of coins, ceramics and archaeological objects at Gedung Artja Museum. Do not miss seeing the morning activity at the Pasar Ikan, a large fish market. The National Mosque. The Museum Kota.

The interesting Dutch houses and the canals in Chinatown. Ride out to Bogoru by bus or taxi to see the old Dutch palace (Merdeka Palace) and the fantastic 275-acre Botanical Garden: 10,000 species of trees and more than 500,000 other plants, including more than 100,000 orchid plants. Nothing in the world to compare with these gardens.

Surabaja

There are 3 railstations. Trains for Jakarta depart from Gubeng. Trains for Bandung depart from Kota. Tasar Turi is the third railstation.

This is a major seaport. A 30-minute ferry-boat ride takes you to Madura, where the major attraction is the racing of bulls. Surabaja is a convenient point for visiting Mount Bromo and seeing live animals sacrificed in the boiling volcano crater there.

There are 2 routes from Jakarta to Surabaja.

Jakarta - Surabaja (via Cirebon)   7410

Dep. Jakarta (Kota)	12:00(1+2+3)	16:00(2+4+5+9)
Arr. Surabaja (Kota)	8:15	9:30
	*	*
Dep. Surabaja (Kota)	13:30(2+3)	16:00(2+4+5+10)
Arr. Jakarta (Kota)	8:30(1)	9:45

(1)Arrive/Depart Jakarta's Gambir railstation. (2)Meal service. (3)Third-class only. (4)Reservation required. Carries sleeping car. (5)Air-conditioned. (6)Second-class only. (7)Arrive/Depart Jakarta's Parsensen railstation. (8)Arrive/Depart Surabaja's Pasarturi railstation. (9)Plus other departures from Jakarta at 16:38(2+5+6) and 17:45(2+3+7+8(. (10)Plus other departures from Surabaja at 16:30(2+5+6+8) and 17:45(2+3+7+8).

Jakarta - Surabaja (via Bandung) 7410

Dep. Jakarta (Kota)	6:15(1)	13:15(3)	15:15(1)	18:35(1+4)
Arr. Bandung	10:05	17:15	19:05	22:10
Change trains.				
Dep. Bandung	17:00(1+2)	-0-	-0-	5:00(5)
Arr. Surabaja (Kota)	10:45	-0-	-0-	23:40
	*	*	*	
Dep. Surabaja (Kota)	5:00(5)	16:50(1+2)	-0-	-0-
Arr. Bandung	0:05	10:15	-0-	-0-
Change trains.				
Dep. Bandung	5:45(1)	10:45(1)	14:45(1)	17:45(1)
Arr. Jakarta (Kota)	9:35	14:45	18:15(4)	22:00

(1)Second-class only. Meal service. (2)Air-conditioned. (3)Second and third-class only. Meal service. (4)Arrive/Depart Jakarta's Gambir railstation. (5)Third-class only. Meal service.

Sights in **Bandung:** This is a much nicer and cooler city than Jakarta. It is the center of Indonesia's quinine industry, with many cinchona tree plantations here. Quinine is derived from cinchona bark. Numerous tea plantations in this area. See the collection of crocodiles, birds and snakes at the Zoological Garden.

Jakarta - Jogjakarta 7410

Dep. Jakarta				
(Gambir)	12:00(1)	13:00(2)	16:00(3)	17:00(1+5)
Arr. Jogjakarta	1:05	2:11	3:20	5:06

Sights in **Jogjakarta:** The batik schools, 2 museums, the mosques and the Sultan's Palace, all inside the walled Kraton complex. Be sure to see the carved teak pillars in the Bengsal Kencono (Golden Pavillion) and the gold pillars, gems and sacred weapons displayed in Gadjah Mada University.

Visit the shops stocked with excellent batik, along Jalan Tirtodipuran. The seated Buddha at the Mendut Temple. The dances at the 10th century Roro Djonggrang Temple, 10 miles from Jogjakarta.

There is an air-conditioned bus tour to the 9th century Borobudor, 35 miles from the city. The lower terraces of this low pyramid have 432 statues and 1,460 reliefs of the Buddha. It is a 15-mile trip to Prambanam, a temple complex dedicated to Shiva, Hindu deity.

Dep. Jogjakarta	18:00(2)	18:42(4)	19:30(2)	20:30(1+6)
Arr. Jakarta				
(Gambir)	6:25	7:00	7:30	8:30

(1)Third-class only. Meal service. (2)Second and third-class only. Meal service. (3)Reservation required. Air-conditioned. Meal service. This train has only first and second-class sleeping cars. (4)Second-class only. Meal service. (5)Plus another departure from Jakarta at 19:00(2). (6)Plus other departures from Jogjakarta at 20:30(1), 21:10(1) and 22:27(3).

Jogjakarta - Solo   7410

This is an easy one-day roundtrip.

Dep. Jogjakarta (Gambir)	5:16	6:07	9:30	16:20	
Arr. Solo	6:25	7:22	10:58	17:40	
	*	*	*		
Dep. Solo	11:00	15:37	17:00	17:46	18:51(1)
Arr. Jogjakarta (Gambir)	12:30	17:15	18:37	19:25	20:25

(1)Plus other departures from Solo at 19:30, 20:55 and 22:30.

Sights in **Solo:** A quite attractive village. Famous for its good batik cloth and its Sriwedai Amusement Park, which has a fine Zoological Garden.

The one rail route on Sumatra is across the bay from Penang. A one-day roundtrip from Medan to Tanjong Balai is possible. There are large oil palm and rubber-tree plantations near Medan.

Medan - Rantau Prapet - Tanjon Balai   7400

All of these trains serve light refreshments and are second and third-class only.

Dep. Medan	7:00	9:30	14:35	21:00
Arr. Rantau Prapet	-0-	16:17	-0-	5:12
Arr. Tanjong Balai	11:05	-0-	18:42	3:20
	*	*	*	
Dep. Tanjong Balai	6:40	-0-	14:20	-0-
Dep. Rantau Prapet	-0-	7:15	-0-	-0-
Arr. Medan	10:51	14:06	18:25	-0-

JAPAN

Children under 6 travel free. Half-fare for children 6-11. Children 12 and over must pay full fare.

Those magical 2 elements that are necessary for top quality rail service both exist in Japan: high population density and short distances.

Japan enacted in 1970 its "Law for Construction of Nationwide High-Speed Railways". This program calls for speeds up to 150 miles per hour on many routes when the entire system is completed, about 1985. Some of the links are already in operation.

When completed, the 22-mile long undersea Seikan Tunnel will connect Tappi and Yoshioka.

Japanese National Railways surpasses all other rail systems in the world as to speed, service and size. It operates more than 26,000 trains a day.

Express trains between Tokyo and Osaka (345 miles) usually run at 125mph, sometimes going as fast as 137 mph. Passengers can follow the trains' speed on speedometers located throughout the trains. On the stretch from Tokyo to Kyush, some trains reach a speed of 156mph.

The most famous Japanese trains are its Shinkansen "bullet trains". The great "Hikari", leaving Tokyo every 15 or 20 minutes, runs the 345 miles from Tokyo to Osaka in 3 hours 10 minutes. The 455-mile run from Tokyo to Okayama is made in 4 hours 10 minutes. From Tokyo to Hakata (735 miles), it is only 6 hours 40 minutes.

Bullet trains have telephone service, while traveling, to 26 cities.

When we rode a bullet train both from Tokyo to Kyoto, and then the next day back to Tokyo, the speed was so great that it was difficult to focus on scenery or objects within 1,000 feet from the train. The interior was immaculately clean. It is one of the world's best travel experiences.

And the bullet trains are very safe. To guard against natural disasters, the Japanese installed seismoscopes, anemometers and rain gauges along the entire line. In case of an earthquake exceeding a certain intensity, the electrical current that runs the trains in the area concerned will automatically cut off.

If there are excessive rains or winds, the running speed of the train is restricted or the train is stopped. Each train window is made of double-layer glass with a dry air space between so as to minimize noise, wind pressure and moisture condensation, as well as guard against flying stones.

Tickets for all Japanese trains which require reservation go on sale one month before travel day and can be purchased at JNR railstations and at major travel agencies throughout Japan.

Passengers are permitted to take 2 suitcases weighing a total of 44 pounds into their car and may also check 3 additional suitcases at a small fee for transit in the baggage car. Also, for little cost, arrangements can be made either to have baggage delivered from the train to one's residence or to be stored at a railstation. Porters are available at all main railstations.

Principal trains have restaurant cars. There are refreshment vendors on almost all other long-distance trains. Both Japanese and "Western" food are provided.

There are 4 classes of trains in Japan: Super-Express (Hikari and Kodama), Limited Express, Ordinary Express and Local. A surcharge is required for all types of express trains. When any express train arrives 2 hours or more late, the express surcharge is refunded at the destination.

Each express train has one or more "Green Cars". Seat reservations, at an additional charge, are required for space in a Green Car.

Sleeping cars have roomettes (for one person) and double compartments in Class "A" cars. Class "B" cars provide 2-berth and 3-berth compartments.

Combination tickets (for both hotel rooms and seats on bullet trains) can be purchased from either Japanese National Railways or from Japan Travel Bureau.

All of Japan's many privately-owned trains are single-class and require seat reservations. Many of these trains serve resort areas.

JAPAN'S TRAIN PASSES

Japan Tour Tickets. These cover a variety of routes listed by Japanese National Railways. Offering reduced-rate excursions, they can be obtained at principal Japanese railstations, or at the Kobe, Kyoto and Tokyo offices of Japan Travel Bureau, and also at all offices of Kinki Nippon Tourist.

Japan Railpass. Unlimited travel on the trains, buses and ferries of the Japanese National Railways System. Does *not* cover travel on private lines. Vouchers are sold only outside Japan, at offices of Japan Air Lines, Nippon Travel Agency and Japan Travel Bureau. After arriving in Japan, the voucher is exchanged for the pass at JNR ticket counters at the New Tokyo International Airport (Narita) and at JNR offices in Hakata, Hiroshima, Kumamoto, Kyoto, Nagoya, Niigata, Osaka, Sapporo, Sendai, Tokyo, Nishi Kagoshima and Yokohama.

Travel must start within 3 months after the voucher is purchased. With a Japan Railpass there is no charge for seat reservations, which can be made only in Japan and at either any Travel Service Center or any railstation. Refundable at a 10% fee before the first day of use if presented at a Travel Service Center in a JNR station that is designated to handle this pass.

The prices effective until September, 1984 are: Y30,000 for 7 days, Y48,000 for 14 days, and Y64,000 for 21 days. Children 6-11: Y15,000, Y24,000 and Y32,000. Second-class prices: Y21,000, Y33,000 and Y44,000. For children 6-11: Y10,500, Y16,500 and Y22,000.

In planning a tour of Japan, keep in mind that the country is 3 major islands: Honshu (Tokyo and Kyoto), Kyushu (Nagasaki) to the south, and Hokkaido (the wild northern land of Japan).

Hiroshima

Rebuilt since 1955. See the monuments at Peace Memorial Park. The interesting exhibits in the Peace Memorial Museum.

Kyoto

You will not see all worth seeing here in a few days. There are more than 600 shrines, over 1400 temples, plus 9 museums, 3 palaces and an imposing castle in Kyoto.

The 17th century Nijo Castle is first on everyone's list. Beautiful gold ceilings, wood sculptures, and murals to see at this complex.

Other sights in Kyoto: the 13th century 393-foot long Sanjusangendo (Hall of 33 Bays). The incredible halls at Nishi Hongan-ji. The 200-acre park in the center of Kyoto, with the Imperial Palace. The 3 large gardens of the 68-acre Shugaku-in. The 22 subtemples at Daitoku-ji, one of the city's many Zen temples. The Library, Zoo, Art Gallery and Heian Jingu Shrine, allOin Okazaki Park. Hundreds of narrow streets, each with interesting shops, food stores and inns.

Kinkaku-ji (Temple of the Golden Pavilion). Ryoan-ji (Temple of the Peaceful Dragon). Kokedera (The Moss Temple), with many different types of moss in its lovely garden. The 17th century Kiyomizu (Clear Spring Temple).

Osaka

The 16th century Osaka Castle, and its fine museum. Shitenno-ji Temple. Nishi Temple. Higashi Hongan-ji Temple. The Kabuki Theater. The view from the top of 338-foot high Tsutenkaku (Tower Leading to Heaven). The view from the top of the 340-foot high observation platform on Osaka Tower, Sumiyoshi Taisha Shrine.

Temmangu Shrine. The Bunraku puppet theater. The dozen different farmhouses with hundreds of utensils in the Museum of Japanese Farmhouses. The Japan Handicraft Museum. Ancient and modern art at the Municipal Art Museum in Tennoji Park, where the Zoo and Botanical Garden are also located.

The Electric Science Museum. The Transportation Museum. The Natural Science Museum. The Fujita Art Museum. A tourist specialty in Osaka is visiting factories: clothing, beverages, ice cream, chocolate, cameras, autos, bread, etc.

Tokyo

Schedules for the 60-minute train ride between Tokyo's Ueno Keisei station and Narita Airport appear later in this section, under "Tokyo-Narita".

There is monorail and bus service between Haneda Airport and the center of Tohyo. A special train goes non-stop between Narita Airport Station (a 6-minute bus ride from the terminal) and Tokyo.

Several English-language daily newspapers list entertainment events.

Any tour of Tokyo must focus on visiting the massive park surrounding the Palace, in the center of the city. Then see: The gardens at the Meiji Shrine. The enormous Zoo, the National Museum of Western Art, and the Tokyo National Museum, all in Ueno Park, next to Ueno Railstation. The tremendous assortment of sealife at the wholesale fish market at Tsukiji, very early in the morning.

Stroll the Ginza, particularly after dark. See the elegant lobby of the Imperial Hotel. The Iris Garden (Shobu-en). The gardens at Shin-juku Gyoen. Kiyosumi Garden. The 60-acre Hama Rikyu Park. Buddhist art at Goto Museum. The collection of ancient Japanese and Chinese art in the Nezu Museum. Koishikawa Botanical Garden.

The city's largest department stores have amusement parks and many restaurants on their roofs Several have undergrounds malls connected to Tokyo Railstation.

Hiroshima - Fukuoka (Hakata)   8070 +   8080

Most of the trains on this route require reservations for first-class seats. All serve either meals or light refreshments.

Dep. Hiroshima	Frequent times from 6:34 to 22:08
Arr. Fukuoka (Hakata)	2 hours later

Sights in **Hakata:** Hakata is the railstation for Fukuoka. This twin-city is famous for Hakata dolls. Much night-life here. Only a few miles from away, there is cormorant fishing at Harazuru.

Dep. Fukuoka (Hakata)	Frequent times from 6:00 to 21:35
Arr. Hiroshima	2 hours later

Hiroshima - Kokura - Beppu   8070

All of these trains have meal service or light refreshments.

Dep. Hiroshima	8:06	9:06	11:08	12:08
Arr. Kokura	9:23	10:18	12:22	13:17

Change trains.
8120

Dep. Kokura	9:25	10:38	12:35	13:35
Arr. Beppu	11:06	12:20	14:16	15:11

Sights in **Beppu:** Noted for its curative mineral baths.

Dep. Beppu	14:48	15:48	17:09	18:39	19:21
Arr. Kokura	16:44	17:45	19:07	20:37	21:17

Change trains.
8070

Dep. Kokura	16:59	17:59	19:24	20:59	21:59
Arr. Hiroshima	18:12	19:12	20:53	22:28	23:26

Hiroshima - Kagoshima

Most of the trains on the Hiroshima-Hakata route require reservations for first-class seats. All serve light refreshments or meals.

8070

Dep. Hiroshima	Frequent times from 6:34 to 22:08
Arr. Fukuoka (Hakata)	2 hours later
Change trains.	

8111

| Dep. Fukuoka (Hakata) | 8:05 | 9:22 | 10:05 | 12:05 | 13:05(2) |
| Arr. Kagoshima | 13:08 | 14:39 | 15:09 | 17:11 | 17:55 |

Sights in **Kagoshima:** A good base for visiting the beautiful crater lake, many live volcanoes and thick forests of Kirishima National Park.

| Dep. Kagoshima | 6:26 | 8:03 | 9:26 | 11:13 | 13:49(3) |
| Arr. Fukuoka (Hakata) | 11:21 | 12:42 | 14:15 | 16:15 | 18:26 |

(1)Carries sleeping car. (2)Plus other departures from Fukuoka (Hakata) at 15:05, 17:05, 18:20, 23:59(1), 5:43 and 7:18.   (3)Plus other departures from Kagoshima at 15:02, 16:16, 17:50, 19:34 and 22:08(1).

Change trains.

8070

| Dep. Fukuoka (Hakata) | Frequent times from 6:00 to 21:35 |
| Arr. Hiroshima | 2 hours later |

Hiroshima - Kumamoto

Most trains on the Hiroshima-Hakata route require reservations. All serve either light refreshments or meals.

8070

Dep. Hiroshima	Frequent times from 6:34 to 22:08
Arr. Fukuoka (Hakata)	2 hours later
Change trains.	

811

| Dep. Fukuoka (Hakata) | Frequent times from 7:18 to 23:59 |
| Arr. Kumamoto | 1¾-2 hours later |

Sights in **Kumamoto:** It is a short drive from here to marvelous Suizenji Park.

Dep. Kumamoto	Frequent times from 6:28 to 22:50
Arr. Fukuoka (Hakata)	1¾-2 hours later
Change trains.	

8070

| Dep. Fukuoka (Hakata) | Frequent times from 6:00 to 21:35 |
| Arr. Hiroshima | 2 hours later |

Hiroshima - Nagasaki

Most trains on the Hiroshima-Hakata route require reservations for first-class seats. All serve either light refreshments or meals.

8070

Dep. Hiroshima	Frequent times from 6:34 to 22:08
Arr. Fukuoka (Hakata)	2 hours later
Change trains.	

There is great scenery of Omura Bay on the ride from Fukuoka (Hakata) to Nagasaki. Sit on the right-hand side for the best view in this direction.

8110

Dep. Fukuoka (Hakata)	9:08	9:35	10:01	10:56	11:58(1)
Arr. Nagasaki	11:49	12:15	12:37	13:25	14:27

* * *

Dep. Nagasaki	4:50	6:50	7:48	8:44	9:27(2)
Arr. Fukuoka (Hakata)	8:20	9:24	10:21	11:25	12:10
Change trains.					

8070

Dep. Fukuoka (Hakata)	Frequent times from 6:00 to 21:35
Arr. Hiroshima	2 hours later

(1)Plus other departures from Fukuoka (Hakata) at frequent times from 12:58 to 20:13, plus 4:43, 6:15, 7:00 and 7:43. (2)Plus other departures from Nagasaki at frequent times from 10:42 to 19:57.

Sights in **Nagasaki:** Japan's first contact with the Western world was here, as well as the country's early traffic with China. That explains both the Chinese and Catholic influence on this area. The local tradition is flying the huge kites that were first flown in China. Two other Chinese influences seen here even now are the annual June racing of large rowboats to the tempo of a drum that is beaten amidship and an annual October festival featuring Chinese-style costumes, floats and dragons.

See: The Catholic Cathedral. (Nearly half of Japan's small Catholic population lives in this area.) The view of the city and harbor from Glover House, the place where Madame Butterfly (in Puccini's imagination) waited for Pinkerton to return. The 17th century Chinese temple (Sofukuji). The 33-foot high bronze torii at the Suwa Shrine. Much marvelous seacoast scenery in this area.

Kyoto - Gifu

All trains on the Kyoto-Nagoya route require reservations for first-class seats.

8070				8082			
Dep. Kyoto	7:29	9:17	11:29	Dep. Gifu	14:21	18:33	19:25
Arr. Nagoya	8:17	10:05	12:17	Arr. Nagoya	14:46	19:02	19:53
Change trains.				Change trains			
8082				8070			
Dep. Nagoya	8:35	10:41	13:00	Dep. Nagoya	15:03	19:39	20:15
Arr. Gifu	9:03	11:08	13:29	Arr. Kyoto	15:51	20:27	21:06

Sights in **Gifu:** There is large production of lovely paper lanterns and paper umbrellas here. Numerous hot springs resorts in this area. See the cormorant fishing, almost every night from mid-May to mid-October.

Kyoto - Kobe   8070

These trains require reservations and serve either light refreshments or meals.

Dep. Kyoto   Frequent times from 7:41 to 21:53
Arr. Kobe   35 minutes later

Sights in **Kobe:** This is Japan's largest seaport. See: Ikuta Shrine. Take a bus tour to Minatogawa Shrine and the ancient Temple in Sumadera. Great cherry tree blossoms there every Spring. Equally beautiful maple tree foliage, every Autumn, at Zenshoji Temple. See the Hakutsuru Gallery of Oriental Art, near Mikage station. Visit the Zoo, Botanical Garden and all-girl opera at nearby Takarazuka.

Dep. Kobe   Frequent times from 7:04 to 21:39
Arr. Kyoto   35 minutes later

Kyoto - Matsuyama

All trains on the Kyoto-Okayama route require reservations and serve light refreshments or meals.

8070			8138		
Dep. Kyoto	7:53	8:43	Dep. Uno	9:56	10:54
Arr. Okayama	9:10	10:00	Arr. Takamatsu	10:56	11:54
Change trains.			Change to train.		
8138			8139		
Dep. Okayama	9:13	10:13	Dep. Takamatsu	11:14	13:04
Arr. Uno	9:46	10:46	Arr. Matsuyama	14:07	16:01
Change to boat.					

Sights in **Matsuyama:** This is a popular hot springs resort. See the lovely maple trees in nearby Omogo Valley. There is a fine castle here. The local sport is bullfighting.

8139			8138		
Dep. Matsuyama	9:07	14:23	Dep. Uno	13:37	18:34
Arr. Takamatsu	12:09	17:14	Arr. Okayama	14:11	19:08
Change to boat.			Change trains.		
8138			8070		
Dep. Takamatsu	12:25	17:28	Dep. Okayama	14:21	19:23
Arr. Uno	13:25	18:28	Arr. Kyoto	15:39	20:51
Change to train.					

Kyoto - Nagoya 8070

These trains require reservation for first-class seats and serve either light refreshments or meals.

Dep. Kyoto   Frequent times from 6:19 to 22:16
Arr. Nagoya   40-50 Minutes later

Sights in **Nagoya:** The art objects in the recently re-built 5-story 17th century castle. The view of Nagoya from the top of the 350-foot high television tower. The modern Nittaiji Temple, a gift from Thailand. The 1700-year old Atsuta Shrine. The Tokugawa Art Museum. Shop for fine Noritake chinaware and Ando cloisonne. It is only a 45-minute train ride to Inuyama to see the 16th century castle and the Kiso rapids there.

There is bus service every 20 minutes at the Nagoya station for the 1½-hour ride to the marvelous preservation park at Meiji, a 172-acre mountain village that has reproduced the lifestyle that existed in Japan at the end of the 19th century. Among the many monuments from the 1868-1912 era are: the railroad coach of the Meiji Emperor, the lobby of the original Frank Lloyd Wright Imperial Hotel (a Tokyo landmark for almost 50 years until it was demolished in the 1960's), a public bath, a merchant's townhouse, a teahouse, a Kabuki theater, antique railway machines, a hand-printing press, and textile spinning, weaving and threading machines. The village is open 10:00-17:00 March-October and 10:00-16:00 November-February.

Dep. Nagoya   Frequent times from 6:42 to 22:15
Arr. Kyoto   40-50 minutes later

Kyoto - Nara 8088

Dep. Kyoto   Frequent times from 5:34 to 22:34
Arr. Nara   60-75 minutes later

Sights in **Nara:** This is a very crowded tourist town. Weekends should be avoided. See the 1250-acre Nara Park and its temples.

Dep. Nara   Frequent times from 4:38 to 22:00
Arr. Kyoto   60-75 minutes later

Kyoto - Okayama 8070

These trains require reservation for first-class seats and serve either light refreshments or meals.

Dep. Kyoto   Frequent times from 7:41 to 21:53
Arr. Okayama   90 minutes later

Sights in **Okayama:** The bamboo groves, tea plantation, streams and ponds in the 28.5-acre Korakuen Park, one of Japan's finest gardens, established in 1700. Nearby, the lovely Kibitsu Shrine and the Saidaiji Temple. There is much extraordinary fruit in this area: white peaches, muscat grapes and unusual pears.

Dep. Okayama   Frequent times from 6:04 to 20:39
Arr. Kyoto   90 minutes later

Kyoto - Takamatsu

All trains on the Kyoto-Okayama route require reservation for first-class seats and serve either light refreshments or meals.

8070				8138			
Dep. Kyoto	9:26	10:17	14:17	Dep. Uno	11:54	12:54	16:54
Arr. Okayama	10:56	11:54	15:52	Arr. Takamatsu	12:54	13:54	17:54

Change trains.

8138

Dep. Okayama	11:13	12:13	16:13
Arr. Uno	11:46	12:46	16:46

Change to boat.

Sights in **Takamatsu:** The museum of 12th century battle relics in Yashima Temple, 5 miles away. The outstanding Ritsurin Park and Zoo. The Kimpira Shrines, only a one-hour ride by electric train to Kotohira. Nearby Kotobiki Park.

8138

Dep. Takamatsu	13:25	14:25	15:25	17:28	18:25
Arr. Uno	14:25	15:25	16:25	18:28	19:25

Change to train.

Dep. Uno	14:31	15:31	16:31	18:34	19:31
Arr. Okayama	15:06	16:06	17:06	19:09	20:36

Change trains.

8070

Dep. Okayama	15:28	16:23	17:23	19:23	20:39
Arr. Kyoto	17:04	17:51	18:51	20:51	22:14

Kyoto - Toba   0000   (Kinki Nippon Rly. Not shown in Cook's.)

Dep. Kyoto	Every 20 minutes	Dep. Toba	Every 20 minutes
Arr. Toba	35 minutes later	Arr. Kyoto	35 minutes later

Sights in **Toba:** See women divers gathering oysters into which an irritant is inserted which starts the process of pearl formation. A program is presented at Pearl Island, near the waterfront. Then continue on to Kashikojima, where you will want to visit the Cultured Pearl Institute to see the exhibition there.

Kyoto - Tottori   8095

These trains require reservations for first-class seats and serve light refreshments.

Dep. Kyoto	4:26(1)	9:20	14:38	16:32
Arr. Tottori	8:43	13:17	19:17	20:38

Sights in **Tottori:** Many hotsprings here. See the sand dunes on the nearby shore.

Dep. Tottori	14:58	18:20(1)	19:51(1)	-0-
Arr. Kyoto	18:54	22:30	0:09	-0-

(1)Train has only sleeping cars.

Osaka - Himeji   8080
Dep. Osaka   Frequent local service (second-class only)
Arr. Himeji   1½ hours later
  Sights in **Himeji:** The 5-story White Herron Castle.
Dep. Himeji   Frequent local service (second-class only)
Arr. Osaka   1½ hours later

Osaka - Kanazawa   8035
  All of these trains have meal service.
Dep. Osaka   Frequent times from 7:05 to 20:15
Arr. Kanazawa   3 hours 10 minutes later
  Sights in **Kanazawa:** A lovely castle city on Japan's seacoast. See Kenroken, the beautiful garden with ponds and waterfalls, next to the castle. Mountain-climbing trips start from here.
Dep. Kanazawa   Frequent times from 6:13 to 19:06
Arr. Osaka   3 hours 20 minutes later

Osaka - Kobe   8070
  All of these trains require reservation.
Dep. Osaka (1)Frequent times from 6:06 to 22:12
Arr. Kobe   17 minutes later
  Sights in **Kobe:** See notes under ''Kyoto-Kobe''.
Dep. Kobe   Frequent times from 7:04 to 23:05
Arr. Osaka (1)   17 minutes later
(1)Shin-Osaka, a commuter station.

Osaka - Nagoya   8070
  These trains require reservation and serve either light refreshments or meals.
Dep. Osaka (1)   Frequent times from 6:00 to 21:57
Arr. Nagoya   90 minutes later
  Sights in **Nagoya:** See notes under ''Kyoto-Nagoya''.
Dep. Nagoya   Frequent times from 6:42 to 22:15
Arr. Osaka (1)   90 minutes later
(1)Shin-Osaka, a commuter station.

Osaka - Okayama   8070
  These trains require reservation and serve either light refreshments or meals.
Dep. Osaka (1)   Frequent times from 6:00 to 22:12
Arr. Okayama   60-90 minutes later
  Sights in **Okayama:** See notes under ''Kyoto-Okayama''.
Dep. Okayama   Frequent times from 6:04 to 22:26
Arr. Osaka (1)60-90 minutes later
(1)Shin-Osaka, a commuter station.

614

Osaka - Tottori   8095

Dep. Osaka   8:00(1)   9:30(2)   12:10(2)   18:00(2)   21:34(2+3)
Arr. Tottori   12:13   13:44   16:28   22:24   3:30

Sights in **Tottori:** See notes about sightseeing in Tottori earlier in this section, under "Kyoto-Tottori".

Dep. Tottori   0:26(2+3)   6:21(2)   9:22(2)   12:44(2)   15:53(2+4)
Arr. Osaka   6:32   10:29   14:38   17:09   20:12

(1)Meal service. (2)Light refreshments. (3)Reservation required. Carries sleeping car. (4)Plus another departure from Tottori at 17:00(1).

Osaka - Toyama   8035

All trains on this route have meal service.

Dep. Osaka   Frequent times from 7:05 to 20:15
Arr. Toyama   4 hours later

Sights in **Toyama:** Famous since the 17th century for its medical powders, pills, drugs and other pharmaceutical items.

Dep. Toyama   Frequent times from 5:27 to 18:20
Arr. Osaka   4 hours later

Tokyo - Kanazawa   8072

Dep. Tokyo (Ueno)   9:00(1)   14:00(1)   16:00(1)   21:50(2)
Arr. Kanazawa   15:49   20:46   22:54   6:39

Sights in **Kanazawa:** See notes about sightseeing in Kanazawa earlier in this section, under "Osaka-Kanazawa".

Dep. Kanazawa   7:34(1)   10:28(1)   15:33(1)   21:40(2)
Arr. Tokyo (Ueno)   14:34   17:34   22:34   6:42

(1)Meal service. (2)This train is all sleeping cars. Light refreshments.

Tokyo - Lake Hakone   8048

Dep. Tokyo (Shinjuku)
    7:30 plus every 30 minutes from 9:30 to 17:00+18:00 and 18:30
    Sundays: above + 8:00, 8:30, 9:00, 17:30 and 19:00
Arr. Hakone-Yumoto   90 minutes later
    Take a taxi or bus from Yumoto to the lake.
    Sights: Beautiful scenery on this easy one-day roundtrip.
Dep. Hakone-Yumoto
    9:12 plus every 30 minutes from 10:42 to 18:42+20:12
    Sundays: above + 9:42, 10:42, 19:12, 19:42 and 20:42
Arr. Tokyo (Shinjuku)   90 minutes later

Tokyo - Kofu - Matsumoto   8050

All of these trains have light refreshments.

Dep. Tokyo (Shinjuku)	7:00	8:00	9:00	10:00	11:00	13:00(1)
Arr. Kofu		8:48	9:52	10:50	11:50	12:48	14:48
Arr. Matsumoto		10:39	11:46	12:40	13:39	14:43	16:41

Sights in **Kofu:** Good views of the Japanese Alps. Fine Summer and Winter sports facilities. From Kofu, there are connections to Lake Suwa.

Sights in **Matsumoto:** Great mountain scenery. Gateway to the Japanese Alps.

Dep. Matsumoto	6:39	8:00	9:47	10:58	12:48	13:48(2)
Dep. Kofu		8:36	9:44	11:39	12:43	14:38	15:40
Arr. Tokyo (Shinjuku)		10:25	11:30	13:25	14:25	16:25	17:25

(1)Plus other departures from Tokyo at 14:00, 15:00, 17:00, 18:00 and 19:00
(2)Plus other departures from Matsumoto at 14:34, 15:55, 16:48, 18:17 and 19:27.

Tokyo - Mito   8019

All of these trains have light refreshments.

Dep. Tokyo (Ueno)   Frequent times from 7:00 to 21:40
Arr. Mito   1½ hours later

Sights in **Mito:** Visit Kairaku-en Park, noted for its plum blossoms, about one mile west of the railstation. The special flowering season is late February to mid-March.

Dep. Mito   Frequent times from 5:01 to 21:30
Arr. Tokyo (Ueno)   1½ hours later

Tokyo - Narita   8016

Here are the connections with the international jet airport that serves Tokyo.

Dep. Tokyo (Ueno Keisei)   Frequent times from 5:00 to 22:10
Arr. Narita   60-90 minutes later

Sights in **Narita:** Located 40 miles from Tokyo and only 15 minutes by taxi from the international airport. Many Buddhist temples here. Be sure to visit the 10th century Shinshoji Temple and see the daily Goma ceremony there. Also: Issaikyodo Temple. The Historical Museum, located behind Naitasan Temple, and the nearby 45-acre park with flowering trees and plants, waterfalls and reflecting ponds. There are many country-inn restaurants on Monzen-Dori, Narita's narrow main street.

Dep. Narita   Frequent times from 6:07 to 23:00
Arr. Tokyo (Ueno Keisei)   60-90 minutes later

Tokyo - Niigata   8045

High-speed trains began operating in 1982 on this route through the 22.3km-long Daishimizu Tunnel. It is the world's longest, followed by Switzerland's 19.8km-long Simplon Tunnel. At 200km (120 miles) per hour, the "bullet train" runs through the Daishimizu in 7 minutes.

Dep. Tokyo (Ueno)   Frequent times from 5:40 to 20:17
Arr. Niigata   3 hours later
   Sights in **Niigata:** The leading Sea of Japan seaport.
Dep. Niigata   Frequent times from 6:45 to 20:00
Arr. Tokyo (Ueno)   3 hours later

Tokyo - Nikko   8047

These trains are first-class only.

Dep. Tokyo (Asakusa)   7:20   8:00   8:40   9:00   11:00(1+2)
Arr. Nikko   2 hours later
   Sights in **Nikko:** A cool retreat from hot Tokyo in Summer. Beautiful foliage in Autumn. Fine Winter sports. Many mountain lakes in this area.
Dep. Nikko   8:41(1)   9:08(1)   10:14(1)   12:01(1)   13:42(1+3)
Arr. Tokyo (Asakusa)   2 hours later
(1)Change trains in Shimoimaichi. (2)Plus other departures from Tokyo at 11:30(1), 12:30(1), 13:30(1), 14:30(1), 16:00(1), 19:40(1) and 20:10   (3)Plus other departures from Nikko at 14:42(1), 16:00, 16:08(1), 16:40, 17:00, 17:40 and 19:40(1).

Tokyo - Sendai   8020

Dep. Tokyo (Ueno)   Frequent times from 6:17 to 20:17
Arr. Sendai   3 hours later
   Sights in **Sendai:** The Osaki Hachiman Shrine. The Star Festival (early August) is the most splendid display of color in Japan. Each year at that time, Sendai's streets are decorated with brilliant paper streamers. The celebration goes 24 hours. Also see the nearby Matsushima National Park. Nearly every night in August, you can see the Summer Dance Festival, illuminated by lanterns painted by school children. Only a 30-minute bus ride from Sendai are many pinetree mountain hot springs resorts with inns. Much beautiful foliage there. Skiing at nearby Mt. Zao.
Dep. Sendai   Frequent times from 6:30 to 20:48
Arr. Tokyo (Ueno)   3 hours later

Tokyo - Karuizawa   8072

Dep. Tokyo (Ueno)   Frequent times from 7:00 to 20:00
Arr. Karuizawa   2¼ hours later

Sights in **Karuizawa:** Japanese Alps scenery. There are connections in Karuizawa for Lake Nojiri and Akakura, where there is good skiing.

Dep. Karuizawa   Frequent times from 7:25 to 20:25
Arr. Tokyo (Ueno)   2¼ hours later

Tokyo - Toyama   8072

Dep. Tokyo (Ueno)   9:00(1)   14:00(1)   16:00(1)   21:50(2)
Arr. Toyama   15:00   20:00   22:05   5:45

Sights in **Toyama:** See notes about sightseeing in Toyama earlier in this section, under "Osaka-Toyama".

Dep. Toyama   8:24(1)   11:16(1)   16:22(1)   22:38(2)
Arr. Tokyo (Ueno)   14:34   17:34   22:34   6:42

(1)Meal service. (2)This train has only sleeping cars. Light refreshments.

Tokyo - Yokohama   0000

Dep. Tokyo   By suburban train, at frequent times.
Arr. Yokohama   30 minutes later

Sights in **Yokohama:** The Chinatown area. The boutiques in the Motomachi section. The 19th century garden, Sankei-en. A stroll outside Myohoji Temple. The thousands of Buddhas in the Taya Caves. The history written on the tombstones in the Foreign Cemetery.

Dep. Yokohama   By suburban trains, at frequent times
Arr. Tokyo   30 minutes later

HOKKAIDO TRAIN TRIPS

What Hokkaido offers tourists is wild, primitive scenery: great lakes, fierce animals, aborigines, large herds of cattle, a severe northern climate, fine Winter sports, scenic mountains and forests. The 2 train routes on Hokkaido are: Hakodate-Kushiro and Hakodate-Abashiri.

Hakodate

This is the starting point for rail trips to Japan's northernmost frontier. See the only Western castle in Japan: Goryokaku fortress, constructed in the form of a 5-pointed star.

Sapporo

Known as "Little Tokyo", this 1.3 million metropolis has marvelous skiing and is also a hot springs resort. Its most famous event is the annual February Show Festival, featuring 10-foot high snow sculptures of subjects ranging from Colonel Sanders to Donald Duck. Visit the Shikotsu-Toya National Park and the Akan National Park, a reservation for Ainu aborigines.

Kushiro

One of the bases for visiting Akan National Park.

Hakodate - Sapporo - Kushiro   8002

All of these trains require reservations for first-class seats, for which there is an extra charge.

Dep. Hakodate	4:50(1)	9:40(2)	11:45(3)	14:32(3+6)
Arr. Sapporo	9:22	13:50(2)	16:27	20:07
Change trains.				
Dep. Sapporo	12:20(1)	13:56(2)	17:15(3)	22:10(4+7)
Arr. Kushiro	18:53	19:15	22:14	6:15
		*	*	*
Dep. Kushiro	7:20(2)	11:55(3)	22:35(4)	-0-
Arr. Sapporo	12:19(2)	18:14	6:25	-0-
Change trains.				
Dep. Sapporo	12:25(2)	19:20(3)	10:20(3)	-0-
Arr. Hakodate	16:40	23:55	16:08	-0-

(1)Meal service. (2)Direct train. No train change in Sapporo. Light refreshments. (3)Light refreshments. (4)Carries sleeping car. Light refreshments. (5)Second-class only. (6)Plus another departure from Hakodate at 23:51(5).   (7)Plus another departure from Sapporo at 7:05(3).

Hakodate - Sapporo - Asahigawa - Abashiri

These trains require reservations for first-class seats, for which there is an extra charge.

8000 + 8002

Dep. Hakodate	-0-	4:45(1)	7:40(1)	11:40(3+6)
Arr. Sapporo	-0-	8:57	11:59	15:55

Change trains.

8007

Dep. Sapporo	7:00(2)	9:28(2)	13:40(4)	16:00(3+7)
Dep. Asahigawa	8:48(2)	11:16(2)	15:40(4)	17:51
Arr. Abashiri	12:48	15:39	23:07	21:57

Sights in **Abashiri:** Take a sightseeing bus or taxi to view the magnificent seacoast. See the unique igloo sculptures during February Snow Festival—blocks of ice containing frozen fish.

Sights in **Asahigawa:** The aborigine Ainu village at Chikabumi, a few minutes away. Instead of stopping in Asahigawa, many tourists drive by rental car to the hot spring resorts a few hours away (Shirogane and Sounkyo), where there are good inns, skiing and beautiful mountain scenery. This is in the excellent Daisetsuzan National Park. There is good fishing in this area.

8007

Dep. Abashiri	5:40(2)	8:58(3)	13:54(2)	17:02(2+8)
Arr. Asahigawa	9:56(2)	13:07(3)	17:57(2)	21:16(2)
Arr. Sapporo	12:11	14:59(3)	19:53	23:04

Change trains.

8000 + 8002

Dep. Sapporo	12:25(2)	15:05(1)	20:00(1+9)	-0-
Arr. Hakodate	16:40	19:24	0:20	-0-

(1)Meal service. (2)Light refreshments. (3)Direct train. No train change in Sapporo. Meal service. (4)Second-class only. (5)Carries second-class sleeping car. Light refreshments. (6)Plus another departure from Hakodate at 14:55(1), connecting with a departure from Sapporo at 22:15(5). (7)Plus other departures from Sapporo at 17:10(2) and 22:15(5). (8)Plus another departure from Abashiri at 21:14(5). (9)For other departures from Sapporo (to Hakodate), see page 618.

DISTANCE TRAIN TRIPS FROM TOKYO

Tokyo - Kyoto and Osaka   8070

These trains require reservation and serve either light refreshments or meals.

Dep. Tokyo	Frequent times from 6:00 to 20:12
Arr. Kyoto	3 hours later
Arr. Osaka	18 minutes after departing Kyoto

*   *   *

Dep. Osaka	Frequent times from 6:00 to 20:34
Dep. Kyoto	18 minutes later
Arr. Tokyo	3 hours 18 minutes after departing Osaka

Tokyo - Aomori (via Niigate)
8045

Dep. Tokyo (Ueno)	6:17(1)	9:18(1)	11:47(1)	13:47(1)	16:25(1)
Arr. Niigata	8:50	11:50	14:45	16:45	18:50

Change trains.
8018

Dep. Niigata	10:10(2)	12:15(2)	15:05(2)	17:00(2)	19:40(1)
Arr. Aomori	14:00	16:05	18:55	20:50	23:30

*   *   *

Dep. Aomori	5:25(2)	7:30(2)	10:15(2)	12:15(2)	14:55(2)
Arr. Niigata	9:15	11:20	14:05	16:05	18:45

Change trains.
8045

Dep. Niigata	9:55(1)	12:00(1)	15:00(1)	16:45(1)	19:55(1)
Arr. Tokyo (Ueno)	12:27	14:57	17:47	19:17	22:21

(1)Light refreshments. (2)Meal service.

Tokyo - Aomori (via Sendai)   8019

Unless otherwise designated, a supplement is charged. All of these trains serve light refreshments.

Dep. Tokyo (Ueno)	19:10(1)	19:50(2)	20:50(1)	22:20(1)	23:00(2+4)
Arr. Aomori	6:15	5:03	9:08	7:15	8:21

*   *   *

Dep. Aomori	18:45(3)	19:20(3)	19:44(1)	21:10(2)	21:15(2+5)
Arr. Tokyo (Ueno)	5:41	6:08	7:24	6:35	6:52

(1)Second-class only. (2)Carries second-class sleeping car. (3)Carries only sleeping cars.

Tokyo - Aomori (via Akita)   8018

Dep. Tokyo (Ueno)	7:20(1)	10:30(2+3)	20:50(2+4)	21:40(4+5)
Arr. Akita	15:15	-0-	-0-	8:20
Change trains.				
Dep. Akita	15:23(1)	-0-	-0-	8:55(1)
Arr. Aomori	18:03	21:13	9:09	11:56
	*	*	*	
Dep. Aomori	7:56(2+3)	9:55(1)	13:02(1)	18:06(2+4+6)
Arr. Akita	-0-	12:32	15:43	-0-
Change trains.				
Dep. Akita	-0-	13:02(1)	18:05(4)	-0-
Arr. Tokyo (Ueno)	18:34	21:24	5:55	6:33

(1)Light refreshments. (2)Direct train. No train changein Akita. (3)Meal service. (4)Carries only sleeping cars. Light refreshments. (5)Plus another departure from Tokyo at 22:00(2+4).   (6)Plus another departure from Aomori at 20:15(2+4).

THE TRANS-SIBERIAN RAIL TRIP

This is the westward ride on the Trans-Siberian Express.

Yokohama - Khabarovsk - Moscow

5050			5020		
Dep. Yokohama	11:00(1)	Day 1	Dep. Khabarovsk	6:55(3)	Day 4
Arr. Nakhodka	17:00	Day 3	Arr. Moscow		
Change to train.			(Yar.)	15:05	Day 10
5045					
Dep. Nakhodka	12:50(2)	Day 3			
Arr. Khabarovsk	4:10	Day 4			
Change trains.					

(1)For specific sailing dates, check a current Cooks International Timetable. (2)Runs only on arrival days of ships from Yokohama. Carries sleeping car. Has only second-class coach cars. Meal service. (3)Runs daily. Carries sleeping car. Has both first and second-class coach cars. Meal service.

KAMPUCHEA
(formerly called Khmer Republic and Cambodia)

The one rail route in Kampuchea links the seaport of Kompong Sam with the capital, Phnom Penh, and then extends westward from there to Aranyaprathet, just inside Thailand's border, and on to Bangkok.

Phnom Penh - Kompong Sam   7101

Dep. Phnom Penh	N/A(1)	Dep. Kompong Sam	N/A(1)
Arr. Kompong Sam	N/A(1)	Arr. Phnom Penh	N/A(1)

Sights in **Phnom Penh:** The diamond encrusted black derby at the Royal Museum in the Royal Palace. Also there: The Throne Hall, Silver Pagoda (with its solid silver floors and Golden Buddha), Pavilion of the Holy Sword, and the open-air Chanchhaya Hall, where royal ballets once were performed. Also see, nearby, The National Museum and the Khmer Art School, with its arts and handicrafts (silk sarongs, small figures of dancers and musicians, and silver carriages).

Phnom Penh - Aranyaprathet - Bangkok   7100

Dep. Phnom Penh	N/A(1)		
Arr. Aranyaprathet	N/A(1)		

  Change trains.
  7059

Dep. Aranyaprathet	5:35(2)	7:10(2)	13:15(2)
Arr. Bangkok	10:55	12:40	18:35

(1)Service has been suspended since the Kampuchea-Thailand frontier closed in 1977.   (2)Third-class only.

LAO PEOPLE'S DEMOCRATIC REPUBLIC

There is no passenger train service in Lao.

MALAYSIA

Children under 4 travel free. Half-fare for children 4-11. Children 12 and over must pay full fare.

There is passenger rail service from Kuala Lumpur to 4 Malayan seaports: Penang and Padang Besar on its westcoast, and to Tumpat and Kuantan on its eastcoast. Kota Bahru, 8 miles inland from the South China Sea, is also served by trains from Kuala Lumpur.

There is also train service from Kuala Lumpur south to Singapore.

The views through Malaysia include pepper-vine farms, rice paddies, colorfully clothed people at small railstations, water buffalo, and many different tree farms: rubber, banana, tapioca, coconut and palm oil nut, used in making soap and margarine.

Malayan Railway Pass

Unlimited train travel on all classes of coach on all rail lines within Peninsular Malaysia, including travel to and from Singapore. The 1984 prices are: M$70 for 10 days, M$150 for 30 days. Space in first-class air-conditioned coaches must be reserved. (The single air-conditioned coach operated between Kuala Lumpur and Singapore has seats for only 22 people.) Reservations for first-class space can be made up to 3 months in advance of travel date from: Director of Commerce, Malayan Railway, Jalan Sultan Hishamuddin, Kuala Lumpur. This pass is sold at stations in Kuala Lumpur, Penang, Padang Besar, Johore Baru, Butterworth, Pelabuhan Kelang, Rantau Panjang, Wakaf Bharu and Singapore.

Kuala Lumpur

See the marvelous collection of dioramas portraying primitive Malay life, costumes, ancient vehicles, silver, brass and weapons in the National Museum (Muzium Negara). Parliament House. Rubber and pewter factories. Tin mines. The old Central Mosque. The National Art Gallery. The Zoo. The Batu Caves, a Hindu shrine, 8 miles away. The breathtaking modern Majid Negara (National Mosque). The Chan See Shu Yuen Society Temple.

The Sunday Market (to be visited Saturday night) on Jalan Raja Muda Musa, to sample Malay food. The antiques and art in Wisma Loke, formerly the residence of a wealthy Chinese merchant, on Jalan Medan Tuanku.

Kuala Lumpur - Butterworth (Penang) - Padang Besar

7005
Dep. Kuala Lumpur	7:30(1)	9:00(1)	15:00(1+2)	20:10(3+8)
Arr. Butterworth	13:25	17:30	21:25	5:40

Change trains.
7016
Dep. Butterworth	6:40(4)	7:55(5)
Arr. Padang Besar	10:40	11:35

*   *   *

Dep. Padang Besar	15:00(6)	15:30(7)
Arr. Butterworth	18:45	19:40

Change trains.
7005
Dep. Butterworth	20:35(3)	22:00(1+7)	8:15(1+2)	8:45(1+9)
Arr. Kuala Lumpur	5:55	7:00	14:35	17:25

(1)Air-conditioned in first-class. Meal service. (2)Reservation required. (3)Second and third-class only. (4)Third-class only. Meal service. (5)Runs Monday, Wednesday and Friday. Meal service. (6)Runs Tuesday, Thursday and Sunday. Meal ture from Kuala Lumpur at 22:00(7).   (9)Plus another departure from Butterworth at 13:55(1).

Sights in **Penang:** An island, just off Butterworth. See the Snake Temple. Ayer Hitami Temple. Khoo Kongsi Temple. The view of the island from the top (2500 feet) of Penang Hill, reached by a funicular. Siva Temple. Goddess of Mercy Temple. The sociable monkeys at the Botanical Gardens. The shops on Campbell Street. The pagoda at Kek Lok Si Temple. Kapitan Kling Mosque.

Kuala Lumpur - Mentakab - Kuantan - Kota Bahru   7015

Dep. Kuala			Dep.		
Lumpur	8:00	19:30	Kota Bahru	8:00	19:30
Dep. Mentakab	N/A(1)	N/A(1)	Dep. Kuantan	N/A(1)	N/A(1)
Dep. Kuantan	N/A(1)	N/A(1)	Dep. Mentakab	N/A(1)	N/A(1)
Arr.			Arr. Kuala		
Kota Bahru	18:00	7:30		18:00	7:30

(1)Time has not been available since 1980.

Kuala Lumpur - Mentakab - Tumpat

7015		7006	
Dep. Kuala Lumpur	15:30	Dep. Tumpat	9:00(2)
Arr. Mentakab	17:30(1)	Arr. Mentakab	20:53
Change trains.		Change trains.	
7006		7015	
Dep. Mentakab	6:14(2)	Dep. Mentakab	5:30(1)
Arr. Tumpat	19:00	Arr. Kuala Lumpur	7:30

(1)Estimated time. (2)Meal service.

INTERNATIONAL ROUTES FROM MALAYSIA

Butterworth is Malaysia's train gateway to Thailand. Kuala Lumpur is the starting point for rail trips to Singapore.

Butterworth - Bangkok   7050
Dep. Butterworth   7:55(1)
Arr. Bangkok   6:45 Day 2
(1)Runs Monday, Wednesday and Friday. Carries sleeping car. Meal service.

Kuala Lumpur - Singapore   7005

Dep. Kuala Lumpur	7:30	9:00(1)	15:05(1+2)	20:15(3)	22:00(4)
Arr. Singapore	13:35	17:30	21:35	5:55	7:25

(1)Air-conditioned in first-class. Meal service. (2)Reservation required. (3)Second and third-class only. (4)Air-conditioned in first-class. Carries sleeping car.

NORTH KOREA

In overnight trains, the first-class seats convert to berths with complete bedding; second-class seats convert to couchettes. Children under 3 travel free. Half-fare for children 3-9. Children 10 and over must pay full fare.

The 16-car train from Pyonyang to Pekin is pulled by an electric engine. About half of the cars have sleeping facilities. These are occupied mainly by non-Koreans. The other cars have 4-seat benches. Passage between the 2 classes of cars is prevented by locked doors.

A restaurant car is accessible to the first-class sleeping cars. In it, passengers can buy food, beer and Pullosul, a yellow liqueur containing an alcohol-preserved pit viper snake.

The scenery on this route is mostly rice paddies.

Before reaching the Chinese border, the train crosses the Yalu River. On the other side of the Yalu, a steam engine replaces the electric Korean locomotive. Chinese immigration officers board the train when it stops in Dandong, where a Chinese restaurant car replaces the Korean one.

After reaching Pekin, there are connections by train from there to both Moscow and to Hanoi (and on from there to Ho Chi Minh City, formerly called Saigon).

Chongjin - Pyongyang   5205

Dep. Chongjin	N/A(1)	Dep. Pyongyang	N/A(1)
Arr. Pyongyang	N/A(1)	Arr. Chongjin	N/A(1)

(1)Times have not been available since 1977.

Pyongyang - Pekin

5200

Dep. Pyongyang	12:00	Wednesdy and Saturday
Arr. Dandong	16:23	

5306

Dep. Dandong	17:54	Wednesday and Saturday
Arr. Shenyang	22:15	

5307

Dep. Shenyang	22:30	Wednesday and Saturday
Arr. Pekin	9:40	Thursday and Sunday

PEOPLE'S REPUBLIC OF CHINA

In overnight trains, the first-class seats convert to berths with complete bedding; second-class seats convert to couchettes. Children 1 metre tall or less travel free. Quarter-fare for children 1.00 to 1.29 metres. Children 1.30 metres and taller must pay full fare.

The 3 categories of Chinese National Railways trains are Express, Fast and Ordinary. Short-distance trains have soft and hard (first and second-class) seat accommodations. Long-distance trains provide soft-class compartment berths and hard-class sleeping berths. We learned on our 1980 rail trips (Shanghai-Changsha, Changsha-Guilin and Canton-Hong Kong) that Chinese trains do not provide drinking water, toilet paper, or soap, although each sleeping compartment is supplied with a thermos of hot water, tea and cups. There is enough storage space in each 4-person compartment for 6 large suitcases. Each berth has a reading lamp.

You can count on 2 things when touring China: the government will keep you on the go 10-14 hours every day, and you will be placed in a Friendship Store from one to 3 hours almost every day. These emporiums sell every possible souvenir you could want to bring home from China: jade, ivory, fabrics, furniture, porcelain, clothing, lacquerware, jewelry, books, etc.

Canton (Guangzhou, pronounced "Kwang-chow")

In the 64-acre Memorial Garden to the Martyrs (also called Red Uprising (the 1927 massacre of many Chinese Communist Party members by government soldiers), holding more than 5,000 bodies. Also: The Pavillion of Sino-Korean Friendship and the Memorial Pavillion. The Tomb of the 72 Martyrs, honoring leaders of the unsuccessful 1911 revolution, located at Huanghuagang (Yellow Flower Hill Park). The Sun Yat-sen Memorial Hall.

At the enormous Yuexiu Park, go to the top of the 600-year-old Zhen Hai Tower (also called Five-Storied Building) for a view of all of the city. Also located in this park are the Museum of Liberation and many other museums: prehistory, Ming Dynasty, the Manchu era, the Opium Wars, and one on the industrialization of Canton.

At the west side of Yuexiu Park, there is an excellent Chinese Orchid Garden. The 82-acre Zoo, with more than 200 varieties of birds and animals, is considered one of the best in Asia and is famous for its Panda bears.

Other notable sights: the 6th century Lu Yung Temple (Temple of the Six Banyan Trees). The 7th century Huaisheng Mosque. The 4th century (B.C.) Kwang Shiao Temple. Many parks and lakes. The view from White Cloud Mountain. The Monument to the Struggle Against the British Invasion, at San-yuanli, north of the city.

Pekin (Beijing)

It is said that everyone starts a tour of Pekin from the enormous Tian'anmen Square (nearly 100 acres), where Chairman Mao Zedong first raised the flag of the People's Republic of China and initiated the contemporary era of China.

At the north side of the Square is Tian'anmen (Gate of Heavenly Peace), the entrance to the fabled Forbidden City, a 250-acre compound containing many palaces, museums, pavillions and gardens.

You walk first through the Upright Gate, then down Sightseer's Route to Meridian Gate and then through Gate of Supreme Harmony, next reaching the exhibits inside Hall of Supreme Harmony, followed by Hall of Complete Harmony, Hall of Preserving Harmony, Gate of Heavenly Purity, Palace of Heavenly Purity, Hall of Union, Hall of Earthly Peace, Gate of Earthly Peace, and finally reach Hall of Imperial Peace, surrounded by the Imperial Garden.

East of Tian'anmen Square are the Chinese History Museum and the Museum of the Chinese Revolution. West of the Square is the Great Hall of the People. Its banquet room seats 5,000 people. A theater near it holds 10,000. At the south side of the Square is the magnificent Chairman Mao Memorial Hall and the Monument to the People's Heroes.

Other important sights in Pekin are: The large Zoo, featuring Giant Pandas. The 770-foot long white marble Marco Polo Bridge, spanning the Yungting River. The National Art Gallery. The fantastic 15th century Temple of Heaven, located in a complex measuring 16 square miles.

It is a 90-minute bus ride from Pekin to the Great Wall, the mightiest human construction in history. Although a special excursion train departs Pekin daily at 7:03 (arriving back in Pekin at 13:30), the train leaves passengers about ¼-mile from the Great Wall. Buses from Pekin take you directly to the section of the Great Wall at Badaling that was restored in 1957 for visitors.

Most of the 3,600-mile long wall was built 476-221(B.C.), with more than another 100 years of work performed to restore and reinforce it in the 14th-15th century(A.D.).

Seven miles from Pekin is the Summer Palace, set in a 700-acre park that includes the lovely Kunming Lake and many museums. The walk down the beautifully decorated ''Long Corridor'', along the lakeshore, is memorable.

Thirty miles from Pekin, the Ming Tombs cover an area of several square miles. The sculptured animals along the road leading to the exhibit tomb are very interesting.

Canton - Kowloon - Hong Kong   5400

Prior to 1979, it was always necessary to walk from Shenzhen across the bridge spanning the Shum Chun River, to the Lo Wu railstation on the south side of the river before boarding a second train in Lo Wu and proceeding on to Kowloon and Hong Kong.

Since 1979, 2 trains per day make a direct ride from Canton to Kowloon, without requiring passengers to change trains at Shenzhen-Lo Wu.

Departures for the short ferry-boat ride from Kowloon to Hong Kong are frequent.

Dep. Canton	6:25(1)	7:32(1)	8:30(3)	9:15(4)	10:10(3)
Arr. Shenzhen	8:36(2)	9:49(2)	10:20(3)	11:14(2)	12:00
Dep. Shenzhen	-0-	-0-	10:23(3)	-0-	12:03
Arr. Lo Wu	-0-	-0-	10:28(3)	-0-	12:08
Change trains.					
Dep. Lo Wu	9:39	10:52	10:31	12:36	12:11
Arr. Kowloon	10:50	12:09	11:26	13:49	13:07

(1)Second-class only. (2)Walk across the frontier bridge. (3)First-class only. Reservation required. Meal service. Air-conditioned. Direct train to Kowloon. No train change in Lo Wu. (4)First-class only. Air-conditioned.

Canton - Shanghai   5330

Dep. Canton		Dep. Shanghai	9:18
(Guangzhou)	14:25	Arr. Canton	
Arr. Shanghai	23:10 Day 2	(Guangzhou)	19:10 Day 2

Sights in **Shanghai:** This is the largest city in the world (more than 11,000,000 population). See Chung Shan Lu Street, on the waterfront, called "the Bund", with its European-style buildings, from the period when foreigners controlled the city. You will want to visit the Number One Department Store while strolling this famous street.

Also see People's Park, once a race track. The enormous People's Square. The goods displayed at the Industrial Exhibit, everything from jade to ship-building.

Next to the City God Temple are the Yueyuan Gardens and the Temple of the Town Gods and the Garden of the Purple Clouds of Autumn.

Do not miss the 3rd century pagoda, rebuilt in the 10th century, located in Lung Hua Park. The laughing Buddha in the temple there is a major attraction.

Visit the large natural exhibit Zoo in Si Jiao Park and the smaller Zoo in Fu Hsing Park. The vast collection of artwork in the Museum of Shanghai. The white jade Buddha in the Jade Buddha Temple. The antiques for sale at the Antique and Curio Branch of Shanghai Friendship Store. The Children's Palace. Swan Lake in West Suburb Park.

Shanghai - Pekin   5330

Stops are made at Nanking, Tsinan, Tientsin and many towns not on the Cooks timetable: Soochow, Wusih, Pengpu, etc. At most stops, passengers alight to buy local food items sold along the platforms. At Tientsin, the favorite is meat-filled dumplings that the Chinese regard as the best in their country.

The route actually originates in Foochow. This is a critical military area and, as the case of Vladivostok with the Soviets, is closed to most foreigners.

Compartments are fitted with loudspeakers from which pour a steady combination of propaganda and music, the same as we experienced on the "Trans Siberia Express".

However, where the Soviet off-switch is in plain sight, the Chinese have placed theirs more obscurely under a small reading table.

The compartments on the Shanghai-Peking Express have a fin de siecle elegance: potted plants, porcelain cups, and tea bags. An acupuncturist is available for anyone requiring that service. As on most Chinese express trains, women workers are constantly scrubbing and mopping the interior. Boiling water is provided free in large thermos containers.

Each compartment has 4 berths. However, foreigners traveling in pairs are usually given an entire compartment. Early in the trip the train goes along the Grand Canal that was being used before Marco Polo saw it 6 centuries ago. It still has heavy boat traffic. Arrivals below are on Day 2.

Dep. Shanghai	9:13	11:54	14:46	19:03(1)
Arr. Pekin	5:35	13:03	10:04	14:24
		*	*	*
Dep. Pekin	12:50(1)	17:12	19:10	21:08(1)
Arr. Shanghai	8:01	13:50	18:09	16:21

(1)Air-conditioned in first-class.

Pekin - Guilin   5320

Dep. Pekin (Beijing)	23:59	Dep. Guilin	1:28
Arr. Guilin	7:10 Day 3	Arr. Pekin (Beijing)	9:10 Day 2

Sights in **Guilin:** The most magnificent scenery in China. Green fields of rice and sugar cane. Hundreds of weird shart karst peaks. Take the popular half-day boat ride down the meandering Li Jiang River. Visit Huanchu Cave, Seven Star Cave, Reed Flute Cave, Banyan Lake, Pagoda Hill. See the incredible view from the top of Tuhsiu Peak.

INTERNATIONAL ROUTES FROM PEOPLE'S REPUBLIC OF CHINA

Here are the routes from Pekin to Russia, Vietnam and North Korea.

Pekin - Moscow   5100
Dep. Pekin   7:40 Wednesday
Arr. Moscow   16:40 Monday (Day 6)
This is one of the special Russian Intourist trains for foreign travelers. Carries sleeping car. Meal service.

Pekin - Hanoi   5320
Dep. Pekin	23:59	Dep. Nanning	N/A(1)
Arr. Nanning	14:50 Day 3	Arr. Hanoi	N/A(1)

(1)Service was "temporarily" suspended in 1980.

Pekin - Pyonyang - Chongjin
In Dandong, a Korean restaurant car replaces the Chinese one. It is accessible to the first-class sleeping cars. Passengers can buy food, beer and Pullosul, a yellow liqueur containing an alcohol preserved pit viper snake. An electric Korean locomotive replaces the Chinese steam engine, and the train crosses the Yalu River.

About half of the cars have sleeping facilities. These are occupied mainly by non-Koreans. The other cars have 4-seat benches. Passage between the 2 classes of cars is prevented by locked doors.

5307
Dep. Pekin   16:48(1)
Arr. Shenyang   3:31
  5306
Dep. Shenyang   3:46(2+3)
Arr. Dandong*   8:05
  5200
Dep. Dandong   9:35(2+3)
Arr. Pyongyang   15:55
*The revised spelling of Antung.

(1)Runs Monday and Thursday. (runs Tuesday and Friday. (3)Carries sleeping car on Friday only. (4)Times have not been available since 19:77.

PHILIPPINES

The rail system on Luzon is 2 lines, north from Manila to San Fernando and south from Manila to Camalig.

Children under 3 travel free. Half-fare for children 3-9. Children 10 and over must pay full fare.

Manila

See: Representations of the country's major regions (Visayas, Mindanao, Vigan and the Mountain Provinces) at the Philippine Village, next to the airport. Excellent souvenirs are sold there. Visit the complex of Cultural Center, Folks Art Theater and Convention Center. The sidewalk cafes, Chinese and Japanese gardens, planetarium and the lagoon with "dancing" fountains, all in Rizal Park. For Santiago, San Augustine Church (which has artifacts from the era of Spanish rule) and Manila Cathedral, all in the 16th century walled city called Intramuros. Near it, Chinatown and the marble tombs in the Chinese cemetery. The Zoological and Botanical Garden. Take a hydrofoil for the short trip to see the ruins of Corregidor, the famous World War II fort. The 18th century 12-foot wide Bamboo Organ of Las Pinas is only a few miles from Manila.

Manila - San Fernando   7700

Dep. Manila (Tutuban)	6:00(1)	13:00(2)
Arr. San Fernando	12:45	20:00
	*	* *
Dep. San Fernando	7:50(2)	13:45(1)
Arr. Manila (Tutuban)	15:10	20:45

(1)Has first and third-class coach cars. Meal service. (2)Has second and third-class coach cars.

Manila - Camalig   7700

There are great views of Mayon Volcano from Camalig to Naga and of Pagsanjan Falls and Rapids.

Dep. Manila	9:00(1)	15:00(2)	19:00(1)
Dep. Naga	13:15(1)	7:00(2)	11:25(1)
Arr. Camalig	14:15	9:20	14:05
	*	*	*
Dep. Camalig	9:00(1)	15:00(2)	17:10(1)
Dep. Naga	11:05(1)	18:53(2)	20:00(1)
Arr. Manila	14:10	9:20	11:00

(1)Has second and third-class coach cars. (2)Has first and third-class coach cars. Also has third-class couchettes. Meal service.

REPUBLIC OF CHINA (TAIWAN)

Children under 3 travel free. Half-fare for children 3-13. Children 14 and over must pay full fare.

Express service starts at the northern top of Taiwan, at Kee-Lung, and extends south along western Taiwain to Kaohsiung and Pingtung. From Pingtung, local trains run to a fork at Chen-an. From Chen-an, one local spur goes to Tung-chiang and another to Fanh-liao. Another rail line runs from Kee-Lung along the eastern side of the island, south to Hualien and Tai-tung Hai-an.

Taipei

Among the leading sights to see in Taipei are the fabulous art treasures from mainland China in the National Palace Museum. Also see: The Monument of the Martyrs. The Memorial to Dr. Sun Yat Sen. Luan Shen Temple, and the street of food stores across from the Temple. The lobby and halls of the world's most extravagant and most beautiful hotel, The Grand Hotel, atop a hill that overlooks all of Taipei. Art objects and Chinese currency exhibited at the National Museum of History. Aboriginal artifacts at the Taiwan Provincial Museum.

Taipei - Taichung - Kaohsiung   7800

These trains are air-conditioned, unless designated otherwise.

Dep. Taipei	7:00(1)	8:00	9:00	10:00(2)
Arr. Taichung	9:18(1)	10:09	11:18	12:11(3)
Arr. Kaohsiung	11:52	12:20	13:49	14:22
		*	*	*
Dep. Kaohsiung	8:00	9:10(1)	10:00	10:30(4)
Dep. Taichung	10:11	11:17(1)	12:32	13:15(5)
Arr. Taipei	12:27	13:17	14:50	15:51

(1)This train is *not* air-conditioned. (2)Plus other departures from Taipei at frequent times from 11:00 to 23:30. (3)Plus other departures from Taichung at frequent times from 13:44 to 2:48. (4)Plus other departures from Kaohsiung at frequent times from 11:00 to 23:00. (5)Plus other departures from Taichung at frequent times from 13:42 to 2:29.

We had the advantage of being escorted for 9 days in the Republic of China by the prominent Taiwan engineer and orchid expert, Mr. L. F. King, whose comments and knowledge illuminated everything we saw. His kindness made our travels in Taiwan the most idyllic touring we have ever had in our travel throughout the world.

Taiwan's railstations and other of its public places have enormous mirrors. Personal appearance is very important to the Taiwanese, who like to inspect themselves when starting and ending a journey.

No one could become mussed on the air-conditioned, non-stop ride we made from Taipei to Taichung. A few minutes after leaving Taipei, Chinese-language newspapers are given to each passenger without charge. Next, an attendant brings hot, damp wash-cloths, and everyone washes face and hands. Meanwhile, recorded Western and Chinese music is played over the train's public address system. Other train employees place tea bags and hot water into large glasses that fit into holders along the wall, next to where one is sitting and within easy reach. More hot water is served frequently during the trip.

Mr. King, whose taste in art, orchids and food is impeccable, carries with him when he travels a special blend of tea, which he brought on our trip in sufficient quantity for us so that we might have it to enjoy in place of the tea that the train serves.

During the ride, he alerted us to various brick and ceramic factories, the construction of a new super-highway which his company was then building, and other interesting sights. Halfway to Taichung, the train goes along the Formosa Strait.

Vendors come through the train with sandwiches, candies and cigarettes. An hour before arriving in Taichung, a hot meal of beef, rice and a hardboiled egg flavored with tea can be purchased at one's seat for $1.00 (U.S.).

This train has airplane style seating, all passengers facing forward. Each car has separate lavatories for men and women. The price for that journey from Taipei to Taichung on that all first-class express train is $7.00 (U.S.).

Taichung - Sun Moon Lake

One of Taiwan's 2 most famous tourist attractions is the incredibly beautiful Sun Moon Lake, a 50-mile bus trip from Taichung. Motor launches offer cruises on the lake.

Government Timetable

Dep. Taichung	7:30	8:30	9:50	13:30	15:30
Arr. Sun Moon Lake	9:20	10:30	11:40	15:20	17:20
	*	*	*		
Dep. Sun Moon Lake	10:30	12:30	-0-	16:00	18:00
Arr. Taichung	12:20	14:20	-0-	17:50	19:50

Here is an easy stopover in Taichung, en route from Taipei to Kaohsiung or vice versa, with a side-trip to Sun Moon Lake.

Dep. Taipei	10:00	Dep. Kaohsiung		10:00
Arr. Taichung	12:09	Arr. Taichung		12:32
Take bus to Sun Moon Lake.		Take bus to Sun Moon Lake.		
Dep. Taichung	13:30	Dep. Taichung		13:30
Arr. Sun Moon Lake	15:20	Arr. Sun Moon Lake		15:20
Dep. Sun Moon Lake	16:00	Dep. Sun Moon Lake		16:00
Arr. Taichung	17:50	Arr. Taichung		17:50
Continue on train.		Continue on train.		
Dep. Taichung	18:21	Dep. Taichung		18:44
Arr. Kaohsiung	20:40	Arr. Taipei		20:52

Chia I - Alishan   7800

This spur off the Kaohsiung-Taipei line has great mountain scenery. The station at Alishan (7,461 feet) is the highest railstation in East Asia.

Dep. Kaohsiung	6:20	Dep. Chia I	8:00
Arr. Chia I	7:50	Arr. Alishan	12:00
Change trains		* * *	
		Dep. Alishan	13:30
		Arr. Chia I	17:15

Dep. Chia I	18:12	Dep. Chia I	19:18
Arr. Taipei	22:06	Arr. Kaohsiung	20:40

Taipei - Su Ao New - New Hualien - Taitung   7801

A very scenic train ride down the East Coat of Taiwan.

Dep. Taipei	7:00(1)	7:43(1)	9:00(1)	9:40(2+6)
Dep. Su Ao New	-0-	10:48(1)	-0-	12:23
Arr. New Hualien	10:15	12:19	12:25	13:44
Change trains.				
Dep. New Hualien	10:55	12:37(2)	13:40	-0-(7)
Arr. Taitung	14:34	16:13	17:11	-0-
		*	*	*
Dep. Taitung	0:50	6:25	10:02	12:20(8)
Arr. New Hualien	5:45	10:00	13:35	15:56
Change trains.				
Dep. New Hualien	6:45	10:17(1)	13:46(1)	17:00(1+9)
Dep. Su Ao New	18:18	11:58(1)	15:21(1)	-0-
Arr. Taipei	11:15	15:03	18:26	20:23

(1)Air-conditioned. (2)Second-class only. (3)Terminates in Su Ao New. (4)Does not stop in Su Ao New. (5)Terminates in New Hualien. (6)Plus other departures from Taipei at 9:40(2), 12:30(1+3), 13:10(3), 13:50(1), 17:40(3), 19:30 and 20:30(3).   (7)Plus other departures from New Hualien at 15:25, 17:40, 18:45, 0:35 and 7:45.   (8)Plus other departures from Taitung at 13:00, 15:30(4) and 18:45(5).   (9)Plus other departures from New Hualien at 7:35(1), 8:20(1), 15:35(1) and 19:15(1).

Only a 20-minute auto (or bus) ride from Hualien is the eastern end of Taiwan's most fantastic scenic subject: Taroko Gorge.

Spectacular marble mountains and, in the river along which you drive, marble boulders of various colors and patterns, larger than a sightseeing bus.

Within an hour, the road comes to a long, carved marble bridge. Do not drive over it. Instead, be sure you get out of your car and walk across this bridge in order to get a good view under the bridge of a raging waterfall and the massive boulders that have been polished by the extremely heavy and fast-falling watercourse.

The 3,000-foot-high cliffs along this 12-mile ride contain millions of tons of marble.

There are many marble factories on the outskirts of Hualien. We went through the largest, RSEA Marble Plant. It is well worth visiting. You can watch blocks of unpolished raw marble the size of a large automobile being sawed into smaller pieces and then see the smaller pieces being carved and buffed into ornamental vases, urns, tables, chairs, ash trays, wine glasses, lamps, chessboards, dragons, etc.

The other great attraction in Hualien is the marvelous show presented 2 times during the day and once at night that features dancing and singing by very attractive, beautifully-costumed aborigine Taiwanese.

SABAH

Children under 4 travel free. Half-fare for children 4-11. Children 12 and over must pay full fare.

Extraordinary scenery of dense jungles, wild animals and high mountains is seen on the short rail trips in Sabah, one north from Beaufort and the other south from Beaufort.

Beaufort - Koto Kinabalu   7500

Dep. Beaufort	5:45(1+3)	7:30(2+3)	8:12(1+4)	9:02(2+4+5)
Arr. Kota Kinabalu	8:21	10:16	9:55	11:01

Sights in **Kota Kinabalu:** The small museum on Gaya Street. Visit nearby Kinabalu National Park. The marvelous beach resort at Tanjong Aru.

Dep. Kota Kinabalu	6:30(1+4)	7:20(2+4)	7:30(1+3)	7:59(2+3+6)
Arr. Beaufort	8:13	9:10	10:06	10:50

(1)Daily, except Sundays and holidays. (2)Sundays and holidays only. (3)Third-class only. (4)First-class only. (5)Plus other departures from Beaufort at 9:23(1+3), 10:50(1+3), 11:00(2+3), 13:40(1+3), 14:30(2+3), 14:56(1+3), 15:36(2+4) and 16:24(1+4)   (6)Plus other departures from Kota Kinabalu at 7:45(1+3), 11:00(1+3), 11:24(2+3), 13:30(1+3), 13:44(2+3), 14:40(1+4), 14:54(2+3) and 16:35(1+3).

Beaufort - Tenom   7500

Dep. Beaufort	6:45(1+3)	8:13(2+4)	9:10(1+4)	12:15(2+3+5)
Arr. Tenom	8:45	9:45	10:45	14:54
		*	*	*

Dep. Tenom	6:40(2+4)	7:20(1+4)	7:50(2+3)	7:55(1+3+6)
Arr. Beaufort	8:12	9:02	10:50	10:10

(1)Sundays and holidays only. (2)Daily, except Sundays and holidays. (3)Third-class only. (4)First-class only. (5)Plus other departures fromBeaufort at 13:38(2+3), 14:30(1+3), 15:40(1+4) and 16:26(2+4).   (6)Plus other departures from Tenom at 12:50(2+3), 13:55(1+4) and 14:55(2+4).

SINGAPORE

The long train ride from Singapore is to Kuala Lumpur, and on to Butterworth (Penang) and Bangkok. The short trip from Singapore is to Johore Bahru.

Singapore

A great seaport and the most modern city in Asia. See: the excellent exhibit of Malay culture at the National Museum. The food markets in Chinatown, soon to be relegated to oblivion as this section is demolished in order to make way for modern high-rise apartment buildings. The view of the city and harbor from the top of Fort Canning Hill.

The 50-foot tall, 300-ton statue of Buddha and other wonders in the Temple of 1,000 Lights in the Indian section, near Serangoon Road. The Thian Hock Keng Taoist temple. The ornately-carved Sri Mariammon Hindu Temple. The wood and marble carvings in Sian Lim Sian Si temple.

The orchids (some of which we contributed) and the monkeys at the excellent Botanical Garden. The Chettiar Hindu temple. The Sultan Mosque. Twin Grove temple. Sakya Muni Gaya temple.

Take a one-hour cruise to see the hundreds of ships anchored in the world's fourth busiest harbor, only 77 miles north of the Equator. The cable car or ferry trip to Sentosa Island, to see its beaches, the museum of corals and shells, and the 18-hole golf course. A 3-hour out-of-town tour, visiting the nearby Malay villages, rubber and coconut plantations, temples and a crocodile farm.

Participate in the open-air eating that starts at 17:00 at the dozens of food stalls and pushcarts which vend Chinese, Indonesian and Malaysian delicacies at the Ras Singapura Food Centre (next door to the Singapore Arts and Crafts Centre) and also at Car Park on Orchard Road, near many hotels. There are similar food facilities at Newton Eating Stalla, Albert Street, Hokkien Street and Bugis Street. Prawn fritters, fried pork, satay, beef curry, fish-head fried rice, carrot cake, exotic fruits, a rice dish called Nasi Goreng, and on and on. The gourmet can find in Singapore 9 styles of Chinese cuisine plus Thai, Indian, Malay, Italian, German, French and Japanese Food.

See the many Chinese and Indian shops on narrow, twisting Change Alley. The more than 7,000 birds of 350 species in aviaries (some so large that visitors can walk through them) in Jurong Bird Park. Near it, the elaborately landscaped Chinese and Japanese Gardens.

Also see the tremendous collection of jade from every important Chinese dynasty, in the House of Jade. The daily cultural show at Instant Asia. The exhibit of more than 3,000 fish and the many corals at Van Kleef Aquarium. Over 600 animals in the 70-acre Zoological Garden. Souvenirs and antiques in the stalls at Thieves' Market.

Singapore - Kuala Lumpur - Butterworth (Penang) - Bangkok   7005

Dep. Singapore	8:00(1)	8:45(2+3)	13:55	22:00(2+5)
Arr. Kuala Lumpur	14:30(1)	17:20	19:55	7:05
Change trains.				
Dep. Kuala Lumpur	15:00(1)	21:10(4)	22:00(2+3+5)	7:30(2+3)
Arr. Butterworth				
(Penang)	21:25	5:40	7:15	13:25
Change trains.				
7050				
Dep. Butterworth	-0-	-0-	7:55(3+6)	-0-
Arr. Bangkok	-0-	-0-	6:45(7)	-0-

(1)Direct train. No train change in Kuala Lumpur. Air-conditioned in first-class. Meal service. (2)Air-conditioned in first-class. (3)Meal service. (4)Runs daily. Has only second and third-class coach cars except on Thursday, when this train also has an air-conditioned first-class car. (6)Runs daily. Carries sleeping car only on Monday, Wednesday and Friday. (7)Day 2 from Butterworth.

Singapore - Johore Bahru   Bus   7008

Dep. Singapore	Frequent times from 6:00 to 23:00
Arr. Johore Bahru	45 minutes later

*   *   *

Dep. Johore Bahru	Frequent times from 6:00 to 23:00
Arr. Singapore	45 minutes later

Sights in **Johore Bahru:** Do not forget to bring your passport. This short trip takes you from the Republic of Singapore to Malaysia. See: The Hindu Mariamman Temple. The Sultan Suleiman Mosque. The Chinese Goddess of Mercy Temple. The National Museum collection of arts, crafts and Malaysian culture.

Singapore - Kota Bharu

Very beautiful jungle and high mountain scenery on this route.

7005 (Train)		7015 (Bus)	
Dep. Singapore	22:00(1)	Dep. Kota Bharu	8:00
Arr. Gemas	2:57	Arr. Mentakab	N/A(3)
Change trains.		Change to train.	
7006		7006	
Dep. Gemas	3:30(2)	Dep. Mentakab	20:53
Arr. Mentakab	6:14	Arr. Gemas	23:46
Change to bus.		Change trains.	
7015		7005	
Dep. Mentakab	N/A(3)	Dep. Gemas	2:25(1+4)
Arr. Kota Bharu	18:00(4)	Arr. Singapore	7:25(4)

(1)Air-conditioned in first-class. Carries sleeping car. (2)Meal service. (3)Time has not been available since 1980. Distance: 511km (307 miles). (4)Day 2.

SOUTH KOREA

First-class sleeping compartments have one berth. Second-class sleeping compartments have 2 berths. A supplement is charged for all of the many categories of express trains, refundable if the train's arrival is more than one hour later than scheduled. Children under 3 travel free. Half-fare for children 3-11. Children 12 and over must pay full fare.

Seoul is the focal point for rail trips in South Korea, to 3 different seaports: Gangreung, Mokpo and Pusan.

Seoul

See: The Kyonghweru Banquet Hall and the Throne Hall in the 14th century Kyongbok (Great Happiness) Palace, rebuilt in 1867 after a 16th century Japanese invasion destroyed it. Nearby, the beautiful Pagoda, the Folklore Museum and Kwanghwa Gate. The collection of metal craft, pottery, paintings and sculpture in the National Museum.

The fantastic 78-acre Secret Garden in the 17th century Changdok (Illustrious Virtue) Palace, with its museum. Nearby, the Yun Kyung Dang residence, Changgyongwon (Garden of Bright Happiness), the Zoo and the Chongmyo Royal Shrine.

In the center of Seoul, the Duksoo (Virtuous Longevity) Palace. The view from the 763-foot high hill in the park on Namsan. The exhibits of music, dance, architecture and art at Korea House. The colorful Chogye-sa Buddhist Temple. Tong Myo Shrine. The great silks, jewelry, antiques, fresh fish and lacquerware on sale at the 2-mile-long East Gate Market. The folk dances and reproduction of rural Yi-dynasty lifestyles at Korean Folk Village, a one-hour drive south of Seoul.

Seoul - Jeoniu - Yeosu   5502

Dep. Seoul (Main)	9:45	12:10(1)	13:45	21:00(2)
Dep. Jeonju	13:42	15:49	17:40	1:54
Arr. Yeosu	16:58	18:45	20:55	5:30

Sights in **Jeonju:** The Tourist Information Office is in front of the railstation. This city is also spelled "Kyonju" and "Gyeongiu". It is South Korea's most popular tourist resort and has been called "a museum without walls" because of the number of historical attractions here, including 20 ancient tombs in Tumuli Park. See the ceramics, bejeweled sword hilts, elaborate gold jewelry, and the gold Silla crown and helmets in the National Museum. On the outskirts of Jeonju are many interesting sculptures, temples and royal tombs. The hotels have rental cars for driving to many such nearby places of interest.

Dep. Yeosu	8:00	10:45(1)	13:10	19:35(2)
Dep. Jeonju	11:20	13:43	16:40	23:29
Arr. Seoul (Main)	15:20	17:30	20:50	4:35

(1)Air-conditioned. Meal service. (2)Carries first-class sleeping car and second-class coach car.

Seoul - Mogpo 5500

Dep. Seoul	7:30	11:10(1)	12:30	14:30	17:10(1+2+4)
Arr. Mogpo	13:55	17:15	18:55	20:55	22:45

*   *   *

Dep. Megpo	8:20(1+2)	9:20	10:55(1)	13:55	14:55(5)
Arr. Seoul	13:55	16:00	17:10	20:30	21:35

(1)Air-conditioned. (2)Neal service. (3)Carries sleeping car. (4)Plus another departure from Seoul at 21:30(3).   (5)Plus another departure from Mogpo at 20:35(3).

Seoul - Pusan (via Andong) 5505

Dep. Seoul			Dep. Pusan	8:40	20:44(1)
(Cheon.)	10:30	21:30(1)	Arr. Andong	13:17	1:34(1)
Arr. Andong	15:57	2:59(1)	Change trains.		
Change trains.			Dep. Andong	15:15(2)	1:44(1)
Dep. Andong	16:30	3:09(1)	Arr. Seoul		
Arr. Pusan	21:05	8:00	(Cheon)	19:53	7:15

(1)Direct train. No train change in Andong. Carries first-class sleeping car and second-class coach car. (2)Air-conditioned. Meal service.

Sights in **Pusan:** This is South Korea's principal seaport. Many beaches, monasteries and hot springs resorts a few miles from here.

See the museums and temple at the Chung-Yol Shrine (open during daylight hours), where brightly-costumed dancers, singers and musicians perform. This Shrine honors 16th century patriots who resisted Japanese invaders.

The view of the city and harbor from the Pusan Observation Tower in Youngdusan (Dragonhead) Park. The enormous range of fish sold at "Visit The Fisheries" in the downtown dock area, amounting to an outdoor aquarium. The busy shopping center, called Kuk-Je to buy jewelry, silk items, masks and ginseng.

The marvelous wood tile and the many carvings in Pomosa Temple. The Zoo, Botanical Gardens and ancient fort in Kumgang Park. Pusan has the world's only United Nations Military Cemetery, where graves are decorated with the flags of the many nations that contributed soldiers to the battles in Korea in the 1950's. Visit Boma-Sa (15 miles north of Pusan), a temple complex with 30 buildings.

Seoul - Pusan (via Daejeon) 5501

Most of these trains are air-conditioned and have meal service. Some overnight trains carry sleeping cars.

Dep. Seoul	
(Main)	Frequent times from 7:40 to 17:00 and 22:00 to 23:20
Arr. Pusan	5-7 hours later

*   *   *

Dep. Pusan	Frequent times from 7:40 to 17:00 and 22:00 to 23:40
Arr. Seoul	
(Main)	5-7 hours later

Seoul - Onyang   5502

Dep. Seoul (Main)	7:45(1)	10:05(1)	14:05(2)	16:05(1+4)
Arr. Onyang	9:15	11:35	15:31	17:39
		*	*	*
Dep. Onyang	10:41(1)	12:51(1+3)	15:31(1)	18:05(1+5)
Arr. Seoul (Main)	12:20	14:25	17:05	19:45

(1)Second-class only. (2)Air-conditioned. Meal service. (3)Air-conditioned. (4)Plus another departure from Seoul at 18:00(1+3).   (5)Plus another departure from Onyang at 21:11(2).

Sights in **Onyang:** A major hot springs resort, surrounded by beautiful scenery.

SRI LANKA (CEYLON)

Rail travel cannot be much more exotic than the 32 package tours that Sri Lanka Government Railways offers year-round in its air-conditioned trains throughout the tiny (270-mile by 140-mile) island off the southern tip of India. Among the sights to see in Sri Lanka are ancient palaces, shrines, temples, libraries and pleasure-gardens.

The tours range from one to 3 days and include bus transportation between hotel and railstation, all meals, hotel rooms, guides and sightseeing.

Origin points are Alutgama, Bentota, Colombo Fort, Hendala, Miragama, Mount Lavinia and Negombo.

Children under 3 travel free. Half-fare for children 3-13. Children 14 and over must pay full fare.

Colombo

See: the exhibit of stone and bronze sculptures at the Museum. Nearby, the performing elephants at the Zoo. Also a short distance away, the Buddhist murals in Kelaniya, at Raja Maha Vihara Temple.

Bentota, Mount Lavinia and Negombo are beach resorts a short distance from Colombo.

Colombo - Colombo Airport   6302

All of these trains are third-class only.

Dep. Colombo	5:10	5:26	13:40	15:20
Arr. Colombo Airport	6:59	7:26	15:10	16:54
	*	*	*	
Dep. Colombo Airport	7:56	8:30	16:32	17:20
Arr. Colombo	9:16	9:48	17:47	18:54

Colombo - Badulla   6304

Dep. Colombo Fort	6:35(1)	9:30(1)	20:15(2)
Dep. Nanu Oya	14:00(1)	15:31(1)	3:56(2)
Arr. Badulla	17:40	18:50	7:48

This extremely scenic rail trip is through mountains and tea plantations. The area at Nanu Oya (6,000 feet) is cool and green. Badulla is 5,000-foot altitude.

Dep. Badulla	5:55(1)	10:05(1)	18:15(2)
Dep. Nanu Oya	9:39(1)	14:06(1)	22:46(2)
Arr. Colombo Fort	15:28	21:30	6:15

(1)Carries observation car. Has second and third-class coach cars. (2)Carries sleeping car. Also has third-class couchettes and both first and second-class coach cars.

Colombo - Polonnaruwa - Batticaloa   6301

Dep. Colombo Fort	6:05(1+2)	12:45(1)	20:00(1+2+3)
Dep. Polonnaruwa	1:14(1+2)	19:05(1)	3:07(1+2+3)
Arr. Batticaloa	13:41	21:08	5:20

* * *

Dep. Batticaloa	5:00(1)	14:00(1+2)	19:40(1+2+3)
Dep. Polonnaruwa	6:51(1)	15:51(1+2)	22:12(1+2+3)
Arr. Colombo Fort	13:18	22:06	5:50

(1)Has second and third-class coach cars. (2)Meal service. (3)Carries sleeping car.

Sights in **Polonnaruwa:** The ruins from this city's greatest era, in the 10th century.

Sights in **Batticaloa:** The singing fish.

Colombo - Kandy   6304

For the best views on this ride, sit on the right-hand side en route to Kandy, on the left-hand side when going to Colombo. These trains have second and third-class coach cars.

Dep. Colombo Fort	5:55	6:35	10:15	13:35	17:10	20:15
Arr. Kandy	3-3½ hours later					

* * *

Dep. Kandy	2:10	6:45	9:37	14:57	17:00	18:03
Arr. Colombo Fort	3-3½ hours later					

Sights in **Kandy:** The praying and ceremonies at the pink-domed Dalada Maligawa (Temple of the Tooth), so-named because it claims to have an authentic tooth of Buddha. See wonderful orchids displayed at the 147-acre Botanical Gardens in nearby Peradeniya. The Tea Factory. Elephants taking baths, nearly all afternoon.

Colombo - Galle - Matara   6305

This very scenic train ride, along Sri Lanka's coastline, offers many miles of palm-fringed beaches washed by turquoise ocean.

These trains have only second and third-class coach cars.

Dep. Colombo Fort	6:20	8:40	13:35	15:45(1)	16:50(2+3)
Dep. Galle	9:48	11:28	16:32	17:45	20:09
Arr. Matara	11:02	13:00	17:26	-0-	-0-
		*	*	*	
Dep. Matara	-0-	5:50	-0-	-0-	12:10(4)
Dep. Galle	5:00(2)	6:56	7:50(2)	8:20(1)	13:35(5)
Arr. Colombo Fort	8:09	9:15	9:50	12:20	16:25

(1)Supplement charged. (2)Daily, except Sundays and holidays. (3)Plus another departure from Colombo Fort at 19:00.   (4)Plus another departure from Matara at 15:15.   (5)Plus another departure from Galle at 16:40.

Sights in **Galle:** A Portuguese seaport before the Dutch seized it and then Sri Lanka's chief port until Colombo was developed in the 1880's.

Sights in **Matara:** An ancient fort town. See the old Dutch Reformed Church. Swim and snorkel at nearby Polhena.

Colombo - Negombo   6305

These trains are third-class only.

Dep. Colombo Fort	4:45	10:40(1+2)	16:30	16:55(1)	17:35
Arr. Negombo	6:54	12:16	17:52	17:54	18:52

Sights in **Negombo:** A fishing port. See the remarkable murals in Raja Maha Vihara, a famous temple. Visit the old Dutch fort.

Dep. Negombo	4:44(1)	6:25	7:00(1)	8:10	14:22
Arr. Colombo Fort	6:24	7:50	8:05	9:34	16:16(2)

(1)Runs Monday-Friday, except holidays. (2)Arrive/Depart Colombo's Maradena railstation.

Colombo - Trincomalee   6301

The coach cars on these trains are second and third-class.

Dep. Colombo Fort	6:05(1)	12:45	21:20(1+2)
Arr. Trincomalee	12:50	20:22	5:15

Sights in **Trincomalee:** One of the world's finest natural harbors. The 17th century fort constructed by Portuguese invaders from the ancient Temple of a Thousand Columns.

Dep. Trincomalee	6:00	14:05(1)	20:00(1+2)
Arr. Colombo Fort	13:18	22:06	5:00

(1)Meal service. (2)Carries sleeping car and coach car.

Jaffna - Talaimannar - Anuradhapura - Colombo Fort   6300
The fantastic Elephant's Pass is on this route.

Dep. Jaffna   6:32(1)   12:21(2)   18:18(1)   -0-
Dep. Talaimannar
  Pier   -0-   -0-   -0-   20:43(1+3+7)
Dep. Anuradahapura   10:22(1)   16:15(2)   22:40(1)   2:07(1+4+8)
Arr. Colombo Fort   14:30   20:32   4:10   8:36

(1)Second and third-class only. (2)Air-conditioned in first-class. Meal service.
(3)Runs Tues., Thurs. Sat. and Sun. (4)Runs Mon., Wed., Fri. and Sun. (5)Runs
Mon., Wed. and Fri. (6)Runs Tues., Thurs. and Sat. (7)Plus another departure
from Talaimannar Pier at 22:30(1+5).   ((8)Plus another departure from
Anuradahapura at 2:55(1+6).

Sights in **Anuradhapura:** Ruins of many ancient palaces and temples. The
sacred Bo Tree. The 300-foot diameter dome of the Ruwanveliseya.

Sights in **Jaffna:** Many ancient ruins. An outstanding exhibit at the Archaeological Museum.

INTERNATIONAL ROUTE FROM SRI LANKA
There is ferry service from Talaimannar to Rameswaram in southern India.
(Rail service is provided from Rameswaram to Bombay and Calcutta, via Madras.)

Colombo Fort - Anuradahapura - Talaimannar - Jaffna   6300
Dep. Colombo Fort
     6:42(1)   11:50(1)   18:50(1+2+3)   19:25(1+2+5+9)
Dep. Anuradahapura
    13:05(1)   16:17(1)   1:03(1+2+4)   1:03(1+2+6+10)
Arr. Talaimannar Pier
     -0-   -0-   4:45(4)   4:45(6)
Arr. Jaffna
    17:41   19:34   -0-   -0-

(1)Second and third-class only. (2)Carries sleeping car. Meal service. (3)Runs
Mon., Wed. and Fri. (4)Runs Tues., Thurs. and Sat. (5)Runs Tues., Thurs.,
Sat. and Sun. (6)Runs Mon., Wed., Fri. and Sun. (7)Air-conditioned in first-
class. Meal service. (8)Has second and third-class couchettes. Meal service.
(9)Plus other departures from Colombo Fort (which do *not* stop at Talaimannar
Pier)   at   5:45(7)   and
21:05(8).   (10)Plus other departures from Anuradahapura (which do *not* stop
at Talaimannar Pier) at 9:46(7) and 2:15(8).

6180		6182	
Dep. Talaimannar Pier	9:00(1)	Dep. Rameswaram	13:45(2)
Arr. Rameswaram	12:00	Arr. Madras (Egmore)	8:10

(1)Runs Tuesday, Thursday and Saturday. (2)Runs daily.

THAILAND

Children under 4 travel free. Half-fare for children 4-11. Children 12 and over must pay full fare. In 1981, the State Railway of Thailand began replacing first-class coach cars with new air-conditioned second-class cars.

Reservations in Thailand can be made only in person (or by a local travel agent) and no more than 10 days before travel date. A supplement is charged for fast trains, sleeping berths and air-conditioned coaches.

The rail lines from Bangkok to Chiang Mai and to Nam Tok come close to Burma's border. The routes to Nong Khai and to Ubon Ratchathani go to Laos' border. The ride to Aranyaprathet is on the border of Kampuchea (Cambodia, Khmer) and ran to Phnom Penh prior to the 1976 closing of the frontier.

Thailand's sixth rail route is to Butterworth (Penang) and then through the length of Malaysia to Singapore.

Bangkok

A boat ride on the klongs (canals) to a floating market and a visit to the Royal Palace are the 2 major tourist attractions in Bangkok. The best place to hire a boat is at the pier in back of the Oriental Hotel. Cruises on the Chao Phya River also start from there.

In the Royal Palace complex, see: Chakri Palace, the gold thrones in the Amarin, Dusit Hall, the Chapel of the Emerald Buddha. Nearby, the Temple of the 160-foot long Reclining Buddha. The exhibit of the history of this area since 4,000 B.C., at Southeast Asia's largest museum, the excellent Thai National Museum (closed Monday and Friday).

Also in Bangkok: The Weekend Market at Pramane Ground. The carrara Marble Wat. The Pasteur Institute Snake Farm. The collection of Thai paintings and pottery at James Thompson's House. Another collection of Thai art at Kamthiang House. Suan Pakkad Palace.

Bangkok - Chiang Mai   7060

Dep. Bangkok	15:45(1)	18:00(2)	Dep.		
Arr.			Chiang Mai	14:45(1)	16:50(2)
Chiang Mai	6:20	7:50	Arr. Bangkok	5:40	6:30

(1)Second and third-class. Air-conditioned in second-class. Meal service. (2)Carries sleeping car. Also has air-conditioned second-class coach car. Meal service.

Sights in **Chiang Mai:** An abundance of Thai handicrafts are available here: lacquerware, woodcarving, pottery, weaving, batik cloth, silk and pottery. See: the 14th century temple, Wat Chian Man. The porcelain decorated 17th century Wat Koo Tao. The 14th century Wat Phra Singh. The beautiful bronze Buddha in Wat Kao Tue. The view from the mountain-top Wat Doi Suthrep, 3500 feet above Chiang Mai. Climbing its 290 steep steps is an exertion on a hot, sultry day. The display of fruits and vegetables at Varoros Market. The 7 spires at Wat Ched Yod Temple. take a tour outside the city to see local aborigines. Another tour, a 30-minute drive, to watch elephants perform.

Bangkok - Thon Buri - River Khwae Bridge - Nam Tok   7057
Take the 5-minute ferry from Bangkok to Thon Buri, a suburb.
The bridge, rebuilt after World War II, is a plate girder bridge. To see timber bridges such as the one in the famous motion picture, continue the ride through the jungle, past the River Kwae Bridge, all the way to Nam Tok. This is an easy one-day roundtrip.

Dep. Thon Buri	8:00	Dep. Nam Tok	12:35
Arr. River Khwae Bridge	10:33	Arr. River Khwae Bridge	14:24
Arr. Nam Tok	12:20	Arr. Thon Buri	16:55

Bangkok - Ubon Ratchathani   7065

Dep. Bangkok	6:50(1)	7:15(1)	15:25(1)	18:45(1+3)
Arr.				
Ubon Ratchathani	17:35	19:55	3:35	5:25
		*	*	*
Dep.				
Ubon Ratchathani	6:35(1)	7:00(1)	15:30(1)	18:25(1+4)
Arr. Bangkok	17:20	19:20	4:20	5:15

(1)Second and third-class coach cars. Meal service. (2)Carries first and second-class sleeping cars. (3)Plus other departures from Bangkok at 20:30(1+2) and 23:20(1).   (4)Plus other departures from Ubon Ratchathani at 19:35(1+2) and 23:20(1).

Bangkok - Aranyaprathet   7059
These trains have only third-class coach cars.

Dep. Bangkok	6:00	13:10	14:25
Arr. Aranyaprathet	11:20	18:40	19:40
	*	*	*
Dep. Aranyaprathet	5:35	7:10	13:15
Arr. Bangkok	10:55	12:40	18:35

Bangkok - Butterworth (Penang) - Kuala Lumpur - Singapore

7050		7005		
Dep. Bangkok	16:10(1)	Dep. Kuala Lumpur	7:30	9:00(3)
Arr Butterworth	18:45 Day 2	Arr. Singapore	13:25	17:30
Change trains.				
7005				
Dep. Butterworth	22:00(2)			
Arr. Kuala Lumpur	7:00 Day 3			
Change trains.				

(1)Runs Monday, Wednesday and Saturday. Carries air-conditioned sleeping car and air-conditioned first-class coach cars. Meal service. (2)Air-conditioned in first-class coach cars. Carries sleeping car. (3)Air-conditioned in first-class coach cars. Meal service.

VIETNAM

Children under 5 travel free. Half-fare for children 5-9. Children 10 and over must pay full fare.

The single rail route in Vietnam is from Hanoi to Ho Chi Minh City (formerly Saigon). This train's name is "Reunification Train".

Hanoi - Hue - Da Nang - Ho Chi Minh City   7305

Dep. Hanoi	21:20	Dep.	
Arr. Hue	3:16 Day 3	Ho Chi Minh City	20:23
Arr. Da Nang	8:22 Day 3	Arr. Da Nang	3:55(1) Day 3
Arr.		Arr. Hue	8:30(1) Day 3
Ho Chi Minh City.	19:27 Day 4	Arr. Hanoi	11:31 Day 4

(1)Estimated. Time has not been confirmed since 1980.

This trip involves an overnight stop in Hue and in Da Nang in both directions.

Sights in **Ho Chi Minh City:** Chinese, Japanese, Vietnamese, Cham and Khmer art objects in the National Museum. The Zoo. The Cho Ben Thanh Market. The Botanical Garden. The Flower Market. The Chinese temples in Cholon, the city's Chinatown suburb.

Sights in **Danang:** The Buddhist monastery at Marble Mountain.

Sights in **Hue:** Thai Hoa (Palace of the Full Peace). Dien Tho (Everlasting Longevity) Palace. The-Mieu Temple. Ngu Phung (Five Phoenix Building). Tin Tam (Serenity of Heart) Lake. The 7-story Phuoc Duyen Tower. The imperial tombs of the Nguyen emperors.

INTERNATIONAL ROUTE FROM VIETNAM

The Vietnam gateway for rail service to the People's Republic of China is Hanoi.

Hanoi - Pekin   5320

Dep. Hanoi	N/A(1)	N/A(1)	N/A(1)	N/A(1)
Dep. Hankou*	13:59	16:39	17:45	21:35
Arr. Pekin	6:01	9:10	10:32	17:00

*The revised spelling of Hankow.

(1)Service was "temporarily" suspended in 1980 between Hanoi and the Chinese border at Nanning.

Chapter 13

AUSTRALIA

Summer here is December 21 to March 20. Winter is June 21 to September 20.

Children under 4 travel free if space has *not* been reserved for them. Half-fare for children 4-15. Children 16 and over must pay full fare.

To make advance reservations, write to: The Booking Officer, P.T.C. Travel & Tours Centre, 11 York Street, Sydney, N.S.W. 2000, Australia.

The State Rail Authority of New South Wales offers more than 20 different special one-day train tours that leave Sydney between 7:40 and 9:20, arriving back in Sydney between 16:30 and 21:45.

Typical of a day's outing is the "Wine Tasting Tour" that has been offered every year. The air-conditioned train takes a scenic route to Broadmeadow, where passengers transfer to a motorcoach which drives through the wine-producing area of Pokolbin. At the Wyndham Estate Winery, passengers are given a wine-tasting with a barbecue lunch. After lunch, the bus continues through scenic countryside to Newcastle, where the tourists board the train for the return ride to Sydney.

Other one-day tours go to lakes, seashores, mountains, caves and sheep stations.

The 3 most outstanding train rides in Australia are luxurious and long.

"Indian Pacific", Australia's most elegant train, makes a 63-hour run between Sydney and Perth, a 2,461-mile journey from Australia's East Coast to its West Coast, and return. This trip involves 3 nights on board.

Fully air-conditioned and sound-proofed, this *first-class onlu* train carries 144 sleeping-berth passengers.

Two types of sleeping accommodations are available. Twinette cabins (2 berths) have private shower and toilet, wash basin, refrigerated water dispenser, and choice of radio or taped music. Roomettes (for one person) have all this, except they lack the private shower. However, there are shower rooms at both ends of the Roomette carriage.

This train has one deluxe compartment, a luxurious bed-sitting room with armchairs.

"Indian Pacific" carries a restaurant car, lounge car (with piano, taped music and bar service), and a cafeteria club car that serves morning and afternoon teas, ice cream sandwiches and liquor.

All food served on this train is prepared on board. The "Indian Pacific" is famous for its lavish breakfast: fruit juice, cereal, bacon and eggs, steak or sausage, potatoes, toast and beverage.

On this route, temperatures outside the train average 109 degrees Fafrenheit in February.

Overseas tourists are allowed up to 336 pounds of free luggage for first-class, 224 pounds if traveling economy-class.

Reservations can and should be made one year in advance. Stops may be made at any station en route and journey resumed later at no extra cost provided that the whole journey is completed within 3 months.

Another sensational train ride in Australia (covering part of the same route as "Indian Pacific" does) is on the air-conditioned "Trans-Australian Railway Express", making a 35-hour run between Port Pirie and Perth, a trip of 1,464 miles. Reservations can and should be made as much as one year in advance of travel date on this train.

This train carries a lounge car for first-class passengers that is divided into 2 sections: a smoking area and a music salon with piano.

Music, news and announcements are piped into each compartment's individually-controlled speakers. Among many other amenities, each car has showers. First-class passengers receive a breakfast tray in their "cabin". Economy passengers are served a Continental breakfast in the restaurant car. Afternoon tea is served to all passengers in their cabin. Sleeping berths, meals and teas are included in the fares.

The third extraordinary Australian rail trip is the one made by "Sunlander", the 1,043 miles from subtropical Brisbane across many coastal estuaries to Cairns, gateway to several Barrier Reef resorts. The sleeping cars have shower facilities, and the train is fully air-conditioned.

The variety of landscapes is so interesting that Queensland Railways offers a 5-day version of this 37-hour trip (with 4 overnight stays en route) so that all of the scenery can be observed during daylight.

AUSTRALIAN TRAIN PASS

Austrailpass. Unlimited first-class travel on all Australian railways, including suburban and metropolitan lines (except in Adelaide). Use of this pass must begin within 6 months of the date it is issued (within 12 months when issued in New Zealand).

Cannot be purchased in Australia. (Exception: a 7-day extension to the 14-day pass can be purchased after arriving in Australia.)

Austrailpass is sold worldwide by travel agents and Tour Pacific/Australian Travel Service (phone for all U.S.A., except California: 800-423-2880 . . . for Cal.: 800-232-2121). The prices from April 1, 1984 through March 31, 1985 are: 14 days A$319, 7-day extension A$143, 21 days A$402, one month A$511, 2 months A$715, and 3 months A$825. Although sleeping berths and meals are included in the price of some Australian *tickets*, they are *not* covered by Austrailpass.

The state railways of New South Wales, Victoria and Western Australia offer separate train passes, valid for travel within their state borders.

Sydney

See the view from the observation deck on the 48th floor of one of Australia's tallest buildings, Australia Square on George Street. Take the guided tour of Sydney Opera House. Go on a walking tour around The Rocks, the oldest part of Sydney, after obtaining information from the Visitors' Centre in George Street North.

Visit the collection of Australian and European art at the Art Gallery of New South Wales. The exhibit of Aboriginal artifacts and relics in Australia Museum, College Street, open Tuesday-Saturday 10:00-17:00 and on Sunday and Monday 12:00-17:00. The planetarium at the Museum of Applied Arts and Sciences, Harris Street. The craft, gift and curio shops at Argyle Arts Center, open daily 10:00-18:00. Lush tropical plants and exotic trees at Royal Botanic Gardens, open daily 8:00 to sunset. The changing of the guard every Thursday at 13:30 at the ANZAC Memorial in beautiful Hyde Park. Take a day tour to visit nearby sheep and cattle stations.

See the sharks and other Australian fish at Marineland. Take the ferry or hydrofoil from Circular Quay, also the departure point for visits to Taronga Zoo Park. There are many excellent beaches, easy to reach from the center of Sydney.

Rail tours operate to Old Sydney Town, 44 miles to the north, where the settlement of 1810 has been re-created complete with convict dwellings, jail, church, shops and 2 old ships.

Sydney - Port Pirie - Kalgoorlie - Perth   9000

This is the all-sleeping car "Indian Pacific". Reservation required. Air-conditioned train. Meal service.

Dep. Sydney (Cent.)	15:15(1)		Dep. Perth (Ter.)	21:00(2)
Set watch back one hour.			Dep. Kalgoorlie	7:00 Day 2
Arr. Broken Hill	9:05 Day 2		Arr. Cook	19:15
Dep. Broken Hill	9:30		Set watch forward 1½ hours.	
Arr. Port Pirie	15:16		Dep. Cook	21:15
Dep. Port Pirie	17:00		Arr. Port Pirie	13:00 Day 3
Arr. Cook	8:10 Day 3		Dep. Port Pirie	13:40
Set watch back 1½ hours.			Set watch forward one hour.	
Dep. Cook	7:10		Arr. Broken Hill	19:54
Dep. Kalgoorlie	20:30		Dep. Broken Hill	20:24
Arr. Perth (Term.)	7:00 Day 4		Arr. Sydney (Cent.)	15:50 Day 4

(1)Runs Thursday and Saturday. (2)Runs Thursday and Sunday.

Sights in **Broken Hill:** This is the area of the dry, sunburnt "outback". The city is built over huge silver, lead and zinc deposits. Visits to mines can be arranged. Also see the collection of coins, minerals, shells and Aboriginal artifacts at Carlton Gardens and Art Gallery. The restored Afghan Mosque, once used by the camel drivers imported to carry supplies through the region.

Scenic air tours operate from here to various nearby points of interest such as the diggings of the world's only source of black opals at White Cliffs, plus trips to Kinchega National Park, Menindee Lakes and several outback stations. Only 82 miles northeast are ancient Aboriginal rock carvings, at Mootwingee. The restored Silverton ghost town is also nearby.

Sights in **Kalgoorlie:** This famous goldrush town is still Australia's largest producer of gold. Tours of a mine can be arranged.

Sights in **Perth:** Wide sandy beaches on the Indian Ocean, with good surfing. Tours to wildflower and forest areas nearby from August to November, when it is Spring here. See: The marvelous display of wildflowers in the 1,000-acre King's Park. London Court, a shopping area re-created as a 16th century English street. The folk museum of early pioneering days, Old Mill.

The exhibit of the large Blue Whale skeletons, meteorites, Aborigine culture and paintings in the Western Australian Art Gallery. The lovely Georgian-style Old Court House, in Stirling Gardens.

The marvelous horses 37 miles away at El Caballo Blanco, where Andalusian dancing horses are bred. Skin-diving at the popular Rottnest Island resort, 12 miles offshore. (Ferries operate 5 days a week, daily in Summer.) The 6,000-acre Yanchep Park, only 37 miles away, with its koalas, black swans, limestone caves and profusion of wildflowers.

The Maritime Museum and Art Center in nearby Fremantle, and the great views of the city and harbor from the Round House there. *   *   *

Adelaide

The coin collection and paintings at the Art Gallery of South Australia, open 10:00-17:00. The Australian birds and animals in the South Australian Museum. The spectacular water-lilies at the Botanic Gardens. The view of Adelaide from Light's Vision. The sealife at Marineland. Australian native animals in nearby Cleland Wildlife Reserve.

Winery tours in the nearby McLaren Vale and Southern Wine District. Coach and 4-wheel drive vehicle tours go from Adelaide to the Andamooka and Coober Pedy opal fields, often visiting Alice Springs and Ayers Rock.

Adelaide - Port Pirie - Kalgoorlie - Perth   9001

The "Trans-Australian Railway Express". All sleeping car Port Pirie-Perth and v.v. Reservation required. Meal service. Air-conditioned train.

Dep. Adelaide	12:50	Dep. Perth (Ter.)	21:00	
Arr. Port Pirie	16:09	Dep. Kalgoorlie	7:00 Day 2	
Change trains.		Arr. Cook	19:15	
Dep. Port Pirie	17:00	Set watch forward 1½ hours.		
Arr. Cook	8:10 Day 2	Dep. Cook	21:15	
Set watch back 1½ hours.		Arr. Port Pirie	13:00 Day 3	
Dep. Cook	7:10	Change trains.		
Dep. Kalgoorlie	19:30	Dep. Port Pirie	14:00	
Arr. Perth (Ter.)	6:00 Day 3	Arr. Adelaide	17:23	

Adelaide - Mount Gambier   9080

Dep. Adelaide	8:00(1)	21:15(2)
Arr. Mount Gambier	15:56	8:00

*   *   *

Dep. Mount Gambier	8:05(1)	20:35(3)
Arr. Adelaide	16:05	7:30

(1)Daily, except Sundays and holidays. Light refreshments. (2)Reservation required. Runs Tuesday, Thursday and Sunday. (3)Reservation required. Runs Monday, Wednesday and Friday.

Sights in **Mount Gambier:** The remarkable Blue Lake. Australia's largest pine forests. Skin-diving in Little Blue Lake.

Eastern Australia Rail Routes

An extensive rail system in eastern Australia radiates west and north from Melbourne.

Melbourne

The view from the top of the ICI Building, Nicholas Street, with a guide there pointing out the main features of the area. Also see: The largest plant collection in the Southern Hemisphere, at the Royal Botanic Gardens. The Zoological Gardens in Royal Park. Treasury Gardens, near Parliament House. The superb collection of Australian trees, shrubs and plants at Maranoa Gardens.

Australia's largest art collection, at National Gallery, St. Kilda Road. Old Melbourne Gaol and Penal Museum, Russell Street. Institute of Applied Science Museum, Swanston Street. Australian birds, animals and minerals, as well as Aborigine artifacts, at the National Museum, Russell Street. The exhibit of Australian ceramics, weaving and hand-made jewelry in the Galaxy of Handicrafts, 99 Cardigan Street.

Captain Cook's Cottage, in Fitzroy Gardens, honoring the discoverer of eastern Australia. The kangaroos, koalas, emus, wombats and platypuses at Healesville Sanctuary, 39 miles east of Melbourne. Take a ride on one of Melbourne's old-fashioned trams.

See the Rhododendron garden at 100-acre Olinda. The demonstrations of sheep dogs working, sheep shearing, wool classing and freeze branding of cattle of Grevisfield, 24 miles from Melbourne.

Take the bus to Philip Island to see the "Penguin Parade", a large number of Penguins coming onto the shore to feed their young.

Suburban electric trains run frequently from Melbourne's Flinders Street station for the 70-minute ride to Belgrave. Several different 2-hour roundtrip steam-train excursions on "Puffing Billy" offer fine mountain scenery on the 8-mile ride between Belgrave and beautiful Emerald Lake Reserve. A collection of early steam locomotives can be seen at the Steam Museum in Menzies Creek, one of the stops on that line.

Melbourne - Adelaide   9080

Both trains require reservations, are air-conditioned, carry sleeping cars and a club car, and have meal service.

Dep. Melbourne(Spencer St.)	20:55	Dep. Adelaide		19:40
Arr. Adelaide	8:50	Arr. Melbourne(Spencer St.)		9:15

Melbourne - Sydney   9070

All of these trains are air-conditioned, require reservation and have meal service.

Dep. Melbourne (Spencer St.)	9:00(1)	18:45(2)	20:00(3)
Arr. Sydney (Central)	2:45	8:45	9:00
	*	*	*
Dep. Sydney (Central)	7:45(1)	20:00(3)	20:10(2)
Arr. Melbourne (Spencer St.)	20:20	8:55	9:55

(1)Late January to late December: runs daily, except Sundays and holidays. Late December to late January: runs daily. (2)Carries sleeping car. Also has coach car. (3)Carries only sleeping cars. Has Club Car. The Restaurant Car opens at 19:00, reservation recommended.

Sydney - Canberra - Cooma   9065

It is an easy one-day roundtrip to visit Canberra.

Dep. Sydney (Cent.)	7:30(1)	17:23(2)	21:10(3)
Arr. Canberra	12:19	23:12	-0-
Arr. Cooma	14:26	-0-	5:50

Sights in **Canberra:** The modern art exhibit at National Library. The 6 tons of water jetting 450 feet into the air by the Captain Cook Memorial Water Jet on Lake Burley Griffin (10:00-12:00 and 14:00-16:00). The Sunday afternoon (14:45-15:30) concerts of the 53-bell carillon on Aspen Island. The daily exhibits at the Indonesian Pavilion. The view of the marvelous surroundings of Canberra from Mt. Ainslie, Mt. Pleasant or Red Hill Lookout. All Saints' Anglican Church in a railway station that was built in 1868. Its bell is from an old locomotive.

The 98-acre Botanic Gardens, containing 6,000 native Australian plants representing 2,000 species. Parliament House. The Royal Australian Mint. The Tidbinbilla Nature Reserve collection of kangaroos, emus and koalas, 24 miles away.

Dep. Cooma	-0-	8:50(5)	15:15(6)	-0-
Dep. Canberra	6:55(4)	10:40(5)	17:25(6)	17:25(7)
Arr. Sydney (Cent.)	11:45	17:28	22:17	22:53

(1)Runs daily, except Sundays and holidays. Reservation required. Air-conditioned train. Meal service. (2)Runs daily, except Saturday. Air-conditioned train. Meal service. (3)Runs Tuesday, Thursday, Friday and Sunday. Second-class only. (4)Runs daily, except Sundays and holidays. Air-conditioned train. Meal service. (5)Runs Monday, Wednesday, Friday and Saturday. (6)Runs daily, except Sundays and holidays. Reservation required. Air-conditioned train. Light refreshments. (7)Runs Sundays and holidays only.

Melbourne - Bendigo - Swan Hill   9078

All of these trains require reservation and are air-conditioned.

Dep. Melbourne (Spen.)	9:35(1)	17:40(2+3)	18:05(3+4)
Dep. Bendigo	12:05(1)	19:55(2+3)	20:15(3+4)
Arr. Swan Hill	14:25	22:20	22:35

Sights in **Bendigo:** Central Deborah Gold Mine. Pottery Centre. Joss House. The Historical Museum and Art Gallery at nearby Castlemaine.

Sights in **Swan Hill:** The re-creation of pioneer days at the Folk Museum.

Dep. Swan Hill	6:40(3+5)	16:30(1)	-0-
Dep. Bendigo	9:00(3+5)	19:00(1)	-0-
Arr. Melbourne (Spen.)	11:05	21:20	-0-

(1)Runs Sundays and holidays only. (2)Runs Monday-Friday, except holidays..(3)Light refreshments. (4)Runs Saturday only. (5)Runs daily, except Sundays and holidays.

Sydney - Brisbane   9050

Watch for the outstanding forest and river scenery between Gosford and Sydney en route from Brisbane. This area comes in view about 90 minutes before arriving Sydney. The best way to see this area is by taking a ride on a suburban train from Sydney, returning to Sydney the same day.

Both of these trains require reservation, are air-conditioned, carry sleeping cars, and have meal service.

Dep. Sydney (Cent.)	18:30	Dep. South Brisbane	15:20(1)
Arr. South Brisbane	10:25(1)	Arr. Sydney (Cent.)	7:32

(1)One hour earlier from late October to early March

Sights in **Brisbane:** The view from the observation platform of the clock tower at City Hall. Sub-tropical flowers and shrubs in the 50-acre Botanic Gardens. The Queensland Museum. Queensland Art Gallery. The lovely lake and the native animals and plants at Alma Park Zoo and Tropical Palm Gardens.

The 12,000 rose trees in bloom from September through November in New Farm Park, along Brisbane River. The Miegunyah Folk Museum.

You can hold a koala and watch the kangaroos and wallabies at the Lone Pine Koala Sanctuary. Take the 2½-hour boat trip to Moreton Island, or a day cruise to Stradbroke Island.

Sydney - Lithgow - Sydney

Marvelous Blue Mountain scenery on this easy one-day roundtrip by frequent suburban service.

Interurban trains depart from Sydney's Terminal railstation frequently for the 3-hour trip to Lithgow.

Sydney - Murwillumbah   9050

Both trains require reservations, carry sleeping cars, are air-conditioned, haul autos and have meal service.

Dep. Sydney (Central)	18:00	Dep. Murwillumbah	15:00
Arr. Murwillumbah	9:40	Arr. Sydney (Central)	6:55

Sights in **Murwillumbah:** This is Australia's "Gold Coast" land development, similar to the USA's Florida coastline resort area.

Sydney - Newcastle - Sydney   9045

It is an easy one-day roundtrip to take Australia's most scenic rail route. This line travels through the Ku-ring-gai National Park, the Hawkesbury River estuary (famous for its oyster farms), Australia's longest rail tunnel and the Lake McQuarie district.

Dep. Sydney (Cent.)	6:30(1)	8:15(1)	8:25(2+3)	8:50(3+8)
Arr. Newcastle	2¾-3½ hours later			

*   *   *

Dep. Newcastle	6:50(2+6)	7:36(1)	8:10(7)	9:20(3+9)
Arr. Sydney (Cent.)	2¾-3½ hours later			

(1)Runs Monday-Friday, except holidays. (2)Reservation required. Air-conditioned train. (3)Runs Saturday only. (4)Runs daily, except Saturday. (5)Runs Saturdays, Sundays and holidays. (6)Runs daily, except Sundays and holidays. (7)Runs Sunday only. (8)Plus other departures from Sydney at 9:00(2+4), 9:50(5), 12:50(1+6). 13:33(1), 13:50(3), 14:07(7), 15:03(1), 16:05(3) and 16:53(1+2). (9)Plus other departures from Newcastle at 10:30(3), 11:55(3), 12:35(1+2), 12:45(3), 12:50(1), 13:10(7), 13:35(2+3), 15:25(7), 15:50(1), 16:40(1+2) and 16:45(2+7).

Brisbane - Rockhampton - Townsville - Cairns   9040

All of these trains require reservations, are air-conditioned, carry sleeping cars and have meal service.

Dep. Brisbane (Roma St.)	7:15(1)	16:00(3)
Arr. Rockhampton	20:38	5:31(2)
Arr. Townsville	12:45(2)	21:25(2)
Arr. Cairns	20:55(2)	6:00(4)
	*	*	*
Dep. Cairns	6:45(5)	15:00(6)
Dep. Townsville	14:30	23:15
Dep. Rockhampton	6:00(2)	15:25(2)
Arr. Brisbane (Roma St.)	19:40(2)	5:45(4)

(1)Runs Monday, Tuesday, Wednesday and Thursday. (2)Day 2.   (3)Runs Friday and Saturday. (4)Day 3.   (5)Runs Wednesday, Thursday, Friday and Saturday. (6)Runs Sunday and Monday.

Sights in **Cairns:** Visitors can study coral gardens and colorful marine life from the Underwater Observatory or from a glass-bottomed boat at Green Island, only 17 miles from Cairns. The Atherton Tableland Rainforest, teeming with birdlife, is to the west of Cairns. Aerial tours of the Great Barrier Reef take tourists from Cairns along the jungle coastline and over many cattle stations.

Brisbane - Toowoomba   9031

The ascent through the Great Dividing Range offers outstanding scenery on this easy one-day roundtrip.

Dep. Brisbane (Roma St.)	6:46(1)	7:02(2)	8:13(3)	9:02(2+6)
Arr. Toowoomba	9:00	9:10	10:25	11:10

Sights in **Toowoomba:** This is a garden city in the center of the very rich 8,500,000-acre Darling Downs agricultural area. A week-long Carnival of Flowers takes place here every September. The dense rainforest with many species of birds in Ravensbourne National Park is 28 miles from here.

Dep. Toowoomba	6:25(1)	6:45(3)	7:45(2)	8:40(1+7)
Arr. Brisbane (Roma St.)	8:43	9:00	10:00	11:00

(1)Runs Monday-Friday, except holidays. (2)Runs Sundays and holidays only. (3)Runs Saturday only. (4)Runs daily. (5)Runs daily, except Sundays and holidays. (6)Plus other departures from Brisbane at 9:32(1), 12:13(3), 12:32(1), 16:02(2), 16:54(1), 17:02(3), 18:02(4) and 20:02(2).   (7)Plus other departures from Toowomba at 10:40(5), 12:40(3), 15:00(1), 15:45(2), 16:45(2), 17:40(5) and 18:45(2).

Rockhampton - Winton   9025

All of these trains require reservation, are air-conditioned, carry sleeping cars and have meal service.

Dep. Rockhampton	17:55(1)	Dep. Winton	14:00(2)	17:00(3)
Arr. Winton	14:06	Arr. Rockhampton	9:45	12:45

(1)Runs Tuesday and Friday. (2)Runs Thursday only. (3)Runs Saturday only.

Townsville - Mount Isa   9020

Dep. Townsville	10:30(1)	12:00(2)	16:30(3)	16:45(4+5)
Arr. Mount Isa	3:10(6)	15:01(7)	1:15(6)	13:45(7)

Sights in **Mount Isa:** Visitors may inspect one of the world's richest copper, silver-lead and zinc mines.

Dep. Mount Isa	11:45(8)	14:00(5+9)	16:00(10)	22:00(5+10)
Arr. Townsville	2:58(6)	10:30(7)	8:48(6)	18:30(7)

(1)Runs daily. Departs 13:35 on Monday and Friday. (2)Runs Wednesday and Thursday. (3)Runs Saturday only. (4)Runs Tuesday and Friday. (5)Reservation required. Air-conditioned train. Carries sleeping car. Meal service. (6)Day 3. (7)Day 2. (8)Runs daily, except Saturday. Departs 12:30 on Thursday and Friday, at 16:00 on Sunday. (9)Runs Thursday only. (10)Runs Saturday only.

Cairns - Kuranda - Cairns   9010

Excellent scenery of the most lush, tropical rain forests in Australia on this easy one-day roundtrip.

The 9:00 departure from Cairns is a special tourist train that makes stops along the way for passengers to take photos and enjoy waterfall scenes. People on this special excursion may either return to Cairns on the same train or go back to Cairns on a special bus tour.

Dep. Cairns	5:15(1)	9:00(2)	9:30(2)	13:45(3)	15:40(2)
Arr. Kuranda	7:00	10:28	11:06	15:13	16:58
		*	*	*	
Dep. Kuranda	7:05(2)	11:20(2)	16:05(4)	16:53(4)	19:12(2)
Arr. Cairns	8:23	12:40	17:25	18:38	20:30

(1)Runs Wednesday only. (2)Runs daily, except Sundays and holidays. (3)Runs Sundays and holidays. (4)Runs Thursday only.

The Central Australian Rail Route

Adelaide - Port Pirie - Alice Springs   9004

Called "The Ghan", this standard-gauge train is the successor to the original narrow-gauge operation of the same name that ran from Port Pirie to Alice Springs from 1930 to 1980. The name is in tribute to the Afghan traders who in the 19th century carried passengers and goods on camels between Port Pirie and Oodnatta, the end of the original rail line.

This train is air-conditioned. Carries sleeping car. Also has second-class coach car. Meal service for sleeping car passengers. Light refreshments for coach car passengers. Carries motor vehicles.

Dep. Adelaide	10:40(1)		Dep. Alice Springs	15:30(3)
Arr. Port Pirie	13:55		Arr. Port Pirie	11:55 Day 2
Dep. Port Pirie	14:30		Dep. Port Pirie	14:00
Arr. Alice Springs	10:30(2) Day 2		Arr. Adelaide	17:35(4)

(1)Early May to late October: Thursday and Sunday. Late October to early May: Thursday only. (2)Arrives 9:30 early November to early March. (3)Early May to late October: Tuesday and Saturday. Late October to early May: Saturday only. (4)Arrives 17:23 on Tuesday.

Sights in **Alice Springs:** This is the ideal base for tours to the "Great Outback". It is a frontier town with modern homes and wide, tree-lined streets. Alice Springs is the headquarters for both the Royal Flying Doctor Service and the unique School of the Air, the sole means of education for those living in the deserted areas of Australia.

Visitors can listen to the children and the teachers, and visit the Flying Doctor facility.

See the museum in the Old Telegraph Station. Many art galleries and souvenir shops. The Pitchi-Richi Bird Sanctuary, 2 miles from Alice Springs, has a collection of Aboriginal sculptures and implements, also Australian gemstones.

Take a tour to awe-inspiring Ayers Rock to see it change color at sunset and sunrise.

Adelaide - Port Pirie   9107

Here is the complete list of schedules for train services between these 2 cities. All of these trains require reservation and are air-conditioned.

Dep. Adelaide	10:40(1)	12:00(2)	18:05(3)
Arr. Port Pirie	13:55	16:09	21:22
	*	*	*
Dep. Port Pirie	7:55(4)	14:00(2)	17:45(5)
Arr. Adelaide	01:10	17:35	21:19

(1)Early May to late October: Thursday and Sunday. Late October to early May: Thursday only. (2)Runs daily. (3)Runs daily, except Saturday. (4)Runs daily, except Sundays and holidays. (5)Runs Friday only.

Western Australian Routes

Perth - Albany   9138   (Bus)
All of these buses require reservation.

Dep. Perth (Ter.)	9:00(1)	9:00(2)	15:00(4)	18:00(5)
Arr. Albany	15:25	16:15(3)	20:50	23:50

Sights in **Albany:** A magnificent harbor. This is the starting point for tours through the Porongurup and Stirling mountain ranges for scenic walks and viewing marvelous wildflowers August-November.

Dep. Albany	9:00(6)	9:00(7)	15:00(8)	15:00(4+9)
Arr. Perth (Ter.)	15:20	17:30	22:45	20:50

(1)Via Kojunup. Runs Monday-Friday, except holidays. (2)Via Katanning. Runs Monday, Thursday, Friday and Saturday. (3)Arrives Albany 16:55 on Friday, at 17:35 on Monday and Thursday. (4)Via Kojunup. Runs Sundays and holidays only. (5)Via Kojunup. Runs Friday only. (6)Via Kojunup. Runs daily, except Sundays and holidays. (7)Via Katanning. Runs Thursday and Friday. (8)Via Katanning. Runs Sunday only. (9)Plus another departure from Albany at 17:30(5)

Perth - Bunbury   9131
This is an easy one-day roundtrip.

Dep. Perth	9:30(1)	Dep. Bunbury	15:00(1)
Arr. Bunbury	12:40	Arr. Perth	18:10

(1)Runs daily, except Sundays and holidays. Meal service.

Sights in **Bunbury:** An important port. Good fishing and surfing here.

Perth - Fremantle   9145   (Bus)

Dep. Perth	Frequent departures Mon-Sat 5:20-23:20,Sun 9:15-19:30
Arr. Fremantle	35 minutes later

*   *   *

Dep. Fremantle	Frequent departures Mon-Sat 5:50-23:20,Sun 7:55-19:15
Arr. Perth	35 minutes later

Sights in **Fremantle:** This is Western Australia's principal port. See: The Maritime Museum and Art Center. The great views of the city and harbor from The Round House.

Perth - Kalgoorlie   9130

The "Prospector" trains are Australia's fastest, making their 395-mile (655km) trip in 7 hours 45 minutes. Reservations are required. Stewardesses bring hot meals to the passengers' seats: lunches at 12:30, dinners at 18:30.

All of the trains listed below are air-conditioned.

Dep. Perth (Ter.)   9:00(1+2)   15:00(1+3)   16:15(1+4)   21:00(5)
Arr. Kalgoorlie   16:35   22:35   23:45   6:30

Sights in **Kalgoorlie:** See notes about sightseeing in Kalgoorlie earlier in this chapter, under "Sydney-Port Pirie-Kalgoorlie-Perth".

Dep. Kalgoorlie   12:20(1+4)   14:25(1+5)   15:30(1+3)   19:30(6+8)
Arr. Perth (Ter.)   20:00   22:05   23:15   6:00

(1)"Prospector". (2)Runs Tuesday and Thursday. (3)Runs Monday, Wednesday and Sunday. (4)Runs Friday only. (5)This train has only sleeping cars on Tuesday and Thursday. On Sunday, it carries a sleeping car and also a second-class coach car. Does *not* run on other days. (6)Runs Tuesday, Thursday and Sunday. Carries sleeping car and second-class coach car. (7)This train has only sleeping cars on Tuesday and Sunday. On Saturday, it carries a sleeping car and also a second-class coach car. Does *not* run on other days. (8)Plus another departure from Kalgoorlie at 20:30(7).

Sydney - Alice Springs   0000

"The Alice" was innaugurated in late 1983. This train is air-conditioned, has sleeping cars with both roomette and twinette facilities and also convertible day/night berths, and has meal service. Its lounge car has a piano and offers radio and television programs.

Scenic stops are made at Broken Hill, the South Australia/Northern Territory border, Kulgera, the Iron Man and the famous Finke River.

Dep. Sydney	13:40 Mon.	Dep. Alice Springs	17:00 Wed.
Arr. Alice Springs	12:25 Wed.	Arr. Sydney	15:50 Fri.

Tasmania

Australia's island state, 150 miles south of mainland Victoria, measures 190 miles from east to west and 180 miles from north to south. Visitors can inspect historic homes and folk museums, stay at old inns, see the ruins of old penal colonies, enjoy fine beaches, swimming and excellent mountain and rural scenery.

Tasmania's one rail route ceased operating in 1978. It ran north from Hobart to Launceston and then west to Devonport and Wynyard.

Chapter 14

NEW ZEALAND

Sleeping cars have 2-berth compartments. Children under 4 travel free. Half-fare for children 4-14. Children 15 and over must pay full fare.

The country is 2 islands: North Island and South Island. There is ferry service between the 2 islands, connecting Wellington (at the southern tip of North Island) with Picton (the north tip of South Island).

NEW ZEALAND'S TRAIN PASS

New Zealand Railways/Road Service Tourist Pass. Unlimited travel for 8, 15 or 22 consecutive days on all trains, buses (except suburban ones) and inter-island ferries. Can be extended to a maximum of 28 days. Not transferable or refundable. The 8-day pass is sold only *outside* New Zealand and only by travel agents. The 15 and 22-day passes are sold outside N.Z. by travel agents and are *also* available from bus and train depots in New Zealand and from any New Zealand Government Tourist Bureau or accredited travel agent in New Zealand. Valid only from February 1 to December 14.

The 1984 prices are: NZ$120 for 8 days, NZ$180 for 15 days, NZ$240 for 22 days, and NZ$15 for each additional day up to a maximum of 28 days. Half-fare for children 4-14 years old. Children under 4 travel free.

North Island Rail Routes

The rail system on North Island is 4 lines running north from Wellington.

Auckland

Walking tours are so popular here that the city publishes 2 brochures: "Go Strolling in Your Lunch Hour" and "Coast to Coast Walking". (It is only an 8-mile walk from the Pacific Ocean on the east side of Auckland to the Tasman Sea on the west side of the city.) All interesting sights are outlined in a free map, and the routes are marked clearly.

See: The sculptures and fountains in Queen Elizabeth II Square. Parnell Rose Gardens. Westheaven Mariba. The view of Waitemata Harbor from the War Memorial Mueseum, which has a good collection of Maori artifacts, native New Zealand animals and plants, and relics of both wars.

The exhibits and Pioneer Village at the Museum of Transport and Technology, reached by free double-decker buses from and to major downtown hotels. The outstanding collection of mammals, fish, reptiles and birds (including the local non-flying Kiwi) at the Zoo.

Marvelous views of Auckland, its beaches and harbors as well as many streams and waterfalls, at Centennial Memorial Park. The Cathedral of the Holy Trinity. The Waitakere Scenic Reserve. The view of the city from Mt. Eden, a dormant volcano.

The Emily Nixon Garden of Memories. The views of Hauraki Gulf from Musick Point. Tour the Earth Satellite Tracking Station. Swim in the thermal pools at nearby Waiwera. Take a 2-day motorcoach tour to **Waitomo** and *Rotorua,* an interesting place with thermal swimming pools, the beautiful Government Gardens, the Maori Arts and Crafts Institute, trout fishing, St. Faith's Maori Church, TeWairoa (an excavated Maori village), the exhibits at Agrodome, and the overall Polynesian ambiance.

Visit some of the 19 wineries in West Auckland's Henderson Valley.

Sights in **Hamilton:** This is only 68 miles from Rotorua (see notes above).

Sights in **Wellington:** The view of the city, harbor and Hutt Valley from the 648-foot high Mount Victoria. The 62-acre Botanical Gardens. Lady Norwood Rose Gardens. The Zoological Gardens. The crafts at the New Zealand Display Center. Conducted tours of the marble-faced House of Parliament.

Government Building, one of the largest wood structures in the Southern Hemisphere. The collection of Maori exhibits at Dominion Museum and National Art Gallery. Nearby, the Carillon and Hall of Memories. The Carter Observatory. Many fine beaches. Freyberg Tepid Pool.

Wellington - Hamilton - Auckland   9760

This scenic trip includes the breathtaking Raurimu Spiral, and rivers, forests, seascapes and 3 high volcanoes: Ngauruhoe (7,515 feet), Ruapehu (9,175) and Tongariro (6,517).

The morning departure from both Wellington and Auckland is "Silver Fern". Passengers on it can have morning and afternoon teas, softdrinks and liquor served to their seats, airline style.

The night departures from both cities are "Northerner", which carries 5 day cars with reclining seats and one sleeping car that has eight 2-berth "cabins". The attendant brings a light supper and morning tea-and-biscuit with a newspaper to the cabins. A full dinner is served in the restaurant car 19:30-21:30. Light refreshments are available through the night. Reservations for the night trains can be made as much as 6 months before travel date.

Both "Silver Fern" and "Northerner" require reservations.

Dep. Wellington	8:20(1)	19:30(3)
Dep. Hamilton	17:37(1+2)	6:13(3)
Arr. Auckland	19:30(2)	8:35
	*	*
Dep. Auckland	8:00(1)	19:30(3)
Dep. Hamilton	9:56(1)	21:45(3)
Arr. Wellington	19:02(4)	8:30

(1)Reservation required. Runs daily, except Sunday. Air-conditioned train. Light refreshments. (2)One hour later on Wednesday. (3)Reservation required. Carries sleeping car. Meal service. (4)Arrive 19:56 on Wednesday.

Wellington - Palmerston North - Napier - Gisborne   9760

This route includes the scenic shoreline of Hawkes Bay (Wairoa-Gisborne). These trains stop for refreshments at Palmerston North and Napier. South of Gisbourne, the track crosses an airport runway, a popular "shot" for photographers. All of these trains require reservation and have meal service.

Dep. Wellington	7:45(1)	8:30(2)
Dep. Palmerston North	10:15(1)	11:00(2)
Dep. Napier	13:55(1)	14:45(2)
Arr. Gisborne	18:30	19:20

Sights in **Napier:** The exhibit of dolphins, sea lions, sea leopards, penguins and other animals and sea birds at Marineland. The assortment of birds in the Botanic Gardens. The fine swimming and fishing beaches. The beautiful Sunken Garden and lovely Golden Mile Park, along the shore.

Dep. Gisborne	9:00(2)	9:55(1)
Dep. Napier	14:00(2)	14:55(1)
Dep. Palmerston North	17:37(2)	18:35(1)
Arr. Wellington	19:45	20:48

(1)Runs Sundays and holidays only. (2)Runs daily, except Sundays and holidays.

Wellington - Otaki - Levin - Shannon   9760

Dep. Wellington	7:45(1)	8:30(2)	19:30(3)
Dep. Otaki	8:59(1)	-0-	20:54(3)
Arr. Levin	9:20(1)	10:04	21:17
Arr. Shannon	9:33	-0-	-0-
	*	*	*
Dep. Shannon	-0-	-0-	18:57(3)
Dep. Levin	6:45(3)	18:16(2)	19:16(3)
Dep. Otaki	7:08(3)	18:33(2)	19:33(3)
Arr. Wellington	8:30	19:45	20:48

(1)Reservation required. (2)Reservation required. Runs daily, except Sundays and holidays. Meal service. (3)Reservation required. Meal service.

Wellington - Masterton - Palmerston North   9760

All of these trains are second-class pnly.

Dep. Wellington	14:30(1)	16:00(1)	16:35(2)	17:20(1+4)
Arr. Masterton	16:21(1)	17:42	18:18	19:05
Arr. Palmerston North	18:28	-0-	-0-	-0-
	*	*	*	
Dep. Palmerston North	-0-	-0-	6:40(1)	-0-
Dep. Masterton	5:55(1)	6:55(1)	8:55(1)	9:10(2+5)
Arr. Wellington	7:40	8:33	10:35	10:52

(1)Sundays and holidays only. (2)Saturday only. (3)Friday only. (4)Plus other departures from Wellington at 17:33(1) and 21:30(3), terminating in Masterton. (5)Plus other departures from Masterton at 18:35(3) and 19:40(1).

Wellington - Picton   9780

This ferry service connects North Island and South Island. These ships carry both automobiles and passengers. They have food and beverage service. Bus and taxi service is available between Wellington's railstation and the pier there.

Dep. Wellington	7:20(1)	10:00	16:00(1)	18:40
Arr. Picton	10:40	13:20	19:20	22:00
		*	*	*
Dep. Picton	11:40(1)	14:20	20:00(1)	22:40
Arr. Wellington	15:00	17:40	23:20	2:00

(1)Runs daily, except Wednesday.

South Island Rail Routes

The rail system on South Island is one route along the South Pacific shoreline due south from Picton via Christchurch and terminating in Invercargill, plus a single cross-island line running from Christchurch to Greymouth.

Wellington - Picton - Christchurch

A daylight journey from Wellington to Christchurch (and v.v.) is possible with the following schedule. The good scenery on this ride includes views of the man-made lakes of Grassmere Saltworks, ocean surf, many attractive beaches, and the Kaikoura mountain range.

The Christchurch railstation restaurant opens at 6:15. Snacks can be purchased during the refreshment stop at Kaikoura.

9780 (Boat)		980 (train)	
Dep. Wellington	10:00	Dep. Christchurh	7:30
Arr. Picton	13:20	Dep. Kaikoura	11:05
Change to train.		Arr. Picton	13:40
9800		Change to boat.	
Dep. Picton	14:10	9780	
Dep. Kaikoura	16:50	Dep. Picton	14:20
Arr. Christchurch	20:05	Arr. Wellington	17:40

Sights in **Christchurch:** Takahe, the carved Maori meeting house. The Botanical Gardens. Cathedral Square. Beautiful Hagley Park. The view from Summit Road. The mementoes from Captain Cook's 3 voyages, displays on Antarctica explorations, and the exhibit of Maori articles (including a 47-foot wood war canoe) in the Canterbury Museum on the side of Hagley Park.

Christchurch - Timaru - Dunedin - Invercargill   9800

There is fine scenery of the South Pacific coastline and the Canterbury Plains on this ride. Looking to the west, one can see the New Zealand Alps. Other views: rivers, sheep runs and wheatfields. The Dunedin-Invercargill portion of this route is the most southerly train ride in the world (latitude 46 degrees south).

The schedules below are for "Southerner", a luxury train with meal service. Reservation is required. Seats can be reserved up to 6 months prior to travel date. As you board, you are given a folder about the journey, with a map and notes on points of interest en route. This service operates daily, except Sundays and holidays.

A hostess will serve morning and afternoon teas and light meals to anyone who is physically unable to eat in the buffet car and to mothers traveling with young children. Arrangements can be made to have a rental car or taxi waiting for one's arrival. In the smoking carriage, passengers are served wine, cocktails and liquor at their seat.

Dep. Christchurch	8:40	Dep. Invercargill	8:40
Dep. Timaru	11:02	Arr. Dunedin	12:16
Arr. Dunedin	15:00	Dep. Dunedin	12:21
Dep. Dunedin	15:05	Dep. Timaru	16:19
Arr. Invercargill	18:45	Arr. Christchurch	18:35

Sights in **Timaru:** A large port. A great beach. Good fishing in this area. Nearby, the National Park with its many mile-high mountains.

Sights in **Dunedin:** Attractive old stone buildings such as the Railstation. Larnach Castle on Otago Peninsula. Nearby, Mount Aspiring National Park and several lovely lakes: Manapouri, Te Anau, Ohau, Pukaki and Tepako. Enjoy miles of beaches.

Sights in **Invercargill:** The view of the city from the seventh floor of the Kelvin Hotel. The collection of Maori exhibits and art gallery at the Southland Centennial Museum in the 200-acre Queen's Park, located in the center of Invercargill. The park features a display of native and exotic trees and plants, a group of statues for children, a large sunken rose garden surrounded by flowering prunus and cherry trees, and a special iris garden.

At the eastern side of this park is a wide variety of tropical plants, a large pond containing aquatic plants and fish, a large lily pond, and a well-stocked aviary, all in the Steans Memorial Winter Garden.

Also see the City Gardens, along the Otepuni stream that runs through the center of Invercargill. The 85-acre Waihopai Scenic Reserve. The City Art Gallery in the 60-acre Anderson Park. The 25-mile long sandy Oreti Beach, fine for swimming.

Christchurch - Arthur's Pass - Greymouth 9800

This is the most scenic rail trip in New Zealand. After departing Christchurch, the train climbs to 2,500 feet at Arthur's Pass before going through the 5½-mile Otira Tunnel. Some grades are as great as 4% on this steep ride. On the approach to Greymouth, there are splendid views of the Tasman Coast.

Dep. Christchurch	9:40(1)	18:40(2)	-0-
Dep. Arthur's Pass	12:40(1)	21:37(2)	-0-
Arr. Greymouth	14:40	23:35	-0-
	*	*	*
Dep. Greymouth	6:00(3)	8:00(4)	18:15(2)
Dep. Arthur's Pass	8:03(3)	10:22(4)	21:31(2)
Arr. Christchurch	10:37	13:13	23:15

(1)Runs daily, except Sundays and holidays. (2)Runs Friday and Sunday. (3)Runs Saturday only. (4)Runs Monday-Friday, except holidays.

Sights in **Greymouth:** Visit a coal mine. Take a jet-boat ride up the Taramakau River to the Kaniere gold dredge and see the little museum of the gold-rush days at Hokitaka. Trout fishing at nearby Brunner.

Lumsden - Kingston 9806

This 42-mile steam train trip on "Kingston Flyer" to the south shore of Lake Wakatipu is a very popular special excursion that runs only from mid-December to Easter Monday. Advance reservations are advisable. The service between Invercargill and Lumsden is by bus.

Dep. Invercargill	10:45(1)	Dep. Kingston	11:20
Arr. Lumsden	12:25	Arr. Lumsden	12:25
Change to train.		Change to bus.	
Dep. Lumsden	13:10	Dep. Lumsden	13:10(1)
Arr. Kingston	14:10	Arr. Invercargill	14:30

November 1 to April 30: daily. May 1 to October 31: daily, except Sundays and holidays.

Chapter 15   NORTH AMERICA

Winter in North America is from December 21 to March 20. Summer is from June 21 to September 20.

CANADA

First-class includes use of a Club Car on day trains or any sleeping accommodation (berth, roomette, bedroom, etc. for which there is an extra charge) on a night train. Bedrooms have 2 berths, toilet and wash basin. Second-class is use of a seat in a coach car, day or night. On major trains, coach seats recline and food is provided both in restaurant cars and by tray meals served to the passengers' seats, airline style.

One child under 5 travels free if *not* occupying a separate seat or separate sleeping accommodation, but only if accompanied by a passenger who is 18 or older. Children 5-11 pay half-fare but must pay all of the charge for any sleeping accommodation. Children 12 and over must pay full fare.

The major Canadian passenger train operation functions under the name "VIA Rail Canada".

Canada's other train systems are: Algoma Central Railway, British Columbia Railway, Ontario Northland Railway, Quebec North Shore & Labrador Railways, and Toronto Hamilton & Buffalo Railway.

The Canrailpass described below is valid only on VIA routes.

Three Canadian cities have 2 or more railstations: Edmonton, Montreal and Saint John.

In order to cross all of Canada by rail, one need change trains only once, in Montreal.

Reservation agents of Amtrak in the U.S.A. and of VIA Rail Canada make reservations and issue tickets on each other's lines. Amtrak operates trains to and from Montreal and Seattle. (There is Trailways bus service from Seattle to Vancouver.) VIA Rail Canada has service to Windsor, which connects by taxi with Amtrak's Detroit railstation.

CANADA'S TRAIN PASS

Canrailpass.   Unlimited train travel in Standard Coaches on VIA trains. The pass can be purchased both in Canada and worldwide. It is issued for 4 different areas: (1) Entire System (coast-to-coast), (2) Winnipeg and east of Winnipeg, (3) Winnipeg and west of Winnipeg, and (4) the Quebec City-Toronto-Windsor Corridor.

The 1984 prices in Canadian dollars for travel June 1 to September 30 are:

AREA	8 days	15 days	22 days	30 days
(1)			$400	$435
(2)		$245	$280	
(3)		$245	$270	
(4)	$110	$140		

The 1984 prices in Canadian dollars for travel any day October 1 to December 14 and January 5 to May 31 (except the Thursday before Easter and the Monday after Easter) were:

AREA	8 days	15 days	22 days	30 days
(1)			$290	$315
(2)		$195	$225	
(3)		$190	$210	
(4)	$110	$140		

Children 5-11 years old travel at half the rates above.

Holders of the Canrailpass can obtain accommodations higher than Standard Coach on any ride by paying a supplement.

Group Fare Reduction. Available every day (except from December 15 through January 4) when the ride is at least $4.00(Can.). Groups of 3 or more persons are allowed the following discounts on ticket prices, including sleeping car space: Groups of 3-6 adults 15%, 7-29 receive 20% discount, 30 or more receive 30% discount. For group fare computation, 2 children each paying half-fare qualify as one adult. Advance reservations are essential for groups of 7 or more. Group discounts are not given for sleeping space from June 1 through September 30.

65 Plus. Available every day of the year when the ride is at least $4.00(Can.). People 65 and over can purchase tickets at a 33% discount.

Under 5. One child under 5, accompanied by a parent or guardian who has purchased a ticket (is *not* using Canrailpass or some other discount), travel free in Standard Coach. Each additional child under 5, accompanied by the same parent or guardian, can travel in Standard Coach at one-half the ticket price.

CANADIAN RAIL TOURS

VIA Rail Canada offers many tour packages, available through travel agents or VIA Passenger Sales Offices.

"Explorer Tours" are escorted and include: sleeping car accommodations on overnight trains, luxury seats on daylight runs, the best available hotels, some meals on and off trains, city sightseeing and narrated bus trips with selected stops for photography. These tours are available only to groups of 20 or more passengers.

"Discoverer Tours" are independent, are for one or more persons, and are not escorted. They are available in 2 qualities: deluxe and economy.

The tour packages range from the 2-day, 1-night "Opera Train Tour" (round-trip train Montreal-Toronto-Montreal, one night at a hotel in Toronto, and a choice seat at the opera) to the 19-day,20-night "Transcontinental Discoverer" (a cruise from Vancouver City to Vancouver Island and return, then train to Jasper, bus to Banff, train to Montreal, train to Quebec City, and train to Toronto, including 17 nights in hotels and sightseeing in all cities).

Montreal

Take this walking tour that starts and ends at Place d'Armes: The Sulpician Seminary, built in 1685, the oldest building in Montreal. The oldest wood clock in North America is exhibited there. Then to see the 10-ton bell ("Le Gros Bourdon") and marvelous stained-glass windows in the Notre Dame Cathedral, completed in 1829. It resembles Westminster Abbey. See the gifts from Louis XIV in the tiny museum next to the Chapel.

Other sights: the Chateau de Ramezay, the most interesting museum in Montreal. St. Joseph's Oratory. The Place des Arts complex of concert and theater halls. The vast underground shopping malls in the ultramodern center of the city, called Place Ville-Marie. Take the short trip to Mount Royal.

Ottawa

See: The Parliament buildings, particularly the 53-bell carillon in the 291-foot high Peace Tower. The National Arts Center. The Arboretum at the Central Experimental Farm. The Governor General's Residence. Hog's Back Falls, located in the city. The Royal Canadian Mint. The Canadian War Museum. The Indian Burial Grounds. The Centennial Cabin Museum. The Old Depot Museum. Superb art dating back to the 13th century, in the National Gallery of Canada.

Quebec City

See: The Plains of Abraham. Parliament buildings. The old gates and fortifications of the walled city, The Citadel. The ancient narrow streets. Place Royale. The 25-minute son-et-lumiere recreation of the 6 sieges to which Quebec City has been subjected, in the Musee du Fort, at 10 Rue Ste. Anne.

The collection of antique furniture in Chevalier House at Place Champlain. The 3-week Winter Carnival, ending on the night of Mardi Gras. Take the 4-hour cruise on the St. Lawrence Seaway.

Toronto

A major port. See: The astounding view from the top of Canadian National's Tower, the tallest (1,800 feet) free-standing structure in the world. City Hall. The Art Gallery of Ontario. The Marine Museum of Upper Canada. Fort York. Casa Loma Castle. Ontario Science Center. The 19th century MacKenzie House, home of Toronto's first mayor. The Royal Ontario Museum and McLaughlin Planetarium. Black Creek Pioneer Village. The Ontario Place recreation complex, at the waterfront.

The Hockey Museum. Ride the special train through the 710-acre Metro Zoo for a view of the 4,000 animals exhibited there. Visit The Islands, a 612-acre complex of amusement rides, bike paths, parks, beaches and lagooons. Go on one of the boats that tour the harbor, departing from next to the Hilton Hotel. Some of these have dinner-dancing cruises.

Vancouver

See: The Zoo and the killer whales in 1,000-acre Stanley Park. The view while walking across Capilano Suspension Bridge. The exhibit of the history of British Columbia from the ice age to today, at the Centennial Museum. The Shakespearean Gardens. Nitobe Gardens. Chinatown. The Maritime Museum.

Nearby, the shows in the MacMillan Planetarium. The Museum of Anthropology at the University of British Columbia.

Halifax - Montreal 3

All of these trains carry sleeping cars, have meal service and are air-conditioned.

Dep. Halifax	12:55	Dep. Montreal (Cent.)	19:00
Dep. Truro	14:30	Set watch forward 2 hours.	
Dep. Moncton	18:05	Dep. Moncton	11:50
Set watch back 2 hours.		Dep. Truro	14:55
Arr. Montreal (Centr.)	8:30	Arr. Halifax	16:20

Moncton - Saint John 92

Dep. Moncton	12:20	Dep. Saint John	16:00(1)
Arr. Saint John	14:05	Arr. Moncton	17:45

(1)Second-class only. Air-conditioned train. Light refreshments.

Montreal - Toronto - Winnipeg - Calgary - Lake Louise - Vancouver 1 + 28

The "Canadian". Reservation required. Meal service. Air-conditioned. Carries sleeping car. Has dome car Winnipeg-Vancouver and v.v.

During the 2-hour layover in Winnipeg, travelers can bathe in a "Fresh-Up Room" in the old Hotel Fort Gary. The charge for 2 hours is about $15(U.S.) for one person, $22 for 2 people. During the more than 2 hours in Calgary (en route to Vancouver), it is a nice diversion to visit the 3-story-high hanging gardens in the Devonian.

West of Calgary, the train travels through the stunning scenery of the Rocky Mountains and the Selkirk Mountains, glaciers near Lake Louise, the Spiral Tunnels at Yoho, across Stoney Creek Bridge, and through the 5-mile Connaught Tunnel.

Trailways provides bus transfer between the Vancouver and Seattle railstations.

Dep. Montreal		Dep. Vancouver	21:45
(Central)	16:30	Set watch forward one hour.	
Arr. Toronto		Dep. Lake Louise	17:40 Day 2
(Union)	22:10	Dep. Banff	18:35
Dep. Toronto		Arr. Calgary	20:40
(Union)	23:59	Dep. Calgary	21:50
Set watch back one hour.		Set watch forward one hour.	
Arr. Winnipeg	10:00 Day 3	Dep. Regina	8:20 Day 3
Dep. Winnipeg	13:30	Set watch forward one hour.	
Dep. Regina	21:15	Arr. Winnipeg	18:00
Set watch back one hour.		Dep. Winnipeg	20:10
Arr. Calgary	8:10 Day 4	Arr. Toronto	
Dep. Calgary	10:30	(Union)	7:00 Day 5
Dep. Banff	12:50	Dep. Toronto	
Dep. Lake Louise	13:35	(Union)	9:00
Set watch back one hour.		Arr. Montreal	
Arr. Vancouver	7:00 Day 5	(Central)	15:10

Rail Routes From Toronto

Train travel to both Canada's eastern and western frontiers can originate from Toronto, which is also the major gateway for rail connections to northeastern U.S. cities (Buffalo, and on to New York or Cleveland; or to Detroit, and on to Chicago . . . see "International Routes From Canada" later in this section).

Toronto - Montreal   85

All of these trains are air-conditioned.

Dep. Toronto (Union)	7:30(1)	10:45(2)	13:00(3)	15:45(2+6)
Arr. Montreal (Cent.)	12:00	15:50	17:40	20:15

*   *   *

Dep. Montreal (Cent.)	7:30(1)	10:45(2)	13:00(3)	15:45(2+7)
Arr. Toronto (Union)	12:00	15:00	17:40	20:15

(1)Reservation required. Runs daily, except Sundays and holidays. Light refreshments. (2)Reservation required. Light refreshments. (3)Light refreshments. (4)Reservation required. Runs daily, except Saturday. Light refreshments. (5)Reservation required. Carries sleeping car and club car. (6)Plus other departures from Toronto at 16:30(3), 17:50(4) and 23:35(5).   (7)Plus other departures from Montreal at 16:30(3), 17:50(4) and 23:35(5).

Toronto - Ottawa   85

All of these trains are air-conditioned and serve light refreshments.

Dep. Toronto (Union)   9:00(1)   17:30   23:35(2)
Arr. Ottawa (Union)   15:00   22:25   6:30

*   *   *

Dep. Ottawa (Union)   8:30   16:25   23:35(2)
Arr. Toronto (Union)   14:40   21:15   7:30

(1)Res. required. (2)Daily, except Sat. Carries sleeping car.

Toronto - Winnipeg - Saskatoon - Edmonton - Jasper - Vancouver

Prior to 1983, a daytime rail service operated between Edmonton and Vancouver. The spectacular scenery of 3 mountain ranges (Rockies, Selkirks and Coast), many ancient glaciers, large lakes and waterfalls attracted many tourists to this route instead of crossing the continent via Regina.

This itinerary now requires en route to Vancouver very long layovers in both Saskatoon and Kamloops plus having to take a night bus ride Edmonton-Kamloops . . . and en route to Toronto very long layovers in both Edmonton and Saskatoon plus having to take a daytime bus Kamloops-Edmonton.

All trains here are air-conditioned and have light refreshments or meal service. An Amtrak bus provides transfer between Vancouver and Seattle railstations.

1

Dep. Toronto
  (Union)   23:59(1)
  Set watch back one hour.
Arr. Winnipeg   10:00 Day 3
  Change trains.
25
Dep. Winnipeg   10:40(2)
Arr. Saskatoon   21:15
  Change trains.
Dep. Saskatoon   8:00(2) Day 4
  Set watch back one hour.
Arr. Edmonton   14:40
  Change to bus.
30
Dep. Edmonton   20:15
Dep. Jasper   1:30 Day 5
  Set watch back one hour.
Arr. Kamloops   7:25
  Change to train.
28
Dep. Kamloops   22:45(1+3)
Arr. Vancouver   7:00 Day 6

28

Dep. Vancouver   21:45(1+3)
Arr. Kamloops   6:20 Day 2
  Change to bus.
30
Dep. Kamloops   7:05
  Set watch forward one hour.
Dep. Jasper   14:55
Arr. Edmonton   19:45
  Change to train.
25
Dep. Edmonton   13:30(2) Day 3
  Set watch forward one hour.
Arr. Saskatoon   20:20
  Change trains.
Dep. Saskatoon   7:00(2) Day 4
Arr. Winnipeg   19:20
  Change trains.
1
Dep. Winnipeg   20:10(1)
  Set watch forward one hour.
Arr. Toronto
  (Union)   7:00 Day 6

(1)Carries sleeping car. (2)Second-class only. (3)Reservation required.

Northern Canadian Rail Routes

In addition to train service in Nova Scotia, to be covered later in this section, there are 17 rail routes on the mainland extending north from Canada's transcontinental lines.

Moncton - Mont Joli - Matapedia - Gaspe 92

All of these trains require reservation, carry a first-class sleeping car and second-class coach car, are air-conditioned and have meal service.

3		92	
Dep. Moncton	18:05	Dep. Gaspe	20:50
Arr. Mont Joli	0:15	Dep. Matapedia	3:15
Change trains.		Arr. Mont Joli	5:40
92		Change trains.	
Dep. Mont Joli	7:40	3	
Dep. Matapedia	10:05	Dep. Mont Joli	3:00
Arr. Gaspe	16:20	Arr. Moncton	11:15

Sept Iles - Schefferville 96

There is meal service on all these trains.

Dep. Sept Iles	8:00(1)	8:00(2)	Dep. Schefferville	8:00(3)
Arr.			Arr. Sept Iles	19:15
Schefferville	19:15	21:00		

(1)Runs Friday only. (2)Runs Tuesday only. (3)Runs Wednesday and Saturday.

Montreal - Quebec City 91

All of these trains are air-conditioned.

Dep. Montreal (Cent.)	-0-	8:30(2)	12:30(2+4)	-0-
Dep. Montreal (Wind.)	7:15(1)	-0-	-0-	13:10(3+5)
Arr. Quebec (Ste. Foy)	10:45	11:00	15:30	16:40

*   *   *

Dep. Quebec (Ste. Foy)	7:15(2)	7:25(1)	11:30(3)	12:20(2+6)
Arr. Montreal (Wind.)	-0-	11:05	15:10	-0-
Arr. Montreal (Cent.)	9:45	-0-	-0-	15:00

(1)Runs daily, except Sundays and holidays. Second-class only. (2)Light refreshments. (3)Second-class only. (4)Plus another departure from Montreal (central) at 17:00(2). (5)Plus another departure from Montreal (Windsor) at 18:05(3). (6)Plus other departures from Quebec City at 17:30(2), arriving Montreal (central) at 20:25, and at 18:15(3), arriving Montreal (Windsor) at 21:55.

Montreal - Hervey - Chicoutimi 88

These trains are air-conditioned and have light refreshments.

Dep. Montreal		Dep. Chicoutimi	10:35(2)	13:00(3)
(Cent.)	14:15(1)	Dep. Hervey	16:45	19:15
Dep. Hervey	17:25	Arr. Monbtreal		
Arr. Chicoutimi	23:40	(Cent.)	20:00	22:25

Runs Monday, Wednesday and Friday. (2)Runs Tuesday and Thursday. (3)Runs Sunday only.

Montreal - Hervey - Senneterre - Cochrane 88

All of these trains are air-conditioned.

Dep. Montreal (Cent.)	18:30(1+2)	20:00(1+4)
Arr. Hervey	21:59(1+2)	23:29(1+4)
Arr. Senneterre	8:30(3)	10:00(5)
Change trains.		
Dep. Senneterre	8:55(3)	10:25(5)
Arr. Cochrane	14:30	16:00
	*	*	*
Dep. Cochrane	11:10(6)	16:05(3)
Arr. Senneterre	16:45	21:40
Change trains.		
Dep. Senneterre	17:20(1+6)	22:15(1+3)
Dep. Hervey	3:02(1+7)	7:57(1+8)
Arr. Montreal (Cent.)	6:20(7)	11:15(8)

(1)Carries first-class sleeping carand second-class coach car. Light refreshments. (2)Runs Monday and Wednesday. (3)Runs Tuesday and Thursday. (4)Runs Friday only. (5)Runs Saturday only. (6)Runs Sunday only. (7)Runs Monday only. (8)Runs Wednesday and Friday.

Toronto - North Bay - Cochrane - Moosonee 63

"Polar Bear Express" makes one-day excursion roundtrips into the Canadian wilderness daily except Friday, from late June to early September, to Moosonee, a trading post since 1673. There are 2 hotels in Moosonee for travelers wishing to stay overnight. For further information regarding this excursion, contact Ontario Northwest Railway, 195 Regina Street, North Bay, Ontario, Canada.

All of these trains are air-conditioned and have meal service.

Dep. Toronto (Union)	21:25(1)	-0-
Dep. North Bay (C.N.)	2:50(1)	-0-
Arr. Cochrane	9:50	-0-
Change trains.		
Dep. Cochrane	10:40(2)	8:30(3)
Arr. Moosonee	16:15	12:50

Dep. Moosonee	9:00(4)	17:15(3)
Arr. Cochrane	14:30	21:20
Change trains.		
Dep. Cochrane	20:05(1)	-0-
Arr. North Bay (C.N.)	2:50(1)	-0-
Arr. Toronto (Union)	8:10	-0-

(1)Air-conditioned train. Carries sleeping car. (2)Runs Monday, Wednesday and Friday. (3)"Polar Bear Express". Reservation required. Operates late June to early September. Runs daily, except Friday. (4)Runs Tuesday, Thursday and Saturday.

Cochrane - Kapuskasing   63

This is a short spur off the North Bay-Moosonee line. These trains are air-conditioned.

Dep. Cochrane	9:50
Arr. Kapuskasing	11:30

Dep. Kapuskasing	17:55
Arr. Cochrane	20:05

Sault Ste. Marie - Hearst   58

These trains are air-conditioned and have meal service.

Dep. Sault Ste. Marie	8:30(1+2)	9:30(3+4)
Arr. Hearst	17:50	19:15

*   *   *

Dep. Hearst	7:15(1+5)	8:15(3+6)
Arr. Sault Ste. Marie	16:30	18:10

(1)Operates mid-October to late May. (2)Runs Friday, Saturday and Sunday. Meal service until 12:19   (3)Operates late May to mid-October. (4)Runs daily, except Monday. Meal service until 13:40.   (5)Runs Monday, Saturday and Sunday. Meal service 12:29 to 16:30.   (6)Runs daily, except Tuesday. Meal service 13:50 to 18:10.

Sights in **Sault Ste. Marie:** The marvelous scenery on the one-day (8:00-17:00) Agawa Canyon sightseeing excursion train operated by Algoma Central Railway. Fall foliage is particularly outstanding, attracting up to 1,500 people daily. About 86,000 passengers make the ride during the late May to mid-October operation. The view of the Montreal River from a 130-foot high and 1,550-foot long bridge and of hundreds of lakes are some of the interesting sights on this ride. Comments are broadcast on the train's public address system. Before making the return ride to Sault Ste. Marie, passengers have time to climb to lookout points above the canyon and walk into the canyon. Hot lunches are sold on the train. The Canadian meat pie and strawberry shortcake are favorites.

Winnipeg - Hudson Bay - Churchill   52

This is a mind-boggling train trip, 992 miles from Winnipeg to the chilly, distant Churchill. VIA Rail Canada offers an escorted 6-day "Hudson Bay Explorer Tour", a package that includes rail fare, berth and all meals.

Passengers are provided sightseeing in 2 mining communities (Flin Flon and Thompson), a night in Churchill, then sightseeing in The Pas (one of the oldest outposts in Manitoba) on the return trip.

These trains require reservation, carry sleeping cars, are air-conditioned and have meal service.

Dep. Winnipeg		Dep. Churchill	18:00(2)
(C.N)	17:50(1)	Dep. Gillam	2:40 Day 2
Dep. Dauphin	22:05	Dep. Thompson	9:15
Arr. Hudson Bay	4:30 Day 2	Arr. The Pas	16:30
Arr. Hudson Bay	4:50	Dep. The Pas	18:15
Arr. The Pas	7:00	Arr. Hudson Bay	20:10
Dep. The Pas	8:30	Dep. Hudson Bay	20:30
Dep. Thompson	17:15	Dep. Dauphin	3:15 Day 3
Dep. Gillam	0:01 Day 3	Arr. Winnipeg	
Arr. Churchill	7:00	(C.N.)	7:30

(1)Runs Tuesday, Thursday and Sunday. (2)Runs, Tuesday, Thursday and Saturday.

Sights in **Churchill:** This is the only town in the world that is located on a polar bear migratory route. They can be seen here during September and October. Seals can be viewed here May-June and white beluga whales from mid-June to mid-September. The grain elevator in Churchill fills ships from all over the world. See the 18th century Fort Prince of Wales and the Eskimo Museum.

Sights in **Thompson:** The huge International Nickel Company mining complex.

Sights in **Flin Flon:** The beautiful scenery at Beaver Lake.

Hudson - Prince Albert - Saskatoon - Regina

When going west across Canada and detouring north to Churchill, it is not necessary to return to Winnipeg in order to rejoin the transcontinental line. One can return from Churchill to the cross-country line on a different route than that taken to Churchill by changing to a bus at Hudson Bay and proceeding from there to Prince Albert, Saskatoon and Regina. The train from Prince Albert to Saskatoon was discontinued in 1982, and the train departure from Saskatoon to Regina is not matched with the bus arrival in Saskatoon.

When going east across Canada, the detour to Churchill can start at Regina, and one can return from Churchill by continuing from Hudson Bay on to Winnipeg, rather than returning to Regina.

38 (Bus)				
Dep. Hudson Bay	-0-	-0-	6:05	-0-
Arr. Prince Albert	-0-	-0-	10:55	-0-
Change buses.				
Dep. Prince Albert	9:50	10:30	14:00	18:00
Arr. Saskatoon	12:45	12:35	15:50	19:55
Change buses.				
42				
Dep. Saskatoon	8:00	13:30	17:30	19:30
Arr. Regina	10:50	16:25	20:20	22:20
	*	*	*	
Dep. Regina	8:00	13:30	17:30	20:00
Arr. Saskatoon	10:50	16:20	20:20	22:50
Change buses.				
38				
Dep. Saskatoon	14:00	17:25	18:00	9:00
Arr. Prince Albert	15:50	20:40	20:05	10:55
Change buses.				
Dep. Prince Albert	19:30	-0-	-0-	-0-
Arr. Hudson Bay	0:35	-0-	-0-	-0-

Saskatoon - Regina - Winnipeg   25

These trains are air-conditioned.

Dep. Saskatoon	7:00	Dep. Winnipeg	10:40
Arr. Regina	10:55	Dep. Regina	17:20
Arr. Winnipeg	19:20	Arr. Saskatoon	21:15

Winnipeg - Hudson Bay - The Pas - Lynn Lake

Bring food with you on these rides. These trains, which are air-conditioned, have *no* food service. The days in early April when we made the trip, the temperature was below zero Fahrenheit. The area north of Winnipeg was under 4 feet of snow.

A good place to rest and eat in The Pas is the Wescana Inn, a few blocks from the railstation. On our trip, they had a good restaurant and treated travelers considerately.

52		50	
Dep. Winnipeg (C.N.)	17:50(1+2)	Dep. Lynn Lake	7:30(4)
Dep. Dauphin	22:05	Arr. The Pas	17:50(4)
Arr. Hudson Bay	3:30	Change trains.	
Dep. Hudson Bay	3:50	52	
Arr. The Pas	7:00	Dep. The Pas	18:15(2+5)Day 2
Change trains.		Arr. Hudson	
50		Bay	19:10
Dep. The Pas	11:00(3)	Dep. Hudson	
Arr. Lynn Lake	21:15	Bay	19:30(2+5)
		Dep. Dauphin	3:15 Day 3
		Arr. Winnipeg	
		(C.N.)	7:30

Runs Tuesday, Thursday and Sunday. (2)Reservation required. Carries sleeping car. Meal service. Air-conditioned train. (3)Runs Wednesday, Friday and Monday. (4)Runs Tuesday, Thursday and Saturday. Requires staying overnight in The Pas before taking the train the next day to Hudson Bay. (5)Runs Wednesday, Friday and Sunday.

Sights in **The Pas:** The hand-carved pews and the Ten Commandments in the Cree Indian language. The Museum. The Cathedral of Our Lady of the Sacred Heart.

The Pas, and most of the land north of it, is a massive reservation for Indians, a few of whom trap for furs.

The train from The Pas to Lynn Lake will stop at any point to let passengers board or get off. On our ride, it stopped in a completely deserted area so that a very old Indian man whose house could be seen on a hill a mile away from the track could get off. As the train started, we could see him beginning his long walk from the track to his house, on the other side of a frozen lake.

Our train for the 233-mile ride from The Pas to Lynn Lake was 23 freight cars, 2 passengers cars and a caboose, hauled by 4 locomotives. Only a few of the seats were filled, mostly by Indians.

The track goes alongside more than 20 very large lakes after the 12:25 stop in Cranberry Portage, and nearly all of this route is heavily forested. Much ore is transported out of here in open gondola freight cars.

Some cabins of fur trappers are only a few feet from the rail track.

In Winter, you can also see the snowmobile paths leading from the train track into the forest, to trapper cabins located away from the rail line.

From October to May, while there is snow on the ground, footprints of moose, deer, lynx, foxes and rabbits can be seen for hundreds of miles, only a few feet from the railway track.

In June, July and August, the splendid fishing and wilderness camping in this area attract many tourists. It is possible to camp and hike only a short distance from either the rail track or the well-traveled highway running between Lynn Lake and Pukatawagan.

Calgary - Edmonton   37

These trains are air-conditioned and have light refreshments.

Dep. Calgary (C.P.)   9:00   17:30(1)
Arr. South Edmonton   12:10   20:40
                                          *   *   *
Dep. South Edmonton   8:00(2)   17:25
Arr. Calgary (C.P.)   11:10   20:25

(1)Runs daily, except Saturday. (2)Runs daily, except Sundays and holidays.

Edmonton - Jasper - Prince George - Prince Rupert   15

These trains require reservation, carry sleeping car and coach car, have meal service and are air-conditioned. There is very beautiful scenery between Burns Lake and Prince Rupert.

Dep. Edmonton	17:00(1)	Dep. Prince Rupert	9:00(1)
Dep. Jasper	22:45(1)	Arr. Prince George	
Arr. Prince George		(VIA)	21:15
(VIA)	5:50(2)	Dep. Prince George	
Dep. Prince George		(VIA)	21:40(1)
(VIA)	6:30	Dep. Jasper	6:40(2+3)
Arr. Prince Rupert	19:00	Arr. Edmonton	12:00

(1)Reservation required. Runs Wednesday, Friday and Sunday. (2)Day 2.
(3)Reservation required. Runs Thursday, Saturday and Monday.

Vancouver - Squamish - Lillooet - Prince George   16

All of these trains are air-conditioned.

This is one of the most scenic rail trips in Canada. The train travels the entire length of Lord Howe Sound before climbing the steep and heavily-timbered Cheakamus Valley to Alta Lake. After Pemberton, it passes through wilderness along the shore of fjord-like Anderson and Seton Lakes. Then, it drops down to Lillooet in the Fraser River Valley.

Dep. North			Dep. Prince George		
Vancouver	7:30(1)	7:30(2)	(BCR(	7:30(3)	-0-
Dep. Squamish	8:44(1)	8:44(2)	Dep. Lillooet	15:25(3)	15:25(4)
Dep. Pemberton	10:27(1)	10:27(2)	Dep. Pemberton	17:30(3)	17:30(4)
Arr. Lillooet	12:35	12:40(2)	Dep. Squamish	19:11(3)	19:11(4)
Arr. Prince George			Arr. North		
(BCR	-0-	20:30	Vancouver	20:30	20:30

(1)Runs Monday, Tuesday, Thursday and Saturday. (2)Reservation required. Runs Wednesday, Friday and Sunday. (3)Reservation required. Runs Monday, Thursday and Saturday. (4)Runs Tuesday, Wednesday, Friday and Sunday.

Nova Scotia Rail Routes
The rail route southwest from Halifax connects in Digby with ferry service to and from Saint John, New Brunswick.

Halifax - Yarmouth 92
All of these trains are air-conditioned and have light refreshments.

Dep. Halifax (C.N.)	17:30(1)	19:00(2)
Dep. Kentville	19:25	20:55
Dep. Digby	21:19	22:49
Arr. Yarmouth	22:50	0:20

* * *

Dep. Yarmouth	7:00(1)	13:00(2)
Dep. Digby	8:26	14:26
Dep. Kentville	10:30	16:30
Arr. Halifax (C.N.)	12:20	18:20

(1)Runs daily, except Sundays and holidays. (2)Runs Sundays and holidays only.

Digby - Saint John 113
Ferry service.

Dep. Digby	4:45(1)	5:00(2)	12:30(3)	14:30(4+8)
Arr. Saint John	3 hours later			

* * *

Dep. Saint John	0:01(2)	0:15(1)	8:45(3)	10:30(5+9)
Arr. Digby	3 hours later			

(1)Early May to mid-June: runs Tuesday-Saturday. Mid-June to early October: runs daily, except Sunday. Early October to late October: runs Tuesday-Saturday. (2)Operates early January to early May and late October to late December. Runs Tuesday-Saturday. (3)Operates mid-June to early October. Runs daily. (4)Operates early May to mid-June and most of October. Runs Saturday and Sunday. (5)Early January to early May: runs daily, except Sunday. Early May to mid-June: runs daily. Most of October: runs daily. Late October to late December: runs daily, except Sunday. (6)Early January to early May: runs daily, except Sunday. Early May to mid-June: runs Monday-Friday. Late

October to late December: runs daily, except Sunday. (7)Operates early January to early May and late October to late December. Runs Sunday only. (8)Plus other departures from Digby at 15:30(6), 17:00(7), 20:00(3) and 21:30(4).
   (9)Plus other departures from Saint John at 12:30(7), 16:15(3) and 18:00(4).

Halifax - Truro - Sydney   92
   The rail route north from Halifax connects in North Sydney with the ferry service to Port aux Basques, Newfoundland.
   These trains have light refreshments and are air-conditioned.

Dep. Halifax	8:10	17:10(1)		Dep. Sydney	8:30(1)	15:00
Arr. Truro	9:25	18:30(1)		Dep. No. Sydney	8:59(1)	15:25
Change trains.				Arr. Truro	14:00(1)	20:35
Dep. Truro	15:10	18:40		Change trains.		
Arr. No. Sydney	20:14	23:40		Dep. Truro	14:10	20:45
Arr. Sydney	20:45	0:10		Arr. Halifax	15:50	22:05

(1)Direct train. No train change in Truro

North Sydney - Port aux Basques   114 (Ferry Boat)
Dep. North Sydney   8:00(1) 11:30(2) 17:45(3) 23:30(4)
   Set your watch forward one hour.
Arr. Port aux Basques   15:30   19:00   1:15   7:00
                                              *   *   *
Dep. Port aux Basques   8:00(5) 12:30(2) 17:30(1) 23:59(4)
   Set your watch back one hour.
Arr. North Sydney   15:00   19:30   0:30   7:00
(1)Operates from mid-June to late August. (2)Operates early May to early June and early July to late August. (4)Reservation required. Operates early May to early January. (5)Operates early July to late August.

Glace Bay - Port Morien   0000
   The Cape Breton Steam Railway offers visitors a 10-mile trip from Glace Bay, a mining town, to Port Morien, a small fishing village. Passengers can visit the Miner's Museum at Glace Bay.

Dep. Glace Bay	N/A	Dep. Port Morien	N/A
Arr. Port Morien	N/A	Arr. Glace Bay	N/A

Bus Service in Newfoundland
   There is cross-island bus service, connecting with the arrival of the ferry from Nova Scotia, and its return trip.
   130

Dep. Port aux Basques	8:30	Dep. St. John's	8:00
Dep. Gander Airport	17:50	Dep. Gander Airport	12:00
Arr. St. John's	17:50	Arr. Port aux Basques	22:10

Special Canadian Train Excursions

Here are schedules for special rail trips featuring steam locomotives.

North Vancouver - Squamish - North Vancouver British Columbia
Timetable

This is an easy one-day roundtrip (27 miles each way), featuring a steam locomotive tour of scenic Howe Sound. Scenery on this trip includes forests, waterfalls and the seacoast. Squamish is a logging town. Visitors can see logging and sports shows, musical performances and sidewalk markets. There are tours of pulp mills.

The excursion train operates mid-May to early September. The train runs Wednesday-Saturday from mid-May to the end of June. Daily, except Tuesday, from July 1 to early September.

A bus departs from the downtown Vancouver bus depot at 9:00, making several stops on the way to the train (front of the Hudson Bay Department Store, front of The Royal Bank, etc.). Look for the bus that displays a sign reading "Train Connection".

Reservations are recommended. Telephone or write: B.C. Railway, 1311 W. First St., North Vancouver, B.C. V7P 1A7. Tel: (604) 987-5211.

| Dep. North Vancouver | 10:00 | Dep. Squamish | 13:30 |
| Arr. Squamish | 11:45 | Arr. North Vancouver | 15:45 |

Toronto - Niagara Falls - Toronto 67

Dep. Toronto (Union)	9:05(1)	18:00	23:05
Arr. Niagara Falls	11:00	19:55	0:50
	*	*	*
Dep. Niagara Falls	6:40	13:10	18:35(1)
Arr. Toronto (Union)	8:35	15:05	20:30

(1)Meal service.

Victoria - Courtenay - Victoria 8

Good views of Vancouver Island scenery as this line winds along sheer cliffs high above Finlayson Arm, en route to Malahat Summit. There are spectacular vistas from many high trestles before the train begins its descent along Shawnigan Lake, en route to Nanaimo.

The station 13 minutes before arriving Courtenay is Union Bay. Many prefer to get off the train there in order to have a more leisurely lunch than is possible when going all the way to Courtenay.

A 2-day circle-trip can be made by taking the bus ferry Vancouver-Victoria (with a night in Victoria), and then the next day the Victoria-Nanaimo train and the Nanaimo-Vancouver ferry.

| Dep. Victoria | 8:15 | Dep. Courtenay | 13:05 |
| Arr. Courtenay | 12:35 | Arr. Victoria | 17:15 |

INTERNATIONAL ROUTES FROM CANADA

The gateways for travel from Canada to the United States are: Montreal (to Boston, New York and south along the eastern U.S. seaboard), Toronto (to Buffalo and on to New York City or Cleveland, or to Detroit and on to Chicago), and Vancouver (to Seattle).

Montreal - New York City - Philadelphia - Baltimore - Washington

Both of these trains have meal service and are air-conditioned.

	180	181
Dep. Montreal (Windsor)	-0-	10:05
Dep. Montreal (Central)	19:40	-0-
Arr. New York (Grand Central	-0-	18:57
Arr. New York (Penn.)	7:15	-0-
Arr. Philadelphia (30th St.)	9:01	-0-
Arr. Baltimore (Penn.)	10:26	-0-
Arr. Washington (Union)	11:10	-0-

Toronto - Buffalo - New York (or Cleveland)   67

Dep. Toronto (Union)	9:05(1)	240 + 186	
Arr. Buffalo (Depew)	12:50	Dep. Buffalo (Depew)	3:37(2)
Arr. New York		Arr. Cleveland	
(Grand Central)	20:37	(Lakefront)	6:54

(1)Meal service. (2)Reservation required. Carries sleeping car. Also has Slumbercoach and coach cars.

Toronto - Windsor - Detroit   67

All of these trains are air-conditioned and have light refreshments.

Dep. Toronto (Union)	9:00	12:30	15:30(1)	17:30	19:30
Arr. Windsor		13:05	16:35	19:30	21:45	23:40

Take a taxi from Windsor through the International Tunnel to Detroit.

Toronto - Brantford - Toronto   67

Dep. Toronto (Union)	8:10	13:00	17:30	19:30	20:45	23:15
Arr. Brantford	9:26	14:13	18:41	20:42	21:50	0:25

Sights in **Brantford:** The home of Alexander Graham Bell, with the world's first telephone business office. The history of Brant County, from Paleo-Indian culture to the days of the Six Nations Indians and Canadian pioneers, in the Brant Historical Museum. The exhibit of Woodland Indian artifacts at the Wood and Indian Museum.

Dep. Brantford	13:12	14:48	15:24	17:51	20:38	21:05
Arr. Toronto (Union)	14:30	16:00	16:35	19:10	21:50	22:25

Vancouver - Seattle

In 1981, this train service was replaced by bus transportation between VIA Rail Canada's terminal in Vancouver and Amtrak's station in Seattle, allowing for connection between the Montreal-Vancouver train and the Seattle-L.A. train.

MEXICO

Mexico's passenger railroads are operated by these 5 companies: Ferrocarril Chihuahua al Pacifico (CH-P), Ferrocarriles Nacionales de Mexico (NdeM), Ferrocarril del Pacifico (FCP), Ferrocarril Unidos del Sureste (FUS), and Ferrocarril Sonora-Baja California (S-BC).

Nacionales de Mexico is the principal line, with routes along the U.S. border from Juarez (El Paso), Piedras Negras, Nuevo Laredo (Laredo), and Matamoros (Brownsville), all of these providing service to Mexico City. Other N de M gateways to Mexico City are Tampico, Veracruz, Coatzacoalos, Oaxaca, Uruapan, Durango, Manzanillo and Guadalajara.

All Mexican railway schedules use the same time as U.S. Central Standard Time (same as Chicago). Children under 5 travel free when accompanied by a parent. Half-fare for children 5-11. Children 12 and over must pay full fare.

Several U.S. and Mexican tour operators offer escorted private train tours of Mexico. Check your travel agent for details. Because Mexican railways do not pay travel agents a commission, an agent who assists you in obtaining train reservations is entitled to a fee of 15% of the ticket price. Advance reservations are advisable.

Mexico City

Altitude of 7.350 feet (2,240 meters) limits activity for many tourists. Cool and dry weather except during the May-September rainy season. Railways link Mexico City with 5 Gulf of Mexico seaports (Matamoros, Tampico, Veracruz, Coatzacoalcos and Campeche) and 4 Pacific ports (Los Mochis, Mazatlan, Manzanillo and Ciudad Hidalgo).

The art, sculpture, movies and scale models of ancient cities at the National Museum of Anthropology and History in Chapultepec Park are the major attractions. You will see the results of more than 15,000 discovery sites, including the 167-ton statue of Tlatloc, the Aztec rain god, and a 30-ton Aztec calendar stone.

All the major Indian tribes of Mexico are represented at this fabulous museum (jewelry, paintings, furniture, sculpture). Guided tours are conducted in many languages, including English.

Also see: The Museum of Modern Art. The 16th century Basilica de Guadalupe, most sacred shrine in Mexico. The mariachi bands in Plaza de Garibaldi. The daily markets, Centro de Abastos and San Juan. Window-shop the displays of silver jewelry on Juarez and Madero Streets. The shops in Zona Rosa. The textiles at the Londres Street Market.

Visit Zocalo (or Plaza Mayor), the main square. The Cathedral, oldest and largest church in Latin America. The National Pawnshop (Monte de Piedad). Palacio Nacional. The Palace of Fine Arts. The goode collection of European paintings at the School of Fine Arts. Plaza Mexico, largest bullfighting ring in the world.

Jai-Alai at Fronton Mexico. The largest of many parks here (almost 1,000 acres) is Bosque de Chapultepec.

There are several splendid one-day excursions from Mexico City. It is only 40 miles to the pre-Aztec pyramids at Teotihuacan. Take the short ride to Cuernavaca and the Popocatepetl and Ixtaccihuati national parks. Do not miss seeing the floating gardens at Xochimilco.

Information about many special one-day train excursions from Mexico City can be obtained from Club Amigos del Ferrocarril, Apartado Postal 7-1373, Mexico 7, D.F., Mexico.

Unless indicated otherwise, Mexico City departure and arrival times are for its Buenavista railstation.

U.S. RAIL GATEWAYS TO MEXICO

Brownsville - Matamoros - Monterrey - Mexico City   1056
Take a taxi from Brownsville, Tex. to Matamoros.

| Dep. Matamoros | 6:50 | Dep. Monterrey | 6:00 |
| Arr. Monterrey | 13:55 | Arr. Matamoros | 13:05 |

Sights in **Matamoros:** The cannon, walls and turrets of old Fort Mata, site of the Casa Mata Museum. The Cathedral. The leather, jewelry and souvenirs for sale in the city's 2 street markets. The handwork of Tamaulipas artisans on sale at the Arts and Crafts Center, near the International Bridge.

Sights in **Monterrey:** The collection of rare books in Indian languages and more than 2,000 editions of Don Quixote in many languages at the regional museum in the 200-year-old El Obispado, originally a bishop's palace. The painting and sculpture gallery in the Casa de la Cultura arts center, formerly a railstation. Sunday bullfights and Mexican-style rodeos.

Sampling free cerveza at the Carta Blanca brewery. The 18th century Cathedral in Plaza Zaragosa, where band concerts are performed. El Obispado (the Bishop's Palace), once occupied by Pancho Villa. Visit nearby Horseshoe Falls, scenic Huasteca Canyon, the subterranean lagoons, grottoes and stalactites at Garcia Caves, and see the views from the pine-covered slopes of Chipinique Mesa.

Monterrey was founded in 1579.

Monterrey - Mexico City   1065

Dep. Monterrey	9:08	18:00(1)	0:01(2)
Arr. Mexico City	6:23	9:00	20:04
	*	*	*
Dep. Mexico City	8:00(2)	18:00(1)	21:15
Arr. Monterrey	2:20	9:00	17:59

(1)Air-conditioned train that is sleeping cars only. Also has observation car. Meal service. (2)Air-conditioned train. Carries sleeping cars. Also has coach cars. Meal service.

Laredo - Mexico City   1020

Many package tours of Mexico (transportation, hotels, sightseeing, entertainment and meals) start and end in Laredo. Check your travel agent for details. Several connections can be made from Monterrey.

Dep. Nuevo Laredo	18:55(1)	Dep. Mexico City	8:00(1)
Arr. Monterrey	23:30	Dep. San Luis Potosi	17:38
Dep. Monterrey	0:01	Arr. Monterrey	2:20
Dep. San Luis Potosi	10:35	Dep. Monterrey	2:50
Arr. Mexico City	20:04	Arr. Nuevo Laredo	7:20

(1)Air-conditioned train. Carries sleeping car. Light refreshments.

Monterrey - Torreon - Durango

1040		1043	
Dep. Monterrey	8:10	Dep. Durango	7:00
Arr. Torreon	14:42	Arr. Torreon	11:30
Change trains.		Change trains.	
1043		1040	
Dep. Torreon	15:10	Dep. Torreon	12:05
Arr. Durango	20:10	Arr. Monterrey	18:50

Attractions in **Torreon:** Many wineries. The famous Willie's ice cream. Charcoal-broiled baby goat is a regional specialty here.

Sights in **Durango:** Very popular for hunting game (wolves, bears, deer, ducks). The 17th century Cathedral. The iron-water spring. The Government Palace. Sunday concerts in Plaza de Armas. The display of handblown glass, ceramics, textiles and sculpture at the Arts and Crafts School in Guardiana Park

San Luis Potosi - Tampico   1080

Between Cardenas and Valles, the track follows a small stream that widens into a rushing river. Watch to the left for the spectacular Micos Waterfall.

Dep. San Luis Potosi	7:50	Dep. Tampico	6:30
Arr. Tampico	20:45	Arr. San Luis Potosi	20:20

Sights in **San Luis Potosi:** The frescoes at the modern railstation. The Cathedral. The ornate tower of San Agustin Church. The suspended glass boat and the beautiful white and blue tiled dome of San Francisco Church. The Capilla de Aranzazu in the museum behind San Francisco Church. The lovely altar and pulpit of Carmen Church, as well as its tiled dome.

Sights in **Tampico:** Great sea and river fishing here. Playa de Miramar, nearby, is a popular beach resort.

El Paso - Ciudad Juarez - Mexico City   1023

Passengers transferring from or to Amtrak in El Paso have to make their own provision for crossing the border. There is taxi service. At Chihuahua, there is a connection for taking the "Copper Canyon Ride" to Los Mochis. At Torreon, a feeder line runs to Durango. At Irapuato, there is a connection for Guadalajara.

Dep. Ciudad Juarez	18:25(1)		Dep. Mexico City	19:50(1)
Arr. Chihuahua	23:25		Arr. Irapuato	2:50 Day 2
Dep. Chihuahua	23:55		Dep. Zacatecas	10:33
Arr. Torreon	8:03 Day 2		Arr. Torreon	17:20
Dep. Torreon	8:30		Dep. Torreon	17:50
Dep. Zacatecas	15:48		Arr. Chihuahua	1:47 Day 3
Arr. Irapuato	23:00		Dep. Chihuahua	2:17
Arr. Mexico City	6:55 Day 3		Arr. Ciudad Juarez	7:20

(1)Air-conditioned train. Carries sleeping car. Meal service.

Sights in **Ciudad Juarez:** The statues of Abraham Lincoln and Mexico's counterpart of him, Benito Juarez. Visit the Museum of Art and History in Juarez Cultural Center.

Sights in **Chihuahua City:** The dungeon of Miguel Hidalgo, Mexico's George Washington, at the Federal Palace. The Cathedral, built from 1724 to 1826 because Indian wars interrupted its construction. The museum at Quinta Gameros, an old private residence. Quinta Luz, Pancho Villa's home, now a museum about him and his exploits. The 18th century Chihuahua Aqueduct. The murals in Government Palace, depicting the history of Chihuahua. Plaza de la Constitucion.

Sights in **Zacatecas:** The images of St. Peter and St. Francis, made from hummingbird feathers, in the Church de Nuestra Senora Guadalupe, and the hundreds of paintings there as well as the Christ on the Cross made of cornstalks and the porcelain Virgin Mary. The outstanding wrought-iron in Pension Tacuba. The marvelous Cathedral. You can visit the tremendous El Bote Silver Mine by obtaining a permit and guide at the Tourist Office. It is only a 30-mile drive south to La Quemada to see the prehistoric Chicomoztoc Ruins.

These are the schedules for making a detour from Torreon to Durango en route from Ciudad Juarez to Mexico City.

Torreon - Durango

1023			1043	
Dep. Ciudad Juarez	18:25(1)		Dep. Durango	7:00
Arr. Torreon	8:03(2)		Arr. Torreon	11:30
Change trains.			Spend night in Torreon	
1043			1023	
Dep. Torreon	15:10(2)		Dep. Torreon	8:30(1+2)
Arr. Durango	20:10(2)		Arr. Mexico City	6:55(3)

(1)Air-conditioned. Carries sleeping car. Meal service. (2)Day 2. (3)Day 3.

Sights in **Durango:** See notes earlier in this section, under "Monterrey-Durango".

Durango - Regocijo   1045

Considered by many to be the most beautiful rail trip in Mexico. An easy one-day excursion that provides great mountain scenery. Be sure to see the last 3 miles going into Regocijo from the rear of the last car.

Dep. Durango	6:30(1)	Dep. Regocijo	11:55(1)
Arr. Regocijo	11:30	Arr. Durango	16:37

(1)Runs Tuesday, Wednesday, Friday and Saturday.

Chihuahua - Los Mochis   1035

This is the Copper Canyon scenic ride. One of the most exciting train trips in the world. A veritable roller coaster. Highest point of the journey is 8,071 feet at Los Ojitos.

Both 8:20 departures carry a Vistadome car and an observation-restaurant car. They have broad windows for picture taking.

Completed only in 1962, the rail line to Los Mochis crosses 39 very tall bridges and passes through 8½ miles of 73 tunnels. The bridge over Septentron River is 335 feet high. At several points, the route is so rugged that the track must double back in a complete circle.

Scenery includes spectacular deserts, mountains and subtropical landscape. What is regarded as the most impressive part of the journey begins as the line leaves the plateau west of Chihuahua City and climbs into the Sierra Madres. Upon reaching Creel, the aborigine Tarahumara Indians can be observed.

Halfway between Chihuahua and Los Mochis, the train comes into Divisadero. Meaning "look-out point", Divisadero stands on the rim of Urique Canyon. The train stops here for 20 minutes of viewing down 6,000 feet into the canyon.

Then the train proceeds into a mile-long tunnel, making a 180-degree turn inside the mountain so that when it emerges it is heading back in the direction from which it came as it passes a 400-foot waterfall.

The next large town is El Fuerte, once a very rich mining town. Another 50 miles, and the destination of Los Mochis is reached.

Dep. Chihuahua	8:00(1+2)	8:20(3+4)	22:30(1+5)
Dep. Dep. Creel	12:58	13:37	4:07
Dep. Divisadero	14:05	14:52	5:42
Arr. Los Mochis	20:20	21:51	13:00
	*	*	*
Dep. Los Mochis	8:00(2+6)	8:00(5+7)	8:00(4+8)
Dep Divisadero	14:07	15:25	15:00
Dep. Creel	15:40	17:15	16:34
Arr. Chihuahua	20:30	22:55	21:50

(1)Runs Tues. and Fri. (2)Has parlor car. Light refreshments. (3)Runs Mon., Thurs., Sat. and Sun. (4)"Vista Train". Has dome car and parlor car. Meal service. (5)Train has only sleeping cars. Meal service. (6)Runs Wed. and Sat. (7)Runs Mon. and Thurs. (8)Runs Tues., Fri. and Sun.

Ciudad Juarez - Irapuato - Mexico City

Here are the schedules for making a detour from Irapuato to Guadalajara en route from Ciudad Juarez to Mexico City.

1023		1024	
Dep. Ciudad Juarez	18:25(1)	Dep. Guadalajara	20:55(1)
Arr. Irapuato	23:00 Day 2	Dep. Irapuato	1:37
Change trains.		Arr. Mexico City	8:45
1024			
Dep. Irapuato	3:59(1)		
Arr. Guadalajara	8:10		

(1)Air-conditioned train. Carries sleeping car. Meal service.

Irapuato - Guanajuato   1074

Another interesting detour from the Ciudad Juarez-Mexico City route. These trains have only second-class coach cars.

Dep. Irapuato	6:30	Dep. Guanajuato	8:20
Arr. Guanajuato	8:05	Arr. Irapuato	9:50

Sights in **Guanajuato:** Many ornate 17th century churches that were endowed by the wealth of the richest silver mine in the world. Much late Renaissance architecture here. A museum of mummified corpses. An old underground aqueduct that is now used as a subterranean road.

Nogales - Mazatlan - Guadalajara - Mexico City   1024

Dep. Nogales	16:30(1)	Dep. Mexico City	20:30(1)
Arr. Mazatlan	8:25(2)	Arr. Guadalajara	8:10(2)
Dep. Mazatlan	8:35	Dep. Guadalajara	8:50
Arr. Guadalajara	19:00	Arr. Mazatland	18:30
Dep. Guadalajara	20:55	Dep. Mazatlan	18:40
Arr. Mexico City	8:45(3)	Arr. Nogales	10:20(3)

(1)Air-conditioned train. Carries sleeping car. Meal service. (2)Day 2. (3)Day 3.

Sights in **Mazatlan:** A marvelous seashore resort. Ride a 3-wheel "pneumonia" past the hotels, boutiques and shopping centers that line the seaside Avenida de Mar. Prize billfish and marlin are caught here. Much hunting for wild boar, deer, rabbit, ducks, quail and pheasant in the nearby mountains.

Sights in **Guadalajara:** The 16th century Cathedral, surrounded by 4 plazas in the shape of a cross. The Cabanas Institute arts center and its marvelous Orozco murals, at the former Orphanage. Near there, the sculpture and fountains at the new Plaza Tapatia. Municipal Palace. The State Museum. The Library. Mercado Libertad, Mexico's largest public market. Casa de las Artesianas de Jalisco, a state-run arts and crafts exhibition and shop.

Guadalajara - Manzanillo 1061

This sensational ride down the steep sides of the Sierra Madre is very uncomfortable, dusty and hot (no air-conditioning).

Dep. Guadalajara	10:00	Dep. Manzanillo	8:00
Arr. Manzanillo	18:16	Arr. Guadalajara	16:45

Sights in **Manzanillo:** Mexico's principal Pacific seaport. Excellent beaches and great deep-sea fishing here. Much hunting in the nearby hills. The fabulous Las Hadas resort complex.

The California connection with rail travel to Mexico City begins by walking or driving from Calexico across the border to Mexicali and taking Sonora Baja California Railways' short line from there to Benjamin Hill, where a connection can be made with the Nogales-Mexico City line operated by Ferrocarril Nacionales de Mexico.

Mexicali - Benjamin Hill - Mazatlan - Guadalajara - Mexico City 1024

There are air-conditioned sleeping cars Mexicali-Mexico City and v.v., and also Guadalajara-Mexico City and v.v. First and second-class coach space is provided Mexicali-Benjamin Hill and v.v., as well as Guadalajara-Mexico City and v.v. There are *no* coach cars Benjamin Hill-Guadalajara and v.v.

There is *no* meal service Mexicali-Guadalajara and v.v. The train has meal service and an Observation Car only Guadalajara-Mexico City and v.v.

Dep. Mexicali	8:00	Dep. Mexico City	20:30
Arr. Benjamin Hill	17:30	Arr. Guadalajara	8:10 Day 2
Through cars switched here.		Dep. Guadalajara	8:50
Dep. Benjamin Hill	18:46	Arr. Mazatlan	18:30
Arr. Mazatlan	8:25 Day 2	Dep. Mazatlan	18:40
Dep. Mazatlan	8:35	Arr. Benjamin Hill	7:25 Day 3
Arr. Guadalajara	19:00	Through cars switched here.	
Dep. Guadalajara	20:55	Dep. Benjamin Hill	7:40
Arr. Mexico City	8:45 Day 3	Arr. Mexicali	13:35

Mazatlan - Tepic - San Blas - Guadalajara 1030

It is a one-hour bus ride from Tepic to San Blas.

Dep. Mazatlan	8:35	Dep. Guadalajara	8:50
Arr. Tepic	13:25	Arr. Tepic	14:00
Arr. Guadalajara	19:00	Arr. Mazatlan	18:40

Sights in **San Blas:** A popular resort.

Mexico City - Morelia 1086

Excellent Michoacan farm scenery is viewed on this ride.

Dep. Mexico City	6:55	21:29(1)	Dep. Morelia	10:33	23:12(1)
Arr. Morelia	17:30	6:20	Arr. Mexico City	20:50	7:50

(1)Air-conditioned train. Carries sleeping car.

Monterrey - Tampico   1055

These trains are second-class only.

Dep. Monterrey	8:00	Dep. Tampico	7:48
Arr. Tampico	18:45	Arr. Monterrey	18:40

Nogales - Guaymas - Guadalajara Mexico City   1030

Dep. Nogales	7:15(1)	16:30(5)
Arr. Guaymas	N/A(2)	N/A(2)
Arr. Guadalajara	17:20(3)	19:00(5+6)
Arr. Mexico City	8:34(4)	8:45(4)

Sights in **Guaymas:** A beautiful city and great beach resort on a bay of the Gulf of California, surrounded by colorful mountains. There is sensational sportsfishing (marlin, sailfish) here with peak catches from June to October. An unusual variety of seashells, best found during low tides November to March.

Dep. Mexico City	20:30(5+6)	20:30(1)
Dep. Guadalajara	12:00(3)	12:00(1+3)
Arr. Guaymas	N/A(2+4+5)	N/A(1+2+4)
Arr. Nogales	10:20(4)	23:15(4)

(1)Light refreshments. (2)Time not available in 1983. (3)Day 2. (4)Day 3. (5)"El Costeno". Carries air-conditioned sleeping car. (6)Has meal service. Carries dome car Guadalajara-Mexico City and v.v.

Routes South of Mexico City

There are 4 principal train routes south from Mexico City: to Veracruz, Oaxaca, Merida and Ciudad Hidalgo.

Mexico City - Veracruz   1025 + 1101 + 1105

The excellent tropical mountain scenery on this route, including Orizaba Volcano (Mexico's tallest), warrants taking this trip during daylight. It is necessary to bring your own food. Box lunches can be purchased on the lower level of Mexico City's Buenavista Railstation.

Dep. Mexico City   7:18(1+2)   7:34(1+3)   21:32(3+4)
Arr. Veracruz   19:25   19:00   7:00

Sights in **Veracruz:** A very picturesque resort. See the excellent 17th century Palacio Municipal. Look for the silver-decorated tortoise-shell jewelry that is a specialty here. The beautiful Isla de Sacrificios beach. Take the bus marked "Ulua" to see the 16th century San Juan de Ulua Castle on Gallega Island (reached by a road).

Dep. Veracruz   7:25(1+2)   8:00(1+3)   21:30(3+4)
Arr. Mexico City   19:45   19:12   7:37

(1)Has only second-class coach cars. (2)Takes the route via Jalapa. (3)Takes the route via Esperanza. (4)Air-conditioned train. Carries sleeping car.

Mexico City - Uruapan   1086

Dep. Mexico City   6:55   21:29(1) | Dep. Uruapan   6:35   19:15(1)
Arr. Uruapan   21:05 10:07 | Arr. Mexico City   20:50   7:50

(1)Air-conditioned train. Carries a sleeping car,

Sights in **Uruapan:** Founded in 1540. Tjarascan Indians are native to this area. Their crafts, including outstanding lacquerware, are exhibited at the Guatapara Museum, a 16th century structure noted for its lovely patio.

· Visit Eduardo Ruiz National Park (called "Cupatitzio"), a municipal woodland filled with rustic walks, bubbling streams, ferns and palm trees.

Mexico City - Puebla - Oaxaca 1095

Dep. Mexico City	17:32(1)		Dep. Oaxaca	18:20(1)
Arr. Puebla	22:15(1)		Arr. Puebla	3:30(1)
Arr. Oaxaca	8:05		Arr. Mexico City	8:52

(1)Air-conditioned train. Carries sleeping car and second-class coach car.

Sights in **Puebla:** The beautiful tiles at the Patio de los Azulejos. The great view of many snow-capped volcanoes from the top of Avenida Internacional, and a similar view from the Cathedral's bell-tower.

The marvelous onyx and marble statues, marble floors and gold leaf decor in the Cathedral. Nearby, Casa del Alfenique (Sugar Candy House). The outstanding museum of Mexican history near the forts of Guadalupe and Loreto. The sensational 16th century Talavera tiles in the Museo de Santa Rosa. The 17th century Church of San Critobal.

The fascinating architecture, Indian statues in Santa Maria de Tonantzintla Church, and the excavated pyramid at nearby Cholula. The courtyard and tiled entrance at the Consejo de Justicia. The Cinco de Mayo civic center. The 16th century Theater, oldest in the western hemisphere.

The collection of Talavera pottery and Chinese porcelain in the Museo de Bello. The onyx and souvenir stores on Plaza Parian.

Sights in **Oaxaca:** The arcaded Zocalo Plaza, with the 16th century Cathedral built of pale green stone and, nearby, the fantastic gold leaf and the national museum in Santo Domingo Church. The Saturday Indian market. Do not miss seeing the sculpture and ironwork in the 17th century La Soledad Church. See the view from the monument to Juarez on Cerro de Fortin. Shop for woolen zarapes, gold and silver jewelry, blankets made from cane, green and black pottery, embroidered blankets and clothing, rugs, etc.

The Regional Museum has exhibits of ZapotecIndian treasures from the nearby Monte Alban tombs and Mixtec art from Mitla, another archaeological site on the outskirts of Oaxaca.

Mexico City - Merida 1026 + 1115

Stopovers en route at Palenque and Campeche (to see Mayan ruins) can be arranged. Short excursions from Merida to Uxmal and Chichen-Itza are recommended. A first-class bus to Uxmal leaves Merida at 8:00, returning there at 15:00. Uxmal is an hour drive southwest from Merida. Chichen-Itza is a 2-hour drive east.

Dep. Mexico City	20:10(1)		Dep. Merida	20:00(1)
Dep.			Arr. Campeche	23:10
Coatzacoalcos	14:40(2)		Arr. Palenque	7:56(2)
Arr. Palenque	21:50		Arr.	
Arr. Campeche	5:52(3)		Coatzacoalcos	15:25
Arr. Merida	9:05		Arr. Mexico City	9:15(3)

(1)Air-conditioned train. Carries sleeping car. Also has first and second-class coach car. Meal service Coatzacoalcos-Merida and v.v. (2)Day 2. (3)Day 3.

Sights in **Coatzacoalcos:** An important river and ocean port.

Sights in **Palenque;** Interesting ruins of stone buildings from the 7th and 8th centuries are located only 5 miles from this lovely orchard village. One of these, the pyramid-like Temple of the Inscriptions, was built into the side of a hill. Visitors can descend 65 feet below the entrance to the tomb of a Mayan ruler and see the 12½-foot long carved stone slab that covered a sarcaphagous. The fireflies in this area are so large that a newspaper can be read by the light of a few captured ones.

Sights in **Campeche:** A fortified city, walled in the 17th century for protection from marauding pirates. See the white and vermillion painted wood altars in the 16th century San Francisquito Church. The excellent museum. The rocky seacoast. The museums at the 18th century San Miquel Fort. About 25 miles by road, the Edzna pyramid.

Sights in **Merida:** It is great to sightsee here in a horse-drawn carriage (about $3.00 U.S. per hour). See: The marvelous wrought-iron on the mansions on Paseo de Montejo. The massive Monument of the Flags, the entire history of Mexico in bas-relief. Casa Montejo, home of the man who founded this city in 1542.

The 16th century Cathedral, built from stones of Mayan ruins found on the site. Buy souvenirs at the tremendous public market (traditional Yucatan costumes, embroidered cotton smocks, huaraches, hammocks, mountains of fruit). Maps and advice can be obtained from the English-speaking employees of the Tourist Office on Zocalo Plaza. Take the short bus ride to Progreso Beach to swim and to eat fish, turtle and shrimp. Try the mild regional Yucatan cuisine.

Sights in **Uxmal:** Ruins of the perfectly-proportioned 11th century Mayan buildings that are decorated with intricate stone carvings. One week here might be adequate.

Sights in **Chichen Itza:** The best-preserved Mayan City, spread over an area of 6 square miles.

Mexico City - Tapachula - Ciudad Hidalgo 1025 + 1105

Dep. Mexico City	21:32(1)		Dep. Ciudad Hidalgo	8:30(3)
Arr. Veracruz	7:00(2)		Arr. Tapachula	9:50
Change trains.			Change trains.	
Dep. Veracruz	9:05(3)		Dep. Tapachula	18:10(2)
Arr. Tapachula	8:20(4)		Arr. Veracruz	17:20(3)
Change trains.			Change trains.	
Dep. Tapachula	13:15(3)		Dep. Veracruz	21:30(1)
Arr. Ciudad Hidalgo	14:35		Arr. Mexico City	7:37(4)

(1)Air-conditioned train. Carries sleeping car. Also has first and second-class coach car. (2)Day 2. (3)Second-class only. (4)Day 3.

Sights in **Tapachula:** The extinct Taconah Volcano that towers above the city. Fifteen miles south is the Puerto Madero beach resort.

INTERNATIONAL CONNECTIONS FROM MEXICO

All the schedules for rail travel between Mexico and the United States appear at the start of this section.

The only train connection from Mexico to Guatemala is very difficult, and we advise against attempting this trip until the conditions improve. There is no acceptable lodging in either primitive Ciudad Hidalgo or in equally primitive Tecun Uman, the Guatemalan city on the other side of the border. Furthermore, there is a 16-hour overnight layover and no place for tourists to stay. The final obstacle is that passengers attempting to transfer from Ciudad Hidalgo to Tecun Uman must walk more than one mile in great heat and mucho dust, and a substantial toll charge is exacted to cross the border bridge.

Mexico City - Guatemala City

1105		1151	
Dep. Mexico City	21:32(1)	Dep. Tecun Uman	6:00(3)
Arr. Ciudad Hidalgo	14:35(2)	Arr. Guatemala City	17:30
Change			trains.

(1)Air-conditioned train. Carries sleeping car. (2)Day 2. (3)Second-class only.

Information and Reservations

Because few travel agents book Mexican train travel, you will find the following sources of information and reservations helpful.

LAREDO
Ferrocarril Nacionales de Mexico
P.O. Box 595
Laredo, Tex.

EL PASO
Ferrocarril Nacionales de Mexico
P.O. Box 2220
El Paso, Tex. 79951

NOGALES
Ferrocarril del Pacifico
Calle Internacional No. 10
Nogales, Sonora
Mexico

CALEXICO
Sonora-Baja California Ry.
P.O. Box 3-182
Mexicali, B.C.
Mexico (TEL: 7-21-63 7-21-01)

CHIHUAHUA - LOS MOCHIS
Ferrocarril Chihuahua al Pacifico
P.O. Box 46
Chihuahua, Chih.
Mexico (TEL: 2-22-84)

For return reservations from Mexico City to the U.S., contact: Passenger Traffic Dept., Ferrocarril Nacionales de Mexico, Buenavista Central Station, Mexico 3, D.F., Mexico (TEL: 547-31-90).

UNITED STATES OF AMERICA

There are 2 classes of trains in the U.S.A.: first-class and coach class. Children under 2 travel free. Half-fare for children 2-11 in coach class only. Children over 12 must pay full fare.

On some day trains, first-class service consists of reserved-seat club cars with 2 seats on one side of the aisle and one seat on the other side.

Night trains have variable sleeping accommodations. Most are complete with private wash and toilet facilities. All have doors that can be locked. All sleeping spaces must be reserved in advance.

Roomettes are for one person. The seat used during the day folds over at night, making room for a bed that is lowered from a recess in the wall.

Bedroom is available in 2 different daytime styles, one with a 2-person divan, the other with 2 chairs. At night, the porter makes up one upper bed and one lower bed. Each is 30 inches wide.

Bedroom Suite results when the dividing partition between 2 adjoining bedrooms is removed. Accommodates up to 4 persons and has 2 wash basins and 2 toilets.

Slumbercoach costs much less than other sleeping spaces. Rooms for one or 2 persons are available. Much smaller than other sleeper spaces. Has one upper and one lower bed (each less than 27 inches wide) and private lavatory.

New 2-level Superliner sleeping cars have deluxe, economy, family and special bedrooms. Deluxe sleeps 2 persons and has private wash and toilet facilities. Some have a shower. Economy accommodates one or 2 persons but does not have either private wash or toilet. Family bedroom sleeps 3 adults and 2 children. Special bedrooms with private bath and toilet are available for handicapped persons.

Coaches have 2 seats on each side of the aisle. These seats are adjustable to a semi-reclining position, similar to airplane reclining seats. Certain long-distance trains have reserved-seat coaches with reclining seats and leg rests for overnight journeys.

All Amtrak trains are air-conditioned. Most long-distance trains carry a restaurant car. Some short-distance trains have a snack bar or lounge car with counter food service. Most Amtrak long-distance trains operating west of Chicago carry 2-level Superliner observation-lounge cars with large wrap-around windows for viewing the scenery.

Amtrak's fares are shown in its free timetables, available by writing to: Timetable Dept., Amtrak Distribution Center, P.O. Box 7717, Itasca, Ill. 60143, U.S.A.

Trains in the U.S.A. run through 4 time zones: Eastern, Central, Mountain and Pacific. There is a one-hour difference between each adjacent time zone. Summer schedules are in effect from late April to late October.

U.S.A. TRAIN PASSES

Both U.S.A. National Railpass and U.S.A. Regional Railpasses are sold only *outside* North America. Residents of North America are *not* eligible to buy them. These passes offer unlimited coach travel on all Amtrak trains other than Metroliners and Auto Trains. Coach seats can be upgraded by paying an additional fee for reserved-seat club car or for sleeping car space. For more information, write to: Amtrak International Sales, 400 No. Capitol St., N.W., Washington, D.C. 20001, U.S.A.

U.S.A. National Railpass.   7 days \$265(U.S.), 14 days \$400, 21 days \$535, 30 days \$665. Children under 2 not occupying a separate seat travel free. Half-fare for children 2-11. Children 12 and over must pay full fare.

U.S.A. Regional Railpass.   Unlimited travel for 14 days, allowing unlimited stopovers. One adult pays full price. His or her spouse and children 12-21 pay 50% of the pass price. Children 2-11 pay 25%. The eastern pass is priced at \$125. The price for the western, central and southern passes is \$215 each.

Family U.S.A. Rail Pass.   This pass was cancelled in 1984.

Senior Citizens and Handicapped Persons Roundtrip Discount.   A 25% discount on roundtrip ticket prices for those who prove they are 65 or older and those who offer certification from a physician, a government agency or an organization of handicapped persons that the applicant is handicapped. *Not* offered on many days in holiday periods

Packaged Tours.   Amtrak offers more than 200 different packaged tours (some escorted, some independent), that include transportation and, in some cases, hotels.
Amtrak tour books can be obtained from travel agents or by writing to: Amtrak Distribution Center, P.O. Box 7717, Itasca, Ill. 60143, U.S.A.

Notes for sightseeing in 9 principal U.S. cities appear below.

Boston

The collection of Oriental and Egyptian art at the Museum of Fine Arts. The splendid Italian Renaissance paintings in the Isabella Stewart Gardner Museum. The many outstanding museums of science and industry at Harvard University. The elegant 19th century architecture of the Boston Public Library, which has many fine murals.

The New England Aquarium. Arnold Arboretum. The Massachusetts Institute of Technology. The Museum of Science and the Hayden Planetarium, both in Science Park. The Christian Science Mother Church. Take the Bay Cruise.

Many historic places: Boston Massacre Site. Old South Church. Bunker Hill. The Tea Party Site. Boston Common. Haymarket Square. The Paul Revere House. The ship "Old Ironsides". Old South Meeting House. King's Chapel. Benjamin Franklin's birthplace.

Chicago

The Field Museum of Natural History. Shedd Aquarium, world's largest collection of sealife. Adler Planetarium. The collection of Near East art at Chicago University's Oriental Institute and, near it, a World War II submarine and the Apollo-8 spacecraft in the enormous Museum of Science and Industry. Lincoln Park Zoo. The Picasso statue at Civic Center Plaza. The Chagall mosaic at First National Bank Plaza. The Museum of Contemporary Art. The exhibit of impressionist art at the splendid Art Institute of Chicago.

Los Angeles

You cannot depend on public transportation to sightsee in Los Angeles. To do so by taxi is extremely expensive. Car rental is the solution. See: Olvera Street, across from the railstation. This is where the city began. The incomparable Music Center complex of 3 outstanding theaters and the City Mall, leading from it to City Hall and the Civic Center of city, county, state of California and Federal buildings.

The marvelous interior of the 19th century Bradbury Building. The Coliseum. Site of the 1932 Olympics and also where the 1984 ceremonies and many games will be held. Near it, a splendid Natural History Museum.

Heading west on Wilshire Boulevard toward the Pacific Ocean, the Los Angeles County Museum of Art and, a 2-minute walk from it, the Page Museum of prehistoric mammals and birds at the La Brea Tar Pits. Nearby, Farmers' Market for the finest fruits, vegetables, meats and seafood in the world, also restaurants serving Mexican, Chinese, Italian and American food.

In the Hollywood area: The interesting forecourt at the Chinese Theater, with footprints and handprints of Hollywood's greatest stars from Mary Pickford to Sylvester Stallone. The great musical events at the Hollywood Bowl all Summer.

The many wealthy residential estates in Beverly Hills, Bel Air, Westwood and Brentwood. The Alcoa "Century City" complex, between Beverly Hills and Westwood. Window-shopping the row of high-priced stores on Rodeo Drive in Beverly Hills. The University of California at Los Angeles campus, in Westwood.

The expanse of great beaches on the Pacific Ocean shoreline, from Santa Monica north to Malibu and Oxnard, and south to Newport Beach, Laguna, La Jolla and San Diego. Marineland. The spectacular array of private yachts at both Marina Del Rey (near Los Angeles International Airport) and at Balboa.

For the best chocolate candy in the world, stop at The Nutty Chocolatier, 17200 Ventura Blvd., Encino (in the Town & Country Shopping Center). Nearby, take the guided tours of both Universal Studios (Universal City) and the National Broadcasting Company (Burbank).

Visit the Rose Bowl Stadium, Norton Simon Museum of Art, and Huntington Art Museum, all in Pasadena. Hearst's Castle in San Simeon is a 2½-hour drive by auto from Los Angeles. Disneyland, in Anaheim, is a one-hour drive by auto.

New Orleans

Jazz on Bourbon Street and the Spanish-French architecture in the French Quarter. Absinthe House. Audubon's Little House. Boat tours of the harbor. The view from the top of the 400-foot high International Trade Mart, at the foot of Canal Street. Mardi Gras.

New York City

The Statue of Liberty. The United Nations complex. The view from the top of the Empire State Building. The New York Stock Exchange. The Rockefeller Center complex. The Metropolitan Museum of Art, greatest art museum in the United States. The Whitney Museum of American Art. The Solomon R. Guggenheim Museum. The American Museum of Natural History.

The International Center of Photography. Central Park, but never after dark. The Museum of the City of New York. The Cathedral of St. John the Divine, far more interesting than St. Patrick's, but often neglected by tourists. The exhibition rooms and movies at the country's first capitol, at 26 Wall Street. The museum of Revolutionary War relics and Washington memorabilia at Fraunces Tavern. Guided tours at the Federal Reserve Bank. Chinatown. The Bronx Zoo and Botanical Garden.

Philadelphia

The Liberty Bell and Independence Hall, on Independence Square. Stroll down Elfreth's Alley, one of America's oldest streets, to the Betsy Ross House. Nearby, the grave of Benjamin Franklin. See the hundreds of fine portraits at The Historical Society of Pennsylvania.

The War Library and Museum. Rosenbach Museum. The Pennsylvania Academy of Fine Arts. The Academy of Natural Sciences. The Rodin Museum, largest collection of Rodin sculptures outside Paris. The Philadelphia Museum of Art. The 388-acre food industry park (stores, warehouses, processing plants) called Food Distribution Center.

Performances of the Philadelphia Orchestra at the Academy of Music. The Civic Center Museum. The Franklin Institute of Science Museum. The University Museum.

San Francisco

Fisherman's Wharf. Watch them making chocolate at nearby Ghirardelli Square. The Maritime Museum. The Chinese Museum. The treasures for sale at Gump's store. Chinatown. North Beach. The Presidio. Golden Gate Bridge. The Arboretum and the spectacular exhibits of Far Eastern art at the de Young Memorial Museum, both in the 1,017-acre Golden Gate Park. Fleischacker Zoo, one of the world's best zoos. The pyramidal Transamerica Building. San Francisco Museum of Art. Nob Hill and the cable car ride from there, down California Street.

Seattle

The monorail ride to the 605-foot high tripod Space Needle tower. The Aquarium at Waterfront Park. The 200-acre Arboretum. A tour of Boeing's 747 assembly plant (phone 206-342-4801 for reservations and directions).

The Seattle Art Museum. The more than 1,000,000 used books for sale at Shorey Bookstore. The granite sculptures at Myrtle Edwards Park. The crafts in the specialty shops at Pioneer Square. The pleasure boats anchored along Shilshole Bay Marina.

Take the 2½-hour sightseeing cruise of Puget Sound, from Pier 51 at 10:30 and 13:00. Or go on the ferry-boat ride, starting at the foot of Marion Street.

Washington, D.C.

There is rail service between Washington's Union Station and its National Airport. Take the "Red Line" Subway from the railstation to Metro Center (heart of the city's business district). At Metro Center, transfer to the "Blue Line" Subway, in the direction which services both the Pentagon and the National Airport.

For subway service from Union Station to the Smithsonian complex and to RFK Stadium, take the "Blue Line" at Metro Center, in the opposite direction from the "Blue Line" route to National Airport.

Sights in **Washington:** The many great museums in the Smithsonian Institution complex: The exhibit of balloons, dirigibles, primitive propellor airplanes and on to the Apollo II space ship in the Air & Space wing. The many displays (dinosaurs, Hope Diamond and other gems, etc.) in the Natural History Museum. The many old machines and clothing in the Museum of History & Technology. The marvelous French Impressionist and Italian Renaissance paintings at the National Gallery of Art. The sculptures and mobiles in the circular Hirschorn Museum. The collection of art in the Freer Gallery. Most of the museums are open 10:00-17:30.

See Congress in session. Tours of the House of Representatives and the Senate operate every 15 minutes from 9:00 to 15:45 daily, starting from the Rotunda. Walk up the 897 steps to the top of the 555-foot high Washington Monument obelisk, open 9:00-17:00 daily (also 20:00-24:00 in the Summer). The Reflecting Pool in West Potomac Park. The Jefferson Memorial, open 24 hours. The Lincoln Memorial, always open.

The National Zoo. The National Arboretum, with its large display of azaleas, daffodils and magnolias. The eternal-flame tomb of John F. Kennedy, the Greek Revival Arlington House, and the Tomb of the Unknowns, all in Arlington National Cemetery.

The largest collection of books, maps, newspapers, documents and manuscripts in the world, at the Library of Congress. Guided tours are conducted there Monday-Friday 9:00-16:00.

See the art collections at Corcoran Gallery, Phillips Collection, the National Portrait Gallery and the National Collection of Fine Arts. Take a tour of Federal Bureau of Investigation, every 15 minutes (9:15-16:15, Monday-

Friday) at 13th Street and Pennsylvania Avenue. There is a 25-minute tour of the Bureau of Engraving & Printing (where money is *not* printed as fast as it is spent) Monday-Friday 8:00-11:30 and 12:30-14:00 at 14th and "C" Streets, SW.

Visit the White House for a 40-minute tour Tuesday-Saturday, 10:00-12:00. Tour the Supreme Court when the Court is not in session, Monday-Friday 9:00-16:30 and, when it is in session, 10:00-14:30. Take the short guided bus trip to Mt. Vernon.

MAJOR U.S. RAILSTATIONS

Reservation and Information Telephone Numbers

Albany	(518) 465-9971	Kanasas City (Mo.)	(816) 421-4725
Albuquerque	(505) 242-7816	Las Vegas	(800) 421-8320
Atlanta	(404) 688-4417	Los Angeles	(213) 624-0171
Baltimore	(301) 539-2112	Miami	(305) 371-7738
Boston	(617) 482-3660	Milwaukee	(414) 933-3081
Buffalo	(716) 856-1229	Minneapolis	(612) 339-2382
Chicago	(312) 558-1075	New Orleans	(504) 525-1179
Cininnati	(513) 579-8506	New York City	(212) 736-4545
Cleveland	(216) 861-0105	Oklahoma City	(405) 943-5337
Dallas	(800) 421-8320	Orlando	(305) 843-8460
Denver	(303) 893-3911	Philadelphia	(215) 824-1600
Detroit	(313) 963-7396	Reno	(702) 323-4375
Fort Worth	(817) 336-1010	St. Lous	(314) 241-8806
Houston	(713) 757-1713	San Francisco	(415) 982-8512
Indianapolis	(317) 632-1905	Seattle	(206) 464-1930
Jacksonville	(904) 731-1600	Washington, D.C.	(202) 484-7540

A toll-free phone number for the contiguous 48 states is: **1-800-USA-RAIL.**

TRANSCONTINENTAL RAIL ROUTES

There is a rail route from New York City to Chicago. From Chicago, there are 4 different train routes to the West Coast of the United States.

Another route to the West is from New York City, the long ride via New Orleans.

NEW YORK ROUTES WEST

New York - Albany - Buffalo - Cleveland - Chicago   186 + 240
This route can also be started in Boston, by connecting in Albany.

These trains require reservations, are air-conditioned, have meal service, and carry sleeping cars, Slumbercoach and ordinary coach.

Dep. New York (Gr. Cent.)	19:30	Dep. Chicago (Union)	18:20
Dep. Albany	22:48	Dep. Cleveland (Lakefront)	1:49
Dep. Buffalo (Depew)	3:37	Set your watch forward one hour.	
Set your watch back one hour,		Dep. Buffalo (Depew)	5:04
Dep. Cleveland (Lakefront)	7:04	Arr. Albany	10:00
Arr. Chicago (Union)	12:51	Arr. New York (Gr. Cent.)	13:15

Boston - Albany   186 + 240
These trains require reservations and have meal service.

Dep. Boston (South)	17:14	Dep. Albany	10:00
Arr. Albany	22:38	Arr. Boston (South)	15:30

Detroit - Chicago   300
All of these trains are air-conditioned, have a club car and serve light refreshments.

Dep. Detroit (Mich. Ave.)	8:30	12:30	17:25
Arr. Chicago (Union)	13:05	17:15	22:00
	*	*	*
Dep. Chicago (Union)	9:05	14:05	17:15
Arr. Detroit (Mich. Ave.)	15:35	20:38	23:45

New York - Pittsburgh - Chicago   185 + 310
This route can be started in Washington, with a connection in Philadelphia.

These trains require reservations, are air-conditioned, have meal service, and carry sleeping car, Slumbercoach and ordinary coach.

Dep. New York (Penn.)	14:15	Dep. Chicago (Union)	16:50
Dep. Philadelphia (30th St.)	16:05	Set watch forward one hour.	
Dep. Pittsburgh (Penn.)	23:45	Dep. Pittsburgh (Penn.)	4:15
Set your watch back one hour.		Arr. Philadelphia (30th St.)	11:32(1)
Arr. Chicago (Union)	8:53	Arr. New York (Penn.)	13:22

(1)Stops only for passengers getting off train.

Washington - Cincinnati - Chicago   276
These trains require reservation, are air-conditioned, carry a sleeping car and have meal service.

Both trains run from their origin cities on Wednesday, Friday and Sunday, arriving at their destinations the following day.

Dep. Washington (Union)	21:05	Dep. Chicago (Union)	8:10
		Dep. Cincinnati	16:59
Dep. Cincinnati	10:54	Arr. Washington (Union)	
Arr. Chicago (Union)	17:50		6:56

New York - New Orleans - Houston - Los Angeles

A long (3,417 miles) but interesting route from New York to the West Coast is via New Orleans, where there is more than a 19-hour layover on the trip West and nearly 12 hours when going from Los Angeles to New York. Passengers were once allowed to occupy sleeping space on the train during each overnight stop, but now must make other provision.

Between Phoenix and Los Angeles, "Sunset Limited" rides at the lowest altitude of the Amtrak system: 231 feet (70 meters) *below* sea level, near Niland, California.

These trains require reservation, are air-conditioned, carry a sleeping car and have meal service.

190

Dep. New York
(Penn.) 14:30(1)
Arr. Philaedlphia
(30th St.) 16:01
Dep. Philadelphia
(30th St.) 16:02(1)
Arr. Washington
(Union) 18:00
Dep. Washington
(Union) 18:30(1)
Arr. Atlanta
(Peachtree St.) 7:30(1)Day 2
Dep. Atlanta
(Peachtree St.) 7:45
Set your watch back one hour.
Arr. New Orleans 18:20
Change trains.

193

Dep. New Orleans 13:55(Day 3)
Dep. Houston 22:30(2)
Dep. San Antonio 3:45(3)Day 4
(East Com. St.)
Dep. El Paso 15:30(3)
Set your watch back one hour.
Dep. Phoenix 22:50(3)
Set your watch back one hour.
Arr. Los Angeles 7:40 Day 5

193

Dep. Los Angeles 22:30(4)
Set watch forward one hour.
Dep. Phoenix 6:45(5)Day 2
Set watch forward one hour.
Dep. El Paso 16:45(5)
Dep. San Antonio
(East Com. St.) 5:50(6)Day 3
Dep. Houston 10:25(6)
Arr. New Orleans 20:05
Change trains.

190

Dep. New Orleans 7:30(1)Day 4
Set watch forward one hour.
Arr. Atlanta
(Peachtree St.) 19:15
Dep. Atlanta
(Peachtree St.) 19:35
Arr. Washington
(Union) 8:55 Day 5
Dep. Washington
(Union) 9:30
Arr. Philadelphia
(30th St.) 11:24
Dep. Philadelphia
(30th St.) 11:25
Arr. New York
(Penn.) 12:52

(1)Runs daily. (2)Runs Monday, Wednesday and Saturday. (3)Runs Tuesday, Thursday and Sunday. (4)Runs Wednesday, Friday and Sunday. (5)Runs Thursday, Saturday and Monday. (6)Runs Friday, Sunday and Tuesday.

CHICAGO ROUTES WEST

Here are the schedules for the 5 train services west from Chicago.

Chicago - Minneapolis - Glacier Park - Spokane - Seattle   194 + 412

These trains require reservations, carry a sleeping car, have meal service and are air-conditioned.

Dep. Chicago		Dep. Seattle		
(Union)	14:30	(King St.)	16:50	
Dep. Milwaukee	16:05	Dep. Spokane	0:40	Day 2
Dep. Minneapolis	23:05	Set watch forward one hour.		
Dep. Fargo	3:47 Day 2	Dep. Glacier Park	8:53(1)	
Set your watch back one hour.		Set watch forward one hour.		
Dep. Glacier Park	17:45(1)	Dep. Fargo	2:04	Day 3
Set your watch back one hour.		Dep. Minneapolis	7:25	
Arr. Spokane	1:15 Day 3	Arr. Milwaukee	14:14	
Arr. Seattle		Arr. Chicago		
(King St.)	9:15	(Union)	15:50	

(1)Stops only from late May to mid-September.

Chicago - Denver - Salt Lake City - Reno - Oakland - San Francisco   189+501

Many regard the Denver-Salt Lake City portion of this route to be the most scenic train ride in the U.S.A.   The train reaches heights of more than 9,000 feet, offering marvelous views of the Rocky Mountains.

These trains require reservations, carry a sleeping car, have meal service and are air-conditioned.

Dep. Chicago (Union)	14:50	Dep. San Francisco	11:55(1)	
Dep. Omaha	23:20	Dep. Oakland	12:25	
Set your watch back one hour.		Dep. Reno	18:42	
Dep. Denver (Union)	8:00 Day 2	Set watch forward one hour.		
Dep.		Dep.		
Salt Lake City	22:30	Salt Lake City	6:50	Day 2
Set your watch back one hour.		Dep. Denver	21:20	
Arr. Reno	8:05 Day 3	Set watch forward one hour.		
Arr. Oakland	15:35(1)	Dep. Omaha	7:00	Day 3
Arr. San Francisco	16:05	Arr. Chicago (Union)	15:50	

(1)Bus service Oakland-San Francisco and v.v.

Sights in **Salt Lake City:** The temple and tabernacle of the Mormon Church, in 10-acre Temple Square, at the center of the city.

Visitors can attend recitals on the 11,000-pipe tabernacle organ in a building considered accoustically perfect since it is entirely wood, even to the wood nails that were used in its construction. Performances are offered Monday-Friday at 12:00; on Monday, Tuesday and Wednesday at 19:30; and on Saturday and Sunday at 16:00.

Every day except Sunday, more than 5,000 people of every faith use the Mormon Genealogical Library (50 East North Temple St.), containing statistics on more than one *billion* people who lived and died in 60 countries since 1538. It is open Monday 7:30-18:00, Tuesday-Thursday 7:30-22:00, and Saturday 7:30-17:00.

Chicago - St. Louis - Dallas - San Antonio - Los Angeles   187

These trains require reservations, carry a sleeping car, have meal service and are air-conditioned.

Dep. Chicago		Dep. Los Angeles	22:30
(Union)	17:20	Set watch forward one hour.	
Dep. St. Louis	23:05	Dep. Phoenix	6:45 Day 2
Dep. Dallas	13:15 Day 2	Set watch forward one hour.	
Dep. Fort Worth	14:40	Dep. El Paso	16:45
Arr. San Antonio	21:25	Arr. San Antonio	5:25 Day 3
Dep. San Antonio	3:45 Day 3	Dep. San Antonio	8:45
Dep. El Paso	15:30	Dep. Fort Worth	15:40
Set your watch back one hour.		Dep. Dallas	16:45
Dep. Phoenix	22:50	Dep. St. Louis	7:35 Day 4
Set your watch back one hour.		Arr. Chicago	
Arr. Los Angeles	7:40 Day 4	(Union)	12:55

Chicago - Kansas City - Albuquerque - Los Angeles   188+470

At Flagstaff, there is bus service to the Grand Canyon (see page 718).
These trains require reservations, carry a sleeping car, have meal service and are air-conditioned.

Dep. Chicago		Dep. Los Angeles	19:45
(Union)	17:45	Set watch forward one hour.	
Dep. Kansas City	1:25 Day 2	Dep. Flagstaff	6:26 Day 2
Dep. Dodge City	7:45	Dep. Albuquerque	13:05
Set your watch back one hour.		Set watch forward one hour.	
Dep. Albuquerque	17:30	Dep. Dodge City	0:11 Day 3
Dep. Flagstaff	21:46	Dep. Kansas City	6:55
Set your watch back one hour.		Arr. Chicago	
Arr. Los Angeles	9:00 Day 3	(Union)	15:00

Chicago - New Orleans   184

These trains require reservations, carry a sleeping car, have meal service and are air-conditioned.

Dep. Chicago		Dep. New Orleans	15:20
(Union)	18:35	Dep. Memphis	22:41
Dep. Memphis	5:05 Day 2	Arr. Chicago	
Arr. New Orleans	12:40	(Union)	9:25 Day 2

EASTERN SEABOARD TRAIN ROUTES

Boston - New York City - Philadelphia - Washington   220

Note: There are departures not listed here (Cook's Table 260) on the hour and half-hour from New York City to Washington 6:30-21:00 and from Washington to New York City 6:00-20:30.

Dep. Boston (South)	Dep. New York (Penn.)	Dep. Philadelphia (30th St.)	Arr. Washington (Union)
6:35(1+2)	11:25	12:54	14:55
7:40(2+3)	12:25	13:52	15:53
7:45(1+4)	11:45	13:13	14:49
8:35(4+5)	13:20	15:04	17:05
10:30(2+5)	15:25	17:05	19:12
12:40(2+5)	17:25	18:58	21:03
15:45(2+5	20:32	22:17	0:15
17:00(4+6)	20:55	-0-	-0-
17:30(1+2)	22:25	23:58(11)	-0-
29:15(2+3)	24:00	1:41(11)	-0-
22:30(5+7)	3:27	5:32	8:30
-0-	7:20(5+8)	9:06	11:10
-0-	8:52(2+9)	10:13	11:49
-0-	9:25(1+2)	10:58	12:44
-0-	10:25(2+10)	11:50	13:41

Washington - Philadelphia - New York City - Boston   220

Dep. Washington (Union)	Dep. Philadelphia (30th St.)	Dep. New York (Penn.)	Arr. Boston (South)
6:30(1+2)	8:37	10:30	15:15
7:30(2+12)	9:36	11:20	16:04
8:30(2+5)	10:33	12:10	16:48
11:30(5+13)	13:33	15:13	19:58
12:30(2+5)	14:24	15:59	20:32
-0-	-0-	17:16(16+17)	21:11
14:30(2+5)	16:25	18:00(15)	-0-
15:30(2+5)	17:28	19:01	23:44
17:00(14)	18:42	19:59(15)	-0-
17:20(5+8)	19:55	21:45(15)	-0-
22:30(7)	0:39	3:00	8:05
-0-	5:55(1+4)	8:00	11:15

(1)Daily, except Sun. and holidays. (2)Has parlor car. Light refreshments. (3)Sun. and holidays only. (4)Res. required. Light refreshments. (5)Daily. (6)Daily, except Sat. Terminates in N.Y. (7)Carries sleeping car. Light refreshments. (8)Res. required. Meal service. (9)Mon.-Fri., except holidays. (10)Sat. only. (11)Terminates in Phil. (12)Sun. only. (13)Has parlor car. (14)Res. req. Daily, except Sat. Terminates in New Haven. (15)Terminates in New Haven. (16)Light refreshments. (17)Res. required. Daily, except Sat.

New York - Philadelphia - Washington - Miami   182+183
These trains require reservations, carry a sleeping car, have meal service and are air-conditioned.

	183	182
Dep. New York (Penn.)	9:25	15:35
Dep. Philadelphia (30th St.)	11:02(1)	17:18(1)
Dep. Washington (Union)	13:50(1)	19:50(1)
Arr. Miami	12:39(2)	16:43(2)

*   *   *

	182	183
Dep. Miami	9:04	14:32
Arr. Washington (Union)	6:05(2+3)	13:45(2+3)
Arr. Philadelphia (30th St.)	8:55(3)	16:30(3)
Arr. New York (Penn.)	10:32	18:03

(1)Stops only to take boarding passengers. (2)Day 2.   (3)Stops only to allow passengers to get off train.

Western Train Routes

Los Angeles - Las Vegas - Salt Lake City   191+535
"Desert Wind" eastbound connects in Salt Lake City with "Zephyr" heading east to Denver and Chicago. "Zephyr" westbound from Chicago and Denver connects in Salt Lake City with "Desert Wind" heading west to Las Vegas and Los Angeles.

These trains require reservations, carry a sleeping car, have meal service and are air-conditioned.

Dep. Los Angeles 13:55	Dep. Salt Lake City 22:35
Arr. Las Vegas 20:35	Set watch back one hour.
Set watch forward one hour.	Arr. Las Vegas 6:10 Day 2
Arr. Salt Lake City 6:20 Day 2	Arr. Los Angeles 13:30

Los Angeles - San Diego   571
Amtrak has a one-day independent tour package from Los Angeles to San Diego and return, which includes rail fare, transfers between the San Diego railstation and the exceptional San Diego Zoo, admission to the Zoo, a 40-minute guided bus tour of the 100-acre wildlife facility, and a ride on the Zoo's aerial tram. Another San Diego attraction: Sea World.

These trains are air-conditioned and have light refreshments.

Dep. Los Angeles	8:00	10:10	13:00	14:50	17:00(3)
Arr. San Diego	10:45	12:55	15:45	17:35	19:45

*   *   *

Dep. San Diego	5:15(1)	7:00	9:10	11:20(2)	13:00(4)
Arr. Los Angeles	7:55	9:40	11:55	14:05	15:45

(1)Runs Monday-Friday, except holidays. (2)Runs Saturdays, Sundays and holidays. (3)Plus other departures from Los Angeles at 17:55(1), 18:55(2) and 19:45. (4)Plus other departures from San Diego at 16:00, 17:15 and 19:40

Los Angeles - Oakland (San Francisco) - Portland - Seattle   192

A very Scenic route: seacoast, forests, snow-capped mountains.

These trains carry sleeping cars, are air-conditioned and have meal service.

Dep. Los Angeles	10:15		Dep. Seattle	
Arr. Oakland	20:25(1)		(King St.)	11:05
Dep. Oakland	20:50		Arr. Portland	15:05
Arr. Portland	14:15(2)		Dep. Portland	15:15
Dep. Portland	14:25		Arr. Oakland	7:55(1+2)
Arr. Seattle (King St.)	18:25		Dep. Oakland	8:30
			Arr. Los Angeles	18:55

(1)Bus service to/from San Francisco connects with arrival/departure. (2)Day 2.

Portland - Seattle   585

Here are all the schedules for this route. These trains are air-conditioned.

Dep. Portland	8:00(1)	14:25(2)	16:40(3)
Arr. Seattle (King St.)	11:50	18:25	20:30
	*	*	*
Dep. Seattle (King St.)	7:00(3)	11:05(2)	17:30(1)
Arr. Portland	10:50	15:05	21:20

(1)Light refreshments. (2)Reservation required. Meal service. (3)Meal service.

Portland - Spokane   194

This is a spur off the Seattle-Spokane-Chicago route. The train passes through the historic Columbia River Gorge, following the path of the Lewis and Clark expedition. Unfortunately, the best scenery is passed during night hours. The train unites in Spokane with the Seattle-Chicago service.

These trains require reservations, carry a sleeping car, are air-conditioned and have meal service.

Dep. Portland	16:50		Dep. Spokane	1:45
Arr. Spokane	0:01		Arr. Portland	8:35

Salt Lake City - Boise - Portland - Seattle   195+530

Dep. Salt Lake City			Dep. Seattle (King St.)	7:00
(4th West St.)	22:30		Dep. Portland	10:55
Dep. Boise	6:25		Set watch forward one hour.	
Set your watch back one hour			Dep. Boise	22:40
Arr. Portland	16:35		Arr. Salt Lake City	
Arr. Seattle (King St.)	20:30		(4th West St.)	6:35

San Francisco - Oakland - Reno   501

These trains require reservations, are air-conditioned and have meal service.

Bus		Train	
Dep. San Francisco		Dep. Reno	8:05
(Transbay Ter.)	11:35	Arr. Oakland	15:35
Arr. Oakland	11:55	Change to bus.	
Change to train.		Dep. Oakland	15:50
Dep. Oakland	12:25	Arr. San Francisco	
Arr. Reno	18:42	(Transbay Ter.)	16:10

Sights in **Reno:** Many gambling casinos. Nearby are gold-mining ghost towns and beautiful Lake Tahoe.

SCENIC RAIL TRIPS

The schedules for these 8 scenic train rides appear earlier in this section.

Salt Lake City - Denver (501)
This route reaches a height of more than 9,000 feet and provides marvelous views of the Rocky Mountains.

Salt Lake City - Seattle (530)
This route goes through 2 of the most scenic river valleys in North America: the Snake River Valley in southern Idaho and the Columbia River Valley through Oregon and Washington State.

Reno - Oakland - San Francisco (501)
Excellent mountain scenery of the High Sierra can be seen on this portion of the Ogden-San Francisco ride.

Los Angeles - Seattle (192)
Very fine views of the Pacific seacoast, forests and snow-capped mountains.

Raton Pass (470)
Crossing the Colorado-New Mexico state line (Chicago-Albuquerque-Los Angeles route), the train goes over the 7,588-foot high Raton Pass.

Glacier National Park (412)
Fifty-six miles of glaciers and soaring peaks can be seen as the Chicago-Havre-Seattle route passes through Glacier National Park.

New York City - Albany (186+240)
The train follows the beautiful Hudson River for 142 miles on this trip. You also travel along Lake Champlain.

Washington - Cincinnati (276)
Beautiful mountain scenery on the West Virginia portion of this ride. Unfortunately, most of that area is traveled at night on Amtrak's schedule.

Two Alaskan Scenic Rail Trips

The last run of the "White Pass" was on October 8, 1982 as a consequence of the closing of all mines in the Yukon during 1982 (which caused severe unemployment in the area) and the simultaneous decrease in tourism that year. The following description has been retained in the hopes that the line will re-open after this edition has been published.

One of the most scenic rail trips in the U.S. and Canada required a bit of doing to get on board. It is the Skagway-Lake Bennett portion of the White Pass Railway's route in Alaska and British Columbia, which connects Whitehorse on the Alcan Highway with the port of Skagway.

The scenery equals many of the most glorious train trips in Europe.

A special roundtrip excursion train operated daily from early June to late September.

We made this 41-mile, narrow-gauge ride by taking a cruise ship from Vancouver, B.C. up the West Coast of Canada and then north to Ketchikan and Juneau, before reaching Skagway.

Cruise ships docked in Skagway in early morning so that passengers could connect with the train's 10:00 departure. After arriving in Bennett, there was adequate time to visit the old Gold Rush church and take pictures of the lakeshore. Included in the tour fee was a prospector's lunch of beef stew, baked beans, apple pie and beverage served in the large Bennett station restaurant, which can accommodate 900 persons.

The train, varying from 5 to 10 cars long depending on the day's passenger volume, arrived back in Skagway early enough to allow a few hours for wandering Skagway's dismal streets, haunting its "frontier" bars, and selecting cheap souvenirs before one's ship pulled anchor.

A few minutes after leaving Skagway, watch out the right-hand side of the train for the very small goldrush graveyard, only a few feet to the side of the track. The train climbs along the edge of mountains for an hour before reaching a plateau at the summit. This ascent of 2,885 feet is made in only 21 miles, with a grade of 4% at one point. During the ascent, there is a great view looking down at Skagway and up at the snow-topped mountains.

The final stretch, into Bennett, has excellent scenery, including many cold-blue indigo ponds and dwarfed pine trees. Other sights en route are the 100-ton granite Black Cross Rock, Bridal Veil Falls, Dead Horse Gulch (where 3,000 pack animals died while carrying the prospectors' supplies) and Beaver Lake.

Now deserted, except for a few railstation employees, Bennett was where more than 10,000 men built rafts and crude boats in 1898 to get themselves and their equipment up the Yukon River to the Klondike gold fields. Highest point on the complete Skagway-Whitehorse route is 2,916 feet, at Log Cabin, B.C.

Because Alaska coastal ferries carry vehicles, tourists could reach the White

Pass Railway without being on an Inland Passage cruise as we wereᶜeither by auto, auto plus trailer, or camper.

Vehicles must be delivered to the railway station in Skagway before 7:30 and in Whitehorse no later than 6:00 on the day of travel on the railroad, and passengers must travel on the same train. Advance reservations are mandatory. Write to: White Pass & Yukon Route, P.O. Box 2147, Seattle, WA. 98111, U.S.A.

Vehicles are *not* accepted for transportation that are over 30 feet long, or over 11'6" high, or over 7'6" wide. Also unacceptable are Fifth Wheel trailer units and motorcycles, canoes or boats that are not attached to a vehicle.

This service allows motoring up the Alcan Highway to Whitehorse, traveling to Skagway by train, and then continuing from Skagway by ferry south to Juneau, Sitka, Petersburg, Wrangell, Ketchikan or Prince Rupert.

Or, one can first ferry to Skagway, train to Whitehorse, and then proceed by auto or camper either north to Mayo, Dawson, Tok, Fairbanks and Anchorage . . . or south to Prince George and Vancouver.

Ferry and train space for vehicles is far less than the demand. Arrangements should be made far in advance through a travel agent.

After gold was discovered in the Klondike Valley, early prospectors landed at Skagway and carried their outfits the 40-mile walk (mostly uphill) to Lake Bennett, proceeding from there to the gold fields by boat on the Yukon River. It soon became impossible to provide the growing population in the Klondike with adequate supplies.

Construction of the White Pass and Yukon Route started on May 27, 1898. The summit was reached on February 18, 1899, and transportation from Skagway to Bennett was completed on July 6 of that year, the first train to run in Alaska. Rail service from Bennett to Whitehorse began on July 29, 1900.

This was one of the most difficult railroad constructions ever engineered. Supplies had to be brought 1,000 miles, from Seattle, on small coastal steamships. There was no heavy construction equipment. Workers had only horses, shovels and black powder to cut through barriers of solid rock.

Skagway - Bennett - Whitehorse   905

These were the schedules in 1982.

Trains have a 60-minute meal stop in Bennett.

Dep. Skagway	8:00(1+3)	10:00(2+3)	19:45(2)
Arr. Bennett	11:20	12:45	22:55
Dep. Bennett	12:20	13:45	23:55
Arr. Whitehorse	15:30	17:00	3:30
	*	*	*
Dep. Whitehorse	8:00(1+3)	9:45(2+3)	19:45(2)
Arr. Bennett	11:30	12:50	22:55
Dep. Bennett	12:30	13:50	23:55
Arr. Skagway	15:30	16:15	3:30

(1)Runs Monday-Friday, except holidays. Operates early October to late May. (2)Runs daily. Operates early June to late September. (3)Has parlor car. Carries passengers' vehicles (autos, campers, trailers, etc.), which may *not* exceed 7'6" in width, 30' in length and 11'6" in height.

All persons with the vehicle must travel on the same train that transports the vehicle. Space for vehicles must be reserved in advance of travel date. Vehicles must be delivered to the railstation before 8:00 and are not carried on Sundays.

Mt. McKinley Park Rail Route

Completed in 1923, the Alaska Railroad's 356-mile line from Anchorage to Fairbanks with Vistadome cars ranks among the world's most exotic train journeys. Fairbanks is only 160 miles south of the Arctic Circle. In Summer, there are 20 hours of daylight every day here.

Reservations are required at least 2 weeks in advance of travel date. Write to: Pouch 7-2111, Anchorage, Alaska 99510, U.S.A. Telephone: (907) 265-2685

This railway, first surveyed in 1914, provides access to North America's highest mountain, Mt. McKinley (20,320 feet). Construction began in 1915. The temperature on this route ranges from 100(F) in Summer to -70(F) in Winter. Seventy-pound cabbages are produced in the Matanuska Valley.

Connected with this line is another that proceeds south from Anchorage to Portage, running east from Portage to Whittier. Only freight service is operated Anchorage-Seward, with the exception of special charter passenger trains. The shuttle service between Portage and Whittier is run for the State of Alaska.

The Anchorage-Fairbanks line affords many interesting travel possibilities: an easy one-day roundtrip Anchorage-McKinley Park-Anchorage, another easy one-day roundtrip Fairbanks-McKinley Park-Fairbanks, the complete ride from Anchorage to Fairbanks (and vice versa), and the complete Anchorage-Fairbanks or Fairbanks-Anchorage ride with a stopover at the McKinley Park resort.

Inside the 3,030 square mile national park are 3 other prominent mountains: Mt. Foraker (17,000 feet), Mt. Hunter (14,960 feet) and Mt. Russell (11,500 feet). On some Summer days, Mt. McKinley and Mr. Foraker are clearly visible from Anchorage, more than 150 miles to the South. .

Headquarters for park activities is the McKinley Park Station Hotel, built in 1972 and operated by a private firm, with accommodations for 275 guests. The hotel is open from late May to late September. A highway links the hotel with such points of interest as Sable Pass, Polychrome Pass, Caribou Pass, Toklat Creek, Igloo Creek, Camp Eilson, Wonder Lake, Camp Denali and Richardson Highway.

If making hotel reservations *prior* to April 15, write to: Outdoor World Ltd., 451 Park View Dr., Suite 9, Sacramento, CA 95825, U.S.A. If making reservations *after* April 15, write to: McKinley Park, Alaska 99755, U.S.A.

Caribou, giant Alaska moose, 33 other mammals and 112 kinds of birds comprise the animal life in the park. There are grizzly bears and 200-pound mountain sheep to be seen there. Salmon and trout abound in the nearby lakes, streams and rivers.

The hotel offers 2 guided tours. One starts at 6:00, so as to have maximum opportunity to observe wildlife. For late sleepers, a second tour starts at 15:00.

Both McKinley Park Station Hotel and McKinley Village provide free transportation from the train station to the free shuttle bus, which runs through the park on an hourly basis.

A 2-hour "Hills of Fire Tour" leaves McKinley Park Station Hotel at 16:30. Pack trips in and around the park are also available.

Some of the interesting points along the route from Fairbanks to Anchorage are: College, where the northernmost institution of higher education in the world is located, the University of Alaska. Dunbar, from which trails lead to a gold-mining district. (It is F 70 degrees below zero here in the Winter.) Clear, a military post. Mountain sheep, between Healy and McKinley Park, Honolulu, with many beaver dams, on the western side of the track. Hurricane Gulch, which the train crosses on a bridge that is 296 feet above the creek. From Mt. McKinley Station to Chulitna, there are (weather permitting) splendid views of Mt. McKinley, and then such views again from Curry to Nancy.

Anchorage

Alaska's largest city (200,000 population). Named for Captain Cook having anchored his ships here in 1778. See the National Park Service movies 12:15 and 14:30 at the NPS Information Center at 540 West Fifth Ave. Subjects covered in the film are park lands, Alaskan history and the northern environment (Canada and Alaska).

Also see the traditional prospector's log cabin, which houses the Visitor Information Center at Fourth Ave. and "F" Street. The 139-foot high Sitka spruce flagpole at the City Hall. Eskimo, Aleut and Athabascan Indian artifacts at the Historical and Fine Arts Museum, 121 West Seventh Ave.

There are good buys here in fox, mink, seal, beaver, muskrat, wolf and coyote furs. Also Eskimo carvings (scrimshaw) in whalebone, walrus ivory, jade and soapstone.

Anchorage - McKinley Park - Fairbanks   900

All of these trains have meal service and are air-conditioned. Sixty thousand people ride this route every year.

Dep. Anchorage	8:00(1+2)	9:00(2+3+4)	9:45(1+5)
Dep. McKinley Park	14:05(1+2)	16:45(2+3+4)	16:25(1+5)
Arr. Fairbanks	17:30	20:55	20:15
	*	*	*
Dep. Fairbanks	9:00(2+3+6)	10:00(1+2)	11:30(1+7)
Dep. McKinley Park	13:00(2+3+6)	13:25(1+2)	15:00(1+7)
Arr. Anchorage	20:40	19:30	22:15

(1)Operates mid-May to mid-September. (2)Has domecar. (3)Operates mid-September to mid-May. (4)Runs Saturday only. (5)Runs Monday, Thursday and Saturday. (6)Runs Sunday only. (7)Runs Tuesday, Friday and Sunday.

Anchorage - Portage - Whittier   902

All of these trains run only Wednesday, Friday and Sunday, have light refreshments and carry autos.

About 100,000 people ride this route every year, along the Portage Glacier.

Dep. Anchorage	13:00	-0-		Dep. Whittier	17:10	19:30
Dep. Portage	15:20	18:20		Dep. Portage	17:45	20:10
Arr. Whittier	15:55	18:55		Arr. Anchorage	-0-	21:40

INTERNATIONAL ROUTES FROM THE UNITED STATES

All of the schedules for train trips to Mexico appear earlier in this chapter, in the section on "Mexico".

U.S. gateways for train trips to Canada are: Boston, New York, Detroit and Seattle.

Boston - Springfield - Montreal
These trains require reservations, are air-conditioned and have meal service.

214		215	
Dep. Boston (South)	17:15	Dep. Springfield	1:12(1)
Arr. Springfield	19:30	Arr. Montreal (Cent.)	10:05
Change trains.			

(1)Carries a sleeping car. Also has Slumbercoach.

New York - Montreal
Both trains have meal service and are air-conditioned.

	229	215
Dep. New York (Grand Central)	10:35	-0-
Dep. New York (Penn.)	-0-	21:45(1)
Arr. Montreal (Windsor)	19:23	-0-
Arr. Montreal (Central)	-0-	10:05

(1)Reservation required. Carries a sleeping car. Also has Slumbercoach.

New York - Toronto   67
There is excellent Hudson River scenery for 142 miles after leaving New York City. You also travel along Lake Champlain. Sit on the left side of the train when going to Toronto, on the right side when going to New York City. The train crosses the gorge below Niagara Falls.

These trains have meal service and are air-conditioned.

Dep. New York (G.C.)	8:45	Dep. Toronto		9:05
Dep. Niagara Falls (USA)	17:40	Arr. Niagara Falls (USA)		11:50
Arr. Toronto	20:30	Arr. New York (G.C.)		20:37

Detroit - Windsor - Toronto   67
These trains have light refreshments.

Take a taxi from Detroit through the International Tunnel to Windsor.

Dep. Windsor (Walkerville)	7:00(1)	8:30	10:10(2)
Arr. Toronto (Union)	11:05	12:35	14:30

(1)Runs daily, except Sundays and holidays. (2)Plus other departures from Windsor at 12:35, 14:50 and 18:00.

Seattle - Vancouver

In 1981, this train service was replaced by bus transportation between Amtrak's Seattle terminal and VIA Rail Canada's station in Vancouver, allowing for connection with the Vancouver-Montreal train.

ADDENDUM

Earlier in this section, schedules appear for the Chicago-Albuquerque-Los Angeles route, including a stop at Flagstaff. Here are the bus services between Flagstaff and the Grand Canyon.

There are guided tours at Grand Canyon.

Flagstaff - Grand Canyon   (Bus) 542

| Dep. Flagstaff | 9:15 | Dep. Grand Canyon | 17:00 |
| Arr. Grand Canyon | 11:20 | Arr. Flagstaff | 18:50 |

Chapter 16

CENTRAL AMERICA and WEST INDIES

COSTA RICA

Children under 3 travel free. Half-fare for children 3-10. Children 11 and over must pay full fare.

There are no train connections from Costa Rica to adjacent countries. It is possible to travel by train in Costa Rica from the Caribbean (Limon) to the Pacific Ocean (Puntarenas). This is the only rail route in Costa Rica for which reliable timetables are available. En route, the train passes through Cartago and San Jose, the country's capital. All tracks in Costa Rica are narrow-gauge.

Cartago

See the tiny (under 6 inches tall) statue of La Negrita, the legendary Indian Virgin, in the Basilica of Our Lady of the Angels. This is the location where a primitive structure was built in 1715 on the place where the Virgin Mary is believed to have appeared to a peasant girl. Pilgrims come from all over Central America to see "La Negrita". The Sunday market in Cartago is an interesting event. Take the short bus trip to see the crater of Irazu Volcano.

Limon

Millions of bunches of bananas are exported from this seaport every year. See the gardens in Vargas Park.

San Jose

The capital of Costa Rica. See: The National Theater, with its statues, gold-decorated foyer and marble staircases. The excellent collection of pre-Columbian (as far back as 10,000 B.C.) ceramic and stone vases, figurines, tools and other antiques in the National Museum, open daily except Monday, 9:00-17:00. Thousands of pre-Columbian jade birds, ornaments, musical instruments and human figures at the Jade Museum (in the Insurance Building on Calle 17), open daily except Monday, 10:00-16:00. The National Liquor Factory, in Parque Espana. Frescoes of Costa Rican life in the Salon Dorado at the old La Sabana Airport, now an enormous park.

See the colored glassware and carved wood pieces sold at the government craft center, next to Soledad Church. The leather goods for sale at Caballo Blanco on Moravia Church Plaza. There are all-day bus tours to the Monteverde Cloud Forest, a 4,000-acre biological reserve. Cool at its 4,500-foot altitude, the reserve has 2,000 species of plants and 320 of birds.

San Jose - Cartago - Limon   1402

NOTE: This trip leaves from the San Jose railstation that is located on the northeast side of Parque Nacional !

There is extraordinary scenery on this 102-mile train trip, which takes about 7 hours partly because of the nature of the route (scores of tunnels, bridges and hairpin curves as you descend 5,000 feet to sea level) and partly due to the fact that there are 52 scheduled stops in addition to some unscheduled ones.

It cost thousands of lives (yellow fever, dysentery, beriberi) to build this line between 1871 and 1890. In the area of the 20 miles leading into Limon, it has rained as much as 35 inches in a 30-hour period.

Tres Rios, the first stop on the ride from San Jose, is in the heart of the coffee country. Then come dense rain forest jungles, swamps, waterfalls, hibiscus, poinciana trees, sugar cane, the rampaging Reventazon River, coconut trees, orchids and many other wildflowers. The train makes one 3,000-foot descent in 30 minutes.

You can visit a Chinese general store during a 5-minute stop in Bataan, a Chinese community. White, sandy beaches along the Caribbean come into view during the last 12 miles, before arriving in Limon.

En route, Indian vendors offer hot coffee, watermelon slices, cashews, corn on the cob, mangoes, hard-boiled eggs, cold chicken and guava juice. There is a 26-minute airplane flight (about $10 U.S.) you can take for the return to San Jose.

Dep. San Jose (Atlantico)	8:10	12:20	17:30(1)
Dep. Cartago	9:15	13:15	18:20
Arr. Limon	14:55	17:40	23:15
	*	*	*
Dep. Limon	6:10	8:15	18:25(1)
Dep. Cartago	11:15	14:06	23:46
Arr. San Jose (Atlantico)	12:00	15:00	0:35

(1)Runs Friday, Saturday and Sunday.

San Jose - Puntarenas   1400

NOTE: This train departs from the San Jose railstation that is located at the south end of the city !

Dep. San Jose (Pacifico)	6:00	9:15	15:15	17:15
Arr. Puntarenas	9:00	13:15	19:15	20:15

Sights in **Puntarenas:** Good sea bathing and fishing (shark and tuna) here. An inexpensive boat ride ($1.00 U.S.) takes you on Sunday mornings to San Lucas Island, with its great El Coro beach. Because it is a penal colony, your guide on San Lucas will be an English-speaking prisoner !

Dep. Puntarenas	6:00	10:00	15:00	18:00
Arr. San Jose (Pacifico)	9:00	14:00	19:00	21:00

CUBA

Children under 5 travel free. Half-fare for children 5-11. Children 12 and over must pay full fare.

The 4 rail trips from Habana are west to Pinar del Rio and Guane, a short trip east to Matanzas, and the route southeast to both Cienfuegos and to Santiago de Cuba.

Habana

This is the largest, most cosmopolitan and most beautiful city in the Caribbean.

See: El Morro Castle. The view from the tower of the city's oldest fort, La Fuerza. Marvelous gardens in Parque Central. Vermay paintings in El Templete on Plaza Carlos Manuel Cespedes. The patio at the former palace of the Captain's General, on the west side of the Plaza Cespedes.

The lovely interior of La Merced Church. The view from the east tower of the Cathedral. The National Museum in Palacio de Bellas Artes. The Botanical Gardens on Avenida Allende. The Museum of Natural Sciences, in the Capitol building. The Museum of the Revolution, in the Presidential Palace. The statues and mausoleums in the outstanding Colon Cemetery. Ernest Hemingway's home, maintained as it was when he lived there in 1960. The art gallery, carnival rides, equestrian center and restaurants in the enormous Lenin Park. The tremendous monument to Jose Marti, a leader of the last century's revolution against Spain, in the Plaza of the Revolution, competing with the enormous picture on a government building of Che Guevara, who helped Fidel Castro overthrow Batista in this century.

Santiago de Cuba

See The Colonial Museum.

Habana - Pinar del Rio - Guane   1511

Dep. Habana (Central)	5:55(1)	-0-	-0-	-0-
Dep. Habana (Tulipan)	-0-	9:55(2)	14:00(1+2)	21:00(2)
Arr. Pinar del Rio	N/A(1)	13:32	N/A(1)	0:41
Change trains.				
Dep. Pinar del Rio	12:30	18:05	17:50(2)	7:30
Arr. Guane	14:37	20:34	19:25	9:51
	*	*	*	
Dep. Guane	5:10(1)	10:37	15:30	20:10(1+2)
Arr. Pinar del Rio	N/A(1)	13:02	17:45	N/A(1)
Change trains.				
Dep. Pinar del Rio	7:53	15:25(2)	4:15(2)	21:50(2)
Arr. Habana (Tulipan)	-0-	19:16	8:06	1:44
Arr. Habana (Central)	15:20	-0-	-0-	-0-

(1)Direct train. No train change in Pinar del Rio. (2)Air-conditioned train. Light refreshments.

Habana - Matanzas 1510

Dep. Habana (C.B.)	4:50	8:00	11:35	14:55	18:12	21:25
Arr. Matanzas	7:30	10:45	14:20	17:41	20:53	0:05

*   *   *

Dep. Matanzas	4:45	7:57	11:35	14:51	18:09	21:20
Arr. Habana (C.B.)	7:27	10:40	14:20	17:39	21:51	0:03

Habana - Cienfuegos 1515

Dep. Habana (Tulipan)	7:00(1)	-0-	13:00(1)	23:17(1)
Dep. Habana (Central)	-0-	7:30	-0-	-0-
Arr. Cienfuegos	12:26	16:46	18:25	4:30

*   *   *

Dep. Cienfuegos	0:05(1)	6:35(1)	7:27	15:22(1)
Arr. Habana (Central)	-0-	-0.	16:40	-0-
Arr. Habana (Tulipan)	5:23	12:09	-0-	20:55

Air-conditioned train. Light refreshments.

Habana - Santiago de Cuba 1520

Dep. Habana (Central)	2:00(1)	18:00(2)
Arr. Santiago de Cuba	20:20	8:47

*   *   *

Dep. Santiago de Cuba	12:15(1)	18:14(2)
Arr. Habana (Central)	6:18	9:01

(1)First-class only. Light refreshments. (2)Air-conditioned train. Meal service.

EL SALVADOR

Children under 3 travel free. Half-fare for children 3-9. Children 10 and over must pay full fare.

The principal train line in El Salvador is from Cutuco, a seaport on the Pacific Ocean, to inland San Salvador. The only international rail route from El Salvador is a continuation of the Cutuco-San Salvador line into Guatemala. Because El Salvador is largely 2 rows of volcanoes, many volcanoes can be seen on the trips listed here.

Cutuco

This is a popular resort for swimming and fishing.

San Salvador

See Casa Presidencial. The Zoo. Many beautiful parks. The view from the top of Mount Chulul, looking through 2 tremendous vertical rocks called Puerta del Diablo (Devil's Door). Recommended short excursions: to Panchimalco and Lake Ilopango, the crater of San Salvador Volcano, Izalco Volcano and Atecosol Park, Ichanmichen Park, Lake Coatepeque, and Cerro Verde.

Cutuco - San Salvador   1200

Dep. Cutuco	6:30	Dep. San Salvador	6:45
Dep. San Miguel	8:53	Dep. San Vicente	9:05
Dep. Zacatecoluca	11:45	Dep. Zacatecoluca	9:57
Dep. San Vicente	12:43	Dep. San Miguel	12:45
Arr. San Salvador	15:10	Arr. Cutuco	14:50

Sights in **San Miguel:** Fine parks. The statues and fountains at Chinameca Church.

Sights in **Zacatecoluca:** Inchanmichen, the garden park.

Sights in **San Vicente:** El Pilar, the most unique church in El Salvador.

Three other rail routes in El Salvador are: San Salvador-San Jeronimo, San Salvador-Ahuachapan, and San Salvador.Sonsonate.

San Salvador - San Jeronimo   1200

Dep. San Salvador	6:15	Dep. San Jeronimo	12:55
Arr. San Jeronimo	12:20	Arr. San Salvador	18:50

San Salvador - Ahuachapan   1200

Dep. San Salvador	6:15	Dep. Ahuachapan	12:45
Arr. Texis Junction	9:35	Arr. Texis Junction	15:20
Change trains.		Change trains.	
Dep. Texis Junction	9:45	Dep. Texis Junction	15:25
Arr. Ahuachapan	12:20	Arr. San Salvador	18:50

Sights in **Ahuachapan:** The Atehuezian waterfalls. Many geysers. Two lakes draw visitors: Laguna Verde and Apaneca.

San Salvador - Sonsonate   1200

Dep. San Salvador	6:25	14:20	Dep. Sonsonate	6:00	14:00
Arr. Sonsonate	9:55	17:50	Arr. San Salvador	9:40	17:40

Sights in **Sonsonate:** The Sunday market (dairy products, tropical fruits, hides). El Pilar Church. The white porcelain cupola on the Cathedral. It is a 30-minute bus ride from Sosonate to the fine beaches at Acajutla, El Salvador's main seaport.

INTERNATIONAL ROUTE FROM EL SALVADOR

Here is the route from El Salvador to western Guatemala.

San Salvador - San Jeronimo - Anguiatu - Zacapa - Guatemala City

1200

Dep. San Salvador   6:15
Arr. San Jeronimo   12:20(1)
Change trains.

1154

Dep. Anguiatu   13:00(2)
Arr. Zacapa   17:40
Stay overnight in Zacapa.

1152

Dep. Zacapa   13:35(3)
Arr. Guatemala City   19:30

(1)Walk or take bus or taxi ½-mile to Anguiatu. (2)Runs Monday, Wednesday and Friday. (3)Runs Tuesday, Thursday and Saturday.

GUATEMALA

Children under 3 travel free. Half-fare for children 3-11. Children 12 and over must pay full fare.

It is possible to travel in Guatemala by train from the Caribbean (Puerto Barrios) to the Pacific Ocean (Tecun Uman).

Guatemala City

See Mayan treasures in the Archaeological Museum in La Aurora Park, open daily except Monday. A very large collection of Mayan figurines, masks and pottery at Popol Vuh Museum (9 Calle 3-62), open daily except Sunday. Museo Ixchel (4 Avenue 6-27) has a good exhibit of Indian textiles and clothing, open daily except Monday.

The murals, stained-glass and tiled patios and fountains in the National Palace, near Central Park. Next door is the Metropolitan Cathedral. The gold and mahogany altar at Cerro del Carmen Church, and the splendid view of the city from the gardens there.

The marvelous assortment of fabrics at the Central Market. The Botanical Gardens. The Zoo. The National Museum of History and Fine Arts. A display of products made in Guatemala, at the Popular Arts and Handicrafts Center (10 Avenue and 11 Calle). The fish-shaped Templo de la Expiacion. These churches: La Merced, San Francisco, Santa Domingo, Las Capuchinas, and Santa Rosa.

The slide lecture on Mayan archaeology, every night at 19:00 Camino Real Hotel, 9 Calle 4-69.

Take a local bus to the western side of the city to see the Mayan ruins of Kaminal Juyu (Valley of Death). It is a short bus ride to see these nearby Indian villages: Chinautla, San Pedro Sacatepequez and San Juan Sacatepequez.

Visit nearby (28 miles) **Antigua** to see many colonial churches, plazas, fountains and walled palaces where 70,000 people lived before Antigua was destroyed by earthquake in the 18th century. One of the many giant volcanos here is still very active.

Visit nearby (90 miles) **Chichicastenango** for fabulous bargains in strawgoods, fabrics (tablecloths, napkins, etc.) and pottery at the extraordinary Thursday and Sunday markets.

Visit nearby (134 miles) **Quirigua** to see excellent remains of the Mayan Old Empire.

Visit nearby 50-square-mile **Lake Atitlan** to see its beautiful setting amid mountains and volcanos. The lake's color changes constantly.

Puerto Barrios

Nearby beaches are very popular: Escabas and Santo Tomas de Castilla.

Guatemala City - Puerto Barrios   1152

This route goes through many banana plantations and dense jungles. Watch for 3 volcano cones, a short distance from Guatemala City.

Dep. Guatemala City	6:45	Dep. Puerto Barrios	7:00
Dep. Jalapa	9:57	Dep. Zacapa	13:35
Dep. Zacapa	13:25	Dep. Jalapa	16:32
Arr. Puerto Barrios	19:05	Arr. Guatemala City	19:05

Sights in **Jalapa:** The Valley of Monjas, one of the country's most fertile valleys, is near Jalapa.

Sights in **Zacapa:** En route from Guatemala City, a stop is made here for dining at the railstation. This is the junction for the train service to and from El Salvador.

Guatemala City - Esquintla - Mazatenango - Tecun Uman   1151

Dep. Guatemala City	7:05	Dep. Tecun Uman	6:00
Dep. Escuintla	10:19	Dep. Mazatenango	9:55
Dep. Mazatenango	14:35	Dep. Escuintla	14:40
Arr. Tecun Uman	18:35	Arr. Guatemala City	17:30

Sights in **Escuintla:** Famous for fruits and medicinal baths. Nearby are giant sculptures in La Democracia (an archaeological park) and the 13th century ruins at Mixco Viejo.

Sights in **Mazatenango:** The production of tropical fruits, coffee, sugar and cacao.

INTERNATIONAL ROUTES FROM GUATEMALA
There are train connections from Guatemala to El Salvador and Mexico.

Guatemala City - Zacapa - Anguiatu - San Jeronimo - San Salvador

1152		1154	
Dep. Guatemala City	7:00(1)	Dep. Zacapa	6:30(2)
Arr. Zacapa	13:15	Arr. Anguiatu	11:25(3)
Stay overnight in Zacapa.		Change trains.	
		1200	
		Dep. San Jeronimo	12:55
		Arr. San Salvador	18:50

(1)Runs Tuesday, Thursday and Saturday. (2)Runs Monday, Wednesday and Friday. (3)Walk or take bus or taxi ½-mile to San Jeronimo.

Guatemala City - Tecun Uman - Ciudad Hidalgo - Mexico City   1151
Dep. Guatemala City   7:05
Arr. Tecun Uman   18:35

It is possible, although very difficult, to travel by train from Guatemala City into southern Mexico. The reasons we always advise against attempting this trip until conditions improve are:

There is no acceptable lodging in either primitive Tecun Uman or in equally primitive Cuidad Hidalgo, the 2 border cities where a transfer is necessary.

Further, there is an *overnight* interval of 14 hours between arriving in Tecun Uman and departing from Ciudad Hidalgo for Tapachula and on to Vera Cruz and Mexico City.

The final obstacle is that passengers attempting this transfer have to walk more than a mile in great heat and mucho dust from Tecun Uman to Ciudad Hidalgo, and pay a substantial toll charge to cross the border bridge.

1105			
Dep. Ciudad Hidalgo	8:30	Dep. Vera Cruz	21:30(2)
Arr. Tapachula	9:50	Arr. Mexico City	7:37(3)
Change trains.			
Dep. Tapachula	18:10	(1)Day 2. (2)Air-conditioned. Carries	
Arr. Vera Cruz	17:20(1)	a sleeping car. (3)Day 3 from	
Change trains.		Ciudad Hidalgo.	

HONDURAS

The country's rail lines serve banana plantations and 2 seaports.

Children under 3 travel free. Half-fare for children 3-11. Children 12 and over must pay full fare.

Puerto Cortes

Honduras' main port. Very hot climate here. Take the bus ride to see the castle at Omoa.

San Pedro Sula

This is the gateway (by air or bus) for travel to Tegucigalpa. Terribly hot here. The population is cosmopolitan: North American, Irish, Cuban, Russian. Fabulous Mayan ruins are located at Copan, 112 miles by road from San Pedro Sula.

Tela

This seaport ships mountains of bananas. See United Fruit Company's experimental farm in nearby Lancetilla.

San Pedro Sula - Baracoa - Puerto Cortes   1250

Dep. San Pedro Sula	7:00		Dep. Puerto Cortes	15:15
Dep. Baracoa	8:15		Dep. Baracoa	16:15
Arr. Puerto Cortes	9:15		Arr. San Pedro Sula	17:30

San Pedro Sula - Baracoa - Tela   1250

Dep. San Pedro Sula	15:00		Dep. Tela	6:00
Arr. Baracoa	16:05		Arr. Baracoa	7:40
Change trains.			Change trains.	
Dep. Baracoa	16:15		Dep. Baracoa	7:45
Arr. Tela	18:00		Arr. San Pedro Sula	9:00

Tela - Baracoa - Puerto Cortes   1250

Dep. Tela	13:45		Dep. Puerto Cortes	7:00
Dep. Baracoa	16:15		Dep. Baracoa	8:15
Arr. Puerto Cortes	17:15		Arr. Tela	10:30

JAMAICA

Jamaica has 3 rail lines: one from Kingston to Port Antonio, one from Kingston to Montego Bay, and a short line for one-day excursions from Montego Bay to the Appleton Rum Distillery.

Children under 4 travel free. Half-fare for children 4-13. Children 14 and over must pay full fare.

Kingston

The capital and commercial center of Jamaica. Shopping for duty-free items is the key tourist attraction here. See: The carvings and historical items at the Institute of Jamaica. The Royal Botanical Gardens at Hope, only a few minutes away, a fine collection of tropical plants, including many orchids.

Montego Bay

Also popular for its duty-free goods. Take the glass-bottom boat to see the beautiful coral gardens. Much deep-sea fishing, sailing, water skiing, golf and tennis here.

Kingston - Spanish Town - Port Antonio   1550

Dep. Kingston	8:20(1)	13:30(3)	16:15
Arr. Spanish Town	8:52	14:15	16:36
Arr. Port Antonio	-0-(2)	-0-(2)	-0-(2)

Sights in **Spanish Town:** The Cathedral. A broad canvas of Jamaican history and good ethnic exhibits at the Museum. Much fine 18th century English architecture.

Sights in **Port Antonio:** Every ocean sport is excellent here. Try a ride on a bamboo raft, down the Rio Grande, to see lush jungle scenery.

Dep. Port Antonio	-0-(2)	-0-(2)	-0-(2)
Dep. Spanish Town	9:00	11:12(3)	19:40(1)
Arr. Kingston	9:30	11:45	20:20

(1)Runs Saturdays, Sundays and holidays. (2)Service was suspended in 1983. (3)Runs daily, except Sundays and holidays.

Kingston - Montego Bay   1550

Dep. Kingston	7:10	10:40(1)	15:40
Dep. Spanish Town	7:43	11:21(1)	16:14
Arr. Montego Bay	13:00	18:10	21:24

Sights in **Spanish Town:** See notes above, under "Kingston-Spanish Town-Port Antonio".

Dep. Montego Bay	6:45	8:15(1)	15:30
Dep. Spanish Town	12:18	14:55(1)	20:42
Arr. Kingston	12:50	15:30	21:15

(1)Runs daily, except Sundays and holidays.

Montego Bay - Appleton Rum Distillery 1550

The one-day excursion to Appleton and the rum distillery there is very popular. Although there are 3 morning departures from Montego Bay, be sure to take the 9:30 "Catapuda Choo-Choo", for which it is advisable to reserve seats well in advance through either hotels or travel agents in Montego Bay.

This tour package includes the only train on the 34-mile route that has a bar, a guide and calypso band on board, and a layover en route of nearly 2 hours in Catapuda for souvenir shopping. The full-day outing also features a tour of the Appleton Distillery, rum drinks and lunch, plus transportation from your Montego Bay hotel to the railstation and, at end of day, from the railstation back to hotels.

Dep. Montego Bay	6:45	8:15(1)	9:30(2)	15:30
Arr. Catapuda	7:53	9:36	10:15	16:37
Dep. Catapuda	7:56	9:39(1)	12:06(2)	16:40
Arr. Appleton	8:53	10:54	13:55	17:27
		*	*	*
Dep. Appleton	10:57	14:10(3)	15:31(1)	19:21
Arr. Catapuda	11:54	15:14	16:43	20:18
Dep. Catapuda	11:57	15:17(3)	16:46(1)	20:21
Arr. Montego Bay	13:00	16:20	18:10	21:25

(1)Runs daily, except Sundays and holidays. (2)Catapuda Choo-Choo special excursion train. (3)Light refreshments.

NICARAGUA

The only rail route in Nicaragua once went from Corinto on the Pacific Ocean to Leon, Managua, and then to Granada on the shore of Lake Nicaragua. It now runs only from Leon to Granada. There are no rail connections between Nicaragua and adjacent countries.

Children under 3 travel free. Half-fare for children 3-11. Children 12 and over must pay full fare.

Corinto

Nicaragua's main seaport.

Leon

See: The largest Cathedral in Central America. Ancient streets and buildings. The 16th century Subtiava Church. Do not miss the iron cannon at the old colonial bridge, Guadalupe. En route from Leon to Managua, there is a short spur to El Sauce, for which timetables are not available.

Managua

Most of this city was totally destroyed in the 1972 earthquake and has been in the process of being rebuilt since then. Be sure to stroll through the beautiful Parque Central (fountains, statues, stately trees). See the Cathedral and the nearby National Palace.

Masaya

Much Indian handicrafts here. Between Managua and Masaya there is a short spur to Jinotepe and Diriamba, for which timetables are not available.

Granada

This city is at the end of the 114-mile rail line that once began in Corinto. Boats leave from the center of Granada for excursions to islands on Lake Nicaragua, one of the world's most unique phenomenon.

The area of this lake was once part of the Pacific Ocean. Volcano lava formed a fill, separating this area from the ocean, but not until after salt-water species of fish had been cut off from the ocean. Over millions of years, the water changed slowly from salt-water to fresh-water, allowing the sea life time to adapt to the new environment. The only fresh-water sharks in the world inhabit this lake.

Sights to see in Granada: The Jalteva and San Francisco churches. The turtles and baby crocodiles in the fountains at Parque Central. A very interesting cemetery. Ride in a horse-drawn carriage.

Leon - Managua - Masaya - Granada 1300

Dep. Leon	-0-	4:55(1)	-0-	10:35(3)	12:00
Arr. Managua	-0-	7:10(1+2)	-0-	14:05	14:15
Change trains.					
Dep. Managua	5:10	7:15	12:00	-0-	16:00
Dep. Masaya	6:11	8:06	12:51	-0-	17:20
Arr. Granada	6:45	8:40	13:25	-0-	18:05
		*	*	*	
Dep. Granada	-0-	4:45	5:20(1)	10:00	14:00
Dep. Masaya	-0-	5:35	6:05	10:35	14:37
Arr. Managua	-0-	6:50	7:02(1+2)	11:25	15:30
Change trains.					
Dep. Managua	5:00(4)	-0-	7:12	-0-	17:10
Arr. Leon	8:20	-0-	9:30	-0-	19:25

(1)Direct train. No train change in Managua. (2)Estimated arrival time. (3)Runs Wednesday, Friday and Sunday. (4)Runs Tuesday, Thursday and Saturday.

PANAMA

It is possible to travel by train from the Caribbean (Colon) to the Pacific Ocean (Panama City) in 90 minutes. There are on this trip excellent views of the jungle, the canal and the ships passing through the Canal. Sit on the left side for the best view. There are no rail connections between Panama and adjacent countries.

Children under 5 travel free. Half-fare for children 5-14. Children 15 and over must pay full fare. A supplement is charged both children and adults for air-conditioned space.

Panama City

Stroll down Paseo de las Bovedas and see the view from there of the Bay of Panama and the islands offshore (Flamenco, Naos and Perico). See: The President's Palace, called Palacio de las Garzas. The egrets there are worth the visit. The gold altar and famous organ in San Jose Church. The view of the bay from the top of La Cresta. Inca and Spanish treasures in the National Museum. The monument dedicated to the Canal, at Plaza de Francia. Instituto Bolivar. The 17th century Cathedral, facing Plaza de la Independencia.

Panama City - Colon   1500

All of these trains have both air-conditioned class and second-class.

Dep. Panama City   5:00(1)   6:45(1)   8:30(2)   9:50(1) 11:40(1)
                     12:35(2) 15:20(1) 17:05(1) 17:50(2) 21:50(1)
Arr. Colon   90 minutes later

Sights in **Colon:** This is one of the world's busiest ports. See: The old Spanish ruins of Portobelo. The statues on Paseo Centenario. The Cathedral. The Casino. Many nightclubs. Shop for English bone china, ivory, furniture and perfume on Front Street. There are 3 good excursions from Colon: To Gatun Locks and the nearby jungle. To Fort San Lorenzo, at the mouth of the Chagres River. And a boat trip to the San Blas archipelago.

Dep. Colon   4:50(1)   6:40(2)   6:55(1)   9:40(1) 10:45(2)
                    11:50(1) 15:10(1) 16:00(2) 17:15(1) 21:00(2)
Arr. Panama City   90 minutes later

(1)Runs Monday-Friday, except holidays. (2)Runs Saturdays, Sundays and holidays.

Concepcion - Puerto Armuelles   0000 (LTR)

Dep. Concepcion	N/A	Dep. Puerto Armuelles	N/A
Arr. Puerto Armuelles	N/A	Arr. Concepcion	N/A

Chapter 17

SOUTH AMERICA

Winter in South America (south of Colombia and Venezuela) is from June 21 to September 20. Summer is from December 21 to March 20.

AMERAILPASS

Much like the Eurailpass that is valid for 16 countries in Europe, the Amerailpass provides unlimited train travel on first-class, second-class and one-class passenger trains in the 6 countries which are members of The Association of Latin American Railways: Argentina, Bolivia, Brazil, Chile, Paraguay and Uruguay.

The Association recommends 2 major "circuits" that offer extensive variety. Complete details on each leg of these appear in this chapter.

The first circle rail trip includes Buenos Aires, the fantastic Transandine route to Santiago and Valparaiso, then south to Puerto Mont, from which the balance of the journey is the southern transcontinental trip to Bariloche and on to Bahia Blanca, and then north to Buenos Aires.

The second "circuit" consists of Buenos Aires to La Paz, then the transcontinental trip to Sao Paulo and Rio de Janeiro, completed by proceeding south from Sao Paulo to Montevideo and Buenos Aires.

Amerailpass becomes valid on the first day it is used, must be used for the first time within 6 months after the day it is issued, and it stops being valid at Midnight the last day of the validity period. It can be purchased from any of the 6-nation member railroads.

If one's rail itinerary involves a relatively short train ride on the first day and a fairly long ride on the day after the pass ceases to be valid (or vice versa), it can be worthwhile to purchase a ticket for the short ride.

There is no refund if the pass is lost or stolen. An unused pass can be returned to the office where it was purchased for a refund of 85% of the price.

The 1983 prices were: $120(U.S.) for 16 days, $140 for 23 days, $175 for 30 days, and $260 for 60 days. Children 3 to under 12 (based on age as of the first day of using the pass) pay half-fare but can travel only when accompanied by an adult. Children under 3 travel free if they are held and do not Toccupy a separate seat.

Information about Amerailpass can be obtained from the offices listed on the next page.

ARGENTINA

Centro Informaciones de
Ferrocarriles Argentinos
Florida 753
Buenos Aires

ALAF
Av. Cordoda, 883
6 Piso
Buenos Aires 1054

BOLIVA

Empresa Nacional de Ferracarriles, Estacion Central, La Paz

BRASIL

Red Ferroviaria Federal S.A.
Plaza Procopio Ferreira, 86
Rio de Janeiro

Red Ferroviaria Federal S.A.
Plaza de Luz 1
San Pablo

CHILE

Ferrocarriles del Estado de Chile
Subdepartamento de Comercio
Balmaceda 1215=2 Piso
Santiago

Ferrocarriles de Antofagas a Bolivia
Gerencia de Trafico
Antofagasta

PARAGUAY

F.C. "Pte Carlos A. Lopez"
Eligio Ayala y Mexico
Asuncion

URUGUAY

Secretaria de Prensa,
   Publicidad y Turismo
La Paz 1057
Montevideo

In planning trips based on information in this chapter, readers are advised to consider the fact that throughout Eastern Europe, Asia, Africa and Latin America, second-class space is usually primitive and almost always extremely crowded. It is best to reserve first-class space when traveling these areas by train.

As is true of countries in Western Europe, train schedules and ticket prices are always subject to change. **All over the world, departure and arrival times should be re-checked at each leg of a trip.** Where changes have occurred, usually the changes will be slight and have little effect on one's itinerary. Re-checking will help you avoid arriving at a railstation after your train has departed.

Another point that has been repeated throughout this book is that many cities all over the world have 2 or more railstations.

Throughout this book, we have taken pains to tell you the name of the railstation (in parentheses immediately after the name of a city) whenever a city has more than one railstation, so you will not miss a departure by going to the wrong station.

ARGENTINA

Children under 3 travel free. Half-fare for children 3-11. Children 12 and over must pay full fare.

There are 27,000 miles of rail service in Argentina, radiating out from Buenos Aires.

The 6 major rail routes from Buenos Aires are to Rosario (from where one branch continues to Tucuman and Jujuy, via Cordoba, and a second goes to Tucuman and Jujuy via La Banda), the transcontinental route to Mendoza (and on to Valparaiso, Chile, the most exciting rail trip in South America before this was substituted by bus in 1980), and the lines to Santa Rosa, Bahia Blanca (from where one branch continues to Zapala and a second branch goes to Viedma and from there on to San Carlos de Bariloche, gateway to the Lake District), Mar del Plata, and to Posadas.

The connection with Uruguay (and on to Brazil) involves using hydrofoil boat service from Buenos Aires to Colonia and then bus service from Colonia to Montevideo, from where rail service resumes.

There is also connection by rail from Buenos Aires to Asuncion Paraguay.

ARGENTINA'S DISCOUNT RAIL PASS

Boletos de Libre Circulacion.   *Not* transferable. Unlimited first-class train travel. Can be upgraded for sleeping car accommodation by paying the supplemental charge for sleeper space. The validity period begins on the first day the pass is used and ends at 24:00 on the final day.

There is a very small charge for obtaining a refund before starting to use the pass. When a 60-day or 90-day pass has been used any part of the first 30 days, it can be returned to the Argentine Railways for a refund that results in the passenger paying only for a 30-day pass. Similarly, if the 90-day pass is used 31-60 days, it can be returned for a refund that results in paying only the price for a 60-day pass.

The prices for this pass have increased frequently since the end of 1978, as they are indexed to Argentina's inflation. The prices charged in September of 1979 were: 30 days 215,600 Argentine Pesos, 60 days 360,000 (AP), and 90 days 505,700(AP). In November of 1979, those prices in U.S. dollars were: $140, $234 and $328.

Buenos Aires

The railstations here and the routes they serve are: Constitucion (southern), Lacroze (northeastern Paraguay), Once (western), Puente Alsina, Retiro (Chile and Bolivia), and Velez Sarsfield (northwestern).

Stroll the magnificent Avenida 9 Julio. See Colon Opera House. The Museum of Modern Art. Palermo Park and the nearby Zoological and Botanical Gardens. The excellent statues and paintings in the Cathedral. The Museum of Fine Arts. See and hear the inimitable tango in San Telmo, the oldest section of the city, where a fair takes place every Sunday.

Eva Peron's mausoleum, in Recoleta Cemetery. The collection of gaucho artifacts, silver and iron objects, musical instruments and tapestries in the Museo de Motivos de Jose Hernandez (Avenida de Libertador 2373). The tapestries and antiques at the Museum of Decorative Arts and the National Museum of Oriental Art (both at Ave. de Libertador 1902).

The Museo de Bellas Artes (Ave. de Libertador 1473), open Tuesday-Saturday 9:00-13:00 and 15:00-19:00. The Natural Sciences Museum (Avenida Angel Gallardo 470). The Isaac Fernandez Blanco Museum of Spanish-American Art (Suipacha 1422). El Pilar Church (Junin 1904). The Municipal Museum. The Numismatic Museum at the Banco Central.

Buenos Aires - Rosario Norte   2270

Dep. B.A. (Retiro)	7:30(1)	10:00(2)	13:00(1+11)
Arr. Rosario Norte	11:30	14:25	17:30

Sights in **Rosario:** The Juan B. Castagnino Municipal Museum and the Provincial Historical Museum, both in Parque Independencia. The Cathedral (Calle 25 de Mayo). Stroll on Boulevard Orono. The Monument of The Flag, along the river bank.

Dep. Rosario Norte	3:45(1+7)	4:45(8)	5:45(1+5+9+12)
Arr. B.A. (Retiro)	8:15	9:15	10:15

(1)Meal service. Has air-conditioned Pullman car. (2)Light refreshments. (3)"Independencia". Operates all year. Has a cinema car. (4)Runs Tues. and Fri. (5)"Ciudad de Tucuman". Operates late December to mid-March. (6)Runs daily, except Tues. and Fri. (7)Carries air-conditioned sleeping car. (8)Operates late December to mid-March. Light refreshments. (9)Runs daily, except Wed. and Sun. (10)Runs Wed. and Sun. (11)Plus other departures from Buenos Aires at 16:00(1+3+4), 16:00(1+5+6), 17:00(2), 18:00(1), 19:00(1), 21:00(1+7) and 22:00(8).   (12)Plus other departures from Rosario Norte at 5:45(1+3+10), 7:30(1), 8:40(1), 10:00(2), 13:00(1), 17:00(2) and 19:00(1).

Buenos Aires - Rosario - Tucuman - Guemes - Salta or Jujuy   2257

Dep. B.A. (Ret.)	10:00(1)	18:00(3)	Dep. Jujuy	10:08(4)	12:40(5)
Dep. Rosario	15:09(1)	22:15(3)	Dep. Salta	-0-	12:25(5)
Dep. Tucuman			Dep. Guemes	11:46(4)	14:35
(G.M.)	-0-	13:40(2)	Arr. Tucuman		
Dep. Tucuman			(Norte)	-0-	20:25
(Norte)	10:30(2)	-0-	Arr. Tucuman		
Arr. Guemes	16:31(2)	19:37	(G.M.)	17:35	-0-
Arr. Salta	18:43(2)	-0-	Arr. Rosario	8:25(2)	15:45(2)
Arr. Jujuy	18:35(2)	21:20	Arr. B.A. (Ret.)	13:15(2)	21:00(2)

(1)Mid-December to early March: runs Mon., Wed., Thurs. and Sat. Early March to mid-December: runs Mon. and Thurs. Train is divided into 2 sections. At Guemes, one section goes to Salta, the other to Jujuy. (2)Day 2. (3)Runs Thurs. and Sun. (4)Runs Wed. and Sun. (5)Mid-December to early March: runs Tues., Thurs., Fri. and Sun. Early March to mid-December: runs

Tues. and Fri. Train starts as 2 sections. One begins in Jujuy, the other in Salta. The 2 sections combine in Guemes.

Sights in **Alta Cordoba:** The Cathedral. The Jesuit church. The College of Monserrat. The 17th century university. The Historical and Colonial Museum in the Viceroy's House, on Calle Rosario. The lovely doorway at the Church and Convent of Santa Teresa, on Calle Independencia. The cedar vault and cupola in the 17th century La Merced Church, on Calle Rivadavia. The serpent collection at the excellent Zoological Garden, and the view of Alta Cordoba from there. The Museum of Fine Arts at the Plaza Centenario. The Academy of Fine Arts, near the Plaza Velez Sarsfield. Sacred Heart Church.

Sights in **Tucuman:** Government Palace. At Plaza Independencia: The Church of San Francisco, the Cathedral, Government Palace, and the statue of Liberty, surrounded by orange and palm trees. The Museum at Casa Historica, on Calle Congresso, and the "son et lumiere" programs presented there every night. The menhir stone in beautiful Parque 9 de Julio. The herbarium, animals and insects in the Instituto Miguel Lillo. The lovely Parque Avellaneda and Parque Quebrada de Lules. The Folklore Museum. The Anthropological Museum at 25 de Mayo 492. Nearby: the outstanding Villa Nougues residential area.

Sights in **Salta:** The 16th century images of Cristo del Milagro and the Virgin Mary, in the Cathedral. The Museum of Colonial History and Fine Arts, at Caseros 575. The historical museum, Cabildo, at Caseros 549. Shopping for handicraft, particularly onyx. The view of Salta from Cerro San Bernardo, a short walk or drive. There is train service from Salta to Resistencia, Posadas, La Paz and Antofagasta.

Sights in **Jujuy:** The superb wood pulpit in the Cathedral at Plaza Belgrano. The Palacio de Tribunales. Parque San Martin. Nearby: numerous ancient Franciscan, Dominican and Jesuit churches.

Here is the second route between Rosario and Tucuman.

Buenos Aires - Rosario Norte - Tucuman (via La Banda)   2270

Dep. B.A. (Ret.)	10:00(1)	16:00(3+4+5)	16:00(3+6+7+14)
Arr. Rosario Norte	14:25	19:55(3)	19:55(3)
Change trains.			
Dep. Rosario Norte	15:45(2)	20:10(3+4+5)	20:10(3+6+7)
Arr. Tucuman (GM)	8:45	8:30	9:30
	*	*	*
Dep. Tucuman (GM)	16:40(3+6+8)	17:15(3+4+10)	18:50(3+12+15)
Arr. Rosario Norte	5:40(3)	5:40(3)	8:39(3)
Change trains.			
Dep. Rosario Norte	5:45(6+9)	5:45(3+4+11)	8:40(12)
Arr. B.A. (Ret.)	10:15	10:15	13:15

(1)Second-class only. Light refreshments. (2)Second-class only. Mid-December to mid-March: runs daily. Mid-March to mid-December: runs Tues., Thurs. and Sun. (3)Direct train. No train change in Rosario. (4)"Independencia".

Operates all year. Has a cinema car. Carries an air-conditioned sleeping car and an air-conditioned Pullman car. Meal service. (5)Runs Tues. and Fri. (6)"Ciudad de Tucuman". Operates late December to mid-March. Has air-conditioned Pullman car. Meal service. (7)Runs daily, except Tues. and Fri. (8)Runs daily, except Wed. and Sun. (9)Runs daily, except Thurs. and Mon. (10)Runs Wed. and Sun. (11)Runs Thurs. and Mon. (12)Has air-conditioned Pullman car. Meal service. (13)Second-class only. Mid-December to mid-March: runs daily. Mid-March to mid-December: runs Mon., Wed. and Fri. (14)Plus another departure from Buenos Aires at 18:00(12). (15)Plus another departure from Tucuman at 22:45(13).

Buenos Aires - Santa Fe - Resistencia   2266

All of these trains have meal service.

Dep. B.A. (Ret.)	8:45(1)	8:45(3)	Dep. Resistencia	8:45(4)	18:00(5)
Dep. Santa Fe	18:22(1)	18:40(3)	Arr. Santa Fe	7:35(2)	7:35(2)
Arr. Resistencia	7:45(2)	17:00(2)	Arr. B.A. (Ret.)	17:35(2)	17:35(2)

(1)"El Litoral". Mid-December to early March: runs Mon., Wed. and Fri. Early March to mid-December: runs Wed. only. (2)Day 2.   (3)"El Chaqueno". Mid-December to early March: runs Tues., Thurs., Sat. and Sun. Early March to mid-December: runs Tues., Thurs. and Sat. (4)"El Chequeno". Mid-December to early March: runs Mon., Wed., Fri. and Sun. Early March to mid-December: runs Mon., Wed. and Fri. (5)"El Litoral". Mid-December to early March: runs Tues., Thurs. and Sat. Early March to mid-December: runs Thurs. only.

Sights in **Santa Fe:** The 17th century La Merced Church on Plaza Mayo. Nearby, Casa de Gobierno. The marvelous 17th century San Francisco Church. Across from it, the Provincial Historical Museum. The Rosa Galisteo de Rodriguez Museum of Fine Arts on Calle General.

Buenos Aires - Santa Rosa   2300

Dep. Buenos Aires		Dep. Santa Rosa	20:35(1)
(Once)	21:05(1)	Arr. Buenos Aires	
Arr. Santa Rosa	8:32	(Once)	8:10

(1)Runs daily, except Saturday. Meal service. Has air-conditioned Pullman car.

Buenos Aires - Bahia Blanca   2305

Dep. B.A. (P.Con.)	8:20(1+2)	12:30(1+3)	21:50(1+3+4)
Arr. Bahia Blanca	18:07	22:26	8:20(5)

Sights in **Bahia Blanca:** The statues and lakes in Parque de Mayo. The Zoological Garden in Parque Independencia.

Dep. Bahia Blanca	9:20(1+2)	13:25(1+6)	19:10(1+7+9)
Arr. B.A. (P. Con.)	19:40	23:20	8:25

(1)Has air-conditioned Pullman. Meal service. (2)Runs Wed., Fri. and Sun. (3)Runs daily. (4)Mid-March to mid-December: carries air-conditioned sleeping car every day. Mid-December to mid-March: carries air-conditioned sleeping car only Tues. and Thurs. (5)Arrives 10:01 on Wed. and Fri. (6)Runs Tues., Thurs. and Sat. (7)Runs Tues. and Thurs. Carries air-conditioned sleeping car.

(8)Air-conditioned sleeping car daily, except Tues. and Thurs. Arrives B.A. at 8:25 on Day 2.   (9)Plus another departure from Bahia Blanca at 21:30(1+8).

Buenos Aires - Bahia Blanca - San Carlos de Bariloche   2325
All arrivals shown are on Day 2.

Dep. B.A. (P. Con.)	8:20(1+2)	Dep. San Carlos de B.	17:30(1+4)
Dep. Bahia Blanca	18:22(1+2)	Arr. Bahia Blanca	13:10(1)
Arr. San Carlos de B.	14:20(3)	Arr. B.A. (P. Con.)	23:20

(1)Carries air-conditioned sleeping car and air-conditioned Pullman car. Meal service. (2)Runs Wed., Fri. and Sun. (3)Mid-December to mid-March: arrives 17:05. Mid-March to mid-December: arrives 18:20.   (4)Runs Mon., Wed. and Fri. Mid-December to mid-March: departs 17:30 on Mon., at 14:45 on Wed. and Fri. Mid-March to mid-December: departs 17:30 on Mon., at 13:30 on Wed. and Fri.

Sights in **San Carlos de Bariloche:** This is the biggest ski area in South America (7 different chairlifts). Similar to an Alpine village. Much mountain climbing here, also. See the collection of Indian artifacts in the Nahuel Huapi Museum. Take the cable car from Cerro Cathedral. Many tours of Argentina's Lake District orginate in Bariloche.

THE PATAGONIAN EXPRESS
The southernmost rail trip in the Western Hemisphere is this spur from the Bariloche-Buenos Aires line, the ride from Ing. Jacobacci to Esquel, a ranch town that attracts skiers in September and October. There are 70mph cyclones here in July and August. During harvest period, that train operates at different times and on different days than the schedule published by Argentina.

San Carlos de Bariloche - Buenos Aires   2325+2331

Dep. San Carlos de B.	13:30(1+2)	14:45(1+3)	17:30(4)
Arr. Ing. Jacobacci	18:20	19:35	21:49
Change trains.			
Dep. Ing. Jacobacci	11:00(2+5)	13:30(3+6)	-0-
Arr. Esquel	1:05	3:35	-0-
	*	*	*
Dep. Esquel	2:50(2+7)	3:50(3+8)	-0-
Arr. Ing. Jacobacci	17:05	18:05	-0-
Change trains.			
Dep. Ing. Jacobacci	18:20(1+2+9)	19:35(1+3+9)	21:49(4+9)
Arr. Buenos Aires			
(P.Con.)	23:20	23:20	23:20

(1)Runs Wed. and Fri. Meal service. (2)Operates mid-March to mid-December. (3)Operates mid-December to mid-March. (4)Runs Mon. only. Meal service. (5)Runs Mon. only. (6)Runs Sat. only. (7)Runs Fri. only. (8)Runs Wed. only. (9)Carries an air-conditioned sleeping car.

Buenos Aires - San Carlos de Bariloche   2325+2331

Dep. Buenos Aires			
(P. Con.)	8:20(1+2)	8:20(1+4+5)	8:20(1+4+6)
Arr. Ing. Jacobacci	9:59(3)	12:14(3)	13:27(3)
Change trains.			
Dep. Ing. Jacobacci	11:00(6+7)	13:30(5+8)	-0-
Arr. Esquel	1:05	3:35	-0-
	*	*	*
Dep. Esquel	2:50(6+9)	3:50(5+10)	-0-
Arr. Ing. Jacobacci	17:05	18:03	-0-
Change trains.			
Dep. Ing. Jacobacci	9:59(1+7)	12:14(1+5+11)	13:27(1+6+11)
Arr. San Carlos			
de Bariloche	14:20	17:05	18:20

(1)Carries air-conditioned sleeping car. Meal service. (2)Runs Sun. only. (3)Day 2. (4)Runs Wed. and Fri. (5)Operates mid-December to mid-March. (6)Operates mid-March to mid-December. (7)Runs Mon. only. (8)Runs Sat. only. (9)Runs Fri. only. (10)Runs Wed. only. (11)Runs Thurs. and Sat.

LAKE DISTRICT BUS CONNECTIONS

Bariloche - Puerto Montt   2334

Dep. Bariloche	8:00	8:30(2)	Dep. Puerto Montt		8:00(3)
Dep. Osorno	14:30(1)	15:00(2)	Dep. Osorno		10:00(3)
Arr.			Arr. Bariloche		17:30
Puerto Montt	16:30	17:00			

(1)Runs Tues. and Thurs. (2)Runs daily. (3)Runs daily, except Mon. and Sat.

The interesting lakes in this area are: Argentino, Nahuel Huapi, Correntoso, Espejo, Traful, Gutierrez, Mascardi, Futulafquen, Meliquina, Falkner, Villarino, Epulafquen and Tromen. There is much outstanding trout fishing in many of these lakes.

Buenos Aires - Mar del Plata   2320

All of these trains have meal service, unless designated otherwise.

Dep. B.A. (P.Con.)	7:00(1)	8:00(2)	9:10(1)	10:30(1+3+14)
Arr. Mar del Plata	11:33	12:55	13:45	14:58

Sights in **Mar del Plata:** Five miles of attractive sandy beaches. A very large casino.

Dep. Mar del Plata	7:00(1)	8:45(1)	9:45(1)	9:50(4+15)
Arr. B.A. (P.Con.)	12:20	14:08	17:30	14:55

(1)Operates mid-December to mid-March. (2)Operates all year. (3)Runs daily, except Mon. and Tues. (4)Operates mid-March to mid-December. (5)Runs Fri. only. (6)Runs daily, except Sat. (7)Second-class only. *No* meal service. (8)Runs Mon., Wed. and Fri. (9)Runs Sun. and holidays only. (10)Runs Tues., Thurs., Sun. and holidays. (11)Runs daily, except Mon. and Sat. (12)Runs Sun. only.

(13)Runs daily, except Sundays and holidays. (14)Plus other departures from Buenos Aires at 11:45(1), 15:15(2), 16:55(4+5), 18:35(4+5), 18:35(1+6), 18:55(1+7), 20:20(4+7+8), 23:00(1+5), 23:55(2), 1:00(1) and 1:45(1).

(15(Plus other departures from Mar del Plata at 15:20(1), 16:05(4+9), 17:00(2), 17:50(4+9), 18:05(1), 18:40(1), 20:25(4+7+10), 20:40(1+11), 21:35(1+12), 23:45(2) and 1:35(1+13)

INTERNATIONAL ROUTES FROM ARGENTINA

Argentina's gateways for rail travel to Bolivia, central Brazil, northern Chile and southern Peru are Tucuman and Salta.

From Tucuman, there is rail service to La Paz (with spurs to Potosi, Sucre and Cochabamba), to Santa Cruz (and on across Brazil to Sao Paulo, Brasilia and Rio de Janeiro), and also a beautiful valley ride to Antofagasta.

The starting point for 2 train trips to southern Chile, Paraguay and Uruguay (and on to southern Brazil) is Buenos Aires.

Tucuman - La Paz   1910

Dep. Tucuman
(GM)   13:40 Mon. and Fri. Meal service.
Arr. La Quiaca   4:35 Tues. and Sat.
Walk 3km across border to Villazon.
Dep. Villazon   13:40 Daily, except Mon. and Thurs. Meal service.
Arr. La Paz   10:45 Day 2.

Salta - Yacuiba - Santa Cruz

2255		1915		
Dep. Salta	20:05(1)	Dep. Yacuiba	8:50(3)	17:00(4)	22:00(5)
Arr. Pocitos	7:50(2)	Arr. Santa Cruz	22:25	11:34	6:32
Change trains.				

(1)Runs Wed. only. Light refreshments. (2)It is 4km Pocitos to Yacuiba. (3)Runs Tues., Thurs. and Sat. Meal service. (4)Runs Wed. and Sun. Second-class only. (5)Supplement charged. First-class only. Meal service. Runs Mon., Wed., Fri. and Sun.

Tucuman - Antofagasta

This is a very scenic valley train ride.

2257		2256	
Dep. Tucuman (Norte)	10:30(1)	Dep. Salta	N/A(4)
Arr. Guemes	16:31(2)	Arr. Socompa	N/A(4)
Dep. Guemes	17:06(3)	Arr. Antofagasta	N/A(4)
Arr. Salta	18:43		
Change to bus.			

(1)Mid-December to early March: runs Tues., Thurs., Fri. and Sun. Early March to mid-December: runs Tues and Fri. (2)Day 2.   (3)Runs daily. (4)Time was not available in 1983.

Buenos Aires - Mendoza - Valparaiso (Santiago)

Before it was discontinued in 1980, the Mendoza-Los Andes portion of this rail trip was the most exciting train ride in South America.

Altitudes (in feet) En Route

ASCENT		DESCENT	
Mendoza	2,518	Caracoles (tunnel exit)	10,420
Paso de los Andes	3,069	El Portillo	9,408
Blanco Encalda	3,502	El Juncal	7,321
Cacheuta	4,080	Guardia Vieja	5,397
Portrerillos	4,443	Rio Blanco	4,764
Guido	4,957	Salta del Soldado	4,141
Uspallata	5,741	San Pablo	3,174
Rio Blanco	7,000	Los Andes	2,669
Zanjon Amarillo	7,236	Valparaiso	-0-
Punta de las vacas	7,852		
Puente del Inca	8,915		
Las Cuevas	10,331		
Tunnel Entrance	10,452	(the summit is 13,082.)	

Breakfast was served at the railstation in Mendoza before boarding a narrow-gauge train that went through a scenic valley to Paso de Los Andes. There is much snow in this area from May to November. The ride from Puente del Inca to Las Cuevas was by rack railway. It is a deep descent from Las Cuevas to Portillo. At Llay Llay there is a fork, and one branch of the train route went to Santiago, the other to Valparaiso.

Here is the current train + bus schedule:

2290 Train					
Dep. Buenos Aires	20:00(1)	20:00(3)	21:00(4)		
Arr. Mendoza	9:00	9:00	12:50		
Change to bus. 2423					
Dep. Mendoza	8:00	8:00	8:30	11:00	12:00
Dep. Puente del Inca	N/A(2)	N/A(2)	-0-	N/A(2)	N/A(2)
Dep. Los Andes	N/A(2)	N/A(2)	-0-	N/A(2)	N/A(2)
Set your watch back one hour.					
Arr. Santiago	N/A(2)	N/A(2)	15:30	18:00	22:00
Arr. Valparaiso	15:30	19:00	-0-	-0-	-0-

(1)Operates all year. Runs Thurs. and Sun. First-class only. Carries air-conditioned sleeping car, air-conditioned Pullman, first-class coach and cinema car. Meal service. (2)Time has not been available since 1980. (3)Operates late December to mid-March. Runs daily, except Thurs. and Sun. Has air-conditioned Pullman. Meal service. (4)Carries air-conditioned sleeping car, air-conditioned Pullman, and first and second-class coach. Meal service.

Sights En Route

Mendoza is a large, modern city, having been completely rebuilt after it was destroyed by earthquake and fire in 1861. Its proliferation of gardens make the city extremely beautiful. A 24-hour stopover here is well worthwhile. Do not miss seeing the public park with the splendid monument to Jose de San Martin, the liberator of Chile and Peru. It has an incredible collection of statues and bas-reliefs. Then walk to the lake and streams in the nearby Zoological Gardens.

Also see: The San Martin Museum (Av. General San Martin). The exhibit of Argentine animals and plants in the Moyano Museum of Natural History (Calle Belgrano). The beautiful Romanesque Law Courts building. Window-shop on Calle Las Heras.

There is a splendid all-day bus trip to see the famous Christ the Redeemer statue, which cannot be seen on the train trip. Great scenery on this ride, with a stop for lunch at **Las Cuevas.** Particularly recommended for those not making the complete train trip to Chile.

From **Cacheuta,** the train follows an old Spanish trail called Camino de los Andes. After **Uspallata,** a desolate and vast plain comes into view. There are many rushing mountain streams in the area of **Rio Blanco.** Next in sight is Aconcagua, highest (22,834 feet) mountain in the Western hemisphere.

Puente del Inca is a popular Winter sports resort, attracting the largest crowds of visitors from November to May. It is named for the natural stone bridge spanning the Mendoza River and is one of South America's most marvelous sights. This city is also popular as a base for excursions by foot and horseback to many high valleys in the Andes.

Next in sight is the Horcones River, before arriving at **Las Cuevas** on the Chilean border. This is another popular ski resort.

Extremely good rock scenery can be seen after emerging from the tunnel at **Caracoles.** Next, you will see the Aconcagua River. Here, on the Pacific side of the Andes, the ground is covered by foliage, including many flowers.

Portillo, another Andean ski resort, has many attractive lodges and hotels. The views from the ski lifts and at the 10,824-foot peak are so superb, it's worthwhile visiting here even if you don't ski. The best ski weather is from mid-August to mid-September.

Only 4,000 people are allowed to use this facility each season. Of these, there are 3,000 who have permanent privilege. The few hundred newcomers are culled from over 8,000 applicants, permitting entry only to those who come here on a package tour (check the tour desk of Braniff International). There is much farming in the valley that continues from Portillo to Valparaiso.

Buenos Aires - Puerto Montt

For this transcontinental train trip across southern Argentina, please refer to separate schedules earlier in this section for (1) Buenos Aires-Bahia Blanca, (2) Bahia Blanca-San Carlos de Bariloche, and (3) Bariloche-Puerto Montt.

Buenos Aires - Posadas - Villa Encarnacion - Asuncion   2230

The 40-hour trip from Buenos Aires to Asuncion is a very rough ride, 930 miles through dense brush and jungle. The inconveniences include hard wood seats, stifling heat, swarms of mosquitoes and much dust.

From Encarnacion to Asuncion at night the station platforms at villages along the route are lined with people who, sitting at tables while eating and singing, enjoy watching the train pass by. The locomotive on this portion of the route was built in 1912. The train is said to be the oldest train in South America.

Be sure to have an inexpensive (about $1.00 U.S.) ''through ticket'' before departing Buenos Aires. Passengers without it are required to leave the train at Posadas, carry their luggage to the auto ferry pier, take the auto ferry across the river, and re-board the train on the other side of the river, in Encarnacion. With a ''through ticket'', passengers can remain on the train as it is carried across the river.

Dep.

Buenos Aires (F.LaCroze)	12:00	Tues. and Thurs.
Dep. Posadas (Train Ferry)	9:30	Day 2 (Wed. and Fri.)

Set your watch back one hour from April 1 to September 30.

Arr. Encarnacion	12:00	
Dep. Encarnacion	12:35	Meal service.
Arr. Asuncion	4:30	Day 3 (Thurs. and Sat.)

Sights in **Posadas:** Make the 210-mile bus trip to see one of South America's most impressive sights, Iguazu Falls, much grander than Victoria Falls or Niagara Falls. The biggest flow is August to November.

Buenos Aires - Corrientes   2263

These trains carry sleeping cars and have meal service.

Dep. B.A. (F. La Croze)	11:00(1)	Dep. Corrientes	13:00(3)
Arr. Corrientes	6:45(2)	Arr. B.A. (F. La Croze)	8:45(2)

(1)Late December to mid-March: runs Monday, Wednesday, Friday and Saturday. Mid-March to late December: runs Monday, Wednesday and Saturday. (2)Day 2.   (3)Late December to mid-March: runs Tuesday, Thursday, Saturday and Sunday. Mid-March to late December: runs Tuesday, Thursday and Saturday.

Sights in **Corrientes:** The Colonial Historical and Fine Arts Museum. The Church of La Cruz. Government Palace on Plaza 25 de Mayo. The Cathedral

Buenos Aires - Montevideo   2217

Dep. Buenos Aires	7:50	8:00	10:50	11:00	14:50(1)
Arr. Colonia	8:50	9:00	11:50	12:00	15:50

Change to bus.

Dep. Colonia	9:00	9:10	12:00	12:10	16:00
Arr. Montevideo	11:50	11:45	14:40	14:45	18:45

(1)Plus other departures from Buenos Aires at 17:50 and 18:00.

Buenos Aires - Rio de Janeiro   2125 Bus

Dep. Buenos Aires	16:30
Arr. Rio de Janeiro	16:30 Day 3

BOLIVIA

Children under 3 travel free. Half-fare for children 3-11. Children 12 and over must pay full fare.

All of Bolivia's scant 1,400 miles of railway are narrow-guage, one metre wide.

La Paz

This is the world's highest capital (11,735-foot altitude). See: The National Art Museum, across from the Cathedral, in the Palace of the Condes do Arana. Window-shop on Calle Comercio. See the Central Food Market, largest one in South America. Stroll Calle Sagarnaga, called "Street of the Indians" to examine the assortment of handicrafts sold there. The view of La Paz from Monticulo Park. Walk on The Prado and on Avenida Buenos Aires. See ancient Indian arts and crafts in The National Museum (Calle Don Bosco 93). The furniture and paintings exhibited at Casa de Murillo. Visit The House of Culture. Go to the Tiahuanco ruins, 49 miles from La Paz.

La Paz - Cochabamba   1910

Dep. La Paz	8:20(1)	Dep. Cochabamba	8:00(1)
Arr. Cochabamba	19:25	Arr. La Paz	19:13

(1)Meal service.

Sights in **Cochabamba:** This is the most comfortable area in Bolivia, a mere 8,500 feet altitude. See: The former home of tin baron Simon Patino, now a museum. The several museums in the Palace of Culture. Colorful stalls in the Municipal Market.

La Paz - Potosi - Sucre   1900

This train ride over the Andes is both the highest meter-gauge track in the world (15,705 feet at El Condor, between Rio Mulato and Potosi), and it is also the world's highest passenger train run on any gauge.

Dep. La Paz	18:00(1)	Dep. Sucre	15:40(1)
Arr. Potosi	8:14 Day 2	Dep. Potosi	21:25(1)
Arr. Sucre	13:54	Arr. La Paz	11:50 Day 2

(1)Runs Monday and Thursday. Meal service.

Sights in **Potosi:** The silver and silk statue of Christ in San Francisco Cathedral. The silver altar in San Lorenzo Church. Half-day tours of the tin mine are offered weekdays at 9:00, starting at the headquarters of COMIBOL. The mine can be reached by taxi or by taking the 7:45 bus from Plaza 10 de Noviembre.

After the tin mine tour, you can see the nearby ancient Inca hot springs. Do not fail to visit the Royal House of Money, built in 1773, for a 2-hour tour of this ancient mint. Visit the small shops near the mint, on Calle Bustillos.

Sights in **Sucre:** This city is 10,300 feet high. See the marvelous 16th and 17th century architecture. Many interesting palaces, museums and churches. The ancient University of San Francisco Xavier. The Palace of Justice. The Monastery of La Recoleta.

La Paz - Puno   1826

Dep. La Paz	14:40 Friday	Boat	
Arr. Guaqui	17:49 Friday	Dep. Puno	20:00 Wednesday
Change to boat.		Arr. Guaqui	7:00 Thursday
Dep. Guaqui	19:00 Friday	Change to train.	
Arr. Puno	7:00 Saturday	Dep. Guaqui	10:45 Thursday
		Arr. La Paz	13:45 Thursday

Sights in **Lake Titicaca:** See notes on page 777.

INTERNATIONAL ROUTES FROM BOLIVIA

La Paz - La Quiaca - Jujuy - Tucuman - Buenos Aires   1910+2257

On this 1500-mile route to Argentina, there is an approximately 13-hour wait at La Quiaca, involving a search for drugs by Argentine customs officials before they allow the train to proceed to Tucuman. A Monday departure from La Paz brings you into Buenos Aires on Friday. If you leave La Paz on Friday, you arrive Buenos Aires the next Tuesday.

(Timetable notes appear on next page.)

Dep. La Paz 16:00(1)	Dep. La Quiaca 3:15(2) Day 3
Set watch forward 2 hours.	Arr. Jujuy 9:53
Arr. Villazon 12:20 Day 2	Dep. Jujuy 10:08(2)
Walk 3km across border	Arr. Tucuman (G.M.) 17:35
to La Quiaca	Arr. Rosario 825(3) Day 4
	Arr. Buenos Aires 13:15

(1)Runs daily, except Wednesday and Sunday. Meal service. (2)Runs Wednesday and Sunday. Meal service. (3)Runs Thursday and Monday.

The route to Peru is via Cuzco.

La Paz - Cuzco - Lima

1815 Bus	1814 Bus
Dep. La Paz 8:00(1)	Dep. Cuzco 7:30(4)
Arr. Puno 20:00	Arr. Huancavelica N/A(5)
Change to train.	Change to train.
1825	1816
Dep. Puno 20:45(2)	Dep. Huancavelica 7:00(6)
Arr. Juliaca 21:55	Arr. Huancayo 10:10
Change trains.	Change trains.
1810	1821
Dep. Juliaca 9:25	Dep. Huancayo 7:00(6)
Arr. Cuzco 17:30	Arr. La Oroya 10:06
Change to bus.	Arr. Lima (Des.) N/A(7)

(1)Runs Tues., Thurs. and Sat. (2)Runs daily. (3)Runs daily, except Sun. and holidays. Meal service. May be replaced in 1984 by a 22:30 departure. (4)Runs Mon. and Fri. (5)Time has not been available since 1980. (6)Runs daily, except Sun. and holidays. Supplement charged. (7)Sevice west of La Oroya, to Lima, was by 5-hour bus in 1982 due to damaged bridge near Matucana and in 1983 because of landslides west of La Oroya.

There are 2 rail routes from La Paz to Chile.

La Paz - Charana - Arica   1901

Dep. La Paz	12:00 Tuesday
Arr. Charana	19:46
Change trains.	
Dep. Charana	22:50 second and fourth Tuesday of each month
Arr. Arica	8:05

Marvelous Andean scenery while riding on an excellent train.

You travel on 30 miles of rack and pinion track during a portion of this 270-mile trip. The highest place on this route is 14,000 feet at General Lagos. The best scenery is at the start of the trip, during the descent from La Paz.

The Chilean border is only 5 minutes from Charana, at Visviri, where the passport control procedure takes more than one hour. Many herds of llamas roam here. Because military installations are nearby, photo-taking is not permitted at the frontier area.

Seventy miles before reaching Arica, the track plunges from 11,000 feet to sea level. The scenery on this stretch is a jumble of brown lava rocks.

Passengers are surprised by the amazingly elegant complimentary service of tea, sandwiches and cookies on individual silver trays.

La Paz - Antofagasta 1910

From La Paz to Ollague, for more than 22 hours, the train is constantly at more than 12,000-feet altitude.

Dep. La Paz	12:10(1)	Fri.	Dep. Calama	17:00	Sat.
Dep. Ollague	10:30(1)	Sat.	Arr. Antofagasta	20:00	Sat.
Arr. Calama	16:10	Sat.			

Change to bus.
(1)Meal service.

Santa Cruz - Sao Paulo - Rio de Janeiro

There is great jungle scenery on the Santa Cruz-Corumba portion of this train trip to Brazil.

1915

Dep. Santa Cruz	18:20(1)	14:40(2)		
Arr. Corumba	6:28	8:17		

Change trains.
2068

Dep. Corumba	8:00(3)	
Arr. Bauru	13:05	Day 2 from Corumba

Change trains.
2097

Dep. Bauru	13:43(4)	22:42(3)	4:15(4)	7:53(4)
Arr. Sao Paulo (Luz)	20:01	6:00(5)	10:45	14:53

Change trains.
2075

Dep. Sao Paulo (Luz)	23:20(6+7)	8:00(7)	-0-	-0-
Arr. Rio de Jan. (D.Ped.)	8:27	17:03	-0-	-0-

(1)Runs Thurs. only. First-class only. Supplement charged. Meal service. (2)Runs daily, except Thurs. Meal service. (3)Carries sleeping car. Meal service. (4)Meal service. (5)Day 2 from Bauru. (6)First-class only. Carries sleeping car. Also has couchettes. (7)Air-conditioned train. Meal service.

Santa Cruz - Yacuiba - Pocitos - Salta

1915				225		
Dep. Sta. Cruz	10:00(1)	11:55(2)	16:40(3)	Dep. Pocitos	0:20(5)	
Arr. Yacuiba	19:22(4)	20:25(4)	11:03(4)	Arr. Salta	12:10	

(1)Runs Tues., Thurs. and Sat. Meal service. (2)Runs Mon., Wed., Fri. and Sun. First-class only. Supplement charged. Meal service. (3)Runs Wed. and Sun. Second-class only. (4)It is 4km Yacuiba to Pocitos. (5)Runs Fri. only. Light refreshments.

BRAZIL

Children under 3 travel free. Half-fare for children 3-9. Children 10 and over must pay full fare.

Nearly all (91%) of Brazil's 23,000 miles of rail lines are located within 300 miles of its shoreline on the Atlantic Ocean. Brazil employs 5 different rail gauges. However, most of its tracks are one metre. The only route for train travel to the unique capital, Brasilia, is from Sao Paulo.

Belo Horizonte

See the odd-shaped church at Pampulha, on the edge of the city. Palacio de Liberdade, in Praca de Liberdade. The City Museum. The collection of lamps, photographs, tools, maps and crystal in the Tassini Museum. The 2,000 varieties of trees in the Municipal Park gardens. The marble and glass Museum of Modern Art. The Governor's Palace. The enormous (110,000 seats) soccer stadium. The Fantastic rock shapes in the 22-million-year-old Lapinha Cavern.

Brasilia

In existence only since 1960, this has been Brazil's capital since then. See: The lovely water gardens at the Ministry of Foreign Affairs, the most beautiful structure in Brazil. Across from it, the Palacio de Justica. The blue glass Church of Dom Bosco. Great sculptures throughout the city. The view at night of the white marble federal buildings, sparkling in the glow of spotlights.

The unique housing units, each containing expensive apartments, buildings for middle-income workers, and a complete shopping center. The National Cathedral. Nearby, the 18 buildings that are each for a different government department. Plenalto Palace, where the President's office is located. Alvorada Palace, residence of the President. Arcos Palace. The Metropolitan Cathedral. The 600-foot-long Gallery of States shopping mall, featuring handicrafts from each of Brazil's 22 states. Take the 50-mile drive around Paranoa.

The Museum. The Hall of Mirrors, scene of formal state receptions. The exquisite interior of Alvorada Palace. The National Theater.

Rio de Janeiro

Perhaps the most beautiful city in the world. See: Copacabana Beach. Take the funicular from Rua Cosme Velho 513 to see the incredible 100-foot-high 700-ton statue, Christ The Redeemer, at the 2400-foot-high top of Corcovado. It is a short walk from the Cosme Velho station to the 5 marvelous colonial-style houses in the little square called Largo do Boticario.

Ride the cablecar to the top of Sugar Loaf for the fine view from there. See the concrete and steel Candelaria Cathedral (styled after Mayan temples). Next to the Cathedral is a stop for the city's last streetcar. Ride it for a one-hour roundtrip on its route through the hilly Santa Teresa residential area.

Take bus #206 from Largo da Carioca to Silvestre. Visit Ipanema, Barra da Tijuca and Leblon beaches. Sao Bento Monastery. The Church of Penha. Gloria Church. The Museum of Modern Art on Avenida Presidente Vargas. The Museum of Fine Arts (Avenida Rio Branco 100). The collection of movie theaters, called Cinelandia.

See the photos, jewels and costumes of the great Brazilian entertainer of the 1930's, at the Carmen Miranda Museum. The collection of weaving, stone works, leather and ceramics in the Indian Museum (Rua Mata Machado).

Gems and precious stones at the Museum of Geology and Mineralogy (Avenida Pasteur 404). The Museum of Villa-Lobos (Rua da Imprensa 16). The Museum of the Republic (Rua do Catete 153) in the granite and rose-colored marble Catete Palace. The Museum of Sacred Arts. The Museum of Pictures and Sound. The Municipal Theater.

The enormous collection of plants and trees at the Botanical Gardens (Rua Jardim Botanico). The National Library (Avenida Rio Branco). Fine colonial art in the Convent of Santa Antonio. The Church of Candelaria. Quinta da Boa Vista Museum, with one of the world's best collections of birds, reptiles and insects. Nearby, the Zoo.

Salvador

Called "Bahia" by Brazilians. English-speaking guides are available at the Tourist Office at Praca da Se. To its left is the 18th century Archbishop's Palace. On the other side of the Tourist Office is the 18th century Holy House of Mary Church.

See: The Sao Damaso Seminary. The absolutely beautiful Church of Sao Francisco Convent, filled with gold-leaf decorations. The picturesque market near Praca Cairu. Take the ride on the Lacerda elevator, from Praca Cairu to Praca Municipal to see the Government Palace and Municipal Library, and to window-shop on Rua Chile.

The 17th century furniture in Sao Bento Church. The Instituto Geografico e Historico. Sao Pedro Fort. The Zoo, in the Botanical Gardens at Ondina. The view from Ondina Hill.

The 16th century Basilica Cathedral and the church of St. Peter of the Clerics, in the square of Terreiro de Jesus. The silver altar and the tiles in the Museum of Sacred Art in the 17th century Santa Teresa Church. Do not miss seeing Largo do Pelourinho, Alfredo de Brito Street. The 17th century Convent of the Desterro, most beautiful of all of Brazil's convents.

Dique, the 17th century artificial lake below the Tororo steps. The blue tiles inside University Rectory, en route to Lagoa do Abaete. The beach at Itaparica. The lofty coconut trees at Itapoa Beach. The forts of Santa Maria and Sao Diogo. Igreja da Graco, Salvador's first church. The stalls of fish, pork, beef and tropical fruits at the Agua de Meninos market.

See the Fratelli Vita glassblowing factory. The fort of Mont Serrat and, nearby, Mont Serrat Church. The Cacao Institute, for a look at the processing of chocolate from seed to candy.

Sao Paulo

Largest city in Latin America. See the view while standing on the bridge that spans Avenida Anhangabau. The Municipal Theater, across from Praca Ramos de Azevedo. Instituto Butantan, South America's largest snake farm. Nearby, the collection of antique pottery and furniture in Casa do Bandeirante.

Stroll through Ibirapuera Park, with its statues, Japanese Pavillion (an exact copy of Japan's Katura Palace), the various museums (Science, Aeronautics and Technical Arts) in the History Pavillion, contemporary art in the Pavillion Pereira, and the Planetarium. Visit Praca de la Republica. Window-shop on Rua Augusta.

The Zoological Park (Avenida Miguel Estefeno), considered to be the world's largest. Nearby, the world-famed orchid collection (over 35,000 species). To visit the orchids and Zoo, take Bus #546 from Praca da Liberdade or from Anhangabau. The Art Museum (Avenida Paulista 1578), an outstanding collection of Renoir, Lautrec, Rembrandt, Frans Hals, and many modern Brazilian painters. The Sound and Image Museum (Avenida Europa 158). South America's largest cathedral, in Cathedral Plaza. Liberdade, the city's oriental district (rock gardens, herb stores and many restaurants).

The Museum of Brazilian Art (Rua Alagoas 903), with its collection of copies of all the statues and monuments in the buildings and parks of Brazil. The Museum of Sacred Art in Convento da Luz. The State Art Collection (Avenida Tiradentes 141). The collection of Indian artifacts at Casa do Sertanista (Avenida Francisco Morato 2200).

If you want to learn to dance the samba, there are 44 samba schools here, and Sao Paulo's annual Carnival features their students.

ROUTES IN NORTHERN BRAZIL

The principal seaports north of Salvador (Sao Luiz, Parnaiba, Fortaleza, Natal and Recife) are connected by train service.

There is also rail service from Rio de Janeiro, north to the ports of Campos and Vitoria as well as from Rio, south to Santos, Paranagua, Porto Alegre, Pelotas and Rio Grande do Sul.

The southernmost rail connections are to Quaraio and to Santana do Livramento, both at the border with Uruguay.

Sao Paulo - Brasilia

2097		2062	
Dep. Sao Paulo	10:05(1)	Dep. Brasilia	20:50(3+5)
Arr. Campinas	11:40	2063	
Change trains.		Dep. Araguari	5:45(3+4+6)
2063		Arr. Campinas	17:20
Dep. Campinas	12:00(2+3)	Change trains.	
2062		2097	
Dep. Araguari	23:53(2+3)	Dep. Campinas	18:20
Arr. Brasilia	8:30(4)	Arr. Sao Paulo	20:01

(1)Meal service. (2)Runs Sunday only. (3)First-class only. Carries sleeping car and air-conditioned Pullman. Meal service. (4)Day 2. (5)Runs Friday only. (6)Runs Saturday only.

Rio de Janeiro - Salvador   2039+2042+2043   Bus
Dep. Rio de Janeiro   N/A(1)
Arr. Salvador   N/A(1)
   Sights in **Salvador:** See notes about sightseeing in Salvador earlier in this section.
Dep. Salvador   N/A(1)
Arr. Rio de Janeiro   N/A(1)
(1)Time has not been available since 1980.

Salvador - Recife   2039   Bus

Dep. Salvador	N/A(1)	Dep. Reife	N/A(1)
Arr. Recife	N/A(1)	Arr. Salvador	N/A(1)

(1)Time has not been available since 1980.

   Sights in **Recife:** Named for the reefs along its coastline. Called "the Venice of Brazil" because it is on 3 rivers. The churches to see here are: the 17th century Capela Dourada (with its gold carved altar), the 17th century Santo Antonio, the 18th century Sao Pedro dos Clerigos, Convento de Sao Francisco, Madre de Deus, and Conceicao dos Militares.

   Visit the Museum of Sugar and Alcohol. The Anthropological Museum of Instituto Joaquim Nabuco. Olinda, 5 miles away, is the arts and crafts capital of this region. Attracting many tourists is the faithful reproduction of Jerusalem at Nova Jerusalem, 115 miles to the west.

Recife - Caruaru - Salgueiro   2035

Dep. Recife	7:45(1)	Dep. Salgueiro	5:00(2)
Dep. Caruaru	11:35(1)	Dep. Caruaru	17:05(2)
Arr. Salgueiro	23:32	Arr. Recife	20:49

(1)Runs Tues. and Sat. Meal service. (2)Runs Wed. and Sun. Meal service.
   Sights in **Caruaru:** Great leather, straw articles and pottery bargains at the Wednesday and Saturday market.

Recife - Fortaleza

2027 Bus		2026	
Dep. Recife	N/A(1)	Dep. Fortaleza (Felipe)	17:05(2)
Arr. Lavras	N/A(1)	Arr. Lavras	
Change to train		Change to bus.	
Dep. Lavras	16:42(2)	Dep. Lavras	N/A(1)
Arr. Fortaleza (Felipe)	5:10	Arr. Recife	N/A(1)

(1)Time has not been available since 1980. (2)Meal service.
   Sights in **Fortaleza:** The best lobsters in Brazil. The museum and shops in the Tourist Center. Excellent beaches. Good textiles are sold here, including exquisite hand-made laces.

Fortaleza - Teresina   2005
  This is a very scenic rail trip.

Dep. Fortaleza (Felipe)	19:45(1)	Dep. Teresina	10:50(2)
Arr. Teresina	13:25	Arr. Fortaleza (Felipe)	4:25

(1)Runs Monday and Friday. Meal service. (2)Runs Thursday and Sunday. Meal service.
  Sights in **Teresina:** See the washed clothing laid out to dry on the river bank. The open market.

Teresina - Parnaiba   2006
  This is a freight train that has limited accommodation for passengers.

Dep. Teresina	6:00(1)	Dep. Parnaiba	6:00(2)
Arr. Parnaiba	16:09	Arr. Teresina	16:09

(1)Runs Tuesday, Thursday and Saturday. (2)Runs Monday, Wednesday and Friday.

Teresina - Sao Luis   2007
  This freight train has limited passenger accommodation.

Dep. Teresina	4:00(1)	Dep. Sao Luis	4:00(2)
Arr. Sao Luis	20:17	Arr. Teresina	20:17

(1)Runs Tuesday, Thursday and Saturday. (2)Runs Monday, Wednesday and Friday.

Rio de Janeiro - Niteroi

2050 Train			2043 Bus	
Dep. Rio de Janeiro			Dep. Niteroi	N/A(3)
(B. de Maua)	23:00(1)		Arr. Cachoeira do	
Arr. Campos	6:30(2)		Itapemirim	N/A(3)
Arr. Cachoeira do			Change to train.	
Itapemirim	N/A(2)		2050	
Change to bus.			Dep. Cachoeira do	
2043			Itapemirim	N/A(2)
Dep. Cachoeira do			Dep. Campos	22:30(1)
Itapemirim	N/A(3)		Arr. Rio de Janeiro	
Arr. Niteroi	N/A(3)		(B. de Maua)	6:00

(1)(1)First-class only. Carries sleeping car. Meal service. (2)Service between Campos and Cachoeira was suspended "temporarily" in 1982. (3)Time has not been available since 1980.

Sights in **Niteroi:** The 17th century Boa Viagem Church. The Antonio Parreira Museum. Take the very pretty ride on bus #33 to the Icarai, Sao Francisco and Jurujuba beaches.

Rio de Janeiro - Vitoria   2050

Dep. Rio de Janeiro			Dep. Vitoria	4:40(4)
(B. de Maua)	23:00(1)		Arr. C. do Itapemirim	12:35(2)
Arr. Campos	6:30(2)		Arr. Campos	N/A(2)
Arr. C. do Itapemirim	N/A(2)		Change trains.	
Change trains.			Dep. Campos	22:30(1)
Dep. C. do Itapemirim	5:20(3)		Arr. Rio de Janeiro	
Arr. Vitoria (RFFSA)	13:25		(B. de Maua)	6:00

(1)First-class only. Carries sleeping car. Meal service. (2)Service between Campos and Cachoeira was "temporarily" suspended in 1982. (3)Runs Tuesday, Thursday and Saturday. (4)Runs Monday, Wednesday and Friday.

Sights in **Vitoria:** A beautiful seaport. Marvelous beaches.

Rio de Janeiro - Belo Horizonte   2072

Dep. Rio de Janeiro			Dep. Belo Horizonte	20:15(1)
(D.Pedro)	20:15(1)		Arr. Rio de Janeiro	
Arr. Belo Horizonte	8:45		(D. Pedro)	8:45

(1)Runs Friday and Sunday. First-class only. Air-conditioned train. Carries sleeping car. Has Club Car. Meal service.

Sights in **Belo Horizonte:** See notes on page 748.

Belo Horizonte - Brasilia   Bus 2060

Dep. Belo Horizonte	7:00	8:00	17:00	19:00	20:00	21:45
Arr. Brasilia	18:00	N/A(1)	N/A(1)	N/A(1)	N/A(1)	8:45
			*	*	*	
Dep. Brasilia	7:00	19:00	20:00	21:45	22:00	22:30
Arr. Belo Horizonte	18:00	N/A(1)	N/A(1)	N/A(1)	N/A(1)	

(1)Time has not been available since 1980.

ROUTES IN SOUTHERN BRAZIL

Sao Paulo - Curitiba - Paranagua

The ride from Curitiba to the coastal town of Paranagua is down a steep mountainside.

Bus service.
2100

Dep. Sao Paulo	Frequent times.
Arr. Curitiba	7 hours later
Change to train.	

2102

Dep. Curitiba	7:00	8:10(1)
Arr. Paranagua	10:30	11:00

Train.
2102

Dep. Paranagua	15:30(1)	16:30
Arr. Curitiba	18:05	20:20
Change to bus.		

2100

Dep. Curitiba	Frequent times.
Arr. Sao Paulo	7 hours later

(1)First-class only. Air-conditioned train.

Sights in **Curitiba:** This is Brazil's melting-pot: Italian, Polish, German, Slav, Japanese and Syrian settlers galore. See: The Cathedral, patterned after the one in Barcelona. The Civic Center. The tropical fish collection at the Aquarium in Passeio Publico, a public park in the center of the city. The Çoronel David Carneiro Museum. The Paranaense Museum, in the old city hall. Trips to Iguassu Falls originate from here.

Sights in **Paranagua:** Much of Brazil's coffee is shipped from this seaport. See: The Museum of Archaeology and Popular Art in the wonderful Colegio dos Jesuitas building. The fascinating market near the waterfront. The Church of Sao Benedito. The 17th century fountain. Nearby, the Nossa Senhora do Rocio shrine. Take the one-hour boat trip to see the 18th century Nossa Senhora dos Orazeres Prazeres fort.

Sao Paulo - Curitiba - Porto Alegre   Bus   2100

Dep. Sao Paulo	8:00(1)	Dep. Porto Alegre	8:00(3)
Arr. Curitiba	N/A(2)	Arr. Curitiba	N/A(2)
Dep. Curitiba	N/A(2)	Dep. Curitiba	N/A(2)
Arr. Porto Alegre	4:00	Arr. Sao Paulo	4:00

(1)Plus frequent additional departures 14:00-21:00. (2)Time has not been available since 1980. (3)Plus frequent additional departures 13:00-20:00.

Sights in **Porto Alegre:** A marvelous modern seaport city, at the junction of 5 rivers. Very Germanic here. See: Farroupilha Park. The Zoological Gardens. The Julio de Castilhos Museum. Rua dos Andradas, a strolling street.

Santa Maria - Porto Alegre   2112

Dep. Santa Maria	1:56(1)	9:00(2)	22:15(3)
Arr. Porto Alegre	7:15	16:55	5:45
	*	*	*
Dep. Porto Alegre	8:15(2)	19:00(2)	22:30(3)
Arr. Santa Maria	16:05	0:19	6:05

(1)First-class only. Air-conditioned train. Meal service. (2)Meal service. (3)Carries sleeping car. Has parlor car. Meal service.

Porto Alegre - Santa Maria - Uruguaiana   2112

All of these trains have meal service.

Dep. P. Alegre	19:00(1)	22:30(2)	Dep.		
Arr. Santa Maria	0:18(1)	6:02	Uruguiana	11:15(4)	19:20(1)
Change trains.			Arr.		
Dep. Santa Maria	0:26(1)	7:00(3)	Santa Maria	21:13	1:50(1)
Arr. Uruguaiana	7:00	17:12	Change trains.		
			Dep.		
			Santa Maria	22:15(2)	1:56(1)
			Arr. P. Alegre	5:45	7:15

(1)Direct train. No train change in Santa Maria. First-class only. Air-conditioned train. (2)Carries sleeping car. (3)Runs Tuesday, Thursday and Saturday. (4)Runs Monday, Wednesday and Friday.

Rio Grande - Cacequi   2113

Both of these trains have light refreshments.

Dep. Rio Grande	7:30(1)	Dep. Cacequi	11:30(2)
Arr. Cacequi	17:55	Arr. Rio Grande	22:00

(1)Runs Monday, Wednesday and Friday. (2)Runs Tuesday, Thursday and Saturday.

SCENIC RAIL TRIPS IN BRAZIL

There is a spectacular 67-mile rail trip from Paranagua to Curitiba. The train ascends in 4 hours from sea level to 3,000 feet. Along the way, there is great mountain, gorge, waterfall and jungle scenery.

Paranagua - Curitiba   2102

Dep. Paranagua   15:30(1) 16:30
Arr. Curitiba   18:05   20:20

Sights in **Curitiba and Paranagua:** See notes about sightseeing in Curitiba and Paranagua earlier in this section, under "Sao Paulo-Curitiba-Paranagua". (See: "Routes in Southern Brazil".)

Dep. Curitiba   7:00   8:10(1) 13:30(2)
Arr. Paranagua   10:30   11:00   17:20

(1)First-class only. Air-conditioned train. (2)Runs Saturday only.

Santos - Sao Paulo   2095

One of the rail wonders of the world can be experienced on the 50-mile trip from Santos to Sao Paulo. At 5 separate locations, the entire train is lifted by wire cables from one elevation to another until the train reaches the top of the 2300-foot high Serra do Mar escarpment.

Dep. Santos   5:40(1) 6:50(2) 15:50(1) 18:15(2)
Arr. Sao Paulo (Luz)   7:27   8:37   17:40   20:03
                          *   *   *
Dep. Sao Paulo (Luz)   6:00   16:10(1) 18:20(2) -0-
Arr. Santos   7:57   18:05   20:16   -0-

(1)Runs daily, except Sundays and holidays. (2)Runs Sundays and holidays only.

Sights in **Santos:** A very popular holiday resort and Brazil's most active seaport. Many monuments in the various parks: Praca da Republica, Praca Rui Barbosa, Praca Jose Bonifacio. Night-life activities in the Gonzaga area.

INTERNATIONAL ROUTES FROM BRAZIL

Brazil's international train routes are from Rio de Janeiro south to Uruguay and Argentina, and from Sao Paulo west to Bolivia and Chile.

Rio de Janeiro - Sao Paulo - Buenos Aires   2125   Bus

Dep. Rio de Janeiro	18:00		Dep. Uruguiana	N/A	Day 3
Dep. Sao Paulo	0:15	Day 2	Dep. Paso de		
Dep. Curitiba	6:30	Day 2	los Libres	4:40	Day 3
Dep. Porto Alegre	19:45	Day 2	Dep. Santa Fe	11:10	Day 3
Arr. Uruguaiana	N/A(1)		Arr. Buenos Aires	19:45	Day 4

(1)Time has not been available since 1980.

Rio de Janeiro - Sao Paulo - Montevideo

2075

Dep. Rio de Janeiro (D.Pedro)	8:00(1)	23:00(1+2)	-0-
Arr. Sao Paulo	16:27	8:05	-0-

Change to bus.

2100

Dep. Sao Paulo	8:00	14:00	16:00(5)
Arr. Porto Alegre	N/A(3)	N/A(3)	N/A(3)

Change buses.

2120

Dep. Porto Alegre	20:00	21:00	22:00
Arr. Montevideo	9:15	9:35	10:00

(1)First-class only. Air-conditioned. Meal service. (2)Carries sleeping car. Aldo has couchettes. (3)Time has not been available since 1980. (4)Direct bus. No bus change in Porto Alegre. (5)Plus other departures from Sao Paulo at 18:00, 18:30, 20:00 and 22:00(4).

Sao Paulo - Corumba - Santa Cruz - La Paz

2085

Dep. Sao Paulo (Luz)	9:00(1)	12:05(1)	19:25(1)	22:25(2)
Arr. Bauru	15:05(3)	18:50(3)	1:43(3)	5:00(3)

(1)Meal service. (2)Carries sleeping car. Meal service. (3)Estimated time.

Change trains. You cross the Mato Grosso mountain range going from Bauru to Corumba.

2068

Dep. Bauru	15:45(1)
Arr. Corumba	19:17(2)

(1)Carries sleeping car. Meal service. (2)Day 2.

Change trains.

1915

Dep. Corumba	11:20(1)	13:00(2)	20:00(3)
Arr. Santa Cruz	23:19	7:00	19:48

Change to bus

1911

Dep. Santa Cruz	6:00
Arr. Cochabamba	12 hours later

Change to train

1910

Dep. Cochabamba	8:00(4)
Arr. La Paz	19:13

(1)Runs Friday only. Meal service. (2)Runs daily, except Friday. Meal service. (3)Runs Wednesday and Sunday. Second-class only. (4)Runs daily. Meal service.

Sao Paulo - Antofagasta

1915

Arr. Santa Cruz
  from Sao Paulo (see preceding timetable)   23:19(1)   7:00(2)   19:48(3)
    Change trains.

Dep. Santa Cruz	10:00(4)	11:55(5)	16:40(6)
Arr. Yacuiba	19:22	20:25	11:03

    Change trains. It is 4km to Pocitos

2255

Dep. Pocitos   N/A(7)
Arr. Salta   21:25
    Change to bus.

2256

Dep. Salta   N/A(8)
Arr. Antofagasta   N/A(8)

(1)Runs Friday only. (2)Runs daily, except Saturday. (3)Runs Monday and Thursday. (4)Runs Tuesday, Thursday and Saturday. Meal service. (5)Runs Monday, Wednesday, Friday and Sunday. First-class only. Supplement charged. Meal service. (6)Runs Wednesday and Sunday. Second-class only. (7)Runs Friday only. Light refreshments. (8)Time has not been available since 1980.

CHILE

Children under 1m.20 travel free. Children 1m.20 and taller must pay full fare.

From September to March, first-class train tickets in Chile are difficult to obtain. It is advisable to reserve space far in advance of travel date through a prominent travel agency in Santiago or Antofagasta.

Train service runs from Antofagasta to Puerto Montt, on the shore of the Gulf of Ancud. Feeder lines branch off the main north-south line, eastward to great resorts at Lake Villarrica, Lake Panguipulli, Lake Ranco, Lake Puyehul and Lake Llanquihue. The Lake District is the area east of the rail line from Temuco to Puerto Montt. The connecting point is Puerto Varas.

The average width of Chile is a scant 120 miles, ranging from 312 miles at its widest to 56 miles where it is the most narrow.

Antofagasta

There are many beautiful beaches, parks and plazas in this city.

Santiago

See: The Presidential Palace. The view of the city from the terrace of Castillo Gonzalez on Santa Lucia Hill. The Popular Arts Museum in Castillo Hidalgo. The Cathedral, near Plaza de Armas, with its fine painting of The Last Supper. These churches: Santo Domingo, San Francisco, San Augustin, La Merced, Santa Ana, Recoleta Dominica and Recoleta Franciscana.

The foods and souvenirs (saddles, baskets, ceramics, dolls, rugs) in the central market. The Palace of Fine Arts at Parque Forestal. The National Library and the Historical Museum, both in the same building at Alameda, between Miraflores and McIver streets. The Natural History Museum and Modern Art Museum, both in the Quinta Normal.

Take the funicular to the top of San Cristobal Hill for a spectacular view of Santiago, stopping on the ascent to see the Zoo that is about one-third of the way up.

Valparaiso

See: The Beaux Arts Museum. Severin Public Library. The view from Miradero O'Higgins, in Alto del Puerto. Take the 20-minute ride to the beaches at Vina del Mar, called "The Pearl of the Pacific" and "The Garden City". Also in Vina: The Academy and Museum of Fine Arts in the Quinta Vergara, the Naval History Museum, and the Municipal Casino.

Valparaiso - Santiago - Concepcion

Marvelous scenery: fertile farms (first colonized by Germans in the early 19th century), snow-capped mountains, shimmering lakes, mile after mile of wildflowers, vineyards and pine forests.

2426

Dep. Valparaiso (Puerto)	7:25(1)	11:30(1)	14:30(1)	18:40(1)
Dep. Vina del Mar	7:38(1)	11:44(1)	14:45(1)	18:53(1)
Arr. Santiago (Mapocho)	10:18	14:23	17:20	21:30

Change trains . . . and change railstations.

2430

Dep. Santiago (Alameda)	13:30(2)	8:30(2)	-0-	23:00(2)
Arr. Concepcion	21:15	16:55	-0-	7:15

*   *   *

Dep. Concepcion	23:00(2)	9:30(2)	1:33(2)	-0-
Arr. Santiago (Alameda)	7:20	18:30	21:15	-0-

Change trains . . . and change railstations.

2426

Dep. Santiago (Mapocho)	8:35(1)	12:40(1)	14:40(1)	16:40(1+3)
Arr. Vina del Mar	11:16	15:17	17:17	19:18
Arr. Valparaiso (Puerto)	13 minutes later			

(1)First-class only. (2)Train consists of only an air-conditioned parlor car. (3)Plus another departure from Santiago at 19:25(1).

Sights in **Concepcion:** The Pedro del Rio Zanartu Museum. The view of the city from Cerro Amarillo. A lovely view of valleys and Bio-Bio, Chile's largest river, from Cerro Caracol.

Arica - Antofagasta - Santiago   Bus   2425

Rail passenger service for this 1,300-mile trip, basically a freight train with limited passenger accommodation, is considered to be so appalling that the state railway refuses to publish information about the journey. Here is the schedule for a 2-day bus trip.

Dep. Arica	9:00(1)		Dep. Santiago	9:00	18:00
Arr. Antofagasta	N/A(2)		Arr. Antofagasta	N/A(2)	N/A(2)
Dep. Antofagasta	N/A(2)		Dep. Antofagasta	N/A(2)	N/A(2)
Arr. Santiago	18:00		Arr. Arica	18:00	6:00

(1)Plus other departures from Arica at 10:30, 18:00, 22:00 and 22:35.
(2)Time has not been available since 1980.

Antofagasta - Santiago   Bus   2425

Schedules in addition to those shown on the Arica-Antofagasta-Santiago table.

Dep. Antofagasta	17:00(1)		Dep. Santiago	10:00(2)
Arr. Santiago	13:10		Arr. Antofagasta	6:40(3)

(1)Runs daily, except Sunday. Departs 16:00 on Wednesday. (2)Runs daily, except Sundays and holidays. (3)Arrives 7:40 on Friday.

Antofagasta - Arica   Bus   2425

Schedules in addition to those shown on the Arica-Antofagata-Santiago table.

Dep. Antofagasta	8:00	19:00	Dep. Arica	9:00	18:00
Arr. Arica	18:00	6:00	Arr. Antofagasta	19:00	5:00

Santiago - Puerto Montt   2430

Dep. Santiago (Alameda)	18:30(1)		Dep. Puerto Montt	16:00(1)
Arr. Puerto Montt	12:15		Arr. Santiago (Alameda)	9:55

(1)First-class only. Carries sleeping car. Meal service.

LAKE DISTRICT BUS CONNECTIONS

Puerto Montt - Bariloche   2334

Dep. Puerto Montt	8:00(1)
Arr. Bariloche	17:30

*   *   *

Dep. Bariloche	8:00(2)	8:30(3)	8:30(4)
Arr. Puerto Montt	16:30	N/A(5)	17:00

(1)Runs daily, except Monday and Saturday. (2)Runs Tuesday and Thursday. (3)Runs Tuesday, Thursday, Friday and Saturday. (4)Runs Monday, Wednesday and Saturday. (5)Time has not been available since 1980.

SPECIAL ONE-DAY ANDEAN SCENIC TRAIN TRIP

Schedules permit an exciting one-day glimpse at the overwhelming Andes range, both from Valparaiso and Santiago.

Valparaiso - Los Andes   2422

Dep. Valparaiso			Dep. Los Andes	8:00(2)	12:00(3)
(Puerto)	9:00(1)	12:40(2)	Arr. Llay Llay	9:00	13:01
Dep. Llay Llay	10:54(1)	14:18(2)	Arr. Valparaiso		
Arr. Los Andes	11:46	15:12	(Puerto)	10:40	14:50

(1)Second-class only. (2)First-class only. Plus another first-class only train departing at 18:00. (3)Second-class only. Plus a first-class only train departing at 19:10.

Santiago - Llay Llay   2426

All of these trains are first-class only.

Dep. Santiago (Mapocho)	8:35	12:40	14:40	16:40	19:25
Arr. Llay Llay	1½ hours later				

*   *   *

Dep. Llay Llay	7:37	8:59	13:03	16:04	20:12
Arr. Santiago (Mapocho)	1½ hours later				

INTERNATIONAL ROUTES FROM CHILE

There is train service from both Arica and Antofagasta to La Paz. One can cross the continent by rail from Antofagasta, to either Rio de Janeiro or Buenos Aires. Until 1980, there was transcontinental train service from Valparaiso to Buenos Aires.

Valparaiso (Santiago) - Mendoza - Buenos Aires

The Los Andes-Mendoza portion of this rail trip was the most exciting train ride in South America before the train was replaced by bus.

Altitudes (in feet) En Route

ASCENT		DESCENT	
Valparaiso	-0-	Tunnel Exit	10,452
Los Andes	2,669	Las Cuevas	10,331
San Pablo	3,174	Puente del Inca	8,915
Salto del Soldado	4,141	Punta de las Vacas	7,852
Rio Blanco	4,764	Zanjon Amarillo	7,236
Guardia Vieja	5,397	Rio Blanco	7,000
El Juncal	7,321	Uspallata	5,741
El Portillo	9,408	Guido	4,957
Caracoles (tunnel entrance)	10,420	Portrerillos	4,443
(The summit is 13,082.)		Cacheuta	4,080
		Blanco Encalda	3,502
		Paso de los Andes	3,069
		Mendoza	2,518

On the original train ride, there were great amounts of snow Los Andes-Mendoza from May to November. It was a steep descent from Portillo (a Winter sports resort) to Las Cuevas, another ski resort. Then, it was a rack railway from Las Cuevas to Puente del Inca. The ride from there to Mendoza was by narrow-gauge, through a scenic valley.

2423 Bus				
Dep. Valparaiso	7:30	-0-	8:30	-0-
Dep. Santiago	-0-	8:15	-0-	9:00
Set your watch forward one hour.				
Dep. Los Andes	N/A(1)	N/A(1)	N/A(1)	N/A(1)
Dep. Puente del Inca	N/A(1)	N/A(1)	N/A(1)	N/A(1)
Arr. Mendoza	16:00	16:30	18:00	18:00
Change to train.				
2290				
Dep. Mendoza	-0-	16:20(2)	20:00(3)	-0-
Arr. Buenos Aires (Ret.)	-0-	8:00	9:00	-0-

(1)Time has not been available since 1980. (2)Runs daily. Carries air-conditioned sleeping car and parlor car. Meal service. (3)Late December to mid-March: runs daily. Carries air-conditioned sleeping car and cinema car only on Monday and Friday. Carries sleeping cars that are *not* air-conditioned on the other 5 days. Also has parlor car. Meal service. Mid-March to late December: Runs Monday and Friday only. Carries air-conditioned sleeping car. Also has parlor car and cinema car. Meal service.

Sights En Route

The train traveled through a fertile valley until beginning the ascent to **Portillo,** a popular ski resort with many hotels. Mountain slopes on the Pacific side of the Andes are covered with foliage, including many flowers. You saw the Aconcagua River and excellent rock scenery before entering the tunnel at Caracoles. See notes about skiing at Portillo, earlier in this chapter under "Buenos Aires-Valparaiso"

The next arrival was at **Las Cuevas,** another popular ski resort. After leaving Las Cuevas, you had a view of the Horcones River before arriving at **Puente del Inca,** a popular Winter sports resort area, attracting the greatest crowds from November to May. It is named for its natural stone bridge spanning the Mendoza River and is one of South America's most marvelous sights. This city is also popular as a base for excursions by foot and horseback to many high valleys in the Andes: Los Penitentes, Laguna de los Horcones, etc.

After leaving Puente del Inca, Aconcagua was next in sight. It is the highest (22,834 feet) mountain in the western hemisphere. Many rushing mountain streams can be seen in the area of Rio Blanco. Then, a desolate and vast plain came into view before reaching **Uspallata.** The train followed an old Spanish trail called Camino de los Andes between Upsallata and **Cacheuta.**

The next stop was **Mendoza.** If you left Valparaiso or Santiago on a Saturday, a 48-hour stopover here was well worthwhile, continuing on to Buenos Aires the following Monday.

Completely rebuilt after it was destroyed by earthquake and fire in 1861, Mendoza is a large, modern city. Its proliferation of gardens makes the city extremely beautiful.

Do not miss seeing the public park with the splendid monument to Jose de San Martin, the liberator of Chile and Peru. It is an incredible collection of statues and bas-reliefs. Then walk to the lake and streams in the nearby Zoological Gardens.

Also see: The San Martin Museum (Av. General San Martin). The exhibit of Argentine animals and plants in the Moyano Museum of Natural History (Calle Belgrano). The beautiful Romanesque Law Courts building. Window-shop on Calle Las Heras.

There is a splendid all-day bus trip from Mendoza to see the famous Christ the Redeemer statue, which cannot be seen on the train trip. Great scenery on this ride, with a stop for lunch at Las Cuevas.

There are 4 rail routes from Chile to Bolivia. The first we list includes the great Transandine ride from Valparaiso (or Santiago) to Mendoza. Instead of going from Mendoza east to Buenos Aires, however, you proceed from Mendoza north to Tucuman and then on from there to either La Paz or Santa Cruz. The one rail route from Chile to Brazil is from Antofagasta to Sao Paulo.

Mendoza - Tucuman

2423
Arr. Mendoza   16:00, 16:30 and 18:00 (by bus from
                      Valparaiso or Santiago)
  Change buses.
  2267
Dep. Mendoza   13:00 14:00(1) 20:00
Arr. Tucuman   9:05 8:19   13:34
(1)Runs Monday and Friday.

Tucuman - La Paz   1910

Dep. Tucuman	13:40(1)	Dep. Villazon 13:40(2)
Arr. La Quiaca	4:31	Arr. La Paz 10:45
Walk 3km across border.		

Runs Monday and Friday. Meal service. (2)Runs daily, except Monday and Thursday. Meal service.

Tucuman - Salta - Pocitos - Yacuiba - Santa Cruz

2257		2255			
Dep. Tucuman		Dep. Salta	20:05(2)	-0-	-0-
(Norte)	10:30(1)	Arr. Pocitos	7:50	-0-	-0-
Arr. Guemes	16:31	Change trains. It is 4km to Yacuiba.			
Change trains.		1915			
Dep. Guemes	17:06	Dep. Yacuiba	8:50(3)	17:00(4)	22:00(5)
Arr. Salta	18:43	Arr. Santa Cruz	22:25	11:34	6:32

(1)Late December to early March: runs Mon., Wed., Thurs. and Sat. Early March to late December: runs Tues. and Fri. (2)Runs Wed. only. Light refreshments. (3)Runs Tues., Thurs. and Sat. Meal service. (4)Runs Wed. and Sun. Second-class only. (5)Runs Mon., Wed., Fri. and Sun. First-class only. Supplement charged. Meal service.

Arica - La Paz   1901

There are 30 miles of rack and pinion track during this 270-mile rail trip. The highest place on this route is 14,000 feet, at General Lagos. The best scenery is during the last portion of the trip, on the descent into La Paz. During the last 6 miles, a series of loops traveled very slowly, there is excellent scenery of 3 tremendous Andean peaks: Illampu (21,490 feet), Illiman (21,315 feet) and Huayna-Potosi (20,407 feet).

Dep. Arica	11:00(1+2)	11:30(1+3)
Arr. Charana	20:10	20:30
Change trains.		
Dep. Charana	17:00(4)	22:00(5)
Arr. La Paz	0:22	6:15

(1)Runs only 2nd and 4th Tues. of each month. (2)Operates mid-March to mid-Oct. (3)Operates mid-Oct. to mid-March. (4)Runs Fri. only. (5)Runs Tues. only.

Antofagasta - La Paz   1910

Bus			Train		
Dep. Antofagasta	9:00	Wed.	Dep. Calama	12:55(1)	Wed.
Arr. Calama	12:00	Wed.	Arr. La Paz	14:40	Thurs.
Change to train.			(1)Meal service.		

It is easy to understand why this train trip of 705 miles takes 36 hours. The first 18 miles out of Antofagasta, there is an ascent of 1,800 feet as the route crosses the Atacama Desert. In the next 211 miles, the train climbs to the summit of the Chilean section of the ride: 13,000 feet above sea level, at Ascotan. There is generally a 3 to 4-hour wait at the Chile-Bolivia border (Ollague) while Bolivian customs officers go through the train to check passports and inspect baggage.

One of the most unusual sights on this trip occurs on the second day, just before reaching Poopo. Thousands of flamingos can be seen on a lake that is 12,000 feet above sea level.

The top of 21,000-foot Illimani can be seen if there are no clouds or fog. The train descends 1,000 feet to the highest capital in the world. La Paz is nearly 12,000 feet above sea level.

Antofagasta - Salta - Yacuiba - Bauru - Sao Paulo

2420	Bus		1915	Train	
Dep. Antofagasta	15:00(1)		Dep. Santa Cruz	14:40(7)	
Arr. Salta	9:00(2)		Arr. P. Suarez	8:17(8)	
Change buses.			It is 11km to Corumba.		
2255			Change trains.		
Dep. Salta	20:05(3)		2068		
Arr. Pocitos	7:50(4)		Dep. Corumba	21:00(9)	
It is 4km to Yacuiba.			Arr. Campo Grande	6:40	
Change to train.			Change trains.		
1915			Dep. Campo Grande	19:04(9)	
Dep. Yacuiba	22:00(5)		Arr. Bauru	13:05(10)	
Arr. Santa Cruz	6:32(6)				
Change trains.					

(1)Runs Wed. and Sat. (2)Runs Thurs. and Sun. (3)Runs Wed. only. Light refreshments. (4)Arrives Thurs. Overnight layover required. (5)Runs Fri., Sun., Mon. and Wed. Meal service. Plus other departures from Yacuiba at 8:50 Tues., Thurs. and Sat., and also at 17:00 Fri. and Sat. (6)Day 2 after Yacuiba departure: Sat., Mon., Tues. and Thurs. (7)Runs daily, except Thurs. Meal service. (8)Train has not continued to Corumba since 1980. (9)Runs daily. Carries sleeping car. Meal service. (10)Day after departing Campo Grande.

2097				
Dep. Bauru	4:15(1)	7:53(1)	13:43(1)	22:42(2)
Arr. Sao Paulo (Luz)	10:45	14:53	20:01	6:00

(1)Meal service. (2)Carries sleeping car. Meal service.

COLOMBIA

Children under 3 travel free. Half-fare for children 3-11. Children 12 and over must pay full fare.

This is the only South American country with a coast on both the Atlantic and Pacific oceans. There is no train service between Colombia and adjacent countries, only a few short internal narrow-gauge rail routes.

Bogota

Capital of Colombia. Founded in 1538 at 8,460-feet altitude. Population is nearly 5,000,000. See 20,000 pre-Colombian gold items and the world's largest emerald in the Museo del Oro in Santander Park on Carrera 7. It is an indescribable thrill to stand in the totally dark room on the Gold Museum's third floor and instantly see more than 10,000 gold objects when the lights are switched on.

Of the city's more than 300 churches, be sure to see the ceiling of Islamic designs in La Concepcion, Bogota's oldest church (late 16th century). The panelled ceiling and the main altar in the very beautiful Moorish-style 17th century San Francisco Church. The carved oak-and-cedar altar in the 18th century La Tercera Church. The colonial paintings by Vasquez and the columns inlaid with turquoise in the lovely El Sagrario Chapel, next door to the Cathedral. The outstanding stained-glass in the Church of Maria del Carmen. The 16th century Veracruz Church. Also visit San Diego, San Augustin, San Ignacio and Santa Ines churches.

See exceptional art and history collections at the National Museum. The Museum of Natural History and the sidereal projection room, both in the City Planetarium. Take the cable car to the top of Montserrate, 2000 feet above the city, for a spectacular view of Bogota. Seeing the pilgrims climb the mountain on their knees during Holy Week is a fantastic spectacle.

Nearby is Yequendama Falls, set in lush jungle foliage. Quinta de Bolivar, the villa given to the liberator by a wealthy man, now a museum of Napoleonic-style furniture and Bolivar relics. Its gardens are decorated with busts of heroes and heavy bronze cannons used in the country's War of Independence (1810).

The Palace of San Carlos. The Municipal Palace. The coin presses and wood balconies in the Mint House Museum. The pre-Colombian pottery in the mansion of the Marques de Jan Jorge. The incredible carved ceiling in the Presidential Palace. The Museum of July 20, 1810 (Independence Day). The Museum of Folk Art. The excellent collection of paintings in the Museum of Colonial Art. Teatro Colon. Luis Angel Arango Library.

Exceptional art and history collections at the National Museum. Many rare coins at Casa de la Moneda. Rare manuscripts at Hierba Buena Literary Museum. The craftwork at the Handicrafts and Traditional Arts Museum. Religious art at the Theological Seminary Museum. The elegant police uniforms. The ramshackle huts in the suburbs.

Shop for emeralds, reptile leatherwork (alligator, crocodile, snake) and beautiful linen shirts. The handicrafts of more than 1,000,000 artisans are sold at Artesanias de Colombia. Stroll the cobbled streets of the La Candelaria area to see the 17th century colonial homes with red tile roofs, overhanging balconies and interior patios. Celebrate the tradition of afternoon "Chocolate Santaferreno".

Bogota - Barrancabermeja - Santa Marta   1710

Some meal stops are made during this trip. Most of the journey offers great jungle, river and mountain scenery. Particularly scenic is the descent at Puerto Salgar to the Magdalena River.

These trains are first-class only.

Dep. Bogota	8:00(1+2)	10:00(2+3)
Dep. Barrancabermeja	20:52	23:22
Arr. Santa Marta	8:06	11:23

Dep. Santa Marta   10:00(2+4)   13:00(2+5)
Dep. Barrancabermeja   21:45   0:23
Arr. Bogota   12:17   13:37

(1)Operates Dec. 1 through Jan. 31. Runs Monday and Friday. Carries sleeping car. (2)Meal service. (3)Operates all year. Runs Tuesday and Saturday. (4)Operates all year. Runs Mon. and Thurs. (5)Operates Dec. 1 through Jan. 31. Runs Tuesday. and Saturday. Carries sleeping car.

Sights in **Barrancabermeja:** The Cathedral of the Sacred Heart of Jesus.

Sights in **Santa Marta:** This was the first European city in South America. It is now a banana center. Founded in 1525, it is Colombia's important commercial Atlantic seaport. Simon Bolivar, South America's great liberator, died here. You can visit the plantation where he lived his last days, 3 miles southeast of the city.

Also see: The Gaira and Rodadero beaches. The Cathedral. The Church of San Francisco. Two nearby fishing villages: Taganga and La Concha. The marine biology institute at Punta de Betin.

Bogota - Grecia - Medellin

All of these trains are first-class only and have meal service unless designated otherwise.

1710
Dep. Bogota   8:00(1+2)   10:00(3)
Arr. Grecia (P. Berrio) 17:42   20:02
  Change trains.
  1715 .
Dep. Grecia (P. Berrio) 1:09(4)   10:56(5)
Arr. Medellin   7:33   18:40
                   *   *   *
Dep. Medellin   7:10(5)   13:00(6)
Arr. Grecia (P. Berrio) 14:38   19:01
  Change trains.
  1710
Dep. Grecia (P. Berrio) 1:09(1+7) 2:25(3)
Arr. Bogota   12:17   13:37

(1)Operates Dec. 1 through Jan. 31. (2)Runs Monday and Friday. (3)Runs Tuesday and Saturday. (4)Runs Tuesday only. (5)Second-class only. *No* meal service. (6)Runs Saturday only.(7)Runs Monday and Thursday.

Sights in **Medellin:** The 17th century churches: San Benito, La Veracruz, San Jose and the Old Cathedral. The cattle auctions on Tuesday and Thursday. The South American animals and birds in the Zoo. The Museum of Folk Art. The Museo Zea. The Botanical Garden, with its world-famous collection of orchids.

Cauca Valley Scenic Train Rides

There are 2 beautiful short rail trips in the scenic Cauca Valley.

Cali - Armenia 1730

Dep. Cali	13:00	Dep. Armenia	6:30
Arr. Armenia	17:45	Arr. Cali	11:21

Sights in **Cali:** See relics of the city's last Royal Sheriff in the colonial ranchhouse called Canasgordas. The Museum of Natural History. Plaza de Caicedo, with the Cathedral and National Palace. There are great views of Cali from San Fernando Mountain. See the 3,000 different types of orchids at "El Orquideal". There is excellent deep-sea fishing at Buenaventura, a 2-hour ride from Cali.

Sights in **Armenia:** A modern city. See Quindio University.

Cali - Cartago 1730

Dep. Cali	6:00	9:30	11:30	16:35	18:20
Arr. Cartago	9:09	13:14	14:37	19:42	22:04

Sights in **Cartago:** Many fine colonial buildings. See Casa de Los Virreyes (House of the Viceroys).

Dep. Cartago	4:55	6:15	9:30	13:55	16:15
Arr. Cali	8:38	9:21	12:44	17:39	19:25

ECUADOR

Children under 3 travel free. Half-fare for children 3-11. Children 12 and over must pay full fare. There is no train service between Ecuador and adjacent countries.

The 288-mile ride from Guayaquil (Duran Alfaro) is one of the world's most thrilling train trips ¢ and advance reservations are essential. The former antique bus on rail wheels that provided 30 uncomfortable wood seats was replaced in 1980 by a new autoferro that has 43 upholstered seats.

No food is sold en route. There is time for breakfast in a restaurant at the first of many stops where food and beverages can be purchased.

The ride begins with a 20-minute ferryboat trip from Guayaquil to Duran. You ascend a 5.5 percent gradient, climbing in one 50-mile stretch (Bucay-Palmira) from 975 feet to 10,600 feet. At a point called "Devil's Nose", there is a double switchback zig-zag, carved out of a rock mountain.

Highest point on the route is 11,841 feet, at Urbina. Watch for Mt. Chimborazo, rising an additional 8,000 feet above the train. This 12-hour train trip involves hundreds of bridges and tunnels. You can make the return trip by airplane in 35 minutes. A popular stopover is at Riobamba.

Here are the stations and their altitudes:

MILES FROM GUAYAQUIL		ALTITUDE IN FEET	MILES FROM GUAYAQUIL		ALTITUDE IN FEET
	Guayaquil	15	142	Luisa	10,379
14	Yaguachi	20	150	Riobamba	9,020
21	Milagro	42	170	Urbina	11,841
31	Naranjito	100	178	Mocha	10,346
43	Barranganeta	300	186	Cevallos	9,100
54	Bucay	975	196	Ambato	8,435
72	Huigra	4,000	219	San Miguel	8,645
76	Chunchi	4,875	227	Latacunga	9,055
81	Sibambe	5,925	239	Lasso	10,375
89	Alausi	8,553	250	Cotopaxi	11,653
95	Tixan	9,200	263	Machachi	10,118
103	Palmira	10,626	266	Aloag	9,090
112	Guamote	10,000	273	Tambillo	9,891
132	Cajabamba	10,388	288	Quito	9,375

Guayaquil - Quito   1755

These trains require reservation, are first-class only and run daily, except Sundays and holidays.

Dep. Guayaquil		Dep. Quito	6:00
(Duran)	6:15	Dep. Latacunga	8:05
Dep. Milagro	6:58	Dep. Ambato	8:57
Dep. Sibambe	9:08	Dep. Riobamba	11:05
Dep. Alausi	9:32	Dep. Alausi	13:01
Dep. Riobamba	11:55	Dep. Sibambe	13:21
Dep. Ambato	13:30	Dep. Milagro	15:29
Dep. Latacunga	14:23	Arr. Guayaquil	
Arr. Quito	18:15	(Duran)	18:00

On the route from Guayaquil to Quito, Indian women meet the train's arrival in Milagro, hawking fruits and native bread. Lush foliage can be seen after leaving Bucay. Then the train ascends the Chanchan River gorge as it approaches Huigra and finally climbs 1,000 feet above the river, up the Devil's Nose (Nariz del Diablo).

Many small Indian mountain villages line the track en route to Sibambe. In Alausi, a resort village, bus connections to Quito are available. At Palmira, there is a view of many high mountain peaks: Altar, Carihuairazo, Chimborazo, Sangay, Tungurahua.

Next, the train skirts the shoreline of Lake Colta before coming into Riobamba. Highest point of the trip (11,841 feet) is shortly after leaving Riobamba, at Urbina Pass. The Indian market at Ambato is worth seeing. Nine volcanoes can be seen from Latacunga.

Guayaquil

This is the largest city (800,000 population) in Ecuador as well as the country's financial and commercial center. See: The City Museum. La Rotunda. Government Palace. San Carlos Fort. The Municipal Tower. The tombs and monuments at "White City", the major cemetery. Santo Domingo Church. Colon Park. Do not miss the view of the city from El Mirador, or a visit to the world's largest balsa wood factory.

Riobamba

There are wonderful views from here of the peaks of Altar, Chimborazo and Tungurahua. See: The Saturday fair, in 9 different plazas (leather articles, rope sandals, embroidered belts, etc.). Nearby, see the carpets in Guano.

Quito

Ecuador's capital. See: The marvelous sculptures at the San Francisco Convent. The gold leaf in La Compania Church. Fine art in the Cathedral. The campus at the Central University. The National Palace. The view of Quito from the top of the 600-foot high Panecillo Hill. Colonial homes along La Ronda.

Some of Ecuador's best art, in the Municipal Art and History Museum at the Real de Lima. Stroll in 2 suburbs: Guapulo and San Roque. You can stand on the equator by taking a 15-mile auto trip north of Quito, where you can place one foot in the northern hemisphere and the other in the southern hemisphere.

Take the very scenic 2½-hour $1.20 bus ride to Otalvo, particularly on Friday in order to see the early-morning opening of the Saturday market with its many concessions (merchandise, food, beverages) and the colorful Indian costumes worn there.

Sibambe - Cuenca   1761

| Dep. Sibambe | 11:00 | Dep. Cuenca | 6:00 |
| Arr. Cuenca | 16:00 | Arr. Sibambe | 11:00 |

Sights in **Cuenca:** Founded by Spaniards in the 16th century on the ruins of the residence of a former Inca ruler. The major tourist attraction here is the Indian market. See the 16th century La Concepcion Convent and the 17th century Las Carmelitas Descalzas Convent. The Municipal Museum.

Quito - San Lorenzo   1750

Dep. Quito	N/A(1)	Dep. San Lorenzo	7:00(2)
Arr. Ibarra	N/A(1)	Arr. Ibarra	13:00
Change trains.		Overnight in Ibarra.	
Dep. Ibarra	7:00(2)	Dep. Ibarra	N/A(1)
Arr. San Lorenzo	13:00	Arr. Quito	N/A(1)

(1)Service "temporarily" suspended in 1982.   (2)Second-class only.

Sights in **San Lorenzo:** Ecuador's second rail-connected seaport, linked by train service (via Quito) with the other port, Guayaquil.

GUYANA

There is no train service between Guyana and adjacent countries. The 2 rail lines in Guyana have been replaced by bus service.

Georgetown

See the collection of orchids, palms and birds at the 120-acre Botanic Gardens. Local animals at the Zoo. Guyanese objects in the Natural History Museum. The world's tallest wood building, the Anglican Cathedral. The assortment of sundries at the Stabroek Market. The tiny, 216-seat Playhouse Theater.

Georgetown - Rosignol   1643   Bus

Dep. Georgetown	Frequent times	Dep. Rosignol	Frequent times
Arr. Rosignol	3 hours later	Arr. Georgetown	3 hours later

Vreed-en-Hoop - Parika   1642 Bus

Dep. Vreed	Frequent times	Dep. Parika	Frequent times
Arr. Parika	70-90 minutes later	Arr. Vreed	70-90 minutes later

GUYANE (French Guiana)

There are no passenger trains in Guyane.

PARAGUAY

Children under 3 travel free. Half-fare for children 3-9. Children 10 and over must pay full fare. Paraguay's only rail route is from Asuncion to Encarnacion. Its only passenger train service to an adjacent country is the extension from Encarnacion to Argentina.

Asuncion

The capital of Paraguay. Linked by rail (via Encarnacion) with Buenos Aires. See: Government Palace, on Calle El Paraguayo Independiente. The Pantheon of Heroes, the national shrine designed to emulate the Invalides in Paris. The Gran Hotel del Paraguay. The view of Asuncion from Parque Carlos Antonio Lopez. The Botanical and Zoological Garden, location of the Museum of Natural Science.

Window-shop on Calle Palma. Take a ride on one of the old trolleys, maintained for tourists as San Francisco, California's cable cars are.

Encarnacion

A busy river port. This is a base for taking auto or airplane trips to see the Iguazu Falls, most spectacular from August to November.

Asuncion - Encarnacion   2230

This route is through dense brush and jungle. The inconveniences include hard wood seats, stifling heat, swarms of mosquitoes and much dust. The locomotive was built in 1912, and the train is said to be the oldest in South America.

At night, the station platforms at villages along the route are lined with people who, sitting at tables while eating and singing, enjoy watching the train pass by.

Dep. Asuncion	20:00(1)	Dep.		
Arr. Encarnacion	12:00(2)	Encarnacion	5:00(3)	12:35(4)
		Arr. Asuncion	21:00	4:30(2)

(1)Runs Tuesday, Thursday and Friday. Meal service. (2)Day 2. (3)Runs Sunday only. Meal service. (4)Runs Wednesday and Friday. Meal service.

Encarnacion - Posadas - Buenos Aires   2230

Be sure to have an inexpensive (about $1.00 U.S.) "through ticket" before departing Asuncion for Encarnacion. Passengers from Asuncion who do not have a "through ticket" are required to leave the train at Encarnacion, carry their luggage to the auto ferry pier, take the auto ferry across the river, and re-board the train on the other side of the river, in Posadas.

Passengers with a "through ticket" can remain on the train as the train is ferried across the river.

Dep. Encarnacion	14:30(1)
Dep. Pacu Cua (Train Ferry)	17:30(1)
Arr. Posadas	18:20(1)
Arr. Buenos Aires (F. LaCroze)	14:10(2)

(1)Runs Wednesday and Friday. Meal service. (2)Day 2.

PERU

Children under 4 travel free. Half-fare for children 4-11. Children 12 and over must pay full fare.

Many rail routes in Peru are at such high altitudes that several trains provide passengers with free oxygen. Details on trips follow a description of interesting sights in 6 cities which can be visited by train.

Arequipa

This is called "The White City" because it is built mostly of white volcanic rock. It lies at the foot of 19,200-foot high El Misti Volcano. See: The beautiful furniture in the 17th century Santa Cataline Convent, reflecting medieval architecture and life. The flowery Plaza de Armas. The colonial residences: Casa del Moral, Casa Ricketts and Casa Gibbs. Leatherwork is a specialty here. At an altitude of 7,500 feet, much lower than Cuzco, Arequipa has a splendid climate.

Cuzco

November to March is the rainy season. The rest of the year, this is the popular tourist spot in Peru. At 11,400 feet altitude, it is often cold here in what was once the capital of the Inca Empire. Many Inca remains in this area. See: The Palace of Manco Capac, the first Inca ruler and founder of Cuzco. The famous stone of Twelve Anles, in the walls of the Palace of Inca Roca. Main Square, where Incas held their celebrations and ceremonies. Stroll Callejon Loreto, a perfectly preserved Inca street. Visit the unusually quiet Indian market.

The base of the ancient Temple of the Sun, now in the foundation of the Church of Santa Domingo. The gold and bejeweled pulpit in the 17th century Cathedral. The House of the Chosen Women, now the Convent of Santa Catalina. Five colonial churchs: El Triunfo, La Merced, Santa Domingo, Jesuite, and Jesus and Maria.

The excellent murals, carved altars and paintings in La Compania de Jesus, Cuzco's most beautiful church. The magnificent main altar in Belen de los Reyes Church, outside the city. The Inca stonework throughout the city's streets. The prominent colonial residences: La Casa de Garcilaso de la Vega Inca, La Casa de los Marqueses de Buenavista, La Casa de Diego Maldonado, and La Casa de Concha.

The museums: Art, Anthropological and Archaeological, Culture, Larco Heriera, and Viceregal. Two ancient forts nearby: Puca Pucara (the "red fort") and the enormous Sacsayhuaman (pronounced "sexy woman") with its 3 tremendous parallel walls. The ruins of Quenko, Tambomachay and Pucara.

The great excursion from Cuzco is the trip to Machu-Picchu, the large ancient Inca city-fortress. Details for that train ride appear later in this section.

Huancayo

Located where an Inca highway once existed, in a wide valley at 10,696 feet altitude. Sunday fairs is the event that attracts tourists here (herbs, fruits, embroidered skirts and petticoats, vegetables, furs, silver jewelry, gourds, etc.). This is the most famous market in Peru, attracting both Peruvian and Bolivian Indians.

Juliaca

Great woolen goods, leather items and alpaca knits are offered in the Sunday and Monday markets in the enormous Plaza Melgar.

Lima

In Summer, stores and offices here are closed from 12:30 to 16:00 so that loca people can go to the beaches. Shopping for silver and gold jewelry, alpaca and llama furs, and colonial antiques is a key tourist activity in Lima.

See: Much fine 16th and 17th century colonial architecture. Torre Tagle Palace and these churches: Santa Domingo (one block west of Government Palace), La Merced (on Jiron de la Union, 2 blocks from Plaza de Armas), San Francisco (one block east of Government Palace), San Augustin (2 blocks from Plaza de Armas), and San Pedro (2 blocks east and one block south of Plaza de Armas).

The curved mahogany ceiling in the main hall at the Court of the Inquisition. The city's famous bullring. Plaza San Martin, a lovely park. The centuries-old, 15-minute ritual of Changing of the Guard at Government Palace, daily except Sunday at 13:00.

The Museum of Art (5,000 years of Peruvian culture) in the 1868 Exposition Palace on Paseo Colon. Pre-Hispanic relics (back to 500 B.C.) in the Museum of Anthropology and Archaeology, and the adjoining Museum of the Republic, both at Plaza Bolivar. The Museum of Peruvian Culture at 650 Alfonso Ugarte Ave.

Colonial paintings, furniture and costumes in the Museum of Vice-royalty in the Quinta de Presa mansion. The Museum of Italian Art on Paseo de la Republica. The gold and silver collection at the Rafael Larco Herrera Museum. The Gold of Peru collection at the residence of Sr. Mujica Callo in nearby Monterrico. The mosaic tiles at La Punta, along the beach. The Military Museum at Fort Felipe Real.

The fantastic gold and silver items in the Gold Museum at Monterrico, a suburb. The 3½-hour tour (operated every day by Lima Tours, located near Hotel Bolivar) to the nearby Pachacamac ruins. Sunday afternoon fights in the Plaza de Acho bullring.

Puno (and Lake Titicaca)

It is cold and windy here, at 12,648 feet. The legend is that the Sun God created the first Inca king and his queen on the Island of the Sun in Lake Titicaca, on Peru's western border with Bolivia.

Today, 37-pound trout are the monarchs of a lake that is more than 2 miles above sea level, 35 miles wide and 95 miles long. There are many hydrofoil boat excursions to small "floating islands" of reeds, populated by Uru Indians

Lima - Huancayo   1821

The Lima-La Oroya portion of this train journey is the highest standard gauge rail trip in the world (built in 1893 and reaching a height of 15,681 feet) and carries a staff doctor. The descent to 10,696-foot high Huancayo becomes a relief ! The altitude is so debilitating that most passengers sleep or take oxygen inhalation.

For optimum experience, depart Lima on Saturday morning, spend that night in Huancayo, see the weekly Indian market there on Sunday (silver, llama wool blankets, hides, etc.), and return to Lima on Monday morning.

At the early part of the trip is Chosica, a popular Winter resort. Then, the train goes through scenic valleys and passes Indian farmhouses and rustic railstations where Indian women sell fruits and flowers. The track follows the Rimac River as it crosses 59 bridges, goes through 66 tunnels and makes 22 switchbacks. The "descent" into Huancayo is along small wheat farms.

Dep. Lima		Dep. Huancayo	7:00(2)
(Desamparados)	N/A(1)	Arr. La Oroya	10:06(1)
Dep. La Oroya	13:40(2)	Arr. Lima	
Arr. Huancayo	16:38	(Desamparados)	N/A(1)

(1)Service west of La Oroya was suspended in 1982 due to a damaged bridge and in 1983 because of landslides. (2)Daily, except Sundays and holidays. Meal service.

La Oroya - Cerro de Pasco   1817

Dep. La Oroya	14:00(1)	Dep. Cerro de Pasco	6:30(1)
Arr. Cerro de Pasco	17:42	Arr. La Oroya	9:35

(1)Daily, except Sundays and holidays. Meal service.

Sights in **Cerro de Pasco:** At 14,232-feet altitude, this is one of the world's highest towns. There are many metal mines here (copper, gold, zinc, lead). The town was rebuilt in the early 1970's.

*   *   *

Huancayo - Huancavelica   1816

All of these trains run daily, except Sundays and holidays.

Dep. Huancayo	7:00(1)	7:30(2)	13:00(1)
Arr. Huancavelica	10:10	13:55	16:10

*   *   *

Dep. Huancavelica	7:00(1)	7:30(2)	13:00(1)
Arr. Huancayo	10:10	13:50	16:10

(1)First-class only. (2)Has both first and second-class coach. Meal service.

Cuzco to Machu Picchu and Inca City   1810

One of the most popular train journeys in Peru is from Cuzco to Machu-Picchu, paralleling the turbulent Urubamba River. The 5,000-foot descent from Cuzco through the verdant jungle is considered by many as one of the most scenic rail trips in the world.

The other attraction, of course, is seeing the incredible 15th century Inca ruins at Machu-Picchu, an 8,000-foot high plateau surrounded by snow-covered mountains, not discovered until the early 20th century by Hiram Bingham, a Yale University professor.

In his book "The Lost City of the Incas", Bingham wrote: "I know of no other place in the world that can compare to this sight."

At some train stops, native women go through the train, selling tortillas. En route, the train goes through a fertile valley at Ollantaytambo. A bus provides transportation from the Machu-Picchu railstation 1,000 feet up to the ruins. The small (14 rooms) Hotel Turista accommodates visitors who want to stay overnight before returning to Cuzco.

All of these trains have a parlor car.

Dep. Cuzco (S.Pedro)	6:00	7:00(1)	14:25	22:15
Dep. Machu-Picchu	9:33	-0-	18:17	1:29
Arr. Pte. Ruinos	9:40	10:25	18:24	1:36
	*	*	*	
Dep. Pte. Ruinos	1:24	8:15	15:20(1)	15:44
Dep. Machu-Picchu	1:31	8:22	-0-	15:51
Arr. Cuzco (S.Pedro)	5:25	12:25	19:00	19:50

(1)Special tourist train. Supplement charged. There is bus service for the 8km trip Pte. Ruinos-Inca City and v.v.

Cuzco - Juliaca   1810

This extremely scenic route is along the heights of the Andes. Indian women sell colorful knitted garments at the Juliaca railstation.

These trains may be replaced in 1984 by new equipment, with departures from Cuzco at 14:00 and from Juliaca at 22:30.

Dep. Cuzco (Main)	9:40(1)	Dep. Juliaca	9:25(1)
Arr. Juliaca	17:42	Arr. Cuzco (Main)	17:30

(1)Runs daily, except Sundays and holidays. Meal service.

Juliaca - Arequipa   1825

The train passes along many grain fields. Highest place on the route is 14,688-feet high Crucero Alto. After it, all water flows toward the Pacific Ocean.

Many tall mountains can be seen as well as grazing vicunas, sheep, llamas and alpacas. The train descends in 189 miles from Juliaca (12,500 feet) to Arequipa (7,500 feet).

These trains may be replaced in 1984 by new equipment, with departure from Arequipa at 14:00 and from Juliaca at approximately 22:30.

All of these trains have meal service.

Dep. Juliaca	9:35(1)	21:55(2+3)
Arr. Arequipa	16:35	6:00

*   *   *

Dep. Arequipa	9:30(4)	22:00(2+5)
Arr. Juliaca	17:13	5:45

(1)Runs Tuesday, Thursday and Saturday. (2)Carries sleeping car daily. (3)Has coach cars daily, except Sunday. (4)Runs Monday, Wednesday and Friday. (5)Has coach cars daily, except Saturday.

Chimbote - Huallanca   0000

This is an 88-mile ride up Santa Valley to the del Pato canyon.

Dep. Chimbote	N/A	Dep. Huallanca	N/A
Arr. Huallanca	N/A	Arr. Chimbote	N/A

INTERNATIONAL ROUTES FROM PERU

Rail connections are available from both Cuzco and Arequipa to both Bolivia and Chile. Puno, on the shore of Lake Titicaca, is 12,648 feet high. These trains may be replaced in 1984 by new equipment, with departures from Cuzco at 14:00, Juliaca 22:30 and Arequipa 14:00.

Cuzco-Puno
1810

Dep. Cuzco	9:40(1)
Arr. Juliaca	17:42
Change trains.	

1825

Dep. Juliaca	17:55(2)
Arr. Puno	19:00

Arequipa-Puno
1825

Dep. Arequipa	9:30(3)	22:00(4)
Dep. Juliaca	17:18(3)	5:50(4)
Arr. Puno	19:00	7:20

(1)Runs daily, except Sundays and holidays. Meal service. (2)Runs Tuesday, Thursday and Saturday. Meal service. (3)Runs Monday, Wednesday and Friday. Meal service. (4)Carries sleeping car. Meal service.

Puno - Guaqui - La Paz   1826   Boat trip.

Dep. Puno	20:00 Wed.	Dep. Guaqui	10:45 Thurs.
Arr. Guaqui	7:00 Thurs.	Arr. La Paz	13:45 Thurs.
Change to bus.			

Arequipa - Guaqui - Viacha . . . and on to Arica or Antofagasta 1826
Arr. Guaqui from Puno   7:00 Thursday
(See preceding schedules: "Puno-Guaqui-La Paz".)
  Change from boat to Bus.
  1815
  This was a 2-hour daytime train ride in 1977.
Dep. Guaqui   N/A(1)
Arr. Viacha   2 hours later
(1)Time has not been available since 1977.

Viacha - Arica	1901	**Viacha - Antofagasta**	1910
Dep. Viacha	13:46(1)	Dep. Viacha	13:33(3)
Arr. Charana	19:46	Arr. Calama	16:10(4)
Change trains.		Change to bus.	
Dep. Charana	22:50(2)	Dep. Calama	17:00(5)
Arr. Arica	8:05	Arr. Antofagasta	20:00

(1)Runs Tuesday only. (2)Runs only on the 2nd and 4th Tuesday of the month.
(3)Runs Friday only. (4)Arrival on Saturday. (5)Runs Saturday only.

SURINAM

Children under 3 travel free. Half-fare for children 3-14. Children 15 and over must pay full fare. The only passenger rail line in Surinam is Onverwacht-Brownsweg. There is good forest and mountain scenery on that route.
Paramaribo
See the lovely 18th and 19th century Dutch building on Oranjeplein. The Museum in Fort Zeelandia. The Zoo in Cultuurtuin Park. The picturesque waterfront.

Paramaribo - Onverwacht - Brownsweg		1635	
Bus		Train	
Dep. Paramaribo	6:30(1)	Dep. Brownsweg	13:00(2)
Arr. Beekhuizen	6:59	Arr. Onverwacht	17:00
Change buses.		Change to bus.	
Dep. Beekhuizen	7:00(1)	Dep. Onverwacht	17:30(2)
Arr. Onverwacht	7:30	Arr. Beekhuizen	17:59
Change to train.		Change buses.	
Dep. Onverwacht	8:00(1)	Dep. Beekhuizen	18:00(2)
Arr. Brownsweg	12:30	Arr. Paramaribo	18:30

(1)Runs Friday only. (2)Runs Saturday only.

URUGUAY

Children under 3 travel free. Half-fare for children 3-9. Children 10 and over must pay full fare.

Montevideo is the hub for Uruguay's 1,874 miles of rail service. The 4 lines from there are to Colonia, Mercedes, Rio Branco and Rivera. A branch off the line to Rivera leads to Salto and Artigas.

Colonia

See: The Municipal Museum. The Mansion of the Viceroy. The beautiful plaza. The Parochial Church.

Montevideo

Peak tourist season here is January and February. The major attraction is the city's big beaches. See: The enormous marble Legislative Palace. The National Historical Museum (Rincom 437). Plaza Independencia and the nearby Natural History Museum (Buenos Aires 652). The large lake and National Fine Arts Museum in Rodo Park.

The Oceanography and Fish Museum (Rambla Republica de Chile 4215). The Zoo on Avenida de Rivera. The Military Museum (Montevideo Hill), and the view from there. The Pre-Columbian Museum (Mateo Vidal 3249). The collection of paintings and sculptures at the Joaguin Torres Garcia Museum (Constitujente 1467). The outstanding Rose Garden (850 varieties) and Municipal Museum of Fine Arts and History, both in El Prado Park. The Sunday morning flea market on Calle Tristen Narvaja, across from the University's statue of David.

The many fine statues in Batlle y Ordonez Park. The Cathedral, on Plaza Constitucion. Stroll down Avenida 18 de Julio. East of Plaza Zabala, see the Customs House, the Bolsa (Stock Exchange) and Banco de la Republica. Lunch at the stand-up bars (barbecued meats, fruits, soups, sandwiches, fish) at Mercado del Puerto, at the waterfront. Then walk to the breakwater at Punta Santa Teresa to see ships coming into port, or walk along the beaches bordered by Rio de Plata.

The nearby Punta del Este beach resort, during the peak season (mid-December to mid-March). The Casa Pueblo Museum, featuring the work of Uruguayan painter Carlos Paez Vilaro, the Picasso of South America. Night life centers at the local gambling casino. Stroll Avenida Gorlero to see its antique shops, notable for American and European Art Nouveau items from the early years of this century. Take a boat to Isla de Lobos to see the seal colony there.

Rivera

See: Canapiru Dam. Plaza Internacional. Stroll the street which is the border with Brazil. On the other side of the street is the Brazilian city Santa Ana do Livramento.

Salto

See: Lovely Solari Park. The walkway along the Uruguay River.

Montevideo - Colonia   2213

Dep. Montevideo		Dep. Colonia	16:00(1)
(Gen. Artigas)	6:55(1)	Arr. Montevideo	
Arr. Colonia	12:19	(Gen. Artigas)	21:35

(1)Runs Monday, Wednesday and Friday.

Montevideo - Mercedes   2213

Dep. Montevideo		Dep. Mercedes	5:20(1)
(Gen Artigas)	16:20(1)	Arr. Montevideo	
Arr. Mercedes	23:05	(Gen. Artigas)	11:50

(1)Runs daily, except Sundays and holidays. Meal service.

Montevideo - Rio Branco   2203

Dep. Montevideo		Dep. Rio Branco	22:58(1)
(Gen Artigas)	7:10(1)	Arr. Montevideo	
Arr. Rio Branco	15:19	(Gen. Artigas)	7:08

(1)Supplement charged. Meal service.

Montevideo - Rivera   2205

Dep. Montevideo		Dep. Rivera	22:00(1)
(Gen. Artigas)	22:35(1)	Arr. Montevideo	
Arr. Rivera	8:14	(Gen. Artigas)	7:55

(1)Supplement charged. Meal service.

Montevideo - Salto - Artigas   2210

Dep. Montevideo		Dep. Artigas	8:00(1+4)
(Gen. Artigas)	19:20(1+2)	Dep. Salto	17:40(1+4)
Dep. Salto	11:30(3)	Arr. Montevideo	
Arr. Artigas	21:03(3)	(Gen. Artigas)	9:50(2)

(1)Carries sleeping car. Light refreshments. (2)Runs Wednesday only. (3)Day 2.   (4)Runs Friday only.

INTERNATIONAL ROUTES FROM URUGUAY

Montevideo - Buenos Aires 2217

Dep. Montevideo by Bus	6:15	6:30	9:00	9:40	13:15(1)
Arr. Colonia	9:05	9:15	12:05	12:15	16:05
Dep. Colonia by Hydrofoil	9:20	9:30	12:20	12:30	16:20
Arr. Buenos Aires	60 minutes later				

(1)Plus another departure from Montevideo at 16:15.

Montevideo - Sao Paulo 2120 Bus

Dep. Montevideo	20:00	21:00	22:00	23:30(2)
Arr. Porto Alegre	7:59(1)	9:20(1)	11:10(1)	12:05(1+2)

Change buses.
2100

Dep. Porto Alegre	8:00	-0-	17:00(4)	N/A(2+5)
Arr. Sao Paulo	4:00(3)	-0-	14:00(3)	6:55(3)

(1)Day 3 from Montevideo. (2)Direct bus. No bus change in Porto Alegre. (3)Day 5 from Montevideo. (4)Change trains in Curitiba. (5)Time has not been available since 1980.

VENEZUELA

Children under 3 travel free. Half-fare for children 3-11. Children 12 and over must pay full fare.

There is no train service between Venezuela and adjacent countries. The only rail service for which timetables are available is the 105-mile route from Puerto Cabello to Barquisimeto.

Puerto Cabello - Barquisimeto 1655

Dep. Puerto Cabello	6:11	9:11(1)	13:11(1)	17:40
Arr. Barquisimeto	8:56	11:56	15:56	20:25
	*	*	*	
Dep. Barquisimeto	6:00	9:00(1)	13:00(1)	17:26
Arr. Puerto Cabello	8:45	11:45	15:45	20:11

(1)Runs Saturdays, Sundays and holidays.

Sights in **Puerto Cabello:** A heavily industrialized city.

Sights in **Barquisimeto:** A collecting point for sugar, cacao, cereals, coffee and cattle.

Chapter 18

EURAIL® GUIDE ROUTE CHART

In view of the fact that there are over 100,000 miles of railroad lines in just the 16 Eurailpass countries, it would be impossible to list every conceivable trip one could make by train in Western Europe. We do provide you in this chapter a list of 734 trips that most people touring Europe might make, giving the travel time and first-class fare for each.

We have condensed route descriptions by listing them only in alphabetical priority. For example, the first route is Aix-en-Provence to Marseille. If you were looking for the trip from Marseille to Aix-en-Provence, you would refer to the name that has alphabetical priority: Aix-en-Provence. Similarly, the trip Rome-Paris will be found as Paris-Rome, etc.

The rates listed are first-class fares, in U.S. dollars. To compute second-class fares, figure 66% of the first-class fare shown. While this will not always be the exact second-class fare, it will be very close to it. Also remember that European train fares, like all other European goods and services, are subject to change relative to U.S. dollar devaluation (or the reverse). On the other hand, once a Eurailpass has been issued to you, you are spared the possibility of any dollar devaluation increasing the cost of your train transportation ¢ another hidden plus to having a Eurailpass.

All the fares listed in this chapter are subject to a seat reservation fee of $2.00 per person (if you want to be sure of having a seat). This charge is made whether traveling with a ticket or with Eurailpass. However, a Eurailpass holder does *not* have to pay the supplement that is charged in addition to the ticket price when riding on a Trans Europ Express, International Inter-City or TGV train, ranging from $3 to $18.

We have listed a few TEE and IIC ticket prices to illustrate that cost and to show how much is saved when traveling with a Eurailpass. Many TEE, IIC and TGV prices are *not* included here. The complete list of those special trains and their routes appear in Chapter 7.

Keep in mind that trips between Eurailpass countries and non-Eurailpass countries are only partly covered by Eurailpass. A passenger holding a Eurailpass has to pay the non-Eurailpass portion of such a fare.

Because Paris has 6 different railstations, we indicate in parenthesis after the name ''Paris'' the name of the Paris railstation at which a train is arriving.

EURAIL® GUIDE ROUTE CHART
1984 first-class train fares, *not* including seat reservation fee.

	Travel Time	Fare
AIX-EN-PROVENCE		
Marseille	½	6.00
ALBORG		
Copenhagen	6	34.00
ALGECIRAS		
Corodoba	5½	22.00
Granada	6½	21.00
Madrid	10	51.00
Malaga	5	17.00
Seville	7½	24.00
ALICANTE		
Valencia	3	14.00
ALKMAAR		
Amsterdam	½	5.00
AMSTERDAM		
Antwerp	2½	24.00
Basel (via Roosendaal)	9½	103.00
Berlin	8½	83.00
Bremen	4	46.00
Brussels	3½	29.00
TEE	2½	37.00
Cologne (Koln)	3	35.00
Copenhagen (Kobenhavn)	12	109.00
Dusseldorf	2½	31.00
Frankfurt	6	63.00
Hamburg	6	61.00
Hannover	5½	48.00
Heidelberg	6½	71.00
Hoek Van Holland	2	13.00

Luxembourg (via Roosendaal)	5	52.00
Munich (Munchen)	12	111.00
Paris (Nord)	5½	64.00
TEE	5	78.00
Rotterdam	1	12.00
Salzburg	13	132.00
Utrecht	½	5.00
Vienna (Wien)		
(via Passau)	15	144.00
Wiesbaden	6	58.00
Zurich	11	118.00

ANDALSNES

Oslo	8	68.00
Trondheim	5½	49.00

ANDERMATT

Brig	2	17.00
Chur	2½	22.00
Lugano	2	24.00
Luzern	2	20.00
Zurich	2	24.00

ANTWERP

Brussels	1	5.00
Paris (Nord)	3½	40.00
Rotterdam	1½	15.00

AOSTA

Milan	3½	16.00
Turin (Torino)	1½	9.00

ARHUS

Copenhagen (Kobenhavn)	5	29.00

ARLES

Marseille	1	11.00
Nimes	½	6.00

AROSA

Chur	1	6.00
Zurich	3	27.00

ASSISI

Florence (Firenze)	3	13.00
Rome	2½	13.00

ATHENS

Patras	3	14.00
Thessaloniki	9	26.00

AVIGNON

Barcelona	6½	46.00
Cannes	3½	35.00
Carcassone	2½	29.00
Geneva	4½	45.00
Lourdes	7	58.00
Lyon	2½	27.00
Marseille	1	15.00
Nice	4	39.00
Nimes	1	7.00
Paris (Lyon)	7	82.00
Paris (Lyon) TGV. Sup. on some rides.	4	82.00
Port Bou	4	34.00

BARCELONA

Bilboa	9½	51.00
Carcassone	6	32.00
Geneva	12	89.00
IIC	9½	99.00
Genoa	13½	93.00
Lourdes	10	60.00
Lyon	10	71.00
Madrid	8	50.00
Marseille	8	55.00
Nice	10	78.00
Paris (Austerlitz)	12	117.00
Rome	20	129.00
Seville	22	72.00
Toulouse	7	41.00
Valencia	5	26.00
Vigo	27	88.00
Zaragoza	4½	27.00

BARI

Bologna	7½	45.00
Brindisi	1½	8.00
Messina	9	40.00
Milan	10	58.00
Naples	4	23.00
Pescara	3½	21.00
Rome	6	38.00
Taranto	1½	8.00
Turin (Torino)	13	63.00
Venice	13	56.00

BASEL

Bern	1½	22.00
Brig	3½	36.00
Brussels	7	65.00
Bucharest (Partly covered by Eurailpass)	29	163.00
Budapest (Partly covered by Eurailpass)	16	107.00
Cologne (Koln)	6	66.00
Copenhagen (Kobenhavn)	15	155.00
Florence (Firenze)	10	68.00
Frankfurt	3½	45.00
Geneva	3½	36.00
Genoa	9	57.00
Hamburg	9	109.00
Hannover	7½	88.00
Heidelberg	3	35.00
Innsbruck	6	48.00
Interlaken	2½	30.00
Lausanne	2½	31.00
Locarno	4½	39.00
Lugano	4½	40.00
Luxembourg	4	41.00
Luzern	1½	17.00
Milan	6	46.00
Montreux	3	33.00
Paris (Est)	6	58.00
Rome	14½	91.00
Rotterdam (via Brussels)	8½	84.00
Salzburg	9	68.00
Strasbourg	1	17.00
Venice	10	64.00
Vienna (Wien)	12	85.00
Wiesbaden	4	47.00
Zurich	1	15.00

BAYONNE

Hendaye	1	6.00
Madrid	6½	51.00

BAYREUTH

Nurnberg	1½	12.00

BERGEN

Bodo	26½	163.00
Flam	3½	23.00
Goteborg	12	104.00
Myrdal	2½	22.00
Oslo	7	69.00
Trondheim	14½	110.00
Voss	1½	14.00

BERLIN

Bremen	5½	52.00
Brussels	10	97.00
Cologne (Koln)	7	75.00
Copenhagen (Kobenhavn)	8	49.00
Dusseldorf	6½	69.00
Frankfurt	7	62.00
Hamburg	3½	34.00
Hannover	4	34.00
Leipzig	1½	20.00
Luxembourg	11	102.00
Malmo	8½	47.00
Munich (Munchen)	9	81.00
Nurnburg	7	55.00
Oslo	19½	117.00
Paris (Nord)	14	128.00
Rotterdam	10	85.00
Stockholm	15½	97.00
Vienna (Wien) (Sudbf.) via Prague	14	71.00

BERN

Brig	2	26.00
Geneva	2	27.00
Interlaken	1	13.00
Lausanne	1	17.00
Lugano	4½	40.00
Luzern	1½	22.00
Milan (via Lotschberg)	4½	39.00

Montreux	3½	30.00
Paris (Lyon) via Verrieres	5	69.00
Zurich	1½	23.00

BILBAO

Hendaye	4	20.00
Madrid	5½	39.00
Vigo	12	55.00
Zaragoza	5	24.00

BODEN

Stockholm	16	69.00

BODO

Goteborg		
via Stockholm	34	164.00
via Oslo	24½	162.00
Oslo	19½	130.00
Trondheim	12	89.00

BOLOGNA

Florence (Firenze)	1½	7.00
TEE	1	11.00
Genoa	4½	21.00
Innsbruck	6½	31.00
Milan	2½	15.00
TEE	2	22.00
Naples	6½	45.00
TEE	6	62.00
Paris (Lyon)	12½	110.00
Ravenna	1½	6.00
Rimini	1½	8.00
Rome	4	30.00
TEE	4	41.00
Turin (Torino)	4½	24.00
Venice	2	11.00
Verona	1½	8.00

BONN

Cologne (Koln)	½	5.00
Frankfurt	2	24.00
Koblenz	1	7.00

BORDEAUX

Geneva	10	88.00
Hendaye	3	27.00
Lourdes	3½	31.00
Lyon	9	70.00
Marseille	7	75.00
Nice	12	99.00
Paris (Austerlitz)	5	64.00
TEE	4	79.00
Toulouse	3½	29.00
Tours	3½	39.00

BREMEN

Budapest (Partly covered by Eurailpass)	19½	147.00
Cologne (Koln)	3	43.00
Copenhagen (Kobenhavn)	7	64.00
Dusseldorf	3	37.00
Essen	2½	33.00
Frankfurt	6	60.00
Hamburg	2	15.00
Hannover	1	15.00
Heidelberg	7	72.00
Munich (Munchen)	8½	96.00
Stuttgart	8½	83.00
Vienna (Wien)	14	126.00

BRIG

Chur	4½	40.00
Interlaken	1½	23.00
Lausanne	1½	26.00
Zermatt	1½	21.00

BRUGGE

Brussels	1½	10.00

BRUSSELS

Budapest (Partly covered by Eurailpass)	20½	155.00
Calais	3	25.00
Cologne (Koln)	2½	25.00
Copenhagen (Kobenhavn)	13½	129.00
Frankfurt	5½	55.00
Ghent	½	6.00
Hamburg	8	82.00
Liege	1	11.00
Luxembourg	3	24.00

Munich (Munchen)	10	104.00
Paris (Nord)	3	35.00
TEE	2½	44.00
Rotterdam	2	20.00
Vienna (Wien) (via Frankfurt)	15	134.00
Zurich	13	80.00

BUCHS

Innsbruck	3	17.00
Zurich	1½	20.00

BUDAPEST

These trips are only partly covered by Eurailpass.

Cologne (Koln)	18	133.00
Frankfurt	15½	104.00
Hamburg	19½	154.00
Milan	16½	91.00
Munich (Munchen)	11	69.00
Paris (Est)		
via Nancy	21	178.00
via Basel	25	165.00
Rome	25½	112.00
Trieste	15	69.00
Venice	13	73.00
Vienna (Wien)	4	26.00
Zurich	18	96.00

CADIZ

Madrid	8	50.00
Seville	2	11.00

CALAIS

Paris (Nord)	4	35.00
Strasbourg	9½	69.00

CANNES

Florence (Firenze)	11	38.00
Geneva	9	78.00
Genoa	3	19.00
Marseille	2	22.00
Milan	7½	30.00
Nice	1	5.00
Paris (Lyon)	11	115.00
Rome	13	55.00
San Remo	3	10.00

CARCASSONE

Lourdes	4	31.00
Marseille	4	38.00
Nice	7	61.00
Paris (Austerlitz)	8	88.00
Port Bou	2½	20.00
Toulouse	1	12.00

CHAMONIX-MONT BLANC

Geneva	2½	14.00
Grenoble	2¼	28.00
Martigny (Second-class only)	3	10.00
Paris (Lyon)	8	78.00

CHARTRES

Paris (Montparnasee)	1	11.00

CHERBOURG

Paris (St. Lazare)	3½	42.00

CHUR

St. Moritz	2½	22.00
Zurich	1½	22.00

COLOGNE (KOLN)

Copenhagen (Kobenhavn)	11	104.00
Dortmund	1	15.00
Dusseldorf	½	7.00
Essen	1	11.00
Frankfurt	2½	30.00
Hamburg	5	60.00
Hannover	3	40.00
Heidelberg	3	37.00
Koblenz	1	12.00
Luxembourg	3½	31.00
Luzern	7½	83.00
Mainz	2	24.00
Mannheim	3	33.00
Milan	12	112.00
Munich (Munchen)	7	79.00
Paris (Nord)	7	56.00
Rotterdam	3½	33.00
Salzburg	8½	96.00

Stuttgart	4½	50.00
Vienna (Wien)	12	112.00
Wiesbaden	2	24.00
Zurich	7½	81.00

COIMBRA
| Lisbon | 2½ | 13.00 |

COMO
Lugano	½	6.00
Luzern	4	34.00
Milan	1	4.00
Venice	4	22.00
Zurich	4	39.00

COPENHAGEN (KOBENHAVN)
Frankfurt	11½	110.00
Fredrickshavn	7	36.00
Hamburg (via Puttgarden)	5	48.00
Helsinki (Ship)	24	95.00
Kristiansand (Ship)	15	57.00
Luxemburg	14½	132.00
Malmo (Hydrofoil)	½	7.00
(Not covered by Eurailpass.)		
Milan	22½	197.00
Munich (Munchen) (via Berlin)	19	123.00
Narvik	32½	103.00
Odense	3	16.00
Oslo (via Goteberg)	10	74.00
Paris (Nord)	14	160.00
Rome	31½	246.00
Rotterdam	13	111.00
Stockholm (via Hassleholm)	8	57.00
Trondheim (via Goteborg)	18	136.00
Venice	26	195.00
Vienna (Wien)	21	179.00
Wiesbaden	13	128.00

CORDOBA
Granada	4½	17.00
Madrid	5½	31.00
Malaga	3	14.00
Seville	1½	10.00

DAVOS
| Zurich | 3 | 29.00 |

DIJON
Lausanne	3	25.00
Lyon	2	23.00
Paris (Lyon) TGV. Sup. on some rides.	2	35.00
Strasbourg (via Belfort)	4	39.00

DORTMUND
Paris (Nord)	7	70.00

DUNKERQUE
Lille	1½	13.00
Paris (Nord)	3½	33.00
Strasbourg	8	68.00

DUSSELDORF
Essen	½	5.00
Frankfurt	3	34.00
Hamburg	4	53.00
Hannover	3	37.00
Munich (Munchen)	11	86.00
Paris (Nord)	6	60.00

ESSEN
Hamburg	4	50.00

FLAM
Myrdal (2nd class fare)	1	3.00
Oslo	7	53.00

FLORENCE (FIRENZE)
Geneva	10	66.00
Genoa	4	18.00
Innsbruck	8	38.00
Lausanne	9	61.00
Leghorn (Livorno)	1½	8.00
Luzern	9	59.00
Marseille	12	59.00
Milan	3	22.00
TEE	3	31.00
Munich (Munchen)	10	55.00
Naples	6	38.00
TEE	5	52.00
Nice	9½	33.00
Paris		
(Est) via Chiasso	18	126.00
(Lyon) via Iselle	15	117.00
(Lyon) via Pisa	18	112.00
(Lyon) via Turin (Torino)	18	113.00

Perugia	2½	12.00
Pisa	1½	6.00
Ravenna	3	11.00
Rome	3	22.00
TEE	2½	31.00
Siena	2½	7.00
Turin (Torino)	6	30.00
Venice	3	18.00
Vienna (Wien)	13	68.00

FRANKFURT

Hamburg	5½	67.00
Hannover	3½	45.00
Heidelberg	1	12.00
Innsbruck	7½	77.00
Luxembourg	4½	37.00
Mainz	½	5.00
Mannheim	1	11.00
Munich (Munchen)	5	53.00
Nurnberg	2½	30.00
Paris (Est)	7	74.00
Rotterdam	6	61.00
Salzburg	7	72.00
Stuttgart	2½	27.00
Vienna (Wien)	9	83.00
Wiesbaden	½	7.00
Zurich	5	60.00

FREDRICKSHAVN

Hamburg	8½	56.00
Oslo (Ship) (*Not* covered by Eurailpass.)	10	58.00
Stockholm (Ship) (*Not* covered by Eurailpass.)	11½	55.00

GARMISCH-PARTENKIRCHEN

Innsbruck	1½	10.00
Munich (Munchen)	1½	14.00

GAVLE

Stockholm	2	18.00

GENEVA
    Genoa
        via Milan   7½   53.00
        via Turin (Torino)   7   43.00
    Grenoble   3½   20.00
    Gstaad   2½   26.00
    Interlaken (via Bern)   3   33.00
    Lausanne   ½   11.00
    Locarno   4½   45.00
    Lourdes   10   101.00
    Luzern   3½   35.00
    Lyon   3   20.00
    Marseille (via Lyon)   6½   58.00
    Milan   6   44.00
        IIC   4   47.00
    Montreux   1   15.00
    Nice (via Lyon)   10½   82.00
    Paris (Lyon) TGV.   Sup. on some rides.   3¾   69.00
    Rome   10   87.00
    Turin (Torino)   5   32.00
    Venice   8   63.00
    Zurich   3   38.00

GENOA
    Lausanne   7   49.00
    Luzern   7½   48.00
    Marseille   7½   40.00
    Milan   2   11.00
        IIC   1½   14.00
    Monaco-Monte Carlo   3   13.00
    Munich (Munchen)   11½   61.00
    Naples   8½   51.00
    Nice   3½   16.00
    Paris (Lyon) (via Torino)   12   93.00
    Pisa   2½   12.00
    Rome   7   37.00
    Salzburg   14   64.00
    San Remo   2   10.00
    Turin (Torino)   2½   12.00
    Venice   7   30.00

GOTEBORG

Copehagen (Kobenhavn)	4½	30.00
Hamburg	10	75.00
Helsingborg	3	25.00
Kalmar	7	36.00
Oslo	5	47.00
Stockholm	4½	44.00
Trondheim	21	87.00

GRANDA

Madrid	6½	34.00
Malaga	3½	14.00
Seville	5½	20.00
Valencia	12½	42.00

GRANVIN

Voss (Second-class only)	1	3.00

GRAZ

Vienna (Wien)	3½	19.00

GRENOBLE

Marseille	5½	35.00

GRINDELWALD

Interlaken (*Not* covered by Eurailpass)	1	5.00
Zurich (Only partially covered by Eurailpass)	3	36.00

HAMBURG

Hannover	2	23.00
Heidelberg	7	79.00
Helsinki	33	140.00
Luxembourg	8½	90.00
Malmo (Hydrofoil) (*Not* covered by Eurailpass.)	5½	55.00
Munich (Munchen)	8½	100.00
Oslo	15	119.00
Paris (Nord)	11	113.00
Rotterdam	6½	63.00
Salzburg	10	118.00
Stockholm	14½	102.00
Stuttgart	8	89.00
Vienna (Wien)	13	133.00

HANNOVER

Munich (Munchen)	6	79.00
Paris (Nord)	10	96.00
Rotterdam	5	50.00
Wurzburg	4	47.00

HAPARANDA

Helsinki	12	50.00
Narvik	11	58.00
Stockholm	19	80.00

HEIDELBERG

Koblenz	2	24.00
Luzern	4½	52.00
Mainz	1	12.00
Munich (Munchen)	4	45.00
Nurnberg	4	35.00
Paris (Est)	7	67.00
Rothenburg	3	30.00
Stuttgart	1	15.00
Wiesbaden	1½	14.00

HELSINKI

Kuopio	6	33.00
Oslo (Ship) (*Not* covered by Eurailpass.)	22	102.00
Oulu	7½	44.00
Stockholm (Ship)	12½	38.00
Turku	3	16.00

HENDAYE

Lisbon	17	67.00
Lourdes	3½	21.00
Madrid	7	45.00
Paris (Austerlitz)	8	89.00
Zaragoza	5½	24.00

HOEK VAN HOLLAND

Copenhagen	12	112.00
Innsbruck	13	136.00
Munich (Munchen)	12	112.00
Rotterdam	½	6.00

INNSBRUCK
Kitzbuhel	1	11.00
Luzern	6	42.00
Milan	6½	34.00
Munich (Munchen)	4	22.00
Paris (Est)	21	106.00
Rome	12½	60.00
Salzburg	4	22.00
Venice	5	32.00
Verona	5	23.00
Vienna (Wien)	8	47.00
Zurich	5	37.00

INTERLAKEN
Jungfraujoch (*Not* covered by Eurailpass.)	2	34.00
Kleine Scheidegg (*Not* covered by Eurailpass.)	1½	13.00
Lausanne	2	30.00
Luzern	2	13.00
Milan	5	37.00
Montreux	3	28.00
Paris (Lyon) via Verrieres	8½	80.00
Paris (Est) via Grenchen	8	83.00
Schilthorn (*Not* covered by Eurailpass.)	2	19.00
Price shown is for roundtrip.		
Zurich	2¾	31.00

KARLSTAD
Oslo	3	34.00
Stockholm	3½	33.00

KLAGENFURT
Salzburg	4	21.00
Venice	4½	25.00
Vienna (Wein)	6	28.00

KLOSTERS
Zurich	2½	26.00

KOBLENZ
Luxemburg	2½	21.00
Munich (Munchen)	6½	67.00
Paris (via Reims)	7½	65.00
Vienna (Wien)	10	102.00
Wiesbaden	1	12.00

KONSTANZ
    Zurich   1   16.00

KRISTIANSAND
    Oslo   5   54.00
    Stavanger   3½   36.00

LAUSANNE
    Locarno   4   40.00
    Luzern   3   33.00
    Milan   4½   39.00
    Montreux   ½   5.00
    Paris (Lyon) TGV.   Sup. on some rides.   3¾   60.00
    Rome   14   82.00
    Venice   8½   58.00
    Zurich   2½   33.00

LEGHORN (LIVORNO)
    Pisa   ½   2.00
    Rome   3   22.00

LE HAVRE
    Paris (St. Lazare)   2½   26.00

LIEGE
    Luxemburg   3   17.00
    Paris (Nord)   4   41.00

LINZ
    Salzburg   2   13.00
    Vienna (Wien)   2   17.00

LISBON
    Madrid (Atocha)   9   45.00
    Paris (Austerlitz)   25   156.00
    Porto   4   19.00
    Santiago de Compostela   9   33.00
    Seville   12   38.00
    Vigo   9   27.00

LOCARNO
    Lugano   1   8.00
    Luzern   3   30.00
    Milan   1   17.00
    Zurich   3½   31.00

LOURDES

Madrid	12	66.00
Nice	12	90.00
Paris (Austerlitz)	8½	93.00
Toulouse	2½	21.00

LUGANO

Luzern	3	31.00
Milan	1½	9.00
Venice	6	27.00
Zurich	3½	32.00

LUXEMBOURG

Marseille	10	96.00
Metz	1	9.00
Munich (Munchen)	9	83.00
Nurnberg	7	68.00
Paris (Est) via Bettembourg	4	48.00
Salzburg (via Strasbourg)	11	99.00
Strasbourg	3	26.00
Stuttgart	6	49.00
Vienna (Wien)	13	119.00
Zurich	5	56.00

LUZERN

Milan	4½	37.00
Montreux	5½	34.00
Munich (Munchen)	6½	62.00
Paris (Est)	10	75.00
Pilatus	1½	16.00
Rigi	1½	16.00
Rome	13	82.00
Venice	8	55.00
Vienna (Wein)	13	79.00
Zurich	1	10.00

LYON

Marseille	4	40.00
Milan	4½	47.00
Nice	5	63.00
Paris (Lyon)	4	57.00
Paris (Lyon) TGV. Sup. on some rides.	2	57.00
Strasbourg	6	53.00
Turin (Torino)	4½	36.00
Tours	7	50.00

MADRID
Pamplona	7	31.00
Paris (Austerlitz)	16	134.00
Port Bou	19	59.00
Rome	34	176.00
San Sebastian	7	44.00
Santiago de Compostela	9	47.00
Seville	6	40.00
Toledo	2	7.00
Valencia	5½	28.00
Vigo	9	47.00
Zaragoza	4	24.00

MAINZ
Munich (Munchen)	5	57.00

MALAGA
Seville	4	17.00

MALMO
Stockholm	6	53.00

MARSEILLE
Milan	11	51.00
Nice	3	26.00
Paris (Lyon)	8	94.00
Port Bou	4½	43.00
Rome	15	76.00
Toulouse	5	47.00
Venice	17	71.00

MILAN
Montreux	4	37.00
Munich (Munchen)	8½	51.00
TEE	6¾	65.00
Naples	8	56.00
TEE	8	77.00
Nice	6	27.00
Padua	3	16.00
Paris (Est) via Basel	13	104.00
Paris (Lyon) via Vallorbe	10	95.00
Rome	7	45.00
TEE	6	62.00

Stuttgart	9	71.00
Turin (Torino)	2	11.00
Trieste	6	30.00
Venice	3	19.00
Verona	1½	11.00
Vienna	15½	68.00
Zurich	4½	42.00
TEE	4	51.00

MONTREUX

Paris (Lyon)	6½	65.00
Zurich	3¼	35.00

MOSJOEN

Oslo	14	109.00

MUNICH (MUNCHEN)

Nurnberg	1½	25.00
Oberammergau	2	12.00
Paris (Est)	10	110.00
Rome	14	77.00
Rotterdam	11	109.00
Salzburg	2	20.00
Stockholm	20	174.00
Stuttgart	3	30.00
Venice (via Innsbruck)	9	49.00
Vienna (Wien)	6	47.00
Wiesbaden	5	57.00
Wurzburg	3	37.00
Zurich	5	54.00

MYRDAL

Oslo	5½	50.00

NANCY

Paris (Est)	3	40.00

NAPLES

Nice	14	66.00
Paris (Lyon)		
via Rome-Florence	21	147.00
via Rome-Genoa	23½	138.00
Reggio Calabria	5½	33.00
Rome	2	15.00

Taranto	5	22.00
Turin (Torino)	10	58.00
Venice	9	54.00
Vienna (Wien)	19	97.00

NARVIK

Oslo	33	117.00
Stockholm	22	87.00

NICE

Paris (Lyon)	11½	118.00
Rome	11½	52.00
Turin (Torino)	4½	24.00
Venice	11½	47.00

OSLO

Stavanger	9	81.00
Stockholm	6½	64.00
Trondheim	8	78.00
Voss	5½	57.00

PALERMO

Paris (Lyon)	32	146.00
Rome	13	61.00

PARIS

(Parentheses indicate Paris station)

Port Bou (Austerlitz)	12	105.00
Reims (Est)	2	19.00
Rome (Lyon) via Culoz	17	129.00
Salzburg (Est)		
(via Nancy)	11½	129.00
(via Basel)	16	126.00
San Sebastian (Austerlitz)	9½	90.00
Stockholm (Nord)	24	214.00
Strasbourg (Est)	4½	56.00
TEE	4	69.00
Stuttgart (Est)	7½	79.00
Toulouse (Austerlitz)	7	78.00
TEE	6	97.00
Trieste (Lyon)	15½	124.00
Turin (Torino) - (Lyon)	11	82.00
Venice (Est) via Basel	15	122.00
Venice (Lyon) via Vallorbe	13	114.00
Vienna (Wein) - (Est)	15	156.00
Zurich (Est)	7½	73.00

PERUGIA
Rome 3 15.00

PISA
Rome 3½ 24.00
Siena 2½ 8.00

RATTVIK
Stockholm 4 29.00

RAVENNA
Venice 3 13.00

ROME
Siena 4½ 18.00
Trieste 8 51.00
Turin (Torino) 7 47.00
Venice 6 40.00
Vienna (Wien) 20 89.00
Zurich 10 87.00

ROTTERDAM
Vienna (Wein) 19 142.00

SALZBURG
Trieste 7½ 32.00
Venice 7½ 36.00
Vienna (Wien) 4 27.00
Villach 3 17.00
Zurich 8½ 57.00

STOCKHOLM
Trondheim 12½ 73.00
Turku (boat) 12½ 21.00
Uppsala 1 8.00

STUTTGART
Vienna (Wien) 9 77.00
Zurich 4 33.00

TRIESTE
    Venice   2½   11.00
    Vienna (Wien)   10   46.00

TURIN (TORINO)
    Venice   5   30.00

VENICE
    Verona   2   8.00
    Vienna (Wien)   10   50.00
    Zurich   7   60.00

VIENNA (WIEN)
    Zurich   12   74.00

INDEX OF CITIES

247 Aarhus
498 Abadan
444 Aberdeen
541 Abidjan
528 Abomey
538 Accra
519 Adana
536 Addis Abeba
651 Adelaide
597 Agra
227 Agrigento
593 Ahmadabad
723 Ahuachapen
770 Alausi
659 Albany (Aust.)
702 Albany (U.S.A.)
246 Alborg
706 Albuquerque
511 Aleppo (Halab)
553 Alexandria
521 Algiers
172 Alicante
658 Alice Springs
634 Alishan
83 Alkmaar
593 Allahabad
175 Almeria
312 Alpnachstad
736 Alta Cordoba
544 Ambatosoratra
505 Amman
510 Amritsar
82 Amsterdam
715 Anchorage
270 Andalsnes
299 Andermatt
724 Anguiatu
514 Ankara
522 Annaba
116 Annecy
544 Antananarivo
725 Antigua
759 Antofagasta
545 Antsirabe
84 Antwerp
214 Anzio
620 Aomori
238 Aosta
729 Appleton
162 Aranjuez
646 Aranyaprathet
775 Arequipa
202 Arezzo
142 Arghos
761 Arica
114 Arles
769 Armenia
229 Arona
302 Arosa
330 Arth Goldau
666 Arthur's Pass
782 Artigas
421 Arundel
619 Asahigawa
537 Asmara

203 Assisi
773 Asuncion
535 Aswan
141 Athens
725 Atitlan, Lake
704 Atlanta
710 Atlantic City
661 Auckland
369 Augsburg
112 Avignon
163 Avila

64 Baden
288 Baden Baden
642 Badulla
499 Baghdad
737 Bahia Blanca
466 Balanton-
     szentgyorgy
547 Bamako
516 Bandirma
602 Bandung
671 Banff
594 Bangalore
645 Bangkok
491 Bar
727 Baracoa
154 Barcelona
219 Bari
219 Barletta
783 Barquisimeto
768 Barrancabermeja
286 Basle
499 Basra
720 Bataan (Costa Rica)
321 Bath
642 Batticaloa
766 Bauru
120 Bayeux
167 Bayonne
364 Bayreuth
636 Beaufort
525 Bechar
503 Beersheeva
552 Beira
506 Beirut
523 Bejaia
187 Belfast
488 Belgrade
748 Belo Horizonte
654 Bendigo
690 Benjamin Hill
713 Bennett
607 Beppu
265 Bergen
457 Berlin (East)
348 Berlin (West)
286 Bern
168 Bilbao
525 Biskra
562 Bitterfontein
575 Bizerte
741 Blanco Encalda
157 Blanes
546 Blantyre

431 Blenheim Palace
573 Blitta
560 Bloemfontein
121 Blois
171 Bobadilla
540 Bobo Dioulasso
270 Bodo
766 Bogota
710 Boise
195 Bologna
230 Bolzano
592 Bombay
353 Bonn
122 Bordeaux
697 Boston
541 Bouake
422 Bournemouth
683 Brantford
748 Brasilia
474 Brasov
452 Bratislava
531 Brazzaville
60 Bregenz
359 Bremen
230 Brennero
310 Brienz
309 Brig
422 Brighton
219 Brindisi
655 Brisbane
422 Bristol
452 Brno
651 Broken Hill
685 Brownsville
780 Brownsweg
68 Bruck an der Mur
91 Bruges
82 Brussels
473 Bucharest
68 Buchs
465 Budapest
734 Buenos Aires
702 Buffalo
585 Bulawayo
659 Bunbury
449 Burgas
163 Burgos
623 Butterworth

755 Cacequi
742 Cacheuta
168 Cadiz
120 Caen
656 Cairns
533 Cairo
592 Calcutta
670 Calgary
769 Cali
227 Caltanisetta
632 Camalig
423 Cambridge
325 Camedo
693 Campeche
753 Campos
653 Canberra

118 Cannes
424 Canterbury
626 Canton
561 Cape Town
742 Caracoles
133 Carcassone
423 Cardiff
719 Cartago
575 Carthage
751 Caruaru
549 Casablanca
160 Cascais
527 Cassinga
223 Catania
219 Catanzaro
366 Celle
777 Cerro de Pasco
452 Ceske Budejovice
320 Chamonix
124 Chantilly
124 Chartres
424 Chartwell
424 Chester
634 Chia I
645 Chiang Mai
698 Chicago
475 Chichester
725 Chichicastenango
674 Chicoutimi
553 Chicualacuala
687 Chihuahua City
779 Chimbote
546 Chipoka
587 Chittagong
217 Chiusi
625 Chongjin
777 Chosica
664 Christchurch
303 Chur
676 Churchill
722 Cienfuegos
691 Ciudad Guatemala
693 Ciudad Hidalgo
686 Ciudad Juarez
95 Clervaux
702 Cleveland
744 Cochabamba
599 Cochin
674 Cochrane
160 Coimbra
350 Cologne
641 Colombo
731 Colon
781 Colonia
210 Como
124 Compeigne
539 Conakry
760 Concepcion (Chile)
731 Concepcion
     (Panama)
521 Constantine
474 Constantza
653 Cooma
245 Copenhagen
169 Cordoba

142 Corinth
729 Corinto
187 Cork
743 Corrientes
757 Corumba
528 Cotonou
425 Coventry
688 Creel
207 Cremona
771 Cuenca (Equador)
164 Cuenca (Spain)
231 Cuneo
754 Curitiba
722 Cutuco
775 Cuzco
469 Czestochowa

587 Dacca
557 Dakar
706 Dallas
512 Damascus
511 Dammam
647 Da Nang
570 Dar es-Salaam
596 Darjeeling
676 Dauphin
303 Davos
564 De Aar
130 Deauville
85 Delft
592 Delhi
86 Den Haag
705 Denver
512 Deraa
703 Detroit
660 Devonport
418 Dieppe
680 Digby
134 Digne
116 Dijon
583 Dilolo
503 Dimona
101 Dinant
383 Dinkelsbuhl
537 Diredawa
332 Disentis
688 Divisadero
532 Djibouti
497 Djulfa
230 Dobaccio
706 Dodge City
572 Dodoma
269 Dombas
309 Domodossola
377 Donauschingen
527 Dondo
354 Dortmund
530 Douala
574 Dougga
425 Dover
144 Drama
264 Drammen
457 Dresden
187 Dublin
493 Dubrovnik
446 Dunbar
444 Dundee
665 Dunedin
441 Dun Laoghaire
686 Durango
559 Durban

448 Durres
354 Dusseldorf

560 East London
    (So. Af.)
567 Ed Damazine
443 Edinburgh
515 Edirne
672 Edmonton
474 Eforie Nord
69 Eibsee
534 El Alamein
448 Elbasan
543 Eldoret
579 El Jem
741 El Juncal
686 El Paso
741 El Portillo
773 Encarnacion
329 Engelberg
546 Entre Lagos
500 Erbil
459 Erfurt
517 Erzurum
164 Escorial
497 Esfahan
278 Eskilstuna
738 Esquel
725 Esquintia
354 Essen
160 Estoril
125 Evreux
426 Exeter

716 Fairbanks
517 Fevzipasa
549 Fez
545 Fianarantsoa
161 Figueira da Foz
440 Fishguard Harbor
718 Flagstaff
267 Flam
676 Flin Flon
195 Florence
219 Foggia
214 Foligno
125 Fontainbleau
752 Fortaleza
230 Fortezza
537 Franceville
350 Frankfurt
251 Fredericia
377 Freiburg
660 Fremantle
292 Fribourg
338 Friedrichshafen
383 Fussen

579 Gabes
474 Galati
643 Galle
189 Galway
68 Garmisch
673 Gaspe
279 Gavle
469 Gdansk
469 Gdynia
287 Geneva
195 Genoa
92 Gent
772 Georgetown

157 Gerona
576 Ghardimaou
378 Giessen
610 Gifu
663 Gisborne
681 Glace Bay
705 Glacier Park
446 Glasgow
497 Gorgan
317 Gornergrat
299 Goschenen
367 Goslar
277 Goteborg
86 Gouda
730 Granada (Nicaragua)
169 Granada (Spain)
718 Grand Canyon
273 Granvin
118 Grasse
65 Graz
427 Greenwich
117 Grenoble
666 Greymouth
768 Grecia
324 Grindelwald
689 Guadalajara
721 Guane
745 Guaqui
741 Guardia Vieja
724 Guatemala City
771 Guayaquil
735 Guemes
741 Guido
629 Guilin

83 Haarlem
721 Habana
502 Haifa
607 Hakata
618 Hakodate
614 Hakone, Lake
511 Halab (Aleppo)
670 Halifax
262 Hamar
355 Hamburg
256 Hameenlinna
368 Hameln
662 Hamilton
576 Hammamet
427 Hampton Court
256 Hanko
350 Hannover
647 Hanoi
259 Haparanda
427 Hastings
428 Hatfield
721 Havana
515 Haydarpasa
675 Hearst
355 Heidelberg
71 Heiflau
379 Heilbronn
246 Helsingborg
249 Helsingor
255 Helsinki
183 Hendaye
674 Hervey
368 Hildesheim
249 Hillerod
613 Himeji
606 Hiroshima

658 Hobart
647 Ho Chi Minh City
441 Holyhead
590 Hong Kong
87 Hoorn
704 Houston
634 Hualien
779 Huallanca
778 Huancavelica
776 Huancayo
676 Hudson Bay
647 Hue
507 Hyderabad

555 Ibadan
582 Ilebo
555 Ilorin
778 Inca City
738 Ing. Jacobacci
59 Innsbruck
289 Interlaken
665 Invercargill
445 Inverness
689 Irapuato
484 Irkutsk
428 Isle of Wight
534 Ismailia
514 Istanbul
516 Izmir
519 Izmit

599 Jaipur
601 Jakarta
725 Jalapa
672 Jasper
100 Jemelle
639 Jeonju
170 Jerez
504 Jerusalem
492 Jesenice
602 Jogjakarta
559 Johannesburg
638 Johor Bahru
568 Juba
736 Jujuy
776 Juliaca
298 Jungfraujoch

547 Kadira
555 Kaduna
608 Kagoshima
577 Kairouan
584 Kapiri Mposhi
142 Kalamata
582 Kalemie
651 Kalgoorlie
278 Kalmar
247 Kalundborg
512 Kamechlie
581 Kamina
580 Kampala
613 Kanazawa
642 Kandy
539 Kankan
555 Kano
706 Kansas City
632 Kaohsiung
675 Kapuskasing
507 Karachi
256 Karjaa
458 Karl Marx Stadt

453 Karlovy Vary
517 Kars
617 Karuizawa
368 Kassel
145 Katerini
144 Kavala
517 Kayseri
466 Kecksmet
565 Keetmanshoop
574 Kerkouane
486 Khabarovsk
517 Kharkov
567 Khartoum
496 Khorramshahr
478 Kiev
572 Kigoma
189 Killarney
562 Kimberley
728 Kingston (Jamaica)
666 Kingston (N.Z.)
582 Kinshasa
500 Kirkuk
61 Kitzbuhl
72 Klagenfurt
610 Kobe
356 Koblenz
615 Kofu
607 Kokura
622 Kompong Sam
263 Kongsberg
380 Konstanz
520 Konya
571 Korogwe
454 Kosice
568 Kosti
636 Kota Kinabalu
590 Kowloon
573 Kpalime
470 Krakow
492 Kranj
273 Kristiansand
623 Kuala Lumpur
608 Kumamoto
538 Kumasi
657 Kuranda
618 Kushiro
445 Kyle of Lochalsh
606 Kyoto

554 Lagos
508 Lahore
256 Lahti
725 Lake Atitlan
614 Lake Hakone
670 Lake Louise
777 Lake Titicaca
509 Landi Kotal
303 Landquart
293 Langnau
777 La Oroya
744 La Paz
686 Laredo
265 Larvik
742 Las Cuevas
589 Lashio
708 Las Vegas
178 La Tour-de-Carol
660 Launceston
291 Laussane
435 Leemington Spa
429 Leicester

87 Leiden
457 Leipzig
478 Leningrad
729 Leon (Nic.)
175 Leon (Spain)
158 Lerida
492 Lesce-Bled
92 Liege
261 Lillehammer
776 Lima
546 Limbe
190 Limerick
127 Limoges
719 Limon
429 Lincoln
59 Linz
155 Lisbon
655 Lithgow
583 Livingstone
203 Livorno
489 Ljubljana
762 Llay Llay
554 Llorin
527 Lobito
211 Locarno
504 Lod
573 Lome
683 London (Can.)
417 London (Eng.)
762 Los Andes
698 Los Angeles
688 Los Mochis
670 Louise, Lake
590 Lo Wu
526 Luanda
527 Luau
470 Lublin
566 Luderitz
212 Lugano
581 Lubumbashi
666 Lumsden
369 Luneburg
584 Lusaka
82 Luxembourg City
535 Luxor
287 Luzern
678 Lynn Lake
112 Lyon

87 Maastricht
778 Machu-Picchu
593 Madras
155 Madrid
586 Mafeking
579 Mahdia
556 Maiduguri
357 Mainz
579 Maktar
160 Malaga
526 Malanje
513 Malatya
447 Mallaig
249 Malmo
229 Malta
474 Mangalia
730 Managua
545 Manakara
589 Mandalay
631 Manila
516 Manisa
358 Mannheim

690 Manzanillo
553 Maputo
739 Mar del Plata
453 Marianske Lazne
548 Marrakech
114 Marseille
238 Martigny
730 Masaya
497 Mashhad
537 Massawa
685 Matamoros
722 Matanzas
673 Matapedia
643 Matara
579 Matmata
615 Matsumoto
610 Matsuyama
61 Mayrhofen
725 Mazatenango
689 Mazatlan
531 M'Binda
714 McKinley Park
603 Medan
768 Medellin
549 Meknes
652 Melbourne
66 Melk
742 Mendoza
782 Mercedes
693 Merida (Mexico)
170 Merida (Spain)
519 Mersin
223 Messina
98 Metz
690 Mexicali
684 Mexico City
708 Miami
196 Milan
226 Milazzo
555 Minna
705 Minneapolis
594 Miraj
615 Mito
527 Mocamedes
640 Mogpo
579 Moknine
541 Mombasa
579 Monastir
673 Moncton
175 Monforte
115 Monte Carlo
728 Montego Bay
685 Monterrey
781 Montevideo
669 Montreal
296 Montreux
158 Montserrat
674 Moosenee
279 Mora
544 Moramanga
175 Moreda
690 Morelia
479 Moscow
571 Moshi
561 Mossel Bay
493 Mostar
500 Mosul
652 Mount Gambier
657 Mount Isa
323 Mt. Pilatus
330 Mt. Rigi

126 Mt. St. Michel
329 Mt. Titlis
351 Munich
172 Murcia
479 Murmansk
373 Murnau
655 Murwillumbah
571 Mwanza
589 Myitkyina
267 Mydral

576 Nabeul
546 Nacala
631 Naga
609 Nagasaki
611 Nagoya
542 Nairobi
543 Nakuru
646 Nam Tok
93 Namur
642 Nanu Oya
127 Nancy
663 Napier
197 Naples
611 Nara
134 Narbonne
615 Narita
272 Narvik
462 Naumberg
585 Ndola
293 Neuchatel
655 Newcastle
592 New Delhi
596 New Jalpaiguri
699 New Orleans
663 New Plymouth
699 Ney York City
497 Neyshabur
530 N'Gaoundere
682 Niagara Falls
113 Nice
616 Niigata
616 Nikko
115 Nimes
753 Niteroi
546 Nkaya
530 Nkongsamba
263 Nordagutu
368 Nordstemmen
280 Norrkoping
674 North Bay
429 Norwich
430 Nottingham
484 Novosibirsk
564 Nurnberg
568 Nyala

705 Oakland
692 Oaxaca
447 Oban
373 Oberammergau
250 Odense
478 Odessa
380 Offenburg
708 Ogden
611 Okayama
143 Olympia
780 Onverwacht
641 Onyang
524 Oran
739 Osorno

215 Orvieto
606 Osaka
261 Oslo
281 Ostersund
565 Otavi
669 Ottawa
524 Oued Tlelat
540 Ougadougou
528 Ouida
528 Ouidah
259 Oulu
175 Oviedo
537 Owendo
431 Oxford

204 Padua
177 Palencia
693 Palenque
225 Palermo
771 Palmira
168 Pamplona
731 Panama City
528 Parakou
780 Paramaribo
754 Paranagua
772 Parika
110 Paris
198 Parma
741 Paso de Los Andes
143 Patras
627 Pekin
624 Penang
432 Penzance
651 Perth (Aust.)
445 Perth (Scot.)
205 Perugia
216 Pescara
509 Peshawar
699 Philadelphia
622 Phnom Penh
704 Phoenix
664 Picton
559 Pietermaritzburg
312 Pilatus Kulm
721 Pinar del Rio
143 Piraeus
145 Pirghos
199 Pisa
703 Pittsburgh
449 Plovdiv
529 Plumtree
453 Plzen
531 Pointe Noir
642 Polonnauruwa
213 Pompeii
454 Poprad Tatry
728 Port Antomo
681 Port aux Basques
561 Port Elizabeth
741 Porterillos
556 Port Harcourt
681 Port Morien
650 Port Pirie
534 Port Said
567 Port Sudan
716 Portage
742 Portillo
709 Portland
161 Porto
755 Porto Alegre
432 Portsmouth

743 Posadas
492 Postojna
745 Potosi
460 Potsdam
471 Poznan
451 Prague
559 Pretoria
677 Prince Albert
679 Prince George
679 Prince Rupert
692 Puebla
742 Puente del Inca
731 Puerto Armuelles
725 Puerto Barrios
783 Puerto Cabello
727 Puerto Cortes
739 Puerto Montt
174 Puigcerda
595 Pune
777 Puno
741 Punta de las Vacas
720 Puntarenas
640 Pusan
438 Pwllheli
625 Pyongyang

669 Quebec City
162 Queluz
510 Quetta
726 Quirigua
771 Quito

550 Rabat
529 Ramagthabama
523 Ramdane Djamal
600 Rameswaram
588 Rangoon
545 Ranomena
603 Rantau Prapet
280 Rattvik
200 Ravenna
751 Recife
220 Reggio di Calabria
677 Regina
688 Regocijo
177 Regua
128 Reims
710 Reno
737 Resistencia
290 Rheinfelden
480 Riga
257 Riihimaki
206 Rimini
771 Riobamba
742 Rio Blanco
782 Rio Branco
748 Rio de Janeiro
755 Rio Grande
781 Rivera
646 River Khwae Bridge
511 Riyadh
433 Rochester
656 Rockhampton
338 Romanshorn
197 Rome
84 Roosendaal
735 Rosario
772 Rosignol
250 Roskilde
440 Rosslare Harbor
460 Rostock

482 Rostov
282 Rothenburg
375 Rottach-Egern
88 Rotterdam
128 Rouen
434 Rye

99 Saarbrucken
536 Sadd el Ali
647 Saigon (see Ho
    Chi Minh City)
435 St. Albans
338 St. Gallen
557 St. Louis (Sen.)
706 St. Louis (U.S.A.)
306 St. Moritz
670 Saint John
119 Saint Raphael
165 Salamanca
751 Salgueiro
434 Salisbury (Eng.)
586 Salisbury (Zim.)
736 Salta
741 Salta del Soldado
708 Salt Lake City
781 Salto
749 Salvador
59 Salzburg
481 Samarkand
518 Samsun
706 San Antonio
738 San Carlos de
    Bariloche
264 Sandefjord
708 San Diego
631 San Fernando
700 San Francisco
723 San Jeronimo
719 San Jose
772 San Lorenzo
686 San Luis Potosi
723 San Miguel
741 San Pablo
727 San Pedro Sula
208 San Remo
723 San Salvador
156 San Sebastian
737 Santa Fe (Arg.)
755 Santa Maria
768 Santa Marta
177 Santander
737 Santa Rosa
759 Santiago
180 Santiago de
    Compostela
721 Santiago de Cuba
178 Sant Julia de Loria
756 Santos
723 Sao Vicente
752 Sao Luiz
750 Sao Paulo
618 Sapporo
488 Sarajevo
333 Sargans
672 Saskatoon
675 Sault Ste. Marie
579 Sbeitla
338 Schaffhausen
673 Schefferville
310 Scheidegg
374 Schliersee

69 Schneefernhaus
463 Schwerin
301 Schwyz
700 Seattle
498 Seeba
165 Segovia
71 Selzthal
546 Sena
616 Sendai
674 Senneterre
639 Seoul
673 Sept Iles
161 Setubal
481 Sevastopol
156 Seville
492 Sezana
579 Sfax
626 Shanghai
440 Shannon
439 Shrewsbury
589 Shwenyaung
771 Sibambe
357 Siegen
200 Siena
475 Sighisoara
475 Sinaia
637 Singapore
380 Singen
162 Sintra
466 Siofok
299 Sion
224 Siracusa
159 Sitges
713 Skagway
264 Skien
523 Skikda
491 Skopje
481 Sochi
740 Socompa
449 Sofia
603 Solo
307 Solothurn
234 Sondrio
723 Sonsonate
471 Sopot
235 Sorrento
525 Souk-Ahras
579 Sousse
728 Spanish Town
318 Spiez
488 Split
705 Spokane
217 Spoleto
682 Squamish
266 Stalheim
454 Stary Smokovec
273 Stavanger
277 Stockholm
434 Stonehenge
460 Stralsund
447 Stranraer
129 Strasbourg
435 Stratford on Avon
455 Strbske Pleso
365 Stuttgart
635 Su Ao
769 Suarez
745 Sucre
534 Suez
497 Sufian
481 Sukhumi

633 Sun Moon Lake
601 Surabaja
566 Swakopmund
654 Swan Hill
439 Swansea
650 Sydney (Aust.)
681 Sydney (Can.)
587 Sylhet
466 Szeged

453 Tabor
572 Tabora
496 Tabriz
632 Taichung
632 Taipei
635 Taitung
612 Takamatsu
539 Takoradi
644 Talaimannar
479 Tallinn
544 Tamatave
257 Tampere
686 Tampico
571 Tanga
548 Tangier
603 Tanjong Balai
226 Taormina
693 Tapachula
220 Taranto
538 Tarkwa
159 Tarragona
481 Tashkent
454 Tatranska Lomnica
663 Taumarunui
589 Taunggyi
525 Tebessa
694 Tecun Uman
374 Tegernsee
495 Tehran
727 Tela
503 Tel Aviv
581 Tenke
636 Tenom
752 Teresina
205 Terontola
589 Thazi

678 The Pas
144 Thessaloniki
676 Thompson
646 Thon Buri
574 Thuburo Majus
665 Timaru
448 Tirana
331 Tirano
777 Titicaca, Lake
612 Toba
606 Tokyo
166 Toledo
264 Tonsberg
656 Toowoomba
209 Torino
670 Toronto
543 Tororo
436 Torquay
171 Torremolinos
686 Torreon
172 Tortosa
471 Torun
612 Tottori
525 Touggourt
132 Toulouse
94 Tournai
117 Tours
656 Townsville
614 Toyama
189 Tralee
228 Trapani
720 Tres Rios
99 Trier
73 Trieste
643 Trincomalee
506 Tripoli
272 Trondheim
130 Trouville
130 Troyes
681 Truro
736 Tucuman
624 Tumpat
584 Tunduma
574 Tunis
258 Turku

646 Ubon Ratchathani
73 Udine
375 Ulm
586 Umtali
476 Ungen
280 Uppsala
742 Upsallata
755 Uruguaiana
575 Utica
86 Utrecht
693 Uxmal

156 Valencia
166 Valladolid
131 Valorcine
759 Valparaiso
518 Van
670 Vancouver
449 Varna
201 Venice
691 Veracruz
202 Verona
131 Versailles
780 Viacha
585 Victoria Falls
60 Vienna
118 Vienne
176 Vigo
70 Villach
743 Villa Encarnacion
220 Villa San Giovanni
261 Vinstra
753 Vitoria
330 Vitznau
482 Volgograd
251 Vordingborg
273 Voss
772 Vreed-en-Hoop

568 Wadi Halfa
682 Wakefield
566 Walvis Bay
461 Warnemunde
468 Warsaw
700 Washington, D.C.

568 Waw
461 Weimar
662 Wellington
713 Whitehorse
716 Whittier
445 Wick
366 Wiesbaden
428 Wight, Isle of
436 Winchester
439 Windermere
565 Windhoek
683 Windsor (Can.)
436 Windsor (Eng.)
671 Winnipeg
308 Winterthur
657 Winton
438 Wolverhampton
375 Wurzburg
660 Wynyard

530 Yaounde
680 Yarmouth
639 Yeosu
617 Yokohama
437 York

722 Zacapa
687 Zacatecas
723 Zacatecoluca
490 Zadar
489 Zagreb
499 Zahedan
471 Zakopane
741 Zanjon Amarillo
737 Zapala
167 Zaragoza
496 Zarand
579 Zarzis
62 Zell am See
308 Zug
68 Zugspitze
288 Zurich
322 Zweisimmen

NOTES

NOTES

NOTES

1984

January 1984	February 1984	March 1984
S M T W T F S	S M T W T F S	S M T W T F S
1 2 3 4 5 6 7	1 2 3 4	1 2 3
8 9 10 11 12 13 14	5 6 7 8 9 10 11	4 5 6 7 8 9 10
15 16 17 18 19 20 21	12 13 14 15 16 17 18	11 12 13 14 15 16 17
22 23 24 25 26 27 28	19 20 21 22 23 24 25	18 19 20 21 22 23 24
29 30 31	26 27 28 29	25 26 27 28 29 30 31

April 1984	May 1984	June 1984
S M T W T F S	S M T W T F S	S M T W T F S
1 2 3 4 5 6 7	1 2 3 4 5	1 2
8 9 10 11 12 13 14	6 7 8 9 10 11 12	3 4 5 6 7 8 9
15 16 17 18 19 20 21	13 14 15 16 17 18 19	10 11 12 13 14 15 16
22 23 24 25 26 27 28	20 21 22 23 24 25 26	17 18 19 20 21 22 23
29 30	27 28 29 30 31	24 25 26 27 28 29 30

July 1984	August 1984	September 1984
S M T W T F S	S M T W T F S	S M T W T F S
1 2 3 4 5 6 7	1 2 3 4	1
8 9 10 11 12 13 14	5 6 7 8 9 10 11	2 3 4 5 6 7 8
15 16 17 18 19 20 21	12 13 14 15 16 17 18	9 10 11 12 13 14 15
22 23 24 25 26 27 28	19 20 21 22 23 24 25	16 17 18 19 20 21 22
29 30 31	26 27 28 29 30 31	23 24 25 26 27 28 29
		30

October 1984	November 1984	December 1984
S M T W T F S	S M T W T F S	S M T W T F S
1 2 3 4 5 6	1 2 3	1
7 8 9 10 11 12 13	4 5 6 7 8 9 10	2 3 4 5 6 7 8
14 15 16 17 18 19 20	11 12 13 14 15 16 17	9 10 11 12 13 14 15
21 22 23 24 25 26 27	18 19 20 21 22 23 24	16 17 18 19 20 21 22
28 29 30 31	25 26 27 28 29 30	23 24 25 26 27 28 29
		30 31

1985

January 1985	February 1985	March 1985
S M T W T F S	S M T W T F S	S M T W T F S
1 2 3 4 5	1 2	1 2
6 7 8 9 10 11 12	3 4 5 6 7 8 9	3 4 5 6 7 8 9
13 14 15 16 17 18 19	10 11 12 13 14 15 16	10 11 12 13 14 15 16
20 21 22 23 24 25 26	17 18 19 20 21 22 23	17 18 19 20 21 22 23
27 28 29 30 31	24 25 26 27 28	24 25 26 27 28 29 30
		31

April 1985	May 1985	June 1985
S M T W T F S	S M T W T F S	S M T W T F S
1 2 3 4 5 6	1 2 3 4	1
7 8 9 10 11 12 13	5 6 7 8 9 10 11	2 3 4 5 6 7 8
14 15 16 17 18 19 20	12 13 14 15 16 17 18	9 10 11 12 13 14 15
21 22 23 24 25 26 27	19 20 21 22 23 24 25	16 17 18 19 20 21 22
28 29 30	26 27 28 29 30 31	23 24 25 26 27 28 29
		30

July 1985	August 1985	September 1985
S M T W T F S	S M T W T F S	S M T W T F S
1 2 3 4 5 6	1 2 3	1 2 3 4 5 6 7
7 8 9 10 11 12 13	4 5 6 7 8 9 10	8 9 10 11 12 13 14
14 15 16 17 18 19 20	11 12 13 14 15 16 17	15 16 17 18 19 20 21
21 22 23 24 25 26 27	18 19 20 21 22 23 24	22 23 24 25 26 27 28
28 29 30 31	25 26 27 28 29 30 31	29 30

October 1985	November 1985	December 1985
S M T W T F S	S M T W T F S	S M T W T F S
1 2 3 4 5	1 2	1 2 3 4 5 6 7
6 7 8 9 10 11 12	3 4 5 6 7 8 9	8 9 10 11 12 13 14
13 14 15 16 17 18 19	10 11 12 13 14 15 16	15 16 17 18 19 20 21
20 21 22 23 24 25 26	17 18 19 20 21 22 23	22 23 24 25 26 27 28
27 28 29 30 31	24 25 26 27 28 29 30	29 30 31